# THE STATISTICS PROBLEM SOLVER®

REGISTERED TRADEMARK

## A Complete Solution Guide to Any Textbook

**Staff of Research and Education Association**
**Dr. M. Fogiel, Director**

Research and Education Association
61 Ethel Road West
Piscataway, New Jersey 08854

# THE STATISTICS PROBLEM SOLVER ®

Copyright © 1994 by Research & Education Association

Printed in the United States of America

Library of Congress Catalog Card Number 78-64581

International Standard Book Number 0–87891-515-X

PROBLEM SOLVER is a registered trademark of
Research and Education Association, Piscataway, New Jersey

# WHAT THIS BOOK IS FOR

For as long as statistics has been taught in schools, students have found this subject difficult to understand and learn because of its unusually complex and abstract nature. Despite the publication of hundreds of textbooks in this field, each one intended to provide an improvement over previous textbooks, statistics remains particularly perplexing and the subject is often taken in class only to meet school/departmental requirements for a selected course of study.

In a study of the problem, REA found the following basic reasons underlying students' difficulties with statistics taught in schools:

(a) No systematic rules of analysis have been developed which students may follow in a step-by-step manner to solve the usual problems encountered. This results from the fact that the numerous different conditions and principles which may be involved in a problem, lead to many possible different methods of solution. To prescribe a set of rules to be followed for each of the possible variations, would involve an enormous number of rules and steps to be searched through by students, and this task would perhaps be more burdensome than solving the problem directly with some accompanying trial and error to find the correct solution route.

(b) Textbooks currently available will usually explain a given principle in a few pages written by a professional who has an insight into the subject matter that is not shared by students. The explanations are often written in an abstract manner which leave the student confused as to the application of the principle. The explanations given are not sufficiently detailed and extensive to make the student aware of the wide range of applications and different aspects of the principle being studied. The numerous possible variations of principles and their applications are usually not discussed, and it is left for the students to discover these for themselves while doing the exercises. Accordingly, the average student is expected to rediscover that which has been long known and practiced, but not published or explained extensively.

(c) The examples usually following the explanation of a topic are too few in number and too simple to enable the student to obtain a thorough grasp of the principles involved. The explanations do not provide sufficient basis to enable a student to solve problems that may be subsequently assigned for homework or given on examinations.

The examples are presented in abbreviated form which leaves out much material between steps, and requires that students derive the omitted material themselves. As a result, students find the examples difficult to understand--contrary to the purpose of the examples.

Examples are, furthermore, often worded in a confusing manner. They do not state the problem and then present the solution. Instead, they pass through a general discussion, never revealing what is to be solved for.

Examples, also, do not always include diagrams/graphs, wherever appropriate, and students do not obtain the training to draw diagrams or graphs to simplify and organize their thinking.

(d) Students can learn the subject only by doing the exercises themselves and reviewing them in class, to obtain experience in applying the principles with their different ramifications.

In doing the exercises by themselves, students find that they are required to devote considerably more time to statistics than to other subjects of comparable credits, because they are uncertain with regard to the selection and application of the theorems and principles involved. It is also often necessary for students to discover those "tricks" not revealed in their texts (or review books), that make it possible to solve problems easily. Students must usually resort to methods of trial-and-error to discover these "tricks," and as a result they find that they may sometimes spend several hours in solving a single problem.

(e) When reviewing the exercises in classrooms, instructors

usually request students to take turns in writing solutions on the board and explaining them to the class. Students often find it difficult to explain in a manner that holds the interest of the class, and enables the remaining students to follow the material written on the board. The remaining students seated in the class are, furthermore, too occupied with copying the material from the board, to listen to the oral explanations and concentrate on the methods of solution.

This book is intended to aid students in statistics in overcoming the difficulties described, by supplying detailed illustrations of the solution methods which are usually not apparent to students. The solution methods are illustrated by problems selected from those that are most often assigned for class work and given on examinations. The problems are arranged in order of complexity to enable students to learn and understand a particular topic by reviewing the problems in sequence. The problems are illustrated with detailed step-by-step explanations, to save the student the large amount of time that is often needed to fill in the gaps that are usually found between steps of illustrations in the textbooks or review/outline books.

The staff of REA considers statistics a subject that is best learned by allowing students to view the methods of analysis and solution techniques themselves. This approach to learning the subject matter is similar to that practiced in various laboratories, particularly in the medical fields.

In using this book, students may review and study the illustrated problems at their own pace; they are not limited to the time allowed for explaining problems on the board in class.

When students want to look up a particular type of problem and solution, they can readily locate it in the book by referring to the index which has been extensively prepared. It is also possible to locate a particular type of problem by glancing at just the material within the boxed portions. To facilitate rapid scanning of the problems, each problem has a heavy border around it. Furthermore, each problem is identified with a number immediately above the problem at the right-hand margin.

To obtain maximum benefit from the book, students should familiarize themselves with the section, "How To Use This Book," located in the front pages.

To meet the objectives of this book, staff members of REA have selected problems usually encountered in assignments and examinations, and have solved each problem meticulously to illustrate the steps which are usually difficult for students to comprehend. For outstanding effort and competence in this area, special gratitude is due to David Bernklau, Alfred Brothers, R. Kannan, Jeffrey Shaw, and Joel Steckel. Thanks are, furthermore, due to several contributors who devoted brief periods of time to this work.

Gratitude is also expressed to the many persons involved in the difficult task of typing the manuscript with its endless changes, and to the REA art staff who prepared the numerous detailed illustrations together with the layout and physical features of the book.

Finally, special thanks are due to Helen Kaufmann for her unique talents in rendering those difficult border-line decisions and in making constructive suggestions related to the design and organization of the book.

Max Fogiel, Ph.D.
Program Director

# HOW TO USE THIS BOOK

This book can be an invaluable aid to students in statistics as a supplement to their textbooks. The book is subdivided into 24 chapters, each dealing with a separate topic. The subject matter is developed beginning with basic probability and extending through binomial, normal, joint, discrete, and continous distributions. Other sections deal with sampling and sampling theory, confidence intervals, hypothesis testing, regression and correlation analysis, analysis of variance, and non-parametric methods. An extensive number of applications have been included since these appear to be most troublesome to students.

# TO LEARN AND UNDERSTAND
# A TOPIC THOROUGHLY

1. Refer to your class text and read the section pertaining to the topic. You should become acquainted with the principles discussed there. These principles, however, may not be clear to you at that time.

2. Then locate the topic you are looking for by referring to the "Table of Contents" in the front of this book, "The Statistics Problem Solver."

3. Turn to the page where the topic begins and review the problems under each topic, in the order given. For each topic, the problems are arranged in order of complexity, from the simplest to the more difficult. Some problems may appear similar to others, but each problem has been selected to illustrate a different point or solution method.

To learn and understand a topic thoroughly and retain its contents, it will generally be necessary for students to review the problems several times. Repeated review is essential in order to gain experience in recognizing the principles that should be applied, and in selecting the best solution technique.

# TO FIND A PARTICULAR PROBLEM

To locate one or more problems related to a particular subject matter, refer to the index. In using the index, be certain to note that the numbers given there refer to problem numbers, not to page numbers. This arrangement of the index is intended to facilitate finding a problem more rapidly, since two or more problems may appear on a page.

If a particular type of problem cannot be found readily, it is recommended that the student refer to the "Table of Contents" in the front pages, and then turn to the chapter which is applicable to the problem being sought. By scanning or glancing at the material that is boxed, it will generally be possible to find problems related to the one being sought, without consuming considerable time. After the problems have been located, the solutions can be reviewed and studied in detail. For this purpose of locating problems rapidly, students should acquaint themselves with the organization of the book as found in the "Table of Contents".

In preparing for an exam, it is useful to find the topics to be covered on the exam, in the "Table of Contents", and then review the problems under those topics several times. This should equip the student with what might be needed for the exam.

# CONTENTS

**Chapter No.**                                                    **Page No.**

UNITS CONVERSION FACTORS    xiii

1  DESCRIPTIVE STATISTICS    1
   Graphs and Frequency Distributions    1
   Measures of Central Tendency    9
   Measures of Dispersion    16
   Measures of Grouped Data    30
   Moments, Skewness, Kurtosis    51

2  ELEMENTARY PROBABILITY AND STATISTICS    56
   Fundamental Principle of Counting    56
   Permutations    57
   Combinations    60
   Venn Diagrams    62
   Classical Model of Probability    65
   Conditional Probability    76
   Bayes' Theorem    96
   Random Sampling    99

3  PROBABILITY DISTRIBUTIONS    103
   Discrete Distributions    103
   Geometric Density Function    106
   Poisson Density Function    108
   Continuous Distributions    109
   Uniform Density Function    114
   Exponential Density Function    116

4  THE BINOMIAL DISTRIBUTION    118
   Derivation of the Binomial Distribution    118
   Cumulative Binomial Probabilities    146
   Multinomial Distribution    151

5  JOINT DISTRIBUTIONS    158
   Discrete Joint Distributions    158
   Continuous Joint Distributions    165

6  FUNCTIONS OF RANDOM VARIABLES    177
   Change of Variable Technique    177
   Moment Generating Function Technique    183
   Distribution Functions    186

Convolutions    203
Multivariate Functions    206

**7 EXPECTED VALUE**    219
For Discrete Random Variables    219
For Continuous Random Variables    228
For Functions of Random Variables    238
General Rules of Expectation    244
Conditional Expectation and Expected Value of
Multivariate Densities    247
Variance of Discrete Random Variables    255
Variance of Continuous Random Variables    261
Covariance and Correlation    266

**8 MOMENT GENERATING FUNCTION**    275
Discrete Random Variables    275
Continuous Random Variables 283

**9 CHEBYSHEV'S INEQUALITY**    289

**10 SPECIAL DISCRETE DISTRIBUTIONS**    295
Uniform Distribution    295
Geometric Distribution    296
Poisson Distribution    299
Hypergeomtric Distribution    313

**11 NORMAL DISTRIBUTIONS**    317
Areas Under the Standard Normal Curve    317
Conversions  and Applications of
Standard Normal Variables    320
Normal Approximation to the Binomial Distribution    346
Additional Applications    364

**12 SPECIAL CONTINUOUS DISTRIBUTIONS**    369
Uniform Distribution    369
Exponential Distribution    374
Gamma Distribution    379

**13 SAMPLING THEORY**    382
Random Samples    382
Weak Law of Large Numbers    386
The Central Limit Theorem and Distribution of
the Sample Mean    387
The Chi-Square, t, and F Distributions    396
The t-Test    404
The F-Distribution    407
The Sampling of Order Statistics    415

**14 CONFIDENCE INTERVALS**    420
Mean of a Normal Distribution With Known Variance    423
Difference of Means of Normal Populations
With Known Variance    430

Large Samples With Mean of Unknown Variance   437
Small Samples With Mean of Unknown Variance   447
Difference of Means With Unknown Variances   460
Variances   470
Ratio of Variances   476
Proportions   480
Difference of Proportions   494
Bayesian Confidence Interval   502

**15  POINT ESTIMATION**   506

Estimating the Population Variance   506
The Method of Moments   509
Maximum Likelihood Estimators   512
Unbiased Estimators   530
Sufficient Statistics   539
Consistent Statistics   553
Completeness   556
The Cramer-Rao Inequality and Efficiency   557
Bayesian Estimation   566

**16  HYPOTHESIS TESTING**   570

Level of Significance   570
Means: Large Samples   571
Means: Small Samples   580
Differences Between Means: Z Tests   587
Differences Between Means: t-Tests   594
Proportions   608
Differences Between Proportions   613
The Normal Approximation to the Binomial   621
Variances   626
Differences Between Variances   630
Tests Involving the Poisson Distribution   637
Combining Results of Different Samples   638
Type II Errors   640
The Power of a Test   655
Likelihood Ratio Test for the Best Critical Region   659

**17  REGRESSION AND CORRELATION ANALYSIS**   665

Simple Regression   665
Linear Correlation   680
Spearman's Rank Correlation   699
Fisher's Z-Transformation   708
Properties of the Regression Coefficients   720
Applications of Regression and Correlation Analysis   734
Factor Analysis   760

**18  ANALYSIS OF VARIANCE**   767

One-Way Anova   767
Two-Way Anova   787
Random Effects Model   803

**19  CHI-SQUARE AND CONTINGENCY TABLES**   809

Contingency Tables    809
Chi-Square Tests and Contingency Tables    811
Fisher's Test and 2 X 2 Tables    823
Yate's Correction and 2 X 2 Tables    827
Chi-Square Tests    833

**20 NON-PARAMETRIC METHODS**    864
Sign Test    864
Confidence Intervals for Quantiles    868
Tolerance Limits    871
Kolmogorov-Smirnov Statistic    876
Wilcoxon's Sum of Ranks Test (Mann-Whitney
Rank Sum Test)    883
The Wilcoxon Signed-Rank Test    894
The Wilcoxon Stratified Test    894
Spearman's Rank Correlation Test    904
The Kruskal-Wallis Test    914
Cochran's Test 924
Runs Test    928

**21 TIME-SERIES AND INDEX NUMBERS**    933
Period Ratios    933
Price Indices    935
Time-Series    940

**22 BUSINESS AND ECONOMIC APPLICATIONS**    955

**23 BIOLOGICAL APPLICATIONS**    984

**24 MISCELLANEOUS APPLICATIONS**    1004

**INDEX**    1030

# UNITS CONVERSION FACTORS

This section includes a particularly useful and comprehensive table to aid students and teachers in converting between systems of units.

The problems and their solutions in this book use SI (International System) as well as English units. Both of these units are in extensive use throughout the world, and therefore students should develop a good facility to work with both sets of units until a single standard of units has been found acceptable internationally.

In working out or solving a problem in one system of units or the other, essentially only the numbers change. Also, the conversion from one unit system to another is easily achieved through the use of conversion factors that are given in the subsequent table. Accordingly, the units are one of the least important aspects of a problem. For these reasons, a student should not be concerned mainly with which units are used in any particular problem. Instead, a student should obtain from that problem and its solution an understanding of the underlying principles and solution techniques that are illustrated there.

| To convert | To | Multiply by | For the reverse, multiply by |
|---|---|---|---|
| acres | square feet | $4.356 \times 10^4$ | $2.296 \times 10^{-5}$ |
| acres | square meters | 4047 | $2.471 \times 10^{-4}$ |
| ampere-hours | coulombs | 3600 | $2.778 \times 10^{-4}$ |
| ampere-turns | gilberts | 1.257 | 0.7958 |
| ampere-turns per cm. | ampere-turns per inch | 2.54 | 0.3937 |
| angstrom units | inches | $3.937 \times 10^{-9}$ | $2.54 \times 10^8$ |
| angstrom units | meters | $10^{-10}$ | $10^{10}$ |
| atmospheres | feet of water | 33.90 | 0.02950 |
| atmospheres | inch of mercury at 0°C | 29.92 | $3.342 \times 10^{-2}$ |
| atmospheres | kilogram per square meter | $1.033 \times 10^4$ | $9.678 \times 10^{-5}$ |
| atmospheres | millimeter of mercury at 0°C | 760 | $1.316 \times 10^{-3}$ |
| atmospheres | pascals | $1.0133 \times 10^5$ | $0.9869 \times 10^{-5}$ |
| atmospheres | pounds per square inch | 14.70 | 0.06804 |
| bars | atmospheres | $9.870 \times 10^{-7}$ | 1.0133 |
| bars | dynes per square cm. | $10^6$ | $10^{-6}$ |
| bars | pascals | $10^5$ | $10^{-5}$ |
| bars | pounds per square inch | 14.504 | $6.8947 \times 10^{-2}$ |
| Btu | ergs | $1.0548 \times 10^{10}$ | $9.486 \times 10^{-11}$ |
| Btu | foot-pounds | 778.3 | $1.285 \times 10^{-3}$ |
| Btu | joules | 1054.8 | $9.480 \times 10^{-4}$ |
| Btu | kilogram-calories | 0.252 | 3.969 |
| calories, gram | Btu | $3.968 \times 10^{-3}$ | 252 |
| calories, gram | foot-pounds | 3.087 | 0.324 |
| calories, gram | joules | 4.185 | 0.2389 |
| Celsius | Fahrenheit | (°C × 9/5) + 32 = °F | (°F − 32) × 5/9 = °C |

| To convert | To | Multiply | For the reverse, multiply by |
|---|---|---|---|
| Celsius | kelvin | $°C + 273.1 = K$ | $K - 273.1 = °C$ |
| centimeters | angstrom units | $1 \times 10^8$ | $1 \times 10^{-8}$ |
| centimeters | feet | 0.03281 | 30.479 |
| centistokes | square meters per second | $1 \times 10^{-6}$ | $1 \times 10^6$ |
| circular mils | square centimeters | $5.067 \times 10^{-6}$ | $1.973 \times 10^5$ |
| circular mils | square mils | 0.7854 | 1.273 |
| cubic feet | gallons (liquid U.S.) | 7.481 | 0.1337 |
| cubic feet | liters | 28.32 | $3.531 \times 10^{-2}$ |
| cubic inches | cubic centimeters | 16.39 | $6.102 \times 10^{-2}$ |
| cubic inches | cubic feet | $5.787 \times 10^{-4}$ | 1728 |
| cubic inches | cubic meters | $1.639 \times 10^{-5}$ | $6.102 \times 10^4$ |
| cubic inches | gallons (liquid U.S.) | $4.329 \times 10^{-3}$ | 231 |
| cubic meters | cubic feet | 35.31 | $2.832 \times 10^{-2}$ |
| cubic meters | cubic yards | 1.308 | 0.7646 |
| curies | coulombs per minute | $1.1 \times 10^{12}$ | $0.91 \times 10^{-12}$ |
| cycles per second | hertz | 1 | 1 |
| degrees (angle) | mils | 17.45 | $5.73 \times 10^{-2}$ |
| degrees (angle) | radians | $1.745 \times 10^{-2}$ | 57.3 |
| dynes | pounds | $2.248 \times 10^{-6}$ | $4.448 \times 10^5$ |
| electron volts | joules | $1.602 \times 10^{-19}$ | $0.624 \times 10^{18}$ |
| ergs | foot-pounds | $7.376 \times 10^{-8}$ | $1.356 \times 10^7$ |
| ergs | joules | $10^{-7}$ | $10^7$ |
| ergs per second | watts | $10^{-7}$ | $10^7$ |
| ergs per square cm. | watts per square cm. | $10^{-3}$ | $10^3$ |
| Fahrenheit | kelvin | $(°F + 459.67)/1.8$ | $1.8K - 459.67$ |
| Fahrenheit | Rankine | $°F + 459.67 = °R$ | $°R - 459.67 = °F$ |
| faradays | ampere-hours | 26.8 | $3.731 \times 10^{-2}$ |
| feet | centimeters | 30.48 | $3.281 \times 10^{-2}$ |
| feet | meters | 0.3048 | 3.281 |
| feet | mils | $1.2 \times 10^4$ | $8.333 \times 10^{-5}$ |
| fermis | meters | $10^{-15}$ | $10^{15}$ |
| foot candles | lux | 10.764 | 0.0929 |
| foot lamberts | candelas per square meter | 3.4263 | 0.2918 |
| foot-pounds | gram-centimeters | $1.383 \times 10^4$ | $1.235 \times 10^{-5}$ |
| foot-pounds | horsepower-hours | $5.05 \times 10^{-7}$ | $1.98 \times 10^6$ |
| foot-pounds | kilogram-meters | 0.1383 | 7.233 |
| foot-pounds | kilowatt-hours | $3.766 \times 10^{-7}$ | $2.655 \times 10^6$ |
| foot-pounds | ounce-inches | 192 | $5.208 \times 10^{-3}$ |
| gallons (liquid U.S.) | cubic meters | $3.785 \times 10^{-3}$ | 264.2 |
| gallons (liquid U.S.) | gallons (liquid British Imperial) | 0.8327 | 1.201 |
| gammas | teslas | $10^{-9}$ | $10^9$ |
| gausses | lines per square cm. | 1.0 | 1.0 |
| gausses | lines per square inch | 6.452 | 0.155 |
| gausses | teslas | $10^{-4}$ | $10^4$ |
| gausses | webers per square inch | $6.452 \times 10^{-8}$ | $1.55 \times 10^7$ |
| gilberts | amperes | 0.7958 | 1.257 |
| grads | radians | $1.571 \times 10^{-2}$ | 63.65 |
| grains | grams | 0.06480 | 15.432 |
| grains | pounds | $^1/_{7000}$ | 7000 |
| grams | dynes | 980.7 | $1.02 \times 10^{-3}$ |
| grams | grains | 15.43 | $6.481 \times 10^{-2}$ |

| To convert | To | Multiply | For the reverse, multiply by |
|---|---|---|---|
| grams | ounces (avdp) | $3.527 \times 10^{-2}$ | 28.35 |
| grams | poundals | $7.093 \times 10^{-2}$ | 14.1 |
| hectares | acres | 2.471 | 0.4047 |
| horsepower | Btu per minute | 42.418 | $2.357 \times 10^{-2}$ |
| horsepower | foot-pounds per minute | $3.3 \times 10^4$ | $3.03 \times 10^{-5}$ |
| horsepower | foot-pounds per second | 550 | $1.182 \times 10^{-3}$ |
| horsepower | horsepower (metric) | 1.014 | 0.9863 |
| horsepower | kilowatts | 0.746 | 1.341 |
| inches | centimeters | 2.54 | 0.3937 |
| inches | feet | $8.333 \times 10^{-2}$ | 12 |
| inches | meters | $2.54 \times 10^{-2}$ | 39.37 |
| inches | miles | $1.578 \times 10^{-5}$ | $6.336 \times 10^4$ |
| inches | mils | $10^3$ | $10^{-3}$ |
| inches | yards | $2.778 \times 10^{-2}$ | 36 |
| joules | foot-pounds | 0.7376 | 1.356 |
| joules | watt-hours | $2.778 \times 10^{-4}$ | 3600 |
| kilograms | tons (long) | $9.842 \times 10^{-4}$ | 1016 |
| kilograms | tons (short) | $1.102 \times 10^{-3}$ | 907.2 |
| kilograms | pounds (avdp) | 2.205 | 0.4536 |
| kilometers | feet | 3281 | $3.408 \times 10^{-4}$ |
| kilometers | inches | $3.937 \times 10^4$ | $2.54 \times 10^{-5}$ |
| kilometers per hour | feet per minute | 54.68 | $1.829 \times 10^{-2}$ |
| kilowatt-hours | Btu | 3413 | $2.93 \times 10^{-4}$ |
| kilowatt-hours | foot-pounds | $2.655 \times 10^6$ | $3.766 \times 10^{-7}$ |
| kilowatt-hours | horsepower-hours | 1.341 | 0.7457 |
| kilowatt-hours | joules | $3.6 \times 10^6$ | $2.778 \times 10^{-7}$ |
| knots | feet per second | 1.688 | 0.5925 |
| knots | miles per hour | 1.1508 | 0.869 |
| lamberts | candles per square cm. | 0.3183 | 3.142 |
| lamberts | candles per square inch | 2.054 | 0.4869 |
| liters | cubic centimeters | $10^3$ | $10^{-3}$ |
| liters | cubic inches | 61.02 | $1.639 \times 10^{-2}$ |
| liters | gallons (liquid U.S.) | 0.2642 | 3.785 |
| liters | pints (liquid U.S.) | 2.113 | 0.4732 |
| lumens per square foot | foot-candles | 1 | 1 |
| lumens per square meter | foot-candles | 0.0929 | 10.764 |
| lux | foot-candles | 0.0929 | 10.764 |
| maxwells | kilolines | $10^{-3}$ | $10^3$ |
| maxwells | webers | $10^{-8}$ | $10^8$ |
| meters | feet | 3.28 | $30.48 \times 10^{-2}$ |
| meters | inches | 39.37 | $2.54 \times 10^{-2}$ |
| meters | miles | $6.214 \times 10^{-4}$ | 1609.35 |
| meters | yards | 1.094 | 0.9144 |
| miles (nautical) | feet | 6076.1 | $1.646 \times 10^{-4}$ |
| miles (nautical) | meters | 1852 | $5.4 \times 10^{-4}$ |
| miles (statute) | feet | 5280 | $1.894 \times 10^{-4}$ |
| miles (statute) | kilometers | 1.609 | 0.6214 |
| miles (statute) | miles (nautical) | 0.869 | 1.1508 |
| miles per hour | feet per second | 1.467 | 0.6818 |
| miles per hour | knots | 0.8684 | 1.152 |
| millimeters | microns | $10^3$ | $10^{-3}$ |

| To convert | To | Multiply | For the reverse, multiply by |
|---|---|---|---|
| mils | meters | $2.54 \times 10^{-5}$ | $3.94 \times 10^4$ |
| mils | minutes | 3.438 | 0.2909 |
| minutes (angle) | degrees | $1.666 \times 10^{-2}$ | 60 |
| minutes (angle) | radians | $2.909 \times 10^{-4}$ | 3484 |
| newtons | dynes | $10^5$ | $10^{-5}$ |
| newtons | kilograms | 0.1020 | 9.807 |
| newtons per sq. meter | pascals | 1 | 1 |
| newtons | pounds (avdp) | 0.2248 | 4.448 |
| oersteds | amperes per meter | $7.9577 \times 10$ | $1.257 \times 10^{-2}$ |
| ounces (fluid) | quarts | $3.125 \times 10^{-2}$ | 32 |
| ounces (avdp) | pounds | $6.25 \times 10^{-2}$ | 16 |
| pints | quarts (liquid U.S.) | 0.50 | 2 |
| poundals | dynes | $1.383 \times 10^4$ | $7.233 \times 10^{-5}$ |
| poundals | pounds (avdp) | $3.108 \times 10^{-2}$ | 32.17 |
| pounds | grams | 453.6 | $2.205 \times 10^{-3}$ |
| pounds (force) | newtons | 4.4482 | 0.2288 |
| pounds per square inch | dynes per square cm. | $6.8946 \times 10^4$ | $1.450 \times 10^{-5}$ |
| pounds per square inch | pascals | $6.895 \times 10^3$ | $1.45 \times 10^{-4}$ |
| quarts (U.S. liquid) | cubic centimeters | 946.4 | $1.057 \times 10^{-3}$ |
| radians | mils | $10^3$ | $10^{-3}$ |
| radians | minutes of arc | $3.438 \times 10^3$ | $2.909 \times 10^{-4}$ |
| radians | seconds of arc | $2.06265 \times 10^5$ | $4.848 \times 10^{-6}$ |
| revolutions per minute | radians per second | 0.1047 | 9.549 |
| roentgens | coulombs per kilogram | $2.58 \times 10^{-4}$ | $3.876 \times 10^3$ |
| slugs | kilograms | 1.459 | 0.6854 |
| slugs | pounds (avdp) | 32.174 | $3.108 \times 10^{-2}$ |
| square feet | square centimeters | 929.034 | $1.076 \times 10^{-3}$ |
| square feet | square inches | 144 | $6.944 \times 10^{-3}$ |
| square feet | square miles | $3.587 \times 10^{-8}$ | $27.88 \times 10^6$ |
| square inches | square centimeters | 6.452 | 0.155 |
| square kilometers | square miles | 0.3861 | 2.59 |
| stokes | square meter per second | $10^{-4}$ | $10^{-4}$ |
| tons (metric) | kilograms | $10^3$ | $10^{-3}$ |
| tons (short) | pounds | 2000 | $5 \times 10^{-4}$ |
| torrs | newtons per square meter | 133.32 | $7.5 \times 10^{-3}$ |
| watts | Btu per hour | 3.413 | 0.293 |
| watts | foot-pounds per minute | 44.26 | $2.26 \times 10^{-2}$ |
| watts | horsepower | $1.341 \times 10^{-3}$ | 746 |
| watt-seconds | joules | 1 | 1 |
| webers | maxwells | $10^8$ | $10^{-8}$ |
| webers per square meter | gausses | $10^4$ | $10^{-4}$ |

# CHAPTER 1

# DESCRIPTIVE STATISTICS

## GRAPHS AND FREQUENCY DISTRIBUTIONS

● **PROBLEM** 1-1

Discuss and distinguish between discrete and continuous values.

<u>Solution:</u>    The kinds of numbers that can take on any fractional or integer value between specified limits are categorized as continuous, whereas values that are usually restricted to whole-number values are called discrete. Thus, if we identify the number of people who use each of several brands of toothpaste, the data generated must be discrete. If we determine the heights and weights of a group of college men, the data generated is continuous.

However, in certain situations, fractional values are also integers. For example, stock prices are generally quoted to the one-eighth of a dollar. Since other fractional values between, say, 24.5 and 24.37 cannot occur, these values can be considered discrete. However, the discrete values that we consider are usually integers.

● **PROBLEM** 1-2

(a) Suppose a manufacturer conducts a study to determine the average retail price being charged for his product in a particular market area. Is such a variable discrete or continuous? (b) In conjunction with the previous study the manufacturer also wants to determine the number of units sold in the area during the week in which an advertising campaign was conducted. Is this variable discrete or continuous?

<u>Solution:</u>    (a) Since an average may take any fractional value, the average retail price is continuous.
    (b) We have a count. This variable must be discrete. The number of units sold is a discrete variable.

● **PROBLEM** 1-3

Twenty students are enrolled in the foreign language department, and their major fields are as follows:
Spanish, Spanish, French, Italian, French, Spanish, German, German, Russian, Russian, French, German, German, German, Spanish, Russian, German, Italian,

German, Spanish.

(a)  Make a frequency distribution table.
(b)  Make a frequency histogram.

Solution:    The frequency distribution table is constructed by writing down the major field and next to it
the number of students.

| Major Field | Number of Students |
|-------------|--------------------|
| German      | 7                  |
| Russian     | 3                  |
| Spanish     | 5                  |
| French      | 3                  |
| Italian     | 2                  |
| Total       | $\overline{20}$    |

A histogram follows:

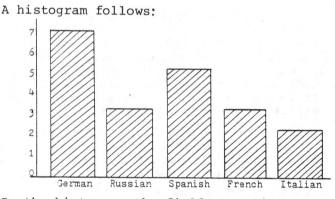

In the histogram, the fields are listed and spaced
evenly along the horizontal axis. Each specific field
is represented by a rectangle, and all have the same
width. The height of each, identified by a number on the
vertical axis, corresponds to the frequency of that field.

● **PROBLEM** 1-4

The IQ scores for a sample of 24 students who are entering
their first year of high school are:

| | | | |
|---|---|---|---|
| 115 | 119 | 119 | 134 |
| 121 | 128 | 128 | 152 |
| 97  | 108 | 98  | 130 |
| 108 | 110 | 111 | 122 |
| 106 | 142 | 143 | 140 |
| 141 | 151 | 125 | 126 |

(a) Make a cumulative percentage graph using classes of
seven points starting with 96 - 102.
(b) What scores are below the 25th percentile?
(C) What scores are above the 75th?
(d) What is the median score?

Solution:

| Interval | Interval Midpoint | Frequency | Cumulative Frequency | Cumulative Percentage |
|----------|-------------------|-----------|----------------------|-----------------------|
| 96-102   | 99   | 2 | 2  | 8.34   |
| 103-109  | 106  | 3 | 5  | 20.83  |
| 110-116  | 113  | 3 | 8  | 33.33  |
| 117-123  | 120  | 4 | 12 | 50.00  |
| 124-130  | 127  | 5 | 17 | 71.00  |
| 131-137  | 134  | 1 | 18 | 75.00  |
| 138-144  | 141  | 4 | 22 | 91.33  |
| 145-151  | 148  | 1 | 23 | 96.00  |
| 152-158  | 155  | 1 | 24 | 100.00 |

The frequency is the number of students in that interval. The cumulative frequency is the number of students in intervals up to and including that interval. The cumulative percentage is the percentage of students whose IQ's are at that level or below.

$$\text{Cumulative Percentage} = \frac{\text{Cumulative Frequency}}{24} \times 100 \text{ \%}.$$

We, will plot our graph using the interval midpoint as the x coordinate and the cumulative percentage as the y coordinate.

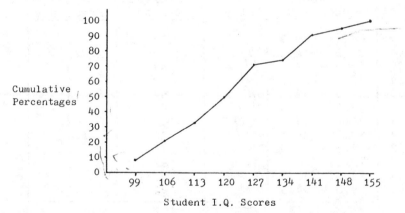

Student I.Q. Scores

(b)   The 25th percentile is defined to be a number that is exactly greater than the lowest 25 % of the scores. We want to know the score that is at least greater than (.25)24=6 other students. The 6 lowest scores are 97, 98, 106, 108, 108 and 110. We cannot use 111 as a 25th percentile since another student has that score so we use 110.5.

(c)   The 75th percentile is the score which exceeds the lowest 75% of the population but is less than the top 25 % of scores. We want the score below 6 students and above 18. The 6 highest scores are 152, 151, 143, 142, 141, 140. The next highest is 134. As our 75 % percentile we can take any value between 134 and 140. We will take 137, the average of 134 and 140.

(d) The median is the value which half of the values of the population exced and half do not. There are 12 values ≤ 123

3

and 12 values $\geq$ 124. Therefore we take as our median 123.5, the average of these two values. The median is the 50th percentile.

The following data is a sample of the accounts receivable of a small merchandising firm.

| 37 | 42 | 44 | 47 | 46 | 50 | 48 | 52 | 90 |
| 54 | 56 | 55 | 53 | 58 | 59 | 60 | 62 | 92 |
| 60 | 61 | 62 | 63 | 67 | 64 | 64 | 68 | |
| 67 | 65 | 66 | 68 | 69 | 66 | 70 | 72 | |
| 73 | 75 | 74 | 72 | 71 | 76 | 81 | 80 | |
| 79 | 80 | 78 | 82 | 83 | 85 | 86 | 88 | |

Using a class interval of 5, i.e. 35 - 39,

(a)  Make a frequency distribution table.
(b)  Construct a histogram.
(c)  Draw a frequency polygon.
(d)  Make a cumulative frequency distribution.
(e)  Construct a cumulative percentage ogive.

| Class Interval | Class Boundaries | Tally | Interval Median | Frequency |
|---|---|---|---|---|
| 35 - 39 | 34.5 - 39.5 | / | 37 | 1 |
| 40 - 44 | 39.5 - 44.5 | // | 42 | 2 |
| 45 - 49 | 44.5 - 49.5 | /// | 47 | 3 |
| 50 - 54 | 49.5 - 54.5 | //// | 52 | 4 |
| 55 - 59 | 54.5 - 59.5 | //// | 57 | 4 |
| 60 - 64 | 59.5 - 64.5 | //// /// | 62 | 8 |
| 65 - 69 | 64.5 - 69.5 | //// /// | 67 | 8 |
| 70 - 74 | 69.5 - 74.5 | //// / | 72 | 6 |
| 75 - 79 | 74.5 - 79.5 | //// | 77 | 4 |
| 80 - 84 | 79.5 - 84.5 | //// | 82 | 5 |
| 85 - 89 | 84.5 - 89.5 | /// | 87 | 3 |
| 90 - 94 | 89.5 - 94.5 | // | 92 | 2 |

We use fractional class boundaries. One reason for this is that we cannot break up the horizontal axis of the histogram into only integral values. We must do something with the fractional parts. The usual thing to do is to assign all values to the closest integer. Hence our above class boundaries. The appropriate histogram follows.

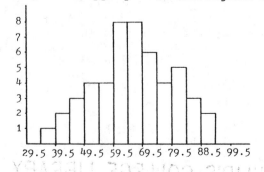

We now construct a frequency polygon as follows:

Plot points $(x_i, f_i)$, where $x_i$ is the interval median and $f_i$, the class frequency. Connect the points by successive line segments.

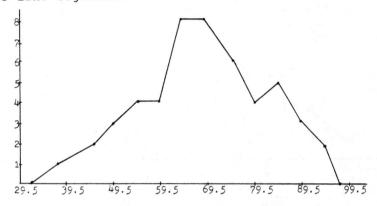

Accounts Receivable

| Interval | Interval Median | Frequency $(f_i)$ | Cumulative Frequency | Cumulative Percentage |
|---|---|---|---|---|
| 35 - 39 | 37 | 1 | 1 | 2 |
| 40 - 44 | 42 | 2 | 3 | 6 |
| 45 - 49 | 47 | 3 | 6 | 12 |
| 50 - 54 | 52 | 4 | 10 | 20 |
| 55 - 59 | 57 | 4 | 14 | 28 |
| 60 - 64 | 62 | 8 | 22 | 44 |
| 65 - 69 | 67 | 8 | 30 | 60 |
| 70 - 74 | 72 | 6 | 36 | 72 |
| 75 - 79 | 77 | 4 | 40 | 80 |
| 80 - 84 | 82 | 5 | 45 | 90 |
| 85 - 89 | 87 | 3 | 48 | 96 |
| 90 - 94 | 92 | 2 | 50 | 100 |

The cumulative frequency is the number of values in all classes up to and including that class. It is obtained by addition. For example, the cumulative frequency for 65 - 69 is 1 + 2 + 3 + 4 + 4 + 8 + 8 = 30. The cumulative percentage is the percent of all observed values found in that class or below. We can use the formula -

$$\text{cumulative percentage} = \frac{\text{cumulative frequency}}{\text{total observations}} \times 100 \ \%.$$

For example, Cum. per. (65-69) $= \frac{30}{50} \times 100 \ \% = 60 \ \%.$

We construct the cumulative percentage ogive by plotting points $(x_i, f_i)$ where $x_i$ is the interval median and $f_i$ is the cumulative frequency. Finally we connect the points with successive line segments.

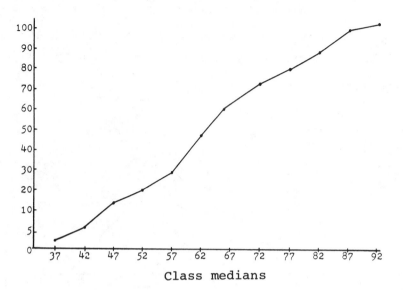

Class medians

In the following chart, make 2 additional columns and fill in the cumulative frequencies and cumulative percentages. Also draw a histogram and a cumulative frequency diagram.

Relative Frequency Distribution of 100 Sixth-Grade Students and their Weights

| Class | Frequency $(f_i)$ | Relative Frequency | Percentage Distribution |
|---|---|---|---|
| 59-61 | 4 | 4/100 | 4 |
| 62-64 | 8 | 8/100 | 8 |
| 65-67 | 12 | 12/100 | 12 |
| 68-70 | 13 | 13/100 | 13 |
| 71-73 | 21 | 21/100 | 21 |
| 74-76 | 15 | 15/100 | 15 |
| 77-79 | 12 | 12/100 | 12 |
| 80-82 | 9 | 9/100 | 9 |
| 83-85 | 4 | 4/100 | 4 |
| 86-88 | 2 | 2/100 | 2 |
| | 100 | | 100% |

Solution:    The relative frequency of a class is found by dividing the class frequency by the total number of observations in the sample. The results, when multiplied by 100, form a percentage distribution. The class relative frequencies and the percentage distribution of the weights of 100 sixth grade students are given in the above table.

The relative frequency of a class is the empirical probability that a random observation from the population will fall into that class. For example, the relative frequency of the class 59-61 in the table is 4/100, and therefore, the empirical probability that a random observation falling in this interval is 4/100.

The table allows us to determine the percentage of the observations in a sample that lie in a particular class. When we want to know the percentage of observations that is above or below a specified interval, the cumulative frequency distribution can be used to advantage. The cumulative frequency distribution is obtained by adding the frequencies in all classes less than or equal to the class with which we are concerned. To find the percentage in each class just divide the frequency by the total number of observations and multiply by 100 %. In this example, $\frac{x}{100} \times 100$ % = x %. Now we can find the cumulative percentages by taking the cumulative frequencies.

$$\text{Cum. percentage} = \frac{y \text{ cumulative frequency}}{\text{total observations}} \times 100 \text{ \%} =$$

$$= \frac{y}{100} \times 100\% = y\%.$$

Cumulative Frequency and Cumulative Percentage Distribution of the 100 Sixth-Grade Students

| Class | Frequency $(f_i)$ | Cumulative Frequency | Cumulative Percentage |
|-------|-----------|------------|------------|
| 59-61 | 4 | 4 | 4 |
| 62-64 | 8 | 12 | 12 |
| 65-67 | 12 | 24 | 24 |
| 68-70 | 13 | 37 | 37 |
| 71-73 | 21 | 58 | 58 |
| 74-76 | 15 | 73 | 73 |
| 77-79 | 12 | 85 | 85 |
| 80-82 | 9 | 94 | 94 |
| 83-85 | 4 | 98 | 98 |
| 86-89 | 2 | 100 | 100 % |
| | 100 | | |

The data in a frequency distribution may be represented graphically by a histogram. The histogram is constructed by marking off the class boundaries along a horizontal axis and drawing a rectangle to represent each class. The base of the rectangle corresponds to the class width, and the height to that class' frequency. See the accompanying histogram depicting the data on the table in the beginning of the problem. Note that the areas above the various classes are proportional to the frequency of those classes.

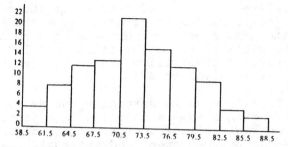

Frequency Histogram of the Weights of the 100
Sixth-Grade Students

Often a frequency polygon is used instead of a
histogram. In constructing a frequency polygon, the
points $(x_i, f_i)$ are plotted on horizontal and vertical
axes. The polygon is completed by adding a class mark with
zero    frequency to each end of the distribution and
joining all the points with line segments. The frequency
diagram for the data in this problem follows:

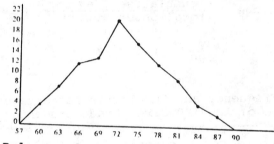

Frequency Polygon of the Weights of 100 Sixth-Grade
Students

A frequency polygon may also be constructed by
connecting the midpoints of the bars in a frequency
histogram by a series of line segments. The main advantage of the frequency polygon compared to the frequency
histogram is that it indicates that the observations in
the interval are not all the same. Also, when several
sets of data are to be shown on the same graph, it is
clearer to superimpose frequency polygons than histograms,
especially if class boundaries coincide.

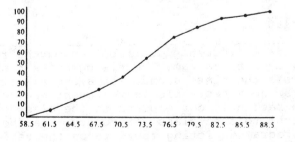

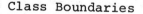

Class Boundaries

Cumulative Frequency Graph of the Weights of 100 Sixth-
Grade Students

It is often advantageous and desirable to make a graph showing the cumulative frequency within a sample. The data for such a graph depicting the cumulative frequency of the weights of the 100 sixth grade students are found in column three of the table in the solution. The graph, called an ogive, is illustrated below. To avoid the confusion of less than or greater than, the class boundaries are plotted on the horizontal axis rather than the interval medians.

A cumulative frequency graph makes it easy to read such items as the percentage of students whose weights are less than or greater than a specified weight. If the cumulative percentage had been plotted, the graph would appear the same as above but would be called a percentage ogive.

# MEASURES OF CENTRAL TENDENCY

● **PROBLEM** 1-7

Find the mean salary for four company employees who make $ 5/hr., $ 8/hr., $ 12/hr., and $ 15/hr.

Solution:  The mean salary is the average.

$$\bar{X} = \frac{\Sigma\ x_i}{n} = \frac{\$\ 5 + \$\ 8 + \$\ 12 + \$\ 15}{4} = \frac{\$\ 40}{4} = \$\ 10/hr.$$

● **PROBLEM** 1-8

Find the mean weight of the sample of trout that weighed 2 lbs., 3 lbs., 6 lbs., 8 lbs., and 9 lbs.

Solution:  The mean weight is the average.

Let $x_1 = 2$, $x_2 = 3$, $x_3 = 6$, $x_4 = 8$, $x_5 = 9$. Therefore,

$$\bar{X} = \frac{\Sigma\ x_i}{n} = \frac{x_1 + x_2 + x_3 + x_4 + x_5}{5} = \frac{2 + 3 + 6 + 8 + 9}{5}$$

$$= \frac{28}{5} = 5.6\ lbs.$$

● **PROBLEM** 1-9

Find the mean length of five fish with lengths of 7.5 in., 7.75 in., 8.5 in., 8.5 in., 8.25 in.

Solution:   The mean length is the average length.

$$\bar{X} = \frac{\Sigma\ x_i}{n} = \frac{7.5 + 7.75 + 8.5 + 8.5 + 8.25}{5} = \frac{40.5}{5} = 8.1\ in.$$

9

A motor car traveled 3 consecutive miles, the first mile at $x_1 = 35$ miles per hour (mph), the second at $x_2 = 48$ mph, and the third at $x_3 = 40$ mph. Find the average speed of the car in miles per hour.

**Solution:** Distance = Rate × Time. Therefore,

$$\text{Time} = \frac{\text{Distance}}{\text{Rate}}.$$

For the first mile, $\text{Time} = \dfrac{1 \text{ mile}}{35 \text{ miles/hour}} = \dfrac{1}{35}$ hour.

For the second mile, $\text{Time} = \dfrac{1 \text{ mile}}{48 \text{ miles/hour}} = \dfrac{1}{48}$ hour.

For the third mile, $\text{Time} = \dfrac{1 \text{ mile}}{40 \text{ miles/hour}} = \dfrac{1}{40}$ hour.

Total time $= T_1 + T_2 + T_3 = \dfrac{1}{35} + \dfrac{1}{48} + \dfrac{1}{40}$.

Converting to decimals, $\text{Time}_{tot} = .0286 + .0208 + .025$

$$= .0744 \text{ hours}.$$

The average speed can be computed by the following formula:

$$\text{Average Speed} = \frac{\text{Total distance}}{\text{Total time}} = \frac{3 \text{ miles}}{.0744 \text{ hours}} = 40.32 \text{ mph}.$$

Average speed is an example of a harmonic mean. The harmonic is,

$$H = \frac{3}{\dfrac{1}{T_1} + \dfrac{1}{T_2} + \dfrac{1}{T_3}}.$$

Find the median of the sample 34, 29, 26, 37, 31.

**Solution:** The median, a measure of central tendency, is the middle number. The number of observations that lie above the median is the same as the number of observations that lie below it.

Arranged in order we have 26, 29, 31, 34 and 37. The number of observations is odd and thus the median is 31. Note that there are two numbers in the sample above 31 and two below 31.

● **PROBLEM** 1-12

Find the median of the sample 34, 29, 26, 37, 31 and 34.

Solution:    The sample arranged in order is 26, 29, 31, 34, 34, and 37. The number of observations is even and thus the median, or middle number is chosen halfway between the third and fourth number. In this case the median is

$$\frac{31 + 34}{2} = 32.5.$$

● **PROBLEM** 1-13

What is the value of the median for the numbers 5, 8, 12, 3, 9?

Solution:    In ascending order, the values are

3, 5, 8, 9, 12.

We have a sample of 5. The median is the middle or third value 8.

● **PROBLEM** 1-14

Find the median age in a sample of 6 children with ages 3, 6, 4, 7, 9, 8.

Solution:    Arranging the observations in order, we have 3, 4, 6, 7, 8, 9. There are six observations in the sample so the median will be the average of the third and fourth observations, 6 and 7. The median is

$$\frac{6 + 7}{2} = 6\frac{1}{2}.$$

● **PROBLEM** 1-15

Arrange the values 7, 8, 5, 10, 3 in ascending order and identify the value of the median.

Solution:    In ascending order the numbers are

3, 5, 7, 8, 10.

The median is the middle value. In the case of 5 observations, it will be the third, 7.

11

What is the value of the median for the numbers
(a) 7, 9, 2, 2, 8, 11? (b) 3, 5, 6, 6, 8, 9?

Solution:      (a) We first arrange the values in ascending
order; 2, 2, 7, 8, 9, 11. We have six observations. When
there is an even number of measurements, there is no one
middle value. We assume that the median can be found midway between the 2 middle values. The 2 middle values are
7 and 8. Hence,

$$\frac{7 + 8}{2} = 7.5 \text{ is the median.}$$

(b) Since the values are already in ascending order, we see
the two middle values are 6 and 6; the median is also 6.

● **PROBLEM** 1-17

What is the median of the following set of observations?
What is the mode?  55,      55, 50, 53, 54, 53, 54, 55, 56,
58, 60, 54, 54, 55, 58, 52, 54, 56, 57, 59.

Solution:      Let us first write the observations in
ascending order.

50, 52, 53, 53, 54, 54, 54, 54, 54, 55, 55, 55,
55, 56, 56, 57, 58, 58, 59, 60.

There are 20 observations. The median is the one in the
middle, however, since there are an even number of observations, the median is the average of the two middle values.
Both the tenth and the eleventh equal 55, so the median is
55. The mode is the observation that occurs the most frequently. Here it is 54, which occurs five times.

● **PROBLEM** 1-18

Find the mode of the sample 14, 19, 16, 21, 18, 19, 24, 15
and 19.

Solution:      The mode is another measure of central tendency in a data set. It is the observation or observations
that occur with the greatest frequency. The number 19 is
observed three times in this sample and no other observation
appears as frequently.      The mode of this sample is 19.

● **PROBLEM** 1-19

Find the mode or modes of the sample 6, 7, 7, 3, 8, 5,
3, 9.

Solution:     In this sample the numbers 7 and 3 both
appear twice. There are no other observations that appear
as frequently as these two. Therefore 3 and 7 are the
modes of this sample. The sample is called "bimodal".

● **PROBLEM** 1-20

Find the mode of the sample 14, 16, 21, 19, 18, 24 and
17.

Solution:     In this sample all the numbers occur with
the same frequency. There is no single number which is
observed more frequently than any other. Thus there is
no mode or all observations are modes. The mode is not a
useful concept here.

● **PROBLEM** 1-21

Find the mode for the sample composed of the observations
4, 5, 6, 6, 6, 7, 7, 8.

Solution:     The mode is the observation that appears most
often. That is 6.

● **PROBLEM** 1-22

A sample of 9 patients in the intensive care unit of
Mt. Sinai Hospital were questioned. The number of heart
attacks that they had suffered numbered 2, 3, 4, 5, 5,
6, 7, 7, 10. Find the mode.

Solution:     The mode is the observation that appears
most often in the sample. Both 5 and 7 appear twice in
the data while the other observations appear only once.
Both observations, 5 and 7, are modes. This sample is
called "bimodal".

● **PROBLEM** 1-23

The number of home runs the Boston Red Sox hit in eight
consecutive games were 2, 3, 0, 3, 4, 1, 3, 0.

(a) What is the mean number of home runs hit?
(b) What is the median?
(c) What is the mode?

Solution:     (a) The mean number of home runs hit is the
average per game.

$$\bar{X} = \frac{\Sigma\ x_i}{n} = \frac{2 + 3 + 0 + 3 + 4 + 1 + 3 + 0}{8} = \frac{16}{8} = 2.$$

13

(b)   The median is the middle value. Since we have an even numbered sample we take the value halfway between the two central values, the fourth and fifth. We must put the data in ascending order,

$$0, \ 0, \ 1, \ 2, \ 3, \ 3, \ 3, \ 4 \ .$$
$$\uparrow \ \uparrow$$

The median will be 2.5, the value which is halfway between 2 and 3.

(c)   The observation 3 appears most often, three times, and is the mode.

● PROBLEM 1-24

Given the following set of ungrouped measurements

3, 5, 6, 6, 7, and 9,

determine the mean, median, and mode.

Solution:   The mean is the average value of the measurements,

$$\bar{X} = \frac{\sum_i x_i}{n} = \frac{3 + 5 + 6 + 6 + 7 + 9}{6} = \frac{36}{6} = 6.$$

The median is the middle value. Since we have an even number of measurements, we take as the median the value halfway between the 2 middle values. In this case the 2 middle values are both 6 and hence the median is

$$\frac{6 + 6}{2} = 6.$$

The mode is the most common value. Therefore, it is 6, the same as the mean and the median.

● PROBLEM 1-25

Consider the distribution of the previous problem. Let us add 2 relatively high values in order to observe the differential effect on the three measures of central tendency. Use the following eight ordered values: 3, 5, 6, 6, 7, 9, 16, 20.

Solution:   (a) First the mean.

$$\bar{X} = \frac{\sum_i x_i}{n} = \frac{3 + 5 + 6 + 6 + 7 + 9 + 16 + 20}{8} = \frac{72}{8} = 9.$$

We have 8 (an even number) observations. The median will be halfway between the two middle ones, the fourth and fifth. Halfway between 6 and 7 is 6.5. The mode is still easily found. The only value that appears more than once is still 6.

Comparing the measures of central tendency for the data of the last two problems, we find that the measure which is most affected by the addition of extreme measurements is the mean; the measure which is only somewhat affected is the median; the measure which is unaffected is the mode.

● **PROBLEM** 1-26

For this series of observations find the mean, median, and mode.

500, 600, 800, 800, 900, 900, 900, 900, 900, 1000, 1100

Solution:    The mean is the value obtained by adding all the measurements and dividing by the numbers of measurements.

$$\overline{X} = \frac{\sum_i x_i}{n}$$

$$\overline{X} = \frac{500+600+800+800+900+900+900+900+900+1000+1100}{11}$$

$$\overline{X} = \frac{9300}{11} = 845.45.$$

The median is the observation in the middle. We have 11, so here it is the sixth, 900.

The mode is the observation that appears most frequently. That is also 900, which has 5 appearances.

All three of these numbers are measures of central tendency. They describe the "middle" or "center" of the data.

● **PROBLEM** 1-27

Nine rats run through a maze. The time each rat took to traverse the maze is recorded and these times are listed below.

1 min., 2.5 min., 3 min., 1.5 min., 2 min., 1.25 min., 1 min., .9 min., 30 min.

Which of the three measures of central tendency would be the most appropriate in this case?

Solution: We will calculate the three measures of central tendency and then compare them to determine which would be the most appropriate in describing these data.

The mean, $\overline{X}$, is the sum of observations divided by

15

the number of observations. In this case,

$$\bar{X} = \frac{1 + 2.5 + 3 + 1.5 + 2 + 1.25 + 1 + .9 + 30}{9}$$

$$= \frac{43.15}{9} = 4.79.$$

The median is the "middle number" in an array of the observations from the lowest to the highest.

0.9, 1.0, 1.0, 1.25, 1.5, 2.0, 2.5, 3.0, 30.0

The median is the fifth observation in this array or 1.5. There are four observations larger than 1.5 and four observations smaller than 1.5.

The mode is the most frequently occurring observation in the sample. In this data set the mode is 1.0.

mean, $\bar{X}$ = 4.79

median  = 1.5

mode   = 1.0

The mean is not appropriate here. Only one rat took more than    4.79 minutes to run the maze and this rat took 30 minutes. We see that the mean has been distorted by this one large observation.

The median or mode seem to describe this data set better and        would be more appropriate to use.

# MEASURES OF DISPERSION

● PROBLEM 1-28

A family had eight children. The ages were 9, 11, 8, 15, 14, 12, 17, 14.

(a) Find the measures of central tendency for the data.
(b) Find the range of the data.

Solution:    (a) The mean is the average age.

$$\bar{X} = \frac{\Sigma x_i}{n} = \frac{9 + 11 + 8 + 15 + 14 + 12 + 17 + 14}{8}$$

$$= \frac{100}{8} = 12.5 \text{ years.}$$

The median is the middle value. To find it, first we must arrange our data in ascending order;

8, 9, 11, 12, 14, 14, 15, 17.

We have an even number of measurements, eight.

The median will be the midway point between the fourth and fifth observations, 12 and 14. The median is 13.

The mode is the most common age. Only one age, 14, appears more than once. 14 must be the mode.

(b)   Often we want to know how spread out the observations of data were . The range of the sample is a quantity which measures dispersion. We define the range to be the difference between the largest and smallest observations in our sample. In this case, R      = 17 - 8 = 9.

● **PROBLEM** 1-29

The staff of a small company sign a timesheet indicating the time they leave the office.

These times for a randomly chosen day are given below,

|       |       |       |
|-------|-------|-------|
| 5:15  | 4:50  | 1:50  |
| 5:30  | 2:45  | 5:15  |
| 5:00  | 5:30  | 5:30  |
| 5:30  | 4:55  | 4:20  |
| 5:20  | 5:30  | 5:20  |
| 5:25  | 5:00  |       |

How do the three measures of central tendency describe the data? How variable is the data? What is the variance and standard deviation?

Solution:      The following table, lists the departure times in ascending order. It also aids in the computation of the moments. In order to compute averages, we must first convert each departure time to a score which can be meaningfully added and multiplied. We will then convert back to a time after the computations. Let 12:00 noon be zero and convert each departure time to the number of hours from 12 noon. Thus 5:00 PM would be converted to 5. 5:20 PM would be converted to $5 \frac{1}{3}$ hours or 5.33, etc.

The median is the middle observation, in this case the 9th observation. Thus the median is 5.25 = 5 1/4 or 5:15 PM.

The mode is the most frequent observation. For our sample, the mode is 5:30 PM which appears 5 times.

The variance and standard deviation describe the variation or dispersion in a sample. The formula for the sample variance is,

$$ s^2 = \frac{\Sigma (X_i - \bar{X})^2}{n} = \frac{\Sigma X_i^2 - n\bar{X}^2}{n} = \frac{\Sigma X_i^2}{n} - \bar{X}^2 $$

| Converted Departure Time $X_i$ | $X_i^2$ |
|---|---|
| $1 + \frac{50}{60} = 1.83$ | 3.35 |
| 2.75 | 7.56 |
| 4.34 | 18.83 |
| 4.83 | 23.32 |
| 4.92 | 24.21 |
| 5.00 | 25.00 |
| 5.00 | 25.00 |
| 5.25 | 27.56 |
| 5.25 | 27.56 |
| 5.34 | 28.52 |
| 5.34 | 28.52 |
| 5.42 | 29.38 |
| 5.5 | 30.25 |
| 5.5 | 30.25 |
| 5.5 | 30.25 |
| 5.5 | 30.25 |
| 5.5 | 30.25 |

We can now compute the three measures of central tendency:

$$\bar{X} = \frac{\Sigma X_i}{n}$$

$$= \frac{\text{sum of observations}}{\text{number of observations}}$$

$$= \frac{82.77}{17} = 4.87$$

$$= 4 \frac{87}{100} = 4 \frac{52}{60} \text{ PM}$$

$$= 4:52 \text{ PM}$$

$\Sigma X_i = 82.77$  $\Sigma X_i^2 = 420.06$.  Thus,

$$s^2 = \frac{420.06}{17} - (4.87)^2$$

$$= .9925 \text{ (hours)}^2 = 3573 \text{ (min.)}^2.$$

The standard deviation is

$$s = \sqrt{s^2} = \sqrt{\frac{\Sigma X_i^2}{n} - \bar{X}^2} = \sqrt{.9925} = .9962 \text{ hours}$$

$$= 59.7 \text{ minutes}.$$

Note that the standard deviation is slightly preferable because it is expressed in meaningful units, minutes. The variance is expressed in $(\text{minutes})^2$.

● **PROBLEM** 1-30

Find the range of the sample composed of the observations: 33, 53, 35, 37, 49.

Solution:    The range is a measure of dispersion of the sample and is defined to be the difference between the largest and smallest observations.

In our sample, the largest observation is 53 and the smallest is 33. The difference is 53 - 33 = 20 and the range is 20.

The range is not a very satisfactory measure of
dispersion as it involves only two of the observations in
the sample.

● **PROBLEM** 1-31

Find the range of the sample composed of the observations
3, 12, 15, 7, 9.

Solution:    The range is the difference between the largest
and smallest observations. The largest observation is 15
and the smallest is 3.        The range is 15 - 3 = 12.

● **PROBLEM** 1-32

Find the midrange of this sample of SAT-Verbal scores.
The sample had the smallest observation of 426 and the
largest at 740.

Solution:    The midrange is the number halfway between
the largest and smallest observations. In this case;

$$\text{midrange} = \frac{426 + 740}{2} = \frac{1166}{2} = 583.$$

● **PROBLEM** 1-33

Given the values 4, 4, 6, 7, 9 give the deviation of each
from the mean.

Solution:    First find the mean.

$$\overline{X} = \frac{\Sigma \, x_i}{n} = \frac{4 + 4 + 6 + 7 + 9}{5} = \frac{30}{5} = 6.$$

$X - \overline{X}$ = the deviation from the mean.

We will provide the deviations in tabular form.

| X | $X - \overline{X}$ |
|---|---|
| 4 | 4 - 6 = - 2 |
| 4 | 4 - 6 = - 2 |
| 6 | 6 - 6 =   0 |
| 7 | 7 - 6 = + 1 |
| 9 | 9 - 6 = + 3 |

● **PROBLEM** 1-34

Compute the average deviation for the following sample
representing the age at which men in a Chataqua bowling
club scored their first game over 175.

19

```
29
36
42
48
49
56
59
62
64
65
```

Solution:    The average deviation is the average absolute
deviation from the mean. The average deviation is an alternate measure of variation, in a sample. It is defined as

$$A.D. = \frac{\Sigma |X_i - \overline{X}|}{n},$$

where $X_i$ are the individual observations, $\overline{X}$ the sample
mean and n the number of observations.

$|X_i - \overline{X}|$ = the absolute value of the difference between
the ith observation and $\overline{X}$.

$$\overline{X} = \frac{\Sigma X_i}{n} = \frac{29+36+42+48+49+56+59+62+64+65}{10} = \frac{510}{10} = 51.$$

$$\Sigma |X_i - \overline{X}| = |29-51| + |36-51| + |42-51| + |48-51|$$
$$+ |49-51| + |56-51| + |59-51| + |62-51|$$
$$+ |64-51| + |65-51|$$
$$= 22 + 15 + 9 + 3 + 2 + 5 + 8 + 11 + 13 + 14 = 102.$$

Thus,   A.D. $= \frac{102}{n} = \frac{102}{10} = 10.2.$

● PROBLEM 1-35

Find the variance of the sample of observations 2, 5, 7,
9, 12.

Solution:    The variance of the sample is defined as

$$s^2 = \frac{\Sigma (X_i - \overline{X})^2}{n}.$$ This is an average of the squared

deviations from the sample mean, $\overline{X}$.

$$\overline{X} = \frac{\Sigma X_i}{n} = \frac{2 + 5 + 7 + 9 + 12}{5} = \frac{35}{5} = 7$$

and   $s^2 = \frac{(2-7)^2 + (5-7)^2 + (7-7)^2 + (9-7)^2 + (12-7)^2}{5}$

20

$$= \frac{25 + 4 + 0 + 4 + 25}{5} = \frac{58}{5} = 11.6.$$

### ● PROBLEM 1-36

A couple has six children whose ages are 6, 8, 10, 12, 14, and 16. Find the variance in ages.

Solution:    The variance in ages is a measure of the spread or dispersion of ages about the sample mean.

To compute the variance we first calculate the sample mean.

$$\overline{X} = \frac{\Sigma X_i}{n} = \frac{\text{sum of observations}}{\text{number of observations}}$$

$$= \frac{6 + 8 + 10 + 12 + 14 + 16}{6} = \frac{66}{6} = 11.$$

The variance is defined to be

$$s^2 = \frac{\sum\limits_{i=1}^{n} (X_i - \overline{X})^2}{n}$$

$$= \frac{(6-11)^2+(8-11)^2+(10-11)^2+(12-11)^2+(14-11)^2+(16-11)^2}{6}$$

$$= \frac{25 + 9 + 1 + 1 + 9 + 25}{6} = \frac{70}{6} = 11.7.$$

### ● PROBLEM 1-37

From the sample of data 5, 8, 2, 1, compute the standard deviation of the sample.

Solution:    The degree to which numerical data tends to spread about an average value is usually called dispersion or variation of the data. One way to measure the degree of dispersion is with the standard deviation. We define it as

$$s = \sqrt{\frac{\sum\limits_{i} (X_i - \overline{X})^2}{n}} .$$

It gives a feeling for how far away from the mean we can expect an observation to be. Sometimes the standard deviation for the data of a sample is defined with n - 1 replacing n in the denominator of our expression. The resulting value represents a "better" estimate of the true standard deviation of the entire population. For large n (n > 30) there is practically no difference between the 2 values. Let us find the mean for our sample.

21

$$\overline{X} = \frac{\Sigma X_i}{n} = \frac{5 + 8 + 2 + 1}{n} = \frac{16}{4} = 4 \ .$$

| $X_i$ | $X_i - \overline{X}$ | $(X_i - \overline{X})^2$ |
|-------|----------------------|--------------------------|
| 5 | $5 - 4 = 1$ | $1^2 = 1$ |
| 8 | $8 - 4 = 4$ | $4^2 = 16$ |
| 2 | $2 - 4 = -2$ | $(-2)^2 = 4$ |
| 1 | $1 - 4 = -3$ | $(-3)^2 = 9$ |

$$\Sigma (X_i - \overline{X})^2 = 1 + 16 + 4 + 9 = 30$$

$$n = 4$$

$$s = \sqrt{\frac{\Sigma (X_i - \overline{X})^2}{n}} = \sqrt{\frac{30}{4}} = \sqrt{\frac{15}{2}} = \sqrt{7.5} = 2.74.$$

● **PROBLEM** 1-38

In 1976, the top eight male tennis players won the following number of tournaments:

| | | | |
|---|---|---|---|
| Jimmy Connors | 4 | Manolo Orantes | 3 |
| Bjorn Borg | 4 | Raul Ramirez | 2 |
| Ilie Nastase | 4 | Adriano Panotta | 2 |
| Guillermo Vilas | 3 | Roscoe Tanner | 2 |

Find the standard deviation of the number of tournaments won by the top eight players.

Solution: The basic formula for the standard deviation is:

$$S_x = \sqrt{\frac{\Sigma (X - \overline{X})^2}{n}} \ .$$

Let us first find the mean, $\overline{X}$.

$$\overline{X} = \frac{\Sigma X_i}{n} = \frac{2 + 2 + 2 + 3 + 3 + 4 + 4 + 4}{8} = \frac{24}{8} = 3 \ .$$

Computations in the following table will be helpful.

| $X$ | $(X - \overline{X})$ | $(X - \overline{X})^2$ |
|-----|----------------------|------------------------|
| 2 | $2 - 3 = -1$ | $(-1)^2 = 1$ |
| 2 | $2 - 3 = -1$ | $(-1)^2 = 1$ |
| 2 | $2 - 3 = -1$ | $(-1)^2 = 1$ |
| 3 | $3 - 3 = 0$ | $(0)^2 = 0$ |
| 3 | $3 - 3 = 0$ | $(0)^2 = 0$ |
| 4 | $4 - 3 = 1$ | $1^2 = 1$ |
| 4 | $4 - 3 = 1$ | $1^2 = 1$ |
| 4 | $4 - 3 = 1$ | $1^2 = 1$ |

$$\Sigma (X - \mu)^2 = 6; \ (\mu = \overline{X})$$

Dividing $\Sigma(X - u)^2$ by n yields $\dfrac{\Sigma(X - \mu)^2}{n} = \dfrac{6}{8} = .75.$

Taking the square root, $S_x = \sqrt{\dfrac{\Sigma(X - \mu)^2}{n}} = \sqrt{0.75} = .866.$

● **PROBLEM** 1-39

Compute the standard deviations for the following sample of measurements, given that $\overline{X} = 8.0$ and

$$s = \sqrt{\dfrac{\displaystyle\sum_{i=1}^{n}(X_i - \overline{X})^2}{n}} \quad \text{and } X = 5, 7, 8, 9, 11.$$

<u>Solution:</u> The standard deviation is a measure of <u>dispersion</u> about the sample mean $\overline{X}$.

$$s = \sqrt{\dfrac{\displaystyle\sum_{i=1}^{n}(X_i - \overline{X})^2}{n}}$$

is one formula for the standard deviation, where the $X_i$ are the actual observations and n is the number of observations in the sample.

In this case

$$s = \sqrt{\dfrac{(5-8)^2 + (7-8)^2 + (8-8)^2 + (9-8)^2 + (11-8)^2}{5}}$$

$$= \sqrt{\dfrac{3^2 + 1^2 + 0^2 + 1^2 + 3^2}{5}} = \sqrt{\dfrac{20}{5}} = \sqrt{4} = 2.$$

● **PROBLEM** 1-40

Find the standard deviation of the sample of measurements 1, 3, 7, 10, 14.

<u>Solution:</u> We first compute,

$$\overline{X} = \dfrac{\Sigma X_i}{n} = \dfrac{1 + 3 + 7 + 10 + 14}{5} = \dfrac{35}{5} = 7,$$

the sample mean. Next we compute the standard deviation, s, a measure of dispersion about the sample mean.

$$s = \sqrt{\dfrac{\displaystyle\sum_{i=1}^{n}(X_i - \overline{X})^2}{n}}$$

$$= \sqrt{\frac{(1-7)^2+(3-7)^2+(7-7)^2+(10-7)^2+(14-7)^2}{5}}$$

$$= \sqrt{\frac{36 + 16 + 0 + 9 + 49}{5}} = \sqrt{22} = 4.69.$$

● **PROBLEM** 1-41

Find the standard deviation of the sample of measurements
3, 10, 10, 11, 15, 15, 26, 30.

Solution: To find the standard deviation of this sample
we first compute the sample mean $\overline{X}$.

$$\overline{X} = \frac{\text{sum of observations}}{\text{number of observations}} = \frac{\Sigma X_i}{n} .$$

In this problem, n = 8 so

$$\overline{X} = \frac{3 + 10 + 10 + 11 + 15 + 15 + 26 + 30}{8} = \frac{120}{8} = 15 .$$

The standard deviation is

$$s = \sqrt{\frac{\Sigma (X_i - \overline{X})^2}{n}}$$

$$= \sqrt{\frac{(3-15)^2+(10-15)^2+(10-15)^2+(11-15)^2+(15-15)^2+(15-15)^2}{8}}$$

$$\overline{+(26-15)^2+(30-15)^2}$$

$$= \sqrt{\frac{556}{8}} = \sqrt{69.5} = 8.34 .$$

● **PROBLEM** 1-42

A survey asking for the number of times toast is burned
during one week was distributed to eight randomly selected
households. The survey yielded the following results:

2, 3, 0, 3, 4, 1, 3, 0.

What is the range, variance and standard deviation for
this data set?

Solution: The range is the difference between the
largest and smallest observations is 4 - 0 = 4.

The variance is the mean or average squared
deviation from $\overline{X}$. To compute the variance of this sample

we use the formula

$$s^2 = \frac{\Sigma X^2 - n\bar{X}^2}{n} \quad .$$

To facilitate the computation we use the following table,

| X | $X^2$ |
|---|---|
| 2 | 4 |
| 3 | 9 |
| 0 | 0 |
| 3 | 9 |
| 4 | 16 |
| 1 | 1 |
| 3 | 9 |
| 0 | 0 |
| $\Sigma X = 16$ | $\Sigma X^2 = 48$ |

Thus $\quad \bar{X} = \frac{\Sigma X}{n} = \frac{16}{8} = 2 \quad$ and

$$s^2 = \frac{48 - 8(2)^2}{8} = \frac{48 - 8(4)}{8} = \frac{16}{8} = 2 \quad .$$

The standard deviation is

$$s = \sqrt{s^2} = \sqrt{2} = 1.414 .$$

● **PROBLEM 1-43**

Find the sample variance and sample standard deviation for the sample data 21, 17, 13, 25, 9, 19, 6 and 10. Remember the sample variance $s^2$ is defined to be

$$s^2 = \frac{\sum\limits_{i=1}^{n} (X_i - \bar{X})^2}{n} \quad .$$

Solution: The computation can be conveniently shown in a table:

| $X_i$ | $X_i - \bar{X}$ | $(X_i - \bar{X})^2$ |
|---|---|---|
| 21 | 6 | 36 |
| 17 | 2 | 4 |
| 13 | - 2 | 4 |
| 25 | 10 | 100 |
| 9 | - 6 | 36 |
| 19 | 4 | 16 |
| 6 | - 9 | 81 |
| 10 | - 5 | 25 |

$$\bar{X} = \frac{\sum\limits_{i=1}^{n} X_i}{n} = \frac{21 + 17 + 13 + 25 + 9 + 19 + 6 + 10}{8} = 15.$$

Adding the entries in the last column

$\sum\limits_{i=1}^{8} (X_i - \bar{X}) = 302$, thus the sample variance is

$$s^2 = \frac{302}{8} = 37.75$$

and the standard deviation $= \sqrt{s^2} = \sqrt{37.75} = 6.14$.

● **PROBLEM** 1-44

What can be said about a sample of observations whose standard deviation is zero?

Solution: The standard deviation is a measure of dispersion in the sample. If the standard deviation is zero we expect little or no variation in the sample. In fact, a standard deviation of zero is the most extreme example of lack of variation in a sample possible.

$$s = \sqrt{\frac{\sum\limits_{i=1}^{n} (X_i - \bar{X})^2}{n}} \qquad \text{by definition.}$$

If $s = 0$, then $\sqrt{\dfrac{\sum\limits_{i=1}^{n} (X_i - \bar{X})^2}{n}} = 0$

squaring both sides and multiplying by n we see that,

$$\sum\limits_{i=1}^{n} (X_i - \bar{X})^2 = 0.$$

Any number squared is positive or zero. Thus, in order for the sum of squared numbers to be zero each term in the sum must be zero. Thus,

$(X_i - \bar{X})^2 = 0$ for $i = 1, \ldots n$

squaring and adding $\bar{X}$ to each of these n equations we see that

$X_i = \bar{X}$ for $i = 1, \ldots n.$

The n observations are identical and equal to the sample mean. The observations are all the same, the most extreme example of lack of dispersion in a sample.

● **PROBLEM** 1-45

The radii of five different brands of softballs (in inches) are 2.03, 1.98, 2.24, 2.17, 2.08. Find the range, variance, standard deviation, mean deviation about the median, and coefficient of variation.

<u>Solution:</u>    The range gives a measure of how dispersed our sample may be. It is defined as the difference between the smallest and largest observations. In this case the range equals 2.24 in. - 1.98 in. = 0.26 in.

To compute the variance, $s^2 = \frac{1}{n} \Sigma(X - \overline{X})^2$, we first need the mean, $\overline{X}$.

$$\overline{X} = \frac{\Sigma X}{n} = \frac{2.03 + 1.98 + 2.24 + 2.17 + 2.08}{5} = 2.10.$$

Variance = $\frac{1}{n} \Sigma(X - \overline{X})^2$. The computations involved are represented in tabular form.

| X | X - $\overline{X}$ | $(X - \overline{X})^2$ |
|---|---|---|
| 2.03 | 2.03 - 2.10 = - .07 | $(- .07)^2$ = .0049 |
| 1.98 | 1.98 - 2.10 = - .12 | $(- .12)^2$ = .0144 |
| 2.24 | 2.24 - 2.10 = .14 | $(+ .14)^2$ = .0196 |
| 2.17 | 2.17 - 2.10 = .07 | $( .07)^2$ = .0049 |
| 2.08 | 2.08 - 2.10 = - .02 | $(- .02)^2$ = .0004 |
| | | $\Sigma(X - \overline{X})^2$ = .0442 |

$$\frac{1}{n} \Sigma(X - \overline{X})^2 = \frac{.0442}{5} = .00884.$$

The standard deviation is the square root of the variance $s = \sqrt{.00884} = .094$.

Since we have 5 observations, the third from the lowest, 2.08, is the median. We will compute the mean deviation about the median with the aid of a table:

| X | X - n | \|X - n\| |
|---|---|---|
| 2.03 | 2.03 - 2.08 = - .05 | \|- .05\| = .05 |
| 1.98 | 1.98 - 2.08 = - .10 | \|- .10\| = .10 |
| 2.24 | 2.24 - 2.08 = .16 | \| .16\| = .16 |
| 2.17 | 2.17 - 2.08 = .09 | \| .09\| = .09 |
| 2.08 | 2.08 - 2.08 = 0 | \|0\| = 0 |

Mean deviation about median = $\frac{\Sigma |X - n|}{n}$

27

$$= \frac{.05 + .10 + .16 + .09 + 0}{5} = \frac{.4}{5} = .08.$$

The Coefficient of Variation is defined as

$$V = \frac{s}{\overline{X}}.$$

Sometimes we want to compare sets of data which are measured differently. Suppose we have a sample of executives with a mean age of 51 and a standard deviation of 11.74 years. Suppose also we know their average IQ is 125 with a standard deviation of 20 points. How can be compare deviations? We use the coefficient of variation:

$$V_{age} = \frac{s}{\overline{X}} = \frac{11.74}{51} - .23; \quad V_{IQ} = \frac{s}{\overline{X}} = \frac{20}{125} = .16.$$

We now know that there is more variation with respect to age.

In our example, $V = \frac{s}{\overline{X}} = \frac{0.094}{2.10} = .045.$

● **PROBLEM** 1-46

A manufacturer of outboard motors receives a shipment of shearpins to be used in the assembly of its motors. A random sample of ten pins is selected and tested to determine the amount of pressure required to cause the pin to break. When tested, the required pressures to the nearest pound are 19, 23, 27, 19, 23, 28, 27, 28, 29, 27.

(a) Calculate the measures of central tendency.
(b) Calculate the measures of variation.

Solution:     (a) The measures of central tendency, most commonly used are the mean, the median and the mode. These measures give an indication of the "middle" or "center" of the data set. A measure of central tendency attempts to identify the point that the data clusters around.

The mean, $\overline{X}$, is an average of the observations and is defined to be

$$\overline{X} = \frac{\Sigma X_i}{n} = \frac{\text{sum of observations}}{\text{number of observations}}$$

$$= \frac{19+23+27+19+23+28+27+28+29+27}{10}$$

$$= \frac{250}{10} = 25.$$

The median is another measure of central tendency. It is the "middle" number in a sample and is defined to be a number such that an equal number of observations lie above and below it.

To compute the median we first order the observations in the sample. This has been down below.

19  19  23  23  27  27  27  28  28  29

In the case of an even number of observations, n, the median is defined to be the average of the $\frac{n}{2}$ and $\frac{n}{2}$ + 1 observations. In our example the $\frac{n}{2} = \frac{10}{2}$ = 5th and the $\frac{n}{2}$ + 1 = 6th observations are both 27.

The average is $\frac{27 + 27}{2}$ = 27.

Thus the median of this sample is 27.

The mode is another measure of central tendency and is defined as the most frequently occurring observation in the sample. The mode in this sample is the observation 27 which occurs three times, more than any other observation.

(b)  The range, the sample variance and the standard deviation are three commonly used measures of variation or dispersion in a sample.

The range is the difference between the largest and smallest observation in a sample. This is 29 = 19 = 10, thus the range is 10.

The variance is an average of squared deviation about the mean. It is sometimes defined to be

$$s^2 = \frac{\sum\limits_{i=1}^{n} (X_i - \bar{X})^2}{n}$$  and can be computed from the

equivalent formula    $s^2 = \frac{\sum X^2 - n\bar{X}^2}{n}$

For our sample,

$$\sum X^2 = 19^2 + 19^2 + 23^2 + 23^2 + 27^2 + 27^2 + 27^2 + 28^2 + 28^2 + 29^2$$

= 6376,        n = 10 and $\bar{X}$ = 25

Thus, $s^2 = \frac{6376 - 10\ (25)^2}{10} = \frac{6376 - 6250}{10} = 12.6.$

The standard deviation is the square root of the variance and is thus

$s = \sqrt{s^2} = \sqrt{12.6} = 3.55.$

In an office, the employer notices his employees spend more time drinking coffee than working. He counts the number of coffee breaks each of his seven employees takes in the course of a day. The data are

1 , 1 , 2 , 2 , 3 , 5 , and 7 .

Find the mean, variance, standard deviation and the median number of coffee breaks a day.

Solution:    To aid in these computations we present the following table,

| $X_i$ | $X_i - \overline{X}$ | $(X_i - \overline{X})^2$ |
|---|---|---|
| 1 | - 2 | 4 |
| 1 | - 2 | 4 |
| 2 | - 1 | 1 |
| 2 | - 1 | 1 |
| 3 | 0 | 0 |
| 5 | 2 | 4 |
| 7 | 4 | 16 |

$$\overline{X} = \frac{\Sigma X_i}{n} = \frac{21}{7} = 3.$$

The median is the fourth observation, 2, the observation such that 3 other observations are higher and 3 are lower.

$$s^2 = \frac{\Sigma (X_i - \overline{X})^2}{n} = \frac{4 + 4 + 1 + 1 + 4 + 16}{7}$$

$$= \frac{30}{7} = 4.29.$$

Thus the variance is 4.29 and the standard deviation is,

$$s = \sqrt{s^2} = \sqrt{4.29} = 2.07.$$

# MEASURES OF GROUPED DATA

The following measurements were taken by an antique dealer as he weighed to the nearest pound his prized collection of anvils. The weights were,

84, 92, 37, 50, 50, 84, 40, 98.

What was the mean weight of the anvils?

Solution:    The average or mean weight of the anvils is

$$\overline{X} = \frac{\text{sum of observations}}{\text{number of observations}}$$

$$= \frac{84 + 92 + 37 + 50 + 50 + 84 + 40 + 98}{8}$$

$$= \frac{535}{8} = 66.88 \approx 67 \text{ pounds.}$$

An alternate way to compute the sample mean is to rearrange the terms in the numerator, grouping the numbers that are the same. Thus,

$$\overline{X} = \frac{(84 + 84) + (50 + 50) + 37 + 40 + 92 + 98}{8} .$$

We see that we can express the mean in terms of the frequency of observations. The frequency of an observation is the number of times a number appears in a sample.

$$\overline{X} = \frac{2 (84) + 2 (50) + 37 + 40 + 92 + 98}{8} .$$

The observations 84 and 50 appear in the sample twice and thus each observation has frequency 2.

In more general terms, the mean can be expressed as,

$$\overline{X} = \frac{\Sigma \ f_i \ X_i}{\text{number of observations}} ,$$

where $X_i$ is the ith observation and $f_i$ is the frequency of the ith observations.

The sum of the frequencies is equal to the total number of observations, $\Sigma f_i = n$.

Thus,         $$\overline{X} = \frac{\Sigma f_i \ X_i}{\Sigma f_i} .$$

● PROBLEM 1-49

Find the mean age of the mothers of students at the Philadelphia School of Music.

The data are:

| Mothers' Ages | Class Boundaries | Frequency |
|---|---|---|
| 35 - 39 | 34.5 - 39.5 | 5 |
| 40 - 44 | 39.5 - 44.5 | 15 |
| 45 - 49 | 44.5 - 49.5 | 38 |
| 50 - 54 | 49.5 - 54.5 | 29 |
| 55 - 59 | 54.5 - 59.5 | 13 |

Solution:    We determine the mean age by calculating the sample mean $\bar{X}$.

$$\bar{X} = \frac{\Sigma f_i X_i}{\Sigma f_i} \qquad \text{where } f_i \text{ is the frequency in class } i$$

and $X_i$ is the midpoint of class i.

We first calculate the midpoints of the 5 classes. This is done below,

$$\frac{39.5 + 34.5}{2} = 37 \qquad\qquad \frac{49.5 + 54.5}{2} = 52$$

$$\frac{39.5 + 44.5}{2} = 42 \qquad\qquad \frac{54.5 + 59.5}{2} = 57.$$

$$\frac{44.5 + 49.5}{2} = 47$$

The mean is then,

$$\bar{X} = \frac{(37)5 + (42)15 + (38)(47) + 52(29) + (57)13}{100}$$

$$= \frac{4850}{100} = 48.5.$$

The average age of the mothers is 48.5 years.

● **PROBLEM** 1-50

Compute the arithmetic mean for the following grouped data.

| Class Limits | Class Mark $X_i$ | $f_i$ |
|:---:|:---:|:---:|
| 6 - 8 | 7 | 4 |
| 9 - 11 | 10 | 6 |
| 12 - 14 | 13 | 7 |
| 15 - 17 | 16 | 4 |
| 18 - 20 | 19 | 3 |

Solution:    We know that the arithmetic mean is

$$\bar{X} = \frac{\Sigma f_i X_i}{\Sigma f_i} .$$

$$\Sigma f_i = 4 + 6 + 7 + 4 + 3 = 24$$

and $\Sigma f_i X_i = (4)(7) + (6)(10) + (13)(7) + (16)(4) + (19)(3)$

$$= 300$$

Thus, $\overline{X} = \frac{300}{24} = 12.5.$

● **PROBLEM** 1-51

Using the formula $\overline{X} = \Sigma fX/\Sigma f$, determine the value of the mean for the grouped data below.

| Class | $f_i$ | $X_i$ |
|-------|-------|-------|
| 1 - 5 | 2 | 3 |
| 6 - 10 | 5 | 8 |
| 11 - 15 | 2 | 13 |
| 16 - 20 | 1 | 18 |

Solution:    The mean is

$$\overline{X} = \frac{\Sigma f_i X_i}{\Sigma f_i} \quad .$$

We let $X_i$ be the class mark or class midpoint.

$$\Sigma f_i = 2 + 5 + 2 + 1 = 10$$

and $\Sigma f_i X_i = (2)(3) + (5)(8) + (2)(13) + (1)(18)$

$$= 6 + 40 + 26 + 18 = 90 \ .$$

Thus,    $\overline{X} = \frac{90}{10} = 9.$

● **PROBLEM** 1-52

Find the mean of the data given in the frequency distribution below.

| Class | Class Mark $X_i'$ | Frequency $f_i$ | $X_i' f_i$ |
|-------|-------------------|-----------------|-------------|
| 1 | 46 | 4 | 184 |
| 2 | 51 | 1 | 51 |
| 3 | 56 | 2 | 112 |
| 4 | 61 | 2 | 122 |
| 5 | 66 | 2 | 132 |
| 6 | 71 | 9 | 639 |
| 7 | 76 | 5 | 380 |
| 8 | 81 | 10 | 810 |

| 9 | 86 | 4 | 344 |
| 10 | 91 | 8 | 728 |
| 11 | 96 | 3 | 288 |
| Totals: | | 50 | 3790 |

Solution: The sample mean or average of the data is

$$\bar{X} = \frac{1}{n} \sum_{i=1}^{K} X_i' f_i \qquad \text{where}$$

$X_i'$ = class mark or midpoint of class

$f_i$ = frequency or number of observations in a particular class

$n$ = total observations = $\sum_{i=1}^{K} f_i$

$K$ = number of classes .

We wish to obtain some measure of central tendency in the data. However we do not have all the observations available to us. Instead we have the class marks and frequencies.

One possibility would be a straight average of the class marks or $\frac{1}{11} \sum_{i=1}^{11} X_i'$ . The drawback to this method is that if one class has a greater frequency, more observations, than another class this difference will not be reflected. Each class mark will be weighted the same.

A better way would be to weight each class mark by its relative frequency, $\frac{f_i}{n}$ . This weighting system will cause the classes with more observations to receive greater weight.

The sample mean

$$\bar{X} = X_1' \cdot \frac{f_1}{n} + X_2' \cdot \frac{f_2}{n} + \ldots X_K' \cdot \frac{f_K}{n} = \sum_{i=1}^{K} \frac{X_i' \cdot f_i}{n}$$

$$= \frac{1}{n} \sum_{i=1}^{K} X_i' f_i .$$

Referring to our table, $X_i' f_i$ = 3790 and n = 50,

$$\bar{X} = \frac{3790}{50} = 75.8 .$$

Find the mean weight of the 100 sixth- grade students as as tabulated below.

| Class Boundaries | Class Weights | Frequencies |
|---|---|---|
| 58.5 - 61.5 | 60 | 4 |
| 61.5 - 64.5 | 63 | 8 |
| 64.5 - 67.5 | 66 | 12 |
| 67.5 - 70.5 | 69 | 13 |
| 70.5 - 73.5 | 72 | 21 |
| 73.5 - 76.5 | 75 | 15 |
| 76.5 - 79.5 | 78 | 12 |
| 79.5 - 82.5 | 81 | 9 |
| 82.5 - 85.5 | 84 | 4 |
| 85.5 - 88.5 | 87 | 2 |

Solution: We use a different formula to compute the mean weight of the sixth-graders. We do not have all the observations but do have the classweightsor class mid-points and the frequencies or number of observations in each class.

The mean weight of the sixth-graders is

$$\overline{X} = \frac{\text{sum of observations}}{\text{number of observations}} .$$

The number of observations in the sample is the sum of the number of observations in each class or the sum of the frequency in each class.

Thus, n = number of observations

$$= \sum_{i=1}^{10} f_i = 4 + 8 + 12 + 13 + 21 + 15$$

$$+ 12 + 9 + 4 + 2$$

$$= 100 .$$

The sum of observations is the product of the class mark and the frequency, summed for each class. Thus, the sum of observations is $\sum_i f_i X_i$, where $f_i$ and $X_i$ are the frequency and class mark in class i.

$$\sum_{i=1}^{10} X_i f_i = (60)4+ (63)8 + (66)12 + (69)13 + (72)21$$

$$+ (75)15 + (78)12 + (81)9 + (84)4 + (87)2$$

$$= 7,245$$

and $\overline{X} = \frac{7245}{100} = 72.45$ is the sample mean weight of the sixth-graders.

Find the median weight of the 100 sixth-grade students.
Use the data given in the previous problem.

Solution:     There are 100 observations in the sample.
The median will be the 50th observation. When using an
even numbered sample of grouped data, the convention is
to call the $\left(\frac{N}{2}\right)^{th}$ observation the median. There are 37
observations in the first four intervals
        and the first five intervals contain 58 ob-
servations. The 50th observation is in the fifth class
interval.

     We use the technique of linear interpolation to
estimate the position of the 50th observation within the
class interval.

     The width of the fifth class is three and there are
21 observations in the class. To interpolate we imagine
that each observation takes up $\frac{3}{21}$ units of the interval.
There are 37 observations in the first four intervals and
thus the 13th observation in the fifth class will be the
median. This 13th observation will be approximately $13\left(\frac{3}{21}\right)$
units from the lower boundary of the fifth class interval.
The median is thus the lower boundary of the fifth class
plus $13\left(\frac{3}{21}\right)$ or

$$\text{median} = 70.5 + \frac{13}{7} = 72.35.$$

Find the variance and standard deviation of the weights of
the sixth-grade students as given in the preceeding problem.

Solution:     The variance of a grouped data is similar to
the variance for ungrouped data. In both cases, the
variance is an average of the squared deviation from $\overline{X}$.

     We have seen that for grouped data

$$\overline{X} = \frac{\Sigma f_i X_i}{\Sigma f_i} \; .$$

     The variance for grouped data is

$$s^2 = \frac{\Sigma f_i (X_i - \overline{X})^2}{\Sigma f_i} \; ,$$

where $f_i$ is the frequency or number of observations in
the ith class, $X_i$ is the midpoint of the ith class, and $\overline{X}$

is the sample mean of the grouped data.

This variance can be computed more conveniently using the computational formula derived below,

$$s^2 = \frac{\Sigma f_i (X_i - \bar{X})^2}{\Sigma f_i} = \frac{\Sigma f_i (X_i^2 - 2X_i\bar{X} + \bar{X}^2)}{\Sigma f_i}$$

$$= \frac{\Sigma f_i X_i^2 - 2\bar{X}\Sigma f_i X_i + \bar{X}^2 \Sigma f_i}{\Sigma f_i}$$

(because $\Sigma f_i X_i = \bar{X}\Sigma f_i$)

$$= \frac{\Sigma f_i X_i^2 - 2(\Sigma f_i)\bar{X}^2 + \bar{X}^2\Sigma f_i}{\Sigma f_i}$$

$$= \frac{\Sigma f_i X_i^2}{\Sigma f_i} - \bar{X}^2 .$$

We have computed $\bar{X}$ to be 72.45.

This table is convenient in computing $\Sigma f_i X_i^2$.

| Class mark $X_i$ | Frequency $f_i$ | $X_i^2$ | $f_i X_i^2$ |
|---|---|---|---|
| 60 | 4 | 3600 | 14,400 |
| 63 | 8 | 3969 | 31,752 |
| 66 | 12 | 4356 | 52,272 |
| 69 | 13 | 4761 | 61,893 |
| 72 | 21 | 5184 | 108,864 |
| 75 | 15 | 5625 | 84,375 |
| 78 | 12 | 6084 | 73,008 |
| 81 | 9 | 6561 | 59,049 |
| 84 | 4 | 7056 | 28,224 |
| 87 | 2 | 7569 | 15,138 |

$$\sum_{i=1}^{10} f_i X_i^2 = 528,975$$

and

$$s^2 = \frac{\Sigma f_i X_i^2}{\Sigma f_i} - (\bar{X})^2$$

$$= \frac{528,975}{100} - (72.45)^2$$

$$= 5289.75 - 5249.0025 = 40.75.$$

The standard deviation is

$$s = \sqrt{s^2} = \sqrt{40.75} = 6.38.$$

| Class | Class Boundaries | Frequencies |
|-------|------------------|-------------|
| 1 | 49.5 - 99.5 | 17 |
| 2 | 99.5 - 149.5 | 38 |
| 3 | 149.5 - 199.5 | 61 |
| 4 | 199.5 - 249.5 | 73 |
| 5 | 249.5 - 299.5 | 56 |
| 6 | 299.5 - 349.5 | 29 |
| 7 | 349.5 - 399.5 | 16 |
| 8 | 399.5 - 449.5 | 10 |
|   |   | 300 |

Consider this Table. What is the median class? Estimate the median by linear interpolation.

Solution:    The Table does not supply enough information to allow us to read off the median. Rather than observing the individual data, the observations have been grouped into classes. We are given the boundaries of each class, the range of numbers which are included in each class, and the frequencies or number of observations in each class.

The median class is the class which contains the median of the entire data set. In this case there are 300 total observations, 116 observations in the first three classes and 189 observations in the first four classes. The median will be the 150th observation and will be in the fourth class. Thus, the median class is the fourth class.

To estimate the median by linear interpolation we must assume that the observations are distributed uniformly throughout the fourth class. To see what this means, consider the following; If the interval from 199.5 to 249.5 is marked off as on a scale, the scale will be 50 units long. The observations will be distributed uniformly if they are spread out evenly over the 50 units.

In this case, there are 73 observations and by assuming that the observations are distributed uniformly, we are assuming that the observations are $\frac{50}{73}$ units apart. That is, if the 50 units were divided into 73 equal intervals, each interval would contain one observation.

If we make this assumption, then we can estimate the median. There are 116 observations in the first three classes and we wish to find the 150th observation. To do this we divide the fourth class into 73 intervals, by our assumption we know that each observation is in an interval $\frac{50}{73}$ units long. The 34th observation in the fourth class will be the median and this observation will be $34 \cdot \left(\frac{50}{73}\right)$ units from the lower boundary of the fourth class.

The median = 199.5 (the lower boundary of the fourth class + $34 \cdot \left(\frac{50}{73}\right)$ = 199.5 + 23.3 = 222.8.

What is the value of the median for the data in the
following frequency distribution?

| Class Limits | Class Boundaries | Class Mark $X_i$ | Frequency $f_i$ |
|---|---|---|---|
| 1 - 2 | .5 - 2.5 | 1.5 | 2 |
| 3 - 4 | 2.5 - 4.5 | 3.5 | 5 |
| 5 - 6 | 4.5 - 6.5 | 5.5 | 15 |
| 7 - 8 | 6.5 - 8.5 | 7.5 | 10 |
| 9 - 10 | 8.5 - 10.5 | 9.5 | 5 |

Solution:     The median is the 50th-percentile or the
number such that 50% of the cumulative frequency lies
below it. This corresponds to $\frac{37}{2}$ = 18.5.

There are 7 observations in the first two classes
and 22 observations in the first three classes thus the
median will be the 18.5 - 7 = 11.5th  "observation" in
the third class.

Through linear interpolation we assume that each
observation in the third class lies in an interval that is

$$\frac{\text{length of class}}{\text{number of observations in class}} = \frac{2}{15} \quad \text{units.} \qquad \text{The}$$

11.5th "observation" in the class lies $(11.5)\left(\frac{2}{15}\right)$ units
from the lower boundary of the third class.

The median is

$$4.5 + (11.5) \left(\frac{2}{15}\right) = 6.0.$$

Take the following distribution as a set of classroom
test scores (N=30). The test had 55 possible points. In
assigning letter grades to the test papers, the teacher
might follow any one of several procedures. Examine the
consequences of each of the following procedures, determining the number of students getting each grade in part
a, and the numbers getting A or B versus C, D, or F in
parts b and c.

(a) Converting the scores to "percent correct out of
55," and giving A's to those with 90 to 100 percent correct,
B's for 80 to 89 percent, C's for 70 to 79 percent, D's
for 60 to 69 percent, F's to those below 60 percent.

(b) Finding the mean, and giving B or A to those
above the mean and C, D, or F to those below the mean.

(c) Finding the median, and giving B or A to those above it and C, D, or F to those below it.

| Score | Frequency | Score | Frequency | Score | Frequency |
|-------|-----------|-------|-----------|-------|-----------|
| 52 | 1 | 43 | 2 | 34 | 0 |
| 51 | 1 | 42 | 1 | 33 | 1 |
| 50 | 0 | 41 | 0 | 32 | 1 |
| 49 | 3 | 40 | 2 | 31 | 0 |
| 48 | 2 | 39 | 1 | 30 | 1 |
| 47 | 4 | 38 | 1 | 29 | 0 |
| 46 | 3 | 37 | 0 | 28 | 1 |
| 45 | 1 | 36 | 0 | 27 | 2 |
| 44 | 1 | 35 | 1 | | |

Solution:    (a) To convert the scores to "percent correct out of 55" we divide each score by 55 and multiply by 100 to determine the percentage correct.

For example to compute the score 52 to a percentage we have, % correct = $\left(\dfrac{52}{55}\right) \cdot 100 = 94.5\%$.

This has been done for each score and the revised table is below:

| % correct of 55 | Frequency | |
|-----------------|-----------|---|
| 94.5 | 1 | |
| 92.7 | 1 | |
| 90.9 | 0 | A's – 2 students |
| 89.09 | 3 | |
| 87.27 | 2 | |
| 85.45 | 4 | |
| 83.63 | 3 | |
| 81.81 | 1 | |
| 80.00 | 1 | B's – 14 students |
| 78.18 | 2 | |
| 76.36 | 1 | |
| 74.54 | 0 | |
| 72.72 | 2 | |
| 70.90 | 1 | C's – 6 students |
| 69.09 | 1 | |
| 67.27 | 0 | |
| 65.45 | 0 | |
| 63.63 | 1 | |
| 61.81 | 0 | |
| 60.00 | 1 | D's – 3 students |
| 58.18 | 1 | |
| 56.36 | 0 | |
| 54.54 | 1 | |
| 52.72 | 0 | |
| 50.90 | 1 | |
| 49.09 | 2 | F's – 5 students |

(b) The mean is

$$\overline{X} = \frac{\Sigma f_i \ X_i}{\Sigma f_i} \qquad \text{where } f_i \text{ is the frequency of the ith}$$

score and $X_i$ is the ith score.

$$\Sigma f_i = 30$$

$$\Sigma f_i \ X_i = 52 + 51 + 3(49) + 2(48) + 4(47) + 3(46) +$$
$$+ (45)1 + 44 + (43)2 + 42 + (40)2 + 39 +$$
$$+ 38 + 35 + 33 + 32 + 30 + 28 + 2(27)$$
$$= 1258.$$

Thus, $\quad \overline{X} = \frac{1258}{30} = 41.93.$

There are 19 scores above 41.93 and 11 scores below 41.93. 19 students will get A's and B's and 11 students will get C, D or F.

(c) The median is the average of the 15th and 16th largest score. The 15th score from the bottom is 44 and the 16th score from the bottom is 45. The median score is $\frac{44 + 45}{2} = 44.5$

There are 15 scores above 44.5 and these 15 students will have A's and B's. There are 15 scores below 44.5 and the students with these scores will receive C's, D's and F's.

● **PROBLEM** 1-59

What is the modal age of the fathers of students at this Junior High School?

| Age | Frequency |
|---------|-----------|
| 35 - 39 | 5 |
| 40 - 44 | 15 |
| 45 - 49 | 38 |
| 50 - 54 | 29 |
| 55 - 59 | 13 |

Solution: The mode is a measure of central tendency and if all the observations are available the mode is defined to be the most frequently occurring observation.

If the data is grouped into classes, the modal class will be the class with the most observations in it. The mode can be arbitrarily chosen to be the midpoint of the modal class.

From our data, the modal class is 45 - 49. This class has a frequency of 38 which is higher than that of any other class.

The midpoint of the model class is

$$\frac{49 + 45}{2} = 47.$$ Thus the mode is 47.

● **PROBLEM** 1-60

Given the following distribution of per-family income in a small community, which measure of central tendency would be most representative if we wish to use average family income as one basis for deciding whether or not to locate a retail outlet in the community, the mean, median or mode?

| Annual Family Income | Number of Families |
|---|---|
| Under 5,000 | 25 |
| 5,000 -  7,999 | 40 |
| 8,000 - 10,999 | 50 |
| 11,000 - 13,999 | 30 |
| 14,000 - 16,999 | 20 |
| 17,000 - 19,999 | 10 |
| 20,000 - 24,999 | 5 |
| 25,000 - 49,999 | 0 |
| 50,000 - 99,999 | 15 |
| 100,000 + | 5 |

Solution:    The median or mode would be the most appropriate measures of central tendency in this situation.

The mean is the measure that is the most sensitive to extreme observations. If the mean were used to estimate a central tendency of family income, the few families with very high incomes would tend to raise the mean. A large number of families would have incomes less than the mean.

If the median or mode were employed as measures of central tendency, this distortion due to the extreme values would not take place.

● **PROBLEM** 1-61

Find the average deviation for the grouped data given below:

| Class | Frequency $f_i$ | Class Mark $X_i$ | $\bar{X}$ | $|X_i - \bar{X}|$ | $f_i|X_i - \bar{X}|$ |
|---|---|---|---|---|---|
| 49 - 54 | 6 | 51.5 | 66.5 | 15 | 90 |
| 55 - 60 | 15 | 57.5 | 66.75 | 9 | 135 |
| 61 - 66 | 24 | 63.5 | 66.5 | 3 | 72 |

| 67 - 72 | 33 | 69.5 | 66.5 | 3 | 99 |
| 73 - 78 | 22 | 75.5 | 66.5 | 9 | 198 |

**Solution:** In the above table the frequency represents the number of observations in a particular class. The class mark is the midpoint of each class. The sample mean $\overline{X}$ is defined as

$$\overline{X} = \frac{\Sigma f_i X_i}{\Sigma f_i} = [6(51.5) + 15(57.5) + 24(63.5) + 33(69.5)$$

$$+ 22(75.5)] \div 100$$

$$= \frac{6650}{100} = 66.5.$$

$X_i - \overline{X}$ is the absolute value of the difference between the class mark and the sample mean for each class i.

We wish to compute the measure of dispersion known as the average deviation. This measure gives an indication of the spread of the observations around the sample mean. The average deviation is defined to be,

$$A.D. = \frac{\Sigma f_i |X_i - \overline{X}|}{\Sigma f_i}$$

$$= \frac{90 + 135 + 72 + 99 + 198}{100} = \frac{594}{100} = 5.94.$$

● **PROBLEM** 1-62

The distribution below represents the numbers of students in a sample of 212 who arrived at class at various times after the scheduled class hour.

| Frequency | Minutes Late | Frequency | Minutes Late |
|-----------|--------------|-----------|--------------|
| 181 | 0 | 2 | 5 |
| 13 | 1 | 1 | 6 |
| 6 | 2 | 1 | 7 |
| 4 | 3 | 1 | 8 |
| 3 | 4 | | |

Consider how the mean and standard deviation, on the one hand, and the median and AAD from the median, on the other, would differ as methods of describing the variability in these data.

**Solution:** We calculate the mean and standard deviation from this data with the aid of the following table.

| Minutes Late $X_i$ | Frequency $f_i$ | $X_i f_i$ | $X_i^2 f_i$ |
|---|---|---|---|
| 0 | 181 | 0 | 0 |
| 1 | 13 | 13 | 13 |
| 2 | 6 | 12 | 24 |
| 3 | 4 | 12 | 36 |
| 4 | 3 | 12 | 48 |
| 5 | 2 | 10 | 50 |
| 6 | 1 | 6 | 36 |
| 7 | 1 | 7 | 49 |
| 8 | 1 | 8 | 64 |

$$\Sigma X_i f_i = 80 \qquad\qquad \Sigma X_i^2 f_i = 320$$

The mean is,

$$\bar{X} = \frac{\Sigma X_i f_i}{\Sigma f_i} = \frac{80}{212} = .377.$$

And the standard deviation is,

$$s = \sqrt{s^2} = \sqrt{\frac{\Sigma f_i X_i^2}{\Sigma f_i} - \bar{X}^2}$$

$$= \sqrt{\frac{320}{212} - (.377)^2}$$

$$= \sqrt{1.367} = 1.169.$$

The median in this problem is the average of the 106th and 107th observations. Both of these observations are 0 and thus the median is 0.

The average deviation from the median is defined as

$$A.D. = \frac{\Sigma f_i |X_i - \bar{X}|}{n}$$

$$= 181|0-0| + 13|1-0| + 6|2-0| + 4|3-0|$$

$$+ 3|4-0| + 2|5-0| + |6-0| + |7-0| + |8-0|$$

$$= \frac{13 + 12 + 12 + 12 + 10 + 6 + 7 + 8}{212}$$

$$= \frac{80}{212} = .377.$$

The mean and standard deviation are distorted by the few extremely high values. Thus, the median and average deviation from the median give a truer picture of this sample.

A history test was taken by 51 students. The scores ranged from 50 to 95 and were classified into 8 classes of width 6 units. The resulting frequency distribution appears below. Find $s^2$ by applying the definition for $s^2$. Then find s.

| Class i | Class Mark $X_i'$ | Frequency $f_i$ | $X_i' f_i$ |
|---|---|---|---|
| 1 | 51 | 2 | 102 |
| 2 | 57 | 3 | 171 |
| 3 | 63 | 5 | 315 |
| 4 | 69 | 8 | 552 |
| 5 | 75 | 10 | 750 |
| 6 | 81 | 12 | 972 |
| 7 | 87 | 10 | 870 |
| 8 | 93 | 1 | 93 |
|  |  | 51 | $3825 = \sum_{i=1}^{8} X_i' f_i$ |

Solution:    We wish to find $s^2$, the measure of dispersion of the observations about the sample mean for this classified data.

In the table we are given:

$X_i'$ = the midpoint (class mark) of the ith class

$f_i$ = the number of observations in the ith class

   n = the toal number of observations = $\sum_{i=1}^{n} f_i$

By definition, the sample variance for classified data is

$$s^2 = \frac{\sum_{i=1}^{K} (X_i' - \bar{X})^2 f_i}{n}$$

where K is tne number of classes. First find $\bar{X}$,

$$\bar{X} = \frac{\sum_{i=1}^{K} X_i' f_i}{n} = \frac{3825}{51} = 75.$$

The computations used in finding $s^2$ are displayed in the following table.

| Class | $X_i'$ | $f_i$ | $X_i' - \bar{X}$ | $(X_i' - \bar{X})^2$ | $(X_i' - \bar{X})^2 f_i$ |
|---|---|---|---|---|---|
| 1 | 51 | 2 | - 24 | 576 | 1152 |
| 2 | 57 | 3 | - 18 | 324 | 972 |
| 3 | 63 | 5 | - 12 | 144 | 720 |
| 4 | 69 | 8 | - 6 | 36 | 288 |
| 5 | 75 | 10 | 0 | 0 | 0 |
| 6 | 81 | 12 | 6 | 36 | 432 |
| 7 | 87 | 10 | 12 | 144 | 1440 |
| 8 | 93 | 1 | 18 | 324 | 324 |

$$\sum_{i=1}^{8} f_i = 51, \qquad \sum_{i=1}^{8} (X_i' - \overline{X}) f_i = 5328.$$

$$s^2 = \frac{1}{n} \sum_{i=1}^{8} (X_i' - \overline{X})^2 f_i = \frac{1}{51} (5328) = 104.47.$$

and the standard deviation,

$$s = \sqrt{s^2} = 10.22.$$

The data are the scores of 50 freshman students on a mathematics test. Classify the data, and then find the sample variance by applying the computing formula:

$$s^2 = \frac{1}{n} \left[ \sum_{i=1}^{K} X_i'^2 \cdot f_i - \frac{\left( \sum_{i=1}^{K} X_i' f_i \right)^2}{n} \right].$$

| | | | | |
|----|----|----|----|----|
| 67 | 92 | 98 | 49 | 80 |
| 45 | 93 | 80 | 81 | 72 |
| 95 | 97 | 92 | 78 | 76 |
| 79 | 72 | 84 | 69 | 88 |
| 70 | 60 | 74 | 74 | 83 |
| 82 | 57 | 47 | 90 | 70 |
| 83 | 48 | 60 | 71 | 71 |
| 84 | 86 | 57 | 82 | 91 |
| 71 | 44 | 78 | 73 | 90 |
| 93 | 93 | 79 | 65 | 83 |

Solution:    First determine the number of classes which will be appropriate for covering the range of the sample. The range, a measure of dispersion, is defined to be the difference between the maximum and minimum observations.

| Class | Class Boundaries | Class Midpoint $(X_i')$ | $f_i$ | $X_i'^2$ | $X_i' f_i$ | $X_i'^2 f_i$ |
|-------|------------------|-------------------------|-------|----------|------------|--------------|
| 1  | 43.5–48.5 | 46 | 4  | 2116 | 184 | 8,464 |
| 2  | 48.5–53,5 | 51 | 1  | 2601 | 51  | 2,601 |
| 3  | 53.5–58.5 | 56 | 2  | 3136 | 112 | 6,272 |
| 4  | 58.5–63.5 | 61 | 2  | 3721 | 122 | 7,442 |
| 5  | 63.5–68.5 | 66 | 2  | 4356 | 132 | 8,712 |
| 6  | 68.5–73.5 | 71 | 9  | 5041 | 639 | 45,369 |
| 7  | 73.5–78.5 | 76 | 5  | 5776 | 380 | 28,880 |
| 8  | 78.5–83.5 | 81 | 10 | 6561 | 810 | 65,610 |
| 9  | 83.5–88.5 | 86 | 4  | 7396 | 344 | 29,584 |
| 10 | 88.5–93.5 | 91 | 8  | 8281 | 728 | 66,248 |
| 11 | 93.5–99.5 | 96 | 3  | 9216 | 288 | 27,648 |
| Totals: | | | 50 | | 3790 | 296,830 |

In this case the range = 98 - 44 = 54. Some possibilities for classifying the data are eleven classes of width 5 units, fourteen classes of width 4 units, or eight classes of width 7 units. Choosing the first option of eleven classes each of width 5 units we next select the boundary values for our classes. It is convenient to select a lower boundary of 43.5 as this yields integral values for the class mid-points. The upper boundary will be 43.5 + 5(11) = 98.5. The computations are shown in the table above:

For our formula we need

$$\sum_{i=1}^{11} X_i' f_i = 3790 \quad \text{and} \quad \sum_{i=1}^{11} X_i'^2 f_i = 296,830.$$

$$s^2 = \frac{1}{50} \left[ 296,830 - \frac{(3790)^2}{50} \right] = \frac{1}{50} [296,830 - 287,282]$$

$$= \frac{1}{50} [9548]$$

so $\quad s^2 = 190.96$ and

$$s = \sqrt{s^2} = \sqrt{194.9} = 13.82.$$

● **PROBLEM** 1-65

Find $s^2$ and $s$, the sample variance and standard deviation for the previous problem when the data are unclassified. Is this answer the same as the sample variance and standard deviation for classified data? Why or why not?

Solution:    Using our computational formula for $s^2$,

$$s^2 = \frac{1}{n} \left[ \sum_{i=1}^{50} X_i^2 - \frac{\left( \sum_{i=1}^{50} X_i \right)^2}{n} \right].$$

From the data in the previous problem,

$$\sum_{i=1}^{50} X_i^2 = 298,168 \qquad \sum_{i=1}^{50} X_i = 3796$$

$$s^2 = \frac{1}{50} \left[ 298,168 - \frac{(3796)^2}{50} \right]$$

$$= \frac{1}{50} [298,168 - 288,192]$$

$$= \frac{1}{50} [9976] = 199.52$$

and    $s = 14.125.$

Comparing this answer with that of the previous problem we see that the values of $s^2$ for classified and unclassified data differ slightly. They are not in general the same number. The reason for this is that when $s^2$ is calculated for classified data there is a simplification, or a reduction of the data. All the data in a particular class are represented by a class mark or class midpoint and a frequency. That is, when the sample variance is computed with classified data, we are reducing every data point in the class to the midpoint. This simplification results in a different sample variance than that computed using the entire unclassified sample.

● **PROBLEM** 1-66

The highway patrol set up a radar checkpoint and recorded the speed in miles per hour of a random sample of 50 cars that passed the checkpoint in one hour. The speeds of the cars were recorded as follows.

| | | | | |
|----|----|----|----|----|
| 74 | 66 | 65 | 55 | 48 |
| 56 | 50 | 65 | 75 | 67 |
| 76 | 68 | 50 | 65 | 60 |
| 65 | 60 | 51 | 68 | 76 |
| 68 | 77 | 63 | 65 | 52 |
| 52 | 63 | 65 | 80 | 70 |
| 65 | 81 | 70 | 63 | 53 |
| 45 | 65 | 55 | 71 | 64 |
| 55 | 70 | 64 | 45 | 66 |
| 64 | 40 | 66 | 55 | 71 |

(a) Make a frequency distribution chart, using 5 as a class width, e.g., 39.5 - 44.5.
(b) Find the mean and standard deviation.
(c) What value represents the median? The 40th percentile?

Solution: We must first decide how many classes will be necessary. We compute the range of the scores and find it to be $81 - 40 = 41$. Thus 9 classes, each 5 units in width, are necessary to contain all the observations.

(a)

| Class Interval | Class Boundary | Class Mark $X_i$ | Tally | Frequency |
|----------------|----------------|------------------|-------|-----------|
| 40-44 | 39.5-44.5 | 42 | \| | 1 |
| 45-49 | 44.5-49.5 | 47 | \|\|\| | 3 |
| 50-54 | 49.5-54.5 | 52 | 卌 \| | 6 |
| 55-59 | 54.5-59.5 | 57 | 卌 | 5 |
| 60-64 | 59.5-64.5 | 62 | 卌 \|\|\| | 8 |
| 65-69 | 64.5-69.5 | 67 | 卌 卌 卌 | 15 |
| 70-74 | 69.5-74.5 | 72 | 卌 \| | 6 |
| 75-79 | 74.5-79.5 | 77 | \|\|\|\| | 4 |
| 80-84 | 79.5-84.5 | 82 | \|\| | 2 |

We now use a tally sheet to compute the number of observations in each class. The class midpoint can also be computed at this step. We choose the class boundaries, starting with 39.5, to insure integer values of the class midpoints.

(b)   To find the mean and standard deviation we use the formulas developed in previous problems.

$$\overline{X} = \frac{\Sigma f_i \, X_i}{f_i} \quad \text{for the mean; and}$$

$$s = \sqrt{s^2} = \sqrt{\frac{\Sigma f_i \, X_i^2}{\Sigma f_i} - \overline{X}^2} \quad \text{for the standard deviation.}$$

$\Sigma f_i = 50$ and the other quantities are computed in the table below.

| Class Mark $X_i$ | Frequency $f_i$ | $X_i f_i$ | $X_i^2$ | $f_i X_i^2$ |
|---|---|---|---|---|
| 42 | 1 | 42 | 1764 | 1764 |
| 47 | 3 | 141 | 2209 | 6627 |
| 52 | 6 | 312 | 2704 | 16224 |
| 57 | 5 | 285 | 3249 | 16245 |
| 62 | 8 | 496 | 3844 | 30752 |
| 67 | 15 | 1005 | 4489 | 67335 |
| 72 | 6 | 432 | 5184 | 31104 |
| 77 | 4 | 308 | 5929 | 23716 |
| 82 | 2 | 164 | 6724 | 13448 |

$$\Sigma X_i f_i = 3,185 \qquad\qquad \Sigma f_i \, X_i^2 = 207,215$$

Thus $\overline{X} = \dfrac{3185}{50} = 63.7$   and

$$s = \sqrt{s^2} = \sqrt{\frac{207215}{50} - (63.7)^2}$$

$$= \sqrt{4144.3 - 4057.69}$$

$$= \sqrt{86.61} = 9.3$$

(c)   In using an even numbered sample of grouped data we use the convention that the $\left(\frac{N}{2}\right)$th observation will be the median.

The median will be the 25th observation, the mid-point of the sample. There are 23 observations in the first 5 classes and 38 observations in the first 6 classes hence the median lies in the 6th class. We will use linear inter-polation to estimate the position of the median in this class.

The 6th class contains 15 observations and has a width of 5 units. Each observation in the class can be assumed to lie in an interval of length $\frac{5}{15}$ units. The 25th observation will be the 2nd observation from the lower boundary of the 6th class and will lie $2\left(\frac{5}{15}\right)$ units from this boundary.

The median is thus the lower boundary $+ 2\left(\frac{5}{15}\right)$ or

$$64.5 + 2\left(\frac{5}{15}\right) = 64.5 + .67 = 65.17.$$

The 40th percentile is the observation or number such that 40% of the other observations lie on or below it. 40% of 50 is $(.4)50 = 20$, so we wish to find the 20th observation.

There are 15 observations in the first four classes and 23 observations in the first 5 classes. The 20th observation lies in the 5th interval with class boundaries 59.5 - 64.5. The 20th observation will be the 5th observation in the 5th class.

Using linear interpolation, we see that each observation in the 5th class lies in an interval of length $\frac{5}{8}$, hence the 5th observation lies $5\left(\frac{5}{8}\right)$ units from the lower boundary, and the 20th observation or 40th percentile is

$$59.5 + 5\left(\frac{5}{8}\right) = 62.63.$$

Therefore the 40th percentile does not represent the median value for this data.

● **PROBLEM** 1-67

The word "moment" is used quite often in a statistical context. It refers to the sum of the deviations from the mean in respect to sample size. The first moment is defined then as $\dfrac{\Sigma(X_i - \bar{X})}{n}$ $\left(\dfrac{\Sigma f_i(X_i - \bar{X})}{\Sigma f_i} \text{ for grouped data}\right)$.

What numerical value does the first moment always have?

Solution:     Let us perform some algebraic manipulations on the definition of the first moment:

$$m_1 = \frac{\sum\limits^{n}(X_i - \bar{X})}{n} \quad . \quad \text{Substitute} \quad \frac{\sum\limits^{n}X_i}{n} \quad \text{for } \bar{X} \text{ and obtain}$$

$$\frac{\sum\limits^{n}\left(X_i - \dfrac{\sum\limits^{n}X_i}{n}\right)}{n} \quad . \quad \text{We now examine the numerator,}$$

$$\sum_{i}^{n} \left( X_i - \frac{\sum_{i}^{n} X_i}{n} \right).$$ The second term is a constant so we subtract it once for each of the n terms in the summation. Consequently,

$$m_1 = \frac{\left( X_1 - \frac{\sum X_i}{n} \right) + \left( X_2 - \frac{\sum X_i}{n} \right) + \left( X_3 - \frac{\sum X_i}{n} \right) + \ldots + \left( X_n - \frac{\sum X_i}{n} \right)}{n}$$

$$= \frac{(X_1 + X_2 + \ldots + X_n) - \frac{\sum X_i}{n} - \frac{\sum X_i}{n} - \ldots - \frac{\sum X_i}{n}}{n}$$

$$= \frac{\sum X_i - n \frac{\sum X_i}{n}}{n}$$

$$= \frac{\sum X_i - \sum X_i}{n} = \frac{0}{n} = 0.$$

# MOMENTS, SKEWNESS, KURTOSIS

● PROBLEM 1-68

What is the relative measure of skewness for the data listed below? This data represents the waist measurements of six randomly selected chocolate rabbits.

3 inches,  2 inches,  3.7 inches,  5 inches,
2.7 inches,  3 inches.

Solution:  The relative measure of symmetry is defined to be  $a_3 = \frac{m_3}{s^3}$  where $s^3$ is the standard deviation cubed and $m_3$ is the third moment.

The third moment is defined as;
$$m_3 = \frac{\sum (X_i - \overline{X})^3}{n} .$$

We have encountered other examples of moments. The first moment is

$$m_1 = \frac{\sum (X_i - \overline{X})^1}{n} .$$

We can see that this moment has only one value.

$$m_1 = \frac{\sum (X_i - \overline{X})^1}{n} = \frac{\sum X_i}{n} - \frac{n\overline{X}}{n} = \frac{\sum X_i}{n} - \overline{X}$$

but  $\overline{X} = \frac{\sum X_i}{n}$  thus  $m_1 = 0.$

The second moment is $\dfrac{\Sigma(X_i - \bar{X})^2}{n}$ or the sample variance.

The fourth moment is defined as

$$m_4 = \dfrac{\Sigma(X_i - \bar{X})^4}{n} .$$

The measure of symmetry has the following interpretation, if $a_3 = \dfrac{m_3}{s^3}$ is equal to zero, the distribution is symmetrical. If $a_3 < 0$ then the distribution is negatively skewed. If $a_3 > 0$ the distribution is positively skewed.

To calculate the measure of symmetry we use the table below:

| $X_i$ | $\bar{X}$ | $(X_i - \bar{X})$ | $(X_i - \bar{X})^2$ | $(X_i - \bar{X})^3$ |
|---|---|---|---|---|
| 3 | 3.23 | $-$ .23 | .053 | $-$ .012 |
| 2 | 3.23 | $-$ 1.23 | 1.51 | $-$ 1.86 |
| 3.7 | 3.23 | .47 | .22 | .103 |
| 5 | 3.23 | 1.77 | 3.13 | 5.54 |
| 2.7 | 3.23 | $-$ .53 | .28 | $-$ .148 |
| 3 | 3.23 | $-$ .23 | .053 | $-$ .012 |

$$\Sigma(X_i - \bar{X})^2 = 5.246 \qquad \Sigma(X_i - \bar{X})^3 = 3.611$$

$$s^2 = \dfrac{\Sigma(X_i - \bar{X})^2}{n} = \dfrac{5.246}{6} = .8743$$

$$s = \sqrt{s^2} = .9351$$

$$s^3 = .817$$

$$m_3 = \dfrac{\Sigma(X_i - \bar{X})^3}{n} = \dfrac{3.611}{6} = .6018$$

and $a_3 = \dfrac{m_3}{s^3} = \dfrac{.6018}{.817} = .73659$ .

The distribution of the chocolate rabbits' waist measurements is skewed to the right or positively skewed.

● **PROBLEM** 1-69

What are two ways to describe the form of a frequency distribution? How would the following distributions be described?

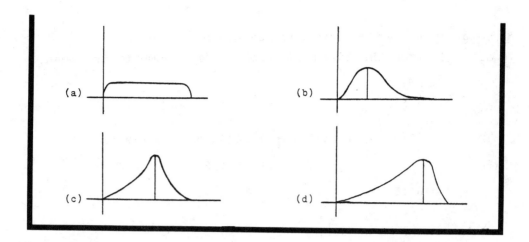

Solution:    The form of a frequency distribution can be described by its departure from symmetry or skewness and its degree of peakedness or kurtosis.

If the few extreme values are higher than most of the others, we say that the distribution is "positively skewed" or "skewed" to the right.

If the few extreme values are lower than most of the others, we say that the distribution is "negatively skewed" or "skewed" to the left.

A distribution that is very flat is called "platykurtic" and a distribution that has a high peak is called "leptokurtic".

(a) This curve is quite flat indicating a wide dispersion of measurements. Thus it is platykurtic.

(b) This distribution has extreme values in the upper half of the curve and is skewed to the right or positively skewed.

(c) This frequency distribution is very peaked and is    leptokurtic.

(d) The extreme values of this distribution are in the lower half of the curve. Thus the distribution is negatively skewed or skewed to the left.

● PROBLEM 1-70

Find the degree of skewness of the distribution representing these data.

| Class Limit | Frequency | Class Midpoint |
|-------------|-----------|----------------|
| 49-54 | 6 | 51.5 |
| 55-60 | 15 | 57.5 |
| 61-66 | 24 | 63.5 |
| 67-72 | 33 | 69.5 |
| 73-78 | 22 | 75.5 |

Solution:    We compute our measure of skewness $a_3 = \frac{m_3}{s^3}$ from the following table. First compute the mean, $\overline{X}$.

$$X = \frac{\Sigma f_i X_i}{\Sigma f_i}$$

$$= [6(51.5) + 15(57.5) + 24(63.5) + 33(69.5)$$

$$+ 22(75.5)] \div 100$$

$$= 66.5.$$

In tabular form we see;

| Class | Frequency $f_i$ | Class Mark $X_i$ | $\overline{X}$ | $(X_i - \overline{X})$ | $f_i(X_i - \overline{X})^2$ | $f_i(X_i - \overline{X})^3$ |
|---|---|---|---|---|---|---|
| 49–54 | 6 | 51.5 | 66.5 | − 15 | 6(225)=1350 | − 20250 |
| 55–60 | 15 | 57.5 | 66.5 | − 9 | 15(81)=1215 | − 10935 |
| 61–66 | 24 | 63.5 | 66.5 | − 3 | 24(9)=216 | − 648 |
| 67–72 | 33 | 69.5 | 66.5 | 3 | 33(9)=297 | 891 |
| 73–78 | 22 | 75.5 | 66.5 | 9 | 22(81)=1782 | 16038 |

$$\Sigma f_i = 100 \qquad \Sigma f_i(X_i - \overline{X})^2 = 4860$$

$$\Sigma f_i(X_i - \overline{X})^3 = -14904 .$$

It is now possible to compute the standard deviation, s, and the third moment, $m_3$.

$$s = \sqrt{s^2} = \sqrt{\frac{\Sigma f_i(X_i - \overline{X})^2}{\Sigma f_i}} = \sqrt{\frac{4860}{100}}$$

$$= \sqrt{48.60} = 6.97$$

$$s^3 = (6.97)^3 = 338.675$$

$$m_3 = \frac{\Sigma f_i(X_i - \overline{X})^3}{\Sigma f_i} = \frac{-14904}{100} = -149.04$$

$$a_3 = \frac{m_3}{s^3} = \frac{-149.04}{338.675} = -.44$$

The distribution from which these observations are drawn is slightly negatively skewed.

The following are the highest continental altitudes:

| Continent | Highest Point | Altitude |
|-----------|---------------|----------|
| Asia | Mt. Everest | 29,028 |
| South America | Mt. Aconcagua | 22,834 |
| North America | Mt. McKinley | 20,320 |
| Africa | Kibo (Kilimanjaro) | 19,340 |
| Europe | Mt. El'brus | 18,510 |
| Antartica | Vinson Massif | 16,860 |
| Australia | Mt. Kosciusko | 7,310 |

Describe the frequency distribution of the altitudes of these peaks. What is the "peakedness" or kurtosis of the distribution of heights based on this sample of observations.

Solution:     The measure of kurtosis or "peakedness" is

$$a_4 = \frac{m_4}{s^4} \qquad \text{where} \qquad m_4 = \frac{\Sigma (X_i - \overline{X})^4}{n}$$

is the fourth moment and $s^4$ is the standard deviation raised to the fourth power.

If $a_4 = 3$ the distribution is neither excessively peaked or flat. If $a_4 > 3$, the distribution is leptokurtic or sharply peaked. If $a_4 < 3$, the distribution is platykurtic or flattened.

We calculate $a_4$ with the aid of the following table.

| $X_i$ | $\overline{X}$ | $X_i - \overline{X}$ | $(X_i - \overline{X})^2$ | $(X_i - \overline{X})^4$ |
|-------|-----|------|------------|------------|
| 29028 | 19172 | 9856 | $97.141 \times 10^6$ | $9436.4 \times 10^{12}$ |
| 22834 | 19172 | 3662 | $13.410 \times 10^6$ | $179.82 \times 10^{12}$ |
| 20320 | 19172 | 1148 | $1.3179 \times 10^6$ | $1.7368 \times 10^{12}$ |
| 19340 | 19172 | 168 | $.028224 \times 10^6$ | $.0007965 \times 10^{12}$ |
| 18510 | 19172 | -662 | $.43824 \times 10^6$ | $.192054 \times 10^{12}$ |
| 16860 | 19172 | -2312 | $5.3453 \times 10^6$ | $28.572 \times 10^{12}$ |
| 7310 | 19172 | -11862 | $140.71 \times 10^6$ | $19799 \times 10^{12}$ |

$$s^2 = \frac{\Sigma (X_i - \overline{X})^2}{n} = \frac{258.39 \times 10^6}{7} = 36.912 \times 10^6$$

$$s = \sqrt{s^2} = 6.0756 \times 10^3$$

$$m_4 = \frac{\Sigma (X_i - \overline{X})^4}{n} = \frac{29445.7}{7} \times 10^{12} = 4206.5 \times 10^{12}.$$

Thus $a_4 = \frac{m_4}{s^4} = \frac{4206.5 \times 10^{12}}{(6.0756)^4 \times 10^{12}} = \frac{4206.5}{1362.6} = 3.087$

Thus the true distribution from which these peak altitudes are drawn seems neither platykurtic (flat) nor leptokurtic (peaked) but very nearly in between.

# CHAPTER 2

# ELEMENTARY PROBABILITY AND STATISTICS

## FUNDAMENTAL PRINCIPLE OF COUNTING

● PROBLEM 2-1

There are two roads between towns A and B. There are three roads between towns B and C. How many different routes may one travel between towns A and C.

Solution:

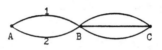

If we take road 1 from town A to town B and then any road from B to C there are three ways to travel from A to C. If we take road 2 from A to B and then any road from B to C there are again three ways to travel from A to C. These two possibilities are the only ones available to us. Thus there are 3 + 3 = 6 ways to travel from A to C.

This problem illustrates the fundamental principle of counting. This principle states that if an event can be divided into k components, and there are $n_1$ ways to carry out the first component, $n_2$ ways to carry out the second, $n_i$ ways to carry out the ith, and $n_k$ ways to carry out the kth then there are $n_1 \cdot n_2 \cdot n_3 \cdot \ldots \cdot n_k$ ways for the original event to take place.

● PROBLEM 2-2

How many ways can r different balls be placed in n different boxes? Consider the balls and boxes distinguishable.

Solution:    If the balls are placed one at a time, then each ball may be placed in one of n (provided there is ample room) boxes. That is, there are n boxes in which to place the first ball, n boxes for the second, n boxes for the third and finally n boxes for the rth.

By the fundamental principle of counting there are

$$\underbrace{n \cdot n \cdot n \cdot \ldots \cdot n}_{r \text{ terms}} \text{ or } n^r \text{ ways to place r different balls in n boxes.}$$

How many different numbers of 3 digits can be formed from
the numbers 1, 2, 3, 4, 5 (a) If repetitions are allowed?
(b) If repetitions are not allowed? How many of these
numbers are even in either case?

Solution:      (a) If repetitions are allowed, there are
5 choices for the first digit, 5 choices for the second
and 5 choices for the third. By the Fundamental Principle
of counting, there are 5 × 5 × 5 = 125 possible three digit
numbers. If the number is even, the final digit must be
either 2 or 4, 2 choices. So there will be  5 choices for
the first digit, 5 choices for the second and 2  for the
third, 5 × 5 × 2 = 50 such numbers.

      (b) If repetitions are not allowed, there are 5
choices for the first digit. After this has been picked,
there will be 4 choices for the second digit, and 3
choices for the third. Hence, 5 × 4 × 3 = 60 such numbers
can be selected.

      If the number must be even, then there are 2 choices
for the final digits, 2 or 4. This leaves 4 choices for
the next digit and 3 choices for the first digit. Hence
there are 4 × 3 × 2 = 24 possible even numbers that can be
selected in this way.

# PERMUTATIONS

Calculate the number of permutations of the letters a,b,c,d
taken two at a time.

Solution:  The first of the two letters may be taken in 4
ways (a,b,c, or d).  The second letter may therefore be
selected from the remaining three letters in 3 ways.  By
the fundamental principle the total number of ways of
selecting two letters is equal to the product of the number
of ways of selecting each letter, hence

$$p(4,2) = 4 \cdot 3 = 12.$$

The list of these permutations is:

        ab  ba  ca  da

        ac  bc  cb  db

        ad  bd  cd  dc.

Calculate the number of permutations of the letters
a,b,c,d taken four at a time.

<u>Solution:</u>  The number of permutations of the four letters
taken four at a time equals the number of ways the four
letters can be arranged or ordered.  Consider four places
to be filled by the four letters.  The first place can be
filled in four ways choosing from the four letters.  The
second place may be filled in three ways selecting one of
the three remaining letters.  The third place may be filled
in two ways with one of the two still remaining.  The fourth
place  is filled one way with the last letter.  By the
fundamental principle, the total number of ways of ordering
the letters equals the product of the number of ways of
filling each ordered place, or $4 \cdot 3 \cdot 2 \cdot 1 = 24 = P(4,4) = 4!$
(read 'four factorial').
    In general, for n objects taken r at a time,

$$P(n,r) = n(n-1)(n-2)...(n-r+1) = \frac{n!}{(n-r)!} \quad (r < n).$$

For the special case where $r = n$,

$$P(n,n) = n(n-1)(n-2)...(3)(2)(1) = n!,$$

since $(n-r)! = 0!$ which $= 1$ by definition.

● **PROBLEM** 2-6

In how many ways may 3 books be placed next to each other
on a shelf?

<u>Solution:</u>  We construct a pattern of 3 boxes to represent
the places where the 3 books are to be placed next to each
other on the shelf:

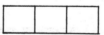

Since there are 3 books, the first place may be filled in 3
ways.  There are then 2 books left, so that the second place
may be filled in 2 ways.  There is only 1 book left to fill
the last place.  Hence our boxes take the following form:

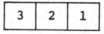

The Fundamental Principle of Counting states that if one
thing can be done in a different ways and, when it is done
in any one of these ways, a second thing can be done in b
different ways, and a third thing can be done in c ways, ...
then all the things in succession can be done in a×b×c ...
different ways.  Thus the books can be arranged in $3 \cdot 2 \cdot 1 = 6$
ways.
    This can also be seen using the following approach.
Since the arrangement of books on the shelf is important,
this is a permutations problem. Recalling the general
formula for the number of permutations of n things taken r
at a time, $_nP_r = n!/(n-r)!$, we replace n by 3 and r by 3
to obtain

$$_3P_3 = \frac{3!}{(3-3)!} = \frac{3!}{0!} = \frac{3 \cdot 2 \cdot 1}{1} = 6 .$$

Determine the number of permutations of the letters in the word BANANA.

Solution: In solving this problem we use the fact that the number of permutations P of n things taken all at a time [P(n,n)], of which $n_1$ are alike, $n_2$ others are alike, $n_3$ others are alike, etc. is

$$P = \frac{n!}{n_1! n_2! n_3! \ldots} \text{, with } n_1 + n_2 + n_3 + \ldots = n.$$

In the given problem there are six letters (n = 6), of which two are alike, (there are two N's so that $n_1 = 2$), three others are alike (there are three A's, so that $n_2 = 3$), and one is left (there is one B, so $n_3 = 1$). Notice that $n_1 + n_2 + n_3 = 2 + 3 + 1 = 6 = n$; thus,

$$P = \frac{6!}{2!3!1!} = \frac{6 \cdot 5 \cdot \overset{2}{\cancel{4}} \cdot 3!}{\cancel{2} \cdot 1 \cdot \cancel{3!} \cdot 1} = 60.$$

Thus, there are 60 permutations of the letters in the word BANANA.

Find the number of permutations of the seven letters of the word "algebra."

Solution: A permutation is an ordered arrangement of a set of objects. For example, if you are given 4 letters a,b,c,d and you choose two at a time, some permutations you can obtain are: ab, ac, ad, ba, bc, bd, ca, cb.

For n things, we can arrange the first object in n different ways, the second in n-1 different ways, the third can be done in n-2 different ways, etc. Thus the n objects can be arranged in order in  n! = n · n-1 · n-2 ... 1 ways.

Temporarily place subscripts, 1 and 2, on the a's to distinguish them, so that we now have  7! = 5040 possible permutations of the seven distinct objects. Of these 5040 arrangements, half will contain the a's in the order $a_1$, $a_2$ and the other half will contain them in the order $a_2$, $a_1$. If we assume the two a's are indistinct, then we apply the following theorem. The number P of distinct permutations of n objects taken at a time, of which $n_1$ are alike, $n_2$ are alike of another kind,. . . ,$n_k$ are alike of still another kind, with $n_1 + n_2 + .. + n_k = n$ is $P = \frac{n!}{n_1! \, n_2! \, \ldots \, n_k!}$ Then, here in this example, the 2 a's are alike so

$$P = \frac{7!}{2!} = 2520 \text{ permutations of the letters of}$$

the word algebra, when the a's are indistinguishable.

In how many ways may a party of four women and four men

be seated at a round table if the women and men are to occupy alternate seats?

Solution:   If we consider the seats indistinguishable, then this is a problem in circular permutations, as opposed to linear permutations. In the standard linear permutation approach each chair is distinguishable from the others. Thus, if a woman is seated first, she may be chosen 4 ways, then a man seated next to her may be chosen 4 ways, the next woman can be chosen 3 ways and the man next to her can be chosen in 3 ways ... Our diagram to the linear approach shows the number of ways each seat can be occupied.

| 4 | 4 | 3 | 3 | 2 | 2 | 1 | 1 |
|---|---|---|---|---|---|---|---|

By the Fundamental Principle of Counting there are thus $4 \cdot 4 \cdot 3 \cdot 3 \cdot 2 \cdot 2 \cdot 1 \cdot 1 = 576$ ways to seat the people.

However, if the seats are indistinguishable then so long as each person has the same two people on each side, the seating arrangement is considered the same. Thus we may suppose one person, say a woman is seated in a part- icular place, and then arrange the remaining three women and four men relative to her. Because of the alternate seating scheme, there are three possible places for the remaining three women, so that there are $3! = 6$ ways of seating them. There are four possible places for the four men, whence there are $4! = 24$ ways in which the men may be seated. Hence the total number of arrangements is $6 \cdot 24 = 144$. In general, the formula for circular per- mutations of n things and n other things which are alter- nating is $(n - 1)!n!$. In our case we have

$$(4 - 1)!4! = 3!4! = 3 \cdot 2 \cdot 4 \cdot 3 \cdot 2 = 144.$$

# COMBINATIONS

● **PROBLEM** 2-10

How many different sums of money can be obtained by choosing two coins from a box containing a penny, a nickel, a dime, a quarter, and a half dollar?

Solution:   The order makes no difference here, since a selection of a penny and a dime is the same as a selection of a dime and a penny, insofar as a sum of money is con- cerned.   This is a case of combinations, then, rather than permutations.   Then the number of combinations of n differ- ent objects taken r at a time is equal to:

$$\frac{n(n-1)\ldots(n-r+1)}{1 \cdot 2 \cdots r}.$$

In this example, $n = 5$, $r = 2$, therefore

$$C(5,2) = \frac{5 \cdot 4}{1 \cdot 2} = 10.$$

As in the problem of selecting four committee members from a group of seven people, a distinct two coins can be selected from five coins in

$$\frac{5 \cdot 4}{1 \cdot 2} = 10 \text{ ways (applying the fundamental principle)}.$$

● **PROBLEM** 2-11

How many baseball teams of nine members can be chosen from among twelve boys, without regard to the position played by each member?

Solution: Since there is no regard to position, this is a combinations problem (if order or arrangement had been important it would have been a permutations problem). The general formula for the number of combinations of n things taken r at a time is

$$C(n,r) = \frac{n!}{r!(n-r)!} \quad .$$

We have to find the number of combinations of 12 things taken 9 at a time. Hence we have

$$C(12,9) = \frac{12!}{9!(12-9)!} = \frac{12!}{9!3!} = \frac{12 \cdot 11 \cdot 10 \cdot \cancel{9!}}{3 \cdot 2 \cdot 1 \cdot \cancel{9!}} = 220$$

Therefore, there are 220 possible teams.

● **PROBLEM** 2-12

How many "words" each consisting of two vowels and three consonants, can be formed from the letters of the word "integral"?

Solution: To find the number of ways to choose vowels or consonants from letters, we use combinations. The number of combinations of n different objects taken r at a time is defined to be

$$C(n,r) = \frac{n!}{r!(n-r)!} \quad .$$

Then, we first select the two vowels to be used, from among the three vowels in integral; this can be done in $C(3,2) = 3$ ways. Next, we select the three consonants from the five in integral; this yields $C(5,3) = 10$ possible choices. To find the number of ordered arrangements of 5 letters selected five at a time, we need to find the number of permutations of choosing r from n objects. Symbolically, it is $P(n,r)$ which is defined to be

$$P(n,r) = \frac{n!}{(n-r)!}$$

We permute the five chosen letters in all possible ways, of which there are $P(5,5) = 5! = 120$ arrangements. Finally, to find the total number of words which can be formed, we apply the Fundamental Counting Principle which states that if one event can be performed in m ways, another one in n ways, and another in k ways, then the total number of ways in which all events can occur is m × n × k ways. Hence the total number of possible words is, by the fundamental principle

$$C(3,2)C(5,3)P(5,5) = 3 \cdot 10 \cdot 120 = 3600.$$

How many different bridge hands are there?

Solution:    A bridge hand contains thirteen cards dealt from a 52 card deck. The order in which the cards are dealt is not important. The number of hands that might be dealt is the same as the number of hands it is possible to select, if one were allowed to select 13 cards at random from a standard deck. The question now becomes: how many ways may 52 objects be taken in combinations of 13 at a time? Let us denote this number by $_{52}C_{13}$.

To solve this problem, first find the number of ordered samples of 13 taken from 52. This can be found in two ways.

The first way is to count the number of unordered samples, $_{52}C_{13}$, and then count the number of ways an unordered sample of 13 may be ordered, 13!. By the Fundamental Principle of counting, the product of these two quantities will be the number of ordered samples. This number is $_{52}C_{13} \cdot 13!$.

The second way to count the ordered samples is the following: There are 52 ways to choose the first card, 51 ways to choose the second, 50 ways to choose the third, ... and 40 ways to choose the thirteenth. The total number of unordered samples is thus $52 \cdot 51 \cdot ... \cdot 40$ which can be written as

$$\frac{52 \cdot 51 \cdot 50 \cdot 49 \cdot 48 \cdot ... \cdot 40 \cdot 39!}{39!} = \frac{52!}{39!} \cdot$$

Our two ways of counting the same thing yield two

equal numbers   $_{52}C_{13} \cdot 13! = \frac{52!}{39!}$   or   $_{52}C_{13} = \frac{52!}{13! \; 39!} \cdot$

This number, the number of combinations of n objects taken r at a time is called a binomial coefficient and is

commonly written $n^C r$, $\binom{n}{r}$  or $C(n, r)$.

With the help of tables for n! we find the number of possible bridge hands to be about 635,000,000,000.

# VENN DIAGRAMS

In a survey carried out in a school snack shop, the following results were obtained. Of 100 boys questioned, 78 liked sweets, 74 ice-cream, 53 cake, 57 liked both sweets and ice-cream. 46 liked both sweets and cake while only 31 boys liked all three. If all the boys interviewed liked at least one item, draw a Venn diagram to illustrate the results. How many boys liked both ice-cream and cake?

<u>Solution</u>:    A Venn diagram is a pictorial representation
of the relationship between sets. A set is a collection of
objects. The number of objects in a particular set is the
cardinality of a set.

To draw a Venn diagram we start with the following
picture:

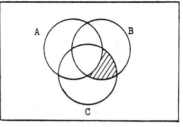

Each circle represents set A, B or C respectively. Let

A = set of boys who like ice-cream

B = set of boys who like cake

C = set of boys who like sweets.

The sections of overlap between circles represents
the members of one set who are also members of another set.
For example, the shaded region in the picture indicates the
set of boys who are in sets B and C but not A. This is the
set of boys who like both cake and sweets but not ice-
cream. The inner section common to all three circles indicates the set of boys who belong to all three sets simultaneously.

We wish to find the number of boys who liked both
ice-cream and cake. Let us label the sections of the diagram
with the cardinality of these sections. The cardinality of
the region common to all three sets is the number of boys
who liked all three items or 31.

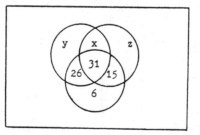

The number of boys who liked ice-cream and sweets
was 57. Of these 57, 31 like all three leaving 26 boys in
set A and set C but not set B. Similarly there are 15 boys
in B and C, but not in A. 78 - 26 - 31 - 15 = 6 boys in C
but not in A or B.

Let  x = number of boys who are in A and B but not C

     y = number of boys are in A but not B or C

z = number of boys who are in B but not A or C.

We know that the sum of all the labeled areas is 100 or

$$26 + 31 + 15 + 6 + x + y + z = 100$$

$$78 + x + y + z = 100.$$

Also, there are 74 boys total in set A or

$$x + y + 31 + 26 = 74 \quad \text{and 53 total in}$$

set B or $\quad x + z + 46 = 53.$

Combining: $\quad x + y + z = 100 - 78 = 22$

$$x + y = 74 - 57 = 17$$

$$x + z = 53 - 46 = 7.$$

Substracting the second equation from the first gives z = 5 implying x = 2 and y = 15. Our answer is the number of boys in sets A and B = x + 31 = 33.

● **PROBLEM** 2-15

Of 37 men and 33 women, 36 are teetotalers. Nine of the women are non-smokers and 18 of the men smoke but do not drink. 13 of the men and seven of the women drink but do not smoke. How many, at most, both drink and smoke.

Solution:  A = set of all smokers

B = set of all drinkers

C = set of all women

D = set of all men.

We construct two Venn diagrams and label it in the following way:

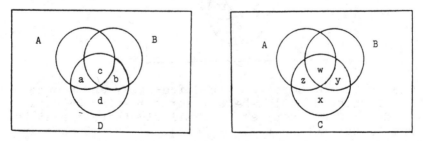

Each section on the graph indicates a subset of the group of men and women. For example, the section labeled "z" is the subset including all women who smoke but do not drink. The section labeled "b" is the subset including all

64

men who drink but do not smoke.

In addition to labels, these letters also will indicate the cardinality, the number of objects, in the subset. We are told there are 37 men; thus, $a + b + c + d = 37$. There are 33 women; thus, $x + y + z + w = 33$. There are 9 women non-smokers which includes $x + y$. $d = 18$ the number of non-drinking, smoking men.

Similarly, $x + z + a + d = 36$, the teetotalers

$b = 13$, the drinking, non-smoking men

$y = 7$, the drinking, non-smoking women.

Collecting all these equations, we wish to find the maximum value of $c + w$, the number of drinkers and smokers.

$$x + z + a + d = 36, \qquad a + b + c + d = 37$$

$$b = 13, \; d = 18, \qquad x + y + z + w = 33$$

$$y = 7, \qquad x + y = 9 \; .$$

Substituting we see that:

$$x + y = x + 7 = 9 \quad \text{or} \quad x = 2 \qquad \text{from this we have}$$

$$2 + z + a + 18 = 36 \qquad a + 13 + c + 18 = 37$$

$$a + z = 16 \qquad\qquad a + c = 6$$

$$2 + 7 + z + w = 33$$

$$z + w = 24 \; .$$

We now solve for $c + w$:

$$a = 6 - c \qquad \text{and thus} \quad z + 6 - c = 16 \quad \text{or} \quad z - c = 10$$

$$c = z - 10 \qquad\qquad \text{and} \qquad w = 24 - z$$

thus, $\qquad c + w = z - 10 + 24 - z = 14$.

The maximum number of drinkers and smokers is 14.

# CLASSICAL MODEL OF PROBABILITY

● **PROBLEM** 2-16

What is the probability of throwing a "six" with a single die?

<u>Solution:</u>  The die may land in any of 6 ways:

1,  2,  3,  4,  5,  6

The probability of throwing a six,

$$P(6) = \frac{\text{number of ways to get a six}}{\text{number of ways the die may land}}$$

Thus $P(6) = \frac{1}{6}$.

● **PROBLEM** 2-17

A deck of playing cards is thoroughly shuffled and a card is drawn from the deck. What is the probability that the card drawn is the ace of diamonds?

Solution:  The probability of an event occurring is

$$\frac{\text{the number of ways the event can occur}}{\text{the number of possible outcomes}}$$

In our case there is one way the event can occur, for there is only one ace of diamonds and there are fifty two possible outcomes (for there are 52 cards in the deck).Hence the probability that the card drawn is the ace of diamonds is 1/52.

● **PROBLEM** 2-18

A box contains 7 red, 5 white, and 4 black balls.  What is the probability of your drawing at random one red ball? One black ball?

Solution:  There are 7 + 5 + 4 = 16 balls in the box.   The probability of drawing one red ball,

$$P(R) = \frac{\text{number of possible ways of drawing a red ball}}{\text{number of ways of drawing any ball}}$$

$$P(R) = \frac{7}{16}.$$

Similarly, the probability of drawing one black ball

$$P(B) = \frac{\text{number of possible ways of drawing a black ball}}{\text{number of ways of drawing any ball}}$$

Thus,

$$P(B) = \frac{4}{16} = \frac{1}{4}$$

● **PROBLEM** 2-19

Find the probability of drawing a black card in a single random draw from a well-shuffled deck of ordinary playing cards.

Solution:    There are 52 cards and since the cards are well-shuffled, each card is equally likely to be drawn. There are 26 black cards in the deck and thus the number of outcomes leading to the event a black card being drawn is 26.  Therefore   $\text{Pr (drawing a black card)} = \frac{26}{52} = \frac{1}{2}$

Find the probability of drawing a spade on a single random draw from a well-shuffled deck of cards.

Solution:    There are 52 possible outcomes to the experiment of drawing a card. There are 13 spades in a deck and hence 13 possible outcomes to the experiment which lead to the event drawing a spade.

Thus,   P (drawing a spade) $= \frac{13}{52} = \frac{1}{4}$ .

● **PROBLEM** 2-21

What is the probability of making a 7 in one throw of a pair of dice?

Solution:  There are 6 X 6 = 36 ways that two dice can be thrown, as shown in the accompanying figure.

The number of possible ways that a 7 will appear are circled in the figure.  Let us call this set B.  Thus,

$$B = \{(1,6),(2,5),(3,4),(4,3),(5,2),(6,1)\}.$$

● **PROBLEM** 2-22

In a single throw of a single die, find the probability of obtaining either a 2 or a 5.

Solution:  In a single throw, the die may land in any of 6 ways:

    1  2  3  4  5  6.

The probability of obtaining a 2,

$$P(2) = \frac{\text{number of ways of obtaining a 2}}{\text{numbers of ways the die may land}} , \quad P(2) = \frac{1}{6}.$$

Similarly, the probability of obtaining a 5,

$$P(5) = \frac{\text{number of ways of obtaining a 5}}{\text{number of ways the die may land}} , \quad P(5) = \frac{1}{6}.$$

The probability that either one of two mutually exclusive events will occur is the sum of the probabilities of the separate events.  Thus the probability of obtaining either a 2 or a 5, P(2) or P(5), is

$$P(2) + P(5) = \frac{1}{6} + \frac{1}{6} = \frac{2}{6} = \frac{1}{3}$$

If a card is drawn from a deck of playing cards, what is the probability that it will be a jack or a ten?

__Solution:__ The probability that an event A or B occurs, but not both at the same time, is $P(A \cup B) = P(A) + P(B)$. Here the symbol "$\cup$" stands for "or."

In this particular example, we only select one card at a time. Thus, we either choose a jack "or" a ten. P(a jack or a ten) = P(a jack) + P(a ten).

$$P(\text{a jack}) = \frac{\text{number of ways to select a jack}}{\text{number of ways to choose a card}} = \frac{4}{52} = \frac{1}{13}.$$

$$P(\text{a ten}) = \frac{\text{number of ways to choose a ten}}{\text{number of ways to choose a card}} = \frac{4}{52} = \frac{1}{13}.$$

$$P(\text{a jack or a ten}) = P(\text{a jack}) + P(\text{a ten}) = \frac{1}{13} + \frac{1}{13} = \frac{2}{13}.$$

Suppose that we have a bag containing two red balls, three white balls, and six blue balls. What is the probability of obtaining a red or a white ball on one withdrawal?

Solution:

Fig. A

Fig. B

The bag is shown in figure A.

There are two favorable possibilities: drawing a red ball and drawing a white ball. The universal set of equally likely possibilities contains eleven elements; the number of red balls is two, and the number of white balls is three. Refer to figure B.

Hence the probability of drawing a red ball is $\frac{2}{11}$ and the probability of drawing a white ball is $\frac{3}{11}$.

In the set notation, the probability of A, P(A), or the probability of B, P(B), is P(A) + P(B) therefore the probability of drawing a red, or a white ball is the probability of drawing a red ball plus the probability of drawing a white ball

$$P(\text{red}) = \frac{2}{11} \qquad\qquad P(\text{white}) = \frac{3}{11}$$

$$P(\text{red or white}) = \frac{2}{11} + \frac{3}{11} = \frac{5}{11} \ .$$

Note: In the above example the probability of drawing a blue ball would be $\frac{6}{11}$ . Therefore the sum of the probability of a red ball, the probability of a white ball, and the probability of a blue ball is $\frac{2}{11} + \frac{3}{11} + \frac{6}{11} = 1$ .

If there are no possible results that are considered favorable, then the probability P(F) is obviously 0. If every result is considered favorable, then P(F) = 1. Hence the probability P(F) of a favorable result F always satisfies the inequality

$$0 \leq P(F) \leq 1.$$

● **PROBLEM** 2-25

A bag contains 4 white balls, 6 black balls, 3 red balls, and 8 green balls. If one ball is drawn from the bag, find the probability that it will be either white or green.

Solution: The probability that it will be either white or green is:
P(a white ball or a green ball) = P(a white ball) + P(a green ball).
This is true because if we are given two mutually exclusive events A or B, then P(A or B) = P(A) + P(B). Note that two events, A and B, are mutually exclusive events if their intersection is the null or empty set. In this case the intersection of choosing a white ball and of choosing a green ball is the empty set. There are no elements in common.

$$P \text{ (a white ball)} = \frac{\text{number of ways to choose a white ball}}{\text{number of ways to select a ball}}$$

$$= \frac{4}{21}$$

$$P \text{(a green ball)} = \frac{\text{number of ways to choose a green ball}}{\text{number of ways to select a ball}}$$

$$= \frac{8}{21}$$

Thus,
P(a white ball or a green ball) = $\frac{4}{21} + \frac{8}{21} = \frac{12}{21} = \frac{4}{7}$ .

● **PROBLEM** 2-26

Determine the probability of getting 6 or 7 in a toss of

69

two dice.

Solution:   Let A = the event that a 6 is obtained in a toss
                  of two dice

                  B = the event that a 7 is obtained in a toss
                  of two dice.

Then, the probability of getting 6 or 7 in a toss of two
dice is

$$P(A \text{ or } B) = P(A \cup B).$$

The union symbol "$\cup$" means that A and/or B can occur.   Now
$P(A \cup B) = P(A) + P(B)$ if A and B are mutually exclusive.
Two or more events are said to be mutually exclusive if the
occurrence of any one of them excludes the occurrence of
the others.   In this case, we cannot obtain a six and a
seven in a single toss of two dice.   Thus, A and B are
mutually exclusive.
        To calculate $P(A)$ and $P(B)$, use the following table.

Note:   There are 36 different tosses of two dice.

A = a 6 is obtained in a toss of two dice

   $= \left\{ (1,5), \ (2,4), \ (3,3), \ (4,2), \ (5,1) \right\}$

B = a 7 is obtained in a toss of two dice

   $= \left\{ (1,6), \ (2,5), \ (3,4), \ (4,3), \ (5,2), \ (6,1) \right\}.$

$P(A) = \dfrac{\text{number of ways to obtain a 6 in a toss of two dice}}{\text{number of ways to toss two dice}}$

   $= \dfrac{5}{36}$

$P(B) = \dfrac{\text{number of ways to obtain a 7 in a toss of two dice}}{\text{number of ways to toss two dice}}$

   $= \dfrac{6}{36} = \dfrac{1}{6}.$

Therefore, $P(A \cup B) = P(A) + P(B) = \dfrac{5}{36} + \dfrac{6}{36} = \dfrac{11}{36}.$

● PROBLEM 2-27

A coin is tossed nine times. What is the total number of
possible outcomes of the nine-toss experiment? How many
elements are in the subset "6 heads and 3 tails"? What is
the probability of getting exactly 6 heads and 3 tails in
nine tosses of thus unbiased coin?

Solution:     There are 2 possible outcomes for each toss,

that is, $\underbrace{2\cdot2\cdot\ldots\cdot2}_{\text{nine terms}}$ $=2^9$ possible outcomes in 9 tosses,

or 512 outcomes.

To count the number of elements in the subset "6 heads and 3 tails" is equivalent to counting the number of ways 6 objects can be selected from 9. These objects will then be labeled "heads" and the remaining 3 objects will be labeled tails. There are

$$\binom{9}{6} = \frac{9!}{6! \; 3!} = 84 \qquad \text{ways to do this and hence the}$$

probability of observing this configuration is

$$\frac{\text{the number of ways 6 heads and 3 tails can occur}}{\text{the total possible outcomes}}$$

$$= \frac{\binom{9}{6}}{2^9} = \frac{84}{512} = .164.$$

● **PROBLEM** 2-28

Suppose a die has been loaded so that the ⚀ face lands uppermost 3 times as often as any other face while all the other faces occur equally often. What is the probability of a ⚁ on a single toss" What is the probability of a ⚀ ?

Solution:    Let p equal the probability of the ⚀ face landing uppermost. We know that    Pr ( ⚀ face landing uppermost) = 3 Pr(any other face landing uppermost). We also know that faces with j dots, j = 2, 3, 4, 5, 6 occur equally often. Thus

$$\sum_{j=1}^{6} \text{Pr (Face with j dots landing uppermost)} = 1,$$

and Pr (face with 1 dot appears) +

$$\sum_{j=2}^{6} \text{Pr (face with j dots appears)} = 1$$

or        $p + 5 \; (1/3 \; P) = 1$.

Thus        $p = 3/8$    and Pr (face with 2 dots landing uppermost)    $= 1/3 \; P = 1/8$.

The probability of a ⚀ is $3/8$.

● **PROBLEM** 2-29

In a single throw of a pair of dice, find the probability

of obtaining a total of 4 or less.

**Solution:** Each die may land in 6 ways. By the Fundamental Principle of Counting the pair of dice may thus land in 6 X 6 = 36 ways:

| 1,1 | 1,2 | 1,3 | 1,4 | 1,5 | 1,6 |
|-----|-----|-----|-----|-----|-----|
| 2,1 | 2,2 | 2,3 | 2,4 | 2,5 | 2,6 |
| 3,1 | 3,2 | 3,3 | 3,4 | 3,5 | 3,6 |
| 4,1 | 4,2 | 4,3 | 4,4 | 4,5 | 4,6 |
| 5,1 | 5,2 | 5,3 | 5,4 | 5,5 | 5,6 |
| 6,1 | 6,2 | 6,3 | 6,4 | 6,5 | 6,6 |

Let us call the possible outcomes which are circled above set A. Then the elements of set A, A = { (1,1), (1,2), (1,3), (2,1), (2,2), (3,1)} are all the possible ways of obtaining four or less.

The probability of obtaining 4 or less, (number of elements in set A)

$$P[(x,y) \le 4] = \frac{\text{number of ways of obtaining 4 or less}}{\text{number of ways the dice may land}}$$

$$= \frac{6}{36} = \frac{1}{6}.$$

$$P(BC) = \frac{\text{number of non-face cards that are divisible by 3}}{\text{number of cards}}$$

$$= \frac{12}{52} .$$

$$P(ABC) = \frac{\text{number of hearts that are non-face cards \& divisible by 3}}{\text{number of cards}}$$

$$= \frac{3}{52} .$$

We have shown informally that

$$P(A \cup B \cup C) = P(A) + P(B) + P(C) - P(AB) - P(AC) - P(BC) + P(ABC).$$

● **PROBLEM 2-30**

A card is drawn at random from a deck of cards. Find the probability that at least one of the following three events will occur:

Event A : a heart is drawn.
Event B: a card which is not a face card is drawn.
Event C: the number of spots (if any) on the drawn card is divisible by 3.

**Solution:**    Let A∪B∪C = the event that at least one of the three events above will occur. We wish to find P(A∪B∪C), the probability of the event A∪B∪C. Let us count the number of ways that at least A, B or C will occur. There are 13 hearts, 40 non-face cards, and 12 cards such that the number of spots is divisible by 3. (Cards numbered 3, 6, or 9 are all divisible by 3 and there are 4 suits each with 3 such cards, 3 × 4 = 12). If we add 40 + 13 + 12 we will have counted too many times. There are 10 cards which are hearts and non-face cards. 3 cards divisible by 3 and hearts, 12 cards which are non-face cards and divisible by 3. We must subtract each of these from our total of 40 + 13 + 12 giving 40 + 13 + 12 - 10 - 3 - 12. But we have subtracted too much; we have subtracted the 3 cards which are hearts and non-face cards and divisible by 3. We must add these cards to our total making

$$P(A∪B∪C) = \frac{40 + 13 + 12 - 10 - 3 - 12 + 3}{52} = \frac{43}{52} .$$

Our counting technique used was called the principle of inclusion/exclusion and is useful for problems of this sort. Also look again at our answer,

$$P(A∪B∪C) = \frac{13 + 40 + 12 - 10 - 3 - 12 + 3}{52}$$

$$= \frac{13}{52} + \frac{40}{52} + \frac{12}{52} - \frac{10}{52} - \frac{3}{52} - \frac{12}{52} + \frac{3}{52} .$$

Note that $P(A) = \frac{\text{number of hearts}}{\text{number of cards}} = \frac{13}{52}$

$$P(B) = \frac{\text{number of non-face cards}}{\text{number of cards}} = \frac{40}{52}$$

$$P(C) = \frac{\text{number of cards divisible by 3}}{\text{number of cards}} = \frac{12}{52}$$

$$P(AB) = \frac{\text{number of hearts and non-face cards}}{\text{number of cards}} = \frac{10}{52}$$

$$P(AC) = \frac{\text{number of hearts and cards divisible by 3}}{\text{number of cards}}$$

$$= \frac{3}{52} .$$

● PROBLEM 2-31

Find the probability of throwing at least one of the following totals on a single throw of a pair of dice: a total 5, a total of 6, a total of 7.

Define the events A, B, and C as follows:

Event A: a total of 5 is thrown,

Event B: a total of 6 is thrown,
Event C: a total of 7 is thrown.

Solution:    Only one of these three events can occur at
one time. The occurrence of any one excludes the occurrence
of any of the others. Such events are called mutually
exclusive.

Let $A \cup B \cup C$ = the event that at least a 5, 6 or 7 is
thrown. $P(A \cup B \cup C) = P(A) + P(B) + P(C)$ because the events
are mutually exclusive.

Referring to  a  previous table we see that

$P(A) = \frac{4}{36}$, $P(B) = \frac{5}{36}$, and $P(C) = \frac{6}{36}$ . Therefore,

$$P(A \cup B \cup C) = \frac{4}{36} + \frac{5}{36} + \frac{6}{36} = \frac{15}{36} = \frac{5}{12} .$$

● **PROBLEM** 2-32

What is the probability of getting a 5 on each of two
successive rolls of a balanced die?

Solution:    We are dealing with separate rolls of a
balanced die. The 2 rolls are independent, therefore we
invoke the following multiplication rule: The probability
of getting any particular combination in two or more
independent trials will be the product of their individual
probabilities. The probability of getting a 5 on any single
toss is $\frac{1}{6}$ and by the multiplication rule

$$P \text{ (5 and 5)} = \frac{1}{6} \cdot \frac{1}{6} = \frac{1}{36} .$$

Note also the problem could have been stated as
follows: What is the probability of rolling 2 balanced dice
simultaneously and getting a 5 on each?

● **PROBLEM** 2-33

If a pair of dice is tossed twice, find the probability of obtaining 5 on both tosses.

Solution:  We obtain 5 in one toss of the two dice if they fall with
either 3 and 2 or 4 and 1 uppermost, and each of these combinations
can appear in two ways.  The ways to obtain 5 in one toss of the two
dice are:

$$(1,4), (4,1), (3,2), \text{ and } (2,3).$$

Hence we can throw 5 in one toss in four ways.  Each die has six faces
and there are six ways for a die to fall.  Then the pair of dice can
fall in 6·6 = 36 ways.  The probability of throwing 5 in one toss is:

$$\frac{\text{the number of ways to throw a 5 in one toss}}{\text{the number of ways that a pair of dice can fall}} = \frac{4}{36} = \frac{1}{9} .$$

Now the probability of throwing a 5 on both tosses is:

P(throwing five on first toss and throwing five on second toss).

"And" implies multiplication if events are independent, thus
p(throwing 5 on first toss and throwing 5 on second toss)

= p(throwing 5 on first toss) × p(throwing 5 on second toss)

Since the results of the two tosses are independent. Consequently, the probability of obtaining 5 on both tosses is

$$\left(\frac{1}{9}\right)\left(\frac{1}{9}\right) = \frac{1}{81} \ .$$

● **PROBLEM** 2-34

A penny is to be tossed 3 times. What is the probability there will be 2 heads and 1 tail?

<u>Solution:</u>　　We start this problem by constructing a set of all possible outcomes:

We can have heads on all 3 tosses:               (HHH)
head on first 2 tosses, tail on the third:   (HHT)     (1)
head on first toss, tail on next two:       (HTT)
                      ●                  (HTH)     (2)
                      ●                  (THH)     (3)
                                     (THT)
                      ●                  (TTH)
                                     (TTT)

Hence there are eight possible outcomes (2 possibilities on first toss x 2 on second x 2 on third = 2 x 2 x 2 = 8).

We assume that these outcomes are all equally likely and assign the probability 1/8 to each. Now we look for the set of outcomes that produce 2 heads and 1 tail. We see there are 3 such outcomes out of the 8 possibilities (numbered (1), (2), (3) in our listing). Hence the probability of 2 heads and 1 tail is 3/8.

● **PROBLEM** 2-35

Of the approximately 635,000,000,000 different bridge hands, how many contain a ten card suit?

Solution: As before, the number of ways a hand could be dealt can be thought of as the number of ways one can select such a hand. We will select a 13 card bridge hand with ten cards of the same suit in three steps. First let us select the suit of the 10 cards; there are $\binom{4}{1}$ or 4 ways to do this. Next let us select 10 of the thirteen possible cards in the suit which will be in our bridge hand. There are $\binom{13}{10}$ or $_{13}C_{10}$ ways to do this,

$$\binom{13}{10} = \frac{13!}{10! \ 3!} = \frac{13 \cdot 12 \cdot 11}{3 \cdot 2 \cdot 1} = 286 \quad \text{ways to}$$

choose the 10 cards.

Last we must select the 3 remaining cards. These three cards must not be in the same suit as the 10 cards we have previously chosen. Instead they must be from the remaining 3 suits or 39 cards. There are $\binom{39}{3}$ ways to select these cards and

$$\binom{39}{3} = \frac{39!}{3! \; 36!} = \frac{39 \cdot 38 \cdot 37}{3 \cdot 2 \cdot 1} = 9139.$$

By the Fundamental Principle of counting the number of different hands containing 10 cards in the same suit is the product of the number of ways in which each of these steps might be carried out. This product is

$$\binom{4}{1} \cdot \binom{13}{10} \cdot \binom{39}{3} = 4 \cdot 286 \cdot 9139 = 10,455,016.$$

This is the number of all the possible bridge hands which have 10 cards all of the same suit.

From this problem and an earlier one (counting the total number of bridge hands), we can calculate the probability of being dealt a hand with 10 cards in the same suit. This probability is the

$$\frac{\text{number of hands with 10 cards in the same suit}}{\text{total number of possible bridge hands}} \; .$$

This equals $\dfrac{\binom{4}{1}\binom{13}{10}\binom{39}{3}}{\binom{52}{13}} = .000016.$

# CONDITIONAL PROBABILITY

● PROBLEM 2-36

Find the probability that a face card is drawn on the first draw and an ace on the second in two consecutive draws, without replacement, from a standard deck of cards.

Solution:   This problem illustrates the notion of conditional probability. The conditional probability of an event, say event B, given the occurrence of a previous event, say event A, is written $P(B|A)$. This is the conditional probability of B given A.

$P(B|A)$ is defined to be $\dfrac{P(AB)}{P(A)}$, where $P(AB) =$ Probability of the joint occurrence of events A and B.

Let  A = event that a face card is drawn on the first draw

B = event that an ace is drawn on the second draw.

We wish to find the probability of the joint occurrence of these events, P(AB).

We know that $P(AB) = P(A) \cdot P(B|A)$.

P(A) = probability that a face card is drawn on the

first draw $= \dfrac{12}{52} = \dfrac{3}{13}$ .

P(B|A) = probability that an ace is drawn on the second draw given that a face card is drawn on the first

= number of ways an ace can be drawn on the second draw given a face card is drawn on the first divided by the total number of possible outcomes of the second draw.

$= \dfrac{4}{51}$ ; remember there will be only 51 cards left in the

deck after the face card is drawn.

Thus $P(AB) = \dfrac{3}{13} \cdot \dfrac{4}{51} = \dfrac{4}{13 \times 17} = \dfrac{4}{221}$ .

● **PROBLEM  2-37**

A survey was made of 100 customers in a department store. Sixty of the 100 indicated they visited the store because of a newspaper advertisement. The remainder had not seen the ad. A total of 40 customers made purchases; of these customers, 30 had seen the ad. What is the probability that a person who did not see the ad made a purchase? What is the probability that a person who saw the ad made a purchase?

Solution:    In these two questions we have to deal with conditional probability, the probability that an event occurred given that another event occurred. In symbols, P(A|B) means "the probability of A given B". This is defined as the probability of A and B, divided by the probability of B. Symbolically,

$$P(A|B) = \dfrac{P(A \cap B)}{P(B)}$$ .

In the problem, we are told that only 40 customers made purchases. Of these 40, only 30 had seen the ad. Thus, 10 of 100 customers made purchases without seeing the ad. The probability of selecting such a customer at random is

$\dfrac{10}{100} = \dfrac{1}{10}$ .

Let A represent the event of "a  purchase", B the

event of "having seen the ad", and $\bar{B}$ the event of "not having seen the ad."

Symbolically, $P(A \cap \bar{B}) = \frac{1}{10}$ . We are told that 40 of the customers did not see the ad. Thus $P(\bar{B}) = \frac{40}{100} = \frac{4}{10}$ .

Dividing, we obtain $\frac{1/10}{4/10} = \frac{1}{4}$ , and, by definition of conditional probability, $P(A|\bar{B}) = \frac{1}{4}$ . Thus the probability that a customer purchased given they did not see the ad is $\frac{1}{4}$ .

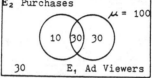

To solve the second problem, note that 30 purchasers saw the ad. The probability that a randomly selected customer saw the ad and made a purchase is $\frac{30}{100} = \frac{3}{10}$ . Since 60 of the 100 customers saw the ad, the probability that a randomly-picked customer saw the ad is $\frac{60}{100} = \frac{6}{10}$ . Dividing we obtain

$$P(A|B) = \frac{P(A \cap B)}{P(B)} = \frac{\frac{3}{10}}{\frac{6}{10}} = \frac{3}{6} = \frac{1}{2} .$$

● **PROBLEM** 2-38

A coin is tossed 3 times, and 2 heads and 1 tail fall. What is the probability that the first toss was heads?

Solution: This problem is one of conditional probability. Given two events, $P_1$ and $P_2$, the probability that event $P_2$ will occur on the condition that we have event $P_1$ is

$$P(P_2/P_1) = \frac{P(P_1 \text{ and } P_2)}{P(P_1)} = \frac{P(P_1 P_2)}{P(P_1)}$$

Define

$P_1$: 2 heads and 1 tail fall,

$P_2$: the first toss is heads.

$$P(P_1) = \frac{\text{number of ways to obtain 2 heads and 1 tail}}{\text{number of possibilities resulting from 3 tosses}}$$

$$= \Big(\{H,H,T\},\{H,T,H\},\{T,H,H\}\Big) / \Big(\{H,H,H\},\{H,H,T\},\{H,T,T\},\{H,T,H\}, \{T,T,H\},\{T,H,T\},\{T,H,H\},\{T,T,T\}\Big)$$

$$= 3/8$$

$$P\left(p_1 p_2\right) = P(2 \text{ heads and } 1 \text{ tail and the first toss is heads})$$

$$= \frac{\text{number of ways to obtain } p_1 \text{ and } p_2}{\text{number of possibilities resulting from 3 tosses}}$$

$$= \frac{\left(\{H,H,T\}, \{H,T,H\}\right)}{8} = 2/8 = 1/4$$

$$P\left(p_2 / p_1\right) = \frac{P\left(p_1 p_2\right)}{P\left(p_1\right)} = \frac{1/4}{3/8} = 2/3$$

● **PROBLEM** 2-39

A coin is tossed 3 times.  Find the probability that all
3 are heads,
   (a) if it is known that the first is heads,
   (b) if it is known that the first 2 are heads,
   (c) if it is known that 2 of them are heads.

Solution:  This problem is one of conditional probability.
If we have two events, A and B, the probability of event
A given that event B has occurred is

$$P(A/B) = \frac{P(AB)}{P(B)}.$$

(a)  We are asked to find the probability that all
three tosses are heads given that the first toss is heads.
The first event is A and the second is B.

P(AB) = probability that all three tosses are heads
        given that the first toss is heads

$$= \frac{\text{the number of ways that all three tosses are heads given that the first toss is a head}}{\text{the number of possibilities resulting from 3 tosses}}$$

$$= \frac{\{H, HH\}}{\{\{H,H,H\}, \{H,H,T\}, \{H,T,H\}, \{H,T,T\}, \{T,T,T\}, \{T,T,H\}, \{T,H,T\}, \{T,H,H\}\}}$$

$$= \frac{1}{8}.$$

P(B) = P(first toss is a head)

$$= \frac{\text{the number of ways to obtain a head on the first toss}}{\text{the number of ways to obtain a head or a tail on the first of 3 tosses}}$$

$$= \frac{\{H,H,H\}, \{H,H,T\}, \{H,T,H\}, \{H,T,T\}}{8}$$

$$= \frac{4}{8} \quad = \frac{1}{2}.$$

$$P(A/B) = \frac{P(AB)}{P(B)} = \frac{\frac{1}{8}}{\frac{1}{2}} = \frac{1}{8} \quad \frac{2}{1} = \frac{1}{4}.$$

To see what happens, in detail, we note that if the first toss is heads, the logical possibilities are HHH, HHT, HTH, HTT. There is only one of these for which the second and third are heads. Hence,

$$P(A/B) = \frac{1}{4}.$$

(b)   The problem here is to find the probability that all 3 tosses are heads given that the first two tosses are heads.

$P(AB)$ = the probability that all three tosees are heads given that the first two are heads

= $\dfrac{\text{the number of ways to obtain 3 heads given that the first two tosses are heads}}{\text{the number of possibilities resulting from 3 tosses}}$

= $\dfrac{1}{8}$.

$P(B)$ = the probability that the first two are heads

= $\dfrac{\text{number of ways to obtain heads on the first two tosses}}{\text{number of possibilities resulting from three tosses}}$

= $\dfrac{\{H,H,H\}, \{H,H,T\}}{8}$ = $\dfrac{2}{8}$ = $\dfrac{1}{4}$.

$$P(A/B) = \frac{P(AB)}{P(B)} = \frac{\frac{1}{8}}{\frac{1}{4}} = \frac{4}{8} = \frac{1}{2}.$$

(c)   In this last part, we are asked to find the probability that all 3 are heads on the condition that any 2 of them are heads.
Define:

A = the event that all three are heads

B = the event that two of them are heads

$P(AB)$ = the probability that all three tosses are heads knowing that two of them are heads

= $\dfrac{1}{8}$.

$P(B)$ = the probability that two tosses are heads

= $\dfrac{\text{number of ways to obtain at least two heads out of three tosses}}{\text{number of possibilities resulting from 3 tosses}}$

$$= \frac{\{H,H,T\}, \ \{H,H,H\}, \ \{H,T,H\}, \ \{T,H,H\}}{8}$$

$$= \frac{4}{8} \qquad = \frac{1}{2}.$$

$$P(A/B) = \frac{P(AB)}{P(B)} = \frac{\frac{1}{8}}{\frac{1}{2}} = \frac{2}{8} = \frac{1}{4}.$$

● **PROBLEM** 2-40

A committee is composed of six Democrats and five Republicans. Three of the Democrats are men, and three of the Republicans are men. If a man is chosen for chairman, what is the probability that he is a Republican?

**Solution:** Let $E_1$ be the event that a man is chosen, and $E_2$ the event that the man is a Republican.

We are looking for $P(E_2|E_1)$. From the definition of conditional probability $P(E_2|E_1) = \frac{P(E_1 \cap E_2)}{P(E_1)}$.

Of the eleven committee members, 3 are both male and Republican, hence

$$P(E_1 \cap E_2) = \frac{\text{number of male Republicans}}{\text{number of committee members}} = \frac{3}{11}.$$

Of all the members, 6 are men (3 Democrats and 3 Republicans), therefore

$$P(E_1) = \frac{6}{11}.$$

Furthermore, $P(E_2|E_1) = \frac{P(E_1 \cap E_2)}{P(E_1)} = \frac{3/11}{6/11} = \frac{3}{6} = \frac{1}{2}.$

● **PROBLEM** 2-41

A hand of five cards is to be dealt at random and without replacement from an ordinary deck of 52 playing cards. Find the conditional probability of an all spade hand given that there will be at least 4 spades in the hand.

**Solution:** Let $C_1$ be the event that there are at least 4 spades in the hand and $C_2$ that there are five. We want $P(C_2|C_1)$.

$C_1 \cap C_2$ is the intersection of the events that there are at least 4 and there are five spades. Since $C_2$ is contained in $C_1$, $C_1 \cap C_2 = C_2$. Therefore

$$P(C_2|C_1) = \frac{P(C_1 \cap C_2)}{P(C_1)} = \frac{P(C_2)}{P(C_1)};$$

$$P(C_2) = P \text{ (5 spades)} = \frac{\text{number of possible 5 spade hands}}{\text{number of total hands}}.$$

The denominator is $\binom{52}{5}$ since we can choose any 5 out of 52 cards. For the numerator we can have only spades, of which there are 13. We must choose 5, hence we have $\binom{13}{5}$ and $P(C_2) = \binom{13}{5} / \binom{52}{5}$.

$$P(C_1) = P(4 \text{ or } 5 \text{ spades}) = \frac{\text{\# of possible 4 or 5 spades}}{\text{\# of total hands}}$$

The denominator is still $\binom{52}{5}$. The numerator is $\binom{13}{5}$ + (number of 4 spade hands). To obtain a hand with 4 spades we can choose any 4 of the 13, $\binom{13}{4}$. We must also choose one of the 39 other cards, $\binom{39}{1}$. By the Fundamental Principle of Counting, the number of four spade hands is $\binom{13}{4}\binom{39}{1}$. Hence the numerator is $\binom{13}{5} + \binom{13}{4}\binom{39}{1}$ and

$$P(C_1) = \frac{\binom{13}{5} + \binom{13}{4}\binom{39}{1}}{\binom{52}{5}}. \text{ Thus}$$

$$P(C_2|C_1) = \frac{P(C_2)}{P(C_1)} = \frac{\dfrac{\binom{13}{5}}{\binom{52}{5}}}{\dfrac{\binom{13}{5} + \binom{13}{4}\binom{39}{1}}{\binom{52}{5}}}$$

$$= \frac{\binom{13}{5}}{\binom{13}{5} + \binom{13}{4}\binom{39}{1}} = .044.$$

● **PROBLEM** 2-42

A bag contains two balls, each of which may be either red or white. A ball is drawn at random and found to be red. What is the probability that the other ball is red?

Solution: To start with, the bag could contain 0, 1 or 2 red balls. We must assume something about the probabilities of these three conjectures. Before any ball is drawn it seems reasonable that any of these hypotheses $H_0$, $H_1$, $H_2$ are equally likely to be true and should each be assigned a probability of 1/3. If each hypothesis is equally likely, then Pr (drawing a red) = Pr (Red is drawn and $H_0$ is true) + Pr(Red is drawn and $H_1$ is true) + Pr(Red is drawn and $H_2$ is true). Each of these probabilities Pr(Red is drawn and $H_i$ is true) = Pr(Red is drawn $\mid$ $H_i$ true) Pr($H_i$ is true).

Thus   $\Pr(\text{Red is drawn}) = \sum_{i=o}^{2} \Pr(\text{Red drawn} \mid H_i \text{ true})\Pr(H_i \text{ true}).$

But   $\Pr(\text{Red drawn} \mid H_0 \text{ true}) = 0$

   $\Pr(\text{Red drawn} \mid H_1 \text{ true}) = \dfrac{1}{2}$

   $\Pr(\text{Red drawn} \mid H_2 \text{ true}) = 1 \,.$

If   $\Pr(H_1) = \Pr(H_2) = \Pr(H_3) = \dfrac{1}{3}$

then $\Pr(\text{Red is drawn}) = 0 \cdot \dfrac{1}{3} + \dfrac{1}{2} \cdot \dfrac{1}{3} + 1 \cdot \dfrac{1}{3}$

   $= \dfrac{1}{6} + \dfrac{1}{3} = \dfrac{3}{6} = \dfrac{1}{2} \,.$

We wish to find the $\Pr(H_i$ is true $\mid$ Red is drawn) for i = 0, 1, 2. $\Pr(H_2$ is true $\mid$ Red is drawn) will be the probability that the other ball in the bag is red given the drawn ball was red. The only way the other ball could be red is if both balls were red to begin with.

$\Pr(H_2 \text{ true} \mid \text{Red ball drawn}) = \dfrac{\Pr(H_2 \text{ true and Red drawn})}{\Pr(\text{Red ball drawn})}$

$= \dfrac{\Pr(\text{Red drawn} \mid H_2 \text{ true}) \Pr(H_2 \text{ true})}{\Pr(\text{Red ball is drawn})} = \dfrac{1 \times \dfrac{1}{3}}{\dfrac{1}{2}} = \dfrac{2}{3} \,.$

So, if we assume that the occurrences of 0, 1 or 2 red balls are equally likely at the start, then Pr(there were two at beginning $\mid$ a red ball is drawn) = $\dfrac{2}{3}$ .

● **PROBLEM 2-43**

Find the probability that Event A, drawing a spade on a single draw from a deck of cards, and Event B, rolling a total of 7 on a single roll of a pair of dice, will both occur.

<u>Solution</u>:   Pr (Event A) = $\dfrac{13}{52}$ , We have previously that

Pr (rolling 7) = $\dfrac{1}{6}$, Pr(Event B) = $\dfrac{1}{6}$. = $\dfrac{1}{6}$ .

We must now somehow combine these two probabilities

to compute the joint probability of the two events A and B. To do this we assume that the conditional probability of event A given B, $P(A|B) = P(A)$.

Because drawing a spade is physically unconnected to rolling a seven, the probabilities of these two events should be unrelated. This is reflected in the statement that $P(A|B) = P(A)$. By our rule for conditional probability this implies that $P(AB) = P(B)P(A|B) = P(B) \times P(A)$.

Two events with this property are called independent and in general the probability of the joint occurrence of independent events is equal to the product of the probability that the events occur in isolation.

In our example, $P(AB) = P(A)P(B)$

$$= \frac{13}{52} \cdot \frac{1}{6}$$

$$= \frac{1}{4} \cdot \frac{1}{6} = \frac{1}{24} .$$

● **PROBLEM** 2-44

A bowl contains eight chips. Three of the chips are red and the remaining five are blue. If two chips are drawn success-ively, at random and without replacement, what is the probability that the first chip drawn is red and the second drawn is blue?

Solution:    The probability that the first chip drawn is red is denoted $P(R_1)$. Since sampling is performed at random and without replacement, the classical probability model is applicable. Thus,

$$Pr(R_1) = \frac{\text{number of red chips}}{\text{total number of chips}} = \frac{3}{8} .$$

We now wish to calculate the conditional probability that a blue chip is drawn on the second draw given a red chip was drawn on the first. Denote this by $P(B_2|R_1)$. The second chip is sampled without replacement. Thus,

$$P(B_2|R_1) = \frac{\text{Number of blue chips}}{\text{total of chips after 1 red chip is drawn}}$$

$$= \frac{5}{8 - 1} = \frac{5}{7} ,$$

The probability we wish to find is $P(R_1 \text{ and } B_2)$. By the multiplication rule,

$$P(R_1 \text{ and } B_2) = P(R_1)P(B_2|R_1)$$

$$= \left(\frac{3}{8}\right)\left(\frac{5}{7}\right) = \frac{15}{56} .$$

Thus the probability that a red chip and than a blue chip are respectively drawn is $\frac{15}{56}$ .

From an ordinary deck of playing cards, cards are drawn successively at random and without replacement. Compute the probability that the third spade appears on the sixth draw.

Solution:    Recall the following form of the multiplication rule: $P(C_1 \cap C_2) = P(C_1) \ P(C_2 | C_1)$ .

Let $C_1$ be the event of 2 spades in the first five draws and let $C_2$ be the event of a spade on the sixth draw. Thus the probability that we wish to compute is $P(C_1 \cap C_2)$ .

After 5 cards have been picked there are $52 - 5 = 47$ cards left. We also have $13 - 2 = 11$ spades left after 2 spades have been picked in the first 5 cards. Thus, by the classical model of probability,

$$P(C_2 | C_1) = \frac{\text{favorable outcomes}}{\text{total possibilities}} = \frac{11}{47} \ .$$

To compute $P(C_1)$, use the classical model of probability. $P(C_1) = \dfrac{\text{ways of drawing 2 spades in 5}}{\text{All ways of drawing 5}} \ .$

The number of ways to choose 5 cards from 52 is $\binom{52}{5}$ . Now count how many ways one can select two spades in five draws. We can take any 2 of 13 spades, $\binom{13}{2}$ . The other 3 cards can be chosen from any of the 39 non-spades, there are $\binom{39}{3}$ ways to choose 3 from 39.

To determine the total number of ways of drawing 2 spades and 3 non-spades we invoke the basic principle of counting and obtain $\binom{13}{2}\binom{39}{3}$ . Hence

$$P(C_1) = \frac{\binom{13}{2}\binom{39}{3}}{\binom{52}{5}} \ .$$

$$P(C_1 \cap C_2) = P(C_1)P(C_2 | C_1) = \frac{\binom{13}{2}\binom{39}{3}}{\binom{52}{5}} \cdot \frac{11}{47} = 0.274$$

More generally, suppose X is the number of draws required to produce the 3rd spade. Let $C_1$ be the event of 2 spades in the first X - 1 draws and let $C_2$ be the event that a spade is drawn on the Xth draw. Again we want to compute the probability $P(C_1 \cap C_2)$. To find $P(C_2 | C_1)$ note that after X-1 cards have been picked, 2 of which were spades, 11 of the remaining 52-(X-1) cards are spades. The classical model of probability gives

$$P(C_2 | C_1) = \frac{11}{52 - (x - 1)} .$$

Again by the classical model,

$$P(C_1) = \frac{\text{ways of 2 spaced in X-1}}{\text{All ways of X-1 cards}} . \text{ The denominator}$$

is the number of ways to choose X-1 from 52 or $\binom{52}{X-1}$. Now determine the number of ways of choosing 2 spades in X-1 cards.

There are still only 13 spades in the deck, 2 of which we must choose. Hence we still have a $\binom{13}{2}$ term. The other (X-1) - 2 = X - 3 cards must be non-spades. Thus we must choose X - 3 out of 39 possibilities. This is $\binom{39}{X-3}$. The basic principle of counting says that to get the number of ways of choosing 2 spades and X - 3 non-spades we must multiply the two terms, $\binom{13}{2} \times \binom{39}{X-3}$.

Therefore, $P(C_1) = \dfrac{\binom{13}{2}\binom{39}{X-3}}{\binom{52}{X-1}}$ and the probability of

drawing the third spade on the Xth card is

$$P(C_1 \cap C_2) = P(C_1) \times P(C_2 | C_1) = \frac{\binom{13}{2}\binom{39}{X-3}}{\binom{52}{X-1}} \times \frac{11}{52-(X-1)}$$

● **PROBLEM 2-46**

Columbia University has 2 major undergraduate divisions, Columbia College and Barnard College. Columbia College comprises 60% of the undergraduate population and Barnard 40%. The percent of Columbia College students that commit suicide is 2%, while 1% of the Barnard women take their own life. Taking one student at random, what is the probability that it is a

(a) Columbia College student staying alive?
(b) Barnard student remaining alive?
(c) Columbia student about to commit suicide?
(d) Barnard girl about to kill herself?

Solution:     The problem gives us the following information P (Columbia) = 60% = .6, P (Barnard) = 40% = .4,
P (Suicide|Columbia) = 2% = .02, and P (Suicide|Barnard) =
.01.

(a)   Recall the definition of conditional probability

$$P(A|B) = \frac{P(A \cap B)}{P(B)} \text{ or } P(A \cap B) = P(A|B)P(B).$$

    Accordingly, P(Columbia $\cap$ alive) =

$$P(alive|Columbia)P(Columbia)$$

$$= (1 - P(suicide|Columbia))P(Columbia)$$

$$= (.98)(.6) = .588.$$

(b)   P(Barnard $\cap$ alive) = P(alive|Barnard)P(Barnard)

$$= (1 - P(suicide|Barnard))P(Barnard)$$

$$= (.99)(.4) = .396.$$

(c)  P(Columbia $\cap$ suicide) = P(suicide|Columbia)P(Columbia)

$$= (.02)(.6) = .012.$$

(d)  P(Barnard $\cap$ suicide) = P(suicide|Barnard)P(Barnard)

$$= (.01)(.4) = .004.$$

● **PROBLEM** 2-47

Find the probability that three successive face cards are
drawn in three successive draws (without replacement) from
a deck of cards.

    Define Events A, B, and C as follows:

    Event A: a face card is drawn on the first draw,
    Event B: a face card is drawn on the second draw,
    Event C: a face card is drawn on the third draw.

Solution:     Let ABC = the event that three successive
face cards are drawn on three successive draws.

    Let D = AB = the event that two successive face
cards are drawn on the first two draws.

Then P(ABC) = P(CD) = P(D) P(C|D) by the properties of
conditional probability. But

    P(D) = P(AB) = P(A)P(B|A).

    We have shown that P(ABC) = P(A)P(B|A)P(C|AB). Now
that the event is broken down into these component parts
we can solve this problem.

$$P(A) = \frac{\text{number of face cards}}{\text{total number of cards}} = \frac{12}{52} .$$

$$P(B|A) = \frac{\text{number of face cards} - 1}{\text{total number of cards in the deck} - 1} = \frac{11}{51} .$$

$$P(C|AB) = \frac{12 - 2}{52 - 2} = \frac{10}{50}$$

$$\text{and } P(ABC) = \frac{12}{52} \cdot \frac{11}{51} \cdot \frac{10}{50} = \frac{11}{1105} = .010.$$

It is important to note that this is an example of sampling without replacement.

● **PROBLEM** 2-48

If 4 cards are drawn at random and without replacement from a deck of 52 playing cards, what is the chance of drawing the 4 aces as the first 4 cards?

Solution:    We will do this problem in two ways. First we will use the classical model of probability which tells us

$$\text{Probability} = \frac{\text{Number of favorable outcomes}}{\text{All possible outcomes}} , \text{ assuming all}$$

outcomes are equally likely.

There are four aces we can draw first. Once that is gone any one of 3 can be taken second.  We have 2 choices for third and only one for fourth. Using the Fundamental Principle of Counting we see that there are 4 × 3 × 2 × 1 possible favorable outcomes. Also we can choose any one of 52 cards first. There are 51 possibilitites for second, etc. The Fundamental Principle of Counting tells us that there are 52 × 51 × 50 × 49  possible outcomes in the drawing of four cards. Thus,

$$\text{Probability} = \frac{4 \times 3 \times 2 \times 1}{52 \times 51 \times 50 \times 49} = \frac{1}{270,725} = .0000037.$$

Our second method of solution involves the multiplication rule and shows some insights into its origin and its relation to conditional probability.

The  formula  for conditional probability $P(A|B) = \frac{P(A \cap B)}{P(B)}$  can be extended as follows:

$$P(A|B \cap C \cap D) = \frac{P(A \cap B \cap C \cap D)}{P(B \cap C \cap D)} ; \qquad \text{thus}$$

$$P(A \cap B \cap C \cap D) = P(A|B \cap C \cap D) \ P(B \cap C \cap D) \text{ but}$$

$$P(B \cap C \cap D) = P(B|C \cap D) \ P(C \cap D) \qquad \text{therefore}$$

$$P(A \cap B \cap C \cap D) = P(A|B \cap C \cap D) \ P(B|C \cap D) \ P(C \cap D) \qquad \text{but}$$

$$P(C \cap D) = P(C|D) \ P(D) \qquad \text{hence}$$

$$P(A \cap B \cap C \cap D) = P(A|B \cap C \cap D) \ P(B|C \cap D) \ P(C|D) \ P(D) .$$

Let event D = drawing an ace on the first card

C = drawing an ace on second card

B = ace on third draw

A = ace on fourth card .

Our conditional probability extension becomes

P (4 aces) = P (on 4th|first 3) × P(3rd|first 2) ×

P(2nd|on first) × P(on first).

Assuming all outcomes are equally likely;

P (on 1st draw) = $\frac{4}{52}$. There are 4 ways of success in

52 possibilities. Once we pick an ace there are 51 remaining cards, 3 of which are aces. This leaves a probability of $\frac{3}{51}$ for picking a second ace once we have chosen the first. Once we have 2 aces there are 50 remaining cards, 2 of which are aces, thus P(on 3rd|first 2) = $\frac{2}{50}$ . Similarly P(4th ace|first 3) = $\frac{1}{49}$ . According to our formula above

$$P(4 \text{ aces}) = \frac{1}{49} \times \frac{2}{50} \times \frac{3}{51} \times \frac{4}{52} = .000037.$$

● PROBLEM 2-49

Four cards are to be dealt successively, at random and without replacement, from an ordinary deck of playing cards. Find the probability of receiving a spade, a heart, a diamond, and a club, in that order.

Solution: Let the events of drawing a spade, heart, diamond, or club be denoted by S, H, D, or C. We wish to find P (S, H, D, C) where the order of the symbols indicates the order in which the cards are drawn. This can be rewritten as

$$P(S, H, D, C) = P(S,H,D,) \ P(C/S,H,D)$$

by the multiplication rule.

Continuing to apply the multiplication rule yields

$$P(S, H, D, C) = P(S) \ P(H|S) \ P(D|S, H) \ P(C|S, H, D).$$

The product of these conditional probabilites will

yield the joint probability.

Because each card is drawn at random, the classical model is an apt one.

Pr (drawing a spade on the first draw)

$$= \frac{\text{number of spades}}{\text{number of cards in deck}} .$$

$$P(S) = \frac{13}{52} .$$

$$Pr(H|S) = \frac{\text{number of hearts}}{\text{number of cards after spade is drawn}}$$

$$= \frac{13}{52 - 1} = \frac{13}{51} .$$

$$Pr(D|S,H) = \frac{\text{number of diamonds}}{\text{number of cards after a heart and spade are drawn}}$$

$$= \frac{13}{52 - 2} = \frac{13}{50} .$$

$$Pr(C|S,H, D)$$

$$= \frac{\text{number of clubs}}{\text{number of cards after heart, spade and diamond are drawn}}$$

$$= \frac{13}{52 - 3} = \frac{13}{49} .$$

Thus, $Pr(S, H, D, C) = \frac{13}{52} \cdot \frac{13}{51} \cdot \frac{13}{50} \cdot \frac{13}{49} .$

● **PROBLEM** 2-50

Find the probability that on a single draw from a deck of playing cards we draw a spade or a face card or both. Define Events A and B as follows:

Event A: drawing a spade,
Event B: drawing a face card.

Solution:    We wish to find the probability of drawing a spade or a face card or both.

Let $A \cup B$ = the event of drawing a spade or face card or both.

$$P(A \cup B) = \frac{\text{number of ways a spade can occur}}{\text{total number of possible outcomes}} +$$

$$+ \frac{\text{number of ways a face card can occur}}{\text{total number of possible outcomes}} .$$

But we have counted too much. Some cards are spades and face cards so we must subtract from the above expression the $\dfrac{\text{number of ways a spade and face card can occur}}{\text{total number of possible outcomes}}$ .

This can be rewritten as

$P(A \cup B) = P(A) + P(B) - P(AB)$ .

$P(A) = \dfrac{13}{52}$ , $P(B) = \dfrac{12}{52}$

$P(AB) = P(B)P(A|B)$ .

$P(A|B)$ = Probability that a spade is drawn given that a face card is drawn.

$= \dfrac{\text{number of spades that are face cards}}{\text{total number of face cards which could be drawn}}$

$= \dfrac{3}{12}$ .

$P(AB) = \dfrac{12}{52} \cdot \dfrac{3}{12} = \dfrac{3}{52}$ .

We could have found $P(AB)$ directly by counting the number of spades that are face cards and then dividing by the total possibilities.

Thus $P(A \cup B) = P(A) + P(B) - P(AB)$

$= \dfrac{13}{52} + \dfrac{12}{52} - \dfrac{3}{52} = \dfrac{22}{52} = \dfrac{11}{26}$ .

We could have found the answer more directly in the following way.

$P(A \cup B) = \dfrac{\text{number of spades or face cards or both}}{\text{total number of cards}}$

$= \dfrac{22}{52} = \dfrac{11}{26}$ .

● **PROBLEM** 2-51

Your company uses a pre-employment test to screen applicants for the job of repairman. The test is passed by 60% of the applicants. Among those who pass the test 80% complete training successfully. In an experiment, a random sample of applicants who do not pass the test is also employed. Training is successfully completed by only 50% of this group. If no pre-employment test is used, what percentage of applicants would you expect to complete training successfully?

Solution: This is an exercise in conditional probability. We can make a tree diagram:

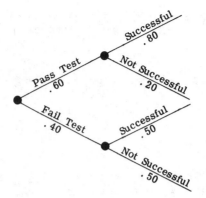

From the definition of conditional probability and the multiplication rule:

P(Successful ∩ Pass) = P(Successful|Pass) P(pass)

= (.80)(.60) = .48.

Similarly, P(Successful∩Fail) = P(Successful|Fail) P(Fail)

= (.50)(.40) = .20.

The event "an applicant is successful" is composed of two mutually exclusive events. These events are; "an applicant passed the test and was successful" (denoted by S∩P) and "an applicant failed the test and was successful" (denoted S∩F). Thus

Pr (Success) = P(S∩P) + P(S∩F)

= .48 + .20 = .68.

Thus we would expect 68 percent of the applicants to successfully complete the training.

● **PROBLEM 2-52**

An electronic device contains two easily removed sub-assemblies, A and B. If the device fails, the probability that it will be necessary to replace A is 0.50. Some failures of A will damage B. If A must be replaced, the probability that B will also have to be replaced is 0.70. If it is not necessary to replace A, the probability that B will have to be replaced is only 0.10. What percentage of all failures will you require to replace both A and B?

Solution:     This situation may be pictured by the following tree diagram. Each "branch" of the tree denotes a possible event which might occur if device A fails.

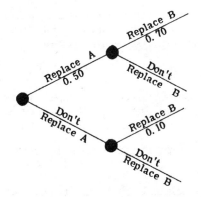

If device A fails, A will be replaced or not re-placed. These first two outcomes are represented by the first two branches of the tree diagram. The branches are labeled with their respective probabilities.

Given that A is replaced, the behavior of B is described by the two secondary branches emanating from the primary branch denoting replacement of A.

If A is not replaced, B's possible behavior is described by the secondary branches emanating from the branch denoting non-replacement of A.

The tree diagram, each branch labeled by its respective probability, is thus:

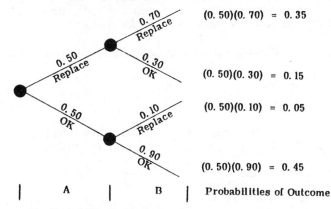

| | A | | B | | Probabilities of Outcome |

The Probability that both A and B must be replaced is 0. 35.

Three probabilities are given but there are six branches to the tree. The probabilities of the remaining branches can be found. If an experiment has only two outcomes, denoted R and DR, and these outcomes are mutually exclusive and exhaustive, the sum

P(R) + P(DR) equals 1.

If P(R) or P(DR) is known, then the other unknown probability may be found.

P(R) = 1 - P(DR).

Let $P(R)$ = probability that component A is replaced. Then $P(DR)$ = probability that A is not replaced = $1 - P(DR)$. Substituting for $P(R)$ gives

$$P(DR) = 1 - P(R) = 1 - .5 = .5.$$

The conditional probabilities that B is not replaced given A is replaced and that B is not replaced given A is not replaced can also be found in this way.

Denote these probabilities by $P(B'|A)$ and $P(B'|A')$. Also let

$P(B|A)$ = probability B is replaced given A is replaced and

$P(B|A')$ = probability B is replaced given A is not replaced.

If A is replaced, then B can be replaced or not replaced. These events are mutually exclusive and exhaustive; thus

$$P(B'|A) + P(B|A) = 1$$

$$P(B|A) = .7$$

thus $P(B'|A) = 1 - P(B|A) = 1 - .7 = .3.$

Similarly, if A is not replaced, B may be replaced or not replaced. Given that A is not replaced, these events are mutually exclusive and exhaustive, thus

$$P(B'|A') + P(B|A') = 1$$

But $P(B|A') = .1$ ;

thus $P(B'|A') = 1 - .1 = .9.$

The problem asks for the probability that both A and B are replaced. Using the multiplication rule,

$P$(A and B are replaced)

$= P$(A is replaced) $P$(B is replaced $|$ A replaced)

$= P$(A is replaced) $P(B|A)$

$= (.5)(.7) = .35.$

The probability that both A and B are replaced is .35.

● **PROBLEM** 2-53

A bag contains 1 white ball and 2 red balls. A ball is drawn at random. If the ball is white then it is put back in the bag along with another white ball. If the ball is red then it is put back in the bag with two extra red balls. Find the probability that the second ball drawn

is red. If the second ball drawn is red, what is the
probability that the first ball drawn was red?

<u>Solution:</u>    Let $W_i$ or $R_i$ = the event that the ball chosen
on the ith draw is white or red.

Assuming that each ball is chosen at random, a tree
diagram of this problem can be drawn showing the possible
outcomes.

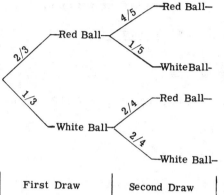

| First Draw | Second Draw |

The probabilities of different outcomes are labeled
on the "branches" of this tree. These probabilities depend
on the number of balls of each color in the bag at the time
of the draw. For example, before the first draw there are
2 red balls and 1 white ball. Thus 2 of 3 balls on the
average will result in a red ball being chosen or
$P(R_1)$ = 2/3.

If a red ball is chosen on the first draw then 2 more
red balls are added to the bag. There are now 4 red balls
and 1 white ball in the bag so on the average 4 of 5 balls
chosen will result in a red ball. Thus Pr($R_2$ given a red
ball on the first draw) = $Pr(R_2|R_1)$ = 4/5. The other
probabilitites are computed in a similar fashion.

We wish to compute $Pr(R_2)$, the probability that the
second ball drawn is red. As we see from the tree diagram
there are two ways this can happen; thus, $Pr(R_2)$ =
$Pr(R_1$ and $R_2$ or $W_1$ and $R_2)$. The events $R_1$ and $R_2$ and $W_1$
and $R_2$ are mutually exclusive.

Thus $Pr(R_2)$ = $Pr(R_1$ and $R_2)$ + $Pr(W_1$ and $R_2)$.

But  $Pr(R_1$ and $R_2)$ = $Pr(R_2|R_1) \times Pr(R_1)$

and  $Pr(W_1$ and $R_2)$ = $Pr(R_2|W_1) \times Pr(W_1)$

by the definition of conditional probability.

From our diagram,

$Pr(R_2|R_1)$ = 4/5  and   $Pr(R_2|W_1)$ = 2/4

also   $Pr(R_1)$ = 2/3        and       $Pr(W_1)$ = 1/3.

Thus $\text{Pr}(R_2) = \text{Pr}(R_2|R_1)\text{Pr}(R_1) + \text{Pr}(R_2|W_1)\text{Pr}(W_1)$

$$= \frac{4}{5} \cdot \frac{2}{3} + \frac{2}{4} \cdot \frac{1}{3}$$

$$= \frac{8}{15} + \frac{1}{6} = \frac{16 + 5}{30} = \frac{21}{30} = \frac{7}{10} \;.$$

Now we wish to find $\text{Pr}(R_1|R_2)$.

From the definition of conditional probability

$$\text{Pr}(R_1|R_2) = \frac{\text{Pr}(R_1 \text{ and } R_2)}{\text{Pr}(R_2)} \;.$$

We also know that

$\text{Pr}(R_2) = \text{Pr}(R_2|R_1)\text{Pr}(R_1) + \text{Pr}(R_2|W_1)\text{Pr}(W_1)$   by the

previous problem.

We also know that

$\text{Pr}(R_1 \text{ and } R_2) = \text{Pr}(R_2|R_1) \times \text{Pr}(R_1)$.

Putting these together we see that

$$\text{Pr}(R_1|R_2) = \frac{\text{Pr}(R_2|R_1)\ \text{Pr}(R_1)}{\text{Pr}(R_2|R_1)\text{Pr}(R_1)\ +\ \text{Pr}(R_2|W_1)\text{Pr}(W_1)}$$

$$= \frac{\dfrac{4}{5} \cdot \dfrac{2}{3}}{\dfrac{4}{5} \cdot \dfrac{2}{3} + \dfrac{2}{4} \cdot \dfrac{1}{3}}$$

$$= \frac{\dfrac{8}{15}}{\dfrac{7}{10}} = \frac{10 \cdot 8}{7 \cdot 15} = \frac{16}{21} \;.$$

Note that in order to compute these probabilities we needed to know the number of red and white balls in the bag at the beginning.

# BAYES' THEOREM

● PROBLEM 2-54

Twenty percent of the employees of a company are college graduates. Of these, 75% are in supervisory position. Of those who did not attend college, 20% are in supervisory positions. What is the probability that a randomly selected supervisor is a college graduate?

Solution:    Let the events be as followed:

E  : The person selected is a supervisor

$E_1$ : The person is a college graduate.

$E_2$ : The person is not a college graduate.

We are searching for $P(E_1|E)$.

By the definition of conditional probability

$$P(E_1|E) = \frac{P(E_1 \cap E)}{P(E)} \; .$$

But also by conditional probability $P(E_1 \cap E) = P(E|E_1) \cdot P(E_1)$. Since, E is composed of mutually exclusive events, $E_1$ and $E_2$, $P(E) = P(E_1 \cap E) + P(E_2 \cap E)$. Furthermore, $P(E_2 \cap E) = P(E|E_2) P(E_2)$, by conditional probability. Inserting these expressions into $\frac{P(E_1 \cap E)}{P(E)}$ , we obtain

$$P(E_1|E) = \frac{P(E_1)P(E|E_1)}{P(E_1)P(E|E_1) + P(E_2)P(E|E_2)} \; .$$

This formula is a special case of the well-known Bayes' Theorem. The general formula is

$$P(E_1|E) = \frac{P(E_1) \; P(E|E_1)}{\sum_{1}^{n} P(E_n)P(E|E_n)} \; .$$

In our problem,

$P(E_1)$ = P(College graduate) = 20% = .20

$P(E_2)$ = P(Not graduate) = 1 - P(Graduate) = 1 - .2 = .80

$P(E|E_1)$ = P(Supervisor|Graduate) = 75% = .75.

$P(E|E_2)$ = P(Supervisor|Not a graduate) = 20% = .20.

Substituting,

$$P(E_1|E) = \frac{(.20)(.75)}{(.20)(.75) + (.80)(.20)} = \frac{.15}{.15 + .16}$$

$$= \frac{15}{31} \; .$$

● **PROBLEM** 2-55

In a factory four machines produce the same product. Machine A produces 10% of the output, machine B, 20%, machine C, 30%, and machine D, 40%. The proportion of defective items produced by these follows: Machine A: .001; Machine B: .0005; Machine C: .005; Machine D: .002. An item selected at random is found to be defective. What is the probability that the item was produced by A? by B? by C? by D?

Solution:    Each question requires us to find the
probability that a defective item was produced by a
particular machine. Bayes' Rule allows us to calculate
this using known (given) probabilities. First we define
the necessary symbols: $M_1$ means the item was produced at
A, $M_2$ means it was produced at B, and $M_3$ and $M_4$ refer
to machines C and D, respectively. Let M mean that an
item is defective. Using Bayes' Rule,

$$P(M_1|M) = \frac{P(M_1)\ P(M|M_1)}{P(M_1)P(M|M_1)+P(M_2)P(M|M_2)+P(M_3)P(M|M_3)+P(M_4)P(M|M_4)}$$

we substitute the given proportions as follows:

$$P(M_1|M) = \frac{(.1)(.001)}{(.1)(.001)+(.2)(.0005)+(.3)(.005)+(.4)(.002)}$$

$$= \frac{.0001}{.0001 + .0001 + .0015 + .0008} = \frac{.0001}{.0025} = \frac{1}{25}.$$

To compute $P(M_2|M)$ we need only change the
numerator to $P(M_2)P(M|M_2)$. Substituting given proportions,
we have $(.20)(.0005) = .0001$. We see that $P(M_2|M) =$
$\frac{1}{25} = P(M_1|M)$. By the same procedure we find that $P(M_3|M) =$
$\frac{3}{5}$ and $P(M_4|M) = \frac{8}{25}$.

To check our work, note that a defective item can be
produced by any one of the 4 machines and that the four
events "produced by machine i and defective" (i=1,2,3,4)
are mutually exclusive. Thus

$$P(M) = \sum_{i=1}^{4} P(M \text{ and } M_i) \quad \text{or} \quad 1 = \sum_{i=1}^{4} \frac{P(M \text{ and } M_i)}{P(M)} ;$$

but       $\frac{P(M \text{ and } M_i)}{P(M)} = P(M_i|M)$.

Thus      $\sum_{i=1}^{4} P(M_i|M) = 1$. Adding we see that

$$\frac{1}{25} + \frac{1}{25} + \frac{15}{25} + \frac{8}{25} = \frac{25}{25} = 1.$$

● **PROBLEM** 2-56

In the St. Petersburg Community College, 30% of the men
and 20% of the women are studying mathematics. Further,
45% of the students are women. If a student selected at
random is studying mathematics, what is the probability
that the student is a woman?

Solution:    This problem involves conditional probabilities.
The first two percentages given can be thought of as con-

ditional probabilitites; "30% of the men are studying mathematics" means that the probability that a male student selected at random is studying mathematics, is .3. Bayes' formula allows us to use the probabilities we know to compute the probability that a mathematics student is a woman. Using the symbols M (the student is studying mathematics); W (the sudent is a woman); and N (the student is not a woman), we write:

$$P(W|M) = \frac{P(W)\ P(M|W)}{P(W)\ P(M|W) + P(N)\ P(M|N)} \text{ , substituting}$$

$$= \frac{(.45)(0.2)}{(.45)(0.2) + (.55)(0.3)} = \frac{.09}{.09 + 0.165}$$

$$= \frac{.09}{.255} = \frac{6}{17} .$$

Thus, the probability that a randomly selected math student is a woman equals

$$\frac{6}{17} = .353 .$$

# RANDOM SAMPLING

● PROBLEM 2-57

Find the probability of drawing three consecutive face cards on three consecutive draws (with replacement) from a deck of cards.

Let:   Event A: face card on first draw,
       Event B: face card on second draw, and
       Event C: face card on third draw.

Solution:   This problem illustrates sampling with replacement. After each draw, the card drawn is returned to the deck. The deck, or "population" from which we draw the second card is identical to the original deck. Thus the drawing of a face card on the second draw is independent of the first draw. Similarly, the result of the third drawing is independent of the first or second drawings. This sampling without replacement implies that

   $P(ABC) = P(A) \cdot P(B) \cdot P(C)$.

But we know that the probability of drawing a face card on any draw is

$$\frac{\text{number of face cards in deck}}{\text{number of cards in deck}} \quad \text{or} \quad \frac{12}{52} .$$

Therefore   $P(ABC) = P(A)P(B)P(C)$

$$= \frac{12}{52} \cdot \frac{12}{52} \cdot \frac{12}{52} = \frac{27}{2197} = .012 .$$

If 4 different balls are placed at random in 3 different cells, find the probability that no cell is empty. Assume that there is ample room in each cell for all 4 balls.

Solution:    There are 3 ways to place each of the 4 balls into a cell. Thus, $3 \times 3 \times 3 \times 3 = 3^4$ ways to put the 4 balls into three cells. If each arrangement is equally likely, then any 1 arrangement will occur with the probability

$$\frac{1}{3^4} = \frac{1}{81} .$$

We now must count the number of ways the balls can be placed in the cells so that none of the cells are empty.

First, we know that one cell will have two balls in it. Choose these two balls from the four; there are $\binom{4}{2}$ ways to do this. Now place these two balls in a cell; there are three ways to do this. There are 2 ways and 1 way respectively to place the two remaining balls in the two remaining cells to insure that all the cells are filled. Together, by the Fundamental Counting Principle, there are $\binom{4}{2} \cdot 3 \cdot 2 \cdot 1$ or 36 arrangements. Thus the probability of observing an arrangement with 0 cells empty if the balls are dropped in at random is $\frac{36}{81} = \frac{4}{9}$ .

A box contains 4 black marbles, 3 red marbles, and 2 white marbles. What is the probability that a black marble, then a red marble, then a white marble is drawn without replacement?

Solution:  Here we have three dependent events. There is a total of 9 marbles from which to draw. We assume on the first draw we will get a black marble. Since the probability of drawing a black marble is the

$$\frac{\text{number of ways of drawing a black marble}}{\text{number of ways of drawing 1 out of (4+3+2) marbles}} ,$$

$$P(A) = \frac{4}{4 + 3 + 2} = \frac{4}{9} .$$

There are now 8 marbles left in the box.

On the second draw we get a red marble.  Since the probability of drawing a red marble is

$$\frac{\text{number of ways of drawing a red marble}}{\text{number of ways of drawing 1 out of the 8 remaining marbles}} ,$$

$$P(B) = \frac{3}{8}$$

There are now 7 marbles remaining in the box.

On the last draw we get a white marble. Since the probability of drawing a white marble is

$$\frac{\text{number of ways of drawing a white marble}}{\text{number of ways of drawing 1 out of the 7 remaining marbles}},$$

$$P(C) = \frac{2}{7}$$

When dealing with two or more dependent events, if $P_1$ is the probability of a first event, $P_2$ the probability that, after the first has happened, the second will occur, $P_3$ the probability that, after the first and second have happened, the third will occur, etc., then the probability that all events will happen in the given order is the product $P_1 \cdot P_2 \cdot P_3 \ldots$

Thus, $P(A \cap B \cap C) = P(A) \cdot P(B) \cdot P(C)$

$$= \frac{4}{9} \cdot \frac{3}{8} \cdot \frac{2}{7} = \frac{1}{21}.$$

● **PROBLEM** 2-60

There is a box containing 5 white balls, 4 black balls, and 7 red balls. If two balls are drawn one at a time from the box and neither is replaced, find the probability that
(a)    both balls will be white.
(b)    the first ball will be white and the second red.
(c)    if a third ball is drawn, find the probability that the three balls will be drawn in the order white, black, red.

Solution: This problem involves dependent events. Two or more events are said to be dependent if the occurrence of one event has an effect upon the occurrence or non-occurrence of the other. If you are drawing objects without replacement, the second draw is dependent on the occurrence of the first draw. We apply the following theorem for this type of problem. If the probability of occurrence of one event is p and the probability of the occurrence of a second event is q, then the probability that both events will happen in the order stated is pq.

(a)  To find the probability that both balls will be white, we express it symbolically.
p (both balls will be white) =
p (first ball will be white and the second ball will be white) =
p (first ball will be white)·p(second ball will be white) =

$$= \left(\frac{\text{number of ways to choose a white ball}}{\text{number of ways to choose a ball}}\right) \cdot \left(\frac{\text{number of ways to choose a second white ball after removal of the first white ball}}{\text{number of ways to choose a ball after removal of the first ball}}\right)$$

$$= \quad \frac{\overset{1}{\cancel{5}}}{\underset{4}{\cancel{16}}} \cdot \frac{\overset{1}{\cancel{4}}}{\underset{3}{\cancel{15}}} = \frac{1}{12}$$

(b)  p (first ball will be white and the second red)

= p (first ball will be white)·p(the second ball will be red)

$$= \begin{pmatrix} \dfrac{\text{number of ways to choose a white ball}}{\text{number of ways to choose a ball}} \end{pmatrix} \cdot \begin{pmatrix} \dfrac{\text{number of ways to choose a red ball}}{\begin{matrix}\text{number of ways to choose a}\\\text{ball after the removal of the}\\\text{first}\end{matrix}} \end{pmatrix}$$

$$= \frac{\overset{1}{\cancel{5}}}{16} \cdot \frac{7}{\underset{3}{\cancel{15}}} = \frac{7}{48}$$

(c)  p (three balls drawn in the order white, black, red)

=   p (first ball is white) p(second ball is black) p(third ball is red)

$$= \begin{pmatrix} \dfrac{\begin{matrix}\text{number of ways to choose that}\\\text{the first ball is white}\end{matrix}}{\begin{matrix}\text{number of ways to choose the}\\\text{first ball}\end{matrix}} \end{pmatrix} \cdot \begin{pmatrix} \dfrac{\begin{matrix}\text{number of ways to choose that}\\\text{second one is black}\end{matrix}}{\begin{matrix}\text{number of ways to choose the}\\\text{second one}\end{matrix}} \end{pmatrix}$$

$$\cdot \begin{pmatrix} \dfrac{\begin{matrix}\text{number of ways to choose that the}\\\text{third one is red}\end{matrix}}{\begin{matrix}\text{number of ways to choose the third}\\\text{one}\end{matrix}} \end{pmatrix}$$

$$= \quad \frac{\overset{1}{\cancel{5}}}{\underset{4}{\cancel{16}}} \cdot \frac{\overset{1}{\cancel{4}}}{\underset{3}{\cancel{15}}} \cdot \frac{\overset{1}{\cancel{7}}}{\underset{2}{\cancel{14}}} = \frac{1}{24}$$

# CHAPTER 3

# PROBABILITY DISTRIBUTIONS

## DISCRETE DISTRIBUTIONS

Let X be the random variable denoting the result of the single toss of a fair coin. If the toss is heads, X = 1. If the toss results in tails, X = 0.
What is the probability distribution of X?

Solution: The probability distribution of X is a function which assigns probabilities to the values X may assume.

This function will have the following properties if it defines a proper probability distribution.

Let $f(x) = Pr(X = x)$. Then $\Sigma\, Pr(X = x) = 1$ and $Pr(X = x) \geq 0$ for all x.

We have assumed that X is a discrete random variable. That is, X takes on discrete values.

The variable X in this problem is discrete as it only takes on the values 0 and 1.

To find the probability distribution of X, we must find $Pr(X = 0)$ and $Pr(X = 1)$.

Let $p_0 = Pr(X = 0)$ and $Pr(X = 1) = p_1$. If the coin is fair, the events X = 0 and X = 1 are equally likely. Thus $p_0 = p_1 = p$ . We must have $p_0 > 0$ and $p_1 > 0$ .

In addition,
$$Pr(X = 0) + Pr(X = 1) = 1$$
or
$$p_0 + p_1 = p + p = 1$$
or
$$2p = 1$$

and
$$p_0 = p_1 = p = \tfrac{1}{2} ,$$
thus the probability distribution of X is $f(x)$: where
$$f(0) = Pr(X = 0) = \tfrac{1}{2} \text{ and}$$
$$f(1) = Pr(X = 1) = \tfrac{1}{2}$$

f (anything else) = Pr(X = anything else) = 0 . We see that this is a proper probability distribution for our variable X.

$$\Sigma\, f(x) = 1 \quad \text{and}$$
$$f(x) \geq 0 .$$

Determine the probability distribution of the number of spades in a 5 card poker hand from an ordinary deck of 52 cards.

**Solution:** Let $X$ = number of spades in a 5 card poker hand. $X$ can take on 6 values; 0,1,2,3,4 or 5.

To find the probability distribution of $X$, we ask, what is the probability that $X = k$.

The classical model of probability applies in finding this probability. Thus,

$$Pr(X = k) = \frac{\text{number of poker hands with k spades}}{\text{total number of poker hands}}.$$

The total number of poker hands is the number of ways 5 objects may be selected from 52 objects. Thus, the total number of poker hands is

$$\binom{52}{5}.$$

To count the number of poker hands with $k$ spades we first count the number of ways $k$ spades may be chosen from the 13 spades available. There are

$$\binom{13}{k}$$

ways to do this. If $k$ of the cards in the hand are spades, $5-k$ cards must be non-spades. The number of ways the remaining $5-k$ cards may be selected from the available non-spades is

$$\binom{52 - 13}{5 - k} = \binom{39}{5-k}.$$

Thus, the total number of poker hands with $k$ spades is the product of these two expressions or

$$\binom{13}{k}\binom{39}{5-k}.$$

Thus

$$Pr(X = k) = \frac{\binom{13}{k}\binom{39}{5-k}}{\binom{52}{5}} \quad \text{for} \quad k = 0,1,2,3,4,5 .$$

If $f(x) = 1/4$, $x = 0,1,2,3$ is a probability mass function, find $F(t)$, the cumulative distribution function and sketch its graph.

**Solution:** $F(t) = \sum\limits_{x=0}^{t} f(x) = Pr(X \le t)$. $F(t)$ changes for integer values of $t$. We have:

$$F(t) = 0 \qquad\qquad t < 0$$
$$F(t) = f(0) = 1/4, \quad 0 \le t < 1$$
$$F(t) = f(0) + f(1) = 1/4 + 1/4 = 1/2 ,$$
$$1 \le t < 2$$

$$F(t) = f(0) + f(1) + f(2) \qquad 2 \le t < 3$$
$$= \tfrac{1}{4} + \tfrac{1}{4} + \tfrac{1}{4} = 3/4 .$$

$$F(t) = \sum_{x=0}^{t} f(x) = 1 \qquad\qquad\qquad 3 \le t .$$

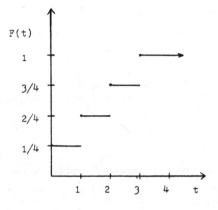

Given that the discrete random variable  X  has mass function,

$$Pr(X = x) = \begin{cases} x/6 & \text{where } x = 1,2,3 \\ 0 & \text{elsewhere,} \end{cases}$$

describe and graph its cumulative distribution function, F(x).

<u>Solution</u>:  The cumulative distribution function  F(x)  is defined to be  Pr(X ≤ x).  Pr(X = x) = 0  except when  x = 1,2 or 3, hence P(X < 1) = 0.  Since the events  "X = 1"  and  "1 < x < 2"  are exclusive, we can add their probabilities: P(X = 1) + P(1 < x < 2) = P(1 ≤ x < 2).

P(X = 1) = 1/6  and  P(1 < x < 2) = 0  because  F(x) = 0  for 1 < x < 2.  Thus  P(1 ≤ x < 2) = 1/6 + 0 = 1/6 .

By the same reasoning, P(2 ≤ x < 3) = P(x = 2) + P(2 < x < 3) = 2/6 + 0 = 2/6.  For  2 ≤ x < 3, F(x) = P(x < 1) + P(1 ≤ x < 2) + P(2 ≤ x < 3) = 0 + 1/6 + 2/6 = 3/6 = 1/2.

Finally, Pr(x = 3) = 3/6 = 1/2.  For  3 ≤ x, F(x) = 1/2 + 1/2 = 1.

Now we summarize and graph

$$F(x) = \begin{cases} 0 & x < 1 \\ 1/6 & 1 \le x < 2 \\ 3/6 & 2 \le x < 3 \\ 1 & 3 \le x \quad . \end{cases}$$

105

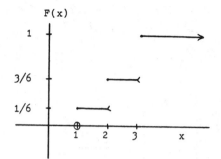

The graph shows that  F(x)  is a step function with steps of heights  1/6, 2/6 and 3/6.  It is constant and continuous in every interval not containing  1,2 or 3.

● **PROBLEM 3-5**

Convert the function  $g(x) = 1/x^2$  to a probability density function  f(x)  of a discrete random variable X.  Let  f(x)  have a non-zero value when  x  is a positive integer, and  f(x) = 0  when  x  is not a positive integer.

<u>Solution</u>:  For  $x = 1,2,3,\ldots, \sum\limits_{x=1}^{\infty} \frac{1}{x^2} = \frac{1}{1^2} + \frac{1}{2^2} + \frac{1}{3^2} + \ldots = \frac{\pi^2}{6}$ .

A discrete function  f(x)  must by definition satisfy  $\sum\limits_{\text{all x}} f(x) = 1$.

To obtain  f(x), multiply  $\sum\limits_{x=1}^{\infty} g(x) = \sum\limits_{x=1}^{\infty} \frac{1}{x^2} = \frac{\pi^2}{6}$  by the reciprocal of

$\frac{\pi^2}{6}$ :     $\frac{6}{\pi^2} \cdot \sum\limits_{x=1}^{\infty} \frac{1}{x^2} = \frac{6}{\pi^2}\left(\frac{\pi^2}{6}\right) = 1$ .

By the distributive property of multiplication,  $\frac{6}{\pi^2}$  can be moved

inside the summation sign:     $\frac{6}{\pi^2} \sum\limits_{x=1}^{\infty} \frac{1}{x^2} = \sum\limits_{x=1}^{\infty} \frac{6}{\pi^2 x^2} = 1$ .

It follows that     $f(x) = \begin{cases} \dfrac{6}{\pi^2 x^2}, & x = 1,2,3,\ldots \\ 0 & \text{when } x \neq 1,2,\ldots \end{cases}$

# GEOMETRIC DENSITY FUNCTION

● **PROBLEM 3-6**

An absent-minded professor has 5 keys.  One of the keys opens the door to his apartment.  One night he arrives at his building, reaches into his pocket and selects a key at random from those on his chain. He tries it in the lock.  If it doesn't work, he replaces the key and again selects at random from the 5 keys.  He continues this process until he finally finds his key, then stops. Let X = the number of attempts the professor makes. What is the probability distribution of X?

Solution: X is a special type of binomial random variable. Each time the professor reaches into his pocket can be considered a trial. The professor always replaces the key so we assume that the trials are independent except if the correct key is chosen.

There are 5 keys and he is selecting at random. The probability of "success" on a given trial is thus 1/5 and the probability that he selects the wrong key is 4/5.

We are not sure how many attempts he will make, but we know that if he selects the correct key he will stop the process.

Let's compute some of the probability distribution of X,

Pr(X = 1) = probability that he picks the right key on the first draw = 1/5.

Pr(X = 2) = probability that he picks a wrong key first and the right key second

$$= (4/5)(1/5).$$

Pr(X = 3) = probability that he picks two wrong keys first and the right key third

$$= (4/5)(4/5)(1/5).$$

In general, Pr(X = k) = probability that k-1 wrong keys are tried and the kth key selected is the correct one.

$$Pr(X = k) = (4/5)^{k-1}(1/5).$$

This distribution is known as the geometric distribution and is a special case of the binomial distribution.

● PROBLEM 3-7

X is a discrete random variable with probability distribution

$$f(x) = (\tfrac{1}{2})^{X} \quad , x = 1,2,\ldots$$
$$= 0 \qquad \text{otherwise.}$$

Find the Pr(X is even).

Solution: X has an infinite but countable number of values with positive probability.

$$Pr(X \text{ is even}) = Pr(X = 2) + Pr(X = 4) + \ldots + Pr(X = 2n) + \ldots$$

$$= \sum_{n=1}^{\infty} Pr(X = 2n)$$

$$= \sum_{n=1}^{\infty} (\tfrac{1}{2})^{2n} = \sum_{n=1}^{\infty} (\tfrac{1}{4})^{n}$$

$$= \tfrac{1}{4} \sum_{n=1}^{\infty} (\tfrac{1}{4})^{n-1}$$

$$= (\tfrac{1}{4}) \sum_{n-1=0}^{\infty} (\tfrac{1}{4})^{n-1} .$$

Let $n-1 = m$ then

$$Pr(X \text{ is even}) = (\tfrac{1}{4}) \sum_{m=0}^{\infty} (\tfrac{1}{4})^{m}$$

but this is now $\tfrac{1}{4}$ times the familiar geometric series.  In general

$$\sum_{m=0}^{\infty} r^{m} = \frac{1}{1-r} \text{ if } |r| < 1 .$$

In our case $r = \tfrac{1}{4} < 1$, thus

$$Pr(X \text{ is even}) = (\tfrac{1}{4}) \sum_{m=0}^{\infty} (\tfrac{1}{4})^{m} = \tfrac{1}{4}\left( \frac{1}{1-\tfrac{1}{4}} \right)$$

$$= \tfrac{1}{4}\left( \frac{1}{3/4} \right) = 1/3 .$$

Since all positive integers are even or odd but not both

$$Pr(X \text{ is even}) + Pr(X \text{ is odd}) = 1$$

and

$$Pr(X \text{ is odd}) = 1 - Pr(X \text{ is even})$$

$$= 1 - 1/3 = 2/3 .$$

# POISSON DENSITY FUNCTION

● **PROBLEM** 3-8

Defects occur along the length of a cable at an average of 6 defects per 4000 feet.  Assume that the probability of k defects in t feet of cable is given by the probability mass function:

$$Pr(k \text{ defects}) = \frac{e^{-\frac{6t}{4000}} \left(\frac{6t}{4000}\right)^{k}}{k!}$$

for $k = 0,1,2,\ldots$ .  Find the probability that a 3000-foot cable will have at most two defects.

Solution:  The probability of exactly k defects in 3000 feet is determined by the given discrete probability distribution as
$Pr(k \text{ defects in 3000 ft.})$

$$= \frac{e^{-\frac{6(3000)}{4000}} \left(\frac{6(3000)}{4000}\right)^{k}}{k!}$$

$$= \frac{e^{-4.5}(4.5)^{k}}{k!} , \quad k = 0,1,2,\ldots .$$

We use the probability distribution to find the probability of at most two defects.

$Pr(\text{at most two defects}) = Pr(0,1 \text{ or } 2 \text{ defects}).$

The events "0 defects", "1 defect" and "2 defects" are all mutually exclusive, thus,

$Pr(\text{at most two defects}) = Pr(0 \text{ defects}) + Pr(1 \text{ defect}) + Pr(2 \text{ defects})$

$$= \frac{e^{-4.5}(4.5)^0}{0!} + \frac{e^{-4.5}(4.5)^1}{1!} + \frac{e^{-4.5}(4.5)^2}{2!}$$

$$= e^{-4.5}(1 + 4.5 + \frac{(4.5)^2}{2!})$$

$$= .1736 .$$

# CONTINUOUS DISTRIBUTIONS

● **PROBLEM** 3-9

Let X be a continuous random variable. We wish to find probabilities concerning X. These probabilities are determined by a density function. Find a density function such that the probability that X falls in an interval (a,b) (0 < a < b < 1) is proportional to the length of the interval (a,b). Check that this is a proper probability density function.

<u>Solution</u>: The probabilities of a continuous random variable are computed from a continuous function called a density function in the following way. If f(x) is graphed and is

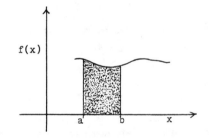

then, $Pr(a \le X \le b)$ = the area under the curve f(x) from a to b.

With this definition some conditions on f(x) must be imposed. f(x) must be positive and the total area between f(x) and the x-axis must be equal to 1.

We also see that if probability is defined in terms of area under a curve, the probability that a continuous random variable is equal to a particular value, $Pr(X = a)$ is the area under f(x) at the point a. The area of a line is 0, thus $Pr(X = a) = 0$. Therefore

$$Pr(a < X < b) = Pr(a \le X \le b).$$

To find a density function for $0 < X < 1$, such that $Pr(a < X < b)$ is proportional to the length of (a,b), we look for a function f(x) that is positive and the area under f(x) between 0 and 1 is equal to 1. It is reasonable to expect that the larger the interval the larger the probability that x is in the interval.

A density function that satisfies these criteria is

$$f(x) = \begin{cases} 1 & 0 < x < 1 \\ 0 & \text{otherwise} . \end{cases}$$

A graph of this density function is

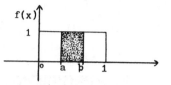

The probability that X is between a and b is the area of the shaded region. This is the area of a rectangle. The area of a rectangle is base × height.

Thus  Pr(a ≤ X ≤ b) = (b - a) × 1 = b - a . Similarly

Pr(X ≤ k) = (k - 0) × 1 = k  for  0 < k < 1.

Often the density function is more complicated and integration must be used to calculate the area under the density function.

To check that this is a proper probability density function, we must check that the total area under f(x) is 1. The total area under this density function is (1 - 0) × 1 = 1.

● **PROBLEM 3-10**

Given that the random variable X has density function

$$f(x) = \begin{cases} 2x & 0 < x < 1 \\ 0 & \text{otherwise} \end{cases}$$

Find  Pr($\frac{1}{2}$ < x < 3/4)  and  Pr($-\frac{1}{2}$ < x < $\frac{1}{2}$).

**Solution:** Since  f(x) = 2x  is the density function of a continuous random variable, Pr($\frac{1}{2}$ < x < 3/4) = area under  f(x)  from $\frac{1}{2}$ to  3/4.

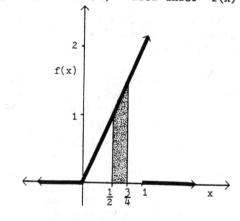

f(x)  is indicated by the heavy line.

The area under  f(x)  is the area of the triangle with vertices at  (0,0), (1,0) and (1,2).
The area of this triangle is  A = $\frac{1}{2}$ bh  where  b = base of the triangle and  h  is the altitude.

Thus,    $A = \frac{1}{2}(1) \times 2 = \frac{2}{2} = 1$

proving that  f(x)  is a proper probability density function.

To find the probability that  $\frac{1}{2} < x < 3/4$  we find the area of the shaded region in the diagram.  This shaded region is the difference in areas of the              right triangle with vertices  (0,0),  $(\frac{1}{2},0)$ and  $(\frac{1}{2}, f(\frac{1}{2}))$  and the area of the triangle with vertices  (0,0), (3/4,0)  and  (3/4, f(3/4)).

This difference is  $Pr(\frac{1}{2} < x < 3/4) = \frac{1}{2}(3/4)f(3/4) - \frac{1}{2}(\frac{1}{2})f(\frac{1}{2})$

$$= \frac{1}{2}[\frac{3}{4} \cdot \frac{6}{4} - \frac{1}{2} \cdot 1]$$

$$= \frac{1}{2}[\frac{9}{8} - \frac{1}{2}] = \frac{1}{2} \cdot \frac{5}{8} = \frac{5}{16} \quad .$$

The probability that  $-\frac{1}{2} < x < \frac{1}{2}$  is

$Pr(-\frac{1}{2} < x < \frac{1}{2})$ = Area under  f(x)  from  $-\frac{1}{2}$  to  $\frac{1}{2}$ .

Because  f(x) = 0  from  $-\frac{1}{2}$  to  0, the area under  f(x)  from $-\frac{1}{2}$  to  0  is  0.  Thus

$Pr(-\frac{1}{2} < x < \frac{1}{2}) = Pr(0 < x < \frac{1}{2})$ = area under  f(x)  from  0  to  $\frac{1}{2}$

$$= \frac{1}{2}(\frac{1}{2}) \; f(\frac{1}{2})$$

$$= \frac{1}{2}(\frac{1}{2}) \cdot 1 = \frac{1}{4} \; .$$

● **PROBLEM 3-11**

Given that the continuous random variable  X  has distribution function  $F(x) = 0$  when  x < 1  and  $F(x) = 1 - 1/x^2$  when  x ≥ 1, graph  F(x), find the density function  f(x)  of  X, and show how F(x)  can be obtained from  f(x).

Solution:  To graph  F(x), observe that as  x  approaches  1  from the right side,  $1 - 1/x^2$  approaches  0.  As  x  approaches  + ∞, $1 - 1/x^2$  approaches  1  because  $\lim_{x \to \infty} 1/x^2 = 0$ .

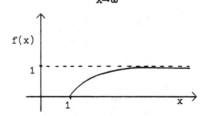

The curve is said to be asymptotic to the line  F(x) = 1  because it comes closer and closer to it, as  x  increases without limit, but never touches it.  F(x)  is a continuous function for all real numbers x  because it satisfies 2 conditions:  (1)  F(x)  is defined for all values of  x;  (2)  the function's value at any point  c  equals the left and right limits:

limit of  F(x) = F(c) = limit of  F(x)
(as  x → c from the left)      (as  x → c from the right) .

111

Differentiating $F(x) = 1 - 1/x^2$ $(1 \le x)$ yields
$$F'(x) = 0 - (-2x^{-3}) = 2/x^3 .$$
When $x < 1$, $F'(x) = d(0)/dx = 0$. The derivative does not exist at $x = 1$ because
$$\text{limit of } F'(x) = 0 \ne 2 = \frac{2}{1^3} = \text{limit of } F'(x)$$
$$\text{(as } x \to 1 \text{ from left)} \qquad (x \to 1 \text{ from right)} .$$

$$F'(x) = f(x) = \frac{2}{x^3} \text{ when } 1 \le x < \infty = 0 \text{ when } x < 1$$

is the density function of X.

We can obtain $F(x)$ by integrating $f(x)$ from 1 to x when $x \ge 1$, and from $-\infty$ to x when $x < 1$. When $x \ge 1$,

$$F(x) = \int_1^x \frac{2}{t^3} dt = 2 \int_1^x t^{-3} dt = 2 \left. \frac{t^{-2}}{-2} \right]_1^x$$

$$= \left. \frac{-1}{t^2} \right]_1^x = -\frac{1}{x^2} - (-1) = -\frac{1}{x^2} + 1 = 1 - \frac{1}{x^2} = F(x).$$

When $x < 1$, $F(x) = \int_{-\infty}^x 0 \, dt = 0$ .

Let a distribution function F, be given by
$$F(x) = 0 ; \qquad x < 0$$
$$= (x+1)/2 ; \quad 0 \le x < 1$$
$$= 1 ; \qquad 1 \le x .$$
Find $\Pr(-3 < x \le \frac{1}{2})$ and sketch F.

Solution: First note that

$$\Pr(-3 < x \le \tfrac{1}{2}) = \Pr(x \le \tfrac{1}{2}) - \Pr(x \le -3) .$$

By definition, this is

$$F(\tfrac{1}{2}) - F(-3) = \frac{\tfrac{1}{2}+1}{2} - 0 = \frac{\tfrac{1}{2}+1}{2}$$

$$= \frac{3/2}{2} = \frac{3}{4} .$$

The graph of F follows:

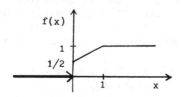

● **PROBLEM** 3-13

Let X be a continuous random variable where $f(x) = cx^2$ ; $0 < x < 1$. Find c.

**Solution:** We want the total probability to sum or integrate to one.

$$1 = \int_{-\infty}^{\infty} f(x) \, dx = \int_{0}^{1} cx^2 \, dx = \left.\frac{cx^3}{3}\right|_{x=0}^{1}$$

$$= c(1/3 - 0) = c/3 .$$

Hence $c = 3$.

● **PROBLEM** 3-14

The cumulative distribution functions of the latitude angle $\theta(w)$ and the longitude angle $\phi(w)$ of the random orientation on the earth's surface are

$$F_\theta(\lambda) = \begin{cases} 0 & ; \ \lambda < 0 \\ 1-\cos\lambda & ; \ 0 \le \lambda \le \pi/2 \\ 1 & ; \ \lambda > \pi/2 \end{cases}$$

$$F_\phi(\lambda) = \begin{cases} 0 & ; \ \lambda < 0 \\ \lambda/2\pi & ; \ 0 \le \lambda \le 2\pi \\ 1 & ; \ \lambda > 2\pi \end{cases}$$

Find the corresponding density functions.

**Solution:** We know that $F(x) = \int_{-\infty}^{x} f(t) \, dt$. But by the Fundamental

Theorem of Integral Calculus: $\dfrac{dF(x)}{dx} = f(x)$ .

Hence $F_\theta(\lambda) = \dfrac{dF_\theta(\lambda)}{d\lambda}$

$$= \begin{cases} \dfrac{d}{d\lambda}(0) & ; \ \lambda < 0 \\ \dfrac{d}{d\lambda}(1-\cos \lambda) & ; \ 0 \le \lambda \le 2\pi \\ \dfrac{d}{d\lambda}(1) & ; \ \lambda > 2\pi \end{cases}$$

$$= \begin{cases} 0 & ; \ \lambda < 0 \\ \sin \lambda & ; \ 0 \le \lambda \le 2\pi \\ 0 & ; \ \lambda > 2\pi . \end{cases}$$

Also $F_\phi(\lambda) = \dfrac{dF(\lambda)}{d\lambda}$

$$= \begin{cases} \dfrac{d(0)}{d\lambda} & ; \ \lambda < 0 \\ \dfrac{d}{d\lambda}\left(\dfrac{\lambda}{2\pi}\right) & ; \ 0 \le \lambda \le 2\pi \\ \dfrac{d}{d\lambda}(1) & ; \ \lambda > 2\pi \end{cases}$$

$$= \begin{cases} 0 & ; \ \lambda < 0 \\ \dfrac{1}{2\pi} & ; \ 0 \le \lambda \le 2\pi \\ 0 & ; \ \lambda > 2\pi . \end{cases}$$

Consider the function, $g(x) = (1 + x^2)^{-1}$ . Determine a constant k such that $f(x) = k(1 + x^2)^{-1}$ is a proper probability density for $-\infty < x < \infty$ . Find $F(x) = Pr(X \leq x)$ if X is distributed with density function $f(x)$.

**Solution:** We see immediately that $f(x)$ is integrable, continuous and $f(x) > 0$ for all x.

To ensure that $f(x)$ is a proper probability function we must

find a constant k such that $\int_{-\infty}^{\infty} f(x)\ dx = 1$ .

Thus

$$\int_{-\infty}^{\infty} k(1 + x^2)^{-1}\ dx = k \int_{-\infty}^{\infty} \frac{1}{1 + x^2}\ dx$$

$$= k[\tan^{-1}x]_{-\infty}^{\infty}$$

$$= k[\tan^{-1}\infty - \tan^{-1}-\infty]$$

$$= k\pi\ .$$

Thus in order for $\int_{-\infty}^{\infty} f(x)\ dx$ to equal 1, k must be equal to $1/\pi$ .

Then, $\quad f(x) = \dfrac{1/\pi}{(1 + x^2)} = \dfrac{1}{\pi(1 + x^2)}$

$$F(x) = \int_{-\infty}^{x} f(t)\ dt = \int_{-\infty}^{x} \frac{1}{\pi(1 + t^2)}\ dt$$

$$= \frac{1}{\pi}\ [\tan^{-1}x - \tan^{-1}(-\infty)]$$

$$= \frac{1}{\pi}\ [\tan^{-1}x + \frac{\pi}{2}]\ .$$

# UNIFORM DENSITY FUNCTION

Let the probability density function for X be given as $f(x) = 1/k$ for $0 < x < k$ and 0 otherwise. Find $Pr(X \leq t) = F(t)$ and sketch $F(t)$.

**Solution:** $F(t) = Pr(X \leq t)$ is defined as the cumulative distribution

function, $\quad F(t) = \int_{-\infty}^{t} f(x)\ dx$ .

In this case $F(t) = \int_{-\infty}^{t} 1/k\ dx \quad$ and

$$F(t) = \begin{cases} 0 & t \leq 0 \\ \int_{0}^{t} 1/k\ dx\ , & 0 < t < k \\ 1 & k \leq t \end{cases}$$

$$F(t) = \begin{cases} 0 & t \le 0 \\ t/k & 0 < t < k \\ 1 & k \le t . \end{cases}$$

This function is graphed below:

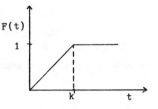

X is a continuous random variable with probability density function

$$f(x) = \begin{array}{ll} 1/k & 0 \le x \le k \\ 0 & \text{otherwise.} \end{array}$$

Show that this is a proper density function and find $Pr(a \le X \le b)$ for $0 \le a < b \le k$ .

Solution: To show that $f(x)$ is a proper probability density function we must show that $f(x) \ge 0$ for all $x$ and that $\int_{-\infty}^{\infty} f(x)dx = 1$ .

From the way $f(x)$ is defined, for any value of $k > 0$ , $f(x) = 1/k \ge 0$ .

Furthermore, $\int_{-\infty}^{\infty} f(x)\,dx = \int_{0}^{k} f(x)\,dx$

because $f(x) = 0$ for $x \ge k$ or $x \le 0$ .

$\int_{0}^{k} f(x)\,dx = \int_{0}^{k} 1/k\,dx = 1/k \cdot x]_{0}^{k} = 1/k[k - 0] = 1$ .

$Pr(a \le X \le b)$ for $0 \le a < b \le k$ is defined to be $\int_{a}^{b} f(x)\,dx.$

Thus $Pr(a \le X \le b) = \int_{a}^{b} f(x)\,dx$

$= \int_{a}^{b} 1/k\,dx = 1/k\ x\ ]_{a}^{b}$

$= \dfrac{b - a}{k}$ .

A graph of $f(x)$ is shown below:

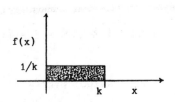

Consider the hardness of steel as a random variable, X, with values between 50 and 70 on the Rockwell B scale. We can assume that the hardness has density function

$$f(x) = 0 \qquad \text{when} \qquad x < 50 \, ,$$

$$f(x) = \frac{1}{20} \qquad \text{when} \qquad 50 \le x \le 70 \, ,$$

$$f(x) = 0 \qquad \text{when} \qquad x > 70 \, .$$

Graph this density function. Compute the probability that the hardness of a randomly selected steel specimen is less than 65.

**Solution:**    Graph of f(x).

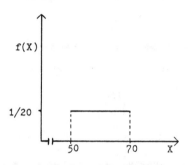

We use the cumulative distribution function $F(a) = P(X \le a)$ to compute $P(X < 65)$.

$$F(a) = \int_{-\infty}^{a} f(x)dx = \int_{50}^{a} \frac{1}{20} \, dx = \frac{1}{20} x\Big]_{50}^{a} = \frac{a - 50}{20} = F(a)$$

when $50 \le a \le 70$. (When $b < 50$, $F(b) = \int_{-\infty}^{b} 0 \, dx = 0$. When $b > 70$,

$$F(b) = \int_{-\infty}^{50} f(x)dx + \int_{50}^{70} f(x)dx + \int_{70}^{b} f(x)dx = 0 + \frac{20}{20} + 0 = 1.)$$ We **find**

that    $P(X < 65) = F(65) = \frac{65 - 50}{20} = \frac{15}{20} = \frac{3}{4}$ .

# EXPONENTIAL DENSITY FUNCTION

● **PROBLEM** 3-19

Suppose the length of time an electric bulb lasts, X, is a random variable with cumulative distribution

$$F(x) = Pr(X \le x) = \begin{cases} 0 & x < 0 \\ 1 - e^{-x/500} & x \ge 0 \, . \end{cases}$$

Find the probability that the bulb lasts    (a) between 100 and 200 hours (b)  beyond 300 hours.

**Solution:**    (a)    $Pr(100 \le X \le 200) = 1 - [Pr(X \ge 200) + Pr(X \le 100)]$

$$= 1 - Pr(X \ge 200) - Pr(X \le 100) \, ;$$

but            $1 - Pr(X \ge 200) = Pr(X \le 200)$

116

thus,    $\Pr(100 \le X \le 200)$ = $\Pr(X \le 200) - \Pr(X \le 100)$

$$= F(200) - F(100)$$

$$= 1 - e^{-200/500} - (1 - e^{-100/500})$$

$$= e^{-1/5} - e^{-2/5}$$

$$= .1484 \ .$$

Similarly,    $\Pr(X \ge 300)$ = $\Pr(\text{bulb lasts longer than 300 hours})$

$$= 1 - \Pr(X < 300)$$

$$= 1 - F(300)$$

$$= 1 - (1 - e^{-300/500})$$

$$= e^{-3/5} = .5488 \ .$$

● **PROBLEM** 3-20

Let  x  be the random variable representing the length of a telephone conversation.  Let  $f(x) = \lambda e^{-\lambda x}$ , $0 \le x < \infty$ .  Find the c.d.f., $F(x)$, and find  $\Pr(5 < x \le 10)$.

Solution:    The c.d.f. is the probability that an observation of a random variable will be less than or equal to  x.  The probability is equal to the following shaded area.

Area can be found by integration:

$$A = \int_0^x \lambda e^{-\lambda t} \, dt = - \left. e^{-\lambda t} \right|_{t=0}^x = 1 - e^{-\lambda x} = F(x).$$

$\Pr(5 < x \le 10)$  is represented by the following shaded area.

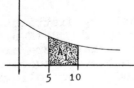

We find  $A_1$  by integration,

$$A_1 = \int_{x=5}^{10} \lambda e^{-\lambda t} \, dt = -e^{-\lambda t} \Big|_{x=5}^{x=10} = e^{-5\lambda} - e^{10\lambda} \ .$$

# CHAPTER 4

# THE BINOMIAL DISTRIBUTION

## DERIVATION OF THE BINOMIAL DISTRIBUTION

PROBLEM 4-1

Find the probabilities that X, the number of "successes" of a binomial experiment with 4 independent trials and $\pi$ = probability of "success" = $\frac{1}{3}$, equals 0, 1, 2, 3, or 4. Sketch a histogram for the distribution.

Solution:    A binomial experiment is an experiment made up of a certain number of independent trials. Independence of the trials implies that the results of the later trials are not influenced in any way by the results of the earlier trials. Each of these trials has two possible outcomes, denoted "success" and "failure." The probability of "success" in any particular trial is denoted by the Greek letter $\pi$.

We are often interested in the probability of a certain number of "successes" throughout the course of a particular experiment. The number of successes is denoted by the capital letter 'X'. X can take on the values from 0 to n, where n is the total number of trials performed in a binomial experiment.

What is the probability distribution of X? That is, what is Pr(X=0), Pr(X=1), ..., Pr(X=n)? Consider first Pr(X=0), the probability that there are no "successes" in n trials and the probability of success equals $\pi$. Each trial can be represented by the following tree diagram,

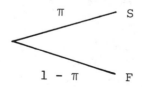

Here S represents the outcome "success" and will occur with probability $\pi$, F represents the outcome failure and will occur with probability $1 - \pi$. The only way that X will be equal to zero is if there is a failure on each of the n trials. Since the trials are independent, Pr (failure on each trial)= Pr (failure on the first trial) × Pr (failure on the second) × Pr (failure on the third) ... × Pr (failure on the nth)

$$= \underbrace{(1 - \pi) \cdot (1 - \pi) \cdot \ldots \cdot (1 - \pi)}_{n \text{ terms}} = (1 - \pi)^n$$

The probability of exactly 1 "success" in n trials Pr (X=1), is found in a similar way.

A "success" in the first trial and "failures" thereafter will occur with probability

$$\pi \cdot \underbrace{(1 - \pi) \cdot \ldots \cdot (1 - \pi)}_{n - 1 \text{ terms}} = \pi (1 - \pi)^{n-1}.$$

Another possibility for X = 1 will be if there is a "failure" on the first trial, a "success" on the second and "failures" thereafter. This will occur with probability

$$(1 - \pi) \cdot \pi \cdot \underbrace{(1 - \pi) \cdot \ldots \cdot (1 - \pi)}_{n - 2 \text{ terms}} = \pi (1 - \pi)^{n-1}.$$

There are n possible trials on which the single "success" might take place. Each of these events is mutually exclusive. Therefore Pr (X = 1) = Pr (the single success is on the first trial) + Pr (success is on second) + ... +

Pr (success is on the nth trial) $= \pi (1 - \pi)^{n-1} + \pi (1 - \pi)^{n-1} + \ldots + \pi (1 - \pi)^{n-1} = n \pi (1 - \pi)^{n-1}.$

To find the probability that X = 2 we select the two trials on which successes will take place. This is "the number of ways 2 objects can be chosen from n" or $\binom{n}{2}$. The probability of two "successes" and n - 2 "failures" in n independent trials is thus

$$\binom{n}{2} \pi \cdot \pi \cdot \underbrace{(1 - \pi) \cdot \ldots \cdot (1 - \pi)}_{n - 2 \text{ terms}}$$

$$Pr \ (X = 2) = \binom{n}{2} \pi^2 (1 - \pi)^{n-2}, \text{ in general}$$

$$Pr \ (X = j) = \binom{n}{j} \pi^j (1 - \pi)^{n-j} \quad j = 0, 1, 2, \ldots n.$$

In our problem $n = 4$ and $\pi = \frac{1}{3}$ and

$$\text{Pr }(X=0) = \binom{4}{0}\left(\frac{1}{3}\right)^0\left(\frac{2}{3}\right)^4 = 1 \cdot 1 \cdot \frac{16}{81} = \frac{16}{81}$$

$$\text{Pr }(X=1) = \binom{4}{1}\left(\frac{1}{3}\right)^1\left(\frac{2}{3}\right)^3 = 4 \cdot \frac{1}{3} \cdot \frac{8}{27} = \frac{32}{81}$$

$$\text{Pr }(X=2) = \binom{4}{2}\left(\frac{1}{3}\right)^2\left(\frac{2}{3}\right)^2 = 6 \cdot \frac{1}{9} \cdot \frac{4}{9} = \frac{24}{81}$$

$$\text{Pr }(X=3) = \binom{4}{3}\left(\frac{1}{3}\right)^3\left(\frac{2}{3}\right)^1 = 4 \cdot \frac{1}{27} \cdot \frac{2}{3} = \frac{8}{81}$$

$$\text{Pr }(X=4) = \binom{4}{4}\left(\frac{1}{3}\right)^4\left(\frac{2}{3}\right)^0 = 1 \cdot \frac{1}{81} \cdot 1 = \frac{1}{81}.$$

Note that $\sum\limits_{j=0}^{4} \text{Pr }(X = j) = \frac{16}{81} + \frac{32}{81} + \frac{24}{81} + \frac{8}{81} + \frac{1}{81}$

$$= \frac{81}{81} = 1 \quad.$$

as it must in order for this to be a proper probability distribution.

Histogram

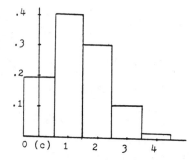

● PROBLEM 4-2

Calculate the binomial probability distribution for $n = 10$ and $p = \frac{1}{8}$ . Compare this distribution with the distribution for $n = 10$ and $p = \frac{1}{2}$ . Do they differ in degree of dispersion? Position of peak? Maximum height of peak? Degree of symmetry?

Solution:    The binomial distribution formula is $P(X = k) =$ $\binom{n}{k} p^k (1 - p)^{n-k}$ where n is the number of trials, k the number of "successes", and p the probability of a "success."

For n = 10  p = $\frac{1}{8}$ ,

$$P(X = k) = \binom{10}{k}\left(\frac{1}{8}\right)^k \left(1 - \frac{1}{8}\right)^{10-k} = \binom{10}{k}\left(\frac{1}{8}\right)^k \left(\frac{7}{8}\right)^{10-k}$$

$$P(X = 0) = \binom{10}{0}\left(\frac{1}{8}\right)^0 \left(\frac{7}{8}\right)^{10} = \frac{10!}{10!0!} \times \left(\frac{7}{8}\right)^{10} = \left(\frac{7}{8}\right)^{10} ,$$

since by definition 0! and any quantity to the zero power is one.

$$P(X = 1) = \binom{10}{1}\left(\frac{1}{8}\right)^1 \left(\frac{7}{8}\right)^9 = \frac{10!}{9!1!}\frac{1}{8}\left(\frac{7}{8}\right)^9 = 10\left(\frac{1}{8}\right)\left(\frac{7}{8}\right)^9$$

$$= 10\ (.125)(.3007) = .376$$

$$P(X = 2) = \binom{10}{2}\left(\frac{1}{8}\right)^2 \left(\frac{7}{8}\right)^8 = \frac{10!}{8!2!}\left(\frac{1}{8}\right)^2\left(\frac{7}{8}\right)^8$$

$$= 90\ \left(\frac{1}{8}\right)^2\left(\frac{7}{8}\right)^8 = 45\ (.016)(.3436) = .247$$

$$P(X = 3) = \binom{10}{3}\left(\frac{1}{8}\right)^3 \left(\frac{7}{8}\right)^7 = \frac{10!}{7!3!}(\frac{1}{8})^3(\frac{7}{8})^7$$

$$= 120\ (.002)\ (.3927) = .094$$

$$P(X = 4) = \binom{10}{4}\left(\frac{1}{8}\right)^4 \left(\frac{7}{8}\right)^6 = \frac{10!}{6!4!}\left(\frac{1}{8}\right)^4\left(\frac{7}{8}\right)^6$$

$$= 210\ (.00024)(.4488) = .023$$

$$P(X = 5) = \binom{10}{5}\left(\frac{1}{8}\right)^5 \left(\frac{7}{8}\right)^5 = \frac{10!}{5!5!}\left(\frac{1}{8}\right)^5\left(\frac{7}{8}\right)^5$$

$$= 252\ (.000016) = .004$$

$$P(X = 6) = \binom{10}{6}\left(\frac{1}{8}\right)^6 \left(\frac{7}{8}\right)^4 = \frac{10!}{6!4!}\left(\frac{1}{8}\right)^6\left(\frac{7}{8}\right)^4$$

$$= 210\ (.000004)(.5862) = .0005$$

$$P(X = 7) = \binom{10}{7}\left(\frac{1}{8}\right)^7 \left(\frac{7}{8}\right)^3 = \frac{10!}{7!3!}\left(\frac{1}{8}\right)^7\left(\frac{7}{8}\right)^3 = .00004$$

$$P(X = 8) = \binom{10}{8}\left(\frac{1}{8}\right)^8 \left(\frac{7}{8}\right)^2 = \frac{10!}{8!2!}\left(\frac{1}{8}\right)^8\left(\frac{7}{8}\right)^2$$

$$= .000002$$

$$P(X = 9) = \binom{10}{9}\left(\frac{1}{8}\right)^9 \left(\frac{7}{8}\right)^1 = \frac{10!}{9!1!}\left(\frac{1}{8}\right)^9\left(\frac{7}{8}\right)^1$$

$$= .00000006$$

$$P(X = 10) = \binom{10}{10}\left(\frac{1}{8}\right)^{10}\left(\frac{7}{8}\right)^{0} = \frac{10!}{10!0!}\left(\frac{1}{8}\right)^{10}\left(\frac{7}{8}\right)^{0}$$

$$= .000000001 \; .$$

The probabilities total 1.007542061. The discrepancy from 1 is due to approximations and rounding off.

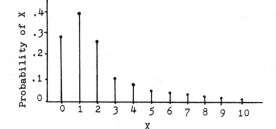

This graph shows the previous distribution. Now consider the binomial distribution for $n = 10$   $p = \frac{7}{8}$ .

$$P\left(X_{\frac{7}{8}} = r\right) = \binom{10}{r}\left(\frac{7}{8}\right)^{r}\left(\frac{1}{8}\right)^{10-r} \; .$$

Recall that $\binom{n}{r} = \dfrac{n!}{(n-r)!\,r!} = \dfrac{n!}{r!\,(n-r)!} = \binom{n}{n-r}$ so that

$$P\left(X_{\frac{7}{8}} = r\right) = \binom{10}{r}\left(\frac{7}{8}\right)^{r}\left(\frac{1}{8}\right)^{10-r} = \binom{10}{10-r}\left(\frac{1}{8}\right)^{10-r}\left(\frac{7}{8}\right)^{r} =$$

$$P\left(X_{\frac{1}{8}} = 10 - r\right). \quad \text{Therefore}$$

$$P_{\frac{1}{8}}(X = 0) = P_{\frac{7}{8}}(X = 10) \qquad P_{\frac{1}{8}}(X = 5) = P_{\frac{7}{8}}(X = 5)$$

$$P_{\frac{1}{8}}(X = 1) = P_{\frac{7}{8}}(X = 9) \qquad P_{\frac{1}{8}}(X = 6) = P_{\frac{7}{8}}(X = 4)$$

$$P_{\frac{1}{8}}(X = 2) = P_{\frac{7}{8}}(X = 8) \qquad P_{\frac{1}{8}}(X = 7) = P_{\frac{7}{8}}(X = 3)$$

$$P_{\frac{1}{8}}(X = 3) = P_{\frac{7}{8}}(X = 7) \qquad P_{\frac{1}{8}}(X = 8) = P_{\frac{7}{8}}(X = 2)$$

$$P_{\frac{1}{8}}(X = 4) = P_{\frac{7}{8}}(X = 6) \qquad P_{\frac{1}{8}}(X = 9) = P_{\frac{7}{8}}(X = 1)$$

$$P_{\frac{1}{8}}(X = 10) = P_{\frac{7}{8}}(X = 0).$$

Hence the probability density function for $n = 10$ and $p = \frac{7}{8}$ is the mirror image of $n = 10$ and $p = \frac{1}{8}$, as shown

122

below:

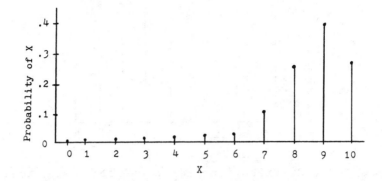

Let us proceed to calculate the binomial density function for $n = 10$, $p = \frac{1}{2}$ .

$$P(X=k) = \binom{n}{k} p^k (1 - p)^{n-k} = \binom{10}{k} \left(\frac{1}{2}\right)^k \left(1 - \frac{1}{2}\right)^{10-k}$$

$$= \binom{10}{k} \left(\frac{1}{2}\right)^k \left(\frac{1}{2}\right)^{10-k} = \binom{10}{k} \left(\frac{1}{2}\right)^{10} = \binom{10}{k} \frac{1}{1024} \quad .$$

A few representative calculations;

$$P(X = 0) = \binom{10}{0} \frac{1}{1024} = \binom{10}{10} \frac{1}{1024} = P(X = 10) = .0010$$

$$P(X = 1) = \binom{10}{1} \frac{1}{1024} = \frac{10!}{9!1!} \frac{1}{1024} = \binom{10}{9} \frac{1}{1024}$$

$$= P(X = 9) = .0098$$

$$P(X = 2) = \binom{10}{2} \frac{1}{1024} = \frac{10!}{8!2! \cdot 1024} = \binom{10}{8} \frac{1}{1024}$$

$$= P(X = 8) = .0439$$

$$P(X = 3) = \binom{10}{3} \frac{1}{1024} = \frac{10!}{7!3! \cdot 1024} = \binom{10}{7} \frac{1}{1024}$$

$$= P(X = 7) = .1172$$

$$P(X = 4) = \binom{10}{4} \frac{1}{1024} = \frac{10!}{6!4! \cdot 1024} = \binom{10}{6} \frac{1}{1024}$$

$$= P(X = 6) = .2051$$

$$P(X = 5) = \binom{10}{5} \frac{1}{1024} = \frac{10!}{5!5! \ 1024} = .2460.$$

The graph follows:

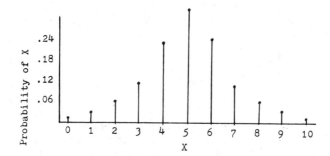

The distributions for $p = \frac{1}{8}$ and $p = \frac{7}{8}$ are mirror images. They are skewed with peaks at X = 1 and X = 9 respectively. The peaks are relatively high (.376). The functions are concentrated near the peaks and are asymmetric. On the other hand, the distribution for $p = \frac{1}{2}$ is completely symmetric. The peak is lower (.2460) and the function is more widely dispersed.

● **PROBLEM** 4-3

John Reeves completed 60% of his passes one season. Assuming he is as good a quarterback the next fall, what is the probability that he will complete 80 of his first 100 passes?

Solution: Since we are working with sequences of independent successes and failures, the binomial distribution is the correct one to use.

The probability of 80% success is given by substitution in the formula $\binom{n}{x} p^x (1 - p)^{n - x}$ where n is the number of trials. In this case n = 100, x is the number of desired successes (X=80 here) and p the probability of success in any trial ($p = \frac{6}{10}$ here).

$\binom{n}{x}$ is the number of combinations of n trials taken x at a time. This is defined to be $\frac{n!}{x!(n-x)!}$ .

The distribution $p(x) = \binom{n}{x} p^x (1 - p)^{n - x}$ is called binomial since for each integer value of x, the probability of x corresponds to a term in the binomial expansion

$$(q + p)^n = q^n + \binom{n}{1} q^{n-1} p + \binom{n}{2} q^{n-2} p + \ldots + p^n.$$

We interpret p to be the probability of success in any trial and q = 1 - p the probability of failure because p + q = p + 1 - p = (p - p) + 1 = 1.

We have, therefore,

$$p(x) = \binom{n}{x} p^x (1 - p)^{n-x} = \binom{100}{80}\binom{60}{100}^{80}\left(\frac{40}{100}\right)^{20}$$

$$= \frac{100!}{80!20!}\left(\frac{6}{10}\right)^{80}\left(\frac{4}{10}\right)^{20} = 1.053(10^{-5}).$$

Thus the probability that Reeves completes Exactly 80 of his first 100 passes in the upcoming football season is about $10^{-5}$.

The binomial theorem provides a convenient way to compute binomial probabilities. The following three examples provide the statement of this theorem and examples of its use.

● **PROBLEM 4-4**

Expand $(x + 2y)^5$.

<u>Solution:</u> Apply the binomial theorem. If n is a positive integer, then

$$(a + b)^n = \binom{n}{0}a^n b^0 + \binom{n}{1}a^{n-1}b + \binom{n}{2}a^{n-2}b^2 + \cdots + \binom{n}{r}a^{n-r}b^r$$

$$+ \cdots + \binom{n}{n}b^n.$$

Note that $\binom{n}{r} = \frac{n!}{r!(n-r)!}$ and that $0! = 1$. Then, we obtain:

$$(x + 2y)^5 = \binom{5}{0}x^5(2y)^0 + \binom{5}{1}x^4(2y)^1 + \binom{5}{2}x^3(2y)^2$$

$$+ \binom{5}{3}x^2(2y)^3 + \binom{5}{4}x^1(2y)^4 + \binom{5}{5}x^0(2y)^5$$

$$= \frac{5!}{0!5!}x^5 + \frac{5!}{1!4!}x^4 2y + \frac{5!}{2!3!}x^3\left(4y^2\right)$$

$$+ \frac{5!}{3!2!}x^2\left(8y^3\right) + \frac{5!}{4!1!}x\left(16y^4\right) + \frac{5!}{5!0!}1\left(32y^5\right)$$

$$= x^5 + \frac{5 \cdot 4!}{4!}x^4 2y + \frac{5 \cdot 4 \cdot 3!}{2 \cdot 1 \cdot 3!}x^3\left(4y^2\right)$$

$$+ \frac{5 \cdot 4 \cdot 3!}{3! \cdot 2 \cdot 1}x^2\left(8y^3\right) + \frac{5 \cdot 4!}{4!1!}x\left(16y^4\right) + \frac{5!}{5!0!}\left(32y^5\right)$$

$$= x^5 + 10x^4 y + 40x^3 y^2 + 80x^2 y^3 + 80xy^4 + 32y^5.$$

Find the expansion of $(x + y)^6$.

<u>Solution:</u> Use the Binomial Theorem which states that

$$(a+b)^n = \frac{1}{0!} a^n + \frac{n}{1!} a^{n-1}b + \frac{n(n-1)}{2!} a^{n-2}b^2 + \ldots + nab^{n-1} + b^n .$$

Replacing a by x and b by y:

$$(x+y)^6 = \frac{1}{0!} x^6 + \frac{6}{1!}x^5 y + \frac{6\cdot5}{2!} x^4 y^2 + \frac{6\cdot5\cdot4}{3!} x^3 y^3 + \frac{6\cdot5\cdot4\cdot3}{4!} x^2 y^4$$

$$+ \frac{6\cdot5\cdot4\cdot3\cdot2}{5!} x^1 y^5 + \frac{6\cdot5\cdot4\cdot3\cdot2\cdot1}{6!} x^0 y^6$$

$$= \frac{1}{1} x^6 + \frac{6}{1} x^5 y + \frac{6\cdot5}{2\cdot1} x^4 y^2 + \frac{6\cdot5\cdot4}{3\cdot2\cdot1} x^3 y^3 + \frac{6\cdot5\cdot4\cdot3}{4\cdot3\cdot2\cdot1} x^2 y^4$$

$$+ \frac{6\cdot5\cdot4\cdot3\cdot2}{5\cdot4\cdot3\cdot2\cdot1} xy^5 + \frac{6\cdot5\cdot4\cdot3\cdot2\cdot1}{6\cdot5\cdot4\cdot3\cdot2\cdot1} y^6$$

$$(x+y)^6 = x^6 + 6x^5 y + 15x^4 y^2 + 20x^3 y^3 + 15x^2 y^4 + 6xy^5 + y^6 .$$

Give the expansion of $\left(r^2 - \frac{1}{s}\right)^5$.

<u>Solution:</u> Write the given expression as the sum of two terms raised to the 5th power:

$$\left(r^2 - \frac{1}{s}\right)^5 = \left[r^2 + \left(-\frac{1}{s}\right)\right]^5 . \qquad (1)$$

The Binomial Theorem can be used to expand the expression on the right side of equation (1). The Binomial Theorem is stated as:

$$(a+b)^n = a^n + na^{n-1}b + \frac{n(n-1)}{1\cdot2}a^{n-2}b^2 + \frac{n(n-1)(n-2)}{1\cdot2\cdot3}a^{n-3}b^3$$

$$+ \ldots + nab^{n-1} + b^n,$$ where a and b are any two numbers.

Let $a = r^2$, $b = -\frac{1}{s}$, and $n = 5$. Then, using the Binomial Theorem:

$$\left(r^2 - \frac{1}{s}\right)^5 = \left[r^2 + \left(-\frac{1}{s}\right)\right]^5$$

$$= \left(r^2\right)^5 + 5\left(r^2\right)^{5-1}\left(-\frac{1}{s}\right) + \frac{5(5-1)}{1 \cdot 2}\left(r^2\right)^{5-2}\left(-\frac{1}{s}\right)^2$$

$$+ \frac{5(5-1)(5-2)}{1 \cdot 2 \cdot 3}\left(r^2\right)^{5-3}\left(-\frac{1}{s}\right)^3$$

$$+ \frac{5(5-1)(5-2)(5-3)}{1 \cdot 2 \cdot 3 \cdot 4}\left(r^2\right)^{5-4}\left(-\frac{1}{s}\right)^4$$

$$+ \frac{5(5-1)(5-2)(5-3)(5-4)}{1 \cdot 2 \cdot 3 \cdot 4 \cdot 5}\left(r^2\right)^{5-5}\left(-\frac{1}{s}\right)^5$$

$$= r^{10} - \frac{5\left(r^2\right)^4}{s} + \frac{5(\cancel{4})}{1 \cdot \cancel{2}}\left(r^2\right)^3\left(\frac{1}{s^2}\right) - \frac{5(\cancel{4})(\cancel{3})}{1 \cdot 2 \cdot \cancel{3}}\left(r^2\right)^2\left(\frac{1}{s^3}\right)$$

$$+ \frac{5(\cancel{4})(\cancel{3})(\cancel{2})}{1 \cdot \cancel{2} \cdot \cancel{3} \cdot \cancel{4}}\left(r^2\right)^1\left(\frac{1}{s^4}\right) - \frac{\cancel{5}(\cancel{4})(\cancel{3})(\cancel{2})(\cancel{1})}{\cancel{1} \cdot \cancel{2} \cdot \cancel{3} \cdot \cancel{4} \cdot \cancel{5}}\left(r^2\right)^0\left(\frac{1}{s^5}\right)$$

$$= r^{10} - \frac{5r^8}{s} + \frac{10r^6}{s^2} - \frac{10r^4}{s^3} + \frac{5r^2}{s^4} - (1)(1)\left(\frac{1}{s^5}\right)$$

$$\left(r^2 - \frac{1}{s}\right)^5 = r^{10} - \frac{5r^8}{s} + \frac{10r^6}{s^2} - \frac{10r^4}{s^3} + \frac{5r^2}{s^4} - \frac{1}{s^5}$$

● **PROBLEM** 4-7

Thirteen machines are in operation. The probability that at the end of one day a machine is still in operation is 0.6. If the machines function independently, find the most probable number of machines in operation at the end of that day and the probability that these many machines are operating.

Solution: Let X = the number of machines in operation at the end of the day. With the assumption of independence, X is binomially distributed with parameters n = 13 and p = .6. A graph of the probability distribution of X is below:

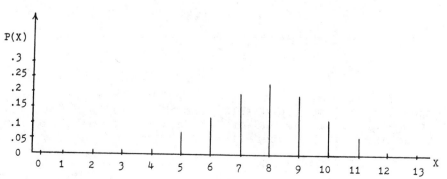

| Number of machines in operation, X | Probability Pr(X = n) |
|:---:|:---:|
| 0 | $\binom{13}{0}(.6)^0(.4)^{13} = 6.6 \times 10^{-6}$ |
| 1 | $\binom{13}{1}(.6)^1(.4)^{12} = .0001287$ |
| 2 | $\binom{13}{2}(.6)^2(.4)^{11} = .0011544$ |
| 3 | $\binom{13}{3}(.6)^3(.4)^{10} = .0063606$ |
| 4 | $\binom{13}{4}(.6)^4(.4)^9 = .0238609$ |
| 5 | $\binom{13}{5}(.6)^5(.4)^8 = .06435$ |
| 6 | $\binom{13}{6}(.6)^6(.4)^7 = .1287$ |
| 7 | $\binom{13}{7}(.6)^7(.4)^6 = .1932289$ |
| 8 | $\binom{13}{8}(.6)^8(.4)^5 = .21737$ |
| 9 | $\binom{13}{9}(.6)^9(.4)^4 = .1811095$ |
| 10 | $\binom{13}{10}(.6)^{10}(.4)^3 = .10868$ |
| 11 | $\binom{13}{11}(.6)^{11}(.4)^2 = .04446$ |
| 12 | $\binom{13}{12}(.6)^{12}(.4)^1 = .0113178$ |
| 13 | $\binom{13}{13}(.6)^{13}(.4)^0 = .001306$ |

The highest probability is $Pr(X = 8) = .21737$ and thus 8 is the most probable number of machines that will be operating at the end of the day. The probability that 8 machines will be operating at the end of the day is .21737.

What is the probability of getting exactly 3 heads in 5 flips of a balanced coin?

Solution:     We have here the situation often referred to as a Bernoulli trial. There are two possible outcomes, head or tail, each with a finite probability. Each flip is independent. This is the type of situation to which the binomial distribution,

$$P(X = k) = \binom{n}{k} p^k (1 - p)^{n-k},$$

applies. The a priori probability of tossing a head is $p = \frac{1}{2}$. the probability of a tail is $q = 1 - p = 1 - \frac{1}{2} = \frac{1}{2}$ . Also $n = 5$ and $k = 3$ (number of heads required). we have

$$P(X = 3) = \binom{5}{3} \left(\frac{1}{2}\right)^3 \left(1 - \frac{1}{2}\right)^2 = \frac{5!}{3!2!} \left(\frac{1}{2}\right)^3 \left(\frac{1}{2}\right)^2$$

$$= \frac{5 \cdot 4 \cdot 3 \cdot 2 \cdot 1}{3 \cdot 2 \cdot 1 \cdot 2 \cdot 1} \left(\frac{1}{2}\right)^5 = \frac{10}{2^5} = \frac{10}{32} = \frac{5}{16} .$$

On three successive flips of a fair coin, what is the probability of observing 3 heads? 3 tails?

Solution:     The three successive flips of the coin are three independent events. Since the coin is fair, the probability of throwing a head on any particular toss is $p = \frac{1}{2}$ .

Let $X =$ the number of heads observed in three tosses of the coin. We wish to find $Pr(X = 3)$. By our assumptions, $X$ is binomially distributed with parameters $n = 3$ and $p = \frac{1}{2}$ .

Thus,          $Pr(X = 3) = \binom{3}{3} \left(\frac{1}{2}\right)^3 \left(\frac{1}{2}\right)^0 = 1 \left(\frac{1}{2}\right)^3 \left(\frac{1}{2}\right)^0 = \frac{1}{8} .$

Similarly, let $T =$ the number of tails observed in three successive flips of a fair coin. $T$ is distributed binomially with parameters $n = 3$ and $p = \frac{1}{2} =$ the probability that a tail is observed on a particular toss of the coin.

Thus          $Pr(T = 3) = \binom{3}{3} \left(\frac{1}{2}\right)^3 \left(\frac{1}{2}\right)^0 = 1 \cdot \frac{1}{8} \cdot 1 = \frac{1}{8} .$

Find the probability that in three rolls of a pair of dice, exactly one total of 7 is rolled.

Solution: Consider each of the three rolls of the 3 pairs as a trial and the probability of rolling a total of s seven as a "success." Assume that each roll is independent o of the others. If X = the number of successes, then we want to find

$$Pr(X = 1) = \binom{3}{1} p^1 (1 - p)^2$$

where p = probability of rolling a total of 7 on a single roll. We have earlier found in the Probability Chapter this probability to be $\frac{6}{36} = \frac{1}{6}$ and hence the probability of rolling a total of 7 exactly once in three rolls is

$$Pr(X = 1) = \binom{3}{1} \left(\frac{1}{6}\right)^1 \left(\frac{5}{6}\right)^2 = 3 \cdot \frac{1}{6} \cdot \frac{25}{36} = \frac{25}{72} .$$

What is the probability of getting exactly 4 "sixes" when a die is rolled 7 times?

Solution: Let X = the number of "sixes" observed when a die is rolled 7 times. If we assume that each roll is independent of each other roll and that the probability of rolling a six on one roll is $= \frac{1}{6}$, the X is binomially distributed with parameters n = 7 and p = $\frac{1}{6}$ .

Thus, $\quad Pr(X = 4) = Pr(\text{exactly 4 "sixes" on 7 rolls})$

$$= \binom{7}{4} \left(\frac{1}{6}\right)^4 \left(\frac{5}{6}\right)^{7-4} =$$

$$= \frac{7 \cdot 6 \cdot 5 \cdot 4 \cdot 3 \cdot 2 \cdot 1}{4 \cdot 3 \cdot 2 \cdot 3 \cdot 2 \cdot 1} \left(\frac{1}{6}\right)^4 \left(\frac{5}{6}\right)^3$$

$$= 35 \left(\frac{1}{6}\right)^4 \left(\frac{5}{6}\right)^3 .$$

$$Pr(X = 4) = 35 \left(\frac{1}{1296}\right) \left(\frac{125}{216}\right) = \frac{4375}{279936} = .0156.$$

A deck of cards can be dichotomized into black cards and red cards. If p is the probability of a black card on a single draw and q the probability of a red card, p = 1/2 and q = 1/2. Six cards are sampled with replacement. What is the probability on six draws of getting 4 black and 2 red cards? Of getting all black cards?

**Solution:** Let X = the number of black cards observed in six draws from this deck.

$Pr(X = 4)$ = the probability that 4 black cards and 2 red cards are in this sample of 6. The probability of drawing a black card on a single draw is $p = 1/2$ and since each draw is independent, X is distributed binomially with parameters 6 and 1/2.

Thus $Pr(X = 4) = \binom{6}{4}\left(\frac{1}{2}\right)^4\left(\frac{1}{2}\right)^2 = 15\left(\frac{1}{2}\right)^6 = \frac{15}{64}$

and $Pr(X = 6) = \binom{6}{6}\left(\frac{1}{2}\right)^6\left(\frac{1}{2}\right)^0 = \left(\frac{1}{2}\right)^6 = \frac{1}{64}$ .

● **PROBLEM** 4-13

In a family of 4 children, what is the probability that there will be exactly two boys?

**Solution:** The case of the sex of a born child is classically described by the binomial distribution. There are 2 possible outcomes, boy or girl. The probability of giving birth to a boy is $p = \frac{1}{2}$ . The probability of having a girl is $q = 1 - p = 1 - \frac{1}{2} = \frac{1}{2}$ . Also n = 4 (number of children) and k = 2 (number of boys). Furthermore,

$$P(X = k) = \binom{n}{k} p^k (1 - p)^{n-k}$$

$$P(X = 2) = \binom{4}{2}\left(\frac{1}{2}\right)^2\left(\frac{1}{2}\right)^{4-2} = \frac{4!}{2!2!}\left(\frac{1}{2}\right)^2\left(\frac{1}{2}\right)^2$$

$$= \frac{4 \cdot 3 \cdot 2 \cdot 1}{2 \cdot 1 \cdot 2 \cdot 1}\left(\frac{1}{2}\right)^4 = \frac{6}{2^4}$$

$$= \frac{3 \cdot 2}{2^3 \cdot 2} = \frac{3}{2^3} = \frac{3}{8} .$$

● **PROBLEM** 4-14

Suppose that the probability of parents to have a child with blond hair is $\frac{1}{4}$ . If there are four children in the family, what is the probability that exactly half of them have blond hair?

**Solution:** We assume that the probability of parents having a blond child is $\frac{1}{4}$ . In order to compute the probability that 2 of 4 children have blond hair we must make another assumption. We must assume that the event consisting of a child being blond when it is born is independent of whether any of the other children are blond. The genetic determination of each child's hair color can be considered one of four independent trials with the probability of success, observing a blond child, equal to $\frac{1}{4}$.

If X = the number of children in the family with blond hair, we are interested in finding Pr(X = 2). By our assumptions X is binomially distributed with n = 4 and p = $\frac{1}{4}$.

Thus Pr(X = 2) = Pr(exactly half the children are blond)

$$= \binom{4}{2}\left(\frac{1}{4}\right)^2\left(\frac{3}{4}\right)^2 = \frac{4!}{2!2!} \cdot \left(\frac{1}{4}\right)^2\left(\frac{3}{4}\right)^2$$

$$= \frac{4 \cdot 3}{2 \cdot 1} \cdot \left(\frac{1}{16}\right)\left(\frac{9}{16}\right) = \frac{27}{128} = .21.$$

● **PROBLEM** 4-15

If a fair coin is tossed four times, what is the probability of at least two heads?

Solution: Let X = the number of heads observed in 4 tosses of a fair coin. X is binomially distributed if we assume that each toss is independent. If the coin is fair, p = Pr (a head is observed on a single toss) = $\frac{1}{2}$.

Thus Pr (at least two heads in 4 tosses)

$$= Pr(X \geq 2) = \sum_{x = 2}^{4} \binom{4}{x}\left(\frac{1}{2}\right)^x\left(\frac{1}{2}\right)^{4-x}$$

$$= \binom{4}{2}\left(\frac{1}{2}\right)^2\left(\frac{1}{2}\right)^2 + \binom{4}{3}\left(\frac{1}{2}\right)^3\left(\frac{1}{2}\right) + \binom{4}{4}\left(\frac{1}{2}\right)^4\left(\frac{1}{2}\right)^0$$

$$= \frac{6}{16} + \frac{4}{16} + \frac{1}{16} = \frac{11}{16}.$$

● **PROBLEM** 4-16

A baseball player has a .250 batting average (one base hit every four times, on the average). Assuming that the binomial distribution is applicable, if he is at bat four times on a particular day, what is (a) the probability that he will get exactly one hit? (b) the probability that he will get at least one hit?

<u>Solution:</u>    Considering a hit as a "success", we have

$= Pr \text{ (success)} = \frac{1}{4}$ ,

(a) Pr (exactly 1 hit in 4 trials) $= \binom{4}{1}\left(\frac{1}{4}\right)^1\left(\frac{3}{4}\right)^3$

$$= 4 \left(\frac{1}{4}\right)\left(\frac{27}{64}\right) = \frac{27}{64} \ .$$

(b) Pr (1 hit or 2 hits or 3 hits or 4 hits)

since these are mutually exclusive events Pr (at least 1 hit), using the addition rule

$$= 4 \left(\frac{1}{4}\right)^1\left(\frac{3}{4}\right)^3 + \binom{4}{2}\left(\frac{1}{4}\right)^2\left(\frac{3}{4}\right)^2 + \binom{4}{3}\left(\frac{1}{4}\right)^3\left(\frac{3}{4}\right) + \binom{4}{4}\left(\frac{1}{4}\right)^4\left(\frac{3}{4}\right)^0$$

$$= \frac{27}{64} + 6 \cdot \frac{1}{16} \cdot \frac{9}{16} + 4 \cdot \left(\frac{1}{64}\right) \cdot \frac{3}{4} + 1 \cdot \frac{1}{256} \cdot 1$$

$$= \frac{27}{64} + \frac{27}{128} + \frac{3}{64} + \frac{1}{256} = \frac{30}{64} + \frac{27}{128} + \frac{1}{256} = \frac{175}{256} \ .$$

There is a simpler way if we notice that the batter getting at least one hit and the batter going hitless are two mutually exclusive and exhaustive events. Because of this fact we know that

Pr(1 hit) + Pr(2 hits) + Pr(3 hits) + Pr(4 hits) +

+ Pr(0 hits) = 1

thus       Pr(at least 1 hit) + Pr(0 hits) = 1

or         Pr(at least 1 hit) = 1 - Pr(0 hits).

But     Pr(0 hits) $= \binom{4}{0}\left(\frac{1}{4}\right)^0\left(\frac{3}{4}\right)^4 = 1 \cdot 1 \cdot \frac{81}{256}$       and

Pr(at least 1 hit) $= 1 - \frac{81}{256} = \frac{175}{256}$ .

● **PROBLEM 4-17**

If a deck of cards is dichotomized into hearts and all other cards, what is the probability p of getting a heart on a single draw? What is the probability q of getting a spade, club, or diamond? When 7 cards are sampled with replacement, what is the probability of getting no hearts at all? What is the probability of getting 4 hearts? What is the probability of getting 2 hearts out of the first 4 draws and then 2 hearts out of the next 3? Is this result more or less probable than "4 hearts out of 7"? Why?

Solution: Using the classical model of probability, $P = \dfrac{\text{favorable outcomes}}{\text{total outcomes}}$ . Of the 52 cards (total possible outcomes), 13 are hearts (favorable outcomes). Therefore $P(\text{heart}) = \dfrac{13}{52} = \dfrac{1}{4}$ .

The total probability of all events must add up to 1. Hence

$$P(\text{spade, club, or diamond}) = 1 - P(\text{heart}) = 1 - \frac{1}{4} = \frac{3}{4}\ .$$

Since there is replacement, the probability of not drawing a heart remains $\dfrac{3}{4}$ on each draw. Therefore, by the multiplication rule

$$P(\text{no hearts in 7}) = \frac{3}{4} \times \frac{3}{4} \times \frac{3}{4} \times \frac{3}{4} \times \frac{3}{4} \times \frac{3}{4} \times \frac{3}{4} = \left(\frac{3}{4}\right)^7\ .$$

For the probability of getting 4 hearts we use the binomial distribution. We do this since we have independent trials with 2 possible outcomes, success or failure, each with constant probabilities, 1/4 and 3/4. According to the binomial distribution,

$$P(X = k) = \binom{n}{k} p^k (1 - p)^{n-k}. \text{ In our case}$$

$$P(X = 4) = \binom{7}{4}\left(\frac{1}{4}\right)^4 \left(\frac{3}{4}\right)^3\ .$$

Again we use the binomial distribution for the same reasons.

$$P(X = 2 \text{ (out of 4)}) = \binom{4}{2}\left(\frac{1}{4}\right)^2 \left(\frac{3}{4}\right)^2\ ;$$

$$P(X = 2 \text{ (out of 3)}) = \binom{3}{2}\left(\frac{1}{4}\right)^2 \left(\frac{3}{4}\right)^1\ .$$

By the multiplication rule for independent events,

$$P(\text{2 of first 4 and 2 of last 3}) = P(\text{2 of first 4}) \times$$
$$P(\text{2 of last 3})$$

$$= \binom{4}{2}\left(\frac{1}{4}\right)^2 \left(\frac{3}{4}\right)^2 \binom{3}{2}\left(\frac{1}{4}\right)^2 \left(\frac{3}{4}\right)^1.$$

The second result is less because it restricts the number of ways the total of 4 hearts can be arranged. The first probability includes such arrangements as 3 in the first 4 and 1 in the second 3 and so on.

If the probability of your hitting a target on a single shot is .8, what is the probability that in four shots you will hit the target at least twice?

Solution:    Each shot at the target is an independent trial with constant probability, $p = .8$, of a success. The only other possibility is failure. This type of situation calls for the binomial distribution,

$$P(X = k \text{ successes}) = \binom{n}{k} p^k (1 - p)^{n-k}.$$

Since the events of 2, 3, or 4 successes are mutually disjoint we use the addition rule for probabilities and

$$P(2 \text{ or } 3 \text{ or } 4) = P(2) + P(3) + P(4)$$

$$P(X = 2) = \frac{4!}{2!(4-2)!} (.8)^2 (.2)^{4-2} = \frac{4!}{2!2!} (.8)^2 (.2)^2$$

$$= \frac{\overset{2}{4}}{2} \frac{3}{1} \frac{2}{2} \frac{1}{1} (.064)(0.04)$$

$$= 6 (.0256) = 0.1536$$

$$P(X = 3) = \frac{4!}{3!(4-3)!} (.8)^3 (.2)^{4-3} = \frac{4!}{3!1!} (.8)^3 .2$$

$$= 4 (0.512)(0.2) = 0.4096$$

$$P(X = 4) = \frac{4!}{4!(4-4)!} (.8)^4 (.2)^{4-4} = \frac{4!}{4!0!} (.8)^4 (.2)^0$$

$$= (0.8)^4 \quad \text{since } \frac{4!}{4!} = 1 \quad \text{and } 0! = 1 \text{ (by}$$

definition) and any number raised to the zero power $= 1$.

$$= 0.4096.$$

Thus $P(2 \text{ or } 3 \text{ or } 4) = 0.1536 + 0.4096 + 0.4096 = 0.9728$.

Records of an insurance company show that 3/1000 of the accidents reported to the company involve a fatality. Determine:

(a)  the probability that no fatality is involved in thirty accidents reported.
(b)  the probability that four fatal accidents are included in twenty accidents reported.

**Solution:** Let X be the number of fatalities involved in n accidents. X may be assumed to be binomially distributed with parameters n and $\pi = 3/1000$. This assumption will be a valid one if the number of fatalities observed can be considered the sum of the results of n independent trials. On each trial (or accident) a fatality will occur with probability 3/1000.

(a) The probability that there are no fatalities in thirty accidents is $Pr(X = 0)$ with $n = 30$.

$$Pr(X = 0) = \binom{30}{0} \left(\frac{3}{1000}\right)^0 \left(\frac{997}{1000}\right)^{30}$$

$$= (1)\,(1)\,(.997)^{30} = .9138.$$

(b) The probability that there are four fatalities in twenty accidents is $Pr(X = 4)$ with $n = 20$.

$$Pr(X = 4) = \binom{20}{4} \left(\frac{3}{1000}\right)^4 \left(\frac{997}{1000}\right)^{16}$$

$$= .374 \times 10^{-6}.$$

● **PROBLEM** 4-20

Given that 40% of entering college students do not complete their degree programs, what is the probability that out of 6 randomly selected students, more than half will get their degrees?

**Solution:** Since 40% of the entering students drop out, 100% − 40% = 60% receive their degrees. We use the binomial probability function because (1) the selection of 6 students can be thought of as a sequence of success-failure trials, where success means graduation from college; (2) each trial is independent of the result of the other 5 trials; (3) the probability of success is the same in every trial.

The probability that 4 students out of 6 will graduate is $P(4) = \binom{6}{4}(.6)^4(.4)^{6-4}$. Note $60\% = \frac{60}{100} = .6$ and we write 0.6 because probabilities range between 0 and 1.

$$P(4) = \binom{6}{4}(0.6)^4(0.4)^2 = \frac{6!}{4!(6-4)!}(0.6)^4(0.4)^2$$

$$= (15)(0.1296)(0.16) = 0.311040 .$$

$$P(5) = \frac{6!}{5!(6-5)!}(0.6)^5(0.4)^{6-5} = 6\,(0.7776)(0.4)$$

$$= 0.186624 .$$

$$P(6) = \frac{6!}{6!(6-6)!}(0.6)^6(0.4)^0 = (0.6)^6 = 0.046656 .$$

No two of the events (that 4 or 5 or 6 students out of the 6 selected graduate) can occur together. We say they are mutually exclusive. Therefore we can add their individual probabilities to find P(4 or 5 or 6) =

$$= 0.311040 + 0.186624 + 0.046656 = 0.54432.$$

● **PROBLEM** 4-21

The probability that a basketball player makes at least one of six free throws is equal to 0.999936. Find: (a) the probability function of X, the number of times he scores; (b) the probability that he makes at least three baskets.

Solution:     This problem involves the binomial distribution for three reasons: (1) there are six independent trials (the outcome of each throw is independent of the others); (2) each throw has only 2 outcomes - score or no score; (3) since the player is shooting "free throws" (from a standing position) we can assume that the probability of a score remains the same from throw to throw.

In order to determine the probability function of the number of scores, we need to know the probability that any free throw will score. The event that no free throw scores is the complement of the event that one or more throws score. By the binomial distribution,

$$P(\underline{no} \text{ scores}) = \binom{6}{0} p^0 (1 - p)^{6-0} = 1 \cdot 1 \cdot (1 - p)^6$$

$$= (1 - p)^6,$$

since $\binom{6}{0} = \dfrac{6!}{(0!)(6-0)!} = \dfrac{6!}{1 \cdot 6!} = 1$     and

$p^0 = 1.$

P(at least one score) + P(no scores) = 1 since the events are complementary. Substituting $(1 - p)^6$ for P(no scores), the equation becomes

P(at least one score) + $(1 - p)^6 = 1$. Using the given information, this becomes p (at least one score)= .999936 = 1 - $(1-p)^6$

$$= (1 - p)^6 = 0.000064, \text{ so}$$

$$1 - p = \sqrt[6]{0.000064} = .2 \text{ and so } p = .8$$

Adding p to both sides and subtracting .2 from both sides, we have 1 - .2 = .8 = p.

Again using the binomial distribution, where r is the number of scores in 6 throws,

$$P(r) = \binom{6}{r} (.8)^r (.2)^{6-r}.$$

Substitution of any integer from 1 to 6 inclusive for r will yield the probability of that number of scores in 6 free throws.

Part (b) asks for the probability of at least three scores. This includes 4 possibilities: exactly 3 scores; exactly 4 scores; exactly 5 scores; or exactly 6 scores in 6 throws. Since only one of these events can occur, they are mutually exclusive. It follows that their probabilities can be added to give the probability that any one event will occur. Using summation notation,

P (3 or more scores in 6 throws) =

$$= \sum_{r=3}^{6} \binom{6}{r} (.8)^r (.2)^{6-r}.$$

By the table, P (3 scores) = .082, P(4) = .246, P(5) = .393, and P(6) = .262. Then

P(3 or more) = .082 + .246 + .393 + .262 = .983.

Many binomial tables give values for $p \leq .5$. Since in our example p = .8, we would have to convert the binomial distribution to an equivalent form in the following way:

Let $Pr(X=k) = \binom{n}{k} p^k (1 - p)^{n-k}$ with $p \geq .5$. If $p \geq .5$ then $1 - p \leq .5$.

We will find a probability for a new random variable Y with probability of success, $1 - p \leq .5$.

$$Pr(X=k) = \binom{n}{k} p^k (1 - p)^{n-k}$$

$$= \binom{n}{n-k} p^k (1 - p)^{n-k} = Pr(Y = n-k).$$

Remember that $\binom{n}{k} = \frac{n!}{(n-k)!k!} = \binom{n}{n-k}$.

We can thus use the table to find $Pr(Y=n-k)$ where the probability of success is $1 - p$ and we can thus find the $Pr(X=k)$ when the probability of success is p.

● PROBLEM 4-22

If 40 percent of a company's employees are in favor of a proposed new incentive-pay system, develop the probability distribution for the number of employees out of a sample of two employees who would be in favor of the incentive system by the use of a tree diagram. Use F for a favorable reaction and F' for an unfavorable reaction.

<u>Solution</u>:    Imagine that the two employees are sampled in succession. The tree diagram describing the possible outcomes is

Because 40 percent of the employees favor the new incentive-pay system, the probability of selecting a single employee who favors the new plan is .4, P(F) = .4 and P(F') = 1 - P(F) = 1 - .4 = .6.

The tree diagram for a single employee with the probabilities labeled is;

After one employee is picked and his opinion is recorded, the second employee will be picked. The probabilities for the second employee will be the same.

Using the multiplication rule, the extended tree diagram is

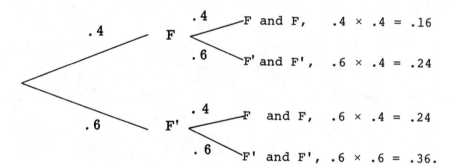

This diagram lists all the probabilities and possible outcomes of this sampling procedure.

Let X be the number of people in the sample who favor the new plan. X can take  on the values 0, 1 or 2. We will compute the probability distribution of X from the tree diagram.

Pr(X =0) = Pr(both sampled do not favor the new plan)

= Pr(F' and F') = .6 × .6 = .36

Pr(X =1) = Pr(1 favors and 1 does not)

= Pr(F and F' or F' and F) = .24 + .24 = .48

Pr(X =2) = Pr(both favor the new plan)

= Pr(F and F) = .16.

An alternative method is to notice that X is bi-nomially distributed with parameters n = 2 and $\pi$ = .4.

Thus, $\Pr(X=0) = \binom{2}{0} (.4)^0 (.6)^2 = (1)(1)(.36) = .36$

$\Pr(X=1) = \binom{2}{1} (.4)^1 (.6)^1 = (2)(.4)(.6) = .48$

$\Pr(X=2) = \binom{2}{2} (.4)^2 (.6)^0 = (1)(.4)^2 (1) = .16.$

● **PROBLEM** 4-23

Over a long period of time a certain drug has been effective in 30 percent of the cases in which it has been prescribed. If a doctor is now administering this drug to four patients, what is the probability that it will be effective for at least three of the patients?

Solution: Let X = the number of patients on which the drug is effective. X is binomially distributed. There are assumed to be 4 independent trials, the administration of the drug to the 4 patients. The probability of "success" in a particular trial is the probability that the drug is effective on a patient and Pr(drug is effective on a patient) = $\pi$ = .30.

The probability that the drug is effective on at least 3 patients is the probability that X is equal to 3 or 4. Since these two events are mutually exclusive,

$\Pr(X = 3 \text{ or } X = 4) = \Pr(X = 3) + \Pr(X = 4)$

by the addition rule. X is distributed binomially with parameters 4 and .3 thus

$\Pr(X=3) = \binom{4}{3} (.3)^3 (.7)^1 = 4(.027)(.7) = .0756$

$\Pr(X=4) = \binom{4}{4} (.3)^4 (.7)^0 = 1 \cdot (.0081) \cdot 1 = .0081$

and $\Pr(X = 3 \text{ or } 4) = .0756 + .0081 = .0837.$

This means that 8.37% of the time this drug will be effective on at least three patients.

● **PROBLEM** 4-24

You are told that 9 out of 10 doctors recommend Potter's Pills. Assuming this is true, suppose you plan to choose 4 doctors at random. What is the probability that no more than two of these 4 doctors will recommend Potter's Pills?

Solution:    Let X = the number of doctors among the 4 chosen that will recommend Potter's Pills. If each doctor is selected at random and the probability of selecting a doctor that recommends Potter's Pills is .9, then X is a binomially distributed random variable with parameters n = 4 and p = .9.

In order to make this assumption we needed to know that each trial on which a doctor was selected was independent of any other trial. This is guaranteed by our selection of doctors at random.

We wish to find Pr(no more than two of these 4 doctors will recommend Potter's Pills). This equals the probability that X = 0, 1 or 2, or Pr(X = 0, 1 or 2). Each of these outcomes is mutually exclusive thus

$$\Pr(X = 0, 1, \text{ or } 2) = \Pr(X = 0) + \Pr(X = 1) + \Pr(X = 2)$$

$$= \binom{4}{0} (.9)^0 (.1)^4 + \binom{4}{1} (.9)^1 (.1)^3 + \binom{4}{2} (.9)^2 (.1)^3$$

$$\Pr(X=0,1, \text{ or } 2) = (.1)^4 + 4(.9)(.1)^3 + \frac{4 \cdot 3 \cdot 2 \cdot 1}{2 \cdot 1 \cdot 2 \cdot 1} (.9)^2 (.1)^2$$

$$= (.1)^4 + (3.6)(.1)^3 + 6(.9)^2 (.1)^2$$

$$= (1 \times 10^{-1})^4 + 3.6(1 \times 10^{-1})^3 + 6(.81)(1 \times 10^{-1})^2$$

$$= 1 \times 10^{-4} + 36 \times 10^{-4} + 486. \times 10^{-4}$$

$$= 523 \times 10^{-4} = .0523.$$

● **PROBLEM** 4-25

The most common application of the binomial theorem in industrial work is in lot-by-lot acceptance inspection. If there are a certain number of defectives in the lot, the lot will be rejected as unsatisfactory.

It is natural to wish to find the probability that the lot is acceptable even though a certain number of defectives are observed. Let p be the fraction of defectives in the lot. Assume that the size of the sample is small  compared to the lot size. This will insure that the probability of selecting a defective item remains constant from trial to trial. Now choose a sample of size 18 from a lot where 10% of the items are defective. What is the probability of observing 0, 1 or 2 defectives in the sample.

Solution:    Imagine that the items are drawn successively from the lot until 18 have been chosen. The probability of selecting a defective item is p = .10, the fraction of defectives in the lot. Hence the probability of selecting a non-defective item is 1 - .10 = .90. If X is the number of defective items observed, X is the sum of the number of defective items observed on 18 independent trials. X is hence binomially distributed with parameters n = 18 and p = .10.

We wish to determine the $\Pr(X = 0, 1 \text{ or } 2)$.

This probability is the sum of the probabilities of three mutually exclusive events. Hence $\Pr(X = 0, 1, \text{ or } 2) = \Pr(X = 0) = \Pr(X = 1) + \Pr(X = 2)$.

X is binomially distributed thus

$$\Pr(X=0) = \binom{18}{0} (.10)^0 (.90)^{18} = .150$$

$$\Pr(X=1) = \binom{18}{1} (.10)^1 (.90)^{17} = .300$$

$$\Pr(X=2) = \binom{18}{2} (.10)^2 (.90)^{16} = .284$$

and $\Pr(X = 0, 1 \text{ or } 2) = .150 + .300 + .284 = .734$.

● **PROBLEM** 4-26

Over a period of some years, a car manufacturing firm finds that 18% of their cars develop body squeaks within the guarantee period. In a randomly selected shipment, 20 cars reach the end of the guarantee period and none develop squeaks. What is the probability of this?

Solution:    The car can either squeak or not squeak. The probability of a car squeaking is 18% or .18. The probability of not squeaking is $q = 1 - p = 1 - .18 = .82$. The situation we have here is a dichotomy of the type that fits the binomial distribution. There are independent trials with two possible outcomes each with a finite, constant probability.

According to the binomial distribution,

$$P(X=k) = \binom{n}{k} p^k (1 - p)^{n-k} .$$

Here, $p = .18$, $1 - p = .82$, $n = 20$, and $k = 0$. Hence,

$$P(X = 0) = \binom{20}{0} (.18)^0 (.82)^{20} = \frac{20!}{20!0!} (.18)^0 (.82)^{20}$$

$$= (.82)^{20} = .019.$$

(since any quantity to the zero power and 0! are both defined to be one.)

● **PROBLEM** 4-27

A sample of 4 fuses is selected without replacement from a lot consisting of 5000 fuses. Assuming that 20% of the fuses in the lot are known to be defective, what is the probability that the sample would contain exactly 2 defective items?

Solution:     Since the sample constitutes a very small
fraction of the population, the probability of getting a
defective fuse, $\pi$, is approximately the same on each
selection. The probability of selecting a defective fuse is
.20, since 20% of the fuses are known to be defective. If
the probability of getting a defective fuse is the same on
each draw, it follows that the outcome of each selection
is independent from the outcome of any other selection.

Let X = the number of defective fuses observed in a
sample of 4 fuses. By our assumptions, X is binomially
distributed with parameters n = 4 and p = .2.

Pr(sample contains exactly 2 defective fuses)

$$= Pr(X = 2) = \binom{4}{2} (.2)^2 (.8)^2 = \frac{4!}{2!2!} (.2)^2 (.8)^2$$

$$= 6(.04)(.64) = .1536.$$

● **PROBLEM 4-28**

An industrial process produces items of which 1% are defective. If a random sample of 100 of these are drawn from
a large consignment, calculate the probability that the
sample contains no defectives.

Solution:     If X = the number of defectives in a sample
of 100, then X is distributed binomially with parameters
n = 100 and p 1% or .01. Thus

$$Pr(X = 0) = Pr(\text{no defectives in sample})$$

$$= \binom{100}{0} (.01)^0 (1 - .01)^{100}$$

$$= (0.99)^{100} = .366.$$

● **PROBLEM 4-29**

A proportion p of a large number of items  in a batch is
defective. A sample of n items is drawn and if it contains
no defective items the batch is accepted  while if it
contains more than two defective items  the batch is
rejected. If, on the other hand, it contains one or two
defectives, an independent sample of m is drawn, and if
the combined number of defectives in the samples does not
exceed two, the batch is accepted. Calculate the possibility
of accepting this batch.

Solution:     The batch will be accepted only if

(1) the first sample contains no defectives.

(2) The first sample contains 1 defective and the
second sample contains 0 or 1 defective.

(3) The first sample contains 2 defectives and the second sample contains 0 defectives.

These three probabilities are mutually exclusive. If one occurs then none of the others can occur. Thus if we compute the probability of each of these events, the sum of the three will be the probability of acceptance.

Let: X = the number of defectives in the first sample.

Y = the number of defectives in the second sample.

If the sampling is done with replacement, X will be binomially distributed with the parameter n equal to the number of trials (or size of sample) and p = probability of selecting a defective on 1 trial. Similarly, Y is binomially distributed with parameters m and p.

Again by the addition law, Pr(acceptance) = Pr(0 defectives in first batch) + Pr( 1 in first and 0 or 1 in second) + Pr(2 in first and 0 in second) = Pr(X=0) + Pr(X=1, Y=0 or 1) + Pr(X = 2, Y=0).

$$Pr(X=0) = \binom{n}{0} p^0 (1 - p)^{n-0}.$$

$$Pr(X=1, Y=0 \text{ or } 1) = Pr(X=1, Y=0) + Pr(X=1, Y=1)$$

by the addition rule, since we are dealing with mutually exclusive events. $Pr(X=1, Y=0) = Pr(X=1) \cdot Pr(Y=0)$ by the multiplication law.   Hence

$$Pr(X=1, Y=0) = \binom{n}{1} p^1 (1 - p)^{n-1} \cdot \binom{m}{0} p^0 (1 - p)^m.$$

Similarly, $Pr(X=1, Y=1) = Pr(X=1) \cdot Pr(Y=1)$

$$= \binom{n}{1} p^1 (1 - p)^{n-1} \cdot \binom{m}{1} p^1 (1 - p)^{m-1},$$

For   similar   reasons,   $Pr(X=2, Y=0) = Pr(X=2) \cdot$

$$Pr(Y=0) = \binom{n}{2} p^2 (1 - p)^{n-2} \binom{m}{0} p^0 (1 - p)^m.$$

Hence Pr(acceptance) =

$$= \binom{n}{0} p^0 (1-p)^{n-0} + \binom{n}{1} p^1 (1-p)^{n-1} \binom{m}{0} p^0 (1-p)^m + \binom{n}{1} p^1 (1-p)^{n-1}$$

$$\binom{m}{1} p^1 (1-p)^{m-1} + \binom{n}{2} p^2 (1-p)^{n-2} \binom{m}{0} p^0 (1-p)^m$$

$$= (1-p)^n + np(1-p)^{m+n-1} + nmp^2 (1-p)^{m+n-2}$$
$$+ \tfrac{1}{2} n(n=1) p^2 (1-p)^{m=n-2}.$$

Letting 1-p=q, we can write this more concisely as

$$pr(\text{acceptance}) = q^n \quad 1 = npq^{m-1} + mnp^2q^{m-2} + \tfrac{1}{2}n(n-1)\,p^2q^{m-2} \quad .$$

| x | $\pi=$ 01 | 02 | 03 | 04 | 05 | 06 | 07 | 08 | 09 | 10 | |
|---|---|---|---|---|---|---|---|---|---|---|---|
| 1 | 0394 | 0776 | 1147 | 1507 | 1855 | 2193 | 2519 | 2836 | 3143 | 3439 | 3 |
| 2 | 0006 | 0023 | 0052 | 0091 | 0140 | 0199 | 0267 | 0344 | 0430 | 0523 | 2 |
| 3 | | | 0001 | 0002 | 0005 | 0008 | 0013 | 0019 | 0027 | 0037 | 1 |
| 4 | | | | | | | | | 0001 | 0001 | 0 |
| x | 99 | 98 | 97 | 96 | 95 | 94 | 93 | 92 | 91 | 90 $=\pi$ | x |

$$n = 4$$

| x | $\pi=$ 11 | 12 | 13 | 14 | 15 | 16 | 17 | 18 | 19 | 20 | |
|---|---|---|---|---|---|---|---|---|---|---|---|
| 1 | 3726 | 4003 | 4271 | 4530 | 4780 | 5021 | 5254 | 5479 | 5695 | 5904 | 3 |
| 2 | 0624 | 0732 | 0847 | 0968 | 1095 | 1228 | 1366 | 1509 | 1656 | 1808 | 2 |
| 3 | 0049 | 0063 | 0079 | 0098 | 0120 | 0144 | 0171 | 0202 | 0235 | 0272 | 1 |
| 4 | 0001 | 0002 | 0003 | 0004 | 0005 | 0007 | 0008 | 0010 | 0013 | 0016 | 0 |
| x | 89 | 88 | 87 | 86 | 85 | 84 | 83 | 82 | 81 | 80 $=\pi$ | x |

$$n = 4$$

| x | $\pi=$ 21 | 22 | 23 | 24 | 25 | 26 | 27 | 28 | 29 | 30 | |
|---|---|---|---|---|---|---|---|---|---|---|---|
| 1 | 6105 | 6298 | 6485 | 6664 | 6836 | 7001 | 7160 | 7313 | 7459 | 7599 | 3 |
| 2 | 1963 | 2122 | 2285 | 2450 | 2617 | 2787 | 2959 | 3132 | 3307 | 3483 | 2 |
| 3 | 0312 | 0356 | 0403 | 0453 | 0508 | 0566 | 0628 | 0694 | 0763 | 0837 | 1 |
| 4 | 0019 | 0023 | 0028 | 0033 | 0039 | 0046 | 0053 | 0061 | 0071 | 0081 | 0 |
| x | 79 | 78 | 77 | 76 | 75 | 74 | 73 | 72 | 71 | 70 = | x |

$$n = 4$$

| x | $\pi=$ 31 | 32 | 33 | 34 | 35 | 36 | 37 | 38 | 39 | 40 | |
|---|---|---|---|---|---|---|---|---|---|---|---|
| 1 | 7733 | 7862 | 7985 | 8103 | 8215 | 8322 | 8425 | 8522 | 8615 | 8704 | 3 |
| 2 | 3660 | 3837 | 4015 | 4193 | 4370 | 4547 | 4724 | 4900 | 5075 | 5248 | 2 |
| 3 | 0915 | 0996 | 1082 | 1171 | 1265 | 1362 | 1464 | 1596 | 1679 | 1792 | 1 |
| 4 | 0092 | 0105 | 0119 | 0134 | 0150 | 0168 | 0187 | 0209 | 0231 | 0256 | 0 |
| x | 69 | 68 | 67 | 66 | 65 | 64 | 63 | 62 | 61 | 60 $=\pi$ | x |

$$n = 4$$

| x | $\pi=$ 41 | 42 | 43 | 44 | 45 | 46 | 47 | 48 | 49 | 50 | |
|---|---|---|---|---|---|---|---|---|---|---|---|
| 1 | 8788 | 8868 | 8944 | 9017 | 9085 | 9150 | 9211 | 9269 | 9323 | 9375 | 3 |
| 2 | 5420 | 5590 | 5759 | 5926 | 6090 | 6252 | 6412 | 6569 | 6724 | 6875 | 2 |
| 3 | 1909 | 2030 | 2155 | 2283 | 2415 | 2550 | 2689 | 2831 | 2977 | 3125 | 1 |
| 4 | 0283 | 0311 | 0342 | 0375 | 0410 | 0448 | 0488 | 0531 | 0576 | 0625 | 0 |
| x | 59 | 58 | 57 | 56 | 55 | 54 | 53 | 52 | 51 | 50 $=\pi$ | x |

# CUMULATIVE BINOMIAL PROBABILITIES

● PROBLEM 4-30

Let X be a binomially distributed random variable with parameters n and π. where n = the number of independent trials and π is the probability of success on a particular trial.

Use the table above to find Pr(X≥2) and Pr(X=2) if n = 4 and π = .23.

Solution:    Pr(X≤2) = Pr(X = 2 or 3 or 4). To find this possibility, we resort to the table of cumulative binomial probabilities.

First find π =.23 in the body of this table. Then read down the left side of the table until x = 2. The number in the row of x = 2 and π = 23 is the Pr(X≥2). We see that Pr(X≥2) = .2285.

To find the Pr(X=2) from the cumulative binomial table we must first express an exact probability in terms of a cumulative probability.

$$Pr(X=2) = Pr(X=2) + Pr(X=3) + Pr(X=4) - [Pr(X=3+Pr(X=4)]$$

$$= Pr(X \geq 2) - Pr(X \geq 3).$$

We now find the two cumulative probabilities, Pr(X>2) and Pr(X>3) from the table. Reading down the column headed by π = 23 and from the left across the row labeled x = 3 we find Pr(X≥3) = .0403.

Thus, Pr(X=2) = Pr(X≥2) - Pr(X≥3)

$$= .2285 - .0403 = .1882.$$

● PROBLEM 4-31

For n = 4 and π = 0.73, find (a) P(X≤2) and (b) P(X=2).

Solution:    The table used in the previous problem can be used again here.

First read through the body of the table until π = 73 (or .73) is found. This is in the third section from the top.

We wish to find Pr(X≤2) where X is binomially distributed with parameters n = 4 independent trials and π = .73, the probability of success on any particular trial.

$$Pr(X \leq 2) = Pr(X=0) + Pr(X=1) + Pr(X=2).$$

We can find this probability in two ways.

(1) In the section where $\pi$ = 73, read up the column on the right until x = 2 is reached. Then read across from right to left until the column labeled $\pi$ = 73 is found. This gives Pr(X$\leq$2) = .2959.

(2) The second method is as follows. Notice that a binomial probability is really two probabilities. To illustrate this let X be a binomially distributed random variable with n = 4 and $\pi$ = .73. Let Y be a binomially distributed random variable with n = 4 and $\pi$ = .27.

A probability about X is also a probability about Y.

$$Pr(X=1) = \binom{4}{1}(.73)^1(.27)^3 = \binom{4}{3}(.27)^3(.73)^1$$

$$= Pr(Y=3) .$$

$$\binom{4}{1} = \frac{4!}{1!3!} = \binom{4}{3} .$$

A cumulative probability for X is also a cumulative probability for Y.

$$Pr(X = 0, 1 \text{ or } 2) = Pr(X\leq2) = \sum_{x=0}^{2} \binom{4}{x}(.73)^x(.27)^{4-x}$$

Let y = 4 - x, then x = 4 - y and $\sum_{x=0}^{2} \binom{4}{x}(.73)^x(.27)^{4-x}$

$$Pr(X\leq2) = \binom{4}{0}(.73)^0(.27)^4 + \binom{4}{1}(.73)^1(.27)^3 + \binom{4}{2}(.73)^2(.27)^2$$

$$= \binom{4}{4}(.27)^4(.73)^0 + \binom{4}{3}(.27)^3(.73)^1 + \binom{4}{2}(.27)^2(.73)^2$$

because $\binom{4}{0} = \binom{4}{4}$, $\binom{4}{1} = \binom{4}{3}$, $\binom{4}{2} = \binom{4}{2}$

$$= Pr(Y=4) + Pr(Y=3) + (Pr(Y=2) .$$

We have shown that

$$Pr(X\leq2) = Pr(Y\geq2).$$

The second method of using a table of cumulative binomial probabilities uses this fact. We wish to find Pr(X$\leq$2) where X is distributed with parameters n = 4 and $\pi$ = .73. This is equal to Pr(Y$\geq$2) where Y is distributed with parameters n = 4 and $\pi$ = .27. We find Pr(Y$\geq$2). To do this we read through the table until we find $\pi$ = .27 and then read down the column on the right until we reach the row headed by 2. Reading from left to right across this row and down the column headed by $\pi$ = 27, our answer is found to be the intersection of this row and column or Pr(X$\leq$2) = Pr(Y$\geq$2) = .2959.

To find Pr(X=2) from this table we convert from
cumulative probabilities to single probabilities.

$$Pr(X=2) = Pr(X=0) + Pr(X=1) + Pr(X=2)$$

$$- [Pr(X=0) + Pr(X=1)] .$$

Thus, $PR(X=2) = Pr(X \le 2) - Pr(X \le 1)$ .

To find the $Pr(X \le 1)$ we read up the column in which
$\pi$ = 73 and across the row from right to left labeled 1. We
see that $Pr(X \le 1)$ = .0628. Hence,

$$Pr(X=2) = .2959 - .0628 = .2331.$$

● PROBLEM 4-32

Given the following cumulative binomial distribution,
find (a) $P(X = 1)$; (b) $P(X = 4)$; (c) $P(X = 5)$.

$$(n = 5, p = 0.31)$$

| x | $P(X \ge x)$ |
|---|---|
| 0 | 1.0000 |
| 1 | 0.8436 |
| 2 | 0.4923 |
| 3 | 0.1766 |
| 4 | 0.0347 |
| 5 | 0.0029 |

Solution:     (a) The probabilities on the table, $P(X \ge x)$,
give the values of the probabilities that a specific
occurrence of a random variable will be at least as great
as the given x. For example, 1 is the only value at least
as great as 1, but not at least as great as 2. Therefore
the probability that X = 1 is the probability that X is at
least 1 but NOT at least 2.

The addition rule for mutually exclusive probabilities
therefore says, $P(X \ge 1) = P(X=1) + P(X \ge 2)$.

Equivalently, $P(X=1) = P(X \ge 1) - P(X \ge 2)$

$$= .8436 - .4923 = .3513.$$

(b)   $P(X=4) = P(X \ge 4) - P(X \ge 5) = .0347 - .0029 = .0318$.

(c)   5 is the only possible value at least as large as 5,
hence $P(X=5) = P(X \ge 5) = .0029$.

Given the following binomial distribution, find (a) P(X=4); (b) P(X=1); (c) P(X=0).

$$(n = 5, \; p = 0.69)$$

| x | $P(X \leq x)$ |
|---|---|
| 0 | 0.0029 |
| 1 | 0.0347 |
| 2 | 0.1766 |
| 3 | 0.4923 |
| 4 | 0.8436 |
| 5 | 1.0000 |

Solution: (a) The events $P(X<3)$ and $P(X=4)$ are disjoint therefore $P(X=4 \cup X \leq 3) = P(X \leq 3) + P(X=4)$ by the addition rule or

$$P(X \leq 4) = P(X \leq 3) + P(X=4)$$

equivalently, $P(X=4) = P(X \leq 4) - P(X \leq 3)$

$$= .8437 - .4923 = .3513.$$

(b) Similarly, $P(X=1) = P(X \leq 1) - P(X \leq 0)$

$$= .0347 - .0029 = .0318.$$

(c) $P(X=0) = P(X \leq 0) = .0029.$

You might notice that the previous problem had the same solution. The similarity can be explained if the binomial formula,

$$P(X=k) = \binom{n}{k} p^k (1 - p)^{n-k}$$

is used to solve both examples. In the first one where $n = 5$ and $p = .31$, $1 - p = .69$ and

$$P(X=1) = \binom{5}{1} (.31)^1 (.69)^4 = \frac{5!}{1!4!} (.31)^1 (.69)^4 = .3513.$$

In this example where $n = 5$ and $p = 0.69$, $1 - p = .31$ and

$$P(X=4) = \binom{5}{4} (.69)^4 (.31)^1 = .3513.$$

Similar operations can be performed on (b) and (c).

The probability of hitting a target on a shot is $\frac{2}{3}$ . If a person fires 8 shots at a target, Let X denote the number of times he hits the target, and find:

(a) $P(X = 3)$    (b) $P(1 < X \leq 6)$    (c) $P(X > 3)$ .

**Solution:** If we assume that each shot is independent of any other shot then X is a binomially distributed random variable with parameters $n = 8$ and $\pi = \frac{2}{3}$ . ($\pi$ equals the probability of hitting the target on any particular shot and n = the number of shots.)

Thus, $\Pr(X=3) = \binom{8}{3}\left(\frac{2}{3}\right)^3\left(\frac{1}{8}\right)^{8-3} = \frac{8!}{3!5!}\left(\frac{2}{3}\right)^3\left(\frac{1}{3}\right)^5$

$$= \frac{8 \cdot 7 \cdot 6}{3 \cdot 2 \cdot 1}\left(\frac{8}{27}\right)\left(\frac{1}{243}\right) = \frac{448}{6561} = .06828$$

$\Pr(1 < X \leq 6) = \Pr(X = 2, 3, 4, 5 \text{ or } 6)$ .

Each of these events is mutually exclusive and thus,

$\Pr(X = 2, 3, 4, 5, \text{ or } 6) = \Pr(X=2) + \Pr(X=3) + \Pr(X=4)$

$$+ \Pr(X=5) + \Pr(X=6)$$

$$= \sum_{n=2}^{6} \Pr(X=n) .$$

$$\Pr(1 < X \leq 6) = \sum_{n=2}^{6} \binom{8}{n}\left(\frac{2}{3}\right)^n\left(\frac{1}{3}\right)^{8-n} .$$

Using tables of cumulative probabilities and the fact that $\Pr(1 < X \leq 6) = \Pr(X \leq 6) - \Pr(X \leq 1)$, or calculating single probabilities and adding, we see that $\Pr(1 < X \leq 6) = .8023$.

$\Pr(X > 3) = \Pr(X = 4, 5, 6, 7 \text{ or } 8)$

$$= \Pr(X=4) + \Pr(X=5) + \Pr(X=6) + \Pr(X=7)$$

$$+ \Pr(X=8)$$

$$= \sum_{n=4}^{8} \Pr(X = n)$$

$$= \sum_{n=4}^{8} \binom{8}{n}\left(\frac{2}{3}\right)^n\left(\frac{1}{3}\right)^{8-n} .$$

Again, using a table of cumulative probabilities or calculating each single probability we see that

$$\Pr(X > 3) = .912.$$

# MULTINOMIAL DISTRIBUTION

If a bag contains three white  two black, and four red balls  and four balls are drawn at random with replacement, calculate the probabilities that

(a) The sample contains just one white ball.
(b) The sample contains just one white ball given that it contains just one red ball.

Solution: Since there are nine balls and we are sampling with replacement and choosing the balls at random, on each draw

$$Pr(white\ ball) = \frac{3}{9} = \frac{1}{3} .$$

$$Pr(black\ ball) = \frac{2}{9} .$$

$$Pr(red\ ball)\quad = \frac{4}{9} .$$

(a)  On each draw, Pr(white) + Pr(black or red) = 1. Let X = number of white balls. Then X is distributed binomially with n = 4 trials and Pr(white ball) = $\frac{1}{3}$ . Thus

$$Pr(just\ one\ white) = Pr(X=1) = \binom{4}{1}\left(\frac{1}{3}\right)^1\left(1 - \frac{1}{3}\right)^{4-1}$$

$$= 4\ \left(\frac{1}{3}\right)\left(\frac{2}{3}\right)^3 = \frac{32}{81} .$$

(b)  Pr(just 1 white | just 1 red)

$$= \frac{Pr(just\ 1\ white\ and\ just\ 1\ red)}{Pr(just\ 1\ red)} .$$

If Y = number of red balls then Y is distributed binomially with parameters n = 4 and p = $\frac{4}{9}$.

Thus  $Pr(just\ 1\ red) = Pr(Y = 1) = \binom{4}{1}\left(\frac{4}{9}\right)^1\left(1 - \frac{4}{9}\right)^{4-1}$

$$= 4\ \binom{4}{9}\left(\frac{5}{9}\right)^3 .$$

Pr(just 1 white and just 1 red)

= Pr(1 white, 1 red and 2 blacks).

Any particular sequence of outcomes in which 1 white ball is chosen, 1 red ball is chosen and 2 black balls are chosen has probability $\left(\frac{3}{9}\right)^1 \left(\frac{2}{9}\right)^2 \left(\frac{4}{9}\right)^1$. We now must find the number of such distinguishable arrangements. There are $\binom{4}{1}$ ways to select the position of the white ball. There are now three positions available to select the position of the red ball and $\binom{3}{1}$ ways to do this. The position of the black balls are now fixed. There are thus

$$\binom{4}{1}\binom{3}{1} = \frac{4!}{1!3!}\ \frac{3!}{1!2!} = \frac{4!}{1!2!1!} \quad \text{distinguishable arrange-}$$

ments.

Thus the Pr(1 red ball, 1 white ball and 2 black balls)

$$= \frac{4!}{1!2!1!} \cdot \left(\frac{3}{9}\right)\left(\frac{2}{9}\right)^2\left(\frac{4}{9}\right)^1 = \frac{4 \cdot 3 \cdot 3 \cdot 4 \cdot 4}{9^4},$$

$$\text{Pr(just 1 white}\,|\,\text{just 1 red)} = \frac{\dfrac{4 \cdot 3 \cdot 3 \cdot 4 \cdot 4}{9^4}}{4\left(\frac{4}{9}\right)\left(\frac{5}{9}\right)^3}$$

$$= \frac{4 \cdot 3 \cdot 3 \cdot 4 \cdot 4}{4 \cdot 4 \cdot 5 \cdot 5 \cdot 5} = \frac{36}{125}.$$

● **PROBLEM** 4-36

Three electric motors from a factory are tested. A motor is either discarded, returned to the factory or accepted. If the probability of acceptance is .7, the probability of return is .2 and the probability of discard is .1, what is the probability that of three randomly selected motors 1 will be returned 1 will be accepted and 1 will be discarded? What is the probability that 2 motors will be accepted, 1 returned and 0 discarded?

Solution:    Let the probability that 1 is returned, 1 accepted and 1 discarded be denoted by P(1, 1, 1). Since the motors are selected at random, each selection is independent and the probability that an arrangement consisting of 1 returned, 1 accepted, and 1 discarded is observed is (.7)(.2)(.1) = .014. We now count the number of possible arrangements in which 1 engine is discarded, 1 returned and 1 accepted.

Let us count the number of arrangements in the following way. First choose the 1 motor from three that will be returned.

There are $\binom{3}{1}$ ways to do this. Now choose 1 motor from the remaining 2 which will be accepted. There are $\binom{2}{1}$ ways to do this. Once the 1 motor that will be accepted is chosen from the remaining 2, the motor that will be discarded is left over and hence selected automatically. Altogether there are $\binom{3}{1}\binom{2}{1}$ arrangements of motors that will consist of 1 accepted 1 returned and 1 discarded.

Hence $P(1,1,1) = \binom{3}{1}\binom{2}{1}(.7)(.2)(.1) = \frac{3!}{1!2!}\frac{2!}{1!1!}(.014)$

$$= 6(.014) = .084.$$

Similarly, the probability of selecting 2 motors that will be accepted, 1 returned, and 0 discarded is computed in two steps. The probability of observing one particular arrangement of this form is $(.7)^2(.2)^1(.1)^0$. We now count the number of arrangements which lead to this observation. First choose the 2 motors that will be accepted. There are $\binom{3}{2}$ ways to do this, from the remaining 1, choose the 1 motor that will be returned. There are $\binom{1}{1}$ ways to do this. Multiplying we see that there are $\binom{3}{2}\binom{1}{1} = \frac{3!}{2!1!0!}$ possible arrangements.

The probability of observing a sample where 2 motors are accepted is thus $\frac{3!}{2!1!0!}(.7)^2(.2)^1(.1)^0 = 3(.7)^2(.2)^1(.1)^0 = .294$.

The coefficient $\begin{pmatrix} & n & \\ k_1, & k_2, & \ldots & k_r \end{pmatrix}$ is called the multinomial coefficient and counts the number of ways n objects can be labeled in r ways, $k_1$ in the first category, $k_2$ in the second up to $k_r$ in the rth. $k_1 + k_2 + \ldots + k_r$ must equal n.

$$\begin{pmatrix} & n & \\ k_1, & k_2, & \ldots & k_r \end{pmatrix} = \frac{n!}{k_1!k_2! \ldots k_r!} .$$

The probability distribution associated with this coefficient is called the multinomial distribution. This problem demonstrates a possible use for the multinomial distribution.

● **PROBLEM** 4-37

A survey was made of the number of people who read classified ads in a newspaper. Thirty people were asked to indicate which one of the following best applies to them: (1) read no ads (N); (2) read "articles for sale" ads (S); (3) read "help wanted" ads (H); (4) read all ads (A).

(a) Use the multinomial theorem for the expansion of

$$(N + S + H + A)^{30}$$

to find the coeffients of the terms involving

$$(1) \underline{\hspace{1cm}} N^{10}A^{10}H^{10}$$
$$(2) \underline{\hspace{1cm}} N^{5}S^{10}H^{10}A^{5} .$$

(b) Assuming the following probabilities, what is the probability that 10 read no ads, 10 read "Help Wanted" ads, and 10 read all ads?

$$P\{N\} = \frac{30}{100}$$

$$P\{S\} = \frac{40}{100}$$

$$P\{H\} = \frac{20}{100}$$

$$P\{A\} = \frac{10}{100} .$$

Solution:   (a) We can generalize the binomial distribution to instances in which the independent, identical "trials" have more than just 2 possible outcomes. Recall that the binomial distribution had its origins in connection with a sequence of "Bernoulli trials," each of which had only two possibilities for an outcome. Now consider a sequence of independent trials, each trial having k possible outcomes, $O_1$, $O_2$, $O_3$, ... $O_k$ with respective probabilities $p_1$, $p_2$, $p_3$, ..., $p_k$. There is the relation $p_1 + p_2 + p_3 + ... + P_k = 1$, so that any one probability can be obtained from the remaining k - 1. Consider the random variables $X_1$, ... $X_k$ , where $X_i$ = frequency of $O_i$ among n trials. Note that $X_1 + X_2 + ... + X_k$ = n since all trials must have some outcome. The joint distribution of $(X_1, ..., X_k)$ is called MULTINOMIAL.

We can derive the probability function of the k-nomial distribution by a method similar to the binomial. For a particular sequence of results, $f_1$ $A_1$`s, $f_2$ $A_2$`s, etc., the probability, according to the multiplication rule, is simply the product of the corresponding probabilitites:

$$p_1^{f_1} p_2^{f_2} ... p_k^{f_k} .$$

Such a sequence can come in many orders - the number of which is the number of ways of arranging n objects, $f_1$ of one kind, ..., and $f_k$ of the kth kind. This is n! divided by a factorial for each group of like objects. Hence the total probability for all sequences with the given frequencies is

$$P(X_1=f_1, \ldots \text{ and } X_k = f_k) = \frac{n'}{r_1! \ldots r_k!} \; p_1{}^{f_1} \; p_2{}^{f_2} \ldots p_k{}^{fk},$$

provided $\Sigma\limits_i f_i = n$. We use the term "multinomial" since (as in the particular case $k = 2$) the probabilities we have are the terms in a multinomial expansion

$$(p_1 + \ldots + p_k)^n = \sum \frac{n!}{f_1! \ldots f_k!} \; p_1{}^{f_1} \ldots p_k{}^{fk} = 1.$$

The sum extends to all sets of nonnegative integers that sum to n.

In our problem, we have 4 possible outcomes N, A, S, H. Just imagine $N = p_1$, $A = p_2$, $S = p_3$, and $H = p_4$.

(1) – We are looking for the coefficient of $p_1{}^{10} \; p_2{}^{10} \; p_3{}^{0} \; p_4{}^{10}$. It is $\frac{30!}{10!10!10! \; 0!}$ but since $0!$ is 1, we have $\frac{30!}{10!10!10!} \; N^{10}A^{10}H^{10}$.

(2) – We are looking for the coefficient of $p_1{}^5 p_2{}^5 p_3{}^{10} p_4{}^{10}$. By our multinomial derivation it is $\frac{30!}{5!5!10!10!}$. We obtain

$$\frac{30!}{5!5!10!10!} \; N^5 A^5 S^{10} H^{10}.$$

(b)   In part (a) – (1) we substitute

$$p_1 = \frac{30}{100} = .3, \; p_2 = \frac{10}{100} = .1, \; p_3 = \frac{40}{100} = .4, \text{ and}$$

$$p_4 = \frac{20}{100} = .2.$$

$$\frac{30!}{10!10!10!} \; N^{10}A^{10}H^{10} = \frac{30!}{10!10!10!} \; (.3)^{10}(.1)^{10}(.2)^{10}.$$

Just as the binomial expansion generates binomial probabilities, the multinomial expansion generates multinomial probabilities. The following problem illustrates a multinomial expansion.

● **PROBLEM** 4-38

Find the coefficient of $a_1^2 a_2 a_3$ in the expansion of $\left(a_1 + a_2 + a_3\right)^4$.

Solution:   The binomial theorem states that, if n is a positive integer, then

$$(a + b)^n = a^n + na^{n-1}b + \frac{n(n-1)}{1 \cdot 2} a^{n-2}b^2 + \frac{n(n-1)(n-2)}{1 \cdot 2 \cdot 3} a^{n-3}b^3$$

$$+ \ldots + nab^{n-1} + b^n.$$

155

Use the binomial theorem, but for convenience, associate the terms $(a_2 + a_3)$, then expand the expression.

$$\left[a_1 + (a_2 + a_3)\right]^4 = a_1^4 + 4a_1^3(a_2 + a_3) + \frac{4 \cdot 3}{1 \cdot 2} a_1^2(a_2 + a_3)^2$$

$$+ \frac{4 \cdot 3 \cdot 2}{1 \cdot 2 \cdot 3} a_1(a_2 + a_3)^3 + (a_2 + a_3)^4.$$

Notice that the only term involving $a_1^2 a_2 a_3$ is the third term with coefficient $\frac{4 \cdot 3}{2}$ and, further, that $(a_2 + a_3)^2$ must be expanded also.

$$(a_2 + a_3)^2 = a_2^2 + 2a_2 a_3 + a_3^2 .$$

Therefore, the third term becomes:

$$\frac{4 \cdot 3}{1 \cdot 2} a_1^2(a_2 + a_3)^2 = \frac{4 \cdot 3}{1 \cdot 2} a_1^2(a_2^2 + 2a_2 a_3 + a_3^2)$$

$$= 6a_1^2 a_2^2 + 12a_1^2 a_2 a_3 + 6a_1^2 a_3^2$$

Hence, the coefficient of $a_1^2 a_2 a_3$ is 12.

● **PROBLEM 4-39**

A package in the mail can either be lost, delivered or damaged while being delivered. If the probability of loss is .2, the probability of damage is .1 and the probability of delivery is .7 and 10 packages are sent to Galveston, Texas, what is the probability that 6 arrive safely 2 are lost and 2 are damaged?

Solution:    If each package being sent can be considered an independent trial with three outcomes, the event of 6 safe arrivals, 2 losses and 2 smashed packages can be assumed to have a multinomial probability. Thus,

$$\Pr(6,\ 2 \text{ and } 2) = \begin{pmatrix} 10 \\ 6,\ 2,\ 2 \end{pmatrix} (.7)^6 \ (.2)^2 \ (.1)^2$$

$$= \frac{10!}{6!2!2!} \ (.7)^6 \ (.2)^2 \ (.1)^2 = .059.$$

The probability of 6 safe arrivals, 2 losses and 2 damaged packages is .059.

● **PROBLEM 4-40**

A die is tossed 12 times. Let $X_i$ denote the number of tosses in which i dots come up   for i = 1, 2, 3, 4, 5, and 6. What is the probability that we obtain two of each value.

Solution:    We have a series of independent successive trials with 6 possible outcomes each with    constant probability $\frac{1}{6}$ . The multinomial distribution,

$$P(X_1=f_1, \ X_2= f_2, \ \ldots X_k = f_k) =$$

$$= \frac{n!}{f_1!f_2!,\ldots f_k!} \ p_1^{f_1} \ p_2^{f_2} \ \ldots \ p_k^{f_k} \ ,$$

is called for.  Hence

$$P(X_1=2, \ X_2=2, \ X_3=2, \ X_4=2, \ X_5=2, \ X_6=2)$$

$$= \frac{12!}{2!2!2!2!2!2!} \ \left(\frac{1}{6}\right)^2 \left(\frac{1}{6}\right)^2 \ \ldots \ \left(\frac{1}{6}\right)^2$$

$$= \frac{12!}{2^6} \ \left[ \left(\frac{1}{6}\right)^2 \right]^6 = \frac{1925}{559872} = .0034.$$

# CHAPTER 5

# JOINT DISTRIBUTIONS

## DISCRETE JOINT DISTRIBUTIONS

● **PROBLEM** 5-1

Consider the joint distribution of X and Y given in the form of a table below. The cell (i,j) corresponds to the joint probability that X = i, Y = j, for i = 1,2,3, j = 1,2,3.

| Y \ X | 1 | 2 | 3 |
|---|---|---|---|
| 1 | 0 | 1/6 | 1/6 |
| 2 | 1/6 | 0 | 1/6 |
| 3 | 1/6 | 1/6 | 0 |

Check that this is a proper probability distribution. What is the marginal distribution of X? What is the marginal distribution of Y?

<u>Solution</u>: A joint probability mass function gives the probabilities of events. These events are composed of the results of two (or more) experiments. An example might be the toss of two dice. In this case, each event or outcome has two numbers associated with it. The numbers are the outcomes from the toss of each die. The probability distribution of the pair (X,Y) is

$$\Pr(X = i, \ X = j) = \frac{1}{36} \qquad \begin{array}{l} i = 1,2,3,4,5,6 \\ j = 1,2,3,4,5,6 \ . \end{array}$$

Another example is the toss of two dice where X = number observed on first die ; Y = the larger of the two numbers.

In order for f(x,y) = Pr(X = x, Y = y) to be a proper joint probability, the sum of Pr(X = x, Y = y) over all (x,y), over all points in the sample space must equal 1.

In the case of the pair of tossed dice,

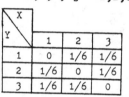

$$\sum_{x} \sum_{y} \Pr(X = x, Y = y) = \sum_{i=1}^{6} \sum_{j=1}^{6} \frac{1}{36} = \sum_{i=1}^{6} \frac{6}{36} = \frac{6 \cdot 6}{36} = 1 \ .$$

Thus, this is a proper probability distribution.

In our original example,

$$\sum_{i=1}^{3} \sum_{j=1}^{3} \Pr(X = i, Y = j) = \sum_{i=1}^{3} [\Pr(X=i,Y=1) + \Pr(X=i,Y=2) + \Pr(X=i,Y=3)]$$

$$= \sum_{i=1}^{3} \Pr(X=i,Y=1) + \sum_{i=1}^{3} \Pr(X=i,Y=2) + \sum_{i=1}^{3} \Pr(X=i,Y=3)$$

$$= (0 + 1/6 + 1/6) + (1/6 + 0 + 1/6) + (1/6 + 1/6 + 0)$$

$$= 1/3 + 1/3 + 1/3 = 1 .$$

Thus, the probability distribution specified in the table is a proper distribution.

We can compute the individual probability distributions of X and Y. These are called the marginal distributions of X and Y and are calculated in the following way.

We wish to find the probability that X = 1,2,3,

$$\Pr(X = 1) = \Pr(X = 1, Y = 1,2, \text{ or } 3) .$$

Because the events "X = 1, Y = 1", "X = 1, Y = 2" ,"X = 1, Y = 3" are mutually exclusive,

$$\Pr(X=1) = \Pr(X=1,Y=1) + \Pr(X=1,Y=2) + \Pr(X=1,Y=3)$$

$$= \sum_{i=1}^{3} \Pr(X=1,Y=i).$$

Thus, $\quad \Pr(X=1) = 0 + 1/6 + 1/6 = 1/3 .$

Similarly, $\quad \Pr(X=2) = \sum_{i=1}^{3} \Pr(X=2,Y=i) = 1/6 + 0 + 1/6 = 1/3$

and $\quad \Pr(X=3) = \sum_{i=1}^{3} \Pr(X=3,Y=i) = 1/6 + 1/6 + 0 = 1/3 .$

We compute the marginal probabilities of Y in a similar way.

$$\Pr(Y=1) = \Pr(X=1,Y=1) + \Pr(X=2,Y=1) + \Pr(X=3,Y=1)$$

$$= 0 + 1/6 + 1/6 = 2/6 = 1/3$$

$$\Pr(Y=2) = \sum_{j=1}^{3} \Pr(X=j,Y=2) = 1/6 + 0 + 1/6 = 1/3 .$$

$$\Pr(Y=3) = \sum_{j=1}^{3} \Pr(X=j,Y=3) = 1/6 + 1/6 + 0 .$$

To see why these are called marginal probabilities we examine the way they were computed.

The marginal probabilities of X were found by summing along the rows of the table of the joint distribution. The marginal probabilities of Y were found by summing along the columns of the table of the joint distribution.

The probabilities resulting from these summations are often placed in the margins, as in the table below, hence the name marginal probabilities.

● **PROBLEM** 5-2

Consider the table representing the joint distribution between X' and Y'.

| X' Y' | 1 | 2 | 3 |
|---|---|---|---|
| 1 | 1/9 | 1/9 | 1/9 |
| 2 | 1/9 | 1/9 | 1/9 |
| 3 | 1/9 | 1/9 | 1/9 |

Find the marginal distributions of X' and Y'. Are X' and Y' independent? In the previous problem, were X and Y independent?

**Solution:** The marginal distributions of X' and Y' are found by summing across the rows and columns of the table above.

$$Pr(X'=1) = \sum_{i=1}^{3} Pr(X'=1,Y'=i) \quad = 1/9 + 1/9 + 1/9 = 1/3 \;.$$

$$Pr(X'=2) = \sum_{i=1}^{3} Pr(X'=2,Y'=i) \quad = 1/9 + 1/9 + 1/9 = 1/3 \;.$$

$$Pr(X'=3) = \sum_{i=1}^{3} Pr(X'=3,Y'=i) \quad = 1/9 + 1/9 + 1/9 = 1/3 \;.$$

Similarly, $Pr(Y'=1) = \sum_{j=1}^{3} Pr(X'=j,Y'=i) \quad = 1/9 + 1/9 + 1/9 = 1/3 \;.$

$$Pr(Y'=2) = \sum_{j=1}^{3} Pr(X'=j,Y'=2) \quad = 1/9 + 1/9 + 1/9 = 1/3.$$

$$Pr(Y'=3) = \sum_{j=1}^{3} Pr(X'=j,Y=3) = 1/3.$$

The marginal distributions are hence

$$Pr(X'=x) = \begin{cases} 1/3 & x = 1,2,3 \\ 0 & \text{otherwise} \end{cases}$$

and

$$Pr(Y'=y) = \begin{cases} 1/3 & y = 1,2,3 \\ 0 & \text{otherwise} . \end{cases}$$

Two random variables, X and Y, will be independent if and only if $Pr(X=x,Y=y) = Pr(X=x) Pr(Y=y)$, for all x and y.

Checking X' and Y' we see that for all x and y,

$$Pr(X'=x,Y'=y) = 1/9 = Pr(X'=x)Pr(Y'=y) \quad = 1/3 \cdot 1/3 \quad = 1/9 \;.$$

In the previous problem, we see that X and Y are not independent but dependent. To see this, consider $Pr(X=i,Y=i)$ for i = 1,2,3.

$$Pr(X=i)Pr(Y=i) = 1/3 \cdot 1/3 = 1/9$$

for i = 1,2,3 but the joint probability function specifies that $Pr(X=i,Y=i) = 0$ for i = 1,2, and 3. Thus

$$Pr(X=i)Pr(Y=i) \neq Pr(X=i,Y=i)$$

and X and Y are not independent.

Consider the experiment of tossing two tetrahedra (regular four-sided polyhedron) each with sides labeled 1 to 4.

Let X denote the number on the downturned face of the first tetrahedron and Y the larger of the two downturned numbers. Find the joint density of X and Y.

**Solution:** The values that a pair (X,Y) may assume are:

$$\begin{array}{llll} (1,1) & (1,2) & (1,3) & (1,4) \\ (2,2) & (2,3) & (2,4) \\ (3,3) & (3,4) \\ (4,4) \end{array}$$

The probability that two numbers are observed as the downturned faces of the tetrahedra is $\Pr(X_1 = x, X_2 = t)$ for $\begin{array}{l} x = 1,2,3,4 \\ t = 1,2,3,4 \end{array}$.

Let $X_1$ = the result of the toss of the first tetrahedron,

$X_2$ = the result of the toss of the second tetrahedron.

If all outcomes of $X_1$ and $X_2$ are equally likely, then

$$\Pr(X_1 = x, X_2 = t) = \frac{1}{16} \text{ for } \begin{array}{l} x = 1,2,3,4 \\ t = 1,2,3,4 \end{array}.$$

We calculate the probabilities of X and Y in terms of the probabilities for $X_1$ and $X_2$.

$$\Pr(X=1,Y=1) = \Pr(X_1=1,X_2=1) = 1/16 .$$

$$\begin{aligned} \Pr(X=1,Y=2) &= \Pr(1 \text{ die is } 1 \text{ and } Y = \max\{X_1,X_2\} = 2) \\ &= \Pr(X_1 = 1, X_2 = 2) = 1/16. \end{aligned}$$

Similarly,
$$\begin{aligned} \Pr(X=1,Y=3) &= \Pr(1 \text{ die is } 1 \text{ and } \max\{X_1,X_2\} = 3) \\ &= \Pr(X_1 = 1, X_2 = 3) = 1/16 \end{aligned}$$

and
$$\begin{aligned} \Pr(X=1,Y=4) &= \Pr(1 \text{ die is } 1 \text{ and } \max\{X_1,X_2) = 4) \\ &= \Pr(X_1 = 1, X_2 = 4) = 1/16. \end{aligned}$$

$\Pr(X=2,Y=1) = 0$: it is impossible for 1 toss to be 2 and the larger of the two tosses to be 1.

$\Pr(X=3,Y=1) = 0$ and $\Pr(X=4,Y=1) = 0$ for the same reasons. Also, $\Pr(X=3,Y=2) = \Pr(X=4,Y=3) = \Pr(X=4,Y=2) = 0$. Continuing,

$$\begin{aligned} \Pr(X=2,Y=2) &= \Pr(X_1=2, \max\{X_1,X_2\} = 2) = \Pr(X_1=2, X_2 = 1 \text{ or } 2) \\ &= \Pr(X_1=2, X_2=1) + \Pr(X_1=2, X_2 = 2) = 1/16 + 1/16 = 1/8 . \end{aligned}$$

$$\Pr(X=2,Y=3) = \Pr(X_1=2, \max\{X_1,X_2\} = 3) = \Pr(X_1=2, X_2=3) = 1/16 .$$

$$\Pr(X=2,Y=4) = \Pr(X_1=2, \max\{X_1,X_2\} = 4) = \Pr(X_1=2, X_2=4) = 1/16 .$$

$$\begin{aligned} \Pr(X=3,Y=3) &= \Pr(X_1=3, \max\{X_1,X_2\} = 3) = \Pr(X_1=3, X_2=1,2, \text{ or } 3) \\ &= \Pr(X_1=3,X_2=1) + \Pr(X_1=3,X_2=2) + \Pr(X_1=3,X_3=3) \end{aligned}$$

$$= 1/16 + 1/16 + 1/16 = 3/16 \ .$$

$$\Pr(X_1=3, Y=4) = \Pr(X_1=3, \max\{X_1,X_2\} = 4) \quad = \Pr(X_1=3, X_2=4) = 1/16 \ .$$

$$\Pr(X_1=4, X_2=4) = \Pr(X_1=4, \max\{X_1,X_2\} = 4) \quad = \Pr(X_1=4, X_2=1,2,3 \text{ or } 4)$$

$$\Pr(X_1=4, X_2=1,2,3 \text{ or } 4)$$

$$= \Pr(X_1=4, X_2=1) + \Pr(X_1=4, X_2=2) + \Pr(X_1=4, X_2=3) + \Pr(X_1=4, X_2=$$
$$= 4/16 = 1/4 \ .$$

Thus the distribution for X and Y is:

| Y' \ X | 1 | 2 | 3 | 4 | Pr(Y = y) |
|---|---|---|---|---|---|
| 1 | 1/16 | 0 | 0 | 0 | 1/16 |
| 2 | 1/16 | 2/16 | 0 | 0 | 3/16 |
| 3 | 1/16 | 1/16 | 3/16 | 0 | 5/16 |
| 4 | 1/16 | 1/16 | 1/16 | 4/16 | 7/16 |
| Pr(X = x) | 4/16 | 4/16 | 4/16 | 4/16 | |

The marginal probabilities of X and Y are given and we see that X and Y are dependent random variables because

$$\Pr(X=x, Y=y) \neq \Pr(X=x) \, \Pr(Y=y) \ .$$

● **PROBLEM** 5-4

Show, by altering the joint density of X and Y in the previous problem, that it is not always possible to construct a unique joint distribution from a pair of given marginal distributions.

Solution: The joint density of X and Y with its marginal distributions is given by the table below:

| Y \ X | 1 | 2 | 3 | 4 |
|---|---|---|---|---|
| 1 | 1/16 | 0 | 0 | 0 |
| 2 | 1/16 | 2/16 | 0 | 0 |
| 3 | 1/16 | 1/16 | 3/16 | 0 |
| 4 | 1/16 | 1/16 | 1/16 | 4/16 |
| Pr(X = x) | 4/16 | 4/16 | 4/16 | 4/16 |

Imagine we are given the marginal distributions of X and Y above and asked to construct the joint distributioi of X and Y. There are an infinite number of possibilities for this distribution as seen by the table below.

For any $\epsilon$ , $0 < \epsilon < 1/16$, this joint distribution will yield the given marginal distributions. Thus, these marginal distributions do not specify a unique joint distribution.

● **PROBLEM** 5-5

Consider a bag containing two white and 4 black balls. If two balls are drawn at random without replacement from the bag, let X and Y be random variables representing the results of these two drawings. Let 0 correspond to drawing a black ball and 1 correspond to drawing a white ball. Find the joint, marginal, and conditional distributions of X and Y.

Solution: $Pr(X=0)$ = Pr(a black ball is drawn first)

$$= \frac{\text{number of black balls}}{\text{total number of balls}} \quad = \frac{4}{6} = \frac{2}{3} .$$

$Pr(X=1)$ = Pr(a white ball is drawn first)

$$= \frac{\text{number of white balls}}{\text{total number of balls}} \quad = \frac{2}{6} = \frac{1}{3} .$$

We may use the notion of conditional probability to find the probability of a particular event on the second draw given a particular event on the first. We may talk about conditional distribution for the variable Y given X. A conditional distribution is defined in terms of conditional probability.

$Pr(Y=y|X=x) = f(y|x)$ = conditional distribution of Y given X, $f(x,y) = Pr(X=x, Y=y)$ = joint distribution of X and Y and $f(x) = Pr(X=x)$ is the marginal distribution of X.

The conditional probabilities may be calculated directly from the problem. We then use the conditional probabilities and marginal distribution of X to find the joint distribution of X and Y.

$Pr(Y=0|X=0)$ = Pr(black ball is second|black ball first)

$$= \frac{\text{number of black balls - 1}}{\text{total number of balls - 1}} = \frac{4-1}{6-1} = \frac{3}{5}$$

$Pr(Y=1|X=0)$ = Pr(white second|black first)

$$= \frac{\text{number of white balls}}{\text{total number of balls - 1}} = \frac{2}{6-1} = \frac{2}{5}$$

$Pr(Y=0|X=1)$ = Pr(black ball second|white ball first)

$$= \frac{\text{number of black balls}}{\text{total number of balls - 1}} = \frac{4}{6-1} = \frac{4}{5}$$

$Pr(Y=1|X=1)$ = Pr(white ball second|white first)

$$= \frac{\text{number of white balls -1}}{\text{number of balls - 1}} = \frac{2-1}{6-1} = \frac{1}{5} .$$

We now calculate the joint probabilities of X and Y.

$$\frac{Pr(X=0, Y=0)}{Pr(X=0)} = Pr(Y=0|X=0) , \text{ or,}$$

$Pr(X=0,Y=0) = Pr(X=0)Pr(Y=0|X=0) = \frac{2}{3} \cdot \frac{3}{5} = \frac{6}{15}$ . Similarly,

$Pr(X=1,Y=0) = Pr(Y=0|X=1)Pr(X=1) = \frac{4}{5} \cdot \frac{1}{3} = \frac{4}{15}$

$Pr(X=0,Y=1) = Pr(Y=1|X=0)Pr(X=0) = \frac{2}{5} \cdot \frac{2}{3} = \frac{4}{15}$

$Pr(X=1,Y=1) = Pr(Y=1|X=1)Pr(X=1) = \frac{1}{5} \cdot \frac{1}{3} = \frac{1}{15}$ .

Summarizing these results in the following table, we see:

| X<br>Y | 0 | 1 | Pr(Y = y) |
|---|---|---|---|
| 0 | 6/15 | 4/15 | 10/15 |
| 1 | 4/15 | 1/15 | 5/15 |
| Pr(X = x) | 10/15 | 5/15 | |

This is the joint distribution of X and Y, with the marginal distribution indicated.

The conditional distribution of Y given X is

$$Pr(Y=y \mid X=x) = \frac{Pr(Y=y, X=x)}{Pr(X=x)} = \begin{cases} \dfrac{6/15}{10/15} = 3/5 & x = y = 0 \\[2mm] \dfrac{4/15}{5/15} = 4/5 & x = 1; \ y = 0 \\[2mm] \dfrac{4/15}{10/15} = 2/5 & x = 0; \ y = 1 \\[2mm] \dfrac{1/15}{5/15} = 1/5 & x = y = 1 . \end{cases}$$

For any fixed value of X, we see that $f(y \mid x) = Pr(Y=y \mid X=x)$ is a proper probability distribution for Y.

$$\sum_{y=0}^{1} Pr(Y=y \mid X=0) = Pr(Y=0 \mid X=0) + Pr(Y=1 \mid X=0) = 3/5 + 2/5 = 1$$

and

$$\sum_{y=0}^{1} Pr(Y=y \mid X=1) = Pr(Y=0 \mid X=1) + Pr(Y=1 \mid X=1) = 1/5 + 4/5 = 1 .$$

● PROBLEM 5-6

A loom stops from time to time and the number X of stops in unit running time is assumed to have a Poisson distribution with parameter $\mu$. For each stop, there is a probability $\theta$ that a fault will be produced in the fabric being woven. Occurrences associated with different stops may be assumed independent. Let Y be the number of fabric faults so produced in unit running time. What is the distribution of Y?

Solution:

$$Pr(Y=k) = \sum_{x=0}^{\infty} Pr(Y=k \mid X=x) \, Pr(X=x)$$

$$= \sum_{x=0}^{\infty} Pr(Y=k \mid X=x) \, \frac{(\mu t)^x e^{-\mu t}}{x!}$$

because X is distributed Poisson with parameter $\mu$.

Each time there is a stop, Pr(fault in the cloth) = $\theta$. In the interval [0,t] if there are x stops, the probability that k of these stops result in faults is $\binom{x}{k} \theta^k (1 - \theta)^{x-k}$.

Hence for k = 0,1,2,...

164

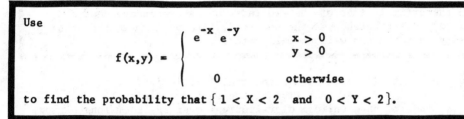

$$Pr(Y=k) = \sum_{x=k}^{\infty} \binom{x}{k} \theta^k (1-\theta)^{x-k} \frac{(\mu t)^x e^{-\mu t}}{x!} = \sum_{x-k=0}^{\infty} \frac{x! \theta^k (1-\theta)^{x-k}}{(x-k)! k!} \frac{(\mu t)^x e^{-\mu t}}{x!}$$

$$= \frac{\theta^k e^{-\mu t} (\mu t)^k}{k!} \sum_{x-k=0}^{\infty} \frac{[(1-\theta)\mu t]^{x-k}}{(x-k)!}$$

$$= \frac{(\theta\mu t)^k e^{-\mu t}}{k!} e^{(1-\theta)\mu t} = \frac{(\theta\mu t)^k e^{-\theta\mu t}}{k!} \quad .$$

Thus, Y, the number of fabric faults produced in time t is distributed Poisson with parameter $\theta\mu$ .

# CONTINUOUS JOINT DISTRIBUTIONS

● **PROBLEM** 5-7

Use

$$f(x,y) = \begin{cases} e^{-x} e^{-y} & \begin{array}{l} x > 0 \\ y > 0 \end{array} \\ 0 & \text{otherwise} \end{cases}$$

to find the probability that $\{ 1 < X < 2 \text{ and } 0 < Y < 2 \}$.

<u>Solution</u>: $Pr(1 < X < 2 \text{ and } 0 < Y < 2)$ is the volume over the shaded rectangle:

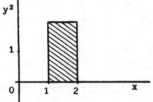

This volume over the rectangle and under f(x,y) is pictured below:

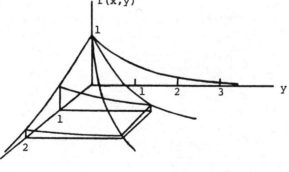

To find this volume we integrate X from 1 to 2 and Y from 0 to 2. Thus,

$$Pr(1 < X < 2 \text{ and } 0 < Y < 2) = \int_0^2 \int_1^2 f(x,y) \, dx \, dy$$

$$= \int_0^2 e^{-y} \left( \int_1^2 e^{-x} \, dx \right) dy$$

165

$$= \int_0^2 e^{-y} dy \left[ -e^{-x} \Big|_1^2 \right] = \int_0^2 e^{-y} dy \, (e^{-1} - e^{-2})$$

$$= -e^{-y} \Big|_0^2 \, (e^{-1} - e^{-2})$$

$$= (e^0 - e^{-2})(e^{-1} - e^{-2}) = (1 - e^{-2})(e^{-1} - e^{-2})$$

$$= (.865)(.233) = .20 \ .$$

● **PROBLEM** 5-8

Two individuals agree to meet at a certain spot sometime between 5:00 and 6:00 P.M. They will each wait 10 minutes starting from when they arrive. If the other person does not show up, they will leave. Assume the arrival times of the two individuals are independent and uniformly distributed over the hour-long interval , find the probability that the two will actually meet.

<u>Solution</u>: Let  X = arrival time of the first individual and
Y = arrival time of the second individual.
     X  and  Y  have uniform distributions over any hour-long period, thus in minutes the densities are:

$$f(x) = \frac{1}{60} \qquad 0 < x < 60$$

$$g(y) = \frac{1}{60} \qquad 0 < y < 60 \ .$$

Furthermore  X  and  Y  are independent.  Thus the joint density of  X  and  Y  will be the product of the individual density functions.

$$h(x,y) = f(x)g(y) \qquad = \begin{cases} (\frac{1}{60})(\frac{1}{60}) = \frac{1}{3600} & \begin{matrix} 0 < x < 60 \\ 0 < y < 60 \end{matrix} \\ \\ 0 & \text{otherwise.} \end{cases}$$

We now try to formulate the event "a meeting takes place" in terms of  X  and  Y.

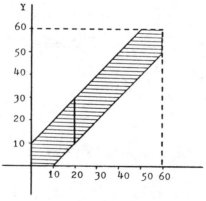

Consider the shaded region above.  If the point  (x,y)  lies within this shaded region a meeting will take place.  To see that this is true, we arbitrarily test the point  X = 20.  If  X = 20,

166

the first individual arrives at 5:20.  If the second individual
arrived at any time between 5:10 and 5:30 there will be a meeting.
Thus  Y  may take on a value between  10  and  30.  This region is
described mathematically by  $|X-Y| < 10$.  The absolute value signs
reflect the fact that the order of arrival is unimportant in assur-
ing a meeting, only the proximity or closeness of the arrival times
is important.  Thus,

$$\text{Pr(a meeting)} = \text{Pr}(|X-Y| < 10)$$
$$= \text{volume over the shaded region in the } x\text{-}y \text{ plane}$$
$$\text{under } f(x,y).$$

This volume can be divided into three regions, $A_1, A_2, A_3$ .

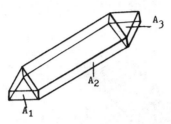

The volume of  $A_2$  is the volume of a rectangular parellelapiped,
(box-shaped region) and  $A_1$  and  $A_3$  are right prisms of equal
volume.

The volume of  $A_2$  is length $\times$ width $\times$ height $= (10\sqrt{2})(50\sqrt{2})(\frac{1}{3600})$

$$= 2(500)(\frac{1}{3600}) .$$

And the volume of  $A_3$  and  $A_1$  each is (Area of base) $\times$ height

$$= \tfrac{1}{2}(10)(10) \cdot \frac{1}{3600}$$

$$= \frac{50}{3600} .$$

$$\text{Pr}(|X-Y| < 10) = \text{Volume of } A_2 + \text{Volume of } A_1 + \text{Volume of } A_3$$

$$= \frac{1000}{3600} + \frac{50}{3600} + \frac{50}{3600} \quad = \frac{1100}{3600} = \frac{11}{36} .$$

● **PROBLEM** 5-9

Consider the bivariate function

$$f(x,y) = K(x+y)I_{(0,1)}(x)I_{(0,1)}(y) = K(x+y)I_U(x,y) ,$$

where  $U = \{(x,y): 0 < x < 1 \text{ and } 0 < y < 1\}$, a unit square.  Can
the constant  K  be selected so that  $f(x,y)$  will be a joint probability density function?  If  K  is positive, $f(x,y) \geq 0$.

Solution:  $I_u(x,y)$  is a function of  x  and  y  such that

$$I_u(x,y) = \begin{cases} 1 & (x,y) \in U \\ 0 & (x,y) \notin U . \end{cases}$$

In order for  $f(x,y)$  to be a joint probability density the
volume over  U  must be equal to  1.  Thus,

$$1 = \int_{-\infty}^{\infty} \int_{-\infty}^{\infty} K\, f(x,y)dx\, dy \qquad = \int_{0}^{1} \int_{0}^{1} K(x+y)dx\, dy$$

$$= K \int_{0}^{1} \left[\tfrac{1}{2} x^2 + yx\right]_{0}^{1} dy \qquad = K \int_{0}^{1} (\tfrac{1}{2}+y)dy = K(\tfrac{1}{2}y+\tfrac{1}{2}y^2)_{0}^{1}$$

$$= K(\tfrac{1}{2}+\tfrac{1}{2}) = K .$$

Thus $K = 1$ will make $f(x,y)$ a joint probability density.

This joint density is pictured below:

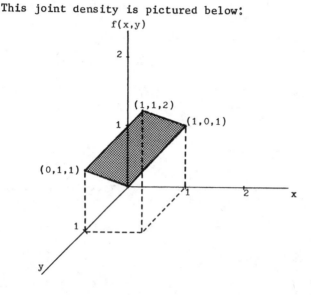

● **PROBLEM** 5-10

Two continuous random variables $X$ and $Y$ may also be jointly distributed. Suppose $(X,Y)$ has a distribution which is uniform over a unit circle centered at $(0,0)$. Find the joint density of $(X,Y)$ and the marginal densities of $X$ and $Y$. Are X and Y independent?

<u>Solution:</u> The pairs of points $(X,Y)$ lie in the unit circle with center at $(0,0)$.

The probability that a random point $(X,Y)$ lies in a particular region of this circle is given by the volume over the region, A, and under a joint density function $f(x,y)$.

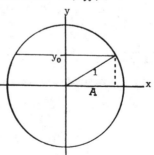

In the case of the uniform joint density function, the density function is a constant such that the total volume over some area in the $(x,y)$ plane and under $f(x,y) = c > 0$ is 1.

168

The total area of the unit circle is $\pi r^2$ where $r = 1$. Thus the area is $\pi$. In order for the total volume to equal 1,

$$c\pi = 1 \quad \text{or} \quad c = 1/\pi .$$

Thus,
$$f(x,y) = \begin{cases} 1/\pi & \text{for } x^2 + y^2 < 1 \\ 0 & \text{otherwise .} \end{cases}$$

The marginal distributions are found by "summing" over all values of the other variable after one variable is fixed. Because the variables are continuous, the "summing" must be performed by integration. Thus the marginal distributions of X and Y are respectively:

$$g(x) = \int_{\text{all } y} f(x,y)dy \qquad x^2 + y^2 < 1$$

and

$$h(y) = \int_{\text{all } x} f(x,y)dx \qquad x^2 + y^2 < 1 .$$

In our problem, let $x$ be fixed, $x = x_0$, then $y^2 < 1-x_0^2$ or $y < \sqrt{1-x_0^2}$ or $y < \sqrt{1-x_0^2}$ and $-y > \sqrt{1-x_0^2}$. Thus

$$g(x_0) = \int_{-\sqrt{1-x_0^2}}^{\sqrt{1-x_0^2}} f(x,y)dy = \int_{-\sqrt{1-x_0^2}}^{\sqrt{1-x_0^2}} \frac{1}{\pi} dy$$

$$= \frac{2\sqrt{1-x_0^2}}{\pi} , \qquad 1 < x_0 < -1 .$$

Similarly, for fixed $y = y_0$, $-\sqrt{1-y_0^2} < x < \sqrt{1-y_0^2}$

$$h(y_0) = \int_{-\sqrt{1-y_0^2}}^{\sqrt{1-y_0^2}} f(x,y)dx = \int_{-\sqrt{1-y_0^2}}^{-\sqrt{1-y_0^2}} \frac{1}{\pi} dx = \frac{x}{\pi} \Big]_{-\sqrt{1-y_0^2}}^{\sqrt{1-y_0^2}}$$

$$= \frac{2\sqrt{1-y_0^2}}{\pi} \qquad -1 < y < 1 .$$

X and Y will be independent if and only if the joint density is the product of the marginal densities or $f(x,y) = g(x)h(y)$.

In this problem, we see that $$g(x_0)h(y_0) = \frac{2\sqrt{1-x_0^2}}{\pi} \cdot \frac{2\sqrt{1-y_0^2}}{\pi}$$

$$= \frac{4}{\pi^2} \sqrt{1-x_0^2} \sqrt{1-y_0^2}$$

$$\neq \frac{1}{\pi} = f(x,y) .$$

Thus X and Y are dependent.

● **PROBLEM** 5-11

Given that the joint density function of X and Y is

$$f(x,y) = 6x^2 y \quad \text{where} \begin{cases} 0 < x < 1 \text{ and} \\ 0 < y < 1, \end{cases}$$
$$= 0 \quad \text{elsewhere,}$$

find $\Pr(0 < x < 3/4, \ 1/3 < y < 2)$.

Solution: The joint density function of two random variables represents a surface over the region on which it is defined. The volume under the surface is always 1. We need to find the volume over the region bounded by the given limits. We construct a double integral:

$$\int_{y=1/3}^{y=2} \int_{x=0}^{x=3/4} f(x,y)dx\, dy = \int_{y=1/3}^{y=1} \int_{x=0}^{x=3/4} 6x^2 y \; dx\, dy$$

$$+ \int_{y=1}^{2} \int_{x=0}^{x=3/4} 0 \; dx\, dy \ ;$$

because $f(x,y) = 0$ where $y \geq 1$), this becomes

$$\int_{y=1/3}^{y=2} \int_{x=0}^{x=3/4} f(x,y)dxdy = 6\int_{y=1/3}^{y=1} \frac{x^3}{3}y \Big]_0^{3/4} dy = 6\int_{y=1/3}^{y=1} \frac{9}{64} y \; dy$$

$$= \frac{54}{64} \frac{y^2}{2} \Big]_{1/3}^{1} = \frac{27}{32}\left(\frac{1}{2} - \frac{1}{18}\right)$$

$$= \frac{27}{32}\left(\frac{8}{18}\right) = \frac{27}{32}\left(\frac{4}{9}\right)$$

$$= \frac{3}{8} = \Pr(0 < x < 3/4, \ 1/3 < y < 2).$$

● **PROBLEM** 5-12

Given that the continuous random variables X and Y have joint probability density function $f(x,y) = x + y$ when $0 < x < 1$ and $0 < y < 1$, and $f(x,y) = 0$, otherwise, use the marginal probability functions to decide whether or not X and Y are stochastically independent.

Solution: The marginal probability density function of X is found by integrating the joint density function, over the entire domain of Y, with respect to y. This produces a function of x:

$$f_x(x) = \int_{-\infty}^{\infty} f(x,y)dy = \int_0^1 (x+y)dy = \int_0^1 xdy + \int_0^1 ydy$$

$$= (x)y\Big]_0^1 + \frac{y^2}{2}\Big]_0^1 = x(1-0) + (\tfrac{1}{2}-0) = \begin{cases} x + \tfrac{1}{2}, \ 0 < x < 1 \\ 0 \quad \text{elsewhere} \end{cases}$$

Similarly,
$$f_y(y) = \int_{-\infty}^{\infty} f(x,y)dx = \int_0^1 (x+y)dx = \int_0^1 xdx + \int_0^1 ydx$$

$$= \frac{x^2}{2}\Big]_0^1 + (y)x\Big]_0^1 = (\tfrac{1}{2}-0) + y(1-0) = \tfrac{1}{2} + y, \ 0 < y < 1$$
$$= 0 \quad \text{elsewhere.}$$

By definition, X and Y are stochastically independent if and only if $f(x,y) = f(x) \cdot f(y)$. If $f(x,y) \neq f_x(x) \cdot f_y(y)$, X and Y are said to be stochastically dependent.

$$f_x(x) \cdot f_y(y) = (x+\tfrac{1}{2})(y+\tfrac{1}{2}) = xy + \tfrac{1}{2}y + \tfrac{1}{2}x + \tfrac{1}{4} \neq x+y = f(x,y).$$

Therefore, X and Y are stochastically dependent.

● **PROBLEM** 5-13

Given that the joint density function of the random variables X, Y and Z is $f(x,y,z) = e^{-(x+y+z)}$ when $0 < x < \infty$, $0 < y < \infty$, $0 < z < \infty$, find the cumulative distribution function $F(x,y,z)$ of X,Y, and Z.

Solution: $F(x,y,z)$ is defined to be $\Pr(X \leq x, Y \leq y, Z \leq z)$. Here we have extended the concept of cumulative probability from one random variable to three. The cumulative distribution function of one variable gives the area under the density curve to the left of the particular value of x. The distribution function of two variables gives the volume under the surface represented by the bivariate density function over the region bounded by the specified values of x and y.

This is obtained by integration with respect to each variable. The number given by a distribution function of three variables can be interpreted as a 4-dimensional volume. It is obtained by constructing an iterated triple integral and integrating with respect to each variable.

$$F(x,y,z) = \int_0^z \int_0^y \int_0^x e^{-u-v-w} \, du \, dv \, dw$$

$$= \int_0^z \int_0^y \int_0^x e^{-u}(e^{-v-w}) \, du \, dv \, dw$$

$$= \int_0^z \int_0^y (e^{-v-w})(1-e^{-x}) \, dv \, dw = (1-e^{-x})\int_0^z e^{-w}\int_0^y e^{-v} \, dv \, dw$$

$$= (1-e^{-x}) \int_0^z e^{-w}(1-e^{-y}) \, dw$$

$$= (1-e^{-x})(1-e^{-y}) \int_0^z e^{-w} \, dw = (1-e^{-x})(1-e^{-y})(1-e^{-z})$$

for $x,y,z > 0$.

● **PROBLEM** 5-14

Let (X,Y) have the distribution defined by the joint density function,

$$f(x,y) = \begin{cases} e^{-x-y} & \begin{array}{l} x > 0 \\ y > 0 \end{array} \\ 0 & \text{otherwise}. \end{cases}$$

Find the marginal and conditional densities of Y and X. Are X and Y independent?

Solution: The marginal distributions of X and Y are:

$$g(x) = \int_0^\infty f(x,y)dy = \int_0^\infty e^{-x-y} dy$$

and

$$h(y) = \int_0^\infty f(x,y) \, dx = \int_0^\infty e^{-x-y} \, dx \, .$$

Thus

$$g(x) = e^{-x}(-e^{-y})\Big|_0^\infty = e^{-x} \qquad x > 0$$

and

$$h(y) = e^{-y}(-e^{-x})\Big|_0^\infty = e^{-y} \qquad y > 0 \, .$$

We see that $f(x,y) = g(x)h(y)$ because $e^{-x-y} = e^{-x}e^{-y}$. Thus X and Y are independent.

The conditional densities of X and Y are defined by analogy to conditional probability.

$f(x|y)$ = conditional density of x given y is by definition

$$= \frac{f(x,y)}{h(y)}$$

for fixed y and

$f(y|x)$ = conditional density of y given x is

$$= \frac{f(x,y)}{g(x)}$$

for fixed y.

The conditional densities in this example are

$$f(x|y) = \frac{e^{-x-y}}{e^{-y}} \qquad x > 0$$

and

$$f(y|x) = \frac{e^{-x-y}}{e^{-x}} \qquad y > 0 \, .$$

Hence

$$f(x|y) = g(x) = e^{-x} \quad \text{and} \quad f(y|x) = h(y) = e^{-y} \, .$$

Another alternate condition for independence is that the conditional density function is equal to the marginal density function.

● **PROBLEM** 5-15

A random vector $(X,Y)$ has a density,

$$f(x,y) = \begin{cases} 2 & x + y < 1, \ x \geq 0 \\ & \qquad\qquad y > 0 \\ 0 & \text{otherwise.} \end{cases}$$

Find the marginal density of X and the conditional density of Y given X.

Solution: The marginal density of X is the area under the cross-section at $X = x$ as a function of x:

$$f(x) = \int_{-\infty}^\infty f(x,y)dy = \int_0^{1-x} 2dy = 2(1-x)$$

for $0 \leq x \leq 1$ .

The conditional distribution of Y given $X = x$ is

$$f(y|x) = \frac{f(x,y)}{f(x)} = \frac{2}{2(1-x)} \quad \text{for} \quad \begin{array}{l} x + y < 1 \\ 1 > x \geq 0 \\ y > 0 \end{array}$$

or for fixed  x,                   $0 < x < 1$ ,

$$f(y|x) = \begin{cases} \dfrac{1}{1-x} & 0 < y < 1-x \\ \\ 0 & \text{otherwise .} \end{cases}$$

Note that for some fixed  x  such that  $0 < x < 1$, $f(y|x)$  is a constant density for  $0 < y < 1-x$ .

Let  X  and  Y  be jointly distributed with density function

$$f(x,y) = \begin{array}{ll} 1 & \begin{array}{l} 0 < x < 1 \\ 0 < y < 1 \end{array} \\ 0 & \text{otherwise .} \end{array}$$

Find
$$F(\lambda|X > Y) = Pr(X \leq \lambda|X > Y).$$

Solution:  By the definition of conditional probability,

$$Pr(A|B) = \frac{Pr(A \text{ and } B)}{Pr(B)} .$$

Thus,

$$F(\lambda|X > Y) = Pr(X \leq \lambda|X > Y)$$

$$= \frac{Pr(X \leq \lambda \text{ and } X > Y)}{Pr(X > Y)} .$$

The shaded region represents the area where  $X \leq \lambda$  and  $X > Y$. Thus the  $Pr(X \leq \lambda \text{ and } X > Y)$  is the volume over the shaded area under the curve  $f(x,y) = 1$.

This volume is that of a right prism.  Thus  $Pr(X \leq \lambda \text{ and } X > Y) =$ volume of right prism whose base is the shaded region in the figure and whose height is  1.

$Pr(X \leq \lambda$ and $X > Y) = $ (Area of base) x height $= \frac{1}{2}\lambda$ x $\lambda$ x 1 $= \frac{\lambda^2}{2}$.

$Pr(X > Y) = $ the volume over the triangle with vertices $(0,0)$, $(1,1)$ and $(1,0)$ and under $f(x,y) = 1$.

This volume is an the shape of a right prism with a base of area $\frac{1}{2}$ and a height of 1.

The volume of this region is thus $\frac{1}{2} \cdot 1 = \frac{1}{2}$ and $Pr(X > Y) = \frac{1}{2}$.

Thus $\frac{Pr(X \leq \lambda \text{ and } X > Y)}{Pr(X > Y)} = \frac{\lambda^2/2}{\frac{1}{2}} = \lambda^2$.

The conditional cumulative distribution function for X given

X > Y is therefore $Pr(X \leq \lambda | X > Y) = \begin{cases} \lambda^2 & 0 < \lambda < 1 \\ 0 & \lambda < 0 \\ 1 & \lambda > 1 . \end{cases}$

● **PROBLEM 5-17**

Let
$$f(x,y) = \begin{cases} 2 - x - y & \begin{array}{l} 0 < x < 1 \\ 0 < y < 1 \end{array} \\ 0 & \text{otherwise} . \end{cases}$$
Find the conditional distribution of Y given X.

Solution: The conditional distribution of Y given X = x is de-

fined to be $f(y | X = x) = \frac{f(x,y)}{g(x)}$,

where $g(x)$ is the marginal distribution of X and $f(x,y)$ is the joint distribution of X and Y.

The marginal distribution of X is

$$g(x) = \int_{-\infty}^{\infty} f(x,y)dy = \int_{0}^{1} (2-x-y)dy$$

$$= (2-x)y - \frac{y^2}{2} \Big]_0^1 = 2 - x - \frac{1}{2} = \frac{3}{2} - x \text{ for } 0 < x < 1 .$$

Thus the conditional density is
$$f(y|x) = \frac{2-y-x}{3/2 - x} , \quad 0 < y < 1 \quad \text{and} \quad x \text{ fixed.}$$

● **PROBLEM 5-18**

Conditional probabilities can often be used to calculate unconditional probabilities. Show that the marginal distribution of X can be calculated from the conditional distribution of X given Y and the marginal distribution of Y.

Solution: Let $h(y)$ be the marginal density of Y and let $f(X|Y)$ be the conditional density of X given Y. Also let $f(x,y)$ be the joint density of X and Y.

$f(x|y) = \dfrac{f(x,y)}{h(y)}$   by definition or   $f(x,y) = f(x|y)h(y)$ .

But the marginal density of X is   $g(x) = \int_{-\infty}^{\infty} f(x,y)dy$ .

Substituting for f(x,y) we see that,   $g(x) = \int_{-\infty}^{\infty} f(x|y)h(y)dy$ .

Let a random variable Y represent the diameter of a shaft and a random variable X represent the inside diameter of the housing that is intended to support the shaft. By design the shaft is to have diameter 99.5 units and the housing inside diameter 100 units. If the manufacturing process of each of the items is imperfect, so that in fact Y is uniformly distributed over the interval (98.5, 100.5) and X is uniformly distributed over (99, 101), what is the probability that a particular shaft can be successfully paired with a particular housing, when "successfully paired" is taken to mean that X - h < Y < X for some small positive quantity h? Assume that X and Y are independent.

Solution: We wish to find the $\Pr(X - h < Y < X)$ where X is distributed with density $f(x) = \tfrac{1}{2}$,   $99 < x < 101$

and Y is distributed with density $g(y) = \tfrac{1}{2}$,   $98.5 < y < 100.5$.

To find the probability that X - h < Y < X , we condition on the value of X.
Thus,

$$\Pr(X-h<Y<x) = \int_{-\infty}^{\infty} \Pr(X-h<Y<x|X = x)\ f(x)dx$$

$$= \int_{99}^{101} \Pr(x-h<Y<x)\tfrac{1}{2}\ dx .$$

Let h = ½, then since ½ is 25% of the interval (99, 101),

$\Pr(x - \tfrac{1}{2} < Y < x) = \tfrac{1}{4}$ for $99 < x < 100.5$ . Also for x > 100.5, the values close to X are not in the range of Y. We can only consider the interval from X - ½ to 100.5. Hence

$$\Pr(X - \tfrac{1}{2} < Y < X) = (100.5 - (x-.5))\tfrac{1}{2},$$

$105.5 < X < 101$. Thus,

$$\int_{99}^{101} \Pr(x - h < Y < x)\tfrac{1}{2}\ dx = \int_{99}^{100.5} \tfrac{1}{2} \cdot \tfrac{1}{4}\ dx + \int_{100.5}^{101} \frac{100.5-(x-.5)}{2}dx$$

$$= \tfrac{1}{8} x\Big]_{99}^{100.5} + \int_{100.5}^{101} \frac{101 - x}{2}\ dx$$

$$= \tfrac{1}{8} \cdot (100.5-99) + \frac{101x}{2} - \frac{x^2}{4}\Big]_{100.5}^{101}$$

$$= \frac{1.5}{8} + \left(\frac{10201}{2} - \frac{10201}{4}\right) - \left(\frac{10150.5}{2} - \frac{10100.25}{4}\right)$$

175

$$= .1875 + \frac{10201}{4} - \left(\frac{10200.75}{4}\right)$$

$$= .1875 + .0625 = .25 .$$

# CHAPTER 6

# FUNCTIONS OF RANDOM VARIABLES

## CHANGE OF VARIABLE TECHNIQUE

● PROBLEM 6-1

X is a discrete random variable with probability mass function, $f(x) = 1/n$ , $x = 1,2,3,\ldots,n; = 0$ otherwise.

If $Y = X^2$ , find the probability mass function of Y.

Solution: Since $Y = X^2$ as x takes the values $1,2,3,\ldots,n$, y takes the values $1,4,9,\ldots,n^2$ . Thus

$$Pr(Y = r^2) = Pr(X = r) = 1/n, \quad r = 1,2,\ldots,n$$

and so
$$h(y) \begin{cases} = 1/n \;, \quad y = 1,4,\ldots,n^2 \\ = 0 \qquad\qquad \text{otherwise.} \end{cases}$$

● PROBLEM 6-2

If X is a discrete random variable with probability mass function

$$f(x) \begin{cases} = \dfrac{1}{2n} & x = \pm 1, \pm 2, \ldots, \pm n \\ = 0 & \text{otherwise} \end{cases}$$

and $Y = X^2$, then find the probability mass function of Y.

Solution: Since $Y = X^2$ ,

$$Pr(Y = r^2) = Pr(X^2 = r^2) = Pr(X = r \text{ or } X = -r)$$
$$= Pr(X = r) + Pr(X = -r)$$
$$= \frac{1}{2n} + \frac{1}{2n} = \frac{1}{n} \qquad r = 1,2,\ldots,n \;.$$

Thus $h(y) = \dfrac{1}{n}$ , $\begin{cases} y = 1,4,9,\ldots,n^2 \\ = 0 \quad \text{otherwise.} \end{cases}$

● PROBLEM 6-3

Given that the random variable X has probability density function $f(x) = (\frac{1}{2})^x$ when x is a positive integer, find the density function of the random variable

$$Y = \sin\left(\pi \frac{X}{2}\right).$$

**Solution:** Determine the possible values of $Y = \sin\left(\pi \frac{X}{2}\right)$. When $x = 1$, $Y = \sin\left(\pi \cdot \frac{1}{2}\right) = 1$. When $x = 2$, $Y = \sin(\pi) = 0$. When $x = 3$, $Y = \sin\left(\frac{3\pi}{2}\right) = -1$. When $x = 4$, $Y = \sin(2\pi) = 0$. When $x = 5$, $Y = \sin\left(\frac{5}{2}\pi\right) = 1$. The same values $(1, 0, -1)$ will be generated as $x$ increases by $1$, because the sine function is periodic with period $2\pi$.

$Y = 0$ if and only if $\pi\left(\frac{X}{2}\right) = k\pi$, where $k$ is a positive integer. Then $\frac{X}{2} = k$ and $x = 2k$.

$Y = 1$ if and only if $\pi\left(\frac{X}{2}\right) = \frac{1}{2}\pi$ or $\pi\left(\frac{X}{2}\right) = \frac{5}{2}\pi$ or $\pi\left(\frac{X}{2}\right) = \frac{4k+1}{2}\pi$ where $k = 0, 1, 2, \ldots$. Dividing each side of this equation by $\pi/2$, we obtain $x = 4k + 1$.

$Y = -1$ if and only if $\pi\left(\frac{X}{2}\right) = \frac{3}{2}\pi$ or $\pi\left(\frac{X}{2}\right) = \frac{7}{2}\pi$ or $\pi\left(\frac{X}{2}\right) = \frac{11}{2}\pi$ or $\pi\left(\frac{X}{2}\right) = \left(\frac{4k+3}{2}\right)\pi$ where $k = 0, 1, 2, 3, \ldots$. Again dividing each side by $\pi/2$, we find that $X = 4k + 3$, $X = 0, 1, 2, 3, \ldots$.

Now we evaluate the probability that $Y$ takes each of its possible values $(1, 0, -1)$.

We are given that $P(X = x) = \left(\frac{1}{2}\right)^x$ when $x = 1, 2, 3, \ldots$. The event $X = 2k$ for some $k$ is exclusive of any other event $x = 2j$, $k \neq j$. Therefore we can add the probabilities of their occurrence to find

$$P(Y = 0) = \sum_{k=1}^{\infty} P(X = 2k) = \sum_{k=1}^{\infty} \left(\frac{1}{2}\right)^{2k}$$

(by substituting $2k$ for $x$ in the given probability function) and

$$\sum_{k=1}^{\infty} \left(\frac{1}{2}\right)^{2k} = \sum_{k=1}^{\infty} \frac{(1)^{2k}}{2^{2k}} = \sum_{k=1}^{\infty} \frac{1}{4^k} = \sum_{k=1}^{\infty} \left(\frac{1}{4}\right)^k.$$

Factoring $\frac{1}{4}$ from this series, we have

$$\sum_{k=1}^{\infty} \left(\frac{1}{4}\right)^k = \frac{1}{4} \sum_{k=0}^{\infty} \left(\frac{1}{4}\right)^k.$$

The series from $k = 0$ is geometric with sum (limit of sequence of partial sums)

$$\frac{1}{1 - \frac{1}{4}} = \frac{1}{3/4} = \frac{4}{3}.$$

Thus,

$$P(Y = 0) = \frac{1}{4} \sum_{k=0}^{\infty} \left(\frac{1}{4}\right)^k = \frac{1}{4} \cdot \frac{4}{3} = \frac{1}{3}.$$

The events $X = 4k + 1$ are mutually exclusive for different $K$. Thus we can add their probabilities to find

$$P(Y = 1) = \sum_{k=0}^{\infty} P(X = 4k+1) = \sum_{k=0}^{\infty} \left(\frac{1}{2}\right)^{4k+1} = \sum_{k=0}^{\infty} \left(\frac{1}{2}\right)^{4k}\left(\frac{1}{2}\right)^1$$

$$= \frac{1}{2} \sum_{k=0}^{\infty} \left(\frac{1}{2^4}\right)^k = \frac{1}{2} \sum_{k=0}^{\infty} \left(\frac{1}{16}\right)^k$$

by the same reasoning we used to find $P(Y = 0)$. $\sum_{k=0}^{\infty} \left(\frac{1}{16}\right)^k$ is a geo-

metric series and so $\sum_{k=0}^{\infty} \left(\frac{1}{16}\right)^k = \frac{1}{1-1/16} = \frac{1}{15/16} = 16/15$. Therefore,

$P(Y = 1) = \frac{1}{2}\left(\frac{16}{15}\right) = \frac{8}{15}$ .

Exactly the same method is used to find

$$P(Y = -1) = \sum_{k=0}^{\infty} P(X = 4k+3) = \sum_{k=0}^{\infty} (\tfrac{1}{2})^{4k+3}$$

$$= \sum_{k=0}^{\infty} (\tfrac{1}{2})^{4k}(\tfrac{1}{2})^3 = \frac{1}{8} \sum_{k=0}^{\infty} \left(\frac{1}{2^4}\right)^k = \frac{1}{8} \sum_{k=0}^{\infty} \left(\frac{1}{16}\right)^k$$

$$= \frac{1}{8}\left(\frac{16}{15}\right) = \frac{2}{15} .$$

Therefore, the distribution of Y is;

$$h(y) = \begin{cases} \frac{2}{15} & , \; y = -1 \\ \frac{1}{3} & , \; y = 0 \\ \frac{8}{15} & , \; y = 1 \\ 0 & , \; \text{otherwise.} \end{cases}$$

Checking we see that

$$Pr(Y = 0) + Pr(Y = 1) + Pr(Y = -1)$$

$$= 1/3 + 8/15 + 2/15 = \frac{5+8+2}{15} = \frac{15}{15} = 1,$$

as it should to have a proper probability distribution.

● **PROBLEM 6-4**

The length of time a device lasts, X, has probability density function

$$f(x) = \begin{cases} 2e^{-2x} & x > 0 \\ 0 & \text{otherwise .} \end{cases}$$

If the gadget lasts more than three days the profit to the manufacturer is \$1.00. If the gadget lasts at most three days the pro-
fit to the manufacturer is - \$2.00. Let Y represent the profit.
Find the distribution of Y.

**Solution:** Let $F(y) = Pr(Y \le y)$ and $G(x) = Pr(X \le x)$.
Y is defined to be:

$$Y = \begin{cases} 1 & \text{when } x > 3 \\ -2 & \text{when } x \le 3 , \end{cases}$$

A graph of Y is:

179

Thus, $\Pr(Y \leq y) = \begin{cases} 0 & y < -2 \\ \Pr(X \leq 3) & -2 \leq y < 1 \\ 1 & y > 1 \end{cases}$

but $\Pr(X \leq 3) = G(3) = \int_0^3 f(x)dx = \int_0^3 2e^{-2x}dx = -e^{-2x}\Big]_0^3 = 1 - e^{-6}$.

Thus

$$\Pr(Y \leq y) = \begin{cases} 0 & y < -2 \\ 1 - e^{-6} & -2 \leq y < 1 \\ 1 & y > 1 \end{cases}.$$

Y is a discrete random variable with two values, 1 and -2.

$$\Pr(Y = 1) = \Pr(X > 3)$$
$$= 1 - \Pr(X \leq 3)$$
$$= 1 - (1 - e^{-6}) = e^{-6}$$

and

$$\Pr(Y = -2) = \Pr(X < 3)$$
$$= 1 - e^{-6}.$$

Thus Y has distribution,

$$\Pr(Y = y) = \begin{cases} 1 - e^{-6} & y = -2 \\ e^{-6} & y = 1 \end{cases}.$$

The expected value of Y is

$$E(Y) = (-2)\Pr(Y = -2) + (1)\Pr(Y = 1)$$
$$= -2(1 - e^{-6}) + 1(e^{-6})$$
$$= -2 + 3e^{-6}$$
$$= -1.99.$$

● PROBLEM 6-5

Suppose X has the Poisson distribution with parameter $\lambda$. Let

$$Y = \begin{cases} 1 & \text{if } X \text{ is even} \\ -1 & \text{if } X \text{ is odd}. \end{cases}$$

Find the distribution of Y.

Solution: Any even number can be written as $2r$, where $r = 0,1,2,3,\ldots.$

Thus
$$Pr(Y = 1) = Pr(X \text{ is even})$$
$$= Pr(X = 2r) \qquad r = 0,1,2,3,\ldots$$

but the events $X = 0$, $X = 2$, $X = 4,\ldots$ are mutually exclusive, thus
$$Pr(Y = 1) = Pr(X = 2r) = Pr(X = 0) + Pr(X = 2) + \ldots$$
$$= \sum_{r=0}^{\infty} Pr(X = 2r) .$$

Since $X$ is Poisson distributed,
$$Pr(X = k) = \frac{\lambda^k e^{-\lambda}}{k!} \qquad k = 0,1,2,\ldots$$

or
$$Pr(X = 2r) = \frac{\lambda^{(2r)} e^{-\lambda}}{(2r)!}$$

and so
$$Pr(Y = 1) = \sum_{r=0}^{\infty} \frac{\lambda^{2r} e^{-\lambda}}{(2r)!}$$
$$= e^{-\lambda} \sum_{r=0}^{\infty} \frac{\lambda^{2r}}{(2r)!}$$
$$= e^{-\lambda}\left(1 + \frac{\lambda^2}{2!} + \frac{\lambda^4}{4!} + \ldots\right) .$$

But
$$2 \sum_{r=0}^{\infty} \frac{\lambda^{2r}}{(2r)!} = \left(1 + \frac{\lambda}{1!} + \frac{\lambda^2}{2!} + \ldots\right) + \left(1 - \frac{\lambda}{1!} + \frac{\lambda^2}{2!} - \frac{\lambda^3}{3!} + \ldots\right)$$
$$= 2 + \frac{2\lambda^2}{2!} + \frac{2\lambda^4}{4!} + \ldots$$
$$= 2\left(1 + \frac{\lambda^2}{2!} + \frac{\lambda^4}{4!} + \ldots\right)$$

And
$$e^{\lambda} = 1 + \frac{\lambda}{1!} + \frac{\lambda^2}{2!} + \ldots = \sum_{r=0}^{\infty} \frac{\lambda^r}{r!}$$

and
$$e^{-\lambda} = +1 - \frac{\lambda}{1!} + \frac{\lambda^2}{2!} - \ldots = \sum_{r=0}^{\infty} \frac{(-\lambda)^r}{r!} .$$

Thus
$$Pr(Y = 1) = e^{-\lambda}\left(\frac{e^{\lambda} + e^{-\lambda}}{2}\right)$$
$$= \frac{1 + e^{-2\lambda}}{2} .$$

Now consider $Pr(Y = -1)$.
$$Pr(Y = -1) = Pr(X \text{ is odd})$$
$$= Pr(X = 2r + 1) \qquad r = 0,1,2,\ldots$$

because any odd number may be expressed as $2r + 1$.
Since $X = 1$, $X = 3$, $X = 5,\ldots$ are mutually exclusive, then
$$Pr(X \text{ is odd}) = \sum_{r=0}^{\infty} Pr(X = 2r + 1)$$
$$= \sum_{r=0}^{\infty} \frac{(\lambda)^{2r+1} e^{-\lambda}}{(2r+1)!}$$
$$= e^{-\lambda} \sum_{r=0}^{\infty} \frac{\lambda^{2r+1}}{(2r+1)!} .$$

But
$$2 \sum_{r=0}^{\infty} \frac{\lambda^{2r+1}}{(2r+1)!} = 2\left(\lambda + \frac{\lambda^3}{3!} + \frac{\lambda^5}{5!} + \ldots\right)$$

$$= 1 - 1 + \frac{\lambda}{1!} - \frac{(-\lambda)}{1!} + \frac{\lambda^2}{2!} - \frac{\lambda^2}{2!} + \frac{\lambda^3}{3!} - \frac{(-\lambda^3)}{3!} \ldots$$

$$= \left(1 + \frac{\lambda}{1!} + \frac{\lambda^2}{2!} + \ldots\right) - \left(1 - \frac{\lambda}{1!} + \frac{\lambda^2}{2!} - \frac{\lambda^3}{3!} + \ldots\right).$$

Also
$$e^{\lambda} = \left(1 + \frac{\lambda}{1!} + \frac{\lambda^2}{2!} + \ldots\right)$$

and
$$e^{-\lambda} = \left(1 - \frac{\lambda}{1!} + \frac{\lambda^2}{2!} - \frac{\lambda^3}{3!} + \ldots\right).$$

Thus
$$2 \sum_{r=0}^{\infty} \frac{\lambda^{2r+1}}{(2r+1)!} = e^{\lambda} - e^{-\lambda}.$$

Finally
$$\Pr(Y = -1) = \Pr(X \text{ is odd}) = e^{-\lambda}\left(\frac{e^{\lambda} - e^{-\lambda}}{2}\right)$$

$$= \frac{1 - e^{-2\lambda}}{2}.$$

Therefore, the distribution of Y can be written

$$g(y) = \begin{cases} \dfrac{1 + e^{-2\lambda}}{2}, & y = 1 \\ \dfrac{1 - e^{-2\lambda}}{2}, & y = -1 \\ 0, & \text{otherwise.} \end{cases}$$

● **PROBLEM 6-6**

Suppose X takes on the values 0,1,2,3,4,5 with probabilities $P_0$, $P_1$, $P_2$, $P_3$, $P_4$ and $P_5$. If $Y = g(X) = (X-2)^2$, what is the distribution of Y?

Solution: First, examine the values that the random variable Y may assume. If X = 0 or 4,

$$Y = (0-2)^2 = (4-2)^2 = 2^2 = 4.$$

If X = 1 or 3,

$$Y = (1-2)^2 = (3-2)^2 = 1^2 = 1.$$

If X = 2,
$$Y = (2-2)^2 = 0^2 = 0$$

and if X = 5,
$$Y = (5-2)^2 = 3^2 = 9.$$

Thus, Y assumes the values 0,1,4 and 9. We now find the probability distribution of Y.

$$\Pr(Y = 0) = \Pr((X-2)^2 = 0)$$

$$= \Pr(X = 2) = P_2$$

$$Pr(Y = 1) = Pr((X-2)^2 = 1) \quad = Pr(X = 1 \text{ or } X = 3)$$

$$= Pr(X = 1) + Pr(X = 3) \quad = p_1 + p_3$$

$$Pr(Y = 4) = Pr((X-2)^2 = 4) \quad = Pr(X = 0 \text{ or } X = 4)$$

$$= Pr(X = 0) + Pr(X = 4) \quad = p_0 + p_4$$

and

$$Pr(Y = 9) = Pr((X-2)^2 = 9)$$

$$= Pr(X = 5) = p_5.$$

Therefore, the distribution of Y can be written

$$h(y) = \begin{cases} p_2 & , y = 0 \\ p_1 + p_3, & y = 1 \\ p_0 + p_4, & y = 4 \\ p_5 & , y = 9 \\ 0 & , \text{otherwise.} \end{cases}$$

# MOMENT GENERATING FUNCTION TECHNIQUE

● **PROBLEM** 6-7

Suppose $X_1, \ldots, X_n$ are independent Bernoulli random variables, that is, $Pr(X_i = 0) = 1 - p$ and $Pr(X_i = 1) = p$ for $i = 1, \ldots, n$. What is the distribution of
$$Y = \sum_{i=1}^{n} X_i ?$$

Solution: We have a sum of independent and identically distributed random variables. The moment generating technique is useful here. We will find the moment generating function of Y and use the one to one correspondence between moment generating functions and distribution functions to find the distribution of Y.

$$M_Y(t) = E[e^{Yt}] \quad = E[e^{(X_1+\ldots+X_n)t}]$$

$$= E[e^{X_1 t}] E[e^{X_2 t}] \cdot \ldots \cdot E[e^{X_n t}].$$

But for each i,

$$E[e^{X_i t}] = e^{0 \cdot t} Pr(X_i = 0) + e^{1 \cdot t} Pr(X_i = 1)$$

$$= Pr(X_i = 0) + e^t Pr(X_i = 1)$$

$$= 1 - p + pe^t.$$

Thus

$$M_Y(t) = (1 - p + pe^t)^n$$

which we recognize as the moment generating function of a binomially distributed random variable with parameters n and p.

Suppose that $X_1, \ldots, X_n$ are independent Poisson distributed random variables, $X_i$ having parameter $\lambda_i$ . Find the distribution of

$$Y = \sum_{i=1}^{n} X_i .$$

Solution: We will use the moment-generating function technique to find the moment generating function of $Y$, then hope to recognize this moment generating function as corresponding to a particular distribution.

We have found the moment generating function of a Poisson random variable with parameter $\lambda_i$ to be

$$M_{X_i}(t) = \exp\{\lambda_i(e^t - 1)\} .$$

Because the $X_i$ are independent and $Y = \sum_{i=1}^{n} X_i$ ,

$$M_Y(t) = M_{X_1}(t) \cdot M_{X_2}(t) \cdot \ldots \cdot M_{X_n}(t)$$

$$= \exp\{\lambda_1(e^t - 1)\} \exp\{\lambda_2(e^t - 1)\} \ldots$$

$$\cdot \exp\{\lambda_n(e^t - 1)\}$$

and by the properties of the law of exponents,

$$M_Y(t) = \exp\{(\lambda_1 + \lambda_2 + \ldots + \lambda_n)(e^t - 1)\} .$$

We recognize this as the moment generating function of a Poisson random variable with parameter $(\lambda_1 + \lambda_2 + \ldots + \lambda_n) = \sum_{i=1}^{n} \lambda_i$ . Thus $Y$ is distributed as a Poisson random variable with parameter $\sum_{i=1}^{n} \lambda_i$ .

Assume $X_1, \ldots, X_n$ are independent and identically distributed exponential random variables each with parameter $\lambda$ . Find the distribution of $Y = \sum_{i=1}^{n} X_i$ .

Solution: The moment generating function of each of the $X_i$ has been found to be

$$E(e^{tX_i}) = \int_0^\infty e^{ts} \lambda e^{-s\lambda} \, ds = \frac{\lambda}{\lambda - t} \text{ for } t < \lambda .$$

Because the $X_i$ are independent and $Y = \sum_{i=1}^{n} X_i$ , the moment generating function of $Y$,

$$M_Y(t) = M_{X_1}(t) \cdot M_{X_2}(t) \cdot \ldots \cdot M_{X_n}(t)$$

$$= \underbrace{\left(\frac{\lambda}{\lambda - t}\right)\left(\frac{\lambda}{\lambda - t}\right) \ldots \left(\frac{\lambda}{\lambda - t}\right)}_{n \text{ terms}}$$

$$= \left(\frac{\lambda}{\lambda-t}\right)^n \qquad \lambda < t .$$

We recognize $M_Y(t)$ as the moment generating function of a gamma distribution with parameters $n$ and $\lambda$. Hence $Y = \sum_{i=1}^{n} X_i$ is gamma distributed with parameters $n$ and $\lambda$.

● **PROBLEM** 6-10

Suppose $X$ has a normal distribution with mean $0$ and variance $1$. Let $Y = X^2$. Find the distribution of $Y$ using the moment generating function technique.

Solution: We find the moment generating function of $Y$ and then hope to recognize it as the moment generating function of a distribution we know.

The moment generating function of $Y$ is
$$M_Y(t) = E[e^{tY}]$$
but $Y = X^2$ where $X$ is distributed normally with mean $0$ and variance $1$; thus

$$E[e^{tY}] = E[e^{tX^2}]$$

$$= \int_0^\infty e^{tx^2} f(x)dx$$

where $f(x)$ is the density function of a standard normal distribution:

$$f(x) = \frac{1}{\sqrt{2\pi}} e^{-x^2/2} \qquad -\infty < x < \infty .$$

Thus

$$M_Y(t) = \int_{-\infty}^\infty \frac{e^{tx^2} \cdot e^{-x^2/2}}{\sqrt{2\pi}} dx$$

$$M_Y(t) = \int_{-\infty}^\infty \frac{1}{\sqrt{2\pi}} e^{-x^2(1-2t)/2} dx .$$

If $t < \frac{1}{2}$,

$$M_Y(t) = \frac{(1-2t)^{-\frac{1}{2}}}{(1-2t)^{\frac{1}{2}}} \int_{-\infty}^\infty \frac{1}{\sqrt{2\pi}} e^{-x^2(1-2t)/2} dx$$

$$= (1-2t)^{-\frac{1}{2}} \int_{-\infty}^\infty \frac{1}{(1-2t)^{-\frac{1}{2}}\sqrt{2\pi}} e^{-x^2/2(1-2t)^{-1}} dx .$$

But,
$$g(x) = \frac{1}{(1-2t)^{-\frac{1}{2}}\sqrt{2\pi}} e^{-x^2/2(1-2t)^{-1}}$$

is the density function of a normally distributed random variable with mean $0$ and variance $(1-2t)^{-1}$. Thus

$$\int_{-\infty}^\infty g(x)dx = 1$$

185

and

$$M_Y(t) = (1-2t)^{-\frac{1}{2}}$$

$$= \left(\frac{1}{1-2t}\right)^{\frac{1}{2}} = \left(\frac{\frac{1}{2}}{\frac{1}{2}-t}\right)^{\frac{1}{2}} \quad \text{for} \quad t < \frac{1}{2} \ .$$

Thus $M_Y(t)$ is the moment generating function of a gamma distributed random variable with parameters $n = \frac{1}{2}, \lambda = \frac{1}{2}$ .

Thus the density function of $Y$ is;

$$f(y) = \frac{1}{2^{\frac{1}{2}} \Gamma(\frac{1}{2})} x^{\frac{1}{2}-1} e^{-x/2} \qquad x > 0 \ .$$

This distribution is also known as the chi-square distribution with 1 degree of freedom.

# DISTRIBUTION FUNCTIONS

● **PROBLEM** 6-11

Let $T$ be distributed with density function

$$f(t) = \begin{cases} \lambda e^{-\lambda t} & \text{for} \quad t > 0 \\ 0 & \text{otherwise} \ . \end{cases}$$

If $S$ is a new random variable defined as $S = \ln T$, find the density function of $S$.

Solution: The technique we will use to find the density function of $S$ is known as the distribution function technique. If $G(t) = Pr(T < t)$ is known, we can sometimes use it to find $F(x) = Pr(S < x)$. Differentiating $F(s)$ will then yield the density function of the random variable $S$.

$$Pr(S \le x) = Pr(\ln T \le x)$$

because $\ln T = S$ but the natural logarithm function of a variable is one-to-one. That is, if $\ln y = x$, then given $y$ we can find a unique $x$ such that $y = \ln^{-1} x$ .

$\ln^{-1}(x)$ is the inverse of the natural log function and is known to be $e^{(x)}$. Thus $\ln y = x$ if and only if $y = e^x$ .

Similarly, $\ln T \le x$ if and only if $T \le e^x$ . Thus,

$$Pr(S \le x) = Pr(\ln T \le x)$$

$$= Pr(T \le e^x) \qquad x > 0 \ .$$

But $Pr(T \le e^x) = G(e^x)$ , the cumulative distribution function of $T$ evaluated at $e^x$ .

$$Pr(T \le e^x) = \int_{-\infty}^{e^x} f(t)dt \qquad x > 0$$

$$= \int_{-\infty}^{e^x} \lambda e^{-\lambda t} dt \qquad x > 0$$

$$= \int_{0}^{e^x} \lambda e^{-\lambda t} dt \qquad x > 0$$

$$= -e^{-\lambda t}\Big]_0^{e^x} \qquad x > 0$$

$$= -[e^{-\lambda e^x} - 1] \ .$$

Thus,

$$Pr(S \leq x) = 1 - e^{-\lambda e^x} \qquad x > 0 \ .$$

Differentiating we see that

$$f(s) = \begin{cases} (\lambda e^x)e^{-\lambda e^x} & x > 0 \\ 0 & \text{otherwise.} \end{cases}$$

● **PROBLEM** 6-12

Consider the problem of finding the density function of the kinetic energy $Z = \frac{1}{2}mV^2$, given the distribution of the velocity $V$. The density function of $V$, the velocity for a gas molecule, is given by

$$f(v) = av^2 e^{-bv^2}$$

where $v > 0$, $b$ is a constant depending on the gas and $a$ is determined such that

$$\int_0^\infty f(v)dv = 1.$$

Find the density function of $Z$.

Solution: We use the cumulative distribution technique and find

$$F(z) = Pr(Z \leq z).$$

Because $Z = \frac{1}{2}mv^2$ for $v > 0$,

$$Pr(Z \leq z) = Pr(\tfrac{1}{2}mv^2 \leq z) \ .$$

For $v > 0$, $\frac{1}{2}mv^2$ is an increasing function of $v$, thus

$$Pr(\tfrac{1}{2}mv^2 \leq z) = Pr(v \leq \sqrt{2z/m}) \ .$$

But

$$F\left(\sqrt{2z/m}\right) = Pr(V \leq \sqrt{2z/m}) = \int_0^{\sqrt{2z/m}} f(v) \ dv$$

and the density function of $Z$ is

$$g(z) = F'\left(\sqrt{2z/m}\right) = f\left(\sqrt{2z/m}\right) \frac{d}{dz}\left(\sqrt{2z/m}\right)$$

by the fundamental theorem of calculus and the chain-rule. Thus,

$$g(z) = a\left(\sqrt{2z/m}\right)^2 e^{-b\left(\sqrt{2z/m}\right)^2} \cdot \tfrac{1}{2}(2z/m)^{-\frac{1}{2}} \cdot \frac{2}{m}$$

$$= a\frac{2z}{m} e^{-2bz/m} \cdot \left(\frac{m}{2z}\right)^{\frac{1}{2}} \cdot \frac{1}{m} \ ,$$

$$g(z) = \frac{a}{m}\sqrt{2z/m} \ e^{-2bz/m} \qquad z > 0$$

is the density function of the kinetic energy.

Two points, A and B, are chosen on the circumference of a circle so that the angle at the center is uniformly distributed over $(0, \pi)$. What is the probability that the length of AB exceeds the radius of the circle?

Solution: Let $a$ = the radius of the circle and $\emptyset$ be the central angle formed by the chord. O is the center of the circle.

Note that line segment OA will equal OB in every random chord. Both of these segments are radii of the circle and equal to $a$. Thus triangle AOB is an isoceles triangle with angle AOB = $\emptyset$. Bisecting angle AOB produces two congruent right triangles with angles of $\pi/2$, $\emptyset/2$, and $\pi/2 - \emptyset/2$. Thus

$$\sin \frac{\emptyset}{2} = \frac{\frac{1}{2}AB}{a} \quad \text{or} \quad AB = 2a \sin \frac{\emptyset}{2} .$$

We wish to find

$$\Pr (AB \geq a) = \Pr(2a \sin \frac{\emptyset}{2} \geq a)$$

$$= \Pr(\sin \frac{\emptyset}{2} \geq \tfrac{1}{2}) .$$

In the interval $(0, \pi)$ over which $\emptyset$ varies, $\sin \frac{\emptyset}{2}$ is strictly increasing and is thus invertible in this interval.

Therefore,

$$\Pr(\sin \frac{\emptyset}{2} \geq \tfrac{1}{2}) = \Pr(\frac{\emptyset}{2} \geq \sin^{-1}\tfrac{1}{2}) = \Pr( \frac{\emptyset}{2} \geq \frac{\pi}{6})$$

and

$$\Pr (AB \geq a) = \Pr(\emptyset \geq \pi/3) .$$

The probability density function for $\emptyset$ is given as

$$f(x) = \begin{cases} \dfrac{1}{\pi} & 0 \leq x \leq \pi \\ \\ 0 & \text{otherwise .} \end{cases}$$

This is the uniform distribution over $(0, \pi)$. Thus,

$$\Pr(\emptyset \geq \frac{\pi}{3}) = \int_{\pi/3}^{\pi} 1/\pi \, dx = 1/\pi[\pi - \pi/3]$$

$$= 1 - 1/3 = 2/3 .$$

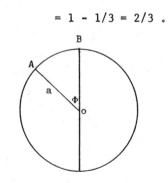

A certain river floods every year. Suppose the low water mark is set at 1 and the high water mark, Y, has the distribution function,

$$F(y) = Pr(Y \le y) = 1 - \frac{1}{y^2} \qquad 1 \le y < \infty .$$

What happens to the distribution if the low water mark is set at 0 instead of 1 and the unit of measuring the height is 1/10 of that used previously?

Solution: If the low water mark is set at 0 and the unit of measuring the water height is 1/10 of that previously used, then a conversion formula between the two systems of measurement may be devised. Let Z be a height measured under the new system and Y the height under the old system. Then

$$Y = \frac{Z}{10} + 1$$

will be an appropriate conversion formula. If the old system measures a height of 1, then we wish a height of 0. Under the new system, if Y = 1, then Z = 0. If Y = 2, Z = 10.

We now use the cumulative distribution function technique to find the distribution Z from the distribution of Y.

$$Pr(Z \le x) = Pr(10(Y-1) \le x) \qquad = Pr(Y \le \frac{x}{10} + 1)$$

$$= 1 - \frac{1}{(x/10 + 1)^2} \qquad \text{for} \quad 1 \le \frac{x}{10} < \infty .$$

$$Pr(Z \le x) = 1 - \frac{100}{(10 + x)^2} \qquad 10 \le x < \infty .$$

● **PROBLEM** 6-15

An earlier example of a function of a random variable was the transformation between a random variable X that is distributed normally with mean $\mu$ and standard deviation $\sigma$ and a random variable Z which is distributed normally with mean 0 and variance 1. Describe this transformation as a special case of the cumulative distribution technique for finding distributions of functions of random variables.

Solution: We wish to find $Pr(X \le a)$, given that we know $Pr(Z \le c)$ for most c. The distributions of X and Z are described above. Recall that to standardize a random variable we subtracted the mean and divided by the standard deviation. Thus

$$Z = \frac{X - \mu}{\sigma} .$$

$$Pr(X \le a) = Pr\left(\frac{X-\mu}{\sigma} \le \frac{a-\mu}{\sigma}\right) \qquad = Pr(Z \le c)$$

$$\text{where} \qquad c = \frac{a-\mu}{\sigma} .$$

● **PROBLEM** 6-16

Let X have the probability distribution defined by

189

$$F(x) = \begin{cases} 1 - e^{-x} & \text{for } x \geq 0 \\ 0 & \text{for } x < 0 . \end{cases}$$

Let $Y = \sqrt{X}$ be a new random variable. Find $G(y)$, the distribution function of $Y$, using the cumulative distribution function technique.

Solution: We find $G(y) = Pr(Y \leq y)$. $Y = \sqrt{X}$ thus

$$Pr(Y \leq y) = Pr(\sqrt{X} \leq y) .$$

Because $X$ takes on only positive values or zero, $\sqrt{X}$ will make sense. $\sqrt{X}$ will always be positive; thus

$$G(Y) = Pr(Y \leq y) = \begin{cases} Pr(\sqrt{X} \leq y) & y \geq 0 \\ 0 & y < 0 \end{cases}$$

$$= \begin{cases} Pr(X \leq y^2) & y \geq 0 \\ 0 & y < 0 . \end{cases}$$

But for $y \geq 0$, $Pr(X \leq y^2) = F(y^2)$, the distribution function of $X$ evaluated at $y^2$. Thus,

$$Pr(X \leq y^2) = 1 - e^{-y^2}$$

and so

$$G(Y) = Pr(Y \leq y) = \begin{cases} 1 - e^{-y^2} & y \geq 0 \\ 0 & y < 0 . \end{cases}$$

The density function of $Y$ is found by differentiating $G(y)$ with respect to $y$. Thus,

$$g(y) = \frac{dG(y)}{dy} = \begin{cases} 2ye^{-y^2} & y \geq 0 \\ 0 & \text{otherwise} . \end{cases}$$

We have shown that the square root of an exponentially distributed random variable is distributed as a Weibull random variable with parameters $a = 1$, $b = 2$.

The general density of a Weibull distribution is

$$f(x) = \begin{cases} abx^{b-1}e^{-ax^b} & \infty > x > 0 \\ 0 & \text{otherwise} . \end{cases}$$

● PROBLEM 6-17

Let $X$ be a random variable with a continuous cumulative distribution function $F(x) = Pr(X \leq x)$. Find the distribution of the random variable $U = F(X)$.

Solution: The random variable $U$ is found in the following way. The $Pr(X \leq x)$ for all $x$ is known. An actual $X$ value is observed, say $X = c$. Then the observed value of $U$ is

$$u = Pr(X \leq c) .$$

To find the distribution of $U$, we wish to find the range of values that $u$ may assume. $F(x) = Pr(X \leq x)$ is between 0 and 1 because it is a probability; hence $U$ ranges between 0 and 1.

Thus,

$$G(u) = Pr(U \le u) = \begin{cases} 0 & u < 0 \\ Pr(F(X) \le u) & 0 \le u < 1 \\ 1 & 1 < u \end{cases} .$$

But $Pr(F(X) \le u) = Pr(X \le F^{-1}(u))$ where $F^{-1}(u) = x$ is the inverse function of $F$ and is the smallest $x$ such that $F(x) \ge u$.

Also,

$$Pr(X \le F^{-1}(u)) = F(F^{-1}(u))$$
$$= u$$

for $0 < u < 1$ and

$$G(u) = \begin{cases} u & 0 < u < 1 \\ 0 & \text{otherwise} \end{cases}$$

and the density function of $U$ is

$$G'(u) = g(u) = \begin{cases} 1 & 0 < u < 1 \\ 0 & \text{otherwise} . \end{cases}$$

Thus $U$ is uniformly distributed over the interval $[0,1]$. This transformation is known as the Probability Integral Transform.

● **PROBLEM** 6-18

Let $X_1,\ldots,X_n$ be independent random variables uniformly distributed over the interval $(0,1)$. Find the distribution of $Y_n = \text{maximum} \{X_1,X_2,\ldots,X_n\}$.

Solution: We wish to find the $Pr(Y_n < y)$. But if the maximum of $X_1,\ldots, X_n$ is less than $y$ then it must be true that $X_1 < y$, $X_2 < y \ldots X_n < y$. Thus

$$Pr(Y_n < y) = Pr(X_1 < y, X_2 < y,\ldots,X_n < y) .$$

By the independence of $X_1,X_2,\ldots,X_n$,

$$Pr(X_1 < y, X_2 < y,\ldots,X_n < y) = Pr(X_1 < y)Pr(X_2 < y)..Pr(X_n < y).$$

For $i = 1,\ldots,n$

$$Pr(X_i < y) = \begin{cases} y & 0 < y < 1 \\ 0 & \text{otherwise} . \end{cases}$$

This is the cumulative distribution of a uniformly distributed random variable, where the random variable is distributed over the interval $(0,1)$. Thus,

$$Pr(Y_n < y) = \begin{cases} \underbrace{y \cdot y \cdot \ldots \cdot y}_{n \text{ terms}} & 0 < y < 1 \\ 0 & \text{otherwise} \end{cases}$$

or

$$Pr(Y_n < y) = \begin{cases} y^n & 0 < y < 1 \\ 0 & \text{otherwise} . \end{cases}$$

191

The density function of $Y_n$ is

$$f(y) = \begin{cases} ny^{n-1} & 0 < y < 1 \\ 0 & \text{otherwise} \end{cases}$$

Let $X_1, \ldots, X_n$ represent the incomes of $n$ randomly selected tax-payers.

Assume that each observation is independent and has probability density function

$$f(x) = \begin{cases} \dfrac{\theta (x_0)^\theta}{x^{\theta+1}} & \text{for } x > x_0 \\ \\ 0 & \text{otherwise.} \end{cases}$$

This is the Pareto distribution. Assume $\theta = 100$ and $x_0 = \$4,000$. Find the density function of the minimum of the $n$ observations.

Solution: We first find $\Pr(Y_1 \leq y)$ where $Y_1 = $ minimum of $\{X_1, X_2, \ldots, X_n\}$. The minimum of the $n$ observations will be the smallest observation in the sample.

$$\Pr(Y_1 \leq y) = \begin{cases} 1 - \Pr(Y_1 \geq y) & y > x_0 \\ 0 & y < x_0 \end{cases}$$

But $Y_1 \geq y$ only if $X_1 \geq y, X_2 \geq y, \ldots, X_n \geq y$. Thus

$$\Pr(Y_1 \geq y) = \Pr(X_1 \geq y, X_2 \geq y, \ldots, X_n \geq y) .$$

By the independence of the $X_i$,

$$\Pr(X_1 \geq y, X_2 \geq y, \ldots, X_n \geq y)$$

$$= \Pr(X_1 \geq y) \Pr(X_2 \geq y), \ldots, \Pr(X_n \geq y) .$$

And for $i = 1, 2, 3, \ldots, n$,

$$\Pr(X_i \geq y) = 1 - \Pr(X_i \leq y)$$

$$\Pr(X_i \leq y) = \int_{x_0}^{y} f(x) dx \qquad y > x_0$$

$$= \int_{x_0}^{y} \frac{\theta x_0^\theta}{x^{\theta+1}} dx \quad = \theta x_0^\theta \int_{x_0}^{y} x^{-(\theta+1)} dx \qquad y > x_0$$

$$= \frac{\theta x_0^\theta}{-(\theta+1)+1} x^{-(\theta+1)+1} \Big]_{x_0}^{y} \quad = \frac{\theta x_0^\theta}{-\theta} \Big[ y^{-\theta} - x_0^{-\theta} \Big]$$

$$= x_0^\theta \left[ x_0^{-\theta} - y^{-\theta} \right] \qquad = 1 - \left( \frac{x_0}{y} \right)^\theta$$

is the cumulative distribution function of each of the observations.
And

$$\Pr(X_i \geq y) = 1 - \Pr(X_i \leq y)$$

$$= 1 - \left[ 1 - \left( \frac{x_0}{y} \right)^\theta \right]$$

$$= \left( \frac{x_0}{y} \right)^\theta .$$

And

$$\Pr(Y_1 \geq y) = \Pr(X_1 \geq y)\Pr(X_2 \geq y) \ \ldots \ \Pr(X_n \geq y) \quad \text{for} \quad y > x_0$$

$$= \underbrace{\left( \frac{x_0}{y} \right)^\theta \cdot \left( \frac{x_0}{y} \right)^\theta \cdot \ldots \cdot \left( \frac{x_0}{y} \right)^\theta}_{n \text{ terms}}$$

or

$$\Pr(Y_1 \leq y) = 1 - \Pr(Y_1 \geq y)$$

$$= 1 - \left( \frac{x_0}{y} \right)^{n\theta} \qquad\qquad y > x_0$$

The density function is found by differentiating $\Pr(Y_1 \leq y)$ with respect to $y$.
Thus,

$$f(y_1) = \begin{cases} \dfrac{d}{dy}\left[ 1 - \left( \dfrac{x_0}{y} \right)^{n\theta} \right] & y > x_0 \\[2ex] 0 & \text{otherwise} \end{cases}$$

$$= \begin{cases} -n\theta \left( \dfrac{x_0}{y} \right)^{n\theta - 1} \left( \dfrac{-x_0}{y^2} \right) & y > x_0 \\[2ex] 0 & \text{otherwise} \end{cases}$$

$$= \begin{cases} \dfrac{n\theta \, x_0^{n\theta}}{y^{n\theta+1}} & y > x_0 \\[2ex] 0 & \text{otherwise} . \end{cases}$$

Substituting our values of $\theta$ and $x_0$ we see that

$$f(y_1) = \begin{cases} \dfrac{(100n)(4,000)^{100n}}{(y_1)^{100n+1}} & y_1 > 4,000 \\[2ex] 0 & \text{otherwise} . \end{cases}$$

● PROBLEM 6-20

A system will function as long as at least one of three components functions. When all three components are functioning, the

distribution of the life of each is exponential with parameter $\frac{1}{3}\lambda$ .
After one of the components fails, the distribution of the life of
each of the two remaining components is exponential with parameter
$\frac{1}{2}\lambda$ .  When only one component is functioning, the distribution of its
life is exponential with parameter $\lambda$ .

    (a)  What is the distribution of the system's lifetime.

    (b)  Suppose only one component is used at a time and it is
replaced when it fails, what is the distribution ?

Solution:  Consider the life of the system, Y, to be composed of three
sections.  These sections are:

$Y_3$ = time when three components are running.

$Y_2$ = time when two components are running.

$Y_1$ = time when one component is running.

$$Y = Y_1 + Y_2 + Y_3 \ .$$

The total life of the system is the sum of these three time
intervals.

If the distributions of $Y_1$, $Y_2$ and $Y_3$ are computed then we
may calculate the distribution of Y.

We assume that after one component fails, the remaining components
"begin life anew".  That is, a component's lifetime after the failure
of another component is independent of the component's life before
the failure.

The time until the first failure, $Y_3$, can be thought of as the
minimum of three independent random variables each distributed with
parameter $\frac{1}{3}\lambda$ .  $Y_3 = \min\{X_1,X_2,X_3\}$ .  Thus,

$$Pr(Y_3 \le t) = 1 - Pr(Y_3 > t)$$

$$= 1 - Pr(\min\{X_1,X_2,X_3\} > t) \ .$$

The $\min\{X_1,X_2,X_3\}$ will be greater than t only if $X_1 > t$,
$X_2 > t$, $X_3 > t$.  Thus

$$Pr(Y_3 \le t) = 1 - Pr(X_1 > t, X_2 > t, X_3 > t) \ .$$

Because the $X_i$ are independent and identically distributed,

$$Pr(Y_3 \le t) = 1 - [Pr(X_i > t)]^3$$

But

$$Pr(X_i > t) = \int_t^\infty \frac{\lambda}{3} e^{-\lambda/3 \ x} \ dx$$

$$= -e^{-\lambda/3 \ x}\Big|_t^\infty$$

$$= e^{-\lambda/3 \ t}$$

and

$$Pr(Y_3 \le t) = 1 - [e^{-\lambda/3 \ t}]^3$$

$$= 1 - e^{-\lambda t} \ .$$

Now we calculate the distribution of $Y_2$.  There are only two
components working.  The random variable $Y_2$, the length of time two
components are operating, will last until one of the two components
fails.  Thus, $Y_2$ can be considered the minimum of two independent and

identically distributed random variables each distributed exponentially
with parameter $\lambda/2$ . $Y_2 = \min\{Z_1, Z_2\}$ .

Thus,

$$Pr(Y_2 \le t) = 1 - Pr(Y_2 > t)$$

$$= 1 - Pr(\min\{Z_1, Z_2\} > t)$$

$\min\{Z_1, Z_2\}$ will be greater than $t$ only if $Z_1 > t$ and $Z_2 > t$.
Thus,

$$Pr(Y_2 \le t) = 1 - Pr(Z_1 > t, Z_2 > t) .$$

But because of independence

$$Pr(Z_1 > t, Z_2 > t) = Pr(Z_1 > t)Pr(Z_2 > t)$$

$$= (e^{-\lambda/2\ t})(e^{-\lambda/2\ t})$$

$\bigg\lvert$ because

$$Pr(Z_1 > t) = Pr(Z_2 > t) = \int_t^\infty \frac{\lambda}{2} e^{-\lambda/2\ x}\ dx$$

$$= -e^{-\lambda/2\ x} \bigg\rvert_t^\infty$$

$$= e^{-\lambda/2\ t}\bigg) .$$

Thus,

$$Pr(Y_2 \le t) = 1 - \left(e^{-\lambda/2\ t}\right)^2$$

$$= 1 - e^{-\lambda t} .$$

After the second component has burned out, the system will last $Y_1$
units of time. The remaining component is exponentially distributed
with parameter $\lambda$ . When the last component burns out, the system
will fail. Thus,

$$Pr(Y_1 < t) = 1 - Pr(Y_1 > t)$$

$$= 1 - \int_t^\infty \lambda e^{-\lambda x}\ dx$$

$$= 1 - e^{-\lambda t} .$$

We have found,

$$Pr(Y_3 < t) = 1 - e^{-\lambda t}$$

$$Pr(Y_2 < t) = 1 - e^{-\lambda t}$$

$$Pr(Y_1 < t) = 1 - e^{-\lambda t}$$

and

$$Y = Y_1 + Y_2 + Y_3 .$$

Differentiating with respect to $t$, we find that the probability
density functions of $Y_1$, $Y_2$, and $Y_3$ are identical and equal to
$\lambda e^{-\lambda t}$ . Thus, $Y_1$, $Y_2$ and $Y_3$ are each exponentially distributed with
parameter $\lambda$ .

To find the distribution of $Y = Y_1 + Y_2 + Y_3$ we use the moment
generating functions of $Y_1$, $Y_2$ and $Y_3$ and the fact that these
random variables are independent.

Let $M_Y(s)$ = the moment generating function of $Y$ and $M_{Y_1}(s)$, $M_{Y_2}(s)$, $M_{Y_3}(s)$ be the moment generating functions of $Y_1$, $Y_2$, $Y_3$ respectively.

By independence, and the fact that $Y = Y_1 + Y_2 + Y_3$ :

$$M_Y(s) = M_{Y_1}(s) \cdot M_{Y_2}(s) \cdot M_{Y_3}(s) .$$

For $i = 1,2,3$

$$M_{Y_i}(s) = E(e^{sT})$$

where $T$ is distributed exponentially with parameter $\lambda$ . Thus,

$$M_{Y_i}(s) = \int_0^\infty \lambda e^{st} e^{-\lambda t} \, dt$$

$$= \int_0^\infty \lambda e^{(s-\lambda)t} \, dt$$

$$= \int_0^\infty \frac{\lambda}{\lambda - s} (\lambda - s) e^{-(\lambda - s)t} \, dt ,$$

If $\lambda - s > 0$, $-(\lambda - s) < 0$ and

$$M_{Y_i}(s) = \frac{-\lambda}{\lambda - s} \int_0^\infty -(\lambda - s) e^{-(\lambda - s)t} \, dt$$

$$= \frac{-\lambda}{\lambda - s} e^{-(\lambda - s)t} \Big|_0^\infty \qquad = \frac{-\lambda}{\lambda - s} [0 - 1] \qquad = \frac{\lambda}{\lambda - s}$$

and so

$$M_Y(s) = \frac{\lambda}{\lambda - s} \cdot \frac{\lambda}{\lambda - s} \cdot \frac{\lambda}{\lambda - s} = \left[\frac{\lambda}{\lambda - s}\right]^3 .$$

The moment-generating function of $Y$ is that of the gamma distribution with parameters 3 and $\lambda$. Thus $Y$ is distributed with density function,

$$f(y) = \frac{\lambda^3}{\Gamma(3)} y^{3-1} e^{-\lambda y} \qquad \text{for } 0 \le y < \infty .$$

In the second situation, the lifetime of the system is the sum of the lifetimes of the three components. Each component is working separately, thus the lifetime of each component is distributed exponentially with parameter $\lambda$.

Let $Y = X_1 + X_2 + X_3$ , where $X_1, X_2$ and $X_3$ are the lifetimes of the individual components. Thus

$$M_Y(s) = M_{X_1}(s) \cdot M_{X_2}(s) \cdot M_{X_3}(s)$$

for the same reasons as before.

$M_{X_i}(s)$ = moment-generating function of a random variable exponentially distributed with parameter $\lambda$.

$$M_{X_i}(s) = \frac{\lambda}{\lambda - s} \quad \text{and hence}$$

$$M_Y(s) = \left[\frac{\lambda}{\lambda - s}\right]^3$$

which implies $Y$ has the gamma distribution with parameters $\lambda$ and 3. The appropriate density is again

$$f_Y(y) = \frac{\lambda^3}{\Gamma(3)} x^{3-1} e^{-\lambda} \qquad 0 < y < \infty .$$

and the distribution of the lifetime of this system is identical under (a) or (b).

● **PROBLEM 6-21**

Let $X$ be a random variable distributed normally with mean 0 and standard deviation 1. If $Y = X^2$ , find the density function of $Y$ using the cumulative distribution function technique.

**Solution:**  Let $F(y) = Pr(Y \le y) = Pr(X^2 \le y)$      $y > 0$ .

If $X^2 \le y$ , then either $0 < X \le \sqrt{y}$ or $-\sqrt{y} \le X < 0$ . Thus

$$F(y) = Pr(X^2 \le y) = Pr(-\sqrt{y} \le X \le \sqrt{y})$$

$$= Pr(-\sqrt{y} \le X < 0) + Pr(0 \le X \le \sqrt{y})$$

But by the symmetry of the standard normal distribution,

$$Pr(-\sqrt{y} \le X < 0) = Pr(0 \le X \le \sqrt{y})$$

Thus

$$F(y) = 2Pr(0 \le X \le \sqrt{y})$$

$$= 2 \int_0^{\sqrt{y}} \frac{1}{\sqrt{2\pi}} e^{-x^2/2} \, dx \qquad y > 0 .$$

Let $x = \sqrt{z}$ ; then $dx = \frac{1}{2} z^{-\frac{1}{2}} dz$ and when $x = 0, \sqrt{z} = x = 0$ .
When $x = \sqrt{y}, \sqrt{z} = \sqrt{y}$ or $z = y, \; y > 0$ .
Thus,

$$F(y) = \int_0^y \frac{2}{\sqrt{2\pi}} e^{-z/2} \cdot \frac{1}{2\sqrt{z}} \, dz$$

$$= \int_0^y \frac{(\frac{1}{2})^{-\frac{1}{2}} z^{-\frac{1}{2}} e^{-z/2}}{\sqrt{\pi}} \, dz.$$

But $\sqrt{\pi} = \Gamma(\frac{1}{2})$ and we recognize the integrand as the density function of a gamma distribution with parameters $\alpha = \frac{1}{2}$ and $\beta = \frac{1}{2}$ .

● **PROBLEM 6-22**

Suppose $X$ has density function:

$$f(X) = [\pi(1+X^2)]^{-1} \qquad -\infty < x < \infty .$$

If $Y = X^2$ , what is the density function of $Y$ ?

**Solution:**  We will use the cumulative distribution technique to find the distribution of $Y$.

$$Pr(Y \le y) = Pr(X^2 \le y) .$$

But $X^2$ has two inverses. If $X^2 = y$, then $X = \sqrt{y}$ and $X = -\sqrt{y}$.
Thus

$$Pr(X^2 \le y) = \begin{cases} Pr(-\sqrt{y} \le X \le \sqrt{y}) & \text{if } y \ge 0 \\ 0 & \text{if } y < 0. \end{cases}$$

To see that this is true, if $-\sqrt{y} \le X$ ,

$$(-\sqrt{y})(-\sqrt{y}) \ge (X)(X)$$

with the inequality reversed because there is multiplication by a negative number.

Thus,

$$(-\sqrt{y})(-\sqrt{y}) = (-1)^2 (\sqrt{y})^2 \ge X^2$$

or

$$y \ge X^2 .$$

Similarly,

$$X \le \sqrt{y}$$

implies

$$(X)(X) \le (\sqrt{y})(\sqrt{y})$$

or

$$X^2 \le y .$$

But

$$Pr(-\sqrt{y} \le X \le \sqrt{y}) = Pr(X \le \sqrt{y}) - Pr(X \le -\sqrt{y}) .$$

If $G(x) = Pr(X \le x)$, then

$$G(X) = \int_{-\infty}^{X} \frac{1}{\pi(1+t^2)} \, dt .$$

And

$$Pr(Y \le y) = G(\sqrt{y}) - G(-\sqrt{y}) .$$

We know that

$$\frac{dG}{dX} = f(x)$$

the density function by the fundamental theorem of calculus.

We also know by the Chain Rule that

$$\frac{dG(f(y))}{dy} = G'(f(y)) \frac{df(y)}{dy} .$$

Thus, differentiating the $Pr(Y \le y)$ with respect to $y$ gives the density function of $Y$ or

$$h(y) = \frac{d(Pr(Y \le y))}{dy} = \frac{d}{dy}\left[ G(\sqrt{y}) - G(-\sqrt{y}) \right]$$

$$= f(\sqrt{y}) \frac{d(\sqrt{y})}{dy} - f(-\sqrt{y}) \frac{d(-\sqrt{y})}{dy}$$

$$= f(\sqrt{y}) \frac{1}{2\sqrt{y}} - f(-\sqrt{y})\left(\frac{-1}{2\sqrt{y}}\right)$$

$$= \frac{1}{\pi(1+(\sqrt{y})^2)} \frac{1}{2\sqrt{y}} - \frac{1}{\pi(1+(-\sqrt{y})^2)} \left(\frac{-1}{2\sqrt{y}}\right)$$

$$= \frac{1}{\pi(1+y)}\left(\frac{1}{2\sqrt{y}}\right) + \frac{1}{\pi(1+y)}\left(\frac{1}{2\sqrt{y}}\right) .$$

Thus $h(y) = \begin{cases} \dfrac{1}{\pi\sqrt{y}\,(1+y)} & y > 0 \\ \\ 0 & \text{otherwise.} \end{cases}$

Suppose $X$ is uniformly distributed over the interval $[-\pi,\pi]$. Find the distribution of
a) $Y = \cos X$     b) $Y = \sin X$     c) $Y = |X|$ .

_Solution:_ The probability density function of $X$ is

$$f(x) = \begin{cases} \dfrac{1}{2\pi} & -\pi < x < \pi \\ 0 & \end{cases}$$

and the cumulative distribution of $X$ is

$$F(x) = \Pr(X \le x) = \int_{-\pi}^{x} \frac{1}{2\pi}\, dt = \frac{t}{2\pi}\Big|_{-\pi}^{x}$$

$$= \begin{cases} 0 & x < -\pi \\ \dfrac{x+\pi}{2\pi} & -\pi < x < \pi \\ 1 & x \ge \pi . \end{cases}$$

a) We will find the probability that $Y \le y$.

$$\Pr(Y \le y) = \Pr(\cos X \le y)$$

but over the interval $(-\pi,\pi)$ the cosine function is not one-to-one. For a single value of $y = \cos x$, there are two values of $x = \cos^{-1}y$. This can be seen from the graph below.
We also see from the graph that $\cos X \le y$ if and only if $\pi > X \ge \cos^{-1}y$ or $-\pi < X \le -\cos^{-1} y$.
Thus,

$$\Pr(Y \le y) = \Pr(\cos X \le y)$$

$$= \begin{cases} 0 & y < -1 \\ \Pr(\pi > X \ge \cos^{-1}y \text{ or} \\ \quad -\pi < X \le -\cos^{-1}y) & -1 < y < 1 \\ 1 & y > 1 \end{cases}$$

For $-1 < y < 1$,

$$\Pr(Y \le y) = \Pr(\pi > X \ge \cos^{-1}y \text{ or } -\pi < X \le -\cos^{-1}y)$$

$$= \Pr(\pi > X \ge \cos^{-1}y) + \Pr(-\pi < X \le -\cos^{-1}y)$$

$$= F(\pi) - F(\cos^{-1}y) + [F(-\cos^{-1}y) - F(-\pi)]$$

$$= 1 - F(\cos^{-1}y) + F(-\cos^{-1}y) - 0$$

$$= 1 - \frac{\cos^{-1}y + \pi}{2\pi} + \frac{-\cos^{-1}y + \pi}{2\pi} = \frac{2\pi - \cos^{-1}y - \pi - \cos^{-1}y + \pi}{2\pi}$$

$$= \frac{2\pi - 2\cos^{-1}y}{2\pi} = \frac{\pi - \cos^{-1}y}{\pi} .$$

Thus,

$$\Pr(Y \le y) = \begin{cases} 0 & y < -1 \\ 1 - \dfrac{\cos^{-1}y}{\pi} & -1 < y < 1 \\ 1 & y > 1 . \end{cases}$$

b) Let $G(u) = Pr(Y = \sin X \le u)$. Then

$$G(u) = Pr(\sin X \le u) = \begin{cases} 0 & u < -1 \\ ? & -1 < u < 1 \\ 1 & u > 1 . \end{cases}$$

If $-1 < u < 1$, there are two possibilities, $-1 < u < 0$, $0 < u < 1$. From the graph of the sine function we see that if $-1 \le u < 0$, then the values of $x$ for which $\sin x \le u$ are $-\pi - \sin^{-1}u \le X \le \sin^{-1}u$.

If $0 \le u \le 1$, then the values of $X$ for which $\sin X \le u$ are $\pi \ge X \ge \pi - \sin^{-1}u$ and $-\pi \le X \le \sin^{-1}u$. Thus,

$$Pr(\sin X \le u) = Pr(-\pi - \sin^{-1}u \le X \le \sin^{-1}u) \quad \text{for } -1 \le u < 0$$

and

$$Pr(\sin X \le u) = Pr(\pi \ge X \ge \pi - \sin^{-1}u \text{ or } -\pi \le X \le \sin^{-1}u)$$

$$\text{for } 0 \le u < 1 .$$

$$G(u) = F(\pi) - F(\pi - \sin^{-1}u) + [F(\sin^{-1}u) - F(-\pi)] \quad \text{for } 0 \le u < 1$$

and

$$G(u) = F(\sin^{-1}u) - F(-\pi - \sin^{-1}u) \quad \text{for } -1 \le u < 0.$$

For $0 \le u \le 1$,

$$G(u) = 1 - \left[\frac{\pi - \sin^{-1}u + \pi}{2\pi}\right] + \left[\frac{\sin^{-1}u + \pi}{2\pi} - 0\right]$$

$$= \frac{2\pi - (2\pi - \sin^{-1}u)}{2\pi} + \frac{\sin^{-1}u + \pi}{2\pi}$$

$$= \frac{\sin^{-1}u}{2\pi} + \frac{\sin^{-1}u + \pi}{2\pi} = \frac{2\sin^{-1}u + \pi}{2\pi}$$

and for $-1 \le u < 0$

$$G(u) = \frac{\sin^{-1}u + \pi}{2\pi} - \left[\frac{-\pi - \sin^{-1}u + \pi}{2\pi}\right] = \frac{2\sin^{-1}u + \pi}{2\pi} .$$

Thus,

$$G(u) = \begin{cases} 0 & u < -1 \\ \dfrac{2\sin^{-1}u + \pi}{2\pi} & -1 < u < 1 \\ 1 & u > 1 . \end{cases}$$

c) To find the distribution of $Y = |X|$, we find

$$H(y) = Pr(Y \le y)$$

$$= \begin{cases} 0 & y < 0 \\ Pr(|X| \le y) & \pi > y > 0 \\ 1 & y > \pi . \end{cases}$$

But $|X| \le y$ only if $-y \le X \le y$, thus for $\pi > y > 0$,

$$Pr(|X| \le y) = Pr(-y \le X \le y) = Pr(X \le y) - Pr(X \le -y)$$

$$= F(y) - F(-y) = \frac{y + \pi}{2\pi} - \left[\frac{-y + \pi}{2\pi}\right] = \frac{2y + \pi - \pi}{2\pi} = \frac{y}{\pi} .$$

And

$$H(y) = Pr(Y = |X| \le y) = \begin{cases} 0 & y < 0 \\ \dfrac{y}{\pi} & \pi > y > 0 \\ 1 & y > \pi . \end{cases}$$

Imagine a radioactive substance which emits radioactive particles. Assume that the number of emissions by time t,Y, is Poisson distributed with parameter $\beta t$, where $\beta > 0$ is the intensity of the radiation. What is distribution of the time of the 1st emission? What is the distribution of the time of the kth emission, where k is a positive integer?

Solution: The probability of j emissions in time t is

$$Pr(Y = j) = \frac{(\beta t)^j e^{-\beta t}}{j!} \qquad j = 0,1,2,\ldots$$

We can relate the probability that $Pr(Y \geq k)$ to the time of the kth emission, denoted by X.

$$Pr(X \leq t) = Pr(Y \geq k) .$$

That is, the time of the kth emission is less than or equal to t if and only if we observe k emissions or more in time interval t. Equivalently,

$$Pr(X \leq t) = 1 - Pr(Y \leq k-1) .$$

$$Pr(Y \leq k-1) = \sum_{j=0}^{k-1} \frac{(\beta t)^j e^{-\beta t}}{j!} .$$

Thus, the probability that $X \leq t$, where X is the time of the first emission is

$$Pr(X \leq t) = 1 - Pr(Y \leq 0)$$

$$= 1 - Pr(Y = 0)$$

$$= 1 - \frac{(\beta t)^0 e^{-\beta t}}{0!}$$

$$= 1 - e^{-\beta t} , \qquad \beta > 0 .$$

Thus the time of the first emission is distributed exponentially with parameter $\beta$.

The distribution of the kth emission is found from

$$F(t) = Pr(X \leq t) = 1 - Pr(Y \leq k-1) \qquad k = 2,3,\ldots$$

$$= 1 - \sum_{j=0}^{k-1} \frac{(\beta t)^j e^{-\beta t}}{j!} ,$$

And the density function of X is

$$\frac{dF}{dt} = -\frac{d}{dt} \left[ \sum_{j=0}^{k-1} \frac{(\beta t)^j e^{-\beta t}}{j!} \right]$$

$$= -\sum_{j=0}^{k-1} \frac{d}{dt} \frac{(\beta t)^j e^{-\beta t}}{j!}$$

Now $\frac{d}{dt}[(\beta t)^j e^{-\beta t}] = (\beta t)^j(-\beta e^{-\beta t}) + e^{-\beta t}(j(\beta t)^{j-1}\beta)$

$$= -\beta^{j+1} t^j e^{-\beta t} + j\beta^j t^{j-1} e^{-\beta t}$$

and so

$$\frac{dF}{dt} = -\sum_{j=0}^{k-1} \frac{[-\beta^{j+1}t^j e^{-\beta t} + j\beta^j t^{j-1} e^{-\beta t}]}{j!} .$$

$$f(t) = \sum_{j=0}^{k-1} \frac{\beta^{j+1} t^j e^{-\beta t}}{j!} - \sum_{j=0}^{k-1} \frac{j\beta^j t^{j-1} e^{-\beta t}}{j!} \; .$$

Compare the ith term in the second sum with the (i-1)st term in the first sum. These are:

$$\frac{i\beta^i t^{i-1} e^{-\beta t}}{i!}$$

and

$$\frac{\beta^{(i-1)+1} t^{(i-1)} e^{-\beta t}}{(i-1)!} = \frac{i\beta^i t^{i-1} e^{-\beta t}}{i!} \; ,$$

Thus the 1st term in the second sum cancels the 0th term in the 1st sum. The 2nd term in the second sum cancels the 1st term in 1st sum. This "telescoping" sum leaves only the (k-1)st term in the first sum and the 0th term in the second sum.

Thus,

$$f(t) = \frac{\beta^{(k-1)+1} t^{k-1} e^{-\beta t}}{(k-1)!} + \frac{0 \cdot \beta^0 t^{0-1} e^{-\beta t}}{o!} \; ;$$

$$f(t) = \frac{\beta^k t^{k-1} e^{-\beta t}}{(k-1)!} + 0 \qquad\qquad \text{for } \; t > 0$$
$$\beta > 0$$
$$k > 0 \; .$$

Thus the time of the kth emission is gamma distributed with parameters $\alpha = k-1$ and $\beta > 0$.

● **PROBLEM** 6-25

Let X and Y be independent, standard normal random variables, and let $R = \sqrt{X^2 + Y^2}$ be the distance of $(X,Y)$ from $(0,0)$. Find the distribution of R.

**Solution:** We shall find the distribution of R by quoting some of the previous results from problems in this chapter.

The random variables $X^2$ and $Y^2$ are independent and both are distributed with a Chi-square distribution with 1 degree of freedom. The density function of $X^2$ and $Y^2$ is

$$f(x) = \frac{1}{2^{\frac{1}{2}} \Gamma(\frac{1}{2})} x^{\frac{1}{2}-1} e^{-x/2} \qquad x > 0 \; .$$

$X^2 + Y^2$ must then be Chi-square distributed with two degrees of freedom. Thus $X^2 + Y^2$ has density,

$$f(x) = \frac{1}{\Gamma(1)} (\tfrac{1}{2})^{2/2} w^{2/2-1} e^{-\frac{1}{2}x} \qquad x > 0$$

$$= \tfrac{1}{2} e^{-\frac{1}{2}x} \qquad x > 0 \; .$$

An exponential density function, $X^2 + Y^2$ is exponentially distributed with parameter $\beta = \frac{1}{2}$.

$R = \sqrt{X^2 + Y^2}$ is the square root of an exponentially distributed random variable. We have shown that such a random variable is dis-

tributed with a Weibull distribution with parameters  a = 1, b = 2.
Thus  R  has density

$$h(r) = 2re^{-r^2} \qquad\qquad r > 0.$$

# CONVOLUTIONS

● **PROBLEM** 6-26

Let  X  and  Y  be jointly distributed continuous random variables with
density  f(x,y).  If  Z = X + Y, find the density function of  Z.

<u>Solution</u>: We will use the cumulative distribution function technique
and integrate to find

$$Pr(Z \le z) = Pr(X+Y \le z)$$

$$= \int\int\limits_{x+y<z} f(x,y)dx\, dy.$$

The range of integration is over the shaded region in the  x,y
plane, i.e., all x,y  such that x + y < z.

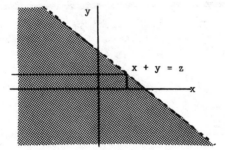

To represent this integral as an iterated integral, we fix  y
and then integrate with respect to  x  from  z-y  to  -∞ .  Next
integrate with respect to  y  from  -∞  to  ∞.  Thus

$$Pr(Z \le z) = Pr(X+Y \le z)$$

$$= \int\int\limits_{x+y<z} f(x,y)dx\, dy$$

$$= \int_{-\infty}^{\infty} \left[ \int_{-\infty}^{z-y} f(x,y)dx \right] dy.$$

Let  u = x+y;  for fixed  y,  du = dx .  If  y  is fixed then when
x = z-y, u = z.  Thus

$$= \int_{-\infty}^{\infty} \left[ \int_{-\infty}^{z} f(u-y,y)du \right] dy$$

We assume that f(x,y) has continuous partial derivatives. Therefore
we exchange the order of integration and

$$F(z) = Pr(Z \le z) = \int_{-\infty}^{z} \left[ \int_{-\infty}^{\infty} f(u-y,y)dy \right] du$$

Differentiating with respect to  z  will yield the density function of the random variable  Z.  Hence,

$$\frac{dF}{dz} = \frac{d}{dz} \left[ \int_{-\infty}^{z} \left( \int_{-\infty}^{\infty} f(u-y,y)dy \right) du \right]$$

$$= \int_{-\infty}^{\infty} f(z-y,y) \ dy$$

This integral is called a convolution.  Thus the density function
of  z  is
$$\int_{-\infty}^{\infty} f(z-y,y) \ dy \ .$$

● **PROBLEM**  6-27

Let  X  and  Y  be independent, exponentially distributed random
variables  with densities

$$f(x) = \beta e^{-\beta x} \qquad\qquad x > 0$$

$$g(y) = \beta e^{-\beta y} \qquad\qquad y > 0 \ .$$

Find the density function of  Z = X + Y.

_Solution:_  We have shown that the density of a sum of two random
variables with joint density given as  $\xi(x,y)$  is the convolution  of
X  and  Y.  The density of  Z = X + Y  is

$$h(z) = \int_{-\infty}^{\infty} \xi(x,z-x)dx \ .$$

In this problem,

$$\xi(x,y) = f(x)g(y) = (\beta e^{-\beta x})(\beta e^{-\beta y}) \quad \text{for} \quad x,y > 0 \ .$$

Hence,

$$h(z) = \int_{-\infty}^{\infty} \beta e^{-\beta x} \ \beta e^{-\beta(z-x)} dx$$

but if  x < 0 ,  h(z) = 0  and if  z-x < 0, or  x > z,  h(z) = 0.  Thus
h(z)  reduces to

$$h(z) = \int_{0}^{z} \beta e^{-\beta x} \ \beta e^{-\beta(z-x)} dx \qquad\qquad z > 0 \ .$$

$$h(z) = \int_{0}^{z} \beta^2 e^{-\beta x} \ e^{\beta x} \ e^{-\beta z} \ dz \qquad\qquad z > 0$$

$$= \beta^2 e^{-\beta z} \int_{0}^{z} dx \qquad\qquad z > 0$$

$$= \frac{\beta^2 \ z^{2-1} \ e^{-\beta z}}{1!} \qquad\qquad z > 0 \ .$$

We recognize  h(z)  as the probability density function of a gamma
distributed random variable with parameters  $\alpha = 2$  and  $\beta$ .

● **PROBLEM**  6-28

Show by the convolution technique that  Z = X + Y, where  X  and  Y
are two independent standard normal random variables, is normally
distributed with mean  0  and variance  2.

<u>Solution</u>: If  X  and  Y  are two independent standard normal random variables, then each has respective density

$$f(x) = \frac{1}{\sqrt{2\pi}} \, e^{-x^2/2} \qquad\qquad -\infty < x < \infty$$

and

$$g(y) = \frac{1}{\sqrt{2\pi}} \, e^{-y^2/2} \qquad\qquad -\infty < y < \infty \, .$$

The joint density of  X  and  Y  is  $f(x)g(y)$.

Thus the density function of  $Z = X + Y$  is

$$h(z) = \int_{-\infty}^{\infty} f(x)g(z-x)\,dx$$

$$= \int_{-\infty}^{\infty} \frac{1}{\sqrt{2\pi}} \, e^{-x^2/2} \, \frac{1}{\sqrt{2\pi}} \, e^{-(z-x)^2/2} \, dx$$

$$= \int_{-\infty}^{\infty} \frac{1}{2\pi} \, e^{-(z-x)^2/2 \, - \, x^2/2} \, dx$$

$$= \int_{-\infty}^{\infty} \frac{1}{2\pi} \, e^{-(z^2-2zx+x^2)/2 \, - \, x^2/2} \, dx \, .$$

But the exponent is

$$\frac{-z^2 + 2zx - x^2 - x^2}{2}$$

$$= -\frac{z^2}{2} - (x^2 - zx)$$

$$= -\frac{z^2}{2} - \left(x^2 - zx + \frac{z^2}{4}\right) + \frac{z^2}{4}$$

$$= -\frac{z^2}{4} - (x - \frac{z}{2})^2 \, .$$

Thus

$$h(z) = \frac{1}{\sqrt{2\pi}} \, e^{-z^2/4} \int_{-\infty}^{\infty} \frac{1}{\sqrt{2\pi}} \, e^{-(x-z/2)^2} \, dx$$

$$= \frac{1}{\sqrt{2\pi}} \, e^{-z^2/4} \cdot \frac{\sqrt{\frac{1}{2}}}{\sqrt{\frac{1}{2}}} \int_{-\infty}^{\infty} \frac{1}{\sqrt{2\pi}} \, e^{-(x-z/2)^2} \, dx$$

$$= \frac{1}{\sqrt{2}\sqrt{2\pi}} \, e^{-z^2/4} \int_{-\infty}^{\infty} \frac{1}{\sqrt{\frac{1}{2}}\sqrt{2\pi}} \, e^{-(x-z/2)^2} \, dx \, .$$

But

$$\nu(x) = \frac{1}{\sqrt{\frac{1}{2}}\sqrt{2\pi}} \, e^{-(x-z/2)^2} \quad \text{is}$$

the density function of a normal random variable with mean  $z/2$  and variance  $\frac{1}{2}$.  Thus

$$\int_{-\infty}^{\infty} \nu(x)\,dx = 1$$

and

$$h(z) = \frac{1}{\sqrt{2}\sqrt{2\pi}} \, e^{-z^2/4} \qquad\qquad -\infty < z < \infty \, .$$

$h(z)$  is the density function of a normally distributed random variable with mean  0  and variance  $(\sqrt{2})^2 = 2$.

# MULTIVARIATE FUNCTIONS

Suppose  X  and  Y  are independent random variables with densities
f(x)  and  g(y).  If  Z = XY, what is the density of  Z?

Solution:  We will use the cumulative distribution function technique.
Let

$$F(z) = Pr(Z \le z) = Pr(XY \le z)$$

$$= \int \int_{xy \le z} f(x)g(y)dx\ dy$$

The range of integration, that is, the region of the  x,y-plane
where  xy ≤ z  is the shaded region below.

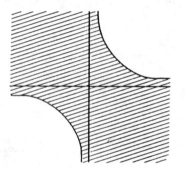

Dividing this region along the y-axis we compute our integral as
the sum of two integrals.

$$Pr(Z \le z) = \int \int_{0 < xy < z} f(x,y)dy\ dx + \int \int_{xy < 0 < z} f(x,y)dy\ dx .$$

$$\int \int_{0 < xy < z} f(x,y)dy\ dx = \int_0^\infty \left[ \int_{-\infty}^{z/x} f(x)g(y)dy \right] dx$$

and

$$\int \int_{xy < 0 < z} f(x,y)dy\ dx = \int_{-\infty}^0 \left[ \int_{z/x}^\infty f(x)g(y)dy \right] dx .$$

Let  $z_1 = xy$   if  x > 0, y > 0; then for fixed  x, $y = z_1/x$ , $dy = dz_1/x$ .
When  $y = z/x$ , $z_1 = z$; when  $y = \infty$ , $z_1 = \infty$. If  x < 0, y < 0  then for
fixed  x , $y = z_1/x$ , $dy = dz_1/x$. When  $y = z/x$, $z_1 = z$  and when  $y = \infty$,
$z_1 = -\infty$ .

The last statement is true because  x < 0.
Substituting yields

$$Pr(Z \le z) = \int_0^\infty \left[ \int_{-\infty}^z f(x)g\left(\frac{z_1}{x}\right) \frac{dz_1}{x} \right] dx$$

$$+ \int_{-\infty}^0 \left[ \int_z^{-\infty} f(x)g\left(\frac{z_1}{x}\right) \frac{dz_1}{x} \right] dx = \int_{-\infty}^z \left[ \int_0^\infty f(x)g\left(\frac{z_1}{x}\right) \frac{dx}{x} \right] dz_1$$

$$+ \int_z^{-\infty} \left[ \int_{-\infty}^0 f(x)g\left(\frac{z_1}{x}\right) \frac{dx}{x} \right] dz_1 = \int_{-\infty}^z \left[ \int_0^\infty f(x)g\left(\frac{z_1}{x}\right) \frac{dx}{x} \right] dz_1$$

$$+ \int_{-\infty}^{z} \left[ \int_{-\infty}^{0} f(x)g\left(\frac{z_1}{x}\right)\left(-\frac{dx}{x}\right)\right] dz_1$$

Differentiating with respect to  $z$  and invoking the fundamental theorem, the density of  $Z$  is

$$h(z) = \int_{0}^{\infty} f(x)g\left(\frac{z}{x}\right)\frac{dx}{x} + \int_{-\infty}^{0} f(x)g\left(\frac{z}{x}\right)\frac{dx}{-x} \, .$$

But we see when  $x > 0$  the integrand is  $f(x)g(z/x)\,dx/x$  and when  $x < 0$  it is  $f(x)g(z/x)\,dx/-x$ . This recalls the absolute value function which is defined as

$$|x| = \begin{cases} x & x > 0 \\ -x & x < 0 \end{cases} .$$

Substituting,

$$h(z) = \int_{-\infty}^{\infty} \frac{1}{|x|} f(x) \, g\left(\frac{z}{x}\right) \, dx \, .$$

● **PROBLEM** 6-30

Suppose that  $X_1$  and  $X_2$  are independent random variables each uniformly distributed over the interval  $(0,1)$ . Let the random variables  $Y_1$  and  $Y_2$  be defined as

$$Y_1 = X_1 + X_2$$

$$Y_2 = X_2 - X_1 \, .$$

Find the joint density function of  $(Y_1, Y_2)$ .

Solution: This transformation between a point  $(X_1, X_2)$  and a point  $(Y_1, Y_2)$ , maps region  1  to region  2  and is pictured below.

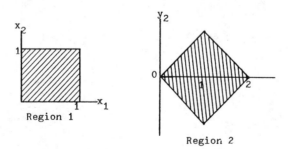

Region 1

Region 2

This transformation is one-to-one. That is, for a single point in region  1  there corresponds a single point in region  2 . Also, to a single point in region  2  there corresponds a single point in region  1 .

Let  A  be a subset of region  1  and  B  be a subset of region  2 .

$$\Pr[(X_1, X_2) \in A] = \int\int_A f(x_1, x_2)dx_1 \, dx_2 \, ,$$

where  $f(x_1, x_2)$  is the joint density of  $X_1$  and  $X_2$ . If we are given functions $u_1(x_1,x_2) = y_1$ and $u_2(x_1,x_2) = y_2$ and $u_1$ and $u_2$ together define a one-to-one mapping from $(X_1,X_2)$ to $(Y_1,Y_2)$, then there exist inverse functions such that

$$w_1(y_1,y_2) = x_1 \quad \text{and} \quad w_2(y_1,y_2) = x_2 \ .$$

We wish to find

$$\Pr((Y_1,Y_2) \in B) = \int\limits_B \int g(y_1,y_2) \ dy_1 \ dy_2$$

and hence $g(y_1,y_2)$, the joint density of $Y_1$ and $Y_2$ .

To find $\Pr((Y_1,Y_2) \in B)$, we will transform $\Pr[(X_1,X_2) \in A]$ by mapping A to B, under the transformations $u_1(x_1,x_2)$ and $u_2(x_1,x_2)$. Thus,

$$\Pr((X_1,X_2) \in A) = \int\limits_A \int f(x_1,x_2) \ dx_1 \ dx_2$$

$$= \int\limits_B \int g(y_1,y_2) \ dy_1 \ dy_2$$

because $(X_1,X_2) \in A$ and $(Y_1,Y_2) \in B$ are equivalent events under the one-to-one mapping from $(X_1,X_2)$ to $(Y_1,Y_2)$.

We are interested in changing variables in

$$\int\limits_A \int f(x_1,x_2) \ dx_1 \ dx_2$$

to transform it to

$$\int\limits_B \int g(y_1,y_2) \ dy_1 \ dy_2 \ .$$

This is a change of variable problem and a result from advanced calculus gives

$$\int\limits_A \int f(x_1,x_2) \ dx_1 \ dx_2 = \int\limits_B \int [f(w_1(y_1,y_2),w_2(y_1,y_2)) \times |J| dy_1 \ dy_2]$$

where $|J|$ is the absolute value of the determinant of the Jacobian matrix, defined by

$$J = \det \begin{bmatrix} \dfrac{\partial w_1}{\partial y_1} & \dfrac{\partial w_1}{\partial y_2} \\[2ex] \dfrac{\partial w_2}{\partial y_1} & \dfrac{\partial w_2}{\partial y_2} \end{bmatrix} \ .$$

Thus the joint density of $Y_1$ and $Y_2$ is

$$g(y_1,y_2) = f(w_1(y_1,y_2) \ , \ w_2(y_1,y_2)) \ |J| \ .$$

To find the joint density of $Y_1, Y_2$ for this problem we find the inverse functions $w_1(y_1,y_2) = x_1$ and $w_2(y_1,y_2) = x_2$ .

We are given

$$Y_1 = X_1 + X_2$$

and
$$Y_2 = X_2 - X_1 .$$

Adding these two equations and dividing by 2 gives
$$X_2 = \tfrac{1}{2}(Y_1 + Y_2) .$$

Subtracting the two equations and dividing by two gives
$$X_1 = \tfrac{1}{2}(Y_1 - Y_2) .$$

Thus,
$$w_1(y_1, y_2) = \tfrac{1}{2}(y_1 - y_2)$$
and
$$w_2(y_1, y_2) = \tfrac{1}{2}(y_1 + y_2)$$

$$\frac{\partial w_1}{\partial y_1} = \frac{\partial w_2}{\partial y_2} = \frac{\partial w_2}{\partial y_1} = \frac{1}{2}$$
and
$$\frac{\partial w_1}{\partial y_2} = -\frac{1}{2} .$$

Thus,
$$J = \begin{bmatrix} \frac{1}{2} & -\frac{1}{2} \\ \frac{1}{2} & \frac{1}{2} \end{bmatrix}$$

and
$$\left| \det J \right| = \left| (\tfrac{1}{2})^2 - (-\tfrac{1}{2})(\tfrac{1}{2}) \right| = \left| \tfrac{1}{4} + \tfrac{1}{4} \right| = \tfrac{1}{2} .$$

The joint density of $X_1$ and $X_2$ is
$$f(x_1 x_2) = \nu(x_1)h(x_2) = \begin{cases} 1 & \begin{matrix} 0 < x_1 < 1 \\ 0 < x_2 < 1 \end{matrix} \\ 0 & \text{otherwise} \end{cases}$$

where $\nu$ and $h$ are the densities of $X_1$ and $X_2$ respectively.

Thus the joint density of $y_1$ and $y_2$ is
$$g(y_1, y_2) = f(w_1(y_1, y_2), w_2(y_1, y_2)) |J|$$
$$= \nu(w_1(y_1, y_2))h(w_2(y_1, y_2)) |J|$$

$$= \begin{cases} \tfrac{1}{2} & \text{if } \begin{matrix} 0 < \tfrac{1}{2}(y_1 - y_2) < 1 \text{ or} \\ 0 < \tfrac{1}{2}(y_1 + y_2) < 1 \end{matrix} \\ 0 & \text{otherwise} \end{cases}$$

or
$$g(y_1, y_2) = \begin{cases} \tfrac{1}{2} & \text{if } \begin{matrix} 0 < y_1 < 2 \\ -1 < y_2 < 1 \end{matrix} \\ 0 & \text{otherwise} . \end{cases}$$

● **PROBLEM 6-31**

If $X_1$ and $X_2$ are two independent standard normal random variables and $Y_1 = X_1 + X_2$, $Y_2 = X_1/X_2$, find the density function of $Y_2$.

<u>Solution</u>:   We will first find the joint density of $Y_1, Y_2$ and then integrate with respect to $Y_1$ to find the marginal density of $Y_2$. The density functions of $x_1$ and $x_2$ are:

$$f_1(x_1) = \frac{1}{\sqrt{2\pi}} e^{-x_1^2/2} \qquad -\infty < x_1 < \infty$$

and

$$f_2(x_2) = \frac{1}{\sqrt{2\pi}} e^{-x_2^2/2} \qquad -\infty < x_2 < \infty .$$

By the independence of $X_1$ and $X_2$, the joint density of $X_1$ and $X_2$ is the product of the individual densities or

$$f(x_1,x_2) = f_1(x_1) f_2(x_2) = \frac{1}{2\pi} e^{-(x_1^2 + x_2^2)/2} \qquad -\infty < x_1, x_2 < \infty .$$

The transformation mapping $(X_1, X_2)$ to $(Y_1, Y_2)$ is one-to-one, hence invertible. We may solve for $Y_1$ and $Y_2$ in terms of $X_1$ and $X_2$. $X_1 = X_2 Y_2$ and $Y_1 = X_1 + X_2$, thus $Y_1 = X_2 Y_2 + X_2$ or

$$X_2 = \frac{Y_1}{Y_2 + 1}$$

Similarly, $X_2 = \dfrac{X_1}{Y_2}$ and thus $Y_1 = X_1 + \dfrac{X_1}{Y_2}$ or

$$X_1 = \frac{Y_1}{1 + 1/Y_2} = \frac{Y_1 Y_2}{1 + Y_2} .$$

Let

$$w_1(y_1, y_2) = \frac{y_1 y_2}{1 + y_2} = x_1 \quad \text{and} \quad w_2(y_1, y_2) = \frac{y_1}{1 + y_2} = x_2 .$$

The Jacobian matrix of this transformation is

$$J = \begin{bmatrix} \dfrac{\partial w_1}{\partial y_1} & \dfrac{\partial w_1}{\partial y_2} \\[2em] \dfrac{\partial w_2}{\partial y_1} & \dfrac{\partial w_2}{\partial y_2} \end{bmatrix} .$$

In this case,

$$\frac{\partial w_1}{\partial y_1} = \frac{y_2}{(1 + y_2)}$$

$$\frac{\partial w_1}{\partial y_2} = \frac{y_1}{(1 + y_2)^2}$$

$$\frac{\partial w_2}{\partial y_1} = \frac{1}{1 + y_2}, \quad \frac{\partial w_2}{\partial y_2} = \frac{-y_1}{(1 + y_2)^2}$$

and

$$|\det J| = \left| \left( \frac{y_2}{1 + y_2} \right) \left( \frac{-y_1}{(1 + y_2)^2} \right) - \left( \frac{y_1}{(1 + y_2)^2} \right) \left( \frac{1}{1 + y_2} \right) \right|$$

$$= \left| \frac{-y_1 y_2 - y_1}{(1 + y_2)^3} \right| = \left| \frac{-y_1(1 + y_2)}{(1 + y_2)^3} \right| = \frac{|y_1|}{(1 + y_2)^2} .$$

The joint density of $Y_1$ and $Y_2$ is

$$g(y_1,y_2) = f(w_1(y_1,y_2), w_2(y_1,y_2)) \, |J|$$

$$= f_1(w_1(y_1,y_2)) \, f_2(w_2(y_1,y_2)) \, |J|$$

$$= \frac{1}{\sqrt{2\pi}} \, e^{-\frac{1}{2}\left(\frac{y_1 y_2}{1+y_2}\right)} \cdot \frac{1}{\sqrt{2\pi}} \, e^{-\frac{1}{2}\left(\frac{y_1}{1+y_2}\right)^2} \cdot \frac{|y_1|}{(1+y_2)^2}$$

$$g(y_1,y_2) = \frac{1}{2\pi} \cdot \frac{|y_1|}{(1+y_2)^2} \cdot e^{-\frac{1}{2}\left[\frac{(y_1 y_2)^2 + y_1^2}{(1+y_2)^2}\right]}$$

$$= \frac{|y_1|}{2\pi(1+y_2)^2} \cdot e^{-\frac{1}{2}\left[\frac{(1+y_2^2)y_1^2}{(1+y_2)^2}\right]}$$

for $-\infty < y_1, y_2 < \infty$.

We wish to find the marginal distribution of $Y_2$; we have

$$g_2(y_2) = \int_{-\infty}^{\infty} g(y_1,y_2) \, dy_1$$

$$= \int_{-\infty}^{\infty} \frac{|y_1|}{2\pi(1+y_2)^2} \exp\left\{-\frac{1}{2} \frac{(1+y_2^2)y_1^2}{(1+y_2)^2}\right\} dy_1 .$$

Let
$$u = \frac{1}{2} \frac{(1+y_2^2)y_1^2}{(1+y_2)^2} \quad \text{then}$$

$$du = \frac{(1+y_2^2)}{(1+y_2)^2} y_1 \, dy_1$$

and

$$\int_0^{\infty} \frac{|y_1|}{2\pi(1+y_2)^2} \exp\left\{-\frac{1}{2} \frac{(1+y_2^2)y_1^2}{(1+y_2)^2}\right\} dy_1$$

$$= \int_0^{\infty} \frac{y_1}{2\pi(1+y_2)^2} \exp\left\{-\frac{1}{2} \frac{(1+y_2^2)y_1^2}{(1+y_2)^2}\right\} dy_1$$

$$= \frac{1}{2\pi(1+y_2^2)} \int_0^{\infty} \frac{(1+y_2^2)y_1}{(1+y_2)^2} \exp\{-u\} \, dy_1$$

$$= \frac{1}{2\pi(1+y_2^2)} \int_0^{\infty} e^{-u} \, du .$$

If $y_1 < 0$, $|y_1| = -y$ ; let $u = -\frac{1}{2}\frac{(1+y_2^2)y_1^2}{(1+y_2)^2}$ then

$$du = \frac{-y_1(1+y_2^2)}{(1+y_2)^2} \, dy_1$$

and

$$\int_{-\infty}^{0} \frac{-y_1}{2\pi(1+y_2)^2} \exp\left\{-\frac{1}{2} \frac{(1+y_2^2)y_1^2}{(1+y_2)^2}\right\} dy_1$$

$$= \frac{1}{2\pi(1+y_2^2)} \int_{-\infty}^{0} e^{u} \, du .$$

Thus,
$$g_2(y_2) = \frac{1}{2\pi(1+y_2^2)} \left[ \int_0^{\infty} e^{-u} \, du + \int_{-\infty}^{0} e^{u} \, du \right]$$

$$= \frac{1}{2\pi(1+y_2^2)}\left[-e^{-u}\Big|_0^\infty + e^u\Big|_{-\infty}^0\right]$$

$$= \frac{1}{2\pi(1+y_2^2)}\left[1 + 1\right]$$

$$= \frac{1}{\pi(1+y_2^2)} \qquad -\infty < y_2 < \infty \ .$$

Consider a probability distribution for random orientations in which the probability of an observation in a region on the surface of the unit hemisphere is proportional to the area of that region. Two angles, u and v, will determine the position of an observation.

It can be shown that the position of an observation is jointly distributed with density function

$$f(u,v) = \frac{\sin u}{2\pi} \qquad \begin{array}{l} 0 < v < 2\pi \\ 0 < u < \pi/2 \ . \end{array}$$

Two new variables, X and Y are defined, where

$$X = \sin u \cos v$$
$$Y = \sin u \sin v.$$

Find the joint density function of X and Y.

**Solution:** In the region $0 < u < \pi/2$ and $0 < v < 2\pi$ this transformation is one-to-one and the mapping is pictured below.

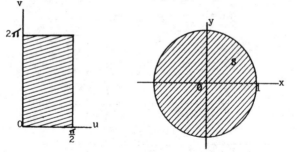

We now find u and v in terms of x and y. Let

$$x^2 = \sin^2 u \cos^2 v$$
$$y^2 = \sin^2 u \sin^2 v \ ;$$

adding we see that

$$x^2 + y^2 = \sin^2 u(\cos^2 v + \sin^2 v)$$
$$= \sin^2 u$$

Thus $\sin u = \sqrt{x^2+y^2}$ and $u = \sin^{-1}\left[\sqrt{x^2+y^2}\right]$.

Also $\dfrac{y}{x} = \dfrac{\sin u \sin v}{\sin u \cos v} = \sin v/\cos v = \tan v.$

Hence

$$v = \tan^{-1}\frac{y}{x} \ .$$

The Jacobian of the original transformation is

$$\frac{\partial(u,v)}{\partial(x,y)} = \frac{1}{\dfrac{\partial(x,y)}{\partial(u,v)}} \ .$$

Thus we find,

$$\frac{\partial(x,y)}{\partial(u,v)} = \begin{bmatrix} \dfrac{\partial x}{\partial u} & \dfrac{\partial x}{\partial v} \\[2mm] \dfrac{\partial y}{\partial u} & \dfrac{\partial y}{\partial v} \end{bmatrix}$$

$$= \left| \det \begin{pmatrix} \cos u \cos v & -\sin u \sin v \\ \sin v \cos u & \cos v \sin u \end{pmatrix} \right|$$

$$= \left| \cos^2 v (\cos u)(\sin u) + \sin^2 v (\cos u)(\sin u) \right|$$

$$= \left| (\cos u)(\sin u) \right|$$

Thus

$$\frac{\partial(u,v)}{\partial(x,y)} = \left[ (\cos u)(\sin u) \right]^{-1}.$$

The joint density of $X$ and $Y$ is

$$g(x,y) = f\!\left( \sin^{-1}(\sqrt{x^2+y^2}),\ \tan^{-1} \frac{y}{x} \right) \cdot \frac{\partial(u,v)}{\partial(x,y)}$$

$$= \frac{\sin\!\left[ \sin^{-1}\sqrt{x^2+y^2} \right]}{2\pi} \cdot \frac{1}{(\cos u)(\sin u)}$$

$$= \frac{\sqrt{x^2+y^2}}{2\pi} \cdot \frac{1}{(\cos u)(\sin u)}$$

But $\sin^2 u = X^2 + Y^2$; thus

$$1 - \cos^2 u = X^2 + Y^2$$

or

$$\cos u = \sqrt{1 - (X^2 + Y^2)}$$

and

$$\sin u = \sqrt{X^2 + Y^2}\,.$$

Thus

$$g(x,y) = \frac{1}{2\pi\sqrt{1-(x^2+y^2)}} \quad \text{for } x^2 + y^2 < 1$$

is the joint density of $X$ and $Y$.

● **PROBLEM 6-33**

Let $X_1$, $X_2$ and $X_3$ be independent standard normal random variables. Define

$$Y_1 = X_1$$

$$Y_2 = \frac{X_1 + X_2}{2}$$

$$Y_3 = \frac{X_1 + X_2 + X_3}{3}\,.$$

Find the marginal distribution of $Y_3$.

Solution: The joint density of the $X_i$ will be

$$f(x_1, x_2, x_3) = \left( \frac{1}{\sqrt{2\pi}} \right)^3 e^{\frac{-(x_1^2 + x_2^2 + x_3^2)}{2}} \qquad -\infty < x_i < \infty$$
$$i = 1,2,3.$$

This is the product of three standard normal density functions.
The transformation of $(X_1, X_2, X_3)$ to $(Y_1, Y_2, Y_3)$ is a one-to-one transformation and the inverse transformation, is

$$X_1 = Y_1$$
$$X_2 = 2Y_2 - Y_1$$
$$X_3 = 3Y_3 - 2Y_2$$

The Jacobian of the inverse transformation is

$$|J| = \det \begin{pmatrix} \dfrac{\partial x_1}{\partial y_1} & \dfrac{\partial x_1}{\partial y_2} & \dfrac{\partial x_1}{\partial y_3} \\[2mm] \dfrac{\partial x_2}{\partial y_1} & \dfrac{\partial x_2}{\partial y_2} & \dfrac{\partial x_2}{\partial y_3} \\[2mm] \dfrac{\partial x_3}{\partial y_1} & \dfrac{\partial x_3}{\partial y_2} & \dfrac{\partial x_3}{\partial y_3} \end{pmatrix}$$

$$= \det \begin{vmatrix} 1 & 0 & 0 \\ -1 & 2 & 0 \\ 0 & -2 & 3 \end{vmatrix}$$

$$= |3 \cdot 2 \cdot 1| = 6 .$$

Thus the joint density function of $Y_1, Y_2, Y_3$ is

$$g(y_1, y_2, y_3) = f(y_1, 2y_2 - y_1, 3y_3 - 2y_2) |J|$$

$$= 6\left(\frac{1}{\sqrt{2\pi}}\right)^3 \exp\left\{\frac{-[y_1^2 + (2y_2 - y_1)^2 + (3y_3 - 2y_2)^2]}{2}\right\} .$$

But

$$-[y_1^2 + 4y_2^2 - 4y_1 y_2 + y_1^2 + 9y_3^2 - 12y_2 y_3 + 4y_2^2]$$

$$= -[2y_1^2 - 4y_1 y_2 + 8y_2^2 - 12y_2 y_3 + 9y_3^2] .$$

We obtain the marginal distributions of $y_1, y_2, y_3$ by integrating. The marginal distribution of $Y_3$ is

$$f_3(y_3) = \int \int_{-\infty}^{\infty} g(y_1, y_2, y_3)\, dy_1\, dy_2$$

$$= 6 \left(\frac{1}{\sqrt{2\pi}}\right)^3 \left[\int_{-\infty}^{\infty} e^{-\frac{1}{2}(8y_2^2 - 12y_2 y_3 + 9y_3^2)}\left(\int_{-\infty}^{\infty} e^{-\frac{1}{2}(2y_1^2 - 4y_1 y_2)}\, dy_1\right) dy_2\right]$$

but

$$\int_{-\infty}^{\infty} e^{-\frac{1}{2}(2y_1^2 - 4y_1 y_2)}\, dy_1 = \int_{-\infty}^{\infty} e^{y_2^2 - [y_1^2 - 2y_1 y_2 + y_2^2]}\, dy_1$$

$$= e^{y_2^2} \int_{-\infty}^{\infty} e^{-(y_1 - y_2)^2}\, dy_1$$

$$= e^{y_2^2} (\sqrt{2\pi})\sqrt{\tfrac{1}{2}} = e^{y_2^2} \sqrt{\pi}$$

because

$$\int_{-\infty}^{\infty} \frac{e^{-\dfrac{(y_1-y_2)^2}{2(\frac{1}{2})}}}{\sqrt{\tfrac{1}{2}} \cdot \sqrt{2\pi}}\, dy_1 = 1 .$$

Thus

$$f_3(y_3) = 6\left(\frac{1}{\sqrt{2\pi}}\right)^3 \cdot \sqrt{\pi} \int_{-\infty}^{\infty} e^{-\frac{1}{2}[8y_2^2 - 12y_2 y_3 + 9y_3^2] + y_2^2}\, dy_2 ;$$

but

$$-\tfrac{1}{2}[8y_2^2 - 12y_2 y_3 + 9y_3^2] + y_2^2 = -\tfrac{1}{2}[6y_2^2 - 12y_2 y_3 + 6y_3^2] - \tfrac{3}{2}y_3^2 .$$

And

$$f_3(y_3) = \frac{6}{\sqrt{2}}\left(\frac{1}{\sqrt{2\pi}}\right)^2 e^{-3y_3^2/2} \int_{-\infty}^{\infty} e^{-\frac{6}{2}[y_2^2 - 2y_2 y_3 + y_3^2]}\, dy_2$$

$$= \frac{6}{\sqrt{2}}\left(\frac{1}{\sqrt{2\pi}}\right)^2 e^{-3y_3^2/2} \int_{-\infty}^{\infty} e^{-3(y_2 - y_3)^2}\, dy_2$$

But

$$\frac{1}{\sqrt{1/6}\,\sqrt{2\pi}} \int_{-\infty}^{\infty} e^{-3(y_2 - y_3)^2} = 1 .$$

Thus

$$f_3(y_3) = \frac{6}{\sqrt{2}}\left(\frac{1}{\sqrt{2\pi}}\right)^2 e^{-3y_3^2/2} \cdot \frac{\sqrt{2\pi}}{\sqrt{6}} = \frac{\sqrt{6}}{\sqrt{2}} \cdot \frac{1}{\sqrt{2\pi}} e^{-3y_3^2/2} \qquad -\infty < y_3 < \infty$$

$$= \frac{1}{\sqrt{2\pi}\sqrt{1/3}} e^{-y_3^2/2(\frac{1}{3})} \qquad\qquad -\infty < y < \infty$$

which is the density function of a normal random variable with mean zero and variance $\tfrac{1}{3}$ .

● **PROBLEM** 6-34

Assume that $X_1$ and $X_2$ are independent standard normal random variables. Find the joint distribution of $Y_1$ and $Y_2$ where

$$Y_1 = X_1^2 + X_2^2$$

and

$$Y_2 = X_2 .$$

<u>Solution</u>: This transformation from $(X_1,X_2)$ to $(Y_1,Y_2)$ is not a one-to-one transformation for all $Y_1,Y_2$ . We see that

$$X_1 = \pm\sqrt{Y_1 - Y_1^2} \quad \text{and} \quad X_2 = Y_2 .$$

Here, the region $D = \{(x_1,x_2)\mid -\infty < x_1 < \infty,\ -\infty < x_2 < \infty\}$ is mapped to the region $R = \{(y_1,y_2)\mid 0 \le y_1 < \infty,\ -\sqrt{y_1} < y_2 < \sqrt{y_1}\}$ . The transformation from $R$ to $D$ is

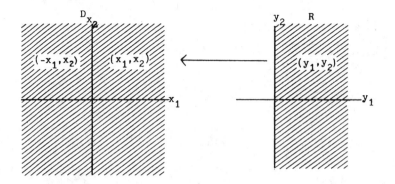

If we divide $D$ into two regions, $D_1 = \{x_1, x_2) \,|\, 0 < x_1 < \infty$, $-\infty < x_2 < \infty\}$ and $D_2 = \{(x_1, x_2) \,|\, -\infty < x_1 < 0, -\infty < x_2 < \infty\}$. Then the transformation from $R$ to $D_1$ and from $R$ to $D_2$ will each be one-to-one transformations. These two transformations are specified by $R \to D_1$, $x_1 = \sqrt{y_1 - y_2^2}$, $x_2 = y_2$ and $R \to D_2$, $x_1 = -\sqrt{y_1 - y_2^2}$, $x_2 = y_2$. And each is one-to-one.

The Jacobian of the transformation from $R \to D_1$ is

$$|\det J_1| = \begin{vmatrix} \frac{1}{2}(y_1 - y_2^2)^{-\frac{1}{2}} & \dfrac{\partial x_1}{\partial y_2} \\ 0 & 1 \end{vmatrix} = \left| \frac{1}{2}(y_1 - y_2^2)^{-\frac{1}{2}} \right| .$$

The Jacobian of the transformation from $R \to D_2$ is

$$|\det J_2| = \begin{vmatrix} -\frac{1}{2}(y_1 - y_2^2)^{-\frac{1}{2}} & \dfrac{\partial x_1}{\partial y_2} \\ 0 & 1 \end{vmatrix}$$

$$= \left| -\frac{1}{2}(y_1 - y_2^2)^{-\frac{1}{2}} \right| .$$

Let $B$ be a region in the $y_1 - y_2$ plane. $\Pr((y_1, y_2) \in B) =$ the probability that the point $(y_1, y_2)$ is in $B$. But each point $(y_1, y_2)$ corresponds to two points in the $(x_1, x_2)$ plane.

By definition,
$$\Pr((x_1, x_2) \in A_1) = \int\int_{A_1} f(x_1, x_2) dx_1\, dx_2$$

and
$$\Pr((x_1, x_2) \in A_2) = \int\int_{A_2} f(x_1, x_2) dx_1\, dx_2$$

where $f(x_1, x_2)$ is the joint density of $X_1$ and $X_2$. We now apply the change of variable technique to each of these integrals.

For the integral over $A_1$, the transformations of $(x_1, x_2)$ to $(y_1, y_2)$ are $x_1 = \sqrt{y_1 - y_2^2}$ and $x_2 = y_2$ with Jacobian

$$|\det J_1| = \left| \frac{1}{2}(y_1 - y_2^2)^{-\frac{1}{2}} \right| .$$

Thus B is mapped to two regions, call them $A_1$ and $A_2$ .

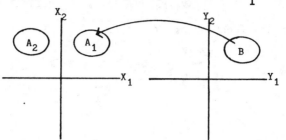

And because the transformation from B to $A_1$ and the transformation from B to $A_2$ are separately one-to-one,

$$\Pr((y_1,y_2) \in B = \Pr((x_1,x_2) \in A_1) + \Pr((x_1,x_2) \in A_2)$$

For the integral over $A_2$, the transformations of $(x_1,x_2)$ to $(y_1,y_2)$ are $x_1 = -\sqrt{y_1 - y_2^2}$ and $x_2 = y_2$ with Jacobian

$$|\det J_2| = \left|-\tfrac{1}{2}(y_1 - y_2^2)^{-\frac{1}{2}}\right| .$$

Note that $y_1 - y_2^2$ must be greater than zero to insure that $\sqrt{y_1 - y_2^2}$ is defined.

$y_1 - y_2^2 > 0$ is equivalent to $-\sqrt{y_1} < y_2 < \sqrt{y_1}$ .

We now change variables in the two integrals, thus

$$\Pr((y_1,y_2) \in B) = \int\int_{A_1} f(x_1,x_2)dx_1\, dx_2 + \int\int_{A_2} f(x_1,x_2)dx_1\, dx_2$$

$$= \int_B\int f(\sqrt{y_1 - y_2^2},y_2)\,|\det J_1|dy_1\, dy_2$$

$$+ \int_B\int f(-\sqrt{y_1 - y_2^2},y_2)\,|\det J_2|\, dy_1\, dy_2 .$$

Now $f(x_1,x_2) = \dfrac{1}{2\pi}\, e^{-\left(\frac{x_1^2 + x_2^2}{2}\right)}$ Thus

$$\Pr((y_1,y_2) \in B) = \int_B\int \frac{1}{2\pi}\, e^{\frac{-(y_1-y_2^2+y_2^2)}{2}} \left|\tfrac{1}{2}(y_1 - y_2^2)^{-\frac{1}{2}}\right| \times dy_1\, dy_2$$

$$+ \int_B\int \frac{1}{2\pi}\, e^{\frac{-(y_1-y_2^2+y_2^2)}{2}} \left|-\tfrac{1}{2}(y_1 - y_2^2)^{-\frac{1}{2}}\right| dy_1\, dy_2$$

$$= \int_B\int \left|\tfrac{1}{2}(y_1-y_2^2)^{-\frac{1}{2}}\right| \left(\frac{e^{-y_1/2} + e^{-y_1/2}}{2\pi}\right) dy_1\, dy_2 ,$$

$$\Pr[(Y_1,Y_2) \in B] = \int_B\int \frac{e^{-y_1/2}}{2\pi(y_1-y_2^2)^{\frac{1}{2}}} dy_1\, dy_2$$

$$= \int_B \int g(y_1, y_2) dy_1 \, dy_2 \, , \quad \text{by definition where} \quad g(y_1, y_2)$$

is the density function of $Y_1$, $Y_2$ .

Thus,

$$g(y_1, y_2) = \frac{e^{-y_1/2}}{2\pi(y_1 - y_2^2)^{\frac{1}{2}}} \quad \text{for} \quad -\infty < y_1 < \infty$$

$$-\sqrt{y_1} < y_2 < \sqrt{y_1} \quad .$$

# CHAPTER 7

# EXPECTED VALUE

## FOR DISCRETE RANDOM VARIABLES

● PROBLEM 7-1

Let X be a random variable whose value is determined by the flip of a fair coin. If the coin lands heads up X = 1, if tails then X = 0. Find the expected value of X.

Solution: The expected value of X, written E(X), is the theoretical average of X. If the coin were flipped many, many times and the random variable X was observed each time, the average of X would be considered the expected value.

The expected value of a discrete variable such as X is defined to be

$$E(X) = x_1 \, Pr(X = x_1) + x_2 \, Pr(X = x_2) \ldots +$$
$$x_n \, Pr(X = x_n)$$

where $x_1$, $x_2$, $x_3$, $\ldots x_n$, are the values X may take on and $Pr(X = x_j)$ is the probability that X actually equals the value $x_j$.

For our problem, the random variable X takes on only two values, 0 and 1. X assumes these values with

$$Pr(X = 1) = Pr(X = 0) = \frac{1}{2} \ .$$

Thus, according to our definition,

$$E(X) = 0 \cdot Pr(X = 0) + 1 \cdot Pr(X = 1)$$
$$= 0 \cdot \frac{1}{2} + 1 \cdot \frac{1}{2} = 0 + \frac{1}{2} = \frac{1}{2} \ .$$

● PROBLEM 7-2

Let X be the random variable defined as the number of dots observed on the upturned face of a fair die after a single toss. Find the expected value of X.

Solution:     X can take on the values 1, 2, 3, 4, 5, or 6. Since the die is fair we assume that each value is observed with equal probability. Thus,

$$\Pr(X = 1) = \Pr(X = 2) = \ldots = \Pr(X = 6)$$

$$= \frac{1}{6} .$$

The expected value of X is

$$E(X) = \Sigma x \Pr(X = x) .\qquad \text{Hence}$$

$$E(X) = 1 \cdot \frac{1}{6} + 2 \cdot \frac{1}{6} + 3 \cdot \frac{1}{6} + 4 \cdot \frac{1}{6} + 5 \cdot \frac{1}{6} + 6 \cdot \frac{1}{6}$$

$$= \frac{1}{6} (1 + 2 + 3 + 4 + 5 + 6)$$

$$= \frac{21}{6} = 3 \frac{1}{2} .$$

● PROBLEM 7-3

Suppose the earnings of a laborer, denoted by X, are given by the following probability function.

| X | 0 | 8 | 12 | 16 |
|---|---|---|----|----|
| Pr(X = x) | 0.3 | 0.2 | 0.3 | 0.2 |

Find the laborer's expected earnings.

Solution:     The laborer's expected earnings are denoted by E(X), the expected value of the random variable X.
The expected value of X is defined to be,

$$E(X) = (0) \Pr(X = 0) + (8) \Pr(X = 8)$$

$$\qquad + (12) \Pr(X = 12) + (16) \Pr(X = 16)$$

$$= (0)(.3) + (8)(.2) + (12)(.3) + (16)(.2)$$

$$= 0 + 1.6 + 3.6 + 3.2$$

$$= 8.4 .$$

Thus the expected earnings are 8.4.

● PROBLEM 7-4

A brush salesman sells door-to-door. His products are short and long brushes. The profit on the long brush is $.30 and on the short one it is $.10. The chances of selling a long brush are one out of ten calls, and the chances of selling a short one are two out of ten calls. The chances of no sales are seven out of ten calls. Find the expected profit per call.

Solution:    Let P be a random variable representing the profit per call. We wish to find E(P).

The probability distribution of P, given in the problem, is summarized in the table below:

|  | P | Pr(P = p) |
|---|---|---|
| long brush | .30 | .1 |
| short brush | .10 | .2 |
| no sale | 0 | .7 |

Thus

$$E(P) = (.30)\ Pr(P = .30) + (.10)\ Pr(P = .10)$$
$$+ (0)\ Pr(P = 0)$$
$$= (.30)\ (.1) + (.10)(.2) + (0)(.7)$$
$$= .03 + .02 + 0 = .05.$$

The expected profit per call is $ .05 or 5 cents.

● PROBLEM 7-5

The State of New Hampshire conducts an annual lottery to raise funds for the school districts in the state. Assume a million tickets are sold. One ticket is the winning ticket and the winner receives $10,000. If each ticket costs $.25, find the expected value of a randomly purchased ticket and the revenue that the lottery generates for the school districts in the state.

Solution:    Let X be the value of a randomly purchased lottery ticket.

$$X = - \$.25 \text{ with probability } \frac{999,999}{1,000,000}.$$

This is because 999,999 of 1,000,000 lottery tickets have no value and the buyers of these tickets lose the $.25 price.

However,

$$X = \$10,000 - \$.25 \text{ with probability } \frac{1}{1,000,000}.$$

221

This reflects the fact that one of the million tickets wins $10,000 minus the purchase price of the ticket, thus the winner receives $10,000 - $.25.

The expected value of the random variable X is the expected value of a randomly purchased lottery ticket. By the definition of expected value,

$$E(X) = \$[10,000 - .25] \cdot \frac{1}{1,000,000}$$

$$+ [- \$.25] \cdot \frac{999,999}{1,000,000} \cdot$$

Rearranging terms we see that

$$E(X) = \$10,000 \cdot \left[ \frac{1}{1,000,000} \right]$$

$$+ \left[ \frac{- \$.25 - (\$.25)(999,999)}{1,000,000} \right]$$

$$= \$10,000 \left[ \frac{1}{1,000,000} \right] - \$.25 \left[ \frac{1,000,000}{1,000,000} \right]$$

$$= \$ \frac{1}{100} - \$.25$$

$$= \$.01 - \$.25 = - \$.24 \ .$$

Thus, the expected value of an average lottery ticket is - $.24. Each buyer loses an average of 24 cents on a lottery ticket.

The total revenue is the number of tickets sold times the price of each ticket or $(.25)(1,000,000) = $250,000. The net revenue, after the prize is paid is

$250,000 - 10,000 = $240,000.

Thus the school districts receive $240,000.

● **PROBLEM** 7-6

Suppose a shipping company buys a new trailer truck for $10,000. If the truck is lost either through accident or theft, it is regarded as a complete loss. The chance of loss is .001; hence, the chance of no loss is .999. Find the expected loss.

Solution:    Let L be the random variable representing the loss that the shipping company takes in the course of a year. L has two values, 0 and 10,000. The probability distribution of L is Pr(L = 0) = .999 and Pr(L=10,000)=.001. This information is summarized in the following table,

|         | $\ell$  | $Pr(L = \ell)$ |
|---------|---------|----------------|
| No loss | 0       | .999           |
| loss    | 10,000  | .001           |

To find the expected loss, we calculate the expected value of the random variable L. This is,

$E(L) = \ell_1 \, Pr(L = \ell_1) + \ell_2 \, Pr(L = \ell_2)$

$\qquad = 0 \quad Pr(L = 0) + 10,000 \, Pr(L = 10,000)$

$\qquad = 0 \quad (.999) + (10,000)(.001)$

$\qquad = 10 .$

Thus the expected loss is 10 dollars.

● **PROBLEM 7-7**

In the previous problem, suppose 1000 shipping companies each having a truck worth $10,000, form an industry association to protect themselves against the loss of a new truck. How much should the firms pay in total to the association to insure its truck?

Solution:    The expected loss for all the companies
combined is

$$L_T = L_1 + L_2 + L_3 + \ldots + L_{1000}$$

where $L_i$ represents the loss of the ith company. The expected loss of all 1000 companies is $E(L_T)$.

By the properties of expectation,

$E(L_T) = E(L_1 + L_2 + \ldots + L_{1000})$

$\qquad = E(L_1) + E(L_2) + \ldots + E(L_{1000}) .$

The expected loss of each company has been found to be $E(L_i) = \$10$. Thus

$$E(L_T) = \underbrace{10 + 10 + \ldots + 10}_{1000 \text{ terms}}$$

$$= (1000) 10 = 10,000 .$$

On the average, there will be a loss of 10,000 a year among the 1000 companies. Some years the loss will be greater than $10,000, some years the loss will be less than $10,000 but on the average the loss will be $10,000 a year.

Dividing this loss equally among all 1000 companies gives the annual premium each company should pay. Thus,

$$\text{premium} = \frac{10,000}{1000} = 10 \text{ dollars} .$$

X is an example of a binomially distributed random variable. We note that for a binomial random variable

$$E(X) \text{ also equals } 4 \cdot \frac{1}{2} = n \cdot p = 2 .$$

This formula $E(X) = np$ is true for all binomially distributed random variables.

● **PROBLEM 7-8**

Find the expected number of boys on a committee of 3 selected at random from 4 boys and 3 girls.

Solution:    Let X represent the number of boys on the committee. X can be equal to 0, 1, 2 or 3. The sampling procedure is without replacement.

To find the probability distribution we calculate the probabilities that X = 0, 1, 2 or 3. The probability that there are zero boys on the committee is

$$\Pr(X = 0)$$

$$= \frac{\text{number of ways 0 boys can be picked}}{\text{number of ways a committee of 3 can be chosen}} .$$

The number of ways a committee of 3 can be chosen from the 4 boys and 3 girls is the number of ways 3 can be selected from 7 or $\binom{7}{3}$ .

The number of ways a committee of 3 can be chosen that contains 0 boys is $\binom{4}{0} \cdot \binom{3}{3}$ , the number of ways 0 boys are chosen from 4 multiplied by the number of ways 3 girls are chosen from the 3 available.

$$\text{Thus, } \Pr(X = 0) = \frac{\binom{4}{0} \binom{3}{3}}{\binom{7}{3}} .$$

Similarly,

$$\Pr(X = 1) = \frac{\binom{4}{1} \binom{3}{2}}{\binom{7}{3}} ,$$

$$Pr(X = 2) = \frac{\binom{4}{2}\binom{3}{1}}{\binom{7}{3}}$$

and

$$Pr(X = 3) = \frac{\binom{4}{3}\binom{3}{0}}{\binom{7}{3}} .$$

By definition, the expected number of boys is

$$E(X) = (0)\ Pr(X = 0) + (1)\ Pr(X = 1) + (2)\ Pr(X = 2)$$
$$+ (3)\ Pr(X = 3)$$

$$= (0)\ \frac{\binom{4}{0}\binom{3}{3}}{\binom{7}{3}} + (1)\ \frac{\binom{4}{1}\binom{3}{2}}{\binom{7}{3}} + (2)\ \frac{\binom{4}{2}\binom{3}{1}}{\binom{7}{3}} + (3)\ \frac{\binom{4}{3}\binom{3}{0}}{\binom{7}{3}}$$

$$= (1)\ \frac{\frac{4!}{3!1!} \cdot \frac{3!}{2!1!}}{\binom{7}{3}} + (2)\ \frac{\frac{4!}{2!2!} \cdot \frac{3!}{2!1!}}{\binom{7}{3}}$$

$$+ (3)\ \frac{\frac{4!}{3!1!} \cdot \frac{3!}{0!3!}}{\binom{7}{3}}$$

$$= \frac{1}{\binom{7}{3}}\ [(4)(3) + (2)(6)(3) + (3)(4)(1)]$$

$$= \frac{12 + 36 + 4}{\binom{7}{3}} = \frac{52}{\frac{7!}{3!4!}}$$

$$= \frac{52}{\frac{7 \cdot 6 \cdot 5}{3 \cdot 2 \cdot 1}} = \frac{52}{35} = 1.5 .$$

Thus, if a comittee of 3 is selected at random over and over it would contain on the average 1.5 boys.

Let the random variable X represent the number of defective radios in a shipment of four radios to a local appliance store. Assume that each radio is equally likely to be defective or non-defective, hence the probability that a radio is defective is $p = \frac{1}{2}$ . Also assume that each radio is defective or non-defective independently of the other radios. Find the expected number of defective radios.

Solution:    First we find the probability distribution of X, the number of defective radios in the shipment of four. X can assume 5 values, 0, 1, 2, 3, or 4.

If X is 0, then 0 radios are defective. This can only take place if each is non-defective. By the independence assumption

$$Pr(X = 0) = \left(\frac{1}{2}\right)\left(\frac{1}{2}\right)\left(\frac{1}{2}\right)\left(\frac{1}{2}\right)$$

$$= \frac{1}{2^4} = \frac{1}{16} \; .$$

Similarly, Pr(X = 1) = Pr(1 radio is defective, 3 are not)

$$= \frac{\text{number of favorable outcomes}}{\text{number of possible outcomes}}$$

$$= \frac{4}{2^4} = \frac{4}{16} = \frac{1}{4} \; .$$

Pr(X = 2)=Pr( 2 radios are defective)

$$= \frac{\text{number of ways two can be chosen from four}}{\text{number of ways to choose 4 radios}}$$

$$= \binom{4}{2}\left(\frac{1}{2}\right)^4 = \frac{6}{16} \; .$$

By symmetry,

$$Pr(X = 1) = Pr(X = 3) = \frac{4}{16} = \frac{1}{4} \qquad \text{and}$$

$$Pr(X = 0) = Pr(X = 4) = \frac{1}{16} \; .$$

The expected number of defective radios is

$$E(X) = 0 \cdot \frac{1}{16} + 1 \cdot \frac{4}{16} + 2 \cdot \frac{6}{16} + 3 \cdot \frac{4}{16} + 4 \cdot \frac{1}{16}$$

$$= \frac{4}{16} + \frac{12}{16} + \frac{12}{16} + \frac{4}{16} = \frac{32}{16} = 2 \; .$$

● **PROBLEM 7-10**

A retailer has the opportunity to sell a portion of slow-moving stock to a liquidator for $1800. Since the items in question are children's toys, he is also aware that he may do better financially by keeping them in stock

226

through the approaching Christmas shopping season and selling them at a discount. The following table indicates the retailer's estimate of the consequences of his decisions given that a certain percentage of stock is sold in the Christmas season.

| Percentage Of Stock Sold | Revenue If Stock Is Kept | Revenue If Stock Is Sold Now |
|---|---|---|
| 70% | $1400 | $1800 |
| 80% | $1600 | $1800 |
| 90% | $1800 | $1800 |
| 100% | $2000 | $1800 |

The retailer has kept good records of previous experience over 25 Christmas seasons and has found that:

$$\text{Pr}(70\% \text{ of stock is sold}) = \frac{4}{25}$$

$$\text{Pr}(80\% \text{ of stock is sold}) = \frac{7}{25}$$

$$\text{Pr}(90\% \text{ of stock is sold}) = \frac{12}{25}$$

$$\text{Pr}(100\% \text{ of stock is sold}) = \frac{2}{25} .$$

Evaluate the decisions using expected revenue as the criterion.

Solution:    Let $X_1$ = the revenue in dollars received by the retailer if he sells his stock now to the liquidator. Let $X_2$ = the revenue in dollars received by the retailer if he keeps his stock and sells it through the Christmas shopping season.

We wish to calculate $E(X_1)$ and $E(X_2)$. If $E(X_1) > E(X_2)$ he should sell now and if $E(X_2) > E(X_1)$ he should keep the stock and sell it through the Christmas shopping season. This exemplifies decision-making based on expected value or the expected value criterion.

The expected value of $X_1$ is computed to be

$$E(X_1) = 1800 \left(\frac{4}{25}\right) + 1800 \left(\frac{7}{25}\right) + 1800 \left(\frac{12}{25}\right) + 1800 \left(\frac{2}{25}\right)$$

$$= 1800 \left(\frac{4 + 7 + 12 + 2}{25}\right) = 1800 \left(\frac{25}{25}\right)$$

$$= 1800 .$$

The expected value of $X_2$ is computed to be

$$E(X_2) = (1400) \, Pr(X_2 = 1400) + 1600 \, Pr(X_2 = 1600)$$
$$+ 1800 \, Pr(X_2 = 1800) + 2000 \, Pr(X_2 = 2000)$$

but

$Pr(X_2 = 1400) = Pr(70\% \text{ of the stock is sold})$

$Pr(X_2 = 1600) = Pr(80\% \text{ of the stock is sold})$

$Pr(X_2 = 1800) = Pr(90\% \text{ of the stock is sold})$

$Pr(X_2 = 2000) = Pr(100\% \text{ of the stock is sold}).$

From previous experience the retailer has estimated these probabilities, thus

$$E(X_2) = (1400) \, \frac{4}{25} + (1600) \, \frac{7}{25} + (1800) \, \frac{12}{25}$$

$$+ 2000 \left(\frac{2}{25}\right)$$

$$= 224 + 448 + 864 + 160$$

$$= 1696.$$

Thus $E(X_2) < E(X_1)$ and the retailer should sell his stock to the liquidator now.

# FOR CONTINUOUS RANDOM VARIABLES

● **PROBLEM** 7-11

Let Y = the Rockwell hardness of a particular alloy of steel. Assume that Y is a continuous random variable that can take on any value between 50 and 70 with equal probability. Find the expected Rockwell hardness.

<u>Solution</u>: The random variable Y has a density function that is sketched below.

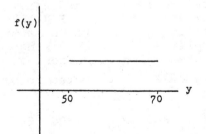

In order for Y to have a proper probability density function, the area under the density function must be 1. The area under the density function of Y is in the shape of a rectangle with length 20. Thus the height of the rectangle must be

$$f(y)(20) = 1 \qquad\qquad 50 < y < 70,$$

where the probability density function $f(y)$ represents the width of this rectangle. Solving for $f(y)$, we find the probability density function to be

$$f(y) = \frac{1}{20} \qquad\qquad 50 < y < 70 .$$

To find the expected value of a continuous random variable we use the technique of integration. Thus

$$E(Y) = \int_{50}^{70} yf(y)\ dy$$

$$E(Y) = \int_{50}^{70} y\ \frac{1}{20}\ dy \qquad = \frac{1}{20}\left(\frac{y^2}{2}\right)\ \bigg|_{50}^{70}$$

$$= \frac{1}{20}\left(\frac{70^2 - 50^2}{2}\right) = \frac{(70 + 50)(70 - 50)}{40}$$

$$= \frac{70 + 50}{2} = \frac{120}{2} = 60 .$$

Thus, the expected Rockwell hardness of this alloy is 60.

● **PROBLEM 7-12**

Let X be a random variable denoting the hours of life in an electric light bulb. Suppose X is distributed with density function

$$f(x) = \frac{1}{1,000}\ e^{-x/1000} \qquad\qquad \text{for } x > 0$$

Find the expected lifetime of such a bulb.

Solution:     The expected value of a continuous random variable is the "sum" of all the values of the random variable multiplied by their probabilities. In the continuous case, this "summing" necessitates integration. Thus

$$E(X) = \int_{\text{all } x} x\ f(x)\ dx .$$

In our problem, x can take all positive values; thus

229

$$E(X) = \int_0^\infty x\, f(x)\, dx$$

$$= \int_0^\infty \frac{x}{1000}\, e^{-\frac{x}{1000}}\, dx.$$

Integrating by parts, let $u = x$ and

$$dv = \frac{1}{1000}\, e^{-\frac{x}{1000}}\, dx; \text{ then } du = dx \text{ and } v = -\, e^{-\frac{x}{1000}}.$$

Thus

$$E(X) = uv \Big|_0^\infty - \int_0^\infty v\, du$$

$$E(X) = -\, xe^{-\frac{x}{1000}} \Big|_0^\infty - \int_0^\infty -\, e^{-\frac{x}{1000}}\, dx$$

$$= 0 - 1000 \int_0^\infty -\frac{1}{1000}\, e^{-\frac{x}{1000}}\, dx$$

$$= -\, 1000 \cdot e^{-\frac{x}{1000}} \Big]_0^\infty$$

$$= -\, 1000\, [0 - 1] = 1000.$$

Thus, the expected lifetime of the bulb is 1000 hours.

● **PROBLEM** 7-13

Find E(X) for the continuous random variables with probability density functions;

a) $f(x) = 2x$, $0 < x < 1$.

b) $f(x) = \frac{1}{(2\sqrt{x})}$, $0 < x < 1$.

c) $f(x) = 6x(1 - x)$, $0 < x < 1$.

d) $f(x) = \frac{1}{2}x^2 e^{-x}$, $0 < x < \infty$.

e) $f(x) = \frac{1}{x^2}$, $1 \le x < \infty$.

f) $f(x) = 1 - |1 - x|$, $0 \le x \le 2$.

<u>Solution:</u>  For a continuous random variable, X,

$$E(X) = \int_{-\infty}^{\infty} x\, f(x)\, dx.$$

It is possible that $f(x) = 0$ for large portions of the real line reducing $E(X)$ to a proper integral.

(a)  $E(X) = \int_{0}^{1} x \cdot 2x\, dx = \int_{0}^{1} 2x^2\, dx = \frac{2}{3}\, x^3 \Big|_{0}^{1}$

$= \frac{2}{3}\, [1 - 0] = \frac{2}{3}$.

(b)  $E(X) = \int_{0}^{1} x\, \frac{1}{2\, \sqrt{x}}\, dx = \frac{1}{2} \int_{0}^{1} \sqrt{x}\, dx$

$= \frac{1}{2}\, \frac{x^{\frac{1}{2} + 1}}{1 + \frac{1}{2}} \Big]_{0}^{1} \quad \frac{1}{2} \cdot \frac{2}{3}\, x^{\frac{3}{2}} \Big]_{0}^{1} = \frac{1}{3}$.

(c)  $E(X) = \int_{0}^{1} x(6x\,(1 - x))\, dx = 6 \int_{0}^{1} (x^2 - x^3)\, dx$

$= 6 \left[ \frac{x^3}{3} - \frac{x^4}{4} \right]_{0}^{1} = 6 \left( \frac{1}{3} - \frac{1}{4} \right) = \frac{6}{12} = \frac{1}{2}$.

(d)  $E(X) = \int_{0}^{\infty} x \cdot f(x)\, dx = \int_{0}^{\infty} \frac{1}{2}\, x^3\, e^{-x}\, dx$.

Using integration by parts,

let        $u = x^3$              thus        $du = 3x^2\, dx$

$dv = e^{-x}\, dx$                    $v = -\, e^{-x}$

and we see that

$$E(X) = \frac{1}{2} \left[ -\, x^3 e^{-x} \Big|_{0}^{\infty} - \int_{0}^{\infty} -\, e^{-x}\, 3x^2\, dx \right]$$

$$= \frac{1}{2} \left[ 0 + 0 + 3 \int_{0}^{\infty} x^2\, e^{-x}\, dx \right]$$

231

$$= \frac{3}{2} \int_0^\infty x^2 e^{-x} dx \qquad = 3 \int_0^\infty \frac{1}{2} x^2 e^{-x} dx,$$

but the integrand is $f(x) = \frac{1}{2} x^2 e^{-x}$ our original density

function and by definition a density function is a positive-valued function $f(x)$ such that

$$\int_0^\infty f(x) \, dx = 1; \qquad\qquad \text{thus}$$

$$E(X) = 3 \int_0^\infty f(x) \, dx = 3.$$

(e) $\quad E(X) = \int_1^\infty x \cdot \frac{1}{x^2} \, dx = \int_1^\infty \frac{1}{x} \, dx = \lim_{b \to \infty} \int_1^b \frac{dx}{x}$

$$= \lim_{b \to \infty} [\log b - \log 1]$$

$$= \lim_{b \to \infty} \log b = \infty;$$

thus the expected value of x does not exist.

(f) $\quad E(X) = \int_0^2 x \, f(x) \, dx$

$$= \int_0^2 x(1 - |1 - x| ) \, dx$$

$$= \int_0^2 [x - x \mid 1 - x \mid] \, dx$$

$$= \frac{1}{2} x^2 \Big|_0^2 - \int_0^2 x \mid 1 - x \mid dx$$

$$= 2 - \int_0^2 x \mid 1 - x \mid dx;$$

but $\quad x \mid 1 - x \mid = \begin{cases} x(1 - x) & \text{for } 0 \le x \le 1 \\ x(x - 1) & \text{for } 1 \le x \le 2 \end{cases}$.

Thus

$$E(X) = 2 - \left[ \int_0^1 x(1 - x) \, dx + \int_1^2 x \, (x - 1) \, dx \right]$$

$$= 2 - \int_0^1 x\,dx + \int_0^1 x^2\,dx - \int_1^2 x^2 + \int_1^2 x\,dx$$

$$= 2 - \frac{1}{2} x^2 \Big|_0^1 + \frac{1}{3} x^3 \Big|_0^1 - \frac{1}{3} x^3 \Big|_1^2 + \frac{1}{2} x^2 \Big|_1^2$$

$$= 2 - \frac{1}{2} + \frac{1}{3} - \frac{8}{3} + \frac{1}{3} + \frac{4}{2} - \frac{1}{2}$$

$$= 1.$$

● **PROBLEM** 7-14

The lifetime x (in hours) of electronic tubes mass-produced by a standard process is a random variable with a probability distribution having the density function

$$\alpha^2 x e^{-\alpha x}$$

for $x \geq 0$. Prove that the expected lifetime of the tubes is $2/\alpha$. Also, show that the probability that a random selected tube will have a lifetime $\geq m$ is

$$(1 + \alpha m) e^{-\alpha m} .$$

A research engineer suggests certain modifications in the production process which would alter the lifetime distribution by increasing the expected lifetime to $2/\beta (\beta < \alpha)$. But because of the cost of introducing the change the manufacturer does not consider it worth while unless the modified process also ensures that the probability of the lifetime of a randomly selected tube being $\geq m$ is increased by a fraction $\lambda (> 0)$. Prove that the manufacturer's condition for introducing the new process is satisfied if

$$\beta < \alpha - \frac{1}{m} \log_e (1 + \lambda).$$

<u>Solution</u>:    The expected lifetime of the electronic tubes X, will be

$$E(X) = \int_0^\infty x\,f(x)\,dx = \int_0^\infty x\,\alpha^2\,x e^{-\alpha x}\,dx$$

$$= \alpha^2 \int_0^\infty x^2 e^{-\alpha x}\,dx .$$

Integrating by parts:        $\int udv = uv - \int v\,du.$

let    $u = x^2$                then            $du = 2x\,dx$

233

$$dv = e^{-\alpha x} \, dx \qquad\qquad v = \frac{-e^{-\alpha x}}{\alpha}$$

and
$$E(X) = \alpha^2 \left[ \frac{-x^2 e^{-\alpha x}}{\alpha} \Bigg|_0^\infty - \int_0^\infty \frac{-e^{-\alpha x}}{\alpha} \cdot 2x \, dx \right]$$

$$= \alpha^2 \left[ 0 + 0 + \frac{2}{\alpha} \int_0^\infty x e^{-\alpha x} \, dx \right]$$

$$= 2\alpha \int_0^\infty x e^{-\alpha x} \, dx \; .$$

Integrate by parts again, letting

$$u = x \qquad\qquad then \qquad\qquad du = dx$$

$$dv = e^{-\alpha x} \, dx \qquad\qquad v = \frac{-e^{-\alpha x}}{\alpha}$$

and
$$E(X) = 2\alpha \left[ \frac{-x e^{-\alpha x}}{\alpha} \Bigg|_0^\infty - \int_0^\infty \frac{-e^{-\alpha x}}{\alpha} \, dx \right]$$

$$= 2\alpha \left[ 0 + \frac{1}{\alpha} \int_0^\infty e^{-\alpha x} \, dx \right]$$

$$= 2 \int_0^\infty e^{-\alpha x} \, dx = \frac{-2}{\alpha} e^{-\alpha x} \Bigg|_0^\infty$$

$$= \frac{-2}{\alpha} [0 - 1] = \frac{2}{\alpha} \; .$$

$$Pr(X \geq m) = \int_m^\infty f(x) \, dx = \int_m^\infty \alpha^2 x e^{-\alpha x} \, dx .$$

Integrating by parts, let

$$u = x \qquad\qquad and \qquad\qquad du = dx$$

$$dv = e^{-\alpha x} \, dx \qquad\qquad v = \frac{-e^{-\alpha x}}{\alpha} \; .$$

Thus
$$Pr(X \geq m) = \alpha^2 \left[ \frac{-x e^{-\alpha x}}{\alpha} \Bigg|_m^\infty - \int_m^\infty \frac{-e^{-\alpha x}}{\alpha} \, dx \right]$$

$$= \alpha^2 \left[ 0 - \left( \frac{-m e^{-m\alpha}}{\alpha} \right) + \frac{1}{\alpha} \int_m^\infty e^{-\alpha x} \, dx \right]$$

234

$$= \alpha m e^{-m\alpha} + \alpha \int_{m}^{\infty} e^{-\alpha x} \, dx$$

$$= \alpha m e^{-m\alpha} + \alpha \left( \frac{-e^{-\alpha x}}{\alpha} \, \bigg|_{m}^{\infty} \right)$$

$$= \alpha m e^{-m\alpha} + \alpha \left[ - \left( \frac{-e^{-m\alpha}}{\alpha} \right) \right].$$

$$\Pr(X \geq m) = \alpha m e^{-m\alpha} + e^{-m\alpha} = e^{-m\alpha} (1 + \alpha m).$$

If the expected lifetime of the tube is increased to $\frac{2}{\beta}$, $(\beta < \alpha)$ this is in effect a change in the probability density function. The density function has been transformed to
$$f(x) = \beta^2 x e^{-\beta x}.$$

Thus $\Pr(X \geq m) = (1 + \beta m) e^{-m\beta}$

using the same calculations as before except that $\alpha$ is replaced by $\beta$.

The plant manager demands that $\Pr(X \geq m)$ be increased by a fraction $\lambda$. This means that

$\Pr(X \geq m,$ before the change$) + \lambda \Pr(X \geq m,$ before the

change$) \leq \Pr(X \geq m,$ after the change$)$.

This condition can be rewritten as

$$(1 + \alpha m) \, e^{-m\alpha} + \lambda(1 + \alpha m)e^{-m\alpha} \leq (1 + \beta m)e^{-m\beta}$$

or $\quad (1 + \lambda)(1 + \alpha m)e^{-m\alpha} \leq (1 + \beta m) \, e^{-m\beta}$

$$(1 + \lambda) \left( \frac{1 + \alpha m}{1 + \beta m} \right) e^{-m\alpha} \leq e^{-m\beta}.$$

235

Any value of $\beta$ that satisfies this inequality will also satisfy the inequality $(1 + \lambda)e^{-m\alpha} < e^{-m\beta}$. This is because $\beta < \alpha$ implies that $\frac{1 + \alpha m}{1 + \beta m} > 1$ and thus

$$(1 + \lambda)e^{-m\alpha} < (1 + \lambda)\left[\frac{1 + \alpha m}{1 + \beta m}\right] e^{-m\alpha} \leq e^{-m\beta}.$$

$(1 + \lambda)e^{-m\alpha} < e^{-m\beta}$ implies

$$\log_e (1 + \lambda) - m\alpha < - m\beta$$

$$m\beta < m\alpha - \log_e (1 + \lambda)$$

or

$$\beta < \alpha - \frac{1}{m} \log_e (1 + \lambda).$$

● **PROBLEM** 7-15

Find the expected value of the random variable X if X is distributed with probability density function

$$f(x) = \lambda e^{-\lambda x} \qquad \text{for} \quad 0 < X < \infty.$$

Solution: To find this expected value we will use another method.

This new method computes the expected value from $F(x) = Pr(X \leq x)$. For our random variable,

$$Pr(X \leq x) = \int_0^x f(t) \, dt = \int_0^x \lambda e^{-\lambda t} \, dt$$

$$= -\int_0^x (-\lambda) e^{-\lambda t} \, dt$$

$$= - e^{-\lambda t} \Big|_0^x = - e^{-\lambda x} - \left(- e^{-\lambda \cdot 0}\right)$$

$$= 1 - e^{-\lambda x}$$

We have defined $E(X) = \int_0^\infty x \, f(x) \, dx = \int_0^\infty x \, \lambda e^{-\lambda x} \, dx$;

but $x = \int_0^x dt$. Thus substituting,

$$E(X) = \int_0^\infty f(x) \left[ \int_0^x dt \right] dx.$$

This is an iterated integration over the shaded region,

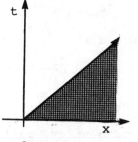

Reversing the order of integration, we integrate with respect to x first. The variable x is integrated from t to ∞ and then t is integrated from 0 to ∞. Thus,

$$\int_0^\infty f(x) \left[ \int_0^x dt \right] dx = \int_0^\infty \left[ \int_t^\infty f(x)\, dx \right] dt .$$

But $\int_t^\infty f(x)\, dx = Pr(X \geq t) = 1 - Pr(X < t) = 1 - F(t)$

or $E(X) = \int_0^\infty [1 - F(t)]\, dt .$

Thus, $E(X) = \int_0^\infty \left[ 1 - \left[ 1 - e^{-\lambda t} \right] \right] dt$

$$= \int_0^\infty e^{-\lambda t} dt = -\frac{1}{\lambda} e^{-\lambda t} \Big|_0^\infty = -\frac{1}{\lambda} [0 - 1] = \frac{1}{\lambda} .$$

● PROBLEM 7-16

Find the expected value of X if X has cumulative distribution $F(X) = \left( 1 - pe^{-\lambda x} \right)$ for x between 0 and ∞, and $P(X = 0)$ is unknown, $0 < p < 1$. This random variable is partly discrete and partly continuous.

Solution:    To find this expectation, we first find the probability density function. Since we are given F(x), then it follows that the pdf is

$$f(x) = F'(x) = \lambda p e^{-\lambda x}.$$

But $\int_0^\infty \lambda p e^{-\lambda x}\, dx = -p \int_0^\infty -\lambda e^{-\lambda x}\, dx$

$$= -pe^{-\lambda x} \Big]_0^\infty = -p [0 - 1] = p.$$

Thus, we must assume that the probability that X

is equal to 0 is 1 - p, because

$$Pr(X = 0) + Pr(0 < X < \infty)$$

must equal 1 for X to have a proper probability distribution or

$$Pr(X = 0) = 1 - Pr(0 < X < \infty) \qquad = 1 - p$$

Thus X has a mixed density, partly discrete and partly continuous.

$$E(X) = 0 \cdot Pr(X = 0) + \int_0^\infty x \ \lambda p e^{-\lambda x} \ dx$$

$$= 0 + p \int_0^\infty x \ \lambda e^{-\lambda x} \ dx \ .$$

Now $\int_0^\infty x \ \lambda e^{-\lambda x} \ dx$ has been calculated several times previously and found to be equal to $\frac{1}{\lambda}$ .

Thus, $E(X) = 0 + \frac{p}{\lambda} = \frac{p}{\lambda}$ .

# FOR FUNCTIONS OF RANDOM VARIABLES

● **PROBLEM** 7-17

Find the expected value of the random variable
Y = f(X), when X is a discrete random variable with
probability mass function g(x). Let $f(X) = X^2 + X + 1$

and $Pr(X = x) = g(x) =$
$$\begin{cases} \frac{1}{2} & x = 1 \\ \frac{1}{3} & x = 2 \\ \frac{1}{6} & x = 3 \ . \end{cases}$$

Solution:    To find the expected value of a function of
a random variable, we define

$$E(Y) = E(f(X)) \quad = \Sigma_x \ f(X) \ g(x) \ = \Sigma_x \ f(X) \ Pr(X = x).$$

As an example, we consider the above problem.

$$E(Y) = f(1) \ Pr(X = 1) + f(2) \ Pr(X = 2) + f(3) \ Pr(X = 3).$$

But   $f(1) = 1^2 + 1 + 1 = 3$

$f(2) = 2^2 + 2 + 1 = 7$

$$f(3) = 3^2 + 3 + 1 = 13.$$

Substituting we see that,

$$E(Y) = 3 \Pr(X = 1) + 7 \Pr(X = 2) + 13\Pr(X = 3)$$

$$= 3 \cdot \frac{1}{2} + 7 \cdot \frac{1}{3} + 13 \cdot \frac{1}{6}$$

$$= \frac{3}{2} + \frac{7}{3} + \frac{13}{6} = \frac{9}{6} + \frac{14}{6} + \frac{13}{6}$$

$$= \frac{36}{6} = 6.$$

● PROBLEM 7-18

A platoon of soldiers is controlling a small cannon. They know that the muzzle velocity of their cannon is $v_0$. Unfortunately the cannon's support apparatus does not allow them to measure precisely the angle the cannon makes with the horizontal plane. They assume that this angle is a continuous random variable, uniformly distributed between the values $\frac{\pi}{4}$ and $\frac{\pi}{2}$. Find the expected horizontal distance which the shell travels.

Solution: This problem requires an elementary knowledge of two-dimensional kinematics.

Let $\theta$ = the random variable representing the angle the cannon makes with the horizontal.

The horizontal distance the shell travels can be computed to be

$$X = (v_0 \cos \theta)t,$$

where t is the time the projectile is in the air.

The time the projectile is in the air is

$$t = \frac{2 v_0 \sin \theta}{g}$$

where g is the acceleration due to gravity.

$$X = (v_0 \cos \theta) \left( \frac{2 v_0 \sin \theta}{g} \right) = 2 v_0^2 \frac{\cos \theta \sin \theta}{g}.$$

The density function of $\theta$ is

$$g(\theta) = \frac{1}{\frac{\pi}{2} - \frac{\pi}{4}} \qquad \frac{\pi}{4} \leq \theta \leq \frac{\pi}{2}$$

or

$$g(\theta) = \frac{4}{\pi} \qquad\qquad \frac{\pi}{4} \leq \theta \leq \frac{\pi}{2} \; .$$

Thus the expected value of X is

$$E(X) = E\left[\frac{2 \; v_0{}^2 \; \sin\theta\cos\theta}{g}\right] = \int_\theta f(\theta) \; g(\theta) \; d\theta$$

where $x = f(\theta) = \dfrac{2 \; v_0{}^2 \; \sin\theta\cos\theta}{g} \; .$

Thus, $\qquad E(X) = \displaystyle\int_{\frac{\pi}{4}}^{\frac{\pi}{2}} \dfrac{2 \; v_0{}^2 \; \sin\theta\cos\theta}{g} \cdot \dfrac{4}{\pi} \; d\theta$

$$= \frac{8 \; v_0{}^2}{\pi g} \int_{\frac{\pi}{4}}^{\frac{\pi}{2}} \sin\theta\cos\theta \; d\theta \; .$$

Let $u = \sin\theta$ then $du = \cos\theta \; d\theta$ and

$$E(X) = \frac{8 \; v_0{}^2}{\pi g} \int_{\frac{\sqrt{2}}{2}}^{1} u \; du = \frac{8 \; v_0{}^2}{\pi g} \cdot \frac{1}{2} \; u^2 \; \Bigg|_{\frac{\sqrt{2}}{2}}^{1}$$

$$= \frac{8 \; v_0{}^2}{\pi g} \cdot \frac{1}{2} \left[ 2 - \left(\frac{\sqrt{2}}{2}\right)^2 \right]$$

$$= \frac{8 \; v_0{}^2}{\pi g} \cdot \frac{1}{2} \left[ 1 - \frac{1}{2} \right]$$

$$= \frac{2 \; v_0{}^2}{\pi g} \; .$$

Thus, if the soldiers fire their cannon many times they can expect the shell to fall a horizontal distance of $\dfrac{2 \; v_0{}^2}{\pi g}$ units away.

● **PROBLEM** 7-19

A factory has to decide the amount y of lengths of a certain cloth to produce. The demand for X lengths is uniformly distributed over the interval (a, b). For each length sold a profit of m dollars is made, while for each length not sold a loss of n dollars is incurred. Find the expected profit and maximize this with respect to y.

Solution:    The form of the profit is related to the value of y, the amount of lengths of cloth produced. If

the demand is greater than the amount produced we will
sell everything made and $P(X)$ = profit when demand is $X = my$.

If we make too many lengths and the demand is less
than y then we will sell X for a profit of mX but will
lose n dollars on each of the extra $y - X$ lengths for a
total loss of $n(y - X)$. The net profit will be
$mX - n(y - X)$.

More succinctly, if $\qquad X \geq y \qquad\qquad P(X) = my$,

$\qquad\qquad$ if $\qquad X < y \qquad\qquad P(X) = mX - n(y - X)$.

The expected profit is $\quad E(P(X)) = \displaystyle\int_a^b P(X)\ f(x)\ dx$

where $f(x)$ is the p.d.f. of X.

X is uniformly distributed over (a, b) thus

$$f(x) = \frac{1}{b - a} \qquad\qquad a \leq x \leq b$$

$$\phantom{f(x)} = 0 \qquad\qquad\qquad \text{otherwise.}$$

Hence $E(P(X)) = \dfrac{1}{b - a} \displaystyle\int_a^b P(x)\ dx$ .

If $y \leq a$ then always $X \geq a \geq y$ and

$$E(P(X)) = \frac{1}{b - a} \int_a^b my\ dx = \frac{my}{b - a}\ x\ \Big|_a^b = my$$

which will increase until $y = a$.

If $y \geq b$ then always $X \leq b \leq y$ and

$$E(P(X)) = \frac{1}{b - a} \int_a^b [mx - n(y - x)]\ dx$$

$$= \frac{1}{b - a} \int_a^b [(m + n)\ x - ny]\ dx$$

$$= \frac{m + n}{2(b - a)}\ x^2\ \Big|_a^b - \frac{ny}{(b - a)}\ x\ \Big|_a^b$$

$$= \frac{m + n}{2(b - a)}\ [b^2 - a^2] - ny$$

$$= \frac{m + n}{2(b - a)}\ (b - a)(b + a) - ny$$

$$= \left(\frac{m + n}{2}\right)(b + a) - ny$$

which is strictly decreasing from y = b.

A graph of our E(Profit (X)) with respect to y so far is

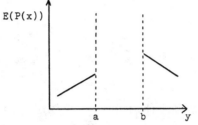

We do not know anything about the expected profit when y is in the interval (a, b) but we can see what the maximum profit with respect to y will be for a $\leq$ y $\leq$ b.

When a $\leq$ y $\leq$ b

$$E(P(X)) = \frac{1}{b - a} \left[ \int_a^b P(x) \, dx \right]$$

$$= \frac{1}{b - a} \left[ \int_a^y P(x) \, dx + \int_y^b P(x) \, dx \right]$$

$$= \frac{1}{b - a} \left[ \int_a^y [mx - n(y - x) \, dx + \int_y^b my \, dx \right]$$

$$= \frac{1}{b - a} \left[ \int_a^y [(m + n)x - ny] \, dx + myx \Big|_y^b \right]$$

$$= \frac{1}{b - a} \left[ \frac{m + n}{2} x^2 \Big|_a^y - nyx \Big|_a^y + my(b - y) \right]$$

$$= \frac{1}{b - a} \left[ \frac{m + n}{2} (y^2 - a^2) - ny(y - a) + mby - my^2 \right]$$

$$E(P(X)) = \frac{1}{b - a} \left[ \frac{-(m + n)}{2} y^2 + (na + mb)y + (\frac{m + n}{2}) a^2 \right].$$

We see that the expected profit is a polynomial in y.

To maximize E(P(X)) we differentiate and then solve for y when $\frac{d \, E(P(X))}{dy} = 0.$

$$\frac{d \, E(P(X))}{dy} = \frac{1}{b - a} [-(m + n)y + (na + mb)] = 0$$

implies that $y = \dfrac{na + mb}{m + n}$ is the amount of cloth lengths

that will maximize the expected profit.

● **PROBLEM** 7-20

A drunk wanders out of a bar thoroughly inebriated. At each step he will move to the right 1 meter with probability p or to the left 1 meter with probability 1 - p. How many meters from the entrance to the bar do you expect the drunk to be after n steps?

Solution:    To help visualize this problem we draw the picture below:

Let $X_n$ = number of meters from entrance after n steps

Let $Z_t = \begin{cases} 1 \text{ with probability p if the drunk moves right} \\ -1 \text{ with probability } 1 - p \text{ if the drunk moves left}. \end{cases}$

We wish to find $E(X_n)$ = expected number of meters from entrance after n steps.

But $X_n = \sum\limits_{t=1}^{n} Z_t$.

To see this let us observe one actualization of this random walk, where n = 4

Step 1:  the drunk moves right, $X_1 = Z_1 = 1$

Step 2:  the drunk moves left, $Z_2 = -1$,

and $X_2 = Z_1 + Z_2 = 1 - 1 = 0$

Step 3:  the drunk moves right, $Z_3 = 1$

and $X_3 = Z_1 + Z_2 + Z_3 = 1 - 1 + 1 = 1$

Step 4:  the drunk moves right, $Z_4 = 1$

and $X_4 = Z_1 + Z_2 + Z_3 + Z_4 = 1 - 1 + 1 + 1 = 2$

Our drunk has wandered 2 meters to the right of the bar and we have charted his position by adding $Z_t$'s.

The $E(X_n) = E\left( \sum\limits_{t=1}^{n} Z_t \right)$

$$= \sum_{t=1}^{n} E(Z_t) \text{ by the rules of expectation.}$$

All we need to solve for the expected position of the drunk is $E(Z_t)$.

$$E(Z_t) = 1 \times p + (-1) \times (1 - p) = 2p - 1$$

$$\text{and } E(X_n) = \sum_{t=1}^{n} (2p - 1) = \underbrace{(2p - 1) + \ldots + (2p - 1)}_{n \text{ times}}$$

$$= n(2p - 1).$$

If $n = 10$ and $p = \frac{1}{3}$ we would expect the drunk to be $10 \left[ 2 \left( \frac{1}{3} \right) - 1 \right] = 10 \left( -\frac{1}{3} \right) = -\frac{10}{3}$ or $\frac{10}{3}$ meters to the left after 10 steps.

If $p = \frac{1}{2}$, $E(X_n) = n \left[ 2 \left( \frac{1}{2} \right) - 1 \right] = n \times 0 = 0$.

No matter how many steps the drunk takes if he is equally likely to move to the right or left $\left( p = \frac{1}{2} \right)$ we can expect him back at the bar.

# GENERAL RULES OF EXPECTATION

● **PROBLEM** 7-21

Find the expected values of the random variables X and Y if $\quad \Pr(X = 0) = \frac{1}{2}\quad$ and $\Pr(X = 1) = \frac{1}{2}$

and $\quad \Pr(Y = 1) = \frac{1}{4}\quad$ and $\Pr(Y = 2) = \frac{3}{4}$.

Compare the sum of $E(X) + E(Y)$ with $E(X + Y)$ if $\Pr(X = x, Y = y) = \Pr(X = x)\Pr(Y = y)$.

Solution: The expected value of X is

$$E(X) = 0 \cdot \Pr(X = 0) + 1 \cdot \Pr(X = 1) = (0)\left(\frac{1}{2}\right) + (1)\left(\frac{1}{2}\right) = \frac{1}{2}$$

The expected value of Y is

$$E(Y) = 1 \cdot \Pr(Y = 1) + 2 \cdot \Pr(Y = 2) = \frac{1}{4} + \frac{6}{4} = \frac{7}{4}.$$

Thus, $\quad E(X) + E(Y) = \frac{1}{2} + \frac{7}{4} = \frac{9}{4}.$

To find the expected value of the random variable (X + Y) we need the joint distribution of X and Y. This has been given to be

$Pr(X = x, Y = y) = Pr(X = x) \ Pr(Y = y).$

The distribution for X and Y is

$Pr(X = 0, Y = 1) = \frac{1}{2} \cdot \frac{1}{4} = \frac{1}{8}$

$Pr(X = 0, Y = 2) = \frac{1}{2} \cdot \frac{3}{4} = \frac{3}{8}$

$Pr(X = 1, Y = 1) = \frac{1}{2} \cdot \frac{1}{4} = \frac{1}{8}$

$Pr(X = 1, Y = 2) = \frac{1}{2} \cdot \frac{3}{4} = \frac{3}{8}$

$E(X + Y) = \sum_{x} \sum_{y} (x + y) \ Pr(X = x, Y = y).$

That is, the expected value of the random variable X + Y is the sum of the possible values that X + Y can assume times the probability that X + Y will assume these values.

Thus, $E(X + Y) = (0 + 1) \ Pr(X = 0, Y = 1) \quad +$

$(0 + 2) \ Pr(X = 0, Y = 2) \quad +$

$(1 + 1) \ Pr(X = 1, Y = 1) \quad +$

$(1 + 2) \ Pr(X = 1, Y = 2) \ ;$

$E(X + Y) = 1 \cdot \frac{1}{8} + 2 \cdot \frac{3}{8} + 2 \cdot \frac{1}{8} + 3 \cdot \frac{3}{8}$

$= \frac{1}{8} + \frac{6}{8} + \frac{2}{8} + \frac{9}{8} = \frac{18}{8} = \frac{9}{4} \ .$

Thus $E(X + Y) = E(X) + E(Y).$

● **PROBLEM** 7-22

Show that the sum of the expected value of two discrete random variables with joint density f(x, y) is equal to the expected value of the sum of these two random variables. That is

$$E(X + Y) = E(X) + E(Y).$$

Solution:      The expected value of X is    $E(X) = \sum_{x} x \ g(x)$

where $g(x) = Pr(X = x) =$ the marginal distribution of X. The marginal distribution of X is   $\sum_{y} f(x, y).$

The expected value of Y is    $E(Y) = \sum_{y} y \ h(y)$

where h(y) is the marginal distribution of Y or $\sum_x f(x, y)$.

The expected value of X + Y is

$$E(X + Y) = \sum_x \sum_y (x + y) f(x, y)$$

but rearranging the terms in this sum we see that

$$E(X + Y) = \sum_x \sum_y x\, f(x, y) + \sum_x \sum_y y\, f(x, y)$$

$$= \sum_x x \left[ \sum_y f(x, y) \right] + \sum_y \sum_x y\, f(x, y)$$

$$= \sum_x x \left[ \sum_y f(x, y) \right] + \sum_y y \left[ \sum_x f(x, y) \right].$$

But $\sum_y f(x, y) = g(x)$ and $\sum_x f(x, y) = h(y)$.

Thus, $E(X + Y) = \sum_x x\, g(x) + \sum_y y\, h(y) = E(X) + E(Y)$.

This result is still valid if X and Y are continuous random variables. The summation signs are replaced by integral signs throughout the proof.

● **PROBLEM 7-23**

Show that $E(aX) = aE(X)$ if a is constant and X is a continuous or discrete random variable with probability density f(x).

Solution: First consider the case where X is a discrete random variable. Here X can take on a finite or countably infinite number of values. The expected value of X, or of a function of X is

$$E(X) = \sum_{\substack{all \\ x}} x\, f(x) \qquad or \qquad E(g(x)) = \sum_{\substack{all \\ x}} g(x)\, f(x).$$

Consider the function of X to be g(X) = aX, then

$$E(g(X)) = E(aX) \qquad but \qquad E(g(x)) = \sum_x g(x)\, f(x) = \sum_x ax\, f(x).$$

Now a is a constant and can be factored out of the sum, thus $E(aX) = a \sum_x x\, f(x) = a\, E(X)$.

If X is a continuous random variable, $E(X) = \int_{\substack{all \\ x}} x\, f(x)\, dx$

and $E(g(X)) = \int_{\substack{\text{all} \\ x}} g(x)\ f(x)\ dx$ .

If $g(X) = aX$, then $E(g(X)) = E(aX) = \int_{\substack{\text{all} \\ x}} ax\ f(x)\ dx$

and by a property of integration   the constant a may
be factored outside the integral sign to obtain

$E(aX) = a \int_{\substack{\text{all} \\ x}} x\ f(x)\ dx = a\ E(X)$ .

● **PROBLEM** 7-24

Find the expected value of the product of two independent
random variables, X and Y.

Solution:   Let f(x, y) be the joint density of the
variables X and Y. Then in the discrete case,

$E(X \cdot Y) = \underset{x}{\Sigma}\ \underset{y}{\Sigma}\ xy\ f(x,\ y)$ .

If X and Y are independent, their joint density
function can be factored into the marginal densities of
X and Y. Thus if g(x) and h(y) are the densities of X and
Y respectively f(x, y) = g(x) h(y).

Substituting we see that: $E(X \cdot Y) = \underset{x}{\Sigma}\ \underset{y}{\Sigma}\ xy\ g(x)\ h(y)$ .

Factoring we see  that: $E(X \cdot Y) = \underset{x}{\Sigma}\ x\ g(x) \left[ \underset{y}{\Sigma}\ y\ h(y) \right]$

but $\underset{y}{\Sigma}\ y\ h(y) = E(y)$   and   $\underset{x}{\Sigma}\ x\ g(x) = E(X)$.

Thus, substituting again we derive:   $E(X \cdot Y) = E(X) \cdot E(Y)$.

This result is also true if X and Y are continuous
random variables and the summation signs are replaced by
integral signs.

# CONDITIONAL EXPECTATION AND EXPECTED VALUE OF  MULTIVARIATE DENSITIES

● **PROBLEM** 7-25

Suppose the random vector (X, Y) is distributed with
probability density,

$$f(x, y) = \begin{cases} x + y & \begin{array}{l} 0 < x < 1 \\ 0 < y < 1 \end{array} \\ \\ 0 & \text{otherwise.} \end{cases}$$

Find $E[XY]$, $E[X + Y]$ and $E(X)$.

Solution:    By definition,

$$E(g(x, y)) = \int \int_{(x, y)} g(x, y)\, f(x, y)\, dx\, dy$$

Thus, if $g(x,y) = xy$, we have: $E(xy) = \int_0^1 \int_0^1 xy\, (x + y)\, dx\, dy$

$$= \int_0^1 \left[ \int_0^1 (x^2 y + xy^2)\, dx \right] dy = \int_0^1 \left[ \frac{x^3 y}{3} + \frac{x^2 y^2}{2} \right]_0^1 dy$$

$$= \int_0^1 \left( \frac{y}{3} + \frac{y^2}{2} \right) dy = \left[ \frac{y^2}{6} + \frac{y^3}{6} \right]_0^1 = \frac{2}{6} = \frac{1}{3} \; .$$

$$E(X + Y) = \int_0^1 \int_0^1 (x + y)(x + y)\, dx\, dy$$

$$= \int_0^1 \int_0^1 (x^2 + 2xy + y^2)\, dx\, dy$$

$$= \int_0^1 \left[ \frac{x^3}{3} + \frac{2\,x^2 y}{2} + y^2 x \right]_0^1 dy$$

$$= \int_0^1 \left[ \frac{1}{3} + y + y^2 \right] dy$$

$$= \left[ \frac{y}{3} + \frac{y^2}{2} + \frac{y^3}{3} \right]_0^1 = \frac{1}{3} + \frac{1}{2} + \frac{1}{3} = \frac{7}{6} \; .$$

$$E(X) = \int_0^1 \int_0^1 x(x + y)\, dx\, dy = \int_0^1 \left[ \frac{x^3}{3} + \frac{x^2 y}{2} \right]_0^1 dy$$

$$= \int_0^1 \left[ \frac{1}{3} + \frac{y}{2} \right] dy = \left[ \frac{y}{3} + \frac{y^2}{4} \right]_0^1$$

$$= \frac{1}{3} + \frac{1}{4} = \frac{7}{12} \; .$$

248

Let the three-dimensional random variable $(X_1, X_2, X_3)$ have the density function

$f(x_1, x_2, x_3) = 8\, x_1 x_2 x_3$ for $0 < x_1 < 1$, $0 < x_2 < 1$

$0 < x_3 < 1$.

Find $E[3X_1 + 2X_2 + 6X_3]$

$E[X_1 X_2 X_3]$ and $E[X_1 X_2]$.

Solution: We know that $E(g(x_1, x_2, x_3)) =$

$$\iiint\limits_{\substack{\text{all} \\ x_i}} \left[ g(x_1, x_2, x_3)\, f(x_1, x_2, x_3)\, dx_1\, dx_2\, dx_3 \right].$$

Thus when $g(x_1, x_2, x_3) = 3 x_1 + 2x_2 + 6x_3$, $E(3x_1 + 2x_2 + 6x_3)$

$$= \int_0^1 \int_0^1 \int_0^1 (3x_1 + 2x_2 + 6x_3)\, 8x_1 x_2 x_3\, dx_1\, dx_2\, dx_3$$

$$= 8 \int_0^1 \int_0^1 x_2 x_3 \left[ \int_0^1 (3x_1^2 + 2x_1 x_2 + 6x_1 x_3)\, dx_1 \right] dx_2 dx_3$$

$$= 8 \int_0^1 \int_0^1 x_2 x_3 \left[ \frac{3x_1^3}{3} + \frac{2x_1^2 x_2}{2} + \frac{6x_1^2 x_3}{2} \right]_0^1 dx_2\, dx_3$$

$$= 8 \int_0^1 \int_0^1 x_2 x_3 [1 + x_2 + 3x_3]\, dx_2\, dx_3$$

$$= 8 \int_0^1 x_3 \left[ \int_0^1 (1 + x_2 + 3x_3)\, x_2\, dx_2 \right] dx_3$$

$$= 8 \int_0^1 x_3 \left| \frac{x_2^2}{2} + \frac{x_2^3}{3} + \frac{3x_2^2 x_3}{2} \right|_0^1 dx_3$$

$$= 8 \int_0^1 x_3 \left[ \frac{1}{2} + \frac{1}{3} + \frac{3x_3}{2} \right] dx_3$$

$$= 8 \int_0^1 \left[ \frac{5}{6} + \frac{3x_3}{2} \right] x_3\, dx_3 = 8 \left[ \frac{5}{12} x_3^2 + \frac{x_3^3}{2} \right]_0^1$$

$$= 8 \left[ \frac{5}{12} + \frac{1}{2} \right] = 8 \left[ \frac{11}{12} \right] = 2 \left[ \frac{11}{3} \right]$$

$$= \frac{22}{3} .$$

$$E[X_1 X_2 X_3] = \int_0^1 \int_0^1 \int_0^1 (x_1 x_2 x_3) \; 8x_1 x_2 x_3 \; [dx_1 \; dx_2 \; dx_3]$$

$$= 8 \int_0^1 \int_0^1 \int_0^1 x_1{}^2 x_2{}^2 x_3{}^2 \; dx_1 \; dx_2 \; dx_3$$

$$= 8 \int_0^1 \int_0^1 x_2{}^2 x_3{}^2 \left[ \int_0^1 x_1{}^2 \; dx_1 \right] dx_2 \; dx_3$$

$$= 8 \int_0^1 \int_0^1 x_2{}^2 x_3{}^2 \left[ \frac{x_1{}^3}{3} \right]_0^1 dx_2 \; dx_3$$

$$= \frac{8}{3} \int_0^1 \int_0^1 x_2{}^2 x_3{}^2 \; dx_2 \; dx_3 \qquad = \frac{8}{3} \int_0^1 x_3{}^2 \left[ \frac{x_2{}^3}{3} \right]_0^1 dx_3$$

$$= \frac{8}{9} \int_0^1 x_3{}^2 \; dx_3 = \frac{8}{27} .$$

$$E(X_1 X_2) = \int_0^1 \int_0^1 \int_0^1 x_1 x_2 \; 8x_1 x_2 x_3 \; dx_1 \; dx_2 \; dx_3$$

$$= 8 \int_0^1 \int_0^1 x_2{}^2 x_3 \left[ \int_0^1 x_1{}^2 \; dx_1 \right] dx_2 \; dx_3$$

$$\frac{8}{3} \int_0^1 x_3 \left[ \int_0^1 x_2{}^2 \; dx_2 \right] dx_3$$

$$= \frac{8}{9} \int_0^1 x_3 \; dx_3 = \frac{8}{9} \left[ \frac{x_3{}^2}{2} \right]_0^1$$

$$= \frac{8}{9} \cdot \frac{1}{2} = \frac{4}{9} .$$

● PROBLEM 7-27

Compute the conditional distribution of Y given X if X and Y are jointly distributed with density

$$f(x,\ y) = \begin{cases} x + y & \begin{array}{l} 0 < x < 1 \\ 0 < y < 1 \end{array} \\ \\ 0 & \text{otherwise.} \end{cases}$$

What is the conditional expectation of Y?

Solution: The conditional distribution of Y given X is defined by analogy with conditional probability to be:

$$f(y|x) = \frac{f(x,\ y)}{f(x)}$$

where $f(x,\ y)$ is the joint density of x and y and $f(x)$ is the marginal distribution of x.

In our example,

$$f(x) = \int_0^1 f(x,\ y)\ dy$$

$$= \int_0^1 (x + y)\ dy = \left[ xy + \frac{y^2}{2} \right]_0^1$$

$$= x + \frac{1}{2} \qquad\qquad 0 < x < 1 .$$

Thus

$$f(y|x) = \frac{f(x,\ y)}{f(x)} = \frac{x + y}{x + \frac{1}{2}} \qquad \begin{array}{l} 0 < y < 1 \\ 0 < x < 1 \end{array} .$$

To see that $f(y|x)$ is a proper density function,

$$\int_0^1 f(y|x)\ dy = \int_0^1 \frac{x + y}{x + \frac{1}{2}}\ dy = \left( \frac{1}{x + \frac{1}{2}} \right) \int_0^1 (x + y)\ dy$$

$$= \left( \frac{1}{x + \frac{1}{2}} \right) \left( xy + \frac{y^2}{2} \right)_0^1 = \frac{x + \frac{1}{2}}{x + \frac{1}{2}} = 1 .$$

The conditional expectation of Y given X is the expectation of y against the conditional density $f(y|x)$.

Thus,

$$E\left(Y\big/X = x\right) = \int_{\text{all } y} y\ f\left(y\big/x\right)\ dy .$$

For our example,

$$E(Y|X = x) = \int_0^1 y \left( \frac{x + y}{x + \frac{1}{2}} \right)\ dy = \left( \frac{1}{x + \frac{1}{2}} \right) \int_0^1 (xy + y^2)\ dy$$

$$= \frac{1}{x + \frac{1}{2}} \left[ \frac{xy^2}{2} + \frac{y^3}{3} \right]_0^1 = \frac{\frac{x}{2} + \frac{1}{3}}{x + \frac{1}{2}}$$

$$= \frac{3x + 2}{3(2x + 1)} \qquad 0 < x < 1 .$$

Conditional expectations may be used to find unconditional expectations. Show that

$$E[E(Y|X=x)] = E(Y).$$

<u>Solution:</u>    Let $f(x)$, $f(y)$ and $f(x, y)$ be the marginal distribution of X, the marginal distribution of Y and the joint density of X and Y respectively.

$E(Y|X=x)$ is in general a function of x, say $E(Y|X=x) = h(x)$, then

$$E[E(Y|X=x)] = E[h(x)]$$

but the expected value of any function of a random variable is that function integrated against the density of X. Thus

$$E[E(Y|X=x)] = E(h(x)) = \int_{-\infty}^{\infty} h(x) \ f(x) \ dx$$

but   $E(Y|X=x) = h(x) = \displaystyle\int_{-\infty}^{\infty} y \ f(y|x) \ dy .$

Thus

$$E[E(Y|X=x)] = \int_{-\infty}^{\infty} \left[ \int_{-\infty}^{\infty} y \ f(y|x) \ dy \right] f(x) \ dx$$

$$= \int_{-\infty}^{\infty} \int_{-\infty}^{\infty} y \ f(y|x) \ f(x) \ dy \ dx .$$

Letting $f(y|x) = \dfrac{f(x, y)}{f(x)}$,

$$E \ E(Y/X=x) = \int_{-\infty}^{\infty} \int_{-\infty}^{\infty} \frac{y \ f(x, y)}{f(x)} f(x) \ dy \ dx$$

$$= \int_{-\infty}^{\infty} \int_{-\infty}^{\infty} y \ f(x, y) \ dy \ dx$$

$$= \int_{-\infty}^{\infty} y \left[ \int_{-\infty}^{\infty} f(x, y) \, dx \right] dy$$

and
$$\int_{-\infty}^{\infty} f(x, y) \, dx = f(y).$$

Thus
$$E[(Y|X=x)] = \int_{-\infty}^{\infty} y \, f(y) \, dy = E(Y).$$

● **PROBLEM** 7-29

Find the theoretical variance of the random variable with the following probability distribution.

| x | Pr(X = x) |
|---|-----------|
| 0 | $\frac{1}{4}$ |
| 1 | $\frac{1}{2}$ |
| 2 | $\frac{1}{8}$ |
| 3 | $\frac{1}{8}$ |

Solution:    The theoretical variance is the expected mean square error. The theoretical variance represents an idealized measure of the spread or dispersion of a probability distribution about its mean.

The variance of a random variable X is denoted $\sigma_x^2$ or Var X. It is defined as

Var $X = E[(X - \mu)^2]$,

where $\mu = E(X)$.

In this example,

$E(X) = (0) \Pr(X = 0) + (1) \Pr(X = 1)$

$+ (2) \Pr(X = 2) + 3\Pr(X = 3)$

$$= 0 \cdot \frac{1}{4} + 1 \cdot \frac{1}{2} + 2 \cdot \frac{1}{8} + 3 \cdot \frac{1}{8}$$

$$= 0 + \frac{1}{2} + \frac{2}{8} + \frac{3}{8} = \frac{9}{8} .$$

We now compute the variance of X.

$$\text{Var } X = E[(X - \mu)^2]$$

$$= E \left[ \left( X - \frac{9}{8} \right)^2 \right]$$

$$= \left( 0 - \frac{9}{8} \right)^2 \Pr(X = 0) + \left( 1 - \frac{9}{8} \right)^2 \Pr(X = 1)$$

$$+ \left( 2 - \frac{9}{8} \right)^2 \Pr(X = 2) + \left( 3 - \frac{9}{8} \right)^2 \Pr(X = 3)$$

$$= \left( \frac{81}{64} \cdot \frac{1}{4} \right) + \left( \frac{1}{64} \cdot \frac{1}{2} \right) + \left( \frac{49}{64} \cdot \frac{1}{8} \right) + \left( \frac{225}{64} \cdot \frac{1}{8} \right)$$

$$= \frac{2 (81) + 4 + 49 + 225}{64 (8)}$$

$$= \frac{440}{(64) 8} = \frac{55}{64} = .859 .$$

A slightly less complicated formula for the theoretical variance is derived below,

$$E[(X - \mu)^2] = E[X^2 - 2X\mu + \mu^2] .$$

By the properties of expectation,

$$E[(X - \mu)^2] = E(X^2) - 2\mu E(X) + E(\mu^2) .$$

$E(\mu^2) = \mu^2$      because the expected value of a constant is a constant. Thus,

$$E[(X - \mu)^2] = E(X^2) - 2\mu E(X) + \mu^2$$

$E(X) = \mu$ ;     thus

$$\text{Var } X = E(X^2) - 2\mu \cdot \mu + \mu^2$$

$$= E(X^2) - 2\mu^2 + \mu^2 \quad = E(X^2) - \mu^2$$

or     $\text{Var } X = E(X^2) - [E(X)]^2 .$

Recomputing Var X we see that

$$\text{Var } X = 0^2 \cdot \Pr(X = 0) + 1^2 \Pr(X = 1) + 2^2 \Pr(X = 2)$$

$$+ 3^2 \Pr(X = 3) - \left[ \frac{9}{8} \right]^2$$

$$= 0 + \frac{1}{2} + \frac{4}{8} + \frac{9}{8} - \left[\frac{9}{8}\right]^2$$

$$= \frac{(17)\ 8 - 81}{64} = \frac{136 - 81}{64} = \frac{55}{64} = .859 \ .$$

# VARIANCE OF DISCRETE RANDOM VARIABLES

● **PROBLEM** 7-30

Given the probability distribution of the random variable X in the table below, compute E(X) and Var (X).

| $x_i$ | $\Pr(X = x_i)$ |
|-------|----------------|
| 0 | $\frac{8}{27}$ |
| 1 | $\frac{12}{27}$ |
| 2 | $\frac{6}{27}$ |
| 3 | $\frac{1}{27}$ |

Solution:

$$E(X) = \sum_i x_i \Pr(X = x_i) \quad \text{and} \quad \text{Var } X = E\left[(X - E(X))^2\right] .$$

Thus, $E(X) = (0)\ \Pr(X = 0) + (1)\ \Pr(X = 1)$

$$+ (2)\ \Pr(X = 2) + (3)\ \Pr(X = 3)$$

$$= (0)\ \frac{8}{27} + (1)\ \frac{12}{27} + (2)\ \frac{6}{27} + 3\ \left(\frac{1}{27}\right)$$

$$= 0 + \frac{12}{27} + \frac{12}{27} + \frac{3}{27} = \frac{27}{27} = 1.$$

Var $X = (0 - 1)^2\ \Pr(X = 0) + (1 - 1)^2\ \Pr(X = 1)$

$$+ (2 - 1)^2\ \Pr(X = 2) + (3 - 1)^2\ \Pr(X = 3)$$

$$= (1^2)\ \frac{8}{27} + (0^2)\ \frac{12}{27} + (1^2)\ \frac{6}{27} + (2^2)\ \frac{1}{27}$$

$$= \frac{8}{27} + \frac{6}{27} + \frac{4}{27} = \frac{18}{27} = \frac{2}{3} \ .$$

Given the following table of probabilities for values $x_i$ of the random variable X, which represents the number of defective radios in a shipment of four, find the variance and standard deviation of X.

| $x_i$ | $P(X = x_i)$ |
|-------|--------------|
| 0 | $\frac{1}{16}$ |
| 1 | $\frac{4}{16}$ |
| 2 | $\frac{6}{16}$ |
| 3 | $\frac{4}{16}$ |
| 4 | $\frac{1}{16}$ |

Solution:    The variance of a random variable X is defined to be

$$E[X - E(X)]^2 = \sigma^2.$$

Since we have a discrete set of data, the most efficient method of finding the variance is to construct a table which will extend the given one. First compute the expected number of defective radios:

$$E(X) = \sum_{i=0}^{4} x_i \Pr(X = x_i)$$

$$= 0 \cdot \left(\frac{1}{16}\right) + 1 \cdot \left(\frac{4}{16}\right) + 2 \cdot \left(\frac{6}{16}\right) + 3 \cdot \left(\frac{4}{16}\right) + 4 \cdot \left(\frac{1}{16}\right)$$

$$= \frac{4}{16} + \frac{12}{16} + \frac{12}{16} + \frac{4}{16} = \frac{32}{16} = 2.$$

| $x_i$ | $P(X = x_i)$ | $E(X) = (x_i - 2)$ | $(x_i - 2)^2$ | $(x_i - 2)^2 P(X = x_i)$ |
|-------|--------------|--------------------|----------------|---------------------------|
| 0 | $\frac{1}{16}$ | $-2$ | 4 | $\frac{4}{16}$ |
| 1 | $\frac{4}{16}$ | $-1$ | 1 | $\frac{4}{16}$ |
| 2 | $\frac{6}{16}$ | 0 | 0 | 0 |

| 3 | $\frac{4}{16}$ | 1 | 1 | $\frac{4}{16}$ |
| 4 | $\frac{1}{16}$ | 2 | 4 | $\frac{4}{16}$ |

The variance of a discrete random variable X is defined to be

$$\sigma^2 = \sum_{i=1}^{n} (x_i - E(X))^2 P(X = x_i).$$

Observe that in this problem $\sigma^2$ is the sum of the entries in the last column of the table

$$\sigma^2 = \frac{4}{16} + \frac{4}{16} + 0 + \frac{4}{16} + \frac{4}{16} = \frac{16}{16} = 1.$$

The standard deviation of $\sigma$ of X is

$$\sigma = \sqrt{\sigma^2} = \sqrt{1} = 1.$$

● **PROBLEM** 7-32

The probability that a certain baseball player will get a hit on any given time at bat is $\frac{3}{10}$ . If he is at bat one hundred times during the next month, find the theoretical mean and variance of x, the number of hits. Assume that the binomial distribution is applicable.

Solution:    The theoretical mean or expected value of X, the number of hits, is an idealized average. The expected value of X is the number of hits we would expect to see over the next 100 times at bat. The expected value of X, written as E(X) or μ is equal to

$$0 \cdot Pr(X = 0) + 1 \cdot Pr(X = 1) + 2 \cdot Pr(X = 2) + \ldots +$$

$$100 \, Pr(X = 100).$$

Since the binomial distribution is applicable

$$Pr(X = j) = \binom{n}{j} p^j (1 - p)^{n-j} \quad j = 0, 1, \ldots n$$

and $n = 100$, $p = \frac{3}{10}$ .

Writing E(X) using summation notation we see that

$$E(X) = \sum_{j=0}^{100} j \binom{100}{j} \left(\frac{3}{10}\right)^j \left(\frac{7}{10}\right)^{100-j}.$$

One way to simplify this expression is to decompose the event X hits in terms of other random variables.

Let $z_i = \begin{cases} 1 & \text{if the ith trial results in a hit} \\ 0 & \text{if the ith trial does not result in a hit.} \end{cases}$

Then $X = z_1 + z_2 + \dots + z_{100}$   or   $X = \sum\limits_{i=1}^{100} z_i$

$$E(X) = E\left(\sum\limits_{i=1}^{100} z_i\right) = \sum\limits_{i=1}^{100} E(z_i)$$

by the rules of expectation. Let

$z_j = \begin{cases} 1 \text{ with probability p the batter hits} \\ 0 \text{ with probability } 1 - p \text{ the batter misses} \end{cases}$

$E(z_i) = 1 \times p + 0 \times (1 - p) = p.$

$$E(X) = \sum\limits_{i=1}^{100} E(z_i) = \sum\limits_{j=1}^{100} p = \underbrace{p + p + \dots + p}_{100 \text{ terms}}$$

$$= 100\,p$$

and since $p = \dfrac{3}{10}$,   $E(X) = 100\left(\dfrac{3}{10}\right) = 30$.

We would expect 30 hits in the next 100 times at bat.

The theoretical variance of X is an idealized measure of the dispersion or spread of X, the number of hits about the idealized average. This theoretical variance is denoted by $\sigma^2$ or Var X and is defined to be

Var $X = E([X - E(X)]^2)$ ;

from this definition follow the rules of variance, especially that if X and Y are independent random variables

Var $(X + Y) = $ Var $X + $ Var $Y$.

Returning to our problem we see that

$$\text{Var } X = \text{Var}\left(\sum\limits_{i=1}^{100} z_i\right)$$

$$= \sum\limits_{i=1}^{100} \text{Var } z_i \quad \text{because the } z_j\text{'s are independent.}$$

Now Var $z_i = E([Z - E(z_i)]^2)$

$$= E([z_i - p]^2) = E(z_i{}^2) - p^2$$

$$E(Z_i{}^2) = 1^2 \cdot p + 0^2 \cdot (1 - p) = p \qquad \text{thus}$$

$$\text{Var } Z_i = p - p^2 = p(1 - p).$$

$$\text{Thus} \qquad \text{Var } X = \sum_{i=1}^{100} \text{Var } Z_i = \sum_{i=1}^{100} (p - p^2)$$

$$= \underbrace{p - p^2 + \ldots + p - p^2}_{100 \text{ terms}}$$

$$= 100 \ (p)(1 - p).$$

Since $p = \dfrac{3}{10}$, $\qquad \text{Var } X = 100 \left(\dfrac{3}{10}\right)\left(\dfrac{7}{10}\right) = 21.$

Thus we would expect the number of hits to be dispersed around the ideal mean with theoretical variance 21.

● **PROBLEM 7-33**

Suppose that 75% of the students taking statistics pass the course. In a class of 40 students, what is the expected number who will pass. Find the variance and standard deviation.

<u>Solution:</u>     Let X be a random variable denoting the number of students in the class of 40 who will pass the course.

If 75% of the students pass the course it is reasonable to assume that a randomly chosen student will pass the course with probability .75 and fail the course with probability .25. It is also reasonable to assume that a student passes or fails the course independently of what other students do.

With these two assumptions, it can be shown that X is a binomially distributed random variable with parameters p = .75 and n = 40. The parameter p indicates the probability of a student passing the course and n represents the number of students in the class.

In the previous problem, we have shown that the expected value of such a random variable is

$E(X) = np$ .          In this case,

$E(X) = (40)(.75) = 30.$

It has also been shown that the variance of X is

$\sigma^2 = \text{Var } X = np(1 - p)$     and substituting we see that:

$\sigma^2 = $ Var X $(40)(.75)(1 - .75) \quad = 7.5$ .

The standard deviation is defined as $\sigma = \sqrt{\text{Var X}}$ ;

thus $\quad \sigma = \sqrt{np(1 - p)} = \sqrt{7.5} = 2.74$.

A new insecticide is advertised as being 90% effective in killing ants with 1 application. If 10,000 ants are treated with one application of the insecticide, find the expected value, variance and standard deviation of the number of ants killed.

Solution: We find the theoretical mean or expected value of a random variable X, by multiplying the outcomes of this random variable by the probability of its occurrence and adding the products.

Thus, $E(X) = \mu = x_1 P(x_1) + x_2 P(x_2) + \ldots + x_n P(x_n)$

$$= \sum_{i=1}^{n} x_i \, Pr(X = x_i) .$$

Let X = the number of ants killed out of the 10,000 ants treated with the insecticide. Each ant is killed with probability p = .90 or survives with probability 1 - p = 1 - .90 = .10. It is reasonable to assume that the effect of the insecticide on a single ant is independent of the insecticide's effect on any of the other ants. With these two assumptions, we see that X is the sum of n = 10,000 independent trials each with probability p = .90 of "success" and probability 1 - p = .10 of "failure". Thus X is by definition a binomially distributed random variable with parameters p = .90 and n = 10,000.

To find the expected value of X, we use our previously derived results namely, $E(X) = np$ and

$\sigma^2 = $ Var X $= np(1 - p)$, $\quad \sigma = \sqrt{\sigma^2} = \sqrt{np(1 - p)}$ .

Substituting we see that:

$E(X) = np = (10,000)(.90) = 9,000$

Var X $= np(1 - p) = (10,000)(.90)(.10) = 900$

$\sigma = \sqrt{\text{Var X}} = \sqrt{900} = 30$.

Use the properties of expectation to find the variance

of the sum of two independent random variables.

<u>Solution:</u>    The variance of the sum of two independent random variables, Var (X + Y), is defined to be

$$\text{Var } (X + Y) = E[(X + Y - E(X + Y))^2] ;$$

squaring inside the square brackets:

$$\text{Var } (X + Y) = E[(X + Y)^2 - 2(X + Y)E(X + Y) - (E(X + Y))^2] .$$

Squaring again yields:

$$\text{Var } (X + Y) = E[X^2 + 2XY + Y^2 - 2(X + Y)E(X + Y) - (E(X + Y))^2] .$$

But    $(E(X + Y))^2 = (E(X) + E(Y))^2$

$$= [E(X)]^2 + 2E(X)E(Y) + [E(Y)]^2 .$$

Substituting we see that:

$$\text{Var } (X + Y) = E[X^2 + 2XY + Y^2 - 2(X + Y)E(X + Y)$$
$$+ E(X)^2 + 2E(X)E(Y) + E(Y)^2] ;$$

but $E(X + Y)$, $E(X^2)$, $E(X)E(Y)$ and $E(Y^2)$ are constants, and E (a constant) = that constant, thus

$$\text{Var } (X + Y) = E(X^2 + 2XY + Y^2) - 2E(X + Y)E(X + Y) + [E(X + Y)]^2$$

$$\text{Var } (X + Y) = E[X^2 + 2XY + Y^2] - 2[E(X + Y)]^2 + [E(X + Y)]^2$$

$$= E[X^2 + 2XY + Y^2] - [E(X + Y)]^2$$

$$= E(X^2) + 2E(XY) + E(Y^2) - [E(X) + E(Y)]^2$$

but since X and Y are independent,   $E(XY) = E(X)E(Y)$.

Thus    $\text{Var}(X + Y) = E(X^2) + 2E(X)E(Y) + E(Y^2) - [E(X)]^2$
$$- 2E(X)E(Y) - [E(Y)]^2$$

$$= E(X^2) - [E(X)]^2 + E(Y^2) - [E(Y)]^2$$

$$= \text{Var } X \qquad\qquad + \text{Var } Y .$$

# VARIANCE OF CONTINUOUS RANDOM VARIABLES

● PROBLEM 7-36

Find the variance of the random variable X + b where X has variance, Var X and b is a constant.

<u>Solution:</u>

$$\text{Var } (X + b) = E[(X + b)^2] - [E(X + b)]^2$$

$$= E[X^2 + 2bX + b^2] - [E(X) + b]^2$$

$$= E(X^2) + 2bE(X) + b^2 - [E(X)]^2 - 2E(X)b - b^2,$$

thus $\text{Var }(X + b) = E(X^2) - [E(X)]^2 = \text{Var } X.$

● **PROBLEM** 7-37

Find the variance of the random variable Y = aX where a is a constant and X has variance, Var X = $\sigma^2$.

Solution:     We wish to find   Var Y = Var aX.

We know that   Var Y = $E(Y^2) - [E(Y)]^2$   but   $Y^2 = a^2 X^2$
and   E(Y) = E(aX) = a E(X).

$$\text{Var }(aX) = E(a^2 X^2) - [a E(X)]^2 \quad = a^2 E(X^2) - a^2 [E(X)]^2$$
$$= a^2 [E(X^2) - E(X)^2] \quad = a^2 \text{ Var } X.$$

● **PROBLEM** 7-38

A population consists of the measurements 2, 3, 3, 4, 4, 4, 5, 5, 5, 6, 6, 7. Compute: (a) $\mu$, (b) $\sigma^2$.

Solution:     Because the entire population is known, we may calculate $\mu$ and $\sigma^2$ directly. This is only possible when the entire population is known. If we have a sample from the entire population, we can only calculate estimates of $\mu$ and $\sigma^2$.

To find $\mu$, we multiply  each value in the population by its frequency of occurrence. Thus,

$$E(X) = \mu = 2\left(\frac{1}{12}\right) + 3\left(\frac{2}{12}\right) + 4\left(\frac{3}{12}\right) + 5\left(\frac{3}{12}\right) + 6\left(\frac{2}{12}\right) + 7\left(\frac{1}{12}\right)$$

$$\mu = \frac{2 + 6 + 12 + 15 + 12 + 7}{12} = \frac{54}{12} = 4.5 \ .$$

We also could have found $\mu$ by adding the population values and dividing by the number of values in the population.

By definition   $E(X - \mu)^2 = \sum_i (X_i - \mu)^2 \Pr(X_i - \mu)$

$$= \sum_i (X_i - \mu)^2 \Pr(X_i) \text{ since } \mu \text{ is invariant}$$

$$= \sum_i (X_i - \mu)^2 \frac{1}{n} \text{ since all } X_i \text{ are equally}$$
$$\text{likely to be chosen}$$

$$= \frac{1}{n} \sum_i (X_i - \mu)^2, \text{ the average squared}$$
$$\text{deviation from the mean } \mu.$$

To find $\sigma^2$, we calculate the average squared deviation from the mean $\mu$. Thus,

$$\sigma^2 = \frac{\sum\limits_{i=1}^{n} (X_i - \mu)^2}{n}$$

$$= \frac{(2 - 4.5)^2 + 2(3 - 4.5)^2 + 3(4 - 4.5)^2}{12}$$

$$+ \frac{3(5 - 4.5)^2 + 2(6 - 4.5)^2 + (7 - 4.5)^2}{12}$$

$$= \frac{(-2.5)^2 + 2(-1.5)^2 + 3(-.5)^2 + 3(.5)^2}{12}$$

$$+ \frac{2(1.5)^2 + (2.5)^2}{12}$$

$$= \frac{2(2.5)^2 + 4(1.5)^2 + 6(.5)^2}{12}$$

$$= \frac{12.5 + 4(2.25) + 1.5}{12} = \frac{12.5 + 10.5}{12} = \frac{23}{12} = 1.9 \ .$$

● **PROBLEM** 7-39

Given a population consisting of the measurements 1, 2, 4, 6, 8 and 9, compute its mean $\overline{X}$, standard deviation, and the expectation of $X$. If 4 numbers are selected at random without replacement from the population, find $\sigma_{\overline{X}}$.

Solution:     Because the entire population is known it is possible to calculate the mean and standard deviation directly.

$$E(X) = x_1 Pr(X = x_1) + \ldots x_n \, Pr(X = x_n) \ .$$

We know the entire population consists of 1, 2, 4, 6, 8 and 9; thus the random variable $X$ will take on each of these values with equal probability. Because there are 6 values, the probability that $X$ equals any of these 6 values is $\frac{1}{6}$ . Thus

$$E(X) = 1 \cdot \frac{1}{6} + 2 \cdot \frac{1}{6} + 4 \cdot \frac{1}{6} + 6 \cdot \frac{1}{6} + 8 \cdot \frac{1}{6} + 9 \cdot \frac{1}{6}$$

$$= \frac{1 + 2 + 4 + 6 + 8 + 9}{6} = \frac{30}{6} = 5 \ .$$

The variance of $X$ is the mean squared error or

$$\sigma_x^2 = Var \, X = E((X - E(X))^2) = E(X^2) - [E(X)]^2 \ ,$$

Thus

$$Var \, X = \left[ 1^2 \cdot \frac{1}{6} + 2^2 \cdot \frac{1}{6} + 4^2 \cdot \frac{1}{6} + 6^2 \cdot \frac{1}{6} + 8^2 \cdot \frac{1}{6} + 9^2 \cdot \frac{1}{6} \right] - (5)^2$$

$$\text{Var } X = \frac{1}{6} + \frac{4}{6} + \frac{16}{6} + \frac{36}{6} + \frac{64}{6} + \frac{81}{6} - 25$$

$$= \frac{202 - 150}{6} = \frac{52}{6} = 8.67$$

and the standard deviation of X is    $\sigma = \sqrt{\text{Var } X} = \sqrt{8.67} = 2.95$.

The random variable $\overline{X}$, is the sum of a random sample of observations from this population divided by the number of observations in the sample. Thus

$$\overline{X} = \frac{X_1 + X_2 + \ldots + X_n}{n} ,$$

where $X_1$, $X_2, \ldots, X_n$ constitutes a random sample from the population. Such a random variable which is a function of observations in a sample  is called a statistic.

$$E(\overline{X}) = E \left[ \frac{X_1 + X_2 + X_3 + \ldots + X_n}{n} \right].$$

By the properties of expectation,

$$E \left( \frac{X_1 + X_2 + \ldots + X_n}{n} \right) = \frac{1}{n} [E(X_1) + \ldots + E(X_n)]$$

but  $E(X_1) = E(X_2) = \ldots = E(X_n) = \mu$,   for all n, thus

$$E(\overline{X}) = \frac{n\mu}{n} = \mu .$$

In our example  $\mu = 5$  thus  $E(\overline{X}) = 5$  for any size random sample drawn from this population.

To find the variance $\overline{X}$, we must proceed with some caution. If the observations in the sample of 4 are each independent, then

$$\text{Var } \overline{X} = \text{Var } \frac{X_1 + X_2 + X_3 + X_4}{n}$$

$$= \frac{1}{n^2} [\text{Var } X_1 + \text{Var } X_2 + \text{Var } X_3 + \text{Var } X_4] .$$

But  $\text{Var } X_1 = \text{Var } X_2 = \text{Var } X_3 = \text{Var } X_4 = \sigma^2 .$

Thus        $\text{Var } \overline{X} = \frac{n\sigma^2}{n^2} = \frac{\sigma^2}{n} .$

In a small sample like the one in this problem, the observations $X_1$, $X_2$, $X_3$, $X_4$ will not be independent if sampling is done without replacement.

If sampling is done without replacement the variance must be corrected. The correction factor is $\frac{N - n}{N - 1}$ where n = the number of observations in the sample and N = the number of elements in the population. Thus for our sample,   $\text{Var } \bar{X} = \left(\dfrac{\sigma^2}{n}\right)\left(\dfrac{N-n}{N-1}\right)$

and the standard deviation is

$$\sigma_{\bar{X}} = \sqrt{\text{Var } \bar{X}} = \sqrt{\frac{N-n}{N-1} \cdot \frac{\sigma^2}{n}} = \frac{\sigma}{\sqrt{n}}\sqrt{\frac{N-n}{N-1}} \;.$$

Substituting we see that:

$$\sqrt{\text{Var } \bar{X}} = \frac{2.95}{\sqrt{4}}\sqrt{\frac{6-4}{6-1}} = \frac{2.95}{2}\sqrt{\frac{2}{5}} = .93 \;.$$

● **PROBLEM** 7-40

If X and Y are independent random variables with variances $\sigma_x{}^2 = 1$ and $\sigma_y^2 = 2$, find the variance of the random variable $Z = 3X - 2Y + 5$.

Solution:    Using the rules of variance,

Var Z = Var (3X - 2Y + 5) = Var 3X + Var(- 2Y) + Var 5

-because X and Y are independent -

$$= 3^2 \text{ Var } X + (-2)^2 \text{ Var } Y + 0$$

because Var aX = $a^2$ Var X and the variance of a constant is zero.

Var Z = 9 Var X + 4 Var Y.

Since Var X = 1        and Var Y = 2,

Var Z = 9·1 + 4·2 = 9 + 8 = 17.

● **PROBLEM** 7-41

Find the expected value and variance of a random variable,

$$Y = a_1 X_1 + a_2 X_2 + \ldots + a_n X_n$$

where the $X_i$ are independent and each have mean $\mu$ and variance $\sigma^2$. The $a_i$ are constants.

Solution:    By a generalization of the property that the expected value of a sum is the sum of the expected values,

$$E(Y) = E\left[a_1 X_1 + \ldots + a_n X_n\right] = E(a_1 X_1) + \ldots + E\left[a_n X_n\right] \;.$$

Also the expected value of a constant multiplied by

265

a random variable is the constant multiplied by the random variable or $E(aX) = a E(X)$. Thus,

$$E\left(a_i X_i\right) = a_i E\left(X_i\right) \qquad \text{and}$$

$$E(Y) = a_1 E(X_1) + a_2 E(X_2) + \ldots + a_n E\left(X_n\right).$$

But $E(X_1) = E(X_2) = E(X_3) \ldots = E\left(X_n\right) = \mu$;

hence $E(Y) = a_1\mu + a_2\mu + a_3\mu + \ldots + a_n\mu$

$$= \mu \left(a_1 + a_2 + a_3 + \ldots + a_n\right).$$

To find the variance of Y we generalize the properties of variance. Remember that if two variables, $X_1$ and $X_2$, are independent then the variance of $X_1 + X_2$ is the variance of $X_1$ + the variance of $X_2$.

Because $X_1, X_2, \ldots X_n$ are independent,

$$\text{Var } Y = \text{Var} \left(a_1 X_1 + \ldots + a_n X_n\right)$$

$$= \text{Var } (a_1 X_1) + \text{Var } (a_2 X_2) + \ldots + \text{Var} \left(a_n X_n\right).$$

Also, the variance of a constant multiplied with a random variable is the constant squared times the variance of the random variable. Equivalently,

$$\text{Var } (aX) = a^2 \text{ Var } X.$$

Thus, $\text{Var } a_i X_i = a_i^2 \text{ Var } X_i$.

But $\text{Var } X_i = \sigma^2$ for all i, hence

$$\text{Var } Y = a_1^2 \text{ Var } X_1 + a_2^2 \text{ Var } X_2 + \ldots + a_n^2 \text{ Var } X_n$$

$$= a_1^2 \sigma^2 + a_2^2 \sigma^2 + \ldots + a_n^2 \sigma^2$$

$$= \sigma^2 \left(a_1^2 + a_2^2 + \ldots + a_n^2\right)$$

# COVARIANCE AND CORRELATION

● PROBLEM 7-42

Find the variance of the random variable, $Z = X + Y$ if X and Y are not independent.

Solution:

$$\text{Var } Z = \text{Var } (X + Y) = E[((X + Y) - E(X + Y))^2]$$

$$= E[(X - E(X) + Y - E(Y))^2]$$

(because $E(X + Y) = E(X) + E(Y)$),

$$= E[(X - E(X))^2 + 2(X - E(X))(Y - E(Y)) + (Y - E(Y))^2],$$

and by the properties of expectation,

$$= E[(X - E(X))^2] + 2E[(X - E(X))(Y - E(Y))] + E[Y - E(Y))^2]$$

Thus $\text{Var } Z = \text{Var } X + \text{Var } Y + 2E[(X - E(X))(Y - E(Y))]$.

If X and Y are independent, $E[(X - E(X))(Y - E(Y))] = 0$ but since X and Y are not independent, we may not assume that this cross product is zero.

$$E[(X - E(X))(Y - E(Y))]$$

is called the covariance of X and Y and is a measure of the linear relation between X and Y. It is a measure in the    sense that  , if X is greater than $E(X)$ at the same time that Y is greater than $E(Y)$ with high probability, then the covariance of X and Y will be positive. If X is below $E(X)$ at the same time Y is above $E(Y)$ with high probability, the covariance of X and Y will be negative.

Related to the covariance is the correlation coefficient defined as;

$$\rho = \frac{\text{Cov } (X, Y)}{\sqrt{\text{Var } X} \sqrt{\text{Var } Y}} .$$

The correlation coefficient gives a clearer picture of the linear relation between X and Y because it takes account of the variation in the individual variables X and Y.

Other properties of covariance are:   $\text{Cov } (X, Y) = 0$, if X and Y are independent. The converse is not true.

$\text{Cov } (X, Y) = \text{Cov } (Y, X)$.

● **PROBLEM** 7-43

Find a formula for the covariance of

$$Y = \sum_{i=1}^{m} a_i Y_i \qquad \text{and} \qquad X = \sum_{j=1}^{n} b_j X_j$$

if $Y_i$ and $X_j$ are random variables and $a_i$ and $b_j$ are constants.

<u>Solution</u>:     $\text{Cov } (X, Y) = \text{Cov } \left( \sum_{j=1}^{n} b_j X_j , \sum_{i=1}^{m} a_i Y_i \right)$

267

$$= E\,[[X - E(X)]]\,[Y - E(Y)]\ ,$$

but $E(X) = E\left[\sum_{j=1}^{n} b_j X_j\right] = \sum_{j=1}^{n} b_j E(X_j)$

and $E(Y) = \sum_{i=1}^{m} a_i E(Y_i)$

by the linearity properties of expectation.

Thus $X - E(X) = \sum_{j=1}^{n} b_j X_j - \sum_{j=1}^{n} b_j E(X_j) = \sum_{j=1}^{n} b_j (X_j - E(X_j))$

similarly, $Y - E(Y) = \sum_{j=1}^{m} a_i Y_i - \sum_{j=1}^{m} a_i E(Y_i) = \sum_{i=1}^{m} a_i (Y_i - E(Y_i))$

and $Cov\,(X, Y) = E\left[\left(\sum_{j=1}^{n} b_j (X_j - E(X_j))\right) \times \left(\sum_{i=1}^{m} a_i (Y_i - E(Y_i))\right)\right]$

$$= E\left[\left(\sum_{j=1}^{m} b_j (X_j - E(X_j))\right)\left[(a_1 (Y_1 - E(Y_1)) + \ldots a_m (Y_m - E(Y_m))\right]\right]$$

$$= E\left[\sum_{j=1}^{m} a_1 b_j (X_j - E(X_j)) (Y_1 - E(Y_1))\right.$$

$$+ \sum_{j=1}^{m} a_2 b_j (X_j - E(X_j)) \cdot (Y_2 - E(Y_2))$$

$$\left. + \ldots + \sum_{j=1}^{m} a_n b_j (X_j - E(X_j)) (Y_n - E(Y_n))\right]$$

$$= E\left[\sum_{j=1}^{m} \sum_{i=1}^{n} a_i b_j (X_j - E(X_j)) (Y_i - E(Y_i))\right]$$

$$= \sum_{j=1}^{m} \sum_{i=1}^{n} a_i b_j\, E\left[(X_j - E(X_j)) (Y_i - E(Y_i))\right]$$

$$= \sum_{j=1}^{m} \sum_{i=1}^{n} a_i b_j\ Cov\,(X_j, Y_i)\ .$$

Find ρ for X and Y if

$$f(x, y) = x + y \qquad \text{for} \qquad 0 < x < 1$$
$$0 < y < 1$$

is the joint density of X and Y.

Solution:    The correlation coefficient, ρ, is defined to be

$$\rho = \frac{\text{Cov } (X, Y)}{\sqrt{\text{Var } X} \sqrt{\text{Var } Y}} ,$$

where    $\text{Cov } (X, Y) = E[(X - E(X))(Y - E(Y))]$

and

$$\text{Var } X = E(X^2) - [E(X)]^2$$

$$\text{Var } Y = E(Y^2) - [E(Y)]^2$$

$$\text{Cov } (X, Y) = E[(X - E(X))(Y - E(Y))]$$

$$= E[XY - E(X)Y - E(Y)X + E(X)E(Y)]$$

$$= E(XY) - E(X)E(Y) - E(Y)E(X) + E(X)E(Y)$$

by the properties of expectation. Thus,

$$\text{Cov. } (X, Y) = E(XY) - E(X)E(Y) .$$

In our problem $E(X) = \iint_R x\, f(x, y)\, dx\, dy$ ,

$$E(X) = \int_0^1 \int_0^1 x(x + y)\, dx\, dy \quad = \int_0^1 \left[ \frac{x^3}{3} + \frac{x^2 y}{2} \right]_0^1 dy$$

$$= \int_0^1 \left[ \frac{1}{3} + \frac{y}{2} \right] dy \quad = \quad \frac{y}{3} + \frac{y^2}{4} \Big|_0^1 \quad = \frac{1}{3} + \frac{1}{4} = \frac{7}{12} .$$

$$E(X^2) = \int_0^1 \int_0^1 x^2 (x + y)\, dx\, dy = \int_0^1 \int_0^1 (x^3 + yx^2)\, dx\, dy$$

$$= \int_0^1 \left| \frac{x^4}{4} + \frac{yx^3}{3} \right|_0^1 dy \quad = \int_0^1 \left( \frac{1}{4} + \frac{y}{3} \right) dy = \left( \frac{y}{4} + \frac{y^2}{6} \right)_0^1$$

$$= \frac{1}{4} + \frac{1}{6} = \frac{10}{24} = \frac{5}{12} .$$

Similarly,  $E(Y^2) = \frac{5}{12}$  and  $E(Y) = \frac{7}{12}$.

Finally,    $E(XY) = \int_0^1 \int_0^1 xy\, (x + y)\, dx\, dy$

$$= \int_0^1 \int_0^1 (x^2y + y^2x) \ dx \ dy = \int_0^1 \left[ \frac{x^3y}{3} \quad \frac{y^2x^2}{2} \right]_0^1 \ dy$$

$$= \int_0^1 \left( \frac{y}{3} + \frac{y^2}{2} \right) \ dy = \left[ \frac{y^2}{6} + \frac{y^3}{6} \right]_0^1 = \frac{1}{6} + \frac{1}{6} = \frac{1}{3} \ .$$

Thus, $\quad \rho = \dfrac{\text{Cov } (X, \ Y)}{\sqrt{\text{Var } X} \ \sqrt{\text{Var } Y}} = \dfrac{E(XY) - E(X)E(Y)}{\sqrt{E(X^2) - [E(X)]^2} \sqrt{E(Y^2) - [E()]^2}}$

$$= \frac{\dfrac{1}{3} - \left(\dfrac{7}{12}\right)\left(\dfrac{7}{12}\right)}{\sqrt{\dfrac{5}{12} - \left(\dfrac{7}{12}\right)^2} \ \sqrt{\dfrac{5}{12} - \left(\dfrac{7}{12}\right)^2}} = \frac{\dfrac{1}{3} - \dfrac{49}{144}}{\dfrac{5}{12} - \left(\dfrac{7}{12}\right)^2}$$

$$= \frac{\dfrac{48}{144} - \dfrac{49}{144}}{\dfrac{60}{144} - \dfrac{49}{144}} = \frac{-\dfrac{1}{144}}{\dfrac{11}{144}} = \frac{-1}{11} \ .$$

● **PROBLEM** 7-45

Find the variance of a random variable X that is uniformly distributed over the interval [0, 3].

Solution:     The variance of X is by definition,

$$E([X - E(X)]^2) = E(X^2) - [E(X)]^2 ,$$

The density function of X is $\ f(x) = \begin{cases} \dfrac{1}{3} & 0 < x < 3 \\ 0 & \text{otherwise} . \end{cases}$

Thus, $E(X) = \displaystyle\int_0^3 xf(x) \, dx = \int_0^3 \frac{x}{3} \, dx = \left. \frac{x^2}{6} \right|_0^3 = \frac{9}{6} = \frac{3}{2} \ .$

$$E(X^2) = \int_0^3 x^2 f(x) \ dx = \int_0^3 \frac{x^2}{3} \ dx = \left. \frac{x^3}{9} \right|_0^3 = \frac{27}{9} = 3 \ .$$

And the variance of X is $\quad \text{Var } X = 3 - \left(\dfrac{3}{2}\right)^2$

$$= 3 - \frac{9}{4} = \frac{12 - 9}{4} = \frac{3}{4} \ .$$

● **PROBLEM** 7-46

Given that the random variable X has density function

$$f(x) = \frac{1}{2} (x + 1) \text{ when } - 1 < x < 1$$

and   f(x) = 0                    elsewhere ;

calculate the mean value or expected value of X and the variance of X.

Solution:      Recall that when X is a discrete random variable, its mean value

$$\mu = E(X) = \Sigma x\, f(x), \text{ where } f(x) = Pr(X = x).$$

This sum of products is a weighted average of the values of X.

In this problem X is a continuous random variable. Therefore we must integrate $xf(x)$ from $-1$ to $+1$, since $f(x) = 0$ when $x \leq -1$ or $x \geq 1$.

$$\mu = \int_{-\infty}^{\infty} xf(x)\ dx = \int_{-1}^{1} x\ \frac{x + 1}{2}\ dx$$

(we have substituted $\frac{x + 1}{2}$ for $f(x)$)

$$= \int_{-1}^{1} \left(\frac{x^2}{2} + \frac{x}{2}\right)\ dx = \frac{1}{2} \int_{-1}^{1} x^2\ dx + \frac{1}{2} \int_{-1}^{1} x\,dx$$

$$= \frac{1}{2} \left.\frac{x^3}{3}\right]_{-1}^{1} + \frac{1}{2} \left.\frac{x^2}{2}\right]_{-1}^{1}$$

$$= \frac{1}{2} \left(\frac{1}{3} + \frac{1}{3}\right) + \frac{1}{2} \left(\frac{1}{2} - \frac{1}{2}\right) = \frac{1}{2} \left(\frac{2}{3}\right) = \frac{1}{3}\ .$$

The variance of X is defined to be

$$\sigma^2 = E[(X - \mu)^2].$$           Since

$$(X - \mu)^2 = (X - \mu)(X - \mu) = X^2 - 2\mu X + \mu^2,$$

we can write,

$$\sigma^2 = E[(X - \mu)^2] = E(X^2 - 2\mu X + \mu^2)$$

$$= \int_{-1}^{1} (X^2 - 2\mu X + \mu^2)\ f(x)\ dx$$

$$= \int_{-1}^{1} X^2\ f(x)\ dx - 2\mu \int_{-1}^{1} xf(x)\,dx + \mu^2 \int_{-1}^{1} 1\ f(x)\ dx$$

$$= E(X^2) - 2\mu E(X) + \mu^2 E(1)$$

$$= E(X^2) - 2\mu^2 + \mu^2 \quad [E(1) = 1 \text{ because } f(x) \text{ is a density}$$

function and must satisfy the condition that $\int_{-\infty}^{\infty} f(x)\ dx = 1$ ].

$$E(X^2) - 2\mu^2 + \mu^2 = E(X^2) - \mu^2$$

$$= \int_{-\infty}^{\infty} X^2\ f(x)\ dx - \left(\frac{1}{3}\right)^2$$

$$= \int_{-1}^{1} X^2 \left(\frac{x + 1}{2}\right)\ dx - \frac{1}{9}$$

$$= \int_{-1}^{1} \frac{x^3}{2}\ dx + \int_{-1}^{1} \frac{x^2}{2}\ dx - \frac{1}{9}$$

$$= \frac{x^4}{8}\ \Big|_{-1}^{1} + \frac{x^3}{6}\ \Big|_{-1}^{1} - \frac{1}{9}$$

$$= \left(\frac{1}{8} - \frac{1}{8}\right) + \frac{1}{6} - \left(\frac{-1}{6}\right) - \frac{1}{9}\ \ = \frac{1}{3} - \frac{1}{9} = \frac{2}{9}\ .$$

● **PROBLEM 7-47**

Let X be a random variable with probability density given by

$$f(x) = \lambda e^{-\lambda x} \qquad\qquad 0 < x < \infty\ \ .$$

Find Var X.

**Solution:**  The variance of X is by definition,

$$\text{Var } X = E[(X - E(X)^2] = E(X^2) - (E(X))^2\ .$$

We have found $E(X)$ to be $\frac{1}{\lambda}$ in previous problems, thus

$$\text{Var } X = E(X^2) - \frac{1}{\lambda^2}\ .$$

We now find $\quad E(X^2) = \int_{0}^{\infty} x^2\ f(x)\ dx = \int_{0}^{\infty} x^2\ \lambda e^{-\lambda x}\ dx\ ;$

let $\quad u = x^2 \quad dv = \lambda e^{-\lambda x}\ dx \quad$ then $du = 2x\ dx \quad$ and

$v = -\ e^{-\lambda x}\ .$

Thus

$$\int_{0}^{\infty} x^2\ \lambda e^{-\lambda x}\ dx = -\ x^2\ e^{-\lambda x}\Big]_{0}^{\infty} - \int_{0}^{\infty} -\ e^{-\lambda x}\ 2x\ dx$$

272

$$= 0 + 2 \int_0^\infty xe^{-\lambda x} \, dx$$

$$= \frac{2}{\lambda} \cdot \int_0^\infty \lambda xe^{-\lambda x} \, dx \; ;$$

but $\int_0^\infty \lambda xe^{-\lambda x} \, dx = E(X) = \frac{1}{\lambda}$. Thus $E(X^2) = \frac{2}{\lambda^2}$.

Therefore, $\text{Var } X = E(X^2) - [E(X)]^2 = \frac{2}{\lambda^2} - \frac{1}{\lambda^2} = \frac{1}{\lambda^2}$.

● **PROBLEM** 7-48

Let Y be distributed with a Pareto distribution with parameters $X_0$ and $\theta$. The density function of such a random variable is:

$$f(y) = \begin{cases} \dfrac{\theta \, X_0^{\theta}}{y^{\theta+1}} & y > X_0 \\ & \text{with } X_0, \; \theta > 0 \\ & \text{otherwise}. \end{cases}$$

What is the variance of Y?

Solution: We first find E(Y), the expected value of Y. By definition,

$$E(Y) = \int_{-\infty}^{\infty} y \, f(y) \, dy = \int_{X_0}^{\infty} \frac{y \, \theta \, X_0^{\theta}}{y^{\theta+1}} \, dy$$

$$= \int_0^\infty \frac{\theta X_0^{\theta}}{y^{\theta}} \, dy = \theta X_0^{\theta} \int_0^\infty \frac{dy}{y^{\theta}}$$

$$= \theta X_0^{\theta} \left[ \frac{y^{-\theta+1}}{-\theta+1} \right]_{X_0}^{\infty} = \theta X_0^{\theta} \, \frac{X_0^{-\theta+1}}{\theta-1}$$

$$= \frac{\theta X_0}{\theta-1} \qquad \text{for} \qquad \theta > 1 \; .$$

Similarly, $E(Y^2) = \int_{X_0}^{\infty} y^2 \, \frac{\theta X_0^{\theta}}{y^{\theta+1}} \, dy = \int_{X_0}^{\infty} \frac{\theta X_0^{\theta}}{y^{\theta-1}} \, dy$

$$= \theta X_0^{\theta} \int_{X_0}^{\infty} y^{-\theta+1} \, dy = \theta X_0^{\theta} \left[ \frac{y^{-\theta+2}}{-\theta+2} \right]_{X_0}^{\infty}$$

273

$$= \frac{\theta X_0 \theta \ X_0{}^{-\theta+2}}{(\theta - 2)} = \frac{\theta X_0{}^2}{\theta-2} \qquad \text{for} \qquad \theta > 2.$$

By definition, the variance of Y is

$$\text{Var } Y = E(Y^2) - [E(Y)]^2$$

$$= \frac{\theta X_0{}^2}{\theta - 2} - \frac{\theta^2 \ X_0{}^2}{(\theta - 1)^2}$$

$$= \frac{[(\theta - 1)^2 \theta - \theta^2 (\theta - 2)] X_0{}^2}{(\theta - 2)(\theta - 1)^2}$$

$$= \frac{[\theta^3 - 2\theta^2 + \theta - \theta^3 + 2\theta^2 ] \ X_0{}^2}{(\theta - 2)(\theta - 1)^2}$$

$$= \frac{\theta \ X_0{}^2}{(\theta - 2)(\theta - 1)^2} \qquad \text{for} \qquad \theta > 2.$$

# CHAPTER 8

# MOMENT GENERATING FUNCTION

## DISCRETE RANDOM VARIABLES

Consider a simple random variable $X$ having just two possible values, $P_r(X = 1) = p$ and $P_r(X = 0) = 1-p$. Find the moment generating function of $X$ and $E(X^k)$ for all $k = 1,2,3,...$

Solution: The moment generating function, $M(t)$, is defined to be

$$M(t) = E(e^{tX})$$

where $t$ is a constant and $e$ is the base of the natural logarithm.

In the case of a discrete, integer-valued random variable, the expected value of $e^{tX}$ is, $M(t) = \sum_{x=0}^{\infty} e^{tx} Pr(X = x)$ .

For this problem, $X$ has only two values, 0 and 1, hence

$$M(t) = e^{t \cdot 0} Pr(X = 0) + e^{t \cdot 1} Pr(X = 1)$$

$$= Pr(X = 0) + e^t Pr(X = 1)$$

$$= (1-p) + e^t p .$$

The moment-generating function has the interesting and useful property that

$$\frac{d^n M(0)}{dt^n} = E(X^n) .$$

That is, the $n$th derivative of the moment-generating function is equal to the expected value of $X^n$.

To see that this is true,

$$M(t) = \sum_{x=0}^{\infty} e^{tx} Pr(X = x)$$

$$\frac{d^n M(t)}{dt^n} = \frac{d^n}{dt^n} \left( \sum_{x=0}^{\infty} e^{tx} Pr(X = x) \right)$$

$$= \sum_{x=0}^{\infty} \frac{d^n}{dt^n} [e^{tx} Pr(X = x)],$$

if

$$\sum_{x=0}^{\infty} \frac{d^n}{dt^n} [e^{tx} Pr(X = x)] \quad \text{converges}$$

uniformly. But, $\frac{d^n}{dt^n} [e^{tx} Pr(X = x)] = Pr(X = x)[x^n e^{tx}]$ .

Thus,

$$\frac{d^n M(t)}{dt^n} = \sum_{x=0}^{\infty} \Pr(X = x) x^n e^{tx}$$

and

$$\frac{d^n M(0)}{dt^n} = \sum_{x=0}^{\infty} \Pr(X = x) x^n e^{x \cdot 0}$$

$$= \sum_{x=0}^{\infty} x^n \Pr(X = x) = E(X^n) .$$

In our example,

$$\frac{d^k M(t)}{dt^k} = \frac{d^k}{dt^k} [(1-p) + pe^t]$$

$$= p \frac{d}{dt^k} [e^t] = pe^t$$

and thus

$$\frac{d^k M(0)}{dt^k} = pe^0 = p$$

or

$$E(X^k) = p \quad \text{for} \quad k = 1, 2, \dots \quad .$$

● **PROBLEM** 8-2

Let $X_1$ and $X_2$ be independent Poisson random variables with parameters $\lambda_1$ and $\lambda_2$. What is the moment generating function of $X_1$; of $X_2$? What is the moment generating function of $X_1 + X_2$?

Solution: The moment generating function of $X_1$ is defined as

$$E(e^{tX_1}) = \sum_{x=0}^{\infty} e^{tx} \Pr(X_1 = x) ;$$

because $X_1$ is Poisson random variable with parameter $\lambda_1$,

$$\Pr(X_1 = x) = \frac{\lambda_1^x e^{-\lambda_1}}{x!} \qquad x = 0, 1, \dots$$

Thus, substituting yields:

$$E(e^{tX_1}) = \sum_{x=0}^{\infty} e^{tx} \Pr(X_1 = x)$$

$$= \sum_{x=0}^{\infty} e^{tx} \frac{\lambda_1^x e^{-\lambda_1}}{x!}$$

$$= e^{-\lambda_1} \sum_{x=0}^{\infty} \frac{(\lambda_1 e^t)^x}{x!}$$

$$= e^{-\lambda_1} \exp\{\lambda_1 e^t\}$$

$$= \exp\{\lambda_1 e^t - \lambda_1\}$$

$$= \exp\{\lambda_1 (e^t - 1)\} \quad .$$

Similarly the moment generating function of $X_2$ is

$$E(e^{tX_2}) = \sum_{x=0}^{\infty} e^{tx} \Pr(X_2 = x)$$

$$= \sum_{x=0}^{\infty} \frac{e^{tx} \lambda_2^x e^{-\lambda_2}}{x!}$$

$$= e^{-\lambda_2} \exp\{\lambda_2 e^t\}$$

$$= \exp\{\lambda_2 (e^t - 1)\} \cdot$$

If $Y = X_1 + X_2$,

$$E[e^{tY}] = E[e^{tX_1}] E[e^{tX_2}]$$

by the independence of $X_1$ and $X_2$. Thus,

$$E[e^{tY}] = \exp\{\lambda_1 (e^t - 1)\} \exp\{\lambda_2 (e^t - 1)\}$$

$$= \exp\{\lambda_1 (e^t - 1) + \lambda_2 (e^t - 1)\} \cdot$$

By the properties of the exponential function,

$$E[e^{tY}] = \exp\{(\lambda_1 + \lambda_2)(e^t - 1)\} \cdot$$

The moment generating function of a distribution is unique to that distribution. The moment generating function of $X_1 + X_2$ is exactly the same as that of $X_1$ with $\lambda_1$ replaced by $\lambda_1 + \lambda_2$. By the unique correspondence of moment generating function to distribution function, we see that $Y = X_1 + X_2$ is a Poisson random variable with parameter $\lambda_1 + \lambda_2$.

● **PROBLEM 8-3**

Given that the probability density function of a discrete random variable $X$ is

$$f(x) = \frac{6}{\pi^2 x^2}, \quad x = 1, 2, \ldots$$

find its moment generating function $M(t)$.

**Solution:** The mathematical expectation of a function $u(X)$ of a discrete random variable $X$, with density function $f(x)$, is defined to be

$$E[u(X)] = \sum_X u(x) f(x).$$

(If $X$ is continuous, $E(u(X)) = \int_{-\infty}^{\infty} u(x) f(x) dx$.) The moment generating function $M(t)$ is defined by $M(t) = E(e^{tX})$. This is obtained by setting $u(X) = e^{tX}$. $E[u(X)] = E(e^{tX}) = \sum_X e^{tX} f(x)$. Given that

$$f(x) = \frac{6}{\pi^2 x^2}, \quad \sum_{x=1}^{\infty} e^{tX} f(x) = \sum_{x=1}^{\infty} \frac{6e^{tx}}{\pi^2 x^2} = M(t).$$

If this series does not converge, then $M(t)$ does not exist. By the ratio test,

$$\frac{\dfrac{6e^{t(X+1)}}{\pi^2 (X+1)^2}}{\dfrac{6e^{tX}}{\pi^2 x^2}} = \frac{6e^{t(X+1)} \pi^2 x^2}{6e^{tX} \pi^2 (X+1)^2} = \frac{e^{t(x+1)}}{e^{tX}} \cdot \frac{x^2}{(X+1)^2} \cdot$$

Observe that: $\dfrac{e^{t(X+1)}}{e^{tX}} = e^{t(X+1) - tX} = e^{tX + t - tX} = e^t.$

277

Substitution yields: $\dfrac{e^{t(X+1)}}{e^{tX}} \cdot \dfrac{X^2}{(X+1)^2} = \dfrac{e^t X^2}{(X+1)^2}$ .

For any positive integer value of $X$, $X + 1 > X$. Thus $(X+1)^2 > X^2$ and $\dfrac{X^2}{(X+1)^2} < 1$. As $X$ increases without bound, the ratio $\dfrac{X}{X+1}$ approaches 1 and $\dfrac{X^2}{(X+1)^2} = \left(\dfrac{X}{X+1}\right)^2$ also approaches 1. For $t = 0$, $e^t = e^0 = 1$. For $t > 0$, $e^t > 1$. It follows that for large values of $x$, the ratio of the $(X+1)$st to the $X^{th}$ term is greater than 1. Thus the series $\displaystyle\sum_{X=1}^{\infty} \dfrac{6e^{tX}}{\pi^2 x^2}$ diverges.

Therefore, $f(x) = \dfrac{6}{\pi^2 x^2}$

does not have a moment generating function.

A rocket-engine igniter system has $n$ separate small igniters. Any one igniter has a probability $\theta$ of firing independently of the other igniters. Since each is small, the firing of a group of igniters may or may not successfully ignite the propellant. It may be assumed that, if $k$ igniters out of $n$ fire, the probability that the propellant ignites has one of two forms:

(a) $\alpha k + \beta k^2$

(b) $1 - \gamma^k$

where $\alpha, \beta$, and $\gamma$ are known constants. Assuming (a) and (b) in turn, prove that the probabilities that the propellant ignites are respectively

(a) $n\theta(\alpha + n\theta\beta + \beta - \beta\theta)$

(b) $1 - (1 - \theta + \gamma\theta)^n$ .

**Solution:** a) We are given two probabilities; $\theta$, the probability that an igniter fires and the conditional probability that given $k$ of $n$ igniters fire, the probability that the propellant ignites is $\alpha k + \beta k^2$ .

To solve this problem we decompose the event "the propellant ignites" into mutually exclusive events. This event can occur if 1 igniter fires and the propellant lights or 2 igniters fire and the propellant lights and so forth up to $n$ igniters fire and the propellant lights.

Since these events are mutually exclusive

$$\text{Pr(the propellant ignites)} = \sum_{k=0}^{n} \text{Pr}(k \text{ igniters fire}$$
$$\text{and the propellant ignites).}$$

But the $\text{Pr}(k$ igniters fire and the propellant ignites) = $\text{Pr}(\text{Propellant ignites} / k$ igniters fire) $\times$ $\text{Pr}(k$ igniters fire). Thus,

$$\text{Pr(the propellant ignites)} = \sum_{k=0}^{n} \text{Pr(propellant ignites} | k \text{ igniters}$$

fire) $\times$ Pr($k$ igniters fire),

$$= \sum_{k=0}^{n} (\alpha k + \beta k^2)\, \Pr(k \text{ igniters fire}).$$

$\Pr(k$ (of $n)$ igniters fire) is a binomial probability. Let $Y =$ the number of igniters that fire. There are $n$ trials and the probability of a "success", of an igniter firing, is $\theta$ .

Thus the $\Pr(k$ igniter fire$) = \Pr(Y = k) = \binom{n}{k}\theta^k(1-\theta)^{n-k}$ and

$$\Pr(\text{the propellent ignites}) = \sum_{k=0}^{n} (\alpha k + \beta k^2)\binom{n}{k}\theta^k(1-\theta)^{n-k}$$

$$= \sum_{k=0}^{n} \alpha k \binom{n}{k}\theta^k(1-\theta)^{n-k} + \sum_{k=0}^{n} \beta k^2 \binom{n}{k}\theta^k(1-\theta)^{n-k}$$

$$= \alpha \sum_{k=0}^{n} k\binom{n}{k}\theta^k(1-\theta)^{n-k} + \beta \sum_{k=0}^{n} k^2 \binom{n}{k}\theta^k(1-\theta)^{n-k} .$$

This rather formidable expression can be interpreted in terms of our random variable $Y$.

$$E(Y) = \sum_{k=0}^{n} k \Pr(Y = k)$$

$$E(Y^2) = \sum_{k=0}^{n} k^2 \Pr(Y = k) .$$

We see that

$$\Pr(\text{propellent ignites}) = \alpha \sum_{k=0}^{n} k \Pr(Y = k) + \beta \sum_{k=0}^{n} k^2 \Pr(Y = k)$$

$$= \alpha\, E(Y) + \beta\, E(Y^2) .$$

We know from previous work that $E(Y) = n \Pr(\text{"success" in one trial}) = n\theta$ .

$$\text{Var } Y = E(Y^2) - [E(Y)]^2 = n\theta(1-\theta)$$

thus

$$E(Y^2) = n\theta(1-\theta) + [n\theta]^2 .$$

Combining these results,

$$\Pr(\text{propellent ignites}) = \alpha n\theta + \beta[n\theta(1-\theta) + n^2\theta^2]$$

$$= n\theta[\alpha + \beta n\theta + \beta - \beta\theta] .$$

b)  If $\Pr(\text{propellent ignites}\,|\,k \text{ igniters fire}) = 1 - \gamma^k$ then

$$\Pr(\text{propellent ignites}) = \sum_{k=0}^{n} (1-\gamma^k)\binom{n}{k}\theta^k(1-\theta)^{n-k}$$

$$= \sum_{k=0}^{n} \binom{n}{k}\theta^k(1-\theta)^{n-k} - \sum_{k=0}^{n} \gamma^k\binom{n}{k}\theta^k(1-\theta)^{n-k} .$$

But the first term is $\sum_{k=0}^{n} \Pr(X = k)$ which equals 1. Hence

$$\Pr(\text{propellent ignites}) = 1 - \sum_{k=0}^{n} \gamma^k\binom{n}{k}\theta^k(1-\theta)^{n-k}$$

where $\sum_{k=0}^{n} \gamma^k\binom{n}{k}\theta^k(1-\theta)^{n-k} = \sum_{k=0}^{n} \gamma^k \Pr(Y = k) = E(\gamma^k)$

This expression is known as a generating function.

To compute a simple form of the generating function we will use the following property. Let $X_1, X_2, X_3,\ldots,X_n$ be $n$ random variables that are independent and have the same identical distribution (i.e., are all normal, all binomially distributed etc.) Then if $Y = X_1 + X_2 + \ldots + X_n$,

$$E(\gamma^Y) = E(\gamma^{X_1}) \cdot E(\gamma^{X_2}) \cdot \ldots \cdot E(\gamma^{X_n}) \; .$$

In particular if $X_i = \begin{cases} 1 & \text{with prob. } p \\ 0 & \text{with prob. } 1-p \end{cases}$ then $Y = \sum_{i=1}^{n} X_i$

will be binomially distributed with parameters $n$ and $p$. In such a case

$$E(\gamma^{X_i}) = \gamma^1 (Pr(X_i = 1) + \gamma^0 Pr(X_i = 0) = \gamma p + 1-p \; .$$

$$E(\gamma^Y) = E(\gamma^{X_1}) \cdot E(\gamma^{X_2}) \cdot \ldots \cdot E(\gamma^{X_n})$$

$$= \underbrace{(\gamma p+1-p) \cdot (\gamma p+1-p) \cdot \ldots \cdot (\gamma p+1-p)}_{n \text{ times}}$$

$$= (\gamma p + 1-p)^n \; .$$

Returning to our problem we see that

$$Pr(\text{propellent ignites}) = 1 - E(\gamma^k)$$

$$= 1 - [\gamma\theta + (1-\theta)]^n$$

$$= 1 - [\gamma\theta + 1-\theta]^n \; .$$

**● PROBLEM** 8-5

Let $X$ denote the number of spots on a fair die. Find the factorial-generating function of $X$.

If this die is tossed three times, with results $X_1, X_2, X_3$, and if the $X_i$ are independent random variables, find the factorial-generating function of the random variable $Y$. $Y$ represents the total number of spots observed in 3 tosses of the die. What is $Pr(Y = 7)$?

Solution: The factorial moment generating function of a discrete, integer-valued random variable $X$ is defined to be:

$$\eta(t) = E(t^X) = \sum_{x=0}^{\infty} t^x Pr(X = x)$$

where $t$ is a constant.

This function is useful in that it produces the factorial moments of $X$.

$$\frac{d^n[\eta(t)]}{dt^n} = \frac{d^n}{dt^n}\left[\sum_{x=0}^{\infty} t^x Pr(X = x)\right]$$

$$= \sum_{x=0}^{\infty} Pr(X = x) \frac{d^n t^x}{dt^n}$$

$$= \sum_{x=0}^{\infty} x(x-1)\ldots(x-n+1)Pr(X = x)t^{x-n} \; .$$

Thus

$$\frac{d^n[\eta(1)]}{dt^n} = \sum_{x=0}^{\infty} x(x-1)\ldots(x-n+1)\Pr(X = x)(1)^{x-n}$$

$$= \sum_{x=0}^{\infty} x(x-1)\ldots(x-n+1)\Pr(X = x)$$

$$= E[X(X-1)\ldots(X-n+1)]$$

$$= E\left[\frac{X!}{(X-n)!}\right],$$

the factorial moment, because $\dfrac{X(X-1)\ldots(X-n+1)(X-n)!}{(X-n)!}$

equals $X(X-1)\ldots(X-n+1)$.

Another useful observation is that the coefficients of $E(t^X)$ provide the probabilities of $X$. Thus given the factorial generating function one can find the $\Pr(X = k)$. $\Pr(X = k)$ is the coefficient of the term $t^k$.

One property of moment generating functions is that $Y = X_1 + X_2 + \ldots + X_n$ where $X_i$, $i = 1,\ldots,n$, are independent random variables has moment generating function:

$$M_Y(t) = M_{X_1}(t) \cdot M_{X_2}(t) \cdot M_{X_3}(t) \ldots \cdot M_{X_n}(t).$$

This type of behavior will extend to the factorial generating function.
To see that this is true for moment generating functions:

$$M_Y(t) = E(e^{tY})$$

$$= E(e^{t(X_1+\ldots+X_n)})$$

$$= E(e^{tX_1+tX_2+\ldots+tX_n})$$

$$= E(e^{tX_1} \cdot e^{tX_2} \cdot \ldots \cdot e^{tX_n})$$

and by the independence of $X_i$,

$$M_Y(t) = E(e^{tX_1}) \cdot E(e^{tX_2}) \cdot \ldots \cdot E(e^{tX_n})$$

$$= M_{X_1}(t) \cdot M_{X_2}(t) \cdot \ldots \cdot M_{X_n}(t) \cdot$$

If $X_1, X_2, \ldots, X_n$ have identical distributions, they will also have identical moment generating functions, say $M_X(t)$. Then
$M_Y(t) = [M_X(t)]^n$.

These results are also true for the factorial moment generating function. Namely if $Y = X_1+\ldots+X_n$ and $X_1, X_2, \ldots, X_n$ are independent random variables then

$$\eta_Y(t) = E(t^Y) = E(t^{X_1+\ldots+X_n})$$

$$= E(t^{X_1})E(t^{X_2})\ldots E(t^{X_n})$$

$$= \eta_{X_1}(t)\, \eta_{X_2}(t)\ldots \eta_{X_n}(t) \cdot$$

We illustrate some of these concepts with our problem.

If $X$ represents the number of spots on a fair die, then $X$ has a probability distribution; $\Pr(X = x) = \begin{cases} 1/6 & \text{for } x = 1, 2, \ldots, 6 \\ 0 & \text{otherwise} \end{cases}$

Thus the factorial moment generating for $X$ is

$$\eta(t) = \sum_{x=0}^{\infty} t^x \Pr(X = x) = E(t^x)$$

$$= \sum_{x=1}^{6} t^x \cdot \frac{1}{6} = \frac{(t+t^2+t^3+t^4+t^5+t^6)}{6}$$

$$= \frac{t(1+t+t^2+t^3+t^4+t^5)}{6} .$$

To simplify this expression, let $S_5 = 1+t+t^2+t^3+t^4+t^5$. Then

$$S_5 - tS_5 = 1 - t^6$$

or

$$S_5(1-t) = 1 - t^6 ,$$
$$S_5 = \frac{1 - t^6}{1 - t} .$$

Thus,

$$\eta_X(t) = \frac{t}{6}\left(\frac{1 - t^6}{1 - t}\right) .$$

Let $Y$ be the number of spots observed in three independent tosses of a fair die. Let $X_1, X_2, X_3$ be random variables indicating the number of spots observed on the first, second and third tosses respectively. Then $Y = X_1 + X_2 + X_3$ and each of the $X_i$ are independent and have moment generating function,

$$\eta_X(t) = \eta_{X_1}(t) = \eta_{X_2}(t) = \eta_{X_3}(t) = \frac{t}{6}\left(\frac{1 - t^6}{1 - t}\right) .$$

Thus

$$\eta_Y(t) = [\eta_X(t)]^3 = \frac{t^3}{6^3}\left(\frac{1 - t^6}{1 - t}\right)^3 .$$

To find the $\Pr(Y = 7)$ we manipulate this expression in order to read off the coefficient on the term $t^7$. Thus,

$$\eta_Y(t) = \frac{t^3}{6^3}(1 - t^6)^3(1 - t)^{-3} ;$$

but

$$(1 - t^6)^3 = 1 - 3t^6 + 3t^{12} + t^{18}$$

$$= \sum_{k=0}^{3} \binom{3}{k}(-1)^k (t)^{6k}$$

and for $|t| < 1$

$$(1 - t)^{-3} = \sum_{j=0}^{\infty} \binom{-3}{j}(-t)^j$$

by a generalization of the binomial theorem.

Here

$$\binom{-3}{j} = \frac{(-3)(-3-1)\ldots(-3-j+1)}{j!} .$$

Thus,

$$\eta_Y(t) = E(t^Y)$$

$$= \frac{t^3}{216}\left[\sum_{k=0}^{3} \binom{3}{k}(-1)^k (t)^{6k}\right]\left[\sum_{j=0}^{\infty} \binom{-3}{j}(-t)^j\right]$$

282

or writing this as a double sum,

$$E(t^Y) = \frac{1}{216} \sum_{k=0}^{3} \sum_{j=0}^{\infty} \binom{3}{k}\binom{-3}{j}(-1)^{k+j}(t)^{6k+j+3} \ .$$

To find the $Pr(Y = 7)$, we first determine the values of $k$ and $j$ so that $6k + j + 3 = 7$, $k = 0,1,2,$ or $3$ and $j = 0,1,2,3,\ldots$ .

If $k$ is any number but $0$, $6k + j + 3$ will be greater than $7$. Thus $k = 0$ and $6 \cdot 0 + j + 3 = 7$ or $j = 4$. The $Pr(Y = 7)$ is

$$= \frac{1}{216} \binom{3}{0}\binom{-3}{4}(-1)^{0+4}$$

$$= \left(\frac{1}{216}\right)\left(\frac{3!}{0!3!}\right)\left(\frac{-3\cdot(-3-1)(-3-2)(-3-4+1)}{4!}\right)$$

$$= \left(\frac{1}{216}\right)\left(\frac{-3\cdot -4\cdot -5\cdot -6}{4!}\right)$$

$$= \frac{12\cdot 30}{(216)(4\cdot 3\cdot 2\cdot 1)} = \frac{15}{216} \ .$$

# CONTINUOUS RANDOM VARIABLES

● PROBLEM 8-6

Find the moment generating function of a standard normal random variable. Use this to calculate the mean and variance of this variable.

Solution: Let $Z$ be a standard normal variable; then $Z$ has density function: $f(z) = \frac{1}{\sqrt{2\pi}} e^{-z^2/2}$    $-\infty < z < \infty$ .

The moment generating function of $Z$ is:

$$M(t) = E(e^{zt}) = \int_{-\infty}^{\infty} \frac{e^{zt} e^{-z^2/2}}{\sqrt{2\pi}} dz$$

$$= \int_{-\infty}^{\infty} \frac{e^{-(z^2-2zt)/2}}{\sqrt{2\pi}} dz \ .$$

Completing the square in the exponent we see that

$$E(e^{zt}) = \int_{-\infty}^{\infty} \frac{e^{-(z^2-2zt+t^2)/2 + t^2/2}}{\sqrt{2\pi}} dz$$

$$= e^{t^2/2} \int_{-\infty}^{\infty} \frac{e^{-(z-t)^2/2}}{\sqrt{2\pi}} dz \ ;$$

but

$$\frac{e^{-(z-t)^2/2}}{\sqrt{2\pi}}$$ is the density function of a normally

distributed random variable with mean $t$ and variance $1$. Thus,

283

$$\int_{-\infty}^{\infty} \frac{e^{-(z-t)^2/2}}{\sqrt{2\pi}} \, dz = 1 \quad \text{and}$$

$$M(t) = E(e^{zt}) = e^{t^2/2}$$

$$E(Z) = \frac{dM(0)}{dt} = \left. e^{t^2/2} \cdot t \right]_{t=0}$$

$$= e^0 \cdot 0 = 0$$

and

$$E(Z^2) = \text{Var } Z \quad (\text{if} \quad E(Z) = 0)$$

$$= \frac{d^2 M(0)}{dt^2} = \frac{d}{dt} \left[ e^{t^2/2} \cdot t \right]_{t=0}$$

$$= \left. e^{t^2/2} + t^2 \, e^{t^2/2} \right]_{t=0}$$

$$= e^0 + 0 \cdot e^0 = 1 + 0 = 1 .$$

● **PROBLEM** 8-7

Given that the random variable $X$ has moment generating function

$$M(t) = e^{t^2/2} ,$$

find $E(X^{2k})$ and $E(X^{2k-1})$ .

**Solution:** We first represent $M(t)$ as a MacLaurin's series. Recall that for all $x$,

$$e^x = \sum_{n=0}^{\infty} \frac{x^n}{n!} .$$

Thus,

$$e^{t^2/2} = \sum_{n=0}^{\infty} \frac{(t^2/2)^n}{n!} = \sum_{n=0}^{\infty} \frac{t^{2n}}{2^n n!}$$

$$= 1 + \frac{1}{2!} t^2 + \frac{t^4}{4 \cdot 2!} + \ldots + \frac{t^{2k}}{2^k \cdot k!} + \ldots$$

but

$$\frac{1}{4 \cdot 2!} = \frac{3 \cdot 1}{4 \cdot 3 \cdot 2 \cdot 1} = \frac{3 \cdot 1}{4!}$$

$$\frac{1}{8 \cdot 3!} = \frac{5 \cdot 3}{(3 \cdot 2) \cdot 5 \cdot 4 \cdot 3!} = \frac{5 \cdot 3}{6!}$$

$$\frac{1}{16 \cdot 4!} = \frac{7 \cdot 5 \cdot 3 \cdot 1}{8 \cdot 2 \cdot 7 \cdot 5 \cdot 3 \cdot 4!} = \frac{7 \cdot 5 \cdot 3 \cdot 1}{8 \cdot 7 \cdot 6 \cdot 5 \cdot 4!} = \frac{7 \cdot 5 \cdot 3 \cdot 1}{8!} .$$

There is a pattern here and it can be shown by induction that

$$\frac{1}{2^k \cdot k!} = \frac{(2k-1)(2k-3)\ldots 3 \cdot 1}{(2k)!} .$$

Thus,

$$M(t) = 1 + 0 \cdot t + \frac{3 \cdot 1}{4!} t^2 + 0 \cdot t^3 + \frac{5 \cdot 3 \cdot 1}{6!} t^4 + \ldots + 0 \cdot t^{(2k-1)}$$

$$+ \frac{(2k-1)(2k-3)\ldots 3 \cdot 1}{(2k)!} t^{2k} + \ldots$$

Thus,

$$E(X^{2k}) = \frac{d^{(2k)}M(0)}{dt^{(2k)}} = 0 + 0 + 0 + \ldots + \frac{[(2k-1)(2k-3)\ldots(3)(1)]}{(2k)!}(2k)!$$

because

$$\frac{d^{(2k)}[t^{2k}]}{dt^{(2k)}} = 2k!$$

Thus,

$$E(X^{2k}) = (2k-1)(2k-3)(2k-5)\ldots(3)\cdot(1)!$$

Also since every odd-powered term is 0, $E(X^{2k-1}) = 0$.

● **PROBLEM** 8-8

Let X be a continuous random variable with probability density function,

$$f(x) = \begin{cases} \lambda e^{-\lambda x} & \infty > x > 0 \\ 0 & \text{otherwise}. \end{cases}$$

Find the moment generating function of X.

Solution:

$$M_X(t) = E(e^{Xt}) = \int_0^\infty e^{xt}\, f(x)dx$$

$$= \int_0^\infty \lambda e^{xt-\lambda x}\, dx$$

$$= \lambda \int_0^\infty e^{-x(\lambda-t)}\, dx$$

$$= \frac{-\lambda}{\lambda-t}\left[\lim_{x\to\infty} e^{-x(\lambda-t)} - 1\right];$$

if $\lambda > t$ then $-x(\lambda-t) < 0$ and $\lim_{x\to\infty} e^{-x(\lambda-t)} = 0$. Thus,

$$M_X(t) = \frac{-\lambda}{\lambda-t}[0 - 1] = \frac{\lambda}{\lambda-t} \qquad \lambda > t.$$

● **PROBLEM** 8-9

Consider the distribution defined by the following distribution function:

$$F(x) = \begin{cases} 0 & \text{if } x < 0 \\ 1-pe^{-x} & \text{if } x \geq 0 \text{ for } 0 < p < 1. \end{cases}$$

This distribution is partly discrete and partly continuous. Find the moment generating function of X and use it to find the mean and variance of X.

Solution: The density function of X is

$$Pr(X = 0) = 1 - p$$

and

$$f(x) = \frac{dF(x)}{dx} = pe^{-x} \qquad x > 0.$$

Thus, the moment generating function of X is

$$M(t) = E(e^{Xt}) = \int_{-\infty}^\infty e^{tx}\, dF(x)$$

285

where this integral is a Riemann-Stieljes integral reflecting both the discrete and continuous nature of X.

$$E(e^{Xt}) = e^{t \cdot 0} \Pr(X = 0) + \int_0^\infty e^{tx} pe^{-x} dx$$

$$= (1-p) + \int_0^\infty pe^{-x(1-t)} dx ;$$

but

$$\int_0^\infty pe^{-x(1-t)} dx = \frac{-p}{1-t} e^{-x(1-t)} \Big]_0^\infty ; \text{ for } |t| < 1$$

this equals

$$\frac{-p}{1-t} [0 - 1] = \frac{p}{1-t} .$$

Thus,

$$M(t) = (1-p) + \frac{p}{1-t} \text{ for } |t| < 1; \frac{1}{1-t} \text{ may be expanded}$$

in a geometric series

$$\frac{1}{1-t} = 1 + t + t^2 + \dots .$$

Hence

$$M(t) = 1-p + p(1 + t + t^2 + \dots)$$

$$= 1 + pt + pt^2 + \dots$$

$$= 1 + \sum_{n=1}^\infty pt^n .$$

$$E(X) = \frac{dM(0)}{dt} = 0 + p \sum_{n=1}^\infty n t^{n-1} \Big]_{t=0}$$

$$= 0 + p + p \sum_{n=1}^\infty (n+1)t^n \Big]_{t=0}$$

$$= p + p \sum_{n=1}^\infty (n+1)(0)^n = p .$$

Thus the mean of X is E(X) = p.

The variance of X is Var X = $E(X^2) - [E(X)]^2$

$$E(X^2) = \frac{d^2 M(0)}{dt^2} = \frac{d^2}{dt^2}\left(1 + p \sum_{n=1}^\infty t^n\right)_{t=0}$$

$$= p \frac{d^2}{dt^2}(t + t^2 + t^3 + \dots)\Big]_{t=0}$$

$$= p \frac{d}{dt}(1 + 2t + 3t^2 + \dots)\Big]_{t=0}$$

$$= p(0 + 2 + 6t + \dots)\Big]_{t=0}$$

$$= 2p .$$

Thus,

$$\text{Var } X = E(X^2) - [E(X)]^2$$

$$= 2p - p^2 = p(2 - p).$$

● **PROBLEM** 8-10

Let X have probability density,

$$f(x) = \begin{cases} \dfrac{1}{x^2} & 1 < x < \infty \\[2mm] 0 & \text{otherwise} . \end{cases}$$

Show that the moment generating function of $X$ does not exist.

Solution: If the moment generating function of $X$ exists, then it is given by:

$$M_X(t) = \int_1^\infty e^{tx} f(x)\ dx = \int_1^\infty \frac{e^{tx}}{x^2}\ dx\ .$$

We investigate the convergence of this integral.

Since the integrand is positive the comparison test may be used. This test is: let $g(X) \geq 0$ for all $x \geq a$ and suppose that $\int_a^\infty g(x) dx$ diverges. Then if $f(x) \geq g(x)$ for all $x \geq a$, $\int_a^\infty f(x)$ diverges.

In this case, let $g(x) = 1/x$; and $f(x) = e^{tx}/x^2$. We must show that $e^{tx}/x^2 \geq 1/x$ for all $x > a$ and for a fixed $t > 0$.

Equivalently, we must show that there is a positive constant 'a' such that $e^{tx}/x > 1$ for all $x > a$.

By L'Hospital's rule,

$$\lim_{x \to \infty} \frac{x}{e^{tx}} = \lim_{x \to \infty} \frac{1}{te^{tx}} = 0\ .$$

By the definition of limit, this means that there exists some $N > 0$ such that for $x > N$,

$$\left| \frac{x}{e^{tx}} - 0 \right| < \epsilon$$

for any given $\epsilon > 0$ and depends on $N$.

This implies that

$$|x| < \epsilon |e^{tx}|\quad \text{for some}\quad x > N,\ \text{but}$$

$x > N > 0$ and $e^{tx} > 0$; hence

$$|x| = x\quad \text{and}\quad |e^{tx}| = e^{tx}\quad \text{and}$$

$$x < \epsilon\, e^{tx}\ .$$

Because $\epsilon$ depends on $N$, we take $N$ large enough so that $\epsilon < 1$ and $x < \epsilon\, e^{tx} < e^{tx}$.

This implies

$$\frac{e^{tx}}{x} > 1\quad \text{for}\quad x > N$$

and hence

$$f(x) = \frac{e^{tx}}{x^2} > \frac{1}{x} = g(x)\quad \text{for all}\quad x > N.$$

But

$$\int_N^\infty g(x) dx = \int_N^\infty \frac{1}{x}\ dx = \lim_{a \to \infty} [\log a - \log N] = \infty\ .$$

Thus $\int_N^\infty \frac{1}{x}\ dx$ is divergent implying $\int_N^\infty \frac{e^{tx}}{x^2}\ dx$ is divergent

or $M_X(t)$ does not exist.

● **PROBLEM** 8-11

Let $X_1$ and $X_2$ be two independent standard normal variables. Let $Y_1 = X_1 + X_2$, $Y_2 = X_2 - X_1$. Find the joint distribution of $Y_1$ and $Y_2$ by finding the joint moment generating function of $Y_1$ and $Y_2$

<u>Solution</u>: The joint moment generating function of two random variables is defined to be

$$M_{Y_1 Y_2}(t_1, t_2) = E[e^{t_1 Y_1 + t_2 Y_2}] .$$

Furthermore, we may use the following result to show independence. $Y_1$ and $Y_2$ are independent if and only if

$$M_{Y_1, Y_2}(t_1, t_2) = M_{Y_1}(t_1) M_{Y_2}(t_2) .$$

$$M_{Y_1, Y_2}(t_1, t_2) = E[e^{t_1 Y_1 + t_2 Y_2}];$$

but

$$Y_1 = X_1 + X_2 \quad \text{and}$$

$$Y_2 = X_2 - X_1$$

thus

$$E[e^{t_1 Y_1 + t_2 Y_2}] = E[e^{t_1(X_1 + X_2) + t_2(X_2 - X_1)}]$$

$$= E[e^{X_1(t_1 - t_2) + X_2(t_1 + t_2)}] .$$

Note $X_1$ and $X_2$ are independent; hence

$$e^{X_1(t_1 - t_2)} \quad \text{and} \quad e^{X_2(t_1 + t_2)}$$

are also independent and

$$E(e^{t_1 Y_1 + t_2 Y_2}) = E[e^{X_1(t_1 - t_2)}] \, E[e^{X_2(t_1 + t_2)}]$$

$$= M_{X_1}(t_1 - t_2) \, M_{X_2}(t_1 + t_2)$$

where $M_{X_1}$ and $M_{X_2}$ are the moment generating functions of $X_1$ and $X_2$ respectively. Because $X_1$ and $X_2$ are normally distributed with mean zero and variance 1,

$$M_{X_1}(t_1 - t_2) = \exp \frac{(t_1 - t_2)^2}{2}$$

and

$$M_{X_2}(t_1 + t_2) = \exp \frac{(t_1 + t_2)^2}{2}$$

and

$$M_{X_1}(t_1 - t_2) M_{X_2}(t_1 + t_2) e = e^{\frac{(t_1 - t_2)^2}{2}} \; e^{\frac{(t_1 + t_2)^2}{2}}$$

$$= e^{\frac{t_1^2 - 2t_1 t_2 + t_2^2 + t_1^2 + 2t_1 t_2 + t_2^2}{2}}$$

$$= e^{\frac{2t_1^2 + 2t_2^2}{2}} .$$

Thus

$$M_{Y_1, Y_2}(t_1, t_2) = e^{\frac{2t_1^2 + 2t_2^2}{2}} = e^{t_1^2 + t_2^2} .$$

This joint moment generating function can be factored into the product of $e^{t_1^2}$ and $e^{t_2^2}$. Thus,

$$M_{Y_1, Y_2}(t_1, t_2) = e^{t_1^2} e^{t_2^2}$$

and

$$M_{Y_1}(t_1) = e^{t_1^2} = e^{2t_1^2/2}$$

$$M_{Y_2}(t_2) = e^{t_2^2} = e^{2t_2^2/2} .$$

# CHAPTER 9

# CHEBYSHEV'S INEQUALITY

● **PROBLEM** 9-1

Show that $\Pr(\mu - k\sigma < X < \mu + k\sigma) \geq 1 - \frac{1}{k^2}$ for $\sigma > 0$ and $k > 0$.

<u>Solution</u>:  This inequality is a form of what is known as Chebyshev's inequality. It provides a lower bound on probabilities when the distribution is unknown.

Let $g(x)$ be a non-negative function of $x$. Consider a set B where

$$g(x) \geq b > 0 \quad \text{for all } x \text{ in B.}$$

The expected value of $g(X)$, where X is a random variable with probability density $f(x)$, is

$$E(g(X)) = \int_{-\infty}^{\infty} g(x) \, f(x) \, dx \, .$$

This integral can be divided into two integrals:

$$\int_{-\infty}^{\infty} g(x) \, f(x) \, dx = \int_{x \epsilon B} g(x) \, f(x) \, dx + \int_{x \notin B} g(x) \, f(x) \, dx;$$

where the first integral is taken over all x belonging to B and the second integral is taken over all x not belonging to B.

Because $g(x) > 0$ for all x, $E(g(x)) \geq \int_{x \epsilon B} g(x) \, f(x) \, dx$ .

And since $b \leq g(x)$ for all $x \in B$, $E(g(x)) \geq b \int_{x \epsilon B} f(x) \, dx$.

But $\int_{x \epsilon B} f(x) \, dx = \Pr(X \epsilon B)$; therefore $\frac{E(g(x))}{b} \geq \Pr(X \epsilon B)$.

To prove Chebyshev's inequality, let

$$g(x) = (x - E(x))^2 = (x - \mu)^2$$

and choose B to be the set where $|X - \mu| \geq b > 0$.

After substituting, we have $\Pr(|X - \mu| \geq b) \leq \frac{1}{b} E\ ([X - E(x)]^2)$ and $E[[X - E(x)]^2] = \text{Var } X = \sigma^2$.

But if $|X - \mu| \geq b > 0$ on the set B, $g(x) = (x - \mu)^2 \geq b^2$

on this interval. Thus $\Pr(|X - \mu| \geq b) \leq \frac{\sigma^2}{b^2}$.

Let $b = k\sigma$, then, $\Pr(|X - \mu| \geq k\sigma) \leq \frac{1}{k^2}$

or $\Pr(- (X - \mu) \leq -k\sigma$ and $(X - \mu) \geq k\sigma) \leq \frac{1}{k^2}$;

but $\Pr(|X - \mu| \geq k\sigma) = 1 - \Pr(|X - \mu| \leq k\sigma)$

and $\Pr(|X - \mu| \leq k\sigma) \geq 1 - \frac{1}{k^2}$

or $\Pr(\mu - k\sigma \leq X \leq \mu + k\sigma) \geq 1 - \frac{1}{k^2}$.

● **PROBLEM** 9-2

Use Chebyshev's inequality to find a lower bound on $\Pr(- 4 < X < 20)$ where the random variable X has a mean $\mu = 8$ and variance $\sigma^2 = 9$.

Solution: Chebyshev's inequality gives

$\Pr(\mu - k\sigma < X < \mu + k\sigma) \geq 1 - \frac{1}{k^2}$. We wish to find k.

Let $\mu - k\sigma = - 4$ and $\mu + k\sigma = 20$

$\mu = 8$ and $\sigma = \sqrt{\sigma^2} = \sqrt{9} = 3$. Thus, k satisfies either

$8 - 3k = - 4$ or $8 + 3k = 20$ Hence $k = 4$.

Then $\Pr(\mu - k\sigma < X < \mu + k\sigma) \geq 1 - \frac{1}{k^2}$

$= \Pr(- 4 < X < 20) \geq 1 - \frac{1}{(4)^2} \doteq 1 - \frac{1}{(4)^2} = 1 - \frac{1}{16} = \frac{15}{16}$.

Thus a lower bound on $\Pr(- 4 < X < 20)$ is $\frac{15}{16}$.

● **PROBLEM** 9-3

Given that the discrete random variable X has density function f(x) given by $f(- 1) = \frac{1}{8}$, $f(0) = \frac{6}{8}$, $f(1) = \frac{1}{8}$, use Chebyshev's inequality,

$\Pr(|X - \mu| \geq k\sigma) \leq \frac{1}{k^2}$,

to find the upper bound when k = 2. What does this tell us about the possibility of improving the inequality to make the upper bound closer to the exact probability?

Solution:     In order to use the inequality, we need to know the mean and variance of X.

$$\mu = E(x) = \sum_x x \, f(x) = (-1)\left(\frac{1}{8}\right) + \left(0 \cdot \frac{6}{8}\right) + \left(1 \cdot \frac{1}{8}\right)$$

$$= \frac{1}{8} - \frac{1}{8} = 0 \, , \quad \sigma^2 = E[(X - \mu)^2] = E[(X - 0)^2] = E(X^2)$$

$$= \sum_x x^2 \, f(x) = (-1)^2 \left(\frac{1}{8}\right) + 0 + (1^2) \left(\frac{1}{8}\right) = \frac{1}{8} + \frac{1}{8} = \frac{1}{4} \, .$$

When k = 2,   $Pr(|X - \mu| \geq k\sigma) =$

$$Pr\left[|X| \geq 2 \sqrt{\frac{1}{4}}\right] = Pr(|X| \geq 1) \leq \frac{1}{2^2} = \frac{1}{4} \, .$$

The exact $Pr(|X| \geq 1) = Pr(X \leq -1 \text{ or } X \geq 1)$.

$Pr(X < 1) = 0 = Pr(X > 1)$, because the sum of the probabilities for x = -1, x = 0, and x = 1 is

$\frac{1}{8} + \frac{6}{8} + \frac{1}{8} = \frac{8}{8} = 1$.   Therefore we need to consider only

$$Pr(X = -1) = \frac{1}{8} \quad \text{and} \quad Pr(X = 1) = \frac{1}{8} \, .$$

Since x = -1 and x = 1 are mutually exclusive events, we can add their probabilities:

$$\frac{1}{8} + \frac{1}{8} = \frac{2}{8} = \frac{1}{4} \, . \quad \text{Therefore, the exact}$$

$Pr(|X| \geq 1) = \frac{1}{4}$ equals the upper bound given by Chebyshev's inequality, so that we cannot improve the inequality for a   random variable  having finite variance $\sigma^2$.

● **PROBLEM 9-4**

Given that the random variable X has density function $f(x) = \dfrac{1}{2\sqrt{3}}$ when $-\sqrt{3} < X < \sqrt{3}$ and $f(x) = 0$ when $X \leq -\sqrt{3}$ or $X \geq \sqrt{3}$, compute $Pr\left[|X| \geq \frac{3}{2}\right]$   and

$Pr(|X| \geq 2)$. Compare these probabilities with the upper bounds given by Chebyshev's inequality.

Solution:     Chebyshev's inequality states that when a

random variable X has finite variance $\sigma^2$,

$$\Pr(|X - \mu| > k\sigma) \le \frac{1}{k^2} \, ,$$

In order to use this we need to know the mean $\mu$ and variance $\sigma^2$.

$$\mu = E(X) = \int_{-\sqrt{3}}^{\sqrt{3}} X \cdot \frac{1}{2\sqrt{3}} \, dx = \frac{1}{2\sqrt{3}} \left. \frac{X^2}{2} \right|_{-\sqrt{3}}^{\sqrt{3}}$$

$$= \frac{1}{2\sqrt{3}} \left( \frac{3}{2} - \frac{3}{2} \right) = 0 = \mu \, .$$

$$\sigma^2 = E(X^2) - \mu^2 = E(X^2) - 0 = E(X^2)$$

$$= \int_{-\sqrt{3}}^{\sqrt{3}} X^2 \, \frac{1}{2\sqrt{3}} \, dx = \frac{1}{2\sqrt{3}} \left. \frac{X^3}{3} \right]_{-\sqrt{3}}^{\sqrt{3}} = \frac{1}{2\sqrt{3}} \left( \frac{3\sqrt{3}}{3} - \frac{3\,(-\sqrt{3})}{3} \right)$$

$$= \frac{1}{2\sqrt{3}} \, (\sqrt{3} + \sqrt{3}) = \frac{2\sqrt{3}}{2\sqrt{3}} = 1 = \sigma^2 \, .$$

Now $\Pr\left( |X| \ge \frac{3}{2} \right) = 1 - \Pr\left( |X| \le \frac{3}{2} \right)$

because the total area under the line represented by $f(x) = \frac{1}{2\sqrt{3}}$, from $-\sqrt{3}$ to $\sqrt{3}$, is 1. (This can be verified by integration:

$$\int_{-\sqrt{3}}^{\sqrt{3}} \frac{1}{2\sqrt{3}} \, dx = \frac{1}{2\sqrt{3}} \left. X \right]_{-\sqrt{3}}^{\sqrt{3}} = \frac{1}{2\sqrt{3}} \, (\sqrt{3} + \sqrt{3}) = \frac{2\sqrt{3}}{2\sqrt{3}} = 1).$$

Then $\Pr\left( |X| \ge \frac{3}{2} \right) = 1 - \Pr\left( |X| \le \frac{3}{2} \right) = 1 - \Pr\left( -\frac{3}{2} \le X \le \frac{3}{2} \right)$

$$= 1 - \int_{-\frac{3}{2}}^{\frac{3}{2}} \frac{1}{2\sqrt{3}} \, dx = 1 - \frac{1}{2\sqrt{3}} \left. X \right]_{-\frac{3}{2}}^{\frac{3}{2}} = 1 - \frac{1}{2\sqrt{3}} \left( \frac{3}{2} + \frac{3}{2} \right)$$

$$= 1 - \frac{2\left(\frac{3}{2}\right)}{2\sqrt{3}} = 1 - \frac{3}{2\sqrt{3}} = 1 - \frac{\sqrt{3}}{2} \, .$$

Using Chebyshev's inequality, with $\mu = 0$, $\sigma^2 = 1$

and $\sigma = \sqrt{\sigma^2} = 1$, $\Pr\left[|X - 0| \geq \frac{3}{2} \cdot 1\right] \leq \dfrac{1}{\left(\frac{3}{2}\right)^2} = \dfrac{1}{\left(\frac{9}{4}\right)} = \dfrac{4}{9}$ .

Hence $\Pr\left[|X| \geq \frac{3}{2}\right] \leq \frac{4}{9}$ .

The exact probability $1 - \dfrac{\sqrt{3}}{2} \cong 0.134$ is much less than the upper bound given by Chebyshev's inequality.

Next $\Pr(|X| \geq 2) = 1 - \Pr(|X| \leq 2) = 1 - \Pr(-2 \leq X \leq 2)$.

Integrate $f(x) = \dfrac{1}{2\sqrt{3}}$ from $x = -\sqrt{3}$ to $x = \sqrt{3}$,

because $-2 < -\sqrt{3}$, $\sqrt{3} < 2$ and $f(x) = 0$ for $X < -\sqrt{3}$ or $X > \sqrt{3}$.

Since the domain of $f(X)$ is $-\sqrt{3} < X < \sqrt{3}$, then $\Pr(-2 \leq X \leq 2) = 1$, since the interval $-2 \leq X \leq 2$ contains the entire domain.

Therefore, $\Pr(X \geq 2) = 1 - \Pr(-2 \leq X \leq 2)$. $= 1 - 1 = 0$.

Using Chebyshev's inequality to find the upper bound for $\Pr(|X| \geq 2)$, with $\mu = 0$, $\sigma^2 = \sigma = 1$, and $k = 2$,

$$\Pr(|X - 0| \geq 2 \cdot 1) = \Pr(|X| \geq 2) \leq \frac{1}{2^2} = \frac{1}{4} .$$

Again, 0 is much less than the upper bound $\frac{1}{4}$ .

● **PROBLEM** 9-5

Suppose that X assumes the values 1 and - 1, each with probability .5. Find and compare the lower bound on $\Pr(-1 < X < 1)$ given by Chebyshev's inequality and the actual probability that $-1 < X < 1$.

Solution:    Chebyshev's inequality gives

$\Pr(\mu - k\sigma < X < \mu + k\sigma) \geq 1 - \dfrac{1}{k^2}$ . For this random variable,

$\mu = E(X) = \Pr(X = 1) \cdot (1) + \Pr(X = -1) \cdot (-1)$
$= .5 - .5 = 0$    and    $\operatorname{Var} X = E(X^2) - [E(X)]^2 = E(X^2)$

$E(X^2) = \Pr(X = 1)(1)^2 + \Pr(X = -1)(-1)^2 = .5 + .5 = 1$ .

Thus, $\operatorname{Var} X = \sigma^2 = 1$ and $\sigma = 1$.

Now $\Pr(0 - k < X < 0 + k) \geq 1 - \dfrac{1}{k^2}$ .

If $k = 1$, then    $\Pr(-1 < X < 1) \geq 1 - \dfrac{1}{1} = 0$ .

Thus   $\Pr(-1 < X < 1) \geq 0$ .

The actual probability that X is between 1 and - 1 is found by

$$Pr(-1 \leq X \leq 1) = Pr(X = 1) + Pr(-1 < X < 1) + Pr(X$$

$$+Pr(X = 1).$$

But $Pr(-1 \leq X \leq 1) = 1$ because $-1$ and $1$ are the values that X assumes with positive probability. That is,

$$1 = .5 + Pr(-1 < X < 1) + .5 \quad \text{or} \quad Pr(-1 < X < 1) = 0 .$$

Thus, in this case the lower bound on this probability equals the true probability when the distribution of X is known.

● **PROBLEM 9-6**

Find a lower bound on $Pr(-3 < X < 3)$ where $\mu = E(X) = 0$ and $Var X = \sigma^2 = 1$.

Solution: From Chebyshev's inequality,

$$Pr(\mu - k\sigma < X < \mu + k\sigma) \geq 1 - \frac{1}{k^2} .$$

We know that $\mu = 0$ and $\sigma = 1$. Thus $\mu - k\sigma = -3$ implies

$$0 - k(1) = -3 \quad \text{or} \quad -k = -3 \quad k = 3 .$$

Thus $Pr(0 - 3 < X < 0 + 3) \geq 1 - \frac{1}{3^2}$

$Pr(-3 < X < 3) > 1 - \frac{1}{9} = \frac{8}{9}$. The lower bound is thus $\frac{8}{9}$.

# CHAPTER 10

# SPECIAL DISCRETE DISTRIBUTIONS

## UNIFORM DISTRIBUTION

The 1977 World Book Encylopedia has 20 volumes. You are to select one volume at random. Find the probability distribution of X, the number of the selected volume.

Solution: The outcomes are all equally likely. If we have N equally likely outcomes of a random variable, integer-valued from 1 to N, the probability of each outcome is $\frac{1}{N}$ . In other words

$$F(x) = \frac{1}{N} \; ; \; x = 1, 2, \ldots, N.$$

This is the Discrete Uniform distribution.

In the present example N = 20. Therefore

$$F(x) = \frac{1}{20} \; ; \; x = 1, 2, \ldots, 20.$$

Find the uniform distribution for the subsets of months of size 3.

Solution:     Since there are 12 possible months, we may choose 3 at random in

$$\binom{12}{3} = 220 \text{ ways. Numbering these subsets from 1}$$

to 220 the probability distribution is given by

$$F(x) = \frac{1}{220}, \; x = 1, 2, \ldots, 220,$$

since any choice is equally likely. Thus the probability of choosing any given subset is:

$$F(92) = \frac{1}{220} \; .$$

If X follows a discrete uniform distribution, i.e.
$F(x) = \frac{1}{N}$ for x = 1, 2, ..., N, find E(x) and Var(x).

Solution:     By definition $E(x) = \sum\limits_{x} x\, F(x)$.

$$E(x) = \sum_{x=1}^{N} x\, \frac{1}{N} = \frac{1}{N} \sum_{x=1}^{N} x, \text{ but}$$

$$\sum_{x=1}^{N} x = \frac{N(N+1)}{2} \text{ algebraically. Therefore}$$

$$E(x) = \frac{1}{N} \frac{N(N+1)}{2} = \frac{N+1}{2}.$$

For the variance, first find

$$E(x^2) = \sum_{x} x^2\, F(x) = \sum_{x=1}^{N} \frac{1}{N} x^2 = \frac{1}{N} \sum_{x=1}^{N} x^2$$

But by a known algebraic formula,

$$\sum_{x=1}^{N} x^2 = \frac{N(2N+1)(N+1)}{6}. \text{ Hence}$$

$$E(x^2) = \frac{N(N+1)(2N+1)}{6N} = \frac{(N+1)(2N+1)}{6}. \text{ But}$$

$$Var(x) = E(x^2) - (E(x))^2$$

$$= \frac{(N+1)(2N+1)}{6} - \left(\frac{N+1}{2}\right)^2$$

$$= \frac{2N^2 + 3N + 1}{6} - \frac{N^2 + 2N + 1}{4}$$

$$= \frac{4N^2 + 6N + 2}{12} - \frac{3N^2 + 6N + 3}{12}$$

$$= \frac{N^2 - 1}{12}.$$

# GEOMETRIC DISTRIBUTION

Find the probability that a person flipping a balanced coin requires four tosses to get a head.

**Solution:** Suppose one performs a series of repeated Bernoulli trials until a success is observed, and then stops. The total number of trials is random and equal to the number of failures + 1 for the success. The probability that there will be K trials is equal to the probability that there are K - 1 failures followed by a success. If the probability of a success is p,

$$Pr(X = K) = \underbrace{(1 - p)(1 - p) \ldots (1 - p)}_{K - 1 \text{ times.}} p$$

In other words $F(x) = (1 - p)^{x - 1} p; \ x = 1, 2, 3, \ldots$

This is called the geometric distribution. Our problem is one of this type. We have $p = 1 - p = \frac{1}{2}$.

We want $F(4) = \left(\frac{1}{2}\right)^{4-1} \frac{1}{2} = \left(\frac{1}{2}\right)^4 = \frac{1}{16}$.

● **PROBLEM** 10-5

In order to attract customers, a grocery store has started a SAVE game. Any person who collects all four letters of the word SAVE gets a prize. A diligent Mrs. Y who has three letters S, A, and E keeps going to the store until she gets the fourth letter V. The probability that she gets the letter V on any visit is 0.002 and remains the same from visit to visit. Let X denote the number of times she visits the store until she gets the letter V for the first time. Find:

    (a) the probability function of X

    (b) the probability that she gets the letter V for the first time on the twentieth visit

    (c) the probability that she will not have to visit more than three times.

**Solution:** The process consists of a number of failures before a success, the obtaining of a V. The distribution is therefore geometric and

$$F(x) = (1 - p)^{x - 1} p; \text{ for } x = 1, 2, \ldots$$

In this case $p = .002$ and $F(x) = (1 - .002)^{x - 1} (.002)$
$$= (.002)(.998)^{x-1}.$$

(a)   $F(x) = (.002)(.998)^{x-1}.$

(b)   We want $F(20) = (.002)(.998)^{19} = .002 \times .963 = .0019.$

(c)   $Pr(x \leq 3) = Pr(x = 1) + Pr(x = 2) + Pr(x = 3)$

$$= F(1) + F(2) + F(3)$$

$$= (.002)(.998)^{1-1} + (.002)(.998)^{2-1}$$

$$+ (.002)(.998)^{3-1}$$

$$= .002 + (.002)(.998) + (.002)(.998)^2$$

$$= .002 + .001996 + .001992$$

$$= .005988.$$

Find the mean and variance of the geometric distribution:

$$F(x) = (1 - p)^{x-1} p; \quad x = 1, 2, 3, \ldots\ldots$$

Solution: By definition $E(x) = \sum\limits_{x} x \, F(x)$

$$E(x) = \sum_{x=1}^{\infty} x (1 - p)^{x-1} p$$

$$= p \sum_{x=1}^{\infty} x (1 - p)^{x-1};$$

recall that $\dfrac{d}{dz} z^n = nz^{n-1}$; thus

$$p \sum_{x=1}^{\infty} x(1-p)^{x-1} = p \sum_{x=1}^{\infty} \frac{d}{d(1 - p)} (1 - p)^x$$

$$= p \left[ \frac{d}{d(1 - p)} \left[ \sum_{x=1}^{\infty} (1 - p)^x \right] \right].$$

We can put back the $x = 0$ term since it is a constant and differentiates to zero anyway. Also note that $\sum\limits_{x=0}^{\infty} (1 - p)^x$ is a geometric series and therefore sums to

$$\frac{1}{1 - (1 - p)} = \frac{1}{p} \quad . \quad \text{Hence} \quad E(x) = p \left[ \frac{d}{d(1 - p)} \left( \frac{1}{p} \right) \right].$$

Let $q = 1 - p$. Then $E(x) = p \left[ \dfrac{d}{dq} \left( \dfrac{1}{1 - q} \right) \right]$

$$= p \left[ \frac{-1}{(1 - q)^2} (-1) \right]$$

$$= p \left[ \frac{-1}{p^2} (-1) \right] = \frac{1}{p} .$$

To find the variance, we must find $E(x(x-1))$.

$$E(x(x - 1) = \sum_x x (x - 1) F(x)$$

$$= \sum_{x=1}^{\infty} x (x - 1) (1 - p)^{x - 1} p$$

$$= p (1 - p) \sum_{x=1}^{\infty} x (x - 1) (1 - p)^{x-2} .$$

Let $q = 1 - p$, then
$$E(x(x - 1)) = pq \sum_{x=1}^{\infty} x (x - 1) q^{x-2}$$

$$= pq \sum_{x=2}^{\infty} \frac{d^2 (q^x)}{dq^2}$$

$$= pq \times \frac{d^2}{dq^2} \sum_{x=0}^{\infty} q^x .$$

We can put in the $x = 0$ and $x = 1$ terms since they are constants and differentiate to zero. The sum is again geometric and sums to $\frac{1}{1 - q}$ , for $0 < q < 1$.

$$E(x(x - 1)) = pq \left[ \frac{d^2}{dq^2} \frac{1}{1 - q} \right] = pq \frac{d}{dq} \left( \frac{+ 1}{(1 - q)^2} \right)$$

$$= pq \frac{+ 2}{(1 - q)^3} = \frac{2 pq}{p^3} = \frac{2 q}{p^2}$$

$$\text{Var} (x) = E(x^2) - (E(x))^2 = E(x(x - 1)) + E(x) - (E(x))^2$$

$$= \frac{2 q}{p^2} + \frac{1}{p} - \left( \frac{1}{p} \right)^2 = \frac{2 q + p - 1}{p^2}$$

$$= \frac{2 (1 - p) + p - 1}{p^2} = \frac{2 - 2p + p - 1}{p^2}$$

$$= \frac{1 - p}{p^2} .$$

# POISSON DISTRIBUTION

• **PROBLEM** 10-7

Suppose that flaws in plywood occur at random with an average of one flaw per 50 square feet. What is the probability that a 4 foot × 8 foot sheet will have no flaws? At most one flaw? To get a solution assume that the number of flaws per unit area is Poisson distributed.

Solution:     This problem will serve to introduce the Poisson distribution. A random variable X is defined to have a Poisson distribution if the density of X is given

by     $\Pr(X = K) = \frac{e^{-\lambda} \lambda^K}{K!}$     for $K = 0, 1, 2, \ldots$
where $\lambda > 0$.

The Poisson distribution has the unique property that

the expectation equals the variance and they equal the value of the parameter $\lambda$. We will prove this by using the moment generating function.

$$m_x(t) = E(e^{tx}) = \sum_{x=0}^{\infty} e^{tx} \, P(X=x) = \sum_{x=0}^{\infty} e^{tx} \, \frac{e^{-\lambda} \lambda^x}{x!}$$

$$= e^{-\lambda} \sum_{x=0}^{\infty} e^{tx} \, \frac{\lambda^x}{x!} = e^{-\lambda} \sum_{x=0}^{\infty} \frac{(\lambda e^t)^x}{x!}$$

$$= e^{-\lambda} e^{\lambda e^t} = e^{\lambda(e^t-1)}.$$

$$m'_x(t) = e^{\lambda(e^t-1)} \frac{d}{dt}(\lambda e^t - \lambda) = e^{\lambda(e^t-1)} \lambda e^t.$$

By the properties of the moment generating function:

$$E(x) = m'_x(0) = e^{\lambda(e^0-1)} \lambda e^0 = e^{\lambda(1-1)} \lambda e^0 = e^0 \lambda e^0 = \lambda.$$

Also $\mathrm{Var}(x) = E(x^2) - (E(x))^2 = m''_x(0) - (m'_x(0))^2$

$$m''_x(t) = \lambda\left[e^{\lambda(e^t-1)} e^t + e^t \left(e^{\lambda(e^t-1)} \lambda e^t\right)\right]$$

$$m''(0) = \lambda\left[e^{\lambda(e^0-1)} e^0 + e^0 \left(e^{\lambda(e^0-1)} \lambda e^0\right)\right]$$

$$= \lambda(1 + \lambda) = \lambda + \lambda^2.$$

So $\quad \mathrm{Var}(x) = (\lambda + \lambda^2) - \lambda^2 = \lambda.$

For our problem, we can calculate the expected value and use that as $\lambda$. We expect 1 flaw per 50 square feet. Hence we expect $\frac{1}{50}$ flaw per square foot. We have $4 \times 8 = 32$ sq. ft. We expect $\lambda = \frac{32}{50}$ flaws.

$$\mathrm{Pr}(\text{no flaws}) = \mathrm{Pr}(x=0) = \frac{e^{-\frac{32}{50}} \left(\frac{32}{50}\right)^0}{0!} = e^{-\frac{32}{50}} = e^{-.64}.$$

$$\mathrm{Pr}(\text{at most one flaw}) = \mathrm{Pr}(\text{no flaws}) + \mathrm{Pr}(1 \text{ flaw})$$

$$= e^{-.64} \frac{e^{-\frac{32}{50}} \left(\frac{32}{50}\right)^1}{1!}$$

$$= e^{-.64} + .64 \, e^{-.64}.$$

● **PROBLEM** 10-8

Given that the random variable X has a Poisson distribution with mean $\mu = 2$, find the variance $\sigma^2$ and compute $\mathrm{Pr}(1 \leq x)$.

Solution:    The density function for a random variable X
with Poisson distribution is

$$F(x) = \frac{\lambda^x e^{-\lambda}}{x!} \quad \text{when } x = 0, 1, 2, \ldots,$$

$F(x) = 0$ when $x \neq 0, 1, 2, \ldots$ $\lambda$ is a constant that is
specified for the particular circumstances. We are given
that the mean $\mu = 2$, but we are not given $\sigma^2$. But recall
that a Poisson random variable has the unique property
that the expectation equals the variance. Hence $\sigma^2 = 2$
also. Note that $\lambda$ now must be 2.  Also

$$Pr(1 \leq x) = 1 - Pr(x = 0)$$

$$= 1 - \frac{e^{-\lambda} \lambda^0}{0!} = 1 - \frac{e^{-2} \cdot 1}{1} = 1 - \frac{1}{e^2}$$

$$= 1 - .135 = .865.$$

● **PROBLEM** 10-9

Harvey the waiter, drops  on the average  2.5 dishes per
hour. Determine, with the aid of a cumulative Poisson
table, that Harv drops (a) at most 4 dishes, (b) exactly
4 dishes.

Solution:    We are told that $E(x) = 2.5$. In a Poisson
Distribution, the parameter $\lambda = E(x)$. Hence $\lambda = 2.5$. In

this case    $Pr(X=x) = \dfrac{e^{-\lambda} \lambda^x}{x!} = \dfrac{e^{-2.5} (2.5)^x}{x!}$ .

Refer to a table of cumulative Poisson probabilities
that should be in the appendix of your text-book.

Look at the table under expected value 2.5. There is
no column for 2.5 so we will have to average the values for
2.4 and 2.6. In the row c = 4, we find $Pr_{2.4} (X \leq 4) = .904$
and $Pr_{2.6} (X \leq 4) = .877$. Therefore

$$Pr_{2.5} (X \leq 4) = \frac{.904 + .877}{2} = .891.$$

To find $Pr(X = 4)$, we will find $Pr(X \leq 4)$ and then
$Pr(X = 4) = Pr(X \leq 4) - Pr(X \leq 3)$. We will find
$Pr_{2.5} (X \leq 3)$ by taking the average of $Pr_{2.4} (X \leq 3)$ and
$Pr_{2.6} (X \leq 3)$. From the table this is

$$\frac{.779 + .736}{2} = .758 \quad . \quad \text{Therefore}$$

$$Pr(X = 4) = .891 - .758 = .133.$$

● **PROBLEM** 10-10

The average number of traffic accidents that take place

on the Hollywood Freeway on a week day between 7:00 A.M.
and 8:00 A.M. is 0.7 accident per hour. Use tables to
determine the probability that more than 2 traffic
accidents would occur on the Hollywood Freeway on Tuesday
morning between 7:00 A.M. and 8:00 A.M. Assume a Poisson
distribution.

Solution:    Note that $P(X > 2) = 1 - P(X \leq 2)$.

Using the cumulative Poisson tables we will find
$P(X \leq 2)$. We look under the column for expected value
.70 and across the row c = 2 to find $Pr(X \leq 2) = .966$.

Hence $P(X > 2) = 1 - .966 = .034$.

● **PROBLEM** 10-11

The table below gives values for each of two binomial
distributions, one in which n = 10 and p = .1. The other
has n = 20 and p = .05. In each case np is given. Derive
corresponding Poisson probabilities with λ = 1.

| K | Binomial (10, .1) | Binomial (20, .05) |
|---|---|---|
| 0 | .349 | .358 |
| 1 | .387 | .377 |
| 2 | .194 | .185 |
| 3 | .057 | .060 |
| 4 | .011 | .013 |
| 5 | .0015 | .0022 |

Solution:    $P(X = K) = \dfrac{e^{-\lambda} \lambda^K}{K!} = \dfrac{e^{-1} 1^K}{K!} = \dfrac{1}{eK!}$ .

$P(X = 0) = \dfrac{1}{e \cdot 0!} = \dfrac{1}{e} = \dfrac{1}{2.718} = .368$ .

$P(X = 1) = \dfrac{1}{e \cdot 1!} = \dfrac{1}{e} = .368$ .

$P(X = 2) = \dfrac{1}{e \cdot 2!} = \dfrac{1}{2.718 \times 2} = .184$ .

$P(X = 3) = \dfrac{1}{e \cdot 3!} = \dfrac{1}{2.718 \times 6} = .061$ .

$P(X = 4) = \dfrac{1}{e \cdot 4!} = \dfrac{1}{2.718 \times 24} = .015$ .

$P(X = 5) = \dfrac{1}{e \cdot 5!} = \dfrac{1}{2.718 \times 120} = .0031$ .

We see that the Poisson probabilities approximate the
binomial ones.

Suppose a lot is accepted if there is 1 or less defective items in a random sample of n = 50. What is the probability of accepting a lot when incoming quality is 2 percent defective?

Solution:   This is a binomial problem with parameters n = 50 and p = 2% = .02.

$$Pr(X \leq 1) = \sum_{k=0}^{1} \binom{50}{K} p^K (1 - p)^{n - K} .$$

But this is a very hard computation. In the last problem we saw that a Poisson distribution can approximate a binomial.

Let us make this more precise . For a binomial distribution

$$Pr(X = x) = \binom{n}{x} p^x (1 - p)^x , \text{ let}$$

$$F(x) = \frac{n (n - 1) \ldots (n - (x + 1))}{x!} p^x (1 - p)^{n - x} .$$

Multiply numerator and denominator by $n^x$:

$$F(x) = \frac{n (n - 1) \ldots (n - (x + 1))}{n^x x!} (np)^x (1 - p)^{n - x}$$

$$= \frac{n (n - 1) \ldots (n - (x + 1))}{n \cdot n \cdot n \cdot \ldots \cdot n} \frac{\mu^x}{x!} (1 - p)^{n - x}$$

where $\mu = np$,

$$= \left(1 - \frac{1}{n}\right)\left(1 - \frac{2}{n}\right) \ldots \left(1 - \frac{x - 1}{n}\right) \frac{\mu^x}{x!} (1 - p)^{n - x}$$

(*)
$$= \frac{\left(1 - \frac{1}{n}\right)\left(1 - \frac{2}{n}\right) \ldots \left(1 - \frac{x - 1}{n}\right)}{(1 - p)^x} \frac{\mu^x}{x!} (1 - p)^{n} .$$

Notice that

$$(1 - p)^n = [(1 - p)^{-\frac{1}{p}}]^{-np} = [(1 - p)^{-\frac{1}{p}}]^{-\mu} .$$

Also, from the definition of e,   $\underset{z \to 0}{Lim} (1 + z)^{\frac{1}{z}} = e$ .

Hence letting z = -p,   $\underset{p \to 0}{Lim} [(1 - p)^{-\frac{1}{p}}]^{-\mu} = e^{-\mu}$ .

Furthermore   $\underset{n \to \infty}{Lim} \dfrac{\left(1 - \frac{1}{n}\right)\left(1 - \frac{2}{n}\right) \ldots \left(1 - \frac{x - 1}{n}\right)}{(1 - p)^x} = 1$

because p → 0 as n → ∞ when np = μ is fixed.

In the limit, (*) becomes $1 \cdot \dfrac{\mu^x}{x!} \cdot e^{-\mu}$ .

We state this result formally: If the probability of success in a single trial p approaches 0 while the number of trials n becomes infinite in such a manner that the mean $\mu = np$ remains fixed, then the binomial distribution will approach the Poisson distribution with mean $\mu$.

We apply this result to the present problem. $\mu = np = 50 \, (.02) = 1$. Hence

$$P(X = K) = \frac{e^{-\mu} \mu^K}{K!} = \frac{1}{e \cdot K!} \; ;$$

$$P(\text{accepting}) = P(x = 0) + P(x = 1)$$

$$= \frac{1}{e \cdot 0!} + \frac{1}{e \cdot 1!} = \frac{1}{e} + \frac{1}{e} = \frac{2}{e}$$

$$= .736.$$

● **PROBLEM** 10-13

Given that 4% of the items in an incoming lot are defective, what is the probability that at most one defective item will be found in a random sample of size 30? Find the Poisson approximation.

Solution:     We use the binomial distribution for 3 reasons: (1) the selection of the 30 items can be considered a sequence of success-failure trials, because each item is either defective or non-defective; (2) the probability that an item is defective (or nondefective) does not change; (3) the outcome of each trial is independent of the results of the other trials.

Since the events {There are no defectives in the sample of 30 items} and {There is exactly one defective in the sample} are exclusive (they cannot both occur), we can add the probabilities of their occurrence to find

$$P(d \leq 1) = P(d = 0) + P(d = 1),$$

where d is the number of defective items.

$$P(d \leq 1) = \sum_{d=0}^{d=1} \binom{30}{d} (.04)^d (0.96)^{30-d}$$

$$= \binom{30}{0} (.04)^0 (0.96)^{30-0} + \binom{30}{1} (.04)^1 (0.96)^{29}$$

$$= \frac{30!}{30!0!} (1)(0.96)^{30} + 30 \, (.04) \, (.96)^{29}$$

$$= (.96)^{30} + 30 \, (.04)(.96)^{29} = 0.661 .$$

Since np = (number of trials) · (prob. that an item is defective)

$$= 30 \cdot 0.04 = 1.2 < 5$$

and a sample of 30 items is not considered small, we can find an approximation for $P(d \leq 1)$ by using the Poisson distribution $F(d) = \dfrac{\lambda^d e^{-\lambda}}{d!}$ . Substitute np = 1.2 for $\lambda$ and add $P(d = 0)$ and $P(d = 1)$:

$$\sum_{d=0}^{d=1} \frac{(1.2)^d e^{-1.2}}{d!} = \frac{1}{e^{1.2}} \left[ \frac{(1.2)^0}{0!} + \frac{1.2}{1} \right]$$

$$= \frac{1}{e^{1.2}} (1 + 1.2) = \frac{2.2}{e^{1.2}} .$$

The table shows that for 1 or less occurrences of a defective item, with np = 1.2, the probability is 0.663, which differs from the exact probability by only 0.002.

● **PROBLEM** 10-14

Consider a production process of making ball bearings where the probability of a defective bearing is .01. What is the probability of having 10 defective bearings out of 1000?

Solution: Since n is very large and p is small, we can use the Poisson approximation to the binomial with $\lambda = E(x) = np = 1000 \times .01 = 10$.

$$P(X = K) = \frac{e^{-10} (10)^K}{K!}$$

$$P(X = 10) = \frac{e^{-10} (10)^{10}}{10!} .$$

● **PROBLEM** 10-15

Let the probability of exactly one blemish in 1 foot of wire be about $\dfrac{1}{1000}$ and let the probability of two or more blemishes in that length be, for all practical purposes, zero. Let the random variable X be the number of blemishes in 3000 feet of wire. Find $Pr(X = 5)$.

Solution:  Let n = 3000 feet of wire and $p = \dfrac{1}{1000}$ of having a blemish in one foot. We are dealing with a binomial random variable with parameters n = 3000 and $p = \dfrac{1}{1000}$ . The exact answer to this is therefore

$$Pr(X = 5) = \binom{3000}{5} \left(\frac{1}{1000}\right)^5 \left(\frac{999}{1000}\right)^{2995}.$$

This is an incredibly tedious computation. Instead, since n is large and p is small we will use a Poisson approximation.

We know that $\lambda$ must equal np.

$$\lambda = 3000 \left(\frac{1}{1000}\right) = 3.$$

Note that $Pr(X = 5) = Pr(X \leq 5) - Pr(X \leq 4)$.

The last two values can be read off the cumulative tables under expectation 3. Hence

$$Pr(X = 5) = .916 - .815 = .101.$$

● PROBLEM 10-16

Suppose X has a Poisson distribution with parameter $\lambda$.

(a)  Show that $p(k + 1) = \frac{\lambda}{k + 1} p(k)$, where $p(k) = P(X = k)$

(b)  If $\lambda = 2$, compute $p(0)$, and then use the recursive relation in (a) to compute $p(1)$, $p(2)$, $p(3)$, and $p(4)$.

Solution:     (a) Note that $P(X = k) = p(k) = \frac{e^{-\lambda} \lambda^k}{k!}$

But   $p(k + 1) = \frac{e^{-\lambda} \lambda^{k + 1}}{(k + 1)!}$ . Factor out $\frac{\lambda}{k + 1}$ ;

$$p(k + 1) = \frac{e^{-\lambda} \lambda^k}{k!} \cdot \frac{\lambda}{k + 1} = \frac{\lambda}{k + 1} p(k)$$

(b)  Since $\lambda = 2$, $p(k) = \frac{e^{-2} 2^k}{k!}$ . In particular

$$p(0) = \frac{e^{-2} 2^0}{0!} = e^{-2}.$$

$$p(1) = \frac{\lambda}{k + 1} p(0) = \frac{2}{0 + 1} p(0) = 2e^{-2},$$

$$p(2) = \frac{\lambda}{1 + 1} p(1) = \frac{2}{2} p(1) = p(1) = 2 e^{-2},$$

$$p(3) = \frac{\lambda}{2 + 1} p(2) = \frac{2}{3} p(2) = \frac{4}{3} e^{-2}, \quad \text{and}$$

$$p(4) = \frac{\lambda}{3 + 1} p(3) = \frac{2}{4} p(3) = \frac{2}{3} e^{-2}.$$

Consider the Poisson distribution $\dfrac{e^{-\lambda}\lambda^k}{k!}$ .

Prove 
$$\frac{e^{-\lambda}\lambda^{k-1}}{(k-1)!} < \frac{e^{-\lambda}\lambda^k}{k!} \qquad \text{for } k < \lambda,$$

$$\frac{e^{-\lambda}\lambda^{k-1}}{(k-1)!} > \frac{e^{-\lambda}\lambda^k}{k!} \qquad \text{for } k > \lambda,$$

$$\frac{e^{-\lambda}\lambda^{k-1}}{(k-1)!} = \frac{e^{-\lambda}\lambda^k}{k!} \qquad \text{if } \lambda \text{ is an integer and}$$

$k = \lambda$.

**Solution:** Consider the following ratio:

$$R = \frac{\dfrac{e^{-\lambda}\lambda^{k-1}}{(k-1)!}}{\dfrac{e^{-\lambda}\lambda^k}{k!}}$$

If $R > 1$ then $\dfrac{e^{-\lambda}\lambda^{k-1}}{(k-1)!} > \dfrac{e^{-\lambda}\lambda^k}{k!}$ .

If $R < 1$ then $\dfrac{e^{-\lambda}\lambda^{k-1}}{(k-1)!} < \dfrac{e^{-\lambda}\lambda^k}{k!}$ .

If $R = 1$ then $\dfrac{e^{-\lambda}\lambda^{k-1}}{(k-1)!} = \dfrac{e^{-\lambda}\lambda^k}{k!}$ .

$$R = \frac{\dfrac{e^{-\lambda}\lambda^{k-1}}{(k-1)!}}{\dfrac{e^{-\lambda}\lambda^k}{k!}} = \frac{\dfrac{\lambda^{k-1}}{(k-1)!}}{\dfrac{\lambda^k}{k!}} = \frac{\lambda^{k-1}}{(k-1)!}\frac{k!}{\lambda^k}$$

$$= \frac{k}{\lambda} .$$

Hence if $k < \lambda$, $R < 1$; if $k > \lambda$ $R > 1$; and if $k = \lambda$, $R = 1$. The result follows immediately. Note that $\lambda$ must be an integer for $\lambda = k$, since $k$ is an integer.

Suppose that the average number of telephone calls arriving at the switchboard of a small corporation is 30 calls per hour. (i) What is the probability that no calls will arrive in a 3-minute period? (ii) What is the probability that more than five calls will arrive in a 5-minute interval? Assume that the number of calls arriving during any time period has a Poisson distribution.

Solution: Assume that we are observing the occurrence of certain happenings in time, space, region or length. A happening might be a fatal traffic accident, a particle emission, the arrival of a telephone call, a meteorite collision, etc. We will talk of happenings in time; although those in space are appropriate as well. Such time happenings could be represented as follows:

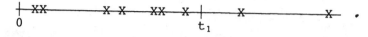

Assume the following: there exists a positive quantity $\nu$ such that:

(i) The probability that exactly one happening will occur in a small time interval of length h is approximately equal to $\nu h$, or Pr[one happening in interval of length h] = $\nu h + o(h)$.

(ii) The probability of more than one happening in a small time interval of length h is negligible when compared to the probability of just one happening in the same interval, or P[two or more happenings] = $o(h)$.

(iii) The number of happenings in nonoverlapping intervals are independent.

The term $o(h)$ denotes an unspecified function which satisfies $\lim\limits_{h \to 0} \dfrac{o(h)}{h} = 0$.

The quantity $\nu$ can be interpreted as the mean rate at which happenings occur per unit of time.

If the above assumptions are satisfied, it can be shown that the number of occurrences of a happening in a period of time of length t has a Poisson distribution with parameter $\lambda = \nu t$. Or if the random variable $Z(t)$ denotes the number of occurrences of the happening in a time interval of length t, then

$$P(Z(t) = z) = \frac{e^{-\nu t} (\nu t)^z}{z!} \qquad \text{for } z = 0, 1, 2, \ldots$$

In the present problem we have 30 calls per hour. This is equivalent to $\dfrac{30}{60} = \dfrac{1}{2}$ calls per minute. Hence $\nu = .5$.

Pr(No calls in 3 minutes)

$$= Pr(Z = 0) = \frac{e^{-\nu t} (\nu t)^0}{0!} = e^{-\nu t} = e^{-(.5)(3)}$$

$$= e^{-1.5} \cong .223.$$

Pr(more than 5 calls in 5 minutes)

$$= \sum_{k=6}^{\infty} \frac{e^{-\nu t} (\nu t)^k}{k!} = \sum_{k=6}^{\infty} \frac{e^{-(.5)(5)} (5(.5))^k}{k!}$$

$$= \sum_{k=6}^{\infty} \frac{e^{-2.5} 2.5^k}{k!} \qquad = 1 - Pr(k \leq 5), (\text{when } E(x) = 2.5)$$

$$= 1 - .958 = .042.$$

● **PROBLEM** 10-19

A merchant knows that the number of a certain kind of item that he can sell in a given period of time is Poisson distributed. How many such items should the merchant stock so that the probability will be .95 that he will have enough items to meet the customer demand for a time period of length T?

Solution: Let $\nu$ denote the mean rate of occurrence per unit time and let k be the unknown number of items the merchant should stock. The problem stipulates that there should be a 95 per cent probability that enough is stocked.

This is an example of the Poisson process discussed in the previous problem. Hence by that discussion the parameter for the Poisson distribution is $\nu T$; and

$Pr(k \text{ items can be sold}) = \dfrac{e^{-\nu T} (\nu T)^k}{k!}$ . Assuming K items

are stocked, Pr(having enough items) = Pr(having a demand

for K items or less) $= \sum_{k=0}^{K} \dfrac{e^{-\nu T} (\nu T)^k}{k!}$ . In general we

have to find K such that this is $\geq$ .95.

In particular, if the merchant sells an average of two such items a day, how many should he stock so that he will have a probability at least .95 of having enough items to meet demand for a 30 day month? Here $\nu = 2$ and $T = 30$, therefore we must find K such that

$$\sum_{x=0}^{K} \frac{e^{-(2)(30)} ((2)(30))^x}{x!} = \sum_{x=0}^{K} \frac{e^{-60} (60)^x}{x!}$$

$= F(K)$ for a parameter of 60.

From cumulative Poisson tables, for $K \geq 73$, $F(K) \geq .95$.

● **PROBLEM** 10-20

Past experience indicates that the ticket office at the

309

Rialto Theatre receives a mean rate of thirty calls per hour. Assuming that the number of calls have the Poisson distribution, find the probability that

(a) during a ten-minute coffee-break, no calls will be received

(b) during a twenty-minute coffee-break, at least two calls will be received.

Solution: The telephone call is a classic example of a Poisson process. We are discussing the occurrence of certain happenings in time and the three conditions of a Poisson process are met. Hence, the distribution of the number of calls received during a time t is

$$Pr(X = k) = \frac{e^{-\lambda t} (\lambda t)^k}{k!} = \frac{e^{-30t} (30t)^k}{k!} .$$

(a) We are interested in a ten-minute period or $\frac{1}{6}$ of an hour. Hence

$$Pr(X = k) = \frac{e^{-30\left(\frac{1}{6}\right)} \left(30 \cdot \frac{1}{6}\right)^k}{k!} = \frac{e^{-5} 5^k}{k!}$$

We want $Pr(X = 0) = \frac{e^{-5} 5^0}{0!} = e^{-5} = .0067.$

(b) We are concerned with a twenty minute period, $\frac{1}{3}$ of an hour. Now $\lambda t = (30)\left(\frac{1}{3}\right) = 10$. Therefore, the probability of k calls is $\frac{e^{-10} 10^k}{k!}$ . Note that

Pr(at least 2 calls) = 1 - Pr(0 or 1 call)

= 1 - Pr(0 calls) = Pr(1 call)

$$= 1 - \frac{e^{-10} 10^0}{0!} - \frac{e^{-10} 10^1}{1!} = 1 - e^{-10} - 10 e^{-10}$$

$$= 1 - 11 e^{-10} \overset{\sim}{=} 1 - .0005 = .9995.$$

● **PROBLEM** 10-21

Customers enter Macy's "at random" at a rate of four per minute. Assume that the number entering Macy's in any given time interval has a Poisson distribution. Determine the probability that at least one customer enters the store in a given half-minute interval.

Solution: We again are discussing the specific occurrence of events in a length of time. The problem describes a Poisson process. The mean rate of occurrence is $\lambda = 4$. Hence the probability that k customers enter Macy's in an interval of time t is $\frac{e^{-\lambda t} (\lambda t)^k}{k!}$ or in our case $\frac{e^{-4t} (4t)^k}{k!}$. Given

$$t = \frac{1}{2} \text{ minute,} \quad Pr(X = k) = \frac{e^{-4(\frac{1}{2})} \left[ 4 \cdot \frac{1}{2} \right]^k}{k!} = \frac{e^{-2} 2^k}{k!}$$

We want $Pr(X \geq 1)$. Note that

$$Pr(X \geq 1) = 1 - Pr(X = 0) = 1 - \frac{e^{-2} 2^0}{0!}$$

$$= 1 - e^{-2} = .865.$$

● **PROBLEM** 10-22

Data on deaths due to a kick from a horse, based on the research of 10 army corps for 20 years are given in the following table:

| Number of deaths in fixed time interval | Number of intervals at that value |
|:---:|:---:|
| 0 | 109 |
| 1 | 65 |
| 2 | 22 |
| 3 | 3 |
| 4 | 1 |
| 5 | 0 |
|  | 200 |

We find that there are 200 readings; that is, 200 fixed intervals. This may be interpreted as 200 repetitions of an experiment.

We are also assuming that the opportunity of an event's (a death due to a kick from a horse) occurring is continually present. This means that if we consider the occurrence of an event as a success and the nonoccurrence as a failure, the proportion of successes is very small.

Let us now divide each fixed interval into n subintervals where n is very large. Then we shall assume the probability of an occurrence or non-occurrence in a subinterval is close to 1. The probability of more than one occurrence is very small. Furthermore, we shall assume that the occurrence of an event in any subinterval is independent of the occurrence in any other subinterval. Thus we have a Poisson process in the fixed interval and hence

$$Pr(X = k) = e^{-\lambda t} \frac{(\lambda t)^k}{k!}$$

311

where k is the number of deaths in the fixed interval.
Estimate λt.

Solution:     The key here is the property of a Poisson
distribution that says that the parameter is the expectation of a single Poisson random variable. Here the
parameter is λt. We will estimate λt, the expectation of
a single observation by the average number of deaths per
interval. Therefore,

$$\lambda t = \frac{\text{Total Number of Deaths}}{\text{Total Number of Fixed Intervals}}$$

$$= \frac{0 \times (\text{no. with 0 deaths}) + 1 \times (\text{no. with 1 death})}{\ldots \times 5 \ (\text{no. with 5 deaths})}$$
$$\frac{}{200}$$

$$= \frac{(0 \times 109) + (1 \times 65) + (2 \times 22) + (3 \times 3) + (4 \times 1) + (5 \times 4)}{200}$$

$$= \frac{122}{200} = 0.61 .$$

Hence the Poisson distribution is

$$\Pr(X = k) = e^{-0.61} \frac{(0.61)^k}{k!} .$$

● PROBLEM 10-23

Suppose $X_t$, the number of phone calls that arrive at an
exchange during a period of length t, has a Poisson distribution with parameter λt. The probability that an
operator answers any given phone call is equal to p,
$0 \leq p \leq 1$. If $Y_t$ denotes the number of phone calls answered, find the distribution of $Y_t$.

Solution:     We want to find $P(Y_t = k)$, k = 0, 1, 2, ...
This is an advanced exercise in conditional probability.
If we are given $X_t = r$, we have r Bernoulli trials and a
success constitutes the operator answering the call. Hence,
given $X_t = r$, $Y_t$ is binomially distributed.

$$\Pr(Y_t = k \mid X_t = r) = \binom{r}{k} p^k (1 - p)^{r-k}, \ k = 0, 1, \ldots, r .$$

By the Law of Total Probability:

$$\Pr(Y_t = k) = \sum_{r=k}^{\infty} \Pr(Y_t = k \cap X_t = r)$$

$$= \sum_{r=k}^{\infty} \Pr(Y_t = k \mid X_t = r) \times \Pr(X_t = r)$$

from the definition of conditional probability;

$$= \sum_{r=k}^{\infty} \binom{r}{k} p^k (1 - p)^{r-k} e^{-\lambda t} \frac{(\lambda t)^r}{r!}$$

$$= \frac{e^{-\lambda t}(\lambda t)^k p^k}{k!} \sum_{r=k}^{\infty} \frac{(1 - p)^{r-k} (\lambda t)^{r-k}}{(r-k)!} .$$

Let $i = r - k$. We see that:

$$\Pr(Y_t = k) = \frac{e^{-\lambda t}(\lambda t)^k p^k}{k!} \sum_{i=0}^{\infty} \frac{(1 - p)^i (\lambda t)^i}{i!}$$

$$= \frac{e^{-\lambda t}(\lambda t)^k p^k}{k!} \sum_{i=0}^{\infty} \frac{[(1 - p)\lambda t]^i}{i!}$$

$$= \frac{e^{-\lambda t}(\lambda t)^k p^k}{k!} e^{(1-p)\lambda t}$$

$$= \frac{e^{-\lambda t} e^{\lambda t} e^{-\lambda p t} (\lambda p t)^k}{k!}$$

$$= \frac{e^{-\lambda p t}(\lambda p t)^k}{k!} .$$

In conclusion we see that $Y_t$ has a Poisson distribution with parameter $p\lambda t$.

# HYPERGEOMETRIC DISTRIBUTION

● **PROBLEM** 10-24

A lot consisting of 100 fuses, is inspected by the following procedure. Five of these fuses are chosen at random and tested; if all 5 "blow" at the correct amperage, the lot is accepted. Find the probability distribution of the number of defectives in a sample of 5 assuming there are 20 in the lot.

Solution: We want to find $\Pr(X = x)$. We will use the classical model of probability;

$$\Pr(X = x) = \frac{\text{no. of ways of getting x defectives in 5 draws}}{\text{total possible draws of 5}}$$

We can draw 5 fuses out of a lot of 100 in $\binom{100}{5}$ ways.

Also we can select x defectives out of the 20 in $\binom{20}{x}$ ways. In addition we must choose 5 - x out of 100 - 20 = 80 nondefectives. We can do this in $\binom{80}{5-x}$ ways. By the multi-plication law we can get x defectives out of a lot of 100 in $\binom{20}{x}\binom{80}{5-x}$ ways.

Hence $F(x) = Pr(X = x) = \dfrac{\binom{20}{x}\binom{80}{5-x}}{\binom{100}{5}}$

for x = 0, 1, 2, 3, 4, 5.

This is an example of the hypergeometric distribution.

● **PROBLEM** 10-25

A random variable X is defined to have a hypergeometric distribution of the discrete density function of X is

$$f(x) = \left\{ \dfrac{\binom{K}{x}\binom{M-K}{n-x}}{\binom{M}{n}} \right. \quad \text{for } x = 0, 1, \ldots, n.$$

The parameters are M, a positive integer, K, a nonnegative integer less than or equal to M, and n, a positive integer at most M. Find E(x) and Var(X).

Solution:

$$E(x) = \sum_{x=0}^{\infty} x\, f(x) \quad = \sum_{x=0}^{n} x\, \dfrac{\binom{K}{x}\binom{M-K}{n-x}}{\binom{M}{n}}$$

$$= \sum_{x=0}^{n} \left[ \dfrac{x\, \dfrac{K!}{(K-x)!\,x!}\, \dfrac{(M-K)!}{(M-K-n+x)!\,(n-x)!}}{\dfrac{M!}{(M-n)!\,n!}} \right]$$

$$= \sum_{x=0}^{n} \dfrac{x\,K!}{(K-x)!\,x!}\, \dfrac{(M-K)!\,(M-n)!\,n!}{(M-K-n+x)!\,(n-x)!\,M!}$$

$$= \sum_{x=1}^{n} \dfrac{K!\,(M-K)!\,(M-n)!\,n!}{(K-x)!\,(x-1)!\,(M-K-n+x)!\,(n-x)!\,M!}$$

$$= \sum_{x=1}^{n} \dfrac{K(K-1)!\,(M-K)!\,(M-n)!\,n\,(n-1)!}{(K-x)!\,(x-1)!\,(M-K-n+x)!\,(n-x)!\,M(M-1)!}$$

314

$$= \frac{nK}{M} \sum_{x=1}^{n} \left[ \frac{\dfrac{(K-1)!}{(K-x)!\,(x-1)!} \cdot \dfrac{(M-K)!}{(n-x)!\,(M-K-n+x)!}}{\dfrac{(M-1)!}{(n-1)!\,(M-n)!}} \right]$$

$$= \frac{nK}{M} \sum_{x=1}^{n} \frac{\dbinom{K-1}{x-1}\dbinom{M-K}{n-x}}{\dbinom{M-1}{n-1}} \ .$$

Now let $y = x - 1$ and we obtain (adding and subtracting 1 to $(M - K)$),

$$\frac{nK}{M} \sum_{y=0}^{n-1} \frac{\dbinom{K-1}{y}\dbinom{M-1-K+1}{n-1-y}}{\dbinom{M-1}{n-1}}$$

but this summation is the sum of a hypergeometric distribution with parameters $M - 1$, $K - 1$, and $n - 1$. Hence the sum is one and $E(x) = \dfrac{nK}{M}$ .

Now for the variance.

$$E[x(x-1)] = \sum_{x=0}^{n} x\,(x-1)\,f(x)$$

$$= \sum_{x=0}^{n} x\,(x-1)\, \frac{\dbinom{K}{x}\dbinom{M-K}{n-x}}{\dbinom{M}{n}} \ .$$

For $x = 0$, $1$ either $x$ or $x - 1 = 0$ so we have

$$\sum_{x=2}^{n} x\,(x-1)\, \frac{\dbinom{K}{x}\dbinom{M-K}{n-x}}{\dbinom{M}{n}}$$

$$= \sum_{x=2}^{n} \left[ \frac{x(x-1)\,\dfrac{K!}{(K-x)!\,x!}\cdot\dfrac{(M-K)!}{(M-K-n+x)!\,(n-x)!}}{\dfrac{M!}{(M-n)!\,n!}} \right]$$

$$= \sum_{x=2}^{n} \frac{x(x-1)\;K!\,(M-K)!\,(M-n)!\,n!}{(K-x)!\,x!\,(M-K-n+x)!\,(n-x)!\,M!}$$

$$= \sum_{x=2}^{n} \frac{K(K-1)(K-2)!\,(M-K)!\,(M-n)!\,n(n-1)(n-2)!}{(K-x)!\,(x-2)!\,(M-K-n+x)!\,(n-x)!\,M(M-1)(M-2)!}$$

$$= n(n-1) \frac{K(K-1)}{M(M-1)} \sum_{x=2}^{n} \left[ \frac{\frac{(K-2)!}{(x-2)!(K-x)!} \frac{(M-K)!}{(M-K-n+x)(n-x)!}}{\frac{M-2)!}{(n-2)!(M-n)!}} \right]$$

$$\frac{n(n-1)K(K-1)}{M(M-1)} \sum_{x=2}^{n} \frac{\binom{K-2}{x-2}\binom{M-K}{n-x}}{\binom{M-2}{n-2}} \quad .$$

Let $y = x - 2$ and obtain

$$n(n-1) \frac{K(K-1)}{M(M-1)} \sum_{y=0}^{n-2} \frac{\binom{K-2}{y}\binom{M-2-K+2}{n-2-y}}{\binom{M-2}{n-2}}$$

which equals $n(n-1)\frac{K(K-1)}{M(M-1)}$ since the sum is the total of all hypergeometric probabilities with parameters $M-2$, $K-2$, and $n-2$.

We know $\text{Var}(x) = E(x^2) - (E(x))^2$

$$= E(x(x-1)) + E(x) - (E(x))^2$$

$$= n(n-1) \frac{K(K-1)}{M(M-1)} + n \frac{K}{M} - n^2 \frac{K^2}{M^2}$$

$$= \frac{nK}{M} \left[ (n-1) \frac{K-1}{M-1} + 1 - \frac{nK}{M} \right]$$

$$= \frac{nK}{M} \left( \frac{(n-1)(K-1)M + (M-1)M - nK(M-1)}{M(M-1)} \right)$$

$$= \frac{nK}{M} \left( \frac{MnK - KM - nM + M + M^2 - M - MnK + nK}{M(M-1)} \right)$$

$$= \frac{nK}{M} \left( \frac{M^2 - KM - Mn + Kn}{M(M-1)} \right)$$

$$= \frac{nK}{M} \left( \frac{(M-K)(M-n)}{M(M-1)} \right) \quad .$$

# CHAPTER 11

# NORMAL DISTRIBUTIONS

## AREAS UNDER THE STANDARD NORMAL CURVE

If Z is a standard normal variable, use the table of
standard normal probabilities to find:

      (a) Pr(Z < 0)
      (b) Pr(- 1 < Z < 1)
      (c) Pr(Z > 2.54) .

Solution:    The normal distribution is the familiar
"bell-shaped" curve. It is a continuous probability
distribution that it widely used to describe the
distribution of heights, weignts, and other characteristics.

    The density function of the standard normal
distribution is

$$f(x) = \frac{1}{\sqrt{2\pi}} \ \exp \ \left[\frac{-x^2}{2}\right] \qquad -\infty < x < \infty \ .$$

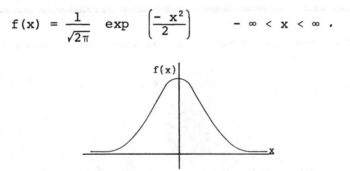

is a graph of this density. The probability of a standard
normal variable being found in a particular interval can be
found with the help of tables found in the backs of most
statistics text books.

    (a) To find the probability Pr(Z < 0) we can take
advantage of the fact that the normal distribution is
symmetric about its mean of zero. Thus

    Pr(Z > 0) = Pr(Z < 0).    We know that

    Pr(Z > 0) + Pr(Z < 0) = 1

because Z > 0 and Z < 0 are exhaustive events.    Thus

$$2\Pr(Z < 0) = 1 \qquad \text{or} \qquad \Pr(Z < 0) = \frac{1}{2}.$$

(b) To find the $\Pr(-1 < Z < 1)$ we use the tables of the standard normal distribution.

$$\Pr(-1 < Z < 1) = \Pr(Z < 1) - \Pr(Z < -1).$$

Reading across the row headed by 1 and down the column labeled .00 we see that $\Pr(Z < 1.0) = .8413$.

$\Pr(Z < -1) = \Pr(Z > 1)$ by the symmetry of the normal distribution. We also know that

$$\Pr(Z > 1) = 1 - \Pr(Z < 1).$$

Substituting we see,

$$\Pr(-1 < Z < 1) = \Pr(Z < 1) - [1 - \Pr(Z < 1)]$$

$$= 2\Pr(Z < 1) - 1 \qquad = 2(.8413) - 1 = .6826.$$

(c) $\Pr(Z > 2.54) = 1 - \Pr(Z < 2.54)$ and reading across the row labeled 2.5 and down the column labeled .04 we see that $\Pr(Z < 2.54) = .9945$.

Substituting,

$$\Pr(Z > 2.54) = 1 - .9945 = .0055.$$

● **PROBLEM** 11-2

Find $\Pr(-.47 < Z < .94)$.

<u>Solution</u>:

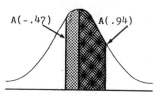

$\Pr(-.47 < Z < .94)$ is equal to the shaded area above. To find the value of the shaded area we add the areas labeled A(- .47) and A(.94).

$$\Pr(-.47 \leq Z \leq .94) = A(-.47) + A(.94).$$

By the symmetry of the normal distribution, $A(-.47) = A(.47) = .18082$ from the table.

Also $A(.94) = .32639$ so

$$\Pr(-.47 < Z < .94) = .18082 + .32639 = .50721.$$

Find $\Phi(-.45)$.

<u>Solution:</u>    $\Phi(-.45) = \Pr(Z \leq -.45)$,

where Z is distributed normally with mean 0 and variance 1.

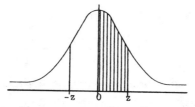

        Let $A(Z)$ = the area under the curve from 0 to Z.
From our table we find $A(.45) = .17364$ and by the symmetry
of the normal distribution,

    $A(-.45) = A(.45) = .17364$.

    We wish to find $\Phi(-.45)$, the shaded area below.

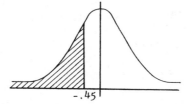

        We know that $\Phi(0) = .5000$ and from the diagram below
we know that $\Phi(0) - A(-.45) = \Phi(-.45)$.

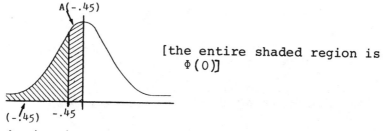

[the entire shaded region is
$\Phi(0)$]

    Substituting,

    $\Phi(0) - A(-.45) = .5000 - .17364 = \Phi(-.45)$

and   $\Phi(-.45) = .32636$.

Find $\Pr(-.47 < Z < .94)$ using $\Phi(-.47)$ and $\Phi(.94)$.

<u>Solution:</u>    $\Phi(-.47) = .5000 - A(-.47)$

                = $.5000 - A(.47)$

and $\Phi(.94) = .5000 + A(.94)$. Hence

$$Pr(- .47 < Z < .94) = \Phi(.94) - \Phi(- .47)$$

$$= [.5000 + A(.94)] - [.5000 - A(.47)]$$

$$= .82639 - .31918 = .50721.$$

# CONVERSIONS AND APPLICATIONS OF STANDARD NORMAL VARIABLES

● **PROBLEM** 11-5

In a normal distribution, what is the Z-score equivalent of the median? What is the Z score above which only 16 percent of the distribution lies? What percentage of the scores lie below a Z score of +2.0?

Solution:    The median is the number such that 1/2 of a probability distribution lies above or below it. Equi-

valently the median is a number $\tilde{m}$ such that a random observation X from a distribution is equally likely to be above or below it. Thus

$$Pr(X \geq \tilde{m}) = Pr(X \leq \tilde{m}) = \frac{1}{2}.$$

To find the Z-score equivalent of the median we

wish to find some number $\tilde{m}$ such that

$$Pr(Z \geq \tilde{m}) = Pr(Z \leq \tilde{m}) = \frac{1}{2}$$

where Z is a normally distributed random variable with mean 0 and variance 1.

From the tables or from the fact that the normal distribution is symmetrical about its mean we have

$$Pr(Z \geq 0) = Pr(Z \leq 0) = \frac{1}{2}.$$

Thus the median is $\tilde{m} = 0$.

To find the Z-score above which 16 percent of the distribution lies we find a constant C such that

$$Pr(Z \geq C) = 16\% = .160 \quad \text{or equivalently}$$

$$Pr(Z \leq C) = 1 - .160 = .840.$$

Searching for .8400 in the body of the table and

then reading up the appropriate row and column we find that

Pr(Z < 1) = .84, thus C = 1.

To find the percentage of scores that lie below a Z-score of 2, we wish to find $\Pr(Z < 2.00)$.

Reading across the column labeled 2.0 and then down the row headed by .00, we find

Pr(Z < 2.00) = .9772,

but .9772 is 97.72% of 1; thus 97.72% of the Z-scores lie below 2.00.

● PROBLEM 11-6

Given that the random variable x has density

$$f(x) = \frac{1}{\sqrt{18\pi}} e^{-(x^2 - 10x + 25)/18}, \quad -\infty < x < \infty.$$

Is this distribution normal? What is its maximum value?

Solution: A normal distribution can be written in the form

$$f(x) = \frac{1}{\sigma\sqrt{2\pi}} \exp\left[-\frac{(x - \mu)^2}{2\sigma^2}\right], \quad \text{when } -\infty < x < \infty.$$

Rewrite $(x^2 - 10x + 25)$ as $(x - 5)^2$ and 18 as $2 \cdot 9 = 2 \cdot 3^2$. Also $\sqrt{18\pi} = \sqrt{9 \cdot 2\pi} = 3\sqrt{2\pi}$. Thus $\mu = 5$ and $\sigma = 3$. Substitution gives

$$f(x) = \frac{1}{3\sqrt{2\pi}} e^{-(x - 5)^2/(2 \cdot 3^2)}.$$

The graph of a normal distribution reaches its maximum at $x = \mu$, so we substitute $x = 5$:

$$f(x) = \frac{1}{3\sqrt{2\pi}} e^{-(5 - 5)^2/2 \cdot 3^2} = \frac{1}{3\sqrt{2\pi}} e^0$$

$$= \frac{1}{3\sqrt{2\pi}}.$$

Thus the maximum value of f(x) is $\frac{1}{3\sqrt{2\pi}}$.

● PROBLEM 11-7

Given that x has a normal distribution with mean 10

Solution:     x is a normal random variable with a mean or location parameter of 10 and a standard deviation or scale parameter of 4. A graph of its density function might look like this:

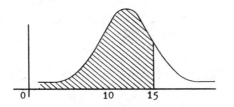

We wish to find the $Pr(x < 15)$ or the area of the shaded area. It would be possible to construct tables which would supply such probabilities for many different values of the mean and standard deviation. Luckily this is not necessary. We may shift and contort our density function in such a way so that only one table is needed. How is such a change accomplished?

First the mean is subtracted from x giving a new random variable, x - 10. This new random variable is normally distributed but $E(x - 10)$, the mean of x - 10, is $E(x) - 10 = 0$. We have shifted our distribution so that it is centered at 0.

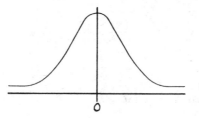

We can contort our new random variable by dividing by the standard deviation creating a new random variable $Z = \dfrac{x - 10}{4}$ ; the variance of Z is

$$\text{Var}\left(\dfrac{x - 10}{4}\right) = \dfrac{\text{Var } x}{16} = \dfrac{(\text{standard deviation of x})^2}{16} = 1.$$

Fortunately, after all this twisting and shifting, our new random variable Z is still normally distributed and has mean 0 and variance 1. This new random variable is referred to as a Z-score or standard random variable and tables for its probabilities are widespread.

To solve our problem we first convert an x-score to a Z-score and then consult the appropriate table.

$$Pr(x < 15) = Pr\left(\dfrac{x - 10}{4} < \dfrac{15 - 10}{4}\right)$$

$$= \Pr\left(Z < \frac{5}{4}\right) = \Phi(1.25) = .5000 + A(1.25)$$

$$= .5000 + .39439 = .89439.$$

● **PROBLEM** 11-8

If a random variable X is normally distributed with a mean of 118 and a standard deviation of 11, what Z-scores correspond to raw scores of 115, 134 and 99.

<u>Solution</u>:     To convert a raw score to a Z-score we subtract the mean and divide by the standard deviation. Thus

$$\text{Z-score} = \frac{\text{Raw score} - \text{mean}}{\text{standard deviation}} .$$

Thus,     $\frac{115 - 118}{11} = \frac{-3}{11} = -.27$ :

a Z-score of - .27 corresponds to a raw score of 115.

$$Z = \frac{134 - 118}{11} = \frac{16}{11} = 1.45 \text{ or}$$

a Z-score of 1.45 corresponds to a raw score of 134. And

$$Z = \frac{99 - 118}{11} = -1.73,$$

or a Z-score of - 1.73 corresponds to a raw score of 99.

● **PROBLEM** 11-9

If X has a normal distribution with mean 9 and standard deviation 3, find P(5 < X < 11).

<u>Solution</u>:     First we convert our X-scores to Z-scores by subtracting the mean and dividing by the standard deviation. Next we consult tables for the standard normal distribution.

Thus,   $P(5 < X < 1) = P\left(\frac{5 - 9}{3} < \frac{X - 9}{3} < \frac{11 - 9}{3}\right)$

$$= P\left(\frac{-4}{3} < Z < \frac{2}{3}\right) = \Phi(.66) - \Phi(-1.33)$$

$$= .74537 - .09176 = .65361 ,$$

Given a mean of 50 and a standard deviation of 10 for a set of measurements that is normally distributed, find the probability that a randomly selected observation is between 50 and 55.

_Solution:_     We wish to find $Pr(50 < X < 55)$ where X is normally distributed with mean 50 and standard deviation 10. We standardize X to convert our distribution of X scores to a distribution of Z-scores. Let $Z = \frac{X - \mu}{\sigma}$ , where $\mu$ is the mean of X scores and $\sigma$ is the standard deviation of the X-scores. Then

$$Pr(50 \le X \le 55) = Pr\left(\frac{50 - \mu}{\sigma} \le \frac{X - \mu}{\sigma} \le \frac{55 - \mu}{\sigma}\right)$$

$$= Pr\left(\frac{50 - 50}{10} \le Z \le \frac{55 - 50}{10}\right) = Pr(0 < Z \le .5).$$

$$Pr(Z \le .5) - Pr(Z \le 0) = Pr(0 \le Z \le .5).$$

From the table of standard normal,

$$Pr(Z \le 0) = .5 \qquad \text{and} \qquad Pr(Z \le .5) = .691.$$

Substituting we see that

$$Pr(50 \le X \le 55) = Pr(0 \le Z \le .5)$$
$$= Pr(Z \le .5) - Pr(Z \le 0) = .691 - .500$$
$$= .191.$$

An electrical firm manufactures light bulbs that have a lifetime that is normally distributed with a mean of 800 hours and a standard deviation of 40 hours. Of 100 bulbs, about how many will have lifetimes between 778 and 834 hours?

_Solution:_     The probability that X, the lifetime of a randomly selected bulb, is between 778 and 834 hours is

$$Pr(778 < X < 834).$$

Standardizing we see that   $Pr(778 < X < 834)$

$$= Pr\left(\frac{778 - \mu}{\sigma} < \frac{X - \mu}{\sigma} < \frac{834 - \mu}{\sigma}\right)$$

$$= Pr\left(\frac{778 - 800}{40} < Z < \frac{834 - 800}{40}\right)$$

$$= \text{Pr} \left[ \frac{-22}{40} < Z < \frac{34}{40} \right] \quad = \text{Pr}(-.55 < Z < .85)$$

$$= \text{Pr}(Z < .85) - \text{Pr}(Z < -.55) \quad = .802 - (1 - .709)$$

$$= .511 \ .$$

Thus 51.1 % of the bulbs manufactured will have lifetimes between 778 and 834 hours. On the average, 51 of 100 light bulbs will have lifetimes between 778 and 834 hours.

● **PROBLEM** 11-12

Given a normal population with $\mu = 25$ and $\sigma = 5$, find the probability that an assumed value of the variable will fall in the interval 20 to 30.

Solution:      We wish to find the probability that a normally distributed random variable, X, mean $\mu = 25$ and standard deviation $\sigma = 5$, will lie in the interval (20, 30), Pr(20 < X < 30). We convert X from a normally distributed variable with mean 25 and standard deviation 5 to Z, a normally distributed random variable with mean 0 and standard deviation 1. The formula for conversion is $Z = \frac{X - \mu}{\sigma}$ . Thus,

$$\text{Pr}(20 < X < 30) = \text{Pr} \left[ \frac{20 - \mu}{\sigma} < \frac{X - \mu}{\sigma} < \frac{30 - \mu}{\sigma} \right]$$

$$= \text{Pr} \left[ \frac{20 - 25}{5} < Z < \frac{30 - 25}{5} \right] \quad = \text{Pr}(-1 < Z < 1) \ .$$

To find this      probability involving the random variable Z, we resort to prepared tables which are usually found in statistics texts. There are a variety of such tables and we find Pr(- 1 < Z < 1) three different ways to illustrate the various types of tables.

(1) This type of table gives Pr(0 < Z < a). To find the Pr(- 1 < Z < 1), we first find Pr(0 < Z < 1). This is Pr(0 < Z < 1) = .341. Next use the fact that the standard normal distribution is symmetrical about 0, hence Pr(0 < Z < a) = Pr(0 > Z > - a).

From this fact,

Pr(0 > Z > - 1) = Pr(0 < Z < 1) = .341

Pr(- 1 < Z < 1) = Pr(0 > Z > - 1) + Pr(0 < Z < 1)

$$= 2(.341) = .682 \ .$$

(2) Another type of table gives Pr(Z ≤ a) for various values of a. To use this table we note that;

325

$$Pr(-1 \leq Z \leq 1) = Pr(Z \leq 1) - Pr(Z \leq -1);$$

from the table we see that

$$Pr(Z \leq 1) = .841 \qquad \text{and} \qquad Pr(Z \leq -1) = .159.$$

Thus,  $Pr(-1 \leq Z \leq 1) = .841 - .159 = .682.$

(3) This type of table gives $Pr(Z \geq a)$ for certain values of a.

$$Pr(-1 \leq Z \leq 1) = Pr(-1 \leq Z) - Pr(1 \leq Z)$$

But  $Pr(-1 \leq Z) = Pr(1 \geq Z)$  by symmetry ;

$$= 1 - Pr(1 \leq Z)$$

Thus,

$$Pr(-1 \leq Z \leq 1) = [1 - Pr(1 \leq Z)] - Pr(1 \leq Z)$$

$$= 1 - 2Pr(1 \leq Z) = 1 - 2(.1587) = .682.$$

● **PROBLEM** 11-13

A television company manufactures transistors that have an average life-span of 1,000 hours and a standard deviation of 100 hours. Find the probability that a transistor selected at random will have a life-span between 875 hours and 1,075 hours. Assume the distribution is normal.

Solution:  The probability that a transistor selected at random will have a life-span between 875 hours and 1,075 hours can be expressed symbolically as P(875 < X < 1075). Life-spans of transistors are normally distributed, but we must standardize X (the random variable which represents life-span) in order to use the standard normal table. We do this by subtracting its mean and dividing the resulting difference by its standard deviation. We are given that the mean (average life-span) is 1000 hours, and that the standard deviation is 100 hours.

Letting Z denote our standard normal random variable, $Z = \dfrac{X - \mu}{\sigma} = \dfrac{X - 1000}{100}$ . We want to find the area under the standard normal curve between the Z-values for X = 875 and X = 1075, so we compute

$$Z(875) = \frac{875 - 1000}{100} = \frac{-125}{100} = -1.25, \qquad \text{and}$$

$$Z(1075) = \frac{1075 - 1000}{100} = \frac{75}{100} = 0.75.$$

In terms of Z,

$$P(875 < X < 1075) = P(- 1.25 < Z < .75).$$

Since some tables give areas under the standard normal curve only for positive Z-values, we put $P(- 1.25 < Z < .75)$ in its equivalent form: $P(0 < Z < 0.75) + P(0 < Z < 1.25)$. The symmetry of the standard normal curve allows us to do this.

Reading the table we find $P(0 < Z < 0.75) = .2734$ and $P(0 < Z < 1.25) = .3944$. The total area between $Z = - 1.25$ and $Z = .75$ is $.2734 + .3944 = .6678$, and this is the probability that a randomly selected transistor will function between 875 and 1075 hours.

● **PROBLEM** 11-14

The true weights of ten-pound sacks of potatoes processed at a certain packaging house have a normal distribution with mean 10 (pounds) and variance 0.01 (square pounds). What is the probability that a sack purchased at the grocery store will weigh at least 9 lbs. 14 oz.?

Solution: Let X = the true weight of a 10-pound sack of potatoes. Our question asks what is the $Pr(9 \text{ lbs. } 14 \text{ ox. } \le X)$?

$$9 \text{ lbs. } 14 \text{ oz. } = 9 \frac{14}{16} \text{ lbs. } = 9.875 \text{ lbs.}$$

We will subtract the mean, 10, and divide by the standard deviation, $\sqrt{.01} = .1$, to standardize and convert the X-score to a Z-score.

$$Pr(9.875 \text{ lbs} < X) = Pr\left(\frac{9.875 - 10}{.1} < \frac{X - 10}{.1}\right)$$

$$= Pr(- 1.25 < Z) \quad = 1 - Pr(Z < -1.25)$$

$$= 1 - \Phi(- 1.25) \quad = 1 - .10565 = .89435.$$

● **PROBLEM** 11-15

If a distribution has a mean of 15 and a standard deviation of 2, what Z score corresponds to a raw score of 19? What Z score corresponds to a raw score of 14?

Solution: Another interpretation of the conversion from X-scores to Z-scores is that taken from the meaning of the standard deviation. If a distribution of X-scores has a certain known mean and standard deviation, the Z-score can be thought of as the number of standard deviations from the mean.

For example, in the above problem, the distribution

has a mean of 15 and a standard deviation of 2. To find
the Z-score equivalent of 19 we can either standardize
score 19 by subtracting the mean and dividing by the
standard deviation or we can find how many standard deviations 19 is from 15.

The standard deviation is 2, and so 19 is a distance
of 2 standard deviations from the mean. 15 + 2(2) = 19.
The Z-score corresponding to 19 is 2 standard deviations
from 15 thus Z = 2 corresponds to 19.

The Z-score that corresponds to an X-score of 14
is the number of standard deviations 14 is from 15. Since
14 is 1 unit below 15 and 1 unit is 1/2 the standard
deviation, then the Z-score corresponding to 14 is -.5.

For a distribution of measurements whose mean is 50 and
standard deviation is 10, what is the probability that
a measurement chosen at random will be between the values
of 35 and 45?

Solution:    We wish to find the $Pr(35 < X < 45)$, where
X is normally distributed with mean 50 and standard deviation of 10. To find the Z-scores we ask how many standard
deviations away is 35 from 50 and 45 from 50.

One standard deviation is a distance of 10 and 1/2
standard deviation is a distance of 5. Thus 35 is 15 units
or 1.5 standard deviations below 50 and 45 is 5 units or
.5 standard deviations below 50. Thus the Z-score corresponding to 35 is - 1.5 and the Z-score corresponding to
45 is - .5. Hence,

$$Pr(35 < X < 45) = Pr(- 1.5 < Z < - .5).$$

But  $Pr(- 1.5 < Z < -.5) = Pr(Z < - .5) - Pr(Z < - 1.5)$

$= .3085 - .0668$    $= .2417.$

Given a population of values for which $\mu = 100$ and $\sigma = 15$,
find the percentage of values that lie within one standard
deviation of the mean.

Solution:    The observations that will lie within one
standard deviation of the mean are those values greater
than 100 - 15 = 85 and less than 100 + 15 = 115.

$$Pr(85 < X < 115) = Pr(- 1 < Z < 1)$$

because 85 is 1 standard deviation below the mean and 115

is 1 standard deviation above the mean.

$$Pr(-1 < Z < 1) = Pr(Z < 1) - Pr(Z < -1)$$
$$= .841 - .159 = .682.$$

Thus 68.2% of the values lie within one standard deviation of the mean.

● PROBLEM 11-18

Let X be a normally distributed random variable with mean $\mu = 2$ and variance $\sigma^2 = 9$. Find the probability that X is less than 8 and greater than 5.

Solution:    The probability of a continuous random variable is defined to be

$$Pr(a < X < b) = \int_a^b f(x)\ dx$$

where f(x) is the density function of the random variable X.

The density function of a normally distributed random variable mean $\mu$ and variance $\sigma^2$ is:

$$f(x) = \frac{1}{\sqrt{2\pi\sigma^2}}\ e^{-\frac{(x-\mu)^2}{2\sigma^2}} \qquad -\infty < X < \infty.$$

Thus

$$Pr(a < X < b) = \int_a^b \frac{1}{\sqrt{2\pi\sigma^2}}\ e^{-\frac{(x-\mu)^2}{2\sigma^2}}\ dx$$

$$= \int_a^\infty \frac{1}{\sqrt{2\pi\sigma^2}}\ e^{-\frac{(x-\mu)^2}{2\sigma^2}}\ dx$$

$$- \int_b^\infty \frac{1}{\sqrt{2\pi\sigma^2}}\ e^{-\frac{(x-\mu)^2}{2\sigma^2}}\ dx$$

$$= Pr(X > a) - Pr(X \geq b).$$

These integrals are quite difficult to evaluate directly so we transform them in the following manner.

Let $Z = \frac{X - \mu}{\sigma}$     $dz = \frac{dx}{\sigma}$

and the lower limits of integration become $\frac{b - \mu}{\sigma}$ and $\frac{a - \mu}{\sigma}$.

Thus,

$$Pr(a < X \le b) = \int_a^\infty \frac{1}{\sqrt{2\pi}} \, e^{-\frac{(x-\mu)^2}{2\sigma^2}} \, \frac{dx}{\sigma}$$

$$- \int_b^\infty \frac{1}{\sqrt{2\pi}} \, e^{-\frac{(x-\mu)^2}{2\sigma^2}} \, \frac{dx}{\sigma}$$

$$= \int_{\frac{a-\mu}{\sigma}}^\infty \frac{1}{\sqrt{2\pi}} \, e^{-\frac{z^2}{2}} \, dz - \int_{\frac{b-\mu}{\sigma}}^\infty \frac{1}{\sqrt{2\pi}} \, e^{-\frac{z^2}{2}} \, dz$$

$$= Pr\left(Z > \frac{a-\mu}{\sigma}\right) - Pr\left(Z > \frac{b-\mu}{\sigma}\right).$$

If the density function of a normal random variable has a mean of 0 and a variance of 1, then the density is written

$$f(Z) = \frac{1}{\sqrt{2\pi}} \, e^{-\frac{z^2}{2}} \qquad -\infty < Z < \infty .$$

This density function is known as the density of a standard normal random variable. The integral of this density has been computed and

$$Pr(Z < a) = \int_{-\infty}^a \frac{1}{\sqrt{2\pi}} \, e^{-\frac{z^2}{2}} \, dz$$

has been found for many constants a.

The procedure of transforming a random variable that is normally distributed with mean $\mu$ and variance $\sigma^2$ to a new random variable that is normally distributed with mean 0 and variance is called "standardizing" or "converting an X-score to a Z-score". Such a transformation is accomplished by subtracting $\mu$ and dividing by $\sigma$. Thus

$$Z = \frac{X - \mu}{\sigma} .$$

To solve our problem we wish to find,

$$Pr(X > 5) \qquad \text{and} \qquad Pr(X > 8)$$

when X is distributed normally with mean $\mu = 2$ and $\sigma^2 = 9$. We have seen that

330

$$Pr(X > 5) = Pr\left(Z \geq \frac{5 - 2}{\sqrt{9}}\right) = Pr\left(Z \geq \frac{3}{3}\right) = Pr(Z \geq 1)$$

and

$$Pr(X > 8) = Pr\left(\frac{X - 2}{3} > \frac{8 - 2}{3}\right)$$

$$= Pr\left(Z > \frac{6}{3}\right) = Pr(Z > 2) .$$

From the table of probabilities for the normal distribution we see that

$$Pr(Z > 1) = .1587 \quad \text{and} \quad Pr(Z > 2) = .0228;$$

thus $\quad Pr(5 < X < 8) = Pr(1 < Z < 2)$

$$= .1587 - .0228 = .1359.$$

● **PROBLEM** 11-19

Suppose a random variable X has the following pdf:

$$f(x) = \frac{1}{2\sqrt{2\pi}} e^{-(x + 4)^2/8} , \quad -\infty < x < \infty .$$

Compute:

(a) $P(X \leq - 2)$        (b) $P(- 5 < X \leq - 2)$

(c) $P(|X + 3| \leq 1)$     (d) $P(X \geq - 6)$ .

Solution:     A random variable with this density function is normally distributed. The general density function of a normally distributed random variable with mean $\mu$ and variance $\sigma^2$ is:

$$f(x) = \frac{1}{\sigma\sqrt{2\pi}} e^{-\frac{(x - \mu)^2}{2\sigma^2}} \quad -\infty < x < \infty .$$

The p.d.f. or probability density function that has been given is identical to this with $\mu = - 4$ and $\sigma = 2$.

To find the probabilities asked for we standardize this distribution and calculate the probabilities from the table of the standard normal distribution.

(a)    $Pr(X \leq - 2) = Pr\left(\frac{X - \mu}{\sigma} \leq \frac{- 2 - \mu}{\sigma}\right)$

$$= Pr\left(Z \leq \frac{- 2 - (- 4)}{2}\right) = Pr(Z \leq 1) = .8413 .$$

(b)  $Pr(-5 \leq X \leq -2) = Pr(X \leq -2) - Pr(X \leq -5)$

$$= Pr\left(\frac{X - \mu}{\sigma} \leq \frac{-2 - \mu}{\sigma}\right) - Pr\left(\frac{X - \mu}{\sigma} \leq \frac{-5 - \mu}{\sigma}\right)$$

$$= Pr\left(Z \leq \frac{-2 - (-4)}{2}\right) - Pr\left(Z \leq \frac{-5 - (-4)}{2}\right)$$

$$= Pr(Z \leq 1) - Pr(Z \leq -.5) \quad = .8413 - .3085 = .5328 .$$

(c)  $|X + 3| \leq 1$  is the set of all X-values such that

| X + 3 $\leq$ 1 | and | $-(X + 3) \leq 1$ |
| or X $\leq$ 1 - 3 | and | $(X + 3) \geq -1$ , |
| X $\leq$ - 2 | and | X $\geq$ - 4 . |

Thus,

$$Pr(|X + 3| \leq 1) = Pr(X \leq -2 \quad \text{and} \quad X \geq -4)$$

$$= Pr(-4 \leq X \leq -2).$$

Converting to Z-scores by subtracting the mean and dividing by the standard deviation we see that

$$Pr(|X + 3| \leq 1) = Pr\left(\frac{-4 - \mu}{\sigma} \leq \frac{X - \mu}{\sigma} \leq \frac{-2 - \mu}{\sigma}\right)$$

$$= Pr\left(\frac{-4 - (-4)}{2} \leq Z \leq \frac{-2 - (-4)}{2}\right)$$

$$= Pr(0 \leq Z \leq 1) \quad = Pr(Z \leq 1) - Pr(Z \leq 0)$$

$$= .8413 - .5000 = .3413 .$$

(d)  $Pr(X \geq -6) = Pr\left(\frac{X - \mu}{\sigma} \geq \frac{-6 - \mu}{\sigma}\right)$

$$= Pr\left(Z \geq \frac{-6 - (-4)}{2}\right) \quad = Pr(Z \geq -1) .$$

By the symmetry of the normal distribution,

$$Pr(Z \geq -1) = Pr(Z \leq 1) \quad = .8413 .$$

Notice that the answer to parts (a) and (d) are the same. This is not surprising because the normal distribution is symmetrical about its mean, $\mu = -4$.

● **PROBLEM** 11-20

The melting point of gold is known to be 1,060°C. This is, of course, an average figure, for unavoidable 'experimental error' causes more or less variation from this figure whenever the test is actually performed. The best measure of these variations is the standard deviation (S). Suppose this has been calculated from a large series of tests, and found to be 3°C.

Now imagine that you are analyzing an unknown metal, and a test shows its melting point to be 1,072°C. Is it likely that this unknown metal is gold? In other words, what is the probability that a sample of gold would show a melting point as different from its average as 1,072°C?

Solution:    Let X be the random variable denoting the observed melting point of gold. X is assumed to be normally distributed with mean 1060°C and standard deviation 3°C.

We wish to know if an unknown sample is melted and has an observed melting point of 1072°C, what is the probability that this unknown is gold.

To compute this probability, we convert the X-observation 1072 into a Z-score.

$$Z = \frac{X - mean}{standard\ deviation} = \frac{1072 - 1060}{3}$$

$$= \frac{12}{3} = 4.$$

That is, this observation of 1,072 is 4 standard deviations from the mean. The probability of an observation lying 4 standard deviations from its mean is very small, virtually zero; 99.8% of the distribution lies within 3 standard deviations of the mean of a normal distribution. It is very unlikely that the unknown sample is in fact gold.

● **PROBLEM** 11-21

A food processor packages instant coffee in small jars. The weights of the jars are normally distributed with a standard deviation of .3 ounces. If 5% of the jars weigh more than 12.492 ounces, what is the mean weight of the jars?

Solution:    Let X = the weight of a randomly selected jar. Five percent of the jars weigh more than 12.492 ounces. Thus Pr(X > 12.492) = the probability that a randomly selected jar weighs more than 12.492 ounces is 5% or .05.

To find the mean of X given a standard deviation of

333

$\sigma = .3$, we convert X scores to Z scores.

We know that

$$Pr(X > 12.492) = Pr\left(\frac{X - \mu}{\sigma} > \frac{12.492 - \mu}{\sigma}\right)$$

$$= Pr\left(Z > \frac{12.492 - \mu}{\sigma}\right) = .05 .$$

From the table of the normal distribution,

$$Pr(Z > 1.64) = .05 .$$

Thus $\frac{12.492 - \mu}{\sigma} = 1.64 .$

$\sigma = .3$, thus $\mu = 12.492 - 1.64 \sigma$

$= 12.492 - (1.64)(.3) = 12.492 - .492$

$\qquad = 12$ ounces.

● **PROBLEM 11-22**

The demand for meat at a grocery store during any week is approximately normally distributed with a mean demand of 5000 lbs and a standard deviation of 300 lbs.

(a) If the store has 5300 lbs of meat in stock, what is the probability that it is overstocked?

(b) How much meat should the store have in stock per week so as to not run short more than 10 percent of the time?

Solution:  (a) Let the random variable X denote the demand for meat. If the demand is less than the quantity of meat the store has in stock, the store will be overstocked. Thus if X < 5300, the store will be overstocked.

The Pr(X < 5300) can be found by converting the X-score to a Z-score.

$$Pr(X < 5300) = Pr\left(\frac{X - \mu}{\sigma} < \frac{5300 - \mu}{\sigma}\right)$$

$$= Pr\left(Z < \frac{5300 - 5000}{300}\right) = Pr(Z < 1)$$

$$= .8413 .$$

Thus if the store keeps 5300 lbs of meat in stock, demand will be less than supply 84.13% of the time.

(b) The store will not run short if X < q. We wish to find the number q such that X < q 90% of the time. Equivalently, we wish to find q such that

$Pr(X < q) = .90$

$$Pr(X < q) = Pr\left[\frac{X - \mu}{\sigma} < \frac{q - \mu}{\sigma}\right] = .90$$

$$= Pr\left[Z < \frac{q - 5000}{300}\right] = .90 .$$

From the table of the standard normal distribution

$Pr(Z < 1.282) = .90 .$  Thus  $\frac{q - 5000}{300} = 1.282$

or    $q = 5000 + (1.282) \ 300 \ = 5384.6 .$

If the store orders 5384.6 pounds of meat a week, they will run short only 10% of the time.

● **PROBLEM** 11-23

A lathe produces washers whose internal diameters are normally distributed with mean equal to .373 inch and standard deviation of .002 inch. If specifications require that the internal diameters be .375 inches plus or minus .004 inch, what percentage of production will be unacceptable?

Solution:    Let X be a random variable representing the internal diameter of a randomly selected washer. X is normally distributed with mean .373 inches and a standard deviation of .002 inches.

If X is greater than .375 + .004 = .379 inches or less than .375 − .004 = .371 inches the washer will be unacceptable.

$Pr(X > .379) + Pr(X < .371) =$

$$Pr\left[\frac{X - \mu}{\sigma} > \frac{.379 - \mu}{\sigma}\right] + Pr\left[\frac{X - \mu}{\sigma} < \frac{.371 - \mu}{\sigma}\right] =$$

$$Pr\left[Z > \frac{.379 - .373}{.002}\right] + Pr\left[Z < \frac{.371 - .373}{.002}\right] =$$

$$Pr\left[Z > \frac{.006}{.002}\right] + Pr\left[Z < \frac{- .002}{.002}\right] =$$

$Pr(Z > 3) + Pr(Z < - 1) =$

$.001 + (1 - .841) = .001 + .159$

$$= .160 .$$

Thus Pr(washer is unacceptable) = .160

or 16% of the washers produced will be unacceptable.

The life of a machine is normally distributed with a mean of 3000 hours. From past experience, 50% of these machines last less than 2632 or more than 3368 hours. What is the standard deviation of the lifetime of a machine?

Solution:    Let X be the random variable denoting the life of this machine. We know that X is normally distributed with mean 3000 and the probability that X is greater than 3368 or less than 2632 is

$$Pr(X < 2632) + Pr(X > 3368) = .5 .$$

Converting X to a standard normal variable with mean 0 and standard deviation 1 we see that

$$Pr(X < 2632) = Pr\left(\frac{X - \mu}{\sigma} < \frac{2632 - \mu}{\sigma}\right)$$

$$= Pr\left(Z < \frac{2632 - \mu}{\sigma}\right)$$

and

$$Pr(X > 3368) = Pr\left(\frac{X - \mu}{\sigma} > \frac{3368 - \mu}{\sigma}\right)$$

$$= Pr\left(Z > \frac{3368 - \mu}{\sigma}\right) .$$

Substituting $\mu = 3000$ into these equations we see that

$$Pr(X < 2632) = Pr\left(Z < \frac{- 368}{\sigma}\right)$$

and

$$Pr(X > 3368) = Pr\left(Z > \frac{368}{\sigma}\right) .$$

By the symmetry of the normal distribution we know that:

$$Pr(Z < - C) = Pr(Z > C) .$$

Thus,   $Pr(X < 2632) = Pr\left(Z < \frac{- 368}{\sigma}\right)$

$= Pr\left(Z > \frac{368}{\sigma}\right)$     $= Pr(X > 3368).$

Taking advantage of this fact we let

$$Pr(X < 2632) = Pr(X > 3368) = Pr\left(Z > \frac{368}{\sigma}\right) .$$

Thus

$$\Pr\left(Z > \frac{368}{\sigma}\right) + \Pr\left(Z > \frac{368}{\sigma}\right) = .5$$

or $\quad \Pr\left(Z > \frac{368}{\sigma}\right) = \frac{.5}{2} = .25$ .

Searching through the table of standardized Z-scores we see that

$$\Pr(Z > .67) = .25 \text{ , very nearly .}$$

Thus $\quad \dfrac{368}{\sigma} = .67 \quad$ or $\quad \sigma = \dfrac{368}{.67} = 549$ hours .

● **PROBLEM** 11-25

The mean height of a soldier in an army regiment is 70 inches. Ten percent of the soldiers in the regiment are taller than 72 inches. Assuming that the heights of the soldiers in this regiment are normally distributed, what is the standard deviation?

Solution: Let X = the height of a randomly selected soldier. We are given that X is normally distributed with mean $\mu = E(X) = 70$ inches and $\Pr(X > 72) = .10$.

To find the standard deviation of X we convert X from an X-score to a Z-score by subtracting the mean and dividing by the unknown standard deviation.

Thus

$$\Pr(X > 72) = \Pr\left(\frac{X - \mu}{\sigma} > \frac{72 - \mu}{\sigma}\right) = .10$$

$$= \Pr\left(Z > \frac{72 - \mu}{\sigma}\right) = .10 .$$

Checking the table of the standard normal distribution, we wish to find the value C such that $\Pr(Z > C) = .10$. To do this we inspect the body of the table until the 4-digit number closest to .10 is located. This is .1003. Reading across the row to the left and up the column we see that C = 1.28. Thus

$$\Pr(X > 1.28) = .10 .$$

We know that

$$\Pr\left(Z > \frac{72 - \mu}{\sigma}\right) = \Pr(Z > 1.28) = .10 .$$

Thus $\quad \dfrac{72 - \mu}{\sigma} = 1.28.$

We have been given that $\mu = 70$; thus substituting for $\mu$ and solving yields;

$$\frac{72 - 70}{\sigma} = 1.28, \quad \sigma = \frac{72 - 70}{1.28} = \frac{2}{1.28} = 1.56 \text{ inches.}$$

The heights of soldiers are normally distributed. If 13.57% of the soldiers are taller than 72.2 inches and 8.08% are shorter than 67.2 inches, what are the mean and the standard deviation of the heights of the soldiers?

Solution:     Let X = the random variable denoting the heights of the soldiers. If 13.57% of the soldiers are taller than 72.2 inches, the probability that a randomly selected soldier's height is greater than 72.2 is:

$$Pr(X > 72.2) = .1357.$$

Similarly, the probability that a randomly selected soldier's height is less than 67.2 inches is:

$$Pr(X < 67.2) = .0808.$$

To find the mean and variance of X from this information, we convert the X-scores to Z-scores by subtracting the mean and dividing by the standard deviation. Thus          $Pr(X > 72.2) = .1357$

$$Pr\left(\frac{X - \mu}{\sigma} > \frac{72.2 - \mu}{\sigma}\right) = .1357 \qquad Pr\left(Z > \frac{72.2 - \mu}{\sigma}\right) = .1357.$$

From the table of Z-scores we know that

$Pr(Z > 1.1) = .1357.$     Thus $\frac{72.2 - \mu}{\sigma} = 1.1$ .

Similarly,   $Pr(X < 67.2) = .0808$                     implies

$$Pr\left(\frac{X - \mu}{\sigma} < \frac{67.2 - \mu}{\sigma}\right) = .0808 \qquad \text{or}$$

$$Pr\left(Z < \frac{67.2 - \mu}{\sigma}\right) = .0808 \quad .$$

By the symmetry of the normal distribution,

$$Pr(Z < - C) = Pr(Z > C) ;$$

thus  $Pr\left(Z < \frac{67.2 - \mu}{\sigma}\right) = Pr\left(Z > \frac{- 67.2 + \mu}{\sigma}\right) .$

From the table we see that $Pr(Z > 1.4) = .0808$

thus          $\frac{- 67.2 + \mu}{\sigma} = 1.4$ .

We now have two equations involving $\mu$ and $\sigma$. These are:

$$\frac{72.2 - \mu}{\sigma} = 1.1 \qquad \text{and} \qquad \frac{- 67.2 + \mu}{\sigma} = 1.4 .$$

Multiplying both equations by $\sigma$ and adding them together gives          $72.2 - \mu = (1.1) \sigma$

and          $- 67.2 + \mu = (1.4) \sigma$

$$5 = (2.5) \sigma .$$

Thus                    $\sigma = \frac{5}{2.5} = 2.$

Substituting 2 into either of our original equations

gives $\mu = 72.2 - (1.1)2 = 70.$

Thus the mean of the distribution of heights is $\mu = 70$ and the standard deviation is $\sigma = 2$.

● **PROBLEM** 11-27

Suppose the weights of adult males are normally distributed and that 6.68 percent are under 130 lbs in weight, and 77.45 percent are between 130 and 180 lbs. Find the parameters of the distribution.

Solution: Let the random variable X denote the weight of adult males. We are given that X is normally distributed and that $Pr(X \leq 130) = 6.68\%$ and $Pr(130 \leq X \leq 180) = 77.45\%$.

Equivalently, $Pr(X \leq 130) = .0668$ and $Pr(130 < X \leq 180) = .7745$. We are asked to find the parameters of this distribution, $\mu$ and $\sigma^2$, the mean and variance.

$$Pr(X \leq 130) + Pr(130 \leq X \leq 180) =$$

$$= Pr(X \leq 130) + [Pr(X \leq 180) - Pr(X \leq 130)]$$

$$= Pr(X \leq 180) .$$

Thus $Pr(X \leq 180) = .0668 + .7745 = .8413 .$

Converting from X scores to Z-scores we see that

$$Pr\left(\frac{X - \mu}{\sigma} \leq \frac{130 - \mu}{\sigma}\right) = .0688$$

and $Pr\left(\frac{X - \mu}{\sigma} \leq \frac{180 - \mu}{\sigma}\right) = .8413$

or $Pr\left(Z \leq \frac{130 - \mu}{\sigma}\right) = .0668$

and $Pr\left(Z \leq \frac{180 - \mu}{\sigma}\right) = .8413 .$

From the table of the standard normal we know that

$Pr(Z < -1.5) = .0668$ and $Pr(Z \leq 1) = .8413 .$

Thus $\frac{130 - \mu}{\sigma} = -1.5$

and $\frac{180 - \mu}{\sigma} = 1$

or $130 = \mu - (1.5)\sigma$

and $180 = \mu + (1)\sigma .$

Subtracting these two equations we see that

$-50 = (-2.5) \ \sigma$     or          $\sigma = 20$                    and

$180 = \mu + 20$          or     $\mu = 180 - 20$

$= 160.$

The average grade on a mathematics test is 82, with a standard deviation of 5. If the instructor assigns A's to the highest 12% and the grades follow a normal distribution, what is the lowest grade that will be assigned A?

Solution:     We relate the given information to the normal curve by thinking of the highest 12% of the grades as 12% of the area under the right side of the curve. Then the lowest grade assigned A is that point on the X-axis for which the area under the curve to its right is 12% of the total area.

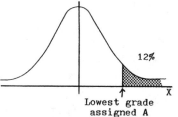

Lowest grade
assigned A

The standard normal curve is symmetric about the Y-axis; this means that if we take the additive inverse of any Z-score, its Y value will be unchanged. For example, the area to the right of Z = 2 is equal to the area to the left of Z = - 2; Pr(Z > 2) = Pr(Z < - 2). It follows that the area under the curve to the right of Z = 0 is exactly half the total area under the curve. Therefore the area between the Y-axis and the desired X-score is 50% - 12% = 38% of the total area, which is 1.
          If we can find a K for which P(0 < Z < K) = .38, K can be converted to an X-score which is the lowest grade assigned A.

Using the table of areas under the standard normal curve, we locate .380 and see that its Z-score is 1.175. This means that P(0 < Z< 1.175) = .380. This is equivalent to P(Z > 1.175) = .500 - .380 = .120.

Now we can convert Z = 1.175 to an X-score by solving the equation

$1.175 = \dfrac{X - \mu}{\sigma}$ for X. We are told that the average

grade on the test is 82 = μ (the mean) and the standard deviation is 5. Substituting we have

$1.175 = \dfrac{X - 82}{5}$ and $5(1.175) = X - 82$, so that

$X = 5(1.175) + 82 \qquad = 87.875$. This means that

$$P(Z > 1.175) = P(X > 87.875) = .120.$$

Since all grades are integers, the integer just above 87.875 is 88, which is the lowest grade assigned an A.

● **PROBLEM** 11-29

A teacher decides that the top 10 percent of students should receive A's and the next 25 percent B's. If the test scores are normally distributed with mean 70 and standard deviation of 10, find the scores that should be assigned A's and B's.

**Solution:** We wish to find two numbers a and b. If X is the random variable denoting a student's test score and X is assumed to be approximately normal then any score such that X > a will get an A. Any score such that b < X < a will get a B.

In addition, only 10% of the students should receive A's. We should choose a to reflect this fact. Thus we wish to find a such that $Pr(X > a) = .10$.

Similarly, if 25% of the students are to receive B's, b must be chosen so that

$$Pr(b < X < a) = .250.$$

But, $Pr(b < X < a) + Pr(x > a) = Pr(X > b)$

$$= .250 + .10 = .350 .$$

Thus our conditions on a and b become

$$Pr(X > b) = .350$$

and $\qquad Pr(X > a) = .10$ .

Since we know the mean and standard deviation of X to be 70 and 10, we can convert X-scores to Z-scores.

$$Pr(X > b) = Pr\left(\frac{X - \mu}{\sigma} > \frac{b - \mu}{\sigma}\right) = .350$$

$$= Pr\left(Z > \frac{b - 70}{10}\right) = .350$$

and $\quad Pr(X > a) = Pr\left(\frac{X - \mu}{\sigma} > \frac{a - \mu}{\sigma}\right) = .10$

$$= Pr\left(Z > \frac{a - 70}{10}\right) = .10 .$$

From the table of the standard normal,

$$Pr(Z > .385) = .35$$

and  $\Pr(Z > 1.282) = .10$ .

Thus,  $\dfrac{b - 70}{10} = .385$  and  $\dfrac{a - 70}{10} = 1.282$

and  $a = 70 + (1.282) \, 10$

$b = 70 + (.385) 10$

or  $a = 82.82$  and  $b = 73.85$ .

Thus if a student scores over 83  he receives an A, while a student who scores between 74  and 83 receives a B.

● **PROBLEM** 11-30

The IQs of the army recruits in a given year are normally distributed with μ = 110 and σ = 8. The army wants to give special training to the 10% of those recruits with the highest IQ scores. What is the lowest IQ score acceptable for this special training?

Solution:    Let X denote the IQ score of a randomly selected recruit. We wish to find the number such that 10% of the distribution of IQ scores is above this number. Thus this number K will be specified by

$$\Pr(X \geq K) = .10 .$$

Standardizing X by subtracting the mean of X, 110, and dividing by the standard deviation, 8, we obtain

$$\Pr(X \geq K) = \Pr\left[\dfrac{X - 110}{8} \geq \dfrac{K - 110}{8}\right] = .10 .$$

But  $\dfrac{X - 110}{8} = Z$  is normally distributed with mean 0 and standard deviation 1. Thus from the table of the standard normal,

$\Pr(Z > 1.282) = .10$ .    Hence  $\dfrac{K - 110}{8} = 1.282$ ,

or  $K = 110 + 8(1.282) = 120.256.$

Thus, the lowest IQ score for this special training is 121.

All recruits with IQ scores of 121 or above will receive this training.

● **PROBLEM** 11-31

Let X be a normally distributed random variable representing the hourly wage in a certain craft. The mean of the hourly wage is $4.25 and the standard deviation is $.75.

<u>Solution:</u>     (a) We seek,

$$Pr(3.50 \leq X \leq 4.90).$$

Converting to Z-scores we see that

$$Pr(3.50 \leq X \leq 4.90) = Pr\left(\frac{3.50 - \mu}{\sigma} \leq Z \leq \frac{4.90 - \mu}{\sigma}\right)$$

$$= Pr\left(\frac{3.50 - 4.25}{.75} \leq Z \leq \frac{4.90 - 4.25}{.75}\right)$$

$$= Pr\left(\frac{- .75}{.75} \leq Z \leq \frac{.65}{.75}\right) \quad = Pr(- 1 \leq Z \leq .87)$$

$$= Pr(Z \leq .87) - Pr(Z \leq - 1) = Pr(Z \leq .87) - (1 - Pr(Z \geq - 1))$$

$$= Pr(Z \leq .87)- [1 - Pr(Z \leq 1)] = .809 - [1 - .841]$$
$$= .650 .$$

Thus 65% of the hourly wages are between $3.50 and $4.90.

(b) The 95th percentile is that number $Z_\alpha$ such that

$$Pr(X \leq K) = .95.$$

To find $Z_\alpha$, we first convert to Z-scores. Thus

$$Pr(X \leq Z_\alpha) = Pr\left(\frac{X - 4.25}{.75} \leq \frac{K - 4.25}{.75}\right) = .95$$

$$= Pr\left(Z \leq \frac{K - 4.25}{.75}\right) = .95 \quad .$$

But   $Pr(Z \leq 1.645) = .95$   thus   $\frac{K - 4.25}{.75} = 1.645$,

$$K = 4.25 + (.75)(1.645) = 5.48.$$

Thus 95% of the craftsmen have hourly wages less than $5.48.

● **PROBLEM** 11-32

(b) if the cups hold exactly 8 ounces, what is the probability that a cup will overflow?
(c) what should be the cup size so that the cups will overflow only 1% of the time?

**Solution:** Let Y be the amount of drink discharged into a cup. Y is assumed to be a normally distributed random variable with a mean of 7 ounces and a standard deviation of .3 ounce.

(a) The fraction of cups which will contain more than 7.1 ounces is found from the $Pr(Y > 7.1)$. Standardizing or converting the Y score to a Z-score we see that,

$$Pr(Y > 7.1) = Pr\left(\frac{Y - \mu}{\sigma} > \frac{7.1 - \mu}{\sigma}\right) =$$

$$Pr\left(Z > \frac{7.1 - 7}{.3}\right) = Pr\left(Z > \frac{.1}{.3}\right)$$

$$= Pr(Z > .33) \qquad = .37 \ .$$

Thus about 37% of the cups will contain more than 7.1 ounces.

(b) A cup will overflow if $Y > 8$. The probability of an overflow is

$$Pr(Y > 8) = Pr\left(\frac{Y - \mu}{\sigma} > \frac{8 - \mu}{\sigma}\right) = Pr\left(Z > \frac{8 - 7}{.3}\right)$$

$$= Pr(Z > 3.33)$$

$$= .0004.$$

Thus .04% of the cups will overflow.

(c) The problem is to find the cup size such that the cups will overflow only 1% of the time. We wish to find some number C, such that

$$Pr(Y > C) = .01.$$

$$Pr(Z > 2.33) = .01 \qquad\qquad \text{and}$$

$$Pr\left(\frac{Y - \mu}{\sigma} > \frac{C - \mu}{\sigma}\right) = Pr\left(Z > \frac{C - 7}{.3}\right) = .01 \ .$$

The proper cup size C, is thus determined by

$$\frac{C - 7}{.3} = 2.33 \ ;$$

$$C = (.3)(2.33) + 7 = 7.699.$$

Thus if the cups hold 7.7 ounces, they will overflow 1% of the time.

Three-hundred college freshmen are observed to have grade
point averages that are approximately normally distributed
with mean 2.1 and a standard deviation of 1.2. How many
of these freshmen would you expect to have grade point
averages between 2.5 and 3.5 if the averages are
recorded to the nearest tenth.

**Solution:**    To find the number of students with averages
between 2.5 and 3.5 we first find the percentage of
students with averages between 2.5 and 3.5. The averages
are continuous random variables that are rounded to become
discrete random variables. For example any average from
2.45 to 2.55 would be recorded as 2.5. An average of 3.45
to 3.55 would be recorded as 3.5.

Thus in computing the probability of an average
lying between 2.5 and 3.5 we must account for this rounding
procedure. Hence,

$$Pr(2.5 < X < 3.5) = Pr(2.45 < X < 3.55).$$

We now find this probability by standardizing the
X-scores and converting them to Z-scores. Thus,

$$Pr(2.45 < X < 3.55) = Pr\left(\frac{2.45 - \mu}{\sigma} < \frac{X - \mu}{\sigma} < \frac{3.55 - \mu}{\sigma}\right)$$

$$= Pr\left(\frac{2.45 - 2.1}{1.2} < Z < \frac{3.55 - 2.1}{1.2}\right)$$

$$= Pr(.292 < Z < 1.21) \quad = Pr(Z < 1.21) - Pr(Z < .292)$$

$$= .8869 - .6141 \quad = .2728 ,$$

or 27.28% of the freshmen have grades between 2.5 and 3.5 So,
27.28% of 300 is 81.84 or approximately 82 students have
grade point averages between 2.5 and 3.5.

Miniature poodles are thought to have a mean height of
12 inches and a standard deviation of 1.8 inches. If
height is measured to the nearest inch, find the percentage
of poodles having a height exceeding 14 inches.

**Solution:**    Let X be the height of a randomly selected
poodle. X has mean 12 and standard deviation 1.8.
Because the heights are measured to the nearest inch any
height that is greater than 13.5 or less than 14.5 is
recorded as 14.

To find the percentage of poodles such that height,
X, is greater than 14, we must find the percentage of
poodles whose heights are greater than 13.5.

$Pr(X > 13.5)$ can be found by converting X to a
random variable Z, that is normally distributed with
mean 0 and variance 1.

$$Pr(X \geq 13.5) = Pr\left(\frac{X - \mu}{\sigma} \geq \frac{13.5 - \mu}{\sigma}\right)$$

$$= Pr\left(Z \geq \frac{13.5 - 12}{1.8}\right) = Pr(Z \geq .83 ) .$$

From the table this is found to be

$$= .2033.$$

Thus about 20% of these miniature poodles have heights that are greater than 14 inches.

# NORMAL APPROXIMATION TO THE BINOMIAL DISTRIBUTION

● **PROBLEM** 11-35

A pair of dice *is* thrown 120 times. What is the approximate probability of throwing at least 15 sevens? Assume that the rolls are independent and remember that the probability of rolling a seven on a single roll is $\frac{6}{36} = \frac{1}{6}$ .

Solution: The answer to this problem is a binomial probability. If X = number of sevens rolled, n = 120, then

$$Pr(X \geq 15) = \sum_{j=15}^{120} \binom{120}{j}\left(\frac{1}{6}\right)^{j}\left(\frac{5}{6}\right)^{120-j} .$$

This sum is quite difficult to calculate. There is an easier way. If n is large, $Pr_B(X \geq 15)$ can be approximated by $Pr_N(X \geq 14.5)$ where X is normally distributed with the same mean and variance as the binomial random variable. Remember that the mean of a binomially distributed random variable is np; n is the number of trials and p is the probability of "success" in a single trial. The variance of a binomially distributed random variable is np(1 - p) and the standard deviation is $\sqrt{np(1 - p)}$.

Because of this fact $\frac{X - np}{\sqrt{np(1 - p)}}$ is normally distributed with mean 0 and variance 1.

$$np = (120)\left(\frac{1}{6}\right) = 20 \qquad \text{and}$$

$$\sqrt{np(1 - p)} = \sqrt{120\left(\frac{1}{6}\right)\left(\frac{5}{6}\right)} = \sqrt{\frac{50}{3}} = 4.08248 .$$

Thus $Pr(X \geq 15) = Pr\left(\frac{X - 20}{4.08248} > \frac{14.5 - 20}{4.08248}\right)$

$$= Pr(Z > - 1.35) = 1 - Pr(Z < - 1.35)$$

$$= 1 - \Phi(- 1.35) = 1 - .0885$$

$$= .9115 .$$

$$Pr_B(X > 15) \overset{\sim}{\sim} Pr_N(X \geq 14.5).$$

The reason 15 has become 14.5 is that a discrete random variable is being approximated by a continuous random variable.

Consider the example below:

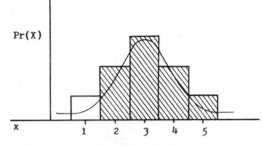

$Pr_B(2 \leq X \leq 5)$ = sum of the areas of the shaded rectangles. In approximating this area with a curve we must start at the edge of the first shaded rectangle and move to the edge of the last shaded rectangle. This implies

$$Pr_B(2 \leq X \leq 5) \overset{\sim}{\sim} Pr_N(1.5 \leq X \leq 5.5).$$

● **PROBLEM** 11-36

Suppose that in a large city it is desired to get an estimate of the proportion of voters in favor of a certain proposal by taking a sample of 200. What is the probability that a majority of the persons in the sample are against the proposal if, in reality, only 45 percent of the electorate is against the proposal.

Note that we must assume that the population is sufficiently large so that the probability of "success" on each trial is constant, and that the trials are independent.

Solution: The desired probability is associated with a binomial experiment. In this problem each independent trial consists of selecting a voter from the electorate and checking to see if they favor the proposal. This procedure is carried out 200 times. Since 45% of the voters favor the proposal, the probability of selecting a voter from the electorate that favors the proposal is .45.

Let X = the number of voters sampled who favor the proposal. As we have seen X is distributed binomially with parameters n = 200 and p = .45. We wish to find the probability that a majority of the sample favors the proposal or Pr(X > 101). Because n is large we may use the normal approximation to the binomial distribution

$$Pr_B(X \geq 101) \underset{\sim}{\sim} Pr_N\left(\frac{X - E(X)}{\sqrt{Var\ X}} > \frac{100.5 - E(X)}{\sqrt{Var\ X}}\right)$$

where $\dfrac{X - E(X)}{\sqrt{Var\ X}}$ is normally distributed with mean 0 and variance 1.

$E(X)$ = expected value of $X = np = (200)(.45) = 90$

$Var\ X$ = variance of $X = np(1 - p) = (200)(.45)(.55) = 49.5$

and $\quad Z = \dfrac{X - E(X)}{\sqrt{Var\ X}} = \dfrac{X - 90}{\sqrt{49.5}}$.

Thus $\quad Pr(X \geq 101) \underset{\sim}{\sim} Pr\left(Z \geq \dfrac{100.5 - 90}{\sqrt{49.5}}\right)$

$= Pr(Z \geq 1.49) \quad = 1 - Pr(Z < 1.49)$

$\qquad\qquad\qquad\qquad = 1 - .9319 = .068.$

● **PROBLEM** 11-37

A binomial random variable has a mean of 6 and a standard deviation of 1.5. What percent of the area under the probability histogram is to the left of 5; to the right of 7.0?

Solution: Let X be the binomial random variable with a mean of 6 and standard deviation of 1.5. The percent of area under the probability histogram to the left of 5 is $Pr_B(X \leq 5)$, a binomial probability.

This probability can be approximated by a normal probability

$$Pr_B(X \leq 5) \overset{\sim}{=} Pr_N(Y \leq 5.5) \text{ where } Pr_N(Y \leq 5.5)$$

is the probability that a normally distributed variable Y is less than 5.5. The addition of .5 is because a discrete distribution is being approximated by a continuous distribution.

The new normally distributed random variable Y has the same mean and standard deviation as X. Thus the mean of Y is 6 and the standard deviation of Y is 1.5. To find

$$Pr(X \leq 5) \underset{\sim}{\sim} Pr(Y \leq 5.5)$$

we standardize the variable Y by subtracting the mean and dividing by the standard deviation. Thus

$$Pr(Y \leq 5.5) = Pr\left(\frac{Y - \mu}{\sigma} \leq \frac{5.5 - \mu}{\sigma}\right)$$

$$= \Pr\left(Z \leq \frac{5.5 - 6}{1.5}\right)$$

where Z is distributed normally with mean zero and variance 1.

Thus, $\Pr\left(Z \leq \frac{5.5 - 6}{1.5}\right) = \Pr(Z \leq -.33)$

and from the table of the standard normal,

$\Pr(Z \leq - .33) = .37.$

Thus the probability that X is less than 5 is approximately $\Pr(X \leq 5) = .37$.

The percentage to the right of 7.0 is the $\Pr(X > 7.0)$ where X is binomially distributed with mean 6 and standard deviation 1.5. To correct for the approximation of a discrete random variable by a continuous random variable, subtract $\frac{1}{2}$ from 7.

Thus $\Pr(X \geq 7) \stackrel{\sim}{=} \Pr\left(Y \geq 7 - \frac{1}{2}\right)$

$$\stackrel{\sim}{=} \Pr(Y \geq 6.5)$$

where Y is normally distributed with mean 6 and standard deviation 1.5.

Standardizing Y by subtracting the mean and dividing by the standard deviation yields,

$$\Pr(Y \geq 6.5) = \Pr\left(\frac{Y - 6}{1.5} \geq \frac{6.5 - 6}{1.5}\right)$$

$$= \Pr\left(Z \geq \frac{.5}{1.5}\right),$$

where Z is normally distributed with mean 0 and standard deviation 1. From the table of the normal distribution

$$\Pr\left(Z \geq \frac{.5}{1.5}\right) = \Pr(Z \geq .33) = .37.$$

$$\Pr(X > 7) \stackrel{\sim}{=} \Pr(Y \geq 6.5) = \Pr(Z > .33)$$

$$= .37.$$

● **PROBLEM** 11-38

A multiple-choice test has 200 questions, each with 4 possible answers, of which only 1 is the correct answer. What is the probability that sheer guesswork yields from 25 to 30 correct answers for 80 of the 200 problems about which the student has no knowledge?

__Solution:__ Let X be the number of correct answers in the 80 questions about which the student has no knowledge. If the student is guessing, the probability of selecting the correct answer is $\frac{1}{4}$. It may also be assumed that random guesswork will imply that each question is answered independently of any other question. With these assumptions, X is binomially distributed with parameters n = 80 and p = $\frac{1}{4}$. Hence E(X) = np = 80 · $\frac{1}{4}$ = 20 and

$$\sqrt{\text{Var } X} = \sqrt{np(1 - p)} = \sqrt{80 \cdot \frac{1}{4} \cdot \frac{3}{4}} = \sqrt{15} = 3.87.$$

We wish to find $\Pr(25 \leq X \leq 30)$. This probability is found exactly to be

$$\Pr(25 \leq X \leq 30) = \sum_{j=25}^{30} \binom{80}{j} \left(\frac{1}{4}\right)^j \left(\frac{3}{4}\right)^{80-j}.$$

This expression is quite tedious to calculate and we thus use the normal approximation to the binomial. Let Y be normally distributed with mean np = 20 and standard deviation $\sqrt{np(1 - p)}$ = 3.87. Then

$$\Pr(25 \leq X \leq 30) \stackrel{\sim}{=} \Pr\left(25 - \frac{1}{2} \leq Y \leq 30 + \frac{1}{2}\right).$$

We add and subtract $\frac{1}{2}$ to improve the approximation of a discrete random variable by a continuous random variable.

To calculate,

$\Pr(24.5 \leq Y \leq 30.5)$ we standardize Y by subtracting the mean and then dividing by the standard deviation. Thus,

$\Pr(24.5 \leq Y \leq 30.5)$

$$= \Pr\left(\frac{24.5 - 20}{3.87} \leq \frac{Y - 20}{3.87} \leq \frac{30.5 - 20}{3.87}\right)$$

$$= \Pr\left(\frac{4.5}{3.87} \leq Z \leq \frac{10.5}{3.87}\right)$$

where Z is normally distributed with mean 0 and standard deviation 1. From the table of the standard normal distribution,

$$\Pr\left(\frac{4.5}{3.87} \leq Z \leq \frac{10.5}{3.87}\right) = \Pr(1.163 \leq Z \leq 2.713)$$

$$= \Pr(Z \leq 2.713) - \Pr(Z \leq 1.163)$$

$$= .9966 - .8776 = .1190.$$

Thus, the approximate probability that the student answers between 25 and 30 questions by sheer guesswork is .1190.

350

The records of a large university show that 40% of the student body are classified as freshmen. A random sample of 50 students is selected. Find (a) the expected number of freshmen in the sample, (b) the standard error of the number of freshmen in the sample, (c) the probability that more than 45% are freshmen.

Solution: Let the random variable X denote the number of freshmen in the random sample. Because 40% of the student body are freshmen, the random variable X is binomially distributed with parameters n = 50 and p = .40.

(a) To find the expected number of freshmen in the sample, we find the E(X). The expected value of a binomially distributed random variable is

E(X) = np = 50(.4) = 20.

(b) The standard error of X is the standard deviation of X.

$$\sqrt{Var\ X} = \sqrt{np(1-p)} = \sqrt{50(.4)(.6)} = 3.46.$$

(c) Pr (more than 45% of the sample are freshmen) is the probability that X > 45% of 50 or X > 22.5. Using the normal approximation to the binomial,

Pr(X > 22.5) $\overset{\sim}{=}$ Pr(Y > 22.5 - .5)

$\overset{\sim}{=}$ Pr(Y > 22)

where Y is normally distributed with mean np = 20 and standard deviation $\sqrt{np(1-p)}$ = 3.46. Standardizing Y by subtracting the mean and dividing by the standard deviation we see that

$$Pr(Y > 22) = Pr\left(\frac{Y-20}{3.46} > \frac{22-20}{3.46}\right)$$

$$= Pr(Z > .578)$$

where Z is normally distributed with mean 0 and standard deviation 1.

From the table of the standard normal distribution

Pr(Z > .578) = 1 - Pr(Z ≤ .578)

= 1 - .7190

= .281 .

Thus, the probability of observing more than 45% freshmen in the sample of 50 is approximately .281.

The student body of a large school has approximately an equal number of boys and girls. If a committee of 8 is selected at random, what is the probability that it will contain exactly 5 girls?

Solution:     Since the probability that a student picked at random is a boy (or girl) is $\frac{1}{2}$ = 0.5, we can use the binomial distribution with n = 8 (the number of committee members selected at random) and p = 0.5. The probability of exactly 5 girls on the comittee is,

$$P(X = 5) = \binom{8}{5}(.5)^5 (1 - .5)^{(8-5)}$$

$$= 56 \ (.5)^5(.5)^3 = .2188 .$$

We can also find an approximate value of the probability by using the normal curve. Computing the standard deviation

$$\sigma = \sqrt{np(1 - p)} = \sqrt{8(.5)(.5)} = \sqrt{8(.25)} = 1.4,$$

we find that $n\sigma = 8(1.4) = 11.2 > 5$ ($n\sigma > 5$ is one "rule of thumb" for the applicability of the normal curve as an approximation to a discrete distribution like the binomial). We will find the area over an interval whose midpoint is 5. It is common practice to add and subtract $\frac{1}{2}$ from (to) the desired value of X (in this case 5) when calculating Z-scores for the standard normal curve. Thus

$$Z_1 = \frac{5 - \frac{1}{2} - \mu}{1.4} \quad \text{and} \quad Z_2 = \frac{5 + \frac{1}{2} - \mu}{1.4}$$

Substitute $\mu = np = 8(.5) = 4$:

$$Z_1 = \frac{5 - \frac{1}{2} - 4}{1.4} \quad \text{and} \quad Z_2 = \frac{5 + \frac{1}{2} - 4}{1.4}$$

$$Z_1 = \frac{4.5 - 4}{1.4} = \frac{.5}{1.4} = .36 \quad \text{and}$$

$$Z_2 = \frac{5.5 - 4}{1.4} = \frac{1.5}{1.4} = 1.07.$$

We are ready to compute

$$P(X = 5) = P(.36 < Z < 1.07)$$

$$= P(0 < Z < 1.07) - P(0 < Z < .36)$$

[subtracting areas]

$$= .3577 - .1406 = .2171,$$

which is only .0017 less than the exact probability given by the binomial distribution.

What is the probability that in 100 throws of an unbiased coin the number of heads obtained will be between 45 and 60?

**Solution:** Let X be the number of heads obtained in n = 100 throws. We wish to find $\Pr(45 \leq X \leq 60)$. This is a binomial probability and may be approximated by a normal probability.

If the coin is unbiased there is a probability $p = \frac{1}{2}$ of a head on any particular toss. Thus the mean number of heads is $E(X) = np = (100)\frac{1}{2} = 50$. The standard deviation is

$$\sqrt{\text{Var } X} = \sqrt{np(1-p)} = \sqrt{100\,\frac{1}{2}\cdot\frac{1}{2}} = \sqrt{\frac{100}{4}} = \sqrt{25} = 5.$$

To correct for the approximation of a discrete random variable X by a continuous random variable Y, we extend the boundaries by adding $\frac{1}{2}$ to 60 and subtracting $\frac{1}{2}$ from 45. Thus

$$\Pr(45 \leq X \leq 60) \cong \Pr\left(45 - \frac{1}{2} \leq Y \leq 60 + \frac{1}{2}\right)$$

where Y is normally distributed with mean np = 50 and standard deviation 5.

To find $\Pr(44.5 \leq Y \leq 60.5)$ we standardize Y by subtracting the mean and dividing by the standard deviation.

Thus

$$\Pr(44.5 \leq Y \leq 60.5)$$
$$= \Pr\left(\frac{44.5 - 50}{5} \leq Z \leq \frac{60.5 - 50}{5}\right)$$
$$= \Pr\left(\frac{-5.5}{5} \leq Z \leq \frac{10.5}{5}\right)$$
$$= \Pr(-1.1 \leq Z \leq 2.1)$$

where Z is normally distributed with mean 0 and standard deviation 1. From the table of the standard normal,

$$\Pr(-1.1 \leq Z \leq 2.1) = \Pr(Z \leq 2.1) - \Pr(Z \leq -1.1)$$
$$= .982 - (1 - \Pr(Z \leq 1.1))$$
$$= .982 - 1 + .864$$
$$= .846 .$$

Thus, there is an approximate probability of .846 that the number of heads will be between 45 and 60.

Forty percent of all graduate students on a campus are married. If 100 graduate students are selected at random, what is the probability that the proportion of married students in this particular sample will be between 32% and 47%?

_Solution:_ Let X be the random variable denoting the number of married students in a random sample of size 100. Because 40% of the students are married, the probability of a randomly selected student being married is p = .4.

The expected number of married students in the sample of size 100 is np = (100)(.4) = 40 and the standard deviation of X is

$$\sqrt{np(1-p)} = \sqrt{100(.4)(1-.4)}$$

$$= \sqrt{100\left(\frac{4}{10}\right)\left(\frac{6}{10}\right)} \quad .$$

Using the normal approximation to the binomial,

$$\frac{X - E(X)}{\sqrt{Var\ X}} = \frac{X - np}{\sqrt{np(1-p)}}$$

is approximately normally distributed with mean 0 and standard deviation 1. But dividing the numerator and denominator by n,

$$\frac{X - np}{\sqrt{Var\ X}} = \frac{\frac{X}{n} - \frac{np}{n}}{\frac{1}{n}\sqrt{np(1-p)}} = \frac{\frac{X}{n} - p}{\sqrt{\frac{p(1-p)}{n}}} \quad .$$

Thus $\dfrac{\frac{X}{n} - p}{\sqrt{\frac{p(1-p)}{n}}}$ is also approximately normally

distributed with mean zero and standard deviation 1.

The quantity $\frac{X}{n}$ is the proportion of married students observed in the sample of size n.

We are interested in the probability that $\frac{X}{n}$, the sample proportion is between the values .32 and .47 or

$$Pr\left(.32 < \frac{X}{n} < .47\right).$$

Substituting n = 100 and p = .40, we standardize $\frac{X}{n}$ and find that

$$\mathrm{Pr}\left[\frac{.32 - p}{\sqrt{\dfrac{p(1 - p)}{n}}} < \frac{\dfrac{X}{n} - p}{\sqrt{\dfrac{p(1 - p)}{n}}} < \frac{.47 - p}{\sqrt{\dfrac{p(1 - p)}{n}}}\right]$$

$$= \mathrm{Pr}\left[\frac{.32 - .4}{\sqrt{\dfrac{(.4)(.6)}{100}}} < \frac{\dfrac{X}{n} - p}{\sqrt{\dfrac{p(1 - p)}{100}}} < \frac{.47 - .4}{\sqrt{\dfrac{.4(.6)}{100}}}\right]$$

But $Z = \dfrac{\dfrac{X}{n} - p}{\sqrt{\dfrac{p(1 - p)}{100}}}$ is approximately a standard

normal variable.

Thus

$$\mathrm{Pr}\left(.32 < \frac{X}{100} < .47\right) = \mathrm{Pr}\left(\frac{-.08}{.049} < Z < \frac{.07}{.049}\right)$$

where Z is standard normal.

From the table of the standard normal distribution

$$\mathrm{Pr}\left(\frac{-.08}{.049} < Z < \frac{.07}{.049}\right) = \mathrm{Pr}(-1.63 < Z < 1.43)$$

$$= .8720 \ .$$

Thus, the probability that $\frac{X}{100}$, the sample proportion, is between .32 and .47, is .8720.

● **PROBLEM 11-43**

The probability that an electronic switch will operate successfully is .98. A random sample of 1,000 switches were tested and 30 were found to be defective. What is the probability of finding 30 or more defective switches in the sample?

Solution: The probability that a randomly selected switch is defective is $(1 - .98) = .02$. Letting $n = 1000$ and $p = .02$, we compute the expected number of defective switches, $np = (1,000)(.02) = 20$ and the standard deviation is $\sqrt{np(1 - p)} = \sqrt{1000(.02)(.98)} = \sqrt{20(.98)} = 4.43$. Thinking of the number of defective switches a a random variable X, we can use the standard normal curve to find an approximate value of the binomial probability, $P(X \geq 30)$. Because a discrete random variable is being approximated by a continuous random variable, $P(X \geq 30)$ is approximated by the normal probability $P(X > 29.5)$. We must convert 29.5 to a Z-score in order to use the table:

$$\frac{29.5 - np}{\sqrt{np(1 - p)}} = \frac{29.5 - 20}{4.43} = \frac{9.5}{4.43} = \frac{950}{443} \cong 2.14$$

It follows that $P(X > 29.5) = P(Z > 2.14)$.

$P(Z > 2.14) = 1 - P(Z \le 2.14)$

$= 1 - \Phi(2.14) \quad = 1 - .9838 = .0162.$

If you are using a table that gives the probabilities from 0 to a positive K,

$$P(Z > 2.14) = 1 - P(Z \le 2.14)$$

$$= 1 - \left[ \frac{1}{2} + \Phi^* (2.14) \right] \quad = 1 - (.5 + .4838)$$

$$= 1 - .9838 = .0162.$$

The probability that 30 or more switches will be defective is .0162.

● **PROBLEM** 11-44

In a random sample of 10,000 claims filed against an automobile insurance company, 75% exceeded $300. What is the probability that of the next 400 claims filed more than 72% will be above $300?

Solution:     Let X be a random variable denoting the number of the claims exceeding $300 that are among the next 400 filed against this insurance company. We have a good idea that the probability of a claim exceeding $300 being filed is .75.

We wish to find the probability that X is greater than 72% of 400. That is, the probability that of the next 400 claims, more than 72% will be above $300.

$$\Pr(X > 72\% \text{ of } 400) = \Pr(X > 288).$$

X is a binomially distributed random variable with mean $np = (400)(.75) = 300$ and standard deviation $\sqrt{np(1 - p)} = \sqrt{400(.75)(.25)} = \sqrt{75} = 8.66$. Using the normal approximation to the binomial, the binomial probability $\Pr(X > 288)$ is closely approximated by $\Pr(Y > 287.5)$ where Y is normally distributed with mean $E(Y) = np = 300$ and standard deviation, $\sqrt{np(1 - p)} = 8.66$.

Thus, we standardize Y to find its probability.

$$\Pr(Y > 287.5) = \Pr\left( \frac{Y - \mu}{\sqrt{\text{Var } Y}} > \frac{287.5 - \mu}{\sqrt{\text{Var } Y}} \right)$$

$$= \Pr\left( Z > \frac{287.5 - 300}{8.66} \right)$$

where Z is normally distributed with mean 0 and standard deviation 1.

$$Pr(Z > - 1.44) = .9251 .$$

Thus the probability that there are more than 288 claims of $300 is .925.

A new car was designed on the assumption that 60% of its sales would be to female customers. If a random sample of 500 purchasers is selected, what is the probability that at least 275 of them are female?

Solution: Let X be the number of female purchasers observed in the random sample of 500 purchasers. X may be assumed to be binomially distributed with parameters n = 500 and p = .60.

We wish to estimate the binomial probability that X > 275. X has mean $E(X) = np = 500(.60) = 300$ and standard deviation of $\sqrt{Var\ X} = \sqrt{np(1 - p)} = 10.9$. Using the normal approximation to the binomial,

$$Pr(X > 275) \overset{\sim}{=} Pr\left(Y > 275 - \frac{1}{2}\right)$$

where Y is normally distributed with mean np = 300 and standard deviation, $\sqrt{np(1 - p)} = 10.9$.

The $\frac{1}{2}$ is subtracted from 275 to correct for a discrete random variable being approximated by a continuous random variable.

To compute the $Pr(Y > 274.5)$ we convert Y to a standard normal random variable by subtracting its mean and dividing by its standard deviation. Thus

$$Pr(Y > 274.5) = Pr\left(\frac{Y - np}{\sqrt{np(1 - p)}} > \frac{274.5 - np}{\sqrt{np(1 - p)}}\right)$$

$$= Pr\left(Z > \frac{274.5 - 300}{10.9}\right)$$

where Z is normally distributed with mean 0 and standard deviation 1. Thus

$$Pr(X > 275) \overset{\sim}{=} Pr(Z > - 2.34)$$

and from the table of the standard normal,

$$Pr(Z > - 2.34) = Pr(Z < 2.34)$$
$$= .99 .$$

Thus, the probability that there are more than 275 female purchasers in a random sample of 500 purchasers given p = .60 is approximately .99.

A company produces light bulbs and knows that, on the average, 10% are defective and will not pass inspection. What is the probability that more than 15% of a random sample of 100 bulbs is defective?

**Solution:** Let X be the number of defective bulbs in a random sample of size 100. If on the average 10% of the bulbs are defective, and each bulb in the sample is selected independently from the entire population of bulbs; X may be assumed to be a binomially distributed random variable with parameters n = 100 and p = .10. Thus the expected number of defective bulbs is $E(X) = np = 10$ and the standard deviation in the number of defective bulbs is $\sqrt{\text{Var } X} = \sqrt{np(1 - p)} = \sqrt{100(.1)(.9)} = \sqrt{9} = 3$.

We wish to find the probability that there are more than 15 defective light bulbs in the sample of size 100. Equivalently, we wish to find the probability that $X \geq 14.5$.

Using the normal approximation to the binomial

$$Pr(X \geq 15) \cong Pr(Y \geq 14.5)$$

where Y is normally distributed with mean np and standard deviation $\sqrt{np(1 - p)}$. To find $Pr(Y > 14.5)$ we standardize Y by subtracting the mean and dividing by the standard deviation. Thus

$$Pr(x \geq 15) \cong Pr(Y \geq 14.5) = Pr\left(Z \geq \frac{14.5 - 10}{3}\right)$$

where $Z = \dfrac{Y - np}{\sqrt{np(1-p)}}$ is normally distributed with mean 0

and variance 1. From the table of the standard normal

$$Pr(Z \geq 1.5) = 1 - Pr(Z < 1.5)$$

$$= 1 - .9332 = .0668.$$

Thus, the probability that the number of defective light bulbs in the sample exceeds 15 is approximately .067 .

The diameters of a large shipment of ball bearings are normally distributed with a mean of 2.0 **cm** and a standard deviation of .01 **cm** . If three ball bearings are selected at random from the shipment, what is the probability that exactly two of the selected ball bearings will have a diameter larger than 2.02 **cm**?

**Solution:** We will solve this problem in 2 steps. First, using the normal distribution we will determine the probability that the diameter of any one ball bearing is greater than 2.02 cm. Second, we will use the binomial formula,

$$P(X = x) = \binom{n}{x} p^x (1 - p)^{n-x} ,$$

to determine the probability that exactly 2 diameters exceed 2.02 cm.

Step 1: We want $p = Pr(X > 2.02)$. Since X is normally distributed, we can standardize it by subtracting the mean and dividing by the standard deviation.

$$p = Pr\left(\frac{X - \mu}{\sigma} > \frac{2.02 - \mu}{\sigma}\right)$$

$$= Pr\left(\text{Standard Normal Quantity} > \frac{2.02 - \mu}{\sigma}\right) .$$

Substituting, $p = Pr\left(\text{Standard Normal} > \frac{2.02 - 2}{.01}\right)$

$$p = Pr(\text{Standard Normal Quantity} > 2).$$

From the standard normal table, $p = .0228$.

Step 2: We want $P(X = 2) = \binom{n}{2} p^2 (1 - p)^{n-2}$. p was found to be .0228 and n, the sample size, is 3. Hence,

$$P(X = 2) = \binom{3}{2} (.0228)^2 (1 - .0228)$$

$$= \frac{3!}{2!1!} (.0228)^2 (.9772) = 3(.00051984)(.9772)$$

$$= .00152.$$

● **PROBLEM** 11-48

A poultry farmer wished to make a comparison between two feed Mixtures. One flock of hens was fed from Mixture 1 and another flock from Mixture 2. In a six-week period, the flock being fed from Mixture 1 increased egg production by 25%, while those fed from Mixture 2 increased egg production by 20%. Random samples of 200 and 300 hens were selected from the respective flocks. Let $\hat{p}_1$ be the proportion of the sample from the first flock with increased egg production, and let $\hat{p}_2$ be the proportion of the sample from the second flock. Find
  (a) the expected difference between the two proportions
  (b) the standard error of this difference,
  (c) the probability that hens fed from Mixture 1 increased their egg production more than those fed from Mixture 2.

Solution: Let $p_1$ and $p_2$ denote the population proportions representing the percentage increase in egg production of hens who were fed Mixtures 1 and 2 respectively. We are given that $p_1 = .25$ and $p_2 = .20$.

After the random samples of size 200 and 300 have been selected, $\hat{p}_1$ and $\hat{p}_2$ will denote the proportions representing the percentage increase in egg production observed in the two samples.

$\hat{p}_1 = \frac{Y_1}{200}$ will be observed increase in egg production ($Y_1$) divided by the size of the first sample population.

$\hat{p}_2 = \frac{Y_2}{300}$ will be the observed increase in egg production ($Y_2$) divided by the size of the second sample population.

(a)  The expected difference between $\hat{p}_1$ and $\hat{p}_2$ is

$$E(\hat{p}_1 - \hat{p}_2) = E(\hat{p}_1) - E(\hat{p}_2)$$

by the properties of expectation. To find $E(\hat{p}_1)$ and $E(\hat{p}_2)$ we need to know something about the distributions of $Y_1$ and $Y_2$, the observed   hens   with increased egg production.

$Y_1$ and $Y_2$ may be assumed to be binomially distributed with parameters $n_1 = 200$ and $p_1 = .25$ and $n_2 = 300$ and $p_2 = .20$ respectively. Thus

$$E(Y_1) = n_1 p_1 = (200)(.25) = 50 \qquad \text{and}$$

$$E(Y_2) = n_2 p_2 = (300)(.20) = 60.$$

$$\text{Var } Y_1 = n_1 p_1 (1 - p_1) = 37.5 \quad \text{and}$$

$$\text{Var } Y_2 = n_2 p_2 (1 - p_2) = 48.$$

Substituting we find the expected value of

$$\hat{p}_1 - \hat{p}_2 = \frac{Y_1}{n_1} - \frac{Y_2}{n_2} ;$$

$$E(\hat{p}_1 - \hat{p}_2) = E(\hat{p}_1) - E(\hat{p}_2)$$

$$= E\left(\frac{Y_1}{200}\right) - E\left(\frac{Y_2}{300}\right) = \frac{E(Y_1)}{200} - \frac{E(Y_2)}{300}$$

$$= \frac{50}{200} - \frac{60}{300} \quad = .25 - .20 = .05.$$

(b)  To find the standard error or standard deviation of this difference, we first find $\text{Var}(\hat{p}_1 - \hat{p}_2)$. Using the properties of variance we see that

$$\text{Var } (ax + by) = a^2 \text{ Var } X + b^2 \text{ Var } Y .$$

Therefore $\text{Var } (\hat{p}_1 - \hat{p}_2) = \text{Var } \hat{p}_1 + (-1)^2 \text{ Var } \hat{p}_2$

$$= \text{Var } \frac{Y_1}{n_1} + \text{Var } \frac{Y_2}{n_2} = \frac{1}{n_1{}^2} \text{Var } Y_1 + \frac{1}{n_2{}^2} \text{Var } Y_2$$

$$= \frac{p_1(1 - p_1)}{n_1} + \frac{p_2(1 - p_2)}{n_2} = \frac{(.25)(.75)}{200} + \frac{(.20)(.80)}{300}$$

$$= .0009375 + .000533 = .00147.$$

The standard error of $\hat{p}_1 - \hat{p}_2$ is

$$\sqrt{\text{Var}(\hat{p}_1 - \hat{p}_2)} = \sqrt{.00147} = .038 .$$

(c) The probability that the sample of hens fed from Mixture 1 increased their egg production more than the sample fed from Mixture 2 is $\Pr(\hat{p}_1 > \hat{p}_2)$ or

$\Pr(\hat{p}_1 - \hat{p}_2 > 0)$.

To compute this probability we use the normal approximation to the binomial. Thus

$$\Pr(\hat{p}_1 - \hat{p}_2 > 0) \stackrel{\sim}{=} \Pr(Y > 0)$$

where Y is distributed normally with mean $E(\hat{p}_1 - \hat{p}_2) = .05$ and standard deviation .038.

Standardizing we see that

$$\Pr(Y > 0) \stackrel{\sim}{=} \Pr\left(\frac{Y - .05}{.038} > \frac{0 - .05}{.038}\right)$$

$$= \Pr\left(z > \frac{-.05}{.038}\right) = \Pr(z \geq -1.31)$$

$$= 1 - \Pr(z > 1.31) = .9049 .$$

● **PROBLEM 11-49**

The receiving department of a large television manufacturer uses the following rule in deciding whether to accept or reject a shipment of 100,000 small parts shipped every week by a supplier: Select a sample of 400 parts from each lot received. If 3% or more of the selected parts are defective, reject the entire lot; if the proportion of defectives is less than 3% accept the lot. What is the probability of rejecting a lot that actually contains 2% defectives?

Solution: Let X be the number of defective parts in a sample of 400. If the probability of selecting a defective item is .02, we want to find the probability that 3% or more of the sample is defective. Equivalently, we wish to find the probability that $X \geq 3\%$ of 400 or $X \geq (.03)(400) = 12$.

The expected number of defectives is $E(X) = (.02)400 = 8$ and the standard deviation of the number of defectives is $\sqrt{\text{Var } X} = \sqrt{np(1 - p)} = \sqrt{400(.02)(.98)} = 2.8$ since X is distributed binomially with parameters n = 400 and p = .02.

We now employ the normal approximation to the binomial to find the probability that X > 12.

$$Pr(X \geq 12) \cong Pr(Y \geq 11.5),$$

where Y is normally distributed with mean np = 8 and standard deviation 2.8.

We standardize Y by subtracting the mean and dividing by the standard deviation. Thus

$$Pr(X \geq 12) \cong Pr(Y \geq 11.5)$$

$$\cong Pr\left(\frac{Y - np}{\sqrt{np(1 - p)}} > \frac{11.5 - np}{\sqrt{np(1 - p)}}\right)$$

where $Z = \dfrac{Y - np}{\sqrt{np(1 - p)}}$ is normally distributed with

mean 0 and standard deviation 1. From the table of the standard normal,

$$Pr(Y \geq 11.5) = Pr\left(Z \geq \frac{11.5 - 8}{2.8}\right)$$

$$= Pr(Z \geq 1.25) = 1 - .8944 = .1056.$$

Thus given that 2% of the population of light bulbs is defective, there is a probability of approximately .1056 of observing 3% defective in the sample of size 400.

This problem is an example of a hypothesis test, a topic to which we will devote much space later.

● **PROBLEM 11-50**

Congressional candidate X will base his decision on whether or not to endorse the Educational Opportunity Act on the results of a poll of a random sample of 200 registered voters from his district. He will endorse the Educational Opportunity Act only if 100 or more voters are in favor if it.

(a) What is the probability that candidate X will endorse the Act if 45% of all registered voters in his district are in favor of it?

(b) What is the probability that candidate X will fail to endorse the Act if 52% of all voters in his district are in favor of it?

Solution:    (a) We will regard the random selection of 200 voters from a district in which 45% of all voters are in favor of the Educational Opportunity Act as a binomial experiment with parameters n = 100 and p = 45. The expected value and the standard deviation of this experiment are computed below.

$$E(X) = np = 200(.45) = 90 \text{ voters}$$

$$\sigma_x = \sqrt{np(1 - p)} = \sqrt{49.5} = 7.04 \text{ voters}.$$

Candidate X will endorse the Act only when 100 or more voters are in favor of it. Using the normal distribution as an approximation to the binomial, the probability that the Act will be endorsed by 100 or more voters is approximated by the area under the normal curve lying to the right of x = 99.5 (see shaded area below).

We want $P(X \geq 99.5)$.

Equivalently we will find after standardizing

$$P\left(\frac{X - \mu}{\sigma} \geq \frac{99.5 - \mu}{\sigma}\right)$$

or $\quad P\left(z \geq \frac{99.5 - \mu}{\sigma}\right).$

Substituting, we obtain

$$P\left(z \geq \frac{99.5 - 90}{7.04}\right) = P(z \geq 1.35).$$

Reading off the table we see the probability that candidate X will endorse the Educational Opportunity Act is .0885.

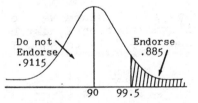

(b) The random selection of 200 voters from a district in which 52% of all voters endorse the Act can be regarded as a binomial experiment with n = 200 and P = .52. The expectation and standard deviation are computed as follows.

$$E(X) = np = 200(.52) = 104 \text{ voters}$$

$$\sigma_x = \sqrt{np(1 - p)} = \sqrt{200(.52)(1 - .52)} = \sqrt{49.92} = 7.07.$$

Candidate X will fail to endorse the Act if less than 100 voters are in favor of it.

We want $P(X \leq 99.5)$.

We standardize and obtain $\quad P\left(\frac{X - \mu}{\sigma} \leq \frac{99.5 - \mu}{\sigma}\right).$

We have $P\left(\text{Standard Normal Quantity} \leq \frac{99.5 - \mu}{\sigma}\right).$

Substituting we have $\quad P\left(z \leq \frac{99.5 - 104}{7.07}\right)$

or $P(z \leq -.636)$. From the tables, this is about .26.

# ADDITIONAL APPLICATIONS

Show by integrating, that

$$f(x) = \frac{1}{\sigma\sqrt{2\pi}} \exp\left[-\frac{1}{2}\left(\frac{x-\mu}{\sigma}\right)^2\right] ,$$

the normal distribution, is an actual probability density function.

**Solution:**    We must show that

$$\text{Total Probability} = \int_{-\infty}^{\infty} \frac{1}{\sigma\sqrt{2\pi}} e^{-\frac{1}{2}\left(\frac{x-\mu}{\sigma}\right)^2} dx = 1.$$

Let $t = \frac{x-\mu}{\sigma}$ , then $x = \sigma t + \mu$ and $dx = \sigma dt$.

Our integral becomes

$$I = \int_{-\infty}^{\infty} \frac{1}{\sigma\sqrt{2\pi}} e^{-\frac{t^2}{2}} \sigma dt = \int_{-\infty}^{\infty} \frac{1}{\sqrt{2\pi}} e^{-\frac{t^2}{2}} dt.$$

We want to show $I = 1$. Since we are taking the integral of a positive function $I$ must be $> 0$. Hence all we need to do to show $I = 1$ is to show $I^2 = 1$.

$$I^2 = \left(\frac{1}{\sqrt{2\pi}} \int_{-\infty}^{\infty} e^{-\frac{t^2}{2}} dt\right)\left(\frac{1}{\sqrt{2\pi}} \int_{-\infty}^{\infty} e^{-\frac{w^2}{2}} dw\right) .$$

Each of the two integrals is a constant, independent of any variables; hence we can take one inside the integral sign of the other.

$$I^2 = \frac{1}{\sqrt{2\pi}} \int_{-\infty}^{\infty} \left(\frac{1}{\sqrt{2\pi}} \int_{-\infty}^{\infty} e^{-\frac{t^2}{2}} dt\right) e^{-\frac{w^2}{2}} dw.$$

We now write the iterated integrals as one double integral.

$$I^2 = \frac{1}{2\pi} \int_{-\infty}^{\infty} \int_{-\infty}^{\infty} e^{-\frac{1}{2}(t^2 + w^2)} dt\, dw .$$

We now transform to polar coordinates by the substitutions $t = r \sin \theta$ and $w = r \cos \theta$. Now $t^2 + w^2 = r^2 \sin^2 \theta + r^2 \cos^2 \theta = r^2(\sin^2 \theta + \cos^2 \theta) = r^2 \times 1 = r^2$. By the change of variables formula

$$dtdw = \left| \det \begin{pmatrix} \dfrac{\delta t}{\delta r} & \dfrac{\delta t}{\delta \theta} \\[6pt] \dfrac{\delta w}{\delta r} & \dfrac{\delta w}{\delta \theta} \end{pmatrix} \right| drd\theta$$

$$= \left| \det \begin{pmatrix} \sin \theta & r \cos \theta \\ \cos \theta & - r \sin \theta \end{pmatrix} \right| drd\theta$$

$$= |- r \sin^2 \theta - r \cos^2 \theta| \; drd\theta$$

$$= |- r (\sin^2 \theta + \cos^2 \theta)| \; drd\theta$$

$$= |- r| drd\theta = rdrd\theta \; .$$

Substituting our derived quantities

$$I^2 = \frac{1}{2\pi} \int_{\theta=0}^{2\pi} \int_{r=0}^{\infty} e^{-\frac{1}{2} r^2} rdrd\theta.$$

There might be some confusion about the limits. $\{- \infty < t < \infty, \; - \infty < w < \infty\}$ covers the entire Euclidean plane.

$r = \sqrt{x^2 + y^2}$, the distance of a point from the origin. For us to cover the entire plane we must include the points at all distances from $(0, 0)$. Hence $0 \leq r < \infty$ . $\theta$ can be shown to equal $\text{Arctan} \left( \dfrac{t}{w} \right)$ or the angle the line connecting the origin with the point makes with the positive x-axis. To cover the entire plane $\theta$ must be allowed to include any value $0 \leq \theta < 2\pi$.

Now

$$I^2 = \frac{1}{2\pi} \int_{\theta=0}^{2\pi} \left( \int_{r=0}^{\infty} re^{-\frac{1}{2} r^2} dr \right) d\theta \; .$$

We must evaluate $\displaystyle\int_{r=0}^{\infty} re^{-\frac{1}{2} r^2} dr$ .

Let $u = - \frac{1}{2} r^2$; then $du = - rdr$ and

$$\int\limits_{r=0}^{\infty} re^{-\frac{r^2}{2}} dr = -\int\limits_{0}^{-\infty} e^u\, du = -e^u \Bigg]_{0}^{-\infty} = -\left[ e^{-\infty} - e^0 \right]$$

$$\rightarrow -[0 - 1] = 1.$$

Now

$$I^2 = \frac{1}{2\pi} \int\limits_{\theta=0}^{2\pi} 1 \cdot d\theta = \frac{1}{2\pi} \int\limits_{0}^{2\pi} d\theta$$

$$= \frac{1}{2\pi} [\theta]_0^{2\pi} = \frac{1}{2\pi} (2\pi - 0) = 1$$

as was to be shown.

● **PROBLEM** 11-52

Find the expected value of a normally distributed random variable with parameters $\mu$ and $\sigma^2$.

Solution: A random variable X with probability density function:

$$f(x) = \frac{1}{\sqrt{2\pi\sigma^2}} e^{-\frac{(x - \mu)^2}{2\sigma^2}} \quad \text{for } -\infty < X < \infty$$

is normally distributed with parameters $\mu$ and $\sigma^2$.

Thus

$$E(X) = \int\limits_{-\infty}^{\infty} \frac{x}{\sqrt{2\pi\sigma^2}} e^{-\frac{(x - \mu)^2}{2\sigma^2}} dx .$$

Let $u = \frac{x - \mu}{\sigma}$ and $du = \frac{dx}{\sigma}$ .

Substituting we see that

$$E(X) = \int\limits_{-\infty}^{\infty} \frac{(\mu + \sigma u)}{\sqrt{2\pi}} e^{-\frac{u^2}{2}} du$$

$$= \int\limits_{-\infty}^{\infty} \frac{\mu}{\sqrt{2\pi}} e^{-\frac{u^2}{2}} du + \int\limits_{-\infty}^{\infty} \frac{\sigma u}{\sqrt{2\pi}} e^{-\frac{u^2}{2}} du$$

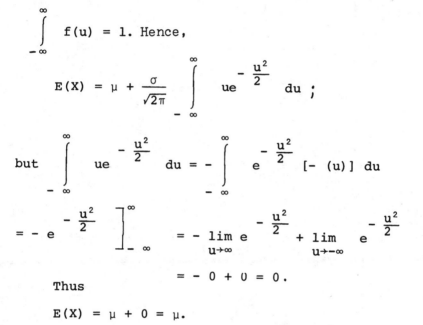

$$= \mu \int_{-\infty}^{\infty} \frac{1}{\sqrt{2\pi}} e^{-\frac{u^2}{2}} du + \frac{\sigma}{\sqrt{2\pi}} \int_{-\infty}^{\infty} u e^{-\frac{u^2}{2}} du ;$$

but $\dfrac{1}{\sqrt{2\pi}} e^{-\frac{u^2}{2}} = f(u)$    $-\infty < u < \infty$

is the probability density function of a normal distribution with parameters $\mu = 0$ and $\sigma^2 = 1$. Thus by the definition of a probability mass function

$$\int_{-\infty}^{\infty} f(u) = 1.$$ Hence,

$$E(X) = \mu + \frac{\sigma}{\sqrt{2\pi}} \int_{-\infty}^{\infty} u e^{-\frac{u^2}{2}} du ;$$

but $$\int_{-\infty}^{\infty} u e^{-\frac{u^2}{2}} du = -\int_{-\infty}^{\infty} e^{-\frac{u^2}{2}} [-(u)] du$$

$$= -e^{-\frac{u^2}{2}} \Bigg]_{-\infty}^{\infty} = -\lim_{u \to \infty} e^{-\frac{u^2}{2}} + \lim_{u \to -\infty} e^{-\frac{u^2}{2}}$$

$$= -0 + 0 = 0.$$

Thus

$$E(X) = \mu + 0 = \mu.$$

● **PROBLEM** 11-53

Show that the normal density function

$$f(x) = \frac{1}{\sigma\sqrt{2\pi}} e^{-\frac{1}{2}\left(\frac{x - \mu}{\sigma}\right)^2} ,$$

has variance $\sigma^2$.

Solution:    We will use the following computational formula for variance;

$$Var(x) = E(x^2) - (E(x))^2.$$

From the last problem, $(E(x))^2 = \mu^2$ .

Therefore all we have to do to show $Var(x) = \sigma^2$ is to show $E(x^2) = \sigma^2 + \mu^2$ .

$$E(x^2) = \int_{-\infty}^{\infty} x^2\ f(x)\ dx,\ \text{by definition}\ .$$

$$E(x^2) = \int_{-\infty}^{\infty} \frac{x^2}{\sigma\sqrt{2\pi}}\ e^{-\frac{1}{2}\left(\frac{x-\mu}{\sigma}\right)^2}\ dx\ .$$

Let $t = \dfrac{x-\mu}{\sigma}$; then $x = \sigma t + \mu$ and $dx = \sigma dt$.

$$E(x^2) = \int_{-\infty}^{\infty} \frac{(\sigma t + \mu)^2}{\sigma\sqrt{2\pi}}\ e^{-\frac{1}{2}t^2}\ \sigma dt$$

$$= \int_{-\infty}^{\infty} \frac{(\sigma t + \mu)^2}{\sqrt{2\pi}}\ e^{-\frac{t^2}{2}}\ dt$$

$$= \int_{-\infty}^{\infty} \frac{(\sigma^2 t^2 + 2\sigma t\mu + \mu^2)}{\sqrt{2\pi}}\ e^{-\frac{t^2}{2}}\ dt$$

$$= \sigma^2 \int_{-\infty}^{\infty} \frac{t^2}{\sqrt{2\pi}}\ e^{-\frac{t^2}{2}}\ dt + 2\sigma\mu \int_{-\infty}^{\infty} \frac{t}{\sqrt{2\pi}}\ e^{-\frac{t^2}{2}}\ dt$$

$$+ \mu^2 \int_{-\infty}^{\infty} \frac{1}{\sqrt{2\pi}}\ e^{-\frac{t^2}{2}}\ dt$$

$$= I_1 + I_2 + I_3\ .$$

$I_2$ is $2\sigma\mu \times$ Expected value of a Standard Normal Random Variable $= 2\sigma\mu \times 0 = 0$. $I_3$ is $\mu^2 \times$ Total Probability under a standard normal curve $= \mu^2 \times 1 = \mu^2$. $I_1$ is $\sigma^2 \times E(x^2)$ of a standard normal random variable. But, by the formula , Var $(x) = E(x^2) - (E(x))^2$, $E(x^2) =$ Var $(x) + (E(x))^2$. In the case of a standard normal random variable $E(x^2) = 1 + 0^2 = 1$. Hence $I_1 = \sigma^2 \times 1 = \sigma^2$.

Finally, $E(x^2) = I_1 + I_2 + I_3$

$$= \sigma^2 + 0 + \mu^2$$

$$= \sigma^2 + \mu^2$$

as was to be shown.

# CHAPTER 12

# SPECIAL CONTINUOUS DISTRIBUTIONS

## UNIFORM DISTRIBUTION

● PROBLEM 12-1

The simplest continuous random variable is the one whose distribution is constant over some interval (a, b) and zero elsewhere. This is the uniform distribution.

$$f(x) = \begin{cases} \dfrac{1}{b-a}, & a \le X \le b \\ 0, & \text{elsewhere} \end{cases}$$

Find the mean and variance of this distribution.

Solution: By definition,

$$E(x) = \int_{-\infty}^{\infty} x\, f(x)\, dx = \int_{a}^{b} \frac{1}{b-a}\, x\, dx$$

$$= \frac{1}{b-a} \int_{a}^{b} x\, dx = \frac{1}{b-a}\, \frac{x^2}{2}\, \Big|_{a}^{b}$$

$$= \frac{b^2 - a^2}{2} \left( \frac{1}{b-a} \right) = \frac{a+b}{2}\ .$$

For the variance we must first find $E(X^2)$. By definition

$$E(X^2) = \int_{-\infty}^{\infty} x^2\, f(x)\, dx$$

$$= \int_{a}^{b} x^2\, \frac{1}{b-a}\, dx$$

$$= \frac{1}{b-a} \int_{a}^{b} x^2\, dx$$

$$= \frac{1}{b-a}\, \frac{x^3}{3}\, \Big|_{a}^{b}$$

$$= \frac{b^3 - a^3}{3(b - a)} \quad .$$

But  Var $(X) = E(X^2) - (E(x))^2$

$$= \frac{b^3 - a^3}{3(b - a)} - \left(\frac{b + a}{2}\right)^2$$

$$= \frac{b^3 - a^3}{3(b - a)} - \frac{(a^2 + 2ab + b^2)}{4}$$

$$= \frac{(b^2 + ab + a^2)(b - a)}{3(b - a)} - \frac{(a^2 + 2ab + b^2)}{4}$$

$$= \frac{(b^2 + ab + a^2)}{3} - \frac{(a^2 + 2ab + b^2)}{4}$$

$$= \frac{(4b^2 + 4ab + 4a^2)}{12} - \frac{(3a^2 + 6ab + 3b^2)}{12}$$

$$= \frac{b^2 - 2ab + a^2}{12} = \frac{(b - a)^2}{12} \quad .$$

● **PROBLEM** 12-2

Spin a needle on a circular dial. When it stops it points at a random angle   (measured from the horizontal, say). Under normal conditions it is reasonable to suppose that $\theta$ is uniformly distributed between 0° and 360°. This means it has the following density function:

$$f(u) = \begin{cases} \dfrac{1}{360} & \text{for } 0 \le u \le 360, \\ 0 & \text{otherwise} . \end{cases}$$

Thus for any $\theta_1 < \theta_2$ we have

$$P(\theta_1 \le X \le \theta_2) = \int_{\theta_1}^{\theta_2} \frac{1}{360} \, du = \frac{\theta_2 - \theta_1}{360} \quad .$$

Discuss this formula.

Solution:    The formula says that the probability of the needle pointing between any two directions is proportional to the angle between them. If the angle $\theta_2 - \theta_1$ shrinks to zero, then so does probability. Hence in the limit the probability of the needle pointing exactly to $\theta_1$ is equal to zero. From an empirical point of view, this event does not really make sense because the needle itself must have a width.

● **PROBLEM** 12-3

The length of hair of female postal employees is uniformly distributed between 4 and 24 inches. Find the probability that Gretchen, a random employee, has hair that is 19 inches long to the nearest inch.

Solution:  To have hair that is 19 inches to the nearest inch, the length must fall in the following interval $18.5 \leq L < 19.5$. By definition then

$$Pr(18.5 \leq L < 19.5) = \int_{18.5}^{19.5} f(x) \, dx .$$

We have a uniform distribution.

$$f(x) = \begin{cases} \dfrac{1}{b-a}, & a \leq L \leq b \\ \\ 0, & \text{otherwise .} \end{cases}$$

In this problem, $a = 4$ and $b = 24$.

$$f(L) = \begin{cases} \dfrac{1}{20}, & 4 \leq L \leq 24 \\ \\ 0, & \text{otherwise .} \end{cases}$$

The probability now becomes

$$\int_{18.5}^{19.5} \frac{1}{20} \, dx = \frac{1}{20} \left. x \right]_{18.5}^{19.5}$$

$$= \frac{19.5 - 18.5}{20} = \frac{1}{20} .$$

● **PROBLEM** 12-4

For the continuous uniform distribution, find the cumulative distribution function and the moment generating function.

Solution:    $$f(x) = \begin{cases} \dfrac{1}{b-a} & a \leq x \leq b \\ \\ 0 & \text{otherwise .} \end{cases}$$

The cumulative distribution $F(x)$ is the function which gives the probability that a single observation of the random variable will be less than or equal to x. It is found by the following integral

$$F(x) = \int_{-\infty}^{x} f(t) \, dt .$$

For the uniform distribution, if $x \leq a$

$$F(x) = \int_{-\infty}^{x} 0 \; dt = 0 .$$

If $a \leq x \leq b$

$$F(x) = \int_{a}^{x} \frac{1}{b-a} \; dt = \frac{x-a}{b-a} .$$

For $x > b$

$$F(x) = \int_{a}^{b} \frac{1}{b-a} \; dt + \int_{b}^{x} 0 \; dt$$

$$= \frac{b-a}{b-a} + 0 = 1 .$$

For the moment generating function $M_x(t) = E(e^{tx})$. By definition, this is

$$\int_{-\infty}^{\infty} e^{tx} F(x) \; dx$$

$$= \int_{a}^{b} e^{tx} \frac{1}{b-a} \; dx$$

$$= \frac{1}{b-a} \int_{a}^{b} e^{tx} \; dx$$

$$= \frac{1}{b-a} \left( \frac{1}{t} e^{tx} \Big|_{a}^{b} \right)$$

$$= \frac{e^{tb} - e^{ta}}{t(b-a)} .$$

● **PROBLEM** 12-5

Find the probability that three random points on the circumference of a circle all lie on a semicircle.

Solution:     Note that the first two points do not matter. There will always be a common semicircle for any two random points. The placement of the third point can cause trouble as in the following diagram:

Let us examine the ways we can place the third point so as to still be in a semicircle.

$\theta$ is the angle formed by the placement of the first two points.

By the previous diagram, we see that if the third point is placed anywhere on the arc of the nonshaded region the three points will lie on a semicircle. There is an arc of angle $2\pi - \theta$ on which we can place the point. We will assume that the probability of placing the point is uniform. Hence

$$\Pr_\theta \text{(Semicircle)} = \frac{\text{Possible angle of placement}}{2\pi}$$

$$\Pr(\text{Semicircle} \mid \theta = \theta) = \frac{2\pi - \theta}{2\pi} \ .$$

If one is bothered by the use of "semicircle" as a random variable, he can set up the following random variable.

$$X = \begin{cases} 0 & \text{if no semicircle} \\ 1 & \text{if a semicircle exists .} \end{cases}$$

Now note the following series of equalities:

$$\Pr(\text{Semicircle}) = \Pr(X = 1)$$

$$= \int \Pr(X = 1 \mid \theta = \theta) \ F(\theta) \ d\theta$$

$$= \int \frac{2\pi - \theta}{2\pi} \ F(\theta) \ d\theta.$$

We will now assume that $\theta$ is uniformly distributed. If the first two points are coincident $\theta = 0$. The largest possible value of $\theta$ is when the first two points are at extreme ends of a diameter. Then $\theta = \pi$. Hence

$$F(\theta) = \frac{1}{\pi - 0} = \frac{1}{\pi} \quad \text{for } 0 \leq \theta \leq \pi.$$

Finally,

$$Pr(X = 1) = \int_0^\pi \frac{2\pi - \theta}{2\pi} \left(\frac{1}{\pi}\right) d\theta$$

$$= \int_0^\pi \left[\frac{1}{\pi} - \frac{\theta}{2\pi^2}\right] d\theta = \left[\frac{\theta}{\pi} - \frac{\theta^2}{4\pi^2}\right]_0^\pi$$

$$= \frac{\pi}{\pi} - \frac{\pi^2}{4\pi^2} - 0 + 0 = 1 - \frac{1}{4} = \frac{3}{4}.$$

# EXPONENTIAL DISTRIBUTION

Consider the exponential distribution $f(x) = \lambda e^{-\lambda x}$ for $x > 0$. Find the moment generating function and from it, the mean and variance of the exponential distribution.

<u>Solution:</u>    By definition    $M_x(t) = E(e^{tx})$

$$= \int_{-\infty}^\infty e^{tx} f(x) dx$$

$$= \int_{x=0}^\infty e^{tx} \lambda e^{-\lambda x} dx$$

$$= \int_0^\infty \lambda e^{(t - \lambda)x} dx = \lambda \int_0^\infty e^{(t - \lambda)x} dx$$

$$= \lambda \left[\frac{-1}{t - \lambda} e^{(t - \lambda)x}\right]_0^\infty$$

$$= \frac{\lambda}{\lambda - t} \left[e^{(t - \lambda)x}\right]_0^\infty.$$

Consider $t < \lambda$. Then $\lambda - t > 0$ and $t - \lambda < 0$. Hence $e^{(t - \lambda)x} = e^{-kx}$ and $M_x(t) = \frac{\lambda}{\lambda - t} (0 - (-1)) = \frac{\lambda}{\lambda - t}$ for $t < \lambda$.

The mean is

$$E(x) = M_x'(t) \Big|_{t=0}$$

$$M_x'(t) = \frac{d}{dt} \left[\frac{\lambda}{\lambda - t}\right] = \lambda \left[\frac{d}{dt} \frac{1}{\lambda - t}\right]$$

$$= \lambda \left[\frac{-1}{(\lambda - t)^2}\right] \frac{d}{dt} (\lambda - t) = \frac{\lambda}{(\lambda - t)^2}$$

$$M_x'(0) = E(x) = \frac{\lambda}{(\lambda - 0)^2} = \frac{\lambda}{\lambda^2} = \frac{1}{\lambda} \ .$$

Also by the moment generating function's properties

$$E(x^2) = M_x''(t) \ \Big|_{t=0}$$

$$M_x''(t) = \frac{d}{dt} \ \frac{\lambda}{(\lambda - t)^2} = \lambda \ \frac{d}{dt} \ \frac{1}{(\lambda - t)^2} \cdot$$

$$= \lambda \ \frac{-2}{(\lambda - t)^3} \ \frac{d}{dt} \ (\lambda - t) = \frac{2\lambda}{(\lambda - t)^3}$$

$$M_x''(0) = E(x^2) = \frac{2\lambda}{\lambda^3} = \frac{2}{\lambda^2} \ ,$$

Now $\quad Var(X) = E(x^2) - (E(x))^2$

$$= \frac{2}{\lambda^2} - \left(\frac{1}{\lambda}\right)^2$$

$$= \frac{1}{\lambda^2} \ .$$

● **PROBLEM** 12-7

Engineers determine that the lifespans of electric light bulbs manufactured by their company have the exponential distribution $f(x) = \frac{1}{1000} \ e^{-x/1000}$ when $x \geq 0$ and $f(x)=0$, $x<0$. Compute the probability that a randomly selected light bulb has a lifespan of less than 1,000 hours. Graph the density function.

Solution:     The cumulative distribution function $F(a) = P(X \leq a)$ is used to compute $P(X < 1000)$. We find the area under the graph of $f(x)$ from 0 to a (the area from $-\infty$ to 0 is 0 because $f(x) = 0$ when $x < 0$).

$$P(X \leq a) = F(a) = \int_0^a f(x) \ dx = \int_0^a \frac{1}{1000} \ e^{-x/1000} \ dx$$

$$= \int_0^a \frac{1}{1000} \ e^{-x/1000} dx = \frac{1}{1000} \left[ - 1000 \ e^{- x/1000} \right]_0^a$$

$$= - e^{- x/1000} \Big]_0^a = - \left[ e^{- a/1000} - e^0 \right]$$

$$= 1 - e^{- a/1000} = F(a)$$

375

$$P(X \leq 1000) = F(1000) = 1 - e^{-1000/1000} = 1 - e^{-1}$$

$$= 1 - \frac{1}{e} \ .$$

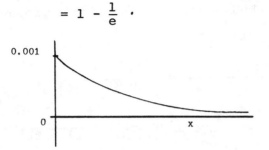

Graph of $f(x) = 0.001 \ e^{-0.001 \ x}$

When $x = 0$, $f(x) = 0.001$. As $x \to \infty$, $f(x) \to 0$.

● **PROBLEM** 12-8

The probability density function of the length of life
of a certain component is given by

$$f(t) = ke^{-kt} \qquad (0 < t < \infty).$$

An apparatus contains three components of this type and
the failure of one may be assumed independent of the
failure of the others.

   Find the probability that

(a)   None will have failed at $t_o$ hours.

(b)   Exactly one will fail in the first $t_o$ hours,
another in the second $t_o$, and the third after more
than 2 $t_o$ hours.

Solution:     First let us find the cumulative distribution
of t.

$$F(t) = \Pr(T \leq t) = \int_{-\infty}^{t} f(x) \ dx$$

$$= \int_{0}^{t} ke^{-kx} \ dx = -e^{-kx} \Big|_{0}^{t} = 1 - e^{-kt}.$$

Note that $\Pr(T \geq t) = 1 - \Pr(T \leq t)$

$$= 1 - (1 - e^{-kt}) = e^{-kt} \ .$$

(a)   For none to have failed at $T = t_o$, the three must

have lifetimes greater than $t_0$. Since the lifetimes are independent, the probability of this is the product

$$Pr(T_1 \geq t_0) \times Pr(T_2 \geq t_0) \times Pr(T_3 \geq t_0)$$

$$= [Pr(T \geq t_0)]^3$$

$$= (e^{-kt_0})^3 = e^{-3kt_0} .$$

(b)   To do part b, we make use of the following calculations:

$$Pr(T_1 \leq t_0) = F(t_0) = 1 - e^{-kt_0},$$

$$Pr(t_0 \leq T_2 \leq 2t_0) = F(2t_0) - F(t_0)$$

$$= 1 - e^{-2kt_0} - (1 - e^{-kt_0})$$

$$= e^{-kt_0} - e^{-2kt_0} , \quad \text{and}$$

$$Pr(T_3 \geq 2t_0) = 1 - F(2t_0) = 1 - (1 - e^{-2kt_0})$$

$$= e^{-2kt_0}.$$

If we simply multiply these three quantities we get the probability that one will fail in the first $t_0$, another in the next $t_0$, and the third after $2t_0$; but in a specific order. We must also account for the fact that the bulbs may burn out in $3 \cdot 2 \cdot 1 = 6$ ways. Hence the probability we want is

$$6 \times Pr(T_1 \leq t_0) \times Pr(t_0 \leq T_2 \leq 2t_0) \times Pr(T_3 \leq 2t_0)$$

$$= 6(1 - e^{-kt_0})(e^{-kt_0} - e^{-2kt_0})(e^{-2kt_0})$$

$$= 6 e^{-3kt_0} (1 - e^{-kt_0})(1 - e^{-kt_0})$$

$$= 6 e^{-3kt_0} (1 - 2e^{-kt_0} + e^{-2kt_0})$$

$$= 6 e^{-3kt_0} - 12e^{-4kt_0} + 6e^{-5kt_0} .$$

● PROBLEM 12-9

If the random variable X has an exponential distribution; i.e., $f(x) = \lambda e^{-\lambda x}$ for $X \geq 0$, show that for a,b positive

$$Pr(X > a + b \mid x > a) = Pr(X > b).$$

Solution:    First let us find

$$Pr(X > x) = \int_x^\infty f(t) \, dt = \int_x^\infty \lambda e^{-\lambda t} \, dt$$

$$= -e^{-\lambda t} \Big|_x^\infty = 0 - (-e^{-\lambda x}) = e^{-\lambda x}.$$

Now, by definition

$$Pr(X > a + b \mid x > a)$$

$$= \frac{Pr(X > a + b \text{ and } x > a)}{Pr(x > a)}.$$

But if $x > a + b$, it will be greater than a also since $b > 0$.

Thus we have

$$\frac{Pr(X > a + b)}{Pr(x > a)} = \frac{e^{-\lambda(a + b)}}{e^{-\lambda a}}$$

$$= \frac{e^{-\lambda a} e^{-\lambda b}}{e^{-\lambda a}} = e^{-\lambda b} = Pr(X > b).$$

● **PROBLEM** 12-10

This problem will show an analogy between the geometric and exponential distributions. Show that the result of the last problem holds if X is distributed geometrically.

Solution:    We want to show that if X has the distribution $Pr(X = x) = (1 - p)^{x - 1} p$, $x = 1, 2, 3, \ldots$, then for non-negative a and b

$$Pr(X > a + b \mid x > a) = Pr(x > b).$$

First find $Pr(X > k)$

$$= \sum_{x=k+1}^\infty Pr(X = x) = \sum_{x=k+1}^\infty (1 - p)^{x - 1} p$$

$$= p \sum_{k+1}^\infty (1 - p)^{x - 1} = p \sum_{k}^\infty (1 - p)^x$$

$$= p \times \text{Sum of geometric series}$$

$$= p \times \frac{\text{1st term}}{1 - (\text{common factor})} = p \frac{(1 - p)^k}{1 - (1 - p)}$$

378

$$= p \ \frac{(1 - p)^k}{p} = (1 - p)^k .$$

By definition, $\Pr(X > a + b \mid x > a)$

$$= \frac{\Pr(X > a + b \text{ and } x > a)}{\Pr(x > a)} .$$

Since $b \geq 0$, if $X > a + b$ then $X > a$ too. Hence we have

$$\frac{\Pr(X > a + b)}{\Pr(X > a)} = \frac{(1 - p)^{a + b}}{(1 - p)^a}$$

$$= \frac{(1 - p)^a (1 - p)^b}{(1 - p)^a} = (1 - p)^b$$

$$= \Pr(X > b) .$$

The last two problems may be interpreted as follows: if we have already spent some time in waiting, the distribution of further waiting time is the same as that of the initial waiting time. It is as if we waited in vain! A suggestive way of saying this is that the random variable X has no memory. This turns out to be a fundamental property of these two distributions and is basic for the theory of Markov processes. Distributions with this property are said to have the Markov property.

# GAMMA DISTRIBUTION

● PROBLEM 12-11

The following density function defines the gamma distribution:

$$f(x) = \frac{\lambda^\alpha}{\Gamma(\alpha)} \ x^{\alpha-1} \ e^{-\lambda x}, \text{ for } X > 0,$$

where $\alpha$ and $\lambda$ are positive parameters. $\Gamma(t)$, the gamma function, is defined by

$$\Gamma(t) = \int_0^\infty x^{t-1} \ e^{-x} \ dx \qquad \text{for } t > 0.$$

Integration by parts yields the following recursion relations: $\Gamma(t + 1) = t \ \Gamma(t)$, and if n is an integer $\Gamma(n + 1) = n!$. Find the moment generating function, mean, and variance of the gamma distribution.

Solution: First find the moment generating function.

$$M_x(t) = E(e^{tx}) = \int_0^\infty e^{tx} \ f(x) \ dx$$

$$= \int_0^\infty e^{tx} \frac{\lambda^\alpha}{\Gamma(\alpha)} x^{\alpha-1} e^{-\lambda x} dx$$

$$= \lambda^\alpha \int_0^\infty \frac{e^{(t-\lambda)x}}{\Gamma(\alpha)} x^{\alpha-1} dx$$

$$= \left(\frac{\lambda}{\lambda - t}\right)^\alpha \int_0^\infty \frac{(\lambda - t)^\alpha}{\Gamma(\alpha)} x^{\alpha-1} e^{-(\lambda-t)x} dx,$$
$$(t < \lambda).$$

The integral is that of a gamma distribution with parameters $\alpha$ and $\lambda - t$ and hence must be 1. Therefore

$$M_x(t) = \left(\frac{\lambda}{\lambda - t}\right)^\alpha.$$

By the properties of the moment generating function,

$$E(x) = M_x'(t) \text{ at } t = 0.$$

$$M_x'(t) = \frac{d}{dt}\left[\frac{\lambda}{\lambda - t}\right]^\alpha = \lambda^\alpha \frac{d}{dt} \frac{1}{(\lambda - t)^\alpha}$$

$$= \lambda^\alpha \frac{-\alpha}{(\lambda - t)^{\alpha+1}} (-1) = \frac{\alpha \lambda^\alpha}{(\lambda - t)^{\alpha+1}}$$

$$E(x) = M_x'(0) = \frac{\alpha \lambda^\alpha}{\lambda^{\alpha+1}} = \frac{\alpha}{\lambda}.$$

We also know

$$E(x^2) = M_x''(t)\Big|_{t=0} .$$

$$M_x''(t) = \frac{d}{dt} \frac{\alpha \lambda^\alpha}{(\lambda - t)^{\alpha+1}} = \alpha\lambda^\alpha \frac{d}{dt} \frac{1}{(\lambda - t)^{\alpha+1}}$$

$$= \alpha\lambda^\alpha \frac{-(\alpha + 1)}{(\lambda - t)^{\alpha+2}} (-1) = \frac{\alpha (\alpha + 1) \lambda^\alpha}{(\lambda - t)^{\alpha+2}}$$

$$E(x^2) = M_x''(0) = \frac{\alpha (\alpha + 1)\lambda^\alpha}{\lambda^{\alpha+2}} = \frac{\alpha (\alpha + 1)}{\lambda^2}.$$

Finally, $\text{Var}(X) = E(x^2) - (E(x))^2$

$$= \frac{\alpha (\alpha + 1)}{\lambda^2} - \frac{\alpha^2}{\lambda^2}$$

$$= \frac{\alpha^2 + \alpha - \alpha^2}{\lambda^2} = \frac{\alpha}{\lambda^2}.$$

The probability density of time between arrivals at Macy's service counter is

$$f(t_i) = 4\ e^{-4t_i} \qquad t_i > 0.$$

Find the probability density for the time to the tenth arrival.

Solution:     If we consider the time to the first arrival as $T_1$; between the first and second as $T_2$; etc., we are looking for the distribution of

$$T = T_1 + T_2 + T_3 + T_4 + T_5 + T_6 + T_7 + T_8 + T_9 + T_{10}\ ,$$

the sum of 10 identically distributed exponential random variables.

In the chapter on Functions of a Random Variable, we will prove, using the moment generating function technique, that the sum of r exponential distributions with identical parameter $\lambda$ is gamma distributed with parameters r and $\lambda$. Hence

$$f(t) = \frac{\lambda^r\ t^{r-1}\ e^{-\lambda t}}{\Gamma\ (r)} \qquad \begin{array}{l} t > 0 \\ r > 1\ . \end{array}$$

But we know r is an integer. (It is the number of distributions added.) For an integer r, we know

$$\Gamma\ (r) = (r-1)!\ . \qquad \text{Therefore}$$

$$f(t) = \frac{\lambda^r\ t^{r-1}\ e^{-\lambda t}}{(r-1)!}\ .$$

In this problem $r = 10$ and $\lambda = 4$

$$f(t) = \frac{4^{10}\ t^{10-1}\ e^{-4t}}{(10-1)!}$$

$$= \frac{4^{10}\ t^9\ e^{-4t}}{9!}\ .$$

# CHAPTER 13

# SAMPLING THEORY

## RANDOM SAMPLES

Suppose that a sociologist desires to study the religious habits of 20-year-old males in the United States. He draws a sample from the 20-year-old males of a large city to make his study. Describe the sampled and target populations. What problems arise in drawing conclusions from this data?

Solution: The sampled population consists of the 20-year-old males in the city which the sociologist samples.

The target population consists of the 20-year-old males in the United States.

In drawing conclusions about the target population, the researcher must be careful. His data may not reflect religious habits of 20-year-old males in the United States but rather the religious habits of 20-year-old males in the city that was surveyed. The reliability of the extrapolation cannot be measured in probabilistic terms.

Each of the following sampling procedures is to be classified as producing a random sample or as producing a biased sample. Consider each case and decide whether the procedure is random or biased.

a. The population about which inference is to be made is a population of scores in dart throwing, and the question to be decided is whether men achieve higher scores than women. The investigator selects 10 men and 10 women at random; he then obtains five scores from each, making a sample of 100 scores. Is this a random sample?

b. In attacking the same problem, the investigator takes 100 averages of five scores, each average coming from a different randomly selected person. Is this sample of average scores a random sample?

c. The population of interest is a population of attitude scores at Alpha College; assume that it is an infinite population. The experimenter whishes to obtain a sample of about 100 scores. He administers the attitude test to four existing groups. In this case they are four classes selected at random whose total enrollment is 100. Is this a random sample?

d. The same investigator interested in attitude scores sends out the attitude test by mail to a sample of 100 students whose names he has selected by taking every seventy-fifth name in the student directory after randomly choosing a starting point. He receives 71 completed tests; the other 29 students fail to respond. Is the original list a random sample? Is the sample of 71 tests random?

Solution: A sample must meet the following conditions in order to be random:

1)   Equal Chance. A sample meets the condition of equal chance if it is selected in such a way that every observation in the entire population has an equal chance of being included in the sample.

2)   Independence. A sample meets this condition when the selection of any single observation does not affect the chances for selection of any other.

Samples that are not random are called biased.

a)   Independence is violated, since each member of a set of 5 scores comes with the other four. This example is important, because it is very common to use repeated measures of the same individual. A set of N observations on K persons, where each person contributes N/K of the N observations, is not a random sample if N is greater than K.

b)   The 100 elements are now independent. When repeated measures can be converted to a single score, so that each individual observed contributes just one summary observation (such as an average), the independence condition is met. Use of an average often helps to reduce the effects of chance variation within an individuals performance. Also any observation would have an equal chance of being chosen. The sample is random.

c)   The sample is biased since any one score is not independent of selection of the other scores from the same class. This example is another common situation. It is more convenient to get measures from existing groups, but such a procedure does not produce independent observations.

d)   The list is random, but the completed test sample is probably biased. It is impossible to know whether the factors determining "response to the requests" were random, and since it is quite possible that both equal chance and independence were violated, it is best to assume that the sample is biased.

● PROBLEM 13-3

A wheat researcher is studying the yield of a certain variety of wheat in the state of Colorado. He has at his disposal five farms scattered throughout the state on which he can plant the wheat and observe the yield. Describe the sampled population and the target population. Under what conditions will this be a random sample?

Solution: The sampled population consists of the wheat yields on the five farms.

The target population consists of the yields of wheat on every farm in the state. This sample will be random if 1) every farm in the state has an equal chance of being selected and 2) the selection of any particular farm is independent of the selection of any other farm.

A population consists of the number of defective transistors in shipments received by an assembly plant.  The number of defectives is 2 in the first, 4 in the second, 6 in the third, and 8 in the fourth.

(a)  Find the mean $\bar{x}$ and the standard deviation $s'_x$ of the given population.

(b)  List all random samples, with replacement, of size 2 that can be formed from the population and find the distribution of the sample mean.

(c)  Find the mean and the standard deviation of the sample mean.

**Solution:**  The population is  2,4,6,8.

a)  $\bar{x} = \dfrac{\sum\limits_{i=1}^{n} x_i}{n} = \dfrac{\sum\limits_{i=1}^{4} x_i}{4} = \dfrac{2 + 4 + 6 + 8}{4} = \dfrac{20}{4} = 5$ .

We will compute

$$s'_x = \sqrt{\dfrac{\sum\limits_{i=1}^{n} (x - \bar{x})^2}{n}} = \sqrt{\dfrac{(2-5)^2 + (4-5)^2 + (6-5)^2 + (8-5)^2}{4}}$$

$$= \sqrt{\dfrac{9 + 1 + 1 + 9}{4}} = \sqrt{\dfrac{20}{4}} = \sqrt{5} .$$

b)  The following table should prove useful.

| | Sample | Sample Mean |
|---|---|---|
| 1. | 2,2 | 2 |
| 2. | 2,4 | 3 |
| 3. | 2,6 | 4 |
| 4. | 2,8 | 5 |
| 5. | 4,2 | 3 |
| 6. | 4,4 | 4 |
| 7. | 4,6 | 5 |
| 8. | 4,8 | 6 |
| 9. | 6,2 | 4 |
| 10. | 6,4 | 5 |
| 11. | 6,6 | 6 |
| 12. | 6,8 | 7 |
| 13. | 8,2 | 5 |
| 14. | 8,4 | 6 |
| 15. | 8,6 | 7 |
| 16. | 8,8 | 8 |

Collating the data we have

| x = Sample Mean | N(x) = Number of times x occurs | F(x) = N(x)/n = N(x)/16 |
|---|---|---|
| 2 | 1 | 1/16 |
| 3 | 2 | 1/8 |
| 4 | 3 | 3/16 |
| 5 | 4 | 1/4 |
| 6 | 3 | 3/16 |
| 7 | 2 | 1/8 |
| 8 | 1 | 1/16 |

c)  Sample Mean $= \dfrac{\sum\limits_{i=1}^{n} i^{th} \text{ Sample Mean}}{n}$

$= \dfrac{2+3+4+5+3+4+5+6+4+5+6+7+5+6+7+8}{16}$

$= \dfrac{80}{16} = 5 .$

$s'_{\bar{x}} = \sqrt{\dfrac{\Sigma(sm - \overline{sm})^2}{n}}$

$= \sqrt{\dfrac{(2-5)^2+2(3-5)^2+3(4-5)^2+4(5-5)^2+3(6-5)^2+2(7-5)^2+(8-5)^2}{16}}$

$= \sqrt{\dfrac{9+8+3+0+3+8+9}{16}} = \sqrt{\dfrac{40}{16}} = \sqrt{\dfrac{5}{2}} .$

● **PROBLEM** 13-5

It helps to remember that the total of all probabilities in a sampling distribution is always 1.      If the probability of a sample mean between 19 and 21 is 0.9544 (i.e., 95% of the time), what is the probability of a sample mean that is not between 19 and 21 (either less than 19 or more than 21)?

Solution: Let $\bar{x}$ be the random variable denoting the sample mean. We are given that

$$\Pr(19 < \bar{x} < 21) = .9544$$

and are asked to find

$$\Pr(\bar{x} \text{ is not between 19 and 21}) .$$

If $\bar{x}$ is not between 19 and 21 then either $\bar{x} < 19$ or $\bar{x} > 21$. These two events are mutually exclusive. That is, if $\bar{x} < 19$ then $\bar{x}$ cannot possibly be greater than 21 and if $\bar{x} > 21$ then $\bar{x}$ cannot be less than 19.  Thus,

$$\Pr(\bar{x} \text{ is not between 19 and 21})$$
$$= \Pr(\bar{x} < 19 \text{ or } \bar{x} > 21)$$
$$= \Pr(\bar{x} < 19) + \Pr(\bar{x} > 21) .$$

We also know that the events $19 < \bar{x} < 21$ and $\bar{x}$ not between 19 and 21 are exhaustive, i.e., they 'exhaust' all the alternatives for the values of $\bar{x}$ .  Thus,

$$\Pr(19 < \bar{x} < 21) + \Pr(\bar{x} \text{ not between 19 and 21}) = 1 .$$

Thus,

$$\Pr(\bar{x} \text{ not between 19 and 21})$$
$$= \Pr(\bar{x} < 19 \text{ or } \bar{x} > 21) = 1 - \Pr(19 < \bar{x} < 21)$$
$$= 1 - .9544$$
$$= .0456 .$$

# WEAK LAW OF LARGE NUMBERS

Suppose that some distribution with an unknown mean has variance equal to 1. How large a sample must be taken in order that the probability will be at least .95 that the sample mean $\bar{X}_n$ will lie within .5 of the population mean?

Solution: This problem involves the Weak Law of Large Numbers. In order to establish the law we must first verify the following lemma.

Lemma: Let X be a random variable and g(X) a non-negative function with the real line as a domain; then

$$\Pr[g(X) \geq K] \leq \frac{E[g(X)]}{K} \quad \text{for all } K > 0 .$$

Proof of Lemma: Assume that X is a continuous random variable.(a similar proof will hold for X discrete ) with probability density f(x); then by definition

$$E(g(x)) = \int_{-\infty}^{\infty} g(x) \ f(x)dx$$

$$= \int_{\{x:g(x)\geq K\}} g(x)f(x)dx + \int_{\{x:g(x)<K\}} g(x)f(x)dx$$

$$\geq \int_{\{x:g(x)\geq K\}} g(x)f(x)dx .$$

Since $g(x) \geq h(x) = K$ in the domain of integration, this is greater than or equal to

$$\int_{\{x:g(x)\geq K} Kf(x)dx = K \int_{\{x:g(x)\geq K} f(x)dx$$

$$= K \Pr(g(x) \geq K) .$$

Now divide by K and obtain

$$\frac{E(g(x))}{K} \geq \Pr(g(x) \geq K) .$$

An equivalent result to this lemma is
$$\Pr(g(x) < K) \geq 1 - \frac{E(g(x))}{K}$$

because
$$\Pr(g(x) < K) = 1 - \Pr(g(x) \geq K) .$$

Now let $g(x) = (\bar{X}_n - \mu)^2$ and $K = \epsilon^2$ ; then

$$\Pr((\bar{X}_n - \mu)^2 < \epsilon^2) \geq 1 - \frac{1}{\epsilon^2} E((\bar{X}_n - \mu)^2) .$$

Equivalently
$$\Pr(-\epsilon < \bar{X}_n - \mu < \epsilon) \geq 1 - \frac{E((\bar{X}_n - \mu)^2)}{\epsilon^2}$$

or
$$\Pr(|\bar{X}_n - \mu| < \epsilon) \geq 1 - \frac{E((\bar{X}_n - \mu)^2)}{\epsilon^2} .$$

But $E((\bar{X}_n - \mu)^2) = Var(\bar{X}) = Var(\frac{\Sigma x}{n}) = Var[\frac{1}{n}(X_1 + X_2 + \ldots + X_n)]$

$$= \frac{1}{n^2} Var(X_1 + \ldots + X_n)$$

since $Var(aX) = a^2 Var(X)$. But the $X_i$ will be assumed independent. Therefore

$$\frac{1}{n^2} Var(X_1 + \ldots + X_n) = \frac{1}{n^2} [Var(X_1) + Var(X_2) + \ldots + Var(X_n)]$$

$$= \frac{1}{n^2} n Var(X) = \frac{\sigma^2}{n} .$$

Thus, $$Pr(|\bar{X}_n - \mu| < \epsilon) \geq 1 - \frac{\sigma^2}{n\epsilon^2} .$$

This is the Weak Law of Large Numbers.
  In the present problem, we want

$$Pr(|\bar{X}_n - \mu| < .5) \geq .95 = 1 - .05.$$

Comparing this with the general statement of the Weak Law of Large Numbers we set $\epsilon = .5$, $\sigma^2/n\epsilon^2 = .05$. Multiplying through by $n/.05$ we see that we would need an $n \geq \sigma^2/.05\epsilon^2$ . Here then

$$n \geq \frac{1}{(.05)(.5)^2} = \frac{1}{.05(.25)} = \frac{1}{.0125}$$

$$n \geq 80.$$

We must therefore choose a sample of at least 80.

● **PROBLEM** 13-7

How large a sample must be taken in order that you are 99 percent certain that $\bar{X}_n$ is within $.5\sigma$ of $\mu$ ?

Solution: The general statement of the Weak Law of Large Numbers is
$$Pr(|\bar{X}_n - \mu| < \epsilon) \geq 1 - \frac{\sigma^2}{n\epsilon^2} .$$
We want
$$Pr(|X_n - \mu| < .5\sigma) \geq 1 - .01 = .99 .$$

We set $\epsilon = .5\sigma$ and $\frac{\sigma^2}{n\epsilon^2} = .01$ . Multiplying through by $\frac{n}{.01}$ we see
$$n = \frac{\sigma^2}{.01\epsilon^2} = \frac{\sigma^2}{.01(.5\sigma)^2} = \frac{\sigma^2}{.01(.25)\sigma^2} = \frac{1}{.0025} = 400 .$$

# THE CENTRAL LIMIT THEOREM AND DISTRIBUTION OF THE SAMPLE MEAN

● **PROBLEM** 13-8

Briefly discuss the Central Limit Theorem.

Solution: The theorem has to do with the means of large (greater than 30) samples. As the sample size increases, the distribution of the sample mean, $\bar{X}$, has a distribution which is approximately normal. This distribution has a mean equal to the population mean and a standard deviation equal to the population standard deviation divided by the square root of the sample size.

Since $\bar{X}$ is approximately normal, $\dfrac{\bar{X} - E(\bar{X})}{\sigma_{\bar{X}}} = \dfrac{\bar{X} - \mu}{\sigma/\sqrt{n}} = \dfrac{\sqrt{n}(\bar{X} - \mu)}{\sigma}$

will have a standard normal distribution.

● **PROBLEM** 13-9

For a large sample, the distribution of $\bar{X}$ is always approximately normal. Find the probability that a random sample mean lies within
a)  one standard error of the mean.
b)  two standard errors.

<u>Solution</u>:  a)  The question asks what is $\Pr(\mu_{\bar{X}} - \sigma_{\bar{X}} < \bar{X} < \mu_{\bar{X}} + \sigma_{\bar{X}})$ ?

If $\bar{X}$ is approximately normally distributed,

$$\dfrac{\bar{X} - \mu_{\bar{X}}}{\sigma_{\bar{X}}}$$

will be standard normal. Let $\mu_{\bar{X}} = \mu, \sigma_{\bar{X}} = \sigma$.

Note $\Pr(\mu - \sigma < \bar{x} < \mu + \sigma)$

$$= \Pr\left(\dfrac{(\mu - \sigma) - \mu}{\sigma} < \dfrac{\bar{x} - \mu}{\sigma} < \dfrac{(\mu + \sigma) - \mu}{\sigma}\right)$$

$$= \Pr(-1 < \text{Standard Normal Quantity} < 1)$$

$$= .6826 \text{ from the tables.}$$

b)  We now want

$$\Pr(\mu_{\bar{X}} - 2\sigma_{\bar{X}} < \bar{X} < \mu_{\bar{X}} + 2\sigma_{\bar{X}}) .$$

Again assuming $\bar{X}$ is approximately normally distributed, $\dfrac{\bar{X} - \mu_{\bar{X}}}{\sigma_{\bar{X}}}$

will be standard normal. Again, for ease of reading, let $\mu_{\bar{X}} = \mu, \sigma_{\bar{X}} = \sigma$.

Using a similar procedure,

$$\Pr(\mu_{\bar{X}} - 2\sigma_{\bar{X}} < \bar{X} < \mu_{\bar{X}} + 2\sigma_{\bar{X}}) = \Pr\left(\dfrac{\mu - 2\sigma - \mu}{\sigma} < \dfrac{\bar{x} - \mu}{\sigma} < \dfrac{\mu + 2\sigma - \mu}{\sigma}\right)$$

$$= \Pr(-2 < \text{Standard Normal Quantity} < 2)$$

$$= .9544 \text{ from the table.}$$

These problems can be completely generalized. Any normal distribution has 68.26 % of the probability within one standard deviation of the mean and 95.44% within two.

A population of Australian Koala bears has a mean height of 20 inches and a standard deviation of 4 inches. You plan to choose a a sample of 64 bears at random. What is the probability of a sample mean between 20 and 21?

Solution: Our method of attack will be to transform 20 and 21 into standard normal statistics. The sample is large enough, 64, so that the Central Limit Theorem will apply and $\sqrt{n}(\bar{X} - \mu)/\sigma$ will approximate a standard normal statistic.

We want to know

$$Pr(20 < \bar{X} < 21).$$

Equivalently we want to know

$$Pr\left(\frac{(20 - \mu)\sqrt{n}}{\sigma} < \frac{\sqrt{n}(\bar{X} - \mu)}{\sigma} < \sqrt{n}(21 - \mu)\right)$$

or

$$Pr\left(\frac{\sqrt{n}(20 - \mu)}{\sigma} < Z < \frac{\sqrt{n}(21 - \mu)}{\sigma}\right).$$

Substituting the values $n = 64$, $\mu = 20$, and $\sigma = 4$, we obtain

$$Pr\left(\frac{\sqrt{64}(20 - 20)}{4} < Z < \frac{\sqrt{64}(21 - 20)}{4}\right)$$

$$= Pr(0 < Z < 2).$$

From the standard normal table, this is .4772.

The mean diameter of marbles manufactured at a particular toy factory is 0.850 cm with a standard deviation of 0.010 cm. What is the probability of selecting a random sample of 100 marbles that has a mean diameter greater than 0.851 cm?

Solution: Our sample is of size 100, certainly large enough for the Central Limit Theorem to apply. We will use this theorem to assume that $\sqrt{n}(\bar{X} - \mu)/\sigma$ is a standard normal statistic.

We want to know $Pr(\bar{X} > .851)$. This is equivalent to

$$Pr\left(\frac{\sqrt{n}(\bar{X} - \mu)}{\sigma} > \frac{\sqrt{n}(.851 - \mu)}{\sigma}\right),$$

or by the Central Limit Theorem

$$Pr\left(Z > \frac{\sqrt{n}(.851 - \mu)}{\sigma}\right).$$

Make the substitutions $\mu = .850$, $\sigma = .01$, and $n = 100$, to obtain

$$Pr\left(Z > \frac{\sqrt{100}(.851 - .850)}{.01}\right) = Pr\left(Z > \frac{10(.001)}{.01}\right) = Pr(Z > 1)$$

$$= 1 - Pr(Z < 1) = 1 - .841 = .159,$$

from the standard normal tables.

An electrical firm manufactures a certain type of light bulb that has a mean life of 1,800 hours and a standard deviation of 200 hours.
(a) Find the probability that a random sample of 100 bulbs will have an average life of more than 1,825 hours.
(b) Find the probability that a random sample of 100 bulbs will have an average life of not more than 1,775 hours and not less than 1,760 hours.

Solution: a) We have a large sample of 100. The Central Limit Theorem can therefore be used. $\sqrt{n}(\bar{X} - \mu)/\sigma$ will be approximately standard normal. We are here asked for

$$Pr(\bar{X} > 1825).$$

This is equivalent to

$$Pr\left( \frac{\sqrt{n}(\bar{X} - \mu)}{\sigma} > \frac{\sqrt{n}(1825 - \mu)}{\sigma} \right).$$

Substituting $n = 100$, $\mu = 1800$, and $\sigma = 200$, we obtain

$$Pr\left( \frac{\sqrt{n}(\bar{X} - \mu)}{\sigma} > \frac{\sqrt{100}(1825 - 1800)}{200} \right)$$

$$= Pr\left( \text{Standard Normal Quantity} > \frac{10(25)}{200} \right)$$

$$= Pr(Z > 1.25) = 1 - .8944 = .1056 ,$$

from the standard normal tables.

b) We now want $Pr(1760 < \bar{x} < 1775)$. We transform into standard normal quantities as follows:

$$Pr \frac{n(1760 - \mu)}{\sigma} < \frac{\sqrt{n}(\bar{x} - \mu)}{\sigma} < \frac{\sqrt{n}(1775 - \mu)}{\sigma} ,$$

which is equal to

$$Pr \frac{\sqrt{n}(1760 - \mu)}{\sigma} < \text{Standard Normal} < \frac{\sqrt{n}(1775 - \mu)}{\sigma} .$$

Substituting $n = 100$, $\mu = 1800$ and $\sigma = 200$, we obtain

$$Pr \frac{100 (1760 - 1800)}{200} < z < \frac{100 (1775 - 1800)}{200}$$

$$= Pr \frac{10(-40)}{200} < z < \frac{10(-25)}{200}$$

$$= Pr( -2 < z < -1.25) = Pr(1.25 < z < 2)$$

by the symmetry of the normal curve. Using the standard normal table, this is found to be .0828.

A manufacturing company receives a shipment of ball bearings each month from a supplier. The inspectors apply the following rule in deciding whether to accept or reject each shipment. A random sample of 36 bearings is selected and measured. If the mean diameter of the sample is between .245 and .255, the shipment is accepted; otherwise it is rejected.

(a) What is the probability of accepting a shipment that has a mean diameter of .24 inches and a standard deviation of .015 inches?

**(b)** What is the probability of accepting a shipment that has a mean diameter of .2515 inches and a standard deviation of .005 inches?

**Solution:** a) The question rephrased is: for a sample of size 36 (n = 36) from a shipment that has $\mu$ = .24 and $\sigma$ = .015, what is $Pr(.245 < \bar{X} < .255)$? This is equivalent to asking, what is

$$Pr\left(\frac{\sqrt{n}(.245 - \mu)}{\sigma} < \frac{\sqrt{n}(\bar{X} - \mu)}{\sigma} < \frac{\sqrt{n}(.255 - \mu)}{\sigma}\right)$$

$$= Pr\left(\frac{\sqrt{36}(.245 - .24)}{.015} < \frac{\sqrt{n}(\bar{X} - \mu)}{\sigma} < \frac{\sqrt{36}(.255 - .24)}{.015}\right)$$

$$= Pr\left(\frac{6(.005)}{.015} < \frac{\sqrt{n}(\bar{X} - \mu)}{\sigma} < \frac{6(.015)}{.015}\right)$$

$$= Pr\left(2 < \frac{\sqrt{n}(\bar{X} - \mu)}{\sigma} < 6\right) .$$

A sample of size 36 is large enough for the Central Limit Theorem to apply. Hence $\sqrt{n}(\bar{X} - \mu)/\sigma$ is a standard normal quantity. We now have

$$Pr(2 < Z < 6) \cong Pr(Z > 2)$$

since $Pr(Z > 6)$ is negligibly small; $Pr(Z > 2)$ = .0228 from the table.

b) We still want $Pr(.245 < \bar{X} < .255)$, but now n = 36, $\mu$ = .2515, and $\sigma$ = .005. We perform the same series of operations,

$$Pr(.245 < \bar{X} < .255) = Pr\left(\frac{\sqrt{n}(.245 - \mu)}{\sigma} < \bar{X} < \frac{\sqrt{n}(.255 - \mu)}{\sigma}\right)$$

$$= Pr\left(\frac{\sqrt{36}(.245 - .2515)}{.005} < \frac{\sqrt{n}(\bar{X} - \mu)}{\sigma} < \frac{\sqrt{36}(.255 - .2515)}{.005}\right)$$

$$= Pr\left(\frac{6(-.0065)}{.005} < \text{Standard Normal Quantity} < \frac{6(.0035)}{.005}\right)$$

$$= Pr(-7.8 < Z < 4.2) = \text{virtually } 1 \text{, from the standard normal}$$
table.

● **PROBLEM** 13-14

Suppose that light bulbs made by a standard process have an average life of 2000 hours, with a standard deviation of 250 hours, and suppose that it is worthwhile to change the process if the mean life can be increased by at least 10 percent. An engineer wishes to test a proposed new process, and he is willing to assume that the standard deviation of the distribution of lives is about the same as for the standard process. How large a sample should he examine if he wishes the probability to be about .01 that he will fail to adopt the new process if in fact it produces bulbs with a mean life of 2250 hours?

**Solution:** For the engineer to adopt the process the new mean must be a ten percent increase over the old. Since 10 percent of 2000 is 200, the new sample mean would have to be at least 2200. Since we know that the true mean is 2250, then $\bar{X}$ - would have to be less than -50 in order to reject it. We want $Pr(\bar{X} - \angle -50)$ = .01. Divide by

$\frac{\sigma}{\sqrt{n}}$ to obtain $Pr\left(\frac{\bar{X} - \mu}{\sigma/\sqrt{n}} < -\frac{50}{\sigma/\sqrt{n}}\right) = .01.$

By the Central Limit Theorem, $\frac{\bar{X} - \mu}{\sigma/\sqrt{n}}$ is a standard normal quantity.

Hence we have $Pr(Z < -\frac{50}{\sigma/\sqrt{n}}) = .01.$ The standard normal table tells

us $Pr(Z < -2.33) = .01$ ; as a result set

Now set $-\frac{50}{\sigma/\sqrt{n}} = -2.33.$ But since $\sigma = 250$, we have

$\left(\frac{50}{250}\right)\sqrt{n} = 2.33$ $\qquad\qquad \sqrt{n} = 11.65$

$$n = 135.7275.$$

The sample should include at least 136 observations.

● **PROBLEM** 13-15

A research worker wishes to estimate the mean of a population using a sample large enough that the probability will be .95 that the sample mean will not differ from the population mean by more than 25 percent of the standard deviation. How large a sample should he take?

<u>Solution</u>: 25 percent of the standard deviation is ¼ of it, $\sigma/4$. We want

$$Pr(|\bar{X} - \mu| < \sigma/4) = .95.$$

Equivalently, $\qquad Pr(-\frac{\sigma}{4} < \bar{X} - \mu < \frac{\sigma}{4}) = .95$ .

Divide through by $\sigma/\sqrt{n}$ :

$$Pr\left(\frac{\bar{X} - \mu}{\sigma/\sqrt{n}} < \frac{\sigma/4}{\sigma/\sqrt{n}}\right) = .95$$

or

$$Pr\left(\frac{\bar{X} - \mu}{\sigma/\sqrt{n}} < \frac{\sqrt{n}}{4}\right) = .95 .$$

By the Central Limit Theorem, $\frac{\bar{X} - \mu}{\sigma/\sqrt{n}}$ has a standard normal distribution.

Therefore $\qquad Pr(\text{Standard Normal Quantity} < \sqrt{n}/4) = .95.$
From the standard normal tables we know,

$$Pr(-1.96 < \text{Standard Normal} < 1.96) = .95.$$

Now set

$$1.96 = \frac{\sqrt{n}}{4}$$

$$4(1.96) = \sqrt{n}$$

$$\sqrt{n} = 7.84$$

$$n = 61.4656.$$

The research worker would have to take a sample of at least 62 observations.

Car batteries produced by company A have a mean life of 3.5 years with a standard deviation of .4 years. A similar battery produced by company B has a mean life of 3.3 years and a standard deviation of .3 years. What is the probability that a random sample of 25 batteries from company A will have a mean life of at least .4 years more than the mean life of a sample of 36 batteries from company B?

<u>Solution</u>: The problem supplies us with the following data:

Propulation A: $\mu_1 = 3.5$  $\sigma_1 = .4$  $n_1 = 25$
Population B: $\mu_2 = 3.3$  $\sigma_2 = .3$  $n_2 = 36$

We are dealing with samples large enough to assume that the sample means, $\bar{X}_1$ and $\bar{X}_2$, are approximately normally distributed. Their difference $\bar{X}_1 - \bar{X}_2$ will then also be approximately normally distributed.

By the linearity properties of expectation

$$E(\bar{X}_1 - \bar{X}_2) = E(\bar{X}_1) + E(-\bar{X}_2) = E(\bar{X}_1) - E(\bar{X}_2) = \mu_1 - \mu_2 \ .$$

By the property $Var(aX + bY) = a^2 Var(X) + b^2 Var(Y)$, for $X$ and $Y$ independent, $Var(\bar{X}_1 - \bar{X}_2) = Var(\bar{X}_1 + (-\bar{X}_2)) = Var(\bar{X}_1) + (-1)^2 Var(\bar{X}_2) = $

$$Var(\bar{X}_1) + Var(\bar{X}_2) = \frac{\sigma_1^2}{n_1} + \frac{\sigma_2^2}{n_2} \ . \quad \sigma_{\bar{X}_1 - \bar{X}_2} = \sqrt{Var(X_1 - X_2)} = \sqrt{\frac{\sigma_1^2}{n_1} + \frac{\sigma_2^2}{n_2}} \ .$$

Applying these general results, we see $\bar{X}_1 - \bar{X}_2$ is normally distributed with mean $\mu_1 - \mu_2 = 3.5 - 3.3 = .2$, and standard deviation

$$\sqrt{\frac{\sigma_1^2}{n_1} + \frac{\sigma_2^2}{n_1}} = \sqrt{\frac{.16}{25} + \frac{.09}{36}} = .094 \ .$$

We are asked for $Pr[(\bar{X}_1 - \bar{X}_2) > .4]$. Subtracting $\mu_1 - \mu_2$ and dividing by $\sqrt{\sigma_1^2/n_1 + \sigma_2^2/n_2}$ we obtain

$$Pr\left[\frac{(\bar{X}_1 - \bar{X}_2) - (\mu_1 - \mu_2)}{\sqrt{\sigma_1^2/n_1 + \sigma_2^2/n_2}} > \frac{.4 - (\mu_1 - \mu_2)}{\sqrt{\sigma_1^2/n_1 + \sigma_2^2/n_2}}\right]$$

The Central Limit Theorem tells us

$$\frac{(\bar{X}_1 - \bar{X}_2) - (\mu_1 - \mu_2)}{\sqrt{\sigma_1^2/n_1 + \sigma_2^2/n_2}} = \frac{(\bar{X}_1 - \bar{X}_2) - E(\bar{X}_1 - \bar{X}_2)}{\sigma_{(\bar{X}_1 - \bar{X}_2)}}$$

is approximately standard normal. We now only want

$$Pr\left(Standard\ Normal > \frac{.4 - (\mu_1 - \mu_2)}{\sqrt{\sigma_1^2/n_1 + \sigma_2^2/n_2}}\right)$$

$$= Pr\left(Z > \frac{.4 - .2}{.094}\right) = Pr(Z > 2.13) = 1 - Pr(Z < 2.13)$$

= 1 - .9834

= .0166 using standard normal tables.

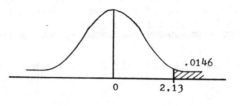

.0146

0    2.13

Random samples of size 100 are drawn, with replacement, from two populations, $P_1$ and $P_2$, and their means, $\bar{X}_1$ and $\bar{X}_2$, computed. If $\mu_1 = 10$, $\sigma_1 = 2$, $\mu_2 = 8$, and $\sigma_2 = 1$, find

(a) $E(\bar{X}_1 - \bar{X}_2)$;

(b) $\sigma_{(\bar{X}_1 - \bar{X}_2)}$ ;

(c) the probability that the difference between a given pair of sample means is less than 1.5;

(d) the probability that the difference between a given pair of sample means is greater than 1.75 but less than 2.5.

**Solution:**  a)  By the linearity properties of the expectation operator
$$E(\bar{X}_1 - \bar{X}_2) = E(\bar{X}_1) - E(\bar{X}_2) = \mu_1 - \mu_2 = 10 - 8 = 2.$$

b)  $\bar{X}_1$ and $\bar{X}_2$ are independent.  In light of this we can say
$$\text{Var}(a\bar{X}_1 + b\bar{X}_2) = a^2 \text{Var}(\bar{X}_1) + b^2 \text{Var}(\bar{X}_2) .$$

In our case  $a = 1$  and  $b = -1$.  $\text{Var}(\bar{X}_1 - \bar{X}_2) = 1^2 \text{Var}(\bar{X}_1) + (-1)^2 \text{Var}(\bar{X}_2)$

$= \text{Var}(\bar{X}_1) + \text{Var}(\bar{X}_2) = \sigma_1^2/n_1 + \sigma_2^2/n_2$ .  Finally

$$\sigma_{(\bar{X}_1 - \bar{X}_2)} = \sqrt{\text{Var}(\bar{X}_1 - \bar{X}_2)} = \sqrt{\sigma_1^2/n_1 + \sigma_2^2/n_2} =$$

$$= \sqrt{\frac{2^2}{100} + \frac{1^2}{100}} = \sqrt{\frac{5}{100}} = \frac{\sqrt{5}}{10} .$$

c)  We want  $\Pr(|\bar{X}_1 - \bar{X}_2| < 1.5)$  or equivalently

$$\Pr(-1.5 < \bar{X}_1 - \bar{X}_2 < 1.5) .$$

Subtract  $E(\bar{X}_1 - \bar{X}_2) = 2$  and divide by  $\sigma_{(\bar{X}_1 - \bar{X}_2)} = \frac{\sqrt{5}}{10}$  to obtain

$$\Pr\left(\frac{-1.5-2}{\sqrt{5}/10} < \frac{(\bar{X}_1 - \bar{X}_2) - E(\bar{X}_1 - \bar{X}_2)}{\sigma_{\bar{X}_1 - \bar{X}_2}} < \frac{1.5-2}{\sqrt{5}/10}\right)$$

$$= \Pr\left(-15.652< \frac{(\bar{X}_1 - \bar{X}_2) - E(\bar{X}_1 - \bar{X}_2)}{\sigma_{\bar{X}_1 - \bar{X}_2}} < -2.236\right) .$$

The Central Limit Theorem tells us that since we have large samples

$$\frac{(\bar{X}_1 - \bar{X}_2) - E(\bar{X}_1 - \bar{X}_2)}{\sigma_{\bar{X}_1 - \bar{X}_2}}$$ is approximately standard normal. We then have

Pr(-15.652< Standard Normal < -2.236) $\cong$ Pr(Standard Normal < -2.236), since the area under the standard normal curve to the left of -15.652 is negligible.

From the standard normal tables
$$\Pr(Z \le -2.236) \cong .0127.$$

d) To solve this, we will follow exactly the method of part c). We want Pr(-1.75 $< \bar{X} - \bar{X}_2 < 2.5$). As in c), this is equivalent to

$$\Pr\left(\frac{1.75-2}{5/10} < \frac{(\bar{X}_1 - \bar{X}_2) - E(\bar{X}_1 - \bar{X}_2)}{\sigma_{\bar{X}_1 - \bar{X}_2}} < \frac{2.5-2}{5/10}\right)$$

= Pr(-1.118< Standard Normal < 2.236)

= Pr(-1.12 < z < 0) + Pr(0 < z < 2.24)

(by the symmetry of the standard normal curve)

= .3686 + .4875 = .8561.

● **PROBLEM 13-18**

A seed company advertises that it has developed an early tomato that will produce ripe tomatoes in 54 days with a standard deviation of 4 days. Another seed company advertises that they have developed an early tomato that will produce ripe tomatoes in 60 days with a standard deviation of 6 days. A gardener makes a number of plantings of seed from each company, and each planting contains 400 seeds. The mean number of days $\bar{X}_1$ before ripe tomatoes for each planting from the first seed company was found. The average number of days $\bar{X}_2$ for each planting from the second company was found. Assume that the conditions were identical for each planting and find the probability that the difference between any one sample mean taken from seeds produced by the first company and any one sample mean taken from seeds developed by the second company is less than 5 days.

<u>Solution</u>: We begin with some preliminary observations: $\mu_1 = 54$, $\sigma_1 = 4$, $\mu_2 = 60$, $\sigma_2 = 6$, $E(\bar{X}_1 - \bar{X}_2) = \mu_1 - \mu_2 = 60 - 54 = 6$, and

$$\sigma_{(\bar{X}_1 - \bar{X}_2)} = \sqrt{\sigma_1^2/n_1 + \sigma_2^2/n_2} = \sqrt{4^2/400 + 6^2/400} = \sqrt{52/400} = .36 .$$

The problem asks for $\Pr(|\bar{X}_1 - \bar{X}_2| < 5)$ or equivalently, what is

Pr(-5 < $\bar{X}_1 - \bar{X}_2$ < 5)? We subtract $E(\bar{X}_1 - \bar{X}_2)$ and divide by $\sigma_{\bar{X}-Y}$ and the result is

$$\Pr\left(\frac{-5-E(\bar{X}_1-\bar{X}_2)}{\sigma_{\bar{X}_1-\bar{X}_2}} < \frac{(\bar{X}_1-\bar{X}_2) - E(\bar{X}_1-\bar{X}_2)}{\sigma_{\bar{X}_1-\bar{X}_2}} < \frac{5 - E(\bar{X}_1-\bar{X}_2)}{\sigma_{\bar{X}_1-\bar{X}_2}}\right) .$$

By the Central Limit Theorem,

$$\frac{(\bar{X}_1-\bar{X}_2) - E(\bar{X}_1-\bar{X}_2)}{\sigma_{\bar{X}_1-\bar{X}_2}}$$

is distributed standard normally. Using this and substituting our preliminary values we obtain

$$\Pr\left(\frac{-5-6}{.36} < \text{Standard Normal} < \frac{5-6}{.36}\right)$$

$$= \Pr(-30.56 < Z < -2.78) \cong \Pr(Z < -2.78)$$

since the area under the standard normal curve to the left of $-30.56$ is negligible.

From the standard normal tables $\Pr(Z < -2.78) \cong .0027$.

# THE CHI-SQUARE, t, AND F DISTRIBUTIONS

● PROBLEM 13-19

Find the expected value of the random variable

$$S_*^2 = \frac{1}{n} \sum_{i=1}^{n} (X_i - \bar{X})^2 , \text{ where } \bar{X} = \sum_{i=1}^{n} X_i/n \text{ and the } X_i \text{ are}$$

independent and identically distributed with $E(X_i) = \mu$, $\text{Var } X_i = \sigma^2$ for $i = 1, 2, \dots n$.

Solution: $E(S_*^2) = E\left[\frac{1}{n} \sum_{i=1}^{n} (X_i - \bar{X})^2\right]$ by definition. We will use the com-

mon mathematical trick of adding and subtracting the same quantity, thereby leaving everything unchanged. Hence,

$$E(S_*^2) = E\left[\frac{1}{n} \sum_{i=1}^{n} ((X_i-\mu) - (\bar{X}-\mu))^2\right] = E\left[\frac{1}{n} \sum_{i=1}^{n} ((X_i-\mu)^2 - 2(\bar{X}-\mu)(X_i-\mu)\right.$$

$$\left. + (\bar{X}-\mu)^2))\right]$$

$$= E\left[\frac{1}{n} \sum_{i=1}^{n} (X_i-\mu)^2 - \frac{2}{n} \sum_{i=1}^{n} (\bar{X}-\mu)(X_i-\mu) + \frac{1}{n} \sum_{i=1}^{n} (\bar{X}-\mu)^2\right]$$

Since $(\bar{X}-\mu)$ is constant with respect to $i$, we have

$$E(S_*^2) = E\left[\frac{1}{n} \sum_{i=1}^{n} (X_i-\mu)^2 - \frac{2}{n}(\bar{X}-\mu) \sum_{i=1}^{n} (X_i-\mu) + \frac{1}{n} (\bar{X}-\mu)^2 \sum_{i=1}^{n} 1\right].$$

Since $\sum X_i = n\bar{X}$, we have

$$E(S_*^2) = E\left[\frac{1}{n} \sum_{i=1}^{n} (X_i-\mu)^2 - \frac{2}{n}(\bar{X}-\mu)(n\bar{X}-n\mu) + \frac{1}{n} (\bar{X}-\mu)^2 \cdot n\right.$$

$$= E\left[\frac{1}{n} \sum_{i=n}^{n} (X_i-\mu)^2 - 2(\bar{X}-\mu)^2 + (\bar{X}-\mu)^2\right]$$

$$= E\left[\frac{1}{n} \sum_{i=1}^{n} (X_i-\mu)^2 - (\bar{X}-\mu)^2\right]$$

$$= \frac{1}{n} \sum_{i=1}^{n} E(X_i-\mu)^2 - E(\bar{X}-\mu)^2 ,$$

by the linearity properties of the expectation operator; then,

$$E(S_*^2) = \frac{1}{n} \sum_{i=1}^{n} \sigma^2 - \sigma_{\bar{X}}^2 ; \quad \sigma_{\bar{X}} = \text{standard deviation of the sample mean,}$$

$$= \frac{1}{n}(n\sigma^2) - \frac{\sigma^2}{n} = \sigma^2 - \frac{\sigma^2}{n} = \frac{n-1}{n} \sigma^2 .$$

If we estimate $\sigma^2$ by $\frac{1}{n} \sum_{i=1}^{n} (X_i-\bar{X})^2$ , we see that $E(S_*^2) \neq \sigma^2$ . The

word given to this type of estimator is biased.

● **PROBLEM** 13-20

Let $X_1, X_2,\ldots,X_n$ be a random sample from a density $F(\cdot)$ and let

$$S^2 = \frac{1}{n-1} \sum_{i=1}^{n} (X_i-\bar{X})^2 .$$

Show $E(S^2) = \sigma^2$ .

Solution: We know from the last problem that

$$E\left(\frac{1}{n} \sum_{i=1}^{n} (X_i-\bar{X})^2\right) = \frac{n-1}{n} \sigma^2 .$$

But $S^2 = \frac{n}{n-1} \left(\frac{1}{n} \sum_{i=1}^{n} (X_i-\bar{X})^2\right)$ .

Hence $E(S^2) = E\left(\frac{n}{n-1} \cdot \frac{1}{n} \sum_{i=1}^{n} (X_i-\bar{X})^2\right)$

$$= \frac{n}{n-1} E\left(\frac{1}{n} \sum_{i=1}^{n} (X_i-\bar{X})^2\right) \qquad = \frac{n}{n-1} \frac{n-1}{n} \sigma^2 = \sigma^2 .$$

Since $E(S^2) = \sigma^2$ , $S^2$ is an unbiased estimate of $\sigma^2$ .

● **PROBLEM** 13-21

The chi-square density function is the special case of a gamma density with parameters $\alpha = K/2$ and $\lambda = \frac{1}{2}$ . Find the mean, variance and moment-generating function of a chi-square random variable.

Solution: Recall the gamma distribution

397

$$f(x) = \frac{\lambda}{\Gamma(\alpha)} (\lambda x)^{\alpha-1} e^{-\lambda x} \quad , \quad x \geq 0 .$$

With $\alpha = K/2$ and $\lambda = \frac{1}{2}$,

$$f(x) = \frac{1}{2\Gamma(K/2)} \left(\frac{x}{2}\right)^{K/2-1} e^{-X/2} = \frac{1}{\Gamma(K/2)} \left(\frac{1}{2}\right)^{K/2} X^{K-2/2} e^{-X/2},$$

for $X \geq 0$. Earlier for the gamma distribution we found

$$M_x(t) = \left(\frac{\lambda}{\lambda-t}\right)^{\alpha} \text{ for } t < \lambda , \quad E(x) = \frac{\alpha}{\lambda} , \text{ and } Var(X) = \frac{\alpha}{\lambda^2} .$$

Making the substitution $\alpha = K/2$ and $\lambda = \frac{1}{2}$ into the formulae for the gamma distribution, we see that the chi-square distribution has

$$M_x(t) = \left[\frac{\frac{1}{2}}{\frac{1}{2}-t}\right]^{K/2} = \left[\frac{1}{1-2t}\right]^{K/2} , \quad t < \frac{1}{2} ,$$

and

$$E(x) = \frac{K/2}{\frac{1}{2}} = \frac{K}{2} \cdot \frac{2}{1} = K ,$$

$$Var(X) = \frac{K/2}{(\frac{1}{2})^2} = \frac{K}{2} \frac{4}{1} = 2K .$$

● **PROBLEM** 13-22

Prove the following: if the random variables $X_i$, $i = 1, 2, \ldots, k$, are normally and independently distributed with means $\mu_i$ and variances $\sigma_i^2$, then

$$U = \sum_{i=1}^{k} \left(\frac{X_i - \mu_i}{\sigma_i}\right)^2$$

has a chi-square distribution with $k$ degrees of freedom.

Solution: We first change variables. Let $Z_i = \frac{X_i - \mu_i}{\sigma_i}$, then $Z_i$ has a standard normal distribution and $U = \sum_{i=1}^{k} Z_i^2$.

We now employ the moment-generating function technique.

$$M_u(t) = E(e^{tu}) = E(e^{t\Sigma Z_i^2})$$

$$= E(e^{tZ_1^2} e^{tZ_2^2} \ldots e^{tZ_K^2})$$

$$= E\left(\prod_{i=1}^{k} e^{tZ_i^2}\right) = \prod_{i=1}^{k} E(e^{tZ_i^2})$$

since the $Z_i$ are all independent. Since $f(z) = \frac{1}{\sqrt{2\pi}} e^{-Z^2/2}$,

$E(e^{tZ_i^2})$ is by definition equal to

$$\int_{-\infty}^{\infty} e^{tZ^2} \frac{1}{\sqrt{2\pi}} e^{-\frac{1}{2} Z^2} dz$$

$$= \int_{-\infty}^{\infty} \frac{1}{\sqrt{2\pi}} e^{-\frac{1}{2}(1-2t)Z^2} dz$$

$$= \frac{1}{\sqrt{1-2t}} \int_{-\infty}^{\infty} \frac{\sqrt{1-2t}}{\sqrt{2\pi}} e^{-\frac{1}{2}(1-2t)Z^2} dz .$$

For $t < \frac{1}{2}$ the integral on the right is the total probability under a normal curve with mean $0$ and variance $1/1-2t$. Hence

$$E(e^{tZ_i^2}) = \frac{1}{\sqrt{1-2t}} \times 1 = \frac{1}{\sqrt{1-2t}} \quad \text{for} \quad t < \frac{1}{2} .$$

Now

$$M_u(t) = \prod_{i=1}^{k} E(e^{tZ_i^2}) = \prod_{i=1}^{k} \frac{1}{\sqrt{1-2t}} = \left(\frac{1}{1-2t}\right)^{k/2}$$

which is the moment generating function of a chi-square $(\chi^2)$ distribution with $k$ degrees of freedom.

Advanced statistics tells us there is a one-to-one correspondence between distribution and moment generating functions. In light of this, since $U$ has the moment generating function of a $\chi^2(k)$, it must be so distributed.

● **PROBLEM** 13-23

If $z_1, z_2, \ldots, z_n$ is a random sample from a standard normal distribution, then show:
(i) $\bar{z}$ has a normal distribution with mean $0$ and variance $1/n$,
(ii) for $n = 2$, $\bar{z}$ and $\sum_{i=1}^{n} (z_i - \bar{z})^2$ are independent, and

(iii) $\sum_{i=1}^{n} (z_i - \bar{z})^2$ has a chi-square distribution with $n-1$ degrees of freedom.

Solution: (i) We will use the moment generating function technique:

$$M_{\bar{z}}(t) = E(\exp t\bar{z}) = E\left(\exp \frac{t\Sigma z_i}{n}\right)$$

$$= E\left(\prod_{i=1}^{n} \exp \frac{tz_i}{n}\right) \quad \text{by the Law of Exponents,}$$

$$= \prod_{i=1}^{n} E\left(\exp \frac{tz_i}{n}\right) \quad \text{since the } z_i \text{ are independent },$$

$$= \prod_{i=1}^{n} M_{z_i}\left(\frac{t}{n}\right) .$$

But for a standard normal random variable $M_z(t) = \exp(\frac{1}{2}t^2)$ .

Therefore

$$M_{z_i}\left(\frac{t}{n}\right) = \exp\left(\frac{t^2}{2n^2}\right) \quad \text{and}$$

$$\prod_{i=1}^{n} M_{z_i}\left(\frac{t}{n}\right) = \prod_{i=1}^{n} \exp\left(\frac{t^2}{2n^2}\right) \quad \text{and therefore}$$

$$M_{\bar{z}}(t) = \exp\left(\frac{t^2}{2n}\right)$$ which we recognize as the moment generating function of a normal random variable with mean $0$ and variance $1/n$. By the one-to-one correspondence between mgf's and distributions $\bar{z}$ must be normally distributed with mean $0$ and variance $1/n$.

(ii)  If $n = 2$, $\bar{z} = (z_1 + z_2)/2$ and it follows that

$$\Sigma(z_i - \bar{z})^2 = \left(z_1 - \frac{z_1 + z_2}{2}\right)^2 + \left(z_2 - \frac{z_1 + z_2}{2}\right)^2$$

$$= \left(\frac{z_1 - z_2}{2}\right)^2 + \left(\frac{z_2 - z_1}{2}\right)^2 = \frac{(z_1 - z_2)^2}{4} + \frac{(z_2 - z_1)^2}{4}$$

$$= \frac{(z_1 - z_2)^2}{4} + \frac{(-(z_1 - z_2))^2}{4} = \frac{(z_1 - z_2)^2}{2} .$$

Note now that $\bar{z}$ is a function of $z_1 + z_2$ and $\Sigma(z_i - \bar{z})^2$ is a function of $z_2 - z_1$; so to prove $\bar{z}$ and $\Sigma(z_i - \bar{z})^2$ are independent, it suffices to show that $z_1 + z_2$ and $z_2 - z_1$ are independent. Note that

$$M_{z_1 + z_2}(t_1) = E\left[e^{t_1(z_1 + z_2)}\right] = E\left[e^{t_1 z_1} e^{t_2 z_2}\right]$$

$$= E\left(e^{t_1 z_1}\right) E\left(e^{t_1 z_2}\right)$$

since $z_1$ and $z_2$ are independent. This is equal to $M_{z_1}(t_1)M_{z_2}(t_1)$ where $z_1$ and $z_2$ are standard normal. Making the substitution of the standard normal mgf's we obtain

$$e^{\frac{1}{2}t_1^2} e^{\frac{1}{2}t_1^2} = e^{t_1^2} .$$

A similar computation yields $M_{z_2 - z_1}(t_2) = e^{t_2^2}$.

Also the joint moment generating function is defined as

$$M_{x_1, \ldots, x_k}(t_1, \ldots, t_k) = E\left(\exp \sum_{j=1}^{k} t_j x_j\right)$$

In our case

$$M_{z_1 + z_2, z_2 - z_1}(t_1, t_2) = E\left(e^{t_1(z_1 + z_2) + t_2(z_2 - z_1)}\right)$$

$$= E\left(e^{z_1(t_1 - t_2) + z_2(t_1 + t_2)}\right)$$

$$= E\left(e^{z_1(t_1 - t_2)}\right) E\left(e^{z_2(t_1 + t_2)}\right) \text{ since } z_1 \text{ and}$$

$z_2$ are independent,

$$= M_{z_1}(t_1 - t_2) \times M_{z_2}(t_1 + t_2)$$

$$= e^{\frac{1}{2}(t_1 - t_2)^2} e^{\frac{1}{2}(t_1 + t_2)^2}$$

$$= e^{\frac{1}{2}(t_1-t_2)^2 + \frac{1}{2}(t_1+t_2)^2}$$

$$= e^{\frac{1}{2}(t_1^2+t_2^2 - 2t_1t_2 + t_1^2 + t_2^2 + 2t_1t_2)}$$

$$= e^{t_1^2 + t_2^2} = e^{t_1^2} e^{t_2^2}$$

$$= M_{z_1+z_2}(t_1) M_{z_1-z_2}(t_2)$$

by what was said earlier.

A well-known but difficult theorem in statistics says that if the joint moment generating function can be factored into the mgf's of the components then the components are independent. The converse is also true. This, combined with our previous computations, yields the desired result.

(iii) We can now accept the independence of $\bar{z}$ and $\sum_1^n (z_i-\bar{z})^2$ for arbitrary n. To show (iii), we will use the trick of adding and subtracting a unique quantity thus leaving the expressions the same.

Note that $\Sigma z_i^2 = \Sigma(z_i-\bar{z}+\bar{z})^2 = \Sigma(z_i-\bar{z})^2 + 2\bar{z}\,\Sigma(z_i-\bar{z}) + \Sigma\bar{z}^2$ .

But $\Sigma(z_i-\bar{z}) = \Sigma z_i - \Sigma\bar{z} = n\bar{z} - n\bar{z}$, since $\Sigma z_i/n = \bar{z}$ , thus $\Sigma(z_i-\bar{z}) = 0$. We now have

$$\Sigma(z_i-\bar{z})^2 + \Sigma\bar{z}^2 = \Sigma(z_i-\bar{z})^2 + n\bar{z}^2 .$$

The two terms $\Sigma(z_i-\bar{z})^2$ and $n\bar{z}^2$ are independent. From this we know that $M_{\Sigma z_i^2}(t) = M_{\Sigma(z_i-\bar{z})^2}(t)$. Since $\Sigma(z_i-\bar{z})^2$ and $n\bar{z}^2$ are independent we have

$$M_{\Sigma(z_i-\bar{z})^2 + n\bar{z}^2}(t) = M_{\Sigma z_i-\bar{z})^2}(t)\, M_{n\bar{z}^2}(t) .$$

Therefore $M_{\Sigma(z_i-\bar{z})^2}(t) = \dfrac{M_{\Sigma z_i^2}(t)}{M_{n\bar{z}^2}(t)}$ .

We know from the last problem that $\Sigma z_i^2$ is chi-square with n degrees of freedom and has mgf $(1/1-2t)^{n/2}$ . Also note that since $\bar{z} = N(0,\frac{1}{n})$, $\sqrt{n}\,\bar{z}$ is standard normal. Therefore $(\sqrt{n}\,\bar{z})^2 = n\bar{z}^2$ is $\chi^2$ with 1 d.o.f. Its mfg is $(1/1-2t)^{\frac{1}{2}}$ .

Hence

$$M_{\Sigma(z_i-\bar{z})^2}(t) = \frac{(1/(1-2t))^{n/2}}{(1/(1-2t))^{\frac{1}{2}}} = \left(\frac{1}{1-2t}\right)^{(n-1)/2} .$$

We recognize this as the mgf of a chi-square random variable with n-1 degree of freedom. Hence

$$\Sigma(x_i-\bar{x})^2 \text{ is } \chi^2_{(n-1)} .$$

If $S^2 = \frac{1}{(n-1)} \sum_{i=1}^{n} (X_i - \bar{X})^2$ is the unbiased sample variance of a random sample from a normal distribution with mean $\mu$ and variance $\sigma^2$, then show

$$U = \frac{(n-1)S^2}{\sigma^2}$$

has a chi-square distribution with $n-1$ degrees of freedom.

**Solution:** $S^2 = \frac{1}{n-1} \sum_{i=1}^{n} (X_i - \bar{X})^2$ .

$$U = \frac{(n-1)S^2}{\sigma^2} = \frac{n-1 \frac{1}{n-1} \Sigma(X_i - \bar{X})^2}{\sigma^2} = \frac{\Sigma(X_i - \bar{X})^2}{\sigma^2} .$$

Now add and subtract $\mu$ within the parentheses.

$$U = \frac{\Sigma(X_i - \mu - \bar{X} + \mu)^2}{\sigma^2} = \frac{\Sigma((X_i - \mu) - (\bar{X} - \mu))^2}{\sigma^2}$$

$$= \Sigma\left(\frac{X_i - \mu}{\sigma} - \frac{\bar{X} - \mu}{\sigma}\right)^2 = \Sigma(Z_i - \bar{Z})^2 \text{ where the } Z_i \text{ are standard normal.}$$

In the last problem this was shown to have a chi-square distribution with $n-1$ degrees of freedom.

A manufacturer of kitchen clocks claims that a certain model will last 5 years on the average with a standard deviation of 1.2 years. A random sample of six of the clocks lasted 6, 5.5, 4, 5.2, 5, and 4.3 years. Compute

$$\frac{(n-1)S^2}{\sigma^2}$$

and use the chi-square tables to find the probability of a $X^2$ value this high.

**Solution:** First we must calculate the sample mean.

$$\bar{X} = \frac{\sum_{i=1}^{6} X_i}{n} = \frac{6 + 5.5 + 4 + 5.2 + 5 + 4.3}{6} = \frac{30}{6} = 5 .$$

$$S^2 = \frac{1}{n-1} \sum_{i=1}^{6} (X_i - \bar{X})^2 = \frac{1}{6-1}((6-5)^2 + (5.5-5)^2 + (4-5)^2 + (5.2-5)^2$$

$$+ (4.3-5)^2)$$

$$= \frac{1}{5}(1^2 + (.5)^2 + (-1)^2 + (.2)^2 + 0^2 + (-.7)^2)$$

$$= \frac{1}{5}(1 + .25 + 1 + .04 + .49) = \frac{1}{5} \cdot 2.78$$

$$= .556$$

The standard deviation, $\sigma$, is 1.2. Hence $\sigma^2 = (1.2)^2 = 1.44$.

Finally

$$U = \frac{(n-1)s^2}{\sigma^2} = \frac{(6-1)(.556)}{1.44} = 1.931.$$

In this case U has a chi-square distribution with $n-1 = 5$ degrees of freedom. On a chi-square table, look down the left side for the row with 5 degrees of freedom. The probabilities on the top row are $\Pr(\chi^2_{(n-1)} \geq U)$. Looking across the rwo for 5 d.o.f., we see that the value for $\Pr = .80$ is 2.343 and that for $\Pr = .90$ is 1.610. To find $\Pr(\chi^2(5) \geq 1.931)$, we use linear interpolation,

$$\frac{1.931 - 1.610}{2.343 - 1.610} = \frac{X - .90}{.80 - .90}$$

Thus, $X = .90 + (.80-.90)\left(\dfrac{1.931 - 1.610}{2.343 - 1.610}\right)$

$$= .90 - .1\left(\frac{.321}{.743}\right) = .90 - .1(.432)$$

$$= .857.$$

Hence $\Pr(\chi^2_{(5)} \geq 1.931) = .857$.

● **PROBLEM** 13-26

Suppose a random sample of 10 observations is to be drawn where $x_1, x_2, \ldots, x_{10}$ are independent normally distributed random variables each with mean $\mu$ and variance $\sigma^2$. Find the $\Pr(\sigma^2 \geq .5319s^2)$ where

$$s^2 = \text{sample variance} = \frac{\sum_{i=1}^{10} (x_i - \bar{x})^2}{9}.$$

Solution: In this problem $s^2 = \dfrac{\sum_{i=1}^{10} (x_i - \bar{x})^2}{9}$ is a random variable.

We must determine the distribution of $s^2$ in order to compute this probability. We here give a different outlook than in the preceding problem.

Let Z = standard normal variable. Z has mean 0 and variance 1. Define the random variable $\chi_1^2 = Z^2$. This new random variable is distributed with a chi-square distribution with 1 degree of freedom. An interesting property of $\chi^2$ is if $Y = \chi_1^2 + \chi_1^2$ then Y is also chi-square but with 2 degrees of freedom, $Y = \chi_2^2$. This property generalizes to

$$\chi_n^2 = \underbrace{\chi_1^2 + \chi_1^2 + \cdots + \chi_1^2}_{n \text{ terms.}}$$

We wish to find $\Pr(\sigma^2 \geq .5319s^2) = \Pr(s^2/\sigma^2 \leq 1/.5319)$

$$= \Pr(s^2/\sigma^2 \leq 1.88).$$

What is the distribution of $s^2/\sigma^2$?

$$(n-1)S^2 = \sum_{i=1}^{10} (x_i - \bar{x})^2 \quad \text{and} \quad \frac{(n-1)S^2}{\sigma^2} = \frac{\sum_{i=1}^{10} (x_i - \bar{x})^2}{\sigma^2} = \sum_{i=1}^{10} \left(\frac{x_i - \bar{x}}{\sigma}\right)^2$$

Intuitively, if we replace $\bar{x}$ by $\mu$ then

$$\frac{(n-1)S^2}{\sigma^2} = \sum_{i=1}^{10} \left(\frac{x_i - \mu}{\sigma}\right)$$

or

$$= \sum_{i=1}^{10} Z_i^2 \quad \text{where} \quad Z \text{ is a standard}$$

normal random variable. Thus $(n-1)S^2/\sigma^2$ will be a chi-square random variable with 10 degrees of freedom. However, we cannot replace $\bar{x}$ by $\mu$ without any justification. This substitution only provides motivation for the following result: $(n-1)S^2/\sigma^2$ is distributed chi-square with n-1 degrees of freedom.

We must now use the table of $\chi^2$-values with 9 degrees of freedom to find,

$$\Pr\left(\frac{9S^2}{\sigma^2} \le 9(1.88)\right) = \Pr\left(\frac{9S^2}{\sigma^2} \le 16.92\right).$$

This equals $1 - .05 = .95$. Thus $\Pr(\sigma^2 \ge .5319S^2) = .95$.

# THE t-TEST

● PROBLEM 13-27

Z is a standard normal random variable. U is chi-square with k degrees of freedom. Assume Z and U are independent. Using the change of variable technique, find the distribution of

$$X = \frac{Z}{\sqrt{u/k}}.$$

Solution: Note that

$$g(z) = \frac{1}{\sqrt{2\pi}} e^{-Z^2/2} \qquad -\infty < Z < \infty$$

$$h(u) = \frac{1}{\Gamma(k/2)} \left(\tfrac{1}{2}\right)^{k/2} u^{k/2 - 1} e^{-(\frac{1}{2})u} \qquad u > 0.$$

Since Z and U are independent, the joint density $f(z,u) = g(z)h(u)$. Therefore

$$f(z,u) = \frac{1}{\sqrt{2\pi}} \frac{1}{\Gamma(k/2)} \left(\tfrac{1}{2}\right)^{k/2} u^{(k/2)-1} e^{-\frac{1}{2}u} e^{-\frac{1}{2}z^2} \quad \text{for} \quad u > 0.$$

We make the change of variables $X = Z/\sqrt{u/k}$ and $Y = U$. The change of variables technique tells us

$$f_{x,y}(x,y) = f_{u,v}(x,y)|J|,$$

where J is the Jacobian determinant of the transformation,

$$J = \det \begin{bmatrix} \frac{\partial x}{\partial z} & \frac{\partial x}{\partial u} \\ \frac{\partial y}{\partial z} & \frac{\partial y}{\partial u} \end{bmatrix} = \det \begin{bmatrix} \frac{1}{\sqrt{u/k}} & -\frac{z}{2}\sqrt{\frac{k}{u^3}} \\ 0 & 1 \end{bmatrix}$$

$$= \sqrt{k/u} \quad \text{but} \quad y = u \quad \text{so} \quad |J| = J = \sqrt{k/y} \; .$$

Hence
$$f(x,y) = \sqrt{y/k} \; \frac{1}{\sqrt{2\pi}} \; \frac{1}{\Gamma(k/2)} \; (\tfrac{1}{2})^{k/2} \; y^{(k/2)-1} e^{-\tfrac{1}{2}y} e^{(-x^2/2)y}$$
$$y > 0 \; .$$

$$f(x) = \int_{-\infty}^{\infty} f(x,y)dy$$

$$= \int_{0}^{\infty} \sqrt{y/k} \; \frac{1}{\sqrt{2\pi}} \; \frac{1}{\Gamma(k/2)} \; (\tfrac{1}{2})^{k/2} \; y^{(k/2)-1} \; e^{-(y/2)} \; e^{-x^2 y/2} \; dy$$

$$= \frac{1}{\sqrt{2k\pi}} \; \frac{1}{\Gamma(k/2)} \; (\tfrac{1}{2})^{k/2} \int_{0}^{\infty} y^{(k/2)-1+\tfrac{1}{2}} \; e^{-\tfrac{1}{2}(1+x^2/k)y} \; dy$$

$$= \frac{1}{\sqrt{k\pi}} \; \frac{1}{\Gamma(k/2)} \; (\tfrac{1}{2})^{(k+1)/2} \int_{0}^{\infty} y^{k-1/2} \; e^{-\tfrac{1}{2}(1+x^2/k)y} \; dy \; .$$

Let
$$r = \tfrac{1}{2}(1+x^2/k) \; y \quad \text{then}$$
$$dr = \tfrac{1}{2}(1+x^2/k)dy \quad \text{and}$$
$$y = \frac{r}{\tfrac{1}{2}(1+x^2/k)} \; .$$

We now have

$$\frac{1}{\sqrt{k\pi}} \; \frac{1}{\Gamma(k/2)}(\tfrac{1}{2})^{k+1/2} \; \frac{1}{(\tfrac{1}{2}(1+\frac{x^2}{k}))^{k-1/2} \cdot \tfrac{1}{2}(1+x^2/k)} \int_{0}^{\infty} r^{\frac{k-1}{2}} e^{-r} \; dr$$

$$= \frac{1}{\sqrt{k\pi}} \; \frac{1}{\Gamma(k/2)} \; \frac{(\tfrac{1}{2})^{k+1/2}}{(\tfrac{1}{2})^{k+1/2} (1+x^2/k)^{k+1/2}} \; \Gamma(\frac{k+1}{2}) \; ,$$

$$= \frac{\Gamma(k+\tfrac{1}{2})}{\Gamma(k/2)} \; \frac{1}{\sqrt{k\pi} \; (1+x^2/k)^{k+1/2}} \; .$$

This is the density function of what is usually called the Student's t distribution.

● **PROBLEM** 13-28

Find the probability that a t-distribution has a t score

(a)  greater than 1.740 when  d.o.f. = 17

(b)  less than - 1.323 when  d.o.f. = 21.

Solution:  This problem involves reading the t-table.

a)  This part involves a t-distribution with 17 degrees of freedom. We want to know $Pr(t(17) > 1.74)$. We look at the row on the t-table which has 17 degrees of freedom. The number 1.74 appears under the column headed by .95. These column headings are the probabilities that $t(n) \leq$ number in the column below. Hence $Pr(t(17) < 1.74) = 0.95$. Finally $Pr(t(17) > 1.74) = 1 - Pr(t(17) < 1.74) = 1 - 0.95 = .05$.

b) We have 21 degrees of freedom. In the row marked 21, 1.323 is under the column headed .90. Hence $Pr(t(21) < 1.323) = .90$. By the symmetry of the t-distribution,

$$Pr(t(21) > -1.323) = Pr(t(21) < 1.323) = .90 .$$

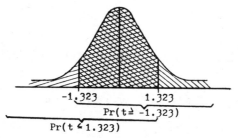

Also note that $Pr(t(21) < -1.323) = 1 - Pr(t(21) > 1.323) = 1 - .90 = .10$.

● **PROBLEM** 13-29

Find $t_{.975}$ (5).

Solution:

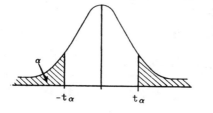

$t_\alpha$ is the number such that $Pr(t(n) > t_\alpha) = \alpha$. Let $\alpha = .975$. By the symmetry of the t-distribution $t_\alpha = -t_{1-\alpha}$ and $t_{.975} = -t_{.025}$. Using the t-table we see that $t_{.025}(5) = 2.57$ and $t_{.975} = -2.57$.

● **PROBLEM** 13-30

A manufacturer of light bulbs claims that his lightbulbs will burn on the average 500 hours. To maintain this average, he tests 25 bulbs each month. If the computed t value falls between $-t_{0.05}$ and $t_{0.05}$, he is satisfied with his claim. What conclusion should he draw from a sample that has a mean $\bar{x} = 518$ hours and a standard deviation $s = 40$ hours? Assume the distribution of burning times to be approximately normal.

Solution: We solve this problem by noting that the statistic $\bar{x}-\mu/s/\sqrt{n}$ has a t distribution with n-1 degrees of freedom. We will show this in the following manner. We will show that $\bar{x}-\mu/s/\sqrt{n}$ is the quotient of a standard normal distribution and the square root of a chi-square random variable divided by its degrees of freedom. From there the result follows since $z/\sqrt{u/k}$ is $t(n-1)$ where $z$ is standard normal and $U$ is $\chi^2(K)$.

We know $Z = \dfrac{\bar{X} - \mu}{\sqrt{\sigma^2/n}}$ is standard normal. We also know $\dfrac{(n-1)s^2}{\sigma^2}$

406

is $\chi^2(n-1)$. But $\dfrac{(n-1)s^2}{\sigma^2} = \dfrac{\sum\limits_{i=1}^{n}(X_i-\bar{X})^2}{\sigma^2}$ . Hence

$$\sqrt{\dfrac{Z}{\dfrac{U}{K}}} = \dfrac{\dfrac{\bar{X}-\mu}{\sqrt{\sigma^2/n}}}{\sqrt{\dfrac{\sum\limits_{i=1}^{n}(X_i-\bar{X})^2}{(n-1)\sigma^2}}} = \dfrac{\dfrac{1}{\sigma}\dfrac{\bar{X}-\mu}{1/\sqrt{n}}}{\dfrac{1}{\sigma}\sqrt{\dfrac{\sum\limits_{i=1}^{n}(X_i-\bar{X})^2}{n-1}}}$$

$$= \dfrac{\bar{X}-\mu}{1/\sqrt{n}} \cdot \dfrac{1}{\sqrt{\dfrac{\sum\limits_{i=1}^{n}(X_i-\bar{X})^2}{n-1}}}$$

$$= \dfrac{\bar{X}-\mu}{1/\sqrt{n}} \dfrac{1}{\sqrt{s^2}} = \dfrac{\bar{X}-\mu}{s/\sqrt{n}}$$

and we are done.

In this problem we have 25 bulbs. Hence n-1 = 24 degrees of freedom. We are also given S = 40, $\bar{X}$ = 518, and $\mu$ = 500. Thus

$$t = \dfrac{\bar{X}-\mu}{s/\sqrt{n}} = \dfrac{518-500}{40/\sqrt{25}} = \dfrac{18}{8} = 2.25 .$$

A look at the t-table shows that for 24 degrees of freedom $t_{.05}$ is 1.711. Since 2.25 is well above 1.711, the manufacturer should assume that his bulbs, on the average, burn more than 500 hours.

# THE F-DISTRIBUTION

● PROBLEM 13-31

Let U be a chi-square random variable with m degrees of freedom. Let V be a chi-square random variable with n degrees of freedom. Consider the quantity

$$X = \dfrac{U/m}{V/n} ,$$ where U and V are independent.

Using the change of variable technique, find the probability density of X.

Solution: We start with

$$g(U) = \dfrac{1}{\Gamma(m/2)} (\tfrac{1}{2})^{m/2} \, U^{m/2-1} \, e^{-u/2} \quad U > 0$$

$$h(V) = \dfrac{1}{\Gamma(n/2)} (\tfrac{1}{2})^{n/2} \, V^{n/2-1} \, e^{-v/2} \quad V > 0 .$$

Since U and V are independent, the joint density f(U,V) equals the product g(u)h(v). Hence

$$f(u,v) = \dfrac{1}{\Gamma(m/2)\Gamma(n/2)2^{m+n/2}} \, U^{m-2/2} \, V^{n-2/2} \, e^{-\frac{1}{2}(u+v)} .$$

Consider the transformation $X = \dfrac{U/m}{V/n}$ , Y = V . By the change of variable formula, $f_{x,y}(x,y) = f_{u,v}(x,y)|J|$ where $J$ is the Jacobian determinant of the transformation,

$$J = \det \begin{bmatrix} \dfrac{\partial x}{\partial u} & \dfrac{\partial x}{\partial v} \\[2ex] \dfrac{\partial y}{\partial u} & \dfrac{\partial y}{\partial v} \end{bmatrix} = \det \begin{bmatrix} \dfrac{mv}{n} & \dfrac{-nu}{mv^2} \\[2ex] 0 & 1 \end{bmatrix}$$

$$= \frac{mv}{n} = \frac{my}{n} \quad \text{since} \quad y = v. \quad \text{Therefore}$$

$$f(x,y) = \frac{my}{n} \; \frac{1}{\Gamma(m/2)\Gamma(n/2)2^{m+n/2}} \left(\frac{mxy}{n}\right)^{m-2/2} y^{n-2/2} \, e^{-\frac{1}{2}\left(\frac{m}{n} xy + y\right)}.$$

Now $f(x) = \displaystyle\int_{-\infty}^{\infty} f(x,y)\,dy = \int_{0}^{\infty} \frac{my}{n} \; \frac{1}{\Gamma(m/2)\Gamma(n/2)2^{m+n/2}} \left(\frac{mxy}{n}\right)^{m-2/2} y^{n-2/2}$

$$e^{-\frac{1}{2}\left(\frac{m}{n} xy + y\right)} \, dy$$

$$= \frac{1}{\Gamma(m/2)\Gamma(n/2)2^{m+n/2}} \left(\frac{m}{n}\right)^{m/2} x^{m-2/2} \int_{0}^{\infty} y^{m+n-2/2} \, e^{-\frac{1}{2}\left(\frac{m}{n} xy + y\right)} dy.$$

Let $r = \frac{1}{2}\left(\frac{m}{n} xy + y\right)$. Then $y = \dfrac{2r}{\frac{m}{n} x + 1}$ and $dy = \dfrac{2}{\frac{m}{n} x + 1} \, dr$.

We now have

$$\frac{1}{\Gamma(m/2)\Gamma(n/2)2^{m+n/2}} \left(\frac{m}{n}\right)^{m/2} x^{m-2/2} \left(\frac{2}{\frac{m}{n} x + 1}\right)^{m+n/2} \int_{0}^{\infty} r^{m+n-2/2} e^{-r} dr$$

$$= \frac{1}{\Gamma(m/2)\Gamma(n/2)2^{m+n/2}} \left(\frac{m}{n}\right)^{\frac{m}{2}} x^{m-2/2} \left(\frac{2}{\frac{m}{n} x + 1}\right)^{m+n/2} \Gamma\left(\frac{m+n}{2}\right)$$

$$= \frac{\Gamma((m+n)/2)}{\Gamma(m/2)\Gamma(n/2)} \left(\frac{m}{n}\right)^{m/2} \frac{x^{(m-2)/2}}{[1 + (m/n)x]^{m+n/2}} \quad X > 0 .$$

The above is called an $F$ distribution with $m$ and $n$ degrees of freedom

● **PROBLEM** 13-32

$X$ is an F-distributed random variable with $m$ and $n$ degrees of freedom. Find $E(X)$.

Solution: We attack this problem in a manner different from any previous expectation problem. We write $X$ as

$$\frac{U/m}{V/n}$$

where $U$ is $\chi^2(m)$ and $V$ is $\chi^2(n)$. Now

$$E(X) = E\left(\frac{U/m}{V/n}\right) = E\left(\frac{n}{m} \cdot \frac{U}{V}\right) = \left(\frac{n}{m}\right) E(U) E\left(\frac{1}{V}\right) .$$

Since the expectation of a chi-square random variable with $k$ degrees of freedom is $K$, $E(U) = m$ and

$$E(X) = \frac{n}{m} m \, E\left(\frac{1}{V}\right) = n \, E\left(\frac{1}{V}\right) .$$

By definition

$$E\left(\frac{1}{V}\right) = \int_{-\infty}^{\infty} \frac{1}{V} h(V)dV = \int_{0}^{\infty} \frac{1}{V} \frac{1}{\Gamma(n/2)} \left(\frac{1}{2}\right)^{n/2} V^{n/2-1} e^{-V/2} dV , V > 0$$

$$= \frac{1}{\Gamma(n/2)} \left(\frac{1}{2}\right)^{n/2} \int_{0}^{\infty} V^{n/2-2} e^{-V/2} dV$$

$$= \frac{1}{\Gamma(n/2)} \left(\frac{1}{2}\right)^{n/2} \int_{0}^{\infty} V^{(n-2)/2-1} e^{-V/2} dV .$$

Let $r = V/2$, then $2r = V$ and $2dr = 1dV$. We now have

$$\frac{1}{\Gamma(n/2)} \left(\frac{1}{2}\right)^{n/2} 2^{n-2/2-1} \cdot 2 \int_{0}^{\infty} r^{(n-2)/2-1} e^{-r} dr$$

$$= \frac{1}{\Gamma(n/2)} \left(\frac{1}{2}\right)^{n/2} 2^{(n-2)/2} \Gamma\left(\frac{n-2}{2}\right)$$

$$= \frac{\Gamma(n-2/2)}{\Gamma(n/2)} \left(\frac{1}{2}\right)^{n/2} \left(\frac{1}{2}\right)^{-(n-2)/2} .$$

By the properties of the gamma function $\Gamma(t+1) = t\Gamma(t)$. Hence

$$\Gamma(n/2) = \Gamma\left(\frac{n-2}{2} + 1\right) = \frac{n-2}{2} \Gamma\left(\frac{n-2}{2}\right) .$$

We now have

$$E\left(\frac{1}{V}\right) = \frac{\Gamma\left(\frac{n-2}{2}\right)}{\frac{n-2}{2}\Gamma\left(\frac{n-2}{2}\right)} \left(\frac{1}{2}\right)^{n/2} \left(\frac{1}{2}\right)^{-\frac{(n-2)}{2}}$$

$$= \frac{2}{n-2} \left(\frac{1}{2}\right)^{(n-(n-2))/2} = \frac{2}{n-2} \frac{1}{2} = \frac{1}{n-2} .$$

Finally $E(X) = n \, E\left(\frac{1}{V}\right) = \frac{n}{n-2} .$

● **PROBLEM** 13-33

Find the probability that $X$ is greater than $3.28$ if $X$ has an F distribution with 12 and 8 degrees of freedom.

Solution: We look on the following cumulative F-table. Look across the top for 12, the degrees of freedom of the numerator. Now we look along the side for 8, the degrees of freedom of the denomonator. Find the block that is in row 8 and column 12. In it the value 3.28 corresponds to the G-value .95 in the extreme left hand column. This signifies $G(3.28) = Pr(X < 3.28) = .95$. Hence

$$Pr(X > 3.28) = 1 - Pr(X < 3.28) = 1 - .95 = .05.$$

● **PROBLEM** 13-34

Find the value $\xi_{0.05}$ such that for an F-distribution with 12 and 8 degrees of freedom $Pr(X < \xi_{0.05}) = .05$ .

<u>Solution</u>:  This problem provides a real exercise in reading the F-table.

Note the following.  If  X  has an  F distribution with  m  and  n  degrees of freedom, X  is of the form

$$\frac{U/m}{V/n}$$

where  U  and  V  are chi-square random variables with  m  and  n  degrees of freedom.  1/X  will then be of the form

$$\frac{V/n}{U/m}$$

and have an  F-distribution with  n  and  m  degrees of freedom.  This allows one to table the  F-distribution for the upper tail only.  For example, if the quantile  $\xi_{.95}$  is given for an  F-distribution with  m  and  n  degrees of freedom, then the quantile  $\xi'_{.05}$  for an  F-distribution with  n  and  m  degrees of freedom is given by  $1/\xi_{.95}$ .

In general, if  X  has an  F-distribution with  m  and  n  degrees of freedom, then the  $p^{th}$ quantile of  X,  $\xi_p$,  is the reciprocal of the  $(1-p)^{th}$  quantile of  Y,  $\xi'_{1-p}$  of an  F-distribution with  n  and  m  degrees of freedom, as the following shows:

$$p = Pr[X \le \xi_p] = Pr[1/X \ge 1/\xi_p]$$

$$= Pr[Y \ge 1/\xi_p] = 1 - Pr[Y \le 1/\xi_p] ;$$

but

$$1 - p = Pr[Y \le \xi'_{1-p}] .$$

1-p  also equals

$$1 - (1 - Pr[Y \le 1/\xi_p])$$

$$= Pr[Y \le 1/\xi_p] .$$

Hence  $1/\xi_p = \xi'_{1-p}$ .  Therefore

$$\xi_{.05}(12,8) = \frac{1}{\xi_{.95}(8,12)} = \frac{1}{2.85} = 0.351 .$$

The results of the last two problems are illustrated below.

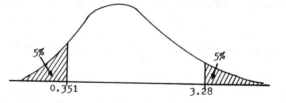

● **PROBLEM 13-35**

Find the tenth quantile point of an F distribution with 15 and seven degrees of freedom.

<u>Solution</u>:  We know that if the  $p^{th}$  quantile  $\xi_p$  is given for an  F-distribution with  m  and  n  degrees of freedom, then the quantile  $\xi'_{1-p}$  for an  F-distribution with  n  and  m  degrees of freedom is given by  $1/\xi_p$ .

Following this, we see

$$\xi_{.10}(15,7) = \frac{1}{\xi_{.90}(7,15)} = \frac{1}{2.16} = .463 .$$

● **PROBLEM** 13-36

Let $X_1$, $X_2$ be a random independent sample from $N(0,1)$.

a)   What is the distribution of

$$\frac{X_2 - X_1}{\sqrt{2}} ?$$

b)   What is the distribution of

$$\frac{(X_1 + X_2)^2}{(X_2 - X_1)^2} ?$$

c)   What is the distribution of

$$\frac{(X_2 + X_1)}{\sqrt{(X_2 - X_1)^2}} ?$$

d)   What is the distribution of $1/Z$ if $Z = X_1^2/X_2^2$ ?

Solution:   First we will establish the distributions of $X_1 + X_2$ and $X_2 - X_1$. $X_1 + X_2$ is the sum of two normal random variables. Hence it is normally distributed with $E(X_1+X_2) = E(X_1) + E(X_2) = 0 + 0 = 0$, and $Var(X_1+X_2) = Var(X_1) + Var(X_2) = 1 + 1 = 2$, since $X_1$, $X_2$, are independent.

Similarly, $X_2 - X_1$ will also be normally distributed with

$$E(X_2 - X_1) = E(X_2) - E(X_1) = 0 - 0 = 0$$

and

$$Var(X_2 - X_1) = Var(X_2) + Var(X_1) = 1 + 1 = 2.$$

a)   We have now $1/\sqrt{2}\ N(0,2)$. A constant times a normal distribution will still be normally distributed. $E(ax) = a\,E(x)$. Therefore the new mean will be $1/\sqrt{2} \cdot 0 = 0$. $Var(ax) = a^2 Var(X)$; hence the new variance will be

$$(1/\sqrt{2})^2(2) = 1.$$

The new distribution is $N(0,1)$.

b)   We start with

$$\frac{(X_1 + X_2)^2}{(X_2 - X_1)^2} .$$

Multiply numerator and denominator by $\frac{1}{2}$ to obtain

$$\frac{\frac{1}{2}(X_1 + X_2)^2}{\frac{1}{2}(X_2 - X_1)^2} = \frac{\left(\dfrac{X_1 + X_2}{\sqrt{2}}\right)^2}{\left(\dfrac{X_2 - X_1}{\sqrt{2}}\right)^2}$$

411

From part a) we know the denomonator is $[N(0,1)]^2$. For similar reasons the numerator is also $[N(0,1)]^2$. But we know that a $[N(0,1)]^2$ is $\chi^2(1)$. We now have

$$\frac{\chi^2(1)}{\chi^2(1)} = \frac{\chi^2(1)/1}{\chi^2(1)/1} \ .$$

By definition this is an $F(1,1)$ random variable.

c) We start with

$$\frac{(X_1 + X_2)}{\sqrt{(X_2 - X_1)^2}} \ .$$

Multiply numerator and denomonator by $1/\sqrt{2}$ to obtain

$$\frac{\frac{1}{\sqrt{2}}(X_1 + X_2)}{\frac{1}{\sqrt{2}}\sqrt{(X_2 - X_1)^2}} = \frac{\left(\dfrac{X_1 + X_2}{\sqrt{2}}\right)}{\sqrt{\left(\dfrac{X_2 - X_1}{\sqrt{2}}\right)^2}} \ .$$

From previous experience $X_1 + X_2/\sqrt{2}$ and $X_2 - X_1/\sqrt{2}$ are both $N(0,1)$. We now have

$$\frac{N(0,1)}{\sqrt{[N(0,1)]^2}} = \frac{N(0,1)}{\sqrt{\chi^2(1)}} \ , \text{ since } [N(0,1)]^2 \text{ is } \chi^2(1) \ ,$$

$$= \frac{N(0,1)}{\sqrt{\dfrac{\chi^2(1)}{1}}} = t(1) \text{ by definition.}$$

d) If $Z = X_1^2/X_2^2$, then $1/Z = X_2^2/X_1^2$. $X_1^2$ and $X_2^2$ are both $[N(0,1)]^2$ and thereby $\chi^2(1)$, $1/Z$ is therefore

$$\frac{\chi^2(1)}{\chi^2(1)} = \frac{\chi^2(1)/1}{\chi^2(1)/1}$$

which is $F(1,1)$ by definition.

● **PROBLEM** 13-37

Let $X_1,\ldots,X_n$ be a random sample from $N(0,1)$. Define

$$\bar{X}_k = \frac{1}{k}\sum_1^k X_i \quad \text{and} \quad \bar{X}_{n-k} = \frac{1}{n-k}\sum_{k+1}^n X_i \ .$$

(a) What is the distribution of $\frac{1}{2}(\bar{X}_k + \bar{X}_{n-k})$ ?

(b) What is the distribution of $k\bar{X}_k^2 + (n-k)\bar{X}_{n-k}^2$ ?

(c) What is the distribution of $X_1^2/X_2^2$ ?

<u>Solution</u>: a) $\bar{X}_k$ and $\bar{X}_{n-k}$ are sample means from a normal distribu-

tion. As such they are normally distributed with means equal to the original distribution mean, 0. Their variances are

$$\frac{\sigma^2 \text{ orig.}}{\text{sample size}} = \frac{1}{k} \text{ and } \frac{1}{n-k} \text{ respectively.}$$

$\bar{X}_k + \bar{X}_{n-k}$ is normally distributed, being the sum of two normal distributions. By the linearity properties of expectation

$$E(\bar{X}_k + \bar{X}_{n-k}) = E(\bar{X}_k) + E(\bar{X}_{n-k}) = 0 + 0 = 0 .$$

$\bar{X}_k$ and $\bar{X}_{n-k}$ are concerned with different observations; hence they are independent. In light of this

$$\text{Var}(\bar{X}_k + \bar{X}_{n-k}) = \text{Var}(\bar{X}_k) + \text{Var}(\bar{X}_{n-k}) = \frac{1}{k} + \frac{1}{n-k} .$$

We now see $Y = \bar{X}_k + \bar{X}_{n-k}$ is distributed $N(0, \frac{1}{k} + \frac{1}{n-k})$. $\frac{1}{2}Y$ will still be normally distributed. By linearity properties

$$E(\tfrac{1}{2}Y) = \tfrac{1}{2}E(Y) = \tfrac{1}{2} \cdot 0 = 0 .$$

Since $\text{Var}(a\,y) = a^2 \text{Var}(y)$, $\text{Var}(\frac{1}{2}\,y) = \frac{1}{4}\text{Var}\,y = \frac{1}{4}(\frac{1}{k} + \frac{1}{n-k}) = \frac{1}{4k} + \frac{1}{4n-4k}$.

Therefore, $\frac{1}{2}(\bar{X}_k + \bar{X}_{n-k})$ has a distribution which is $N(0, \frac{1}{4k} + \frac{1}{4n-4k})$.

b) Here we concern ourselves with $k\bar{X}_k^2 + (n-k)\bar{X}_{n-k}^2$. Note that $\bar{X}_k$ is distributed normally with mean 0 and variance $1/k$. $\sqrt{k}\,\bar{X}_k$ will still be normally distributed with mean zero but the variance will be 1.

$1 (\text{Var}(aX) = a^2\text{Var}(X); \text{Var}(\sqrt{k}\,\bar{X}_k) = k\,\text{Var}(\bar{X}_k) = k\frac{1}{k} = 1)$. $\sqrt{k}\,\bar{X}_k$ is distributed $N(0,1)$. An identical argument applies to $\sqrt{n-k}\,\bar{X}_{n-k}$.

Note that $k\bar{X}_k^2 + (n-k)\bar{X}_{n-k}^2 = (\sqrt{k}\,\bar{X}_k)^2 + (\sqrt{n-k}\,\bar{X}_{n-k})^2$ which is distributed as $[N(0,1)]^2 + [N(0,1)]^2$. Since $[N(0,1)]^2$ is $\chi^2(1)$, we have $\chi^2(1) + \chi^2(1)$. We know that $\chi^2(m) + \chi^2(n) = \chi^2(m+n)$, so our final answer is $\chi^2(1+1) = \chi^2(2)$.

c) $X_1$ is a standard normal random variable as is $X_2$. Hence $X_1^2/X_2^2$ is the quotient of the squares of 2 standard normal quantities. Equivalently it is the quotient of 2 chi-square random variables, each with 1 degree of freedom. But

$$\frac{\chi^2(1)}{\chi^2(1)} = \frac{\chi^2(1)/1}{\chi^2(1)/1}$$

which by definition is distributed $F(1,1)$.

● **PROBLEM** 13-38

Let $X_1, \ldots, X_n$ be a random sample from $N(\mu, \sigma^2)$. Define

$$\bar{X}_k = \frac{1}{k} \sum_1^k X_i ,$$

$$\bar{X}_{n-k} = \frac{1}{n-k} \sum_{k+1}^{n} X_i ,$$

$$\bar{X} = \frac{1}{n} \sum_{1}^{n} X_i .$$

$$S_k^2 = \frac{1}{n-k} \sum_{1}^{k} (X_i - \bar{X}_k)^2 ,$$

$$S_{n-k}^2 = \frac{1}{n-k-1} \sum_{k+1}^{n} (X_i - \bar{X}_{n-k})^2$$

and

$$S^2 = \frac{1}{n-1} \sum_{1}^{n} (X_i - \bar{X})^2 .$$

(a) What is the distribution of $\sigma^{-2}[(k-1)S_k^2 + (n-k-1)S_{n-k}^2]$?

(b) What is the distribution of $(\frac{1}{2})(\bar{X}_k + \bar{X}_{n-k})$?

(c) What is the distribution of $\sigma^{-2}(X_i - \mu)^2$ ?

(d) What is the distribution of $S_k^2/S_{n-k}^2$ ?

Solution: a) We are concerned with

$$\frac{(k-1)S_k^2}{\sigma^2} + \frac{(n-k-1)S_{n-k}^2}{\sigma^2} .$$

From a previous problem and the general theory we know that $\frac{(n-1)S^2}{\sigma^2}$ has a chi-square distribution with $n-1$ degrees of freedom. Applying this to our situation

$$\frac{(k-1)S_k^2}{\sigma^2} \quad \text{and} \quad \frac{(n-k-1)S_{n-k}^2}{\sigma^2}$$

are chi-square distributed with $k-1$ and $n-k-1$ degrees of freedom respectively.

We have $\chi^2(k-1) + \chi^2(n-k-1)$. Since chi-square degrees of freedom are additive our answer is

$$\chi^2(k-1 + n-k-1) = \chi^2(n-2).$$

b) $\bar{X}_k$ and $\bar{X}_{n-k}$ are sample means taken from a normal distribution. They will be normally distributed with mean equal to the original population mean $\mu$ . The variances are found by dividing the population variance by the sample sizes. We obtain $\sigma^2/k$ and $\sigma^2/n-k$ .

A linear combination of normal distributions, such as $\frac{1}{2}(\bar{X}_k + \bar{X}_{n-k})$, will be normally distributed. By the linearity properties of expectation,

$$E[\frac{1}{2}(\bar{X}_k + \bar{X}_{n-k})] = \frac{1}{2}[E(\bar{X}_k) + E(\bar{X}_{n-k})] = \frac{1}{2} 2\mu = \mu . \text{ Since } \bar{X}_k \text{ and}$$

$\bar{X}_{n-k}$ are formed from different observations, they will be independent. The formula $\text{Var}(aX + bY) = a^2 \text{Var}(X) + b^2 \text{Var}(Y)$ will apply. In our example $\text{Var}(\frac{1}{2}[\bar{X}_k + \bar{X}_{n-k}]) = \text{Var}(\frac{1}{2}\bar{X}_k + \frac{1}{2}\bar{X}_{n-k}) = \frac{1}{4}\text{Var } \bar{X}_k + \frac{1}{4}\text{Var } \bar{X}_{n-k} =$

$$= \frac{1}{4}\frac{\sigma^2}{k} + \frac{1}{4}\frac{\sigma^2}{n-k} = \frac{\sigma^2}{4k} + \frac{\sigma^2}{4n-4k} .$$

Our final distribution is

$$N(\mu, \frac{\sigma^2}{4k} + \frac{\sigma^2}{4n-4k}) .$$

c) Since $X_i$ is normally distributed with mean $\mu$ and variance $\sigma^2$,

$$\frac{X_i - \mu}{\sigma}$$

is distributed $N(0,1)$. Note the following:

$$\sigma^{-2}(X_i - \mu)^2 = ((X_i - \mu)/\sigma)^2 \sim [N(0,1)]^2 \quad \text{and we know}$$

that the square of a standard normal random variable follows a chi-square distribution with one degree of freedom.

d) We will manipulate the quantity $S_k^2/S_{n-k}^2$. First divide the numerator and denominator by $\sigma^2$,

$$\frac{S_k^2/\sigma^2}{S_{n-k}^2/\sigma^2} .$$

Now multiply the numerator by $k-1/k-1$ and the denominator by $n-k-1/n-k-1$,

$$\frac{\dfrac{1}{k-1}\left(\dfrac{(k-1)S_k^2}{\sigma^2}\right)}{\dfrac{1}{n-k-1}\left(\dfrac{(n-k-1)S_{n-k}^2}{\sigma^2}\right)} .$$

The quantities in the parentheses we recognize from previous work as chi-square random variables. We have

$$\frac{\chi^2_{(k-1)}/k-1}{\chi^2_{(n-k-1)}/n-k-1} .$$

By definition this ratio has a distribution which is $F(k-1, n-k-1)$.

# THE SAMPLING OF ORDER STATISTICS

● PROBLEM 13-39

Suppose that the life of a certain light bulb is exponentially distributed with mean 100 hours. If 10 such light bulbs are installed simultaneously, what is the distribution of the life of the light bulb that fails first, and what is its expected life? Let $X_i$ denote the life of the ith light bulb; then $Y_1 = \min[X_1, \ldots, X_{10}]$ is the life of the light bulb that fails first. Assume that the $X_i$'s are independent.

Solution: We discuss the case in complete generality first. Let $X_1, \ldots, X_n$ be $n$ given random variables. Define $Y_1 = \min (X_1, \ldots, X_n)$ and $Y_n = \max(X_1, \ldots, X_n)$. $Y_1$ and $Y_n$ are called the first and nth order statistics.

In order to find $f_{y_1}(y)$, we first obtain $F_{y_1}(y)$ and then differentiate to find $F_{y_1}'(y)$.

$$F_{y_1}(y) = \Pr(Y_1 \leq y) = 1 - \Pr(Y_1 > y) = 1 - \Pr(X_1 > y; \ldots; X_n > y)$$

since $Y_1$ is greater than $y$ if and only if every $X_i > y$. And if

$X_1, \ldots, X_n$ are independent, then

$$1 - \Pr(X_1 > y; \ldots; X_n > y) = 1 - \Pr(X_1 > y) \ldots \Pr(X_n > y)$$

$$= 1 - \prod_{i=1}^{n} \Pr(X_i > y) = 1 - \prod_{i=1}^{n} [1 - F_{X_i}(y)].$$

We further assume that $X_1, \ldots, X_n$ are identically distributed with common cumulative distribution function $F_x(\cdot)$; then,

$$1 - \prod_{i=1}^{n} [1 - F_{X_i}(y)] = 1 - [1 - F_x(y)]^n .$$

To find $f_{y_1}(y)$, we note

$$f_{y_1}(y) = \frac{d}{dy} F_{y_1}(y) = \frac{d}{dy}[1 - [1 - F_x(y)]^n]$$

$$= -n[1 - F_x(y)]^{n-1} \frac{d}{dy}[1 - F_x(y)]$$

$$= n[1 - F_x(y)]^{n-1} f_x(y).$$

We now apply this to our example. The mean of an exponential distribution is $1/\lambda$ where $\lambda$ is the parameter of the distribution. We know then that $1/\lambda = 100$ or $\lambda = 1/100$. The distribution of a certain light bulb is exponential with parameter $1/100$;

$$f(y) = \frac{1}{100} e^{-(1/100)y} , \quad y \geq 0 .$$

Also by definition

$$F(y) = \int_{-\infty}^{y} f(t)dt = \int_{0}^{y} \frac{1}{100} e^{-(1/100)t} dt$$

$$= -e^{-\frac{1}{100}t} \Big|_{0}^{y} = 1 - e^{-y/100} .$$

In our problem, $n = 10$; therefore,

$$f_{y_1}(y) = n[1 - F(y)]^{n-1} f(y)$$

$$= 10[1 - (1 - e^{-y/100})]^9 \frac{1}{100} e^{-y/100}$$

$$= \frac{10}{100}(e^{-y/100})^{10} = \frac{1}{10} e^{-y/10} .$$

The first order statistic, $y_1$ is exponentially distributed with parameter $1/10$. Hence $E(y_1) = \frac{1}{1/10} = 10$.

● **PROBLEM 13-40**

Let $Y_1 \leq Y_2 \leq \ldots \leq Y_n$ represent the order statistics of the sample $\{X_1, \ldots, X_n\}$ from a cumulative distribution function $F$. Find the marginal cumulative distribution function of $Y_\alpha$, $\alpha = 1, 2, \ldots, n$.

<u>Solution</u>: For any fixed $y$, let $Z_i = 1$ if $X_i$ is in the interval $(-\infty, y]$ and $0$ if not. The sum $\sum_{i=1}^{n} Z_i$ will then be the number of

the $X_i$ that are less than or equal to y. Note that $F(y)$ is the constant probability that $X_i \leq y$ , and there are n Bernoulli"trials" to see whether $X_i \leq y$ or not.

From this description, we see that $\sum_{i=1}^{n} Z_i$ has a binomial distribution with parameters n and $F(y)$.

We are looking for $F_{y_\alpha}(y)$. $F_{y_\alpha}(y) = \Pr(y_\alpha \leq y) = \Pr[\Sigma Z_i \geq \alpha]$

$$= \sum_{j=\alpha}^{n} \binom{n}{j} [F(y)]^j [1 - F(y)]^{n-j} .$$

The key step in this problem is the equivalence of the two events $\{Y_\alpha \leq y\}$ and $\{\Sigma Z_i \geq \alpha\}$. If the $\alpha$th order statistic is less than or equal to y, then surely the number of $X_i$ less than or equal to y is greater than or equal to $\alpha$ , and conversely.

● **PROBLEM** 13-41

For the density $f(x) = 2x$; $0 \leq x \leq 2$ , find the cumulative distribution for the twelfth order statistic in a sample of 13.

Solution: We know that
$$F_{y_\alpha}(y) = \sum_{j=\alpha}^{n} \binom{n}{j} [F(y)]^j [1 - F(y)]^{n-j} .$$

In our problem $\alpha = 12$, n = 13, and

$F(y) = \int_{-\infty}^{y} f(x)dx = \int_{0}^{y} 2x\,dx$; $0 \leq y \leq 2$

$\quad = y^2$ ; $0 \leq y \leq 2$ .

$F_{y_{12}}(y) = \sum_{j=12}^{13} \binom{13}{j}(y^2)^j (1 - y^2)^{n-j}$

$\quad = \binom{13}{12}(y^2)^{12} (1 - y^2)^{13-12} + \binom{13}{13}(y^2)^{13}(1-y)^{13-13}$

$\quad = 13\,y^{24}(1 - y^2)^1 + y^{26} \quad = 13\,y^{24} - 13y^{26} + y^{26}$

$\quad = 13\,y^{24} - 12\,y^{26} .$

● **PROBLEM** 13-42

This problem is of a theoretical nature.                    Prove all parts of the following theorem: Let $X_1, X_2, \ldots, X_n$ be a random sample from the probability density function $f(\cdot)$ with cumulative distribution $F(\cdot)$. Let $Y_1 \leq Y_2 \leq \ldots \leq Y_n$ denote the corresponding order statistics; then

i) $$f_{y_\alpha}(y) = \frac{n!}{(\alpha-1)!(n-\alpha)!} \, [F(y)]^{\alpha-1}[1 - F(y)]^{n-\alpha} \, f(y) \ .$$

(ii) $$f_{y_\alpha y_\beta}(x,y) = \frac{n!}{(\alpha-1)!(\beta-\alpha-1)!(n-\beta)!} \times [F(x)]^{\alpha-1}$$

$$\times [F(y) - F(x)]^{\beta-\alpha-1} \times [1 - F(y)]^{n-\beta}$$

$$\times f(x)f(y) \ .$$

(iii) $$f_{y_1,\dots,y_n} = n! \, f(y_1)f(y_2)\dots f(y_n) \quad \text{for} \quad y_1 < y_2 < \dots < y_n \ .$$

**Solution:** Assume that the random sample $X_1, X_2, \dots, X_n$ came from a probability density function $f$. The random variables $X_i$ are continuous. We can obtain $f_{y_\alpha}(y)$ by differentiating $F_{y_\alpha}(y)$. Using the definition of a derivative, we have

$$f_{y_\alpha}(y) = \lim_{\Delta y \to 0} \frac{F_{y_\alpha}(y+\Delta y) - F_{y_\alpha}(y)}{\Delta y}$$

$$= \lim_{\Delta y \to 0} \frac{\Pr(y < y_\alpha \le y+\Delta y)}{\Delta y}$$

$$= \lim_{\Delta y \to 0} \frac{\Pr[(\alpha-1) \text{ of the } X_i \le y; \text{ one } X_i \text{ in } (y, y+\Delta y)]; (n-\alpha) \text{ of the } X_i > y+\Delta y]}{\Delta y} \ .$$

By the multinomial distribution this becomes

$$\lim_{\Delta y \to 0} \left( \frac{n!}{(\alpha-1)!1!(n-\alpha)!} \frac{[F(y)]^{\alpha-1}[F(y+\Delta y)-F(y)][1 - F(y+\Delta y)]^{n-\alpha}}{\Delta y} \right)$$

$$= \frac{n!}{(\alpha-1)!(n-\alpha)!} \, [F(y)]^{\alpha-1}[1 - F(y)]^{n-\alpha} \lim_{\Delta y \to 0} \frac{F(y+\Delta y)-F(y)}{\Delta y}$$

$$= \frac{n!}{(\alpha-1)!(n-\alpha)!} \, [F(y)]^{\alpha-1}[1 - F(y)]^{n-\alpha} \, f(y) \ . \qquad \text{(i)}$$

We use a similar method to derive the joint density of $y_\alpha$ and $y_\beta$ for $1 \le \alpha < \beta \le n$.

$$f_{y_\alpha, y_\beta}(x,y) \, \Delta x \Delta y \approx \Pr[x < y_\alpha \le x + \Delta x; \, y \le Y_\beta \le y + \Delta y]$$

$$\approx \Pr[(\alpha-1) \text{ of the } X_i \le X; \text{ one } X_i \text{ in } (X, X+\Delta X);$$
$$(\beta-\alpha-1 \text{ of the } X_i \text{ in } (X + \Delta X, Y);$$
$$\text{one } X_i \text{ in } (y, y+\Delta y); (n-\beta) \text{ of the } X_i > y+\Delta y]$$

$$\approx \frac{n!}{(\alpha-1)!1!(\beta-\alpha-1)!(n-\beta)!} \times [F(x)]^{\alpha-1}$$

$$\times [F(y)-F(x+\Delta x)]^{\beta-\alpha-1}[1-F(y+\Delta y)]^{n-\beta}$$

$$\times \Pr(\text{one } X_i \text{ in}(x, x+\Delta x)) \Pr(\text{one } X_i \text{ in } (y, y+\Delta y))$$

But as $\Delta x$ and $\Delta y$ shrink $F(x+\Delta x)$ and $F(y+\Delta y)$ approach $F(x)$ and $F(y)$. Also note that $\Pr(\text{one } X_i \text{ in } (x+\Delta x])$ is $\approx f(x)\Delta x$.

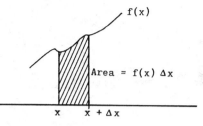

Similarly for $f(y)$. We then have

$$f_{y_\alpha, y_\beta}(x,y)\Delta x \Delta y = \frac{n!}{(\alpha-1)!(\beta-\alpha-1)!(n-\beta)!}[F(x)]^{\alpha-1}[F(y)-F(x)]^{\beta-\alpha-1}$$

$$\times [1 - F(y)]^{n-\beta} f(x)\Delta x \times f(y)\Delta y \ .$$

In the limit theory

$$f_{y_\alpha, y_\beta}(x,y) = \frac{n!}{(\alpha-1)!(\beta-\alpha-1)!(n-\beta)!}[F(x)]^{\alpha-1}[F(y)-F(x)]^{\beta-\alpha-1}[1-F(y)]^{n-\beta}$$

$$\times f(x)f(y). \tag{ii}$$

In general $f_{y_1,\ldots,y_n}(y_1,y_2,\ldots,y_n)$

$$= \lim_{\Delta y_i \to 0} \frac{1}{\prod_{i=1}^{n} \Delta y_i} \Pr[y_1 \le y_1 \le y_1+\Delta y_1;\ldots;y_n \le y_n \le y_n+\Delta y_n]$$

$$= \lim_{\Delta y_i \to 0} \frac{n!}{\prod_{i=1}^{n} \Delta y_i}[F(y_1+\Delta y_1)-F(y_1)]\ldots[F(y_n+\Delta Y_n)-F(Y_n)] \ .$$

The $n!$ accounts for the $n!$ orders in which the observations may be selected. Now

$$f = n! \lim_{\Delta y_i \to 0}\left[\frac{[F(y_1+\Delta y_1)-F(y_1)]}{\Delta y_1} \cdots \frac{[F(y_n+\Delta y_n)-F(y_n)]}{\Delta y_n}\right]$$

$$= n!\frac{dF}{d(y_1)}\frac{dF}{d(y_2)}\cdots\frac{dF}{d(y_n)} = n!\, f(y_1) \ldots f(y_n) \ . \tag{iii}$$

# CHAPTER 14

# CONFIDENCE INTERVALS

Note to the reader: Whenever a sample variance appears in this chapter, it will be understood to be the unbiased estimate $\dfrac{\sum\limits_{i}(X_i - \bar{X})^2}{n - 1}$ , and not the maximum likelihood estimate $\dfrac{\sum\limits_{i}(X_i - \bar{X})^2}{n}$ . Any differences between formulas in this chapter and those with which you are familiar <u>may</u> be due to this.

● **PROBLEM** 14 -1

Let X be $\chi^2(16)$. What is the probability that the random interval $(X, 3.3X)$ contains the point $x = 26.3$? and what is the expected length of the interval?

<u>Solution</u>:    We will begin by trying to transform the interval $X < 26.3 < 3.3 X$ into an equivalent event with which we can more easily deal. It is clear that X must be less than 26.3. Examine now the right hand side of the inequality $26.3 < 3.3 X$.  This is equivalent to $X > \dfrac{26.3}{3.3}$  or $X > 7.97$.

Now we see $\Pr(X < 26.3 < 3.3 X) = \Pr(7.97 < X < 26.3)$. Recall that X is $\chi^2(16)$, therefore:

$\Pr(7.97 < X < 26.3) = \Pr(\chi^2(16) < 26.3) - \Pr(\chi^2(16) < 7.97)$.

From the table of the Chi-square distribution, this equals $.95 - .05 = .90$.

The length of the interval is $3.3X - X = 2.3 X$.

$E \text{ (Length)} = E(2.3 X) = 2.3 E(X)$

by the linearity properties of expectation. Since X is $\chi^2(16)$, $E(X) = 16$ $[E(\chi^2(n)) = n.]$.

$E \text{ (Length)} = 2.3(16) = 36.8$.

Let X be $N(0,\sigma^2)$, $\sigma^2 > 0$. What is the probability that the random interval $(|X|, |10X|)$ includes the point $\sigma$ and what is the expected value of the length of this random interval?

Solution:    Let us try to begin our attack by finding an equivalent more understandable event for $|X| < \sigma < 10|X|$. We have two cases. First consider $X > 0$. Then $|X| = X$ and $X < \sigma < 10X$. We take the reciprocal of the inequality and obtain $\frac{1}{10X} < \frac{1}{\sigma} < \frac{1}{X}$. Multiplying by X yields $\frac{1}{10} < \frac{X}{\sigma} < 1$.

Consider the case where $X < 0$. Then $|X| = -X$ and $-X < \sigma < -10X$. Taking the reciprocal inequality yields $\frac{-1}{10X} < \frac{1}{\sigma} < \frac{-1}{X}$. (Recall         that X is negative.) Multiply by X and obtain $-\frac{1}{10} > \frac{X}{\sigma} > -1$. Finally $|X| < \sigma < 10|X|$ is

equivalent to $\left(\frac{1}{10} < \frac{X}{\sigma} < 1\right) \cup \left(-1 < \frac{X}{\sigma} < -\frac{1}{10}\right)$   . Since

$\frac{1}{10} < \frac{X}{\sigma} < 1$ and $-1 < \frac{X}{\sigma} < -\frac{1}{10}$ are disjoint,

$$\Pr\left[\left(\frac{1}{10} < \frac{X}{\sigma} < 1\right) \cup \left(-1 < \frac{X}{\sigma} < -\frac{1}{10}\right)\right]$$

$$= \Pr\left[\frac{1}{10} < \frac{X}{\sigma} < 1\right] + \Pr\left[-1 < \frac{X}{\sigma} < -\frac{1}{10}\right] \quad .$$

Thus, $\Pr(|X| < \sigma < 10|X|)$

$$= \Pr\left[\frac{1}{10} < \frac{X}{\sigma} < 1\right] + \Pr\left[-1 < \frac{X}{\sigma} < -\frac{1}{10}\right] .$$

But since $N(0, \sigma^2)$ is symmetrical about 0, its mean,

$\Pr\left[\frac{1}{10} < \frac{X}{\sigma} < 1\right] = \Pr\left[-1 < \frac{X}{\sigma} < -\frac{1}{10}\right]$   and thus

$\Pr(|X| < \sigma < 10|X|) = 2\Pr\left[\frac{1}{10} < \frac{X}{\sigma} < 1\right].$

Note that X is normally distributed.    Since its mean is 0 , then $\frac{X}{\sigma}$ is a standard normal quantity.

Hence $2\Pr\left[\frac{1}{10} < \frac{X}{\sigma} < 1\right] = 2(N(1) - N(0.1))$

$$= 2(.84 - .54) = 2(.30) = .60.$$

The random interval's length is $10|X| - |X| = 9|X|$. We want $E(9|X|)$. By linearity properties, $E(9|X|) = 9E(|X|)$.

By definition $E|X| = \int_{-\infty}^{\infty} |X| f(x) = \int_{-\infty}^{0} -xf(x) + \int_{0}^{\infty} xf(x)$

$$= \int\limits^{0} \frac{-x}{\sqrt{2\pi\sigma^2}} e^{-x^2/2\sigma^2} dx + \int\limits_{0}^{\infty} \frac{x \, e^{-x^2/2\sigma^2}}{\sqrt{2\pi\sigma^2}} \, dx.$$

By making the change of variables - x = u, we obtain

$$\int\limits_{u=0}^{\infty} \frac{u \, e^{-u^2/2\sigma^2}}{\sqrt{2\pi\sigma^2}} \, du \text{ and note that}$$

the two integrals are equal; therefore:

$$E(9|X|) = 9 \left[ 2 \int\limits_{0}^{\infty} \frac{x \, e^{-x^2/2\sigma^2}}{\sqrt{2\pi\sigma^2}} \right] dx \ = \frac{18}{\sqrt{2\pi}} \int\limits_{0}^{\infty} \frac{x}{\sigma} e^{-x^2/2\sigma^2} \, dx \ .$$

Let $w = \frac{x^2}{2\sigma^2}$, then $dw = \frac{2x}{2\sigma^2} dx = \frac{xdx}{\sigma^2}$.

Hence $\frac{x}{\sigma} dx = \sigma dw$.

$$E(9|X|) = \frac{18}{\sqrt{2\pi}} \int\limits_{0}^{\infty} \sigma e^{-w} \, dw = \frac{18\sigma}{\sqrt{2\pi}} \int\limits_{0}^{\infty} e^{-w} \, dw$$

$$= \frac{18\sigma}{\sqrt{2\pi}} \left. -e^{-w} \right]_{0}^{\infty} \ = \frac{18\sigma}{\sqrt{2\pi}} (0 + 1)$$

$$= \frac{18\sigma}{\sqrt{2\pi}} \ .$$

● **PROBLEM** 14-3

If $\bar{x}$ denotes the mean of a random sample of size n from a distribution which is $N(\mu, \sigma^2)$, $\sigma^2 > 0$. , then we know that $N(\mu, \sigma^2/n)$. What is the probability that the random interval $(\bar{X} - 2\sigma/\sqrt{n}, \bar{X} + 2\sigma/\sqrt{n})$ includes the point $\mu$, whatever the values of $\mu$, $\sigma^2 > 0$, and the positive integer n?

Solution:    Let us transform the interval $(\bar{X} - 2\sigma/\sqrt{n}$, $\bar{X} + 2\sigma/\sqrt{n})$ into something we can more readily deal with.

We start with $\bar{X} - \frac{2\sigma}{\sqrt{n}} < \mu < \bar{X} + \frac{2\sigma}{\sqrt{n}}$ .

Multiply by - 1: $- \bar{X} - \frac{2\sigma}{\sqrt{n}} < - \mu < - \bar{X} + \frac{2\sigma}{\sqrt{n}}$ .

Add $\bar{X}$: $- \frac{2\sigma}{\sqrt{n}} < \bar{X} - \mu < \frac{2\sigma}{\sqrt{n}}$ .

Divide by $\frac{\sigma}{\sqrt{n}}$ : $- 2 < \frac{\overline{X} - \mu}{\sigma/\sqrt{n}} < 2.$

Now $\frac{\overline{X} - \mu}{\sigma/\sqrt{n}}$ is a standard normal quantity and so

$$Pr\left(- 2 < \begin{array}{l} \text{Standard} \\ \text{Normal} \end{array} < 2\right) = \Phi(2) - \Phi(- 2) = .977 - .023 = .954.$$

Note that in determining the probability .954, no attention was paid to what values $\mu$ and $\sigma^2$ might take on. n didn't come into play either.

Quantities, such as $\frac{\overline{X} - \mu}{\sigma/\sqrt{n}}$ , which have distributions independent of the parameters $\mu$ and $\sigma^2$ are often called pivotal quantities. Examples of pivotal quantities are those that have fixed distributions such as standard normal, t with n degrees of freedom, etc. Algebraic manipulations of pivotal quantities are key factors in establishing confidence intervals.

# MEAN OF A NORMAL DISTRIBUTION WITH KNOWN VARIANCE

● **PROBLEM** 14-4

Find a 95 per cent confidence interval for $\mu$, the true mean of a normal population which has variance $\sigma^2 = 100$. Consider a sample of size 25 with a mean of 67.53.

Solution: We have a sample mean $\overline{X} = 67.53$. We want to transform that into a standard normal quantity, for we know from the standard normal tables that

Pr (- 1.96 < Standard Normal Quantity < 1.96) = .95 .

$\frac{\overline{X} - E(\overline{X})}{\sqrt{Var\ (\overline{X})}}$ is a standard normal quantity.

Recall now that the expectation of a sample mean is $\mu$, the true mean of a population. Also recall that the variance of a sample mean is $\frac{\sigma^2}{n}$ where $\sigma^2$ is the true variance of the population and n is the size of our sample. Applying

this to our case, $E(\overline{X}) = \mu$ and $\sqrt{Var\ (\overline{X})} = \sqrt{\frac{\sigma^2}{n}} = \sqrt{\frac{100}{25}} = 2.$

For our sample: $Pr\left(- 1.96 < \frac{\overline{X} - \mu}{2} < 1.96\right) = .95 .$

Multiplying by 2: Pr(- 3.92 < $\overline{X}$ - $\mu$ < 3.92) = .95.

Transposing:  $\Pr(\overline{X} - 3.92 < \mu < \overline{X} + 3.92) = .95$.

$\overline{X} - 3.92 < \mu < \overline{X} + 3.92$ is our required confidence interval. If we insert our given sample mean, we come up with   $67.53 - 3.92 < \mu < 67.53 + 3.92$

or                $63.61 < \mu < 71.45$.

● **PROBLEM** 14-5

This problem deals with the tensile strength of a new material. Nineteen samples of the new material were tested. The mean tensile strength was found to be 26,100 psi. Find a ninety-five per cent lower confidence limit for $\mu$, the true mean tensile strength, i.e., find a value which we can be 95% certain is lower than $\mu$. Assume tensile strength to be normally distributed with mean $\mu$ and standard deviation $\sigma = 300$ psi.

Solution:   From the Standard Normal Table we see that
$\Pr(\text{Standard Normal Quantity} < 1.645) = .95$ .

Our task is now to find a standard normal pivitol quantity involving $\mu$. Let's try to standardize the sample mean $\overline{X}$. Recall that when sampling from a normal population, the sample mean, $\overline{X}$, is distributed normally and

$$E(\overline{X}) = \mu \qquad \text{and} \qquad \text{Var}(\overline{X}) = \frac{\sigma^2}{n}$$

where $\mu$, $\sigma^2$ are the parameters of the population and n is the sample size. For any normal distribution,

$$\frac{X - E(X)}{\sqrt{\text{Var}(\overline{X})}} \qquad \text{is standard normal. Thus,} \qquad \frac{\overline{X} - E(\overline{X})}{\sqrt{\text{Var }\overline{X}}}$$

is standard normal.

$$\Pr\left[\frac{\overline{X} - E(\overline{X})}{\sqrt{\text{Var }(\overline{X})}} < 1.645\right] = .95 \qquad \text{or} \qquad \Pr\left[\frac{\overline{X} - \mu}{\sqrt{\sigma^2/n}} < 1.645\right] = .95 .$$

Since $\overline{X}$, $\sigma^2$, and n are known we have found our pivitol quantity involving $\mu$,  $\dfrac{\overline{X} - \mu}{\sqrt{\sigma^2/n}}$ or $\dfrac{\overline{X} - \mu}{\sigma/\sqrt{n}}$ .

Therefore,  $\Pr\left[\dfrac{\overline{X} - \mu}{\sigma/\sqrt{n}} < 1.645\right] = .95$ .

$\overline{X}$ is given as 26,100; $\sigma$ is 300; n is 19 ; thus ,

$\dfrac{26,100 - \mu}{300/\sqrt{19}} < 1.645$;  $(\mu < 25,986.8)$;   $A = 25,986.8$.

In the production of size D cells for use as flashlight batteries, the standard deviation of operating life for all batteries is 3.0 hours, based on the known variability of battery ingredients. Distribution of the operating life for all batteries is approximately normal. A random sample has a mean operating life of 20.0 hours. Find a 90% confidence interval for the true mean life of the battery.

Solution:    Let $\mu$ = the true mean life of the battery.

Let $\sigma$ = the standard deviation of operating life.

We know from the standard normal table:

$Pr(-1.645 <$ standard normal quantity $< 1.645) = .90$.

Our main stumbling block now is the lack of an appropriate standard normal quantity involving $\mu$. But we know that if a population is normally distributed with mean $\mu$ and standard deviation $\sigma$, an extracted sample mean will be normally distributed with expectation $\mu$ and standard deviation $\frac{\sigma}{\sqrt{n}}$. (n is the sample size.) Let's standardize the sample mean.

$\frac{\overline{X} - E(\overline{X})}{\sqrt{Var\ \overline{X}}}$ is standard normal. In our case

$\frac{\overline{X} - E(\overline{X})}{\sqrt{Var\ \overline{X}}} = \frac{20.0 - \mu}{3.0/\sqrt{n}}$ . We have obtained a standard

normal quantity involving $\mu$. Therefore

$-1.645 < \frac{20.0 - \mu}{3.0/\sqrt{n}} < 1.645$ is a 90 percent C. I.

Multiplying by $\frac{3.0}{\sqrt{n}}$ :    $-\frac{4.94}{\sqrt{n}} < 20.0 - \mu < \frac{4.94}{\sqrt{n}}$ .

Subtracting 20:    $-\frac{4.94}{\sqrt{n}} - 20 < -\mu < \frac{4.94}{\sqrt{n}} - 20$ .

Multiply by $-1$:    $20 - \frac{4.94}{\sqrt{n}} < \mu < 20 + \frac{4.94}{\sqrt{n}}$

Our required confidence interval is

$20 - \frac{4.94}{\sqrt{n}} < \mu < 20 + \frac{4.94}{\sqrt{n}}$ .

In doing a confidence interval problem involving a standard normal statistic we always choose a quantity k such that

Pr(- k < Standard Normal Quantity < k) = 1 - α.

Why?

Solution:    Consider an example. For 95% confidence intervals we use the values ± 1.96 such that - 1.96 < Z < 1.96. Inspection also tells us that P(- 1.68 < Z < 2.70) = .95. Consider the interval lengths. The first one is 1.96 - (- 1.96) = 3.92; the second is 2.70 - (- 1.68) = 4.38. The first calculation will yield a shorter interval.

It is obvious that any two numbers a and b such that 95% of the area under the standard normal curve lies between a and b will give us a 95% confidence interval. Ordinarily one would want the confidence interval to be as short as possible, and it is made so by making a and b as close together as possible since the relation $P\left(a < \dfrac{\overline{X} - \mu}{\sigma/\sqrt{n}} < b\right)$

gives rise to a confidence interval as follows:

$$a < \frac{\overline{X} - \mu}{\sigma/\sqrt{n}} < b .$$

Multiplying by    $\dfrac{\sigma}{\sqrt{n}}$ : $a \dfrac{\sigma}{\sqrt{n}} < \overline{X} - \mu < b \dfrac{\sigma}{\sqrt{n}}$ .

Multiplying by    - 1: $\overline{X} - b \dfrac{\sigma}{\sqrt{n}} < \mu < \overline{X} - a \dfrac{\sigma}{\sqrt{n}}$ .

The length of the interval is

$$(- a - (- b)) \frac{\sigma}{\sqrt{n}} = (b - a) \frac{\sigma}{\sqrt{n}} .$$

The length of the interval depends on b - a since $\dfrac{\sigma}{\sqrt{n}}$ is a constant. The distance b - a will be minimized for a fixed area when $\Phi(b) = \Phi(a)$, as is evident on referring to the following diagram.

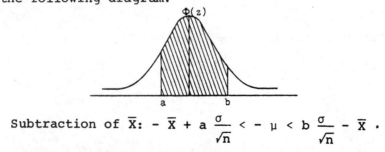

Subtraction of $\overline{X}$: $- \overline{X} + a \dfrac{\sigma}{\sqrt{n}} < - \mu < b \dfrac{\sigma}{\sqrt{n}} - \overline{X}$ .

If the point b is moved a short distance to the left, the point a will need to be moved a lesser distance to the left in order to keep the area the same; this operation decreases the interval length and will continue to do so as long as $\Phi(b) < \Phi(a)$. Since $\Phi(Z)$ is symmetrical about $Z = 0$ in the present example, the minimum value of $b - a$ for a fixed area occurs when $b = -a$.

● **PROBLEM** 14-8

In Grand Central Station, there is a coffee machine which is regulated so that the amount of coffee dispensed is normally distributed with a standard deviation of .5 ounces per cup. A random sample of 50 cups had an average of 5 ounces per cup.

(a) Find the maximum likelihood estimate for the average amount of coffee in each cup dispensed by the machine.
(b) Find a 95% confidence interval for the mean of all cups dispensed.

Solution:      (a) The maximum likelihood estimator has the following underlying idea. Consider every possible value the parameter might have, and for each value compute the probability that the particular sample at hand would have occurred if that were the true value of the parameter. Of all possible values of the parameter, the one to be chosen as the estimate is the one for which the probability of the actual observations is greatest. The maximum likelihood estimate for the mean of a normal distribution is the sample mean. Therefore our answer is 5, the sample mean.

(b) As always, we must search for a standard normal quantity involving $\mu$. Note that the sample mean of a normal distribution is normally distributed with mean $\mu$ and standard deviation $\dfrac{\sigma}{\sqrt{n}}$, where $\mu$ and $\sigma$ are the mean and standard deviation of the population and n is the sample size. Standardizing the sample mean we obtain

$$\frac{\overline{X} - E(\overline{X})}{\sqrt{\text{Var } \overline{X}}} = \frac{\overline{X} - \mu}{\sigma/\sqrt{n}} \quad \text{is standard normal.}$$

This is valid since $\overline{X}$ is normally distributed. We are given $\overline{X}(5)$, $\sigma(.5)$, and n (50) so we have a standard normal quantity depending on $\mu$ alone.

From the standard normal table we know:

Pr(- 1.96 < standard normal < 1.96) = .95 .

Inserting our standard normal variable:

$$\text{Pr}\left(- 1.96 < \frac{\overline{X} - \mu}{\sigma/\sqrt{n}} < 1.96\right) = .95 .$$

427

Substituting our given values into the interval and solving for $\mu$:

$$-1.96 < \frac{5 - \mu}{.5/\sqrt{50}} < 1.96$$

$$-.139 < 5 - \mu < .139.$$

$$-5.139 < -\mu < -4.861)$$

$$4.859 < \mu < 5.139$$

Our required confidence interval is

$$4.859 < \mu < 5.139 .$$

● **PROBLEM** 14-9

In a massive attempt to compete with General Electric, the Acme Light Bulb Company issued a new line of bulb. Acme took 100 bulbs from their new line which had an established standard deviation of 140 hours. The mean measured lifetime was 1 280 hours.

(a) Give an estimate of the mean lifetime and briefly rationalize it. (b) Give a 95 per cent confidence interval estimate of the mean lifetime of Acme's bulbs.

Solution: (a) $\bar{X} = 1\,280$, n = 100. A sample of size 100 is quite large. The Weak Law of Large Numbers tells us that as a sample gets large we can estimate the true population mean by a sample mean. Therefore our answer is 1 280 hours.

(b) We will search for a standard normal pivotal quantity upon which we can construct a confidence interval. Since the lifetime of a bulb is normally distributed, the sample mean, $\bar{X}$, is too. The sample mean will have an expectation $\mu$, and standard deviation $\frac{\sigma}{\sqrt{n}}$ , where $\mu$ and $\sigma$ are the mean and standard deviation of the population and n is the size of the sample.

$\frac{\bar{X} - E(\bar{X})}{\sqrt{Var\ \bar{X}}}$ will be a standard normal quantity since $\bar{X}$

is normally distributed. By use of the standard normal table,

$$Pr\left[-1.96 < \frac{\bar{X} - E(\bar{X})}{\sqrt{Var\ \bar{X}}} = \frac{\bar{X} - \mu}{\sigma/\sqrt{n}} < 1.96\right] = .95 .$$

We are given $\bar{X} = 1\,280$, $\sigma = 140$, and n = 100.

We can construct our interval estimate from the inequality $- 1.96 < \dfrac{1\ 280 - \mu}{140/\sqrt{100}} < 1.96$.

Simplifying the denominator: $- 1.96 < \dfrac{1280 - \mu}{14} < 1.96$ .

Multiplying by 14: $- 27.44 < 1280 - \mu < 27.44$ .

Subtracting 1280: $- 1307.44 < - \mu < - 1252.56$ .

Multiplying by $- 1$: $1252.56 < \mu < 1307.44$ .

Hence $\quad 1252.56 < \mu < 1307.44$ .

● **PROBLEM** 14-10

Suppose that the weights of all toy fox terrier dogs are normally distributed with a standard deviation of 2.5 kilograms, How large a sample should be taken in order to be 95% confident that the sample mean does not differ from the population mean by more than 0.5 kilograms?

Solution: We are given a normal distribution so we know immediately that $\dfrac{(\overline{X} - \mu)}{\sigma/\sqrt{n}}$ is going to be a standard normal random variable. From the normal tables we know that

$$\Pr\left[- 1.96 < \dfrac{(\overline{X} - \mu)}{\sigma/\sqrt{n}} < 1.96\right] = .95 .$$

We only concern ourselves with our interval

$$- 1.96 < \dfrac{(\overline{X} - \mu)}{\sigma/\sqrt{n}} < 1.96 .$$

To get n*, the smallest n such that the conditions of the problem will hold, we set $\dfrac{\overline{X} - \mu}{\sigma/\sqrt{n^*}} = 1.96.$

$(\overline{X} - \mu)$ involves the restriction that we want the sample mean to differ from the true mean by less than .5 pounds. By examining the expression

$\dfrac{\overline{X} - \mu}{\sigma/\sqrt{n}} = \dfrac{(\overline{X} - \mu)\ \sqrt{n}}{\sigma} = 1.96,$ we see that once n exceeds

n* we can make $(\overline{X} - \mu)$ smaller, thereby having a further restriction on the closeness of the sample mean and the true mean. If we do not need a finer restriction, n < n* will produce a smaller value on the right hand side and we can no longer be .95%confident. We can now conclude that n* can be found by setting $\frac{(\overline{X} - \mu)\ \sqrt{n^*}}{\sigma}$ = 1.96.

Multiply through by $\sigma$: $(\overline{X} - \mu)\ \sqrt{n^*}$ = 1.96 $\sigma$ .

Divide by $(\overline{X} - \mu)$ and square: $n^* = \frac{1.96^2\ \sigma^2}{(\overline{X} - \mu)^2}$ .

We know $|\overline{X} - \mu| < .5$. This implies $(\overline{X} - \mu)^2 < .25$.

By using the value .25 for $(\overline{X} - \mu)^2$ we make use of our maximum margin of error for $\overline{X}$.

Hence $n^* = \frac{1.96^2\ \sigma^2}{.25} = \frac{3.84\ (2.5)^2}{.25}$ = 96.

The sample size should be 96 or greater.

# DIFFERENCE OF MEANS OF NORMAL POPULATIONS WITH KNOWN VARIANCE

● PROBLEM 14-11

A group of experts feel that polishing would have a positive effect on the average endurance limit of steel. Eight specimens of polished steel were measured and their average, $\overline{X}$, was computed to be 86,375 psi. Similarly, 8 specimens of unpolished steel were measured and their average, $\overline{Y}$, was computed to be 79,838 psi. Assume all measurements to be normally distributed with standard deviation 4,000 psi (both samples). Find a 90% lower one-sided confidence limit for $\mu_X - \mu_Y$, the difference in means.

Solution: Our plan of attack will be a common one. We will try to construct a standard normal pivotal quantity involving $\mu_X - \mu_Y$ and use the fact, obtainable from the standard normal table, that

Pr (Standard Normal Quantity < 1.28) = .90.

The sample mean, $\overline{X}$, must be normally distributed, since each measurement is. Also $\overline{X}$ is distributed with $E(\overline{X}) = \mu_X$ and $\sqrt{Var\ \overline{X}} = \frac{\sigma_X}{\sqrt{n_X}}$ . ($\mu_X$, $\sigma_X$, and $n_X$ are the mean of population X, its standard deviation, and the size of the sample we draw from X.) A similar discussion applies to population Y. $E(\overline{Y}) = \mu_Y$; $\sqrt{Var\ \overline{Y}} = \frac{\sigma_Y}{\sqrt{n_Y}}$ .

Consider the random variable $\overline{X} - \overline{Y}$.

$$E(\overline{X} - \overline{Y}) = E(\overline{X} + (-\overline{Y})) = E(\overline{X}) + E(-\overline{Y}) = E(\overline{X}) - E(\overline{Y}).$$

This conclusion follows from the linearity properties of expectation (i.e. $E(X + Y) = E(X) + E(Y)$ and $E(aX) = aE(x)$ when a is a constant). Also note that $E(\overline{X} - \overline{y}) = E(\overline{X}) - E(\overline{Y}) = \mu_x - \mu_y$. Furthermore,

$$\sigma_{(\overline{X}-\overline{Y})} = \sigma \sqrt{\frac{1}{n_x} + \frac{1}{n_y}} \quad . \text{ This results from the rule}$$

$Var(ax + by) = a^2 Var(x) + b^2 Var(y)$. In our case $a = 1$ and $b = -1$ therefore

$$\sigma_{(\overline{X}-\overline{Y})} = \sqrt{Var(\overline{X} - \overline{Y})} = \sqrt{Var(x) + Var(\overline{Y})}$$

$$= \sqrt{\frac{\sigma^2}{n_x} + \frac{\sigma^2}{n_y}} = \sigma\sqrt{\frac{1}{n_x} + \frac{1}{n_y}} \quad .$$

$$\frac{(\overline{X} - \overline{Y}) - E(\overline{X} - \overline{Y})}{\sigma_{(\overline{X}-\overline{Y})}} \quad \text{must be standard normal since}$$

$\overline{X} - \overline{Y}$, the difference of 2 normal distributions, is normal.

$$\frac{(\overline{X} - \overline{Y}) - E(\overline{X} - \overline{Y})}{\sigma_{(\overline{X}-\overline{Y})}} = \frac{(\overline{X} - \overline{Y}) - (\mu_x - \mu_y)}{\sigma\left(\sqrt{\frac{1}{n_x} + \frac{1}{n_y}}\right)}$$

by inserting our derived results.

We obtain: $\quad Pr\left[\dfrac{(\overline{X} - \overline{Y}) - (\mu_x - \mu_y)}{\sigma\sqrt{\frac{1}{n_x} + \frac{1}{n_y}}} < 1.28\right] = .90.$

We are given:

$\overline{X} = 86,375;\ \overline{Y} = 79,838;\ n_x = n_y = 8;\ \sigma = 4000.$

Substituting, the inequality becomes

$$\frac{(86,375 - 79,838) - (\mu_x - \mu_y)}{4000\sqrt{\frac{1}{8} + \frac{1}{8}}} < 1.28.$$

Combining: $\quad \dfrac{6537 - (\mu_x - \mu_y)}{2000} < 1.28.$

Multiplying through by 2000: $\quad 6537 - (\mu_x - \mu_y) < 2560.$

Subtracting 6537: $\quad -(\mu_x - \mu_y) < -3977.$

Multiplying by - 1:   $\mu_x - \mu_y > 3\ 977$

Our lower limit is 3 977.

Barnard College is a private institution for women
located in New York City. A random sample of 50 girls
was taken. The sample mean of grade point averages was
3.0. At neighboring Columbia College a sample of 100 men
had an average gpa of 2.5. Assume all sampling is normal
and Barnard's standard deviation is .2, while Columbia's is
.5. Place a 99% confidence interval on $\mu_{Barnard} - \mu_{Columbia}$.

<u>Solution</u>:    The main idea behind all of these problems
is the same. We want to find a standard normal pivotal
quantity involving $\mu_B - \mu_C$ and use the fact, obtainable
from the standard normal tables, that

   Pr(- 2.58 < Standard Normal Quantity < 2.58) = .99.

   We want to find a quantity $\bar{B} - \bar{C}$, where $\bar{B}$ = Barnard's
average and $\bar{C}$ = Columbia's average.

   The sample mean from a normal population is normally
distributed. $\bar{B} - \bar{C}$ is a difference in normal distributions
and is thus also normal. Hence $\dfrac{(\bar{B} - \bar{C}) - E(\bar{B} - \bar{C})}{S.D.\ (\bar{B} - \bar{C})}$ is

standard normal.

   Recall that the expectation of a sample mean is $\mu$,
the expectation of the original distribution. Thus,
$E(\bar{B}) = \mu_B$ and $E(\bar{C}) = \mu_C$.

$E(\bar{B} - \bar{C}) = E(\bar{B} + (- \bar{C})) = E(\bar{B}) + E(- \bar{C}) = E(\bar{B}) - E(\bar{C})$

by the linearity properties of expectation.

   Hence $E(\bar{B} - \bar{C}) = E(\bar{B}) - E(\bar{C}) = \mu_B - \mu_C$.

Also, $\sigma = \sqrt{Var(\bar{B} - \bar{C})} = \sqrt{Var(\bar{B}) + Var(\bar{C})}$ since

   $Var(ax + by) = a^2 Var(X) + b^2 Var(Y)$. Furthermore,

$\sigma = \sqrt{\dfrac{\sigma_B^2}{n_B} + \dfrac{\sigma_C^2}{n_C}}$   since the standard deviation

of a sample mean is $\dfrac{\sigma}{\sqrt{n}}$.

   Now we see   when substituting that

432

$$\Pr\left(-2.58 < \frac{(B - C) - (\mu_B - \mu_C)}{\sqrt{\dfrac{\sigma_B^2}{n_B} + \dfrac{\sigma_C^2}{n_C}}} < 2.58\right) = .99 .$$

We are given

$\bar{B} = 3.0$; $\bar{C} = 2.5$; $\sigma_B = .2$; $\sigma_C = .5$; $n_B = 50$; $n_C = 100$.

Inserting these values into the inequality, we obtain:

$$-2.58 < \frac{(3.0 - 2.5) - (\mu_B - \mu_C)}{\sqrt{\dfrac{(.2)^2}{50} + \dfrac{(.5)^2}{100}}} < 2.58.$$

Combining: 
$$-2.58 < \frac{.5 - (\mu_B - \mu_C)}{\sqrt{.0033}} < 2.58.$$

Multiplying by $\sqrt{.0033}$: $\quad -.148 < .5 - (\mu_B - \mu_C) < .148$.

Subtracting .5: $\quad -.648 < -(\mu_B - \mu_C) < -.352$ .

Multiplying by $-1$: $\quad .352 < \mu_B - \mu_C < .648$

Our required interval is

$.352 < \mu_B - \mu_C < .648.$

Neighboring farmers, Mr. Solinger and Mr. Rottner, were planting different varieties of corn. Each planted 100 acres under similar conditions. Mr. Solinger's yield was 84 bushels per acre with a standard deviation, $\sigma_S$, of 5 bushels. Mr. Rottner had a yield of 80 bushels per acre with a standard deviation, $\sigma_R$, of 6. Assume all sampling normal. (a) What is the maximum likelihood estimate of the difference in means? (b) Make a 90% confidence interval estimate for the mean difference in yield between the two farms.

Solution: (a) The method of maximum likelihood estimates the parameter by determining what value for the unknown parameters gives the highest probability of producing the observed results. For a normal population, the maximum likelihood estimate of the expectation is the sample mean. Our estimates of $\mu_S$ and $\mu_R$ are $\bar{X}_S$ AND $\bar{X}_R$. We estimate

$\mu_S - \mu_R$ by $\bar{X}_S - \bar{X}_R = 84 - 80 = 4.$

(b)  Once again we will try to find a standard normal pivotal quantity involving $\mu_S - \mu_R$, the true mean difference between Solinger's yield and Rottner's yield.

$$Pr(-\ 1.645 < \text{Standard Normal Quantity} < 1.645) = .90.$$

Let's standardize $\overline{X}_S - \overline{X}_R$. The sample mean from a normal population is normally distributed. $\overline{X}_S - \overline{X}_R$ is normally distributed since it is the difference of two normal distributions. Hence $\dfrac{(\overline{X}_S - \overline{X}_R) - E(\overline{X}_S - \overline{X}_R)}{\sqrt{\text{Var}\ (\overline{X}_S - \overline{X}_R)}}$ is standard normal. Remember that the expectation of a sample mean is $\mu$, the expectation of the original distribution. Thus $E(\overline{X}_S) = \mu_S$ and $E(\overline{X}_R) = \mu_R$.

$$E(\overline{X}_S - \overline{X}_R) = E(\overline{X}_S + (-\ \overline{X}_R)) = E(\overline{X}_S) + E(-\ \overline{X}_R)$$

$$= E(\overline{X}_S) - E(\overline{X}_R)$$

by the linearity properties of expectation.

Hence $\qquad E(\overline{X}_S - \overline{X}_R) = E(\overline{X}_S) - E(\overline{X}_R) = \mu_S - \mu_R$ .

Also, $\sigma_{(\overline{X}_S - \overline{X}_R)} = \sqrt{\text{Var}(\overline{X}_S - \overline{X}_R)} = \overline{\text{Var}(\overline{X}_S) + \text{Var}(\overline{X}_R)}$

since $\text{Var}(aX + bY) \quad a^2\,\text{Var}(X) + b^2\,\text{Var}(Y)$. Furthermore,

$$\sigma_{(\overline{X}_S - \overline{X}_R)} = \sqrt{\frac{\sigma^2_S}{n_S} + \frac{\sigma^2_R}{N_R}} \qquad \text{since the standard}$$

deviation of a sample mean is $\dfrac{\sigma}{\sqrt{n}}$ .

Substituting, we see that

$$Pr\left[-\ 1.645 < \frac{(X_S - X_R) - (\mu_S - \mu_R)}{\sqrt{\dfrac{\overline{\sigma}^2_S}{n_S} + \dfrac{\sigma^2_R}{n_R}}} < 1.645\right] = .90 .$$

We are given

$$\overline{X}_S = 84;\ \overline{X}_R = 80;\ \sigma_S = 5;\ \sigma_R = 6;\ n_S = n_R = 100.$$

Inserting these values into the inequality, we obtain

$$- 1.645 < \frac{(84 - 80) - (\mu_S - \mu_R)}{\sqrt{\frac{5^2}{100} + \frac{6^2}{100}}} < 1.645.$$

Combining: $\quad - 1.645 < \dfrac{4 - (\mu_S - \mu_R)}{\sqrt{\frac{61}{100}}} < 1.645 .$

Multiplying by $\sqrt{\frac{61}{100}}$ : $\quad - 1.285 < 4 - (\mu_S - \mu_R) < 1.285.$

Subtracting 4: $\qquad - 5.285 < - (\mu_S - \mu_R) < - 2.715 .$

Multiplying by $- 1$: $\qquad 2.715 < (\mu_S - \mu_R) < 5.285 .$

Our interval is

$2.715 < \mu_S - \mu_R < 5.285 .$

● **PROBLEM** 14-14

There was an old woman who lived in a shoe. She had so many children she didn't know what to do, so she measured their heights. First she sampled 13 girls and found a sample mean $\overline{X}_G$, or 31.4 inches. Next she sampled 7 boys and calculated a sample mean $\overline{X}_B$ of 38.1 inches. From the U.S. Statistical Abstract she found that the variance in girls' heights is 100 in$^2$ and 80 in$^2$ in boys. Help the old girl find a 95 per cent confidence interval for the difference in height between the heights of her boys and her girls, $\mu_B - \mu_G$. Assume normality.

Solution: $\quad \overline{X}_B$ and $\overline{X}_G$, being sample means taken from a normal population are normally distributed with

$$E(\overline{X}_B) = \mu_B, \ E(\overline{X}_G) = \mu_G, \text{Var}(\overline{X}_B) = \frac{\sigma^2_B}{n_B} , \text{ and Var}(\overline{X}_G) = \frac{\sigma^2_G}{n_G} ,$$

where the n's are the sample sizes.

$$E(\overline{X}_B - \overline{X}_G) = E(\overline{X}_B + (- \overline{X}_G)) = E(\overline{X}_B) + E(- \overline{X}_G)$$

$$= E(\overline{X}_B) - E(\overline{X}_G) .$$

This results from the linearity properties of expectation (i.e. $E(X + Y) = E(X) + E(Y)$ and $E(KX) = KE(X)$ when K is a constant). Therefore

$$E(\overline{X}_B - \overline{X}_G) = E(\overline{X}_B) - E(\overline{X}_G) = \mu_B - \mu_G .$$

Note that $Var(aX + bY) = a^2 Var(X) + b^2 Var(Y)$. This implies

$$Var(\bar{X}_B - \bar{X}_G) = Var(\bar{X}_B) + (-1)^2 Var(\bar{X}_G) = Var(\bar{X}_B) + Var(\bar{X}_G)$$

$$= \frac{\sigma_B^2}{n_B} + \frac{\sigma_G^2}{n_G}$$

Since $\bar{X}_B$ and $\bar{X}_G$ are normal, $\bar{X}_B - \bar{X}_G$ is normal also and we can standardize it.

$$\frac{(\bar{X}_B - \bar{X}_G) - E(\bar{X}_B - \bar{X}_G)}{\sqrt{Var\ (\bar{X}_B - \bar{X}_G)}} \quad \text{is a standard normal quantity.}$$

From the standard normal tables, we know

$Pr(-1.96 < \text{Standard Normal Quantity} < 1.96) = .95$.

Therefore

$$Pr\left[-1.96 < \frac{(\bar{X}_B - \bar{X}_G) - E(\bar{X}_B - \bar{X}_G)}{\sqrt{\sigma^2\ (\bar{X}_B - \bar{X}_G)}} < 1.96\right] = .95.$$

Substituting in our derived quantities:

$$Pr\left[-1.96 < \frac{(\bar{X}_B - \bar{X}_G) - (\mu_B - \mu_G)}{\sqrt{\dfrac{\sigma_B^2}{n_B} + \dfrac{\sigma_G^2}{n_G}}} < 1.96\right] = .95 .$$

(Recall the standard deviation is the square root of the variance.)

We are given

$X_B = 3.81$, $X_G = 31.4$, $\sigma^2_B = 80$, $\sigma^2_G = 100$, $n_B = 7$, $n_G = 13$. We now insert these values into the inequality.

$$-1.96 < \frac{(38.1 - 31.4) - (\mu_B - \mu_G)}{\sqrt{\dfrac{80}{7} + \dfrac{100}{13}}} < 1.96:$$

Combining: $\quad -1.96 < \dfrac{6.7 - (\mu_B - \mu_G)}{\sqrt{19.12}} < 1.96.$

Multiplying by $\sqrt{19.12} = 4.37$: $-8.57 < 6.7 - (\mu_B - \mu_G) < 8.57.$

Subtracting 6.7: $\quad -15.27 < -(\mu_B - \mu_G) < 1.87.$

Multiplying through by - 1:     - 1.87 < $(\mu_B - \mu_G)$ < 15.27.

Our 95 per cent confidence interval is

- 1.87 < $\mu_B - \mu_G$ < 15.27 .

# LARGE SAMPLES WITH MEAN OF UNKNOWN VARIANCE

● **PROBLEM** 14-15

The Harvard class of 1927 had a reunion.which 36 attended. Among them they discovered they had been married an average of 2.6 times apiece. From the Harvard Alumni Register Dean Epps learned that the standard deviation for the 1927 alumni was 0.3 marriages. Help Dean Epps construct a 99 per cent confidence interval for the marriage rate of all Harvard alumni.

Solution:     We are not given a standard deviation for the entire population here, but we are given a sample standard deviation. Our sample of 36 is fairly large thus the Laws of Large Numbers tell us that we can use the sample deviation as a good approximation to this real standard deviation. Again we search for a standard normal pivotal quantity upon which we can construct our confidence interval.

Recall the Central Limit Theorem: Let X be a random variable with mean $\mu$ and standard deviation $\sigma$; then the random variable $Z = \dfrac{(\overline{X} - \mu)\ \sqrt{n}}{\sigma}$ has a distribution that approaches standard normal as n gets large. We have n = 36. (That is large enough). We know from the tables that

Pr(- 2.58 < Standard Normal < 2.58) = .99 .

Inserting our standard normal random variable:

$$Pr\left[- 2.58 < \frac{(\overline{X} - \mu)\ \sqrt{n}}{\sigma} < 2.58\right] = .99 .$$

We know $\overline{X}$ = 2.6, $\sqrt{n} = \sqrt{36}$ = 6, and $\sigma$ = 0.3.

Substituting these values, the inequality becomes:

$$- 2.58 < \frac{(2.6 - \mu)\ 6}{0.3} < 2.58 .$$

Multiplying through by $\dfrac{0.3}{6}$     - 0.129 < 2.6 - $\mu$ < 0.129 .

Subtracting 2.6:  - 2.729 < - $\mu$ < 2.471 .

Multiplying through by - 1: 2.471 < $\mu$ < 2.729 .

Tell Dean Epps that he can be 99% sure that Harvard men on the average marry between 2.471 and 2.729 times.

In July, 1969 the first man walked on the moon. Armstrong, Aldren and Collins brought back 64 rock samples. The rocks had an average Earth weight of 172 ounces. The sample variance, $s^2$, was 299 $oz^2$. The moon rock population is known,however,to follow a distribution which is <u>not</u> normal. Find a 99 per cent confidence interval estimate for the mean weight of rocks on the lunar surface.

<u>Solution</u>: That the distribution is not normal does not matter because our sample, being of size 64, is large enough for the Central Limit Theorem to apply. The random variable $Z = \frac{(\overline{X} - \mu)\sqrt{n}}{\sigma}$ can therefore be considered a standard normal random variable. ($\mu$ is the true mean, $\overline{X}$ the sample mean, $\sigma$ is the standard deviation, and n the sample size.) In our example we have only a sample standard deviation, $\sigma_s$ , 17.29 (the sample standard deviation is the square root of the sample variance.) We can use the sample deviation as the true one.(The Law of Large Numbers in combination with our large sample allows this.) We know for all standard normal quantities, Z,

Pr(- 2.58 < Z < 2.58) = .99 .

In our case $Pr\left(- 2.58 < \frac{(\overline{X} - \mu)\sqrt{n}}{\sigma} < 2.58\right) = .99$ .

We know $\overline{X} = 172$, $\sqrt{n} = \sqrt{64} = 8$, $\sigma = 17.29$.

We can construct a confidence interval using the inequality $- 2.58 < \frac{(172 - \mu)8}{17.29} < 2.58$ .

Multiplying through by $\frac{17.29}{8}$ : $- 5.58 < 172 - \mu < 5.58$ .

Subtracting 172: $- 177.58 < - \mu < - 166.42$ .

Multiply by $- 1$: $166.42 < \mu < 177.58$ ·

Thus, $166.42 < \mu < 177.58$ is an approximate 99% confidence interval for the true mean weight of moon rocks.

● **PROBLEM** 14-17

A survey was conducted in 1970 to determine the average hourly earnings of a female sales clerk employed by a department store in metropolitan Los Angeles. A simple random sample of 225 female clerks was selected and the following information obtained:

X = hourly wage rate earned by female sales clerk,

$$\Sigma x = \$450.00, \quad \Sigma(x - \bar{x})^2 = \$2016.00 \ .$$

What is the .99 confidence interval estimate of the average hourly wage rate?

Solution: We have a large sample problem here. Two major theorems facilitate such problems. The Law of Large Numbers will allow us to approximate $\sigma$, the true standard deviation by $s$ the sample deviation. In addition the Central Limit Theorem tells us that $\dfrac{(\bar{X} - \mu) \sqrt{n}}{\sigma}$ is approximately standard normal. Hence we will assume $\dfrac{(\bar{X} - \mu) \sqrt{n}}{s}$ is standard normal. One look at the tables will tell us that,

$$Pr\left(- 2.58 < \frac{(\bar{X} - \mu) \sqrt{n}}{s} < 2.58\right) = .99 \ .$$

We have to compute $\bar{X}$ and $s$ .

$$\bar{X} = \frac{\Sigma X}{n} = \frac{\$450.00}{225} = \$2.00 \ \text{(the sample mean)}.$$

$$s = \sqrt{\frac{\Sigma(X_i - \bar{X})^2}{n - 1}} = \sqrt{\frac{2016.00}{224}} = \sqrt{9.00} = 3.00$$

(the standard deviation of the sample).

Now we can insert these values into the inequality

$$- 2.58 < \frac{(\bar{X} - \mu) \sqrt{n}}{s} < 2.58 \ \text{to obtain}$$

$$- 2.58 < \frac{(2.00 - \mu) \sqrt{225}}{3.00} < 2.58 \ .$$

Multiply by $\dfrac{3.00}{\sqrt{225}}$ : $- 0.516 < 2.00 - \mu < 0.516$ .

Subtracting 2.00: $- 2.516 < - \mu < - 1.484$ .

Multiply by $- 1$: $1.484 < \mu < 2.516$ .

Thus the average hourly earnings of a female sales clerk is 99% interval estimated to be between $ 1.48 and $2.52.

● **PROBLEM** 14-18

A random sample of 100 students from a large college showed an average IQ score of 112 with a standard deviation of 10.

(a) Establish a .95 confidence interval estimate of the mean IQ score of all students attending this college.

(b) Establish a .99 confidence interval estimate of the mean IQ score of all students in this college.

Solution: (a) A random sample of size 100 is certainly large enough for us to approximat the true standard deviation $\sigma$, by the sample standard deviation, $S = 10$. The Central Limit Theorem allows us to assume $\dfrac{(\overline{X} - \mu)\sqrt{n}}{\sigma}$ is approximately distributed standard normal. With our approximation, we will consider $\dfrac{(\overline{X} - \sigma)\sqrt{n}}{S}$ to be standard normal. Therefore from the standard normal table we have that

$$\Pr\left[-1.96 < \frac{(\overline{X} - \mu)\sqrt{n}}{S} < 1.96\right] = .95 .$$

We need only concern ourselves with the inequality

$$-1.96 < \frac{(\overline{X} - \mu)\sqrt{n}}{S} < 1.96 .$$

Substituting $\overline{X} = 112$, $S = 10$, $\sqrt{n} = \sqrt{100} = 10$ we see

$$-1.96 < \frac{(112 - \mu)\,10}{10} < 1.96$$

$$110.04 < \mu < 113.96.$$

(b) From the standard normal table we find that

$$\Pr(-2.58 < \text{Standard Nor.} < 2.58) = .99.$$

Substituting: $-2.58 < \dfrac{(\overline{X} - \mu)\sqrt{n}}{\sigma} < 2.58.$

(We only care about the interval.)

Inserting our values: $-2.58 < \dfrac{(112 - \mu)\,10}{10} < 2.58.$

Subtracting 112: $-114.58 < -\mu < -109.42.$

Our final answer, when we multiply by $-1$, is

$$109.42 < \mu < 114.58.$$

● **PROBLEM 14-19**

The past 400 records tested by Dick Clark on American Bandstand's Rate-a-Record segment resulted in an average score of 74, with a standard deviation of 40.

(a) Establish a .95 confidence interval estimate for the average score awarded on Rate-a-Record.

(b) What can we conclude with .99 confidence about the maximum error of the sample mean if the sample mean is calculated to be 74?

(c) With what degree of confidence can we assert that the average Rate-a-Record score is somewhere between 71 and 77.

**Solution:** (a) We are dealing with a large sample, 400. We can therefore approximate $\sigma$, the population standard deviation, by S, the sample standard deviation.

The Central Limit Theorem tells us that $\frac{(\overline{X} - \mu)\sqrt{n}}{\sigma}$, or our estimate $\frac{(\overline{X} - \mu)\sqrt{n}}{S}$, will be approximately Standard Normal. Then $P\left[-1.96 < \frac{(\overline{X} - \mu)\sqrt{n}}{S} < 1.96\right] = .95$.

Let us concern ourselves only with the interval

$$-1.96 < \frac{(\overline{X} - \mu)\sqrt{n}}{S} < 1.96.$$

Multiply through by $\frac{S}{\sqrt{n}}$ : $-1.96\frac{S}{\sqrt{n}} < \overline{X} - \mu < 1.96\frac{S}{\sqrt{n}}$.

Subtract $\overline{X}$: $-\overline{X} - 1.96\frac{S}{\sqrt{n}} < -\mu < -\overline{X} + 1.96\frac{S}{\sqrt{n}}$.

Multiply by $-1$: $\overline{X} - 1.96\frac{S}{\sqrt{n}} < \mu < \overline{X} + 1.96\frac{S}{\sqrt{n}}$.

Since S = 40 and n = 400, $\sqrt{n} = \sqrt{400} = 20$, and $\overline{X} = 74$ the interval is

$$74 - 1.96\frac{40}{20} < \mu < 74 + 1.96\frac{40}{20}.$$

Equivalently, $74 - 3.92 < \mu < 74 + 3.92$ or

$70.08 < \mu < 77.92$. This is a 95% interval estimate for the average Rate-a-Record score.

(b) First let's find a .99 confidence interval for $\mu$. Note that

$$P\ (-2.58 < \text{Standard Normal Quantity} < 2.58) = .99.$$

Making the same assumptions, substitutions and algebraic manipulations as in part a), we obtain a confidence interval of the form

$$\overline{X} - 2.58 \frac{S}{\sqrt{n}} < \mu < \overline{X} + 2.58 \frac{S}{\sqrt{n}} .$$

Consequently, $74 - 2.58 \frac{40}{20} < \mu < 74 + 2.58 \frac{40}{20}$ or

$74 - 5.16 < \mu < 74 + 5.16$. Simplifying, the .99 interval is $68.84 < \mu < 79.16$.

Since we have added and subtracted the expression $2.58 \left( \frac{40}{\sqrt{400}} \right)$, or $5.16$ from the sample mean, 74, in

order to establish a .99 confidence interval estimate for $\mu$, we can assert with a probability of .99 that our maximum expected error is 5.16 if $\mu$ is estimated by $\overline{X}$ to be 74.

(c) If $\mu$ is estimated to be between 71 and 77, then we must have added and subtracted 3 from the sample mean, 74, in order to obtain this interval estimate of $\mu$.

This confidence interval came from some inequality

$$- z < \frac{(\overline{X} - \mu) \sqrt{n}}{S} < z .$$

Multiplying through by $\frac{S}{\sqrt{n}}$: $\quad - z \frac{S}{\sqrt{n}} < \overline{X} - \mu < z \frac{S}{\sqrt{n}} .$

Subtracting $\overline{X}$: $\quad - \overline{X} - z \frac{S}{\sqrt{n}} < - \mu < - \overline{X} + z \frac{S}{\sqrt{n}} .$

Multiply by $- 1$: $\quad \overline{X} - z \frac{S}{\sqrt{n}} < \mu < \overline{X} + z \frac{S}{\sqrt{n}} .$

$\overline{X} = 74; \quad 74 - z \frac{S}{\sqrt{n}} < \mu < 74 + z \frac{S}{\sqrt{n}} .$

To get (71, 77) we must set $\quad z \frac{S}{\sqrt{n}} = 3 .$

Substituting $\quad z \frac{40}{\sqrt{400}} = 3: \quad z \cdot 2 = 3, \quad z = 1.5 .$

We now look on the standard normal table and find that the area between $Z = 0$ and $Z = 1.5$ is .4332. Hence as in the following diagram:

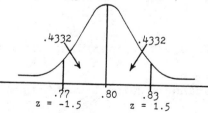

$P(- 1.5 < \text{Standard Normal} < 1.5) = .8664.$
We have a .8664 confidence interval for $\mu$.

A department store has 10,000 customers' charge accounts. To estimate the total amount owed by its customers, it selected a random sample of 36 charge accounts which showed a mean amount of $150 per account and a standard deviation of $60 ($\bar{x}$ = 150, s = 60). Establish a 0.95 confidence interval estimate of the total amount owed by customers to the department store.

**Solution:** We have to solve this problem in two steps. First we have to establish a 0.95 confidence interval estimate of the average amount owed per customer (a 0.95 confidence interval estimate of $\mu$). Second we will multiply the interval estimate for $\mu$ by the number of customers to obtain an interval estimate for the total amount owed by all customers.

To find a 0.95 confidence interval estimate for $\mu$, note that a sample of 36 is large enough for us to be able to apply the Central Limit Theorem and assume $\frac{(x - \mu) \sqrt{n}}{\sigma}$ is standard normal. Also, the Law of Large Numbers will allow us to approximate $\sigma$ by $S$ the sample deviation, 60. $\frac{(\bar{X} - \mu) \sqrt{n}}{S}$ is approximately standard normal and from the tables:
$$Pr\left[- 1.96 < \frac{(\bar{X} - \mu) \sqrt{n}}{S} < 1.96\right] = .95 .$$

Substituting known values into the inequality:
$$- 1.96 < \frac{(150 - \mu) \sqrt{36}}{60} < 1.96 .$$

Simplifying we obtain: $- 1.96 < \frac{(150 - \mu)}{10} < 1.96 .$

Multiply by 10: $- 19.6 < 150 - \mu < 19.6$.

Subtract 150: $- 169.60 < - \mu < -130.40$.

Multiply by $- 1$: $130.40 < \mu < 169.60$.

Now since the department store has 10,000 customers, the 0.95 confidence-interval estimate for the total amount owed by customers can be obtained by multiplying the interval by 10,000.

10,000 ($130.40 < \mu < $169.60)

gives us the interval between $1,304,000 and $1,696,000.

A factory has a machine that cuts spaghetti and noodles into appropriate lengths for packaging. It can be adjusted to cut any given length. The variability of the machine is determined to be a standard deviation of o.lcm. The machine is set to cut pasta 30cm in length and you take a number of 36 noodle samples. According to the normal distribution table, how often will $\bar{X}$ be within 0.0167 cm of $\mu$?

**Solution:** We want to know how often $|\bar{X} - \mu| \leq 0.0167$. We will phrase the question as follows: What is Pr$(- 0.0167 < \bar{X} - \mu < 0.0167)$?

We are dealing with samples of size 36 so we can approximate $\sigma$, the population standard deviation by $S$, the sample one. Also by the Central Limit Theorem, we can assume $\dfrac{\bar{X} - \mu}{S/\sqrt{n}}$ has a standard normal distribution.

We want Pr$(- 0.0167 < \bar{X} - \mu < 0.0167)$.

Divide inside the parentheses by $\dfrac{Sx}{\sqrt{n}}$. We now want

$$Pr\left(\dfrac{- 0.0167}{S_x/\sqrt{3}} < \dfrac{\bar{X} - \mu}{S_x/\sqrt{3}} < \dfrac{0.0167}{S_x/\sqrt{3}}\right) .$$

Since $Sx = .1$ and $n = 36$, $\dfrac{Sx}{\sqrt{n}} = \dfrac{.1}{\sqrt{36}} = \dfrac{.1}{6} = .0167$

We are now after $Pr\left(- \dfrac{.0167}{.0167} < \dfrac{\bar{X} - \mu}{Sx/\sqrt{n}} < \dfrac{.0167}{.0167}\right) .$

Equivalently, we seek P$(- 1 < $ Standard Normal $< 1)$.

From the tables we find this to be 6826. Therefore $\bar{X}$ will be within .0167 cm of $\mu$ 68.26% of the time.

● **PROBLEM 14-22**

You select a random sample of 100 teardrops. The sample has an average salt concentration of .1 with a standard deviation of .01. Establish a 95% confidence interval for the mean saline concentration of the tears.

**Solution:** We have a large sample, 100. The Law of Large Numbers will allow us to use the sample standard deviation, S, as an estimate for the population deviation $\sigma$. The Central Limit Theorem tells us $\dfrac{(\bar{X} - \sigma) \sqrt{n}}{\sigma}$ is approximately standard normal. We will assume then that $\dfrac{(\bar{X} - \mu) \sqrt{n}}{S}$ is standard normal. Therefore, from the table, $Pr\left(- 1.96 < \dfrac{(\bar{X} - \mu) \sqrt{n}}{S} < 1.96\right) = .95.$

Substituting .1 for $\overline{X}$, 100 for n, and .01 for $S$, the inequality within the parenthesis becomes

$$- 1.96 < \frac{(.1 - \mu) \sqrt{100}}{.01} < 1.96 .$$

Multiply through by $\frac{.01}{\sqrt{100}}$:   $-$  .002 $< .1 - \mu <$   .002 .

Subtract .1:   $-$ 1.002 $< - \mu < -$   .098

Multiply by $-$ 1 to obtain the final answer:

.098 $< \mu <$ 1.002.

This is a 95% confidence interval for $\mu$, the true but unknown salt concentration of audience tears.

● **PROBLEM** 14-23

A random sample of 50 workers is taken out of a very large number of workers in a factory; the time that each of the workers in the sample takes to perform the same manufacturing process is recorded. The average time requirement for this sample is 21 minutes and the standard deviation is 3 minutes. Find the 99% confidence interval for the average time requirement to perform this manufacturing process for all the workers in this factory.

Solution:    We have a large sample problem. The Law of Large Numbers allows us to estimate the population standard deviation, $\sigma$, by the sample one, $S$. The Central Limit Theorem will allow us to assume $\frac{(\overline{X} - \mu) \sqrt{n}}{\sigma}$ is standard normal. With our estimation $\frac{(\overline{X} - \mu) \sqrt{n}}{S}$ becomes standard

normal. By the tables,    $P\left(- 2.58 < \frac{(\overline{X} - \mu) \sqrt{n}}{S} < 2.58\right) = .99.$

Multiplying the         inequality by $\frac{S}{\sqrt{n}}$, we obtain

$$- 2.58 \frac{S}{\sqrt{n}} < \overline{X} - \mu < 2.58 \frac{Sx}{\sqrt{n}} .$$

Subtract $\overline{X}$:   $- \overline{X} - 2.58 \frac{S}{\sqrt{n}} < - \mu < - \overline{X} + 2.58 \frac{S}{\sqrt{n}} .$

Multiply by $-$ 1:   $\overline{X} - 2.58 \frac{S}{\sqrt{n}} < \mu < \overline{X} + 2.58 \frac{S}{\sqrt{n}} .$

Now substitute n = 50, $\overline{X}$ = 21 minutes, $S$ = 3 minutes

and the result is      $21 - 2.58 \frac{3}{\sqrt{50}} < \mu < 21 + 2.58 \frac{3}{\sqrt{50}} .$

Simplifying: $21 - 1.09 < \mu < 21 + 1.09$ .

Finally we have 19.91 min. $< \mu < 22.09$ min. as the 99% confidence interval for the true average time for the workers performing this process.

● **PROBLEM 14-24**

What size sample is required to establish a .95 confidence interval for the grade point average of students attending Ponoma State Teachers College if a random sample of 100 students had a mean grade point average of 2.8 with a standard deviation of .4 and if the length of the interval is .1?

Solution: We are dealing with a large sample, 100. We can approximate $\sigma$, the true standard deviation, by S, the sample standard deviation . Also the Central Limit Theorem will apply and therefore $\frac{(\overline{X} - \mu)\ \sqrt{n}}{\sigma}$ can be considered standard normal. In light of this, we have

$$\Pr\left(- 1.96 < \frac{(\overline{X} - \mu)\ \sqrt{n}}{\sigma} < 1.96\right) = .95 .$$

We need only concern ourselves with the interval

$$- 1.96 < \frac{(\overline{X} - \mu)\ \sqrt{n}}{\sigma} < 1.96 .$$

We want the smallest n such that the above inequality will hold uniformly under the conditions of the problem.

Set $\frac{(\overline{X} - \mu)\ \sqrt{n}}{\sigma} = 1.96$. Multply through by $\sigma$.

$(\overline{X} - \mu)\ \sqrt{n} = 1.96\ \sigma$. Next divide by $(\overline{X} - \mu)$ and square both sides. The result, $n = \left(\frac{1.96\ \sigma}{(\overline{X} - \mu)}\right)^2$ . $\sigma$ is given as .4, but to resolve $(\overline{X} - \mu)$ is trickier. The length of $(\overline{X} - \mu)$ will be at most .1. We can minimize $|\overline{X} - \mu|$ by assuming $\mu$ is the center of the interval. $|\overline{X} - \mu|$ now must $\leq .05$. $(.05 = (\frac{1}{2})\ (.1))$. If $\mu$ were not in the center it would have to be further then .5 from one end and $|\overline{X} - \mu|$ could be greater than .05. By minimizing $|\overline{X} - \mu|$, we minimize $(\overline{X} - \mu)^2$ and increase our value of n thereby obtaining a safer estimate for n. With our numbers

$$n = \left(\frac{(1.96)\ (.4)}{(.05)}\right)^2 = 245.86.$$

We can be confident that a random sample of size 246 will provide a 95% interval estimate of $\mu$ with length no more than .1 units.

A random sample of size n is taken from a very large number of army recruits. The average weight for the recruits in the sample ($\overline{X}$) is 160 pounds and the sample standard deviation is 10 pounds. Suppose that we want the 90% confidence interval to be equal at most to 5 pounds. What size random sample greater than 30 (n > 30) should we take?

**Solution:** We are given that $\overline{X} = 160$, $\sigma = 10$, and the size of the 90% confidence interval to be at most 5 lbs. We are told to expect an n > 30. Therefore, the Central Limit Theorem tells us the sampling distribution of $\dfrac{(\overline{X} - \mu)\sqrt{n}}{\sigma}$ is approximately standard normal. The Law of Large Numbers will allow us to estimate $\sigma$, the population standard deviation, by $s$, the sample one. We will assume $\dfrac{(\overline{X} - \mu)\sqrt{n}}{s}$ is standard normal. Hence

$$P\left(-1.64 < \frac{(\overline{X} - \mu)\sqrt{n}}{s} < 1.64\right) = .90.$$

Multiplying the inequality within the parentheses by $\dfrac{s}{\sqrt{n}}$ we obtain: $-1.64 \dfrac{s}{\sqrt{n}} < (\overline{X} - \mu) < 1.64 \dfrac{s}{\sqrt{n}}$.

Subtract $\overline{X}$: $-\overline{X} - 1.64 \dfrac{s}{\sqrt{n}} < -\mu < 1.64 \dfrac{s}{\sqrt{n}} - \overline{X}$.

Multiply by $-1$: $\overline{X} - 1.64 \dfrac{s}{\sqrt{n}} < \mu < \overline{X} + 1.64 \dfrac{s}{\sqrt{n}}$. Now

$5 =$ Length of interval = Upper limit - Lower limit

$= \overline{X} + 1.64 \dfrac{s}{\sqrt{n}} - \left(\overline{X} - 1.64 \dfrac{s}{\sqrt{n}}\right)$

$= 2 \left(1.64 \dfrac{s}{\sqrt{n}}\right) = 3.28 \dfrac{s}{\sqrt{n}}$.

Substitute for $s$ (10) and set equal to 5: $3.28 \dfrac{10}{\sqrt{n}} = 5$.

Transposing: $\sqrt{n} = \dfrac{(3.28)(10)}{5}$.

Squaring: $n = \left(\dfrac{(3.28)(10)}{5}\right)^2 = 43.03$.

Thus, if we take a random sample of 44 recruits, we will get a 90% confidence interval less than 5 lbs. or 5 units in weight.

# SMALL SAMPLES WITH MEAN OF UNKNOWN VARIANCE

● PROBLEM 14-26

During the 1976-77 season Coach Jerry Tarkanian outfitted his University of Nevada at Las Vegas basketball team with new sneakers. The 16 member team had an average size of 14.5 and a standard deviation of 5. Find a 90 percent confidence interval for the mean sneaker size of all collegiate basketball players. Assume the population is normal and the variance is not known.

**Solution:** In confidence interval problems the approch is to find a pivotal quantity, i.e. a function of the observations which has a distribution independent of the parameter we are trying to estimate. For example, the

quantity $\dfrac{(\overline{X} - \mu)\ \sqrt{n}}{\sigma}$ is normal with mean 0 and standard deviation 1, provided that X is normal. This is true regardless of the value of $\mu$. We can now use facts about the standard normal distribution to rearrange our expressionand obtain a confidence interval for $\mu$. In a case such as our present example where $\sigma$ is unknown

$\dfrac{(\overline{X} - \mu)\ \sqrt{n}}{\sigma}$ does us no good in searching for $\mu$. There is no obvious way to rid ourselves of $\sigma$. We look for a pivotal quantity involving only $\mu$.

We know that $\dfrac{\overline{X} - \mu}{\sigma/\sqrt{n}}$ is standard normal.

Recall also that $\dfrac{\Sigma(X_i - \overline{X})^2}{\sigma^2}$ has a Chi-Square distribution with n - 1 degrees of freedom. We also know that if Z is standard normal and U is $\chi^2_{(k)}$, $\dfrac{Z}{\sqrt{\dfrac{U}{k}}}$ follows a t

distribution with k degrees of freedom. In our case then

$$\frac{(\overline{X} - \mu)/(\sigma/\sqrt{n})}{\sqrt{\Sigma(X_i - \overline{X})^2/(n-1)\ \sigma^2}} = \frac{\text{Normal }(0,1)}{\sqrt{\chi^2_{(n-1)}}/n-1}$$

has a t distribution with n - 1 degrees of freedom. Furthermore, $\dfrac{(\overline{X} - \mu)/(\sigma/\sqrt{n})}{\sqrt{\Sigma(X_i - \overline{X})^2/(n-1)\ \sigma^2}} = \dfrac{\overline{X} - \mu}{S/\sqrt{n}}$ where S is the

sample standard deviation, $\sqrt{\dfrac{\Sigma(X_i - \overline{X})}{n-1}}$ . Note that

some books define the sample standard deviation as

$\sqrt{\dfrac{\Sigma(X_i - \overline{X})}{n}}$ . In that case $\dfrac{(\overline{X} - \mu)/(\sigma/\sqrt{n})}{\sqrt{\Sigma(X_i - \overline{X})^2/(n-1)\ \sigma^2}} = \dfrac{\overline{X} - \mu}{S/\sqrt{n-1}}$

and $\dfrac{\overline{X} - \mu}{S/\sqrt{n-1}}$ not $\dfrac{\overline{X} - \mu}{S/\sqrt{n}}$ would have a t distribution

448

with n - 1 degrees of freedom. Notice that in the statistic
$\frac{\overline{X} - \mu}{S/\sqrt{n}}$ there is no mention of $\sigma$. The fact that $\sigma$ is unknown need no longer bother us. A look at the t tables
tells us that $Pr\ (-\ 1.753 < t_{(15)} < 1.753) = .90$ .

We chose 15 degrees of freedom since our sample is
of size 16 and $U = \frac{(n - 1)\ S^2}{\sigma^2}$ is thus $\chi^2$ with n - 1
degrees of freedom. Returning to our problem:

$$Pr\ \left[-\ 1.753 < \frac{\overline{X} - \mu}{S/\sqrt{n}} < 1.753\right]\ = .90\ .$$

We know $\overline{X} = 14.5$, $\sqrt{n} = \sqrt{16} = 4$, and $S = 5$.

Inserting these values, the inequality becomes

$$-\ 1.753 < \frac{14.5 - \mu}{5/4} < 1.753$$

The inequality $-\ 1.753 < \frac{14.5 - \mu}{5/4} < 1.753$ will give
us our confidence interval.

Multiplying by $\frac{5}{4}$ : $-\ 2.19 < 14.5 - \mu < 2.19$ .

Subtracting 14.5: $-\ 16.69 < -\ \mu < -\ 12.31$ .

Multiplying by $-\ 1$: $12.31 < \mu < 16.69$ 

$$12.31 < \mu < 16.69\ .$$

● **PROBLEM** 14-27

Redo the previous problem but assume the distribution is
normal with a known standard deviation of 5.

Solution: The purpose of this problem is to compare the
t statictic with the standard normal. Here we are assuming
something about the distribution of sneaker size, i.e. it
is normal. We should get a "better" interval estimate.

We know that since sneaker size X is normal, the
sample mean, $\overline{X}$, is normally distributed with expectation
$\mu$ and standard deviation $\sigma/\sqrt{n}$. $\mu$ and $\sigma$ are the parameters
of the original distribution of X. Since $\overline{X}$ is normal
$\frac{\overline{X} - E(\overline{X})}{\sqrt{Var\ (\overline{X})}}$ is standard normal.

By checking the standard normal table we see

$$Pr\left[-\ 1.645 < \frac{\overline{X} - E(\overline{X})}{\sqrt{Var\ (\overline{X})}} < 1.645\right]\ = .90\ .$$

Substituting, $Pr\left[-\ 1.645 < \frac{\overline{X} - \mu}{\sigma/\sqrt{n}} < 1.645\right]\ = .90\ .$

It is the inequality $- 1.645 < \dfrac{\bar{X} - \mu}{\sigma/\sqrt{n}} < 1.645$ that will give us our confidence interval. We are given $\bar{X} = 14.5, \sigma = 5$, and $\sqrt{n} = \sqrt{16} = 4$. Inserting these values

$$- 1.645 < \frac{14.5 - \mu}{5/4} < 1.645 \ .$$

Multiplying by $\dfrac{5}{4}$: $- 2.06 < 14.5 - \mu < 2.06$ .

Subtracting 14.5: $-16.56 < - \mu < - 12.44$ .

Multiplying by $- 1$: $12.44 < \mu < 16.56$ .

Here the length of our interval is 4.12 whereas before it was 4.38.

● **PROBLEM** 14-28

Mr. Greenberg owns a gas station in Philadelphia. His busiest hour is from 11 to noon. On May 18th, Mr. Greenberg's daughter Beth surveyed 36 customers. She found that the 36 people bought an average of 12 gallons of gasoline with a standard deviation of 4 gallons.

(a) Find a point estimate for $\mu$, the mean number of gallons of gas people buy.
(b) Establish a .95 confidence interval for $\mu$.
(c) Establish a .99 confidence interval for $\mu$.

Solution:    (a) 36 people constitutes a large sample. The law of large numbers applies. We have taken a large sample and therefore can estimate $\mu$ by $\bar{X} = 12$ gallons.

(b)  Note that we have a sample standard deviation and not the true one. In a large sample, however, we can use the sample deviation as an estimate of $\sigma$, the real one and use the Central Limit Theorem which tells us $\dfrac{\bar{X} - \mu}{S/\sqrt{n}}$ will approach standard normal. We can justify this fairly easily by one look at the t table. To form an inequality using the t-statistic we would consider

$$\Pr(- 2.03 < t_{(35)} < 2.03) = .95$$

while using the standard normal we would use

$$\Pr(- 1.96 < \text{Standard Normal} < 1.96) = .95$$

The accuracy of 2.03 to 1.96 is certainly no less than the accuracy of most of our measurements anyway. To continue we will use the inequality $- 1.96 < \dfrac{\bar{X} - \mu}{\sigma/\sqrt{n}} < 1.96$. Substituting the known quantities $\bar{X} = 12$, $\sigma = 4$, $\sqrt{n} = \sqrt{36} = 6$, we obtain $- 1.96 < \dfrac{12 - \mu}{4/6} < 1.96$.

Multiplying by $\frac{4}{6}$ : $-1.31 < 12 - \mu < 1.31$,

Subtracting 12: $-13.31 < -\mu < -10.69$.

Multiplying through by $-1$: $10.69 < \mu < 13.31$.

(c)  To get a 99 percent confidence interval note

$$Pr\left(-2.58 < \frac{\overline{X} - \mu}{\sigma/\sqrt{n}} < 2.58\right) = .99 \quad \text{for the same}$$

reasons as in (b). Substituting into the central in-equality we obtain; $-2.58 < \dfrac{12 - \mu}{4/6} < 2.58$ .

Multiplying by $\frac{4}{6}$ : $-1.72 < 12 - \mu < 1.72$ .

Subtracting 12: $-13.72 < -\mu < -10.28$ .

Multiplying by $-1$: $10.28 < \mu < 13.72$ .

Our answer is $10.28 < \mu < 13.72$.

The interval (10.28, 13.72) is a 99% confidence interval for the true mean number of gallons of gasoline purchased.

● **PROBLEM** 14-29

Cranston, Rhode Island has the reputation for selling the most expensive bubble gum in the United States. Ten candy stores were surveyed and it was found that the average price in the 10 stores was 4 cents (.04 dollars) with a standard deviation of half a penny (.005 dollars). Find (a) a 95% and (b) a 99% confidence interval for $\mu$, the mean price of bubble gum in Cranston.

Solution:    Ten measurements does not constitute a large sample, so we cannot use the Central Limit Theorem and a normal approximation. We must search for a t statistic as a pivotal quantity.

$\dfrac{\overline{X} - \mu}{\sigma/\sqrt{n}}$   is standard normal.

$\dfrac{\Sigma(X_i - \overline{X})^2}{\sigma^2}$   is Chi-square with $n - 1$ d.o.f.

$$\frac{(\overline{X} - \mu)/(\sigma/\sqrt{n})}{\sqrt{\Sigma(X_i - \overline{X})^2/(n - 1)\,\sigma^2}} = \frac{\overline{X} - \mu}{S/\sqrt{n}}$$

(S is the sample standard deviation) is the quotient of a standard normal quantity divided by the square root of

$\chi^2$ random variable with $n - 1$ degrees of freedom divided by $n - 1$. Therefore $\dfrac{\overline{X} - \mu}{S/\sqrt{n}}$ follows a t distribution with $n - 1$ d.o.f. The equality of

$$\dfrac{(\overline{X} - \mu)/(\sigma/\sqrt{n})}{\sqrt{\Sigma(X_i - \overline{X})^2/(n - 1)\ \sigma^2}}$$

and $\dfrac{\overline{X} - \mu}{S/\sqrt{n}}$ follows with the cancellation of $\sigma$ and $\sqrt{\sigma^2}$

and the definition of S as $\sqrt{\dfrac{\Sigma(X_i - \overline{X})^2}{n - 1}}$ .

In our case $n = 10$ so we are interested in a t distribution with 9 degrees of freedom.

(a)  Looking at the t table we discover

$$\Pr(-\ 2.262 < t_{(9)} < 2.262) = .95 \ .$$

From the inequality $-\ 2.262 < t_{(9)} < 2.262$ we will get our confidence interval. Substituting for $t_{(9)}$

$$-\ 2.262 < \dfrac{\overline{X} - \mu}{S/\sqrt{n}} < 2.262 \ .$$

Now let us insert the known values of $\overline{X}$, $S$, and n. We obtain:  $-\ 2.262 < \dfrac{.04 - \mu}{.005/\sqrt{10}} < 2.262$ .

Multiplying by $\dfrac{.005}{\sqrt{10}}$, our result becomes

$$-\ .0036 < .04 - \mu < .0036$$

Subtracting .04:  $-\ .0436 < -\ \mu < -\ .0364$ .

Multiply by $-\ 1$ for the final answer,

$$.0364 < \mu < .0436$$

(b)  We use the same t-statistic and look at the table for 9 degrees of freedom. We find

$$\Pr\left(-3.25 < \dfrac{\overline{X} - \mu}{S/\sqrt{n}} < 3.25\right) = .99 \ .$$

We will work with the interval:  $-\ 3.25 < \dfrac{\overline{X} - \mu}{S/\sqrt{n}} < 3.25$ .

Substituting our known values  $-\ 3.25 < \dfrac{.04 - \mu}{.005/\sqrt{10}} < 3.25$ .

Multiplying by $\dfrac{.005}{\sqrt{10}}$ $\leftarrow$ $.0051 < .04 - \mu < .0051$ .

Subtracting $.04$: $-.0451 < -\mu < -.0349$ .

Multiplying by $-1$, our final answer now is:

$.0349 < \mu < .0451$.

● **PROBLEM** 14-30

In the Idaho State Home for Runaway Girls, 25 residents were polled as to what age they ran away from home. The sample mean was 16 years old with a standard deviation of 1.8 years. Establish a 95% confidence interval for $\mu$, the mean age at which runaway girls leave home in Idaho.

<u>Solution</u>: We do not know precisely the population standard deviation and our sample is not large, 25. We might be all right in using the sample deviation to approximate the real one, but it is better to be safe and use a t-statistic. We know $\dfrac{\overline{X} - \mu}{\sigma/\sqrt{n}}$ is a standard normal random

variable. Also note that $\sqrt{\dfrac{\Sigma(X_i - \overline{X})^2}{\sigma^2 (n - 1)}}$ is the square

root of a Chi-square random variable with n- 1 degrees of freedom divided by n - 1. The quotient of these two

quantities $\dfrac{(\overline{X} - \mu)/(\sigma/\sqrt{n})}{\sqrt{\Sigma(X_i - \overline{X})^2/\sigma^2(n - 1)}}$ is a t random

variable with n - 1 degrees of freedom. Factoring

$$\frac{(\overline{X} - \mu)/(\sigma/\sqrt{n})}{\sqrt{\Sigma(X_i - \overline{X})^2/\sigma^2 (n - 1)}} = \frac{\dfrac{1}{\sigma} \dfrac{(\overline{X} - \mu)}{1/\sqrt{n}}}{\dfrac{1}{\sigma} \sqrt{\Sigma(X_i - \overline{X})^2/(n - 1)}} .$$

The denominator is now the sample standard deviation, S. A convenient form for our t-statistic (n - 1 d.o.f.) is $\dfrac{\overline{X} - \mu}{S/\sqrt{n}}$ .

In our case n - 1 = 25 - 1 = 24. From t-tables we see that $\Pr(-2.064 < t_{(24)} < 2.064) = .95$ .

Inserting our t-statistic: $\Pr\left(-2.064 < \dfrac{\overline{X} - \mu}{S/\sqrt{n}} < 2.064\right) = .95$.

It is the interval, $-2.064 < \dfrac{\overline{X} - \mu}{S/\sqrt{n}} < 2.064$, with

453

which we are concerned. Substituting our values $\bar{X} = 16$, $S = 1.8$, $\sqrt{n} = \sqrt{25} = 5$, we see the result is

$$- 2.064 < \frac{16 - \mu}{1.8/5} < 2.064 \ .$$

Multiplying through by $\frac{1.8}{5}$: $- .743 < 16 - \mu < .743 \ .$

Subtracting 16: $- 16.743 < - \mu < - 15.267 \ .$

Multiplying by -1: $15.267 < \mu < 16.743 \ .$

Thus a 95% confidence interval for the true mean age at which Idaho girls run away from home is (15.267, 16.743).

● PROBLEM 14-31

Nine students living on the third floor in Burton Hall at Oberlin College did their laundry an average of 19 times during the academic year.         Their standard deviation was 2.7 washes. Establish a .95 confidence interval estimate of the average number of times a year an Oberlin student launders his clothes.

Solution:     Again we have a problem where we are given a small sample with an unknown variance. The t distribution is called for.

The t can be expressed as the ratio of a standard normal random variable and the square root of a chi-square divided by its degrees of freedom. $\dfrac{\bar{X} - \mu}{\sigma/\sqrt{n}}$ is standard normal and as we have seen before $\dfrac{(n - 1)S^2}{\sigma^2}$ is $\chi^2_{(n - 1)}$

where Sx is the sample standard deviation $\sqrt{\dfrac{\Sigma(X_i - \bar{X})^2}{n - 1}}$ .

Their quotient will be t with n - 1 d.o.f. As seen in earlier problems the quotient reduces to $\dfrac{\bar{X} - \mu}{S/\sqrt{n}}$ . Therefore $\dfrac{\bar{X} - \mu}{S/\sqrt{n}}$ is $t_{n-1}$. n - 1 in our case = 9 - 1 = 8.

From the tables:     $- 2.306 < t_{(8)} < 2.306$.

With our t random variable:     $- 2.306 < \dfrac{\bar{X} - \mu}{Sx/\sqrt{n}} < 2.306$.

Substituting for X, $S$ and n:     $- 2.306 < \dfrac{19 - \mu}{2.7/\sqrt{9}} < 2.306$.

Multiplying by $\dfrac{2.7}{\sqrt{9}} = .9$:   $-2.075 < 19 - \mu < 2.075$.

Subtracting 19 yields:   $-21.075 < -\mu < -16.925$.

The final interval estimate is arrived at by multiplying through by $-1$:   $16.925 < \mu < 21.075$ .

● **PROBLEM** 14-32

The nicotine contents of five cigarettes of a certain brand, measured in milligrams, are 21, 19, 23, 19, 23. Establish a .99 confidence interval estimate of the average nicotine content of this brand of cigarette.

<u>Solution</u>:   In this problem we are given specific measurements and must determine the sample mean and standard deviation for ourselves.

For the mean: $\bar{X} = \dfrac{\Sigma X}{n}$

$$= \dfrac{21 + 19 + 23 + 19 + 23}{5} = \dfrac{105}{5}$$

$$= 21 \text{ milligrams.}$$

For the sample standard deviation:

$$S = \sqrt{\dfrac{\Sigma (X - \bar{X})^2}{n - 1}}$$

| X | $(X - \bar{X})$ | $(X - \bar{X})^2$ |
|---|---|---|
| 21 | 0 | 0 |
| 19 | $-2$ | 4 |
| 23 | $+2$ | 4 |
| 19 | $-2$ | 4 |
| 23 | $+2$ | 4 |

$$\Sigma (X - \bar{X})^2 = 16$$

$$S = \sqrt{\dfrac{\Sigma (X - \bar{X})^2}{n - 1}} = \sqrt{\dfrac{16}{5 - 1}} = 2 \text{ milligrams.}$$

We have a small sample with an unknown variance.

We search for the quotient of a standard normal random variable and the square root of a chi-square random variable divided by its degrees of freedom.

Since $\dfrac{\bar{X} - \mu}{\sigma/\sqrt{n}}$ is standard normal and $\dfrac{\Sigma (X_i - \bar{X})^2}{\sigma^2}$ is

455

$\chi^2_{n-1}$ $\dfrac{(\overline{X} - \mu)/(\sigma/\sqrt{n})}{\sqrt{\Sigma(X_i - \overline{X})^2/(n-1)\sigma^2}} = \dfrac{\overline{X} - \mu}{s/\sqrt{n}}$ is such a random

variable and as we have seen in previous problems is t distributed with n - 1 d.o.f. In our case n - 1 = 5 - 1 so $\dfrac{\overline{X} - \mu}{s/\sqrt{n}}$ is $t_{(4)}$. Looking at the t table we see

$Pr(- 4.604 < t_{(4)} < 4.604) = .99$ .

Substituting our t random variable,

$Pr\left(- 4.604 < \dfrac{\overline{X} - \mu}{s/\sqrt{n}} < 4.604\right) = 0.99.$

Since we know $\overline{X} = 21$, $s = 2$, and n = 5, we only need to use the inequality

$- 4.604 < \dfrac{21 - \mu}{2/\sqrt{5}} < 4.604$ .

Multiplying through by $\dfrac{2}{\sqrt{5}}$:  $- 4.118 < 21 - \mu < 4.118$ .

Subtracting 21 yields:$- 25.118 < - \mu < - 16.882.$

Multiplying by - 1 gives the 99% confidence interval for $\mu$:

$16.882 < \mu < 25.118$ .

● **PROBLEM 14-33**

State briefly the assumptions involved in establishing a confidence interval using the standard normal distribution and the t distribution.

Solution:    We use the standard normal when (a) the variance $\sigma^2$ is known and X is normally distributed or (b) the sample is large (> 30) and we can estimate the variance $\sigma^2$ by the sample variance $S^2$. In case (a)

$\dfrac{\overline{X} - \mu}{\sigma/\sqrt{n}}$ is standard normal. In case (b) the Central

Limit Theorem and Law of Large Numbers allow  us to assume

$\dfrac{\overline{X} - \mu}{s/\sqrt{n}}$ is standard normal.

We use the t statistic for a small sample (n<30) with unknown variance, $\sigma^2$. $\sigma$ is never used here, always S.

The following data are a sample selected from a population you assume to be normally distributed. What is your best estimate of $\mu$ and $\sigma$? Establish a 95% confidence interval for $\mu$.

Data: 3, 4, 5, 6, 6, 7, 7, 7, 8, 8, 8, 9, 9, 10, 11, 12.

**Solution:**  We will take $\overline{X}$ as our best estimate of $\mu$.

$$\overline{X} = \frac{\Sigma X}{n}$$

$$= \frac{3+4+5+6+6+7+7+7+8+8+8+9+9+10+11+12}{16} = \frac{120}{16} = 7.5$$

For the best estimate of $\sigma^2$, we will take the un-biased estimator $S^2 = \frac{\Sigma (X - \overline{X})^2}{n - 1}$. We can compute it using the following table.

| X | X − $\overline{X}$ | (X − $\overline{X}$)$^2$ |
|---|---|---|
| 3 | 3 − 7.5 = − 4.5 | (− 4.5)$^2$ = 20.25 |
| 4 | 4 − 7.5 = − 3.5 | (− 3.5)$^2$ = 12.25 |
| 5 | 5 − 7.5 = − 2.5 | (− 2.5)$^2$ = 6.25 |
| 6 | 6 − 7.6 = − 1.5 | (− 1.5)$^2$ = 2.25 |
| 6 | 6 − 7.5 = − 1.5 | (− 1.5)$^2$ = 2.25 |
| 7 | 7 − 7.5 = − 0.5 | (− 0.5)$^2$ = .25 |
| 7 | 7 − 7.5 = − 0.5 | (− 0.5)$^2$ = .25 |
| 7 | 7 − 7.5 = − 0.5 | (− 0.5)$^2$ = .25 |
| 8 | 8 − 7.5 = 0.5 | (+ 0.5)$^2$ = .25 |
| 8 | 8 − 7.5 = 0.5 | ( 0.5)$^2$ = .25 |
| 8 | 8 − 7.5 = 0.5 | ( 0.5)$^2$ = .25 |
| 9 | 9 − 7.5 = 1.5 | ( 1.5)$^2$ = 2.25 |
| 9 | 9 − 7.5 = 1.5 | ( 1.5)$^2$ = 2.25 |
| 10 | 10 − 7.5 = 2.5 | ( 2.5)$^2$ = 6.25 |
| 11 | 11 − 7.5 = 3.5 | ( 3.5)$^2$ = 12.25 |
| 12 | 12 − 7.5 = 4.5 | ( 4.5)$^2$ = 20.25 |

$$\Sigma (X - \overline{X})^2 = 88$$

$$n - 1 = 16 - 1 = 15$$

$$S = \sqrt{S^2} = \sqrt{\frac{\Sigma (X - \overline{X})^2}{n - 1}} = \sqrt{\frac{88}{15}} = \sqrt{5.87} = 2.42$$

Since our sample is small, a normal approximation will not do. We must use a t statistic. We have earlier shown that $\frac{\overline{X} - \mu}{Sx/\sqrt{n}}$ is the quotient of a standard normal random variable and a square root of a $\chi^2_{(n - 1)}$ divided by n − 1. Hence $\frac{\overline{X} - \mu}{Sx/\sqrt{n}}$ is t distributed with n − 1 degrees of freedom. In our example n − 1 = 15. By looking at the t-tables we see; $P(- 2.131 < t_{(15)} < 2.131) = .95$ .

$\dfrac{\overline{X} - \mu}{Sx/\sqrt{n}}$    is $t_{(15)}$, therefore:

$$P\left(- 2.131 < \dfrac{\overline{X} - \mu}{Sx/\sqrt{n}} < 2.131\right) = .95 \ .$$

Let us now manipulate the interval; first multiply by $\dfrac{S}{\sqrt{n}}$ and get $- 2.131 \dfrac{S}{\sqrt{n}} < \overline{X} - \mu < 2.131 \dfrac{S}{\sqrt{n}}$ .

Subtract $\overline{X}$: $\quad - \overline{X} - 2.131 \dfrac{S}{\sqrt{n}} < - \mu < - \overline{X} + 2.131 \dfrac{S}{\sqrt{n}}$ .

Multiply by $- 1$: $\qquad \overline{X} - 2.131 \dfrac{S}{\sqrt{n}} < \mu < \overline{X} + 2.131 \dfrac{S}{\sqrt{n}}$ .

Now substitute 7.5 for $\overline{X}$, 2.42 for $S$, and 16 for n:

$$7.5 - 2.131 \dfrac{2.42}{\sqrt{16}} < \mu < 7.5 + 2.131 \dfrac{2.42}{\sqrt{16}} \ .$$

And consequently

$6.21 < \mu < 8.79$ is a 95% confidence interval for $\mu$.

● **PROBLEM** 14-35

A sample of 10 patients in the intensive care unit of Brothers' Hospital in Frostbite Falls, Minnesota has a mean body temperature of 103.8 degrees. The standard deviation is 1.26 degrees. Establish a 95 per cent confidence interval for $\mu$, the mean temperature of Brothers' intensive care patients.

Solution: We have a small sample and an unknown variance. The t distribution is called for. From previous problems, we know $\dfrac{\overline{X} - \mu}{S/\sqrt{n}}$ is t distributed with $n - 1$ degrees of freedom. Here we are told $\overline{X} = 103.8$, $S = 1.26$, and $n = 10$. Hence $n - 1 = 9$ and $\sqrt{n} = 3.16$. From the t tables we can see that $\quad P(- 2.262 < t_{(9)} < 2.262) = .95.$

With our $t_{(9)}$, the inequality within the parenthesis is $\quad - 2.262 < \dfrac{\overline{X} - \mu}{S/\sqrt{n}} < 2.262.$

Substituting our given values:
$- 2.262 < \dfrac{103.8 - \mu}{1.26/3.16} < 2.262$ .

Multiplying through by $\dfrac{1.26}{3.16}$: $\quad - .902 < 103.8 - \mu < .902$ .

458

Subtracting 103.8:    $- 104.702 < - \mu < - 102.898$ .

Multiply by $- 1$:   $102.898 < \mu < 104.702$.

The mean temperature, with 95% confidence, is between 102.898 and 104.702.

● **PROBLEM** 14-36

When estimating a confidence interval for the mean of a normal distribution with unknown variance, we choose a value b such that $P\left( - b < \dfrac{\bar{X} - \mu}{S/\sqrt{n}} < b \right) = 1 - \alpha$. Why do we choose our bounds symmetrically?

**Solution:**    Recall how the confidence interval is produced;

$$a < \frac{\bar{X} - \mu}{S/\sqrt{n}} < b, \text{ where a, b are such that}$$

$$P(a < t_{(n - 1)} < b) = 1 - \alpha.$$

Multiply the inequality by $\dfrac{S}{\sqrt{n}}$ :    $a\left(\dfrac{S}{\sqrt{n}}\right) < \bar{X} - \mu < b\left(\dfrac{S}{\sqrt{n}}\right)$

Subtract $\bar{X}$:      $- \bar{X} + a\left(\dfrac{S}{\sqrt{n}}\right) < - \mu < - \bar{X} + b\left(\dfrac{S}{\sqrt{n}}\right)$ .

Multiply by $- 1$:      $\bar{X} - b\left(\dfrac{S}{\sqrt{n}}\right) < \mu < \bar{X} - a\left(\dfrac{S}{\sqrt{n}}\right)$ .

Interval Length $=$

$$\bar{X} - a\left(\dfrac{S}{\sqrt{n}}\right) - \left[\bar{X} - b \cdot \dfrac{S}{\sqrt{n}}\right] = \dfrac{S}{\sqrt{n}}(b - a)$$

which depends directly on $b - a$ since $\dfrac{S}{\sqrt{n}}$ is constant.

For any given sample the length will be minimized if $b - a$ is a minimum. We advance the following rigorous argument.

We seek to minimize      $L = \dfrac{S}{\sqrt{n}}(b - a)$        (1)

subject to  $P(a < t_{(n - 1)} < b) = 1 - \alpha$        (2)

or equivalently,  $\displaystyle\int_a^b f(s)\ ds = 1 - \alpha$        (3)

459

where f(s) is the density of the t distribution with n - 1 degrees of freedom. Equation (3) gives b as a function of a.

Differentiating (3) with respect to a yields,

$$f(b) \frac{db}{da} - f(a) = 0 \qquad \text{by the Fundamental Theorem}$$

of Integral Calculus. To minimize L, we set $\frac{dL}{da} = 0$.

Differentiating (1): $\qquad \frac{dL}{da} = \frac{S}{\sqrt{n}} \left( \frac{db}{da} - 1 \right) = 0.$

But $\frac{db}{da} = \frac{f(a)}{f(b)}$ . Substitution yields,

$$\frac{S}{\sqrt{n}} \left( \frac{f(a)}{f(b)} - 1 \right) = 0 \qquad \text{which implies}$$

$$\frac{f(a)}{f(b)} = 1 \qquad \text{or} \quad f(a) = f(b) .$$

This implies that either a = b, in which case

$$P(a < t_{(n - 1)} < b) = 0 \quad \underline{OR} \quad a = -b$$

since the t distribution is symmetric.

Notice that this argument can easily be extended to standard normal problems. Simply substitute Z for $t_{(n - 1)}$ and $\sigma$ for S and the argument carries through in exactly the same manner.

# DIFFERENCE OF MEANS WITH UNKNOWN VARIANCES

● **PROBLEM** 14-37

Assume you have two populations $N(\mu_1, \sigma^2)$ and $N(\mu_2, \sigma^2)$. The distributions have the same, but unknown, variance $\sigma^2$. Derive a method for determining a confidence interval for $\mu_1 - \mu_2$.

<u>Solution</u>: Let $X_1, X_2, \ldots, X_n$ and $Y_1, Y_2, \ldots Y_m$ denote different random samples from the two independent distributions. We shall denote the sample means by $\overline{X}$ and $\overline{Y}$, and the sample variances by $S_1^2$ and $S_2^2$ $\left[ S_1^2 = \frac{\Sigma (X - \overline{X})^2}{n - 1} \right].$

These four statistics are all mutually stochastically independent. Therefore $\overline{X}$ and $\overline{Y}$ are normally distributed and independent with means $\mu_1$ and $\mu_2$ and variances $\frac{\sigma^2}{n}$ and $\frac{\sigma^2}{m}$. The difference, $\overline{X} - \overline{Y}$, is normally distributed with mean

$\mu_1 - \mu_2$ and variance $\dfrac{\sigma^2}{n} + \dfrac{\sigma^2}{m}$ . The random variable

$$\frac{(\bar{X} - \bar{Y}) - (\mu_X - \mu_Y)}{\sqrt{\dfrac{\sigma^2}{n} + \dfrac{\sigma^2}{m}}} \quad \text{will be standard normal and thus may}$$

serve as the numerator of a t random variable.

Also note that

$$\frac{(n - 1)S_1^2}{\sigma^2} = \frac{\Sigma(X - \bar{X})^2}{\sigma^2} \quad \text{and} \quad \frac{(m - 1)S_2^2}{\sigma^2} = \frac{\Sigma(Y - \bar{Y})^2}{\sigma^2} \quad \text{are}$$

stochastically independent chi-square random variables
with $n - 1$ and $m - 1$ degrees of freedom respectively. Their

sum $\dfrac{(n - 1)S_1^2}{\sigma^2} + \dfrac{(m - 1)S_2^2}{\sigma^2}$ will then be chi-square with

$m + n - 2$ degrees of freedom, provided $m + n - 2 > 0$

$$\sqrt{\frac{U}{m + n - 2}} = \sqrt{\frac{\dfrac{(n - 1)S_1^2}{\sigma^2} + \dfrac{(m - 1)S_2^2}{\sigma^2}}{m + n - 2}}$$

is the square root of a chi-square random variable divided
by its degrees of freedom. Thus it can serve as the denominator of a t random variable. Thus

$$T = \frac{(\bar{X} - \bar{Y}) - (\mu_1 - \mu_2)}{\sqrt{\dfrac{\sigma^2}{n} + \dfrac{\sigma^2}{m}}} \div \sqrt{\frac{U}{m + n - 2}}$$

$$= \frac{\dfrac{(\bar{X} - \bar{Y}) - (\mu_1 - \mu_2)}{\sigma \sqrt{\dfrac{1}{m} + \dfrac{1}{n}}}}{\dfrac{1}{\sigma}\sqrt{\dfrac{(n - 1)S_1^2 + (m - 1)S_2^2}{(m + n - 2)}}}$$

$$= \frac{(\bar{X} - \bar{Y}) - (\mu_1 - \mu_2)}{\sqrt{\dfrac{(n - 1)S_1^2 + (m - 1)S_2^2}{m + n - 2}\left[\dfrac{1}{n} + \dfrac{1}{m}\right]}}$$

$$= \frac{(\bar{X} - \bar{Y}) - (\mu_1 - \mu_2)}{\sqrt{W}}$$

$\left(\text{where } \sqrt{W} \text{ is } \sqrt{\dfrac{(n-1)S_1^2 + (m-1)S_2^2}{m+n-2} - \left[\dfrac{1}{n} + \dfrac{1}{m}\right]}\right).$

T is a t random variable with $m + n - 2$ degrees
of freedom.

Say we wanted a $100(1 - \alpha)\%$ confidence interval. We
can examine the tables to find a value b such that

$$\Pr(-b < t_{(m+n-2)} < b) = 1 - \alpha .$$

We have

$$\Pr\left[- b < \frac{(\overline{X} - \overline{Y}) - (\mu_1 - \mu_2)}{\sqrt{W}} < b\right] = 1 - \alpha.$$

Multiplying the inequality within the parentheses through by the denominator we obtain

$$- b \sqrt{W} < (\overline{X} - \overline{Y}) - (\mu_1 - \mu_2) < b \sqrt{W}.$$

We subtract $(\overline{X} - \overline{Y})$ and multiply by $- 1$ to obtain the final confidence interval.

$$(\overline{X} - \overline{Y}) - b \sqrt{\frac{(n - 1)S_1^2 + (m - 1)S_2^2}{n + m - 2} \left[\frac{1}{n} + \frac{1}{m}\right]} \; ,$$

$$(\overline{X} - \overline{Y}) + b \sqrt{\frac{(n - 1)S_1^2 + (m - 1)S_2^2}{n + m - 2} \left[\frac{1}{n} + \frac{1}{m}\right]} \; .$$

This is our $100(1 - \alpha)\%$ confidence interval.

● **PROBLEM** 14-38

Using the result of the preceding problem find a 90% confidence interval for $\mu_1 - \mu_2$ when $n = 10$, $m = 7$, $\overline{X} = 4.2$, $\overline{Y} = 3.4$, $S_1^2 = 49$, $S_2^2 = 32$.

Solution:    First we look at the t table and find

$$\Pr(- 1.753 < t_{(m+n-2=17-2=15)} < 1.753) = .90$$

We have derived a confidence interval for $\mu_1 - \mu_2$ and found it to be

$$(\overline{X} - \overline{Y}) - b \sqrt{\frac{(n - 1)S_1^2 + (m - 1)S_2^2}{n + m - 2} \left[\frac{1}{n} + \frac{1}{m}\right]} \; ,$$

$$(\overline{X} - \overline{Y}) + b \sqrt{\frac{(n - 1)S_1^2 + (m - 1)S_2^2}{n + m - 2} \left[\frac{1}{n} + \frac{1}{m}\right]} \; .$$

Now $b = 1.753$. Let us insert our values

$$(4.2 - 3.4) - 1.753 \sqrt{\frac{(10 - 1)49 + (7 - 1)32}{10 + 7 - 2} \left[\frac{1}{10} + \frac{1}{7}\right]} \; ,$$

$$(4,2 - 3.4) + 1.753 \sqrt{\frac{(10 - 1)49 + (7 - 1)32}{10 + 7 - 2} \left[\frac{1}{10} + \frac{1}{7}\right]} \; .$$

Combining, we obtain    $0.8 - 1.753 \sqrt{\frac{9(49) + 6(32)}{15} \left[\frac{17}{70}\right]} \; ,$

$$0.8 + 1.753 \sqrt{\frac{9(49) + 6(32)}{15} \left[\frac{17}{70}\right]}$$

$$\left(0.8 - 1.753 \sqrt{\frac{633}{15} \left[\frac{17}{70}\right]}, \quad 0.8 + 1.753 \sqrt{\frac{633}{15} \left[\frac{17}{70}\right]}\right).$$

Now we convert to decimals.

$$[0.8 - 1.753 \sqrt{10.25}, \quad 0.8 + 1.753 \sqrt{10.25}]$$

or     $[0.8 - 1.753 (3.202), \quad 0.8 + 1.753 (3.202)]$.

Our final answer is

$(- 4.813, 6.413)$.

● **PROBLEM** 14-39

We are looking for a comparison between the financial states of people leaving Las Vegas and Reno after their vacations. 23 tourists leaving Vegas lost an average $\bar{X}$ of \$551.49. Similarly 23 Reno vacationers came up short an average, $\bar{Y}$, of \$549.93. It is assumed that the losses in each city are independent, normally distributed random variables with common unknown standard deviation. The quantity $\dfrac{\Sigma (X_i - \bar{X})^2 + \Sigma (Y_i - \bar{Y})^2}{n + m - 2}$ was found to be 87.683. Find a 90% confidence interval for the difference in means.

Solution:     We are given small samples with unknown variance. We should immediately recall the result derived two problems ago for confidence intervals under such conditions,

$$\left[(\bar{X} - \bar{Y}) - b \sqrt{\frac{(n - 1)S_1^2 + (m - 1)S_2^2}{n + m - 2} \left[\frac{1}{n} + \frac{1}{m}\right]}, \right.$$

$$\left. (\bar{X} - \bar{Y}) + b \sqrt{\frac{(n - 1)S_1^2 + (m - 1)S_2^2}{n + m - 2} \left[\frac{1}{n} + \frac{1}{m}\right]}\right).$$

Since $n + m - 2 = 23 + 23 - 2 = 44$, b is the value such that     $Pr(- b < t_{(44)} < b) = .90$.

Most t tables do not have a reading for 44 d.o.f; thus we will have to use linear interpolation to find b(44) and - b(44).

$b(40) = 1.684$     and     $b(50) = 1.676$.

$$\frac{b(44) - b(40)}{b(50) - b(40)} = \frac{44 - 40}{50 - 40} = \frac{4}{10}.$$

Solving for b(44) we obtain

$$b(44) = b(40) + \frac{4}{10} [b(50) - b(40)].$$

Substituting:  $b(44) = 1.684 + \frac{4}{10} (1.676 - 1.684)$

$$= 1.684 + .4 (- .008) = 1.681 .$$

Also note that $S_1{}^2 = \frac{\Sigma (X - \bar{X})^2}{n - 1}$ .  Hence $(n - 1)S_1{}^2 =$

$\Sigma (X_i - \bar{X})^2$. Similarly, $(m - 1)S_2{}^2 = \Sigma (Y_i - \bar{Y})^2$. Therefore

$$\frac{\Sigma (X_i - \bar{X})^2 + \Sigma (Y_i - \bar{Y})^2}{n + m - 2} = \frac{(n - 1)S_1{}^2 + (m - 1)S_2{}^2}{n + m - 2}$$

which equals 87.$\underline{6}$83.  In addition, we know  n=m=23, X = 551.49, and $\bar{Y}$ = 549.93.  Inserting all values we obtain

$$\left[ (551.49 - 549.93) - 1.681 \sqrt{87.683 \left( \frac{1}{23} + \frac{1}{23} \right)} , \right.$$

$$\left. (551.49 - 549.93) + 1.681 \sqrt{87.683 \frac{2}{23}} \right] .$$

Combining yields:

$(1.56 - 1.681 (2.761), 1.56 + 1.681 (2.761)$   or

$(1.56 - 4.64,  1.56 + 4.64)$. Our final answer is

$(- 3.08, 6.20)$.

● **PROBLEM** 14-40

The weights of 15 New York models had a sample mean of 107 lbs. and a sample standard deviation of 10 lbs. Twelve Philadelphia models had a mean weight of 112 and a standard deviation of 8. Make a .90 confidence interval estimate of the difference of the mean weights between the two model populations.

**Solution:**    With small samples and an unknown variance we can immediately quote our previously derived result. The interval comes from a t statistic and is

$$\left[ (\bar{X} - \bar{Y}) - b \sqrt{\frac{(n - 1)S_1{}^2 + (m - 1)S_2{}^2}{n + m - 2} \left[ \frac{1}{n} + \frac{1}{m} \right]} , \right.$$

$$\left. (\bar{X} - \bar{Y}) + b \sqrt{\frac{(n - 1)S_1{}^2 + (m - 1)S_2{}^2}{n + m - 2} \left[ \frac{1}{n} + \frac{1}{m} \right]} \right] .$$

The number of degrees of freedom is
    n + m - 2 = 15 + 12 - 2 = 25. Therefore b is the value such that        $Pr(- b < t(25) < b) = .90$.

From the tables, we see that b = 1.708.

The problem tells us $\bar{X}$ = 107, $\bar{Y}$ = 112, $S_1{}^2 = 10^2 = 100$,

$S_2{}^2 = 8^2 = 64$, n = 15, and m = 12. Inserting these values we obtain:

$$\left[ -5 - 1.708 \sqrt{\frac{(14)100 + (11)64}{25} \left[\frac{27}{180}\right]} \; , \right.$$
$$\left. -5 + 1.708 \sqrt{\frac{(14)100 + (11)64}{25} \left[\frac{27}{180}\right]} \; \right] .$$

Further simplification results in

[- 5 - 1.708 (3.553), - 5 + 1.708 (3.553).

Equivalently (- 5 - 6.069, - 5 + 6.069).

Our final confidence interval for the difference in models' weights is (- 11.069, 1.069).

● **PROBLEM 14-41**

The seven dwarfs challenged the Harlem Globetrotters to a basketball game. Besides the obvious difference in height, we are interested in constructing a 95% confidence in ages between dwarfs and basketball players. The respective ages are,

| Dwarfs | | Globetrotters | |
|---|---|---|---|
| Sneezy | 20 | Meadowlark | 43 |
| Grumpy | 39 | Curley | 37 |
| Dopey | 23 | Marques | 45 |
| Doc | 41 | Bobby Joe | 25 |
| Sleepy | 35 | Theodis | 34 |
| Happy | 29 | | |
| Bashful | 31 | | |

Can you construct the interval? Assume the variance in age is the same for dwarfs and Globetrotters.

Solution: We have small samples with a common unknown variance. We have previously solved a problem dealing with such confidence intervals in general. We obtain a t statistic by taking the quotient of a standard normal random variable and the square root of a chi-square random variable with n + m - 2 degrees of freedom divided by n + m - 2. The resulting confidence interval was

$$\left[ (\overline{X} - \overline{Y}) - b \sqrt{\frac{(n-1)S_1{}^2 + (m-1)S_2{}^2}{n + m - 2} \left[\frac{1}{n} + \frac{1}{m}\right]} \; , \right.$$
$$\left. (\overline{X} - \overline{Y}) + b \sqrt{\frac{(n-1)S_1{}^2 + (m-1)S_2{}^2}{n + m - 2} \left[\frac{1}{n} + \frac{1}{m}\right]} \; \right] .$$

We need to compute $\overline{X}$, $\overline{Y}$, $S_1{}^2$, $S_2{}^2$, given n = 7, m = 5.

$$\overline{X} = \frac{\Sigma X}{n} = \frac{20 + 39 + 23 + 41 + 35 + 29 + 31}{7} = \frac{218}{7} = 31.1 \; .$$

$$\bar{Y} = \frac{\Sigma Y}{m} = \frac{43 + 37 + 45 + 25 + 34}{5} = \frac{184}{5} = 36.8 \ .$$

$$S_1{}^2 = \frac{\Sigma (X - \bar{X})^2}{n - 1} \quad . \text{ Use the following table:}$$

| X | X − X̄ | (X − X̄)² |
|---|---|---|
| 20 | − 11.1 | 123.21 |
| 39 | 7.9 | 62.41 |
| 23 | − 8.1 | 65.61 |
| 41 | 9.9 | 98.01 |
| 35 | 3.9 | 15.21 |
| 29 | − 2.1 | 4.41 |
| 31 | − .1 | .01 |

$$\Sigma (X - \bar{X})^2 = 368.87$$

In the problem we are concerned with

$$(n - 1)S_1{}^2 = (n - 1) \frac{\Sigma (X - \bar{X})^2}{n - 1} = \Sigma (X - \bar{X})^2 = 368.87.$$

Similarly, $(m - 1)S_2{}^2 = \Sigma (Y - \bar{Y})^2$ .

| Y | Y − Ȳ | (Y − Ȳ)² |
|---|---|---|
| 43 | 6.2 | 38.44 |
| 37 | 0.2 | .04 |
| 45 | 8.2 | 67.24 |
| 25 | − 11.8 | 139.24 |
| 34 | − 2.8 | 7.84 |

$$\Sigma (Y - \bar{Y})^2 = 252.80$$
$$= (m - 1)S_2{}^2.$$

Now $\sqrt{\dfrac{(n - 1)S_1{}^2 + (m - 1)S_2{}^2}{n + m - 2} \left[\dfrac{1}{n} + \dfrac{1}{m}\right]}$

$$= \sqrt{\frac{368.87 + 252.80}{7 + 5 - 2} \left[\frac{1}{7} + \frac{1}{5}\right]}$$

$$= \sqrt{\frac{621.67}{10} \left[\frac{12}{35}\right]} = \sqrt{21.314} = 4.62 \ .$$

$n + m - 2 = 7 + 5 - 2 = 10$. Our t statistic has 10 degrees of freedom and b is the value such that

$$Pr(- b < t(10) < b) = .95.$$

The t table tells us b = 2.228. Our confidence interval is now

$$((\bar{X} - \bar{Y}) - 2.228 \ (4.62), \ (\bar{X} - \bar{Y}) + 2.228 \ (4.62)).$$

But $\bar{X} - \bar{Y} = 31.1 - 36.8 = - 5.7$ .

The interval is

$$(- 5.7 - 2.228 \ (4.62), \ - 5.7 + 2.228 \ (4.62)),$$

or     $(- 15.99, \ 4.59)$

is a 95% confidence interval for $\mu_1 - \mu_2$, the difference between the dwarfs and Globetrotters' ages.

● **PROBLEM** 14-42

A random sample of 10 Miss America contestants had a mean age of 22.6 years with a standard deviation of 2 years. A random sample of 12 Miss U.S.A. candidates had a mean age of 19.6 with a standard deviation of 1.6. Assume the population variances are equal. Find a 90% confidence interval estimate for the difference between the population means.

<u>Solution</u>:     We have small samples with a common unknown variance. We have already derived the general confidence interval for this type of problem. The interval we obtained was

$$\left( (\overline{X} - \overline{Y}) - b \ \sqrt{\frac{(n - 1)S_1{}^2 + (m - 1)S_2{}^2}{n + m - 2} \left[ \frac{1}{n} + \frac{1}{m} \right]} \ , \right.$$

$$\left. (\overline{X} - \overline{Y}) + b \ \sqrt{\frac{(n - 1)S_1{}^2 + (m - 1)S_2{}^2}{n + m - 2} \left[ \frac{1}{n} + \frac{1}{m} \right]} \ \right).$$

The problem tells us $\overline{X} = 22.6$, $S_1{}^2 = 2^2 = 4$, $n = 10$, $\overline{Y} = 19.6$, $S_2{}^2 = 1.6^2 = 2.56$, and $m = 12$. Since $m + n - 2 = 12 + 10 - 2 = 20$, b will be the value such that

$$Pr(- b < t(20) < b) = .95.$$

A glance at the t tables reveals $b = 1.725$. Inserting the known values, our interval becomes

$$\left( (22.6 - 19.6) - 1.725 \ \sqrt{\frac{(10 - 1)4 + (12 - 1)2.56}{12 + 10 - 2} \left[ \frac{1}{10} + \frac{1}{12} \right]} \ , \right.$$

$$\left. (22.6 - 19.6) + 1.725 \ \sqrt{\frac{(10 - 1)4 + (12 - 1)2.56}{12 + 10 - 2} \left[ \frac{1}{10} + \frac{1}{12} \right]} \ \right).$$

Combining yields:     $\left( 3 - 1.725 \ \sqrt{\frac{36 + (11)2.56}{20} \left[ \frac{22}{120} \right]} \ , \right.$

$$\left. 3 + 1.725 \ \sqrt{\frac{36 + (11)2.56}{20} \left[ \frac{22}{120} \right]} \ \right).$$

Further simplification changes our result to

$$(3 - 1.725 \ (.767), \ \ 3 + 1.725 \ (.767) \ .$$

Equivalently we have $(3 - 1.32, \ 3 + 1.32)$ or     $(1.68, \ 4.32)$.

as the 90% confidence interval for the difference in ages between Miss America contestants and Miss U.S.A. contestants.

● **PROBLEM** 14-43

A standardized chemistry test was given to 50 girls and 75 boys. The girls made an average grade of 76 with a standard deviation of 6, while the boys made an average grade of 82 with a standard deviation of 8. Find a 96% confidence interval for the difference $\mu_X - \mu_Y$ where $\mu_X$ is the mean score of all boys and $\mu_Y$ is the mean score of all girls who might take this test.

Solution:    This problem differs from the ones immediately preceding it in a fundamental way. Here we have large samples (m, n > 30). The Law of Large Numbers will allow us to approximate the population standard deviations ($\sigma_X$, $\sigma_Y$) by the sample ones $s_X$, $s_Y$. Consider the random variable $\overline{X} - \overline{Y}$. We will assume X, Y are normally distributed. In that case, $\overline{X}$ and $\overline{Y}$ will be normal, and therefore $\overline{X} - \overline{Y}$ will

also be normal. Since $\overline{X}-\overline{Y}$ is normal, $\dfrac{(\overline{X} - \overline{Y}) - E(\overline{X} - \overline{Y})}{\text{Standard Dev.}(\overline{X} - \overline{Y})}$

will be a standard normal quantity.

We need $E(\overline{X} - \overline{Y})$ and $\sigma_{\overline{X} - \overline{Y}}$.

Let $E(X) = \mu_X$ and $E(Y) = \mu_Y$. Then $E(\overline{X}) = \mu_X$ and $E(\overline{Y}) = \mu_Y$.

$$E(\overline{X} - \overline{Y}) = E(\overline{X} + (-\overline{Y})) = E(\overline{X}) + E(-\overline{Y}) = E(\overline{X}) - E(\overline{Y})$$

$$= \mu_X - \mu_Y,$$ by the linearity properties of

expectation. $Var(\overline{X} - \overline{Y}) = Var(\overline{X}) + Var(\overline{Y})$ since if X and Y are independent, $Var(aX + bY) = a^2 Var(X) + b^2 Var(Y)$. We also know $Var(\overline{X}) = \dfrac{\sigma_X}{n}$ and $Var(\overline{Y}) = \dfrac{\sigma_Y}{m}$ where n and m are the sizes of samples X and Y.

Thus, $\sigma_{\overline{X} - \overline{Y}} = \sqrt{Var(\overline{X} - \overline{Y})} = \sqrt{\dfrac{\sigma^2_X}{n} + \dfrac{\sigma^2_Y}{m}}$.

With our approximation, we take

$$\sigma_{\overline{X} - \overline{Y}} = \sqrt{\dfrac{s_X^2}{n} + \dfrac{s_y^2}{m}}. \quad \text{Hence}$$

$$\dfrac{(\overline{X} - \overline{Y}) - E(\overline{X} - \overline{Y})}{\sigma_{\overline{X} - \overline{Y}}} = \dfrac{(X - Y) - (\mu_X - \mu_Y)}{\sqrt{\dfrac{s_X^2}{n} + \dfrac{s_y^2}{m}}} \quad \text{is a}$$

standard normal quantity and the normal tables tell us

$$\Pr\left[-2.054 < \frac{(\overline{X} - \overline{Y}) - (\mu_X - \mu_Y)}{\sqrt{\dfrac{s_x^2}{n} + \dfrac{s_y^2}{m}}} < 2.054\right] = .96.$$

We are concerned only with the central inequality. Multiply it through by $\sqrt{\dfrac{s_x^2}{n} + \dfrac{s_y^2}{m}}$ and the result is

$$-2.054 \sqrt{\frac{s_x^2}{n} + \frac{s_y^2}{m}} < (\overline{X} - \overline{Y}) - (u_1 - \mu_2)$$

$$< 2.054 \sqrt{\frac{s_x^2}{n} + \frac{s_y^2}{m}} .$$

Subtract $(\overline{X} - \overline{Y})$ and obtain:

$$-(\overline{X} - \overline{Y}) - 2.054 \sqrt{\frac{s_x^2}{n} + \frac{s_y^2}{m}} < -(\mu_1 - \mu_2) < -(\overline{X} - \overline{Y})$$

$$+2.054 \sqrt{\frac{s_x^2}{n} + \frac{s_y^2}{m}} .$$

Multiply by $-1$:

$$(\overline{X} - \overline{Y}) - 2.054 \sqrt{\frac{s_x^2}{n} + \frac{s_y^2}{m}} < \mu_1 - \mu_2 < (\overline{X} - \overline{Y})$$

$$+2.054 \sqrt{\frac{s_x^2}{n} + \frac{s_y^2}{m}} .$$

Our 96% confidence interval is

$$\left[ (\overline{X} - \overline{Y}) - 2.054 \sqrt{\frac{s_x^2}{n} + \frac{s_y^2}{m}} , \right.$$

$$\left. (\overline{X} - \overline{Y}) + 2.054 \sqrt{\frac{s_x^2}{n} + \frac{s_y^2}{m}} \right] .$$

Now we insert our given values:

$$\overline{X} = 82 \qquad Sx = 8 \qquad n = 75$$
$$\overline{Y} = 76 \qquad Sy = 6 \qquad m = 50$$

$$\left( (82 - 76) - 2.054 \sqrt{\frac{8^2}{75} + \frac{6^2}{50}} , \right.$$

$$\left. (82 - 76) + 2.054 \sqrt{\frac{8^2}{75} + \frac{6^2}{50}} \right) .$$

Simplification yields:

$$\left( 6 - 2.054 \sqrt{\frac{64}{75} + \frac{36}{50}} , \; 6 - 2.054 \sqrt{\frac{64}{75} + \frac{36}{50}} \right) ,$$

$$\left( 6 - 2.054 \sqrt{\frac{128 + 108}{150}} \ , \ 6 - 2.054 \sqrt{\frac{128 + 108}{150}} \right)$$

or $\left( 6 - 2.054 \sqrt{\frac{236}{150}} \ , \quad 6 + 2.054 \sqrt{\frac{236}{150}} \right)$.

Further simplification produces $(6 - 2.58, 6 + 2.58)$ or $(3.42, 8.58)$. Thus a 96% confidence for $\mu_1 - \mu_2$ is $(3.42, 8.58)$.

# VARIANCES

● **PROBLEM 14-44**

Consider a distribution $N(\mu, \sigma^2)$ where $\mu$ is known but $\sigma^2$ is not. Devise a method of producing a confidence interval for $\sigma^2$.

Solution: Let $X_1, X_2, \ldots, X_n$ denote a random sample of a size n from $N(\mu, \sigma^2)$, where $\mu$ is known. The random variable

$$Y = \frac{\sum\limits_{1}^{n} (X_i - \mu)^2}{\sigma^2} \quad \text{is a chi-square with n degrees of}$$

freedom. This is not to be confused with

$$\frac{\sum\limits_{1}^{n}(X_i - \bar{X})^2}{\sigma^2} \quad \text{which is } \chi^2(n - 1). \text{ We select a probability,}$$

$1 - \alpha$, and for the constant n, determine values a and b, with $a < b$ such that

$$\Pr(a < Y < b) = 1 - \alpha .$$

Thus $\quad P \left[ a < \dfrac{\sum\limits_{1}^{n}(X_i - \mu)^2}{\sigma^2} < b \right] = 1 - \alpha.$

We will concern ourselves with the central inequality. Taking reciprocals, we obtain

$$\frac{1}{b} < \frac{\sigma^2}{\dfrac{n}{\sum\limits_{1} (X_i - \mu)^2}} < \frac{1}{a} .$$

Multiply through by $\sum\limits_{1}^{n} (X_i - \mu)^2$ and the interval is

$$\frac{\sum\limits_{1}^{n} (X_i - \mu)^2}{b} < \sigma^2 < \frac{\sum\limits_{1}^{n} (X_i - \mu)^2}{a} .$$

470

The interval $\left( \dfrac{\overset{n}{\underset{1}{\Sigma}}(X_i - \mu)^2}{b}, \dfrac{\overset{n}{\underset{1}{\Sigma}}(X_i - \mu)^2}{a} \right)$ is a

random interval having probability $1 - \alpha$ of including the unknown fixed point (parameter) $\sigma^2$. Once we perform the experiment and find that $X_1 = x_1$, $X_2 = x_2$, ..., $X_n = x_n$, then the particular interval we calculate is a $1 - \alpha$ confidence interval for $\sigma^2$.

You should observe that there are no unique numbers a and b, a < b, such that $Pr(a < Y < b) = 1 - \alpha$. A common convention, one which we will follow, is to find a and b such that $Pr(Y < a) = \dfrac{\alpha}{2}$ and $Pr(Y > b) = \dfrac{\alpha}{2}$. That way

$$Pr(a < Y < b) = 1 - \frac{\alpha}{2} - \frac{\alpha}{2} = 1 - \alpha.$$

● **PROBLEM 14-45**

In the previous problem, assume $n = 10$, $\mu = 0$, $\overset{10}{\underset{1}{\Sigma}} X_i^2 = 106.6$ and $\alpha = .05$. Find a 95% confidence interval for $\sigma^2$.

**Solution:** Since $n = 10$, we are dealing with a $\chi^2(10)$. Since $\alpha = .05$, $\dfrac{\alpha}{2} = .025$. From the chi-square tables

$$P(\chi^2(10) < 3.25) = .025$$

and $\quad P(\chi^2(10) > 20.5) = .025.$

Hence a = 3.25 and b = 20.5.

Since $\mu = 0$, $\overset{10}{\underset{1}{\Sigma}} X_i^2 = \overset{10}{\underset{1}{\Sigma}}(X_i - 0)^2 = \overset{10}{\underset{1}{\Sigma}}(X_i - \mu)^2$

$$= 106.6 ,$$

our interval $\left( \dfrac{\overset{10}{\underset{1}{\Sigma}}(X_i - \mu)^2}{b}, \dfrac{\overset{10}{\underset{1}{\Sigma}}(X_i - \mu)^2}{a} \right)$ becomes

$\left( \dfrac{106.6}{20.5}, \dfrac{106.6}{3.25} \right) \quad$ or $\quad (5.2, 32.8).$

Thus, (5.2, 32.8) is a 95% confidence interval for $\sigma^2$.

● **PROBLEM 14-46**

Derive a method for determining a $100(1 - \alpha)$% confidence interval for the unknown variance, $\sigma^2$, of a normal distribution when the mean is also unknown.

**Solution:** Let $X_1$, $X_2$, ..., $X_n$ be a sample from a normal distribution with both mean and variance unknown. We will let $Y = \dfrac{\Sigma (X_i - \overline{X})^2}{\sigma^2} = \dfrac{(n-1)S^2}{\sigma^2}$

$\left( \text{Recall } S^2 = \dfrac{\Sigma (X_i - \overline{X})^2}{n-1} \right)$. $Y$ is chi-square with $n - 1$ degrees of freedom. For a fixed positive integer $(n \geq 2)$, we can find, from chi-square tables, values of a and b such that $\quad \Pr(a < \chi^2_{(n-1)} < b) = 1 - \alpha$.

Here we would find a and b by using a chi-square distribution with $n - 1$ d.o.f. In accordance with the convention previously adopted we would select a and b so that

$$P\left( \chi^2_{(n-1)} < a \right) = \frac{\alpha}{2}$$

and $\quad P\left( \chi^2_{(n-1)} > b \right) = \frac{\alpha}{2}$. $\quad$ Accordingly,

$$P\left( a < \frac{(n-1)S^2}{\sigma^2} < b \right) = 1 - \alpha.$$

As usual we will only concern ourselves with the inequality $\quad a < \dfrac{(n-1)S^2}{\sigma^2} < b$. First take reciprocals, $\dfrac{1}{b} < \dfrac{\sigma^2}{(n-1)S^2} < \dfrac{1}{a}$. Multiply by $(n-1)S^2$ and obtain

$$\frac{(n-1)S^2}{b} < \sigma^2 < \frac{(n-1)S^2}{a} .$$

$\left( \dfrac{(n-1)S^2}{b}, \dfrac{(n-1)S^2}{a} \right)$ is an interval having probability $1 - \alpha$ of including the unknown parameter $\sigma^2$. After we perform the random experiment, we set values $X_1 = x_1$, $X_2 = x_2$, ..., $X_n = x_n$, with $S^2 = \dfrac{1}{n-1} (\Sigma x_i - \overline{x})^2$ and we have as our $1 - \alpha$ interval $\left( \dfrac{(n-1)S^2}{b}, \dfrac{(n-1)S^2}{a} \right)$.

● **PROBLEM 14-47**

In the previous problem, find a 95% interval using the data n = 9, $S^2 = 7.63$.

**Solution:** Since n = 9, we are dealing with a chi-square statistic with $n - 1 = 8$ degrees of freedom.

We want a 95% (= .95) confidence interval, therefore, .95 = 1 - $\alpha$ or $\alpha$ = .05 and $\alpha/2$ = .025. Hence

$$P(\chi^2_{(8)} < 2.18) = .025 \text{ and } P(\chi^2_{(8)} > 17.5) = .025$$

which implies a = 2.18 and b = 17.5.

Making the required substutitions into

$$\left(\frac{(n-1)S^2}{b}, \frac{(n-1)S^2}{a}\right) \quad \text{yields} \quad \left(\frac{8(7.63)}{17.5}, \frac{8(7.63)}{2.18}\right)$$

or                (3.49, 28).

● **PROBLEM 14-48**

The lengths of a random sample of 10 staples have a sample variance of .32 centimeters squared. Find a .95 confidence interval estimate for the variance of all staple lengths.

Solution:    We have a small sample with an unknown variance. We are looking for a confidence interval for the variance. The statistic of concern here is

$$\frac{(n-1)S^2}{\sigma^2}$$ which is chi-square distributed with n - 1

degrees of freedom. Here n - 1 = 10 - 1 = 9.   Thus

$$\frac{(n-1)S^2}{\sigma^2}$$ is $\chi^2_{(9)}$.

We want values a, b such that    $Pr(a < \chi^2_{(9)} < b) = .95$.
We choose a such that $P(\chi^2_{(9)} < a) = .025$, and b such
that $P(\chi^2_{(9)} > b) = .025$. From the chi-square tables

a = 2.7 and b = 19. Since $\frac{(n-1)S^2}{\sigma^2}$ is $\chi^2_{(9)}$,

$$Pr\left[2.7 < \frac{(n-1)S^2}{\sigma^2} < 19\right] = .95.$$

Substitute n = 10 and $s^2$ = .32 in the central in-equality. Thus

$$2.7 < \frac{(10-1)(.32)}{\sigma^2} < 19 = 2.7 < \frac{2.88}{\sigma^2} < 19.$$

Divide by 2.88 and obtain $\frac{2.7}{2.88} < \frac{1}{\sigma} < \frac{19}{2.88}$

Taking the reciprocal produces $\frac{2.88}{19} < \sigma^2 < \frac{2.88}{2.7}$

or                $.15 < \sigma^2 < 1.06$.

A sample of 10 Jack Nicholson movies produced a mean of 8 Academy Award nominations and a variance $S^2$ of .25 nominations. Establish a .95 confidence interval estimate of the variance of Jack Nicholson movie Oscar nominations.

**Solution:** Recall first that $\frac{(n-1)S^2}{\sigma^2}$ is chi-square distributed with n − 1, in our case 9, degrees of freedom. A .95 confidence interval implies that $\alpha = .05$. Therefore $\frac{\alpha}{2} = .025$.

We want to find a, b such that $\Pr(a < \chi^2_{(9)} < b) = .95$

We will choose a such that $\Pr(\chi^2_{(9)} < a) = .025$ and b such that $\Pr(\chi^2_{(9)} > b) = .025$. This will leave $\Pr(a < \chi^2_{(9)} < b) = 1 - .025 - .025 = .95$. From the chi-square table a = 2.70 and b = 19.0.

Hence $\Pr(2.7 < \chi^2_{(9)} < 19) = .95$ We are concerned with the inequality $2.7 < \chi^2_{(9)} < 19$ or $2.7 < \frac{(n-1)S^2}{\sigma^2} < 19$. Substituting 10 for n and .25 for $S^2$ yields

$$2.7 < \frac{(10-1)\ .25}{\sigma^2} < 19 = 2.7 < \frac{2.25}{\sigma^2} < 19.$$

Taking the reciprocal of the inequality yields

$\frac{1}{19} < \frac{\sigma^2}{2.25} < \frac{1}{2.7}$ . To find the limits, simply multiply by 2.25, $0.118 < \sigma^2 < 0.833$.

We are 95% confident that the true variance is within the interval.

Eight scholars are working on a book. They are scheduled for an eight hour day, but no one works exactly eight hours. Yesterday the totals were 7.9, 7.8, 8.0, 8.1, 8.2, 7.9, 7.7, and 8.3 hours. Find a .95 confidence interval estimate for the variance of all 8 hour days these scholars will put in before their work is published.

**Solution:** We have a small sample with an unknown mean. We want a confidence interval for $\sigma^2$. The statistic we resort to is $\frac{(n-1)S^2}{\sigma^2}$ which is $\chi^2_{(n-1)}$ or $\chi^2_{(7)}$ here.

We must find $(n-1)S^2$. Since $S^2 = \frac{\Sigma(X - \overline{X})^2}{n-1}$ ,

$(n - 1)S^2 = \Sigma(X - \bar{X})^2$.

We must find $\bar{X}$.

$$\bar{X} = \frac{\Sigma X}{n} = \frac{7.9+7.8+8+8.1+8.2+7.9+7.7+8.3}{8} = \frac{63.9}{8} = 7.99.$$

The following table will help us find $\Sigma(X - \bar{X})^2$.

| X | $X - \bar{X}$ | $(X - \bar{X})^2$ |
|-----|------|-------|
| 7.9 | - .09 | .0081 |
| 7.8 | - .19 | .0361 |
| 8.0 | .01 | .0001 |
| 8.1 | .11 | .0121 |
| 8.2 | .21 | .0441 |
| 7.9 | - .09 | .0081 |
| 7.7 | - .29 | .0841 |
| 8.3 | .31 | .0961 |

$$\Sigma(X - \bar{X})^2 = 0.2888 = (n - 1)S^2$$

We know that there exists a and b so that

$\Pr\left(a < \frac{(n - 1)S^2}{\sigma^2} < b\right)$. Since $\frac{(n - 1)S^2}{\sigma^2}$ is $\chi^2_{(7)}$, we

choose a and b such that

$$P(\chi^2_{(7)} < a) = .025 \quad \text{and} \quad P(\chi^2_{(7)} > b) = .025.$$

The chi-square tables tell us a = 1.69 and b = 16.0.

We will construct our confidence interval from the

inequality $\quad a < \frac{(n - 1)S^2}{\sigma^2} < b \quad$ which equals

$1.69 < \frac{.2888}{\sigma^2} < 16$ .

Dividing by .2888 yields: $\quad \frac{1.69}{.2888} < \frac{1}{\sigma^2} < \frac{16}{.2888}$ .

Taking the reciprocal produces the result:

$\frac{.2888}{16} < \sigma^2 < \frac{.2888}{1.69} \quad$ or $\quad .018 < \sigma^2 < .171$.

● **PROBLEM 14-51**

One night New York City was victimized by a power failure. Most homes were without power 12 hours or more. Twenty-five homes were polled as to how long they were without power. It was observed that the variance of the sample was $S^2 = 4$. Find a .98 confidence interval estimate for the variance for all homes in New York.

<u>Solution:</u>    As in the previous problems concerning
confidence intervals of variances when the mean is unknown
we use the statistic $\frac{(n-1)S^2}{\sigma^2}$ which has a chi-square distribution with n - 1 degrees of freedom. We have n - 1 =
25 - 1 = 24. We want a and b so that

$$Pr(a < \chi^2_{(24)} < b) = .98.$$

To obtain this a and b, we set .98 = 1 - $\alpha$ so that
$\alpha$ = .02 and $\frac{\alpha}{2}$ = .01. a is the value such that

$$P\left(\chi^2_{(24)} < a\right) = .01 \text{ and b is the value such that}$$

$$P\chi^2_{(24)} > b = .01. \text{ From chi-square tables a = 10.9}$$

and b = 43.0. Since $\frac{(n-1)S^2}{\sigma^2}$ is $\chi^2_{(24)}$,

$$P\left[10.9 < \frac{(n-1)S^2}{\sigma^2} < 43\right] = .98.$$

Substituting n = 25, $S^2$ = 4 yields the inequality

$$10.9 < \frac{(25-1)\ 4}{\sigma^2} < 43$$

Simplification produces:    $10.9 < \frac{96}{\sigma^2} < 43.$

Divide by 96:    $\frac{10.9}{96} < \frac{1}{\sigma^2} < \frac{43}{96}$.

Take the reciprocal:    $\frac{96}{43} < \sigma^2 < \frac{96}{10.9}$

or    $(2.233 < \sigma^2 < 8.807)$

Thus $(8.807,\ 8.772)$ is our 98% confidence interval for $\sigma^2$.

# RATIO OF VARIANCES

● **PROBLEM 14-52**

Consider the following situation: A normal distribution of
a random variable, X, has a variance $\sigma_1^2$, where $\sigma_1^2$ is unknown. It is found however that experimental values of X
have a wide dispersion indicating that $\sigma_1^2$ must be quite
large. A certain modification in the experiment is made
to reduce the variance. Let the post-modification random
variable be denoted Y, and let Y have a normal distribution
with variance $\sigma_2^2$. Find a completely general method of
determining confidence intervals for ratios of variances,
$\frac{\sigma_1^2}{\sigma_2^2}$.

<u>Solution:</u>    Consider a random sample $X_1$, $X_2$, ..., $X_n$ of

476

size n $\geq$ 2 from the distribution of X and a sample $Y_1$, $Y_2$, ..., $Y_m$ of size m $\geq$ 2. The X's are independent of the Y's and m and n may or may not be equal. Let the two means be denoted $\bar{X}$ and $\bar{Y}$, and the sample variances

$$S_1^2 = \frac{\Sigma (X_i - \bar{X})^2}{n - 1} \quad \text{and} \quad S_2^2 = \frac{\Sigma (Y_i - \bar{Y})^2}{m - 1} .$$

The independent random variables $\frac{(n - 1)S_1^2}{\sigma_1^2}$ and $\frac{(m - 1)S_2^2}{\sigma_2^2}$ have chi-square distributions with n - 1 and m - 1 degrees of freedom, respectively. The quotient of 2 chi-square random variables each divided by their degrees of freedom is called an F random variable. Then

$$\frac{\frac{(n - 1)S_1^2}{\sigma_1^2}/n - 1}{\frac{(m - 1)S_2^2}{\sigma_2^2}/m - 1} = \frac{S_1^2/\sigma_1^2}{S_2^2/\sigma_2^2} \text{ has an F distribution with}$$

n - 1 degrees of freedom in the numerator and m - 1 degrees of freedom in the denominator.

For given values of n and m, a specified probability 1 - $\alpha$, and the use of F tables, we can determine a such that

$$Pr\left[F_{(n - 1, m - 1)} < a\right] = \frac{\alpha}{2}$$

and b such that $Pr\left[F_{(n - 1, m - 1)} > b\right] = \frac{\alpha}{2}$ . With

these values $Pr\left[a < F_{(n - 1, m - 1)} < b\right] = 1 - \frac{\alpha}{2} - \frac{\alpha}{2}$

= 1 - $\alpha$.

We know therefore that $Pr\left[a < \frac{S_1^2/\sigma_1^2}{S_2^2/\sigma_2^2} < b\right] = 1 - \alpha$.

Our confidence interval can be constructed from the

inequality $a < \frac{S_1^2/\sigma_2^2}{S_2^2/\sigma_1^2} < b$. Inverting the fraction,

$a < \frac{S_1^2\sigma_2^2}{S_2^2\sigma_1^2} < b$. Multiply through by $\frac{S_2^2}{S_1^2}$ and the interval is

$a \frac{S_2^2}{S_1^2} < \frac{\sigma_2^2}{\sigma_1^2} < b \frac{S_2^2}{S_1^2}$ .

It is seen that the interval has a probability 1 - $\alpha$ of including the fixed but unknown point $\frac{\sigma_2^2}{\sigma_1^2}$ .

● **PROBLEM** 14-53

A random sample of 10 salt-waterfish had variance, $S_1^2$, in girth of 7.2 inches$^2$, while a random sample of 8 fresh-water fish had a variance $S_2^2$ in girth of 3.6 in$^2$. Find a .90 confidence interval for the ratio between the two variances $\frac{\sigma_2^2}{\sigma_1^2}$ . Assume normal populations.

Solution: From the last problem. we know the interval
is of the form: $a \dfrac{S_2{}^2}{S_1{}^2} < \dfrac{\sigma_2{}^2}{\sigma_1{}^2} < b \dfrac{S_2{}^2}{S_1{}^2}$ .

Since $1 - \alpha = .90$, $\alpha = .10$ and $\alpha/2 = .05$. In this case $m = 8$ and $n = 10$. Thus $n - 1 = 9$ and $m - 1 = 7$. a is the value such that $\Pr(F_{(9,7)} < a) = .05$. b is the value such that $\Pr(F_{(9,7)} > b) = .050$.

From the F tables $a = .304$ and $b = 3.68$.

Since $S_1{}^2 = 7.2$ and $S_2{}^2 = 3.6$, the interval becomes

$.304 \left(\dfrac{3.6}{7.2}\right) < \dfrac{\sigma_2{}^2}{\sigma_1{}^2} < 3.68 \left(\dfrac{3.6}{7.2}\right)$ or $.152 < \dfrac{\sigma_2{}^2}{\sigma_1{}^2} < 1.84$ .

● **PROBLEM** 14-54

The standard deviation of a particular dimension of a metal component is small enough so that it is satisfactory in subsequent assembly; a new supplier of metal plate is under consideration and will be preferred if the standard deviation of his product is lower than that of the present supplier. The new supplier had a sample variance of $S_2{}^2 = .00041$ based on 100 observations, and the current supplier, a sample variance of $S_1{}^2 = .00057$ also based on 100 observations. Find a 90% lower one-sided confidence limit for $\dfrac{\sigma_2}{\sigma_1}$ .

Solution: Consider the distribution of $\dfrac{S_1{}^2/\sigma_1{}^2}{S_2{}^2/\sigma_2{}^2}$ .

We have previously shown that this has an F distribution with $n - 1$ and $m - 1$ degrees of freedom where n and m are the sizes of samples 1 and 2 respectively.

Since $n - 1 = m - 1 = 99$, **c** will be such that

$$\Pr\left[F_{(99,99)} > c\right] = .90$$

The F table does not have any values for 99,99 d.o.f. Due to the proximity of the values when n and m get that high we can safely use the values for 100,100 d.o.f. From the F table,

$c = \dfrac{1}{1.29}$ . We can safely state that

$$\Pr\left[F_{(99,99)} > \dfrac{1}{1.29}\right] = .90$$

Equivalently, $\Pr\left[\left(\dfrac{\sigma_2{}^2}{\sigma_1{}^2}\right)\left(\dfrac{S_1{}^2}{S_2{}^2}\right) > .775\right] = .90$.

Multiplying by $\left(\dfrac{S_2{}^2}{S_1{}^2}\right)$: $\Pr\left[\dfrac{\sigma_2{}^2}{\sigma_1{}^2} > .775 \dfrac{S_2{}^2}{S_1{}^2}\right] = .90$.

Since all values in the inequality
have only positive square roots, an equivalent expression
would be $\quad \Pr\left[\frac{\sigma_2}{\sigma_1} > (\sqrt{.775}) \; \frac{S_2}{S_1}\right] \; = .90$ .

Substituting .00041 for $S_2{}^2$ and .00057 for $S_1{}^2$ yields

$$\Pr\left[\frac{\sigma_2}{\sigma_1} > (.880) \; \left(\frac{\sqrt{.00041}}{\sqrt{.00057}}\right)\right] = .90 \quad \text{or} \quad \Pr\left[\frac{\sigma_2}{\sigma_1} > .747\right] = .90 .$$

We can be 90% confident that $\frac{\sigma_2}{\sigma_1} > .747$. Accordingly,
.747 is a 90% lower confidence limit.

● **PROBLEM** 14-55

The last 21 Mr. Americas' had a variance of 6 in$^2$ in
their chest size while the last 16 Mr. U.S.A.s' had a
variance of 4 in$^2$ in the same category. Assuming normality, find a .98 confidence interval estimate of
$\dfrac{\text{Variance Mr. America}}{\text{Variance Mr. U.S.A.}}$ .

Solution:　　First we will record the pertinent data

| Mr. U.S.A. Data | Mr. America Data | |
|---|---|---|
| $S_1{}^2 = 4$ | $S_2{}^2 = 6$ | $1 - \alpha = .98$ |
| $n = 16$ | $m = 21$ | $\alpha = .02$ |
| $n - 1 = 15$ | $m - 1 = 20$ | $\frac{\alpha}{2} = .01$ |

We want to find a confidence interval for $\frac{\sigma_2{}^2}{\sigma_1{}^2}$ .
Three problems ago we used the quotient of two chi-squares
divided by their degrees of freedom to obtain an F statistic
which yielded the following interval; $\left(a \; \frac{S_2{}^2}{S_1{}^2}, \; b \; \frac{S_2{}^2}{S_1{}^2}\right)$.

a is the value such that

$$\Pr(F_{(n-1, \; m-1)} < a) = .01 \quad \text{or} \quad \Pr(F_{(15, \; 20)} < a) = .01.$$

From the tables a = .297. b is obtainable from inequality

$$\Pr(F_{(15, \; 20)} > b) = .01. \quad b = 3.09.$$

Inserting all our values now the interval is

$$\left[.297 \left(\frac{6}{4}\right), \; 3.09 \left(\frac{6}{4}\right)\right] = (.446, \; 4.64).$$

# PROPORTIONS

Out of a group of 10,000 degree candidates of The University of North Carolina at Chapel Hill, a random sample of 400 showed that 20 per cent of the students have an earning potential exceeding $30,000 annually. Establish a .95 con- fidence-interval estimate of the number of students with a $30,000 plus earning potential.

Solution:     We solve this problem in two steps. First we will establish a 0.95 confidence-interval estimate for the proportion of students with a chance at the $30,000 bracket (a 95% confidence interval estimate of p). Secondly, we will multiply the range established for p by 10,000, the number of degree candidates, to obtain a range for the number of students about to exceed $30,000.

We can assume that there is a population of 10,000 and we are looking for p, the probability of a "success". This is a problem in binomial probabilities. Recall the following theorem relating the normal distribution to the binomial:

Theorem:     If X represents the number of successes in n independent trials of an event for which p is the probability of success in a single trial, then the variable $\dfrac{(x - np)}{\sqrt{npq}}$ has a distribution that approaches the standard

normal distribution as the number of trials, n, approaches infinity.

If we divide both numerator and denominator by  n  we obtain $\dfrac{\frac{x}{n} - p}{\sqrt{pq/n}}$  which is still standard normal. Therefore

$$Pr\left[- 1.96 < \frac{\frac{x}{n} - p}{\sqrt{pq/n}} < 1.96\right] = .95 .$$

Since we have a large sample, 400, the Law of Large Numbers will allow us to estimate p and q in the denominator by the proportions in the population, $\hat{p} = .20$ and $\hat{q} = 1 - .20 = .80$. Also $\frac{x}{n} = 20\% = .20$ and n = 400.

Substitution yields:

$$Pr\left[- 1.96 < \frac{.20 - p}{\sqrt{(.20)(.80)/400}} < 1.96\right] = .95.$$

Manipulate the central inequality as follows:

$$- 1.96 \sqrt{\frac{(.20)(.80)}{400}} < .20 - p < 1.96 \sqrt{\frac{(.20)(.80)}{400}} .$$

Simplification gives us:

$- 1.96 \ (.02) < .20 - p < 1.96 \ (.02)$

or $\quad - .0392 < .20 - p < .0392$ .

Subtract .20 from all terms: $\quad - .2392 < - p < - .1608$ .

For our final confidence interval, multiply by $- 1$:

$.1608 < p < .2392$ .

Since we have 10,000 degree candidates, the .95 confidence interval estimate of the number of students with a \$30,000 earning potential is

$10,000(0.1608 \leq p \leq 0.2392)$;

or between 1608 and 2392 students.

• **PROBLEM** 14-57

Given $X = 60$, construct a central 95% confidence interval for the parameter p of a binomial distribution for which $n = 100$.

Solution:    The random variable X is binomially distributed with mean $E(X) = np$ and Variance $X = np(1 - p)$. We use our best estimate of the Variance of X which is $n\hat{p}(1 - \hat{p})$ where $\hat{p}$ = the sample proportion $= \frac{x}{n} = \frac{60}{100}$ .

Since $n = 100$ is large,

$Z = \dfrac{X - E(X)}{\sqrt{\text{Var } X}}$ is approximately normally distributed

with mean 0 and variance 1.

Thus we want to find c such that

$$\Pr\left[- c \leq \frac{X - E(X)}{\sqrt{\text{Var } X}} \leq c\right] = .95 .$$

$c = 1.96$ will insure us of this because 95% of the standard normal distribution lies between $- 1.96$ and $1.96$. Thus

$$\Pr\left[- 1.96 \leq \frac{X - np}{\sqrt{n\hat{p}(1 - \hat{p})}} \leq 1.96\right] = .95 .$$

Multiply through:

$$\Pr\left[- 1.96\sqrt{n\hat{p}(1 - \hat{p})} \leq X - np \leq 1.96 \sqrt{n\hat{p}(1 - \hat{p})}\right] = .95 .$$

481

$$Pr\left(\frac{x}{n} - \frac{1.96}{n}\sqrt{\frac{x(n-x)}{n}} \leq p \leq \frac{x}{n} + \frac{1.96}{n}\sqrt{\frac{x(n-x)}{n}}\right) = .95$$

and $\frac{x}{n} \pm \frac{1.96}{n}\sqrt{\frac{x(n-x)}{n}}$ will be a 95% confidence interval

for p. When x = 60, n = 100, the limits of the confidence interval will be

$$\frac{60}{100} \pm \frac{1.96}{100}\sqrt{\frac{60(100-60)}{100}} = .6 \pm .096$$

or     .504 < p < .696.

● **PROBLEM** 14-58

In assessing the desirability of windowless schools, officials asked 144 elementary  school children whether or not they like windows in their classrooms. Thirty percent of the children preferred windows. Establish a 0.95 confidence-interval estimate of the proportion of elementary school children who like windows in their classrooms.

Solution:     From the theorem concerning the normal approximation to the binomial distribution, we know that $\frac{x - np}{\sqrt{npq}}$ has a distribution which we can consider to be

standard normal. Divide both numerator and denominator by

n to obtain the standard normal random variable $\frac{\frac{x}{n} - p}{\sqrt{pq/n}}$ . We

will have to estimate $\sqrt{\frac{pq}{n}}$ by $\sqrt{\frac{\hat{p}\hat{q}}{n}}$ where $\hat{p}$ and $\hat{q}$ are

the estimates of p and q from the sample. $\hat{p}$ is the proportion of window-preferrring children, 30% = .30. $\hat{q} = 1 - \hat{p} = 1 - .30 = .70$. Thus

$$\sqrt{\frac{pq}{n}} = \sqrt{\frac{\hat{p}\hat{q}}{n}} = \sqrt{\frac{(.30)(.70)}{144}} = .038.$$ Note also that

$$\frac{x}{n} = 30\% = .30.$$

Since $\frac{\hat{p} - p}{\sqrt{\frac{pq}{n}}}$ is approximately standard normal, $\frac{\hat{p} - p}{\sqrt{\frac{\hat{p}\hat{q}}{n}}} =$

$\frac{.30 - p}{.038}$ will be also. Thus, $Pr\left(-1.96 < \frac{.30 - p}{.038} < 1.96\right) = .95$

Remove the inequality from the parentheses:

$$- 1.96 < \frac{.30 - p}{.038} < 1.96 .$$

Multiply by .038:    $-.075 < .30 - p < .075 .$

Subtract .30:    $- .375 < - p < - .225 .$

Multiply by $- 1$ and the .95 confidence interval is (.225, .375) or (22.6%, 37.4%). Thus (.225, .375) is a 95% confidence interval for the true proportion of students preferring windowless classrooms.

● **PROBLEM** 14-59

In a public opinion poll, 320 out of 400 persons interviewed supported the administration's policy on disarmament.

(a) Establish a 95% confidence interval estimate of the proportion of persons supporting the government's stand on disarmament.

(b) What can be concluded with .99 confidence about the maximum error in our estimate if the proportion of those supporting the administration policy is es-timated as 80%?

(c) With what degree of confidence can we assert that the proportion of persons supporting the administration policy is somewhere between 77% and 83%?

Solution:    First note that the sample proportion is $\hat{p} = \frac{320}{400} = .80.$ $\hat{q} = 1 - \hat{p} = 1 - .80 = .20.$ We have been using a normal approximation to binomial problems and assuming $\frac{x - np}{\sqrt{npq}}$ is standard normal. We divide numerator and denominator by n and obtain the standard normal quantity $\frac{\frac{x}{n} - p}{\sqrt{\frac{pq}{n}}}$ . Since p and q are unknown, we will estimate pq by $\hat{p}\hat{q}$. We can do this because we have a large sample, n = 400. We will assume $\frac{\frac{x}{n} - p}{\sqrt{\frac{\hat{p}\hat{q}}{n}}}$ to be standard normal.

(a)  We can state that    $Pr\left( - 1.96 < \frac{\frac{x}{n} - p}{\sqrt{\frac{\hat{p}\hat{q}}{n}}} < 1.96 \right) = .95 .$

483

We remove the parentheses and multiply the inequality

by $\sqrt{\dfrac{\hat{p}\hat{q}}{n}}$ : $\quad -1.96 \sqrt{\dfrac{\hat{p}\hat{q}}{n}} < \dfrac{x}{n} - p < 1.96 \sqrt{\dfrac{\hat{p}\hat{q}}{n}}$ .

Subtract $\dfrac{x}{n}$: $\quad -\dfrac{x}{n} - 1.96 \sqrt{\dfrac{\hat{p}\hat{q}}{n}} < -p < -\dfrac{x}{n} + 1.96 \sqrt{\dfrac{\hat{p}\hat{q}}{n}}$ .

Multiply by $-1$: $\quad \dfrac{x}{n} - 1.96 \sqrt{\dfrac{\hat{p}\hat{q}}{n}} < p < \dfrac{x}{n} + 1.96 \sqrt{\dfrac{\hat{p}\hat{q}}{n}}$ .

Substituting our values yields:

$$.80 - 1.96 \sqrt{\dfrac{(.8)(.2)}{400}} < p < .80 + 1.96 \sqrt{\dfrac{(.8)(.2)}{400}} .$$

Simplify to obtain a 95% confidence interval for p:

$$.80 - .0392 < p < .80 + .0392 \quad \text{or} \quad .7608 < p < .8392.$$

(b)  We want a .99 confidence error estimate. In other words we want k such that $\Pr\left( \left| \dfrac{x}{n} - p \right| < k \right) = .99$ .

Equivalently: $\quad \Pr\left( -\dfrac{k}{\sqrt{\dfrac{\hat{p}\hat{q}}{n}}} < \dfrac{\dfrac{x}{n} - p}{\sqrt{\dfrac{\hat{p}\hat{q}}{n}}} < \dfrac{k}{\sqrt{\dfrac{\hat{p}\hat{q}}{n}}} \right) = .99$ .

But $\dfrac{\dfrac{x}{n} - p}{\sqrt{\dfrac{\hat{p}\hat{q}}{n}}}$ is a standard normal quantity and for any

standard normal quantity Z, $\Pr(-2.58 < Z < 2.58) = .99$.

Therefore $\quad \dfrac{k}{\sqrt{\dfrac{\hat{p}\hat{q}}{n}}} = 2.58$

and $\quad k = 2.58 \sqrt{\dfrac{\hat{p}\hat{q}}{n}} = 2.58 \sqrt{\dfrac{(.80)(.20)}{400}}$

or $\quad k = 2.58(.02) = .0516.$

We can assert with a probability of .99 that our maximum error is .0516 if p is estimated to be 80%.

(c)  We want to know $\gamma$, the degree of confidence of the interval $.77 < p < .83$, which is equivalent to the interval $.80 - .03 < p < .80 + .03$.

Let us assume the interval originated from a standard normal equality;

$$\Pr\left(-Z_0 < \frac{\frac{x}{n} - p}{\sqrt{\frac{\hat{p}\hat{q}}{n}}} < Z_0\right) = \gamma \ .$$

By manipulating the inequality as in part(a) we obtain

$$\frac{x}{n} - Z_0 \sqrt{\frac{\hat{p}\hat{q}}{n}} < p < \frac{x}{n} + Z_0 \sqrt{\frac{\hat{p}\hat{q}}{n}} \ .$$

Since $\frac{x}{n} = .80$, $\quad Z_0\sqrt{\frac{\hat{p}\hat{q}}{n}} = .03$ .

Substituting yields $Z_0\sqrt{\frac{(.80)(.20)}{400}} = .03$

or $\quad Z_0(.02) = .03 ; \quad Z_0 = \frac{.03}{.02} = 1.5$ .

$\gamma$ equals $\Pr(-1.5 < \text{Standard Normal} < 1.5)$.

From the standard normal table, $\quad \gamma = .8664$.

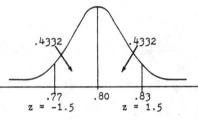

$$\begin{array}{c} .4332 \qquad\qquad .4332 \\ \end{array}$$

$$\begin{array}{ccc} .77 & .80 & .83 \\ z = -1.5 & & z = 1.5 \end{array}$$

● **PROBLEM** 14-60

Harvey of Brooklyn surveyed a random sample of 625 students at SUNY-Stony Brook. Being a pre-medical student, he hoped that most students would major in the social sciences rather than the natural sciences, thus provide him with less competition. To Harvey's dismay, 60% of the students he surveyed were majoring in the natural sciences. Construct a 95% confidence interval for p, the population proportion of students majoring in the natural sciences.

Solution: Let $\hat{p} = .60$, the sample proportion. $\hat{q} = 1 - \hat{p} = .40$. Since the sample size is large, $n = 625$, we can use

the normal approximation to the binomial. $\dfrac{x - np}{\sqrt{npq}} = \dfrac{\frac{x}{n} - p}{\sqrt{\frac{pq}{n}}}$

can be considered a standard normal random variable.

Therefore: $\quad \Pr\left(-1.96 < \dfrac{\frac{x}{n} - p}{\sqrt{\frac{pq}{n}}} < 1.96\right) = .95$ .

We have trouble with p and q however. Since we have a large sample we can estimate them by $\hat{p}$ and $\hat{q}$ for the purpose of computing $\sqrt{\frac{pq}{n}}$. Thus

$$Pr\left(-1.96 < \frac{\frac{x}{n} - p}{\sqrt{\frac{\hat{p}\hat{q}}{n}}} < 1.96\right) = .95 .$$

We multiply the central inequality by $\sqrt{\frac{\hat{p}\hat{q}}{n}}$:

$$-1.96 \sqrt{\frac{\hat{p}\hat{q}}{n}} < \frac{x}{n} - p < 1.96 \sqrt{\frac{\hat{p}\hat{q}}{n}} .$$

Subtract $\frac{x}{n}$: $\quad -\frac{x}{n} - 1.96 \sqrt{\frac{\hat{p}\hat{q}}{n}} < -p < -\frac{x}{n} + 1.96 \sqrt{\frac{\hat{p}\hat{q}}{n}} .$

Multiply by $-1$: $\quad \frac{x}{n} - 1.96 \sqrt{\frac{\hat{p}\hat{q}}{n}} < p < \frac{x}{n} + 1.96 \sqrt{\frac{\hat{p}\hat{q}}{n}} .$

Substitute our given values:

$$.60 - 1.96 \sqrt{\frac{(.60)(.40)}{625}} < p < .60 + 1.96 \sqrt{\frac{(.60(.40)}{625}} .$$

Simplifying yields $.60 - .038 < p < .60 + .038$

or $\qquad .562 < p < .638.$

● **PROBLEM** 14-61

In a sample of 100 cartons of Micheli's milk, 20 had begun to turn sour and 80 had not. Predict the proportion, p, of sour Micheli milk cartons on the market. Use a 95% confidence interval.

Solution: This is another problem which approximates the binomial distribution by the normal. $\frac{x - np}{\sqrt{npq}}$ is approximately standard normal. When we divide both numerator and denominator by n, we see $\frac{\frac{x}{n} - p}{\sqrt{\frac{pq}{n}}}$ is also standard normal.

To estimate $\sqrt{\frac{pq}{n}}$ we will estimate p by $\hat{p} = \frac{x}{n} = \frac{20}{100} = .20$; and q by $\hat{q} = 1 - \hat{p} = 1 - .2 = .80$. We can do this since we have a large sample, 100.

Thus we will assume $\frac{\frac{x}{n} - p}{\sqrt{\frac{\hat{p}\hat{q}}{n}}}$ is a standard normal random variable and hence; $\Pr\left(-1.96 < \dfrac{\dfrac{x}{n} - p}{\sqrt{\dfrac{\hat{p}\hat{q}}{n}}} < 1.96\right) = .95$ .

We remove the parentheses and multiply by $\sqrt{\dfrac{\hat{p}\hat{q}}{n}}$ :

$-1.96\sqrt{\dfrac{\hat{p}\hat{q}}{n}} < \dfrac{x}{n} - p < 1.96\sqrt{\dfrac{\hat{p}\hat{q}}{n}}$ .

Subtract $\dfrac{x}{n}$: $\quad -\dfrac{x}{n} - 1.96\sqrt{\dfrac{\hat{p}\hat{q}}{n}} < -p < -\dfrac{x}{n} + 1.96\sqrt{\dfrac{\hat{p}\hat{q}}{n}}$ .

Multiply by $-1$: $\quad \dfrac{x}{n} - 1.96\sqrt{\dfrac{\hat{p}\hat{q}}{n}} < p < \dfrac{x}{n} + 1.96\sqrt{\dfrac{\hat{p}\hat{q}}{n}}$ .

Substitute our values:

$.20 - 1.96\sqrt{\dfrac{(.20)(.80)}{100}} < p < .20 + 1.96\sqrt{\dfrac{(.20)(.80)}{100}}$ .

Simplifying yields: $\quad .20 - .078 < p < .20 + .078$

or $\quad .122 < p < .278$,

a 95% confidence interval for the true proportion of cartons turning sour.

● **PROBLEM** 14-62

In an appropriately selected sample of 144 members of a fraternal organization 20% are college graduates. Estimate the percentage you would find if you surveyed all 200,000 members. Establish a 99% confidence interval.

Solution: The normal distribution will serve as an approximation to the binomial distribution. We will consider $\dfrac{x - np}{\sqrt{npq}}$ to be standard normal.

After dividing both numerator and denominator by n, we see $\dfrac{\dfrac{x}{n} - p}{\sqrt{\dfrac{pq}{n}}}$ is also standard normal. The quantity $\dfrac{pq}{n}$ is unknown because p and q are unknown. However, since we have a large sample, n = 144, we can estimate $\sqrt{\dfrac{pq}{n}}$ by $\sqrt{\dfrac{\hat{p}\hat{q}}{n}}$ .

With this in mind, we will consider $\dfrac{\dfrac{x}{n} - p}{\sqrt{\dfrac{\hat{p}\hat{q}}{n}}}$ to be a

standard normal random variable.

Hence we can say $\Pr\left(-2.58 < \dfrac{\frac{x}{n} - p}{\sqrt{\frac{\hat{p}\hat{q}}{n}}} < 2.58\right) = .99$ .

We remove the parentheses and multiply by $\sqrt{\dfrac{\hat{p}\hat{q}}{n}}$ to

obtain: $-2.58 \sqrt{\dfrac{\hat{p}\hat{q}}{n}} < \dfrac{x}{n} - p < 2.58 \sqrt{\dfrac{\hat{p}\hat{q}}{n}}$ .

Subtract $\dfrac{x}{n}$ : $-\dfrac{x}{n} - 2.58 \sqrt{\dfrac{\hat{p}\hat{q}}{n}} < -p < -\dfrac{x}{n} + 2.58 \sqrt{\dfrac{\hat{p}\hat{q}}{n}}$ .

Multiply by $-1$: $\dfrac{x}{n} - 2.58 \sqrt{\dfrac{\hat{p}\hat{q}}{n}} < p < \dfrac{x}{n} + 2.58 \sqrt{\dfrac{\hat{p}\hat{q}}{n}}$ .

Substitute our given values:

$.20 - 2.58 \sqrt{\dfrac{(.20)(.80)}{144}} < p < .20 + 2.58 \sqrt{\dfrac{(.20)(.80)}{144}}$ .

Simplifying yields: $.20 - .086 < p < .20 + .086$.

p is therefore between .114 and .286 with 99% confidence.

● **PROBLEM** 14-63

A random sample of 300 Oberlin students were asked if they regularly smoke marijuana. 60 replied in the affirmative. Find an approximate 95% confidence interval on the true proportion, p, of Oberlin marijuana smokers.

Solution:    The theorem concerning the normal approxima-

tion to the binomial distribution tells us that $\dfrac{\frac{x}{n} - p}{\sqrt{\frac{pq}{n}}}$ is

a standard normal quantity. Since p, q are unknown, we will have to use $\hat{p} = \dfrac{x}{n} = \dfrac{60}{300} = .20$ and $\hat{q} = 1 - \hat{p} = 1 - .2 = .80$, in our estimation of $\sqrt{\dfrac{pq}{n}}$ .

We will assume that $\dfrac{\frac{x}{n} - p}{\sqrt{\frac{\hat{p}\hat{q}}{n}}}$ is a standard normal

random variable. Therefore $\Pr\left(-1.96 < \dfrac{\frac{x}{n} - p}{\sqrt{\frac{\hat{p}\hat{q}}{n}}} < 1.96\right) = .95$ .

Remove the parentheses and multiply by $\sqrt{\frac{\hat{p}\hat{q}}{n}}$ to obtain

$$- 1.96 \sqrt{\frac{\hat{p}\hat{q}}{n}} < \frac{x}{n} - p < 1.96 \sqrt{\frac{\hat{p}\hat{q}}{n}} \; .$$

Subtract $\frac{x}{n}$: $\quad - \frac{x}{n} - 1.96 \sqrt{\frac{\hat{p}\hat{q}}{n}} < - p < - \frac{x}{n} + 1.96 \sqrt{\frac{\hat{p}\hat{q}}{n}} \; .$

Multiply by $- 1$: $\quad \frac{x}{n} - 1.96 \sqrt{\frac{\hat{p}\hat{q}}{n}} < p < \frac{x}{n} + 1.96 \sqrt{\frac{\hat{p}\hat{q}}{n}} \; .$

Substitute our given data:

$$.20 - 1.96 \sqrt{\frac{(.20)(.80)}{300}} < p < .20 + 1.96 \sqrt{\frac{(.20)(.80)}{300}} \; .$$

Simplification yields: $\quad .20 - .045 < p < .20 + .045 \; .$

An approximate 95 percent confidence interval for p is (.155, .245).

● **PROBLEM** 14-64

Thanksgiving was coming up and Harvey's Turkey Farm was doing a land-office business. Harvey sold 100 gobblers to Nedicks for their famous Turkey-dogs. Nedicks found that 90 of Harvey's turkeys were in reality peacocks. (a) Estimate the proportion of peacocks at Harvey's Turkey Farm and (b) Find a 95% confidence interval for the true proportion of turkeys that Harvey owns.

Solution:     (a) The estimate we will use is the proportion of peacocks in the sample or

$$\hat{q} = (1 - \hat{p}) = 1 - \frac{x}{n} = 1 - \frac{10}{100} = \frac{90}{100} \; .$$

(b) We want a 95% confidence interval for the proportion of turkeys. The sample proportion is $\hat{p} = \frac{100 - 90}{100} = .10$. $\hat{q} = 1 - p = .90$. From the normal approximation to the binomial we know that

$$\frac{\frac{x}{n} - p}{\sqrt{\frac{pq}{n}}}$$

is approximately a standard normal random variable. But we do not known p and q. However, since we have a large sample, n = 100, we can use $\hat{p}$ and $\hat{q}$ to estimate $\sqrt{\frac{pq}{n}}$ by

$\sqrt{\frac{\hat{p}\hat{q}}{n}}$ . We will consider $\dfrac{\frac{x}{n} - p}{\sqrt{\frac{\hat{p}\hat{q}}{n}}}$ as a standard normal

random variable. Therefore

$$Pr\left[- 1.96 < \frac{\frac{x}{n} - p}{\sqrt{\frac{\hat{p}\hat{q}}{n}}} < 1.96\right] = .95.$$

Remove parentheses and multiply through by $\sqrt{\frac{\hat{p}\hat{q}}{n}}$ :

$$- 1.96 \sqrt{\frac{\hat{p}\hat{q}}{n}} < \frac{x}{n} - p < 1.96 \sqrt{\frac{\hat{p}\hat{q}}{n}} .$$

Subtract $\frac{x}{n}$ : $\quad - \frac{x}{n} - 1.96 \sqrt{\frac{\hat{p}\hat{q}}{n}} < - p < - \frac{x}{n} + 1.96 \sqrt{\frac{\hat{p}\hat{q}}{n}} .$

Multiply by - 1: $\quad \frac{x}{n} - 1.96 \sqrt{\frac{\hat{p}\hat{q}}{n}} < p < \frac{x}{n} + 1.96 \sqrt{\frac{\hat{p}\hat{q}}{n}}$

Now substitute in our data:

$$.10 - 1.96 \sqrt{\frac{(.10)(.90)}{100}} < p < .10 + 1.96 \sqrt{\frac{(.10)(.90)}{100}} .$$

Simplifying: $\quad .10 - .0588 < p < .10 + .0588.$

The true proportion lies in the interval

$$.0412 < p < .1588, \quad \text{with probability .95.}$$

● **PROBLEM** 14-65

A random sample of 225 students at a college showed that 135 had used and benefited from     problem solvers.
(a) Make a point estimate for the proportion of college students who were helped by     problem solvers. (b) Make a .95 confidence interval estimate of the exact proportion.

Solution: (a) We will use as our point estimate, for p, $\hat{p} = \frac{x}{n}$ . One reason for this is that the Weak Law of Large

Numbers tells us that $\quad \underset{n \to \infty}{\text{Lim}} \left|\frac{x}{n} - p\right| \to 0.$

Therefore $\hat{p} = \frac{x}{n} = \frac{135}{225} = .6, \quad \hat{q} = 1 - \hat{p} = 1 - .6 = .4.$

(b) We will approximate a binomial probability with the

normal distribution. We know $\frac{\frac{x}{n} - p}{\sqrt{\frac{\hat{p}\hat{q}}{n}}}$ can be considered a

standard normal distribution for a large sample. Our sample is large, n = 225. The size of the sample will afford us another luxury. We do not know p or q, but our sample size allows us to use point estimates for them in computing $\sqrt{\frac{\hat{p}\hat{q}}{n}}$ .

The rationale is that as the sample size increases, $\sqrt{\frac{\hat{p}\hat{q}}{n}}$ will be very close to $\sqrt{\frac{pq}{n}}$.

Consider $\dfrac{\frac{x}{n} - p}{\sqrt{\frac{\hat{p}\hat{q}}{n}}}$ to be a standard normal random variable. This implies $Pr\left(- 1.96 < \dfrac{\frac{x}{n} - p}{\sqrt{\frac{\hat{p}\hat{q}}{n}}} < 1.96\right) = .95.$

Let us clear the parentheses and multiply by $\sqrt{\frac{\hat{p}\hat{q}}{n}}$,

$$- 1.96 \sqrt{\frac{\hat{p}\hat{q}}{n}} < \frac{x}{n} - p < 1.96 \sqrt{\frac{\hat{p}\hat{q}}{n}}.$$

Subtract $\frac{x}{n}$: $\quad - \frac{x}{n} - 1.96 \sqrt{\frac{\hat{p}\hat{q}}{n}} < - p < - \frac{x}{n} + 1.96 \sqrt{\frac{\hat{p}\hat{q}}{n}}.$

Multiply by $- 1$: $\quad \frac{x}{n} - 1.96 \sqrt{\frac{\hat{p}\hat{q}}{n}} < p < \frac{x}{n} + 1.96 \sqrt{\frac{\hat{p}\hat{q}}{n}}.$

Substitute our given values:

$$.6 - 1.96 \sqrt{\frac{(.6)(.4)}{225}} < p < .6 + 1.96 \sqrt{\frac{(.6)(.4)}{225}}$$

or $\quad .6 - .064 < p < .6 + .064,$

which reduces to $\quad .536 < p < .664.$

● **PROBLEM** 14-66

In Atlanta, a random sample of 400 families contacted by a local TV station showed that 275 owned color TV sets. Make a .90 confidence interval estimate of the proportion of all families living in Atlanta who own color TV sets.

Solution: This problem concerns binomial probabilities. There are two possible outcomes. Either the family has a color TV set or it does not. In the case of large samples, the normal distribution gives a very good approximation for binomial problems. A sample of 400 is large enough to use the normal approximation.

Thus, $\dfrac{\frac{x}{n} - p}{\sqrt{\frac{pq}{n}}}$ can be considered a standard normal random variable. $\sqrt{\frac{pq}{n}}$ poses a bit of a problem since p and q are unknown. The fact that our sample is large, n = 400, allows us to estimate $\sqrt{\frac{pq}{n}}$ by $\sqrt{\frac{\hat{p}\hat{q}}{n}}$ without too much error. $\hat{p}$ is the sample proportion, $\frac{x}{n} = \frac{225}{400} = .56$, $\hat{q} = 1 - \hat{p} = 1 - .56 = .44$.

We will now proceed by assuming $\dfrac{\frac{x}{n} - p}{\sqrt{\frac{\hat{p}\hat{q}}{n}}}$ is a standard

normal random variable. Then $Pr\left[-1.645 < \dfrac{\frac{x}{n} - p}{\sqrt{\frac{\hat{p}\hat{q}}{n}}} < 1.645\right] = .90$

Remove the parentheses and multiply by $\sqrt{\frac{\hat{p}\hat{q}}{n}}$ :

$$- 1.645 \sqrt{\frac{\hat{p}\hat{q}}{n}} < \frac{x}{n} - p < 1.645 \sqrt{\frac{\hat{p}\hat{q}}{n}} \ .$$

Subtract $\frac{x}{n}$: $\ -\frac{x}{n} - 1.645 \sqrt{\frac{\hat{p}\hat{q}}{n}} < - p < - \frac{x}{n} + 1.645 \sqrt{\frac{\hat{p}\hat{q}}{n}}$

Multiply by $- 1$: $\frac{x}{n} - 1.645 \sqrt{\frac{\hat{p}\hat{q}}{n}} < p < \frac{x}{n} + 1.645 \sqrt{\frac{\hat{p}\hat{q}}{n}} \ .$

Substitute our values:

$$\left[.56 - 1.645 \sqrt{\frac{(.56)(.44)}{400}} < p < .56 + 1.645 \sqrt{\frac{(.56)(.44)}{400}}\right]$$

or .56 - .041 < p < .56 + .041 which reduces to (.519, .601). This is a 90% confidence interval for the true proportion that owns color televisions in Atlanta.

● **PROBLEM** 14-67

A political candidate for state office has predicted upon the basis of a poll of the registered voters that he will receive 60% of the vote in the upcoming election. To be 95% confident that he is within 2% of the vote he will actually receive, how many voters should have been polled?

Solution: Since the candidate expects to receive 60% of the vote, we are provided with an estimate for p, $\hat{p} = .60$ and $\hat{q} = 1 - \hat{p} = 1 - .6 = .4$.

The question asks how large a sample must we take to be 95% confident that the absolute difference between the sample proportion $\hat{p}$ and the population proportion p is less than .02. In other words, how large must n be so that the following expression is true.

492

$\Pr(|\hat{p} - p| < .02) = .95.$

This is equivalent to $\Pr\left(\left|\dfrac{x}{n} - p\right| < .02\right) = .95.$

Removing the absolute value signs, we obtain

$\Pr\left(-.02 < \dfrac{x}{n} - p < .02\right) = .95.$

Let us divide through by $\sqrt{\dfrac{\hat{p}\hat{q}}{n}}$ :

$$\Pr\left(\dfrac{-.02}{\sqrt{\dfrac{\hat{p}\hat{q}}{n}}} < \dfrac{\dfrac{x}{n} - p}{\sqrt{\dfrac{\hat{p}\hat{q}}{n}}} < \dfrac{.02}{\sqrt{\dfrac{\hat{p}\hat{q}}{n}}}\right) = .95. \qquad (1)$$

Since we have a large sample $\sqrt{\dfrac{\hat{p}\hat{q}}{n}}$ is an adequate estimation for $\sqrt{\dfrac{pq}{n}}$ .

$\dfrac{\dfrac{x}{n} - p}{\sqrt{\dfrac{\hat{p}\hat{q}}{n}}}$ approximates $\dfrac{\dfrac{x}{n} - p}{\sqrt{\dfrac{pq}{n}}}$ which by the normal

approximation theorem can be considered a standard normal

random variable. We will therefore consider $\dfrac{\dfrac{x}{n} - p}{\sqrt{\dfrac{\hat{p}\hat{q}}{n}}}$ as a

standard normal variable and we know that

$$\Pr\left(-1.96 < \dfrac{\dfrac{x}{n} - p}{\sqrt{\dfrac{\hat{p}\hat{q}}{n}}} < 1.96\right) = .95.$$

This expression must be equivalent to (1). Therefore

$1.96 = \dfrac{.02}{\sqrt{\dfrac{\hat{p}\hat{q}}{n}}}$ .

Squaring: $(1.96)^2 = \dfrac{(.02)^2}{\hat{p}\hat{q}/n}$ .

Combining into a simple fraction: $(1.96)^2 = \dfrac{(.02)^2 \, n}{\hat{p}\hat{q}}$

Multiply by $\hat{p}\hat{q}/(.02)^2$: $n = \dfrac{(1.96)^2 \, \hat{p}\hat{q}}{(.02)^2}$ .

Substituting:    $n = \frac{(1.96)^2 (.6)(.4)}{(.02)^2} = 2\ 304.96.$

If the candidate based his prediction on a random sample of 2,305 registered voters, he can be 95% certain that the sample proportion will not differ from the population proportion by more than 2%.

# DIFFERENCE OF PROPORTIONS

● **PROBLEM** 14-68

Determine a method for constructing a confidence interval for $p_1 - p_2$, the difference of two population proportions.

Solution:    Consider $Y_1$ and $Y_2$ to be two independent random variables with binomial distributions $b(n_1, p_1)$ and $b(n_2, p_2)$. Examine the random variables $\frac{Y_1}{n_1}$ and $\frac{Y_2}{n_2}$. Assume $n_1$ and $n_2$ are known.

The expected values of $\frac{Y_1}{n_1}$ and $\frac{Y_2}{n_2}$ are $p_1$ and $p_2$ respectively. Since    $\text{Var} \left( Y_1 \right) = n_1 p_1 q_1,$

$$\text{Var}\left( \frac{1}{n_1}\ Y_1 \right) = \left( \frac{1}{n_1} \right)^2 \text{Var}(Y_1) = \frac{1}{n_1^2}\ n_1 p_1 q_1 = \frac{p_1 q_1}{n_1}.$$

Similarly for $Y_2$.

The variances of $\frac{Y_1}{n_1}$ and $\frac{Y_2}{n_2}$ are $\frac{p_1 q_1}{n_1}$ and $\frac{p_2 q_2}{n_2}$ or equivalently $\frac{p_1(1 - p_1)}{n_1}$ and $\frac{p_2(1 - p_2)}{n_2}$.

The mean and variance of $\frac{Y_1}{n_1} - \frac{Y_2}{n_2}$, are $p_1 - p_2$, by the linearity properties of expectation, and $\frac{p_1(1 - p_1)}{n_1} + \frac{p_2(1 - p_2)}{n_2}$ by the additive properties of variance.

We will assume that $n_1$ and $n_2$ are large and apply the Central Limit Theorem. We will therefore consider

$$\frac{\left( \frac{Y_1}{n_1} - \frac{Y_2}{n_2} \right) - E\left( \frac{Y_1}{n_1} - \frac{Y_2}{n_2} \right)}{\sqrt{\text{Var}\ \left( \frac{Y_1}{n_1} - \frac{Y_2}{n_2} \right)}}$$

as a standard normal random variable. Hence we find $Z_{\alpha/2}$ such that

$$\text{Pr}\left[ -Z_{\alpha/2} < \frac{\left( \frac{Y_1}{n_1} - \frac{Y_2}{n_2} \right) - E\left( \frac{Y_1}{n_1} - \frac{Y_2}{n_2} \right)}{\sqrt{\text{Var}\ \left( \frac{Y_1}{n_1} - \frac{Y_2}{n_2} \right)}} < Z_{\alpha/2} \right] = 1 - \alpha.$$

Substituting our known expressions, we obtain

$$\Pr\left[-z_{\alpha/2} < \frac{\left(\frac{Y_1}{n_1} - \frac{Y_2}{n_2}\right) - (p_1 - p_2)}{\sqrt{\dfrac{p_1(1 - p_1)}{n_1} + \dfrac{p_2(1 - p_2)}{n_2}}} < z_{\alpha/2}\right] = 1 - \alpha.$$

We do not know $p_1$ and $p_2$ precisely but since our samples are large we can estimate them accurately by

$$\frac{\dfrac{Y_1}{n_1}\left(1 - \dfrac{Y_1}{n_1}\right)}{n_1} \quad \text{and} \quad \frac{\dfrac{Y_2}{n_2}\left(1 - \dfrac{Y_2}{n_2}\right)}{n_2}$$

for the purposes of calculating the square root of the variance. Therefore

$$\Pr\left[-z_{\alpha/2} < \frac{\left(\frac{Y_1}{n_1} - \frac{Y_2}{n_2}\right) - (p_1 - p_2)}{\sqrt{\dfrac{\dfrac{Y_1}{n_1}\left(1 - \dfrac{Y_1}{n_1}\right)}{n_1} + \dfrac{\dfrac{Y_2}{n_2}\left(1 - \dfrac{Y_2}{n_2}\right)}{n_2}}} < z_{\alpha/2}\right] = 1 - \alpha.$$

Multiplying through by the denominator:

$$-z_{\alpha/2}\sqrt{\frac{\dfrac{Y_1}{n_1}\left(1 - \dfrac{Y_1}{n_1}\right)}{n_1} + \dfrac{\dfrac{Y_2}{n_2}\left(1 - \dfrac{Y_2}{n_2}\right)}{n_2}} < \left(\frac{Y_1}{n_1} - \frac{Y_2}{n_2}\right) -$$

$$(p_1 - p_2) < z_{\alpha/2}\sqrt{\frac{\dfrac{Y_1}{n_1}\left(1 - \dfrac{Y_1}{n_1}\right)}{n_1} + \dfrac{\dfrac{Y_2}{n_2}\left(1 - \dfrac{Y_2}{n_2}\right)}{n_2}}$$

Subtracting $\left(\dfrac{Y_1}{n_1} - \dfrac{Y_2}{n_2}\right)$:

$$-\left(\frac{Y_1}{n_1} - \frac{Y_2}{n_2}\right) - z_{\alpha/2}\sqrt{\frac{\dfrac{Y_1}{n_1}\left(1 - \dfrac{Y_1}{n_1}\right)}{n_1} + \dfrac{\dfrac{Y_2}{n_2}\left(1 - \dfrac{Y_2}{n_2}\right)}{n_2}}$$

$$< -(p_1 - p_2) < -\left(\frac{Y_1}{n_1} - \frac{Y_2}{n_2}\right)$$

$$+ z_{\alpha/2}\sqrt{\frac{\dfrac{Y_1}{n_1}\left(1 - \dfrac{Y_1}{n_1}\right)}{n_1} + \dfrac{\dfrac{Y_2}{n_2}\left(1 - \dfrac{Y_2}{n_2}\right)}{n_2}}$$

Multiply by $-1$:

$$\left(\frac{Y_1}{n_1} - \frac{Y_2}{n_2}\right) - Z_{\alpha/2} \sqrt{\frac{\frac{Y_1}{n_1}\left(1 - \frac{Y_1}{n_1}\right)}{n_1} + \frac{\frac{Y_2}{n_2}\left(1 - \frac{Y_2}{n_2}\right)}{n_2}}$$

$$< p_1 - p_2 < \left(\frac{Y_1}{n_1} - \frac{Y_2}{n_2}\right)$$

$$+ \; Z_{\alpha/2} \sqrt{\frac{\frac{Y_1}{n_1}\left(1 - \frac{Y_1}{n_1}\right)}{n_1} + \frac{\frac{Y_2}{n_2}\left(1 - \frac{Y_2}{n_2}\right)}{n_2}} \; .$$

Our $1 - \alpha$ confidence interval is

$$\left[\left(\frac{Y_1}{n_1} - \frac{Y_2}{n_2}\right) - Z_{\alpha/2} \sqrt{\frac{\frac{Y_1}{n_1}\left(1 - \frac{Y_1}{n_1}\right)}{n_1} + \frac{\frac{Y_2}{n_2}\left(1 - \frac{Y_2}{n_2}\right)}{n_2}} \; , \right.$$

$$\left. \left(\frac{Y_1}{n_1} - \frac{Y_2}{n_2}\right) + Z_{\alpha/2} \sqrt{\frac{\frac{Y_1}{n_1}\left(1 - \frac{Y_1}{n_1}\right)}{n_1} + \frac{\frac{Y_2}{n_2}\left(1 - \frac{Y_2}{n_2}\right)}{n_2}}\right]$$

or

$$\left[(\hat{p}_1 - \hat{p}_2) - Z_{\alpha/2} \sqrt{\frac{\hat{p}_1(1 - \hat{p}_1)}{n_1} + \frac{\hat{p}_2(1 - \hat{p}_2)}{n_2}} \; , \right.$$

$$\left. (\hat{p}_1 - \hat{p}_2) + Z_{\alpha/2} \sqrt{\frac{\hat{p}_1(1 - \hat{p}_1)}{n_1} + \frac{\hat{p}_2(1 - \hat{p}_2)}{n_2}}\right] \; .$$

● **PROBLEM 14-69**

In the preceding problem, use the values $n_1 = 100$, $n_2 = 400$, $Y_1 = 30$, $Y_2 = 20$ and $\alpha = .05$.

Solution:     If $\alpha = .05$, $\frac{\alpha}{2} = .025$, and $1 - \alpha = .95$. Therefore $Z_{\alpha/2} = 1.96$.

The interval derived in the last problem was

$$\left[\left(\frac{Y_1}{n_1} - \frac{Y_2}{n_2}\right) - Z_{\alpha/2}\sqrt{\frac{\frac{Y_1}{n_1}\left(1 - \frac{Y_1}{n_1}\right)}{n_1} + \frac{\frac{Y_2}{n_2}\left(1 - \frac{Y_2}{n_2}\right)}{n_2}} \; , \right.$$

$$\left. \left(\frac{Y_1}{n_1} - \frac{Y_2}{n_2}\right) + Z_{\alpha/2}\sqrt{\frac{\frac{Y_1}{n_1}\left(1 - \frac{Y_1}{n_1}\right)}{n_1} + \frac{\frac{Y_2}{n_2}\left(1 - \frac{Y_2}{n_2}\right)}{n_2}}\right] \; .$$

Substitution yields:

$$\left(\left(\frac{30}{100} - \frac{20}{400}\right) - 1.96 \sqrt{\frac{\frac{30}{100}\left(1 - \frac{30}{100}\right)}{100} + \frac{\frac{20}{400}\left(1 - \frac{20}{400}\right)}{400}} \, , \right.$$

$$\left. \left(\frac{30}{100} - \frac{20}{400}\right) + 1.96 \sqrt{\frac{\frac{30}{100}\left(1 - \frac{30}{100}\right)}{100} + \frac{\frac{20}{400}\left(1 - \frac{20}{400}\right)}{400}} \, \right).$$

Combining terms produces:

$$\left(\frac{1}{4}\right) - 1.96 \sqrt{\frac{\frac{30}{100}\left(\frac{70}{100}\right)}{100} + \frac{\frac{20}{400}\left(\frac{380}{400}\right)}{400}} \, ,$$

$$\left(\frac{1}{4}\right) + 1.96 \sqrt{\frac{\frac{30}{100}\left(\frac{70}{100}\right)}{100} + \frac{\frac{20}{400}\left(\frac{380}{400}\right)}{400}} \, .$$

Simplify to obtain:

$(.25 - 1.96 \,(.047), \ .25 + 1.96 \,(.047))$. Equivalently

we have  $(.25 - .092, \ .25 + .092)$  or

$(.158, \ .342)$.

● **PROBLEM** 14-70

A national research institute asked a random sample of 1,000 men and 1,000 women if they were in favor of or against a gentleman offering a Tiparello to a lady. The results showed 60% of the men and 52% of the women were in favor. (a) Find a point estimate of the difference between the true proportions of the men and women. (b) Estimate a .90 confidence interval of $p_m - p_w$.

<u>Solution:</u>　(a) The best estimates of $p_m$ and $p_w$ are the population proportions $p_m = .60$ and $p_w = .52$. We can justify this by appealing to the Weak Law of Large Numbers which tells us

$$\lim_{n \to \infty} \left|\hat{p} - p\right| \to 0 \text{ or as n gets larger } \hat{p} = \frac{Y}{n}$$

approaches p. Thus the point estimate is $.60 - .52 = .08$.

(b) Two problems ago we derived the following confidence interval with the use of the Central Limit Theorem.

$$\left[\left(\frac{Y_m}{n_m} - \frac{Y_w}{n_w}\right) - z_{\alpha/2}\sqrt{\frac{\frac{Y_m}{n_m}\left(1 - \frac{Y_m}{n_m}\right)}{n_m} + \frac{\frac{Y_w}{n_w}\left(1 - \frac{Y_w}{n_w}\right)}{n_w}}\right.,$$

$$\left.\left(\frac{Y_m}{n_m} - \frac{Y_w}{n_w}\right) + z_{\alpha/2}\sqrt{\frac{\frac{Y_m}{n_m}\left(1 - \frac{Y_m}{n_m}\right)}{n_m} + \frac{\frac{Y_w}{n_w}\left(1 - \frac{Y_w}{n_w}\right)}{n_w}}\right].$$

This problem tells us $p_m = \frac{Y_m}{n_m} = .60$, $p_w = .52$

$n_m = n_w = 1000$, $1 - \alpha = .90$, $\alpha = .1$, $\frac{\alpha}{2} = .05$, and then $z_{\alpha/2} = 1.645$.

Inserting these values into our interval, we obtain

$$\left[(.60 - .52) - 1.645\sqrt{\frac{(.60)(1 - .60)}{1000} + \frac{(.52)(1 - .52)}{1000}}\right.,$$

$$\left.(.60 - .52) + 1.645\sqrt{\frac{(.60)(1 - .60)}{1000} + \frac{(.52)(1 - .52)}{1000}}\right].$$

Combining yields: $\left[.08 - 1.645\sqrt{\frac{(.60)(.40) + (.52)(.48)}{1000}}\right.,$

$$\left..08 + 1.645\sqrt{\frac{(.60)(.40) + (.52)(.48)}{1000}}\right]$$

Simplifying:

$(.08 - 1.645(.022), .08 + 1.645(.022))$ or

$(.08 - .036, .08 + .036)$ which reduces to

$(.044, .116)$ .

● **PROBLEM** 14-71

Hospital records show that of 500 men who were admitted for treatment, 60 were admitted because of high blood pressure. Of 500 women who were admitted for treatment, 50 were admitted for high blood pressure. Construct a .95 confidence interval estimate of the difference between the proportion of men and women who have high blood pressure.

<u>Solution</u>: In problem #68 of this chapter, we applied the Central

Limit Theorem to the random variable $\frac{Y_1}{n_1} - \frac{Y_2}{n_2}$ and showed that

$$\frac{\left(\frac{Y_1}{n_1} - \frac{Y_2}{n_2}\right) - E\left(\frac{Y_1}{n_1} - \frac{Y_2}{n_2}\right)}{\sqrt{\text{Var}\left(\frac{Y_1}{n_1} - \frac{Y_2}{n_2}\right)}} = \frac{\left(\frac{Y_1}{n_1} - \frac{Y_2}{n_2}\right)(p_1 - p_2)}{\sqrt{\frac{p_1(1 - p_1)}{n_1} + \frac{p_2(1 - p_2)}{n_2}}}$$

is a standard normal random variable. Since we did not know $p_1$ and $p_2$ we had to estimate them in the denominator b $\hat{p}_1 = \frac{Y_1}{n_1}$ and $\hat{p}_2 = \frac{Y_2}{n_2}$ . We could do this because our sample was large.

We treated $\dfrac{\left(\frac{Y_1}{n_1} - \frac{Y_2}{n_2}\right) - (p_1 - p_2)}{\sqrt{\dfrac{\frac{Y_1}{n_1}\left(1 - \frac{Y_1}{n_1}\right)}{n_1} + \dfrac{\frac{Y_2}{n_2}\left(1 - \frac{Y_2}{n_2}\right)}{n_2}}}$ as a

standard normal random variable. Here we want a .95 interval estimate. Therefore we use the fact that

$$\Pr\left(-1.96 < \frac{\left(\frac{Y_1}{n_1} - \frac{Y_2}{n_2}\right) - (p_1 - p_2)}{\sqrt{\dfrac{\frac{Y_1}{n_1}\left(1 - \frac{Y_1}{n_1}\right)}{n_1} + \dfrac{\frac{Y_2}{n_2}\left(1 - \frac{Y_2}{n_2}\right)}{n_2}}} < 1.96\right) = .95 \,.$$

Multiply through by the denominator:

$$-1.96\sqrt{\dfrac{\frac{Y_1}{n_1}\left(1 - \frac{Y_1}{n_1}\right)}{n_1} + \dfrac{\frac{Y_2}{n_2}\left(1 - \frac{Y_2}{n_2}\right)}{n_2}} < \left(\frac{Y_1}{n_1} - \frac{Y_2}{n_2}\right) - (p_1 - p_2)$$

$$< 1.96\sqrt{\dfrac{\frac{Y_1}{n_1}\left(1 - \frac{Y_1}{n_1}\right)}{n_1} + \dfrac{\frac{Y_2}{n_2}\left(1 - \frac{Y_2}{n_2}\right)}{n_2}} \,.$$

Subtract $\frac{Y_1}{n_1} - \frac{Y_2}{n_2}$:

$$-\left(\frac{Y_1}{n_1} - \frac{Y_2}{n_2}\right) - 1.96\sqrt{\dfrac{\frac{Y_1}{n_1}\left(1 - \frac{Y_1}{n_1}\right)}{n_1} + \dfrac{\frac{Y_2}{n_2}\left(1 - \frac{Y_2}{n_2}\right)}{n_2}}$$

$$< -(p_1 - p_2) < -\left(\frac{Y_1}{n_1} - \frac{Y_2}{n_2}\right) + 1.96$$

$$+ 1.96 \sqrt{\dfrac{\dfrac{Y_1}{n_1}\left(1 - \dfrac{Y_1}{n_1}\right)}{n_1} + \dfrac{\dfrac{Y_2}{n_2}\left(1 - \dfrac{Y_2}{n_2}\right)}{n_2}} \quad .$$

Multiply by $- 1$:

$$\left(\dfrac{Y_1}{n_1} - \dfrac{Y_2}{n_2}\right) - 1.96 \sqrt{\dfrac{\dfrac{Y_1}{n_1}\left(1 - \dfrac{Y_1}{n_1}\right)}{n_1} + \dfrac{\dfrac{Y_2}{n_2}\left(1 - \dfrac{Y_2}{n_2}\right)}{n_2}}$$

$$< p_1 - p_2 < \left(\dfrac{Y_1}{n_1} - \dfrac{Y_2}{n_2}\right) + 1.96$$

$$\sqrt{\dfrac{\dfrac{Y_1}{n_1}\left(1 - \dfrac{Y_1}{n_1}\right)}{n_1} + \dfrac{\dfrac{Y_2}{n_2}\left(1 - \dfrac{Y_2}{n_2}\right)}{n_2}} \quad . \quad (*)$$

In the problem we are given $n_1 = 500$, $Y_1 = 60$, $n_2 = 500$, and $Y_2 = 50$.

Hence $1.96 \sqrt{\dfrac{\dfrac{Y_1}{n_1}\left(1 - \dfrac{Y_1}{n_1}\right)}{n_1} + \dfrac{\dfrac{Y_2}{n_2}\left(1 - \dfrac{Y_2}{n_2}\right)}{n_2}}$

$$= 1.96 \sqrt{\dfrac{\dfrac{60}{500}\left(1 - \dfrac{60}{500}\right)}{500} + \dfrac{\dfrac{50}{500}\left(1 - \dfrac{50}{500}\right)}{500}}$$

$$= 1.96 \sqrt{\dfrac{\dfrac{60}{500}\left(\dfrac{440}{500}\right) + \dfrac{50}{500}\left(\dfrac{450}{500}\right)}{500}}$$

$$= 1.96 \sqrt{\dfrac{60 \cdot 440 + 50 \cdot 450}{500^3}}$$

$$= 1.96 \sqrt{\dfrac{26,400 + 22,500}{125,000,000}} = 1.96 \sqrt{\dfrac{48,900}{125,000,000}}$$

$$= 1.96 \, (.02) = .039 \quad .$$

In addition

$$\dfrac{Y_1}{n_1} - \dfrac{Y_2}{n_2} = \dfrac{60}{500} - \dfrac{50}{500} = \dfrac{60 - 50}{500} = \dfrac{10}{500} = .02.$$

Hence (*) reduces to

$$.02 - .039 < p_1 - p_2 < .02 + .039$$

or $\quad - .019 < p_1 - p_2 < .059.$

Tom and Joe like to throw darts. Tom throws 100 times and hits the target 54 times; Joe throws 100 times and hits the target 49 times. Find a 95 per cent confidence interval for $p_1 - p_2$ where $p_1$ represents the true proportion of hit in Tom's tosses, and $p_2$ represents the true proportion of hits in Joe's tosses.

Solution: In problem #68 of this chapter, we applied the Central Limit Theorem to the statistic $\frac{Y_1}{n_1} - \frac{Y_2}{n_2}$ , we arrived at an approximate standard normal random variable,

$$\frac{\left(\frac{Y_1}{n_1} - \frac{Y_2}{n_2}\right) - (p_1 - p_2)}{\sqrt{\frac{p_1(1 - p_1)}{n_1} + \frac{p_2(1 - p_2)}{n_2}}} \quad . \quad (1)$$

After estimating the denominator by substituting $\frac{Y_1}{n_1}$ for $p_1$ and $\frac{Y_2}{n_2}$ for $p_2$, we "pivoted" (1) into the following confidence interval for $p_1 - p_2$.

$$\left(\left(\frac{Y_1}{n_1} - \frac{Y_2}{n_2}\right) - z_{\alpha/2} \sqrt{\frac{\frac{Y_1}{n_1}\left(1 - \frac{Y_1}{n_1}\right)}{n_1} + \frac{\frac{Y_2}{n_2}\left(1 - \frac{Y_2}{n_2}\right)}{n_2}} \right. ,$$
$$\left. \left(\frac{Y_1}{n_1} - \frac{Y_2}{n_2}\right) + z_{\alpha/2} \sqrt{\frac{\frac{Y_1}{n_1}\left(1 - \frac{Y_1}{n_1}\right)}{n_1} + \frac{\frac{Y_2}{n_2}\left(1 - \frac{Y_2}{n_2}\right)}{n_2}} \right) \quad (2)$$

In the present problem $1 - \alpha = .95$. Hence $\alpha = .05$, $\frac{\alpha}{2} = .025$ and $z_{\alpha/2} = 1.96$. Also $Y_1 = 54$, $Y_2 = 49$, and $n_1 = n_2 = 100$. Therefore

$$z_{\alpha/2} \sqrt{\frac{\frac{Y_1}{n_1}\left(1 - \frac{Y_1}{n_1}\right)}{n_1} + \frac{\frac{Y_2}{n_2}\left(1 - \frac{Y_2}{n_2}\right)}{n_2}}$$

$$= 1.96 \sqrt{\frac{\frac{54}{100}\left(1 - \frac{54}{100}\right)}{100} + \frac{\frac{49}{100}\left(1 - \frac{49}{100}\right)}{100}}$$

$$= 1.96 \sqrt{\frac{\frac{54}{100}\left(\frac{46}{100}\right) + \frac{49}{100}\left(\frac{51}{100}\right)}{100}}$$

$$= 1.96 \sqrt{\frac{(.54)(.46) + (.49)(.51)}{100}}$$

$$= 1.96 \sqrt{\frac{.4983}{100}} = 1.96 \sqrt{.004983} = 1.96 \ (.0706)$$

$$= .138.$$

In addition $\frac{Y_1}{n_1} - \frac{Y_2}{n_2} = \frac{54}{100} - \frac{49}{100} = \frac{5}{100} = .05.$

Therefore (2) reduces to    $(.05 - .138, .05 + .138)$
or          $(- .88, .188)$.

# BAYESIAN CONFIDENCE INTERVAL

Let $X_1$, $X_2$, ... $X_n$ denote a random sample from a distribution which is $N(\theta, \sigma^2)$, where the variance is known. The statistician makes use of prior knowledge  and he takes $h(\theta)$, the prior p.d.f. of $\theta$, to be $N(\mu, \tau^2)$, where $\mu$ and $\tau^2$ are known. Find a 95.4% Bayesian interval estimate for $\theta$.

Solution:     The realm of Bayesian statistics involves different methods than the ones we have been using. It takes into account the prior knowledge of the statistician.

Consider the random variable X. Suppose it has a probability distribution function which depends on $\theta$, where $\theta$ is a member of a well-defined set $\Omega$. For example, if $\theta$ is the mean of a normal distribution, $\Omega$ can be the real line.

We shall now introduce the random variable $\Theta$. Hence, the distribution of X will depend on the random determination of $\Theta$. Note that $\Theta$ has a distribution of probability over $\Omega$. As we look upon x as a possibility for X, $\theta$ is a possible value of $\Theta$. Denote the p.d.f. of $\theta$ by $h(\theta)$ and take $h(\theta) = 0$ when $\theta$ is not an element of $\Omega$.

$X_1$, ..., $X_n$ is a random sample from X's distribution and Y is a statistic which is a function of $X_1$, $X_2$, ..., $X_n$. The p.d.f. of Y, given $\Theta = \theta$ is assumed. Call it $g(Y|\theta)$.

The joint p.d.f. of Y and $\Theta$ is    $k(\theta, Y) = h(\theta) \ g(Y|\theta)$.

If $\theta$ is a continuous random variable, the marginal p.d.f. of Y is      $k(Y) = \int_{-\infty}^{} h(\theta) \ g(Y|\theta) d\theta.$

The conditional p.d.f. of $\theta$ given Y = y, is

$$k(\theta|Y) = \frac{k(Y, \theta)}{k_1(Y)} = \frac{h(\theta) \, g(Y|\theta)}{k_1(Y)} \, .$$

The idea now is to find two functions, $u(y)$ and $v(y)$ so that

$$Pr[u(y) < \theta < v(y) \mid Y=y] = \int_{u(y)}^{v(y)} K(\theta|y) \, d\theta = 1 - \alpha,$$

usually .95. The experimental values of $X_1, \ldots X_n$, say $x_1, \ldots, x_n$, provide us with $y$, an experimental value for $Y$. The interval $(u(y), v(y))$ is an interval estimate in that the conditional probability that $\theta$ belongs to that interval is equal to $1 - \alpha$.

We call the p.d.f. $h(\theta)$, the prior p.d.f. of $\theta$. The conditional p.d.f., $k(\theta|Y)$, is called the posterior p.d.f. of $\theta$. This is because $h(\theta)$ is known prior to the observation of $Y$, while $k(\theta|Y)$ is not. The assignment of $h(\theta)$ is often arbitrary and therefore subjective.

Let us return to the original problem. Let $Y = \bar{X}$, the mean of the random variable. This implies then that $g(Y|\theta)$ is $N(\theta, \frac{\sigma^2}{n})$. Remember that the prior p.d.f. of $\theta$ is $N(\mu, \tau^2)$.

Accordingly, $k(\theta, y) = h(\theta) \, g(y|\theta)$

$$= \frac{1}{\sqrt{2\pi\tau^2}} \exp\left(-\frac{(\theta - \mu)}{2\tau^2}\right) \frac{1}{\sqrt{2\pi\sigma^2/n}} \exp\left(-\frac{(y - \theta)^2}{2\sigma^2/n}\right)$$

$$= \frac{1}{2\pi \, \tau\sigma/\sqrt{n}} \exp\left[\frac{-(\theta - \mu)^2}{2\tau^2} - \frac{(y - \theta)^2}{2\sigma^2/n}\right] \qquad (1)$$

$-\infty < y < \infty, \quad -\infty < \theta < \infty .$

Note that $(y - \theta)^2 = ((y - \mu) + (\mu - \theta))^2$

$$= (\theta - \mu)^2 - 2(\theta - \mu)(y - \mu) + (y - \mu)^2.$$

We can now write the exponent in (1) as

$$-\frac{1}{2}\left[\frac{(\theta - \mu)^2}{\tau^2} + \frac{(\theta - \mu)^2}{\sigma^2/n} - \frac{2(\theta - \mu)(y - \mu)}{\sigma^2/n} + \frac{(y - \mu)^2}{\sigma^2/n}\right]$$

$$= -\frac{1}{2}\left[\left(\frac{1}{\tau^2} + \frac{1}{\sigma^2/n}\right)(\theta - \mu)^2 - \frac{2}{\sigma^2/n}(\theta - \mu)(y - \mu)\right.$$

$$\left. + \frac{1}{\sigma^2/n}(y - \mu)^2\right] \, .$$

By comparing this with the bivariate normal density function,

$$F(x,y) = \frac{1}{2\pi\sigma_1\sigma_2\sqrt{1 - \rho^2}} \exp\left[-\frac{1}{2(1 - \rho^2)}\right.$$

(continues on next page.)

$$\left[\left(\frac{x-\mu_1}{\sigma_1}\right)^2 - 2\rho\left(\frac{x-\mu_1}{\sigma_1}\right)\left(\frac{y-\mu_2}{\sigma_2}\right) + \left(\frac{y-\mu_2}{\sigma_2}\right)^2\right],$$

we seen that $\theta$ and $Y$ have a bivariate normal distribution with $\mu_1 = \mu_2 = \mu$, $\sigma_1^2 = \tau^2$, $\sigma_2^2 = \tau^2 + \sigma^2/n$, and correlation

coefficient $\rho = \dfrac{\tau}{\sqrt{\tau^2 + \sigma^2/n}}$ .

Since $\mu_1 = \mu_2 = \mu$, we assign $\mu_\theta = \mu_y = \mu$. Also, since

we know $\sigma_\theta^2 = \tau^2$, we have no choice but to set $\sigma_y^2 = \tau^2 + \dfrac{\sigma^2}{n}$ .

Before we continue, we will state some results concerning the bivariate normal distribution that will be proven in the chapter on regression and correlation. (1) In a bivariate normal distribution, the conditional density $Y|X = x$ is normally distributed. (2) The mean of

$Y|X = x$ is $\qquad \mu_y + \rho \dfrac{\sigma_y}{\sigma_x} (X - \mu_x)$

and (3) $Y|X = x$ is distributed with a variance of $\sigma_y^2 (1 - \rho^2)$.

In our example $\theta|Y$ will be normally distributed with

mean $\mu_\theta + \rho \dfrac{\sigma_\theta}{\sigma_y} (y - \mu_y)$ and variance $\sigma_\theta^2 (1 - \rho^2)$.

Substituting, the mean for $\theta|Y = y$ becomes

$$\mu + \left(\frac{\tau}{\sqrt{\tau^2 + \sigma^2/n}}\right)\left(\frac{\tau}{\sqrt{\tau^2 + \sigma^2/n}}\right)(y - \mu)$$

$$= \mu + \frac{\tau^2(y - \mu)}{\tau^2 + \sigma^2/n} = \frac{\mu(\sigma^2/n) + y\tau^2}{\tau^2 + \sigma^2/n} .$$

The variance is $\tau^2\left[1 - \dfrac{\tau^2}{\tau^2 + \sigma^2/n}\right] = \dfrac{\tau^2\sigma^2/n}{\tau^2 + \sigma^2/n}$ .

Let us now standardize our normal random variable $\theta|Y = y$. Assume we have observed $y$ already. We will drop the notation $\theta|Y = y$ and call it just $\theta$. This notation makes sense because it is $\theta$ we are making an inference for based on our $y$ observation,

$$\frac{\theta - E(\theta)}{\sqrt{Var\ \theta}} = \frac{\theta - \dfrac{\mu(\sigma^2/n) + y\tau^2}{\tau^2 + \sigma^2/n}}{\sqrt{\dfrac{\tau^2\ \sigma^2/n}{\tau^2 + \sigma^2/n}}} \qquad \text{is a standard normal}$$

random variable.

Hence from the normal tables

$$\Pr\left[- 2 < \cfrac{\cfrac{\theta - \mu(\sigma^2/n) + y\tau^2}{\tau^2 + \sigma^2/n}}{\cfrac{\tau\,\sigma\,\sqrt{n}}{\tau^2 + \cfrac{\sigma^2}{n}}} < 2\right] = .954 .$$

Strip the parentheses and multiply through by the denominator:

$$\frac{- 2\,\tau\,\sigma/\sqrt{n}}{\sqrt{\tau^2 + \cfrac{\sigma^2}{n}}} < \theta - \frac{\mu(\sigma^2/n) + y\tau^2}{\tau^2 + \sigma^2/n} < \frac{2\tau\,\sigma/\sqrt{n}}{\sqrt{\tau^2 + \sigma^2/n}}$$

Add $\dfrac{\mu(\sigma^2/n) + y\tau^2}{\tau^2 + \sigma^2/n}$ to all terms and

$$\frac{\mu\,\sigma^2/n + y\tau^2}{\tau^2 + \sigma^2/n} - \frac{2\,\tau\sigma/\sqrt{n}}{\sqrt{\tau^2 + \sigma^2/n}} < \theta < \frac{\mu\sigma^2/n + y\tau^2}{\tau^2 + \sigma^2/n} + \frac{2\tau\,\sigma/\sqrt{n}}{\sqrt{\tau^2 + \sigma^2/n}} .$$

The above interval serves as an interval estimate in the sense of conditional probability.

It is worthwhile to compare this result with the 95.4 percent "confidence" interval for $\theta$, $(y - 2\,\sigma/\sqrt{n},\ y + 2\,\sigma/\sqrt{n})$. If the sample size is large enough so that $y = \bar{X}$ approximates $\mu$ and so that $\sigma^2/n$ is much smaller than $\tau^2$ then the Bayesian interval estimate approaches

$$\left(\frac{\mu + y\tau^2}{\tau^2 + 0} - \frac{2\,\tau\sigma/\sqrt{n}}{\sqrt{\tau^2 + 0}},\ \frac{\mu + y\tau^2}{\tau^2 + 0} + \frac{2\,\tau\sigma/\sqrt{n}}{\sqrt{\tau^2 + 0}}\right)$$

$$= \left(\frac{y\tau^2}{\tau^2} - \frac{2\,\tau\sigma/\sqrt{n}}{\tau},\ \frac{y\tau^2}{\tau^2} + \frac{2\,\tau\sigma/\sqrt{n}}{\tau}\right)$$

or $(y - 2\sigma/\sqrt{n},\ y + 2\sigma/\sqrt{n})$, the confidence interval.

It is also interesting to compare the interpretation of this confidence interval with those confidence intervals previously constructed. In this confidence interval, the parameter $\theta$ is a random variable and the endpoints are constants. The confidence interval is the interval in which $\theta$ can be expected $100(1 - \alpha)\%$ of the time.

In the previous confidence intervals, the parameter $\theta$ was fixed and the endpoints of the interval were random. These confidence intervals gave the probability that a random interval will include the fixed parameter $100(1 - \alpha)\%$ of the time.

# CHAPTER 15

# POINT ESTIMATION

## ESTIMATING THE POPULATION VARIANCE

● **PROBLEM** 15-1

A psychologist wishes to determine the variation in I.Q.s of the population in his city. He takes many random samples of size 64. The standard error of the mean is found to be equal to 2. What is the population standard deviation?

Solution: The standard error of the mean is defined to be

$$\sigma_{\overline{x}} = \frac{\sigma}{\sqrt{n}} \tag{1}$$

where $\sigma$ is the positive square root of the population variance and n is the size of the sample. Formula (1) is valid when sampling occurs with replacement or when the population is infinite.

We are given n = 64 and $\sigma_{\overline{x}}$ = 2.

Substituting into (1),

$$2 = \frac{\sigma}{\sqrt{64}} \quad \text{or,} \quad \sigma = 16. \tag{2}$$

Thus, the standard deviation of the distribution of I.Q.s in the city is 16.

If we assume that I.Q.s are normally distributed with mean 100, then a standard deviation of 16 tells us that approximately 68% of the population have I.Q.s between 84 and 116.

● **PROBLEM** 15-2

An investigator collected 50 different samples; each sample contained 17 scores. He studied the 50 means and estimated $\sigma_{\overline{x}}^2$ to be 2.9. Estimate $\sigma^2$ of the original population.

Solution:     Consider a population containing a finite number of elements N.  Suppose we wish to take a sample of size n from this population.  How many different samples can we take provided sampling is done with re-placement?  The answer is $N^n$ possible samples.  For there are N ways of choosing the first element of the sample,  N ways of choosing the second element, and pro-ceeding, N ways of choosing the last element.

For each sample of size n, there is a sample mean, $\bar{x}$. We can imagine the means of the samples forming a distri-bution with a mean value and a variance.  The variance of this distribution is given by the formula

$$\sigma_{\bar{x}}^2 = \frac{\sigma^2}{n} , \tag{1}$$

where the subscript $\bar{x}$ indicates that we are dealing with the distribution of sample means and n is the size of the sample.

Substituting the given data into (1),

$$2.9 = \frac{\sigma^2}{17} \quad \text{or,} \quad \sigma^2 = 17(2.9) = 49.3 .$$

Note that we did not use 50, the number of samples taken, for the problem at hand.  This was irrelevant data.

● **PROBLEM** 15-3

An investigator is interested in the physiological effects of sleep.  He selects, at random, a group of 100 people in his city, and determines the mean number of hours spent in sleep during a certain 3-day period.  The sample mean is found to be 7.15 and the sample standard deviation is computed as 1.10.     Find $\sum_{i=1}^{100} (x_i - \bar{x})^2$, i.e., the sum of the squared deviations from the mean.  Use this to estimate the population variance, the variance of the distribution of sample means and the standard error of the mean.

Solution:     The sample mean is computed using the following formula:

$$\bar{x} = \frac{1}{n} \sum_{i=1}^{n} x_i ,$$

where n represents the size of the sample and the $x_i$ represent the sample values.

The sample standard deviation is the positive square root of the sample variance.

$$s = \sqrt{s^2} = \sqrt{\dfrac{\sum\limits_{i=1}^{n}(x_i - \bar{x})^2}{n}} \tag{1}$$

Substituting the given data into (1),

$$1.10 = \sqrt{\dfrac{\sum\limits_{i=1}^{n}(x_i - \bar{x})^2}{100}}$$

Squaring,

$$1.21 = \dfrac{\sum\limits_{i=1}^{n}(x_i - \bar{x})^2}{100} \qquad \text{Hence, the sum of squares is}$$

$$\sum\limits_{i=1}^{n}(x_i - \bar{x})^2 = 121.$$

An unbiased estimator of the population variance is the statistic

$$s^2 = \dfrac{1}{n-1} \sum\limits_{i=1}^{n}(x_i - \bar{x})^2. \tag{2}$$

(2) is known as the sample estimate of the distribution variance. Letting

$$n = 100 \text{ and } \sum\limits_{i=1}^{n}(x_i - \bar{x})^2 = 121 \text{ in (2) we obtain}$$

$$s^2 = \dfrac{1}{99}(121) = 1.22. \tag{3}$$

We may use the above estimate of the population variance to estimate the variance of the sample means distribution. For,

$$\sigma_{\bar{x}}^2 = \dfrac{\sigma^2}{n}. \tag{4}$$

Substituting (3) and n = 100 into (4),

$$\sigma_{\bar{x}}^2 = \dfrac{1.22}{100} = .0122. \tag{5}$$

The square root of (5) yields the estimated standard error of the mean. Thus,

$$\sigma_{\bar{x}} = \sqrt{\sigma_{\bar{x}}^2} = \sqrt{.0122} = .110.$$

# THE METHOD OF MOMENTS

Let $X_1$, ..., $X_n$ be a random sample from a normal distribution with mean $\mu$ and variance $\sigma^2$. Let $(0_1, 0_2) = (\mu, \sigma)$. Estimate the parameters $\mu$ and $\sigma$ by the method of moments.

Solution: Let x be a random variable having the probability density function $f(x; Q_1, ..., Q_k)$ where $Q_1, ..., Q_k$ are parameters that characterize the distribution. The rth moment about the origin, $\mu'_r(Q_1, ..., Q_k)$ is defined as

$$\mu'_r(Q_1, ..., Q_k) = E[x^r].$$

For example, if the distribution is continuous,

$$\mu'_1 = E[x] = \int_{-\infty}^{\infty} xf(x) \, dx,$$

the population expected value, and

$$\mu'_2 = E[x^2] = \int_{-\infty}^{\infty} x^2 f(x) \, dx.$$

Next, consider a random sample, $x_1, ..., x_n$ from the distribution having density function $f(x_1; Q_1, Q_2, ... Q_k)$. Then the jth sample moment is

$$M'_j = \frac{1}{n} \sum_{i=1}^{n} x_i^j \qquad (j = 1, ..., k). \tag{1}$$

These moments are statistics (i.e., functions of the random sample) and hence may be used to estimate the parameters $Q_1, ..., Q_k$. Thus,

$$M'_j = \mu_j(Q_1, ..., Q_k); \qquad j = 1, ...., k \tag{2}$$

in the k variables $Q_1, ..., Q_k$. A solution of (2), say $(\hat{Q}_1, ..., \hat{Q}_k)$ is called the method of moments estimator of $(Q_1, ..., Q_k)$.

In the present problem, we are asked to find the method of moments estimators of the two parameters $\mu$ and $\sigma$ in the normal distribution. Since $\mu = \mu'_1$ and $\sigma^2 = \mu_2 - (\mu_1)^2$, the method of moments equations are

$$M'_1 = \frac{1}{n} \sum_{i=1}^{n} x_i = \mu_1(\mu, \sigma) = \bar{x} \tag{3}$$

509

and $M_2' = \frac{1}{n} \sum_{i=1}^{n} x_i^2 = \mu_2(\mu, \sigma) = \sigma^2 + \mu^2.$ \hfill (4)

From (3), $\bar{x}$ is the method of moments estimator of $\mu$ while from (4)

$$\hat{\sigma} = \sqrt{M_2' - (\mu)^2} = \sqrt{\frac{1}{n} \sum_{i=1}^{n} x_i^2 - (\bar{x})^2}$$

$$= \sqrt{\frac{\sum_{i=1}^{n} (x_i - \bar{x})^2}{n}} \; .$$

Note that the estimator of $\sigma^2$ is biased.

● **PROBLEM 15-5**

Let $X_1, \ldots, X_n$ be a random sample from a Poisson distribution with parameter $\lambda$. Estimate $\lambda$.

Solution: The random variable is said to be Poisson distributed if it has the probability density function

$$f(x) = \frac{e^{-\lambda} \lambda^x}{x!} \qquad x = 0, 1, \ldots \qquad (1)$$

Examining (1), we see that $\mu$ is the only parameter to be estimated. Hence, there is only one method of moments equation,

$$M_1' = \mu_1' = E(X).$$

But the expected value of the random variable X having a Poisson distribution is $\lambda$. Hence the estimator of $\mu$ is the first sample moment about the origin.

$$M_1 = \frac{1}{n} \sum_{i=1}^{n} X_i = \bar{X}. \qquad (2)$$

Equation (2) is the equation for the sample mean.

● **PROBLEM 15-6**

The method of moments does not produce unique estimates. Use the method to produce different estimates of the Poisson parameter $\lambda$.

Solution: Let $x_1, \ldots, x_n$ be a random sample from the Poisson distribution with density

510

$$f(x) = \frac{e^{-\lambda} \lambda^x}{x!} \qquad\qquad x = 0, 1, \ldots \qquad\qquad (1)$$

Using (1), $E(x) = \lambda$. But the parameter $\lambda$ also equals the variance of a Poisson distribution. This may be shown by the following argument

$$V(x) = E[x - E(x)]^2$$

$$= E(x^2) - [E(x)]^2. \qquad\qquad (2)$$

To find (2), we first find $E(x(x - 1))$ for a random variable that is Poisson distributed. Thus,

$$E(x(x - 1)) = \sum_{x=0}^{\infty} x(x - 1) \frac{e^{-\lambda} \lambda^x}{x!}$$

$$= e^{-\lambda} \sum_{x=2}^{\infty} \frac{\lambda^x}{(x - 2)!} = \lambda^2 e^{-\lambda} \sum_{x=2}^{\infty} \frac{\lambda^{x-2}}{(x - 2)!} \;.$$

Replacing the dummy index $x - 2$ by $x$,

$$E(x(x - 1)) = \lambda^2 e^{-\lambda} \sum_{x=0}^{\infty} \frac{\lambda^x}{x!} = \lambda^2 \;.$$

But, using the properties of the expectation operator,

$$E(x(x - 1)) = E(x^2 - x) = E(x^2) - E(x) = E(x^2) - \lambda.$$

Hence, $E(x^2) = \lambda^2 + \lambda$.

Substituting this result into (2),

$V(x) = \lambda^2 + \lambda - \lambda^2 = \lambda$, as was to be shown.

Hence, expressing the parameter in terms of moments

(i) $\qquad\qquad \lambda = E(x) = \mu_1' \;.$

(ii) $\qquad\qquad \lambda = E(x^2) - [E(x)]^2 = \mu_2' - (\mu_1')^2.$

The random sample $x_1, \ldots, x_n$ is used to estimate the sample moments corresponding to (i) and (ii). Thus,

$$M_1' = \frac{1}{n} \sum_{i=1}^{n} x_i \qquad\qquad (3)$$

$$M_2' - (M_1')^2 = \frac{1}{n} \sum_{i=1}^{n} x_i^2 - \left(\frac{1}{n} \Sigma x_i\right)^2$$

$$= \frac{1}{n} \sum_{i=1}^{n} x_i^2 - \bar{x}^2. \qquad\qquad (4)$$

Note that the same parameter $\lambda$ may be estimated by the method of moments as either (3) or (4). Since we will obtain different estimates, the lower order population moment is used.

# MAXIMUM LIKELIHOOD ESTIMATORS

An urn contains a number of black and a number of white balls, the ratio of the numbers being 3 : 1. It is not known, however, which color ball is more numerous. From a random sample of three elements drawn with replacement from the urn, estimate the probability of drawing a black ball.

<u>Solution:</u> Let p be the probability of drawing a black ball, and n the number of balls drawn. Then p is either $\frac{1}{4}$ or $\frac{3}{4}$. Since a drawn ball is either black or white, the number of black balls is given by the binomial distribution

$$f(x; p) = \binom{n}{x} p^x (1 - p)^{n-x} ; \quad x = 0, 1, \ldots, n. \quad (1)$$

Letting $p = \frac{1}{4}$ and then $p = \frac{3}{4}$ we obtain the following table from (1).

| Outcome: x | 0 | 1 | 2 | 3 |
|---|---|---|---|---|
| f(x; 1/4) | 27/64 | 27/64 | 9/64 | 1/64 |
| f(x; 3/4) | 1/64 | 9/64 | 27/64 | 27/64 |

Now assume that we draw a sample and find x = 2. Then, it is more likely that black balls are more numerous in the urn. If, on the other hand, no black balls were drawn, i.e., x = 0, then it is more likely that the white balls are three times more numerous than the black balls.

In general,

$$\hat{p} = \hat{p}(x) = \quad .25 \quad \text{for} \quad x = 0, 1$$

$$.75 \quad \text{for} \quad x = 2, 3.$$

is the estimator of the parameter p. For given sample outcomes it yields the most likely values of the parameter.

Let x be uniformly distributed,

$$f(x; \theta) = \frac{1}{\theta} \quad 0 < x \leq \theta, \ 0 < \theta < \infty \quad (1)$$

$$= 0 \text{ elsewhere.}$$

Find the maximum likelihood estimate for the parameter $\theta$.

<u>Solution</u>: We take a random sample $x_1, \ldots, x_n$ from the above distribution. Using this random sample, construct the likelihood function:

$$L(x_1, \ldots, x_n; \theta) = \frac{1}{\theta^n} \qquad 0 < x_i \leq \theta . \qquad (2)$$

Equation (2) was derived from the facts that i) each random variable has the probability density function $f(x_i; \theta) = \frac{1}{\theta}$; and ii) each member of the sample is statistically independent of the other.

For fixed values of $x_1, x_2, \ldots x_n$, we wish to find that value of $\theta$ which maximizes (2). We cannot use the techniques of calculus to maximize $L(x_1, \ldots, x_n; \theta)$. Note that (2) is largest when $\theta$ is as small as possible. But, examining (1) we see that the smallest value of $\theta$, such that $L(x_1, \ldots, x_n; \theta) > 0$, is equal to the largest value of $x_i$ in the sample. Hence

$$\hat{\theta} = x_{max}. \qquad (3)$$

Let us determine the expected value of (3). First, finding the distribution function,

$$P(x_1, \ldots x_n \leq x) = \prod_{i=1}^{n} P(x_i \leq x) = F^n(x). \qquad (4)$$

Differentiating (4) to obtain the probability density function,

$$\phi(x) = \frac{d}{dx} F^n(x) = nF^{n-1}(x) \frac{d}{dx} F(x) = nF^{n-1}(x)f(x)$$

by the chain-rule. The uniform distribution has

$$f(x) = \frac{1}{\theta}, \qquad F(x) = \frac{x}{\theta} \quad \text{for } 0 < x < \theta. \qquad \text{Hence,}$$

$$\phi(x) = \frac{n}{\theta} \left(\frac{x}{\theta}\right)^{n-1}, \qquad 0 < x < \theta . \qquad (5)$$

Taking the expected value of (5),

$$E[\phi(x)] = \int_0^\theta x \, \phi(x) \, dx = \int_0^\theta \frac{nx^n}{\theta^n} \, dx = \frac{n}{\theta^n} \frac{x^{n+1}}{n+1} \Bigg]_0^\theta$$

$$= \frac{n}{n+1} \theta. \qquad (6)$$

Comparing (6) and (3) we see that $\hat{\theta}$ is a biased estimator of $\theta$. This is an example where the maximum likelihood method yields a biased estimator.

Eight trials are conducted of a given system with the following results: S, F, S, F, S, S, S, S (S = success, F = failure). What is the maximum likelihood estimate of p, the probability of successful operation?

Solution:    If we assume that the trials are independent of each other, the sequence above has the probability

$$L(p) = p^6 (1 - p)^2. \qquad (1)$$

We wish to find that value of p which maximizes (1), the likelihood of this particular sequence. Differentiating (1) with respect to p and setting the derivative equal to zero:

$$L'(p) = 8p^7 - 14p^6 + 6p^5 = 0,$$

or,   $2p^5 (4p^2 - 7p + 3) = 0.$ $\qquad (2)$

From (2) either $\hat{p} = 0$ or

$$\hat{p} = \frac{7 \pm \sqrt{49 - 4(4)(3)}}{8}$$

$$= \frac{7 \pm 1}{8} = 1 \text{ or } \frac{3}{4}.$$

The values $\hat{p} = 0$ and $\hat{p} = 1$ when substituted into (1) yield $L(p) = 0$. Hence the likelihood is maximized when $\hat{p} = \frac{3}{4}$. This is the maximum likelihood estimate of p.

Let a random sample of size n be drawn from a Bernoulli distribution. Find the maximum likelihood estimator for p and sketch the likelihood function for n = 3.

Solution:    The random variable x has the Bernoulli distribution if it has the probability density function

$$f(x; p) = p^x (1 - p)^{1-x}, \quad x = 0, 1, \quad 0 \le p \le 1.$$

Let $x_1, \ldots, x_n$ denote a random sample from this distribution. Then the joint density function of $x_1, \ldots, x_n$ is

$$L(P) = f(x_1; p)f(x_2; p) \ldots f(x_n; p)$$

$$= p^{x_1} (1 - p)^{1-x_1} p^{x_2} (1 - p)^{1-x_2} \ldots p^{x_n}(1 - p)^{1-x_n}$$

$$= \prod_{i=1}^{n} p^{x_i} (1 - p)^{1-x_i}$$

$$= p^{\sum_{i=1}^{n} x_i} (1 - p)^{n - \sum_{i=1}^{n} x_i}. \tag{1}$$

Equation (1) is also known as the likelihood function. A necessary condition for (1) to reach a maximum is

$$L'(p) = 0.$$

$$\ln L(p) = \sum_{i=1}^{n} x_i \ln p + \left( n - \sum_{i=1}^{n} x_i \right) \ln (1 - p). \tag{2}$$

Note that $\ln L(p)$ is a monotone increasing function of $L(p)$ and hence achieves its maximum at the same value of $p$ as $L(p)$. Differentiating (2) with respect to $p$,

$$\frac{d}{dp} \ln L(p) = \frac{\sum_{i=1}^{n} x_i}{p} - \frac{\left( n - \sum_{i=1}^{n} x_i \right)}{1 - p}. \tag{3}$$

Setting (3) equal to zero,

$$(1 - p) \sum_{i=1}^{n} x_i - p \left( n - \sum_{i=1}^{n} x_i \right) = 0,$$

$$\sum_{i=1}^{n} x_i - p \sum_{i=1}^{n} x_i - np + p \sum_{i=1}^{n} x_i = 0,$$

$$p = \sum_{i=1}^{n} \frac{1}{n} (x_i) = \bar{x}.$$

Hence, the maximum likelihood estimator of $p$ given the random sample $x_1, \ldots, x_n$ is the sample mean $\bar{x}$.

Let $n = 3$. Then, the likelihood function is made up of four different possibilities. Thus, using (1),

$$L_0 \left[ p; \sum_{i=1}^{3} x_i = 0 \right] = p^0 (1 - p)^{3-0} = (1 - p)^3 \tag{4}$$

$$L_1 \left[ p; \sum_{i=1}^{3} x_i = 1 \right] = p (1 - p)^{3-1} = p (1 - p)^2 \tag{5}$$

$$L_2 \left[ p; \sum_{i=1}^{3} x_i = 2 \right] = p^2 (1 - p)^{3-2} = p^2 (1 - p) \tag{6}$$

$$L_3 \left[ p; \sum_{i=1}^{3} x_i = 3 \right] = p^3 (1 - p)^{3-3} = p^3. \tag{7}$$

Finally, we must sketch (4) - (7). (See fig.)

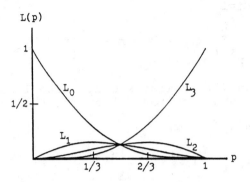

The maximum likelihood estimate of p depends on $\sum\limits_{i=1}^{n} x_i$. Differentiating (4) and setting the result equal to zero we find that when $\sum\limits_{i=1}^{3} x_i = 0$, L(p) is maximized when p = 0. Similarly, (5) is maximimized when $p = \frac{1}{3}$, (6) is maximized when $p = \frac{2}{3}$, and (7) is maximized when p = 1. These facts may be visually grasped from the figure.

• **PROBLEM** 15-11

Use the method of maximum likelihood to find a point estimate of the mean of a random sample from a normally distributed population with unit variance.

<u>Solution</u>: Let $x_1$, $x_2$, ..., $x_n$ be the random sample drawn from the normal distribution n($\theta$, 1), where $-\infty < \theta < \infty$ is the mean of the distribution. We wish to use the sample values to obtain an estimate of the mean.

Each member of the sample has a probability density function f(x; $\theta$). The joint probability density function of the n elements of the sample is, (since they are statistical-ly independent)

$$f(x_1; \theta)f(x_2; \theta) \ldots f(x_n; \theta).\qquad(1)$$

We may view (1) as a function of the parameter $\theta$. Thus,

$$L(\theta; x_1, \ldots x_n) = \left(\frac{1}{\sqrt{2\pi}}\right)^n \exp\left[-\sum_{i=1}^{n}\frac{(x_i - \theta)^2}{2}\right]\qquad(2)$$

since each random variable $x_i$ is distributed

516

$$\frac{1}{\sqrt{2\pi}} \exp \left[ - \frac{(x_i - \theta)^2}{2} \right].$$

Equation (2) is the likelihood function. To find the value of $\theta$ that maximizes (2) we may differentiate (2) with respect to $\theta$ and find $\theta_{max}$. First, however, note that it is possible to simplify the maximization of (2) by taking the logarithm of both sides. We do this because of the monotonic properties of ln. The maximum of ln L will also be the maximum of L.

$$\ln L(\theta; x_1, \ldots, x_n) = - n \ln [\sqrt{2\pi}] - \frac{1}{2} \sum_{i=1}^{n} (x_i - \theta)^2,$$

$$\frac{d[\ln L(\theta; x_1, \ldots, x_n)]}{d\theta} = \sum_{i=1}^{n} (x_i - \theta). \tag{3}$$

Setting (3) equal to 0 we find that

$$\sum_{i=1}^{n} (x_i - \theta) = 0$$

when $\theta = \bar{x}$.

The maximum likelihood method yields $\bar{x}$, the sample mean, as the statistic for the population mean $\theta$.

● **PROBLEM** 15-12

Let $x_1, \ldots, x_n$ be a random sample from a normal distribution with mean $\mu$ and variance $\sigma^2$. Let $\bar{x}$ be the estimate of $\mu$. Find the maximum likelihood estimator of $\sigma^2$.

Solution: The random variable x has the normal distribution if it has the probability density function

$$f(x; \mu, \sigma^2) = \frac{1}{\sqrt{2\pi}\sigma} e^{\frac{-(x - \mu)^2}{2\sigma^2}}.$$

Replacing $\mu$ with $\bar{x}$,

$$f(x; \bar{x}, \sigma^2) = \frac{1}{\sqrt{2\pi}\sigma} e^{\frac{-(x - \bar{x})^2}{2\sigma^2}}. \tag{1}$$

Since the sample is random, the variables are statistically independent. Therefore, the joint probability density function is given by

$$f(x_1, \sigma^2) \ldots f(x_n, \sigma^2)$$

$$= \frac{1}{\sqrt{2\pi\sigma^2}} \, e^{\frac{-(x_1 - \bar{x})^2}{2\sigma^2}} \cdots \frac{1}{\sqrt{2\pi\sigma^2}} \, e^{\frac{-(x_n - \bar{x})^2}{2\sigma^2}}$$

$$= (2\pi\sigma^2)^{-\frac{n}{2}} \exp\left[ -\sum_{i=1}^{n} \frac{(x_i - \bar{x})^2}{2\sigma^2} \right]. \quad (2)$$

Taking the ln of (2)

$$\ln f(x_i; \sigma^2) = -\frac{n}{2} \ln (2\pi) - \frac{n}{2} \ln \sigma^2 - \sum_{i=1}^{n} \frac{(x_i - \bar{x})^2}{2\sigma^2}. \quad (3)$$

We wish to find that value of $\sigma^2$ that maximizes (3). Note that since ln f increases as f does, maximizing ln f is equivalent to maximizing f. First, letting $v = \sigma^2$,

$$\ln f(x_i; v) = -\frac{n}{2} \ln (2\pi) - \frac{n}{2} \ln v - \sum_{i=1}^{n} \frac{(x_i - \bar{x})^2}{2v} \quad (4)$$

Partially differentiating (4) with respect to v and setting the result equal to zero:

$$\frac{\partial}{\partial v} \ln f(x_i; v) = -\frac{n}{2v} + \frac{1}{2} \sum_{i=1}^{n} \frac{(x_i - \bar{x})^2}{v^2} = 0$$

or,

$$\frac{-n2v^2 + 2v \sum_{i=1}^{n} (x_i - \bar{x})^2}{4v^3} = 0$$

or,

$$-nv + \sum_{i=1}^{n} (x_i - \bar{x})^2 = 0$$

or,

$$v = \sum_{i=1}^{n} \frac{(x_i - \bar{x})^2}{n} = s^2, \quad (5)$$

the sample variance. Thus, (5) is the maximum likelihood estimator of v or $\sigma^2$.

● **PROBLEM** 15-13

Consider a normal population with unknown mean $\mu$ and unknown variance $\sigma^2$. A random sample $x_1, \ldots, x_n$ is taken from the population. Find the maximum likelihood estimates for $\mu$ and $\sigma^2$ given this sample.

Solution:     Each member of the sample has the identical distribution

$$f(x;\ \mu,\ \sigma^2) = \frac{1}{\sqrt{2\pi\sigma^2}}\ \exp \frac{(x-\mu)^2}{2\sigma^2}.\qquad(1)$$

Since the sample is a random sample from the same population distribution, the elements of the sample are statistically independent.  The joint probability density function of the sample is therefore

$$L(x_1,\ \ldots,\ x_n;\ \mu;\ \sigma^2) = \frac{1}{[\sqrt{2\pi\sigma^2}]^n}\ \exp\left[-\ n\ \left(\frac{(x-\mu)^2}{2\sigma^2}\right)\right].\ (2)$$

We wish to find values of the parameters $\mu$ and $\sigma^2$ such that (1) is maximized.  Before differentiating (1) we convert it into its logarithm.  This is valid because the logarithm of a function attains its maximum at the logarithm of the value where the function attains its maximum.  Hence (2) becomes

$$\ln L(x_1,\ \ldots,\ x_n;\ \mu;\ \sigma^2)$$

$$= -\frac{n}{2}\ \ln\ (2\pi\sigma^2) - \frac{1}{2\sigma^2}\ \sum_{i=1}^{n}\ (x_i - \mu)^2.\qquad(3)$$

We now compute the partial derivatives of (3) with respect to $\mu$ and $\sigma^2$, and set them equal to zero.  Thus,

$$\frac{\partial \ln [L(x_i;\ \mu;\ \sigma^2)]}{\partial \mu} = \frac{1}{\hat{\sigma}^2}\ \sum_{i=1}^{n}\ (x_i - \hat{\mu}_i) = 0.\qquad(4)$$

$$\frac{\partial \ln [L(x_i;\ \mu;\ \sigma^2)]}{\partial \sigma^2} = -\frac{n}{2\hat{\sigma}^2} + \frac{1}{2(\hat{\sigma}^2)^2}\ \sum_{i=1}^{n}\ (x_i - \hat{\mu})^2 = 0.$$
$$\qquad(5)$$

We place carets on $\mu$ and $\sigma^2$ to indicate that they are estimates.

Recall that for any set of numerical values, $z_1,\ \ldots,$ $z_n$, $\sum_{i=1}^{n}\ (z_i - \bar{z}) = 0$.  Using this fact we see, from (4), that

$$\hat{\mu} = \bar{x}.\qquad(6)$$

Substituting (6) into the other simultaneous equation (5) yields

$$\frac{n}{2\hat{\sigma}^2} = \frac{1}{2(\hat{\sigma}^2)^2}\ \sum_{i=1}^{n}\ (x_i - \bar{x})^2$$

or, $\sigma^2 = \frac{1}{n} \sum\limits_{i=1}^{n} (x_i - \bar{x})^2$ . (7)

Now, the right hand side of (7) is nothing else but the computing formula for the sample variance $s_x^2$. Hence, the maximum likelihood estimates of $\mu$ and $\sigma^2$ are $\bar{x}$ and $s_x^2$, respectively.

● **PROBLEM** 15-14

Consider the geometric distribution

$$f(x) = \begin{cases} p(1 - p)^{x-1}, & x = 1, 2, \ldots \\ \\ 0, & \text{otherwise}, \end{cases} \quad (1)$$

where p denotes the probability that an event A will occur. Find the maximum likelihood estimate of p.

Solution: The geometric distribution yields the probability that the event A occurs after x - 1 failures. The likelihood function is given by (1) since only one experiment is being performed. We wish to find the value of p that will maximize (1). First, taking logarithms

$$\ln f(x; p) = (x - 1) \ln(1 - p) + \ln p. \quad (2)$$

To find $p_{max}$ of (2) we differentiate it with respect to p and set the derivative equal to zero. We are justified in working with $\ln f(x; p)$ since $\ln f(x; p)$ will attain its maximum where $f(x; p)$ does. Thus,

$$\frac{\partial \ln f(x; p)}{\partial p} = -\frac{x - 1}{1 - p} + \frac{1}{p} \quad . \quad (3)$$

Setting (3) equal to zero,

$$-\frac{p(x - 1) + (1 - p)}{p(1 - p)} = 0$$

or, $1 - px = 0$

or, $\hat{p} = \frac{1}{x}$ . (4)

Translated into verbal terms, (4) indicates that the most likely value of $\hat{p}$ given the sample is the reciprocal of the number of failures before the event A occurs. A standard example involves the rolling of a die and obtaining a given number (say 1). The estimate of p, whose value is $\frac{1}{6}$ here, would be the reciprocal of the number of rolls needed before a 1 appeared, i.e., the number of rolls would be 6.

The geometric distribution is used in calculating the probability that an event A (having probability p) will occur after x - 1 trials in which A does not occur. Therefore, the distribution is given by

$$f(x; p) = p(1 - p)^{x-1}.$$

Suppose a series of n such experiments are carried out and let $x_1, \ldots, x_n$ denote the number of trials required before A occurs in each experiment. Find an estimate for p using the method of maximum likelihood.

Solution:    Assuming the experiments are statistically independent, the likelihood function is given by

$$L = \prod_{i=1}^{n} f(x_i; p)$$

$$= (1 - p)^{x_1-1} p \cdot (1 - p)^{x_2-1} p \ldots (1 - p)^{x_n-1} p$$

$$= (1 - p)^{\sum_{i=1}^{n} x_i - n} p^n. \tag{1}$$

We wish to find the value of p that maximizes (1). First, taking logarithms,

$$\ln L(x_1, \ldots, x_n; p) = \left| \sum_{i=1}^{n} x_i - n \right| \ln (1 - p) + n \ln p. \tag{2}$$

$\ln L(x_1, \ldots, x_n; p)$ is monotonically increasing with respect to L.  They will attain their maxima at the same place.

Taking the partial derivative of (2) with respect to p and setting the result equal to zero:

$$\frac{\partial \ln L(x_1, \ldots, x_n; p)}{\partial p} = - \frac{\sum_{i=1}^{n} x_i - n}{1 - p} + \frac{n}{p},$$

$$\frac{- p \left[ \sum_{i=1}^{n} x_i - n \right] + n(1 - p)}{p(1 - p)} = 0,$$

$$- p \sum_{i=1}^{n} x_i + n = 0,$$

$$p = \frac{n}{\displaystyle\sum_{i=1}^{n} x_i} . \qquad (4)$$

Thus, the maximum likelihood estimate of p is the reciprocal of the arithmetic mean of the number of trials in each experiment.

● **PROBLEM** 15-16

Assume that the random variable x has the exponential distribution

$$f(x; \theta) = \theta e^{-\theta x}, \qquad x > 0, \qquad \theta > 0,$$

where $\theta$ is the parameter of the distribution. Use the method of maximum likelihood to estimate $\theta$ if five observations of x were

$$x_1 = .9, \ x_2 = 1.7, \ x_3 = .4, \ x_4 = .3 \text{ and } x_5 = 2.4.$$

Solution: We shall first derive an estimator for $\theta$ of the exponential distribution, using the method of maximum likelihood. Then we shall find an estimate for $\theta$ from the data of the given problem.

Let the variables $x_1, \ldots, x_n$ comprise a random sample from an exponential distribution. Each variable $x_i$ has the distribution

$$f(x_i; \theta) = \theta e^{-\theta x_i}. \qquad (1)$$

Since the members of the sample are statistically independent of each other their joint probability density function is given by, (using (1))

$$L[x_1, \ldots, x_n; \theta] = \theta e^{-\theta x_1} \theta e^{-\theta x_2} \ldots \theta e^{-\theta x_n}$$

$$= \theta^n e^{-\theta \sum_{i=1}^{n} x_i}. \qquad (2)$$

We wish to find the value of $\theta$ that maximizes (2). First, note that ln is a strictly increasing function. Maximizing ln L is equivalent to maximizing L.

$$\ln \{L[x_1, \ldots, x_n; \theta]\} = n \ln \theta - \theta \sum_{i=1}^{n} x_i. \qquad (3)$$

Differentiating (3) with respect to $\theta$ and setting the derivative equal to zero,

$$\frac{n}{\theta} - \sum_{i=1}^{n} x_i = 0 \tag{4}$$

or,

$$\hat{\theta} = \frac{n}{\sum_{i=1}^{n} x_i} \tag{5}$$

To check that (4) is indeed a maximum we differentiate (4) to obtain

$$[\ln \{L[x_1, \ldots, x_n; \theta]\}]'' = -\frac{n}{\theta^2} . \tag{6}$$

Since $\theta > 0$, (6) $< 0$ and (5) is indeed the value of $\hat{\theta}$ that maximizes (2).

We now concentrate on the specific distribution indicated by the given data. Substituting $n = 5$ and $\sum_{i=1}^{5} x_i = 5.7$ into (5),

$$\hat{\theta} = \frac{5}{5.7} = .88.$$

Finally, we note that the maximum likelihood estimator for $\hat{\theta}$ is the reciprocal of the arithmetic mean of the $x_i$, $\frac{1}{n} \sum_{i=1}^{n} x_i$.

● PROBLEM 15-17

Use the method of maximum likelihood to estimate the parameters of the multinomial distribution, $p_1, \ldots, p_k$ where $\sum_{i=1}^{k} p_i = 1$.

Solution: The multinomial distribution is an extension of the binomial distribution. Instead of only two outcomes - "success" or "failure", there are $k$ outcomes,

$A_1, \ldots, A_k$ with probabilities $p_1, \ldots p_k$.

In $n$ independent trials let the outcomes $A_1, \ldots, A_k$ have the frequencies $f_1, \ldots, f_k$. The probability of such a result is the likelihood function

$$L(p_1, \ldots, p_k) = p_1^{f_1} \cdot \ldots \cdot p_k^{f_k} . \tag{1}$$

We wish to find values of p such that (1) is maximized. For ease of computation we take the ln of (1)

$$\ln L (p_1, \ldots, p_k) = \sum_{i=1}^{k} f_i [\ln p_i] . \tag{2}$$

Since ln is a strictly increasing function, maximizing ln L is equivalent to maximizing L. We now note the restriction $\sum_{i=1}^{n} p_i = 1$, which presents the problem of finding a constrained maximum. Forming the Lagrangian multiplier, we must maximize

$$\sum_{i=1}^{k} f_i [\ln p_i] + \lambda \left[ 1 - \sum_{i=1}^{k} p_i \right] . \tag{3}$$

We find the partial derivatives with respect to each $p_i$ of (3). Thus,

$$\frac{\partial}{\partial p_i} \left[ \sum_{i=1}^{k} f_i [\ln p_i] \right] + \lambda \left[ 1 - \sum_{i=1}^{k} p_i \right]$$

$$= \frac{f_i}{p_i} - \lambda, \, (i=1, \ldots, k). \tag{4}$$

A necessary condition for (3) to be maximized is that the partial derivatives given by (4) equal zero. Hence, we obtain:

$$\frac{f_i}{p_i} = \lambda . \tag{5}$$

From (5), $p_i = \lambda f_i$ which means that the maximum likelihood estimates must be proportional to the frequencies $f_i$, the factor of proportionality being given by the multiplier $\lambda$. Since $\sum_{i=1}^{k} p_i = 1$, $\sum_{i=1}^{k} f_i = n$, $\lambda = \frac{1}{n}$ and

$$\hat{p}_i = \frac{f_i}{n}$$

which is the relative frequency of outcomes of type $A_i$.

Consider the probability density function

$$f(x; \theta) = 1, \quad \theta - \frac{1}{2} \leq x \leq \theta + \frac{1}{2}, \quad -\infty < \theta < \infty$$

$$= 0 \text{ elsewhere.}$$

Find a maximum likelihood statistic for the parameter $\theta$.

Solution:     We first take a random sample, $x_1, \ldots, x_n$ from the above distribution. Each member of the sample has the same distribution,

$$f(x; \theta) = 1,$$

and since the sample is random, they are statistically independent. Hence,

$$L(\theta; x_1, \ldots, x_n) = 1, \quad \theta - \frac{1}{2} \leq x \leq \theta + \frac{1}{2} \quad (1)$$

$$= 0 \text{ elsewhere.}$$

We wish to maximize (1), treating it as a function of $\theta$. This is possible when

$$\theta - \frac{1}{2} \leq \min (x_i) \quad \text{and} \quad \max(x_i) \leq \theta + \frac{1}{2}$$

or when

$$\theta \leq \min (x_i) + \frac{1}{2} \quad \text{and} \quad \max (x_i) - \frac{1}{2} \leq \theta.$$

Hence, every statistic $u(x, \ldots, x_n)$ such that

$$\max (x_i) - \frac{1}{2} \leq u(x_1, \ldots, x_n) \leq \min (x_i) + \frac{1}{2} \quad (2)$$

is a maximum likelihood statistic for $\theta$. The length of the interval in which $u(x_1, \ldots, x_n)$ must be, is (from (2)),

$$1 + \min(x_i) - \max (x_i). \quad (3)$$

Then, again from (2),

$$\max(x_i) - \frac{1}{2} + b [1 + \min (x_i) - \max (x_i)]$$

$$= b \min (x_i) + (1 - b) \max (x_i) + b - \frac{1}{2}, \quad (4)$$

$$0 < b < 1,$$

lies in the interval (3).

Since there are infinitely many b for which equation (4) is true, the maximum likelihood statistic for this distribution is not unique. For example, letting b = 1/2 in (4) we obtain the statistic

$$\frac{\min(x_i) + \max(x_i)}{2}$$ . Letting b = 1/4,

$$\frac{\min(x_i) + 3\max(x_i) - 1}{4}$$ , is another maximum

likelihood statistic.

● **PROBLEM** 15-19

Let the random variable x have a uniform distribution given by

$$f(x; \theta) = f(x; \mu, \sigma)$$

$$= \frac{1}{2\sqrt{3}\sigma} \quad , \quad \mu - \sqrt{3}\sigma < x < \mu + \sqrt{3}\sigma, \qquad (1)$$

$\sigma > 0$.

Find the maximum-likelihood estimates of $\mu$ and $\sigma$.

Solution: We first use the indicator function to rewrite (1). Let A be a set. Then

$$I_A(\omega) = \begin{cases} 1 \text{ if } \omega \varepsilon A \\ 0 \text{ if } \omega \notin A \end{cases} \qquad (2)$$

is called the indicator function of A. Using (2), (1) may be rewritten

$$f(x; \mu, \sigma) = \frac{1}{2\sqrt{3}\sigma} I_{(\mu - \sqrt{3}\sigma, \mu + \sqrt{3}\sigma)} x.$$

The likelihood function for the random sample is

$$L(\mu, \sigma; x_1, \ldots, x_n) = f(x; \mu, \sigma) \ldots f(x_n; \mu, \sigma)$$

$$= \left[\frac{1}{2\sqrt{3}\sigma} I_{(\mu - \sqrt{3}\sigma, \mu + \sqrt{3}\sigma)} x_1\right] \cdots \left[\frac{1}{2\sqrt{3}\sigma} I_{(\mu - \sqrt{3}\sigma, \mu + \sqrt{3}\sigma)} x_n\right]$$

$$= \left(\frac{1}{2\sqrt{3}\sigma}\right)^n \prod_{i=1}^{n} I_{(\mu - \sqrt{3}\sigma, \mu + \sqrt{3}\sigma)} (x_i)$$

$$= \left(\frac{1}{2\sqrt{3}\sigma}\right)^n I_{[\mu - \sqrt{3}\sigma, y_n]} (y_1) I_{[y_1, \mu + \sqrt{3}\sigma]} (y_n)$$

526

where $y_1$ is the smallest of the observations and $y_n$ is the largest value.

Since the minimum observation must be less than the maximum and vice versa, the above equals

$$\left(\frac{1}{2\sqrt{3}\sigma}\right)^n I_{[(\mu-y_1)/\sqrt{3},\infty)]}(\sigma)\ I_{[(y_n-\mu)/\sqrt{3},\infty)]}(\sigma)\ I_{[y,\infty]}(y_n)$$

by manipulating $y_1 \geq \mu - \sqrt{3}\sigma$ and $y_n \leq \mu + \sqrt{3}\sigma$.

Hence, the likelihood function is $(2\sqrt{3}\sigma)^{-n}$. Note, that to find the maximum of this function we cannot use the techniques of differential calculus.

The function,

$$f(\sigma) = (2\sqrt{3}\sigma)^{-n}$$

is maximized when $\sigma$ is smallest. This value of $\sigma$ occurs at the intersection of the two lines,

$$\mu - \sqrt{3}\sigma = y_1 \tag{3}$$

$$\text{and} \quad \mu + \sqrt{3}\sigma = y_n. \tag{4}$$

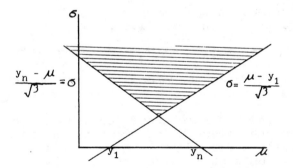

From (3) and (4), we may obtain the maximum likelihood estimates of $\mu$ and $\sigma$. Thus,

$$\mu = y_1 + \sqrt{3}\sigma \tag{3'}$$

$$\mu = y_n - \sqrt{3}\sigma \tag{4'}$$

$$\text{and} \quad \hat{\mu} = \frac{1}{2}(y_1 + y_n). \tag{5}$$

Similarly,

$$\sqrt{3}\sigma = \mu - y_1 \tag{3''}$$

$$\sqrt{3}\sigma = -\mu + y_n \tag{4''}$$

and $\quad \hat{\sigma} = \dfrac{1}{2\sqrt{3}} [y_n - y_1]$. $\hfill (6)$

Equations (5) and (6) are the maximum likelihood estimates of $\mu$ and $\sigma$.

● **PROBLEM** 15-20

---

Consider the negative exponential distribution

$\quad \dfrac{1}{\lambda} \exp \left(- \dfrac{x}{\lambda}\right)$, $x > 0$, $\exp z \equiv e^z$.

Let $x_1, \ldots, x_n$ denote a random sample from this distribution. Using the concept of loss functions, determine the maximum likelihood estimate of $\lambda$.

---

Solution:    We first define what is meant by "loss function." The actual value of the parameter being estimated is called a state of nature, $\theta$. On the basis of the estimate we decide upon a course of action a. Since we do not know the true state of nature, we must expect to lose something by the action we take based on incomplete information. Thus, we obtain the loss function,

$\quad \ell(\theta_0, a)$.

Let us assume, in the given problem, that the loss function is quadratic in form, i.e.,

$\quad \ell(\theta_0, a) = (a - \theta_0)^2$, $\hfill (1)$

the loss incurred upon choosing a as the estimate when the state is $\theta_0$.

Next, we find the likelihood function for the given sample. Since the selection of elements was random, they are statistically independent. Hence, their joint probability density function is given by

$\quad f(x_1; \lambda) \ f(x_2; \lambda) \ \ldots \ f(x_n; \lambda)$

$\quad = \dfrac{1}{\lambda} \exp \left(- \dfrac{x_1}{\lambda}\right) \ \ldots \ \dfrac{1}{\lambda} \exp \left(- \dfrac{x_n}{\lambda}\right)$

$\quad = \prod_{i=1}^{n} \dfrac{1}{\lambda} \exp \left(- \dfrac{x_i}{\lambda}\right)$

$\quad = \dfrac{1}{\lambda^n} \exp \left(\dfrac{-n\bar{x}}{\lambda}\right)$. $\hfill (2)$

Equation (2) is the likelihood function. To find the value of $\lambda$ at which it reaches its maximum we first take the ln of (2) and then differentiate. Thus,

$$\ln f(x; \lambda) = - n \ln \lambda - \frac{n\overline{x}}{\lambda} .$$

$$\frac{d}{d\lambda} \ln f(x; \lambda) = - \frac{n}{\lambda} + \frac{n\overline{x}}{\lambda^2} .$$

Setting (2) equal to zero,

$$\frac{-n\lambda + n\overline{x}}{\lambda^2} = 0$$

or,        $\overline{x} = \lambda$

Hence, the sample mean is the maximum likelihood estimator  of $\lambda$.

Examining (1) we see that it reaches its absolute minimum when $a = \theta_0$.  Hence, taking $\theta$ to be $\overline{x}$ will minimize the loss function relative to the information contained in the sample.

● **PROBLEM** 15-21

Light bulbs come in "lots" of ten, and one is taken from each lot and tested to see how long it burns before fusing. If the bulb is satisfactory, the remaining nine are sold at 15¢ each with a double-your money-back guarantee.  If the bulb is a failure, the lot is junked for 10¢.  Find the maximum likelihood decision function.

Solution:     The state of nature is the number k of defective bulbs among the ten, while there are two actions: sell the lot or junk the whole lot for 10¢.

We obtain the decision functions.

$d_1$ : Sell the lot if the test bulb is good, junk if defective.

$d_2$ : Junk the lot if the test bulb is good; sell if defective.

$d_3$ : Sell the lot if the test bulb is good; sell if defective.

$d_4$ : Junk the lot if the test bulb is good; junk if defective.

Let x denote the outcome of the test.  Then the loss functions are

$\ell(k; d_1(x)) = $    $- 1.35 + (.30)k,$     if x is good,

                .10,                if x is defective

$\ell(k; d_2(x)) = $        .10        if x is good,

$$- 1.35 + (.30)(k - 1) \quad \text{if } x \text{ is defective}$$

$$\ell(k; d_3(x)) = - 1.35 + (.30)k \quad \text{if } x \text{ is good}$$

$$- 1.35 + (.30)(k - 1) \quad \text{if } x \text{ is defective}$$

$$\ell(k; d_4(x)) = \quad .10 \quad \text{if } x \text{ is good}$$

$$.10 \quad \text{if } x \text{ is defective.}$$

Note that the negative sign indicates a negative loss, i.e., a profit.

Next we find the likelihood function. Let $p = \frac{k}{10}$. Then,

$$L(p) = p_p(x=x) = \quad 1 - p, \quad \text{if } x = \text{good} \tag{1}$$

$$p, \quad \text{if } x = \text{defective.}$$

Equation (1) is maximized when

$$\hat{p} = \quad 0, \quad \text{if } x = \text{good,}$$

$$1, \quad \text{if } x = \text{defective.}$$

Hence, the maximum likelihood decision function is to sell the lot if the bulb tested is good and junk the lot if the bulb tested is bad.

# UNBIASED ESTIMATORS

● **PROBLEM** 15-22

Let $x_1, \ldots, x_n$ be a random sample from a distribution having mean $\mu$. Show that the sample mean,

$$\bar{x} = \sum_{i=1}^{n} x_i,$$

is an unbiased estimator of the population mean.

Solution: Let the random variable x have the density function $f(x, \theta)$, where $\theta$ is an unknown parameter and let $x_1, \ldots, x_n$ be a random sample from the distribution having the above density function. Then $\hat{\theta} = \hat{\theta}(x_1, \ldots, x_n)$ is defined to be an unbiased estimator of $\theta$ if

$$E(\hat{\theta}) = \theta, \tag{1}$$

where $E(z)$ is the expected value of z. The expectation operator E has the properties,

$$E[cz] = cE(z) \qquad (2)$$

and $E[z_1 + \ldots + z_n] = E[z_1] + \ldots + E[z_n].$ (3)

In the present problem,

$$\bar{x} = \frac{1}{n} \sum_{i=1}^{n} x_i = \frac{1}{n} (x_1 + x_2 + \ldots + x_n).$$

Hence, $E(\bar{x}) = E\left[\frac{1}{n}(x_1 + x_2 + \ldots + x_n)\right]$

$$= \frac{1}{n} E[x_1 + x_2 + \ldots + x_n],$$

$$= \frac{1}{n} [E(x_1) + \ldots + E(x_n)], \qquad (4)$$

using (2) and (3). But the expected value of a random variable is the mean,

$$E(x) = \mu.$$

Hence, (4) becomes

$$E(\bar{x}) = \frac{1}{n} [n\mu] = \mu. \qquad (5)$$

Comparing (5) and (1), $\bar{x}$, the sample mean, is an unbiased estimator of $\mu$, the population mean.

● **PROBLEM** 15-23

The sample variance is given by the formula:

$$s_x^2 = \frac{1}{n} \sum_{i=1}^{n} (x_i - \bar{x})^2, \qquad (1)$$

where $x_i$ denotes the ith observation in the random sample and $\bar{x}$ denotes the sample mean. (a) Show that (1) is a biased estimate of the population variance $\sigma^2$, (b) Construct an unbiased statistic of $\sigma^2$ and then show that the unbiased statistic is consistent.

Solution: (a) Let $\hat{\theta}$ be an estimate of $\theta$ where $\hat{\theta}$ denotes the sample statistic and $\theta$ denotes the population parameter. $\hat{\theta}$ is defined to be an unbiased estimate of $\theta$ if,

$$E(\hat{\theta}) = \theta.$$

We use the definition (2) to check whether (1) is an unbiased estimate of $\sigma^2$. Thus, taking the expected value of (1),

$$E(s_x^2) = E\left\{ \frac{1}{n} \sum_{i=1}^{n} (x_i - \bar{x})^2 \right\}$$

$$\text{or,} \quad E(s_x^2) = E\left\{ \frac{1}{n} \sum_{i=1}^{n} [(x_i - \mu)^2 - (\bar{x} - \mu)^2] \right\}. \tag{3}$$

Examining (3), note that

$$E\left\{ \frac{1}{n} \sum_{i=1}^{n} (x_i - \mu)^2 \right\} = \sigma^2$$

and $\quad E\left\{ -\frac{1}{n} \sum_{i=1}^{n} (\bar{x} - \mu)^2 \right\} = -\text{var } \bar{x}$.

Since $\quad \text{var } \bar{x} = \dfrac{\sigma^2}{n}, \quad$ (3) becomes

$$E(s_x^2) = \sigma^2 - \frac{\sigma^2}{n} = \sigma^2 \left(1 - \frac{1}{n}\right) = \sigma^2 \left(\frac{n-1}{n}\right)$$

$$= \frac{n-1}{n} \sigma^2. \tag{4}$$

Hence, $s_x^2$ is a biased estimate of $\sigma^2$, the amount of bias being $-\dfrac{\sigma^2}{n}$.

(b) To construct an unbiased estimate of $\sigma^2$ we observe that multiplying (4) by $\dfrac{n}{n-1}$ yields $\sigma^2$. Consider the statistic

$$\bar{s}_x^2 = \frac{1}{n-1} \sum_{i=1}^{n} (x_i - \bar{x})^2. \tag{5}$$

(5) is $\dfrac{n}{n-1}$ times (1). Hence, its expectation is:

$$E(\bar{s}_x^2) = \frac{n}{n-1} E(s_x^2) = \frac{n}{n-1} \frac{n-1}{n} \sigma^2 = \sigma^2.$$

Thus, $\bar{s}_x^2 = \dfrac{1}{n-1} \sum_{i=1}^{n} (x_i - \bar{x})^2$ is an unbiased estimate of $\sigma^2$.

Finally, to judge whether (5) is a consistent estimate of $\sigma^2$ we first lay down the following fact (which may be proven using Tchebychev's theorem):

if $\quad \lim_{n \to \infty} E(\hat{\theta}_n) = \theta \quad$ and $\quad \lim_{n \to \infty} V(\hat{\theta}_n) = 0$

then $\hat{\theta}$ is a consistent estimator of $\theta$. Now the variance of $\bar{s}_x^2$ is

$$\text{var } \bar{s}_x^2 = \frac{2\sigma^4}{n - 1} \cdot$$

(6)

Hence, $\lim_{n \to \infty} V(\bar{s}_x^2) = \lim_{n \to \infty} \frac{2\sigma^4}{n - 1} = 0$

Since $E(\bar{s}_x^2) = \sigma^2$ and $V(\bar{s}_x^2) = 0$, $\bar{s}_x^2$ is a consistent estimate of $\sigma^2$.

● **PROBLEM** 15-24

For a certain sample the sample variance

$$s^2 = \sum_{i=1}^{n} \frac{(x_i - \bar{x})^2}{n}$$

is calculated to be 16. The sample contains 9 elements. Using an unbiased estimator, estimate $\sigma^2$.

<u>Solution:</u>    We must first examine whether $s^2$ is an unbiased estimator of $\sigma^2$. An estimator $\hat{\theta}$ of a population paremeter $\theta$ is said to be unbiased if

$$E(\hat{\theta}) = \theta.$$

Now, $E(s^2) = E\left\{ \frac{1}{n} \sum_{i=1}^{n} (x_i - \bar{x})^2 \right\} \cdot$

(1)

But we may express $\sum_{i=1}^{n} (x_i - \bar{x})^2$ as

$$\left[ \sum_{i=1}^{n} (x_i - \mu)^2 \right] - n(\bar{x} - \mu)^2.$$

(2)

Substituting (2) into (1),

$$E(s^2) = E\left\{ \frac{1}{n} \left[ \sum_{i=1}^{n} (x_i - \mu)^2 - n(\bar{x} - \mu)^2 \right] \right\} \cdot$$ (3)

But $E\left[ \frac{1}{n} \sum_{i=1}^{n} (x_i - \mu)^2 \right] = \sigma^2$ (the population variance)

and $E\left[ \frac{1}{n} (n(\bar{x} - \mu)^2) \right] = \sigma_{\bar{x}}^2$    (the variance of the sampling mean distribution).    Hence,

$$E(s^2) = \sigma^2 - \sigma_{\bar{x}}^2$$

$$= \sigma^2 - \frac{\sigma^2}{n} \tag{4}$$

$$= \sigma^2 \left(1 - \frac{1}{n}\right) = \sigma^2 \left(\frac{n-1}{n}\right). \tag{5}$$

Hence $s^2$ is a biased estimator of $\sigma^2$, the amount of bias being $-\frac{\sigma^2}{n}$. We use (5) to find an unbiased estimator of $\sigma^2$. Define the statistic

$$\overline{s}^2 = \frac{1}{n-1} \sum_{i=1}^{n} (x_i - \overline{x})^2. \tag{6}$$

Note that

$$E(\overline{s}^2) = E\left[\sum_{i=1}^{n} \frac{(x_i - \overline{x})^2}{n-1}\right] = \sigma^2. \tag{7}$$

Hence $\overline{s}^2$ is an unbiased estimator of $\sigma^2$.

We now are ready to estimate $\sigma$ in the given problem. Since $\overline{s}^2 = \frac{n}{n-1} s^2$,

$$\overline{s}^2 = \frac{9}{8} (16) = 18$$

Therefore, an unbiased estimate of $\sigma^2$ for this set of data is $\overline{s}^2 = 18$

● **PROBLEM 15-25**

Let $s_1^2, \ldots, s_k^2$ denote k sample variances based on random samples of sizes $n_1, \ldots, n_k$, respectively. How would you combine several sample variances to obtain a single unbiased estimate of the population variance?

Solution: The sample variance is given by the formula,

$$s_j^2 = \sum_{i=1}^{n_j} \frac{(x_{ji} - \overline{x}_j)^2}{n}, \qquad j = 1, \ldots, k \tag{1}$$

where $\overline{x}_j = \sum_{i=1}^{n_j} \frac{x_{ji}}{n}$, the sample mean. Since

$$E(s_j^2) = \sigma^2 - \frac{\sigma^2}{n}, \qquad \text{(see last problem)} \quad s_j^2 \text{ is a biased estimator of } \sigma^2.$$

When adding together the sample variances a weight must be assigned to $s_i^2$ indicating its importance relative to the sum. Hence, form the sum

$$t = \frac{n_1 \, s_1^2 + \ldots + n_k \, s_k^2}{a} \tag{3}$$

where $n_1, \ldots, n_k$ are the weights and a is a constant that makes (3) unbiased. Taking the expected value of (3),

$$E(t) = \frac{1}{a} \left[ (n_1 - 1)\sigma^2 + \ldots + (n_k - 1)\sigma^2 \right]$$

$$= \frac{\sigma^2}{a} \left[ (n_1 + \ldots + n_k) - k \right], \tag{4}$$

where we used the facts

$$E(s_j^2) = \left( \frac{n-1}{n} \right) \sigma^2 \qquad \text{and}$$

$$E[a_1 x_1 + \ldots + a_n x_n] = a_1 E(x_1) + \ldots + a_n E(x_n).$$

Equation (4) is the desired result.

● **PROBLEM 15-26**

Show that the sample mean is the minimum variance unbiased linear combination of the observations in a random sample.

Solution:     Consider a random sample selected from a distribution with frequency function $f(x; \theta)$. Let $x_1, \ldots, x_n$ be the members of the sample.

A linear combination of the sample elements is

$$a_1 x_1 + a_2 x_2 + \ldots + a_n x_n = \sum_{i=1}^{n} a_i x_i . \tag{1}$$

Recall that the expected value of a random variable is

$$E(x) = \sum_{i=1}^{n} x_i p(x_i), \tag{2}$$

where $\sum_{i=1}^{n} p(x_i) = 1$, the sum of probabilities.

If (1) is to be an unbiased estimator of (2) we must have

$$\sum_{i=1}^{n} a_i = 1. \tag{3}$$

This is because

$$E\left(\sum_{i=1}^{n} a_i x_i\right) = \sum_{i=1}^{n} a_i E(x_i)$$

$$= \sum_{i=1}^{n} a_i E(x)$$

$$= (E(x)) \left(\sum_{i=1}^{n} a_i\right) = E(x).$$

Note that there are many ways of selecting the $a_i$ so that (3) holds. Each of these ways represents an unbiased estimator of $E(x)$, $(\mu)$. Let us seek the estimator with minimum variance, i.e. the most efficient estimator.

The problem is therefore,

$$\text{minimize var} \left(\sum_{i=1}^{n} a_i x_i\right) \tag{4}$$

$$\text{subject to} \qquad \sum_{i=1}^{n} a_i = 1.$$

Since the sample was selected at random, (4) represents the variance of a sum of n independent random variables. It may be rewritten as

$$\text{Var}\left(\sum_{i=1}^{n} a_i x_i\right) = \sum_{i=1}^{n} a_i^2 \text{ Var}(x_i)$$

$$= \text{Var}(x) \sum_{i=1}^{n} a_i^2, \tag{5}$$

where we have used the rule

$$\text{Var}(cx) = c^2 \text{ Var}(x).$$

Substituting (5) into (4),

$$\text{minimize} \quad \text{Var}(x) \sum_{i=1}^{n} a_i^2 \tag{6}$$

$$\text{subject to} \qquad \sum_{i=1}^{n} a_i = 1. \tag{7}$$

The set (6), (7) is a constrained optimization problem. Using the method of Lagrangean multipliers to solve it, we form the objective function

$$H(x, a) = \sum_{i=1}^{n} a_i^2 - \lambda \sum_{i=1}^{n} a_i , \qquad (8)$$

where we neglect Var (x) since it is inessential to the minimization problem.

Differentiating (8) with respect to the $a_j$ and setting the result equal to zero (the necessary condition for a minimum),

$$2a_j - \lambda = 0, \qquad j = 1, \ldots, n.$$

Hence, $\quad a_j = \dfrac{\lambda}{2} .$

The $a_j$ are all equal and from (3), must all equal $\dfrac{1}{n}$. Substituting this result into (1),

$$\sum_{i=1}^{n} a_i x_i = \sum_{i=1}^{n} \frac{1}{n} (x_i) = \frac{1}{n} \sum_{i=1}^{n} x_i = \bar{x}$$

the sample mean.

Hence, the sample mean is indeed the most efficient unbiased linear combination of the observations in a random sample.

● **PROBLEM** 15-27

An investigator is interested in the distribution of weights at a convention of runners. He draws three samples, each sample containing 16 runners. The mean weights were $\bar{x}_1 = 152$, $\bar{x}_2 = 156$ and $\bar{x}_3 = 157$.

(a) Compute the variance using the three sample means and then find the best estimate of $\sigma_{\bar{x}}$. (b) Use this estimate of $\sigma_{\bar{x}}$ to estimate the population variance $\sigma^2$.

Solution:    The variance of a finite set of numbers can be defined as

$$\sigma^2 = \sum_{i=1}^{n} \frac{(x_i - \mu)^2}{n} . \qquad (1)$$

For a sample of numbers, from this set, the corresponding sample variance is

$$s^2 = \sum_{i=1}^{n} \frac{(x_i - \bar{x})^2}{n} .$$

In the given problem, the $x_i$ are the different sample means and the $\bar{x}$ represents the mean of the sample means. For the above set of data,

$$\bar{x} = \frac{\bar{x}_1 + \bar{x}_2 + \bar{x}_3}{3} = \frac{152 + 156 + 157}{3}$$

$$= 155.$$

Hence, $s_{\bar{x}}^2 = \frac{(x_1 - \bar{x}) + (x_2 - \bar{x}) + (x_3 - \bar{x})}{n}$

$$= \frac{[(152 - 155)^2 + (156 - 155)^2 + (157 - 155)^2]}{3}$$

$$= \frac{14}{3} .$$

We know from theoretical statistics that in general, $s^2$ is a biased estimator of $\sigma^2$, the amount of bias being $-\frac{\sigma^2}{n}$. In fact,

$$E(s_{\bar{x}}^2) = \frac{n-1}{n} \sigma_{\bar{x}}^2 . \tag{2}$$

Using (2), we can construct an unbiased estimator of $\sigma_{\bar{x}}^2$,

$$\hat{s}_{\bar{x}}^2 = \frac{1}{n-1} \sum_{i=1}^{n} (x_i - \bar{x})^2 . \tag{3}$$

(3) represents the best estimator of $\sigma_{\bar{x}}^2$ for the following reasons (1) it is unbiased, (2) it is consistent and (3) it has the minimum variance amongst the class of estimators of $\sigma^2$ that are unbiased.

Studying (3), we see that it is equal to

$\frac{n}{n-1} s_{\bar{x}}^2$ . Hence,

$$\text{est } \sigma_{\bar{x}}^2 = \frac{n}{n-1} \sum_{i=1}^{n} \frac{(x_i - \bar{x})^2}{n}$$

$$= \frac{3}{2} \left( \frac{14}{3} \right) = 7.0 .$$

Hence, the best estimate of $\sigma_{\bar{x}}$ is

$$\sqrt{7.0} = 2.6. \tag{4}$$

538

(b)   We now wish to use (4) to estimate the population variance $\sigma^2$.   First we must derive the relationship between $\sigma_{\bar{x}}^2$, (the variance of the sampling mean distribution) and $\sigma^2$, the population variance.

Now,

$$\text{Var } (\bar{x}) = \text{Var } \left( \sum_{i=1}^{n} \frac{x_i}{n} \right)$$

$$= \frac{1}{n^2} \text{Var } \left( \sum_{i=1}^{n} x_i \right) .$$

But since the $x_i$ are independent of each other,

$$\text{Var } \left( \sum_{i=1}^{n} x_i \right) = \sum_{i=1}^{n} \text{Var}(x_i).$$

By definition   $\text{Var } (x_i) = \sigma^2$.

Hence, since the $x_i$ are identically distributed,

$$\sum_{i=1}^{n} \text{Var } (x_i) = n\sigma^2.$$

Thus,      $\text{Var } (\bar{x}) = \frac{1}{n^2} n\sigma^2 = \frac{\sigma^2}{n}$.

This implies that

$$\sigma^2 = n \text{ Var } (\bar{x}) = n\sigma_{\bar{x}}^2 .$$

Since n = 16 (the size of the samples), and $\sigma_{\bar{x}}^2$ has been estimated to be 7, the estimate of the population variance is

$$\sigma^2 = 16(7) = 112.$$

From this, the estimated standard deviation is

$$\sqrt{112} = 10.6 .$$

# SUFFICIENT STATISTICS

● **PROBLEM** 15-28

Give an example of a sufficient statistic.

Solution:    We shall derive a sufficient statistic, T, for the parameter p of the family of Bernoulli distri-

539

butions.  The probability density function of the Bernoulli distribution is

$$f(x) = p^x (1 - p)^{1-x} \qquad\qquad x = 0, 1, \qquad\qquad (1)$$

where $p$ is the probability of success.

Consider now the performance of three Bernoulli trials.  There are then eight distinct samples of size three and the probability function of $(x_1, x_2, x_3)$ is

$$P(X = x) = P(X_1 = x_1, X_2 = x_2, X_3 = x_3)$$

$$= p^k (1 - p)^{3-k} \qquad\qquad (2)$$

where $x_1 + x_2 + x_3 = k$, is the number of 1's among the values $(x_1, x_2, x_3)$.  The number of 1's or successes in three trials is a random variable, (say)

$$T = X_1 + X_2 + X_3,$$

with the probability density function,

$$P(T = k) = P(k \text{ successes in 3 trials})$$

$$= \binom{3}{k} p^k (1 - p)^{3-k} . \qquad\qquad (3)$$

We now ask, what is the conditional probability of obtaining the point $(x_1, x_2, x_3)$ given $T = k$?

$$P(x/T = k) = P(X = x \mid T = k)$$

$$= \frac{P(X = x \text{ and } T = k)}{P(T = k)} , \qquad\qquad (4)$$

using the definition of conditional probability,

$$P(z_2/z_1) = \frac{P(z_2 \cap z_1)}{P(z_1)} , \quad \text{and letting}$$

$$x = x_1 + x_2 + x_3.$$

The conditional probability density function of (4) is given by

$$P(x/T = k) = \begin{cases} 0, & \text{if } x_1 + x_2 + x_3 \neq k \\[2ex] \dfrac{p^k (1 - p)^{3-k}}{\binom{3}{k} p^k (1 - p)^{3-k}} = \dfrac{1}{\binom{3}{k}} & \\[2ex] & \text{if } x_1 + x_2 + x_3 = k \end{cases} \qquad (5)$$

from (2) and (3).

Using (5) we may form the table:

| Sample | T | Prob. | Prob. given T = 0 | Prob. given T = 1 | Prob. given T = 2 | Prob. given T = 3 |
|---|---|---|---|---|---|---|
| (0, 0, 0) | 0 | $(1 - p)^3$ | 1 | 0 | 0 | 0 |
| (0, 0, 1) | 1 | $p(1 - p)^2$ | 0 | 1/3 | 0 | 0 |
| (0, 1, 0) | 1 | $p(1 - p)^2$ | 0 | 1/3 | 0 | 0 |
| (1, 0, 0) | 1 | $p(1 - p)^2$ | 0 | 1/3 | 0 | 0 |
| (0, 1, 1) | 2 | $p^2(1 - p)$ | 0 | 0 | 1/3 | 0 |
| (1, 0, 1) | 2 | $p^2(1 - p)$ | 0 | 0 | 1/3 | 0 |
| (1, 1, 0) | 2 | $p^2(1 - p)$ | 0 | 0 | 1/3 | 0 |
| (1, 1, 1) | 3 | $p^3$ | 0 | 0 | 0 | 1 |

Examining the table we see that the distribution of $(X_1, X_2, X_3)$ given any particular value of T, does not involve the parameter p. That is, we cannot make any inferences about p using the conditional distribution of $(x_1, x_2, x_3)$ given $T = X_1 + X_2 + X_3 = k$. It follows that the statistic T is sufficient for knowledge of the parameter p.

The reader should be aware that the general definition of a sufficient statistic involves the concepts of functional independence and the theory of transformations of a variable. The more modest purpose of this problem was to exhibit a concrete example of a sufficient statistic and how the concept of sufficiency arises.

● **PROBLEM** 15-29

Let $x_1, x_2, x_3$ be a sample of size 3 from the Bernoulli distribution. Show that the statistic

$$S_1 = u(x_1, x_2, x_3) = x_1 + x_2 + x_3$$

is a sufficient statistic but that the statistic

$$S_2 = v(x_1, x_2, x_3) = x_1 x_2 + x_3$$

is not a sufficient statistic.

Solution:   A random variable x has the Bernoulli distribution if it has the frequency function

$$f(x) = p^x (1 - p)^{1-x}; \qquad x = 0, 1,$$

where p is the probability of success. The sample space for the above problem consists of

$$\{\{0, 0, 0\} \ \{0, 0, 1\}\{0, 1, 0\}\{0, 1, 1\}\{1, 0, 0\}$$

$$\{1, 0, 1\}\{1, 1, 0\}\{1, 1, 1\}\} \ .$$

For each sample point we can find the values of the statistics $S_1$ and $S_2$. Thus we may construct the following table:

| (1) | (2) Values of $S_1$ | (3) Values of $S_2$ | (4) $f_{x_1,x_2,x_3/S_1}$ | (5) $f_{x_1,x_2,x_3/S_2}$ |
|---|---|---|---|---|
| (0, 0, 0) | 0 | 0 | 1 | 1 - p/1 + p |
| (0, 0, 1) | 1 | 1 | 1/3 | 1 - p/1 + 2p |
| (0, 1, 0) | 1 | 0 | 1/3 | p/1 + p |
| (1, 0, 0) | 1 | 0 | 1/3 | p/1 + p |
| (0, 1, 1) | 2 | 1 | 1/3 | p/1 + 2p |
| (1, 0, 1) | 2 | 1 | 1/3 | p/1 + 2p |
| (1, 1, 0) | 2 | 1 | 1/3 | p/1 + 2p |
| (1, 1, 1) | 3 | 2 | 1 | 1 |

Since $S_1 = x_1 + x_2 + x_3$, column (2) is found by adding each coordinate of the triple $(x_1, x_2, x_3)$. For example, $(0, 1, 1) = 0 + 1 + 1 = 2$. Similarly, $S_2 = x_1 x_2 + x_3$ and an example is $(1, 0, 0) = (1)(0) + (0) = 0$.

The results of column (4) are calculated as follows. Consider the point $(0, 0, 0)$. The conditional density of $x_1, x_2, x_3 = (0, 0, 0)$ given $S_1 = 0$ is

$$f_{x_1,x_2,x_3/S_1 = 0} (0, 0, 0/0)$$

$$= \frac{P[x_1 = 0; x_2 = 0; x_3 = 0; S_1 = 0]}{P[S_1 = 0]}$$

$$= \frac{(1 - p)^3}{\binom{3}{0}(1 - p)^3} = 1.$$

Similarly,

$$f_{x_1,x_2,x_3/S_1 = 1} (0, 0, 1/S_1 = 1)$$

$$= \frac{P[x_1 = 0; x_2 = 0; x_3 = 1; S_1 = 1]}{P[S_1 = 1]}$$

$$= \frac{(1 - p)^2 p}{\binom{3}{1}(1 - p)^2 p} = \frac{1}{3}.$$

Continuing in this way we obtain column (4). Note that the conditional distribution of the sample given the values of $S_1$ is independent of p. This is in accordance with the definition of a sufficient statistic.

Now consider the construction of column (5). We find that,

$$f_{x_1, x_2, x_3 | S_2 = 0} (0,0,0/0) = \frac{P[x_1 = 0; \ x_2 = 0; \ x_3 = 0; \ S_2 = 0]}{P[S_2 = 0]}$$

$$= \frac{(1 - p)^3}{(1 - p)^3 + 2(1 - p)^2 p}$$

$$= \frac{(1 - p)^3}{(1 - p)^2 [1 - p + 2p]} = \frac{1 - p}{1 + p}.$$

The rest of column (5) is constructed in a similar manner. Note that the conditional distribution of the sample given $S_2$ is not independent of the parameter p. Hence $S_2$ is not a sufficient statistic.

● **PROBLEM** 15-30

Let $x_1, \ldots, x_n$ be a random sample from the Bernoulli density with parameter p. Show that

$$Y = \sum_{i=1}^{n} x_i$$

is a sufficient statistic.

Solution: Let us first define what is meant by a sufficient statistic. Consider a distribution with the probability density function $f(x; \theta)$. Let $x_1, \ldots, x_n$ be a random sample drawn from this distribution and let $Y_1 = u(x_1, x_2, \ldots, x_n)$ denote a function of this sample, i.e., a statistic. Then $Y_1$ is called a sufficient statistic for the parameter $\theta$ if for any other statistics $Y_2 = u(x_1, \ldots, x_n) \ldots Y_n = u(x_1, \ldots, x_n)$ the conditional probability density function $h(y_2, \ldots, y_n)$ of $Y_2, \ldots Y_n$ given $Y_1 = y_1$ does not depend upon the parameter $\theta$. To show that a statistic is sufficient we use the factorization theorem.

This theorem states that if the likelihood function can be factored into two functions, one of which is independent of the parameter and the other a function of the sample only through the statistic, then that statistic is sufficient.

A random variable x that has the Bernoulli distribution has the probability function

$$f(x; p) = p^x (1 - p)^{1-x} ; \qquad x = 0, 1;$$

and $0 \leq p \leq 1$, the parameter describing the distribution.

The joint density function of the random sample is, (since the members of the sample are statistically independent )

$$F(x_1; \theta) \dots f(x_n; \theta) = p^{x_1} (1 - p)^{1-x_1} \dots p^{x_n}(1 - p)^{1-x_n}$$

$$= p^{\sum\limits_{i}^{n} x_i} (1 - p)^{n - \sum\limits_{i=1}^{n} x_i} . \qquad (1)$$

Examining (1), we see that the joint density of the sample depends on the sample values only through $\sum\limits_{i=1}^{n} x_i$. Hence, the statistic $Y = \sum\limits_{i=1}^{n} x_i$ is a sufficient statistic.

● PROBLEM 15-31

Let $x_1, \dots, x_n$ be a random sample from the normal density with mean $\mu$ and variance equal to one. Show that the mean of the sample, $\bar{x} = \sum\limits_{i=1}^{n} \dfrac{x_i}{n}$ is a sufficient statistic for the parameter $\mu$.

<u>Solution</u>: A random variable x is said to be normally distributed when it has the density function,

$$f(x: \mu; \sigma^2) = \frac{1}{\sqrt{2\pi}\sigma} e^{\left[ -\frac{1}{2} \frac{(x - \mu')^2}{\sigma} \right]} \qquad (1)$$

i.e., $x \sim N(\mu, \sigma^2)$, where $\mu$ is the mean and $\sigma^2$ the variance of the distribution. When $\sigma^2 = 1$, (1) reduces to

$$f(x; \mu) = \frac{1}{\sqrt{2\pi}} e^{-\frac{1}{2}(x-\mu)^2} . \qquad (2)$$

The joint density function of the sample is, using (2)

$$f(x_1) \cdot f(x_2) \dots f(x_n)$$

$$= \frac{1}{\sqrt{2\pi}} e^{-\frac{1}{2}(x_1-\mu)^2} \cdot \frac{1}{\sqrt{2\pi}} e^{-\frac{1}{2}(x_2-\mu)^2} \dots \frac{1}{\sqrt{2\pi}} e^{-\frac{1}{2}(x_n-\mu)^2}$$

$$= \prod\limits_{i=1}^{n} \frac{1}{\sqrt{2\pi}} e^{-\frac{(x_i-\mu)^2}{2}} . \qquad (3)$$

544

To show that $\bar{x}$ is a sufficient statistic for $\mu$, we may use the factorization theorem. This states that a statistic $y_1$ is a sufficient statistic of the parameter $\theta$ in the density function $f(x; \theta)$ if the joint density function may be factored into two non-negative functions, one of which does not depend upon $\theta$. Symbolically,

$$f(x_1; \theta)\ f(x_2; \theta)\ \ldots\ f(x_n; \theta)$$

$$= k\ [u_1(x_1, \ldots, x_n); \theta]\ K(x_1, \ldots, x_n)$$

where $\quad y_1 = u_1(x_1, \ldots, x_n)$

Rewriting (3),

$$\prod_{i=1}^{n} \frac{1}{\sqrt{2\pi}}\ e^{-\dfrac{(x_i-\mu)^2}{2}} = \frac{1}{(2\pi)^{n/2}}\ e^{-\dfrac{1}{2}\sum\limits_{i=1}^{n}(x_i-\mu)^2}$$

$$= \frac{1}{(2\pi)^{n/2}}\ e^{-\dfrac{1}{2}\left[\sum\limits_{i=1}^{n} x_i^2 - 2\mu \sum\limits_{i=1}^{n} x_i + n\mu^2\right]}$$

$$= \frac{1}{(2\pi)^{n/2}}\ \exp\left(-\frac{1}{2}\sum_{i=1}^{n} x_i^2 + \mu \sum_{i=1}^{n} x_i - \frac{n}{2}\mu^2\right)$$

$$= \frac{1}{(2\pi)^{n/2}}\ \exp\left[\mu \sum_{i=1}^{n} x_i - \frac{n}{2}\mu^2\right]\ \exp\left[-\frac{1}{2}\sum_{i=1}^{n} x_i^2\right]$$

$$= \exp\left[\mu \sum_{i=1}^{n} x_i - \frac{n}{2}\mu^2\right] \frac{1}{(2\pi)^{n/2}}\ \exp\left[-\frac{1}{2}\sum_{i=1}^{n} x_i^2\right]. \qquad (4)$$

Letting $k[u_1(x_1, \ldots, x_n); \theta] = \exp\left(\mu \sum\limits_{i=1}^{n} x_i - \frac{n}{2}\mu^2\right)$

and $\quad K(x_1, \ldots, x_n) = \dfrac{1}{(2\pi)^{n/2}}\ \exp\left(-\frac{1}{2}\sum\limits_{i=1}^{n} x_i^2\right)$

we see that the joint density has been factored so as to satisfy the factorization theorem. It follows that $v(x_1, \ldots, x_n) = \sum\limits_{i=1}^{n} x_i$ is a sufficient statistic. But this implies that $\sum \dfrac{x_i}{n}$ is also a sufficient statistic, i.e., $\bar{x}$ is a sufficient statistic for $\mu$ as was to be shown.

Consider the probability density function

$$f(x; \theta) = \theta^x (1 - \theta)^{1-x} \qquad x = 0, 1, \quad 0 < \theta < 1,$$

$$= 0 \quad \text{elsewhere}.$$

Let $x_1$, $x_2$, ..., $x_n$ be a random sample from this distribution.

Using the Fisher-Neyman criterion , show that the statistic

$$y_1 = x_1 + x_2 + \ldots + x_n \tag{1}$$

is a sufficient statistic for $\theta$.

Solution:    We may view (1) as a function of the random sample.  Then other statistics that could be calculated from the sample would be

$$y_2 = u_2(x_1, \ldots, x_n)$$
$$\vdots$$
$$y_n = u_n(x_1, \ldots, x_n).$$

The first step is to determine which statistic makes the most use of the random sample.  This statistic is the sufficient statistic.

Descending to particulars, the statistic (1) has the probability density function

$$g_1(y_1; \theta) = \binom{n}{y_1} \theta^{y_1} (1 - \theta)^{n-y_1}$$

$$= \frac{n!}{y_1!(n - y_1)!} \theta^{y_1} (1 - \theta)^{n-y_1}. \tag{2}$$

To justify (2), note that

$$f(x; \theta) = \theta^x (1 - \theta)^{1-x} \qquad x = 0, 1, 0 < \theta < 1$$

is a Bernoulli distribution.  The statistic $Y_1$ assumes the value $y_1$ when k members of the random sample are "successes", i.e., assume the value 1. This "sum" has the binomial distribution given by (2).  We shall use (2) to show that (1) is a sufficient statistic for $\theta$.  But first, recall the Fisher-Neyman condition for a sufficient statistic.  Let $x_1, \ldots, x_n$ be a random sample from a distribution given by $f(x; \theta)$.  Form the statistic $Y_1 = g_1(x_1, \ldots, x_n)$ with probability density function $S_1(y_1; \theta)$.  Then $Y_1 = g_1(x_1, \ldots, x_n)$ is a sufficient statistic for $\theta$ only if,

$$f(x_1; \theta) \; f(x_2; \theta) \; \ldots \; f(x_n; \theta)$$

$$= S_1[g_1(x_1, \ldots, x_n); \theta] \; H(x_1, \ldots, x_n),$$

where $H(x_1, \ldots, x_n)$ is independent of $\theta$.

The joint probability density function of the sample is given by:

$$\left[\theta^{x_1}(1 - \theta)^{1-x_1}\right]\left[\theta^{x_2}(1 -\theta)^{1-x_2}\right] \ldots \left[\theta^{x_n}(1 - \theta)^{1-x_n}\right]$$

$$= \theta^{(x_1+x_2+\ldots+x_n)}\left[(1 -\theta)^{n-(x_1+x_2+\ldots+x_n)}\right]$$

$$= \theta^{y_1}[1 - \theta]^{n-y_1}. \tag{3}$$

But, from (2)

$$\theta^{y_1} [1 - \theta]^{n-y_1} = g_1(y_1; \theta) \cdot \frac{y_1! \; (n - y_1)!}{n!}$$

$$= g_1(x_1, x_2, \ldots, x_n; \theta) \cdot H(x_1, \ldots, x_n).$$

Hence, $\quad f(x_1; \theta) \cdot f(x_2; \theta) \ldots f(x_n; \theta)$

$$= g_1(x_1, \ldots, x_n; \theta) \cdot H(x_1, \ldots, x_n).$$

and, by the Fisher-Neyman criterion, $x_1$ is a sufficient condition for $\theta$.

● **PROBLEM** 15-33

Let x have the probability density function

$$f(x; \theta) = e^{-(x-\theta)}, \qquad \begin{array}{l} \theta < x < \infty, \\ -\infty < \theta < \infty, \end{array}$$

$$= 0 \text{ elsewhere}$$

where $\theta$ is a parameter.

A random sample $x_1, \ldots, x_n$ is chosen from this distribution. The order statistics $Y_1 < Y_2 < \ldots < Y_n$ are then found. Using the Fisher-Neyman criterion, show that the first order statistic $Y_1$ is a sufficient statistic for $\theta$.

Solution:　　To use the Fisher-Neyman criterion, we must show that the joint probability density function of the sample elements may be written as the product of the probability density function of the statistic and a function of the elements of the random sample that is independent of the parameter being estimated. Then, the statistic is a sufficient statistic of the parameter being estimated.

The joint probability density function of the order statistics is given by

$$g(y_1, \ldots, y_n) = (n!) \, f(y_1) \, f(y_2) \ldots f(y_n), \qquad (1)$$

$$a < y_1 < y_2 < \ldots < y_n < b$$

$$= 0 \text{ elswhere.}$$

From (1) we may derive the probability function of $y_1$ as

$$g_1(y_1; \theta) = ne^{-n(y_1 - \theta)}, \qquad \theta < y < \infty \qquad (2)$$

$$= 0 \text{ elswehere.}$$

Next, let us find the joint probability density function of the sample $x_1, \ldots, x_n$. Since the elements are statistically independent, this is

$$e^{-(x_1 - \theta)} \, e^{-(x_2 - \theta)} \ldots e^{-(x_n - \theta)} = e^{-(x_1 + \ldots + x_n - n\theta)}. \qquad (3)$$

Equation (3) is equivalent to

$$e^{n\theta} \, e^{-(x_1 + \ldots + x_n)} = ne^{-n(\min x_i - \theta)} \left\{ \frac{e^{-(x_1 + x_2 + \ldots + x_n)}}{ne^{-n(\min x_i)}} \right\}$$

$$= g_1(\min x_i; \theta) \left\{ \frac{e^{-(x_1 + x_2 + \ldots + x_n)}}{ne^{-n(\min x_i)}} \right\}$$

$$= g_1(y_1; \theta) \, H(x_1, \ldots, x_n), \qquad (4)$$

using (2).

By transforming (3) into (4) we have shown that the order statistic $Y_1 = \min x_i$ satisfies the Fisher-Neyman condition for a sufficient statistic. Hence, $Y_1$ is a sufficient statistic for $\theta$.

● **PROBLEM** 15-34

Let $x_1, \ldots, x_n$ be a random sample from a normal distribution with mean $\mu$ and variance $\sigma^2$. Show that $\bar{x}$ and

$$s^2 = \frac{1}{n-1} \sum_{i=1}^{n} (x_i - \bar{x})^2$$

are jointly sufficient statistics for the parameters $\mu$ and $\sigma^2$.

<u>Solution:</u>    The normal density function is

$$f(x) = \frac{1}{\sqrt{2\pi}\sigma} \exp\left\{ \frac{-(x-\mu)^2}{2\sigma^2} \right\}$$

A random sample of n elements from this distribution, $x_1, \ldots, x_n$ will have the joint density function:

$$f(x_1; \mu; \sigma^2)f(x_2; \mu; \sigma^2) \ldots f(x_n; \mu; \sigma^2)$$

$$= \frac{1}{\sqrt{2\pi\sigma^2}} \exp\left\{ -\frac{(x_1-\mu)^2}{2\sigma^2} \right\} \frac{1}{\sqrt{2\pi\sigma^2}} \exp\left\{ -\frac{(x_2-\mu)^2}{2\sigma^2} \right\}$$

$$\ldots \frac{1}{\sqrt{2\pi\sigma^2}} \exp\left\{ \frac{-(x_n-\mu)^2}{2\sigma^2} \right\}$$

$$= \prod_{i=1}^{n} \frac{1}{\sqrt{2\pi\sigma^2}} \exp\left[ -\frac{1}{2}\left(\frac{x_i-\mu}{\sigma}\right)^2 \right]$$

$$= \frac{1}{(2\pi)^{n/2}} \sigma^{-n} \exp\left[ -\frac{1}{2} \sum_{i=1}^{n}\left(\frac{x_i-\mu}{\sigma}\right)^2 \right]$$

$$= \frac{1}{(2\pi)^{n/2}} \sigma^{-n} \exp\left[ -\frac{1}{2\sigma^2} \sum_{i=1}^{n} x_i^2 - 2\mu \sum_{i=1}^{n} x_i + n\mu^2 \right]. \quad (1)$$

According to the factorization theorem, the statistics $Y_1 = u_1(x_1, \ldots, x_n)$ and $Y_2 = u_2(x_1, \ldots, x_n)$ are joint sufficient statistics for parameters $\theta_1$ and $\theta_2$ if

$$f(x_1; \theta_1, \theta_2)f(x_2; \theta_1, \theta_2) \ldots f(x_n; \theta_1, \theta_2)$$

$$= g[u_1(x_1, \ldots, x_n), u_2(x_1, \ldots, x_n); \theta_1, \theta_2]H(x_1, \ldots, x_n).$$

Consider the statistics,

$$Y_1 = u_1(x_1, \ldots, x_n) = \sum_{i=1}^{n} x_i \qquad (2)$$

and

$$Y_2 = u_2(x_1, \ldots, x_n) = \sum_{i=1}^{n} x_i^2 \qquad (3)$$

where $x_1, \ldots, x_n$ denotes the elements of the random sample.

Equation (1) involves only (2), (3), and the parameters $\sigma^2$ and $\mu$. Hence, $\sum_{i=1}^{n} x_i$ and $\sum_{i=1}^{n} x_i^2$ are jointly

549

sufficient statistics for estimating $\mu$ and $\sigma^2$, letting

$$g \quad [u_1(x_1, \ldots, x_n), u_2(x_1, \ldots, x_n); \theta_1, \theta_2] = (1) \text{ and}$$

$$H(x_1, \ldots, x_n) = 1.$$

Finally, since a one-to-one transformation of a sufficient statistic is a sufficient statistic,

$$\bar{x}_n = \sum_{i=1}^{n} \frac{x_i}{n} \quad \text{and} \quad S_n^2 = \frac{1}{n-1} \sum_{i=1}^{n} (x_i - \bar{x})^2$$

are joint sufficient statistics for estimating $\mu$ and $\sigma^2$.

● **PROBLEM** 15-35

Let $x_1, \ldots, x_n$ be a random sample from a uniform distribution over the interval $[a, b]$. Use the factorization theorem to show that the order statistics

$$Y_1 = \min(x_1, \ldots, x_n) \text{ and } y_n = \max(x_1, \ldots, x_n)$$

are jointly sufficient statistics for the parameters a, b.

Solution:     A random variable x is uniformly distributed if it has the probability density function

$$f(x; a, b) = \frac{1}{b-a}, \quad a < x < b. \tag{1}$$

Let us use the indicator function to rewrite (1). For a set A, and points $\omega \varepsilon A$, the indicator function of A is

$$I_{(A)} = \begin{cases} 1, & \omega \varepsilon A \\ 0, & \omega \notin A, \end{cases} \tag{2}$$

Using (2), (1) becomes

$$f(x; a, b) = \frac{1}{b-a} I_{(a,b)}(x). \tag{3}$$

A random sample, $x_1, \ldots, x_n$ from the distribution (3) will have the joint density function

$$f(x_1; a, b) f(x_2; a, b) \ldots f(x_n; a, b)$$

$$= \frac{1}{b-a} I_{(a,b)}(x_1) \frac{1}{b-a} I_{(a,b)}(x_2) \ldots$$

$$\frac{1}{b-a} I_{(a,b)}(x_n)$$

550

$$= \prod_{i=1}^{n} \frac{1}{b-a} \ I_{(a,b)} \ (x_i)$$

$$= \left(\frac{1}{b-a}\right)^{n} \prod_{i=1}^{n} \ I_{(a,b)} \ (x_i). \qquad (4)$$

Now, recall the factorization theorem for jointly sufficient statistics. A set of statistics $g_1 = u_1(x_1, \ldots, x_n), \ldots g_n = u_n(x_1, \ldots, x_n)$ is jointly sufficient only when the joint density of the random sample generating the statistics can be factored as

$$f_{x_1, \ldots, x_n} (x_1, \ldots, x_n; \theta)$$

$$= g(u_1, \ldots, u_n; \theta) \ h(x_1, \ldots, x_n). \qquad (5)$$

Examining (4) we see that

$$\prod_{i=1}^{n} \ I_{[a,b]} \ (x_i) = I_{[a, \ y_n]} \ (y_1) \ I_{[y_1,b]} \ (y_n),$$

since y , the least member of the sample must be less than or equal to $y_n$, the largest, and vice versa. Hence the joint density depends on $x_1, \ldots, x_n$ only through the statistics $y_1, Y_n$.

Letting $h(x_1, \ldots, x_n) = 1$ in (5), and
$u_1(x_1, \ldots, x_n) = y_1, \quad u_2(x_1, \ldots, x_n) = y_n$

the joint density is factored as required by the theorem. Thus, the statistics $y_1$ and $y_n$ are jointly sufficient.

● **PROBLEM** 15-36

Let x be a random variable having the Beta distribution

$$f(x; a,b) = \frac{1}{B(a, b)} \ x^{a-1} \ (1-x)^{b-1}, \ 0 < x < 1 \qquad (1)$$

where $B(a, b) = \displaystyle\int_{0}^{1} x^{a-1} \ (1-x)^{b-1} \ dx.$

Let $x_1, \ldots, x_n$ denote a random sample from this distribution. Show that

$$\sum_{i=1}^{n} \ln x_i \quad \text{and} \quad \sum_{i=1}^{n} \ln (1-x_i),$$

are jointly sufficient statistics.

Solution:    We first show that the Beta distribution,
(1), belongs to the exponential family of densities and
then we show that the joint density function of the random
sample may be factored in a manner that satisfies the
factorization theorem.

A family of densities belongs to the exponential
family if,

$$f(x; \theta_1, \ldots, \theta_k)$$
$$= a(\theta_1, \ldots, \theta_k)\ b(x)\ \exp \sum_{i=1}^{k} c_i(\theta_1, \ldots, \theta_k) d_i(x)$$

where  $a(\theta_1, \ldots, \theta_k) b(x)$  and  $\exp \sum_{i=1}^{k} c_i(\theta_1, \ldots, \theta_k) di(x)$

are functions of the given parameters.

Now, (1) may be rewritten as

$$f(x; \theta_1, \theta_2) = \frac{1}{B(\theta_1, \theta_2)}\ \exp[(\theta_1-1)\ln x + (\theta_2-1)\ln(1-x)] \quad (2)$$

where $a = \theta_1$, $b = \theta_2$.

Note that in (2) we use the fact,

$$z^{\omega} \equiv \exp[\omega \ln z], \qquad z > 0.$$

Hence, (1) belongs to the exponential family of
densities.

Next, we recall the meaning of the factorization
theorem.  Given a random sample $x_1, \ldots, x_n$ from a density
function $f(x; \theta_1, \ldots, \theta_k)$, the statistics $y_1 = u_1(x_1, \ldots, x_n;$
$\theta_1, \ldots \theta_k)$, $y_2 = u_2(x_1, \ldots, x_n; \theta_1, \ldots, \theta_k) \ldots y_n =$
$u_n(x_1, \ldots, x_n; \theta_1, \ldots, \theta_k)$ are jointly sufficient statistics if the joint density of $x_1, \ldots, x_n$,
$\prod_{i=1}^{n} f(x_j; \theta_1, \ldots, \theta_k)$ can be factored as

$$g[u_1(x_1, \ldots, x_n), u_2(x_1, \ldots, x_n) \ldots, u_n(x_1, \ldots, x_n);$$

$$\theta_1, \ldots, \theta_k]\ h(x_1, \ldots, x_n) \qquad (3)$$

where $g[u_1, \ldots, u_n; \theta_1, \ldots, \theta_k]$ depends on $x_1, \ldots, x_n$
only through the functions $u_1, \ldots, u_n$.

A random sample from an exponential density has the
joint density function

$$\prod_{j=1}^{n} f(x_j; \theta_1, \ldots, \theta_k)$$

$$= a^n(\theta_1,\ldots,\theta_k)\left[\prod_{i=1}^{n} b(x_j)\right] \exp\left[\sum_{i=1}^{k} c_i\ (\theta_1,\ \ldots,\ \theta_k)\right.$$

$$\left.\sum_{j=1}^{n} d_i\ (x_j)\right]. \qquad (4)$$

Using (3), we see that

$$\sum_{j=1}^{n} d_1(x_j),\quad \sum_{j=1}^{n} d_2(x_j),\ \ldots,\ \sum_{j=1}^{n} d_k\ (x_j)$$

are jointly sufficient statistics.

Let us now find the joint density function of a random sample from a distribution having the form (1). We have,

$$f(x_1;\ a,\ b)\ \ldots,\ f(x_n;\ a,\ b)$$

$$= \prod_{j=1}^{n}\ f(x_j;\ a,\ b)$$

$$= \left[\frac{1}{B(a,\ b)}\right]^n \prod_{j=1}^{n} x_j \exp\left[a - 1 \sum_{j=1}^{n} \ln x_j\right.$$

$$\left. + b - 1 \sum_{j=1}^{n}\ \ln(1 - x_j)\right], \qquad (5)$$

using (2).

Comparing (5) with (4), we see that

$$\sum_{j=1}^{n}\ \ln x_j \quad \text{and} \quad \sum_{j=1}^{n}\ \ln\ (1 - x_j) \quad \text{are jointly}$$

sufficient statistics when sampling from a Beta distribution.

# CONSISTENT STATISTICS

● PROBLEM 15-37

Consider a probability distribution having mean $\mu$ and variance $\sigma^2$. Show that

$$\bar{x}_n = \frac{1}{n} \sum_{i=1}^{n}\ x_i \quad \text{and} \quad s_n^2 = \frac{1}{n-1} \sum_{i=1}^{n}\ (x_i - \bar{x}_n)^2$$

are consistent sequences of estimators of $\mu$ and $\sigma^2$.

Solution:   The sample mean and the sample estimate of the distribution variance are unbiased estimates of the population mean $\mu$ and population variance $\sigma^2$. Recall that an estimate $\hat{\theta}$ of a parameter $\theta$ is consistent if

$$\lim_{n \to \infty} E(\hat{\theta}_n) = \theta \quad \text{and} \quad \lim_{n \to \infty} \text{Var} (\hat{\theta}_n) = 0$$

where $\hat{\theta}_n$ represents a sequence of estimators that depend on the sample size n.

Hence, we must show that $\text{Var} [\bar{x}_n]$ and $\text{Var} [s_n^2]$ both tend to zero as $n \to \infty$ .

The variance of a random variable is defined as

$$\text{Var} (\theta) = E [(\theta - E(\theta))^2] \tag{1}$$

From this definition it follows that, for independent random variables $x_1$, $x_2$ and constants a, b,

$$\text{Var} (aX_1 + bX_2) = a^2 \text{Var} (x_1) + b^2 \text{Var} (x_2).$$

In general,

$$\text{Var} \left[ \sum_{i=1}^{n} a_i x_i \right] = \sum_{i=1}^{n} a_i^2 \text{Var} (x_i)$$

Now,   $$\text{Var} (\bar{x}) = \text{Var} \left[ \frac{1}{n} \sum_{i=1}^{n} x_i \right] = \frac{1}{n^2} \text{Var} \left[ \sum_{i=1}^{n} x_i \right]. \tag{2}$$

But since the sample is randomly chosen, the $x_i$ are independent. That is,

$$\text{Var} [x_1 + x_2 + \dots + x_n] = \text{Var} \left[ \sum_{i=1}^{n} x_i \right]$$

$$= \sum_{i=1}^{n} \text{Var} (x_i).$$

Hence, (2) becomes

$$\frac{1}{n^2} \sum_{i=1}^{n} \text{Var} (x_i) = \frac{1}{n^2} n\sigma^2 = \frac{\sigma^2}{n} .$$

Hence,   $$\lim_{n \to \infty} \text{Var} (\bar{x}) = \lim_{n \to \infty} \frac{\sigma^2}{n} = 0$$

and $\bar{x}$ is a consistent estimator of $\mu$.

We now consider $\text{Var} (s_n^2)$. Using (1)

$$\text{Var } (s_n^2) = E \left[ (s_n^2 - \sigma^2)^2 \right]$$

$$= \frac{1}{n} \left[ \mu_4 - \frac{n-3}{n-1} \sigma^4 \right] \tag{3}$$

where $\mu_4$ denotes the fourth moment about the origin. Letting $n \to \infty$ in (3) we find

$$\lim_{n \to \infty} \text{Var } (s_n^2) = \lim_{n \to \infty} \frac{1}{n} \left[ \mu_4 - \frac{n-3}{n-1} \sigma^4 \right] = 0.$$

Hence $s_n^2$ is a consistent estimator of $\sigma^2$.

● **PROBLEM** 15-38

Let $x_1, \ldots, x_n$ be a random sample from the one-parameter Cauchy distribution. Show that the sample mean, $\bar{x}$, is not a mean-square error consistent estimator of the parameter $\theta$.

<u>Solution:</u>    The random variable x is said to have the one-parameter Cauchy distribution of

$$f(x; \theta) = \frac{1}{\pi [(1 + (x - \theta)^2)]} \tag{1}$$

We want to measure the goodness of any estimator of $\theta$. One such measure is to see how the estimator behaves as sample size increases. Consider a sequence of estimators $T_1, \ldots, T_n$. The sequence is said to be a mean-square error consistent if

$$\lim_{n \to \infty} E \{[T_n - \theta]^2\} = 0. \text{ If this condition}$$

is violated, the estimate is not consistent. Let

$$T_n = \frac{\displaystyle\sum_{i=1}^{n} x_i}{n} \quad . \text{ Then}$$

$$(T_n - \theta)^2 = T_n^2 - 2\theta T_n + \theta^2$$

$$= \frac{1}{n^2} \left( \sum_{i=1}^{n} x_i \right)^2 - 2 \frac{\theta}{n} \left( \sum_{i=1}^{n} x_i \right) + \theta^2$$

The expectation of this expression can be easily seen not to exist.

$$E. \left[ 2 \frac{\theta}{n} \sum_{i=1}^{n} x_i \right] = 2 \frac{\theta}{n} n E(x_i)$$

which does not exist since $E(x_i)$ does not.    (It is the mean of a Cauchy distribution.)

# COMPLETENESS

Let $x_1, \ldots, x_n$ be a random sample from the uniform density

$$f(x; a, b) = \frac{1}{b - a} \qquad . \qquad (1)$$

Show that the order statistics

$$y_1 = \min [x_1, \ldots, x_n] \quad \text{and} \quad y_n = \max [x_1, \ldots, x_n]$$

are jointly complete.

Solution: We must first define what jointly complete means. The two statistics $y_1$ and $y_n$ are jointly complete when $E[g(y_1, y_n)] \equiv 0$ for all values of a and b implies $P[g(y_1, y_n) = 0] \equiv 1$, where $g(y_1, y_n)$ is a statistic.

Assume $g(y_1, y_n)$ is an unbiased estimator of 0, i.e.,

$$F[g(y_1, y_n)] \equiv 0. \qquad (1)$$

By the definition of expectation,

$$E[g(y_1, y_n)] \equiv \iint_R g(y_1, y_n) \, f(y_1, y_n) \, dy_1 \, dy_n$$

$$= \int_a^b \left[ \int_0^{y_n} g(y_1, y_n) \, n(n - 1) \left( \frac{y_n - a}{b - a} - \frac{y_1 - a}{b - a} \right)^{n-2} \right.$$

$$\left. \left( \frac{1}{b - a} \cdot \frac{1}{b - a} \right) dy_1 \right] dy_n .$$

Using the uniform density function for $f(y_1, y_n)$ equation (2) may be rewritten

$$E[g(y_1, y_n)]$$

$$\equiv \frac{n(n - 1)}{(b - a)^n} \int_a^b \int_0^{y_n} g(y_1, y_n)(y_n - y_1)^{n-2} \, dy_1 \, dy_n ; \qquad (3)$$

(3) is equal to zero only if

$$\int_a^b \int_0^{y_n} g(y_1, y_n)(y_n - y_1)^{n-2} \, dy_1 \, dy_n \equiv 0. \qquad (4)$$

We differentiate (4) with respect to b using Leibnitz's rule. Thus, we obtain

$$\int_a^b g(y_1, y_n)(b - y_1)^{n-2} dy_1 \equiv 0. \tag{5}$$

Differentiating (5) with respect to the parameter a, (again using Leibnitz's rule for the derivative of an integral)

$$- g(y_1, y_n)(b - a)^{n-2} \equiv 0 \quad \text{for all } a < b.$$

But $a < b$ implies $(b - a)^{n-2} \neq 0$. Hence, we must have $g(y_1, y_n) \equiv 0$, i.e.

$$P[g(y_1, y_n) = 0] \equiv 1.$$

Therefore $y_1$ and $y_n$ are jointly complete.

# THE CRAMÉR-RAO INEQUALITY AND EFFICIENCY

● PROBLEM 15-40

Consider the exponential density $f(x; \theta) = \theta e^{-\theta x}$. Let $x_1, \ldots, x_n$ denote a random sample from this density. Show that the sample mean, $\bar{x}$, is a minimum variance estimator of the mean of the distribution $\frac{1}{\theta}$.

Solution: We use the Cramér-Rao inequality to solve the problem. Let T be an unbiased estimator of the parameter $\frac{1}{\theta}$. Then, by the Cramér-Rao inequality,

$$\text{Var } [T] \geq \frac{\left[ \left( \frac{1}{\theta} \right)' \right]^2}{nE\left[ \left[ \frac{\partial}{\partial \theta} \ln f(x; \theta) \right]^2 \right]} \tag{1}$$

where $\left( \frac{1}{\theta} \right)' = \frac{d}{d\theta} \left( \frac{1}{\theta} \right)$ and $\ln z \equiv \log_e z$.

Verbally, (1) states that the variance of any unbiased estimator of a parameter of a distribution is always greater than the expression on the right side of (1). Equality prevails only when there exists a function $K(\theta, n)$ such that

$$\sum_{i=1}^{n} \frac{\partial}{\partial \theta} \ln f(x_i; \theta)$$

$$= K(\theta, n) \left[ u_1(x_1, \ldots, x_n) - \left( \frac{1}{\theta} \right) \right] \tag{2}$$

When (2) is possible, T is called a minimum variance unbiased estimator.

We first find $\left[ \frac{\partial}{\partial \theta} \ln f(x; \theta) \right]^2$ . Thus,

$$f(x; \theta) = \theta e^{-\theta x}$$

$$\ln f(x; \theta) = \ln \theta - \theta x$$

$$\frac{\partial}{\partial \theta} \ln f(x; \theta) = \frac{1}{\theta} - x.$$  Hence,

$$E \left[ \left[ \frac{\partial}{\partial \theta} \ln f(x; \theta) \right]^2 \right] = E \left[ \left( \frac{1}{\theta} - x \right)^2 \right]$$

$$= E \left[ \left( x - \frac{1}{\theta} \right)^2 \right] = Var \, [x] = \frac{1}{\theta^2} , \tag{3}$$

since the variance of a random variable which has the negative exponential density is $\frac{1}{\theta^2}$ .

Next, we find $\left[ \left( \frac{1}{\theta} \right)' \right]^2$ .   $\frac{d}{d\theta} \left( \frac{1}{\theta} \right) = -\frac{1}{\theta^2}$ .

Hence,   $\left[ \left( \frac{1}{\theta} \right)' \right]^2 = \frac{1}{\theta^4}$ . \tag{4}

Substituting (3) and (4) into (1)

$$Var \, [T] \geq \frac{\frac{1}{\theta^4}}{n \frac{1}{\theta^2}} = \frac{1}{n \, \theta^2} . \tag{5}$$

Changing the inequality in (5) to equality,

$$Var \, [T] = \frac{1}{n \, \theta^2} .$$

Let us try to put the exponential density into the form (2).  Thus

$$\sum_{i=1}^{n} \frac{\partial}{\partial \theta} \ln f(x; \theta) = \sum_{i=1}^{n} \frac{\partial}{\partial \theta} \ln \theta - \theta x_i$$

$$= \sum_{i=1}^{n} \frac{1}{\theta} - x_i = -n \left( \bar{x} - \frac{1}{\theta} \right).$$

Letting $K(\theta, n) = -n$   and $u_1(x_1, \ldots, x_n) = \bar{x}$, we see that (2) is indeed possible for the negative exponential density.

This is a sufficient condition to show that $\bar{x}$ is an unbiased estimator of $\left( \frac{1}{\theta} \right)$ with minimum variance  (equal to the lower bound).

Let $x_1, \ldots, x_n$ be a random sample chosen from a Poisson distribution. Show that the sample mean $\bar{x}$, is an estimator having minimum variance, of the population mean $\lambda$.

Solution:    By the Cramér-Rao inequality, the variances of the class of unbiased estimators of a parameter are bounded from below. More precisely, if $f(x; \theta)$ is a probability density function and T is an estimator of $\theta$, then,

$$\text{Var} [T] \geq \frac{1}{n E\left[\left[\frac{\partial}{\partial \theta} \ln f(x; \theta)\right]^2\right]} , \tag{1}$$

where $\ln z \equiv \log_e z$.

In the present problem,

$$f(x; \theta) = \frac{\lambda^x e^{-\lambda}}{x!} . \tag{2}$$

Taking the logarithm of (2),

$$\ln f(x; \lambda) = x \ln \lambda - \lambda - \ln x! . \tag{3}$$

Differentiating (3) with respect to $\lambda$,

$$\frac{\partial}{\partial \lambda} \ln f(x; \lambda) = \frac{x}{\lambda} - 1. \tag{4}$$

Squaring (4) and substituting the result into the right hand side of (1),

$$n E\left[\left[\frac{\partial}{\partial \lambda} \ln f(x; \lambda)\right]^2\right]$$

$$= n E\left[\frac{(x - \lambda)^2}{\lambda^2}\right] = \frac{n}{\lambda^2} E\left[[x - \lambda]^2\right]. \tag{5}$$

But for a random variable which has the Poisson distribution $E(x) = \lambda$ and $E[x - \lambda]^2 = \text{Var} [x] = \lambda$. Hence, (5) becomes

$$\frac{n}{\lambda^2} \lambda = \frac{n}{\lambda} . \tag{6}$$

Substituting (6) into (1),

$$\text{Var} [T] \geq \frac{\lambda}{n} . \tag{7}$$

If the inequality in (7) becomes an equality then Var [T] equals the lower bound, i.e., it is the minimum variance. In order for equality to prevail, the following condition is required: Let $x_1, \ldots, x_n$ be a random sample from a distribution $f(x; \theta)$ and let $u(x_1, \ldots, x_n)$ be an estimator of $\theta$. Then $u(x_1, \ldots, x_n)$ has minimum variance if

$$\sum_{i=1}^{n} \frac{\partial}{\partial \theta} \ln f(x; \theta) = K(\theta, n) [u(x_1, \ldots, x_n) - \theta]. \qquad (8)$$

In the present problem $u(x_1, \ldots, x_n) = \bar{x}$, the sample mean and $\theta = \lambda$, the population mean of the Poisson distribution. Hence, (8) becomes

$$\sum_{i=1}^{n} \frac{\partial}{\partial \theta} \ln f(x_i; \lambda)$$

$$= \sum_{i=1}^{n} \left[ -1 + \frac{x_i}{\lambda} \right] = \left( \frac{n}{\lambda} \right) (\bar{x} - \lambda). \qquad (9)$$

Comparing (8) and (9), we see that

$$K(\theta, n) = \frac{n}{\lambda}, \quad \theta = \lambda \text{ and } u(x_1, \ldots, x_n) = \bar{x}.$$

Hence, $\bar{x}$ is an unbiased estimator with minimum variance.

● **PROBLEM** 15-42

Consider the normal distribution with known mean $\mu$ and unknown variance $\sigma^2$. Let $x_1, \ldots, x_n$ denote a random sample from this distribution and let $s^2$ be the sample variance. Use the Rao-Cramér inequality to show that $s^2$ is an efficient estimator of $\sigma^2$.

Solution: The Rao-Cramér inequality states that if $y$ is a sufficient statistic of a sample and $z = \omega(y)$ is an unbiased statistic, then

$$\sigma_z^2 \geq \frac{1}{n E \left[ \frac{\partial}{\partial z} \ln(f(x; z)) \right]^2}. \qquad (1)$$

The efficiency of $z$ is then defined to be

$$e(z) \equiv \frac{1/I(z)}{\sigma_z^2},$$

where $I(z) = n E \left[ \frac{\partial}{\partial \theta} \ln f(x; \theta) \right]^2.$

We wish to find $I(z)$ for the given problem. The normal distribution has the probability density function

$$f(x; \sigma^2) = \frac{1}{\sqrt{2\pi\sigma^2}} \ \exp \left\{ \frac{-(x-\mu)^2}{2\sigma^2} \right\} . \tag{2}$$

Taking the logarithms to base e on both sides of (2),

$$\ln f(x; \sigma^2) = -\frac{(\ln 2\pi)}{2} - \ln \frac{\sigma^2}{2} - \frac{(x-\mu)^2}{2\sigma^2} . \tag{3}$$

Differentiating (3),

$$\frac{\partial}{\partial \sigma^2} \ln f(x; \sigma^2) = -\frac{1}{2\sigma^2} + \frac{(x-\mu)^2}{2\sigma^4} . \tag{4}$$

Squaring (4) and letting $v = \sigma^2$,

$$\left[ \frac{\partial}{\partial v} \ln f(x; v) \right]^2 = \left[ \frac{(x-\mu)^2}{2v^2} \right]^2 - \frac{2(x-\mu)^2}{4v^3} + \frac{1}{4v^2}$$

$$= \frac{1}{4v^4} [(x-\mu)^4 - 2v(x-\mu)^2 + v^2]. \tag{5}$$

Taking the expected value of (5),

$$E\left[ \frac{\partial}{\partial v} \ln f(x; v) \right]^2$$

$$= E\left\{ \frac{1}{4v^4} [(x-\mu)^4 - 2v(x-\mu)^2 + v^2] \right\}$$

$$= \frac{1}{4v^4} \left\{ E(x-\mu)^4 - 2vE(x-\mu)^2 + v^2 \right\}$$

$$= \frac{1}{4v^4} (3v^2 - 2v^2 + v^2) = \frac{1}{2v^2} .$$

Hence, $I(v) = \frac{n}{2v^2}$ and $\frac{1}{I(v)} = \frac{2v^2}{n}$ .

Next, we must find the variance of the sample variance. The formula for $s^2$ is

$$s^2 = \sum_{i=1}^{n} \frac{(x_i - \mu)^2}{n} . \tag{6}$$

Since $\mu$ is known,

$$E(s^2) = E\left[ \sum_{i=1}^{n} \frac{(x_i - \mu)^2}{n} \right] = \frac{1}{n} nv = v.$$

Hence, (6) yields an unbiased estimator of $\sigma^2$.

Now, the variance of $s^2$ is given by

$$\text{Var } s^2 = \frac{1}{n^2} \sum_{i=1}^{n} \text{Var } [(x_i - \mu)^2]. \tag{7}$$

Recall that if z is a random variable,

$$\text{Var } (z) = E(z^2) - [E(x)]^2.$$

Thus, (7) becomes

$$\text{Var } s^2 = \frac{1}{n} [E(x_i - \mu)^4 - (E(x_i - \mu)^2)^2]$$

$$= \frac{1}{n} [3v^2 - v^2] = \frac{2v^2}{n}$$

$$= \frac{1}{I(v)} \cdot$$

Hence, the efficiency of $s^2$ is

$$\frac{1/I(v)}{v_{s^2}} = \frac{1/I(v)}{1/I(v)} = 1.$$

When (1) is an equality, z is an efficient estimator. In this problem, we have equality of both sides of the Cramer-Rao inequality. Hence $s^2$ is efficient.

● **PROBLEM 15-43**

Let $x_1, \ldots, x_n$ denote a random sample from a Poisson distribution that has the mean $\theta > 0$. Show, using the Rao-Cramér inequality, that $\frac{y}{n} = \bar{x}$ is an efficient statistic for $\theta$.

Solution:    Consider the parameter $\theta$ of the density function $f(x; \theta)$. Assume that $y = u(x_1, \ldots, x_n)$ is a sufficient statistic for $\theta$ and that $z = r(y)$ is an unbiased statistic for $\theta$. Then, according to the Rao-Cramér inequality,

$$\sigma_z^2 \geq \frac{1}{n \, E\{[\partial \ln f(x; \theta)/\partial\theta]^2\}} \tag{1}$$

where $\sigma_z^2$ denotes the variance of z.

If    $\sigma_z^2 = \dfrac{1}{n \, E\{[\partial \ln f(x; \theta)/\partial\theta]^2\}}$ ,    z is called an efficient statistic.

We shall first show that $y = \sum\limits_{i=1}^{n} x_i$ is a sufficient statistic for $\theta$, the mean of the Poisson distribution,

$$f(x) = \frac{\theta^x e^{-\theta}}{x!} \cdot$$

The joint density function of the elements of the random sample is

$$f(x_1)f(x_2) \ldots f(x_n) = \frac{\theta^{\sum\limits_{i=1}^{n} x_i} e^{-n\theta}}{x_1! \ldots x_n!} \qquad (2)$$

The probability density function of the statistic $y = \sum\limits_{i=1}^{n} x_i$ is found using the theorem for the sum of $n$ independent variables. It is

$$g(x_1 + x_2 + \ldots + x_n) = \frac{e^{-n\theta} (n\theta)^{\sum\limits_{i=1}^{n} x_i}}{\left(\sum\limits_{i=1}^{n} x_i\right)!} . \qquad (3)$$

A statistic $s = g(x_1, \ldots x_n)$ is defined to be a sufficient statistic of $\theta$ if the conditional distribution of $x_1, \ldots, x_n$ given $s = s_1$ does not depend on $\theta$ for any value $s_1$ of $s$.

Using (2) and (3),

$$f(x_1, \ldots, x_n; \theta/s = \Sigma x_i)$$

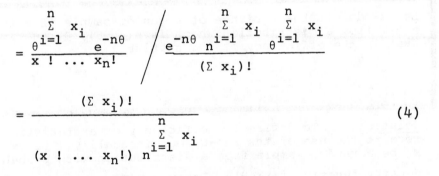

$$= \frac{\theta^{\sum\limits_{i=1}^{n} x_i} e^{-n\theta}}{x_1! \ldots x_n!} \Big/ \frac{e^{-n\theta} n^{\sum\limits_{i=1}^{n} x_i} \theta^{\sum\limits_{i=1}^{n} x_i}}{(\Sigma x_i)!}$$

$$= \frac{(\Sigma x_i)!}{(x_1! \ldots x_n!) \; n^{\sum\limits_{i=1}^{n} x_i}} \qquad (4)$$

Note that (4) does not contain the parameter $\theta$. Hence, $y = \sum\limits_{i=1}^{n} x_i$ is a sufficient statistic for $\theta$. Since any linear function of a sufficient statistic is a sufficient statistic, $z = \frac{y}{n} = \sum\limits_{i=1}^{n} \frac{x_i}{n} = \bar{x}$, the sample mean, is a sufficient statistic. Furthermore, $z$ is an unbiased statistic of $\theta$, i.e., $E(x) = E\left[\sum\limits_{i=1}^{n} \frac{x_i}{n}\right]$

$$= \frac{1}{n} \sum\limits_{i=1}^{n} E(x_i) = \frac{n\theta}{n} = \theta.$$

Examining (1) we see that $\dfrac{\partial \ln f(x;\ \theta)}{\partial \theta}$ is required.

Since $f(x;\ \theta) = \dfrac{\theta^x\ e^{-\theta}}{x!}$ ,

$\ln f(x;\ \theta) = (x \ln \theta - \theta - \ln x!),$

and $\dfrac{\partial \ln f(x;\ \theta)}{\partial \theta} = \left(\dfrac{x}{\theta} - 1\right) = \dfrac{x - \theta}{\theta}$ .

Hence, $E\left[\left(\dfrac{\partial \ln f(x;\ \theta)}{\partial \theta}\right)^2\right] = E \dfrac{(x - \theta)^2}{\theta^2}$ (5)

In (5), $E(x - \theta)^2 = \sigma^2$, the variance. For the Poisson distribution, the variance is $\theta$. Therefore, (5) reduces to

$$E\left[\left(\dfrac{\partial \ln f(x;\ \theta)}{\partial \theta}\right)^2\right] = \dfrac{1}{\theta}\ .$$ (6)

Substituting (6) into (1),

$$\sigma_z^2 \geqq \dfrac{1}{n\left(\dfrac{1}{\theta}\right)} = \dfrac{\theta}{n}\ .$$ (7)

But $\dfrac{\theta}{n} = \text{Var } \overline{x} = \sigma_z^2$. Hence (7) changes to equality, and $z = \overline{x}$ has been shown to be an efficient statistic.

● **PROBLEM 15-44**

Let $s^2$ denote the variance of a random sample of size $n > 1$ from a distribution which is $n(\mu,\ \theta)$, $0 < \theta < \infty$. What is the efficiency of the statistic

$$\dfrac{ns^2}{n - 1}\ ?$$

Solution: To define the efficiency of a statistic, we require the use of the Rao-Cramér inequality. Let $x_1,\ \ldots,\ x_n$ be a random sample from a distribution with probability density function $f(x;\ \theta)$. Let $y = u(x_1,\ x_2,\ \ldots,\ x_n)$ be a sufficient statistic for $\theta$, and $z = v(y)$ an unbiased statistic for $\theta$. Then, the Rao-Cramér inequality states that

$$\sigma_z^2 \geq \dfrac{1}{n\ E\ \{[\partial \ln f(x;\ \theta)/\partial \theta]^2\}}\ .$$ (1)

From (1), the ratio of $\sigma_z^2$ to

$$\dfrac{1}{n\ E\ \{[\partial \ln f(x;\ \theta)/\partial \theta]^2\}}$$ is defined to be the efficiency of z.

Now, $s^2 = \dfrac{1}{n} \sum\limits_{i=1}^{n} (x_i - \overline{x})^2$ and thus,

$$E(s^2) = \theta^2 - \frac{\theta^2}{n} = \frac{(n-1)}{n}\theta .$$

which indicates that $s^2$ is a biased statistic. However, from $s^2$ we can develop an unbiased statistic

$\frac{ns^2}{n-1}$ . That is,

$$E\left[\frac{ns^2}{n-1}\right] = \theta$$

Since $s^2$ is a sufficient statistic for $\theta$ and $z = v(s^2)$ $= \frac{ns^2}{n-1}$ is an unbiased statistic we may use the Rao-Cramér inequality to find the efficiency of z. The normal distribution has the density function

$$f(x; \theta) = \frac{1}{\sqrt{2\pi\theta}} e^{-\frac{(x-\mu)^2}{2\theta}} .$$

Taking the logarithms to base e of both sides.

$$\ln f(x; \theta) = \frac{-\ln (2\pi\theta)}{2} - \frac{(x-\mu)^2}{2\theta} . \tag{2}$$

Differentiating (2) with respect to $\theta$,

$$\frac{\partial \ln f(x; \theta)}{\partial \theta} = -\frac{1}{2\theta} + \frac{(x-\mu)^2}{2\theta^2} .$$

Then, $\left[\frac{\partial \ln f(x; \theta)}{\partial \theta}\right]^2 = \frac{1}{4\theta^2} - \frac{(x-\mu)^2}{2\theta^3} + \frac{(x-\mu)^4}{4\theta^4} . \tag{3}$

Taking the expected value of (3),

$$E\frac{[\partial \ln f(x; \theta)]^2}{\partial \theta} = E\left[\frac{1}{4\theta^2} - \frac{(x-\mu)^2}{2\theta^3} + \frac{(x-\mu)^4}{4\theta^4}\right]$$

$$= \frac{1}{4\theta^2} - \frac{\theta}{2\theta^3} + \frac{3\theta^2}{4\theta^4} = \frac{1}{2\theta^2} . \tag{4}$$

Substituting (4) into (1),

$$\sigma_z^2 \geq \frac{1}{n\left[\frac{1}{2\theta^2}\right]} = \frac{2\theta^2}{n} ,$$

which is the Rao-Cramér lower bound. Next, we must find the variance of $z = \frac{ns^2}{n-1}$ . The ratio $\frac{ns^2}{\theta}$ has the chi-square distribution with n - 1 degrees of freedom. But the variance of a random variable that has the chi-square distribution with k degrees of freedom is 2k. Hence, the variance of $\frac{ns^2}{\theta}$ is 2(n - 1).

Noting that $\frac{ns^2}{n-1} = \frac{ns^2}{\theta}\left(\frac{\theta}{n-1}\right)$ the variance of

$\frac{ns^2}{n-1}$ is given by

$$Var\ z = Var\ \left[ \frac{\theta}{n-1}\ \frac{ns^2}{\theta} \right]$$

$$= \frac{\theta^2}{(n-1)^2}\ Var\ \left( \frac{ns^2}{\theta} \right) = \frac{2\theta^2}{n-1} \ .$$

Hence the efficiency of $\frac{ns^2}{n-1}$ is $\frac{2\theta^2/n}{2\theta^2/n-1} = \frac{n-1}{n} \ .$

# BAYESIAN ESTIMATION

● **PROBLEM** 15-45

A machine manufactures metal screws in a given lot size. Among the lots there is variation in the percentage of defective metal screws, with the distribution below:

| Fraction Defective p | Prior Probability Function P(p) |
|---|---|
| .01 | .25 |
| .02 | .35 |
| .03 | .20 |
| .06 | .15 |
| .10 | .04 |
| .20 | .01 |
| | 1.00 |

A random sample of 10 screws is chosen from the lots and after testing, it is found that one of the screws is defective. Use the prior distribution and the sample evidence to find the posterior probability function of fraction defective.

Solution:     We are given the probability distribution of the random variable p.  Let us use the binomial probability density function to find the various likelihoods.  That is, we ask "what is the likelihood of obtaining one defective in a sample of 10 with the different probabilities in the table?".  A random variable x is said to be binomially distributed if it has the frequency function

$$f(x) = \binom{n}{x}\ p^x\ q^{n-x}. \tag{1}$$

Letting $n = 10$, $x = 1$ and p the different probabilities we obtain the likelihood values.

$$\binom{10}{1}\ (.01)^1\ (.99)^9\ = .0091$$

$$\binom{10}{1}\ (.02)^1\ (.98)^9\ = .167$$

$$\binom{10}{1}\ (.03)^1\ (.97)^9\ = .228 \tag{2}$$

$$\binom{10}{1} (.06)^1 (.94)^9 = .344$$

$$\binom{10}{1} (.10)^1 (.90)^9 = .387$$

$$\binom{10}{1} (.20)^1 (.80)^9 = .268$$

Examining the table (2) we see that the likelihood function achieves its maximum when p = .10.

To find the posterior probabilities we use Bayes' formula:

$$P(A_i|A) = \frac{P(A_i) \ P(A|A_i)}{\sum\limits_{i=1}^{n} P(A_i) \ P(A|A_i)} . \qquad (3)$$

In the present problem, the $A_i$ are the various values that p can take and hence $P(A_i)$ is given by the prior probability function. Consider the term $P(A|A_i)$. The likelihood function defined by (2) gives the probability that $A = \frac{1}{10}$ given the various prior probabilities. Thus, it may be substituted for $P(A|A_i)$. We construct the following table:

| $P(p) = P(A_i)$ | Likelihood $(= P(A|A_i)$ | Joint Probability $P(A_i)P(A|A_i)$ | Posterior Probability $\dfrac{P(A_i)P(A|A_i)}{\sum P(A_i)P(A|A_i)}$ |
|---|---|---|---|
| 1. .25 | .0091 | .023 | .117 |
| 2. .35 | .167 | .058 | .294 |
| 3. .20 | .229 | .046 | .234 |
| 4. .15 | .344 | .052 | .264 |
| 5. .04 | .387 | .016 | .076 |
| 6. .01 | .268 | .003 | .015 |

The entries in the last column of the above table, when substituted into (3) yield $P(A_i|A)$, the posterior probability function.

● **PROBLEM** 15-46

Let $x_1, \ldots, x_n$ denote a random sample from the Bernoulli distribution. Assume that the prior distribution of $\theta$, the parameter, of this distribution is given by $g(\theta) = 1$, $0 < \theta < 1$. Find the posterior Bayes estimator for $\theta$.

Solution:     A random variable x has the Bernoulli distribution if it has the probability density function:

$$f(x; \theta) = \theta^x (1 - \theta)^{1-x}, \qquad x = 0, 1.$$

Now assume that $\theta$, the unknown parameter is no longer a fixed value but itself has a probability distribution. We call this the prior distribution of $\theta$. In the present problem the prior distribution of $\theta$ is the uniform distribution over (0, 1).

The posterior distribution, i.e., the distribution of $\theta$ after selection of the random sample is defined as the conditional distribution of $\theta$ given the values in the sample. Thus,

$$f_{\theta|X = x_1, \ldots X_n = x_n}(\theta\, x_1, \ldots, x_n)$$

$$= \frac{f_{x_1, \ldots, x_n|\theta}(x_1, \ldots, x_n|\theta) g(\theta)}{f_{x_1, \ldots, x_n}(x_1, \ldots, x_n)}$$

$$= \frac{\left[ \prod_{i=1}^{n} f(x_i|\theta) \right] g(\theta)}{\int_a^b \left[ \prod_{i=1}^{n} f(x_i|\theta) \right] g\theta\, d\theta}, \qquad (1)$$

using the conditional probability formula

$$P(Z|Y) = \frac{P(Z)\ P(Y)}{P(Y)}.$$

The mean of the posterior distribution is used to estimate $\theta$. This is the posterior Bayes estimator of $\theta$ and is defined as

$$E\ [\theta|x, \ldots, x_n] \qquad (2)$$

By the definition of the expected value of a continuous random variable,

$$E(Z) = \int_a^b Z\, f(Z)\, dz,$$

$$E[\theta|x_1, \ldots, x_n] = \int \theta\, f_{\theta|x_1, \ldots, x_n}(\theta|x_1, \ldots, x_n)\, d\theta$$

$$= \frac{\int_a^b \theta \left[ \prod_{i=1}^{n} f(x_i|\theta) \right] g(\theta)\, d\theta}{\int_a^b \left[ \prod_{i=1}^{n} f(x_i|\theta) \right] g(\theta)\, d\theta}, \qquad (2)$$

using (1).

568

For the given problem, (1) is

$$f_{\theta|x_1, \ldots, x_n}(\theta|x_1, \ldots, x_n)$$

$$= \frac{\theta^{\sum_{i=1}^{n} x_i} (1 - \theta)^{n - \sum_{i=1}^{n} x_i}}{\int_0^1 \theta^{\sum_{i=1}^{n} x_i} (1 - \theta)^{n - \sum_{i=1}^{n} x_i} d\theta} . \tag{3}$$

To find the posterior Bayes estimator of $\theta$ we compute the expected value of (3).

$$E[\theta|x_1, \ldots, x_n]$$

$$= \frac{\int_0^1 \theta \, \theta^{\sum_{i=1}^{n} x_i} (1 - \theta)^{n - \sum_{i=1}^{n} x_i} d\theta}{\int_0^1 \theta^{\sum x_i} (1 - \theta)^{n - \sum x_i} d\theta} . \tag{4}$$

Recall that the beta function is given by the integral

$$B(a, b) = \int_0^1 x^{a-1} (1 - x)^{b-1} dx; \quad a > 0, b > 0. \tag{5}$$

Comparing (5) and (4) we see that (4) may be rewritten

$$\frac{B\left(\sum_{i=1}^{n} x_i + 2, n - \left(\sum_{i=1}^{n} x_i\right) + 1\right)}{B\left(\sum_{i=1}^{n} x_i + 1, n - \left(\sum_{i=1}^{n} x_i\right) + 1\right)} \tag{6}$$

Recall further, the relationship between the Beta and Gamma functions. Thus,

$$B(a, b) = \frac{\Gamma(a) \Gamma(b)}{\Gamma(a + b)} \tag{7}$$

Using (7), equation (6) may be rewritten

$$\frac{\Gamma(\sum x_i + 2) \Gamma\left(n - \left(\sum_{i=1}^{n} x_i\right) + 1\right)}{\Gamma(n + 3)} \left(\frac{\Gamma(n + 2)}{\Gamma(\sum x_i + 1) \Gamma(n - (\sum x_i) + 1)}\right)$$

$$= \frac{\Gamma(\sum x_i + 2) \Gamma(n + 2)}{\Gamma(\sum x_i + 1) \Gamma(n + 3)} . \tag{8}$$

At this point we must realize

$$\Gamma(Z + 1) = Z \Gamma(Z). \tag{9}$$

Using (9), equation (8) may be rewritten

$$\frac{\sum x_i + 1}{n + 2} . \tag{10}$$

Hence, the posterior Bayes estimator of $\theta$ with respect to the uniform prior distribution is given by (10).

# CHAPTER 16

# HYPOTHESIS TESTING

## LEVEL OF SIGNIFICANCE

● **PROBLEM** 16-1

In testing a hypothesis concerned with the value of a population mean, first the level of significance to be used in the test is specified and then the regions of acceptance and rejection for evaluating the obtained sample mean are determined. If the 1 percent level of significance is used, indicate the percentages of sample means in each of the areas of the normal curve, assuming that the population hypothesis is correct, and the test is two-tailed.

<u>Solution</u>: A level of significance of 1% signifies that when the population mean is correct as specified, the sample mean will fall in the critial areas of rejection only 1% of the time. Referring to the figure below, .005 or .5% of the sample means will fall in each area of rejection and 99% of the sample means will fall in the region of acceptance.

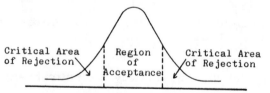

Critical Area of Rejection    Region of Acceptance    Critical Area of Rejection

● **PROBLEM** 16-2

An experimenter tested for differences in attitudes toward smoking before and after a film on lung cancer was shown. He found a difference which was significant between the .05 and .02 levels.

    a. What is the assumed hypothesis in words?

    b. Which level of significance indicates the greater degree of significance, .05 or .02?

    c. If his $\alpha$ level is .05, will he reject $H_1$? Will he reject it if he employs the .02 level? In choosing $\alpha$ = .02 instead of $\alpha$ = .05, he increases the risk of making one of the two types of error. Which type?

<u>Solution</u>: a. The assumed hypothesis $H_0$ is that there are no differences in attitudes toward smoking before and after the film on lung cancer was shown.

b.  The greater degree of significance is .02.  A level of significance of .02 means that the experimenter will be incorrect when he rejects $H_0$ at most 2% of the time.  A level of significance of .05 means he may be incorrect in rejecting $H_0$ as much as 5% of the time.

c.  Since a difference which is significant was found between the .05 and .02 levels, if the $\alpha$ level is .05 the experimenter will reject $H_0$ and accept $H_1$.  At the .02 level of significance he will accept $H_0$ and hence reject $H_1$.  In choosing $\alpha$ = .02 instead of $\alpha$ = .05, the experimenter increases the risk of making a Type II error.  A Type II error is the error of accepting the hypothesis $H_0$ when it is not true.

# MEANS: LARGE SAMPLES

● PROBLEM 16-3

A sample of size 49 yielded the values $\bar{x}$ = 87.3 and $s^2$ = 162. Test the hypothesis that $\mu$ = 95 versus the alternative that it is less.  Let $\alpha$ = .01 .

Solution:  The null and alternative hypotheses are given respectively by

$$H_0 : \mu = 95; \quad H_1 : \mu < 95 .$$

$\alpha$ = .01 is the given level of significance.

Because the sample size is quite large ($\geq$ 30), we can assume that the distribution of $\bar{X}$ is approximately normal.  We are using the sample variance $s^2$ as an estimate of the true but unknown population variance and if the sample were not as large we would use a t-test.

The critical region consists of all z-scores that are less than $z_{.01}$ = -2.33.  The observed z-score is

$$z = \frac{\bar{X} - \mu}{\sqrt{s^2/n}} = \frac{87.3 - 95}{\sqrt{162/49}} = \frac{(-7.7)(7)}{\sqrt{162}} = -4.23 .$$

This observed score is in the critial region; thus we reject the null hypothesis and accept the alternative that $\mu$ < 95.

● PROBLEM 16-4

Past experience has shown that the scores of students who take a certain mathematics test are normally distributed with mean 75 and variance 36.
The Mathematics Department members would like to know whether this year's group of 16 students is typical.  They decide to test the hypothesis that this year's students are typical versus the alternative that they are not typical.  When the students take the test the average score is 82.  What conclusion should be drawn?

Solution:  The hypotheses are

$$H_0 : \mu = 75 , \text{ this year's students are typical.}$$

$H_1 : \mu \neq 75$ , this year's students are atypical.

Specify a level of significance, $\alpha$ . Let $\alpha = .10$ . We are testing a hypothesis about the true mean score of our group of students. It seems reasonable to use $\bar{X}$ , the sample mean, as a test statistic. If the scores are each distributed with mean 75 and variance 36, then the sample mean is distributed normally with mean 75 and variance 36/n.

In this case n = 16. Thus $Z = \dfrac{\bar{X} - 75}{\sqrt{36/16}}$

is distributed normally with mean 0 and variance 1 .

We wish numbers c and -c that will determine a critical region, i.e., where $z < -c$ or $z > c$ will lead to rejecting the null hypothesis. $Pr(z < -c) + Pr(z > c) \leq .10$ . Equivalently $Pr(z > c) = .05$. Using the tables, c = 1.65.

We now calculate z for this example,

$$Z = \frac{82 - 75}{\sqrt{36/16}} = \frac{7}{\sqrt{2.25}} = \frac{7}{1.5} = 4.67 .$$

Since $4.67 > 1.65$, we reject $H_0$ and conclude that this year's students are atypical.

● **PROBLEM 16-5**

Suppose you are a buyer of large supplies of light bulbs. You want to test, at the 5% significance level, the manufacturer's claim that his bulbs last more than 800 hours. You test 36 bulbs and find that the sample mean, $\bar{X}$, is 816 hours and the sample standard deviation s = 70 hours. Should you accept the claim?

Solution: Establish the hypotheses $H_0 : \mu = 800$ hours, and

$H_1 : \mu > 800$ hours. We know by the Central Limit Theorem that the sampling distribution of the sample means is approximately normal, because n = 36 > 30 . The rejection area for $H_0$ is shown in the diagram:

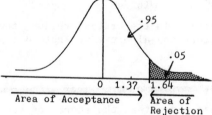

The shaded area represents 5% of the area under the standard normal curve. The table of z-scores gives z = 1.64 for a 5% rejection area. Now compute the z-value corresponding to the sample mean $\bar{X} = 816$.

$$z = \frac{\bar{X} - \mu_0}{\sigma_{\bar{X}}} ,$$

where $\mu_0$ is the mean of the null hypothesis and $\sigma_{\bar{X}}$ is the standard deviation of the sampling distribution of means, which is equal to the quotient of the population standard deviation $\sigma$ and the square root

of the sample size: $\sigma_{\bar{X}} = \sigma/\sqrt{n}$ . We do not know the population standard deviation, so we approximate it by the sample standard deviation
$s = 70$. Making substitutions in the formula for $z$, we have

$$z = \frac{\bar{X} - \mu_0}{\sigma_{\bar{X}}} = \frac{\bar{X} - \mu_0}{\sigma/\sqrt{n}} = \frac{\bar{X} - \mu_0}{s/\sqrt{n}} = \frac{816 - 800}{70/\sqrt{36}} = \frac{16}{11.67} = 1.37 .$$

This z-value falls in the acceptance region $(-\infty, 1.64)$ for $H_0$,
$\mu = 800$ hours. Therefore, you should reject, at the 5% level,
the manufacturer's claim that $\mu > 800$ .

● **PROBLEM** 16-6

For a shipment of cable, suppose that the specifications call for a
mean breaking strength of 2,000 pounds. A sampling of the breaking
strength of a number of segments of the cable has a mean breaking
strength of 1955 pounds with an associated standard error of the mean
of 25 pounds. Using the 5 percent level, test the significance of
the difference found.

<u>Solution</u>: This problem is depicted by the figure below:

$1955 = \bar{X}$    $\mu = 2000$

Since we are looking at the difference but are not concerned
with the direction of this difference we choose

$$H_0 : \mu = 2000; \quad H_1 : \mu \neq 2000 .$$

The statistic $(\bar{X} - \mu)/\sigma_{\bar{X}}$ has a standard normal distribution
with a mean of $0$ and a standard deviation of $1$. We calculate this
value, which is called $Z$ ,

$$Z = \frac{\bar{X} - \mu}{\sigma_{\bar{X}}}$$

and compare the value of $Z$ to a critical value. If $Z$ lies beyond
this critical value, we will reject $H_0$ . For this problem, where we
have $\alpha = 5\%$ and a two-tailed test, our critical value is 1.96, since
for the standard normal distribution, 2.5% of scores will have a
Z-value above 1.96 and 2.5% of scores will have a value below -1.96.

Therefore, we use the following decision rule: reject $H_0$ if
$z > 1.96$ or $z < -1.96$. Accept $H_0$ of $-1.96 \leq z \leq 1.96$.
For this problem,

$$z = \frac{1955 - 2000}{25} = \frac{-45}{25} = -1.8.$$

Since -1.8 lies in the interval (-1.96, 1.96), we accept H  and
conclude that the difference observed is not significant.

A firm producing light bulbs wants to know if it can claim that its light bulbs last 1000 burning hours. To answer this question, the firm takes a random sample of 100 bulbs from those it has produced and finds that the average lifetime for this sample is 970 burning hours. The firm knows that the standard deviation of the lifetime of the bulbs it produces is 80 hours. Can the firm claim that the average lifetime of its bulbs is 1000 hours, at the 5% level of significance?

Solution: Since the firm is claiming that the average lifetime of its bulbs is 1000 hours, we have

$$H_0 : \mu = 1000; \quad H_1 : \mu \neq 1000 .$$

The figure below depicts the data for this problem.

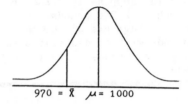

$$970 = \bar{X} \quad \mu = 1000$$

The statistic $(\bar{X} - \mu)/\sigma_{\bar{X}}$ has a standard normal distribution with a mean of 0 and a standard deviation of 1. We calculate this value, which is called z ,

$$z = \frac{\bar{X} - \mu}{\sigma_{\bar{X}}} , \quad \text{where} \quad \sigma_{\bar{X}} = \frac{\sigma}{\sqrt{n}} ,$$

and compare the value of z to a critical value. If Z lies beyond this critical value, we will reject $H_0$ . For this problem, where we have $\alpha$ = 5% and a two-tailed test, our critical value is 1.96, since for the standard normal distribution, 2.5% of scores will have a z-value above 1.96 and 2.5% of scores will have a value below -1.96. Therefore we use the following decision rule: reject $H_0$ if Z > 1.96 or Z < -1.96. Accept $H_0$ if -1.96 ≤ Z ≤ 1.96.

For the data of this problem

$$\sigma_{\bar{X}} = \frac{80}{\sqrt{100}} = 8 \quad \text{and} \quad z = \frac{970 - 1000}{8} = \frac{-30}{8} = -3.75.$$

Since -3.75 < -1.96, we reject $H_0$ and conclude that the average lifetime of the firm's bulbs is not 1000 hours.

In justifying their demand for higher wages, the employees in the shipping department of a large mail order house report that on the average, the department completes an order in 13 minutes. As a general manager for this firm, what can you conclude if a sample of 400 orders shows an average completion time of 14 minutes with a standard deviation of 10 minutes? Use a .05 level of significance.

Solution:

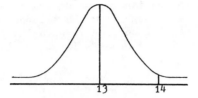

13        14

       Referring to the figure, we desire to see whether the sample mean, 14, is far enough from the alleged population mean, 13, to conclude that the population mean is actually greater than 13 for the given set of data. Therefore, our alternative hypothesis is $\mu > 13$. The null hypothesis is then $\mu = 13$. So we have

$$H_0 : \mu = 13 \; ; \quad H_1 : \mu > 13 .$$

The statistic $(\bar{X} - \mu)/S_{\bar{X}}$ has a t-distribution with a mean of 0 and a standard deviation of 1. Since our sample size, n, is large ($\geq 30$), this statistic may be approximated by the standard normal distribution, also having a mean of 0 and a standard deviation of 1. We calculate this value, which is called Z,

$$Z = \frac{\bar{X} - \mu}{S_{\bar{X}}} , \quad \text{where} \quad S_{\bar{X}} = \frac{S}{\sqrt{n}} ,$$

and compare the value of Z to a critical value. If Z lies beyond this critical value, we will reject $H_0$. For this problem, where we have $\alpha = .05$ and a one-tailed test, our critical value is 1.65, since for the standard normal distribution, 5% of scores will have a z-value above 1.65. Therefore, for our decision rule we will reject $H_0$ if $Z > 1.65$ and accept $H_0$ if $Z \leq 1.65$.

For the data of this example

$$Z = \frac{14 - 13}{10/\sqrt{400}} = \frac{1}{10/20} = \frac{1}{.5} = 2.00 .$$

Since $2.00 > 1.65$, we reject $H_0$ and conclude that the actual average time for the department to complete an order is greater than 13 minutes.

● **PROBLEM 16-9**

All boxes of a particular type of detergent indicate that they contain 21 ounces of detergent. A government agency receives many consumer complaints that the boxes contain less than 21 ounces. To check the consumers' complaints at the 5% level of significance, the government agency buys 100 boxes of this detergent and finds that $\bar{X} = 20.5$ ounces and $S = 2$ ounces. Should the government agency order the seller to put more detergent into its boxes?

Solution:

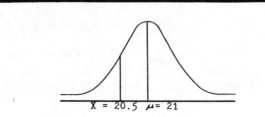

$\bar{X} = 20.5$  $\mu = 21$

Referring to the figure, we desire to see whether the sample mean 20.5, is far enough from the alleged population mean, 21, to conclude that the population mean is actually less than 21. Therefore, our alternative hypothesis is $\mu < 21$. The null hypothesis is then $\mu = 21$. So we have

$$H_0 : \mu = 21; \qquad H_1 : \mu < 21 .$$

The statistic $(\bar{X} - \mu)/S_{\bar{X}}$ has a t-distribution with a mean of 0 and a standard deviation of 1. Since our sample size, n, is large ($\geq 30$), this statistic may be approximated by the standard normal distribution, also having a mean of 0 and a standard deviation of 1. We calculate this value, which is called Z,

$$Z = \frac{\bar{X} - \mu}{S_{\bar{X}}} \qquad \text{where} \qquad S_{\bar{X}} = \frac{S}{\sqrt{n}} ,$$

and compare the value of Z to a critical value. If Z lies beyond this critical value, we will reject $H_0$. For this problem, where we have $\alpha = .05$ and a one-tailed test, our critical value is 1.65, since for the standard normal distribution, 5% of scores will have a Z-value above 1.65. Also 5% of scores will have a Z-value below -1.65.

The decision rule for this problem is: reject $H_0$ if $Z < -1.65$ and accept $H_0$ if $Z \geq -1.65$.

For the data of this problem

$$S_{\bar{X}} = \frac{2}{\sqrt{100}} = \frac{2}{10} = .2$$

and

$$Z = \frac{20.5 - 21}{.2} = \frac{-.5}{.2} = -2.5 .$$

Since $-2.5 < -1.65$, we reject $H_0$ and conclude that the average amount of detergent in the boxes is less than 21 ounces. The government agency should order the seller to put more detergent into its boxes.

● **PROBLEM** 16-10

An official of a trade union reports that the mean yearly wage is $8,000. A random sample of 100 employees in the union produced a mean of $7,875 with a standard deviation of $1,000. Test the null hypothesis at the .05 level of significance that the mean wage is $8,000 against the alternate hypothesis that the wage is greater than or less than $8,000.

Solution: For this problem $H_0$ and $H_1$ are given as follows:

$$H_0 : \mu = \$8,000; \qquad H_1 : \mu \neq \$8,000.$$

For $\alpha = .05$, the critical value is $z = 1.96$ and we accept $H_0$ if z lies between -1.96 and 1.96. This is because the statistic $z = (\bar{X} - \mu)/S_{\bar{X}}$ which has a t-distribution may be approximated by the normal distribution when the sample size, n, is large $(\geq 30)$, and for the standard normal distribution, 2.5% of scores will have a z-value above 1.96 and 2.5% of scores will have a z-value below -1.96. We calculate z using the formula:

$$Z = \frac{\bar{X} - \mu}{S_{\bar{X}}} \quad \text{where}$$

$$\bar{X} = 7875, \quad \mu = 8000$$

and

$$S_{\bar{X}} = S/\sqrt{n} = 1000/\sqrt{100} = 1000/10 = 100 .$$

Therefore Z becomes

$$Z = \frac{7875 - 8000}{100} = \frac{-125}{100} = -1.25.$$

Since -1.25 lies between -1.96 and 1.96, we accept $H_0$ that the mean wage is in reality $8,000.

● PROBLEM 16-11

A certain brand of cigarettes is advertised by the manufacturer as having a mean nicotine content of 15 milligrams per cigarette. A sample of 200 cigarettes is tested by an independent research laboratory and found to have an average of 16.2 milligrams of nicotine content and a standard deviation of 3.6. Using a .01 level of significance, can we conclude based on this sample that the actual mean nicotine content of this brand of cigarettes is greater than 15 milligrams?

Solution:

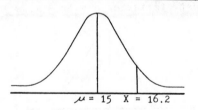

$$\mu = 15 \quad X = 16.2$$

Referring to the figure we wish to determine whether $\bar{X} = 16.2$ is far enough to the right of $\mu = 15$ to be in the critical area and, if so, we will reject the null hypothesis and conclude that $\mu > 15$.
We therefore have:

$$H_0 : \mu = 15; \quad H_1 : \mu > 15.$$

The statistic $Z = (\bar{X} - \mu)/\sigma_{\bar{X}}$ can be approximated by a standard normal distribution with a mean of 0 and a standard deviation of 1, when the sample size, n, is large $(\geq 30)$. We calculate

$$Z = \frac{\bar{X} - \mu}{S_{\bar{X}}} \quad \text{where} \quad S_{\bar{X}} = S/\sqrt{n}$$

and compare the value of Z to a critical value. We reject $H_0$ if Z lies beyond this critical value. For this problem, a one-tailed test with $\alpha = .01$, our critical value is 2.33, since for the standard

577

normal distribution, 1% of scores will have a Z-value above 2.33.
Therefore, we have the following decision rule: Reject $H_0$ if
$Z > 2.33$. Accept $H_0$ if $Z \leq 2.33$.

For the data of this problem

$$S_{\bar{X}} = \frac{3.6}{\sqrt{200}} = .255$$

and

$$Z = \frac{16.2 - 15}{.255} = \frac{1.2}{.255} = 4.71.$$

Since $4.71 > 2.33$, we conclude at a 1% level of significance that
the mean nicotine content of this brand of cigarettes is greater
than 15.

● PROBLEM 16-12

In investigating several complaints concerning the weight of the
"NET WT. 12 OZ." jar of a local brand of peanut butter, the Better
Business Bureau selected a sample of 36 jars. The sample showed an
average net weight of 11.92 ounces and a standard deviation of .3
ounce. Using a .01 level of significance, what would the Bureau
conclude about the operation of the local firm?

Solution: We use a one-tailed test because we are concerned with
whether the actual population mean is 12 ounces or whether it is less
than 12 ounces. Therefore we have

$$H_0 : \mu = 12 ; \quad H_1 : \mu < 12.$$

The figure below depicts this problem. Since the sample size, n, is
large $(\geq 30)$, the test statistic $z = (\bar{x} - \mu)/s_{\bar{x}}$ is normally dis-

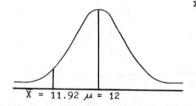

$\bar{X} = 11.92 \quad \mu = 12$

tributed with a mean of 0 and a standard deviation of 1. We must
calculate

$$z = \frac{\bar{x} - \mu}{s_{\bar{x}}} \quad \text{where} \quad s_{\bar{x}} = \frac{s}{\sqrt{n}}$$

and compare the value of z obtained to a critical value. Our
critical value of z for this problem is -2.33 since 1% of scores
of the standard normal distribution have a z-value below -2.33 and we
want to reject $H_0$ for values of $\bar{x}$ less than $\mu$ .

Therefore, we have for our decision rule: reject $H_0$ if $z < -2.33$;
accept $H_0$ if $z \geq -2.33$.
For the data of this problem

$$s_{\bar{x}} = \frac{.3}{\sqrt{36}} = \frac{.3}{6} = .05$$

and

$$Z = \frac{11.92 - 12}{.05} = \frac{-.08}{.05} = -1.60.$$

Since $-1.60 \geq -2.33$, we accept $H_0$ and conclude that at a 1% level of significance the actual population mean of the local brand of peanut butter is 12 ounces.

● **PROBLEM 16-13**

The mean score on a widely given freshman history examination is 75. A history teacher at a very large university wants to determine whether there is statistical evidence for claiming that this year's class is not average.

Given the following scores, and assuming that the students in his class are a random sample from the population of students at the university, test the appropriate hypothesis versus the appropriate alternative. The test scores are:

| 94 | 69 | 89 | 49 | 88 | 89 | 85 |
|----|----|----|-----|----|----|----|
| 95 | 55 | 93 | 86 | 62 | 83 | 96 |
| 48 | 51 | 69 | 74 | 83 | 71 | 89 |
| 58 | 89 | 81 | 79 | 52 | 73 |    |
| 75 | 91 | 68 | 100 | 63 | 81 |    |

_Solution:_    $H_0 : \mu = 75$ , the students are average

$H_1 : \mu \neq 75$ , the students are not average.

This is a two-tailed hypothesis. Arbitrarily select $\alpha = .05$ to be the level of significance for this test. Because $n = 33$ is large we may assume that our test statistic

$$\frac{\bar{x} - \mu}{\sqrt{s^2/n}}$$

is distributed normally with mean 0 and variance 1. The critical region will consist of values of

$$Z = \frac{\bar{x} - \mu}{\sqrt{s^2/n}}$$

such that

$$\Pr(Z < -c) = .025 \quad \text{and} \quad \Pr(Z > c) = .025$$

implying $c = \pm 1.96$; hence the critical region consists of two pieces $Z < -1.96$ and $Z > 1.96$.

$$\sum_{i=1}^{33} x_i = \text{the sum of the test scores} = 2528$$

and

$$\sum_{i=1}^{33} x_i^2 = \text{the sum of squares} = 201,026.$$

$$\bar{X} = \sum_{i=1/n}^{33} x_i = \frac{2528}{33} = 76.6 \; ;$$

579

$$s^2 = \frac{1}{n-1}\left[\sum_{i=1}^{33} x_i^2 - \frac{\left[\sum_{i=1}^{33} x_i\right]^2}{n}\right] = \frac{1}{32}\left[201,026 - \frac{(2528)^2}{33}\right]$$

$$= 230.2 \; ;$$

$$s = \sqrt{230.2} = 15.17.$$

Therefore
$$Z = \frac{76.6 - 75}{15.17/\sqrt{33}} = \frac{1.6}{2.64} = 0.61.$$

.61 does not lie in the critical region so accept $H_0$ and reject $H_1$. There is no statistical basis for concluding that the freshman class this year is not average.

# MEANS: SMALL SAMPLES

● PROBLEM 16-14

Suppose it is required that the mean operating life of size "D" batteries be 22 hours. Suppose also that the operating life of the batteries is normally distributed. It is known that the standard deviation of the operating life of all such batteries produced is 3.0 hours. If a sample of 9 batteries has a mean operating life of 20 hours, can we conclude that the mean operating life of size "D" batteries is not 22 hours? Then suppose the standard deviation of the operating life of all such batteries is not known but that for the sample of 9 batteries the standard deviation is 3.0. What conclusion would we then reach?

Solution: Since the operating life of "D" batteries is normally distributed, and the standard deviation for all batteries is known, the sample mean will have a Z or normal distribution regardless of the sample size.

Hence for the first part of this problem, we will calculate

$$Z = \frac{\bar{X} - \mu}{\sigma_{\bar{X}}} \qquad \text{where} \qquad \sigma_{\bar{X}} = \frac{\sigma}{\sqrt{n}} \; .$$

The diagram for this problem is given below.

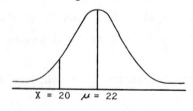

$$X = 20 \quad \mu = 22$$

The null hypothesis and alternate hypothesis are

$$H_0 : \mu = 22 \; ; \qquad H_1 : \mu \neq 22 \; .$$

The decision rule at $\alpha = .05$ is as follows: Reject $H_0$ if $Z > 1.96$ or $Z < -1.96$; accept $H_0$ if $-1.96 \leq Z \leq 1.96$. The value of 1.96 is chosen as the critial value because for this problem we have $\alpha = .05$ and a two-tailed test, and for the standard normal distribution, 2.5% of scores will have a Z-value greater than 1.96 and 2.5% of scores will have a Z-value less than -1.96.

For this set of data

$$\sigma_{\bar{X}} = \frac{3.0}{\sqrt{9}} = 1 \quad \text{and}$$

$$Z = \frac{20 - 22}{1} = -2.0 .$$

Therefore we will reject $H_0$ and conclude that the mean operating life of size "D" batteries is not 22 hours.

When the population standard deviation is not known the sample mean has a t-distribution with n-1 = 8 degrees of freedom. We calculate

$$t = \frac{\bar{X} - \mu}{S_{\bar{X}}}$$

and use the decision rule to reject $H_0$ if $t > 2.306$ or $t < -2.306$ (the critical t for 8 df's $\alpha = .05$, and a two-tailed test is 2.306) and to accept $H_0$ if $-2.306 \leq t \leq 2.306$. For this data

$$t = \frac{20 - 22}{1} = -2.0 .$$

So in this case we will accept $H_0$ that the mean operating life of size "D" batteries is 22 hours.

● **PROBLEM** 16-15

Suppose we have a sample with n = 10 and $\bar{Y} = 50$. We wish to test $H_0 : \mu = 47$ against $H_1 : \mu \neq 47$. We would like to know the probability given $\mu = 47$ of observing a random sample from the population with $\bar{Y} = 50$. We will reject $H_0$ if the probability is less than $\alpha = .05$ that $H_0$ is true when $\bar{Y} = 50$.

Assume for this sample that $\Sigma(Y - \bar{Y})^2 = 99.2250$. Calculate the estimated population variance, the estimated $\sigma_{\bar{Y}}^2$ and the estimated standard error of the mean. Then calculate the t statistic and determine whether $H_0$ can be rejected. Also, suppose $\alpha = .01$. Within what limits may $\bar{Y}$ vary without our having to reject $H_0$?

<u>Solution</u>: The estimated population variance is given by

$$s^2 = \frac{\Sigma(Y - \bar{Y})^2}{n-1} .$$

For the given set of data,

$$s^2 = \frac{99.2250}{9} = 11.025 .$$

The estimated $\sigma_{\bar{Y}}^2$, denoted by $s_{\bar{Y}}^2$ is

$$s_{\bar{Y}}^2 = \frac{s^2}{n} = \frac{11.025}{10} = 1.1025 .$$

The estimated standard error of the mean is $\sqrt{S_{\bar{Y}}^2}$ = 1.05.

The calculated value of t is given by

$$t = \frac{\bar{Y} - \mu}{S_{\bar{Y}}} = \frac{50 - 47}{1.05} = \frac{3}{1.05} = 2.86 \ .$$

For n-1 = 9 degrees of freedom, $t_{.01}$ = 2.821 and $t_{.005}$ = 3.250. Since our calculated value of t lies between $t_{.01}$ and $t_{.005}$, the probability of obtaining a random sample of size 10 with $\bar{Y}$ = 50 when $\mu$ = 47, lies between .02 and .01. (Since for $\alpha/2$ = .01 and .005 respectively, $\alpha$ = .02 and .01.) If we are to reject $H_o$ for $\alpha$ = .05, we would in this case reject $H_o$.

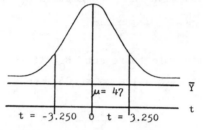

$$\mu = 47$$
$$t = -3.250 \quad 0 \quad t = 3.250$$

If $\alpha$ = .01, $t_{\alpha/2}$ = 3.250. We would not reject $H_0$ if the calculated value of t lies between -3.250 and 3.250.

The corresponding values of $\bar{Y}$ may be obtained by applying the formula

$$t = \frac{\bar{Y} - \mu}{S_{\bar{Y}}}$$

since the statistic $(\bar{Y} - \mu)/S_{\bar{Y}}$ has a t-distribution, and solving for $\bar{Y}$ when t = 3.250 and t = -3.250. For t = 3.250

$$3.250 = \frac{\bar{Y} - 47}{1.05} \ , \quad 3.41 = \bar{Y} - 47 \ , \quad 50.41 = \bar{Y} \ .$$

For t = -3.250

$$-3.250 = \frac{\bar{Y} - 47}{1.05} \ , \quad -3.41 = \bar{Y} - 47 \ , \quad 43.59 = \bar{Y} \ .$$

Therefore, $\bar{Y}$ may vary between 43.59 and 50.41 without rejecting $H_0$ at $\alpha$ = .01 .

● PROBLEM 16-16

For the following given information, find the critical region, compute t, and decide whether the results are significant or not significant.

Sample mean $\bar{X}$ = 26

Sample standard deviation s = 6

Sample size n = 25

Null hypothesis $\mu$ = 30

Alternate hypothesis $\mu$ < 30

Significance level $\alpha$ = .01 .

<u>Solution</u>: The critical region consists of those values of t for which we will reject the null hypothesis, $H_0$. For $\alpha = .01$, df = n-1 = 24, and a one-tailed test, we will reject $H_0$ if t < -2.492. This is because the test statistic, t = $(\bar{X} - \mu)/s_{\bar{X}}$ has a t-distribution with a mean of 0 and a standard deviation of 1, and for 24 degrees of freedom, 1% of scores will have a t-value less than -2.492. We will accept $H_0$ if $t_c \geq -2.492$. We must calculate

$$t = \frac{\bar{X} - \mu}{s_{\bar{X}}} \quad \text{where} \quad s_{\bar{X}} = \frac{s}{\sqrt{n}} .$$

For the data given in this problem,

$$s_{\bar{X}} = \frac{6}{\sqrt{25}} = \frac{6}{5} = 1.2$$

and

$$t_c = \frac{26 - 30}{1.2} = \frac{-4}{1.2} = -3.33.$$

Since -3.33 < -2.492 we reject $H_0$ and conclude the results are significant in this problem.

● **PROBLEM** 16-17

A lathe is adjusted so that the mean of a certain dimension of the parts is 20 cm. A random sample of 10 of the parts produced a mean of 20.3 cm and a standard deviation of .2 cm. Do the results indicate that the machine is out of adjustment? Test at the .05 level of significance.

<u>Solution</u>: Since the question asks whether the machine is out of adjustment but does not ask about the direction of this possible incorrect adjustment a two-tailed test is appropriate. We use a t-test with a null hypothesis that the mean of the population is 20 cm and an alternate hypothesis that the mean is not equal to 20 cm. Thus, we have

$$H_0 : \mu = 20 \; ; \quad H_1 : \mu \neq 20 .$$

The data for this problem are illustrated in the figure below.

For n = 10, we have df = n-1 = 9 degrees of freedom. For 9 df, at a .05 level of significance, and a two-tailed test, the critical value of t is 2.262. This is because of the fact that for a t-distribution with a mean of 0 and a standard deviation of 1, 2.5% of scores will have a t-value above 2.262 and 2.5% of scores will have a t-value below -2.262.

Hence our decision rule is: Reject $H_0$ if $t > 2.262$ or $t < -2.262$; accept $H_0$ if $-2.262 \leq t \leq 2.262$. The test statistic here is

$$t = \frac{\bar{X} - \mu}{(s/\sqrt{n})} \quad .$$

For the given values,

$$t = \frac{20.3 - 20.0}{(.2/\sqrt{10})} = \frac{.3}{.0632} = 4.74.$$

Since $4.74 > 2.262$, we reject $H_0$ and conclude that the machine is in need of adjustment.

● **PROBLEM 16-18**

A manufacturer of transistors claims that its transistors will last an average of 1000 hours. To maintain this average, 25 transistors are tested each month. If the computed value of $t$ lies between $-t_{.025}$ and $t_{.025}$, the manufacturer is satisfied with his claim. What conclusions should be drawn from a sample that has a mean $\bar{x} = 1,010$ and a standard deviation $s = 60$? Assume the distribution of the lifetime of the transistors is normal.

Solution: Since $n = 25$, the number of degrees of freedom for this problem is $n-1 = 24$. For 24 df's, $t_{.025} = 2.064$. Thus the manufacturer will be satisfied if the calculated value of $t$ lies between $-2.064$ and $2.064$ where the calculated value of $t$ is given by

$$t = \frac{\bar{x} - \mu}{(s/\sqrt{n})} \quad \text{since the statistic} \quad \frac{\bar{x} - \mu}{s/\sqrt{n}}$$

has a t-distribution with a mean of 0 and standard deviation of 1. For the given data of this problem, we obtain

$$t = \frac{1010 - 1000}{(60/\sqrt{25})} = -\frac{10}{12} = -.833.$$

Since $.833$ falls between $-2.064$ and $2.064$, the manufacturer will be satisfied that his claim is verified for the given sample.

● **PROBLEM 16-19**

A machine is set to produce metal shims having a thickness of .05 inches. To maintain the proper setting, 10 shims are tested each day. If the computed t-value falls between $-t_{.025}$ and $t_{.025}$, the machinist is satisfied that the machine is in adjustment. What should he conclude about the setting on the basis of a sample that has a mean of .053 inches and a standard deviation of .003?

Solution: He must calculate the value of $t$ for the data of this problem and see whether it falls between $-t_{.025}$ and $t_{.025}$. For

n = 10, the number of degrees of freedom = n-1 = 9, and for 9 df's
$t_{.025} = 2.262$.

The computed value of t is given by

$$t = \frac{\bar{x} - \mu}{(s/\sqrt{n})} \quad , \text{ since the statistic } \frac{\bar{x} - \mu}{(s/\sqrt{n})} \text{ has}$$

a t-distribution with a mean of 0 and a standard deviation of 1.
In this problem, $\bar{x} = .053$, $\mu = .05$, s = .003, and n = 10. So here we have

$$t = \frac{.053 - 05}{(.003/\sqrt{10})} = \sqrt{10} = 3.16.$$

Since 3.16 does not lie between the values $-t_{.025} = -2.262$ and $t_{.025} = 2.262$, we conclude that the machine needs to be adjusted.

● PROBLEM 16-20

A certain printing press is known to turn out an average of 45 copies a minute. In an attempt to increase its output, an altera- tion is made to the machine, and then in 3 short test runs it turns out 46, 47, and 48 copies a minute. Is this increase statistically significant, or is it likely to be simply the result of chance variation? Use a significance level of .05.

Solution: Since the sample size is small (n = 3), we can use a t-test for this problem to determine whether the sample mean number of copies is far enough from 45 for us to conclude that the population mean is greater than 45. We therefore set up our null and alternate hypotheses as follows:

$$H_0 : \mu = 45 ; \quad H_1 : \mu > 45 .$$

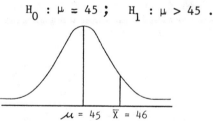

$\mu = 45 \quad \bar{X} = 46$

Our next step in problems of this type is to calculate

$$t = \frac{\bar{X} - \mu}{S_{\bar{X}}} \quad \text{where} \quad S_{\bar{X}} = \frac{S}{\sqrt{n}} .$$

We use the t-distribution because when the sample size is small (n < 30) the statistic $(\bar{X} - \mu)/S_{\bar{X}}$ has a t-statistic with a mean of 0 and a standard deviation of 1. But since $\bar{X}$ and S are not given we must calculate them.

$$\bar{X} = \frac{46+47+48}{3} = 47 ; \quad S = \sqrt{\frac{\Sigma(X - \bar{X})^2}{n-1}}$$

| X | X - $\bar{X}$ | (X - $\bar{X}$)² |
|----|------|------|
| 46 | -1 | 1 |
| 47 | 0 | 0 |
| 48 | 1 | 1 |

$2 = \Sigma(X - \bar{X})^2$

$S = \sqrt{2/2} = \sqrt{1} = 1.$

Now we may calculate $S_{\bar{X}} = \dfrac{1}{\sqrt{3}} = \dfrac{1}{1.732} = .577$

and

$$t = \dfrac{47 - 45}{.577} = \dfrac{2}{.577} = 3.47.$$

For this problem where we have $\alpha = .05$ and a one-tailed test, our critical value of $t$ is 2.92 since for the t-distribution with mean of 0 and standard deviation of 1, 5% of scores will have a t-value above 2.92. Therefore our decision rule is: reject $H_0$ if $t > 2.92$ and accept $H_0$ if $t \leq 2.92$. Since our calculated $t$ of $3.47 > 2.92$ we would reject $H_0$ and conclude that the increase in copies in our sample is statistically significant. If however, we were to choose a 1% level of significance we would obtain for our decision rule: Reject $H_0$ if $t > 6.95$ and accept $H_0$ if $t \leq 6.965$ because 1% of scores will have a t-value above 6.965. Since $3.47 \leq 6.965$, we would accept $H_0$ and conclude that the increase observed was simply the result of chance variation.

● **PROBLEM** 16-21

Given the eight sample observations 31, 29, 26, 33, 40, 28, 30, and 25, test the null hypothesis that the mean equals 35 versus the alternative that it does not. Let $\alpha = .01$.

<u>Solution:</u>     $H_0 : \mu = 35;$   $H_1 : \mu \neq 35.$

The level of significance $\alpha$ is given to be .01. This is a two-tailed test. Since the variance is unknown and must be estimated by the sample variance the t-test is appropriate.

$$\bar{X} = \dfrac{\sum\limits_{i=1}^{n} x_i}{n} = 30.25 \; ; \quad n = 8 \qquad s^2 = \dfrac{1}{n-1} \left[ \sum\limits_{i=1}^{n} x_i^2 - \dfrac{\left(\sum\limits_{i=1}^{n} x_i\right)^2}{n} \right]$$

$$= \dfrac{1}{7} \left[ 7476 - \dfrac{(242)^2}{8} \right] = \dfrac{155.5}{7} = 22.21 \; ; \qquad s = \sqrt{22.2} = 4.71.$$

The t-statistic is

$$t = \dfrac{\bar{x} - \mu}{s/\sqrt{n}} = \dfrac{30.25 - 35}{4.71/\sqrt{8}} = \dfrac{-4.7\sqrt{8}}{4.71} = -2.85.$$

The critical region will be that in which $Pr(c_1 < t < c_2) = 1 - .01$ or $Pr(t < c_1) = .005$ and $Pr(t > c_2) = .005$. Thus,

$$c_1 = -t_{.005}(7) = -3.499$$

$$c_2 = t_{.005}(7) = 3.499 .$$

Thus if our t-statistic lies between $-3.499$ and $3.499$ we will accept $H_0$ and otherwise reject. Our calculated t-statistic is $-2.85$ which leads us to accept the null hypothesis that the mean equals 35 and reject the alternative hypothesis.

586

Ten subjects are randomly drawn from a population. Scores in the population are normally distributed. For the sample $\Sigma X = 1038$ and $\Sigma X^2 = 107888$. Test the hypothesis that $\mu = 100$. Adopt a .05 level of significance. Use a two-tailed test.

Solution: First we must compute S, the standard deviation of the sample.

$$S = \sqrt{\frac{\Sigma X^2 - (\Sigma X)^2/n}{n-1}} = \sqrt{\frac{107888 - (1038)^2/10}{9}}$$

$$= \sqrt{\frac{107888 - 107744.4}{9}} = \sqrt{\frac{143.6}{9}} = 3.99.$$

Next we compute $S_{\bar{X}}$:

$$S_{\bar{X}} = \frac{S}{\sqrt{n}} = \frac{3.99}{\sqrt{10}} = 1.26.$$

The statistic $(\bar{X} - \mu)/S_{\bar{X}}$ has a t-distribution with a mean of 0 and a standard deviation of 1. Now we calculate $t = \dfrac{\bar{X} - \mu}{S_{\bar{X}}}$

where $\bar{X} = \Sigma X/n = 1038/10 = 103.8$. Then

$$t = \frac{103.8 - 100}{1.26} = \frac{3.8}{1.26} = 3.02.$$

We next compare this calculated value of t with $t_{\alpha/2}$. For 9 df's and $\alpha = .05$, $t_{\alpha/2} = 2.262$. Since 3.02 does not lie between $t_{\alpha/2} = -2.262$ and $t_{\alpha/2} = 2.262$, we reject $H_0$ that $\mu = 100$ and conclude that $\mu \neq 100$.

# DIFFERENCES BETWEEN MEANS: Z TESTS

● PROBLEM 16-23

Suppose that you want to decide which of two equally-priced brands of light bulbs lasts longer. You choose a random sample of 100 bulbs of each brand and find that brand A has sample mean of 1180 hours and sample standard deviation of 120 hours, and that brand B has sample mean of 1160 hours and sample standard deviation of 40 hours. What decision should you make at the 5% significance level?

Solution: Arrange the data into a table:

|  | n | $\bar{X}$ | s |
|---|---|---|---|
| Brand A | 100 | 1180 | 120 |
| Brand B | 100 | 1160 | 40 |

Establish two hypotheses: $H_0$ asserts that A and B last the same, on the average, and $H_1$ asserts that A and B have different average lifespans.  Thus:

$$H_0 : \mu_A = \mu_B , \text{ or, } H_1 : \mu_A \neq \mu_B ;$$

equivalently, $H_0 : \mu_A - \mu_B = 0;$    $H_1 : \mu_A - \mu_B \neq 0.$

Now define the acceptance region and rejection region for this test.  We can use the standard normal curve to determine these regions because of the theorem that if two populations from which two independent random samples are taken are normally distributed or if $n_1 + n_2 \geq 30$, then the sampling distribution of the difference between the sample means is normal or approximately normal, and its standard error is

$$\sqrt{\frac{\sigma_1^2}{n_1} + \frac{\sigma_2^2}{n_2}}$$

when $\sigma_1^2$ and $\sigma_2^2$ are the variances of populations 1 and 2 respectively.  In this problem, $n_1 + n_2 = 200 > 30$, so that the sampling distribution of $\bar{X}_1 - \bar{X}_2$ is approximately normal.  The acceptance region is the interval which lies under 95% of the area under the standard normal curve, because your decision will be made at the 5% level of significance.  The acceptance region is therefore $|Z| \leq 1.96$ and the rejection region is $|Z| > 1.96$.

$$\text{Now } Z = \frac{(\bar{X}_A - \bar{X}_B) - (\mu_A - \mu_B)}{\sqrt{\frac{\sigma_A^2}{n_A} + \frac{\sigma_B^2}{n_B}}} = \frac{(\bar{X}_A - \bar{X}_B)}{\sqrt{\frac{\sigma_A^2}{n_A} + \frac{\sigma_B^2}{n_B}}} \text{ by } H_0.$$

$(S_A)^2 = (120)^2$ and $(S_B)^2 = (40)^2$ can be used as estimates for $\sigma_A^2$ and $\sigma_B^2$.  Substituting known values in the formula for Z, we have

$$Z = \frac{1180 - 1160}{\sqrt{\frac{14400}{100} + \frac{1600}{100}}} = \frac{20}{\sqrt{144 + 16}} = \frac{20}{\sqrt{160}} = \frac{20}{\sqrt{12.65}} = 1.58 .$$

Since $- 1.96 < (Z = 1.58) < 1.96$, Z is in the acceptance region.  Therefore, we accept the hypothesis that there is no difference between the average lifespans of the two brands, at the 5% significance level.

● **PROBLEM** 16-24

Suppose a sample of 50 employees in a particular firm has a mean wage rate of $160 per week with a standard error of the mean of $1.44.  Suppose also that a sample of 40 employees taken from another firm has a mean weekly wage rate of $155 and a standard error of the mean of $1.50. Test the difference between these two means at a 5% level of significance.

<u>Solution:</u>    We choose our hypotheses as follows:

$$H_0 : \mu_{X_1} - \mu_{X_2} = 0 \qquad H_1 : \mu_{X_1} - \mu_{X_2} \neq 0 .$$

This problem can be depicted by the following diagram.

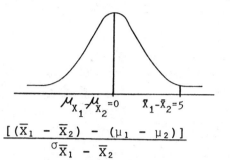

The statistic    $\dfrac{[(\bar{X}_1 - \bar{X}_2) - (\mu_1 - \mu_2)]}{\sigma_{\bar{X}_1 - \bar{X}_2}}$

has a standard normal distribution with a mean of 0 and a standard deviation of 1.  We call this statistic Z and compare its value to a critical value.  If Z lies beyond this critical value, we will reject $H_0$.  For this problem, where we have $\alpha$ = 5% and a two-tailed test, our critical value is 1.96, since for the standard normal distribution, 2.5% of scores will have a Z-value above 1.96 and 2.5% of scores will have a value below - 1.96.

Therefore, our decision rule is:  reject $H_0$ if Z > 1.96 or Z < - 1.96; accept $H_0$ if - 1.96 $\leq$ Z $\leq$ 1.96. We calculate

$$Z = \frac{\bar{X}_1 - \bar{X}_2 - 0}{\sigma_{\bar{X}_1 - \bar{X}_2}} \qquad \text{where}$$

$$\sigma_{\bar{X}_1 - \bar{X}_2} = \sqrt{\sigma_{\bar{X}_1}^2 + \sigma_{\bar{X}_2}^2} .$$

For the data of this problem,

$$\sigma_{\bar{X}_1 - \bar{X}_2} = \sqrt{(1.44)^2 + (1.50)^2}$$

$$= \sqrt{2.07 + 2.25}$$

$$= \sqrt{4.32} = 2.08 \qquad \text{and}$$

$$Z = \frac{160 - 155}{2.08} = \frac{5}{2.08} = 2.40 .$$

Since 2.40 > 1.96, we reject $H_0$ and conclude that there is a difference between the two mean wage rates at a 5% level of significance.

● **PROBLEM** 16-25

A manufacturer suspects a difference in the quality of the spare parts he receives from two suppliers.  He obtains the following data on the service life of random samples of parts from two suppliers.  For supplier A, $n_1$ = 50,

$\bar{X}_1 = 150$, and $S_1 = 10$; for supplier B, $n_2 = 100$, $\bar{X}_2 = 153$, and $S_2 = 5$. Test whether the difference between the 2 samples is statistically significant at the 1% level of significance.

Solution: The statistic $\dfrac{(\bar{X}_1 - \bar{X}_2) - (\mu_1 - \mu_2)}{S_{\bar{X}_1 - \bar{X}_2}}$

is approximately normally distributed with a mean of 0 and a standard deviation of 1. We call this statistic Z.

We must calculate $Z = \dfrac{(\bar{X}_1 - \bar{X}_2) - 0}{S_{\bar{X}_1 - \bar{X}_2}}$ where

$S_{\bar{X}_1 - \bar{X}_2} = \sqrt{\dfrac{S_1{}^2}{n_1} + \dfrac{S_2{}^2}{n_2}}$ Our hypotheses are:

$H_0: \mu_1 - \mu_2 = 0$ $\qquad\qquad H_1: \mu_1 - \mu_2 \neq 0$.

We compare Z to a critical value, and if Z lies beyond this critical value, we will reject $H_0$. For this problem, where we have $\alpha = .01$ and a two-tailed test, our critical value is 2.58, since for the normal distribution with mean of 0 and standard deviation of 1, 0.5% of scores will have a Z-value above 2.58 and 0.5% of scores will have a Z-value below − 2.58.

Therefore, our decision rule is: reject $H_0$ if $Z > 2.58$ or $Z < -2.58$; accept $H_0$ if $-2.58 \leq Z \leq 2.58$.

For the data of this problem

$$S_{\bar{X}_1 - \bar{X}_2} = \sqrt{\dfrac{10^2}{50} + \dfrac{5^2}{100}} = \sqrt{\dfrac{100}{50} + \dfrac{25}{100}}$$

$$= \sqrt{2.25} = 1.5 \qquad \text{and}$$

$$Z = \dfrac{(150 - 153) - 0}{1.5} = \dfrac{-3}{1.5} = -2.$$

Since $-2.58 < -2 < 2.58$, we accept $H_0$ and conclude that there is no significant difference between the two samples at a 1% level of significance.

● **PROBLEM 16-26**

A consumer agency wishes to compare the average life of two brands of batteries. A team of researchers selects 100 batteries of each brand. The first sample has an average life of 47 hours and a standard deviation of 4 hours. The second sample has an average life of 48 hours with standard deviation of 3 hours. Decide whether the difference of sample means is significant at the .05 level.

Solution: We establish the null hypothesis $H_0: \mu_2 - \mu_1 = 0$ and the alternate hypothesis $H_1: \mu_2 - \mu_1 \neq 0$, where $\mu_1$ and $\mu_2$ are the population means from which the

first and second samples were chosen.  Then we compute the
Z-score for the difference of sample means to see whether
it falls in the acceptance region (Z= -1.96, Z = 1.96)
for the .05 significance level.

$$Z = \frac{(\overline{X}_2 - \overline{X}_1) - 0}{S_{\overline{X}_2 - \overline{X}_1}} \qquad \text{where}$$

$$S_{\overline{X}_2 - \overline{X}_1} = \sqrt{\frac{S_1^2}{n_1} + \frac{S_2^2}{n_2}} \; .$$

The figure below depicts this problem:

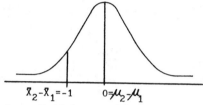

$\overline{X}_2 - \overline{X}_1 = -1 \qquad 0 = \mu_2 - \mu_1$

For the data of this problem:

$$S_{\overline{X}_2 - \overline{X}_1} = \sqrt{\frac{4^2}{100} + \frac{3^2}{100}} = \sqrt{\frac{16}{100} + \frac{9}{100}}$$

$$= \sqrt{\frac{1}{4}} = .5 \qquad \text{and}$$

$$Z = \frac{(4.8 - 4.7) - 0}{.5} = \frac{1}{.5} = 2.$$

Since    2 does not fall in the acceptance region
(- 1.96, 1.96), we reject $H_0$ and conclude that there is a
significant difference between the means of the two samples
at the 5% significance level.

● **PROBLEM** 16-27

A random sample of 120 students attending Florida State
University has a mean age of 20.2 years and a standard
deviation of 1.2 years while a random sample of 100
students attending the University of Florida has a mean
age of 21 years and a standard deviation of 1.5 years.
At a .05 level of significance, can we conclude that the
average age of the students at the two universities are
not the same?

Solution:    We choose as our null and alternate hypotheses
the following.

$H_0 : \mu_2 - \mu_1 = 0$ $\qquad\qquad$ $H_1 : \mu_2 - \mu_1 \neq 0$

where  $\overline{X}_1 = 20.2$, $S_1 = 1.2$, $n_1 = 120$, $\overline{X}_2 = 21$, $S_2 = 1.5$,
$n_2 = 100$, and $\alpha = .05$.  This problem is depicted by the
following figure.

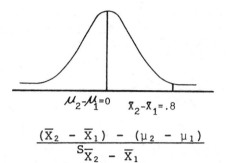

$$\mu_2 - \mu_1 = 0 \qquad \bar{X}_2 - \bar{X}_1 = .8$$

The statistic $\dfrac{(\bar{X}_2 - \bar{X}_1) - (\mu_2 - \mu_1)}{S_{\bar{X}_2 - \bar{X}_1}}$

is approximately normally distributed with a mean of 0 and a standard deviation of 1 when the size of our samples is large ($n_1 + n_2 > 30$).

For a level of significance of $\alpha = .05$ and a two-tailed test, our decision rule is: reject $H_0$ if $Z > 1.96$, or $Z < -1.96$; accept $H_0$ if $1.96 \le Z \le 1.96$. We must calculate

$$Z = \frac{(\bar{X}_2 - \bar{X}_1) - 0}{S_{\bar{X}_2 - \bar{X}_1}} \qquad \text{where}$$

$$S_{\bar{X}_2 - \bar{X}_1} = \sqrt{\frac{S_1^2}{n_1} + \frac{S_2^2}{n_2}} \quad .$$

For the data of this example,

$$S_{\bar{X}_2 - \bar{X}_1} = \sqrt{\frac{(1.2)^2}{120} + \frac{(1.5)^2}{100}} = \sqrt{\frac{1.44}{120} + \frac{2.25}{100}}$$

$$= \sqrt{.012 + .0225} = .186 \qquad \text{and}$$

$$Z = \frac{(21 - 20.2) - 0}{.186} = \frac{.8}{.186} = 4.30 \quad .$$

Since $4.30 > 1.96$, we reject $H_0$ and conclude there is a significant difference at the 5% level of significance between the average ages of the students at the two universities.

● **PROBLEM** 16-28

A recent report claims that college non-graduates get married at an earlier age than college graduates. To support the claim, random samples of size 100 were selected from each group, and the mean age at the time of marriage was recorded. The mean and standard deviation of the college non-graduates were 22.5 years and 1.4 years respectively, while the mean and standard deviation of the college graduates were 23 years and 1.8 years. Test the claims of the report at the .05 level of significance.

Solution: The wording of the problem calls for a one-tailed test. If we let $\mu_1$ = average age at which non-graduates marry and $\mu_2$ = average age at which graduates marry, we have for our hypotheses:

$$H_0: \mu_1 - \mu_2 \geq 0 \qquad\qquad H_1: \mu_1 - \mu_2 < 0 .$$

This problem is depicted in the figure below.

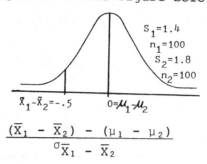

The statistic $\qquad \dfrac{(\overline{X}_1 - \overline{X}_2) - (\mu_1 - \mu_2)}{{}^{\sigma}\overline{X}_1 - \overline{X}_2}$

is approximately normally distributed with a mean of 0 and a standard deviation of 1 when the size of the samples is large ($n_1 + n_2 > 30$).

Our decision rule for a level of significance of $\alpha = .05$ is: reject $H_0$ if $Z < - 1.64$; accept $H_0$ if $Z \geq - 1.64$. We must calculate

$$Z = \frac{(\overline{X}_1 - \overline{X}_2) - 0}{S\overline{X}_1 - \overline{X}_2} \qquad\qquad \text{where}$$

$$S\overline{X}_1 - \overline{X}_2 = \sqrt{\frac{S_1^2}{n_1} + \frac{S_2^2}{n_2}} .$$

For the data of this problem we have

$$S\overline{X}_1 - \overline{X}_2 = \sqrt{\frac{(1.4)^2}{100} + \frac{(1.8)^2}{100}} = \sqrt{\frac{1.96}{100} + \frac{3.24}{100}}$$

$$= \sqrt{.0520} = .229 \qquad\qquad \text{and}$$

$$Z = \frac{(22.5 - 23) - 0}{.229} = \frac{- .5}{.229} = - 2.18 .$$

Since $- 2.18 < - 1.64$, we reject $H_0$ and conclude at a 5% level of significance that college non-graduates do marry at an earlier age than college graduates.

● PROBLEM 16-29

A toothpaste manufacturer wants to determine whether the addition of a certain chemical to his toothpaste will increase its ability to fight tooth decay. Two groups of 100 people each are chosen and an experiment is conducted. Of the 100 people using the toothpaste with the chemical addition for a specified period of time, the manufacturer finds that they have an average of 8 cavities and a standard deviation of 3 cavities. The average number of cavities of the 100 people using the toothpaste without

the chemical addition is 9 with a standard deviation of 4.
Can we conclude at the 1% level of significance that the
addition of the chemical increased the toothpaste's ability
to fight tooth decay?

Solution:    Our hypotheses for this problem are

$H_1: \mu_1 - \mu_2 < 0.$          $H_0: \mu_1 - \mu_2 \geq 0$

The figure below depicts the problem.

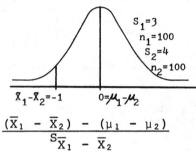

The statistic    $\dfrac{(\bar{X}_1 - \bar{X}_2) - (\mu_1 - \mu_2)}{S_{\bar{X}_1 - \bar{X}_2}}$

is approximately normal with a mean of 0 and a standard
deviation of 1 when the size of the samples is large
$(n_1 + n_2 > 30)$.

Our decision rule for this problem, where $\alpha = .01$
and we have a one-tailed test, is:   reject $H_0$ if $Z < -2.33$;
accept $H_0$ if $Z \geq -2.33$. We must calculate

$$Z = \dfrac{(\bar{X}_1 - \bar{X}_2) - 0}{S_{\bar{X}_1 - \bar{X}_2}}          \text{where}$$

$$S_{\bar{X}_1 - \bar{X}_2} = \sqrt{\dfrac{S_1^2}{n_1} + \dfrac{S_2^2}{n_2}} \, .$$

For the data of this problem

$$S_{\bar{X}_1 - \bar{X}_2} = \sqrt{\dfrac{3^2}{100} + \dfrac{4^2}{100}} = \sqrt{\dfrac{25}{100}} = .5          \text{and}$$

$$Z = \dfrac{(4 - 5) - 0}{.5} = \dfrac{-1}{.5} = -2 .$$

Since $-2 > -2.33$, we accept $H_0$ and conclude at a 1%
level of significance that the addition of the chemical did
not increase the toothpaste's ability to fight tooth decay.

# DIFFERENCES BETWEEN MEANS: t-TESTS

● **PROBLEM** 16-30

A reading test is given to an elementary school class that
consists of 12 Anglo-American children and 10 Mexican-
American children.  The results of the test are - Anglo-
American children: $\bar{X}_1 = 74$, $S_1 = 8$; Mexican-American

children: $\overline{X}_2 = 70$, $S_2 = 10$. Is the difference between the means of the two groups significant at the .05 level of significance?

<u>Solution:</u>     Assuming the test scores are normally distributed, we may use the t-test with $n_1 + n_2 - 2$ degrees of freedom to test the significance of the difference between the means because the statistic

$$\frac{(\overline{X}_2 - \overline{X}_1) - (\mu_2 - \mu_1)}{S_{\overline{X}_2 - \overline{X}_1}}$$

has a t-distribution when $n_1 + n_2 \leq 30$. The figure below depicts this problem.

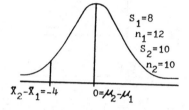

We have for our null and alternate hypotheses

$H_0$: $\mu_2 - \mu_1 = 0$          $H_1$: $\mu_2 - \mu_1 \neq 0$.

We must calculate          $t = \dfrac{(\overline{X}_2 - \overline{X}_1) - 0}{S_{\overline{X}_2 - \overline{X}_1}}$          where

$$S_{\overline{X}_2 - \overline{X}_1} = \sqrt{\frac{(n_1 - 1)S_1^2 + (n_2 - 1)S_2^2}{n_1 + n_2 - 2}} \sqrt{\frac{1}{n_1} + \frac{1}{n_2}}.$$

The critical t for $n_1 + n_2 - 2 = 20$ df's and a two-tailed test at $\alpha = .05$ is 2.09 because for the t-distribution with mean of 0 and standard deviation of 1, 2.5% scores will have a t-value greater than 2.09 and 2.5% of scores will have a t-value less than - 2.09. Therefore, our decision rule is: reject $H_0$ if t > 2.09 or t < - 2.09; accept $H_0$ if - 2.09 $\leq$ t $\leq$ 2.09.

For the data of this problem,

$$S_{\overline{X}_2 - \overline{X}_1} = \sqrt{\frac{11(8)^2 + 9(10)^2}{12 + 10 - 2}} \sqrt{\frac{1}{12} + \frac{1}{10}}$$

$$= \sqrt{\frac{704 + 900}{20}} \sqrt{.0833 + .1}$$

$$= \sqrt{80.2} \sqrt{.1833} = 3.834 \qquad \text{and}$$

$$t = \frac{(70 - 74) - 0}{3.834} = \frac{- 4}{3.834} = - 1.04.$$

Since - 2.09 < - 1.04 < 2.09, we accept $H_0$ and conclude that the difference between the means of the two groups is not significant.

From appropriately selected samples, two sets of IQ scores are obtained. For group 1, $\bar{X} = 104$, $S = 10$, and $n = 16$; for group 2, $\bar{X} = 112$, $S = 8$, and $n = 14$. At the 5% significance level is there a significant difference between the 2 groups?

Solution:   For this problem, we have for our hypotheses

$H_0: \mu_1 - \mu_2 = 0$          $H_1: \mu_1 - \mu_2 \neq 0$.

This problem can be depicted by the following diagram.

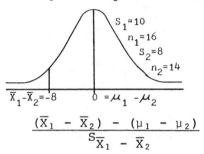

The statistic          $\dfrac{(\bar{X}_1 - \bar{X}_2) - (\mu_1 - \mu_2)}{S_{\bar{X}_1 - \bar{X}_2}}$

has a t-distribution when $n_1 + n_2 \leq 30$.

We have $n_1 + n_2 - 2 = 28$ df's and so our decision rule for $\alpha = .05$ is:   reject $H_0$ if $t > 2.048$ or $t < -2.048$; accept $H_0$ if $-2.048 \leq t \leq 2.048$.   We must calculate

$\quad t = \dfrac{(\bar{X}_1 - \bar{X}_2) - (\mu_1 - \mu_2)}{S_{\bar{X}_1 - \bar{X}_2}}$          where

$S_{\bar{X}_1 - \bar{X}_2} = \sqrt{\dfrac{(n_1 - 1)S_1^2 + (n_2 - 1)S_2^2}{n_1 + n_2 - 2}} \; \sqrt{\dfrac{1}{n_1} + \dfrac{1}{n_2}}$ .

For the data of this problem,

$S_{\bar{X}_1 - \bar{X}_2} = \sqrt{\dfrac{15(10)^2 + (13)(8)^2}{28}} \; \sqrt{\dfrac{1}{16} + \dfrac{1}{14}}$

$\qquad = \sqrt{\dfrac{15(100) + 13(64)}{28}} \; \sqrt{.0625 + .0714}$

$\qquad = \sqrt{\dfrac{1500 + 832}{28}} \; \sqrt{.1339}$

$\qquad = \sqrt{83.29} \; \sqrt{.1339} = 3.34$          and

$\quad t = \dfrac{(105 - 112) - 0}{3.34} = \dfrac{-8}{3.34} = -2.40$ .

Since $-2.40 < -2.048$, we reject $H_0$ and conclude that there is a significant difference between the scores of the 2 groups at the 5% level of significance.

A group of babies all of whom weighed approximately the
same at birth are randomly divided into two groups. The
babies in sample 1 were fed formula A; those in sample 2
were fed formula B. The weight gains attained from birth
to age six months were recorded for each baby. The results
were as follows: sample 1: 5, 7, 8, 9, 6, 7, 10, 8, 6;
sample 2: 9, 10, 8, 6, 8, 7, 9. We desire to know whether
either formula A or formula B is more effective than the
other in producing weight gains. Test for this at the .05
level of significance.

**Solution:** Since we have no preconceived notions about
which formula may be more effective in producing weight
gains, we will use a two-tailed test. We have

$$H_0: \mu_A - \mu_B = 0 \qquad\qquad H_1: \mu_A - \mu_B \neq 0 .$$

The statistic $\dfrac{(\bar{X}_1 - \bar{X}_2) - (\mu_1 - \mu_2)}{S_{\bar{X}_1 - \bar{X}_2}}$

has a t-distribution when $n_1 + n_2 \leq 30$.

At a .05 level of significance our decision rule is:
reject $H_0$ if $t > 2.145$ or $t < -2.145$ (critical t value for
$n_1 + n_2 - 2 = 9 + 7 - 2 = 14$ df's is 2.145); accept $H_0$ if
$-2.145 \leq t \leq 2.145$. We must calculate

$$t = \frac{(\bar{X}_1 - \bar{X}_2) - 0}{S_{\bar{X}_1 - \bar{X}_2}} \qquad \text{where}$$

$$S_{\bar{X}_1 - \bar{X}_2} = \sqrt{\frac{(n_1 - 1)S_1{}^2 + (n_2 - 1)S_2{}^2}{n_1 + n_2 - 2}} \; \sqrt{\frac{1}{n_1} + \frac{1}{n_2}} .$$

But first we must calculate $\bar{X}_1$, $\bar{X}_2$, $S_1$, and $S_2$.

$$\bar{X}_1 = \frac{\Sigma X_1}{n_1} = \frac{5 + 7 + \ldots + 6}{9} = \frac{66}{9} = 7.33 .$$

$$\bar{X}_2 = \frac{\Sigma X_2}{n_2} = \frac{9 + 10 + \ldots + 9}{7} = \frac{57}{7} = 8.14 .$$

To calculate $S_1$ and $S_2$, it is helpful to set up the
following chart.

| $X_1$ | $X_2$ | $X_1{}^2$ | $X_2{}^2$ |
|-------|-------|-----------|-----------|
| 5 | 9 | 25 | 81 |
| 7 | 10 | 49 | 100 |
| 8 | 8 | 64 | 64 |
| 9 | 6 | 81 | 36 |
| 6 | 8 | 36 | 64 |
| 7 | 7 | 49 | 49 |
| 10 | 9 | 100 | 81 |
| 8 | 57 | 64 | 475 |
| 6 | | 36 | |
| 66 | | 504 | |

$$S_1 = \sqrt{\frac{n_1 \Sigma X_1{}^2 - (\Sigma X_1)^2}{n_1(n_1 - 1)}} = \sqrt{\frac{9(504) - (66)^2}{9(8)}}$$

$$= \sqrt{\frac{4536 - 4356}{9(8)}} = \sqrt{\frac{180}{72}} = 1.58;$$

$$S_2 = \sqrt{\frac{n_2 \Sigma X_2{}^2 - (\Sigma X_2)^2}{n_2(n_2 - 1)}} = \sqrt{\frac{7(475) - (57)^2}{7(6)}}$$

$$= \sqrt{\frac{3325 - 3249}{7(6)}} = \sqrt{\frac{76}{42}} = 1.35 .$$

Now we can calculate

$$S_{\overline{X}_1 - \overline{X}_2} = \sqrt{\frac{8(1.58)^2 + 6(1.35)^2}{14}} \sqrt{\frac{1}{9} + \frac{1}{7}}$$

$$= \sqrt{\frac{8(2.50) + 6(1.82)}{14}} \sqrt{.2540}$$

$$= \sqrt{\frac{20 + 10.92}{14}} (.50) = (1.49)(.50)$$

$$= .745 \qquad \text{and}$$

$$t = \frac{(7.33 - 8.14) - 0}{.745} = - \frac{.81}{.745} = - 1.09 .$$

Since $- 2.145 \le - 1.09 \le 2.145$, we accept $H_0$ and conclude that there is no difference in the abilities of formula A and formula B to produce weight gains in babies during the period from birth to age 6 months at a .05 level of significance.

● **PROBLEM** 16-33

A consumer report shows that in testing 8 tires of brand A the mean life of the tires was 20,000 miles with a standard deviation of 2,500 miles. Twelve tires of brand B were tested under similar conditions with a mean life of 23,000 miles and a standard deviation of 2,800 miles. If a .05 level of significance is used, does the data present sufficient evidence to indicate a difference in the average life of the two brands of tires?

Solution:    For this problem, we have for our hypotheses

$H_0: \mu_A - \mu_B = 0$

$H_1: \mu_A - \mu_B \ne 0.$

This problem can be depicted by the following diagram:

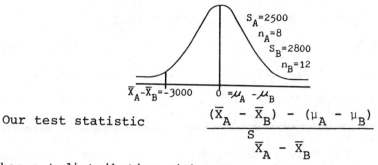

$$S_A = 2500$$
$$n_A = 8$$
$$S_B = 2800$$
$$n_B = 12$$

$$\overline{X}_A - \overline{X}_B = -3000 \qquad 0 = \mu_A - \mu_B$$

Our test statistic
$$\frac{(\overline{X}_A - \overline{X}_B) - (\mu_A - \mu_B)}{S_{\overline{X}_A - \overline{X}_B}}$$

has a t-distribution with a mean of 0 and a standard deviation of 1 since $n_1 + n_2 \leq 30$.

We have $n_A + n_B - 2 = 18$ df's and for $\alpha = .05$ our decision rule is: reject $H_0$ if $t > 2.101$ or $t < -2.101$; accept $H_0$ is $-2.101 \leq t \leq 2.101$.

We must calculate

$$t = \frac{(\overline{X}_A - \overline{X}_B) - (\mu_A - \mu_B)}{S_{\overline{X}_A - \overline{X}_B}} \qquad \text{where}$$

$$S_{\overline{X}_A - \overline{X}_B} = \sqrt{\frac{(n_A - 1)S_A^{\;2} + (n_B - 1)S_B^{\;2}}{n_A + n_B - 2}} \cdot \sqrt{\frac{1}{n_A} + \frac{1}{n_B}} \;.$$

For the data of this problem we have

$$S_{\overline{X}_A - \overline{X}_B} = \sqrt{\frac{7(2500)^2 + 11(2800)^2}{18}} \cdot \sqrt{\frac{1}{8} + \frac{1}{12}}$$

$$= \sqrt{\frac{7(6250000) + 11(7840000)}{18}} \cdot \sqrt{\frac{5}{24}}$$

$$= \sqrt{\frac{43750000 + 86240000}{18}} \cdot \sqrt{\frac{5}{24}}$$

$$= \sqrt{7221666.6} \cdot \sqrt{\frac{5}{24}}$$

$$= 1227 \text{ and}$$

$$t = \frac{(20,000 - 23,000) - 0}{1227} = \frac{-3000}{1227} = -2.44 \;.$$

Since $-2.44 < -2.101$, we reject $H_0$ and conclude that at a 5% level of significance the evidence does indicate a difference in the average life of the two brands of tires.

● PROBLEM 16-34

Two separate groups of subjects were tested. The experimental group (Group E) had 10 subjects; the control group (Group C) had 9 subjects. The data are given below; the scores are assumed to be normally distributed.

Group E: 12, 13, 16, 14, 15, 12, 15, 14, 13, and 16.

Group C: 10, 13, 14, 12, 15, 16, 12, 14, and 11.

Determine whether the means of the two groups differ significantly at the .05 level of significance.

Solution: For this problem, we have for our hypotheses
$H_0: \mu_E - \mu_C = 0$     $H_1: \mu_E - \mu_C \neq 0$ .

The statistic     $\dfrac{(\overline{X}_E - \overline{X}_C) - (\mu_E - \mu_C)}{S_{\overline{X}_E - \overline{X}_C}}$

has a t-distribution because $n_1 + n_2 \leq 30$.

We have $n_1 + n_2 - 2 = 10 + 9 - 2 = 17$ df's and so our decision rule is: reject $H_0$ if $t > 2.110$ or if $t < -2.110$, accept $H_0$ if $-2.110 \leq t \leq 2.110$. We must calculate

$$t = \dfrac{(\overline{X}_E - \overline{X}_C) - 0}{S_{\overline{X}_E - \overline{X}_C}} \qquad \text{where}$$

$$S_{\overline{X}_E - \overline{X}_C} = \sqrt{\dfrac{\left[\Sigma X_E{}^2 - \dfrac{(\Sigma X_E)^2}{n_E}\right] + \left[\Sigma X_C{}^2 - \dfrac{(\Sigma X_C)^2}{n_C}\right]}{n_E + n_C - 2}}$$

$$\cdot \sqrt{\dfrac{1}{n_E} + \dfrac{1}{n_C}} \cdot$$

For the data of this problem, we can construct the following table as aid in finding $S_{\overline{X}_E - \overline{X}_C}$ .

| $X_E$ | $X_E{}^2$ | $X_C$ | $X_C{}^2$ |
|-------|-----------|-------|-----------|
| 12 | 144 | 10 | 100 |
| 13 | 169 | 13 | 169 |
| 16 | 256 | 14 | 196 |
| 14 | 196 | 12 | 144 |
| 15 | 225 | 15 | 225 |
| 12 | 144 | 16 | 256 |
| 15 | 225 | 12 | 144 |
| 14 | 196 | 14 | 196 |
| 13 | 169 | 11 | 121 |
| 16 | 256 | 117 | 1551 |
| 140 | 1980 | | |

$\overline{X}_E = 14$          $\overline{X}_C = 13$

600

Substituting the values obtained from this table in the above formulas, we have

$$S_{\bar{X}_E - \bar{X}_C} = \sqrt{\frac{\left[1980 - \frac{(140)^2}{10}\right] + \left[1551 - \frac{(117)^2}{9}\right]}{10 + 9 - 2}}$$

$$\cdot \sqrt{\frac{1}{10} + \frac{1}{9}}$$

$$= \sqrt{\frac{(1980 - 1960) + (1551 - 1521)}{17}} \sqrt{\frac{19}{90}}$$

$$= \sqrt{\frac{(20) + (30)}{17}} \sqrt{\frac{19}{90}} = (1.71)(.46)$$

$$= .79 \qquad \text{and}$$

$$t = \frac{(14 - 13) - 0}{.79} = \frac{1}{.79} = 1.27.$$

Since $-2.110 < 1.27 < 2.110$, we accept $H_0$ and conclude that the means of the 2 groups do not differ significantly at the 5% level of significance.

● **PROBLEM 16-35**

Suppose we have a type of battery for which we take a sample of 10 batteries. The mean operating life of these batteries is 18.0 hours with a standard deviation of 3.0 hours. Suppose also that we have a new type of battery for which we take a sample of 17 batteries. The mean of this sample is 22.0 hours with a standard deviation of 6.0 hours. Determine for a 1% level of significance whether there is a significant difference between the means of the two samples. Also determine at a 1% level of significance whether we can conclude that the new batteries are superior to the old ones.

Solution:    To test whether there is a significant difference between the two means we have as our hypotheses

$H_0 : \mu_1 - \mu_2 = 0$ $\qquad\qquad$ $H_1 : \mu_1 - \mu_2 \neq 0$ .

This problem can be depicted by the following diagram:

$S_1 = 3.0$
$n_1 = 10$
$S_2 = 6.0$
$n_2 = 17$

$\bar{X}_1 - \bar{X}_2 = -4$ $\qquad 0 = \mu_1 - \mu_2$

The statistic $\qquad\qquad \dfrac{(\bar{X}_1 - \bar{X}_2) - (\mu_1 - \mu_2)}{S_{\bar{X}_1 - \bar{X}_2}}$

has a t-distribution because $n_1 + n_2 \le 30$.

We have $n_1 + n_2 - 2 = 25$ df's and so for $\alpha = .01$ we have for our decision rule: reject $H_0$ if $t > 2.787$ or $t < -2.787$; accept $H_0$ if $-2.787 \le t \le 2.787$.

We must calculate

$$t = \frac{(\bar{X}_1 - \bar{X}_2) - (\mu_1 - \mu_2)}{S_{\bar{X}_1 - \bar{X}_2}} \qquad \text{where}$$

$$S_{\bar{X}_1 - \bar{X}_2} = \sqrt{\frac{(n_1 - 1)S_1^2 + (n_2 - 1)S_2^2}{n_1 + n_2 - 2}} \sqrt{\frac{1}{n_1} + \frac{1}{n_2}} \ .$$

For the data of this problem

$$S_{\bar{X}_1 - \bar{X}_2} = \sqrt{\frac{9(3.0)^2 + 16(6.0)^2}{25}} \cdot \sqrt{\frac{1}{10} + \frac{1}{17}}$$

$$= \sqrt{\frac{9(9) + 16(36)}{25}} \cdot \sqrt{\frac{27}{170}}$$

$$= \sqrt{\frac{81 + 576}{25}} \cdot \sqrt{\frac{27}{170}} = \sqrt{\frac{657}{25}} \cdot \sqrt{\frac{27}{170}}$$

$$= 2.04 \qquad \text{and}$$

$$t = \frac{(\bar{X}_1 - \bar{X}_2) - 0}{S_{\bar{X}_1 - \bar{X}_2}} = \frac{(18 - 22) - 0}{2.04} = \frac{-4}{2.04}$$

$$= -1.96 \ .$$

Since $-2.787 \le -1.96 \le 2.787$, we accept $H_0$, and conclude that there is not a significant difference between the old and the new batteries at a 1% level of significance.

Now to test whether the new batteries are superior to the old ones, our hypotheses become

$$H_0: \mu_1 - \mu_2 > 0$$

$$H_1: \mu_1 - \mu_2 \le 0$$

and our decision rule is: reject $H_0$ if $t < -2.485$; accept $H_0$ if $t > -2.485$. Since our calculated value for t was $-1.96$ and since $-1.96 > -2.485$, we will accept $H_0$. Therefore from this sample of data we cannot conclude that the new batteries are superior to the old ones.

● PROBLEM 16-36

For the following samples of data, compute t and determine whether $\mu_1$ is significantly less than $\mu_2$. For your test use a level of significance of .10. Sample 1: n = 10, $\bar{X}$ = 10.0, S = 5.2; sample 2: n = 10, $\bar{X}$ = 13.3, S = 5.7.

<u>Solution:</u>    For this problem, we have for our hypotheses

$H_0 : \mu_1 - \mu_2 \geq 0$                    $H_1 : \mu_1 - \mu_2 < 0.$

This problem can be depicted by the following diagram:

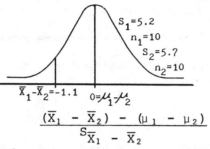

The statistic          $\dfrac{(\bar{X}_1 - \bar{X}_2) - (\mu_1 - \mu_2)}{S_{\bar{X}_1 - \bar{X}_2}}$

has a t-distribution because $n_1 + n_2 \leq 30.$

We have $n_1 + n_2 - 2 = 18$ df's and our decision rule
for $\alpha = .10$ is: reject $H_0$ if $t < -1.330$; accept $H_0$ if
$t \geq -1.330.$

We must calculate

$t = \dfrac{(\bar{X}_1 - \bar{X}_2) - (\mu_1 - \mu_2)}{S_{\bar{X}_1 - \bar{X}_2}}$          where

$S_{\bar{X}_1 - \bar{X}_2} = \sqrt{\dfrac{(n_1 - 1)S_1^2 + (n_2 - 1)S_2^2}{n_1 + n_2 - 2}} \cdot \sqrt{\dfrac{1}{n_1} + \dfrac{1}{n_2}} \ .$

For the data of this problem we have

$S_{\bar{X}_1 - \bar{X}_2} = \sqrt{\dfrac{9(5.2)^2 + 9(5.7)^2}{18}} \cdot \sqrt{\dfrac{1}{10} + \dfrac{1}{10}}$

$= \sqrt{\dfrac{9(27.04) + 9(32.49)}{18}} \cdot \sqrt{\dfrac{1}{5}}$

$= \sqrt{\dfrac{243.36 + 292.41}{18}} \cdot \sqrt{\dfrac{1}{5}}$

$= \sqrt{29.765} \cdot \sqrt{\dfrac{1}{5}} = 2.44$          and

$t = \dfrac{(10.0 - 13.3) - 0}{2.44} = \dfrac{-3.3}{2.44} = -1.35 \ .$

Since $-1.35 < -1.330$, we reject $H_0$ and conclude that
$\mu_2$ is significantly less than $\mu_1$ at a 10% level of significance.

● **PROBLEM 16-37**

A college dean wants to determine if the students entering
the college in a given year have higher IQ's than the
students entering the same college in the previous year.

The IQ's of the college entrants in the two years are known to be normally distributed and to have equal variances. A random sample of four students from this year's entering class gives IQ scores of 110, 113, 116, and 117. Another random sample of four students from last year's entering class gives IQ scores of 109, 111, 112, and 112. At the 5% level of significance, can we conclude that this year's students have a higher IQ than last years?

Solution:  For this problem we have for our hypotheses

$H_0: \mu_1 - \mu_2 \leq 0$   $H_1: \mu_1 - \mu_2 > 0.$

The statistic $\dfrac{(\overline{X}_1 - \overline{X}_2) - (\mu_1 - \mu_2)}{S_{\overline{X}_1 - \overline{X}_2}}$

has a t-distribution because $n_1 + n_2 \leq 30$.

We have $n_1 + n_2 - 2 = 6$ df's and a one-tailed test and so our decision rule is: reject $H_0$ if $t > 1.943$; accept $H_0$ if $t \leq 1.943$.

We must calculate  $t = \dfrac{(\overline{X}_1 - \overline{X}_2) - (\mu_1 - \mu_2)}{S_{\overline{X}_1 - \overline{X}_2}}$    where

$$S_{\overline{X}_1 - \overline{X}_2} = \sqrt{\frac{\Sigma(X_1 - \overline{X}_1)^2 + \Sigma(X_2 - \overline{X}_2)^2}{n_1 + n_2 - 2}} \cdot \sqrt{\frac{1}{n_1} + \frac{1}{n_2}} .$$

For this problem we have the following table of data, used to help compute $S_{\overline{X}_1 - \overline{X}_2}$.

|  | $X_1$ | $X_2$ | $(X_1 - \overline{X}_1)^2$ | $(X_2 - \overline{X}_2)^2$ |
|---|---|---|---|---|
|  | 110 | 109 | 16 | 4 |
|  | 113 | 111 | 1 | 0 |
|  | 116 | 112 | 4 | 1 |
|  | 117 | 112 | 9 | 1 |
| Sums | 456 | 444 | 30 | 6 |

$\overline{X}_1 = 114$    $\overline{X}_2 = 111$

Substituting the results from this table yields

$$S_{\overline{X}_1 - \overline{X}_2} = \sqrt{\frac{30 + 6}{6}} \cdot \sqrt{\frac{1}{4} + \frac{1}{4}}$$

$$= \sqrt{6} \cdot \sqrt{\frac{1}{2}} = 1.732 \qquad \text{and}$$

$$t = \frac{(114 - 111) - 0}{1.732} = \frac{3}{1.732} = 1.732 .$$

Since $1.732 < 1.943$, we accept $H_0$ and conclude that at a 5% level of significance the students entering the college this year do not have IQ's higher than the students entering in the previous year.

Given the following samples, test the hypothesis,
$H_0: \mu_1 - \mu_2 \leq 3$, versus hypothesis, $H_1: \mu_1 - \mu_2 > 3$ at
a 10% level of significance.

Sample 1: 51, 42, 49, 55, 46, 63, 56, 58, 47, 39, 47.

Sample 2: 38, 49, 45, 29, 31, 35.

Solution: The statistic $\dfrac{(\overline{X}_1 - \overline{X}_2) - (\mu_1 - \mu_2)}{S_{\overline{X}_1 - \overline{X}_2}}$
has a t-distribution because $n_1 + n_2 \leq 30$.

For a one-tailed test at a level of significance of
.10 and $n_1 + n_2 - 2 = 15$ df's, our decision rule is:
reject $H_0$ if $t > 1.341$; accept $H_0$ if $t \leq 1.341$. We must
calculate

$$t = \frac{(\overline{X}_1 - \overline{X}_2) - (\mu_1 - \mu_2)}{S_{\overline{X}_1 - \overline{X}_2}} \qquad \text{where}$$

$$S_{\overline{X}_1 - \overline{X}_2} = \sqrt{\frac{(n_1 - 1)S_1^2 + (n_2 - 1)S_2^2}{n_1 + n_2 - 2}} \cdot \sqrt{\frac{1}{n_1} + \frac{1}{n_2}}.$$

Before we apply these formulas however, we must
calculate $\overline{X}_1$, $\overline{X}_2$, $S_1$ and $S_2$. Setting up the following
table is helpful in performing these calculations:

| $X_1$ | $X_1{}^2$ | $X_2$ | $X_2{}^2$ |
|-------|-----------|-------|-----------|
| 51 | 2601 | 38 | 1444 |
| 42 | 1764 | 49 | 2401 |
| 49 | 2401 | 45 | 2025 |
| 55 | 3025 | 29 | 841 |
| 46 | 2116 | 31 | 961 |
| 63 | 3969 | 35 | 1225 |
| 56 | 3136 | 227 | 8897 |
| 58 | 3364 | | |
| 47 | 2209 | | |
| 39 | 1521 | | |
| 47 | 2209 | | |
| 553 | 28315 | | |

Using the table

$$\overline{X}_1 = \frac{\Sigma X_1}{n_1} = \frac{553}{11} = 50.27 \ ;$$

$$\overline{X}_2 = \frac{\Sigma X_2}{n_2} = \frac{227}{6} = 37.83 \ ;$$

$$S_1 = \sqrt{\frac{n_1 \Sigma X_1{}^2 - (\Sigma X_1)^2}{n_1(n_1 - 1)}} = \sqrt{\frac{11(28315) - (553)^2}{11(10)}}$$

$$= \sqrt{\frac{311465 - 305809}{110}} = \sqrt{\frac{5656}{110}} = 7.17$$

$$S_2 = \sqrt{\frac{n_2 \Sigma X_2{}^2 - (\Sigma X_2)^2}{n_2(n_2 - 1)}} = \sqrt{\frac{6(8897) - (227)^2}{6(5)}}$$

$$= \sqrt{\frac{53382 - 51529}{30}} = \sqrt{\frac{1853}{30}} = 7.86.$$

Now we can calculate

$$S_{\overline{X}_1 - \overline{X}_2} = \sqrt{\frac{10(51.41) + 5(61.78)}{15}} \cdot \sqrt{\frac{1}{11} + \frac{1}{6}}$$

$$= \sqrt{\frac{514.1 + 308.9}{15}} \cdot \sqrt{.2576}$$

$$= \sqrt{\frac{823}{15}} \cdot (.508) = 3.76 \qquad \text{and}$$

$$t = \frac{(50.27 - 37.83) - 3}{3.76} = \frac{9.44}{3.76} = 2.51.$$

Since $2.51 > 1.341$, we reject $H_0$ and accept $H_1$ that $\mu_1 - \mu_2 > 3$.

● **PROBLEM 16-39**

A manufacturer of transistors makes two brands, A and B. Brand A is supposed to have an average life of 60 hours more than brand B. To verify whether this is true, each month 9 transistors of each brand are tested and a t-value corresponding to the difference of the sample means is computed. The manufacturer is satisfied if the computed t-value falls between $- t_{.05}$ and $t_{.05}$. During one month, the sample of nine transistors from brand A had a mean life-span of 1000 hours and a standard deviation of 60 hours, while those of brand B had a mean life-span of 925 hours with a standard deviation of 50 hours. Assuming that the life-span of both brand A and brand B is normal, should the manufacturer be satisfied?

Solution:    For this problem, we have for our hypotheses

$H_0: \mu_A - \mu_B = 60$          $H_1: \mu_A - \mu_B \neq 60$.

This problem can be depicted by the following diagram:

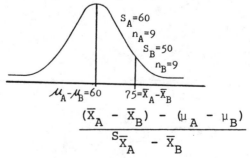

The statistic
$$\frac{(\overline{X}_A - \overline{X}_B) - (\mu_A - \mu_B)}{S_{\overline{X}_A - \overline{X}_B}}$$

has a t-distribution because $n_1 + n_2 \le 30$.

We have $n_A + n_B - 2 = 16$ df's and so our decision rule is: reject $H_0$ if $t > 1.746$ or $t < -1.746$; accept $H_0$ if $-1.746 \le t \le 1.746$. We must calculate

$$t = \frac{(\overline{X}_A - \overline{X}_B) - (\mu_A - \mu_B)}{S_{\overline{X}_A - \overline{X}_B}} \qquad \text{where}$$

$$S_{\overline{X}_A - \overline{X}_B} = \sqrt{\frac{(n_A - 1)S_A^2 + (n_B - 1)S_B^2}{n_A + n_B - 2}} \cdot \sqrt{\frac{1}{n_A} + \frac{1}{n_B}} \cdot$$

For the data of this problem we have

$$S_{\overline{X}_A - \overline{X}_B} = \sqrt{\frac{8(60)^2 + 8(50)^2}{16}} \cdot \sqrt{\frac{1}{9} + \frac{1}{9}}$$

$$= \sqrt{\frac{8(3600) + 8(2500)}{16}} \cdot \sqrt{\frac{2}{9}}$$

$$= \sqrt{\frac{28800 + 20000}{16}} \cdot (.47) = (55.23)(.47)$$

$$= 25.96 \qquad \text{and}$$

$$t = \frac{(1000 - 925) - 60}{25.96} = \frac{75 - 60}{25.96} = \frac{15}{25.96} = .58 \cdot$$

Since $-1.746 < .58 < 1.746$, we accept $H_0$, and conclude that for the month in question the manufacturer should be satisfied that brand A has an average life of 60 hours more than brand B.

● **PROBLEM** 16-40

You are studying problem solving performance using time as a measure. Your subjects usually either solve the problems quickly or take a long time, but only rarely do they take an intermediate amount of time. You select a sample of 10 subjects and give them training that you believe will reduce their mean time for solving the problem set. You wish to compare their performance with that of another sample of 10 who did not receive the instruction. Outline an appropriate statistical test and suggest changes in the plan of the experiment. Use a level of significance of .05.

Solution:    You cannot perform a statistical test for the experiment as planned. The samples are too small to use the normal distribution. To use the t distribution, we must be able to assume that the populations are approximately normally distributed. This is not the case as subjects usually solve the problem quickly or take a long time.

You may use the normal distribution if you change the design of the experiment so that our samples are of size 30 or more because then the statistic

$$\frac{(\bar{X}_1 - \bar{X}_2) - (\mu_1 - \mu_2)}{S_{\bar{X}_1 - \bar{X}_2}}$$

is approximately normally distributed. Then your statistical test becomes the following:

Define $\mu_1$, $\bar{X}_1$, $S_1$, and $n_1$ as the population mean, sample mean, sample standard deviation, and sample size respectively for the group receiving training. Let $\mu_2$, $\bar{X}_2$, $S_2$, and $n_2$ be the population mean, sample mean, sample standard deviation, and sample size respectively for the group not receiving training. Then we have:

Null Hypothesis, $H_0$: $\mu_1 - \mu_2 = 0$

Alternate Hypothesis, $H_1$: $\mu_1 - \mu_2 < 0$

Decision Rule: accept $H_0$ if $Z \geq -1.65$; reject $H_0$ if $Z < -1.65$, where

$$Z = \frac{(\bar{X}_1 - \bar{X}_2) - (\mu_1 - \mu_2)}{\sqrt{(S_1{}^2/n_1) + (S_2{}^2/n_2)}} .$$

# PROPORTIONS

● PROBLEM 16-41

A sports magazine reports that the people who watch Monday night football games on television are evenly divided between men and women. Out of a random sample of 400 people who regularly watch the Monday night game, 220 are men. Using a .10 level of significance, can be conclude that the report is false?

Solution: We have for this problem as our hypotheses:

$H_0$: $p = .50$, where $p$ is the true population proportion.

$H_1$: $p \neq .50$.

The following diagram depicts the data of this problem, where $\bar{p}$ is the sample proportion of men who watch Monday night football.

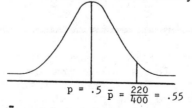

$$p = .5 \quad \bar{p} = \frac{220}{400} = .55$$

The statistic $(\bar{p} - p)/\sigma_p$ is approximately normally distributed with a mean of 0 and a standard deviation of 1. We calculate this

608

value, which is called  Z,

$$Z = \frac{\bar{p} - p}{\sigma_{\bar{p}}} \quad \text{where}$$

$$\sigma_{\bar{p}} = \sqrt{\frac{pq}{n}}$$

and compare the value of  Z  to a critical value.  If  Z  lies beyond
this critical value, we will reject  $H_0$.  For this problem, where we
have  $\alpha = 10\%$  and a two-tailed test, our critical value is 1.645,
since for the normal distribution with mean of  0  and standard deviation of  1,  5% of scores will have a Z-value above 1.645 and 5%
of scores will have a Z-value below -1.645.  Therefore our decision
rule is:  reject  $H_0$  if  $|Z| > 1.645$ , accept  $H_0$  if  $|Z| \leq 1.645$.

For the data of this problem,

$$\sigma_p = \sqrt{\frac{(.50)(.50)}{400}} \approx .025 \quad \text{and}$$

$$Z = \frac{.55 - .50}{.025} = \frac{.05}{.025} = 2.0 \ .$$

Since  $2.0 > 1.645$, we reject  $H_0$  and conclude that the report
of the sports magazine is incorrect at a 10% level of significance.

● PROBLEM 16-42

A college has 500 women students and 1,000 men students.  The
introductory zoology course has 90 students, 50 of whom are women.
It is suspected that more women tend to take zoology than men. In
deciding to test this suspicion with the data of this class, what
would the null and alternate hypotheses be?  Is this a one-sample
or a two-sample case?

Solution: Since it is suspected that women tend to take zoology
more than men, we have a one-tailed test for this problem.

Of the 90 students in the zoology class, 50 or 5/9 are women.
We would like to know if this value of  5/9  is sufficiently
greater than the proportion of women expected to take the course
when men and women have equal preferences for the course.  This
proportion (the expected number) is 1/3  since  1/3  of the students
in the college are women.  Therefore our alternate hypothesis is
p > 1/3.  This leaves for our null hypothesis the possibility of
p ≤ 1/3.
This is a one-sample test; we are comparing a sample proportion
for the number of women to a hypothesized population proportion.
We are not comparing two sample proportions.

● PROBLEM 16-43

In 1964, 40% of shipments of U.S. cotton to Germany were sent
to arbitration because of complaints about the quality being sub-
standard, according to Time Magazine.  Would it signify a real

worsening of the situation if 20 out of the first 40 shipments in 1965 were likewise the cause of complaint, or might this difference be attributed to chance?

Solution: The sample proportion, $\bar{p}$, for this problem is $20/40 = .5$ and we wish to test whether this value is significantly greater than 40% or .4. We then let $H_0$, the null hypothesis, and $H_1$, the alternate hypothesis, be

$$H_0: \bar{p} = .40 , \quad \text{and}$$

$$H_1: \bar{p} > .40 .$$

The statistic $(\bar{p} - p)/\sigma_p$ is approximately equal to the normal distribution with a mean of 0 and a standard deviation of 1. We then test the statistic

$$Z = \frac{\bar{p} - p}{\sigma_{\bar{p}}} \quad \text{where}$$

$$\sigma_{\bar{p}} = \sqrt{\frac{pq}{n}} .$$

Under $H_0$, $p = .40$, $1 - p = 2 = .60$ and

$$\sigma_{\bar{p}} = \sqrt{\frac{(.40)(.60)}{40}} = \sqrt{.006} = .077 .$$

Therefore

$$Z = \frac{.50 - .40}{.077} = \frac{.10}{.077} = 1.30 .$$

At $\alpha = .05$ and a one-tailed test, we would accept $H_0$ if the calculated value of Z is less than 1.96 Since 1.30 is less than 1.96, we accept H in this case and conclude that the difference between the 1965 value of 50% and the 1964 value of 40% can be attributed to chance.

● PROBLEM 16-44

An electrical repair service claims that 10% of the service calls made result solely from appliances not having been plugged properly into the receptacle. A random sample of 200 work invoices produced 15 in which the only "repairs" were the plugging in of the appliance. Do the results indicate that the repair service's claim is justified? Test at the .01 level of significance.

Solution: We have as our hypotheses for this problem:
$$H_0: p = .10 \qquad\qquad H_1: p \neq .10 .$$
The problem may be depicted by the following diagram:

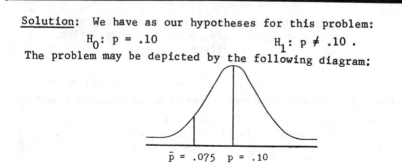

$$\bar{p} = .075 \quad p = .10$$

The statistic $(\bar{p} - p)/\sigma_{\bar{p}}$ is approximately normally distributed with a mean of $0$ and a standard deviation of $1$. For $\alpha = .01$ and a two-tailed test, then our decision rule is: reject $H_0$ if $Z > 2.57$ or $Z < -2.57$; accept $H_0$ if $-2.57 \leq Z \leq 2.57$.

We must calculate

$$Z = \frac{\bar{p} - p}{\sigma_{\bar{p}}} \quad \text{where}$$

$$\sigma_{\bar{p}} = \sqrt{\frac{pq}{n}} .$$

For the data of this problem we have

$$\sigma_{\bar{p}} = \sqrt{\frac{(.1)(.9)}{200}} = .0212 \quad \text{and}$$

$$Z = \frac{.075 - .10}{.0212} = \frac{-.025}{.0212} = -1.18 .$$

Since $-2.57 \leq -1.18 \leq 2.57$, we accept $H_0$ and conclude that the repair service's claim is justified.

● **PROBLEM** 16-45

An electrical company claimed that at least 95% of the parts which they supplied on a government contract conformed to specifications. A sample of 400 parts was tested, and 45 did not meet specifications. Can we accept the company's claim at a .05 level of significance?

Solution: In this problem we wish to determine whether the sample proportion of parts which did meet specifications,

$$\bar{p} = \frac{355}{400} = .8875,$$

is significantly small so as to reject the company's claim that at least 95% of the parts conformed to specifications. Therefore we have for our alternate hypothesis,

$$H_1 : p < .95 .$$

Our null hypothesis is thus

$$H_0 : p = .95 .$$

This problem may be depicted by the following diagram. The statistic $(\bar{p} - p)/\sigma_p$ has approximately a normal distribution with a mean of $0$ and a standard deviation of $1$.

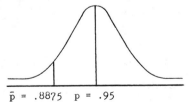

$\bar{p} = .8875 \quad p = .95$

We must calculate

$$Z = \frac{\bar{p} - p}{\sigma_{\bar{p}}} \quad \text{where} \quad \sigma_{\bar{p}} = \sqrt{\frac{pq}{n}} \; .$$

For the data of this problem we have

$$\sigma_{\bar{p}} = \sqrt{\frac{.95(.05)}{400}} = .011 \quad \text{and}$$

$$Z = \frac{.8875 - .95}{.011} = \frac{-.0625}{.011} = -5.7 .$$

For a level of significance, $\alpha$, of .05, and a one-tailed test, our decision rule is: reject $H_0$ if $Z < -2.33$; accept $H_0$ if $Z \geq -2.33$.

Since $-5.7 < 2.33$ we reject $H_0$ and conclude that the company's claim that at least 95% of the parts conformed to specifications is not justified.

● **PROBLEM** 16-46

It is believed that no more than 40% of the students in a certain college wear glasses. Of 64 students surveyed, 40 or 62.5% are found to wear glasses. Does this contradict the belief that no more than 40% of the students wear glasses? Use a 5% level of significance.

<u>Solution</u>: This is a one-tailed test. We would like to know if the sample proportion is far enough above .40 to reject the claim that no more than 40% of the students wear glasses. Therefore, our alternative hypothesis, $H_1$, is $p > .40$. Thus, our null hypothesis is $p = .40$.

This problem may be depicted by the following diagram.

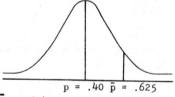

$$p = .40 \quad \bar{p} = .625$$

The statistic $(\bar{p} - p)/\sigma_{\bar{p}}$ is approximately normally distributed with a mean of 0 and a standard deviation of 1. For $\alpha = .05$, and a one-tailed test, our decision rule is: reject $H_0$ if $Z > 1.65$; accept $H_0$ if $Z \leq 1.65$. We must calculate

$$Z = \frac{\bar{p} - p}{\sigma_{\bar{p}}} \quad \text{where}$$

$$\sigma_{\bar{p}} = \sqrt{\frac{pq}{n}} \; .$$

For the data of this problem,

$$\sigma_{\bar{p}} = \sqrt{\frac{(.4)(.6)}{64}} = \sqrt{\frac{.24}{64}} = .0612 \quad \text{and}$$

$$Z = \frac{.625 - .4}{.0612} = \frac{.225}{.0612} = 3.68 .$$

Since $3.68 > 1.64$, we reject $H_0$ and the claim that no more than 40% of the students in the college wear glasses.

● **PROBLEM** 16-47

An opinion survey in town A found that 73% of people considered architect's fees to be too high. A random sample of 30 people in town B were asked the same question 15 thought architect's fees to be too high. Is this proportion significantly different from that of town A?

**Solution:** Let us take as $H_0$, the null hypothesis, that the actual proportion, p, of people in town B who think that architect's fees are too high is .73. That is, we have

$$H_0 : p = .73, \quad \text{and} \qquad H_1 : p \neq .73.$$

But for this sample, $\bar{p} = 15/30 = .5$. We use the test statistic

$$Z = \frac{\bar{p} - p}{\sigma_{\bar{p}}} \qquad \text{where} \qquad \sigma_{\bar{p}} = \sqrt{\frac{pq}{n}}.$$

We do this because the statistic $(\bar{p} - p)/\sigma_{\bar{p}}$ is approximately normally distributed with a mean of 0 and a standard deviation of 1. Since $p = .73$, $q = 1 - p = .27$ and

$$\sigma_p = \sqrt{\frac{(.73)(.27)}{30}} = \sqrt{\frac{.197}{30}} = .081.$$

For $\alpha = .05$ and a two-tailed test, the critical value of Z is 1.96 and we will accept $H_0$ if the calculated value of Z lies between $-1.96$ and $+1.96$. Otherwise we will reject $H_0$.

For this set of data

$$Z = \frac{.50 - .73}{.081} = -\frac{.23}{.081} = -2.84$$

and we reject $H_0$.

For $\alpha = .01$, the critical value of Z is 2.57 and we will accept $H_0$ if the calculated value of Z lies between $-2.57$ and 2.57. Again we reject $H_0$. So for $\alpha = .05$ or $\alpha = .01$, we conclude that there is a significant difference between the proportion of people in town B and the proportion in town A who think that architects' fees are too high.

# DIFFERENCES BETWEEN PROPORTIONS

● **PROBLEM** 16-48

In one income group, 45% of a random sample of people express approval of a product. In another income group, 55% of a random sample of people express approval. The standard errors for these percentages are .04 and .03 respectively. Test at the 10%

level of significance the hypothesis that the percentage of people in the second income group expressing approval of the product exceeds that for the first income group.

Solution: This problem may be depicted by the following diagram.

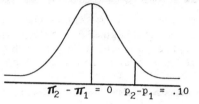

$$\pi_2 - \pi_1 = 0 \qquad P_2 - P_1 = .10$$

We would like to see whether $P_2 - P_1 = .10$ is far enough away from $P_2 - P_1 = 0$ to reject a null hypothesis that $\pi_2 - \pi_1 = 0$. Therefore our hypotheses are:

$$H_0 : \pi_2 - \pi_1 = 0 ,$$

where $\pi_2$ and $\pi_1$ are the population proportions for the second and first income group respectively.

$$H_1 : \pi_2 - \pi_1 > 0 .$$

The statistic

$$\frac{(P_2 - P_1) - (\pi_2 - \pi_1)}{\sigma_{P_2 - P_1}}$$

is approximately normally distributed with a mean of 0 and a standard deviation of 1.

We calculate this value, which is called Z:

$$Z = \frac{(P_2 - P_1) - (\pi_2 - \pi_1)}{\sigma_{P_2 - P_1}} \qquad \text{where} \qquad \sigma_{P_2 - P_1} = \sqrt{S_{P_1}^2 + S_{P_2}^2}$$

and compare the value of Z to a critical value. If Z lies beyond this critical value, we will reject $H_0$. For this problem where we have $\alpha = 10\%$ and a one-tailed test, our critical value is 1.28, since for the normal distribution with mean of 0 and standard deviation of 1 10% of scores will have a Z-value above 1.28.

For $\alpha = .10$ and a one-tailed test our decision rule is: reject $H_0$ if $Z > 1.28$, accept $H_0$ if $Z \leq 1.28$.

We must calculate

$$Z = \frac{(P_2 - P_1) - (\pi_2 - \pi_1)}{\sigma_{P_2 - P_1}} \qquad \text{where} \qquad \sigma_{P_2 - P_1} = \sqrt{S_{P_1}^2 + S_{P_2}^2} .$$

For the data of this problem

$$\sigma_{P_2 - P_1} = \sqrt{(.04)^2 + (.03)^2} = \sqrt{.0016 + .0009}$$

$$= \sqrt{.0025} = .05 \quad \text{and}$$

$$Z = \frac{(.55 - .45) - 0}{.05} = 2.0 .$$

Since $2.0 > 1.28$, we reject $H_0$ and conclude that the percentage of people in the second income group expressing approval of the product exceeds that for the first income group at the 10% level of significance.

● **PROBLEM** 16-49

The student government of a large college polled a random sample of 325 male students and found that 221 were in favor of a new grading system. At the same time, 120 out of a random sample of 200 female students were in favor of the new system. Do the results indicate a significant difference in the proportion of male and female students who favor the new system? Test at the .05 level of significance.

Solution: Our hypotheses for this test are

$$H_0 : P_1 - P_2 = 0,$$

where $P_1$ and $P_2$ are the population proportions for males and females respectively.

$$H_1 : P_1 - P_2 \neq 0 ,$$

The statistic

$$\frac{(\bar{P}_1 - \bar{P}_2) - (P_1 - P_2)}{\sigma_{\bar{P}_1 - \bar{P}_2}}$$

is approximately normally distributed with a mean of 0 and a standard deviation of 1 .

At a 5% level of significance and a two-tailed test, we have for our decision rule: reject $H_0$ if $Z > 1.96$ or $Z < -1.96$, accept $H_0$ if $-1.96 \leq Z \leq 1.96$.

For this problem,

$$\bar{P}_1 = \frac{X_1}{n_1} = \frac{221}{325} = .68$$

and

$$\bar{P}_2 = \frac{X_2}{n_2} = \frac{120}{200} = .60 .$$

This problem may be depicted by the following diagram.

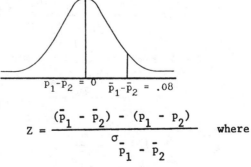

$$P_1 - P_2 = 0 \qquad \bar{P}_1 - \bar{P}_2 = .08$$

We must calculate

$$Z = \frac{(\bar{P}_1 - \bar{P}_2) - (P_1 - P_2)}{\sigma_{\bar{P}_1 - \bar{P}_2}} \qquad \text{where}$$

$$\sigma_{\bar{P}_1 - \bar{P}_2} = \sqrt{\frac{P_1 q_1}{n_1} + \frac{P_2 q_2}{n_2}} .$$

For the data of this problem, using $\bar{P}_1$ and $\bar{P}_2$ as estimates

615

of $p_1$ and $p_2$,

$$\sigma_{\bar{P}_1 - \bar{P}_2} = \sqrt{\frac{(.68)(.32)}{325} + \frac{(.60)(.40)}{200}}$$

$$= \sqrt{\frac{.2176}{325} + \frac{.24}{200}}$$

$$= \sqrt{.0006695 + .0012} = .043$$

and

$$Z = \frac{(.68 - .60) - 0}{.043} = \frac{.08}{.043} = 1.86 \ .$$

Since $-1.96 \le 1.86 \le 1.96$, we accept $H_0$ and conclude that there is not a significant difference between the proportion of male and female students who favor the new system.

● PROBLEM 16-50

Out of 57 men at a weekly college dance, 36 had been at the dance the week before, and of these, 23 had brought the same date on both occasions, and 13 had brought a different date or had come alone. Test whether the number of men who came both weeks with the same date is significantly different from the number who came both weeks but not with the same date. Use a 10% level of significance.

Solution: We test the difference between two proportions, $P_1$ and $P_2$, where $\bar{p}_1 = \frac{23}{57} = .40$ and $\bar{p}_2 = \frac{13}{57} = .23$. Our hypotheses are

$$H_0 : P_1 - P_2 = 0 \qquad\qquad H_1 : P_1 - P_2 \ne 0 \ .$$

This problem may be depicted by the following diagram.

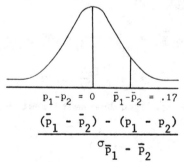

$$p_1 - p_2 = 0 \qquad \bar{p}_1 - \bar{p}_2 = .17$$

The statistic

$$\frac{(\bar{P}_1 - \bar{P}_2) - (P_1 - P_2)}{\sigma_{\bar{P}_1 - \bar{P}_2}}$$

is approximately normally distributed with a mean of 0 and a standard deviation of 1. We must calculate

$$Z = \frac{(\bar{P}_1 - \bar{P}_2) - 0}{\sigma_{\bar{P}_1 - \bar{P}_2}} \qquad \text{where}$$

$$\sigma_{\bar{P}_1 - \bar{P}_2} = \sqrt{\frac{p_1 q_1}{n_1} + \frac{p_2 q_2}{n_2}} \ .$$

For the data of this problem, using $\bar{p}_1$ and $\bar{p}_2$ as estimates of $p_1$ and $p_2$,

$$\sigma_{\bar{P}_1 - \bar{P}_2} = \sqrt{\frac{(.40)(.60)}{57} + \frac{(.23)(.77)}{57}}$$

$$= \sqrt{\frac{.24}{57} + \frac{.176}{57}} = \sqrt{.007310}$$

$$= .0855$$

and

$$Z = \frac{(.40 - .23) - 0}{.0855} = \frac{.1754}{.0855} = 2.05.$$

For a 10% level of significance and a two-tailed test, we have for our decision rule: reject $H_0$ if $Z > 1.65$ or $Z < -1.65$; accept $H_0$ if $-1.65 \le Z \le 1.65$. Since $2.05 > 1.65$, at the 10% level of significance we would reject $H_0$ and conclude that there is a significant difference between the number of men who had brought the same date on both occasions and the number who had brought a different date or came alone.

● **PROBLEM** 16-51

A sample of Democrats and a sample of Republicans were polled on an issue. Of 200 Republicans, 90 would vote yes on the issue; of 100 Democrats, 58 would vote yes. Can we say that more Democrats than Republicans favor the issue at the 1% level of significance?

Solution: For this problem, we have

$$H_0 : \pi_2 - \pi_1 = 0 \qquad\qquad H_1 : \pi_2 - \pi_1 > 0$$

where $\pi_1$ = the proportion of Republicans favoring the issue and $\pi_2$ = the proportion of Democrats favoring the issue. Here, the corresponding sample values, $\bar{p}_1$ and $\bar{p}_2$, are

$$\bar{p}_1 = \frac{90}{200} = .45 \qquad\qquad \bar{p}_2 = \frac{58}{100} = .58 .$$

This problem can be depicted by the following diagram.

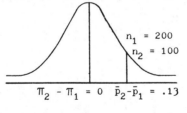

$$n_1 = 200$$
$$n_2 = 100$$

$$\pi_2 - \pi_1 = 0 \qquad \bar{p}_2 - \bar{p}_1 = .13$$

The statistic

$$\frac{(\bar{p}_2 - \bar{p}_1) - (\pi_2 - \pi_1)}{\sigma_{\bar{p}_2 - \bar{p}_1}}$$

is approximately normally distributed with a mean of 0 and a standard deviation of 1.

For $\alpha = .01$ and a one-tailed test our decision rule is: reject $H_0$ if $Z > 2.33$; accept $H_0$ if $Z \le 2.33$.

We must calculate

$$Z = \frac{(\bar{p}_2 - \bar{p}_1) - (\pi_2 - \pi_1)}{\sigma_{\bar{p}_2 - \bar{p}_1}} \qquad \text{where}$$

617

$$S_{\pi_2 - \pi_1} = \sqrt{\bar{p}\,\bar{q}\left(\frac{1}{n_1} + \frac{1}{n_2}\right)} \quad \text{is an estimate of} \quad \sigma_{\bar{p}_2 - \bar{p}_1}$$

and

$$\bar{p} = \frac{X_1 + X_2}{n_1 + n_2} \quad \text{is a 'pooled' estimate of } \pi.$$

For the data of this problem

$$\bar{p} = \frac{90 + 58}{200 + 100} = \frac{148}{300} = .493 \ .$$

So

$$S_{\pi_2 - \pi_1} = \sqrt{(.493)(.507)\left(\frac{1}{200} + \frac{1}{100}\right)}$$

$$= \sqrt{.25(.015)} = .0612,$$

and

$$Z = \frac{(.58 - .45) - 0}{.0612} = \frac{.13}{.0612} = 2.12 \ .$$

Since $2.12 \le 2.33$, we accept $H_0$ and conclude that not more Democrats than Republicans favor the issue at a 1% level of significance.

● **PROBLEM** 16-52

The marketing department of a company that makes brand X laundry detergent found in a random sample of 200 housewives that 20% favored brand X over all others. After an intensive advertising campaign, another random sample of 300 housewives showed that 27% favored brand X. Can the president of the company conclude that the advertising campaign was successful?

Solution: This problem is a one-tailed test because in order to conclude that the advertising campaign was successful, the proportion of housewives favoring brand X after the advertising campaign must be greater than that before.

This problem may be depicted by the following diagram.

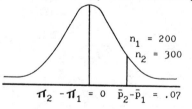

$$\pi_2 - \pi_1 = 0 \quad \bar{p}_2 - \bar{p}_1 = .07$$

$n_1 = 200$
$n_2 = 300$

Our hypotheses are

$$H_0 : \pi_2 - \pi_1 = 0 \qquad H_1 : \pi_2 - \pi_1 > 0$$

where $\pi_2$ = the proportion of housewives favoring brand X before the advertising campaign, and $\pi_1$ = the proportion of housewives favoring brand X after the campaign.

The statistic

$$\frac{(\bar{p}_2 - \bar{p}_1) - (\pi_2 - \pi_1)}{S_{\bar{p}_2 - \bar{p}_1}}$$

618

is approximately normally distributed with a mean of 0 and a standard deviation of 1.

Suppose we choose $\alpha = .05$. Then for a one-tailed test our decision rule is: reject $H_0$ if $Z > 1.65$; accept $H_0$ if $Z \leq 1.65$.

We must calculate

$$Z = \frac{(\bar{p}_2 - \bar{p}_1) - (\pi_2 - \pi_1)}{S_{\bar{p}_2 - \bar{p}_1}} \qquad \text{where}$$

$$S_{\bar{p}_2 - \bar{p}_1} = \sqrt{\frac{\bar{p}_1 \bar{q}_1}{n_1} + \frac{\bar{p}_2 \bar{q}_2}{n_2}} \quad \text{is the estimate of } \sigma_{\bar{p}_2 - \bar{p}_1}.$$

For the data of this problem,

$$S_{\bar{p}_2 - \bar{p}_1} = \sqrt{\frac{(.27)(.73)}{300} + \frac{(.20)(.80)}{200}}$$

$$= \sqrt{.000657 + .0008}$$

$$= .038, \quad \text{and}$$

$$Z = \frac{(.27 - .20)}{.038} = \frac{.07}{.038} = 1.84.$$

Since $1.84 > 1.65$, we would reject $H_0$ and the president of the company could conclude that the advertising campaign was successful.

Now suppose the president wanted to be even more confident in concluding that the advertising campaign was successful. Then an appropriate statistical test would have $\alpha = .01$ instead of .05. In this case our decision rule would be: reject $H_0$ if $Z > 2.33$; accept $H_0$ if $Z \leq 2.33$. Since our calculated $Z$ was 1.84 and $1.84 < 2.33$, we would accept $H_0$, and under these more stringent requirements, the president would not conclude that the advertising campaign was successful.

● **PROBLEM** 16-53

The Selective Service director of a certain state suspects that the proportion of men from urban areas who are physically unfit for military service is more than 5 percentage points greater than the proportion of physically unfit men from rural areas. He decides to treat the men called for a physical examination from urban areas during the next month as a random sample from a binomial population, and those from the rural areas as a random sample from a second binomial population. During the next month 3214 men were called from urban areas and 2011 from rural areas. There were 1078 physical rejects from the urban areas and 543 from rural areas.

Formulate the appropriate null and alternative hypotheses, and test the null hypothesis at the $\alpha = .05$ level.

Solution: Let $\pi_1$ = the true proportion of physically unfit from urban areas, and $\pi_2$ = the true proportion of physically unfit from rural areas.

The null and alternative hypotheses are

$$H_0 : \pi_1 - \pi_2 = .05 \qquad\qquad H_1 : \pi_1 - \pi_2 > .05 .$$

For this problem, the sample statistics, $\bar{P}_1$ and $\bar{P}_2$, are given by

$$\bar{P}_1 = \frac{X_1}{n_1} = \frac{1078}{3214} = .335 \quad \text{and}$$

$$\bar{P}_2 = \frac{X_2}{n_2} = \frac{543}{2011} = .270 \; ;$$

$$\bar{P}_1 - \bar{P}_2 = .335 - .270 = .065.$$

This problem may be depicted by the following diagram.

$$\pi_1 - \pi_2 = 0 \qquad \bar{P}_1 - \bar{P}_2 = .065$$

The statistic

$$\frac{(\bar{P}_1 - \bar{P}_2) - (\pi_1 - \pi_2)}{\sigma_{\bar{P}_1 - \bar{P}_2}}$$

is approximately a normal distribution with mean of $0$ and standard deviation of $1$.

For $\alpha = .05$ and a one-tailed test, we have for our decision rule: reject $H_0$ if $Z > 1.65$; accept $H_0$ if $Z \le 1.65$.

We must calculate

$$Z = \frac{(\bar{P}_1 - \bar{P}_2) - (\pi_1 - \pi_2)}{\sigma_{\bar{P}_1 - \bar{P}_2}} \quad \text{since the true proportions}$$

are unknown.

$\sigma_{\bar{P}_1 - \bar{P}_2}$ is estimated by: $\sqrt{\dfrac{\bar{P}_1(1-\bar{P}_1)}{n_1} + \dfrac{\bar{P}_1(1-\bar{P}_2)}{n_2}}$ .

For the data of this problem we have

$$\sigma_{\bar{P}_1 - \bar{P}_2} = \sqrt{\frac{(.335)(.665)}{3214} + \frac{(.270)(.730)}{2011}}$$

and

$$= \sqrt{\frac{.223}{3214} + \frac{.197}{2011}} = .0130 \quad \text{and}$$

$$Z = \frac{(.335 - .270) - .05}{.0130} = \frac{.065 - .05}{.0130}$$

$$= \frac{.0150}{.0130} = 1.15 .$$

Since $1.15 < 1.65$, we accept $H_0$ and conclude that the proportion of men from urban areas who are physically unfit for military service is <u>not</u> more than 5 percentage points greater than the proportion of physically unfit men from rural areas.

Refer to the data in the previous problem concerning the Selective Service data to test the hypothesis that the proportions are equal against the alternative that $\pi_1 > \pi_2$ . Use $\alpha = .05$ .

Solution: The hypotheses are
$$H_0 : \pi_1 - \pi_2 = 0 ,$$
there is no difference between the true proportions of physically unfit from rural and urban areas, and

$$H_1 : \pi_1 - \pi_2 > 0 ,$$

the proportion of physically unfit men from urban areas is greater than the proportion of physically unfit men from rural areas.

This problem may be depicted by the following diagram.

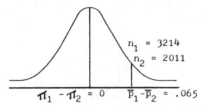

For $\alpha = .05$ , our decision rule is: reject $H_0$ if $Z > 1.65$; accept $H$ if $Z \le 1.65$.

The only difference between this and the previous problem are the hypotheses; as a result, under $H_0$ we replace $\pi_1 - \pi_2 = .05$ in the Z statistic in the preceding problem by $\pi_1 - \pi_2$:

$$Z = \frac{(.335 - .270) - 0}{.0130} = \frac{65}{13} = 5.$$

Since $5 > 1.65$, we reject $H_0$ and conclude that the proportion of physically unfit men from urban areas is greater than the proportion of physically unfit men from rural areas.

# THE NORMAL APPROXIMATION
# TO THE BINOMIAL

A new treatment plan for schizophrenia has been tried for 6 months with 54 randomly chosen patients. At the end of this time, 25 patients are recommended for release from the hospital; the usual proportion released in 6 months is $\frac{1}{3}$ . Using the normal approximation to the binomial distribution, determine whether the new treatment plan has resulted in significantly more releases than the previous plan. Use a 0.05 level of significance.

<u>Solution:</u>     The number of patients recommended for release from the hospital has a binomial distribution.  We have p, the proportion of patients released from the hospital, equal to $\frac{1}{3}$, and q, the proportion of patients not released, equal to $1 - p$ or $\frac{2}{3}$.  Since $np = (54)\left[\frac{1}{3}\right] = 18$ and $nq = (54)\left[\frac{2}{3}\right]$ = 36, are both greater than or equal to 5, we may approximate this binomial distribution by the normal distribution in this case.

We use $\mu = np$ and $\sigma = \sqrt{npq}$ as the mean and standard deviation of this normal approximation.

Since $n = 54$, $p = \frac{1}{3}$ and $q = \frac{2}{3}$, we have $\mu = 54\left[\frac{1}{3}\right] = 18$ and $\sigma = \sqrt{54\left[\frac{1}{3}\right]\left[\frac{2}{3}\right]} = 3.46$.

The problem can now be depicted by the following diagram.

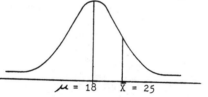

$\mu = 18$     $\overline{X} = 25$

We desire to see whether our sample mean of 25 exceeds 18 by enough for us to conclude that the actual population mean for the new treatment is greater than 18.  Thus we choose as our alternate hypothesis

$H_1$: $\mu > 18$.

Hence, our null hypothesis is

$H_0$: $\mu = 18$.

The statistic $\frac{(x - \mu)}{\sigma}$ has a normal distribution with a mean of 0 and a standard deviation of 1.

We use a critical value of 1.645 for this problem, since we have $\alpha = .05$ and a one-tailed test, and for the normal distribution with mean of 0 and standard deviation of 1, 5% of scores will have a Z-value above 1.645.  Therefore our decision rule is:   reject $H_0$ if $Z > 1.645$; accept $H_0$ if $Z \leq 1.645$.

We must now calculate

$$Z = \frac{x - \mu}{\sigma} .$$

Since the binomial distribution is a discrete distribution and the normal distribution is continuous, we will use 24.5 instead of 25 as the value for x in the above formula.

We calculate Z.

$$Z = \frac{24.5 - 18}{3.46} = \frac{6.5}{3.46} = 1.88.$$

Since $1.88 > 1.645$, we reject $H_0$ and conclude that the population mean for the new treatment is greater than 18, and hence, it has resulted in significantly more releases than the previous plan.

● **PROBLEM** 16-56

A man has just purchased a trick die which was advertised as not yielding the proper proportion of sixes. He wonders whether the advertising was correct, and tests the advertising claim by rolling the die 100 times. The 100 rolls yielded ten sixes. Should he conclude that the advertising was legitimate?

<u>Solution</u>: First formulate the hypotheses to be tested. Let the null and alternate hypotheses be as given below.

$H_0$: The die is like any other die or

$\quad\quad \pi = Pr \text{ (rolling a six)} = \frac{1}{6}$

$H_1$: The die is in fact a trick die and

$\quad\quad \pi = Pr \text{ (rolling a six)} \neq \frac{1}{6}$ .

It is not given in the problem whether the proportion of sixes is greater than or less than $\frac{1}{6}$. Therefore we must test both possibilities and our alternate hypothesis must be two-sided.

The number of sixes rolled in 100 rolls is determined by the binomial distribution. For the distribution, $\pi = \frac{1}{6}$, and $1 - \pi = \frac{5}{6}$, and since $n\pi = 100 \left( \frac{1}{6} \right) = 16.67$ and $n(1 - \pi) = 100 \left( \frac{5}{6} \right) = 83.33$ are both greater than 5, we may approximate this binomial distribution by the normal distribution.

This problem can now be depicted by the following diagram.

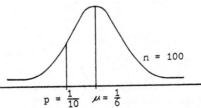

$p = \frac{1}{10} \quad \mu = \frac{1}{6}$

$n = 100$

623

The statistic $\dfrac{(x - \mu)}{\sigma}$ has a normal distribution with a mean of 0 and a standard deviation of 1.

Suppose we choose $\alpha = .05$. Then for this two-tailed test, our decision rule is: reject $H_0$ if $Z > 1.96$ or $Z < -1.96$, accept $H_0$ if $-1.96 \le Z \le 1.96$.

We must calculate

$$Z = \frac{P - \pi}{S_p} \qquad \text{where} \qquad S_p = \sqrt{\frac{\pi(1 - \pi)}{n}} \quad.$$

For the data of this problem we have

$$S_p = \sqrt{\frac{(.167)(.833)}{100}} = .0373 \qquad \text{and}$$

$$Z = \frac{.10 - .167}{.0373} = -1.80.$$

Since $-1.96 < -1.80 \le 1.96$, we accept $H_0$ and conclude at a 5% level of significance that the die is like any other die and that the advertising claim was not legitimate.

● **PROBLEM** 16-57

A coin is tossed 900 times. The owner of the coin alleges that it is biased. How many heads must turn up in 900 tosses for $p = \dfrac{1}{2}$ to be rejected at the 5% level of significance?

Solution:    The number of heads in 900 tosses of a coin has a binomial distribution with p, the probability of obtaining a head on any one toss, equal to 1/2 and q, the probability of obtaining a tail on one toss, equal to $1 - p = \dfrac{1}{2}$. Since $np = (900)\left(\dfrac{1}{2}\right) = 450$ and $nq = (900)\left(\dfrac{1}{2}\right) = 450$ are both greater than 5, we may use the normal approximation to the binomial distribution for this problem.

We have mean, $\mu = np = 900\left(\dfrac{1}{2}\right) = 450$ and standard deviation, $\sigma, = \sqrt{npq} = \sqrt{(900)\left(\dfrac{1}{2}\right)\left(\dfrac{1}{2}\right)} = \sqrt{225} = 15$. This problem may now be depicted by the following diagram.

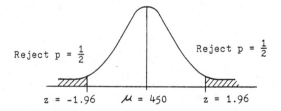

Reject $p = \dfrac{1}{2}$      Reject $p = \dfrac{1}{2}$

$z = -1.96$    $\mu = 450$    $z = 1.96$

We will reject the hypothesis $p = \frac{1}{2}$ at the 5% level of significance if the number of heads obtained is in the top 2.5% or the lowest 2.5% of the normal curve. This will occur if $Z > 1.96$ or $Z < -1.96$, since the statistic $Z = \frac{(x - \mu)}{\sigma}$ is normally distributed with a mean of 0 and a standard deviation of 1. We may now use the formula

$$Z = \frac{x - \mu}{\sigma}$$

to calculate the x values (which stand for the number of heads) for each of these two Z values.

For $Z > 1.96$,

$$\frac{x - \mu}{\sigma} > 1.96$$

$$\frac{x - 450}{15} > 1.96.$$

Multiplying each side by 15,

$$x - 450 > 29.4.$$

Adding 450 to each side yields,

$$x > 479.4.$$

Since the binomial distribution is discrete and the normal distribution is continuous, the interval 478.5 to 479.5 on the normal curve corresponds to 479 for the binomial distribution. Thus we will reject $p = 1/2$ when the number of heads is greater than 479, i.e., 480 or more.

In like fashion, we find the x value corresponding to $Z < -1.96$.

For $Z < -1.96$,

$$\frac{x - \mu}{\sigma} < -1.96,$$

$$\frac{x - 450}{15} < -1.96$$

$$x - 450 < -29.4 \qquad \text{and}$$

$$x < 420.6.$$

This value corresponds to 421 for the normal distribution, so we will also reject $p = 1/2$ when the number of heads is less than 421, i.e., 420 or less.

# VARIANCES

● **PROBLEM** 16-58

A sample of size 10 produced a variance of 14. Is this sufficient to reject the null hypothesis that $\sigma^2 = 6$ when tested using a .05 level of significance? Using a .01 level of significance?

Solution: We use the $\chi^2$ (chi-square) statistic to determine the value of a population variance when given a sample variance. We may do this because the test statistic $\frac{(n-1)s^2}{\sigma^2}$ has a $\chi^2$ distribution with $n - 1$ degrees of freedom. Here we have as our hypotheses:

$H_0: \sigma^2 = 6$ $\qquad\qquad$ $H_1: \sigma^2 \neq 6$.

Since $\alpha = .05$ and this is a two-tailed test, we will reject $H_0$ if our calculated value for $\chi^2$ is $> \chi^2_{.025}$ or $< \chi^2_{.975}$. We will accept $H_0$ if $\chi^2_{.975} \leq$ calculated $\chi^2 \leq \chi^2_{.025}$. The number of degrees of freedom for $\chi^2_{.025}$ and $\chi^2_{.975}$ is $n - 1$, or in this case 9. Therefore, our decision rule is: reject $H_0$ if calculated $\chi^2 > 19.023$ or $\chi^2 < 2.700$; accept $H_0$ if $2.700 \leq \chi^2 \leq 19.023$.

We now calculate $\chi^2$ using the formula

$$\chi^2 = \frac{(n-1)s^2}{\sigma^2} \quad .$$

Since $n = 10$, $s^2 = 14$, and $\sigma^2 = 6$ for this problem, we have

$$\chi^2 = \frac{9(14)}{6} = 21.$$

Since $21 > 19.023$, we reject $H_0$ and conclude that $\sigma^2 \neq 6$ at a 5% level of significance.

For $\alpha = .01$, we must compare our calculated $\chi^2$ to $\chi^2_{.005}$ and $\chi^2_{.995}$, again for 9 degrees of freedom. Our decision rule now becomes: reject $H_0$ if calculated $\chi^2 > 23.589$ or $\chi^2 < 1.735$; accept $H_0$ if $1.735 \leq \chi^2 \leq 23.589$. Since our calculated $\chi^2$ was 21, and $1.735 < 21 < 23.589$, we would accept $H_0$ that $\sigma^2 = 6$ at a 1% level of significance.

● **PROBLEM** 16-59

The makers of a certain brand of car mufflers claim that the life of the mufflers has a variance of .8 year. A random sample of 16 of these mufflers showed a variance of 1 year. Using a 5% level of significance, test whether the variance of all the mufflers of this manufacturer exceeds .8 year.

Solution: Our hypotheses for this problem are:

$$H_0: \sigma^2 = .8 \qquad H_1: \sigma^2 > .8.$$

The statistic $\dfrac{(n-1)s^2}{\sigma^2}$ has a $\chi^2$ distribution with $n-1$ degrees of freedom.

For $\alpha = .05$, a one-tailed test, and $n - 1 = 15$ degrees of freedom, we will have for our decision rule: reject $H_0$ if $\chi^2 > 24.996$; accept $H_0$ if $\chi^2 \leq 24.996$.

We calculate $\chi^2$.

$$\chi^2 = \frac{(n-1)s^2}{\sigma^2} = \frac{15(1)^2}{(.8)} = 18.75.$$

Since $18.75 < 24.996$, we accept $H_0$ and conclude that the variance of all the mufflers of this manufacturer does not exceed .8 year.

● **PROBLEM** 16-60

A manufacturer of car batteries guarantees that his batteries will last, on the average, 3 years with a standard deviation of 1 year. If 5 of these batteries have lifetimes of 1.9, 2.4, 3.0, 3.5, and 4.2 years, is the manufacturer still convinced that his batteries have a standard deviation of 1 year?

Solution: The statistic $\dfrac{(n-1)s^2}{\sigma^2}$ has a $\chi^2$ distribution with $n-1$ degrees of freeom. For this problem our hypotheses are

$$H_0: \sigma^2 = 1 \qquad\qquad H_1: \sigma^2 \neq 1.$$

Since this is a two-tailed test, if we choose $\alpha = .05$, for $n - 1 = 4$ degrees of freedom, our decision rule is: reject $H_0$ if $\chi^2 > 11.143$ or $\chi^2 < .484$; accept $H_0$ if $.484 \leq \chi^2 \leq 11.143$.

We must calculate $\qquad \chi^2 = \dfrac{(n-1)s^2}{\sigma^2}$ .

But first we must calculate $s^2$ for the given data.

$$s^2 = \frac{n\Sigma X^2 - (\Sigma X)^2}{n(n-1)} \quad .$$

We use the following table.

| X | $X^2$ |
|---|---|
| 1.9 | 3.61 |
| 2.4 | 5.76 |
| 3.0 | 9.00 |
| 3.5 | 12.25 |
| 4.2 | 17.64 |
| 15 | 48.26 |

Then we have

$$s^2 = \frac{5(48.26) - (15)^2}{5(4)} = \frac{241.3 - 225}{20}$$

$$= \frac{16.3}{20} = .815 \qquad \text{and}$$

$$\chi^2 = \frac{4(.815)}{1} = 3.26.$$

Since $.484 < 3.26 < 11.143$, we accept $H_0$. The manufactuer should remain convinced that his batteries have a standard deviation of 1 year.

● **PROBLEM 16-61**

Derive a method for determining the appropriate sample size to take for a statistical test designed to test

$\qquad H_0: \sigma^2 = \sigma_1^2 \qquad\qquad$ against

$\qquad H_1: \sigma^2 > \sigma_2^2$

for specified levels of $\alpha$, the type I error, and $\beta$, the type II error, and where $\sigma_2^2 > \sigma_1^2$. Apply this method when $\sigma_1 = .1225$, $\sigma_2 = .2450$, $\alpha = .01$ and $\beta = .01$.

**Solution:** In testing whether $H_0: \sigma^2 = \sigma_1^2$ is true at a level of significance $\alpha$ we will reject $H_0$ if

$$\chi^2 = \frac{(n-1)s^2}{\sigma_1^2} > \chi_{\alpha;\,n-1}^2. \qquad\qquad (1)$$

In testing whether $H_1: \sigma^2 > \sigma_2^2$ is true, we will reject $H_1$ and accept $H_0$ for specified $\beta$ when

$$\chi^2 = \frac{(n-1)s^2}{\sigma_2^2} \le \chi_{1-\beta;\,n-1}^2. \qquad\qquad (2)$$

We solve (1) for $s^2$ and obtain

$$s^2 > \frac{\chi_{\alpha;\,n-1}^2 \; \sigma_1^2}{n-1}. \qquad\qquad (3)$$

We solve (2) for $s^2$ and obtain

$$s^2 \le \frac{\chi_{1-\beta;\,n-1}^2 \; \sigma_2^2}{n-1}. \qquad\qquad (4)$$

Inequality (3) says that we will reject $H_0$ if our sample variance, $s^2$, is greater than some value. Inequality (4) says that we will accept $H_0$ if our sample variance, $s^2$, is less than or equal to some value. In order for our statistical test to be logically consistent, then, the right sides of inequalities (3) and (4) must be equal. Therefore

$$\frac{\chi^2_{\alpha;n-1}\,\sigma_1{}^2}{n-1} = \frac{\chi^2_{1-\beta;n-1}\,\sigma_2{}^2}{n-1} \,. \tag{5}$$

On each side of (5), the $n-1$ terms cancel, and dividing each side by $\sigma_1{}^2\,\chi^2_{1-\beta;n-1}$ yields

$$\frac{\sigma_2{}^2}{\sigma_1{}^2} = \frac{\chi^2_{\alpha;\,n-1}}{\chi^2_{1-\beta;\,n-1}} \,.$$

Finding the required sample size for given $\sigma_1$, $\sigma_2$, $\alpha$, and $\beta$ now reduces to calculating $\sigma_2{}^2/\sigma_1{}^2$ and using a $\chi^2$ table to determine for which value of $n-1$ we have $\dfrac{\chi^2_{\alpha;\,n-1}}{\chi^2_{1-\beta;n-1}}$ equal to $\dfrac{\sigma_2{}^2}{\sigma_1{}^2}$. We then add 1 to get the required sample size.

For $\sigma_1 = .1225$, $\sigma_2 = .2450$, $\alpha = .01$, and $\beta = .01$, we must find that value of $n-1$ for which

$$\frac{\chi^2_{.01;\,n-1}}{\chi^2_{.99;\,n-1}} = \frac{(.2450)^2}{(.1225)^2} = 4 \,.$$

For $n-1 = 24$,

$$\frac{\chi^2_{.01;\,n-1}}{\chi^2_{.99;\,n-1}} = \frac{42.980}{10.856} = 3.959$$

which is closer to 4 than $\dfrac{\chi^2_{.01;\,n-1}}{\chi^2_{.99;\,n-1}}$ is for any other value of $n-1$. Therefore, the appropriate sample size for $\sigma_1 = .1225$, $\sigma_2 = .2450$, $\alpha = .01$ and $\beta = .01$ is $n = 25$.

● **PROBLEM** 16-62

Suppose that a sample of 25 items is taken. The sample variance, $s^2$, is found to be .0384. Can we reject $H_0$: $\sigma = .1225$ in favor of $H_1$: $\sigma > .1225$?

Suppose we take a sample size of $n = 7$. Can we now reject $H_0$ in favor of $H_1$? If we accept $H_0$ when $n = 7$ how certain are we that $\sigma$ is not at least .2450. Refer to the previous problem.

Solution: We will use $\alpha = .01$ as we did in the previous problem.

For a sample size of 25, we have 24 degrees of freedom and since the statistic $\dfrac{(n-1)s^2}{\sigma^2}$ has a $\chi^2$ distribution with 24 degrees of freedom, for a one-tailed test our decision rule is: reject $H_0$ if $\chi^2 > 42.980$; accept $H_0$ if $\chi^2 \leq 42.980$.

We calculate $\chi^2$.

$$\chi^2 = \frac{(n-1)s^2}{\sigma^2} = \frac{24\,(.0384)}{(.1225)^2} = \frac{.9216}{.0150} = 61.44 \ .$$

Since $61.44 > 42.980$, we reject $H_0$ in favor of $H_1$.

For a sample size of 7, $\frac{(n-1)s^2}{\sigma^2}$ has a $\chi^2$ distribution with 6 degrees of freedom and our decision rule becomes: reject $H_0$ if $\chi^2 > 16.812$; accept $H_0$ if $\chi^2 \leq 16.812$.

We calculate $\chi^2$.

$$\chi^2 = \frac{(n-1)s^2}{\sigma^2} = \frac{6\,(.0384)}{(.1225)^2} = \frac{.2304}{.0150} = 15.36.$$

Since $15.36 \leq 16.812$; we accept $H_0$ when $n = 7$.

Now suppose that when $n = 7$, $H_1$ is actually true and that $\sigma = .2450$. How frequently can this occur when $s^2 = .0384$? To find this out, we calculate

$$\chi^2 = \frac{(n-1)s^2}{\sigma^2} \qquad \text{where} \qquad \sigma = .2450$$

We obtain

$$\chi^2 = \frac{6\,(.0384)}{(.2450)^2} = \frac{.2304}{.060025} = 3.838.$$

Now 3.838 lies between $\chi^2_{.75,\ 6} = 3.4546$ and $\chi^2_{.50,\ 6} = 5.3481$. So the probability of obtaining a $\chi^2$ value as low as 3.838, i.e., an $s^2$ value as low as .0384, when $\sigma = .2450$ is between 25 and 50 percent. Thus even though we accept $H_0$ in this case, the probability that $H_1$: $\sigma = .2450$ is true when $s^2 = .0384$ is between 25 and 50 percent and we are only between 50 and 75 percent certain that in reality $\sigma$ is not at least .2450. The reason for this lack of certainty is the small sample size of 7. In the previous problem we showed that for $n = 25$, if we accepted $H_0$: $\sigma = .1225$, we were 99% certain that $H_0$ was indeed true.

# DIFFERENCE BETWEEN VARIANCES

● **PROBLEM 16-63**

A random sample of 20 boys and 15 girls were given a standardized test. The average grade of the boys was 78 with a standard deviation of 6, while the girls made an average grade of 84 with a standard deviation of 8. Test the hypothesis that $\sigma_1^2 = \sigma_2^2$ against the alternate hypothesis $\sigma_1^2 < \sigma_2^2$ where $\sigma_1^2$ and $\sigma_2^2$ are the variances of the population of boys and girls. Use a .05 level of significance.

Solution:    Our hypotheses for this problem are:

$H_0: \sigma_1^2 = \sigma_2^2$

$H_1: \sigma_2^2 > \sigma_1^2$ .

The F random variable is defined as

$$F = V/r_2 \Big/ U/r_1$$

where U and V are chi-square random variables with $r_1$ and $r_2$ degrees of freedom.

Since $(n_1-1)S_1^2/\sigma_1^2$ and $(n_2-1)S_2^2/\sigma_2^2$ have chi-square distributions with $n_1-1$ and $n_2-1$ degrees of freedom, then this becomes,

$$F = (n_2-1)S_2^2/(n_2-1)\sigma_2^2 \Big/ (n_1-1)S_1^2/(n_1-1)\sigma_1^2 = S_2^2/S_1^2,$$

since under $H_0, \sigma_1^2 = \sigma_2^2$.

The statistic $\frac{S_2^2}{S_1^2}$ has an F distribution with $n_2 - 1$ degrees of freedom for the numerator ($df_1$) and $n_1 - 1$ degrees of freedom for the denominator ($df_2$).

To make a decision we must decide whether the calculated F given by $\frac{S_2^2}{S_1^2}$ is greater than $F_{.95}(df_1, df_2)$. Note that $df_1$ represents the degrees of freedom given by the sample size generating $s_2^2$. Similarly, the degrees of freedom in the denominator of the F-ratio, $d.f._2$, are found from the sample size $n_1$.

Since $F_{.95}(14, 19) = 2.26$ our decision rule is: Reject $H_0$ if calculated $F > 2.26$; accept $H_0$ if calculated $F \le 2.26$.

We calculate F.

$$F = \frac{8^2}{6^2} = \frac{64}{36} = 1.78$$

Since $1.78 \le 2.26$, we accept $H_0$ and conclude that the variances of the populations of boys and girls are equal.

● PROBLEM 16-64

The standard deviation of a particular dimension of a metal component is small enough so that it is satisfactory in subsequent assembly. A new supplier of metal plate is under consideration and will be preferred if the standard deviation of his product is not larger, because the cost of his product is lower than that of the present supplier. A sample of 100 items from each supplier is obtained. The results are as follows:

New supplier: $S_1^2 = .0058$.

Old supplier: $S_2^2 = .0041$.

Should the new supplier's metal plates be purchased?  Test at the 5% level of significance.

Solution:    Our hypotheses for this problem are

$H_0: \sigma_1^2 = \sigma_2^2$        $H_1: \sigma_1^2 > \sigma_2^2$.

The statistic $\dfrac{S_1^2}{S_2^2}$ has an F distribution with $df_1$, the number of degrees of freedom for the numerator, equal to $n_1 - 1$, and $df_2$, the number of degrees of freedom for the denominator, equal to $n_2 - 1$.

We will reject $H_0$ if our calculated $F = \dfrac{S_1^2}{S_2^2}$ is greater than $F_{.95}(df_1, df_2)$.  Since $df_1 = 100 - 1 = 99$ and $df_2 = 100 - 1 = 99$, our decision rule is: reject $H_0$ if calculated $F > 1.39$; accept $H_0$ if $F \leq 1.39$.

We calculate F:

$$F = \frac{0.0058}{0.0041} = 1.41.$$

Since $1.41 > 1.39$, we reject $H_0$ and conclude at the 5% level of significance that the variance of the new plates is greater than that of the old plates.  Therefore the new supplier's metal plates should <u>not</u> be purchased.

● **PROBLEM 16-65**

An experimenter produced two kinds of lesions in monkeys - Lesion 1 in one group, Lesion 2 in another group.  Then he observed each animal for a month after surgery and rated the amount of aggression each animal displayed.  He theorized that the two groups would differ primarily in variability.  Here is the data:

Lesion 1              Lesion 2

$\overline{X} = 95.3$            $\overline{X} = 94.8$
$s^2 = 13.7$            $s^2 = 6.13$
$N = 31$              $N = 31$

Do the groups differ in variability?  Assume that the scores are normal, and use the .02 level of significance.

Solution:    Our hypotheses for this problem are:

$H_0: \sigma_1^2 = \sigma_2^2$        $H_1: \sigma_1^2 \neq \sigma_2^2$ .

The statistic $\dfrac{S_1^2}{S_2^2}$ has an F distribution with $df_1$, the number of degrees of freedom for the numerator, equal to $n_1 - 1$, and $df_2$, the number of degrees of freedom for the denominator, equal to $n_2 - 1$.

Since we have a two-tailed test, we must calculate $F = \frac{s_1{}^2}{s_2{}^2}$ and reject $H_0$ if $F > F_{.99}(df_1, df_2)$ or if $F < \frac{1}{F_{.99}(df_2, df_1)}$. Since $df_1 = 30$ and $df_2 = 30$ our decision rule is: reject $H_0$ if $F > 2.38$ or $F < \frac{1}{2.38} = .42$; accept $H_0$ if $.42 \leq F \leq 2.38$.

We calculate F.

$$F = \frac{13.7}{6.13} = 2.23.$$

Since $.42 \leq 2.23 \leq 2.38$, we accept $H_0$ and conclude that the 2 groups do not differ in variability.

● **PROBLEM** 16-66

An investigator tested two samples, one of boys and one of girls. He wanted to know whether the results for girls are significantly more variable than for boys. Test for this at the 5% level of significance using the following sample data.

|  | Sample Size | $S^2$ |
|---|---|---|
| Boys | 8 | 50.21 |
| Girls | 9 | 147.62 |

**Solution:** To solve this problem first we set up the following hypotheses.

$$H_0: \sigma_g{}^2 = \sigma_b{}^2 \qquad H_1: \sigma_g{}^2 > \sigma_b{}^2 .$$

We next calculate the F ratio equal to $\frac{s_g{}^2}{s_b{}^2}$ and compare this value to the critical table value of F for $df_1 = n_g - 1$, $df_2 = n_b - 1$, and $\alpha = .05$.

This is done because the statistic $\frac{s_g{}^2}{s_b{}^2}$ has an F distribution with $n_g - 1$ degrees of freedom for the numerator and $n_b - 1$ degrees of freedom for the denominator. In this case $n_g - 1 = 8$, $n_b - 1 = 7$, and our critical F is

3.73. Therefore our decision rule is: reject $H_0$ if calculated F > 3.73; accept $H_0$ if calculated F is $\leq$ 3.73.

We calculate F.

$$F = \frac{147.62}{50.21} = 2.94.$$

Since 2.94 $\leq$ 3.73, we accept $H_0$ and conclude that girls' results are not more significantly variable than boys' results at the 5% level of significance.

● **PROBLEM 16-67**

Two independent random samples of size $n_1 = 10$ and $n_2 = 7$ were observed to have sample variances of $S_1^2 = 16$ and $S_2^2 = 3$. Using a 10% level of significance, test $H_0: \sigma_1^2 = \sigma_2^2$ against $H_1: \sigma_1^2 \neq \sigma_2^2$. Then using a 5% level of significance, test $H_0$ against $H_1: \sigma_1^2 > \sigma_2^2$ and $H_1: \sigma_1^2 < \sigma_2^2$.

<u>Solution:</u>    The statistic $\frac{S_1^2}{S_2^2}$ has an F distribution with $df_1$, the number of degrees of freedom for the numerator, equal to $n_1 - 1$, and $df_2$, the number of degrees of freedom for the denominator, equal to $n_2 - 1$.

For $H_1: \sigma_1^2 \neq \sigma_2^2$, we have a two-tailed test so we use $\frac{\alpha}{2} = .05$ for each of the two rejection areas. We compare our calculated $F = \frac{S_1^2}{S_2^2}$ to $F_{.95}$ $(df_1, df_2)$ and

$\frac{1}{F_{.95} (df_2, df_1)}$ .    Since $df_1 = n_1 - 1 = 9$ and $n_2 - 1 = 6$, our decision rule is: reject $H_0$ if calculated F > 4.10 or F < .297; accept $H_0$ if .297 $\leq$ F $\leq$ 4.10. We calculate F.

$F = \frac{16}{3} = 5.33$ and since 5.33 > 4.10, we reject $H_0$.

For $H_1: \sigma_1^2 > \sigma_2^2$, our decision rule is for $\alpha = .05$: reject $H_0$ if F > 4.10; accept $H_0$ if F < 4.10. Again we have
$$F = \frac{16}{3} = 5.33 \qquad \text{and so again we reject } H_0.$$
For $H_1: \sigma_1^2 < \sigma_2^2$, we would calculate
$F = \frac{S_2^2}{S_1^2}$ and compare the calculated F to $F_{.95}$ (6, 9) instead of $F_{.95}$ (9, 6). Therefore our decision rule becomes: reject $H_0$ if calculated F > 3.37; accept $H_0$ if F $\leq$ 3.37. We calculate F.

$$F = \frac{3}{16} = .18.$$

Since .18 $\leq$ 3.37, we accept $H_0$.

A laboratory owns two precision measuring devices. The director suspects that there is a slight difference in calibration between the two, so that one of them (he doesn't know which) tends to give slightly higher readings than the other. He proposes to check the two devices by taking readings of 50 different objects on both machines. Outline an appropriate statistical test at the 5% significance level.

<u>Solution</u>: Since the samples are not independent, we cannot use the normal distribution directly. Instead, we may use difference scores. Since we have 50 difference scores, (i.e., more than 30) we may use a Z-test; i.e. the statistic $\frac{\bar{D} - \mu_D}{S_{\bar{D}}}$ is normally distributed with a mean of 0 and a standard deviation of 1. We have

$$H_0: \mu_D = 0 \qquad H_1: \mu_D \neq 0$$

and for $\alpha = .05$ and a two-tailed test, our decision rule is: reject $H_0$ if $Z > 1.96$ or $Z < -1.96$; accept $H_0$ if $-1.96 \leq Z \leq 1.96$.

We calculate $\quad Z = \dfrac{\bar{D} - \mu_D}{S_{\bar{D}}} \quad$ where

$$S_{\bar{D}} = \frac{S_D}{\sqrt{n}} \quad \text{and} \quad S_D = \sqrt{\frac{N\Sigma D^2 - (\Sigma D)^2}{N(N-1)}}$$

where D = the reading given by one of the measuring devices minus the reading given by the other measuring device for each of the 50 different objects.

For the data of this problem,

$$S_D = \sqrt{\frac{50\Sigma D^2 - (\Sigma D)^2}{50(49)}}$$

$$S_{\bar{D}} = \frac{S_D}{\sqrt{50}}, \quad \text{and} \quad Z = \frac{\bar{D} - 0}{S_D/\sqrt{50}} = \frac{\bar{D}}{S/\sqrt{50}}.$$

For given $\bar{D}$ and $S_D$ we can obtain a numerical value for Z and apply the decision rule.

Ten pairs of littermates were studied from birth. One animal of each pair was raised under stress conditions, the other under nonstress conditions. After one year, all the littermates were given tests of motor ability, coordination, and balance. Numerical scores were given to each subject; the scores are given below. Do the means of the nonstress and stress subjects differ significantly?

Use a 5% level of significance.

| Littermate Pair | A | B | C | D | E | F | G | H | I | J |
|---|---|---|---|---|---|---|---|---|---|---|
| Nonstress Subject | 50 | 46 | 50 | 64 | 54 | 70 | 58 | 74 | 58 | 66 |
| Stress Subject | 34 | 42 | 46 | 46 | 50 | 54 | 58 | 58 | 62 | 70 |

Solution: Since the samples represent paired data, we cannot use the normal distribution directly. Instead, we will compute difference scores and test whether the mean difference, $M_D$, is zero or significantly different from zero.

Since n is $\leq$ 30 and $\sigma$ is unknown, the statistic $\dfrac{\overline{D} - \mu_D}{S_{\overline{D}}}$ has a t-distribution with a mean of 0 and a standard deviation of 1.

Our hypotheses for this test are

$H_0: \mu_D = 0$ $\qquad$ $H_1: \mu_D \neq 0$.

Since there are 10 pairs of data, we have 9 df's and our decision rule for $\alpha = .05$ is: reject $H_0$ if $t > 2.262$ or $t < -2.262$; accept $H_0$ if $-2.262 \leq t \leq 2.262$.

We must now calculate

$$t = \frac{\overline{D} - \mu_D}{S_{\overline{D}}} \qquad \text{where} \qquad S_{\overline{D}} = \frac{S_D}{\sqrt{n}} \qquad \text{and}$$

$$S_D \doteq \sqrt{\frac{n\Sigma D^2 - (\Sigma D)^2}{n(n-1)}}.$$

We use the table below to calculate $S_D$.

| Nonstress, X | Stress, Y | D = X - Y | $D^2$ |
|---|---|---|---|
| 50 | 34 | 16 | 256 |
| 46 | 42 | 4 | 16 |
| 50 | 46 | 4 | 16 |
| 64 | 46 | 18 | 324 |
| 54 | 50 | 4 | 16 |
| 70 | 54 | 16 | 256 |
| 58 | 58 | 0 | 0 |
| 74 | 58 | 16 | 256 |
| 58 | 62 | −4 | 16 |
| 66 | 70 | −4 | 16 |
| | | 70 | 1172 |

Using this data, we obtain

$$S_D = \sqrt{\frac{10(1172) - (70)^2}{10(9)}} = \sqrt{\frac{11720 - 4900}{90}}$$

$$= \sqrt{\frac{6820}{90}} = 8.71 \qquad \text{and} \qquad S_{\overline{D}} = \frac{8.71}{\sqrt{10}} = 2.75.$$

Since $\Sigma D = 70$ and $n = 10$, then $\overline{D} = 7.0$ and we may now calculate

$$t = \frac{7.0 - 0}{2.75} = 2.55.$$

Since $2.55 > 2.262$, we reject $H_0$ and conclude that there is a significant difference at the 5% level between the scores of those littermates brought up under stress and those brought up without stress.

# TESTS INVOLVING THE POISSON DISTRIBUTION

● PROBLEM 16-70

A plant manager claims that on the average no more than 5 service calls per hour are made by the plant's workers. Suppose in one particular hour, 9 service calls were required. At a 5% level of significance, could we now reject the plant manager's claim?

Solution: The number of accidents, claims, errors, or other such occurrences in a fixed time interval has a Poisson distribution.

We may use the Poisson distribution for this problem, where the variable in question is the number of service calls.

Our hypotheses in this problem are

$H_0: \lambda = 5$ $\qquad\qquad$ $H_1: \lambda > 5$

where $\lambda$ is the average number of service calls in the fixed time interval of one hour.

For the hypothesized value of $\lambda = 5$, the probability of obtaining 9 or more service calls in one hour is, using a table of Poisson probabilities, given by

$.0363 + .0181 + .0082 + .0034 + .0013 + .0005 + .0002 = .068$

which equals $Pr(9 \text{ service calls}) + Pr(10 \text{ service calls}) + Pr(11 \text{ service calls}) + Pr(12 \text{ service calls}) + Pr(13 \text{ service calls}) + Pr(14 \text{ service calls}) + Pr(15 \text{ service calls})$. (Note: the probability of higher numbers of service calls is virtually 0).

Since this value of .068 is greater than .05, the probability of an hour occurring where 9 or more service calls are required is greater than 5%. Hence at a 5% level of significance, we would not reject $H_0$.

● **PROBLEM** 16-71

If 99% of a certain publisher's books are ordinarily bound perfectly, would the finding of 3 imperfectly bound books in an order of 60 books be significant of a lowered quality, or might this occurrence come about as a result of mere chance?

Solution:    Since a variable such as the number of publisher's books which are bound imperfectly has a Poisson distribution we will use the Poisson distribution to solve this problem. Since 1% of the books are ordinarily found to be bound imperfectly, the expected number, $\lambda$, of books bound imperfectly from a sample of 60 books is

$\lambda = .01 \times 60 = 0.6.$

We choose as our hypotheses for this problem

$H_0: \lambda = 0.6$            $H_1: \lambda > 0.6.$

Under the null hypothesis, $H_0$, the probability of obtaining 3 defective books or more is given by

$.0198 + .0030 + .0004 =$

Pr(3 defective books) + Pr(4 defective books) + Pr(5 defective books) =   .0232.

Note that Pr(6 defective books) and higher numbers of defective books = 0 according to Poisson distribution tables.

Since the probability of 3 or more defective books is .0232, we can reject $H_0$ at a level of significance of .05, but not at a level of significance of .01.

# COMBINING RESULTS OF DIFFERENT SAMPLES

● **PROBLEM** 16-72

Two independent reports on the value of a tincture for treating a disease in camels were available. The first report made on a small pilot series showed the new tincture to be probably superior to the old treatment with a Yates' $\chi^2$ of 3.84, df = 1, $\alpha$ = .05. The second report with a larger trial gave a "not significant" result with a Yates $\chi^2$ = 2.71, df = 1, $\alpha$ = .10. Can the results of the 2 reports be combined to form a new conclusion?

Solution: The statistic $\chi^2$ is additive, so we may combine the results by adding the values of $\chi^2$ and the degrees of freedom. To make the combined result stronger and more accurate, we should recalculate each value of $\chi^2$ from the $2 \times 2$ data tables of the two original studies without the Yates' correction. Since these tables are not available, we must be satisfied with the weaker result obtained by adding the Yates' $\chi^2$ values. We obtain $\chi^2 = 6.55$, df = 2, which is significant at $\alpha = .05$. Thus the difference between the old and new treatments using the combined results of the 2 studies is significant.

● PROBLEM 16-73

A study in which infants were fed baked beans showed that such infants tended to gain more weight than a control group. The Z-value calculated was 1.96, which is equivalent to significance at p = .05. In a second independent study, the Z-value calculated was 1.64, significant only at p = .10. What conclusion can be reached if we combine the results of these 2 studies?

Solution: The Z-values cannot be added together like $\chi^2$ values but we may convert each p-value associated with a Z-value to a $\chi^2$ value by using the following formula

$$\chi^2 \text{(for 2 d.f.)} = -2 \log_e \left(\frac{P \text{ }\%}{100}\right)$$

$$- 2 \log_e 10 \left[\log_{10} \frac{P \text{ }\%}{100}\right]$$

$$= -2(2.3)(\log_{10} P \text{ }\% - \log_{10} 100)$$

$$= -4.6 (\log_{10} P \text{ }\% - 2)$$

$$= 4.6 (2 - \log_{10} P \text{ }\%).$$

For p = 5

$\chi^2 = 4.6(2 - .6990) = 4.6(1.3010) = 5.98$.

For p = 10, we obtain

$\chi^2 = 4.6 (2 - 1) = 4.60$.

In each case df = 2, so our combined

$\chi^2 = 5.98 + 4.60 = 10.58$

with df = 4, which is significant for p < .05. Therefore, combining the results of the 2 studies, we can conclude that a diet of baked beans for a group of infants does cause a greater weight gain than occurs for a control group.

In a recent science fiction novel, aliens invented a death
ray that killed 3 Earthman. The lethal doses were 10, 11,
and 12 units of the ray. The mean lethal dose for Moonmen
is 13.30 units. For this sample of 3 Earthmen $\bar{X}$ = 11 and
S = 1.0 and a test of significance of the difference between
the mean for Earthmen and Moonmen yields t = 3.98, not
significant at the $\alpha$ = .05 level of significance. Then 6
more Earthmen were killed with lethal doses of 9, 10, 11,
12, 13 and 14. For this sample, $\bar{X}$ = 11.5, and S = 1.87,
and a test of significance of the difference between the
mean for Earthmen and Moonmen yields t = 2.36, also not
significant at $\alpha$ = .05. What can be said if we combine
the results of these two samples?

Solution:    Since it is reasonable to assume that both
samples come from the same population we may combine them
directly.    Since for the 9 cases,

$$\Sigma X = 102 \; ; \qquad \Sigma X^2 = 1176 \; ; \qquad \bar{X} = \frac{\Sigma X}{N} \quad \text{and}$$

$$S = \sqrt{\frac{N\Sigma X^2 - (\Sigma X)^2}{N(N-1)}} \; ,$$

this yields in the combined group an $\bar{X}$ = 11.33 and S = 1.58.
Comparing this data to the mean for Moonmen which is 13.3
yields

$$t = \frac{11.33 - 13.3}{1.58/3} = -\frac{1.97}{.527} = -3.74$$

which results in a significant difference at $\alpha$ = .01 and
df = 9 - 1 = 8 since the critical t for 8 df's is 2.896.

# TYPE II ERRORS

Suppose an experimenter is about to analyze some data.  In the data
$\sigma_{\bar{X}_E - \bar{X}_C}$ = 1.0.  The data require a two-tailed test, and the experimenter
adopts the .05 level of significance.

Probability of Accepting $H_0$ and Rejecting $H_0$ for Different Sizes of $\mu_E$-$\mu_C$.

| $\mu_E$-$\mu_C$ (true mean difference) | Probability of accepting $H_0$ | An error to accept $H_0$? | Probability of rejecting $H_0$ | An error to reject $H_0$? |
|---|---|---|---|---|
| 4.0 | .021 | Type II Error | .979 | Not an error: $\mu_0 \neq 0$ |
| 3.5 | .062 | " | .938 | " |
| 3.0 | .149 | " | .851 | " |
| 2.5 | .295 | " | .705 | " |
| 2.0 | ☐ | " | .516 | " |
| 1.5 | .677 | " | .323 | " |
| 1.0 | .830 | " | .170 | " |
| .5 | .921 | " | .079 | " |
| 0 | .950 | Not an error: $\mu_0$= 0 | .050 | Type I Error |
| -.5 | .921 | " | .079 | Not an error: $\mu_0 \neq 0$ |
| -1.0 | .830 | " | .170 | " |
| -1.5 | .677 | " | .323 | " |
| -2.0 | .484 | " | .516 | " |
| -2.5 | .295 | " | .705 | " |
| -3.0 | .149 | " | .851 | " |
| -3.5 | .062 | " | .938 | " |
| -4.0 | .021 | " | .979 | " |

Let us consider differences of various sizes: Let $\mu_E - \mu_C$ range from -4.0 to +4.0. Then for each value, we compute the probability of a Type II error. The table reports all of the probabilities but one. Compute that missing value.

Solution: We will accept $H_0$ at a level of significance of .05 if $\bar{X}_E - \bar{X}_C$ lies within $\pm 1.96$ standard deviations of 0, since $\mu_E - \mu_C = 0$ according to $H_0$. But the standard deviation of the differences between the means $(\sigma_{\bar{X}_E - \bar{X}_C})$ is 1.0. Therefore we will accept $H_0$ if $\bar{X}_E - \bar{X}_C$ lies between -1.96 and +1.96. But when $\mu_E - \mu_C = 2.0$, our normal curve will be as given in the figure below.

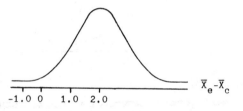

The probability of $\bar{X}_E - \bar{X}_C$ being less than -1.96 in this case is given by using the formula

$$Z = \frac{-1.96 - 2.00}{1.00} = \frac{-3.96}{1.00} = -3.96$$

since the statistic

$$\frac{(\bar{X}_E - \bar{X}_C) - (\mu_E - \mu_C)}{\sigma_{\bar{X}_E - \bar{X}_C}}$$

is normally distributed with a mean of 0 and standard deviation of 1.

Using the table for probabilities associated with the normal curve yields a probability of this occurring to be .00005.

The probability of $\bar{X}_E - \bar{X}_C$ being less than 1.96 is given by the formula

$$Z = \frac{1.96 - 2.00}{1.00} = \frac{-.04}{1.00} = -.04 \; .$$

Using the table for probabilities associated with the normal curve yields  .4840  as the probability of  $\bar{X}_E - \bar{X}_C$  being less than  1.96.  Therefore the probability of  $\bar{X}_E - \bar{X}_C$  lying between  -1.96  and  1.96  when  $\mu_E - \mu_C = 2.00$  is  .4840 -.00005  or approximately  .484.

● **PROBLEM** 16-76

---

Given
$$H_0 : \mu = \mu_0$$
$$H_1 : \mu = \mu_1 ,$$

and $\alpha$ and $\beta$ are probabilities of making type I and type II errors respectively, show that for a two-tailed test the required sample size n is given approximately by

$$n = \frac{(Z_{\alpha/2} + Z_\beta)^2 \; \sigma^2}{(\mu_1 - \mu_0)^2} \quad ,$$

provided that

$$Pr\left(Z < - Z_{\alpha/2} - \frac{\sqrt{n}|\mu_1 - \mu_0|}{\sigma}\right)$$

is small when  $\mu = \mu_1$ .

---

Solution:  Refer to the figure below.

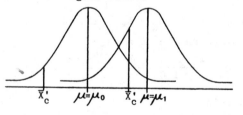

There is a critical value of  $\bar{X}$.  Call it  $\bar{X}_C$.  If our sample mean falls above  $\bar{X}_C$,  we will reject  $H_0$  and accept  $H_1$.  In addition, we will reject  $H_0$  and accept  $H_1$  if our sample mean falls below a value  $\bar{X}'_C$ .

Since  $\alpha$  is specified, we know that

$$Z_{\alpha/2} = \frac{\bar{X}_C - \mu_0}{\sigma/\sqrt{n}} \quad . \tag{1}$$

Also,

$$Z = \frac{\bar{X}_C - \mu_1}{\sigma/\sqrt{n}} \quad . \tag{2}$$

Now if  $Pr(X < \bar{X}'_C)$  is small when  $\mu = \mu_1$ , we may assume the  Z  in equation (2) is actually  $-Z_\beta$ .  So

$$-Z_\beta = \frac{\bar{X}_C - \mu_1}{\sigma/\sqrt{n}} \quad . \tag{3}$$

We solve equation (1) for $\bar{X}_C$. Multiplying both sides by $\sigma/\sqrt{n}$, we obtain

$$\frac{Z_{\alpha/2}\,\sigma}{\sqrt{n}} = \bar{X}_C - \mu_0$$

and

$$\bar{X}_C = \frac{Z_{\alpha/2}\,\sigma}{\sqrt{n}} + \mu_0 .$$

Substituting this value for $\bar{X}_C$ in equation (3) yields

$$-Z_\beta = \frac{\dfrac{Z_{\alpha/2}\sigma}{\sqrt{n}} + \mu_0 - \mu_1}{\sigma/\sqrt{n}} . \qquad (4)$$

Multiplying the numerator and denominator of the right side of equation (4) by $\sqrt{n}$ yields

$$-Z_\beta = \frac{Z_{\alpha/2}\sigma + \mu_0\sqrt{n} - \mu_1\sqrt{n}}{\sigma} .$$

Multiplying both sides by $\sigma$ yields

$$-Z_\beta\,\sigma = Z_{\alpha/2}\,\sigma + \mu_0\sqrt{n} - \mu_1\sqrt{n} .$$

Subtracting $Z_{\alpha/2}\sigma$ from both sides $\quad -Z_\beta\sigma - Z_{\alpha/2}\sigma = \mu_0\sqrt{n} - \mu_1\sqrt{n}$

Multiplying this equation by $-1 \quad Z_\beta\sigma + Z_{\alpha/2}\sigma = \mu_1\sqrt{n} - \mu_0\sqrt{n} .$

Factoring, we obtain

$$\sigma(Z_\beta + Z_{\alpha/2}) = \sqrt{n}(\mu_1 - \mu_0) . \qquad \text{Dividing each side by } (\mu_1 - \mu_0)$$

$$\frac{\sigma(Z_\beta + Z_{\alpha/2})}{\mu_1 - \mu_0} = \sqrt{n} \quad \text{and}$$

$$n = \frac{\sigma^2(Z_\beta + Z_{\alpha/2})^2}{(\mu_1 - \mu_0)^2}$$

as required.

Now what does "$\Pr(X < \bar{X}'_c)$ is small when $\mu = \mu_1$" mean? We have, whenever $X < \bar{X}'_c$

$$Z < \frac{\bar{X}'_c - \mu_1}{\sigma/\sqrt{n}} . \qquad (5)$$

But we know that

$$-Z_{\alpha/2} = \frac{\bar{X}'_c - \mu_0}{\sigma/\sqrt{n}} . \qquad (6)$$

We solve equation (6) for $\bar{X}'_c$. Multiplying both sides of equation (6) by $\sigma/\sqrt{n}$

$$\frac{-Z_{\alpha/2}\sigma}{\sqrt{n}} = \bar{X}'_c - \mu_0 .$$

Adding $\mu_0$ to both sides of this equation yields

$$\bar{X}'_c = \mu_0 - \frac{Z_{\alpha/2}\sigma}{\sqrt{n}} .$$

Substituting this value for $\bar{X}'_c$ in equation (5) yields

$$Z < \frac{\mu_0 - Z_{\alpha/2}\sigma/\sqrt{n} - \mu_1}{\sigma/\sqrt{n}} .$$

Multiplying the numerator and denominator of the right side of this equation by $\sqrt{n}$ yields

$$Z < \frac{\sqrt{n}\,\mu_0 - Z_{\alpha/2}\,\sigma - \sqrt{n}\,\mu_1}{\sigma} .$$

Rearranging terms

$$Z < -Z_{\alpha/2} - \frac{\sqrt{n}(\mu_1 - \mu_0)}{\sigma} .$$

Since $Z < -Z_{\alpha/2} - \dfrac{\sqrt{n}(\mu_1 - \mu_0)}{\sigma}$ whenever $X < \bar{X}'_c$ , our assumption that $Pr(X < \bar{X}'_c)$ is small is equivalent to $Pr(Z < -Z_{\alpha/2} - \dfrac{\sqrt{n}(\mu_1 - \mu_0)}{\sigma})$ as required.

● **PROBLEM 16-77**

Apply the results of the previous problem when $\alpha = .05$, $\beta = .10$, $\mu_0 = 72$, $\mu_1 = 74$ and $\sigma = 2$ to find an appropriate sample size, $n$.

Solution: For $\alpha = .05$, $Z_{\alpha/2} = 1.96$; for $\beta = .10$, $Z_\beta = 1.28$, we have the following.
We may use

$$n = \frac{(Z_{\alpha/2} + Z_\beta)^2 \, \sigma^2}{(\mu_1 - \mu_0)^2}$$

provided that

$$Pr(Z < -Z_{\alpha/2} - \frac{\sqrt{n}(\mu_1 - \mu_0)}{\sigma} )$$

is small when $\mu = \mu_1$ .
For the values given,

$$n = \frac{(1.96 + 1.28)^2 (2)^2}{(74 - 72)^2} = \frac{(3.24)^2 (2)^2}{(2)^2} = 10.50.$$

We round $n$ up to the next integer, 11. Now

$$Pr(Z < -Z_{\alpha/2} - \frac{\sqrt{n}(\mu_1 - \mu_0)}{\sigma})$$

becomes

$$Pr(Z < -1.96 - \frac{\sqrt{11(74 - 72)}}{2} )$$

$$= Pr(Z < -1.96 - \sqrt{11})$$

$$= \Pr(Z < -1.96 - 3.32)$$

$$= \Pr(Z < -5.28)$$

which is certainly small.

Our appropriate sample size  n, is therefore  11.

For a one-sided hypothesis test, where we have

$$H_0 : \mu = \mu_0$$

$$H_1 : \mu = \mu_1$$

with given  $\alpha$  and  $\beta$  explain why the required sample size is given by the expression

$$n = \frac{(Z_\alpha + Z_\beta)^2 \sigma^2}{(\mu_1 - \mu_0)^2} \ .$$

Solution:   The figure below depicts the problem.

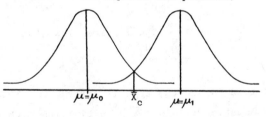

$$\mu = \mu_0 \qquad \bar{X}_c \qquad \mu = \mu_1$$

The critical value of  $\bar{X}$  is  $\bar{X}_c$ .  If our sample mean is above  $\bar{X}_c$  we will reject  $H_0$ .  Otherwise we will accept  $H_0$.

Since  $\alpha$  is specified, we have

$$Z_\alpha = \frac{\bar{X}_c - \mu_0}{\sigma \sqrt{n}} \ , \quad \text{and also} \tag{1}$$

$$-Z_\beta = \frac{\bar{X}_c - \mu_1}{\sigma / \sqrt{n}} \ . \tag{2}$$

As we did 2 problems ago we may solve equation (1) for  $\bar{X}_c$, substitute the value for  $\bar{X}_c$  in equation (2), and then solve the resulting equation for  n.  The algebra is exactly the same as that performed 2 problems ago.  The reader is referred to that problem for details.  The final result gives

$$n = \frac{(Z_\alpha + Z_\beta)^2 \sigma^2}{(\mu_1 - \mu_0)^2}$$

as desired.

A manufacturer produces a special alloy steel with an average tensile strength of 25,800 psi. A change in the composition of the alloy is said to increase the breaking strength but not affect the standard deviation which is known to be 300 psi. The manufacturer wants to conclude that the tensile strength has increased only if he is 99% sure of this ($\alpha = .01$). If the average tensile strength is increased by as much as 250 psi, the manufacturer wants to err by not detecting the change at most 10% of the time ($\beta = .10$). What is the required sample size to meet these conditions?

<u>Solution:</u>  The figure below depicts this problem:

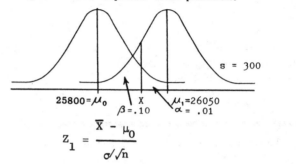

$$Z_1 = \frac{\bar{X} - \mu_0}{\sigma/\sqrt{n}} \tag{1}$$

where  $Z_1 = 2.33$ since the type I error, $\alpha = .01$.  Also

$$Z_2 = \frac{\bar{X} - \mu_1}{\sigma/\sqrt{n}} \tag{2}$$

where  $Z_2 = -1.28$  since the type II error, $\beta = .10$.

We solve equation (1) for $\bar{X}$. Multiplying both sides by $\sigma/\sqrt{n}$.

$$\frac{Z_1 \sigma}{\sqrt{n}} = \bar{X} - \mu_0 \quad \text{and}$$

$$\bar{X} = \frac{Z_1 \sigma}{\sqrt{n}} + \mu_0 .$$

Substituting this value for $\bar{X}$ in equation (2) yields

$$Z_2 = \frac{Z_1 \sigma/\sqrt{n} + \mu_0 - \mu_1}{\sigma/\sqrt{n}} . \tag{3}$$

Multiplying numerator and denominator of the right side of equation (3) by $\sqrt{n}$ yields

$$Z_2 = \frac{Z_1 \sigma + \mu_0 \sqrt{n} - \mu_1 \sqrt{n}}{\sigma}$$

Multiplying both sides by $\sigma$    $Z_2 \sigma = Z_1 \sigma + \mu_0 \sqrt{n} - \mu_1 \sqrt{n} .$

Subtracting $Z_1 \sigma$ from both sides    $Z_2 \sigma - Z_1 \sigma = \mu_0 \sqrt{n} - \mu_1 \sqrt{n} .$

Factoring each side

$$\sigma(Z_2 - Z_1) = \sqrt{n}(\mu_0 - \mu_1) \ .$$

Dividing each side by $(\mu_0 - \mu_1)$

$$\frac{\sigma(Z_2 - Z_1)}{\mu_0 - \mu_1} = \sqrt{n} \quad \text{and}$$

$$n = \frac{\sigma^2(Z_2 - Z_1)^2}{(\mu_0 - \mu_1)^2} \ .$$

But for this problem, $Z_1$ becomes $Z_\alpha$ and $Z_2$ becomes $-Z_\beta$. So we obtain

$$n = \frac{\sigma^2(-Z_\beta - Z_\alpha)^2}{(\mu_0 - \mu_1)^2} \ .$$

Since $(-Z_\beta - Z_\alpha)^2 = (Z_\alpha + Z_\beta)^2$ and $(\mu_0 - \mu_1)^2 = (\mu_1 - \mu_0)^2$. we may rewrite $n$ as

$$n = \frac{\sigma^2(Z_\alpha + Z_\beta)^2}{(\mu_1 - \mu_0)^2} \ .$$

For this particular problem

$$n = \frac{300^2(2.33 + 1.28)^2}{(26,050 - 25,800)^2}$$

$$= \frac{300^2(3.61)^2}{(250)^2} = (4.332)^2$$

$$= 18.77.$$

So the required sample size to meet the criteria of this problem is the next higher integer or 19.

● PROBLEM 16-80

For the previous problem suppose 19 observations were made and that the sample mean is found to be 26,100 psi. Would the manufacturer conclude that the change in the composition of the alloy increased the breaking strength?

Solution: The figure below depicts the problem.

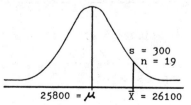

We choose $H_0: \mu \leq 25,800$    $H_1: \mu > 25,800$ .

We calculate

$$Z = \frac{\bar{X} - \mu}{\sigma_{\bar{X}}} \quad \text{where} \quad \sigma_{\bar{X}} = \frac{\sigma}{\sqrt{n}} \ .$$

We use $Z$ in this case instead of $t$ because $\sigma$, the population standard deviation, is known.

For the data of this problem

$$\sigma_{\bar{X}} = \frac{300}{\sqrt{19}} = 68.8 \quad \text{and}$$

$$Z = \frac{26,100 - 25,800}{68.8} = \frac{300}{68.8} = 4.36 \ .$$

At a 1% level of significance we will reject $H_0$ if $Z > 2.33$ and accept $H_0$ if $Z < 2.33$. Since $4.36 > 2.33$, we reject $H_0$ and conclude that the change in composition of the alloy did increase the breaking strength.

● **PROBLEM** 16-81

We desire to perform an experiment to determine whether surface finish has an effect on the endurance limit of steel. There exists a theory that polishing increases the average endurance limit. If in our experiment we wish to detect that polishing fails to have an effect with a probability of 0.99 ($\alpha = .01$) and we also wish to detect a change of 7500 units by a probability of at least 0.9, then if it is known that the standard deviation of the endurance limit of the steel is 4000 units, what sample size would be needed to carry out this experiment?

Solution: The formula for the sample size $n$ for this problem is

$$n = \frac{\sigma^2_{\bar{X}-\bar{Y}}(Z_\alpha + Z_\beta)^2}{(\mu_1 - \mu_0)^2}$$

where $\sigma^2_{\bar{X}-\bar{Y}}$, the square of the standard error of the difference between two means, is given by $\sigma^2_{\bar{X}} + \sigma^2_{\bar{Y}}$ . In this case

$$\sigma^2_{\bar{X}-\bar{Y}} = (4000)^2 + (4000)^2 = 2(4000)^2.$$

For $\alpha = .01$, $Z_\alpha = 2.33$; for $\beta = .10$ ($= 1 - .9$), $Z_\beta = 1.28$. Then

$$n = \frac{2(4000)^2(2.33 + 1.28)^2}{(7500)^2}$$

$$= 2(1.925)^2 = 7.41.$$

We round this value up to the next highest integer value to obtain the required sample size of 8.

648

Suppose the previous problem's experiment was carried out with a sample size of 8. The mean, $\bar{X}$, for the 8 test cases for polished steel was 86,375. The mean, $\bar{Y}$, for the 8 test cases for unpolished steel was 79,838. Can we conclude at a 1% level of significance that the average endurance limit of polished specimens is greater than the average endurance limit for unpolished specimens?

**Solution:** For this problem we have

$$H_0: \mu_X - \mu_Y = 0$$

$$H_1: \mu_X - \mu_Y > 0 .$$

Our decision rule is, for $\alpha = .01$ and a one-tailed test: reject $H_0$ if $Z > 2.33$; accept $H_0$ if $Z \leq 2.33$. We use a Z-test instead of a t-test because the population standard deviation, $\sigma$, is known.

We compute

$$Z = \frac{\bar{X} - \bar{Y} - 0}{\sigma_{\bar{X} - \bar{Y}}} \quad \text{where}$$

$$\sigma_{\bar{X}-\bar{Y}} = \sqrt{\frac{\sigma^2}{n_1} + \frac{\sigma^2}{n_2}} .$$

Since $n_1 = n_2 = 8$ and $\sigma = 4000$, we have in this case

$$\sigma_{\bar{X}-\bar{Y}} = \sqrt{\frac{4000^2}{8} + \frac{4000^2}{8}}$$

$$= \frac{4000}{2}\sqrt{\tfrac{1}{2} + \tfrac{1}{2}} = 2000$$

and

$$Z = \frac{86,375 - 79,838}{2000} = \frac{6537}{2000} = 3.27 .$$

Since $3.27 > 2.33$, we reject $H_0$ and conclude that polished steel specimens <u>do</u> have a higher mean endurance limit than unpolished ones.

A manufacturer of electric irons uses thermostats in the production of its irons. A savings can be made by purchasing thermostats from a new supplier. However, we wish to know whether these new thermostats are as accurate as the old ones about which very few complaints were received. The thermostats are to be tested on the irons on the $550°$ F setting, and the actual temperatures are to be read with a thermocouple. The level of significance, $\alpha$, is chosen to be 5%. The manufacturer feels that a switch is undesirable if the average temperature changes by more than $10.5°$, with the risk of making an incorrect decision not exceeding 0.10. The order of magnitude of the standard deviation is roughly $10°$ for the old supplier, and there is no reason to suspect that it will be different for the new supplier. How many of each type of thermostat should be used to test whether there is a significant difference between the old and the new thermostats?

Solution: The formula for $n$ for this problem is

$$n = \frac{\sigma^2_{\bar{X}-\bar{Y}} (Z_{\alpha/2} + Z_\beta)^2}{(\mu_1 - \mu_0)^2}$$

where $\sigma^2_{\bar{X}-\bar{Y}}$, the square of the standard error of the difference between two means, is given by $\sigma^2_{\bar{X}} + \sigma^2_{\bar{Y}}$. In this case

$$\sigma^2_{\bar{X}-\bar{Y}} = (10)^2 + (10)^2 = 200.$$

Also since $\alpha = .05$, $Z_{\alpha/2} = 1.96$; since $\beta = .10$, $Z_\beta = 1.28$. Then

$$n = \frac{200(1.96 + 1.28)^2}{(10.5)^2}$$

$$= \frac{200(10.5)}{(10.5)^2} = \frac{200}{105} = 19.05.$$

We round this value up to the next highest integer value to obtain the required sample size of 20 for each of the old and the new thermostats.

● **PROBLEM** 16-84

Suppose the previous problem's experiment was carried out with a sample size of 23. The mean, $\bar{X}$, and variance, $S^2_X$, for the old thermostats were 549.93 and 77.415 respectively. The mean, $\bar{Y}$, and variance $S^2_Y$, for the new thermostats were 551.06 and 105.93 respectively. Can we conclude at a 5% level of significance that there is a difference between the average temperature readings of the old and the new thermostats?

Solution: For this problem we have

$$H_0: \mu_X - \mu_Y = 0 \qquad\qquad H_1: \mu_X - \mu_Y \neq 0 .$$

Our decision rule is, for $\alpha = .05$, a two-tailed test, and $n_1 + n_2 - 2 = 44$ df's: reject $H_0$ if $t > 2.02$ or $t < -2.02$; accept $H_0$ if $-2.02 \leq t \leq 2.02$.

We use the t-distribution here because the population standard deviations are unknown. If we had used $Z$, our critical values would have been 1.96 and -1.96, not very different from 2.02 and -2.02 since the number of degrees of freedom, 44 is quite high. We must calculate

$$t = \frac{(\bar{X}-\bar{Y}) - (\mu_X-\mu_Y)}{S_{\bar{X}-\bar{Y}}} \qquad \text{where}$$

$$S_{\bar{X}-\bar{Y}} = \sqrt{\frac{(n_X-1)S^2_X + (n_Y-1)^2 S^2_Y}{n_X + n_Y - 2}} \sqrt{\frac{1}{n_X} + \frac{1}{n_Y}} .$$

For the data of this problem we have

$$S_{\bar{X}-\bar{Y}} = \sqrt{\frac{22(77.45) + 22(105.93)}{44}} \sqrt{\frac{1}{23} + \frac{1}{23}}$$

$$= \sqrt{\frac{1703.13 + 2330.46}{44}} \sqrt{\frac{2}{23}}$$

$$= (9.57)(.295) = 2.82 \quad \text{and}$$

$$t = \frac{549.93 - 551.06}{2.82} = \frac{-1.13}{2.82} = -.40 \; .$$

Since $-2.02 \le -.40 \le 2.02$, we accept $H_0$ and conclude that there is no significant difference between the old and new thermostats at a 5% level of significance.

● **PROBLEM 16-85**

In the manufacture of a food product, the label states the box contains 10 lbs. The boxes are filled by machine and it is of interest to determine whether or not the machine is set properly. Suppose the standard deviation is approximately .05, though this not precisely known. The company feels that the present setting is unsatisfactory if the machine fills the boxes so that the mean weight differs from 10 lbs. by more than .01 lb. and it wants to be able to detect such a difference at least 95% of the time. At a level of significance of $\alpha = .05$, what sample size is needed?

Solution: The figure below depicts this problem.

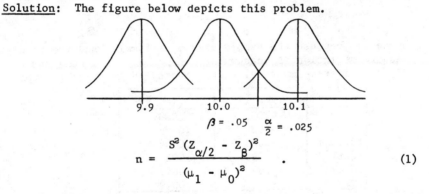

$$n = \frac{S^2 (Z_{\alpha/2} - Z_{\beta})^2}{(\mu_1 - \mu_0)^2} \; . \tag{1}$$

In this problem, $S = .05$, $\mu_0 = 10.0$, and $\mu_1 = 10.1$. Since $\alpha/2 = .025$, $Z_{\alpha/2} = 1.96$; since $\beta = .05$, $Z_{\beta} = -1.65$.

Substituting into (1),

$$n = \frac{(.05)^2 (1.96 + 1.65)^2}{(10.1 - 10.0)^2}$$

$$= \frac{(.05)^2 (3.61)^2}{(.1)^2} = \frac{(.0025)(13.03)}{.01}$$

$$= 3.26.$$

So rounding up to the next highest integer, a sample size of 4 will meet the requirements of the company.

Suppose in the previous problem a sample of 6 boxes is examined. The mean weights of their contents are 9.99 lbs., 9.99 lbs., 10.00 lbs., 10.11 lbs., 10.09 lbs., and 9.95 lbs. Would the company conclude the machine which fills the boxes is set properly?

**Solution:** The figure below depicts this problem:

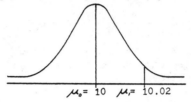

$\mu_0 = 10 \quad \mu_1 = 10.02$

Since we are concerned with whether or not the machine is set properly but are not concerned with the direction of the possible incorrect setting, we let

$$H_0: \mu = 10.0$$
$$H_1: \mu \neq 10.0.$$

We must calculate

$$t = \frac{\bar{X} - \mu}{S_{\bar{X}}} \quad \text{where}$$

$$S_{\bar{X}} = \frac{S}{\sqrt{n}} .$$

We use $t$ because the sample size 6, is small, and the population standard deviation is unknown.

But first we must calculate $\bar{X}$ and $S$.

| X | $(X - \bar{X})$ | $(X - \bar{X})^2$ |
|---|---|---|
| 9.99 | -.03 | .0009 |
| 9.99 | -.03 | .0009 |
| 10.00 | -.02 | .0004 |
| 10.11 | .09 | .0081 |
| 10.09 | .07 | .0049 |
| 9.95 | -.07 | .0049 |

$\Sigma X = 60.13$                      .0201

$\bar{X} = 10.02$

$$S = \sqrt{\frac{\Sigma(X - \bar{X})^2}{n-1}} = \sqrt{\frac{.0201}{5}} = .063.$$

Now

$$S_{\bar{X}} = \frac{.063}{\sqrt{6}} = \frac{.063}{2.45} = .0257 \quad \text{and}$$

$$t = \frac{10.02 - 10.0}{.0257} = \frac{.02}{.0257} = .778 .$$

For $\alpha = .05$, a two-tailed test, and df = 5 we have as a decision rule: reject $H_0$ if $t > 2.57$ or $t < -2.57$; accept $H_0$ if $-2.57 \leq t \leq 2.57$. In this case, .778 lies between -2.57 and 2.57, so we accept $H_0$ and conclude the machine is set properly.

According to a schedule, a given operation is supposed to be performed in 6.4 minutes. A study is to be performed to determine whether a particular worker conforms to this standard or whether his performance deviates from this standard, either higher or lower. If the deviation is as much as 0.5 minute this should be detected 95% of the time. Experience indicates the standard deviation of the distribution of such operations is about 0.4 minute, although this figure is not precisely known. At a level of significance of .01, a sample size of how many operations would be needed to perform the study?

<u>Solution</u>: The figure below depicts this problem.

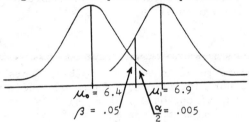

$\mu_0 = 6.4$   $\mu_1 = 6.9$
$\beta = .05$   $\frac{\alpha}{2} = .005$

The required sample size is given by

$$n = \frac{S^2 (Z_{\alpha/2} + Z_\beta)^2}{(\mu_1 - \mu_0)^2} .$$

Since $\alpha/2 = .005$, $Z_{\alpha/2} = 2.57$; since $\beta = .05$, $Z_\beta = 1.65$.

Hence

$$n = \frac{.4^2 (2.57 + 1.65)^2}{(6.9-6.4)^2} = \frac{(.4)^2 (4.22)^2}{(.5)^2}$$

$$= (3.376)^2 = 11.40.$$

Therefore a sample of 12 operations is required.

Suppose for the previous problem a sample of 15 operations is obtained and the sample mean of these operations is 6.87 minutes with a standard deviation of .4 minute. Would these results indicate that the worker deviates from the standard of 6.4 minutes at a 1% level of significance?

<u>Solution</u>: For this problem we must calculate

$t = \dfrac{\bar{X} - \mu}{S_{\bar{X}}}$   where   $S_{\bar{X}} = \dfrac{S}{\sqrt{n}}$ .

We use the t-distribution because the sample size, 15, is small and the population standard deviation is unknown.

The null and alternate hypotheses are

$H_0: \mu = 6.4$                    $H_1: \mu \neq 6.4$ .

Our decision rule for $\alpha = .01$, a two-tailed test, and df = 14 is: reject $H_0$ if $t > 2.98$ or $t < -2.98$. Accept $H_0$ if $-2.98 \leq t \leq 2.98$.

For the data of this problem

$$S_{\bar{X}} = \frac{.4}{\sqrt{15}} = .103 \quad \text{and}$$

$$t = \frac{6.87 - 6.4}{.103} = \frac{.47}{.103} = 4.56 .$$

Since $4.56 > 2.98$, we reject $H_0$ and conclude that this particular worker does not conform to the standard of performing the given operation in 6.4 minutes.

● **PROBLEM** 16-89

Specimens of pipe are to be inspected for the effects of corrosion. The following procedure is outlined. Pairs of specimens are examined for the amount of corrosion. Each pair is buried in the same soil at the same depth but one member of each pair is covered with coating A and one is covered with coating B. The average depth of maximum pit-marks is measured for each specimen. The standard deviation of the depth of maximum pits on similar coatings is known to have a very approximate value of 0.008 inch. If we wish to detect a difference in the average depth of maximum pits for each coating of .011 inch with probability greater than or equal to .95, and if we wish to test for a difference in the corrosion preventing abilities of the two coatings at a .05 level of significance, how many pairs of specimens should be used in the test?

Solution: The formula for the appropriate sample size is

$$n = \frac{\sigma^2 (Z_\beta + Z_{\alpha/2})^2}{(\mu_1 - \mu_0)^2} .$$

Since we wish to detect a difference in the average depth of 0.011 with probability of .95, $\mu_1 - \mu_0 = .011$, $\beta = .05$, and $Z_\beta = 1.65$. Since, $\alpha = .05$, $Z_{\alpha/2} = 1.96$. Since the standard deviation for the depth of maximum pits on similar coatings is .008, the standard deviation of the difference in the average depth of maximum pits for coating A and coating B is

$$\sigma^2 = \sqrt{(.008)^2 + (.008)^2} = .0113.$$

Now we may calculate

$$n = \frac{(.0113)^2 (1.65 + 1.96)^2}{(.011)^2}$$

$$= (3.708)^2 = 13.75.$$

We round this value of n up to the next higher integer and conclude that 14 pairs of specimens should be used in the test.

Suppose that for the preceding problem, we have taken a sample of 15 pairs of specimens. The differences in the average maximum pits for each coating, $\bar{d}$ is 8 with a standard deviation for the differences of 11.03. Test whether there is a significant difference between the corrosion preventing abilities of coatings A and B at a .05 level of significance.

Solution: We have as our hypotheses for this problem

$H_0$: $d = 0$               $H_1$: $d \neq 0$ .

For a two-tailed test, $\alpha = .05$, and 14 df's, our decision rule is:  reject $H_0$ if  $t > 2.145$  or  $t < -2.145$; accept $H_0$ is $-2.145 \leq t \leq 2.145$.  We use a t-test because the sample size in this problem is small (n = 15) and the standard deviation of the population is unknown.  We must calculate

$$t = \frac{\bar{d} - d}{S_{\bar{d}}} , \text{ where } \qquad S_{\bar{d}} = \frac{S}{\sqrt{n}} .$$

For the data of this problem,

$$S_{\bar{d}} = \frac{11.03}{\sqrt{15}} = 2.85 \quad \text{and} \qquad t = \frac{8-0}{2.85} = 2.81.$$

Since  2.81 > 2.145, we reject  $H_0$  and conclude that there is a difference in the corrosion preventing abilities of coatings A and B.

# THE POWER OF A TEST

Suppose we have a binomial distribution for which $H_0$ is $p = \frac{1}{2}$ where  p  is the probability of success on a single trial. Suppose the type I error, $\alpha = .05$ and n = 100.  Calculate the power of this test for each of the following alternate hypotheses, $H_1$: p = .55, p = .60, p = .65, p = .70, and  p = .75.  Do the same when  $\alpha = .01$.

Solution:  Since N(p) and N(q) are both greater than 5, we may use the normal approximation to the binomial distribution for this problem.  For  $p = \frac{1}{2}$, the mean, $\mu$, and standard deviation, $\sigma$, for this data are  $p = \frac{1}{2}$, $\mu = np = 100(\frac{1}{2}) = 50$  and  $\sigma = \sqrt{npq} = \sqrt{100(\frac{1}{2})(\frac{1}{2})} = 5$.

Since  $\alpha = .05$, we will reject  $H_0$  when  Z > 1.65.  Our formula for  Z  is

$$Z = \frac{X - \mu}{\sigma} .$$

Substituting the given values for  Z, $\mu$, and  $\sigma$, we obtain

$$\frac{X - 50}{5} > 1.65.$$

Multiplying both sides of this equation by 5 yields

$$X - 50 > 8.25 .$$

Adding 50 to both sides gives

$$X > 58.25.$$

So we will reject $H_0$ when $X > 58$.

The power of a test is given by the probability of accepting $H_1$ when $H_1$ is true. We must therefore calculate the probability of $X > 58$ for each of the specified $H_1$'s.

We use the formula

$$Z = \frac{X - \mu}{\sigma}$$

where $X = 57.5$ ($58.5 - .5$ because the binomial distribution is discrete and the normal distribution is continuous). Also, for each case $\mu = np$ and $\sigma = \sqrt{npq}$ .

The table below gives the values of $\mu$, $\sigma$, $Z$, and the power of the test for each specified $H_1$.

| $H_1$ | $\mu = np$ | $\sigma = \sqrt{npq}$ | $\frac{X-\mu}{\sigma} = Z$ | Power |
|-------|-----------|----------------------|----------------------------|-------|
| $p = .55$ | 55 | 4.97 | .5 | .308 |
| $p = .60$ | 60 | 4.90 | -.51 | .695 |
| $p = .65$ | 65 | 4.77 | -1.57 | .942 |
| $p = .70$ | 70 | 4.58 | -2.73 | .997 |
| $p = .75$ | 75 | 4.33 | -4.04 | 1.000 |

The power is obtained by using a table for the normal distribution and finding the probability that $Z$ is greater than the value obtained in the prior column.

For $\alpha = .01$, we will reject $H_0$ when $Z > 2.33$. To find the value of $X$ corresponding to $Z = 2.33$, we use

$$Z = \frac{X - \mu}{\sigma}$$

where $Z = 2.33$, $\mu = 50$, and $\sigma = 5$. Substituting $\frac{X - 50}{5} > 2.33$.

Multiplying both sides by 5 yields $X - 50 > 11.65$.

Adding 50 to each side yields $X > 61.65$.

Since 61.65 is in the interval 61.5 to 62.5, we will reject $H_0$ when $X$ is greater than 61.5 for an $\alpha = .01$. Since the binomial distribution is discrete we use the value of $X$ as 61.5, and we may now construct a table to give the power of the test for each specified $H_1$ when $\alpha = .01$.

| $H_1$ | $\mu = np$ | $\sigma = \sqrt{npq}$ | $\frac{X - \mu}{\sigma} = Z$ | Power |
|-------|-----------|----------------------|------------------------------|-------|
| $p = .55$ | 55 | 4.97 | 1.31 | .095 |
| $p = .60$ | 60 | 4.90 | .31 | .378 |
| $p = .65$ | 65 | 4.77 | -.73 | .767 |
| $p = .70$ | 70 | 4.58 | -1.86 | .967 |
| $p = .75$ | 75 | 4.33 | -3.12 | .999 |

Note that a decrease in the size of the critical region from .05 to .01 uniformly reduced the power of the test for all $H_1$.

Suppose we have a binomial distribution for which $H_0$ is that the probability of success on a single trial, $p = \frac{1}{2}$. Suppose also that $H_1$ is $p = 2/3$. Show how the power of the normal approximation to the binomial test increases as $n$ increases by finding the critical value, K, and the type II error, $\beta$, for each of the following values of $n$: 36, 64, 100, 144, and 196. For which of these values of N does $\beta$ first fall as low as .5? Use $\alpha = .01$.

**Solution:** We may use the normal approximation to the binomial distribution because $np$ and $nq$ will exceed 5 in all cases.

For each value of $n$ specified we can calculate $\mu = np$ and $\sigma = \sqrt{npq}$ when $p = \frac{1}{2}$. These results are given in the table below.

| n | $\mu = np$ | $\sigma = \sqrt{npq}$ |
|------|------|------|
| 36 | 18 | 3 |
| 64 | 32 | 4 |
| 100 | 50 | 5 |
| 144 | 72 | 6 |
| 196 | 98 | 7 |

Since the value of $p$ for $H_1$ is greater than the value of $p$ for $H_0$, we will reject $H_0$ in favor of $H_1$ when high values of X occur. More specifically since $\alpha = .01$, we will reject $H_0$ when $Z > 2.33$.

We use the formula

$$Z = \frac{X - \mu}{\sigma} \qquad (1)$$

to find the critical values of X, called K. For each value of $n$, we know $\mu$ and $\sigma$, and $Z = 2.33$ for all values of N. We will solve equation (1) for X.

Multiplying each side by $\sigma$,

$$Z\sigma = X - \mu .$$

Adding $\mu$ to each side yields

$$X = Z\sigma + \mu .$$

Now the critical value K, for each value of $n$ can be found.

$$
\begin{aligned}
n &= 36\text{:} \quad K = 2.33(3) + 18 = 24.99 \quad \text{or} \quad 25 \\
n &= 64\text{:} \quad K = 2.33(4) + 32 = 41.32 \quad \text{or} \quad 41 \\
n &=100\text{:} \quad K = 2.33(5) + 50 = 61.65 \quad \text{or} \quad 62 \\
n &=144\text{:} \quad K = 2.33(6) + 72 = 85.98 \quad \text{or} \quad 86 \\
n &=196\text{:} \quad K = 2.33(7) + 98 = 114.31 \quad \text{or} \quad 114
\end{aligned}
$$

We must now calculate, $\beta$, the probability that $H_1$ is true (p = 2/3) when we accept $H_0$; i.e. when X is less than or equal to the critical value of K. The table below gives these values for each $n$. We add

657

.5 to each value of K to correct for the binomial distribution being a discrete distribution.

| $n$ | $\mu = np$ | $\sigma = \sqrt{npq}$ | K | $Z = \dfrac{K-\mu}{\sigma}$ | $\beta = Pr(X<K)$ |
|---|---|---|---|---|---|
| 36 | 24 | 2.83 | 25.5 | -.53 | .702 |
| 64 | 42.67 | 3.77 | 41.5 | -.31 | .378 |
| 100 | 66.67 | 4.71 | 62.5 | -.86 | .195 |
| 144 | 96 | 5.66 | 86.5 | -1.68 | .047 |
| 196 | 130.67 | 6.60 | 114.5 | -2.45 | .007 |

Since $\beta$ decreases as $n$ increases, the power of the test, $1 - \beta$, increases with increasing $n$. The first value of $n$ for which $\beta$ falls as low as .5 is $n = 64$.

● **PROBLEM 16-93**

In a binomial experiment $H_0$ is that the probability of success on a single trial, $p = 1/3$. Calculate the power of a binomial test with $\alpha = .05$ and $n = 10$ when $H_1$ is $p = \frac{1}{2}$ and when $H_1$ is $p = 2/3$. Do the same for $n = 20$.

Solution: Since the value of $p$ for the alternate hypothesis is greater than that for the null hypothesis, we will reject $H_0$ only when the number of heads we obtain is close to 10. More specifical- ly, we will reject $H_0$ for $\alpha = .05$ when the number of heads is 7 or more since the probability of 6 or more heads from a table of binomial probabilities when $p = 1/3$ is .0764 and the prob- ability of 7 or more heads is less than .05. The power of a test is the probability of rejecting $H_0$ when it is indeed false. Since we reject $H_0$ when the number of heads is 7 or more, the power of this test is given by the probability of obtaining 7 or more heads when $H_1$ is true. When $H_1$ is $p = \frac{1}{2}$, this probability is .1718. When $H_1$ is $p = 2/3$, this probability is .5591.

For $n = 20$, we will reject $H_0$ when the number of heads is 11 or more, since the probability of at least 10 heads out of 20 tosses of a coin is greater than .05, but the probability of at least 11 heads out of 20 tosses of a coin is less than .05 (again from a table of binomial probabilities). When $H_1$ is $p = \frac{1}{2}$, the probability of obtaining at least 11 heads on 20 tosses of a coin, and hence the power of the test, is .4119. When $H_1$ is $p = 2/3$, this same probability, and hence the power of the test, is .9068. It is interesting to note how the power of a test increases when $\alpha$, $H_0$, and $H_1$ remain the same and only the sample size, $n$, is increased.

● **PROBLEM 16-94**

Consider the probability distribution function

$$f(x;\theta) = \frac{1}{\theta} e^{-x/\theta} \qquad 0 < x < \infty$$

= 0 elsewhere.

It is desired to test the hypothesis $H_0: \theta = 2$ against alternate hypothesis $H_1: \theta > 2$. Suppose a random sample $X_1, X_2$ is used and the critical region is $X_1 + X_2 \geq 9.5$. Calculate an expression for the power function, $K(\theta_1)$, for all $\theta_1 > 2$, and specifically for $\theta_1 = 4$.

Solution: The power function is the probability of rejecting $H_0$ when it is false. This is 1 minus the probability of not rejecting $H_0$ when it is false or when $H_1: \theta = \theta_1 > 2$ is true. We do not reject $H_0$ when $X_1 + X_2 < 9.5$. Since $X_1$ and $X_2$ are independent,

$$\Pr(X_1 + X_2 < 9.5) = \int_0^{9.5} \int_0^{9.5-x_2} f(x_1; \theta_1) f(x_2; \theta_1) dx_1 dx_2$$

$$= \int_0^{9.5} \int_0^{9.5-x_2} \frac{1}{\theta_1^2} \exp\left(-\frac{x_1+x_2}{\theta_1}\right) dx_1 dx_2$$

and

$$K(\theta_1) = 1 - \int_0^{9.5} \int_0^{9.5-x_2} \frac{-1}{\theta_1^2} \exp\left(-\frac{x_1 + x_2}{\theta_1}\right) dx_1 dx_2$$

$$= \left(\frac{\theta_1 + 9.5}{\theta_1}\right) e^{-9.5/\theta_1} .$$

For $\theta_1 = 4$, we obtain

$$K(4) = \frac{4 + 9.5}{4} e^{-9.5/4} = \frac{13.5}{4} e^{-2.375}$$

$$= 3.385(.0930) = .31.$$

# LIKELIHOOD RATIO TEST FOR THE BEST CRITICAL REGION

● PROBLEM 16-95

Let $X$ possess a Poisson distribution with mean $\mu$, i.e.

$$f(X, \mu) = e^{-\mu} \frac{\mu^X}{X!}$$

Suppose we want to test the null hypothesis $H_0: \mu = \mu_0$ against the alternative hypothesis, $H_1: \mu = \mu_1$, where $\mu_1 < \mu_0$.

Find the best critical region for this test.

Solution: We use a likelihood ratio test to find the best critical region. This is the method suggested by the Neyman-Pearson theorem.

$$L_1 = \prod_{i=1}^n e^{-\mu_1} \frac{\mu_1^{x_i}}{x_i!} \qquad L_0 = \prod_{i=1}^n e^{-\mu_0} \frac{\mu_0^{x_i}}{x_i!} .$$

The best critical region is therefore given by the region in which

$$\frac{L_1}{L_0} = \frac{\prod\limits_{i=1}^{n} e^{-\mu_1} \frac{\mu_1^{x_i}}{x_i!}}{\prod\limits_{i=1}^{n} e^{-\mu_0} \frac{\mu_0^{x_i}}{x_i!}} = e^{n(\mu_0 - \mu_1)} \left(\frac{\mu_1}{\mu_0}\right)^{\Sigma x_i} \geq k.$$

where $k$ is a constant.

Taking logarithms of each side of this inequality yields

$$n(\mu_0 - \mu_1) + \Sigma x_i (\log \frac{\mu_1}{\mu_0}) \geq \log k. \qquad (1)$$

Since $\log \frac{\mu_1}{\mu_0} = \log \mu_1 - \log \mu_0$, we have

$$n(\mu_0 - \mu_1) + \Sigma x_i ((\log \mu_1 - \log \mu_0) \geq k . \qquad (2)$$

Transposing $n(\mu_0 - \mu_1)$ to the right side of the equation gives

$$\Sigma x_i ((\log \mu_1 - \log \mu_0) \geq \log k + n(\mu_1 - \mu_0). \qquad (3)$$

Dividing both sides of (3) by $\log \mu_1 - \log \mu_0$ yields

$$\Sigma x_i \leq \frac{\log k + n(\mu_1 - \mu_0)}{\log \mu_1 - \log \mu_0} . \qquad (4)$$

The inequality is reversed in (4) because $\log \mu_1 - \log \mu_0$ is negative under our stated assumption of $\mu_1 < \mu_0$ .

Now $x_i$ is a Poisson variable, and since the sum of independent Poisson variables is a Poisson variable with mean equal to the sum of the means, it follows that $Z = \Sigma x_i$ is a Poisson variable with mean $n\mu$ . The critical region determined by (4) is therefore equivalent to a critical region of the type

$$Z \leq \frac{\log k + n(\mu_1 - \mu_0)}{\log \mu_1 - \log \mu_0} \qquad (5)$$

for the Poisson variable $Z$.

By choosing $k$ properly the quantity on the right side of (5) can be made to have a value such that $Z$ will be less than that value when $H_0$ is true $100\alpha$ percent of the time for any specified $\alpha$.

● **PROBLEM 16-96**

Let
$$f(X;\theta) = \frac{e^{-\frac{1}{2}(X-\theta)^2}}{\sqrt{2\pi}}$$

be a probability density function. Assuming $H_0: \theta = \theta_0$, and $H_1: \theta = \theta_1$. where $\theta_0 > \theta_1$, find the best critical region, C, for this test.

Solution: We use a likelihood ratio test to find the best critical region, C. This is in accordance with the Neyman-Pearson theorem which determines the best critical region.

660

$$L_0 = \prod_{i=1}^{n} f(X_i; \theta_0) = (2\pi)^{-\frac{n}{2}} e^{-\frac{1}{2} \Sigma_{i=1}^{n}(X_i - \theta_0)^2}$$

$$L_1 = \prod_{i=1}^{n} f(X_i; \theta_1) = (2\pi)^{-\frac{n}{2}} e^{-\frac{1}{2} \Sigma_{i=1}^{n}(X_i - \theta_1)^2}.$$

The region C, which is desired, is therefore given by the region in which

$$\frac{L_1}{L_0} = \frac{e^{-\frac{1}{2}\Sigma(X_i - \theta_1)^2}}{e^{-\frac{1}{2}\Sigma(X_i - \theta_0)^2}} = e^{\frac{1}{2}[\Sigma(X_i - \theta_1)^2 - \Sigma(X_i - \theta_0)^2]} \geq k.$$

where k is a constant to be determined.

Taking logarithms of each side of this inequality yields

$$\frac{1}{2}[\Sigma(X_i - \theta_0)^2 - \Sigma(X_i - \theta_1)^2] \geq \log k. \tag{1}$$

Multiplying both sides of this inequality by 2 gives

$$\Sigma(X_i - \theta_0)^2 - \Sigma(X_i - \theta_1)^2 \geq 2 \log k. \tag{2}$$

Since

$$\Sigma(X_i - \theta_0)^2 = \Sigma X_i^2 - 2\Sigma X_i \theta_0 + \Sigma \theta_0^2$$

and

$$\Sigma(X_i - \theta_1)^2 = \Sigma X_i^2 - 2\Sigma X_i \theta_1 + \Sigma \theta_1^2,$$

the left side of (2) becomes

$$\Sigma \theta_0^2 - \Sigma \theta_1^2 + 2\Sigma X_i \theta_1 - 2\Sigma X_i \theta_0.$$

Since $\theta_0$ and $\theta_1$ are constants, we obtain for the left side

$$n\theta_0^2 - n\theta_1^2 + \Sigma X_i(2\theta_1 - 2\theta_0).$$

Inequality (2) now becomes

$$n\theta_0^2 - n\theta_1^2 + \Sigma X_i(2\theta_1 - 2\theta_0) \geq 2 \log k. \tag{3}$$

Transposing $n\theta_0^2 - n\theta_1^2$ to the right side of (3) and dividing by $(2\theta_1 - 2\theta_0)$ yields

$$\Sigma X_i \leq \frac{2\log k + (\theta_1^2 - \theta_0^2)n}{2(\theta_1 - \theta_0)} \qquad \text{and} \tag{4}$$

dividing by n,

$$\bar{X} \leq \frac{2\log k + (\theta_1^2 - \theta_0^2)n}{2n(\theta_1 - \theta_0)}. \tag{5}$$

The direction of the inequality was reversed from (3) to (4) because we divided by the negative quantity, $2\theta_1 - 2\theta_0$. (Remember $\theta_1 < \theta_0$ was given.)

From equation (5), we can see that the best critical region is the left tail of the $\bar{X}$ distribution. By choosing k properly the quantity on the right side of (5) can be made to have a value such that $\bar{X}$ will be less than that value when $H_0$ is true $100\alpha\%$ of the time for any specified $\alpha$.

661

Consider the random variable  X  which has a binomial distribution with  n = 5  and the probability of success on a single trial,  $\theta$. Let  $f(x;\theta)$  denote the probability distribution function of  X  and let  $H_0: \theta = \frac{1}{2}$  and  $H_1: \theta = \frac{3}{4}$ .  Let the level of significance  $\alpha = 1/32$.  Determine the best critical region for the test of the null hypothesis  $H_0$  against the alternate hypothesis  $H_1$ .  Do the same for  $\alpha = 6/32$.

**Solution:** We calculate  $f(x;\frac{1}{2})$  for all values of  x = 0,1,2,3,4,5 in the table below.

| x | 0 | 1 | 2 | 3 | 4 | 5 |
|---|---|---|---|---|---|---|
| $f(x;\frac{1}{2})$ | 1/32 | 5/32 | 10/32 | 10/32 | 5/32 | 1/32 |

The values in this table were obtained by direct application of the binomial distribution

$$f(x;\theta) = \binom{n}{x} \theta^x (1-\theta)^{n-x} ,$$

where

$$\binom{n}{x} = \frac{n!}{x!(n-x)!} .$$

For example,

$$f(0;\tfrac{1}{2}) = \binom{5}{0}\left(\tfrac{1}{2}\right)^0\left(\tfrac{1}{2}\right)^5 = \left(\tfrac{1}{2}\right)^5 = \frac{1}{32} .$$

Our candidates for best critical region when  $\alpha = 1/32$  are  $X \leq 0$  and  $X \geq 5$,  i.e.,  x = 0 and x = 5.

When  X = 0, under  $H_1: \theta = \frac{3}{4}$ , we have

$$f(0;\tfrac{3}{4}) = \binom{5}{0}\left(\tfrac{3}{4}\right)^0 \left(\tfrac{1}{4}\right)^5 = \frac{1}{1024} .$$

When  X = 5, under  $H_1: \theta = \frac{3}{4}$ , we have

$$f(5;\tfrac{3}{4}) = \binom{5}{5}\left(\tfrac{3}{4}\right)^5\left(\tfrac{1}{4}\right)^0 = \left(\tfrac{3}{4}\right)^5 = \frac{243}{1024} .$$

We are to choose for our best critical region that value of  X where  $f(x;\frac{1}{2})/f(x;\frac{3}{4})$  is a minimum.

$$\frac{f(0;\tfrac{1}{2})}{f(0;\tfrac{3}{4})} = \frac{1/32}{1/1024} = 32$$

$$\frac{f(5;\tfrac{1}{2})}{f(5;\tfrac{3}{4})} = \frac{1/32}{243/1024} = \frac{1024}{32(243)} = \frac{32}{243} .$$

Hence our best critical region for  $\alpha = 1/32$  is  X = 5.

For  $\alpha = 6/32$, our candidates for best critical region are  X = 4 and 5 as well as  X = 0  and  1,  since  $f(4;\frac{1}{2}) + f(5;\frac{1}{2}) = 6/32$  and  $f(0;\frac{1}{2}) + f(1;\frac{1}{2}) = 6/32$.

Once again we will choose as our best critical region those values of  X  where  $\Sigma f(x;\frac{1}{2})/\Sigma f(x;\frac{3}{4})$  is a minimum, where the summation is over the appropriate values of  X  (either  0  and  1  or  4  and  5 in this case).

Since

$$f(4,\tfrac{3}{4}) = \binom{5}{4}\left(\tfrac{3}{4}\right)^4\tfrac{1}{4} = \frac{(5)(81)}{1024} = \frac{405}{1024} ,$$

$$\sum_{X=4}^{5} f(x;\tfrac{3}{4}) = \frac{405}{1024} + \frac{243}{1024} = \frac{648}{1024} \cdot$$

Also, since

$$f(1;\tfrac{3}{4}) = \binom{5}{1}(\tfrac{3}{4})^1 (\tfrac{1}{4})^4 = \frac{5(3)}{1024} = \frac{15}{1024} ,$$

$$\sum_{X=0}^{1} f(x;\tfrac{3}{4}) = \frac{1}{1024} + \frac{15}{1024} = \frac{16}{1024} \cdot$$

Now we may calculate

$$\frac{\sum\limits_{X=0}^{1} f(x;\tfrac{1}{2})}{\sum\limits_{X=0}^{1} f(x;\tfrac{3}{4})} = \frac{6/32}{16/1024} = \frac{1024(6)}{32(16)} = 12$$

and

$$\frac{\sum\limits_{X=4}^{5} f(x;\tfrac{1}{2})}{\sum\limits_{X=4}^{5} f(x;\tfrac{3}{4})} = \frac{6/32}{648/1024} = \frac{1024(6)}{32(648)} = \frac{24}{81} \cdot$$

Since the second of these last two calculated values is less, the best critical region for $\alpha = 6/32$ is $X = 4$ and $5$.

● **PROBLEM** 16-98

A pharmaceutical company claims that its new vaccine is 90% effective, but the federal drug agency suspects that it is only 40% effective. Devise a procedure to test its effectiveness and use it to find the probability that (a) the government will incorrectly grant the company claim (when the effectiveness is in fact 40%, and (b) the company claim will be incorrectly denied (when the effectiveness is in fact 90%.)

Solution: We establish a discrete random variable $X$ to denote the number of people out of ten who develop immunity following vaccination. $X$ is binomially distributed (with the probability of success on a single trial, $p = .9$ if the company claim is valid, or $p = .4$ if the government claim is valid) for three reasons:
(1)  there are exactly two outcomes, which can be considered success and failure;
(2)  the probability $p$ of success does not change from person to person (it remains either $0.9$ or $0.4$); and
(3)  the vaccinations can be considered a sequence of 10 independent success-failure trials.
   Our procedure to test the company claim is as follows: 10 people are vaccinated. If 8 or more develop immunity, the claim is granted. The government will incorrectly grant the claim if $X \geq 8$ and $p = 0.4$. Since the events $X = 8$, $X = 9$, and $X = 10$ are mutually exclusive (either exactly 8 or exactly 9 or exactly 10 people become immune), we can add their probabilities to find $p(X \geq 8)$:

$$\binom{10}{8}(0.4)^8(0.6)^2 + \binom{10}{9}(0.4)^9(0.6)^1 + \binom{10}{10}(0.4)^{10}(0.6)^0$$

$$= 0.0.106 + 0.0016 + 0.0001 = 0.0123.$$

(b)  The company claim will be denied if (and only if)  X < 8.  The government will incorrectly deny the claim if  X < 8  but  p = 0.9.

$$p(X < 8) = \sum_{k=0}^{7} \binom{10}{k}(0.9)^k(0.1)^{10-k} = 0.0702 .$$

● **PROBLEM** 16-99

Suppose a coin is assumed to be biased and it is believed that the probability, p, of obtaining a head on one toss is  1/10. Suppose the coin is tossed twice.  Is there any value for  k,  the number of heads, for which we can reject the null hypothesis  p = 1/10 in favor of the alternate hypothesis  p > 1/10  at the 1% level of significance?  Suppose the null hypothesis is  p = ½.  Is there any value, k, for which we can reject this null hypothesis in favor of the alternate hypothesis  p < ½  at the 1% level of significance when the coin is tossed twice?

Solution:  For  p = 1/10, we can calculate the probability of  0, 1, or  2 heads in 2 tosses of a coin, using the binomial distribution

$$f(x;p) = \binom{n}{x}p^x(1 - p)^x ,$$

where

$$\binom{n}{x} = \frac{n!}{x!(n-x)!} .$$

$$\text{Prob}(0 \text{ heads}) = \binom{2}{0}\left(\frac{1}{10}\right)^0\left(\frac{9}{10}\right)^2 = (1)(1)\left(\frac{81}{100}\right) = \frac{81}{100}$$

$$\text{Prob}(1 \text{ head}) = \binom{2}{1}\left(\frac{1}{10}\right)^1\left(\frac{9}{10}\right)^1 = (2)\left(\frac{1}{10}\right)\left(\frac{9}{10}\right) = \frac{18}{100}$$

$$\text{Prob}(2 \text{ heads}) = \binom{2}{2}\left(\frac{1}{10}\right)^2\left(\frac{9}{10}\right)^0 = (1)\left(\frac{1}{100}\right)(1) = \frac{1}{100} .$$

Since the probability of 2 heads is  $\frac{1}{100}$ = .01, at the 1% level of significance we may reject the null hypothesis  p = 1/10  in favor of the alternate hypothesis  p > 1/10  when  k, the number of heads is  2.

For  p = ½, we can also calculate the probability of  0,1, or 2 heads in 2 tosses of a coin.

$$\text{Prob}(0 \text{ heads}) = \binom{2}{0}\left(\frac{1}{2}\right)^0\left(\frac{1}{2}\right)^2 = (1)(1)\left(\frac{1}{4}\right) = \frac{1}{4}$$

$$\text{Prob}(1 \text{ head }) = \binom{2}{1}\left(\frac{1}{2}\right)^1\left(\frac{1}{2}\right)^1 = (2)\left(\frac{1}{2}\right)\left(\frac{1}{2}\right) = \frac{1}{2}$$

$$\text{Prob}(2 \text{ heads}) = \binom{2}{2}\left(\frac{1}{2}\right)^2\left(\frac{1}{2}\right)^0 = (1)\left(\frac{1}{4}\right)(1) = \frac{1}{4} .$$

Since there is no value  k  for which  Prob(k heads) ≤ .01, there is no value of  k  for which we can reject the null hypothesis  p = ½ in favor of the alternate hypothesis  p < ½  at the 1% level of significance.

# CHAPTER 17

# REGRESSION AND CORRELATION ANALYSIS

## SIMPLE REGRESSION

● PROBLEM 17-1

| X | Fertilizer | .3 | .6 | .9 | 1.2 | 1.5 | 1.8 | 2.1 | 2.4 |
|---|---|---|---|---|---|---|---|---|---|
| Y | Corn Yield | 10 | 15 | 30 | 35 | 25 | 30 | 50 | 45 |

Plot the dependent variable against the independent variable. Find the least squares line for this data. What is the Y-intercept? If 3.0 units of fertilizer were used what would be a good guess as to the resultant corn yield?

Solution: The dependent variable in this problem is corn yield. The amount of fertilizer used will affect the corn yield that is observed, but the amount of fertilizer used will probably not depend on the corn yield. Fertilizer is used before the corn yield is even observed.

The vertical axis of a coordinate system is usually used to indicate the dependent variable Y and the horizontal axis for the independent variable X. Each point on the graph coincides with a pair of numbers, an X value and a Y value. In this case, the scatter plot, as such a graph is called is given below:

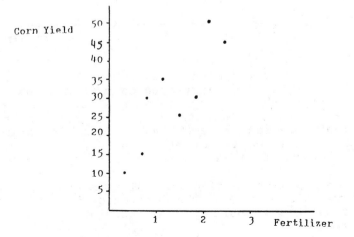

This graph seems to indicate a linear relationship between fertilizer and corn yield.  As more fertilizer is used, more corn is produced.

The general equation of any line is Y = a + bX. Y and X represent the vertical and horizontal distances from the origin.  Given 8 pairs of X and Y values we wish to estimate the Y-intercept a and the slope b.  The Y-intercept, a, is the Y-value that corresponds to an X-value of zero.  The point where the line Y = a + bX intersects the Y-axis is thus the Y-intercept.  The slope b indicates the relative change of Y with respect to X. That is, b = amount Y changes for a unit increase in X.

The points in our scatter plot do not lie precisely on a line but appear to be scattered about a line.  There are many lines that could be chosen to represent the true but unknown relationship between fertilizer and corn yield.

The most common choice of such a line is that line which minimizes the squared distance between the Y-values that lie on the chosen line and the observed Y-values.

Let the estimated values of a and b be denoted by $\hat{a}$ and $\hat{b}$.  From $\hat{a}$ and $\hat{b}$ we can compute a new Y-value, $\hat{Y} = \hat{a} + \hat{b}X$.  This equation denotes a line which is graphed below:

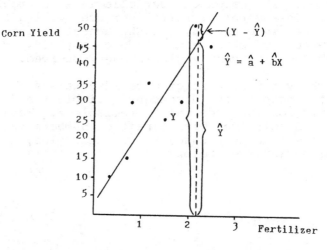

The vertical distances Y, $\hat{Y}$ and (Y - $\hat{Y}$) are indicated on this graph.  The least squares criterion says: estimate the Y-intercept and slope in such a way that the quantity $\Sigma$ (Y - $\hat{Y}$)$^2$ will be minimized.  $\Sigma$ (Y - $\hat{Y}$)$^2$ is the sum of squared deviation of each Y value from the estimated line. If this condition is met, the line $\hat{Y} = \hat{a} + \hat{b}X$ will be the least squares line and will best fit the data.

We now wish to find the values a and b which will achieve this minimum.  The derivation below is included for completeness and may be omitted without loss of continuity.

666

let $\quad \Theta(\hat{a}, \hat{b}) = \Sigma(Y - \hat{Y})^2$

$$= \Sigma\left[Y - (\hat{a} + \hat{b}X)\right]^2$$

$\quad\Theta$ can be considered a function of two variables a and b. To minimize $\Theta(\hat{a}, \hat{b})$ we will find

$$\frac{\delta\Theta(\hat{a},\hat{b})}{\delta\hat{a}} \quad \text{and} \quad \frac{\delta\Theta(\hat{a},\hat{b})}{\delta\hat{b}}$$

and set these partial derivatives equal to zero.

$$\Theta(\hat{a}\ \hat{b}) = \Sigma\left[Y - (\hat{a} + \hat{b}X)\right]^2 ;$$

squaring inside the summation sign and factoring out constants where appropriate,

$$\Theta(\hat{a},\hat{b}) = \Sigma\left[Y^2 - 2Y(\hat{a} + \hat{b}X) + (\hat{a} + \hat{b}X)^2\right]$$

$$= \Sigma Y^2 - 2\Sigma Y(\hat{a} + \hat{b}X) + \Sigma(\hat{a} + \hat{b}X)^2$$

$$= \Sigma Y^2 - 2\hat{a}\Sigma Y - 2\hat{b}\Sigma XY$$

$$+ \Sigma(\hat{a}^2 + 2\hat{a}\hat{b}X + \hat{b}^2 X^2)$$

$$= \Sigma Y^2 - 2\hat{a}\Sigma Y - 2\hat{b}\Sigma XY$$

$$+ \Sigma\hat{a}^2 + 2\hat{a}\hat{b}\Sigma X + \hat{b}^2\Sigma X^2 .$$

Thus $\quad(\hat{a},\hat{b}) = \Sigma Y^2 - 2\hat{a}\ \Sigma Y - 2\hat{b}\Sigma XY + n\hat{a}^2$

$$+ 2\hat{a}\hat{b}\Sigma X + \hat{b}^2\Sigma X^2 .$$

Differentiating with respect to $\hat{a}$ and $\hat{b}$:

$$\frac{\partial\Theta(a,b)}{\partial\hat{a}} = -2\Sigma y + 2\hat{a}n + 2\hat{b}\Sigma x$$

$$\frac{\partial\Theta(a,b)}{\partial\hat{b}} = -2\Sigma xy + 2\hat{a}\Sigma x + 2\hat{b}\Sigma x^2 .$$

Setting these equations equal to zero we get the so-called normal equations:

$$\Sigma y = n\hat{a} + \hat{b}\Sigma x \qquad\qquad (1)$$
$$\Sigma xy = \hat{a}\Sigma x + \hat{b}\Sigma x^2 . \qquad\qquad (2)$$

We now proceed to solve (1) and (2) simultaneously for $\hat{a}$ and $\hat{b}$. Multiply (1) by $\Sigma x$ and (2) by n to obtain

$$(\Sigma x)(\Sigma y) = \hat{a}n\ \Sigma x + \hat{b}(\Sigma x)^2$$

$$n\Sigma xy = \hat{a}n\ \Sigma x + n\hat{b}\Sigma x^2 .$$

Thus, $\quad(\Sigma x)(\Sigma y) - n\Sigma xy = \hat{b}\ [(\Sigma x)^2 - n\Sigma x^2]$

and $\quad\hat{b} = \dfrac{\Sigma x\Sigma y - n\Sigma xy}{(\Sigma x)^2 - n\Sigma x^2} \qquad\qquad (3)$

Substituting (3) for $\hat{b}$ in (2),

$$\hat{a} = \frac{\Sigma y \ \Sigma x^2 - \Sigma x \Sigma xy}{n\Sigma x^2 - (\Sigma x)^2} .$$

(4)

The two formulas (3) and (4) give the values of $\hat{a}$ and $\hat{b}$ and hence the line estimating the linear relationship between corn yield and fertilizer. We can use this line to predict or estimate the corn yield given certain amounts of fertilizer.

The first step in finding $\hat{a}$ and $\hat{b}$ is to find $\Sigma x$, $\Sigma y$, $\Sigma x^2$, $\Sigma xy$ and n. This is done in the table below:

| x | y | $x^2$ | xy |
|---|---|---|---|
| 0.3 | 10 | .09 | 3.0 |
| 0.6 | 15 | .36 | 9.0 |
| 0.9 | 30 | .81 | 27.0 |
| 1.2 | 35 | 1.44 | 42.0 |
| 1.5 | 25 | 2.25 | 37.5 |
| 1.8 | 30 | 3.24 | 54.0 |
| 2.1 | 50 | 4.41 | 105.0 |
| 2.4 | 45 | 5.76 | 108.0 |

$\Sigma = 10.8 \qquad 240 \qquad 18.36 \qquad\qquad 385.5 \qquad\qquad n = 8$

Thus $\quad \hat{a} = \dfrac{(240)(18.36) - (10.8)(385.5)}{8(18.36) - (10.8)^2} = \dfrac{243}{30.24} = 8.03$

and $\quad \hat{b} = \dfrac{(10.8)(240) - 8(385.5)}{(10.8)^2 - 8(18.36)} = \dfrac{-492}{-30.24} = 16.27.$

Thus, $\quad \hat{y} = 8.03 + 16.27x$

(5)

is the least squares line relating fertizilier to corn yield

To predict the corn yield when 3.0 units of fertilizer are used we let x = 3.0 and substitute into (5) giving

$\qquad y = 8.03 + 16.27(3.0) = 56.84.$

56.84 is the corn-yield we would predict based upon our least squares or regression line.

● PROBLEM 17-2

Given the following pairs of measurements for the two variables:

| X | 5 | 8 | 3 | 9 | 10 | 12 |
|---|---|---|---|---|----|----|
| Y | 9 | 12 | 5 | 15 | 18 | 20 |

(a) Construct a scattergram and draw a calculated regression line.

(b) Using the regression line in part (a) estimate the values of Y when:

    (1) X = 4,   (2) X = 1, and   (3) X = 15.

<u>Solution:</u>

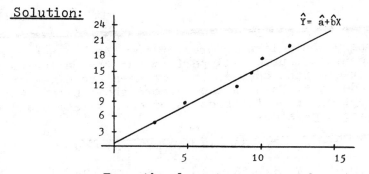

From the data we compute the regression co-efficients $\hat{a}$ and $\hat{b}$.

| X | Y | X$^2$ | XY |
|---|---|---|---|
| 5 | 9 | 25 | 45 |
| 8 | 12 | 64 | 96 |
| 3 | 5 | 9 | 15 |
| 9 | 15 | 81 | 135 |
| 10 | 18 | 100 | 180 |
| 12 | 20 | 144 | 240 |
| $\Sigma X = 47$ | $\Sigma Y = 79$ | $\Sigma X^2 = 423$ | $\Sigma XY = 711$ |

$$\hat{b} = \frac{\Sigma XY - \frac{\Sigma X \ \Sigma Y}{n}}{\Sigma X^2 - n\bar{X}^2}$$

$$= \frac{711 - \frac{(47)(79)}{6}}{423 - 6\left(\frac{47}{6}\right)^2}$$

$$= \frac{711 - 618.833}{423 - 368.16}$$

$$= \frac{92.167}{54.84}$$

$$= 1.68 .$$

The first normal equation is

$$\Sigma Y = n\hat{a} + \hat{b}\Sigma X$$

Divide by n.

$$\frac{\Sigma Y}{n} = \hat{a} + \hat{b} \ \frac{\Sigma X}{n} \quad \text{or equivalently}$$

$$\bar{Y} = \hat{a} + \hat{b} \ \bar{X} .$$

Thus $\quad \hat{a} = \bar{Y} - \hat{b}\bar{X} = \frac{79}{6} - 1.68\left(\frac{47}{6}\right)$

$$= 13.166 - 13.16 = .006 .$$

(b) $\quad \hat{Y} = \hat{a} + \hat{b}X = .006 + 1.68X .$

When $\quad X = 4, \quad \hat{Y} = .006 + 1.68(4) = 6.73$

$\qquad X = 1, \quad \hat{Y} = .006 + 1.68(1) = 1.69$

$\qquad X = 15, \quad \hat{Y} = .006 + 1.68(16) = 25.21.$

A company would like to predict how the trainees in its salesmanship course will perform. At the beginning of their two-months course, the trainees are given an aptitude test. This is the x-score shown below. Records are kept of the sales records of each salesman and these constitute y-values.

| x | 18 | 26 | 28 | 34 | 36 | 42 | 48 | 52 | 54 | 60 |
|---|----|----|----|----|----|----|----|----|----|----|
| y | 54 | 64 | 54 | 62 | 68 | 70 | 76 | 66 | 76 | 74 |

Plot this data and find the regression line relating performance on the test to sales. What levels of sales would you expect from 3 salesman who scored 40, 50 and 70 on the aptitude test?

<u>Solution:</u>    We need the following summary statistics.

$\Sigma X$, $\Sigma Y$, $\Sigma X^2$ and $\Sigma XY$.

These quantities are given in the table below.

| X | Y | $X^2$ | XY |
|---|---|-------|-----|
| 18 | 54 | 324 | 972 |
| 26 | 64 | 676 | 1664 |
| 28 | 54 | 784 | 1512 |
| 34 | 62 | 1156 | 2108 |
| 36 | 68 | 1296 | 2448 |
| 42 | 70 | 1764 | 2940 |
| 48 | 76 | 2304 | 3648 |
| 52 | 66 | 2704 | 3432 |
| 54 | 76 | 2916 | 4104 |
| 60 | 74 | 3600 | 4440 |
| $\Sigma X = 398$ | $\Sigma Y = 664$ | $\Sigma X^2 = 17524$ | $\Sigma XY = 27268$ |

A graph of the aptitude test scores against sales is below.

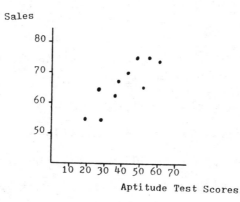

670

The regression coefficients $\hat{a}$ and $\hat{b}$ are those which minimize $\Sigma(Y - \hat{Y})^2$ where $\hat{Y} = \hat{a} + \hat{b}X$. This derivation may be omitted without loss of continuity.

$$Q(\hat{a}, \hat{b}) = \Sigma(Y - \hat{a} - \hat{b}X)^2 \quad \text{will be minimized if}$$

$$\frac{\partial Q}{\partial \hat{a}} = \frac{\partial Q}{\partial \hat{b}} = 0.$$

$$\frac{\partial Q}{\partial \hat{a}} = \frac{\partial}{\partial \hat{a}} [\Sigma(Y - \hat{a} - \hat{b}X)^2]$$

$$= \Sigma \frac{\partial}{\partial \hat{a}} (Y - \hat{a} - \hat{b}X)^2 \quad \text{by the properties of}$$

differentiation.

$$\frac{\partial Q}{\partial \hat{a}} = \Sigma - 2(Y - \hat{a} - \hat{b}X) = -2[\Sigma Y - n\hat{a} - \hat{b}\Sigma X]$$

and $\quad \dfrac{\partial Q}{\partial \hat{b}} = \Sigma \dfrac{\partial}{\partial \hat{b}} (Y - \hat{a} - \hat{b}X)^2 = \Sigma 2(Y - \hat{a} - \hat{b}X)(-X)$

$$= -2[\Sigma XY - \hat{a}\Sigma X - \hat{b}\Sigma X^2].$$

Setting both of these equal to zero we again arrive at the normal equations but in a slightly different form.

$$\hat{a} = \frac{\Sigma Y}{n} - \hat{b} \frac{\Sigma X}{n} = \bar{Y} - \hat{b}\bar{X}$$

and $\quad \hat{b} = \dfrac{\Sigma XY - \left(\dfrac{\Sigma X}{n}\right)\Sigma Y}{\Sigma X^2 - n\left(\dfrac{\Sigma X}{n}\right)^2} = \dfrac{\Sigma XY - \bar{X}\Sigma Y}{\Sigma X^2 - n\bar{X}^2} = \dfrac{\Sigma XY - n\bar{X}\,\bar{Y}}{\Sigma X^2 - n\bar{X}^2} .$

These equations are completely equivalent to the ones we derived earlier. They can be used interchangeably.

From our data, where n = 10, $\bar{X}$ = 39.8   $\bar{Y}$ = 66.4; thus substituting,

$$\hat{b} = \frac{27,268 - 10(39.8)(66.4)}{17,524 - 10(39.8)^2} = \frac{840.8}{1638.6} = .4994$$

and $\hat{a}$ = 66.4 - (.4994)(39.8) = 46.52 .

The least squares regression line relating sales to a score on the aptitude test is

$$\hat{Y} = 46.52 + .4994\, X .$$

The predictions based on scores of 40, 50, 70 are given in the following table:

| Aptitude Score | Predicted Sales |
|---|---|
| 40 | 46.52 + .4994(40) = 66.496 |
| 50 | 46.52 + .4994(50) = 71.49 |
| 70 | 46.52 + .4994(70) = 81.478 |

Given 4 pairs of observations

| X | 6 | 7 | 4 | 3 |
|---|---|---|---|---|
| Y | 8 | 10 | 4 | 2 |

compute and graph the least-squares regression line.

Solution:    We use the table to compute the summary statistics needed.

| X | Y | $X^2$ | XY |
|---|---|---|---|
| 6 | 8 | 36 | 48 |
| 7 | 10 | 49 | 70 |
| 4 | 4 | 16 | 16 |
| 3 | 2 | 9 | 6 |
| $\Sigma X=20$ | $\Sigma Y=24$ | $\Sigma X^2=110$ | $\Sigma XY=140$ |

n = 4

$$\hat{b} = \frac{\Sigma XY - n\bar{X}\,\bar{Y}}{\Sigma X^2 - n\bar{X}^2} = \frac{140 - 4\left(\frac{20}{4}\right)\left(\frac{24}{4}\right)}{110 - 4\left(\frac{20}{4}\right)^2}$$

$$= \frac{140 - 120}{110 - 100} = \frac{20}{10} = 2.0,$$

$$\hat{a} = \bar{Y} - \hat{b}\bar{X} = \frac{24}{4} - (2.0)\left(\frac{20}{4}\right) = 6 - 10$$

$$= -4,$$

$$\hat{Y} = \hat{a} + \hat{b}X$$

$$= -4 + 2X.$$

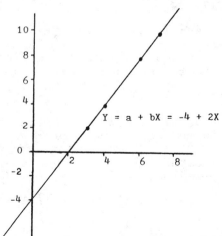

$Y = a + bX = -4 + 2X$

An old farmer had bunions on his feet. He noticed that there seemed to be a relation between the number of bunions and inches of rainfall on his farm. He collected data for a week and then computed the following summary statistics. If X = number of bunions and Y = inches of rainfall, the farmer found that

$$\overline{X} = 4, \quad \overline{Y} = 4, \quad \Sigma XY = 94, \quad \Sigma X^2 = 124.$$

If the farmer wakes up with 5 bunions, how many inches of rain do you predict that day?

Solution:   We compute the least squares regression line relating bunions to inches of rainfall.

$$\hat{b} = \frac{\Sigma XY - n\overline{X}\,\overline{Y}}{\Sigma X^2 - n\overline{X}^2} = \frac{94 - 7(4)(4)}{124 - 7(4)^2},$$

$$\hat{a} = \overline{Y} - \hat{b}\overline{X} \quad = 4 - 4\hat{b}\;; \quad \hat{b} = \frac{-18}{12} = -1.5,$$

$\hat{a} = 4 - (-1.5)\,4 = 10 \cdot$   Thus, $\hat{Y} = 10 - 1.5\,X$ .

If X = 5 then we would predict

$\hat{Y} = 10 - 1.5\,(5) = 2.5$ inches of rainfall.

Graph the pairs of points below. Find the least squares regression line and the standard error of estimate. How many values of Y are within 1 standard deviation or standard error from the regression line?

| X | 9 | 6 | 8 | 5 |
|---|---|---|---|---|
| Y | 5 | 3 | 5 | 3 |

Solution:    The plot of X and Y is

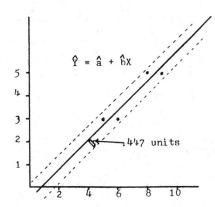

$\hat{Y} = \hat{a} + \hat{b}X$

.447 units

We compute the least-square regression line with the aid of the table.

| X | Y | $X^2$ | $Y^2$ | XY |
|---|---|---|---|---|
| 9 | 5 | 81 | 25 | 45 |
| 6 | 3 | 36 | 9 | 18 |
| 8 | 5 | 64 | 25 | 40 |
| 5 | 3 | 25 | 9 | 15 |

n = 4

$$\Sigma X = 28 \qquad \Sigma Y = 16 \qquad \Sigma X^2 = 206$$

$$\Sigma Y^2 = 68 \qquad \Sigma XY = 118 .$$

The regression line is $\hat{Y} = \hat{a} + \hat{b}X$ where

$$\hat{b} = \frac{\Sigma XY - n\bar{X}\,\bar{Y}}{\Sigma X^2 - n\bar{X}^2} = \frac{118 - 4\left(\frac{28}{4}\right)\left(\frac{16}{4}\right)}{206 - 4\left(\frac{28}{4}\right)^2}$$

$$= \frac{118 - 112}{206 - 196} = \frac{6}{10} = .6 ;$$

$$\hat{a} = \bar{Y} - \hat{b}\bar{X} = \left(\frac{16}{4}\right) - .6\left(\frac{28}{4}\right) = 4 - (.6)7$$

$$= 4 - 4.2 = -.2 ;$$

$$\hat{Y} = -.2 + .6X .$$

The standard error of estimate

$$S_{y\cdot x} = \sqrt{\frac{\Sigma(Y - \hat{Y})^2}{n - 2}} = \sqrt{\frac{\Sigma(Y - \bar{Y})^2 - \hat{b}\Sigma(X - \bar{X})Y}{n - 2}}$$

$$S_{y\cdot x} = \sqrt{\frac{\Sigma Y^2 - n\bar{Y}^2 - \hat{b}(\Sigma XY - \bar{X}\Sigma Y)}{n - 2}}$$

$$= \sqrt{\frac{68 - 4\left(\frac{16}{4}\right)^2 - .6[118 - 7(16)]}{4 - 2}}$$

$$= \sqrt{\frac{4 - .6(6)}{2}}$$

$$= \sqrt{\frac{.4}{2}} = .447$$

All Y values that lie within .447 units from the
regression line lie within 1 standard deviation or
standard error.

| X | Y | $\hat{Y}$ | Distance between (X, Y) and (X, $\hat{Y}$) |
|---|---|-----|---|
| 9 | 5 | 5.2 | .2 |
| 6 | 3 | 3.4 | .4 |
| 8 | 5 | 4.6 | .4 |
| 5 | 3 | 2.8 | .2 |

Referring to the graph the area inside the dotted
lines is all within .447 units or 1 standard error from
the regression line. We see from the graph and the table
of $\hat{Y}$ and Y that all 4 of the Y values differ by less than
1 standard error and hence all 4 Y values lie within 1
standard deviation of the regression line.

● PROBLEM 17-7

Find the standard error of estimate, $S_y.x$ for (problem number
three of this chapter) relating salesmanship to performance
on an aptitude test.
Assume that the population standard error is constant for
all values of X, the aptitude test scores.

Solution:    The standard error of estimate, $S_{y \cdot x}$ ,

measures the dispersion of the observed Y-values about the
regression line.

This quantity is analogous to the standard deviation
which measures the dispersion of the sample about the
sample mean. The standard error of estimate is defined as

$$S_{y \cdot x} = \sqrt{\frac{\Sigma (Y - \hat{Y})^2}{n - 2}}$$

To compute $S_{y \cdot x}$    for our aptitude test score and
sales data we use the following table:

| Y | $\hat{Y}$ | Y - $\hat{Y}$ | $(Y - \hat{Y})^2$ |
|---|-----|-------|---------|
| 54 | 55.5 | - 1.5 | 2.25 |
| 64 | 59.5 | 4.5 | 20.25 |
| 54 | 60.5 | - 6.5 | 42.25 |
| 62 | 63.5 | - 1.5 | 2.25 |
| 68 | 64.5 | 3.5 | 12.25 |
| 70 | 67.5 | 2.5 | 6.25 |
| 76 | 70.5 | 5.5 | 30.25 |
| 66 | 72.4 | - 6.4 | 40.96 |
| 76 | 73.4 | 2.6 | 6.76 |
| 74 | 76.4 | - 2.4 | 5.76 |

$169.23 = \Sigma (Y - \hat{Y})^2$

Thus $S_{y \cdot x}^2 = \dfrac{169.23}{8}$

and $S_{y \cdot x} = \sqrt{21.2} = 4.59$.

An easier way to compute $S_{y \cdot x}$ is to note that

$$\Sigma (Y - \hat{Y})^2 = \Sigma (Y - \overline{Y} + \overline{Y} - \hat{Y})^2$$

$$= \Sigma [(Y - \overline{Y})^2 + 2(Y - \overline{Y})(\overline{Y} - \hat{Y}) + (\overline{Y} - \hat{Y})^2]$$

$$= \Sigma (Y - \overline{Y})^2 + 2 \Sigma (Y - \overline{Y})(\overline{Y} - \hat{Y}) + \Sigma (\overline{Y} - \hat{Y})^2;$$

but $\hat{Y} = \hat{a} + \hat{b}X = \overline{Y} - \hat{b}\overline{X} + \hat{b}X = \overline{Y} + \hat{b}(X - \overline{X})$.
Thus,

$$\Sigma (Y - \hat{Y})^2 = \Sigma (Y - \overline{Y})^2 + 2\Sigma (Y - \overline{Y})[\overline{Y} - \overline{Y} - \hat{b}(X - \overline{X})]$$

$$+ \Sigma [\overline{Y} - \overline{Y} - \hat{b}(X - \overline{X})]^2$$

$$= \Sigma (Y - \overline{Y})^2 + 2\Sigma (Y - \overline{Y})\hat{b}(\overline{X} - X)$$

$$+ \Sigma [(- \hat{b})(X - \overline{X})]^2$$

$$= \Sigma (Y - \overline{Y})^2 - 2\hat{b} \Sigma (Y - \overline{Y})(X - \overline{X})$$

$$+ \hat{b}^2 \Sigma (X - \overline{X})^2.$$

But $\hat{b} = \dfrac{\Sigma (X - \overline{X})(Y - \overline{Y})}{\Sigma (X - \overline{X})^2}$.

Thus $\hat{b}^2 \Sigma (X - \overline{X})^2 = \hat{b} \cdot [\hat{b} \Sigma (X - \overline{X})^2]$

$$= \hat{b} \Sigma (X - \overline{X})(Y - \overline{Y})$$

and

$$\Sigma (Y - \hat{Y})^2 = \Sigma (Y - \overline{Y})^2 - 2\hat{b}[\Sigma (Y - \overline{Y})(X - \overline{X})]$$

$$+ \hat{b} [\Sigma (Y - \overline{Y})(X - \overline{X})$$

$$= \Sigma (Y - \overline{Y})^2 - \hat{b} [\Sigma (Y - \overline{Y})(X - \overline{X})]$$

$$= \Sigma (Y - \overline{Y})^2 - \hat{b} [\Sigma (X - \overline{X})Y - \Sigma (X - \overline{X})\overline{Y}]$$

$$= \Sigma (Y - \overline{Y})^2 - \hat{b}[\Sigma (X - \overline{X})Y - \overline{Y}[\Sigma X - n\overline{X}]]$$

$$= \Sigma (Y - \overline{Y})^2 - \hat{b}[\Sigma (X - \overline{X})Y - \overline{Y}(n\overline{X} - n\overline{X})]$$

$$= \Sigma (Y - \overline{Y})^2 - \hat{b} \Sigma (X - \overline{X})Y .$$

But $\Sigma(X - \bar{X})Y = \Sigma XY - n\bar{X}\bar{Y}$

is the numerator of $\hat{b}$ as may be seen by expanding $\Sigma(X-\bar{X})(Y-\bar{Y})$ and

$$\Sigma(Y - \bar{Y})^2 = \Sigma(Y^2 - 2Y\bar{Y} + \bar{Y}^2)$$
$$= \Sigma Y^2 - 2n\bar{Y}^2 + n\bar{Y}^2$$
$$= \Sigma Y^2 - n\bar{Y}^2 .$$

In the previous problem, we found $\hat{b}, \bar{Y}$ and the numerator of $\hat{b}$. We still need $\Sigma Y^2$. This is found to be 44,680.

Thus $\Sigma(Y - \hat{Y})^2 = 44,680 - 10(66.4)^2 - (.4994)(841)$
$$= 590.4 - 419.99 = 170.4$$

and $S^2_{y \cdot x} = \dfrac{170.4}{8} = 21.3$

or $S_{y \cdot x} = 4.615 .$

The discrepancy between

$$S_{y \cdot x} = \sqrt{\dfrac{\Sigma(Y - \hat{Y})^2}{n - 2}} = 4.59$$

and

$$S_{y \cdot x} = \sqrt{\dfrac{\Sigma Y^2 - n\bar{Y}^2 - \hat{b}[\Sigma XY - n\bar{X}\bar{Y}]}{n - 2}} = 4.615$$

is due to a rounding error.

● **PROBLEM** 17-8

Economists have noticed a relationship between an individual's income and consumption pattern. Describe the functional form such a relationship might take and how linear regression might be used to estimate the consumption function.

Solution: The functional form of a relationship describes the way variables are related. The variables X and Y, if related as $Y = a + bX$ are said to be linearly related.

Another functional relation could be $Y = be^{aX}$, an exponential relation between X and Y. Y and X could also be related as $Y = a + bX^n$ where a, b and n are constants.

$e^Y = a + bX$,     $(b + X)(Y - a) = 1$ are

several other examples of functional forms.

Each of these forms could be used to describe the consumption function, although some functional forms are more consistent with economic theory than others.

$Y = a + bX$ is a functional form that we used in regression analysis. It is very useful for describing the relationship between two variables. A relationship of this type is a prerequisite for regression analysis. All our techniques have been developed for this functional form.

The goal of this problem is to demonstrate the way a data set, consisting of pairs $(X, Y)$ that are not linearly related, may be transformed to assume a linear relationship.

$Y = be^{aX}$ is equivalent to

$\ln Y = \ln b + \ln e^{aX}$   and by the properties of the natural logarithm,

$\ln Y = \ln b + aX$.

If $(X, y)$ is transformed to $(X, \ln Y)$ linear regression may be used.

$Y = a + b X^n$ is not linear in X and Y but is

linear in $X^n$ and Y. If each X observation is raised to the nth power, linear regression may be used to estimate

the relationship between $X^n$ and Y.

$e^Y = a + bX$ is linear in the variables $e^Y$ and X,

thus transforming Y to $e^Y$ will result in a linear relationship.

$(b + X)(Y - a) = 1$ can be transformed algebraically

to $Y = a + \frac{1}{b + X}$ . If each X observation is added to the

constant b and the reciprocal of this quantity is found,

a new variable $S = \frac{1}{b + X}$ is formed and the relationship

between S and Y may be estimated with linear regression.

678

Within certain limits, slime mold is hypothesized to grow at a rate proportional to its size.

That is, if y(t) = size of slime mold at time t,

$\frac{dy}{dt}$ = k y (t) , where $\frac{dy}{dt}$ is the rate of growth.

If the size of the slime mold is measured at time intervals of 1 day for 300 days, we have 300 pairs of data. How could linear regression be used to check the significance of this hypothesized growth model?

Solution: To use linear regression we must transform our equation $\frac{dy}{dt}$ = k y(t) to an equation which is linear in the variables y and t.

Equations of the form $\frac{dy}{dt}$ = k y (t) are called differential equations and frequently arise in mathematical models of growth.

To solve this particular differential equation we use integral calculus. Students who have not studied calculus may skip the following few lines.

$\frac{dy}{dt}$ = k y (t)

$\frac{dy}{y(t)}$ = k dt .

Integrating with respect to t yields

$$\int \frac{dy}{y} = \int k \, dt$$

ln y = k t + c

or $e^{\ln y} = e^{k t + \bar{c}}$

$y = e^{c} \cdot e^{k t}$ .

$e^{c}$ is a constant and will be rewritten $C_1$. Thus

$y(t) = C_1 e^{kt}$ is the solution to our differential equation.

Unfortunately, we still do not have a linear equation in our variables y and t. However, taking the natural logarithm of both sides yields

$$\ln y = \ln [C_1 e^{kt}]$$

$$= \ln C_1 + \ln e^{kt}$$

by the properties of logarithms. Thus,

$$\ln y = \ln C_1 + k t .$$

We still do not have an equation that is linear in the variables y and t. We do have an equation that is linear in the variables ln y and t.

If each observation consisting of (y, t) is transformed to a new observation (ln y, t), linear regression may be used to estimate the constants $\alpha = \ln C_1$ and $\beta = k$. The other techniques of regression such as confidence intervals, hypothesis testing, and tests about the hypothetical correlation coefficient may now be carried out.

In order to make inferences about $\alpha = \ln C_1$ and $\beta = k$, we must assume that ln y is distributed normally, or approximately normally for large samples, with mean $\ln C_1 + kt$ and variance $\sigma^2$.

# LINEAR CORRELATION

● PROBLEM 17-10

Find $r^2$ for the first problem of this chapter. What is $r^2$ and what does it tell us about the regression line?

<u>Solution:</u>   We have found a line which estimates the relationship between corn yield and fertilizer. How good a predictor is this line? How well does the line "fit"? Because we do not know the true line we must compare the least-squares line with another predictor. In the absence of any information about X, the best predictor of Y based on past knowledge is $\overline{Y}$, the sample average. If the regression estimate is a good one, then the

variation explained by $\hat{Y}$ should be greater than the

variation explained by $\overline{Y}$.

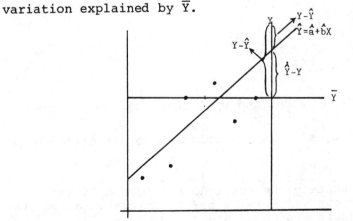

Note that $Y - \overline{Y} = (\hat{Y} - \overline{Y}) + (Y - \hat{Y})$. This can be seen from the above diagram. $\Sigma(Y - \overline{Y})^2 =$ the total variation of Y.

The explained variation of Y is defined as

$$\Sigma(\hat{Y} - \overline{Y})^2.$$

This is the variation from the mean $\overline{Y}$ that is accounted for by the regression line $\hat{Y} = \hat{a} + \hat{b}X$.

The unexplained variation of Y is defined as $\Sigma(Y - \hat{Y})^2$. This is variation in Y that is not accounted for by the regression line.

The coefficient of variation, $r^2$, is defined as the ratio of the variation in the dependent variable (Y) "explained" by the independent variable (X), divided by the total variation of the dependent variable.

Thus

$$r^2 = \frac{\text{Explained variation of Y}}{\text{Total variation of Y}} \quad .$$

The coefficient of determination $r^2$, gives some idea of how well the least-squares line fits the data. If $r^2$ is close to zero, then the variation "explained" by the regression line is very small relative to the variation of Y about the sample mean. If $r^2$ is close to 1, then nearly all the variation of Y is "explained" by the regression line.

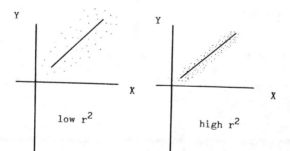

We can compute $r^2$ conveniently from the following identity.

Total variation $\equiv$ Explained variation + unexplained variation

or $\Sigma(Y - \overline{Y})^2 \equiv \Sigma(\hat{Y} - \overline{Y}) + \Sigma(Y - \hat{Y})^2$

Dividing by $\Sigma(Y - \overline{Y})^2$ we see that

$$1 = \frac{\text{Explained variation}}{\text{Total variation}} + \frac{\text{Unexplained variation}}{\text{Total variation}}$$

or $\quad r^2 = \dfrac{\text{Explained variation}}{\text{Total variation}}$

$\quad\quad\quad = 1 - \dfrac{\text{Unexplained variation}}{\text{Total variation}}$ ;

$\quad r^2 = 1 - \dfrac{\Sigma(Y - \hat{Y})^2}{\Sigma(Y - \bar{Y})^2}$ .

To compute $r^2$ for the corn yield - fertilizer data we use the following table.

| X | Y | $\hat{Y}$ | $Y - \hat{Y}$ | $(Y - \hat{Y})^2$ | $Y - \bar{Y}$ | $(Y - \bar{Y})^2$ |
|---|---|---|---|---|---|---|
| .3 | 10 | 12.92 | - 2.92 | 8.53 | - 20 | 400 |
| .6 | 15 | 17.80 | - 2.80 | 7.84 | - 15 | 225 |
| .9 | 30 | 22.68 | 7.32 | 53.58 | 0 | 0 |
| 1.2 | 35 | 27.56 | 7.44 | 55.35 | 5 | 25 |
| 1.5 | 25 | 32.45 | - 7.45 | 55.50 | - 5 | 25 |
| 1.8 | 30 | 37.33 | - 7.33 | 53.73 | 0 | 0 |
| 2.1 | 50 | 42.21 | 7.79 | 60.68 | 20 | 400 |
| 2.4 | 45 | 47.09 | 2.09 | 4.37 | 15 | 225 |
|  | 240 |  |  | 299.58 | 0 | 1,300 |

$$\bar{Y} = \frac{240}{8} = 30$$

$$r^2 = 1 - \frac{\Sigma(Y - \hat{Y})^2}{\Sigma(Y - \bar{Y})^2} = 1 - \frac{299.58}{1300}$$

$$= 1 - .23$$

$$= .77 ,$$

This means that 77% of the variation in Y is accounted for by the regression line while $1 - .77 = .23$, 23% of the variation is due to chance or other factors.

● **PROBLEM** 17-11

What is the coefficient of correlation for the data set given in problem #1 of this chapter?

Solution:     The coefficient of correlation is a measure of the degree of association between an independent and dependent variable. The correlation coefficient is usually denoted by r and measures both the degree and indicates the direction of a relationship. The value of r is closely related to $r^2$, the coefficient of determination. In fact,

$r = \pm \sqrt{r^2}$. The correlation coefficient thus varies from - 1 to 0 to + 1.

The closer r is to 1 or - 1 the stronger the linear association between two variables. The closer r is to zero, the weaker the linear association.

The sign of r indicates the direction of the relationship between an independent and dependent variable. If X and Y denote the independent and dependent variables respectively, than a relationship is said to be positive and $r > 0$ if Y increases as X increases.

If Y decreases as X increases then $r < 0$ and the relationship is said to be negative.

The computational formula for r is:

$$r = \frac{n\Sigma XY - (\Sigma X)(\Sigma Y)}{(\sqrt{n\Sigma X^2 - (\Sigma X)^2})(\sqrt{n\Sigma Y^2 - (\Sigma Y)^2})} .$$

We have calculated

$\Sigma X = 10.8,$ $\qquad \Sigma Y = 240$

$\Sigma X^2 = 18.35,$ $\qquad \Sigma XY = 385.5$

We still need the $\Sigma Y^2$.

$\Sigma(Y - \overline{Y})^2 = \Sigma(Y^2 - 2Y\overline{Y} + \overline{Y}^2) = \Sigma Y^2 - n\overline{Y}^2.$
We know $\Sigma(Y - \overline{Y})^2 = 1300$ ;

hence
Thus $\qquad \Sigma Y^2 = 1300 = 1300 + 8(30)^2 = 8500 .$

$$r = \frac{(8)(385.5) - (10.8)(240)}{(\sqrt{8(18.36) - (10.8)^2})\sqrt{8(8500) - (240)^2}}$$

$$= \frac{492}{(5.499)(101.98)} = .877 .$$

● **PROBLEM** 17-12

Three arctic zoologists spent 5 winters in the Yukon Territory. Their hypothesis was that the number of days on which the temperature dropped below - 50° Fahrenheit affected the length of moose horns. Find the correlation coefficient based on their data.

| X, number of days - 50°F or less | Y, average length of moose Horns (in meters) |
|---|---|
| 30 | .9 |
| 20 | .8 |
| 10 | .5 |
| 30 | 1.0 |
| 10 | .8 |

We compute the correlation coefficient
with the aid of the table below.

| X | Y | $X^2$ | $Y^2$ | XY |
|---|---|---|---|---|
| 30 | .9 | 900 | .81 | 27 |
| 20 | .8 | 400 | .64 | 16 |
| 10 | .5 | 100 | .25 | 5 |
| 30 | 1.0 | 900 | 1.0 | 30 |
| 10 | .8 | 100 | .64 | 8 |

$\Sigma X = 100$ $\qquad \Sigma Y = 4.0$

$\Sigma Y^2 = 3.34$ $\qquad \Sigma X^2 = 2400$

$\Sigma XY = 86$

$$r = \frac{n\Sigma XY - (\Sigma X)(\Sigma Y)}{[\sqrt{n\Sigma X^2 - (\Sigma X)^2}][\sqrt{n\Sigma Y^2 - (\Sigma Y)^2}]}$$

$$= \frac{5(86) - (100)(4.0)}{[\sqrt{5(2400) - (100)^2}][\sqrt{5(3.34) - 4^2}]}$$

$$r = \frac{430 - 400}{[\sqrt{2000}][\sqrt{16.7 - 16}]} = \frac{30}{(44.721)(.8366)} = .80 .$$

It seems there is a high positive correlation
between number of days when the temperature drops to
- 50° F or less and the average length of moose horns.

● **PROBLEM** 17-13

Five people are on a diet reducing plan. Estimate the
regression for the relationship between the number of
pounds of weight lost and the number of weeks each of the
five people were on the plan. Accumulated data consists
of five paired observations: the first element of each
pair indicates the number of weeks the person was on the
diet and the second element indicates the number of pounds
the person lost.      These five paired observations
are given, where X represents the number of weeks on
the diet and Y represents the number of pounds lost.

Quantitative Relationship between Two Variables

| X | Y |
|---|---|
| 3 | 6 |
| 2 | 5 |
| 1 | 4 |
| 4 | 9 |
| 5 | 11 |

The first pair of observations (X = 3, Y = 6) indicates that the first person lost 6 pounds in 3 weeks; the second pair (X = 2, Y = 5) indicates the second person lost 5 pounds in 2 weeks. In like manner, the third pair (X = 1, Y = 4) indicates that the third person lost 4 pounds in 1 week; the fourth pair (X = 4, Y = 9) indicates that the person lost 9 pounds in 4 weeks; and the fifth pair (X = 5, Y = 11) indicates the fifth person lost 11 pounds in 5 weeks.

Find the least squares regression line relating weight loss to weeks on the diet. How many weeks should one diet to expect to lose 20 pounds? How much variation in weight lost is explained by dieting?

Solution:    We plot the independent variable, weeks dieted, on the horizontal axis. The dependent variable, pounds lost, is on the vertical axis. The scatter plot is shown below:

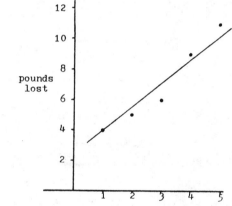

| X | Y | $X^2$ | $Y^2$ | XY |
|---|---|---|---|---|
| 3 | 6 | 9 | 36 | 18 |
| 2 | 5 | 4 | 25 | 10 |
| 1 | 4 | 1 | 16 | 4 |
| 4 | 9 | 16 | 81 | 36 |
| 5 | 11 | 25 | 121 | 55 |

n = 5

$\Sigma X$ = 15    $\Sigma Y$ = 35    $\Sigma Y^2$ = 279    $\Sigma XY$ = 123    $\Sigma X^2$ = 55

The regression coefficients are then found:

$$\hat{b} = \frac{\Sigma XY - n\bar{X}\,\bar{Y}}{\Sigma X^2 - n\bar{X}^2} = \frac{123 - 5\left(\frac{15}{5}\right)\left(\frac{35}{5}\right)}{55 - 5\left(\frac{15}{5}\right)^2}$$

$$= \frac{123 - 3(35)}{55 - 45} = \frac{18}{10} = 1.8 \; ;$$

$$\hat{a} = \overline{Y} - \hat{b}\overline{X} = \frac{35}{5} - 1.8 \left(\frac{15}{5}\right) = 7 - 5.4 = 1.6 \, .$$

$\hat{Y} = 1.6 + 1.8X$ is the least squares regression line.

To lose $\hat{Y} = 20$ pounds one would expect to diet

$$\frac{20 - 1.6}{1.8} = 10.22 \text{ weeks.}$$

To see how well the variation in weight loss is explained by weeks dieted we compute

$$r^2 = 1 - \frac{\text{unexplained variation}}{\text{total variation}}$$

$$= 1 - \frac{\Sigma (Y - \hat{Y})^2}{\Sigma (Y - \overline{Y})^2} \, .$$

To find $r^2$ we first compute $r$, the correlation coefficient, and then square to find $r^2$.

$$r = \hat{b} \frac{S_x}{S_y} = \hat{b} \sqrt{\frac{\Sigma X^2 - n\overline{X}^2}{\Sigma Y^2 - n\overline{Y}^2}}$$

$$= 1.8 \sqrt{\frac{55 - 5(3)^2}{279 - 5(7)^2}}$$

$$= 1.8 \sqrt{\frac{55 - 45}{279 - 5(49)}} = 1.8 \sqrt{\frac{10}{34}} = .976$$

and $r^2 = .952$

95.2% of the variation in weight loss is explained by variation in weeks dieted.

● **PROBLEM** 17-14

A researcher suspects there is a correlation between the number of promises a political candidate makes and the number of promises that are fulfilled once the candidate is elected. He keeps track of several prominent politicians and records the following data:

| Promises made, X | 20 | 30 | 30 | 40 | 50 | 50 | 60 |
|---|---|---|---|---|---|---|---|
| Promises kept, Y | 7 | 6 | 5 | 4 | 3 | 2 | 1 |

What is the correlation between promises made and promises kept?

Solution:    The coefficient of correlation measures the strength of a linear relation between the two variables X and Y.

The sign on the correlation coefficient indicates the direction of the relationship.

| X | $X^2$ | Y | $Y^2$ | XY |
|---|---|---|---|---|
| 20 | 400 | 7 | 49 | 140 |
| 30 | 900 | 6 | 36 | 180 |
| 30 | 900 | 5 | 25 | 150 |
| 40 | 1600 | 4 | 16 | 160 |
| 50 | 2500 | 3 | 9 | 150 |
| 50 | 2500 | 2 | 4 | 100 |
| 60 | 3600 | 1 | 1 | 60 |

n = 7

$\Sigma X$ = 280        $\Sigma Y$ = 28        $\Sigma XY$ = 940 .

$\Sigma X^2$ = 12400        $\Sigma Y^2$ = 140

The coefficient of correlation is

$$r = \frac{n\ \Sigma XY - (\Sigma X)(\Sigma Y)}{[\sqrt{n\Sigma X^2 - (\Sigma X)^2}][\sqrt{n\Sigma Y^2 - (\Sigma Y)^2}]}$$

$$= \frac{7(940) - (280)(28)}{[\sqrt{7(12400) - (280)^2}][\sqrt{7(140) - (28)^2}]}$$

$$= \frac{6580 - 7840}{\sqrt{8400}\ \sqrt{196}} = \frac{-1260}{(91.65)(14)} = -.98 .$$

The coefficient of correlation between promises made and promises kept is - .98, very close to - 1, indicating a very strong negative correlation. On the basis of this data it seems that the politicians who promise the most deliver the least. However it is important to remember that correlation does not imply causality. It seems unlikely that the number of promises made induces or causes a certain number of promises to be kept. Promises made and promises kept are probably both due to the politician's character and hence highly correlated.

● **PROBLEM** 17-15

An independent research team predicts a relationship between birth rate and stork population. In 5 counties they observe the following data.

| X, stork population | 5 | 6 | 1 | 4 | 2 |
|---|---|---|---|---|---|
| Y, births per 1,000 residents | 4 | 3 | 2 | 6 | 3 |

What is the correlation between stork population and births per 1,000?

Solution: We compute the correlation coefficient between X and Y with the aid of the table below,

| X | Y | $X^2$ | $Y^2$ | XY |
|---|---|-------|-------|-----|
| 5 | 4 | 25 | 16 | 20 |
| 6 | 3 | 36 | 9 | 18 |
| 1 | 2 | 1 | 4 | 2 |
| 4 | 6 | 16 | 36 | 24 |
| 2 | 3 | 4 | 9 | 6 |

$n = 5$

$\Sigma X = 18 \quad \Sigma Y = 18 \quad \Sigma X^2 = 82$

$\Sigma Y^2 = 74 \quad \Sigma XY = 70$

The correlation coefficient is

$$r = \frac{n\Sigma XY - (\Sigma X)\, \Sigma Y}{[\sqrt{n\Sigma X^2 - (\Sigma X)^2}]\,[\sqrt{n\Sigma Y^2 - (\Sigma Y)^2}]}$$

$$= \frac{5\,(70) - (18)(18)}{\sqrt{5(82) - (18)^2}\ \sqrt{5(74) - (18)^2}}$$

$$= \frac{350 - 324}{\sqrt{410 - 324}\ \sqrt{370 - 324}}$$

$$= \frac{26}{\sqrt{86}\ \sqrt{46}} = \frac{26}{(9.273)(6.782)} = .41.$$

This correlation of .41 does not provide overwhelming evidence that the number of storks is correlated to birth rate.

This is another example of a problem in which correlation does not imply causation. The number of storks has no causal effect on birth rate.

● PROBLEM 17-16

"There is a complex system of relationships in the business world. As an example, the number of new movies which appear in the course of a week has an appreciable effect on the weekly change in the Dow-Jones Industrial Average."

This is the opinion of a certain armchair economist. This fellow hires you as a consultant and expects you to test his theory. In the first 5 weeks you observe the following:

| X, number of new movies | 1 | 2 | 4 | 5 | 5 |
|---|---|---|---|---|---|
| Y, change in Dow-Jones Industrial Average | - 2 | 4 | - 5 | 7 | - 8 |

What is the correlation between X and Y? What implications does this have for the theory?

Solution: To compute the correlation coefficient r we construct the following table;

| X | Y | $X^2$ | $Y^2$ | XY |
|---|---|---|---|---|
| 1 | - 2 | 1 | 4 | - 2 |
| 2 | 4 | 4 | 16 | 8 |
| 4 | - 5 | 16 | 25 | - 20 |
| 5 | 7 | 25 | 49 | 35 |
| 5 | - 8 | 25 | 64 | - 40 |

n = 5

$\Sigma X = 17$  $\Sigma Y = - 4$  $\Sigma X^2 = 71$

$\Sigma Y^2 = 158$  $\Sigma XY = - 19$

$$r = \frac{n \, \Sigma XY - \Sigma X \Sigma Y}{\sqrt{n\Sigma X^2 - (\Sigma X)^2} \, \sqrt{n\Sigma Y^2 - (\Sigma Y)^2}}$$

$$= \frac{5 \, (- 19) - (17) \, (- 4)}{\sqrt{5(71) - (17)^2} \, \sqrt{5(158) - (- 4)^2}}$$

$$= \frac{- 95 + 68}{\sqrt{66} \, \sqrt{806}}$$

$$= \frac{- 27}{(8.12)(28.39)} = - .117 \, .$$

The coefficient of correlation indicates a weak negative relation between the number of new movies and changes in the Dow-Jones Industrial Average. This seems to cast doubt on the theory.

● **PROBLEM** 17-17

Here are some data that exhibit a strong negative correlation. Compute the regression equation and predict the Y score for someone with X = 164.

$\overline{X} = 200$  $\overline{Y} = 90$  $r_{xy} = - 0.90$

$S_x = 9$  $S_y = 5$

689

<u>Solution:</u>    We are given $\overline{X}$, $\overline{Y}$, $r_{xy}$ and $S_x$ and $S_y$. From these quantities we must compute the regression equation. We know that

$$S_y = \sqrt{\frac{\Sigma(Y - \overline{Y})^2}{n - 1}} \qquad \text{the standard error of the Y scores and}$$

$$S_x = \sqrt{\frac{\Sigma(X - \overline{X})^2}{n - 1}} \qquad \text{the standard error of the X scores} \; ;$$

and $\quad r = \dfrac{n \, \Sigma XY - (\Sigma X)(\Sigma Y)}{(\sqrt{n\Sigma X^2 - (\Sigma X)^2})(\sqrt{n\Sigma Y^2 - (\Sigma Y)^2})}$

$$= \frac{n \, \Sigma XY - (\Sigma X)(\Sigma Y)}{\sqrt{n(\Sigma X^2 - n\overline{X}^2)} \; \sqrt{n(\Sigma Y^2 - n\overline{Y}^2)}}$$

$$= \frac{n \, \Sigma XY - (\Sigma X)(\Sigma Y)}{n \, (\sqrt{\Sigma(X - \overline{X})^2}) \, \sqrt{\Sigma(Y - \overline{Y})^2}} \; .$$

We also know that

$\hat{b}$, the slope coefficient $= \dfrac{\Sigma XY - n\overline{X}\,\overline{Y}}{\Sigma(X - \overline{X})^2}$ .

From these formulas we see that

$$\hat{b} = \frac{\Sigma XY - \dfrac{\Sigma X \Sigma Y}{n}}{\Sigma(X - \overline{X})^2}$$

$$= \frac{n \, \Sigma XY - \Sigma X \Sigma Y}{\sqrt{\Sigma(X - \overline{X})^2} \, \sqrt{\Sigma(Y - \overline{Y})^2}} \cdot \sqrt{\frac{\Sigma(Y - \overline{Y})^2}{\Sigma(X - \overline{X})^2}} = r \cdot \frac{S_y}{S_x} \; .$$

We know that

$\hat{a} = \overline{Y} - \hat{b}\overline{X}$ . Thus $\quad \hat{b} = r \cdot \dfrac{S_y}{S_x} = (-.90) \dfrac{5}{9} = -.5$

and $\quad \hat{a} = \overline{Y} - \hat{b}\overline{X} = 90 - (-.5)(200)$

$$= 190 \; .$$

$\hat{Y} = 190 - .5X \qquad$ is the regression line and an X score of 164 would lead to a prediction of

$$\hat{Y} = 190 - .5(164) = 108.$$

   This problem provides an example of a highly negative correlation between the X-scores and Y-scores. That is, the larger X is the smaller we expect Y to be and the smaller X is the larger we expect Y.

690

The heights of fathers, X, and the heights of their oldest sons when grown, Y, are given as measurements to the nearest inch.

| X | 68 | 64 | 70 | 72 | 69 | 74 |
|---|----|----|----|----|----|----|
| Y | 67 | 68 | 69 | 73 | 66 | 70 |

(a) Construct a scattergram.
(b) Find the equation of the least squares regression line.
(c) Compute the standard error of estimate.
(d) Compute the coefficient of correlation r.

Solution:

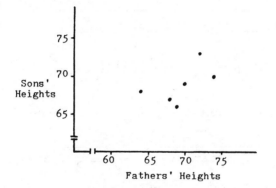

| X | Y | $X^2$ | $Y^2$ | XY |
|---|---|-------|-------|-----|
| 68 | 67 | 4624 | 4489 | 4556 |
| 64 | 68 | 4096 | 4624 | 4352 |
| 70 | 69 | 4900 | 4761 | 4830 |
| 72 | 73 | 5184 | 5329 | 5256 |
| 69 | 66 | 4761 | 4356 | 4554 |
| 74 | 70 | 5476 | 4900 | 5180 |

n = 6

$\Sigma X = 417 \qquad \Sigma Y = 413 \qquad \Sigma XY = 28,728$

$\Sigma X^2 = 29,041 \qquad \Sigma Y^2 = 28,459$

Computing the regression coefficients we see that

$$\hat{b} = \frac{\Sigma XY - n\overline{X}\,\overline{Y}}{\Sigma X^2 - n\overline{X}^2} = \frac{28,728 - 6\left(\frac{417}{6}\right)\left(\frac{413}{6}\right)}{29,041 - 6\left(\frac{417}{6}\right)^2}$$

$$= \frac{6(28,728) - (417)(413)}{6(29,041) - (417)^2} = \frac{172368 - 172221}{174246 - 173889} = \frac{147}{357} = .41$$

and $\hat{a} = \overline{Y} - \hat{b}\overline{X} = \frac{413}{6} - .41 \left(\frac{417}{6}\right) = 40.2$ .

Thus the least squares regression line is
$\hat{Y} = 40.2 + .41X$ .

The standard error of estimate, a measure of dispersion of the Y values about the regression line is defined as

$$S_{y \cdot x} = \sqrt{\frac{\Sigma (Y - \hat{Y})^2}{n - 2}} \quad .$$

As we have previously shown,

$$S_{y \cdot x} = \sqrt{\frac{\Sigma (Y - \overline{Y})^2 - \hat{b} \, \Sigma (X - \overline{X}) Y}{n - 2}}$$

$$= \sqrt{\frac{\Sigma Y^2 - n\overline{Y}^2 - \hat{b} \, [\Sigma XY - n\overline{X} \, \overline{Y}]}{n - 2}} \quad .$$

$$\Sigma XY - n\overline{X} \, \overline{Y} = 28,728 - \frac{(417)(413)}{6} = 24.5$$

and $\Sigma Y^2 - n\overline{Y}^2 = 28,459 - \frac{(413)^2}{6} = 31$ . Hence

$$S_{y \cdot x} = \sqrt{\frac{31 - .41(24.5)}{4}} = \sqrt{\frac{20.95}{4}} = 2.28 \quad .$$

The correlation coefficient is

$$r = \hat{b} \, \frac{S_x}{S_y} = .41 \sqrt{\frac{\Sigma (X - \overline{X})^2}{\Sigma (Y - \overline{Y})^2}} \quad \text{where}$$

$S_x$ = the standard error of X, a measure of the dispersion of the X values about $\overline{X}$.

$S_y$ = the standard error of Y, a measure of the dispersion of the Y values about $\overline{Y}$.

$$\sqrt{(n - 1)} \, S_y = \sqrt{\Sigma (Y - \overline{Y})^2} = \sqrt{\Sigma Y^2 - n\overline{Y}^2} = \sqrt{31} = 5.56$$

and $\sqrt{n - 1} \, S_x = \sqrt{\Sigma (X - \overline{X})^2} = \sqrt{\Sigma X^2 - n\overline{X}^2}$

$$= \sqrt{29041 - 6 \left(\frac{417}{6}\right)^2} = \sqrt{59.5} = 7.71 \quad .$$

Thus

$$r = (.41) \left(\frac{7.71}{5.56}\right) = .57 \quad .$$

57% of the variation about $\overline{Y}$ is explained through the introduction of the variable X

A famous astronomer and sociologist observes the number of sunspots and applications to medical school for 5 successive years. It is his theory that somehow the number of sunspots is responsible for the number of applications to medical school. Find the correlation between these two quantities. How well is the variation in applications explained by the variation in the number of sunspots? If no sunspots are observed in a year, how many applicants to medical school are predicted?

The observations are:

| X, observed sunspots | Y, med school applications (in thousands) |
|---|---|
| 3 | 9 |
| 1 | 5 |
| 2 | 7 |
| 5 | 14 |
| 4 | 10 |

Solution:    We need to calculate three measures. The correlation coefficient, the least-squares regression coefficients and the coefficient of determination $r^2$.

The first step will be to compute the summary statistics.

| X | Y | $X^2$ | $Y^2$ | XY |
|---|---|---|---|---|
| 3 | 9 | 9 | 81 | 27 |
| 1 | 5 | 1 | 25 | 5 |
| 2 | 7 | 4 | 49 | 14 |
| 5 | 14 | 25 | 196 | 70 |
| 4 | 10 | 16 | 100 | 40 |

$n = 5$

$\Sigma X = 15$,   $\Sigma Y = 45$   $\Sigma X^2 = 55$   $\Sigma Y^2 = 451$,   $\Sigma XY = 156$

Now we compute the regression coefficient,

$$\hat{b} = \frac{\Sigma XY - n\bar{X}\ \bar{Y}}{\Sigma X^2 - n\bar{X}^2} = \frac{156 - 5\left(\frac{15}{5}\right)\left(\frac{45}{5}\right)}{55 - 5\left(\frac{15}{5}\right)^2}$$

$$= \frac{156 - 5(3)(9)}{55 - 5(3)^2} = \frac{156 - 135}{55 - 45} = \frac{21}{10} = 2.1$$

and  $\hat{a} = \bar{Y} - \hat{b}\bar{X} = 9 - (2.1)(3) = 2.7.$

Thus the regression line relating observed sunspots to medical school applications is:

$\hat{Y} = 2.7 + 2.1X$ .

If no sunspots are observed, we predict

$$\hat{Y} = 2.7 + (2.1)(0) = 2.7$$

thousand medical school applications.

The correlation coefficient r measures. the direction and strength of linear association between two variables.

$$r = \frac{n\Sigma XY - (\Sigma X)(\Sigma Y)}{\left[\sqrt{n\Sigma X^2 - (\Sigma X)^2}\right]\left[\sqrt{n\Sigma Y^2 - (\Sigma Y)^2}\right]}$$

$$= \frac{5(156) - (15)(45)}{\left[\sqrt{5(55)-(15)^2}\right]\left[\sqrt{5(451)-(45)^2}\right]}$$

$$= \frac{780 - 675}{\sqrt{275-225}\ \sqrt{2255-2025}}$$

$$= \frac{7105}{\sqrt{50}\sqrt{230}} = \frac{105}{(7.071)(15.165)}$$

$$= .979 = .98$$

This correlation is very high but does notimply causality between sunspots and applications to medical school.

The variation in applications to medical school explained by sunspots is indicated by $r^2$, the coefficient of determination.

$$r^2 = (\text{the correlation coefficient})^2$$

$$= (.98)^2 = .96.$$

Hence 96% of the variation in medical school applications is explained by variation in sunspots.

● PROBLEM 17-20

A firm tested 500 new employees on an aptitude test. The score of each employee was X. Three years later they collected supervisor's ratings of each employee's success on the job. These ratings are denoted by Y. The data yielded the following statistics:

$$\bar{X} = 100, \quad S_x = 10, \quad \bar{Y} = 130, \quad S_y = 20 \quad \text{and} \quad r = .70.$$

Compute the least-squares regression line for predicting Y. What ratings would you predict for employees who received test scores of 90 and 125?

Solution:    First compute the regression coefficient $\hat{b}$;

$$\hat{b} = r \frac{S_y}{S_x} = (.70) \left(\frac{20}{10}\right) = 1.40$$

$$\hat{a} = \bar{Y} - \hat{b}\bar{X} = 130 - (1.4)(100) = -10 \ .$$

Thus the least-squares regression line is

$$\hat{Y} = -10 + 1.40X.$$

To predict Y, we substitute values of X into the least-squares regression line.

The predicted rating of an employee with an aptitude test score of 90 is

$$\hat{Y} = -10 + 1.40(90) = 116.$$

The predicted rating of an employee with an aptitude test score of 125 is

$$\hat{Y} = -10 + (1.4)(125) = 165.$$

● **PROBLEM** 17-21

An investigator has data on 1,000 individuals who have been in psychotherapy for five years. Variable X tells the score the individual received on a personality test. Variable Y tells his improvement in psychotherapy over the five years. Here are the data: $\Sigma XY = 30,000$. $\Sigma X = 3,000$. $\Sigma X^2 = 14,000$. $\Sigma Y = 5,000$.

(a) Compute the value of $\hat{b}$ in the regression equation.
(b) What is the regression equation?
(c) Predict the improvement score of a subject with X=4.
(d) If $S_y = 10$, compute r.

Solution:    $\hat{b} = \dfrac{n\Sigma XY - (\Sigma X)(\Sigma Y)}{n \ \Sigma X^2 - (\Sigma X)^2}$

$$= \frac{(1000)(30,000) - (3,000)(5,000)}{(1000)(14,000) - (3,000)^2}$$

$$= \frac{15 \times 10^6}{5 \times 10^6} = 3.0$$

To find the regression line we need

$$\hat{a} = \bar{Y} - \hat{b}\bar{X} = \frac{\Sigma Y}{n} - \hat{b}\left(\frac{\Sigma X}{n}\right) = 5 - (3.0)(3.0) = 5 - 9 = -4.$$

Thus the least-squares regression line is

$$\hat{Y} = \hat{a} + \hat{b}X = -4 + 3X.$$

695

We would predict an improvement score of

$$\hat{Y} = -4 + 3X = -4 + 3(4) = 8$$

from an individual who scores X = 4 on the personality test.

If $S_y$, the standard error or standard deviation of Y, is 10 then we can compute the correlation coefficient r. We know that

$$\hat{b} = r \cdot \frac{S_y}{S_x} \qquad \text{and}$$

$$S_x = \sqrt{\frac{\Sigma(X - \overline{X})^2}{n}} = \sqrt{\frac{\Sigma X^2 - n\overline{X}^2}{n}}$$

$$= \sqrt{\frac{14000 - (1000)\ 3^2}{1000}} = \sqrt{\frac{5000}{1000}} = \sqrt{5} = 2.24 \ . \text{ Hence}$$

$$r = \hat{b} \cdot \frac{S_x}{S_y} = \frac{3(2.24)}{10} = .67$$

● **PROBLEM** 17-22

Plot the following points.

| X | - 1 | - 2 | 0 | 1 | 1.5 |
|---|-----|-----|---|---|-----|
| Y | 1 | 3 | 1 | 2 | 4 |

Use linear regression to estimate the relationship $Y = \alpha + \beta X$. Compute $r^2$. How well does the least squares equation "fit" the data? Now transform each X by squaring. Use linear regression to estimate the relationship between Y and $X^2$. What is $r^2$ for this new regression.

Solution:

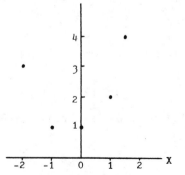

The following table is useful in computing the regression coefficients and r .

| X | Y | $X^2$ | $Y^2$ | XY |
|---|---|---|---|---|
| − 1 | 1 | 1 | 1 | − 1 |
| − 2 | 3 | 4 | 9 | − 6 |
| 0 | 1 | 0 | 1 | 0 |
| 1 | 2 | 1 | 4 | 2 |
| 1.5 | 4 | 2.25 | 16 | 6 |

$$\Sigma X = -.5 \quad \Sigma Y = 11 \quad \Sigma X^2 = 8.25$$

$$\Sigma Y^2 = 31 \quad \Sigma XY = 1 , \quad n = 5$$

$$\hat{\beta} = \frac{\Sigma XY - n \bar{X} \bar{Y}}{\Sigma X^2 - n\bar{X}^2} = \frac{1 - 5\left(\frac{-.5}{5}\right)\left(\frac{11}{5}\right)}{8.25 - 5\left(\frac{-.5}{5}\right)^2}$$

$$= \frac{2.1}{8.2} = .256 .$$

$$\hat{\alpha} = \bar{Y} - \hat{\beta}\bar{X} = \frac{11}{5} - (.256)\left(\frac{-.5}{5}\right) = 2.226 .$$

Thus, the best fitting linear equation is

$$\hat{Y} = \hat{\alpha} + \hat{\beta}X = 2.226 + .256X.$$

$$r = \frac{\Sigma (X - \bar{X})(Y - \bar{Y})}{\sqrt{\Sigma X^2 - n\bar{X}^2} \ \sqrt{\Sigma Y^2 - n\bar{Y}^2}}$$

$$= \frac{\Sigma XY - n\bar{X} \bar{Y}}{\sqrt{\Sigma X^2 - n\bar{X}^2} \ \sqrt{\Sigma Y^2 - n\bar{Y}^2}}$$

$$= \frac{2.1}{\sqrt{8.2} \ \sqrt{31 - 5\left(\frac{11}{5}\right)^2}}$$

$$= \frac{2.1}{\sqrt{8.2} \ \sqrt{6.8}}$$

$$= \frac{2.1}{7.47} = .28$$

$$r^2 = (r)^2 = (.28)^2 = .079 .$$

Approximately 8 percent of the variation in Y is explained by the least squares equation $\hat{Y} = 2.226 + .256X$. This is quite a low correlation between X and Y.

Perhaps there is a significant relationship between X and Y but we have specified the incorrect functional form of this relationship. To check this we regress Y and $X^2$. Let a new variable, S, be created in the following way; let $S = X^2$.

Now we estimate the hypothesized relationship between Y and S.

| S | Y | $S^2$ | $Y^2$ | SY |
|---|---|-------|-------|----|
| 1 | 1 | 1 | 1 | 1 |
| 4 | 3 | 16 | 9 | 12 |
| 0 | 1 | 0 | 1 | 0 |
| 1 | 2 | 1 | 4 | 2 |
| 2.25 | 4 | 5.06 | 16 | 9 |

$\Sigma S = 8.25$      $\Sigma Y = 11$      $\Sigma S^2 = 23.06$

$\Sigma SY = 24,$      $\Sigma Y^2 = 31$

The regression coefficients of the relationship between Y and S are computed in exactly the same way as that used in computing the coefficients between Y and X. Thus,

$$\hat{\beta} = \frac{\Sigma SY - n\bar{S}\,\bar{Y}}{\Sigma S^2 - n\bar{S}^2}$$

$$= \frac{24 - 5\left(\frac{8.25}{5}\right)\left(\frac{11}{5}\right)}{23.06 - 5\left(\frac{8.25}{5}\right)^2}$$

$$= \frac{24 - 18.15}{23.06 - 13.61} = \frac{5.85}{9.45} = .619\ \cdot$$

$$\hat{\alpha} = \bar{Y} - \hat{\beta}\bar{S} = \frac{11}{5} - (.619)\left(\frac{8.25}{5}\right)$$

$$= 2.2 + 1.02 = 3.22\ \cdot$$

The revised least squares equation is

$$\hat{Y} = \hat{\alpha} + \hat{\beta}S = 3.22 + .619X^2\ \cdot$$

$$r = \frac{\Sigma(Y - \bar{Y})(S - \bar{S})}{\sqrt{\Sigma Y^2 - n\bar{Y}^2}\ \sqrt{\Sigma S^2 - n\bar{S}^2}}$$

$$= \frac{24 - 5\left(\frac{8.25}{5}\right)\left(\frac{11}{5}\right)}{\sqrt{31 - 5\left(\frac{11}{5}\right)^2}\ \sqrt{23.06 - 5\left(\frac{8.25}{5}\right)^2}}$$

$$= \frac{5.85}{\sqrt{6.8} \quad \sqrt{9.45}}$$

$$= \frac{5.85}{(2.61)(3.07)}$$

$$= .730$$

and $r^2 = (r)^2 = .53$ .

Thus 53 percent of the variation in Y is explained by the regression line,

$$\hat{Y} = 3.22 + .619X \quad .$$

The functional form of $Y = a + bX^2$ is more appropriate in describing this data than the form $Y = a + bX$. It is necessary that the researcher specify an appropriate functional form before linear regression is used.

# SPEARMAN'S RANK CORRELATION

● PROBLEM 17-23

What is the coefficient of rank-correlation for the first problem of this chapter?

Solution:      Occasionally the correlation coefficient r is not an appropriate measure of association between two variables. Sometimes the variables of interest can be ranked but can not be assigned numerical values on an absolute scale. An example of this situation is a beauty contest in which the contestants are ranked according to their beauty. If two judges provide two different rankings and we wish to determine a measure of correlation between the rankings, r is not an appropriate measure. The correlation coefficient depends on the distance between scores and a ranking provides an order but does not indicate a distance.

A system of measurement that provides an ordering but not an interval scale is called ordinal measurement. Many types of variables in the social sciences such as scales measuring prestige, political efficacy, prejudice or political orientation are ordinal level variables.

One possible way to measure correlation between ordinal level variables is to revise r by replacing the X and Y scores by the rankings of variables X and Y.

To illustrate, let us find the rankings of the variables representing fertilizer and corn yield. To find the rankings, list the independent variable from smallest to largest. Then label the smallest value with rank "1", the next smallest with rank "2", and so on until the largest of the n variables is labeled with rank n. Next label the dependent variables with their ranks.

If there are ties between variables assign each variable the average of the two rankings.

| X, fertilizer | Rank of X | Y, corn yield | Rank of Y |
|---|---|---|---|
| .3<br>.6 | $X_1 = 1$<br>$X_2 = 2$ | 10<br>15 | $Y_1 = 1$<br>$Y_2 = 2$ |
| .9 | $X_3 = 3$ | 30 | $Y_3 = \dfrac{4+5}{2} = 4.5$ |
| 1.2<br>1.5 | $X_4 = 4$<br>$X_5 = 5$ | 35<br>25 | $Y_4 = 6$<br>$Y_5 = 3$ |
| 1.8 | $X_6 = 6$ | 30 | $Y_6 = \dfrac{4+5}{2} = 4.5$ |
| 2.1<br>2.4 | $X_7 = 7$<br>$X_8 = 8$ | 50<br>45 | $Y_7 = 8$<br>$Y_8 = 7$ |

Now we derive the formula for computing a correlation between the ranks. Let $X_i$ = rank of ith X variable and $Y_i$ = rank of the ith Y variable.

$$r = \frac{n\ \Sigma XY - (\Sigma X)(\Sigma Y)}{\sqrt{n\Sigma X^2 - (\Sigma X)^2}\ \sqrt{n\Sigma Y^2 - (\Sigma Y)^2}} \ .$$

This can be rewritten as

$$r = \frac{\Sigma XY - \dfrac{(\Sigma X)(\Sigma Y)}{n}}{\sqrt{\Sigma X^2 - \dfrac{(\Sigma X)^2}{n}}\ \sqrt{\Sigma Y^2 - \dfrac{(\Sigma Y)^2}{n}}} \ ;$$

but $\quad \overline{X} = \dfrac{\Sigma X}{n} \quad$ and $\quad \overline{Y} = \dfrac{\Sigma Y}{n} \ ; \quad$ thus

$$r = \frac{\Sigma\ XY - n\overline{X}\ \overline{Y}}{\sqrt{\Sigma X^2 - n\overline{X}^2}\ \sqrt{\Sigma Y^2 - n\overline{Y}^2}} \ .$$

We now replace the X and Y values with their ranks.

$$\overline{X} = \frac{\Sigma X}{n} = \frac{\sum\limits_{i=1}^{n} X_i}{n} \quad \text{and} \quad \overline{Y} = \frac{\sum\limits_{i=1}^{n} X_i}{n}$$

$$\sum\limits_{i=1}^{n} X_i = 1 + 2 + 3 + 4 + \dots + n$$

$$\sum\limits_{i=1}^{n} Y_i = 1 + 2 + 3 + 4 + \dots + n \quad \text{(after rearranging)}$$

The formula for these expressions is

$$1 + 2 + 3 + 4 + \ldots + n = \frac{n(n + 1)}{2} .$$

We also need to find

$$\Sigma \, X_i{}^2 = 1^2 + 2^2 + 3^2 + \ldots + n^2$$

$$= \frac{n(n + 1)(2n + 1)}{6} .$$

Thus $\quad \Sigma \, X_i{}^2 = \Sigma \, Y_i{}^2 = \dfrac{n(n + 1)(2n + 1)}{6}$

and $\quad \overline{X} = \overline{Y} = \dfrac{\Sigma X_i}{n} = \dfrac{\Sigma Y_i}{n} = \dfrac{\frac{n(n + 1)}{2}}{n}$

$$= \frac{n + 1}{2} .$$

Substituting $X_i$ and $Y_i$ into the formula for r we see that:

$$r_s = \frac{\displaystyle\sum_{i=1}^{n} X_i Y_i - n\left(\frac{n + 1}{2}\right)\left(\frac{n + 1}{2}\right)}{\sqrt{\Sigma X_i{}^2 - n\left(\frac{n + 1}{2}\right)^2} \; \sqrt{\Sigma Y_i{}^2 - n\left(\frac{n + 1}{2}\right)^2}}$$

$$r_s = \frac{\displaystyle\sum_{i=1}^{n} X_i Y_i - n\left(\frac{n + 1}{2}\right)^2}{\displaystyle\sum_{i=1}^{n} X_i^2 - n\left(\frac{n + 1}{2}\right)^2}$$

because $\displaystyle\sum_{i=1}^{n} X_i{}^2 = \sum_{i=1}^{n} Y_i{}^2$; this will be true unless there are ties in the Y ranks.

Adding and subtracting $\Sigma X_i{}^2$ in the numerator we see that

$$r_s = \frac{\displaystyle\sum_{i=1}^{n} X_i{}^2 - n\left(\frac{n + 1}{2}\right)^2}{\Sigma X_i{}^2 - n\left(\frac{n + 1}{2}\right)^2} + \frac{\displaystyle\sum_{i=1}^{n} X_i Y_i - \sum_{i=1}^{n} X_i{}^2}{\Sigma X_i{}^2 - n\left(\frac{n + 1}{2}\right)^2}$$

$$= 1 + \frac{\displaystyle\sum_{i=1}^{n} X_i Y_i - \frac{1}{2}\left[\sum_{i=1}^{n} X_i{}^2 + \sum_{i=1}^{n} Y_i{}^2\right]}{\Sigma X_i{}^2 - n\left(\frac{n + 1}{2}\right)^2}$$

because 
$$\frac{1}{2}\left[\sum_{i=1}^{n} X_i^2 + \sum_{i=1}^{n} Y_i^2\right] = \sum_{i=1}^{n} X_i^2.$$

$$r_s = 1 - \frac{\frac{1}{2}\left[\sum_{i=1}^{n} X_i^2 + \sum_{i=1}^{n} Y_i^2 - 2\sum_{i=1}^{n} X_i Y_i\right]}{\sum_{i=1}^{n} X_i^2 - n\left(\frac{n+1}{2}\right)^2}$$

$$r_s = 1 - \frac{\sum_{i=1}^{n} (X_i^2 - 2X_i Y_i + Y_i^2)}{2\sum_{i=1}^{n} X_i^2 - 2n\left(\frac{n+1}{2}\right)^2}$$

$$r_s = 1 - \frac{\sum_{i=1}^{n} (X_i - Y_i)^2}{2\sum_{i=1}^{n} X_i^2 - 2n\left(\frac{n+1}{2}\right)^2}$$

$$r_s = 1 - \frac{\sum_{i=1}^{n} (X_i - Y_i)^2}{2\,\frac{n(n+1)(2n+1)}{6} - 2n\left(\frac{n+1}{2}\right)^2}$$

$$r_s = 1 - \frac{6\sum_{i=1}^{n} (X_i - Y_i)^2}{2n(n+1)(2n+1) - 3n(n+1)^2}$$

$$r_s = 1 - \frac{6\sum_{i=1}^{n} (X_i - Y_i)^2}{(n+1)[4n^2 + 2n - 3n^2 - 3n]}$$

$$= 1 - \frac{6\sum_{i=1}^{n} (X_i - Y_i)^2}{(n+1)(n^2 - n)}$$

$$r_s = 1 - \frac{6\sum_{i=1}^{n} (X_i - Y_i)^2}{n(n+1)(n-1)} = 1 - \frac{6\sum d^2}{n(n^2 - 1)}$$

where $d^2 = (X_i - Y_i)^2$, the difference in ranks between the ith X score and Y score, squared.

We see if the ranks of X and Y are the same then

702

$$r_s = 1 - \frac{6(0)}{n(n^2 - 1)} = 1$$

a perfect correlation. If the ranks are completely opposite it can be shown that

$$r_s = 1 - \frac{6 \sum\limits_{i=1}^{n} [2i - 1 - n]^2}{n(n^2 - 1)} = -1.$$

a perfect correlation in the opposite direction.

This argument is true if there are no ties between the observed Y values. If there are tied observations, a correction factor must be added to the value of $\Sigma d^2$. This is necessary because each set of ties involving k observations lowers the value of $d^2$ by an amount equal to $\frac{k^3 - k}{12}$. To correct, we proceed as follows:

Let $t_2$ = number of ties involving 2 observations

$t_3$ = number of ties involving 3 observations

$t_k$ = number of ties involving k observations

The correction factor is

$$T = \frac{2^3 - 2}{12} t_2 + \frac{3^3 - 3}{12} t_3 + \ldots + \frac{k^3 - k}{12} t_k$$

where k depends on how many ties are observed. Next add

$$\sum_{i=1}^{n} (X_i - Y_i)^2 + T ,$$

this is the corrected value of $\Sigma d^2$ which is used in the computation of the coefficient of rank-correlation.

Thus in the case of ties,

$$r_s = 1 - \frac{6 [\Sigma (X_i - Y_i)^2 + T]}{n(n^2 - 1)} .$$

We now compute the coefficient of rank correlation for the data relating corn production to fertilizer.

| X | Y | Rank of X | Rank of Y | $X_i - Y_i$ | $(X_i - Y_i)^2$ |
|---|---|---|---|---|---|
| .3 | 10 | 1 | 1 | 0 | 0 |
| .6 | 15 | 2 | 2 | 0 | 0 |
| .9 | 30 | 3 | 4.5 | - 1.5 | 2.25 |
| 1.2 | 35 | 4 | 6 | - 2 | 4 |
| 1.5 | 25 | 5 | 3 | 2 | 4 |
| 1.8 | 30 | 6 | 4.5 | 1.5 | 2.25 |
| 2.1 | 50 | 7 | 8 | - 1 | 1 |
| 2.4 | 45 | 8 | 7 | 1 | 1 |

$$\sum_{i=1}^{8} (X_i - Y_i)^2 = 14.50, \qquad n = 8$$

There is one tie involving two observations, thus the correction factor

$$T = \frac{2^3 - 2}{12} (1) = \frac{8 - 2}{12} = \frac{1}{2}$$

and $\Sigma d^2 = \sum_{i=1}^{8} (X_i - Y_i)^2 + T = 14.5 + .5 = 15.$

$$r_s = 1 - \frac{6 \Sigma d^2}{n(n^2 - 1)} = 1 - \frac{6(15)}{8(63)} = 1 - .178 = .82$$

Comparing $r_s = .82$ with $r = .87$, the correlation coefficient we calculated earlier, we see that $r_s$ and $r$ are fairly close. The discrepancy is due to the fact that the calculation of $r_s$ uses less information about the variables X and Y than does the calculation of $r$.

● **PROBLEM 17-24**

The table below lists the ranks assigned by two securities analysts to 12 investment opportunities in terms of the degree of investor risk involved.

| Investment | Rank by analyst 1 | Rank by analyst 2 |
|------------|-------------------|-------------------|
| A | 7 | 6 |
| B | 8 | 4 |
| C | 2 | 1 |
| D | 1 | 3 |
| E | 9 | 11 |
| F | 3 | 2 |
| G | 12 | 12 |
| H | 11 | 10 |
| I | 4 | 5 |
| J | 10 | 9 |
| K | 6 | 7 |
| L | 5 | 8 |

Find the correlation between the two rankings. What is the relationship between the two rankings?

<u>Solution:</u>    We compute $r_s$, the coefficient of rank correlation between the rankings given by Analyst 1 and Analyst 2.

| Investment | Analyst 1 | Analyst 2 | $X_i - Y_i$ | $(X_i - Y_i)^2$ |
|:---:|:---:|:---:|:---:|:---:|
| A | 7 | 6 | 1 | 1 |
| B | 8 | 4 | 4 | 16 |
| C | 2 | 1 | 1 | 1 |
| D | 1 | 3 | - 2 | 4 |
| E | 9 | 11 | - 2 | 4 |
| F | 3 | 2 | 1 | 1 |
| G | 12 | 12 | 0 | 0 |
| H | 11 | 10 | 1 | 1 |
| I | 4 | 5 | - 1 | 1 |
| J | 10 | 9 | 1 | 1 |
| K | 6 | 7 | - 1 | 1 |
| L | 5 | 8 | - 3 | 9 |

$$r_s = 1 - \frac{6 \sum_{i=1}^{12} (X_i - Y_i)^2}{n(n^2 - 1)} \qquad \sum_{i=1}^{12} (X_i - Y_i)^2 = 40$$

$$n = 12 .$$

$$r_s = 1 - \frac{6(40)}{12(144 - 1)} = 1 - \frac{240}{1716}$$

$$= 1 - .14$$

$$r_s = .86 .$$

The correlation between the rankings given by
Analyst 1 and Analyst 2 is .86. This is a very strong,
positive correlation between the two rankings. It
seems to imply that these two analysts have very similar
ideas about the degree of investor risk involved with
these twelve securities.

● **PROBLEM** 17-25

A large automobile agency wishes to determine the
relationship between a salesman's aptitude test score
and the number of cars sold by the salesman during his
first year of employment. A random sample of 15 sales-
men's files reveals the following information.

| Salesman | Test score x | Number of cars y |
|----------|--------------|------------------|
| A | 72 | 341 |
| B | 88.5 | 422 |
| C | 70 | 322 |
| D | 87 | 440 |
| E | 71 | 287 |
| F | 85 | 415 |
| G | 89 | 463 |
| H | 93 | 497 |
| I | 98 | 510 |
| J | 96 | 512 |
| K | 86 | 432 |
| L | 82 | 390 |
| M | 88 | 453 |
| N | 83 | 374 |
| O | 80 | 385 |

Calculate the coefficient of rank correlation to measure the degree of relationship between test scores and the number of cars sold.

Solution: The first step is to replace the measurements by the two sets of ranks.

| Score x | No. of cars y | Rank x | Rank y | (x-y) | (x-y)$^2$ |
|---------|---------------|--------|--------|-------|-----------|
| 72 | 341 | 13 | 13 | 0 | 0 |
| 88.5 | 422 | 5 | 8 | - 3 | 9 |
| 70 | 322 | 15 | 14 | 1 | 1 |
| 87 | 440 | 7 | 6 | 1 | 1 |
| 71 | 287 | 14 | 15 | - 1 | 1 |
| 85 | 415 | 9 | 9 | 0 | 0 |
| 89 | 463 | 4 | 4 | 0 | 0 |
| 93 | 497 | 3 | 3 | 0 | 0 |
| 98 | 510 | 1 | 2 | - 1 | 1 |
| 96 | 512 | 2 | 1 | 1 | 1 |
| 86 | 432 | 8 | 7 | 1 | 1 |
| 82 | 390 | 11 | 10 | 1 | 1 |
| 88 | 453 | 6 | 5 | 1 | 1 |
| 83 | 374 | 10 | 12 | - 2 | 4 |
| 80 | 385 | 12 | 11 | 1 | 1 |

$$\sum_{i=1}^{15} (x - y)^2 = 22, \qquad n = 15 .$$

Since there are no ties,

$$r_s = 1 - \frac{6 \sum\limits_{i=1}^{15} (x - y)^2}{n(n^2 - 1)} = 1 - \frac{6(22)}{15(225 - 1)}$$

$$= 1 - .039 = .96 \ .$$

This is very strong positive relation. The higher the test score, the higher the number of cars sold by the salesman.

In this problem it would be possible to compute r, the correlation coefficient for interval level data. This would be a very tedious calculation without the aid of high-speed computing equipment.

● **PROBLEM** 17-26

The teaching abilities of a group of 10 college professors are ranked independently by their dean and by their department chairman. Rank 1 is given to the best professor, Rank 2 to the second best, ..., and Rank 10 to the professor with the worst teaching performance. The two sets of ranks are as follows:

| Professor | Dean's ratings | Chairman's ratings |
|-----------|----------------|--------------------|
| A | 5 | 6 |
| B | 4 | 4 |
| C | 3 | 5 |
| D | 1 | 2 |
| E | 2 | 3 |
| F | 6 | 1 |
| G | 7 | 9 |
| H | 10 | 8 |
| I | 9 | 7 |
| J | 8 | 10 |

Calculate the coefficient of rank correlation as a measure of the consistency of the two ratings.

Solution:   We are asked to compute the correlation between ranks and hence must use the rank-correlation coefficient. The table below shows the calculations used to compute $r_s$.

| Professor | Dean's ratings | Chairman's ratings | (x−y) | (x−y)$^2$ |
|-----------|----------------|--------------------|-------|-----------|
| A | 5 | 6 | − 1 | 1 |
| B | 4 | 4 | 0 | 0 |
| C | 3 | 5 | − 2 | 4 |
| D | 1 | 2 | − 1 | 1 |
| E | 2 | 3 | − 1 | 1 |
| F | 6 | 1 | 5 | 25 |
| G | 7 | 9 | − 2 | 4 |
| H | 10 | 8 | 2 | 4 |
| I | 9 | 7 | 2 | 4 |
| J | 8 | 10 | − 2 | 4 |

Since there are no ties:

$$\Sigma d^2 = \sum_{i=1}^{10} (x - y)^2 = 48 \quad , \quad n = 10$$

$$r_s = 1 - \frac{6 \sum_{i=1}^{10} (x - y)^2}{10(10^2 - 1)} = 1 - \frac{6(48)}{10(99)}$$

$$= 1 - .29 = .71 .$$

The rankings are positively correlated with coefficient of rank correlation $r_s$ = .71. This indicates a consistency between the Dean's ratings and the Chairman's ratings.

# FISHER'S Z-TRANSFORMATION

● **PROBLEM** 17-27

| FISHER-z VALUES ($z_f$) | | | | | | | | | |
|---|---|---|---|---|---|---|---|---|---|
| r | .00 | .01 | .02 | .03 | .04 | .05 | .06 | .07 | .08 | .09 |
| .0 | .00000 | .01000 | .02000 | .03001 | .04002 | .05004 | .06007 | .07012 | .08017 | .09024 |
| .1 | .10034 | .11045 | .12508 | .13074 | .14093 | .15114 | .16139 | .17167 | .18198 | .19234 |
| .2 | .20273 | .21317 | .22366 | .23419 | .24477 | .25541 | .26611 | .27686 | .28768 | .29857 |
| .3 | .30952 | .32055 | .33165 | .34283 | .35409 | .36544 | .37689 | .38842 | .40006 | .41180 |
| .4 | .42365 | .43561 | .44769 | .45990 | .47223 | .48470 | .49731 | .51007 | .52298 | .53606 |
| .5 | .54931 | .56273 | .57634 | .59014 | .60415 | .61838 | .63283 | .64752 | .66246 | .67767 |
| .6 | .69315 | .70892 | .72500 | .74142 | .75817 | .77530 | .79281 | .81074 | .82911 | .84795 |
| .7 | .86730 | .88718 | .90764 | .92873 | .95048 | .97295 | .99621 | 1.02033 | 1.04537 | 1.07143 |
| .8 | 1.09861 | 1.12703 | 1.15682 | 1.18813 | 1.22117 | 1.25615 | 1.29334 | 1.33308 | 1.37577 | 1.42192 |
| .9 | 1.47222 | 1.52752 | 1.58902 | 1.65839 | 1.73805 | 1.83178 | 1.94591 | 2.09229 | 2.29756 | 2.64665 |

Using the table above, find $z_f$-values that correspond to r = .48, r = .07, r = .55, r = .80.

<u>Solution:</u>     In order to test hypotheses, construct confidence intervals, or make any inferences about the true but unknown correlation between two variables, we must know something about the distribution of the random variable r.

Unfortunately, the sample correlation coefficient

$$r = \frac{n\Sigma XY - (\Sigma X)(\Sigma Y)}{[\sqrt{n\Sigma X^2 - (\Sigma X)^2}][\sqrt{n\Sigma Y^2 - (\Sigma Y)^2}]}$$

has neither a normal distribution nor a distribution that becomes approximately normal as the sample size increases.

However we can transform this random variable r to another random variable if we assume X and Y are distributed with a bivariate normal distribution.

Let $z_f = (1.1513) \log \frac{1 + r}{1 - r}$ , then $z_f$ is approximately normal with mean $\mu_z = (1.1513) \log \frac{1 + \rho}{1 - \rho}$ where $\rho$ is the true but unknown correlation coefficient.

To compute $z_f$-values from given values of r we can use the above table. To find the $z_f$-value that corresponds to r = .48, read down the first column of digits until .4 is reached. Then read across that row until the column headed by .08 is reached. Then read $z_f$. For r = .48, $z_f$ = .52298.

If r = .55, then we read across the row labeled .5 until we reach the column headed by .05. We read $z_f$ = .61838.

If r = .07, read across the row labled .00 until we reach .07. Read $z_f$ = .07012.

If r = .80, we read down the first column of digits until we reach .80. Then read across this row until the column is headed by .00. We see that for r = .80, $z_f$ = 1.09861.

● **PROBLEM** 17-28

Find the $z_f$ that corresponds to r = - .26.

**Solution:**  $z_f$, the Fischer-z transform, is defined to be $z_f = (1.1513) \log \frac{1 + r}{1 - r}$ , where r = the sample correlation coefficient. The sample correlation coefficient can vary from + 1 to - 1. We have seen how to solve for $z_f$ given r > 0 using the table of Fis her-z values. To find $z_f$ when r < 0, find the $z_f$ value for - r; the $z_f$ value of r < 0 is then - (the $z_f$ value for - r).

Thus to find the $z_f$ value of r = - .26, we find

- (the $z_f$ value for - (- .26))

= - (the $z_f$ for value for .26)

= - (.26611) = - .26611.

Find the $z_f$ that corresponds to r = .73.

Solution:     The first digit of r is 7. We now turn to
the table of Fischer-z Values. Read down the column of
first digits at the left-hand margin until .7 is reached.
Now read across that row until the column headed by .03
is reached. Now read off the $z_f$ value that corresponds
to r = .73. It is .92873.

● PROBLEM 17-30

Find the r that corresponds to $z_f$ = - 1.345.

Solution:     To find the value of r that corresponds to
$z_f$ = - 1.345, first find 1.345 in the body of the $z_f$
table. The closest entry in the table is $z_f$ = 1.33308.

Now read across the row to the left and read the number
there, .8. Reading up the column in which 1.33308 is
located we see that the number is .07. Add the two numbers
found in this way to find the value of r associated with
$z_f$ = 1.345, r = .8 + .07 = .87.

We wish to find the value of r associated with
- 1.345 not the value of r associated with 1.345. But
the value of r associated with - 1.345 is equal to the
negative value of r associated with 1.345. Thus the value
of r associated with - 1.345 is - .87.

● PROBLEM 17-31

From a sample of 103 cases, r = .80. (a) Establish the
95 percent confidence interval for the correlation coefficient. (b) Test the hypothesis that $\rho$ = .90.

Solution:     To establish a 95 percent confidence
interval for $\rho$, we first convert r to $z_f$ and then
standardize by subtracting $\mu_z$ and dividing by $\sigma_z$. The
resulting statistic will be approximately standard
normal.

Thus $\Pr\left[- z_{\alpha/2} \leq \dfrac{z_f - \mu_z}{\sigma_z} \leq z_{\alpha/2}\right] = 1 - \alpha$

will be a 100(1 - $\alpha$)% confidence interval. Multiplying
by $-\sigma_z$ and adding $z_f$ we see that

$\Pr\left[z_f - z_{\alpha/2}\,\sigma_z \leq \mu_z \leq z_f + z_{\alpha/2}\,\sigma_z\right] = \alpha.$

We now have a confidence interval for $\mu_z$ and we can use the Table of Fischer z-transform to find the values of $\rho$ that correspond to the endpoints of this interval. The resulting interval will be a $100(1-\alpha)\%$ confidence interval for $\rho$.

(a) In this example, $n = 103$ and $r = .80$ thus $z_f$ is read from the table to be

$$z_f = 1.099 \quad \text{and} \quad \sigma_z = \frac{1}{\sqrt{n-3}} = \frac{1}{\sqrt{103-3}}$$

$$= \frac{1}{\sqrt{100}} = \frac{1}{10} .$$

Thus $\dfrac{z_f - \mu_z}{\sigma_z} = \dfrac{1.099 - \mu_z}{\frac{1}{10}} .$

For $\alpha = .95$, the critical values of Z are $-Z_{.025}$ and $+Z_{.025}$ or $-1.96$ and $1.96$ .

Our confidence interval for $\mu_z$ is

$$1.099 - \frac{1.96}{10} \le \mu_z \le 1.099 + \frac{1.96}{10}$$

or $\quad 1.099 - .196 = .903 \le \mu_z \le 1.295,$

$$(.903, 1.295).$$

Convert each of these values from $\mu_z$ to $\rho$ via the table of the Fischer z-transform:

$$\mu_z = \frac{1}{2} \ln \frac{1+\rho}{1-\rho} .$$

Solving for $\rho$, when $\mu_z = .903$, we find that $\rho = .72$. When $\mu_z = 1.295$, $\rho = .86$.
Thus $(.72, .86)$ is a 95% confidence interval for $\rho$.

(b) We now test the hypothesis that $\rho = .90$ at the level of significance $\alpha = .05$. Using our confidence interval we see that $.90$ lies outside of the limits we derived in part (a). Thus we reject the hypothesis that $\rho = 0$ at the $\alpha = .05$ level of significance.

● **PROBLEM** 17-32

To check your understanding of the defining and computing formulas, take the following set of paired X, Y
values:

| X | 65 | 55 | 50 | 45 | 35 |
|---|----|----|----|----|----|
| Y | 68 | 52 | 64 | 60 | 76 |

(a)  Find, using a desk calculator, the values of $\Sigma X$, $\Sigma X^2$, $\Sigma Y$, $\Sigma Y^2$, and $\Sigma XY$.

(b)  Use these terms in the computing formulas to find $\overline{X}$, $\overline{Y}$, $s_x$, $s_y$, and the covariance of X and Y.

(c)  Find the value of the Pearson r for these raw scores by each of the following methods: (1) the computing formula; (2) the defining formula for raw scores; and (3) the average cross product of z scores. For method 3, you will have to convert all 10 scores into their z score equivalents. Compare the results of these methods.

Solution:    Use the table to find the summary statistics.

| X | Y | $X^2$ | $Y^2$ | XY |
|---|---|-------|-------|-----|
| 65 | 68 | 4225 | 4624 | 4420 |
| 55 | 52 | 3025 | 2704 | 2860 |
| 50 | 64 | 2500 | 4096 | 3200 |
| 45 | 60 | 2025 | 3600 | 2700 |
| 35 | 76 | 1225 | 5776 | 2660 |

n = 5

$\Sigma X = 250$,       $\Sigma Y = 320$,       $\Sigma X^2 = 13000$

$\Sigma Y^2 = 20800$       $\Sigma XY = 15,840$

$$\overline{X} = \frac{\Sigma X}{n} = \frac{250}{5} = 50$$

$$\overline{Y} = \frac{\Sigma Y}{n} = \frac{320}{5} = 64.$$

$s_x$, the sample standard deviation of the X scores, is

$$s_x = \sqrt{\frac{\Sigma (X - \overline{X})^2}{n}} = \sqrt{\frac{\Sigma X^2 - n\overline{X}^2}{n}}$$

$$= \sqrt{\frac{13000 - 5(50)^2}{5}} = \sqrt{\frac{500}{5}} = \sqrt{100} = 10.$$

$s_y$, the sample standard deviation of the Y scores, is

$$s_y = \sqrt{\frac{\Sigma (Y - \overline{Y})^2}{n}} = \sqrt{\frac{\Sigma Y^2 - n\overline{Y}^2}{n}}$$

$$= \sqrt{\frac{20800 - 5(64)^2}{5}} = \sqrt{\frac{320}{5}} = \sqrt{64} = 8.$$

The covariance of X and Y is

$$\text{Cov}(X, Y) = \frac{\Sigma(X - \bar{X})(Y - \bar{Y})}{n} = \frac{\Sigma(XY - \bar{X}Y - \bar{Y}X + \bar{X}\bar{Y})}{n}$$

$$= \frac{\Sigma XY - \bar{X} \, n\bar{Y} - \bar{Y} \, n\bar{X} + n\bar{Y}\bar{X}}{n}$$

$$= \frac{\Sigma \, XY - n\bar{X} \, \bar{Y}}{n}$$

$$\text{Cov}(X, Y) = \frac{15,840 - 5(50)(64)}{5}$$

$$= \frac{15,840 - 16,000}{5} = \frac{-160}{5} = -32 \, .$$

We now find the value of the Pearson r, the co-efficient of correlation by three similar methods. The computing formula is

$$r = \frac{n \, \Sigma XY - (\Sigma X)(\Sigma Y)}{\sqrt{n\Sigma X^2 - (\Sigma X)^2} \, \sqrt{n\Sigma Y^2 - (\Sigma Y)^2}}$$

$$= \frac{5(15,840) - (250)(320)}{\sqrt{5(13000) - (250)^2} \, \sqrt{5(20,800) - (320)^2}}$$

$$= \frac{79200 - 80000}{\sqrt{2500} \, \sqrt{1600}} = \frac{-800}{(50((40))} = -.4 \, .$$

An alternate computation, once $s_x$ and $s_y$ have been

computed is
$$r = \frac{\Sigma(X - \bar{X})(Y - \bar{Y})}{n \, s_x \, s_y} \, .$$

This comes from a manipulation of the formula

$$r = \frac{n \, \Sigma XY - (\Sigma X)(\Sigma Y)}{\sqrt{n\Sigma X^2 - (\Sigma X)^2} \, \sqrt{n\Sigma Y^2 - (\Sigma Y)^2}}$$

$$= \frac{n \, \Sigma XY - n^2 \, \bar{X} \, \bar{Y}}{\sqrt{n^2 \, S^2 x} \, \sqrt{n^2 \, S^2 y}}$$

$$= \frac{\Sigma XY - n\bar{X} \, \bar{Y}}{n \, Sx \, Sy}$$

$$= \frac{\Sigma XY - n\bar{X} \, \bar{Y} - n\bar{X} \, \bar{Y} + n\bar{X} \, \bar{Y}}{n \, Sx \, Sy}$$

$$= \frac{\Sigma XY - \bar{X}(n\bar{Y}) - \bar{Y}(n\bar{X}) + n\bar{X} \, \bar{Y}}{n \, Sx \, Sy}$$

$$= \frac{\Sigma XY - \bar{X} \, Y - \bar{Y} \, X + n\bar{X} \, \bar{Y}}{n \, Sx \, Sy}$$

$$= \frac{\Sigma(XY - \bar{X}Y - X\bar{Y} + \bar{X} \, \bar{Y})}{n \, Sx \, Sy}$$

$$= \frac{\Sigma(X - \bar{X})(Y - \bar{Y})}{n \, Sx \, Sy} \, .$$

Thus

$$r = \frac{\Sigma (X - \bar{X})(Y - \bar{Y})}{n \, Sx \, Sy} = \frac{Cov(X, Y)}{s_x \, s_y} = \frac{-32}{(10)(8)}$$

$$= -.4 .$$

Another computation involves transforming each of the X and Y scores into z-scores by subtracting the sample means and dividing by the sample standard deviations. Then

$$r = \frac{Z_x \, Z_y}{n}$$

where $Z_x$ is the z-score of each X-score and $Z_y$ is the z-score of each Y-score.

| X | Y | $Z_x = \dfrac{X - \bar{X}}{Sx}$ | $Z_y = \dfrac{Y - \bar{Y}}{Sy}$ | $Z_x \, Z_y$ |
|---|---|---|---|---|
| 65 | 68 | $\dfrac{65-50}{10} = 1.5$ | $\dfrac{68-64}{8} = .5$ | .75 |
| 55 | 52 | $\dfrac{55-50}{10} = .5$ | $\dfrac{52-64}{8} = -1.5$ | -.75 |
| 50 | 64 | $\dfrac{50-50}{10} = 0$ | $\dfrac{64-64}{8} = 0$ | 0 |
| 45 | 60 | $\dfrac{45-50}{10} = -.5$ | $\dfrac{60-64}{8} = -.5$ | .25 |
| 35 | 76 | $\dfrac{35-50}{10} = -1.5$ | $\dfrac{75-64}{8} = 1.5$ | -2.25 |

$$\Sigma \, Z_x \, Z_y = -2$$

$$r = \frac{\Sigma Z_x \, Z_y}{n} = \frac{-2}{5} = -.4 .$$

All of these methods of calculation yield the same value of r.

● **PROBLEM 17-33**

The data in the table below represent the scores on a mathematics placement test and the final averages in a freshman mathematics class. These eleven scores constitute a random sample. Test the usefulness of the placement test in predicting the performance of students in the course.

| Test Score<br>X | Final Average in Math<br>Y |
|:---:|:---:|
| 51 | 75 |
| 52 | 72 |
| 59 | 82 |
| 45 | 67 |
| 61 | 75 |
| 54 | 79 |
| 56 | 78 |
| 67 | 82 |
| 63 | 87 |
| 53 | 72 |
| 60 | 96 |

Solution:    This is a significance test about $\rho$, the theoretical correlation coefficient. If there is no relation between the placement test score and a student's final average, the correlation coefficient will be 0. Thus the null hypothesis will be

$$H_0 : \rho = 0 .$$

If there is a relation between the placement test score and a student's final average, we would expect the relationship to be as follows. If a student does well on the placement test score, then we would expect him to do well in the course. If a student does poorly on the test, we would expect this same student to do poorly in the course. A relation of this type between two variables, X and Y, if such a relation exists, is called positive. The correlation coefficient of positively correlated variables is positive. Thus the alternative hypothesis is,

$$H_A : \rho > 0 .$$

It is natural for the test statistic to be r, the sample correlation coefficient, based on the data.

We have already found a way to derive a normally distributed random variable from r by using Fischer's z-transform. Using r, we let,

$$z_f = 1.153 \log_{10} \frac{1 + r}{1 - r}$$

or    $z_f = \frac{1}{2} \log_e \frac{1 + r}{1 - r} .$

$z_f$ is a normally distributed random variable with

mean $\mu_z = \frac{1}{2} \log_e \frac{1 + \rho}{1 - \rho}$ and variance $\sigma_z^2 = \frac{1}{n - 3} .$

715

We know that

$$z = \frac{z_f - \mu_z}{\sigma_z} \quad \text{is a standard normal random variable.}$$

We next set a level of significance for our test. We choose a common level of significance $\alpha = .01$.

With the level of significance, we determine the critical value of the test. From the table of the standard normal distribution we see that a Z-score of 2.33 or more will appear with probability of .01.

$$Pr(Z \geq 2.33) = .01$$

Thus 2.33 will be the critical value for our test.

To carry out the test we follow this procedure:

(1) Compute r, the sample correlation coefficient.

(2) Use the table of the Fischer z-transform to compute $z_f$.

(3) Let $Z = \frac{z_f - \mu_z}{\sigma_z}$ , this is the calculated z-statistic.

(4) Compare Z with 2.33. If $Z > 2.33$ reject $H_0$. If $Z < 2.33$ accept $H_0$.

These steps are followed below:

(1) $\quad r = \dfrac{\Sigma X_i Y_i - n \bar{X} \bar{Y}}{\sqrt{[\Sigma (X_i^2) - n\bar{X}^2][\Sigma Y_i^2 - n\bar{Y}^2]}}$

| Test score x | Final average y | $x^2$ | $y^2$ | xy |
|---|---|---|---|---|
| 51 | 75 | 2601 | 5625 | 3825 |
| 52 | 72 | 2704 | 5184 | 3744 |
| 59 | 82 | 3481 | 6724 | 4838 |
| 45 | 67 | 2025 | 4489 | 3015 |
| 61 | 75 | 3721 | 5625 | 4575 |
| 54 | 79 | 2916 | 6241 | 4266 |
| 56 | 78 | 3136 | 6084 | 4368 |
| 67 | 82 | 4489 | 6724 | 5494 |
| 63 | 87 | 3969 | 7569 | 5481 |
| 53 | 72 | 2809 | 5184 | 3816 |
| 60 | 96 | 3600 | 9216 | 5760 |

$\Sigma X_i = 621$ $\Sigma X_i^2 = 35,451$

$\Sigma Y_i = 865$ $\Sigma Y_i^2 = 68,665$ $\Sigma XY = 49,182$

$\overline{X} = \dfrac{621}{11} = 56.45$ $\overline{Y} = \dfrac{865}{11} = 78.64$ .

Thus,

$$r = \frac{(49,182) - (11)\ (56.45)\ (78.64)}{\sqrt{[35451 - 11(56.45)^2][68665 - 11(78.64)^2]}}$$

$$= \ \frac{49,182 - 48831.5}{} = \frac{350.5}{\sqrt{(398.4)(638.3)}} = \frac{350.5}{504.3} = .69.$$

(2) We now compute $z_f$ from r. Using the table of Fischer-z values, we see that the $z_f$ that corresponds to r = .69 is .848 (correct to three decimal places).

(3) Under the null hypothesis

$$\mu_z = \frac{1}{2} \log_e \frac{1 + \rho}{1 - \rho} = \frac{1}{2} \log_e \frac{1 + 0}{1 - 0}$$

$$= \frac{1}{2} \log_e 1 = 0 .$$

There are 11 observations thus

$$\sigma_z = \sqrt{\sigma_z^2} = \sqrt{\frac{1}{n - 3}}$$

$$= \sqrt{\frac{1}{11 - 3}} = \frac{1}{\sqrt{8}} .$$

The calculated Z-statistic is

$$Z = \frac{z_f - \mu_z}{\sigma_z} = \frac{.848 - 0}{\dfrac{1}{\sqrt{8}}}$$

$$= (\sqrt{8})\,(.848)$$

$$= 2.398$$

$$= 2.4 .$$

(4) We compare the Z-statistic with the critical value and see that 2.4 > 2.33. Therefore we reject the null hypothesis $\rho = 0$ in favor of the alternative hypothesis $\rho > 0$.

In the data below, let X be the percentage of Lithuanians in Midwestern cities. Let Y be the difference between non-Lithuanian and Lithuanian median incomes. Y is one possible measure of economic discrimination.

| Percent Lithuanian X | Discrimination Y |
|---|---|
| 2.13 | $ 809 |
| 2.52 | 763 |
| 11.86 | 612 |
| 2.55 | 492 |
| 2.87 | 679 |
| 4.23 | 635 |
| 4.62 | 859 |
| 5.19 | 228 |
| 6.43 | 897 |
| 6.70 | 867 |
| 1.53 | 513 |
| 1.87 | 335 |
| 10.38 | 868 |

Draw a scattergram, compute the least-squares line and the correlation between percent Lithuanian and the index of discrimination.

Solution: We draw the scattergram by plotting the pairs of X and Y values on coordinate axis.

We next compute the least squares coefficients with the help of the following table.

| X | Y | $X^2$ | $Y^2$ | XY |
|---|---|---|---|---|
| 2.13 | 809 | 4.54 | 654,500 | 1723.2 |
| 2.52 | 763 | 6.35 | 582,170 | 1922.7 |
| 11.86 | 612 | 140.7 | 374,540 | 7258.32 |
| 2.55 | 492 | 6.50 | 242,064 | 1254.6 |
| 2.87 | 679 | 8.24 | 461,041 | 1948.7 |
| 4.23 | 635 | 17.89 | 403,230 | 2686.1 |
| 4.62 | 859 | 21.3 | 737,881 | 3968.6 |
| 5.19 | 228 | 26.9 | 51,984 | 1183.3 |
| 6.43 | 897 | 41.3 | 804,609 | 5767.71 |
| 6.70 | 867 | 44.9 | 751,689 | 5808.9 |
| 1.53 | 513 | 2.34 | 263,169 | 784.89 |
| 1.87 | 335 | 3.50 | 11,225 | 626.45 |
| 10.38 | 868 | 107.7 | 753,424 | 9009.8 |

n = 13

$\Sigma X = 62.88$

$\Sigma Y = 8,557$

$\Sigma XY = 43,943.32$

$\Sigma X^2 = 432.277$

$\Sigma Y^2 = 6,192,505$

Using the formulas we have previously derived we see that,

$$\hat{b} = \frac{\Sigma XY - n\bar{X}\,\bar{Y}}{\Sigma X^2 - n\bar{X}^2}$$

$$= \frac{43,943.32 - 13\left(\frac{62.88}{13}\right)\left(\frac{8,557}{13}\right)}{432.277 - 13\left(\frac{62.88}{13}\right)^2}$$

$$= \frac{43,943.32 - (62.88)\left(\frac{8,557}{13}\right)}{432.277 - \frac{(62.88)^2}{13}}$$

$$= \frac{43,943.32 - 41,389.55}{432.277 - 304.145} = \frac{2553.77}{128.13} = 19.93 .$$

$$\hat{a} = \bar{Y} - \hat{b}\bar{X}$$

$$= \left(\frac{8,557}{13}\right) - (19.93)\left(\frac{62.88}{13}\right)$$

$$= 658.23 - 96.30 = 561.9 .$$

Thus, $\hat{Y} = \hat{a} + \hat{b}X = 561.9 + 19.93X$ .

To compute the correlation coefficient r, we use the formula

$$r = \frac{n\,\Sigma XY - (\Sigma X)(\Sigma Y)}{\sqrt{[n\Sigma X^2 - (\Sigma X)^2][n\Sigma Y^2 - (\Sigma Y)^2]}}$$

$$= \frac{13(43,943.32) - (62.8)(8557)}{\sqrt{[13(432.28) - (62.88)^2][13(6192505) - (8577)^2]}}$$

$$= \frac{33199}{110,120} = .301.$$

● **PROBLEM** 17-35

Using the data from the previous problem, test the relationship between percent of population Lithuanian and our measure of economic discrimination. Use a level of significance $\alpha = .1$.

Solution:    We follow the test procedure developed previously.

(1) Compute r, the sample correlation coefficient.

(2) Find $z_f$, the Z-value that corresponds to r, from the table of Fischer z-transforms.

(3) Compute $Z = \dfrac{z_f - \mu_z}{\sigma_z}$ , a standard normal random variable where $\mu_z = \dfrac{1}{2} \log_e \dfrac{1 + \rho}{1 - \rho}$ and $\sigma_z = \sqrt{\dfrac{1}{n - 3}}$ .

(4) Find the critical values from the standard normal table that correspond to the level of significance of $\alpha = .1$.

The hypotheses are:

$H_0: \rho = 0$ , there is no correlation between percent Lithuanian and economic discrimination and

$H_A: \rho \neq 0$ , there is a significant correlation.

(1) The observed value of $\rho$ is r = .301 and has been calculated several times before.

(2) The $z_f$ value is found from the table to be approximately $z_f = .310$ (to the nearest 3 digits).

(3) Under the null hypothesis $\rho = 0$; thus

$$\mu_z = \frac{1}{2} \log_e \frac{1 + 0}{1 - 0} = \frac{1}{2} \log_e 1 = 0.$$

Because there are 13 observations: $\sigma_z = \dfrac{1}{\sqrt{n - 3}} = \dfrac{1}{\sqrt{10}} = .316$ .

Thus, $Z = \dfrac{z_f - \mu_z}{\sigma_z} = \dfrac{.310 - 0}{.316} = .981$ .

(4) The critical values of Z are $- Z_{.05}$ and $+ Z_{.05}$ or $- 1.65$ and $1.65$. If the observed statistic is less than $- 1.65$ or greater than $1.65$ we reject $H_0$ and accept $H_A$.

Comparing the Z-statistic of .981 we see that our statistic is less than 1.65 and greater than $- 1.65$. Thus we accept $H_0$, that $\rho = 0$ and thus these two variables are statistically independent.

# PROPERTIES OF THE REGRESSION COEFFICIENTS

● PROBLEM 17-36

Show that if (X, Y) has a bivariate normal distribution, then the marginal distributions of X and Y are univariate normal distributions; that is, X is normally distributed with mean $\mu_x$ and variance $\sigma_x^2$ and Y is normally distributed with mean $\mu_y$ and variance $\sigma_y^2$.

<u>Solution:</u>    This problem involves some slightly advanced mathematical techniques and may be skipped by less advanced students.

The joint distribution of ordered pairs (X, Y) is

$$f(x, y) = \frac{1}{2\pi\sigma_x \sigma_y \sqrt{1 - \rho^2}}$$

$$exp \left\{ - \frac{1}{2(1 - \rho)^2} \left[ \left( \frac{x - \mu_x}{\sigma_x} \right)^2 - 2\rho \left( \frac{x - \mu_x}{\sigma_x} \right) \left( \frac{y - \mu_y}{\sigma_y} \right) \right. \right.$$

$$\left. \left. + \left( \frac{y - \mu_y}{\sigma_y^2} \right)^2 \right] \right\}$$

(where $\mu_x$, $\sigma_x$ are the mean and standard deviation of X, $\mu_x$, $\sigma_y$ are the mean and standard deviation of Y, $\rho$ is the theoretical correlation coefficient between X and Y and exp{ } is $e^{\{\}}$, the exponential function ).

The marginal density of one of the variables, say X, is by definition:

$$f_x(x) = \int_{-\infty}^{\infty} f(x, y) \, dy.$$

Returning to the expression f(x, y) we make the following substitutions,

$$Z = \frac{x - \mu_x}{\sigma_x} \quad \text{and} \quad V = \frac{y - \mu_y}{\sigma_y} \quad .$$

These substitutions are convenient relabelings. Thus

$$\int_{-\infty}^{\infty} f(x, y) \, dy =$$

$$\int_{-\infty}^{\infty} \frac{1}{2\pi \sigma_x \sigma_y \sqrt{1 - \rho^2}} \, exp \left\{ - \frac{1}{2(1 - \rho)^2} [Z^2 - 2\rho ZV + V^2] \right\} dy$$

but $y = \sigma_y V + \mu_y$          hence     $dy = \sigma_y \, dv$ .

Thus, $\int\limits_{\infty}^{\infty} f(x, y)\, dy$

$$= \int\limits_{-\infty}^{\infty} \frac{\sigma y}{2\pi \sigma_x\, \sigma_y\, \sqrt{1 - \rho^2}}\, \exp\left\{\frac{-1}{2(1 - \rho)^2} [Z^2 - 2\rho ZV + V^2]\right\} dv$$

Consider the term contained in the braces
We will complete the square on the variable V.
Thus

$$V^2 - 2\rho ZV + Z^2 = V^2 - 2\rho ZV + (-\rho Z)^2 - (-\rho Z)^2 + Z^2$$

$$= (V - \rho Z)^2 + Z^2 (1 - \rho^2).$$

Our integral becomes, (with cancellation of $\sigma_y$)

$$\int\limits_{-\infty}^{\infty} f(x,y)\,dy$$

$$= \int\limits_{-\infty}^{\infty} \frac{dv}{2\pi\, \sigma_x\, \sqrt{1 - \rho^2}}\, \exp\left\{\frac{-1}{2(1 - \rho^2)} [Z^2(1 - \rho^2) + (V - \rho Z)^2]\right\}$$

$$= \int\limits_{-\infty}^{\infty} \frac{dv}{2\pi\, \sigma_x\, \sqrt{1 - \rho^2}}\, \exp\left\{\frac{-Z^2}{2} - \frac{1}{2(1 - \rho^2)} (V - \rho Z)^2\right\}.$$

We now carry out another relabeling. Let

$$w = \frac{V - \rho Z}{\sqrt{1 - \rho^2}}\quad.\quad \text{Then}$$

$$V = w\sqrt{1 - \rho^2} + \rho Z \quad \text{and}$$

$$dv = dw\sqrt{1 - \rho^2}\quad.\quad \text{Further note that}$$

$$\frac{1}{2(1 - \rho^2)} (V - \rho Z)^2 = \frac{1}{2}\left(\frac{V - \rho Z}{\sqrt{1 - \rho^2}}\right)^2 = \frac{1}{2}\, w^2\quad.$$

Thus, $\int\limits_{-\infty}^{\infty} f(x, y)\, dy$

$$= \int\limits_{-\infty}^{\infty} \frac{dw\, \sqrt{1 - \rho^2}}{2\pi\, \sigma_x\, \sqrt{1 - \rho^2}}\, \exp\left\{-\frac{Z^2}{2} - \frac{w^2}{2}\right\}$$

$$= \int\limits_{-\infty}^{\infty} \frac{dw}{2\pi\, \sigma_x}\, \exp\left\{-\frac{Z^2}{2} - \frac{w^2}{2}\right\}.$$

Because we are integrating with respect to w, we
may factor out the terms which do not involve w.

722

$$= \frac{\exp\left\{\frac{-z^2}{2}\right\}}{2\pi \quad \sigma_x} \int_{-\infty}^{\infty} \exp\left\{\frac{-w^2}{2}\right\} dw \ .$$

The integrand should be familiar. It is the density function of a standard normal variable. We know that

$$\frac{1}{\sqrt{2\pi}} \int_{-\infty}^{\infty} \exp\left\{\frac{-w^2}{2}\right\} dw = 1$$

or

$$\int_{-\infty}^{\infty} \exp\left\{\frac{-w^2}{2}\right\} dw = \sqrt{2\pi} \ .$$

Thus

$$f_x(x) = \int_{-\infty}^{\infty} f(x, y) \, dy = \frac{\exp\left(\frac{-z^2}{2}\right)}{2\pi \quad \sigma_x} \cdot \sqrt{2\pi} \ .$$

Remember $Z = \dfrac{x - \mu_x}{x}$; resubstituting we see

that the marginal density function of a random variable X which is jointly distributed with Y in a bivariate normal distribution is:

$$f_x(x) = \frac{\exp\left\{-\frac{1}{2}\left[\frac{x - \mu_x}{\sigma_x}\right]^2\right\}}{\sigma_x \sqrt{2\pi}} \ .$$

This is the density of a normally distributed random variable with mean $\mu_x$ and variance $\sigma_x^2$.

The marginal density of y, $f_y(y) = \int_{-\infty}^{\infty} f(x,y)dx$, is found by the same argument to be

$$f_y(y) = \frac{\exp\left[-\frac{1}{2}\left(\frac{x-\mu_x}{\sigma_x}\right)^2\right]}{\sigma_x \sqrt{2\pi}} \ .$$

● **PROBLEM** 17-37

---

If (X, Y) has a bivariate normal distribution, find the conditional distribution of Y given X = x.

---

Solution: The density function of the conditional distribution of Y for a given X is,

$$f(y|x) = \frac{f(x,\, y)}{f(x)}$$

where $f(x,\, y)$ is the joint distribution of X and Y and $f(x)$ is the marginal distribution of X.

Substituting the density functions into this expression—we see that

$$f(y|x) = \frac{1}{2\pi\, \sigma_x \sigma_y\, \sqrt{1-\rho^2}}\ \exp\left\{ \frac{1}{2(1-\rho^2)} \right.$$

$$\left[ \left(\frac{x-\mu_x}{\sigma_x}\right)^2 - 2\rho\left[\left(\frac{x-\mu_x}{\sigma_x}\right) \times \left(\frac{y-\mu_y}{\sigma_y}\right)\right] + \left(\frac{y-\mu_y}{\sigma_y}\right)^2 \right]\left.\right\}$$

divided by $\dfrac{1}{\sqrt{2\pi}\ \sigma_x}\ \exp\left\{ -\frac{1}{2}\left(\frac{x-\mu_x}{\sigma_x}\right)^2 \right\}.$

We can write this on one line as

$$\frac{\sqrt{2\pi}\ \sigma_x}{2\pi\sigma_x\sigma_y(1-\rho^2)}\ \exp\left\{ \frac{-1}{2(1-\rho^2)}\left[\left(\frac{x-\mu_x}{\sigma_x}\right)^2\right.\right.$$

$$\left.\left. -2\rho\left(\frac{x-\mu_x}{\sigma_x}\right)\left(\frac{y-\mu_y}{\sigma_y}\right) + \left(\frac{y-\mu_y}{\sigma_y}\right)^2\right] - \left(\frac{-(x-\mu)^2}{2\sigma_x^2}\right)\right\}.$$

We confine our attention to the terms within the braces {}.

$$\left\{ \frac{-1}{2(1-\rho^2)}\left[\left(\frac{x-\mu_x}{\sigma_x}\right)^2 - 2\rho\left(\frac{x-\mu_x}{\sigma_x}\right)\left(\frac{y-\mu_y}{\sigma_y}\right)\right.\right.$$

$$\left.\left. + \left(\frac{y-\mu_y}{\sigma_y}\right)^2\right] - \left[-\frac{1}{2}\left(\frac{x-\mu_x}{\sigma_x}\right)^2\right] \right\}$$

$$= \left\{ \frac{-1}{2(1-\rho^2)}\left[\left(\frac{x-\mu_x}{\sigma_x}\right)^2 - (1-\rho^2)\left(\frac{x-\mu_x}{\sigma_x}\right)^2 - 2\rho\left(\frac{x-\mu_x}{\sigma_x}\right)\right.\right.$$

$$\left.\left. \times\left(\frac{y-\mu_y}{\sigma_y}\right) + \left(\frac{y-\mu_y}{\sigma_y}\right)^2\right] \right\}$$

$$= \left\{ \frac{-1}{2(1-\rho^2)}\left[\rho^2\left(\frac{x-\mu_x}{\sigma_x}\right)^2 - 2\rho\left(\frac{x-\mu_x}{\sigma_x}\right)\left(\frac{y-\mu_y}{\sigma_y}\right) + \left(\frac{y-\mu_y}{\sigma_y}\right)^2\right] \right\}.$$

Let this expression be denoted by *.

Then the marginal distribution of Y given X is

$$\frac{1}{\sqrt{2\pi}\ \sigma_y\ \sqrt{1 - \rho^2}}\ \exp\ \{*\}$$

This density function appears to be a normal density function with variance $\sigma_y^2 (1 - \rho^2)$.

This suggests that we manipulate the expression * by factoring out $\sigma_y^2 (1 - \rho^2)$ in the denominator.

Doing this we see that

$$\{*\} = \left\{ \frac{-1}{2\ \sigma_y^2\ (1 - \rho^2)} \times \left[ \frac{\rho^2 \sigma_y^2 (x - \mu_x)^2}{\sigma_x^2} - \frac{2\rho\ \sigma_y (x - \mu_x)(y - \mu_y)}{\sigma_x} + (y - \mu_y)^2 \right] \right\}.$$

Now let $A = (y - \mu_y)$ and

$$B = \frac{\rho\ \sigma_y}{\sigma_x} (x - \mu_x)\ ;$$

$$(A - B)^2 = A^2 - 2AB + B^2$$

$$= \left[ (Y - \mu_y)^2 - \frac{2\rho\ \sigma_y}{\sigma_x} (X - \mu_x)(Y - \mu_y) \right.$$

$$\left. + \frac{\rho^2\ \sigma_y^2}{\sigma_x^2} (X - \mu_x)^2 \right]$$

Thus, $\{*\} = \left\{ \frac{-1}{2\sigma_y^2 (1 - \rho^2)} \left[ (Y - \mu_y) - \rho \frac{\mu_y}{\sigma_x} (X - \mu_x) \right]^2 \right\}$

The conditional density function is thus,

$$f(y|x) = \frac{1}{\sqrt{2\pi}\ \sigma_y\ \sqrt{1 - \rho^2}}$$

$$\times \exp\ \left\{ \frac{-1}{2\sigma_y^2 (1 - \rho^2)} \left[ (y - \mu_y) - \rho\sigma_y \left( \frac{x - \mu_x}{\sigma_x} \right) \right]^2 \right\}$$

Thus, for a given value of $X = x$, $Y$ is distributed normally with mean

$$\mu_y + \rho \frac{\mu_y}{\sigma_x} (X - \mu_x) \quad \text{and variance} \quad \sigma^2_y (1 - \rho^2).$$

We write $E(Y|X=x)$, the expected value of $Y$ given

$X = x$ as $\quad \mu_y + \rho \frac{\sigma_y}{\sigma_x} (x - \mu_x)$. Thus,

$$E(Y|X = x) = \left[ \mu_y - \rho \frac{\sigma_y}{\sigma_x} \mu_x \right] + \rho \frac{\sigma_y}{\sigma_x} \quad x$$

$$= \mu_y + \rho \sigma_y \left( \frac{x - \mu_x}{\sigma_x} \right)$$

and call this expression the regression curve of $Y$ on $X$. This regression curve is none other than the simple linear regression line. If each of the quantities in this equation are replaced by appropriate point estimates for $\mu_x$, $\mu_y$, $\sigma^2_x$, $\sigma^2_y$ and $\rho^2$, we will have derived formulas for estimating the coefficients of the regression line.

● **PROBLEM** 17-38

In a linear regression problem, find the mean and variance of a Y-value predicted from a given X-value.

<u>Solution</u>: Linear regression is often useful for predicting values of $Y$ from a given value of $X$.

We have previously estimated a linear relationship between corn yield and fertilizer. If we are interested in predicting corn yield if a certain amount of fertilizer ($X_0$ units) is used we substitute $X_0$ into our regression equation, $\hat{\alpha} + \hat{\beta} X_0$ to predict $Y$. The predicted value is denoted by $\hat{Y}$. How good an estimate is $\hat{Y}$? We also may wish to develop confidence intervals or test hypotheses about $\hat{Y}$.

In order to do this, we derived the mean and variance of $\hat{Y}$ given $X_0$ based on our previous assumptions about the observed Y-values.

$$E(\hat{Y}) = E(\hat{\alpha} + \hat{\beta} X_0)$$

where $X_0$ is the value of the independent variable on which the prediction is based. $X_0$ is assumed constant with respect to expectation and variance.

Thus, $\quad E(\hat{Y}) = E(\hat{\alpha} + \hat{\beta} X_0) = E(\hat{\alpha}) + X_0 E(\hat{\beta})$. As

$E(\hat{Y}) = \hat{\alpha} + \hat{\beta}X_0$, we have shown that $\hat{Y}$ is an unbiased point estimate. It can be proven that of all unbiased estimates, $\hat{\alpha} + \hat{\beta}X$ has the smallest variance.

$$\text{Var } \hat{Y} = \text{Var } [\hat{\alpha} + \hat{\beta}X_0]$$

but $\qquad \hat{\alpha} = \overline{Y} - \hat{\beta}\overline{X} \qquad\qquad$ thus

$$\text{Var } \hat{Y} = \text{Var } [\overline{Y} + \hat{\beta}(X_0 - \overline{X})].$$

We have shown that $\overline{Y}$ and $\hat{\beta}$ are independent random variables, thus

$$\text{Var } \hat{Y} = \text{Var } \overline{Y} + (X_0 - \overline{X})^2 \text{ Var } \hat{\beta}$$

$$= \text{Var } \frac{\Sigma Y_i}{n} + (X_0 - \overline{X})^2 \text{ Var } \hat{\beta}$$

$$= \frac{\Sigma \text{Var } Y_i}{n^2} + (X_0 - \overline{X})^2 \text{ Var } \hat{\beta};$$

$$\text{Var } \hat{Y} = \frac{n\,\sigma^2}{n^2} + (X_0 - \overline{X})^2 \text{ Var } \hat{\beta}$$

$$= \frac{\sigma^2}{n} + (X_0 - \overline{X})^2 \frac{\sigma^2}{\Sigma(X_i - \overline{X})^2}$$

$$= \sigma^2 \left[ \frac{1}{n} + \frac{(X_0 - \overline{X})^2}{\Sigma(X_i - \overline{X})^2} \right].$$

● **PROBLEM** 17-39

Compute the maximum likelihood estimators of the three parameters $\alpha$, $\beta$ and $\sigma^2$ in a linear regression problem. Assume each $Y_i$ is distributed normally with means $\alpha + \beta X_i$ and variance $\sigma^2$. Also assume the $Y_i$ form a random sample, that is, each $Y_i$ is independent and normally distributed.

Solution: We first compute the likelihood function of the $Y_i$'s, the Y observations. The likelihood function is the joint probability density of the random sample consisting of the Y values. Let there be n observations in the sample, each observation being normally distributed with density function,

$$\frac{1}{\sqrt{2\pi}\,\sigma} \exp \left\{ -\frac{1}{2\sigma^2} [Y_i - (\alpha + \beta X_i)]^2 \right\}.$$

Because each Y observation is independent, the joint density is the product of the individual density functions. Let $L(y_1, y_2, \ldots y_n)$ = the joint density or the likelihood function.

Thus $L(y_1, \ldots y_n) = \prod_{i=1}^{n} \dfrac{1}{\sqrt{2\pi}\,\sigma} \exp \left\{ -\dfrac{1}{2\sigma^2}[Y_i - (\alpha + \beta X_i)]^2 \right\}$

where $\displaystyle\prod_{i=1}^{n} X_i = X_1 \cdot X_2 \cdot \ldots \cdot X_n$ is

a shorthand way of notating a product in much the same way

that $\displaystyle\sum_{i=1}^{n} X_i = X + \ldots + X_n$ notates a sum.

We can rewrite the product of the joint densities as

$\displaystyle\prod_{i=1}^{n} \dfrac{1}{\sqrt{2\pi}\,\sigma} \exp \left\{ -\dfrac{1}{2\sigma^2} \; [Y_i - (\alpha + \beta X_i)]^2 \right\}$

$= \left[ \dfrac{1}{\sqrt{2\pi}\,\sigma} \right]^n \exp \left\{ -\dfrac{1}{2\sigma^2} \sum_{i=1}^{n} [Y_i - (\alpha + \beta X_i)]^2 \right\}$

$= (2\pi\,\sigma^2)^{-n/2} \exp \left\{ -\dfrac{1}{2\sigma^2} \sum_{i=1}^{n} [Y_i - (\alpha + \beta X_i)]^2 \right\}.$

To compute the maximum likelihood estimators of $\alpha$, $\beta$ and $\sigma^2$, we maximize the likelihood function with respect to these three variables.

Because the natural logarithm is a one to one function we can maximize $\log L(y_1, \ldots y_n)$ with respect to $\alpha$, $\beta$, and $\sigma^2$. This is equivalent to maximizing L.

$$\log L = -\dfrac{n}{2} \log 2\pi\,\sigma^2 - \dfrac{1}{2\sigma^2} \sum_{i=1}^{n} [Y_i - (\alpha + \beta X_i)]^2.$$

Next we differentiate $\log L$ with respect to $\alpha$, $\beta$ and $\sigma^2$. Setting each of these partial derivatives to zero and solving the three equations yields the maximum likelihood estimates of $\alpha$, $\beta$ and $\sigma^2$.

$$\dfrac{\partial \log L}{\partial \alpha} = -\dfrac{1}{2\sigma^2} \sum_{i=1}^{n} (-2)[Y_i - (\alpha + \beta X_i)],$$

$$\dfrac{\partial \log L}{\partial \beta} = -\dfrac{1}{2\sigma^2} \sum_{i=1}^{n} (-2X_i)[Y_i - (\alpha + \beta X_i)],$$

$$\dfrac{\partial \log L}{\partial \sigma^2} = -\dfrac{n}{2}\left(\dfrac{1}{2\pi\,\sigma^2}\right) 2\pi - \tfrac{1}{2}\sum_{i=1}^{n} [Y_i - (\alpha + \beta X_i)]^2 \left[-\dfrac{1}{\sigma^4}\right]$$

$$= \frac{-n}{2\sigma^2} + \frac{1}{2\sigma^4} \sum_{i=1}^{n} [Y_i - (\alpha + \beta X_i)]^2 .$$

We see that the maximum likelihood estimates satisfy the three following equations,

$$\frac{1}{\hat{\sigma}^2} \sum [Y_i - (\hat{\alpha} + \hat{\beta} X_i)] = 0 ,$$

$$\frac{1}{\hat{\sigma}^2} \sum X_i [Y_i - (\hat{\alpha} + \hat{\beta} X_i)] = 0 ,$$

$$\frac{-n}{2\hat{\sigma}^2} + \frac{1}{2\hat{\sigma}^4} \sum [Y_i - (\hat{\alpha} + \hat{\beta} X_i)]^2 = 0 .$$

Solving the first equation for $\hat{\alpha}$ in terms of $\hat{\beta}$ we see that

$$\sum Y_i = n\hat{\alpha} + \hat{\beta} \sum X_i$$

or $\quad \hat{\alpha} = \bar{Y} - \hat{\beta}\bar{X}$ .

Substituting $\hat{\alpha} = \bar{Y} - \hat{\beta}\bar{X}$ into the second equation and solving for $\hat{\beta}$ yields

$$\sum X_i [Y_i - (\bar{Y} - \hat{\beta}\bar{X} + \hat{\beta} X_i)] = 0$$

$$\sum X_i Y_i = \sum [X_i \bar{Y} - \hat{\beta} X_i \bar{X} + \hat{\beta} X_i^2] = \bar{Y} \sum X_i - \hat{\beta}\bar{X} \sum X_i + \hat{\beta} \sum X_i^2$$

$$= n\bar{Y}\,\bar{X} - \hat{\beta} n\bar{X}^2 + \hat{\beta} \sum X_i^2 .$$

$$\sum X_i Y_i - n\bar{X}\,\bar{Y} = \hat{\beta} [\sum X_i^2 - n\bar{X}^2]$$

or $\quad \hat{\beta} = \dfrac{\sum X_i Y_i - n\bar{X}\,\bar{Y}}{\sum X_i^2 - n\bar{X}^2}$

and solving the third equation

$$\frac{1}{\hat{\sigma}^2} \sum [Y_i - (\hat{\alpha} + \hat{\beta} X_i)]^2 = n$$

or $\quad \hat{\sigma}^2 = \dfrac{\sum [Y_i - (\hat{\alpha} + \hat{\beta} X_i)]^2}{n}$ .

The maximum likelihood estimates of $\alpha$ and $\beta$ are the same as the least squares estimates of $\alpha$ and $\beta$!

The least squares principle is applicable even if the distribution of Y given X = x is unknown. The maximum likelihood estimates will differ from those found if the $Y_i$ are not assumed to be distributed normally.

Discover whether the maximum likelihood estimates found in the previous problem are unbiased. That is, does $E(\hat{\alpha}) = \alpha$, $E(\hat{\beta}) = \beta$? Is $E(\hat{\sigma}^2) = \sigma^2$? If an estimate is biased, how can it be adjusted so that it is unbiased?

Solution:

$$E(\hat{\beta}) = E\left[\frac{\Sigma X_i Y_i - n\bar{X}\ \bar{Y}}{\Sigma X_i^2 - n\bar{X}^2}\right].$$

Remember that the $X_i$ are chosen and fixed with respect to this expectation. Thus the $X_i$ are treated as constants.

$$E(\hat{\beta}) = \frac{E\ (\Sigma X_i Y_i - n\bar{X}\ \bar{Y})}{\Sigma X_i^2 - n\bar{X}^2}$$

$$= \frac{\Sigma\ X_i\ E(Y_i) - n\bar{X}\ E(\bar{Y})}{\Sigma (X_i)^2 - n\bar{X}^2}.$$

Remember that each $Y_i$ observation is normally distributed with mean $\alpha + \beta X_i$ and variance $\sigma^2$. Thus,

$$E(Y_i) = \alpha + \beta X_i\ , \qquad E(\bar{Y}) = \frac{\Sigma E(Y_i)}{n} = \frac{\Sigma(\alpha + \beta X_i)}{n}.$$

$$E(\hat{\beta}) = \frac{\Sigma X_i(\alpha + \beta X_i) - n\bar{X}\ \dfrac{\Sigma(\alpha + \beta X_i)}{n}}{\Sigma X_i^2 - n\bar{X}^2}$$

$$= \frac{\alpha\ \Sigma X_i + \beta\Sigma X_i^2 - n\bar{X}\alpha - \beta\bar{X}\ \Sigma X_i}{\Sigma X_i^2 - n\bar{X}^2}$$

$$= \frac{\alpha\ n\bar{X} - n\bar{X}\alpha + \beta\ [\Sigma X_i^2 - n\bar{X}^2]}{\Sigma X_i^2 - n\bar{X}^2}$$

$$= \beta\left[\frac{\Sigma X_i^2 - n\bar{X}^2}{\Sigma X_i^2 - n\bar{X}^2}\right] = \beta\ .$$

Thus $\hat{\beta}$ is unbiased .

$$E(\hat{\alpha}) = E(\overline{Y} - \hat{\beta}\overline{X}) = E(\overline{Y}) - \overline{X} \ E(\hat{\beta})$$

$$= \frac{\Sigma(\alpha + \beta X_i)}{n} - \overline{X}\beta$$

$$= \frac{n\alpha}{n} + \frac{\beta\Sigma \ X_i}{n} - \overline{X} \ \beta$$

$$= \alpha + \beta\overline{X} - \overline{X}\beta$$

$$= \alpha \ .$$

Thus $\hat{\alpha}$ is unbiased.

To find the expected value of $\hat{\sigma}^2$, $E(\hat{\sigma}^2)$, we first find the distribution of

$$\frac{n\hat{\sigma}^2}{\hat{\sigma}^2} = \sum_{i=1}^{n} \left(\frac{Y_i - \hat{\alpha} - \hat{\beta}X_i}{\sigma}\right)^2 \ .$$

It can be shown that

$\dfrac{n\hat{\sigma}^2}{\sigma^2}$ is distributed with a chi-square distribution with $n - 2$ degrees of freedom.

The chi-square is a special case of the gamma distribution with parameters $\alpha = K/2$ and $\beta = 1/2$. K is the number of degrees of freedom. We know that the expected value of X, a gamma distributed random variable, is $E(X) = \alpha/\beta$.

The parameters $\alpha$ and $\beta$ specify the particular distribution in the same way that n and p specify the binomial distribution.

Thus a chi-square distributed random variable X with K degrees of freedom has expected value

$$E(X) = \frac{\alpha}{\beta} = \frac{K/2}{1/2} = K \ .$$

Thus our random variable

$$\frac{n\hat{\sigma}^2}{\sigma^2} = \sum_{i=1}^{n} \left(\frac{Y_i - \hat{\alpha} - \hat{\beta}X_i}{\sigma}\right)^2$$

has expected value $\ E\left(\dfrac{n\hat{\sigma}^2}{\sigma^2}\right) = \dfrac{\frac{n-2}{2}}{\frac{1}{2}} = n - 2$. Equivalently,

$\dfrac{n}{\sigma^2} \ E(\hat{\sigma}^2) = n - 2$ because $\dfrac{n}{\sigma^2}$ is a constant and

$$E(\hat{\sigma}^2) = \left(\frac{n-2}{n}\right) \sigma^2 \ .$$

Our maximum likelihood estimate for $\sigma^2$, $\hat{\sigma}^2$, is a biased estimate. We adjust $\hat{\sigma}^2$ in the following to correct this bias.

Let $\tilde{\sigma}^2 = \dfrac{n}{n-2} \hat{\sigma}^2$, then

$$E(\tilde{\sigma}^2) = \frac{n}{n-2} E(\hat{\sigma}^2) = \frac{n}{n-2} \frac{n-2}{n} \sigma^2 = \sigma^2 . \text{ Hence}$$

$\tilde{\sigma}^2$ is an unbiased estimate of $\sigma^2$.

To compute $\tilde{\sigma}^2$ we let

$$\tilde{\sigma}^2 = \frac{n}{n-2} \hat{\sigma}^2 = \frac{n}{n-2} \frac{\Sigma(Y_i - \hat{\alpha} - \hat{\beta}X_i)^2}{n}$$

$$= \frac{\Sigma(Y_i - \hat{\alpha} - \hat{\beta}X_i)}{n-2} .$$

● **PROBLEM** 17-41

Find the variances of the least squares estimators, $\hat{\alpha}$ and $\hat{\beta}$.

Solution:    We wish to find the var$(\hat{\alpha})$ and the var$(\hat{\beta})$. To do this, we will apply the rules of variance to the computational formulas for $\hat{\alpha}$ and $\hat{\beta}$.

$$\hat{\beta} = \frac{\Sigma X_i Y_i - n\bar{X}\,\bar{Y}}{\Sigma(X_i - \bar{X})^2} = \frac{\Sigma X_i Y_i - \bar{X}\Sigma Y_i}{\Sigma(X_i - \bar{X})^2}$$

$$= \frac{\Sigma Y_i(X_i - \bar{X})}{\Sigma(X - \bar{X})^2} .$$

Thus

$$\text{Var } \hat{\beta} = \text{Var}\left[ \frac{\Sigma Y_i(X_i - \bar{X})}{\Sigma(X - \bar{X})^2} \right]$$

$$= [\Sigma(X_i - \bar{X})^2]^{-2} \Sigma \text{ Var}[Y_i(X_i - \bar{X})]$$

$$= [\Sigma(X_i - \bar{X})^2]^{-2} \Sigma (X_i - \bar{X})^2 \text{ Var } Y_i$$

because the $X_i$ are fixed with respect to the random variable Y. Also the $Y_i$ are independent. Thus,

$$\text{Var } \hat{\beta} = \left[ \sum_{i=1}^{n} (X_i - \bar{X})^2 \right]^{-2} \sum_{i=1}^{n} (X_i - \bar{X})^2 \sigma^2$$

$$= \sigma^2 \left[ \sum_{i=1}^{n} (X_i - \bar{X})^2 \right]^{-1}.$$

To find the variance of $\hat{\alpha}$, we note that $\bar{Y}$ and $\hat{\beta}$ are independent. To show this, we demonstrate that $\text{Cov}(\bar{Y}, \hat{\beta}) = 0$; now $\text{Cov}(\bar{Y}, \hat{\beta}) = E\left[(\bar{Y} - E(\bar{Y})(\hat{\beta} - E(\hat{\beta}))\right]$.

$$\text{Cov}(\bar{Y}, \hat{\beta}) = \text{Cov}\left( \frac{1}{n} \sum_{j=1}^{n} Y_j, \frac{\sum_{i=1}^{n} Y_i (X_i - \bar{X})}{\Sigma(X_i - \bar{X})^2} \right)$$

$$= \sum_{j=1}^{n} \sum_{i=1}^{n} \frac{(X_i - \bar{X})}{n\Sigma(X_i - \bar{X})^2} \text{Cov}(Y_j, Y_i).$$

Reversing the order of summation and summing over j we have

$$\text{Cov}(\bar{Y}, \hat{\beta}) = \sum_{i=1}^{n} \frac{(X_i - \bar{X})}{n\Sigma(X_i - \bar{X})^2} \text{Cov}(Y_i, Y_i)$$

by the independence of the sample $Y, \ldots Y_n$,

$$\text{Cov}(Y_i, Y_j) = \begin{cases} \text{Cov}(Y_i, Y_i) & j = i \\ 0 & j \neq i \end{cases}.$$

Also we know that

$$\text{Cov}(Y_i, Y_i) = E(Y_i - \bar{Y})(Y_i - \bar{Y}) = E(Y_i - \bar{Y})^2 = \sigma^2$$

for all i. Thus

$$\text{Cov}(\bar{Y}, \hat{\beta}) = \frac{\sigma^2}{n \Sigma(X_i - \bar{X})^2} \sum_{i=1}^{n} (X_i - \bar{X})$$

but

$$\sum_{i=1}^{n} (X_i - \bar{X}) = \Sigma X_i - n\bar{X}$$

$$= n\bar{X} - n\bar{X} = 0.$$

Thus, $\text{Cov}(\bar{Y}, \hat{\beta}) = 0$.

A covariance of 0 does not imply independence in general but here $\bar{Y}$ and $\hat{\beta}$ are both normally distributed and jointly distributed with a bivariate normal distribution.

If $\text{Cov}(\overline{Y}, \hat{\beta}) = 0$ then $\rho$, the theoretical correlation coefficient is zero and hence $\overline{Y}$ and $\hat{\beta}$ are independent.

Because $\overline{Y}$ and $\hat{\beta}$ are independent, we can compute the variance of $\hat{\alpha} = \overline{Y} - \hat{\beta}\overline{X}$.

$$\text{Var } \hat{\alpha} = \text{Var}(\overline{Y} - \hat{\beta}\overline{X})$$

$$= \text{Var } \overline{Y} + (\overline{X})^2 \text{ Var } \hat{\beta}$$

$$= \frac{\text{Var } \Sigma Y_i}{n^2} + (\overline{X})^2 \frac{\sigma^2}{\displaystyle\sum_{i=1}^{n} (X_i - \overline{X})^2}$$

$$= \frac{\Sigma \text{ Var } Y_i}{n^2} + \frac{\overline{X}^2 \sigma^2}{\Sigma (X_i - \overline{X})^2}$$

$$= \frac{n \sigma^2}{n^2} + \frac{\overline{X}^2 \sigma^2}{\Sigma (X_i - \overline{X})^2}$$

$$= \frac{\sigma^2 [\Sigma (X_i - \overline{X})^2 + n\overline{X}^2]}{n \Sigma (X_i - \overline{X})^2}$$

$$= \frac{\sigma^2 [\Sigma X_i^2 - n\overline{X}^2 + n\overline{X}^2]}{n \Sigma (X_i - \overline{X})^2}$$

$$= \frac{\sigma^2 \Sigma X_i^2}{n\Sigma (X_i - \overline{X})^2} .$$

Thus, the variance of $\hat{\alpha}$ is $\dfrac{\sigma^2 \Sigma X_i^2}{n \Sigma (X_i - \overline{X})^2}$.

# APPLICATIONS OF REGRESSION AND CORRELATION ANALYSIS

● **PROBLEM** 17-42

Find a 95% confidence interval for $\hat{\alpha}$ in the data set relating to problem number one of this chapter.

Solution: We first derive the confidence intervals for $\hat{\alpha}$ and $\hat{\beta}$. We are making the usual assumptions about the Y observations. That is, each $Y_i$ is independent and distributed normally with mean $\alpha + \beta X_i$ and variance $\sigma^2$.

By our previous work we have found the mean of $\hat{\alpha}$ to be $\alpha$.

We have found the variance of $\hat{\alpha}$ to be

$$\frac{\sigma^2 \, \Sigma \, X_i^2}{n \, \Sigma (X_i - \overline{X})^2} \, .$$

To obtain an estimate for the variance of $\hat{\alpha}$ using the formula above we must first estimate $\sigma^2$. We will use our best unbiased estimate,

$$\hat{\sigma}^2 = s^2 = \frac{1}{n-2} \sqrt{\sum_{i=1}^{n} (Y_i - (\hat{\alpha} + \hat{\beta} X_i))^2} \, .$$

Substituting $\hat{\sigma}^2$ into the formulas for the variances of $\hat{\alpha}$ we can estimate the variance of $\hat{\alpha}$.

It can be shown that $\hat{\alpha}$ is distributed normally and that $(n-2) \frac{\hat{\sigma}^2}{\sigma^2}$ is distributed as a chi-square random variable with $n-2$ degrees of freedom.

We also know that $Z = \dfrac{\hat{\alpha} - E(\hat{\alpha})}{\sqrt{\text{Var } \hat{\alpha}}}$ is distributed as a standard normal variable and that $\dfrac{(n-2) \, \hat{\sigma}^2}{\sigma^2}$ and $Z$ are independent.

$$\text{Var } \hat{\alpha} = \frac{\sigma^2 \, \Sigma X_i^2}{n \Sigma (X_i - \overline{X})^2}$$

and $\sqrt{\text{Var } \hat{\alpha}} = \sigma \sqrt{\dfrac{\Sigma \, X_i^2}{n \, \Sigma (X_i - \overline{X})^2}} \, .$

Thus, $Z = \dfrac{[\hat{\alpha} - E(\hat{\alpha})] \sqrt{\dfrac{n \, \Sigma (X_i - \overline{X})^2}{\Sigma X_i^2}}}{\sigma}$

is standard normal.

If we divide a standard normal variable by the square root of a chi-square random variable with $n-2$ degrees of freedom and then divide again by $n-2$ we obtain a new random variable. This new variable is distributed as Student's t-distribution with $n-2$ degree of freedom.

Let $U = \dfrac{(n - 2)\ \hat{\sigma}^2}{\sigma^2}$ , then $\dfrac{Z}{\sqrt{\dfrac{U}{n - 2}}} = T$, a

Student's random variable with n - 2 degrees of freedom.

$$T = \frac{Z}{\sqrt{\dfrac{U}{n - 2}}} = \frac{[\hat{\alpha} - E(\hat{\alpha})]\ \dfrac{\sqrt{\dfrac{n\ \Sigma(X_i - \overline{X})^2}{\Sigma X_i^2}}}{\sigma}}{\sqrt{\dfrac{(n - 2)\ \hat{\sigma}^2}{\sigma^2}}{n - 2}} \ .$$

We can simplify this rather awesome term. We know
that $E(\hat{\alpha}) = \alpha$. Thus

$$T = \frac{(\hat{\alpha} - \alpha)\ \sqrt{\dfrac{n\ \Sigma(X_i - \overline{X})^2}{\Sigma X_i^2}}}{\hat{\sigma} \ \cdot \ \dfrac{1}{\sigma}} \ \cdot \ \frac{1}{\sigma}$$

$$T = \frac{(\hat{\alpha} - \alpha)\ \sqrt{\dfrac{n\ \Sigma(X_i - \overline{X})^2}{\Sigma X_i^2}}}{\hat{\sigma}}$$

is a t-statistic with n - 2 degrees of freedom.

We can now compute a 95% confidence interval for $\alpha$,
the Y-intercept in our regression problem.

$$Pr(- t_{.025}\ (n - 2) \leq T \leq t_{.025}\ (n - 2)) = .95,$$

where $- t_{.025}\ (n - 2)$ is the value such that 2.5% of
the t-distribution with n - 2 degrees of freedom lies
beneath it. That is,

$$\hat{\alpha} \pm t_{.025}\ (n - 2)\ \frac{\hat{\sigma}}{\sqrt{\dfrac{n\ \Sigma(X_i - \overline{X})^2}{\Sigma X_i^2}}}$$

is a random interval that will contain the true but
unknown parameter $\alpha$ 95% of the time.

We will now construct this confidence interval
for the corn yield - fertilizer data set.

We have found

$$\hat{\alpha} = 8.03$$

$$\Sigma X_i^2 = 18.36 \qquad \text{and} \qquad \Sigma X = 10.8 \ .$$

Thus
$$\sqrt{\frac{n\ \Sigma(X_i - \overline{X})^2}{\Sigma X_i^2}} = \sqrt{\frac{n\ [\Sigma X_i^2 - n\overline{X}^2]}{\Sigma X_i^2}}$$

$$= \sqrt{\frac{8\ [18.36 - 8\cdot1.8225]}{18.36}}$$

$$= \sqrt{\frac{8\ (3.78)}{18.36}} = 1.28 \ .$$

We have found

$$\Sigma(Y - \hat{Y}) = (n - 2)\ \hat{\sigma}^2 \qquad \text{to be}$$

$$= 299.58 \ .$$

Thus $\quad \hat{\sigma}^2 = \dfrac{299.58}{n - 2} = \dfrac{299.58}{8 - 2}$

$$= 49.93$$

and $\quad \hat{\sigma} = \sqrt{\hat{\sigma}^2} = \sqrt{49.93} = 7.06 \ .$

We now consult the tables of the Student's t-distribution and discover that

$$- t_{.025}\ (8 - 2) = - t_{.025}\ (6) = - 2.447$$

and
$$t_{.025}\ (8 - 2) = t_{.025}\ (6) = 2.447 \ ,$$

Our 95% confidence interval is
$$\Pr(T \leq - t_{.025}\ (n - 2)) = .025$$

if T is t-distributed with n - 2 degrees of freedom.

Also $t_{.025}\ (n - 2)$ is the value such that

$$\Pr(t_{.025}\ (n - 2) \leq T) = .025$$

if T is t-distributed with n - 2 degrees of freedom.

In the fertilizer problem, there are n = 8 observations and hence n - 2 = 8 - 2 = 6 degrees of freedom for our calculated t-statistic.

To compute a confidence interval for $\alpha$ we solve in the following manner.

$$\Pr(-t_{.025} \ (n - 2) \le T \le t_{.025} \ (n - 2)) = .95$$

$$\Pr\left[-t_{.025} \ (n - 2) \le \frac{(\hat{\alpha} - \alpha) \, A}{\hat{\sigma}} \le t_{.025} \ (n - 2)\right] = .95$$

where $\qquad A = \sqrt{\dfrac{n \, \Sigma (X_i - \overline{X})^2}{\Sigma \, X_i^{\,2}}}$ .

Multiplying within the inequality by $-\dfrac{\hat{\sigma}}{A}$ and adding $\hat{\alpha}$, we calculate our confidence interval in the usual way.

$$\Pr\left[-t_{.025} \ (n - 2)\left(\frac{-\hat{\sigma}}{A}\right) \ge - (\hat{\alpha} - \alpha) \ge t_{.025} \ (n - 2)\left(\frac{-\hat{\sigma}}{A}\right)\right]$$
$$= .95$$

and

$$\Pr\left[\hat{\alpha} - t_{.025} \ (n - 2)\left(\frac{\hat{\sigma}}{A}\right) \le \alpha \le \hat{\alpha} + t_{.025} \ (n - 2)\left(\frac{\hat{\sigma}}{A}\right)\right]$$

$$= .95 .$$

Thus,

$$\hat{\alpha} - t_{.025} \ (6) \ \frac{\hat{\sigma}}{\sqrt{\dfrac{n \, \Sigma (X_i - \overline{X})^2}{\Sigma X_i^{\,2}}}} \le \alpha \le \hat{\alpha}$$

$$+ \ t_{.025} \ (6) \ \frac{\hat{\sigma}}{\sqrt{\dfrac{n \, \Sigma (X_i - \overline{X})^2}{\Sigma X_i^{\,2}}}} \ .$$

$$8.03 - 2.447 \left(\frac{7.06}{1.28}\right) \le \alpha \le 8.03 + 2.447 \left(\frac{7.06}{1.28}\right)$$

$$8.03 - 2.447 \, (5.52) \le \alpha \le 8.03 + 2.447 \, (5.52)$$

$$8.03 - 13.496 \le \alpha \le 8.03 + 13.49$$

$$(- 5.46 \le \alpha \le 21.52) .$$

This is a 95% confidence interval for $\alpha$, the Y-intercept of the regression line. We see that this interval is quite large. This is primarily because of the rather small number of observations.

Suppose a new method is designed for determining the amount of magnesium in sea water. If the method is a good one, there will be a strong relation between the true amount of magnesium in the water and the amount indicated by this new method. 10 samples of "sea water" are prepared, each sample containing a known amount of magnesium. The samples are then tested by the new method.

The data from this experiment is present in the form of the summary statistics.

X represents the true amount of Mg present and Y the corresponding amount determined by the new method. The data is

$$\Sigma X_i = 311 \qquad \Sigma X_i^2 = 10,100 \qquad \Sigma XY = 10,074$$

$$\Sigma Y_i = 310.1 \qquad \text{and } \Sigma Y_i^2 = 10,055.09 \, .$$

Find the regression equation, the standard error $\hat{\sigma}$ and $r^2$, the coefficient of variation. Develop 95% confidence intervals for $\hat{\alpha}$ and $\hat{\beta}$ and test the hypotehsis that the true equation has parameters $\alpha = 0$ and $\beta = 1$.

Solution:    The regression equation is determined by the coefficients $\hat{\alpha}$ and $\hat{\beta}$.

Computing we see that

$$\hat{\beta} = \frac{\Sigma(X_i Y_i) - n\bar{X}\,\bar{Y}}{\Sigma X_i^2 - n\bar{X}^2}$$

$$= \frac{10,074 - 10\left(\frac{311}{10}\right)\left(\frac{310.1}{10}\right)}{10,100 - 10\left(\frac{311}{10}\right)^2}$$

$$= \frac{10,074 - (311)(31.01)}{10,100 - 10\,(31.1)^2}$$

$$= \frac{10,074 - 9644.11}{10,100 - 9672.1}$$

$$= \frac{429.89}{427.9} = 1.005 \, .$$

$$\hat{\alpha} = \bar{Y} - \hat{\beta}\bar{X} = 31.01 - (1.005)(31.1)$$

$$= -.2455 \, .$$

The standard error is

$$\hat{\sigma} = \sqrt{\hat{\sigma}^2} = \sqrt{\frac{1}{n-2}\left[\Sigma(Y_i - \overline{Y})^2 - (\Sigma XY - N\overline{Y}\,\overline{X})^2\right]}$$

$$= \sqrt{\frac{1}{8}\left[438.89 - (430.69)(1.005)\right]}$$

$$= \sqrt{\frac{6.04}{8}}$$

$$= \sqrt{.7558} = .8693$$

It is possible to calculate r from these values. It has been shown that with the assumption of normality,

$$\hat{\beta} = r\,\frac{S_y}{S_x} \qquad \text{where}$$

$$(\sqrt{n-1})S_y = \sqrt{\Sigma(Y_i - \overline{Y})^2} \quad \text{and} \quad (\sqrt{n-1})\,S_x = \sqrt{\Sigma(X_i - \overline{X})^2}\,.$$

Thus $\quad r = \hat{\beta}\,\dfrac{S_x}{S_y}$

$$= (1.005)\,\frac{\sqrt{427.9}}{\sqrt{438.89}}$$

$$= (1.005)(.9874) = .99\,.$$

and $\qquad r^2 = .9847 \qquad$ indicating a very strong relationship between X and Y. Evidently, this is quite a good method of determining amounts of Mg in sea water.

To construct a 95% confidence interval for $\alpha$ and $\beta$ we use a method similar to that developed in previous problems.

For $\alpha$, we use a standard normal Z and chi-square U,

$$T = \frac{Z}{\sqrt{\dfrac{U}{n-2}}} = \frac{\dfrac{\hat{\alpha} - \alpha}{\sqrt{\text{Var }\hat{\alpha}}}}{\sqrt{\dfrac{(n-2)\,\hat{\sigma}^2}{\sigma^2}}}$$

$$= \frac{\dfrac{\hat{\alpha} - \alpha}{\sqrt{\dfrac{\Sigma X_i{}^2}{\Sigma(X_i - \overline{X})^2}}\,\sigma}}{\dfrac{\hat{\sigma}}{\sigma}}$$

$$= \frac{\hat{\alpha} - \alpha}{\hat{\sigma}}\sqrt{\frac{\Sigma(X_i - \overline{X})^2}{\Sigma X_i{}^2}}\,.$$

T is a t-statistic with n - 2 degrees of freedom.

In this problem,

$$T = \frac{-\ .292 - \alpha}{.8693} \sqrt{\frac{10,100}{10,100 - 10(31.1)^2}}$$

$$= \frac{-\ .292 - \alpha}{.8693} \sqrt{\frac{10,100}{427.9}}$$

$$= \frac{-\ .292 - \alpha}{.8693} \ (4.858)$$

$$= (-\ .292 - \alpha)(5.589) \ .$$

To derive a 95% confidence interval for T, we need $- t_{.025}$ (10 - 2) and $t_{.025}$ (10 - 2).

From the table of the t-distribution we see that $\pm t_{.025}$ (8) = 2.306. Thus our 95% confidence interval is

$$- 2.306 \leq (5.589)(-\ .292 - \alpha) \leq 2.306$$

dividing by - 5.589, and subtracting yields

$$- .292 - \frac{2.306}{5.589} \leq \alpha \leq -\ .292 + \frac{2.306}{5.589}$$

or $\quad - .704 \leq \alpha \leq .121.$

We now find a 95% confidence interval for $\beta$. We use as a t-statistic with 10 - 2 = 8 degrees of freedom,

$$T = \frac{Z}{\sqrt{\dfrac{U}{n - 2}}} = \frac{\dfrac{\hat{\beta} - \beta}{\sqrt{\text{Var } \hat{\beta}}}}{\sqrt{\dfrac{(n - 2)\hat{\sigma}^2}{(n - 2)\sigma^2}}}$$

$$= \frac{\left[\dfrac{\hat{\beta} - \beta}{\dfrac{\sigma}{\sqrt{\Sigma(X_i - \overline{X})^2}}}\right]}{\dfrac{\hat{\sigma}}{\sigma}}$$

$$= \frac{(\hat{\beta} - \beta)\ \sqrt{\Sigma(X_i - \overline{X})^2}}{\hat{\sigma}} \ .$$

The values of t-distribution with 8 degrees of freedom such that

$$\Pr(- t_{.025}(8) \leq T \leq t_{.025}(8)) = .95$$

were found in the previous section to be

$$\pm\, t_{.025}(8) = \pm\, 2.306\;.$$

Thus, a 95% confidence interval for $\beta$ is

$$- 2.306 \leq T \leq + 2.306$$

or $\quad \hat{\beta} - 2.306\; \dfrac{\hat{\sigma}}{\sqrt{\Sigma(X_i - \overline{X})^2}}\; \leq \beta \leq \hat{\beta} + 2.306\; \dfrac{\hat{\sigma}}{\sqrt{\Sigma(X_i - \overline{X})^2}}\;.$

Substituting for $\hat{\beta}$, $\hat{\sigma}$ and $\sqrt{\Sigma(X_i - \overline{X})^2}$ yields

$$\left[\; 1.005 - (2.306)\; \dfrac{.8693}{\sqrt{10,100 - 10(31.1)^2}}\; \leq \beta \right.$$

$$\left. \leq\; 1.005 + (2.306)\; \dfrac{.8693}{\sqrt{10,100 - 10(31.1)^2}}\; \right]$$

equivalently,

$$1.005 - (2.306)\; \dfrac{.8693}{\sqrt{427.9}}\; \leq \beta \leq 1.005 + (2.306)\; \dfrac{.8693}{\sqrt{427.9}}$$

$$1.005 - .0969 \leq \beta \leq 1.005 + .0969$$

$$.908 \leq \beta \leq 1.102\;.$$

Thus $(.908, 1.102)$ is a 95% confidence interval for $\beta$.

To test this hypothesis, we will test separately the hypotheses that $\alpha = 0$ and $\beta = 1$. In order to insure an overall level of significance of .05, we test the separate hypotheses at levels of .025.

We compare the two T statistics for $\alpha$ and $\beta$ with the critical values $- t_{.0125}(8)$ and $t_{.0125}(8)$. If the t-statistics for $\alpha$ and $\beta$ are both between these limits we accept $H_0$, otherwise reject. From a table of Student's t-distribution, $\pm\, t_{.0125}(8)$ is approximately $\pm\, 2.79$.

We now test, at level of significance, $\alpha = .05$, the following hypotheses.

$$H_0: \alpha = 0,\; \beta = 1$$

$$H_A: \alpha \neq 0,\; \beta \neq 1.$$

742

The null hypothesis, if true, implies that the true but unknown regression line passes through the origin and has a slope of 1. If this is in fact the case, the new method of determining Mg in sea-water correlates exactly with the actual amount of Mg in a certain amount of sea water.

Next compute the T statistics for $\alpha$ and $\beta$. Under the null hypothesis, $\alpha = 0$ and $\beta = 1$. Thus the t-statistics for $\alpha$ and $\beta$ respectively are

$$\frac{(\hat{\alpha} - \alpha)}{\hat{\sigma}} \sqrt{\frac{\Sigma (X_i - \overline{X})^2}{\Sigma (X_i)^2}}$$

$$= \frac{\hat{\alpha}}{\hat{\sigma}} \sqrt{\frac{\Sigma X_i^2}{\Sigma (X_i - \overline{X})^2}}$$

and

$$\frac{(\hat{\beta} - \beta) \sqrt{\Sigma (X_i - \overline{X})^2}}{\hat{\sigma}} = \frac{(\hat{\beta} - 1)}{\hat{\sigma}} \sqrt{\Sigma (X_i - \overline{X})^2} \ .$$

Substituting we see that

$$\frac{\hat{\alpha}}{\hat{\sigma}} \sqrt{\frac{\Sigma (X_i - \overline{X})^2}{\Sigma X_i^2}} = \frac{-.292}{.8693} \sqrt{\frac{10,100}{10,100 - 10(31.1)^2}}$$

$$= (-.335) \ 4.858$$

$$= -1.627$$

and

$$\frac{(\hat{\beta} - 1)}{\hat{\sigma}} \sqrt{\Sigma (X_i - \overline{X})^2} = \frac{(1.005 - 1)}{.8693} \sqrt{10,100 - 10(31.1)^2}$$

$$= \left(\frac{.005}{.8693}\right) (20.68)$$

$$= .1189 \ .$$

Because both statistics are between $\pm 2.79$ we accept $H_0$ that the true line passes through the origin and has a slope of 1.

● **PROBLEM** 17-44

Using the data from problem #34 of this chapter, compute a 99% confidence interval for $\hat{\beta}$. Now test the hypothesis that $\beta = 0$ vs. $\beta \neq 0$. If $\beta = 0$, if the null hypothesis is accepted, what possible implications does this have for a theory which relates percent Lithuanians with economic discrimination?

Solution: We have assumed that $\hat{\beta}$ is distributed normally. From this and our other assumptions, we have derived the mean and variance of $\hat{\beta}$ and have found them to be

$$E(\hat{\beta}) = \beta \qquad \text{and}$$

$$\text{Var } \hat{\beta} = \frac{\sigma^2}{\sum_{i=1}^{n} (X_i - \bar{X})^2} .$$

To compute a confidence interval for $\hat{\beta}$ we must first obtain an estimate for Var $\hat{\beta}$. To do this we will use our best estimate of $\sigma^2$.

$$\hat{\sigma}^2 = s^2 = \frac{1}{n-2} \left[ \sum_{i=1}^{n} (Y_i - (\hat{\alpha} + \hat{\beta}X_i))^2 \right] .$$

Substituting $s^2$ into our formula for Var $\hat{\beta}$ we see that we can estimate Var $\hat{\beta}$ by

$$\frac{s^2}{\sum_{i=1}^{n} (X_i - \bar{X})^2} .$$

It can be shown that $U = (n-2)\frac{\hat{\sigma}^2}{\sigma^2}$ is a chi-square random variable and is independent of

$$Z = \frac{\hat{\beta} - E(\hat{\beta})}{\sqrt{\text{Var } \hat{\beta}}} \qquad \text{which is a standard normal}$$

variable.

We also know that $T = \dfrac{Z}{\sqrt{\dfrac{U}{n-2}}}$ is distributed

with Student's t-distribution with $n - 2$ degrees of freedom.

$$\text{Thus} \qquad T = \frac{\dfrac{\hat{\beta} - E(\hat{\beta})}{\sqrt{\dfrac{\sigma^2}{\sum (X_i - \bar{X})^2}}}}{\sqrt{\dfrac{(n-2)\hat{\sigma}^2}{\dfrac{\sigma^2}{n-2}}}} .$$

Simplifying we have,

$$T = \frac{[\hat{\beta} - E(\hat{\beta})] \sqrt{\sum_{i=1}^{n} (X_i - \bar{X})^2}}{\hat{\sigma}}$$

as our t-statistic with n - 2 degrees of freedom.

We wish to make the following probability statement about T,

$$\Pr(- t_{.005} \ (n - 2) \le T \le t_{.005} \ (n - 2)) = .99$$

For this data set, $n = 13$, $\Sigma X = 62.88$  $\Sigma Y = 8,577$
$\Sigma XY = 43,943.32$   $\Sigma X^2 = 432.277$
$\Sigma Y^2 = 6,192,505.$

We have $n - 2 = 13 - 2 = 11$ degrees of freedom and from the tables of the t-distribution we find $- t_{.005} \ (11) = 3.106$.

Computing our confidence interval for $\hat{\beta}$, we see that

$$\Pr(- t_{.005} \ (11) \le T \le t_{.005} \ (11)) = .99$$

$$\Pr(- 3.106 \le T \le 3.106) = .99 \ ;$$

multiplying by $\dfrac{- \hat{\sigma}}{\sqrt{\displaystyle\sum_{i=1}^{n} (X_i - \overline{X})^2}}$  and adding $\hat{\beta}$

we see that

$$\Pr\left( \hat{\beta} - 3.106 \ \frac{\hat{\sigma}}{\sqrt{\Sigma (X_i - \overline{X})^2}} \le \beta \le \hat{\beta} + 3.106 \ \frac{\hat{\sigma}}{\sqrt{\Sigma (X_i - \overline{X})^2}} \right)$$

$$= .99 \ .$$

We know that

$$\hat{\beta} = \frac{\Sigma XY - n\overline{X} \ \overline{Y}}{\Sigma (X_i - \overline{X})^2}$$

$$= \frac{43943.32 - 41389.55}{432.277 - 304.145}$$

$$= 19.93 \ .$$

We also know from the formula for $r^2$ that

$$r^2 = 1 - \frac{\Sigma (Y - \hat{Y})^2}{\Sigma (Y - \overline{Y})^2} \ .$$

Since

$$\hat{\sigma}^2 = \frac{\Sigma (Y - \hat{Y})^2}{n - 2} \quad \text{and} \quad Sy^2 = \frac{\Sigma (Y - \overline{Y})^2}{n - 1}$$

$$r^2 = 1 - \frac{(n - 2)\hat{\sigma}^2}{(n - 1)S_y^2} \quad . \quad \text{Hence}$$

$$\hat{\sigma}^2 = (1 - r^2) \left[\frac{n - 1}{n - 2}\right] S_y^2$$

$$= (1 - r^2) \sum_{i=1}^{n} (Y_i - \overline{Y})^2 \cdot \left(\frac{1}{n - 2}\right) \quad .$$

Thus,

$$\hat{\sigma}^2 = (1 - r^2) \left[\sum_{i=1}^{n} Y_i^2 - n\overline{Y}^2\right] \left(\frac{1}{n - 2}\right) \quad .$$

$$r^2 = \frac{n \Sigma XY - (\Sigma X)(\Sigma Y)}{\sqrt{[n \Sigma X^2 - (\Sigma X)^2][n\Sigma Y^2 - (\Sigma Y)^2]}}$$

$$= \frac{13 (43,943.32) - (62.8)(8557)}{\sqrt{[13(432.28) - (62.88)^2][13(6192505) - (8577)^2]}}$$

$$= \frac{33883.56}{107491.05} = .315$$

and

$$\hat{\sigma}^2 = (1 - .315) \left(\frac{1}{13 - 2}\right) (6,192,505 - (13)(659.8)^2)$$

$$= 33196.5$$

$$\hat{\sigma} = \sqrt{\hat{\sigma}^2} = 182.2 \quad .$$

$$\sqrt{\sum_{i=1}^{n} (X_i - \overline{X})^2} = \sqrt{\sum_{i=1}^{n} X_i^2 - n\overline{X}^2}$$

$$= \sqrt{432.277 - 13 (4.84)^2}$$

$$= \sqrt{432.277 - 304.53}$$

$$= \sqrt{127.7} = 11.3 \quad .$$

Our 99% confidence interval is

$$\Pr\left[19.93 - 3.106 \left(\frac{182.2}{11.3}\right) \le \beta \le 19.93 + 3.106 \left(\frac{182.2}{11.3}\right)\right] = .99$$

or

$$Pr(19.93 - 3.106(16.1) \leq \beta \leq 19.93 + 3.106 \ (16.1))$$

$$= .99$$

$$Pr( \quad -30 \ \leq \beta \leq 69.9) = .99 \ .$$

This is an extremely wide confidence interval. We can use this interval to test the following hypotheses:

$$H_0: \beta = 0 \qquad vs$$

$$H_A: \beta \neq 0.$$

If $\beta = 0$, this implies that there is no relation between the two variables percent Lithuanian and our measure of economic discrimination. If $\beta \neq 0$ then there is a relation of the form $Y = \alpha + \beta X$ between the two variables.

We see that zero lies in the confidence interval, thus we accept the null hypothesis at the level of significance $\alpha = .01$. We accept that $\beta = 0$. This may ·or may not indicate a relationship between these two variables. It does give a primary indication that there is no relation. We might test the hypothesis in other ways at different levels of significance    to be more sure of the conclusion of no relationship between these variables.

The following are 90 and 95% confidence intervals for $\beta$.

$$Pr\left[ 19.93 - 2.20\left(\frac{182.2}{11.3}\right) \leq \beta \leq 19.93 + 2.20\left(\frac{182.2}{11.3}\right) \right]$$

$$= .95$$

$$Pr(19.93 - 35.42 \leq \beta \leq 19.93 + 35.42) = .95$$

$$Pr(- 15.49 \leq \beta \leq 55.35) = .95$$

and

$$Pr\left[ 19.93 - 1.76\left(\frac{182.2}{11.3}\right) \leq \beta \leq 19.93 + 1.76\left(\frac{182.2}{11.3}\right) \right] = .90$$

$$Pr( -8.45 \leq \beta \leq 48.3 ) = .90 \ .$$

Thus we would accept $\beta = 0$ at the levels of significance .05 and .1 also.

● **PROBLEM** 17-45

Twenty samples of sediment from the ocean floor were analyzed for the presence of the metal uranium and the mineral feldspar. The twenty pairs of observations (given in micrograms) are below.

| X, feldspar | Y, Uranium |
|:---:|:---:|
| 10 | 12 |
| 19 | 15 |
| 17 | 12 |
| 8 | 8 |
| 5 | 10 |
| 4 | 7 |
| 8 | 5 |
| 16 | 20 |
| 21 | 19 |
| 26 | 20 |
| 5 | 15 |
| 9 | 5 |
| 12 | 25 |
| 8 | 20 |
| 9 | 12 |
| 26 | 15 |
| 19 | 19 |
| 20 | 24 |
| 2 | 8 |
| 3 | 15 |

You are a statistician brought in to analyze this data. What is the equation of the least square regression? Is there a significant relation between feldspar and uranium?

Solution: The following table is useful for computing $\hat{\alpha}$ and $\hat{\beta}$.

| X | Y | $X^2$ | $Y^2$ | XY |
|:---:|:---:|:---:|:---:|:---:|
| 10 | 12 | 100 | 144 | 120 |
| 19 | 15 | 361 | 225 | 285 |
| 17 | 12 | 289 | 224 | 204 |
| 8 | 8 | 64 | 64 | 64 |
| 5 | 10 | 25 | 100 | 50 |
| 4 | 7 | 16 | 49 | 28 |
| 8 | 5 | 64 | 25 | 40 |
| 16 | 20 | 256 | 400 | 320 |
| 21 | 19 | 441 | 361 | 399 |
| 26 | 20 | 676 | 400 | 520 |
| 5 | 15 | 25 | 225 | 75 |
| 9 | 5 | 81 | 25 | 45 |
| 12 | 25 | 144 | 625 | 300 |
| 8 | 20 | 64 | 400 | 160 |
| 9 | 12 | 81 | 144 | 108 |
| 26 | 15 | 676 | 225 | 390 |
| 19 | 19 | 361 | 361 | 361 |
| 20 | 24 | 400 | 576 | 480 |
| 2 | 8 | 4 | 64 | 16 |
| 3 | 15 | 9 | 225 | 45 |

$\Sigma X = 247 \quad \Sigma Y = 286 \qquad \Sigma X^2 = 4137$

$\Sigma Y^2 = 4862 \qquad\qquad \Sigma XY = 4010 \qquad n = 20.$

$$\hat{\beta} = \frac{\Sigma\, XY - n\bar{X}\,\bar{Y}}{\Sigma X^2 - n\bar{X}^2}$$

$$= \frac{4010 - 20\,(12.35)\,(14.3)}{4137 - 20\,(12.35)^2}$$

$$= \frac{4010 - 3532.1}{4137 - 3050.45} = \frac{477.9}{1086.55}$$

$$= .4398 .$$

$$\hat{\alpha} = \bar{Y} - \hat{\beta}\bar{X} = 14.3 - (.4398)(12.35)$$

$$= 8.868 .$$

Thus the regression equation is

$$\hat{Y} = 8.868 + (.4398)X .$$

To test for the significance of this relationship, we test the hypothesis that

$H_0: \beta = 0 \qquad$ versus

$H_A: \beta \neq 0 .$

If $\beta = 0$ is accepted at a .05 level of significance there is no significant relationship between feldspar and uranium.

We calculate the previously derived t-statistic,

$$T = \frac{\hat{\beta} - \beta}{\hat{\sigma}} \sqrt{\Sigma (X_i - \bar{X})^2}$$

and compare it with the values $\pm t_{.025}$ $(20 - 2)$.

To calculate T, first calculate $\hat{\sigma}^2$.

$$\hat{\sigma}^2 = \frac{1}{n - 2} \left[ \Sigma (Y_i - \bar{Y})^2 - [\Sigma (X_i - \bar{X})(Y_i - \bar{Y})]\,\hat{\beta} \right]$$

$$= \frac{1}{18} [4862 - 20(14.3)^2 - (477.9)(.4398)]$$

$$= \frac{1}{18} [562] = 31.22 .$$

Thus,

$$\hat{\sigma} = \sqrt{\hat{\sigma}^2} = \sqrt{31.22} = 5.58 .$$

$$\sqrt{\Sigma(X_i - \overline{X})^2} = \sqrt{\Sigma X_i^2 - n\overline{X}^2}$$

$$= \sqrt{4137 - 20\,(12.35)^2}$$

$$= \sqrt{4137 - 3050.45}$$

$$= \sqrt{1086.55} = 32.96 \, .$$

Under the null hypothesis, $\beta = 0$. Thus the T statistic is

$$T = \frac{\hat{\beta}}{\hat{\sigma}} \sqrt{\Sigma(X_i - \overline{X})^2} = \frac{(.4398)(32.96)}{5.58} = 2.597 \, .$$

The critical values from the table of the t-distribution are $\pm\, t_{.025}$ (18) $= \pm\, 2.101$. The calculated t-statistic is greater than $+\, 2.101$, thus we reject the null hypothesis, that $\beta = 0$ in favor of $\beta \neq 0$. There is a significant relation between feldspar and uranium.

● **PROBLEM** 17-46

Upon giving the mining company this result, the company is intrigued by the possibility of using feldspar as an indicator of uranium. They ask you to be very sure of your analysis before they invest millions of dollars in an underwater mining scheme. Your professional career may rest on this analysis. What can you do to be more sure of your result?

<u>Solution</u>:    The danger is that we have rejected the null hypothesis when the null hypothesis is in fact true.

Equivalently, we might have accepted the hypothesis that $\beta \neq 0$ when $\beta = 0$. The mining company will lose on its investment and you, the statistician, will be out of a job.

To protect ourselves against such a costly error, we alter the level of significance to $\alpha = .01$. This is decreasing the probability of rejecting the null hypothesis when the null hypothesis is true.

If $\alpha = .01$, the critical values are $\pm\, t_{.005}$ (18).
From the table we see that $\pm\, t_{.005}$ (18) $= \pm\, 2.878$.

Comparing the calculated T-statistic $T = 2.59$ with these new critical values, we are led to reject the alternative and accept $H_0$, that $\beta = 0$ and the relationship is insignificant. Perhaps the mining company should proceed carefully in this venture.

A data set with 37 observations has the following
statistics: $r_{xy}$ = .80, $\bar{X}$ = 200, $S_x$ = 20, $\bar{Y}$ = 150, $S_y$ = 15.

(a) Compute the regression equation. If X = 180, compute
$\hat{Y}$. (b) Suppose the Y-scores are normally distributed.
Describe the distribution of Y scores for subjects with
X = 180. (c) If a subject's X-score is 180, what is the
probability that his Y-score is 150 or more?

Solution:    To compute the regression equation we use
the formulas for the regression coefficients.

$$\hat{b} = r_{xy} \frac{S_y}{S_x} = (.80)\left(\frac{15}{20}\right) = .60$$

and    $\hat{a} = \bar{Y} - \hat{b}\bar{X} = 150 - (.6)(200) = 30$ .

The regression line is $\hat{Y} = \hat{a} + \hat{b}X = 30 + .6X$ .

If X = 180, $\hat{Y} = 30 + .6(180)$ or $\hat{Y} = 138$ .

If we assume that the Y-scores are normally
distributed, what is the mean and variance of Y?

We make the following assumptions:

For a given X, the mean of Y is a + bX and the
variance of Y given X is $\sigma_y^2$.

The best estimate of the mean of Y is our
regression line $\hat{a} + \hat{b}X$. The best estimate of the
variance of Y, the spread of the Y-scores about the
true but unknown regression line, is

$$S_y^{\wedge 2} = \frac{\Sigma(Y - \hat{Y})^2}{n - 2} \quad .$$

To compute $S_y^{\wedge 2}$ we can use some of our previous
computational techniques. Remember that $r^2$, the coefficient of determination was defined in the following
way.
$$r^2 = \frac{\Sigma(\bar{Y} - \hat{Y})^2}{\Sigma(Y - \bar{Y})^2} = \frac{\text{explained variation}}{\text{total variation}}$$

$$r^2 = 1 - \frac{\Sigma(Y - \hat{Y})^2}{\Sigma(Y - \bar{Y})^2} = 1 - \frac{\text{unexplained variation}}{\text{total variation}} \quad .$$

but    $S_y^{\wedge 2} = \frac{\Sigma(Y - \hat{Y})^2}{n - 2}$ ;        thus

$$r^2 = 1 - \frac{(n - 2) S_y^{\wedge 2}}{\Sigma(Y - \bar{Y})^2} \qquad \text{and}$$

$$S_y^2 = \frac{\Sigma (Y - \bar{Y})^2}{n - 1} \; . \qquad \text{Thus}$$

$$r^2 = 1 - \frac{(n - 2) \; S_y^{\wedge 2}}{(n - 1) \; S_y^2} \; .$$

solving for $S_y^{\wedge 2}$ we see that

$$(n - 2) \; S_y^{\wedge 2} = (1 - r^2)(n - 1) \; S_y^2 \qquad \text{and}$$

$$S_y^{\wedge 2} = (1 - r^2) \left( \frac{n - 1}{n - 2} \right) S_y^2 \; .$$

$$r = .80 \qquad \text{and} \quad r^2 = (.80)^2 = .64,$$

$$S_y^{\wedge 2} = (S_y)^2 = (15)^2 = 225 \qquad \text{and}$$

$$S_y^2 = (1 - .64) \left( \frac{37 - 1}{37 - 2} \right) (15)^2 = (.36) \left( \frac{36}{35} \right) (15)^2$$

$$= (.37)(15)^2 = 83.3$$

and $\quad S_y^{\wedge} = \sqrt{83.3} = 9.12 \; .$

The standard deviation of Y-scores that lie about the regression line is 9.12.

To make a probability statement about the Y-scores we standardize the Y-scores and transform them to Z-scores by subtracting the sample mean and dividing by the sample standard deviation $S_y^{\wedge}$ .

$$Z = \frac{Y - \hat{Y}}{\sigma_y^{\wedge}} = \frac{Y - (\hat{a} + \hat{b}X)}{\sigma_y^{\wedge}} \; .$$

$$\Pr (Y > 150 | X = 180)$$

$$= \Pr \left( \frac{Y - \hat{Y}}{\sigma_y^{\wedge}} > \frac{150 - \hat{Y}}{\sigma_y^{\wedge}} \; \Big| \; X = 180 \right)$$

$$= \Pr \left( Z > \frac{150 - [30 + .6(180)]}{9.12} \right) = \Pr \left( Z > \frac{150 - 138}{9.12} \right)$$

$$= \Pr \left( Z > \frac{12}{9.12} \right) = \Pr \; (z > 1.32)$$

$$= \Pr (Z > 0) - \Pr (1.32 > Z > 0)$$

$$= .5000 - .4066$$

$$= .0934$$

Thus $\quad \Pr (Y > 150 | X = 180) = .09.$

A data set relates proportional limit and tensile strength in certain alloys of gold collected for presentation at a Dentistry Convention. (Proportional limit is the load in psi at which the elongation of a sample no longer obeys Hooke's Law.)

Let $(X_i, Y_i)$ be an observed ordered pair consisting of $X_i$, an observed tensile strength, and $Y_i$, an observed proportional limit, each measured in pounds per square inch (psi). After 25 observations of this sort the following summary statistics are:

$\Sigma X_i = 2,991,300$ , $\quad\quad\quad \overline{X} = 119,652$

$\Sigma X_i^2 = 372,419,750,000.$

$\Sigma Y_i = 2,131,200,$ $\quad\quad\quad \overline{Y} = 85,248$

$\Sigma Y_i^2 = 196,195,960,000$

$\Sigma X_i Y_i = 269,069,420,000$

Compute the regression coefficients relating proportional limit and tensile strength.

Solution: If Y is the proportional limit and X the tensile strength we hypothesize a relationship of the form $Y = \alpha + \beta X$.

The regression coefficients are estimated in the usual way

$$\hat{\alpha} = \overline{Y} - \hat{\beta}\overline{X} \quad\quad\quad\quad \text{and}$$

$$\hat{\beta} = \frac{\Sigma XY - n\overline{X}\,\overline{Y}}{\Sigma X^2 - n\overline{X}^2} \, ,$$

Thus,

$$\hat{\beta} = \frac{269,069,420,000 - 25(119,652)(85,248)}{372,419,750,000 - 25(119,652)^2}$$

$$= \frac{1406708 \times 10^4}{14504.73 \times 10^6}$$

$$= 96.9827 \times 10^{-2} = .9698$$

and

$$\hat{\alpha} = \overline{Y} - \hat{\beta}\overline{X} = 85,248 - (.9698)(119652) = -30,790 \, .$$

Thus our regression equation is

$$\hat{Y} = -30,790 + .9698X \, .$$

Test the hypothesis that β, the true but unknown regression coefficient in the equation relating tensile strength to proportional limit, is equal to 1 versus β ≠ 1.

Solution:     Our hypotheses are

$$H_0: \beta = 1 \qquad \text{vs.}$$

$$H_A: \beta \neq 1 .$$

This is a two-tailed rejection region. We set the level of significance to be $\alpha = .05$. The test statistic will be a t-statistic with $n - 2 = 23$ degrees of freedom.

The critical values are those values $- t_{\alpha/2} (23), \quad t_{\alpha/2}(23)$ such that

$$\Pr(- t_{\alpha/2} (23) \leq T \leq t_{\alpha/2} (23)) = 1 - \alpha$$

$$= .95 ,$$

From the tables we see that

$$- t_{.025} (23) = - 2.069 \qquad \text{and}$$

$$t_{.025} (23) = + 2.069 .$$

If the computed t-statistic, T, is greater than 2.069 or less than $- 2.069$ we will reject $H_0$ in favor of $H_A$. It has been shown that

$$T = \frac{Z}{\sqrt{\dfrac{U}{n - 2}}} \qquad \text{where Z is a standard normal}$$

random variable and U is a chi-square random variable with $n - 2$ degrees of freedom. We have seen that

$$U = \frac{n - 2 \; \hat{\sigma}^2}{\sigma^2} . \qquad \text{What is Z in this case?}$$

Under the null hypothesis, $\beta = 1$. The expected value of $\hat{\beta}$ is $E(\hat{\beta}) = \beta$ and $\text{Var } \hat{\beta} = \dfrac{\sigma^2}{\Sigma (X_i - \overline{X})^2}$ . Thus

$$Z = \frac{\hat{\beta} - E(\hat{\beta})}{\sqrt{\text{Var } \hat{\beta}}} = \frac{\hat{\beta} - \beta}{\dfrac{\sigma}{\sqrt{\Sigma (X_i - \overline{X})^2}}} = \frac{\hat{\beta} - 1}{\dfrac{\sigma}{\sqrt{\Sigma (X_i - \overline{X})^2}}}$$

Also

$$T = \frac{Z}{\sqrt{\dfrac{U}{n-2}}} = \frac{\dfrac{(\hat{\beta} - 1)}{\sigma}\left(\sqrt{\Sigma(X_i - \bar{X})^2}\right)}{\dfrac{\hat{\sigma}}{\sigma}}$$

or

$$T = \frac{(\hat{\beta} - 1)\sqrt{\Sigma(X_i - \bar{X})^2}}{\hat{\sigma}} .$$

We compute T by substitution of the numerical values into this formula

$$\underline{T} = \frac{(.9698 - 1)\sqrt{(14,504,722,400)}}{6160} = \frac{-3637}{6160} = -.59 .$$

$-.59$ is greater than $-2.069$ and less than $2.069$ thus the null hypothesis is accepted. That is, $\beta = 1$.

● **PROBLEM** 17-50

Compute 95% confidence intervals for $\hat{\alpha}$ and $\hat{\beta}$, the regression parameters for the data relating proportional limit and tensile strength.

Solution:     We have previously developed the results needed for computing the components needed for the confidence intervals.

The test statistic for $\hat{\alpha}$ is

$$T = \frac{\left(\dfrac{\hat{\alpha} - \alpha}{\sqrt{\text{Var } \hat{\alpha}}}\right)}{\sqrt{\dfrac{(n-2)\hat{\sigma}^2}{\dfrac{\sigma^2}{n-2}}}}$$

and has Student's t-distribution with $n - 2$ degrees of freedom.

The variance of $\hat{\alpha} = \dfrac{\sigma^2 \Sigma X_i^2}{n \sum\limits_{i=1}^{n}(X_i - \bar{X})^2}$

$$\hat{\sigma}^2 = \left[\sum_{i=1}^{n}(Y_i - \bar{Y})^2 - \frac{[\Sigma(X_i - \bar{X})(Y_i - \bar{Y})]^2}{\Sigma(X_i - \bar{X})^2}\right]\frac{1}{n-2} .$$

Since $14,067,077,600 = \Sigma(X_i - \bar{X})(Y_i - \bar{Y})$

and     $\hat{\beta} = \dfrac{\Sigma(X_i - \bar{X})(Y_i - \bar{Y})}{\Sigma(X_i - \bar{X})^2}$ ,

$$\hat{\sigma}^2 = [14{,}515{,}422{,}400 - (14{,}067{,}077{,}600)\hat{\beta}]\,\frac{1}{n-2}$$

$$= \frac{1}{n-2}\,[14{,}515{,}422{,}400 - (14{,}067{,}077{,}600)(.98983)]$$

$$= \frac{1}{25-2}\,[872{,}784{,}730] = 37{,}947{,}162.2$$

$$\hat{\sigma} = \sqrt{\hat{\sigma}^2} = \sqrt{37{,}947{,}162.2} = 6160.1\;.$$

$$T = \frac{\dfrac{\hat{\alpha} - \alpha}{\sqrt{\dfrac{\Sigma X_i^2}{n\,\Sigma(X_i - \overline{X})^2}}}}{\hat{\sigma}\,\sqrt{\dfrac{\hat{\sigma}^2}{\sigma^2}}} = \frac{(\hat{\alpha}-\alpha)}{\hat{\sigma}}\,\sqrt{\frac{n\Sigma(X_i-\overline{X})^2}{\Sigma X_i^2}}\;.$$

Our 95% confidence interval for $\alpha$ is,

$$-t_{.025}\,(n-2) \le T \le t_{.025}\,(n-2)\;.$$

95% of Student's t-distribution with $n-2$ degrees of freedom lies in this interval.

Multiplying each side of these inequalities by

$$\frac{-\hat{\sigma}}{\sqrt{\dfrac{n\Sigma(X_i-\overline{X})^2}{\Sigma X_i^2}}}$$

and then adding $\hat{\alpha}$ we have a 95% confidence interval for $\alpha$ with endpoints

$$\hat{\alpha} - t_{.025}\,(23)\,\frac{\hat{\sigma}}{\sqrt{\dfrac{n\Sigma(X_i-\overline{X})^2}{\Sigma X_i^2}}}\;,$$

$$\hat{\alpha} + t_{.025}\,(23)\,\frac{\hat{\sigma}}{\sqrt{\dfrac{n\,\Sigma(X_i-\overline{X})^2}{\Sigma X_i^2}}}\;.$$

Substituting the numerical values of $\hat{\alpha}$, $\hat{\sigma}$,

$$\sqrt{\frac{n\,\Sigma(X_i-\overline{X})^2}{\Sigma X_i^2}}$$

and finding $t_{.025}\,(23)$ in the table the 95% confidence interval endpoints become after the usual manipulations,

$$\left[\,-30{,}793 - (2.07)\left(\frac{6160.1}{.987}\right)\,,\,-30{,}793 + (2.07)\left(\frac{6160.1}{.987}\right)\,\right]$$

or $\quad(-43{,}710,\quad 17{,}870)\;.$

We follow s aimilar procedure to find a 95% confidence interval for $\hat{\beta}$, the slope parameter of this regression equation.

756

Remember that

$$\frac{\dfrac{\hat{\beta} - \beta}{\sqrt{\text{Var } \hat{\beta}}}}{\sqrt{\dfrac{(n-2)\,\hat{\sigma}^2}{\sigma^2}}{n-2}} = T$$

is distributed with Student's t-distribution with n - 2 = 25 - 2 = 23 degrees of freedom. This implies that

$$\Pr(-\,t_{.025}\,(23) \leq T \leq t_{.025}\,(23)) = .95;$$

equivalently, by simplifying T, multiplying by

$$\frac{-\,\hat{\sigma}}{\sqrt{n\,\Sigma(X_i - \overline{X})^2}}$$

and adding $\hat{\beta}$, we derive a 95% confidence

interval for $\beta$.

$$T = \frac{\dfrac{\hat{\beta} - \beta}{\sqrt{\dfrac{\sigma^2}{\Sigma(X_i - \overline{X})^2}}}}{\dfrac{\sigma}{\hat{\sigma}}} = \frac{(\hat{\beta} - \beta)\sqrt{\Sigma(X_i - \overline{X})^2}}{\hat{\sigma}}$$

and $\pm\,t_{.025}\,(23) = \pm\,2.07$ . Hence the interval is

$$\left[\hat{\beta} - t_{.025}\left(\frac{\hat{\sigma}}{\sqrt{\Sigma(X_i - \overline{X})^2}}\right),\right.$$

$$\left.\hat{\beta} + t_{.025}\left(\frac{\hat{\sigma}}{\sqrt{\Sigma(X_i - \overline{X})^2}}\right)\right].$$

We have calculated

$$\hat{\beta} = .9698$$

$$\hat{\sigma} = 6160$$

$$\sqrt{\Sigma(X_i - \overline{X})^2} = 120435 .$$

The 95% confidence interval for $\beta$ is

$$\left[.9698 - (2.07)\left(\frac{6160}{120435}\right) , .9698 + (2.07)\left(\frac{6160}{120435}\right)\right], \text{ or}$$

$$(.864, 1.076) .$$

Compute a point estimate of the average value of the proportional limit corresponding to a tensile strength of X = 129,000 psi. That is, if a sample is tested and found to have a tensile strength of 129,000 psi, what proportional limit do we expect to observe? Find a 95% confidence interval for the estimated proportional limit.

**Solution:** Our expected proportional limit is the expected Y value given $X = X_0 = 129,000$ psi.

This estimate of proportional limit is found by substituting $X_0 = 129,000$ into our regression equation and computing $\hat{Y} = \hat{\alpha} + \hat{\beta}X$. Thus

$\hat{Y}$ = expected proportional limit given tensile strength of 129,000 psi.

$$= \hat{\alpha} + \hat{\beta}(129,000)$$

$$= -30,793.79 + (.9698)(129,000) = 94,310 \text{ psi}.$$

We have found the mean and variance of $\hat{Y}$ and found them to be $E(\hat{Y}) = \alpha + \beta X_0$ and

$$\text{Var } \hat{Y} = \sigma^2 \left[ \frac{1}{n} + \frac{(X_0 - \bar{X})^2}{\Sigma(X_i - \bar{X})^2} \right] \quad . \text{ Thus}$$

$$Z = \frac{\hat{Y} - E(\hat{Y})}{\sqrt{\text{Var } \hat{Y}}} \qquad \text{is a standard normal}$$

variable and $U = \frac{(n-2)\hat{\sigma}^2}{\sigma^2}$ is a chi-square random variable with n - 2 degrees of freedom.

Thus

$$T = \frac{Z}{\sqrt{\dfrac{U}{n-2}}} \qquad \text{is distributed with Student's}$$

t-distribution with n - 2 degrees of freedom.

$$T = \frac{\dfrac{\hat{Y} - E(\hat{Y})}{\sigma\sqrt{\dfrac{1}{n} + \dfrac{(X_0 - \bar{X})^2}{\Sigma(X_i - \bar{X})^2}}}}{\dfrac{\hat{\sigma}}{\sigma}} = \left[ \frac{\hat{Y} - E(\hat{Y})}{\hat{\sigma}\sqrt{\dfrac{1}{n} + \dfrac{(X_0 - \bar{X})^2}{\Sigma(X_i - \bar{X})^2}}} \right] \quad .$$

Because we know the distribution of T, we can derive a 95% confidence interval

$$E(\hat{Y}) = \alpha + \beta X_0.$$

$$\Pr(- t_{.025}(23) \le T \le t_{.025}(23)) = .95.$$

Equivalently, by multiplying by

$$\left( - \hat{\sigma} \sqrt{\frac{1}{n} + \frac{(X_0 - \bar{X})^2}{\Sigma(X_i - \bar{X})^2}} \right) \quad \text{and adding } \hat{Y} \text{ we derive}$$

$$\Pr\left[ \hat{Y} - t_{.025}(23) \left( \hat{\sigma} \sqrt{\frac{1}{n} + \frac{(X_0 - \bar{X})^2}{\Sigma(X_i - \bar{X})^2}} \right) \le \alpha + \beta X_0 \right.$$

$$\left. \le \hat{Y} + t_{.025}(23) \left( \hat{\sigma} \sqrt{\frac{1}{n} + \frac{(X_0 - \bar{X})^2}{\Sigma(X_i - \bar{X})^2}} \right) \right].$$

From the table of the Student t-distribution we see that $t_{.025}(23) = 2.07$. $\hat{Y}$ has been previously calculated to be 94,310 psi, $\hat{\sigma} = 6,160$ and $\Sigma(X_i - \bar{X})^2 = 14,504,722,000$.

$$(X_0 - \bar{X})^2 = (129,000 - 119,652)^2$$

$$= (9348)^2 = 87,385,100.$$

Substituting these values into the expression representing the confidence interval,

$$\sqrt{\frac{1}{n} + \frac{(X_0 - \bar{X})^2}{\Sigma(X_i - \bar{X})^2}} = \sqrt{\frac{1}{25} + \frac{87,385,100}{14,504,722,000}}$$

$$= \sqrt{\frac{1}{25} + 6.024 \times 10^{-3}}$$

$$= \sqrt{.046}$$

$$= .2145.$$

The 95% confidence interval is derived from

$$\Pr[94,310 - (2.07)(1,321) \le \alpha + \beta X_0 \le 94,310 + 2.07(1,321)]$$

$$= .95.$$

The endpoints of the 95% confidence interval are

(91,575, 97,044).

# FACTOR ANALYSIS

The following is a two variable, one common factor model:

$$X_1 = .8F + .6U_1 \qquad (1)$$
$$X_2 = .6F + .8U_2 \qquad (2)$$

a) Draw a path model for the system.
b) Find the covariance and correlation between $X_1, X_2$ and $F, U_1, U_2$ .

Solution: This is an example of a basic theoretical structure in Factor Analysis. The model (1)-(2) asserts that the observed variables $X_1, X_2$ are linear combinations of an unobserved common factor $F$ and two unobserved unique factors, $U_1$ (uniquely affecting $X_1$) and $U_2$ (uniquely affecting $X_2$). The general form of the model is:

$$X_1 = b_1 F + d_1 U_1 \qquad (3)$$

$$X_2 = b_2 F + d_2 U_2 \qquad (4)$$

a) A path model for the system (3)-(4) consists of the observed and unobserved variables connected by lines showing the causal structure.

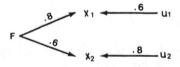

Fig. 1

Applying Fig. 1 to the given model (1)-(2) yields

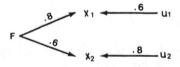

b) The covariance and correlation between the given variables is determined by the assumptions made involving their statistical nature. A convenient set of assumptions is the following:

i) Cov $(F, U_1) =$ Cov $(F, U_2) =$ Cov $(U_1, U_2) = 0$ where

   Cov $(Y, Z) = E[(Y-\bar{Y})(Z-\bar{Z})]$ .

ii) All the variables are normally distributed with mean zero and variance one. In fact, they are standard normal variables.
Note that i) is implicit in the path diagram (Fig. 1) since there are no causal connections between $F$ and $U_1$ or $U_2$ and between $U_1$ and $U_2$ . Using the general model (3)-(4):

$$\begin{aligned}
\text{Var}(X_1) &= E(X_1 - \bar{X})^2 = E(X_1)^2 \\
&= E[b_1 F + d_1 U_1]^2 = E[b_1^2 F^2 + d_1^2 U_1^2 + 2b_1 d_1 FU_1] \\
&= b_1^2 E[F^2] + d_1^2 E[U_1^2] + 2b_1 d_1 E[FU_1] \\
&= b_1^2 \text{ Var}(F) + d_1^2 \text{ Var}(U_1) + 2b_1 d_1 \text{ Cov}(F, U_1)
\end{aligned}$$

$$\left(\text{since} \quad \text{Var}(F) = E(F-\bar{F})^2 = E(F-0)^2 = E(F^2) \quad \text{and} \quad \text{Var}(U_1) = E(U_1-\bar{U}_1)^2\right.$$
$$\left.= E(U_1^2)\right)$$
$$= b_1^2 \ \text{Var}(F) + d_1^2 \ \text{Var}(U_1) \ .$$

(Since $\text{Cov}(FU_1) = 0$ by assumption). (The property of the expectation operator $E[aX + bY] = aE(X) + bE(Y)$ was used in the above derivation).

But $\text{Var}(F) = \text{Var}(U_1) = 1$ (by assumption) and thus $\text{Var}(X_1) = 1 = b_1^2 + d_1^2$. Similarly $\text{Var}(X_2) = 1 = b_2^2 + d_2^2$.

Applying these results to the given model (1)-(2),

$$\text{Var}(X_1) = (.8)^2 + (.6)^2 = 1$$
$$\text{Var}(X_2) = (.6)^2 + (.8)^2 = 1 \ .$$

Thus the proportion of variance in $X_1$ determined by $F$ is .64 and the proportion determined by $U_1$ is .36 . Next, the covariance between a factor and an observed variable is given by

$$\text{Cov}(F,X_1) = E[(F-\bar{F})(X_1-\bar{X})] = E[(F-0)(X_1-0)] = E(FX_1)$$
$$= E[F(b_1F + d_1U_1)] = b_1E(F^2) + d_1E(FU_1)$$

$$= b_1 \ \text{Var}(F) + d_1 \ \text{Cov}(FU_1) = b_1 \ \text{Var}(F) \ .$$

But $\text{Var}(F) = 1$ by assumption and thus $\text{Cov}(F,X_1) = b_1$.

Similarly $\text{Cov}(F,X_2) = b_2$. Now $r_{xy}$ (the correlation coefficient)

$$= \frac{E(X-\bar{X})(Y-\bar{Y})}{\sigma_x \ \sigma_y} = \frac{\text{Cov}(X,Y)}{\sigma_x \ \sigma_y} \ .$$

But here, $\sigma_x, \sigma_y = 1$ and thus $\text{Cov}(F,X_1) = b_1 = r_{F,X_1}$.

The covariance equals the correlation coefficient. For the given model, $\text{Cov}(F,X_1) = .8$ and $\text{Cov}(F,X_2) = .6$.

Also, since $\text{Cov}(X_1,U_1) = r_{X_1U_1} = d_1$ and $\text{Cov}(X_2,U_2) = r_{X_2U_2} = d_2$,

$\text{Cov}(X_1,U_1) = .6$ and $\text{Cov}(X_2,U_2) = .8$.

Finally, the covariance between $X_1$ and $X_2$ is:

$$\text{Cov}(X_1,X_2) = E[(X_1-\bar{X}_1)(X_2-\bar{X}_2)]$$
$$= E[(b_1F + d_1U_1)(b_2F + d_2U_2)]$$
$$= E[b_1b_2F^2 + b_1d_2FU_2 + b_2d_1FU_1 + d_1d_2U_1U_2]$$
$$= b_1b_2\text{Var}(F) + b_1d_2\text{Cov}(FU_2) + b_2d_1\text{Cov}(F,U_1)$$
$$+ d_1d_2\text{Cov}(U_1,U_2)$$
$$= b_1b_2\text{Var}(F) = b_1b_2 \ .$$

Thus the covariance between two observed variables sharing one common factor is equivalent to the variance of the factor times the two respective linear factors involved.

In the given model, $Cov(X_1, X_2) = (.8)(.6) = .48$. This shows that the covariation between the observed variables is completely determined by the common factor; if $F$ were removed, there would be no correlation between $X_1$ and $X_2$.

● **PROBLEM** 17-53

Consider the path model (fig.1) for a two-common factor model:

a) Construct the matrix of factor loadings.

b) What is the correlation matrix?

Solution: The matrix of factor loadings is composed of the linear weights associated with the two common factors. Also, the proportion of variance of an observed variable $(X_i)$ explained by the common factors is listed in a column. This is known as the communality of variable $i$ and is given by

$$h_i^2 = b_{i_1}^2 + b_{i_2}^2 ,$$

where $b_{ij}$ = the correlation between the $j^{th}$ unobserved factor and the $i^{th}$ observed variable.

Finally, the uniqueness component $(1-h_i^2)$ is given in a separate column. The equation system corresponding to the path diagram is

$$X_1 = .8F_1 + .60U_1$$

$$X_2 = .7F_1 + .71U_2$$

$$X_3 = .6F_1 + .6F_2 + .53U_3$$

$$X_4 = .8F_2 + .60U_4$$

$$X_5 = .6F_2 + .80U_5$$

Fig. 1

Therefore the matrix of factor loadings is

| Variables | Common Factors | | $h^2$ | Uniqueness Component $(1-h^2)$ |
|---|---|---|---|---|
| | $F_1$ | $F_2$ | | |
| $X_1$ | .8 | | .64 | .36 |
| $X_2$ | .7 | | .49 | .51 |
| $X_3$ | .6 | .6 | .72 | .28 |
| $X_4$ | | .8 | .64 | .36 |
| $X_5$ | | .6 | .36 | .64 |

The proportion of variance explained by the common factors is given by

762

$$\Sigma\, h_i^2/n_{variables} = \frac{2.85}{5} = .57 \ .$$

This shows that 57% of the variance among the observed variables is determined by the two-common factors.

b) To construct the variance-covariance matrix note that the co-variance between the $i^{th}$ and $j^{th}$ variables is given by

$$r_{ij} = b_{i1}b_{j1} + b_{i2}b_{j2} \ .$$

For example, $\text{Cov}(X_1, X_2) = (.8)(.7) + (0)(0) = .56$ in the given path model.

The variance-covariance matrix is therefore

|        | $X_1$ | $X_2$ | $X_3$ | $X_4$ | $X_5$ |
|--------|-------|-------|-------|-------|-------|
| $X_1$  | 1.00  | .56   | .48   | 0     | 0     |
| $X_2$  |       | 1.00  | .42   | 0     | 0     |
| $X_3$  |       |       | 1.00  | .48   | .36   |
| $X_4$  |       |       |       | 1.00  | .48   |
| $X_5$  |       |       |       |       | 1.00  |

Note that $\text{Cov}(X_1, X_4) = \text{Cov}(X_1, X_5) = \text{Cov}(X_2, X_4) = \text{Cov}(X_2, X_5) = 0$ since these variables have no common factor. Also, since the co-variance matrix is symmetric $(\text{Cov}(X,Y) = \text{Cov}(Y,X))$ only the upper half need be written.

● **PROBLEM** 17-54

Historically, factor analysis arose from the idea that given a covariance matrix that showed how a set of observed variables covaried, the underlying common factors could be deduced.

a) Show by example how this program is carried out.
b) What are some conceptual complications that prevent the idea from being fully realized?

Solution: a) A fundamental theorem of Factor Analysis is that when a set of observed variables corresponds to a set of K common factors then the covariance matrix of the observed variables has rank (number of linearly independent rows or columns) equal to K. Using this theorem the various coefficients relating the factors and variables can be derived and a path model constructed.
For example, suppose the correlation matrix is

|        | $X_1$   | $X_2$   | $X_3$   | $X_4$   |
|--------|---------|---------|---------|---------|
| $X_1$  | $b_1^2$ | .63     | .45     | .27     |
| $X_2$  | .63     | $b_2^2$ | .35     | .21     |
| $X_3$  | .45     | .35     | $b_3^2$ | .15     |
| $X_4$  | .27     | .21     | .15     | $b_4^2$ |

If it is assumed that there is only one common factor, the rank of the matrix is 1. This implies that the determinants of order greater than 1 are equal to zero. Thus, for the first two variables

$$\det \begin{pmatrix} b_1^2 & .63 \\ .63 & b_2^2 \end{pmatrix}$$

$$= b_1^2 \, b_2^2 - (.63)(.63) = 0$$

or, $b_1^2 \, b_2^2 = (.63)^2$ or, $b_1 b_2 = \pm .63$ .

If the various sub-determinants of the correlation matrix are set equal to zero, the resulting set of equations in the variables $b_1, b_2, b_3, b_4$ can be solved to obtain

$b_1 = .9$, $b_2 = .7$, $b_3 = .5$, $b_4 = .3$
and the path diagram

b) But this is an ideal case.
In actual practice the inference from covariance matric to path model is clouded by the following complications:

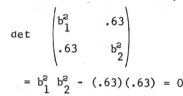

(1) When the number of common factors is two or more, the exact loadings (path coefficients) cannot be found without additional assumptions.

(2) The rank-theorem holds only when the rules for combining factors to create variables meets a certain set of conditions.

(3) The relationships in reality may not fit any factor model exactly.

● **PROBLEM** 17-55

Consider the following path model describing a survey on the mood of the populace regarding government spending:

The observed variables $X_1, X_2,$ $\ldots, X_6$ represent opinions on whether government should control the oil industry, whether government should spend more on elementary and high school education, etc.

a) Derive the correlation matrix.

b) Test whether a one-common factor model could have produced the given correlation matrix.

Use the maximum likelihood method.

Solution: a) The correlation matrix is derived using the relationship $\mathrm{Cov}(X_i, X_j) = r_{ij} = b_{i1}b_{j1} + b_{i2}b_{j2} + \ldots + b_{in}b_{jn}$ where $n$ is the number of assumed common factors. For the given path diagram the correlation matrix is

|       | $X_1$ | $X_2$ | $X_3$ | $X_4$ | $X_5$ | $X_6$ |
|-------|-------|-------|-------|-------|-------|-------|
| $X_1$ | 1.000 | .560  | .480  | .224  | .192  | .160  |

| | | | | | |
|---|---|---|---|---|---|
| $X_2$ | .560 | 1.000 | .420 | .196 | .168 | .140 |
| $X_3$ | .480 | .420 | 1.000 | .168 | .144 | .120 |
| $X_4$ | .224 | .196 | .168 | 1.000 | .420 | .350 |
| $X_5$ | .192 | .168 | .144 | .420 | 1.000 | .300 |
| $X_6$ | .160 | .140 | .120 | .350 | .300 | 1.000 |

b) Now reversing the procedure one attempts to derive the path
model from the correlation matrix. Since the number of factors is
now unknown, the first step is to start with a one-common factor
model. The maximum likelihood method finds the most likely population value that would have produced the given correlation matrix
under the hypothesis that a one-common factor model fits the data.
The assumed path model is:

The maximum likelihood solutions
(calculated on a computer) provide the loadings and the estimated communalities ($h_i^2$). The
total amount of variance explained is given by the sum of
communalities.

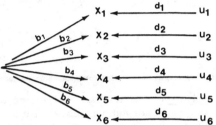

| Variables | $F_1$ | Communalities Implied by model | Actual Communalities |
|---|---|---|---|
| $X_1$ | .774 | .64 | .5995 |
| $X_2$ | .696 | .49 | .4842 |
| $X_3$ | .598 | .36 | .3573 |
| $X_4$ | .345 | .49 | .1193 |
| $X_5$ | .306 | .36 | .0939 |
| $X_6$ | .263 | .25 | .0690 |

Percentage of Variance explained = $\frac{1.723}{6}$ x 100 = 28.7

$X^2$-statistic with 99 d.f (assuming n of 100) = 26.4 .
The coefficients under $F_1$ can be used to calculate the correlation matrix assuming a one-common factor model.
The expected correlations, given the factor loadings, are
$r_{12}$ = (.774)(.696) = .5387, $r_{13}$ = (.774)(.598) = .4259 etc.

| | $X_1$ | $X_2$ | $X_3$ | $X_4$ | $X_5$ | $X_6$ |
|---|---|---|---|---|---|---|
| $X_1$ | 1.0 | .539 | .426 | .267 | .237 | .204 |
| $X_2$ | .539 | 1.0 | .416 | .240 | .213 | .183 |
| | $X_1$ | $X_2$ | $X_3$ | $X_4$ | $X_5$ | $X_6$ |
| $X_3$ | .426 | .416 | 1.0 | .206 | .183 | .157 |
| $X_4$ | .267 | .240 | .206 | 1.0 | .106 | .091 |

765

| | | | | | |
|---|---|---|---|---|---|
| $X_5$ | .237 | .213 | .183 | .106 | 1.0 | .080 |
| $X_6$ | .204 | .183 | .157 | .091 | .080 | 1.0 |

Comparing the expected correlation matrix with the actual correlation matrix, the validity of the one-common factor model appears weak. A more objective test is the Chi-Square test which shows that the maintained hypothesis should be rejected. Thus, using the maximum likelihood method we reject the hypothesis that the correlation matrix could have been generated by a one-common factor. The next stage is to test for a two-common factor model.

● **PROBLEM** 17-56

Use principal component analysis to determine the factor-loadings and the minimum number of common factors that could give rise to the following correlation matrix:

| | $X_1$ | $X_2$ |
|---|---|---|
| $X_1$ | 1.00 | .48 |
| $X_2$ | .48 | 1.00 |

Solution: Principal component analysis is used to transform a given set of observed variables into another set of variables whose variance can be more easily explained.

The nature of principal component analysis can be illustrated graphically. Suppose the set of readings $(X_{1i}, X_{2i})$ $(i = 1, \ldots, n)$ is plotted on the plane. If there is some positive correlation between $X_1$ and $X_2$ then there will be more points in the first and third quadrants than in the second and fourth quadrants. The contour maps will be in the form of ellipses:

The first principal component is the major axis $P_1$ of the ellipse in Fig.1 since it has more data points clustered around it. $P_2$ is the minor axis. Note that the points $(X_1, X_2)$ can now be expressed as coordinates in the axis system $P_1P_2$.

The problem is to determine $P_1$. This is done by a procedure similar to the construction of the least-squares regression line. Here, however, the perpendicular distance of the point $(X_1', X_2')$ from $P_1$ is minimized.

Fig. 1

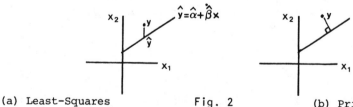

(a) Least-Squares      Fig. 2      (b) Principal Components

In practice, given the correlation matrix, the principal component axes correspond to the eigenvalues of the matrix. The largest eigenvalue corresponds to the first principal axis, the second largest eigenvalue to the second principal axis, etc. Let R be the correlation matrix. Then the eigenvalues of R are real-valued scalars $\lambda_i$ such that

$$R_v = \lambda_v \tag{1}$$

If R is a 2×2 matrix (1) is

$$\begin{bmatrix} 1.00 & r_{12} \\ r_{12} & 1.00 \end{bmatrix} \begin{bmatrix} X_1 \\ X_2 \end{bmatrix} = \lambda \begin{bmatrix} X_1 \\ X_2 \end{bmatrix}$$

or

$$\begin{bmatrix} 1-\lambda & r_{12} \\ r_{12} & 1-\lambda \end{bmatrix} \begin{bmatrix} X_1 \\ X_2 \end{bmatrix} = \begin{bmatrix} 0 \\ 0 \end{bmatrix} \tag{2}$$

Now (2) is true if and only if $\det \begin{bmatrix} 1-\lambda & r_{12} \\ r_{12} & 1-\lambda \end{bmatrix} = 0$ , i.e.,

$(1-\lambda)^2 - r_{12}^2 = 0$ .

Solving this characteristic equation for $\lambda$ yields

$$\lambda_1 = 1 + r_{12} \; ; \; \lambda_2 = 1 - r_{12} \; .$$

In the given problem $R = \begin{bmatrix} 1.00 & .48 \\ .48 & 1.00 \end{bmatrix}$ and hence $\lambda_1 = 1.48$,

$\lambda_2 = .52$. The next step is to find the eigenvectors associated with these eigenvalues, i.e., points $\begin{bmatrix} X_1 \\ X_2 \end{bmatrix}$ such that (1) is true.
When $\lambda = \lambda_1 = 1.48$

$$\begin{bmatrix} 1 & .48 \\ .48 & 1 \end{bmatrix} \begin{bmatrix} X_1 \\ X_2 \end{bmatrix} = 1.48 \begin{bmatrix} X_1 \\ X_2 \end{bmatrix}$$

or, $X_1 + .48X_2 = 1.48 \, X_1$

$\phantom{or,} .48X_1 + X_2 = 1.48 \, X_2$

or

$\phantom{or,} X_1 = X_2 \; .$

Fig. 1

At this point there are an infinite number of possible choices for $X_1$ and thus $X_2$ . The convention is to arbitrarily state the additional condition that $X_1 + X_2 = 1$ . Then $X_1 = X_2 = \frac{1}{2}$ . Since $\lambda_1 = 1.48$ is the eigenvalue that explains the greatest variance, taking the square root will yield the required variation. Thus the first eigenvector is $(\sqrt{\frac{1}{2}}, \sqrt{\frac{1}{2}})$. With $\lambda = \lambda_2 = .52$,

$$\begin{bmatrix} 1 & .48 \\ .48 & 1 \end{bmatrix} \begin{bmatrix} X_1 \\ X_2 \end{bmatrix} = .52 \begin{bmatrix} X_1 \\ X_2 \end{bmatrix}$$

or, $X_1 = -X_2$ . Thus $\left( \dfrac{1}{\sqrt{2}} , - \dfrac{1}{\sqrt{2}} \right)$ is the second eigenvector.

The factor loadings are then given by

$$\begin{bmatrix} 1/\sqrt{2} & 1/\sqrt{2} \\ 1/\sqrt{2} & -1/\sqrt{2} \end{bmatrix} \begin{bmatrix} \dfrac{1}{\sqrt{1.48}} & 0 \\ 0 & 1/\sqrt{.52} \end{bmatrix} = \begin{bmatrix} .86 & .51 \\ .86 & -.51 \end{bmatrix}$$

Thus the path model corresponding to the given correlation matrix has one factor and is given by, (SEE FIG.1).

# CHAPTER 18

# ANALYSIS OF VARIANCE

## ONE-WAY ANOVA

An experimenter compared two groups, an experimental group and a control group. Each group contained 10 subjects. Do the two means of these groups differ significantly?

| Control | Experimental |
|---------|--------------|
| 10 | 7 |
| 5 | 3 |
| 6 | 5 |
| 7 | 7 |
| 10 | 8 |
| 6 | 4 |
| 7 | 5 |
| 8 | 6 |
| 6 | 3 |
| 5 | 2 |

Solution: Let $Y_{ij}$ be the ith observation in the jth population. We can make the following assumptions about $Y_{ij}$.

$$Y_{ij} = \mu_j + \varepsilon_{ij} \qquad i = 1, \ldots n_j$$

$$j = 1, \ldots k$$

where $E(\varepsilon_{ij}) = 0, \qquad \text{Var} (\varepsilon_{ij}) = \sigma^2 .$

In this problem, we have two populations and we wish to compare their means $\mu_1$ and $\mu_2$.

We have previously seen this problem as a test of equality of two means. Using this new notation, we have the following test:

$H_0 : \mu_1 = \mu_2$

$H_A : \mu_1 \neq \mu_2$

and the test statistic for this test will be:

$$\frac{\left[\dfrac{\sum\limits_{i=1}^{n_1} Y_{i1}}{n_1} - \dfrac{\sum\limits_{i=1}^{n_2} Y_{i2}}{n_2}\right] - (\mu_1 - \mu_2)}{\sqrt{s_p^2 \left(\dfrac{1}{n_1} + \dfrac{1}{n_2}\right)}}$$

where $s_p^2$ is an estimate of the pooled population variance. $s_p^2$ is a weighted average of $s_1^2$ and $s_2^2$, the estimates of the individual population variances and it can be shown that

$$s_p^2 = \frac{(n_1 - 1)s_1^2 + (n_2 - 1)s_2^2}{n_1 + n_2 - 2} \, .$$

The following notation is often useful in the analysis of variance.

$$\bar{Y}_{\cdot j} = \frac{\sum\limits_{i=1}^{n_j} Y_{ij}}{n_j} \qquad \text{for } i = 1, \ldots k.$$

This is the average of the observations in the ith popula-tion. Let

$$\bar{Y}_{\cdot\cdot} = \frac{\sum\limits_{j=1}^{k} \sum\limits_{i=1}^{n_j} Y_{ij}}{\sum\limits_{j=1}^{k} n_j} \, .$$

This is the grand average of all the observations.

With this notation,

$$s_1^2 = \frac{\sum\limits_{i=1}^{n_1} (Y_{i1} - \bar{Y}_{\cdot 1})^2}{n_1 - 1} \; ;$$

$$s_2^2 = \frac{\sum\limits_{i=1}^{n_2} (Y_{i2} - \bar{Y}_{\cdot 2})^2}{n_2 - 1} \, .$$

Under the null hypothesis that $\mu_1 = \mu_2$, the test statistic is;

$$\frac{\bar{Y}_{\cdot 1} - \bar{Y}_{\cdot 2} - (\mu_1 - \mu_2)}{\sqrt{s_p^2 \left(\dfrac{1}{n_1} + \dfrac{1}{n_2}\right)}} = \frac{\bar{Y}_{\cdot 1} - \bar{Y}_{\cdot 2}}{s_p \sqrt{\dfrac{1}{n_1} + \dfrac{1}{n_2}}}$$

and will be approximately t-distributed with $n_1 + n_2 - 2$ degrees of freedom. (Ratio of normal and chi-square.)

For this problem, let the control group be population 1 and the experimental group be population 2. Then,

$n_1 = n_2 = 10$

$$\bar{Y}_{.1} = \frac{10+5+6+7+10+6+7+8+6+5}{10} = \frac{70}{10} = 7.$$

$$\bar{Y}_{.2} = \frac{7+3+5+7+8+4+5+6+3+2}{10} = \frac{50}{10} = 5.$$

Also,
$$\sum_{i=1}^{10} Y_{i_1}^2 = 10^2 + 5^2 + 6^2 + \ldots + 6^2 + 5^2 = 520$$

$$\sum_{i=1}^{10} Y_{i_2}^2 = 7^2 + 3^2 + 5^2 + 7^2 + \ldots + 3^2 + 2^2 = 286.$$

We now must compute the pooled variance $s_p^2$.

First find $s_1^2$ and $s_2^2$. We have seen previously that for one sample, the estimate of $\sigma^2$ is

$$s^2 = \frac{\sum\limits_{i=1}^{n} X_i^2 - n\bar{X}^2}{n-1}.$$

Thus,
$$s_1^2 = \frac{\sum\limits_{i=1}^{n_1} Y_{i_1}^2 - n_1 \bar{Y}_{.1}^2}{n_1 - 1} \quad \text{and} \quad s_2^2 = \frac{\sum\limits_{i=1}^{n_2} Y_{i_2}^2 - n_2 \bar{Y}_{.2}^2}{n_2 - 1}$$

Substituting we have,

$$s_1^2 = \frac{520 - 10 \cdot 7^2}{9} \qquad s_2^2 = \frac{286 - 10 \cdot 5^2}{9}$$

$$= 3.33 \qquad\qquad = 4$$

and thus,

$$s_p^2 = \frac{(n_1 - 1)s_1^2 + (n_2 - 1)s_2^2}{n_1 + n_2 - 2} = \frac{30 + 36}{18} = 3.66.$$

Our test statistic is thus,

$$t = \frac{\bar{Y}_1. - \bar{Y}_2.}{s_p \sqrt{\dfrac{1}{n_1} + \dfrac{1}{n_2}}} = \frac{7 - 5}{\sqrt{3.66} \sqrt{\dfrac{1}{10} + \dfrac{1}{10}}}$$

$$= \frac{2}{(1.91)(.447)} = 2.34.$$

From a table of the t-distribution, we see that we will reject $H_0$ at level of significance .05 if $t > 2.101$ or $t < -2.101$. The t-statistic is 2.34 which is greater than 2.101. Thus, we reject the null hypothesis that the mean is the same for both groups and accept that the means are different.

Refer to the previous problem, to test for a difference in population means using an F-test.

Solution:     We will now develop a test for equality of means based on our estimates for variances.  It has already been shown that the pooled variance,

$$s_p^2 = \frac{(n_1 - 1)s_1^2 + (n_2 - 1)s_2^2}{n_1 + n_2 - 2}$$

is a good estimate of $\sigma^2$, the common variance of two populations.  In general,

$$s_p^2 = \frac{(n_1 - 1)s_1^2 + (n_2 - 1)s_2^2 + \ldots + (n_k - 1)s_k^2}{n_1 + n_2 + \ldots + n_k - k}$$

is a good estimate of $\sigma^2$, the common variance of k populations, regardless of the values of $\mu_1$, $\mu_2$, $\ldots$ $\mu_k$.

If $\mu_1 = \mu_2 = \ldots = \mu_k$, i.e., all the population means are the same, then an equally good estimate of the common

variance $\sigma^2$ is     $s_c^2 = \dfrac{\sum\limits_{j=1}^{k} n_j (\overline{Y}._j - \overline{Y}..)^2}{k - 1}$ .

That is, if all the means are equal, we may compute the variance from the dispersion of the population means about the overall mean.

If all the means are equal then $s_c^2 \sim s_p^2$ or $\dfrac{s_c^2}{s_p^2} \sim 1$.

If the means are not equal, then $s_c^2 > s_p^2$ and $\dfrac{s_c^2}{s_p^2} > 1$. Also, when the null hypothesis is true, the statistic

$F = \dfrac{s_c^2}{s_p^2}$ is distributed approximately with an F-distribution, with $k - 1$ and $\displaystyle\sum_{j=1}^{k} n_j - k$ degrees of freedom in the numerator and denominator, respectively. In the previous problem

$$n_1 = 27 \qquad\qquad\qquad n_2 = 25$$

$$\overline{Y}._1 = 4.15 \qquad\qquad\qquad \overline{Y}._2 = 4.38$$

$$\sum_{i=1}^{27} Y_{i_1}^{\,2} = 24.37 \qquad\qquad \sum_{i=1}^{25} Y_{i_2}^{\,2} = 42.25 \ .$$

We need to find $\overline{Y}..$ and $\displaystyle\sum_{j=1}^{2} n_j \, \overline{Y}._j^{\,2}$ .

$$\overline{Y}.. = \frac{\displaystyle\sum_{j=1}^{2}\sum_{i=1}^{n_j} Y_{ij}}{n_1 + n_2} = \frac{\displaystyle\sum_{i=1}^{27} Y_{i_1} + \sum_{i=1}^{25} Y_{i_2}}{52}$$

$$= \frac{27 \cdot \overline{Y}._1 + 25 \cdot \overline{Y}._2}{52} = \frac{112.05 + 109.5}{52}$$

$$= 4.26$$

and $\displaystyle\sum_{j=1}^{2} n_j \, \overline{Y}._j^{\,2} = (4.15)^2 27 + (.438)^2 25$

$$= 465 + 479.61 = 944.61$$

and $s_c^2 = \dfrac{\displaystyle\sum_{j=1}^{2} n_j \, \overline{Y}._j^{\,2} - (n_1 + n_2)\overline{Y}..^{\,2}}{k - 1}$

$$= \frac{944.61 - 943.93}{2 - 1} = .68672 \ .$$

Thus, $F = \dfrac{s_c^2}{s_p^2} = \dfrac{.68672}{1.33} = .5163$ .

Note that $\sqrt{F} = |t| = .719$ where t is the t-statistic from the previous problem. This is true in general and shows the equivalence of these two tests for a two-sample one-way analysis of variance.

The hypothesis $\mu_1 = \mu_2$ will be rejected at level of significance $\alpha = .05$ if $F > F(.95, 1, 50) \cong 4.04$.

The F-statistic is $.5163 < 4.04$ which leads to the conclusion that $\mu_1 = \mu_2$.

● **PROBLEM** 18-4

Decompose the total sum of squares $\displaystyle\sum_{j=1}^{k} \sum_{i=1}^{n_j} (Y_{ij} - \overline{Y}..)^2$

into the error sum of squares and treatment sum of squares. Find the number of degrees of freedom associated with each of these expressions.

Solution: The deviation of an observation $Y_{ij}$ from the overall mean $\overline{Y}..$ can be decomposed in the following way;

$$(Y_{ij} - \overline{Y}..) = (Y_{ij} - \overline{Y}_{ij}) + (\overline{Y}_{ij} - \overline{Y}..)$$

It is an interesting fact that squaring both sides of this expression and summing on i and j gives the equality:

$$\sum_{j=1}^{k} \sum_{i=1}^{n_j} (Y_{ij} - \overline{Y}..)^2 = \sum_{j=1}^{k} \sum_{i=1}^{n_j} (Y_{ij} - \overline{Y}._j)^2$$

$$+ \sum_{j=1}^{k} \sum_{i=1}^{n_j} (\overline{Y}._j - \overline{Y}..)^2.$$

These sums of squares are known as:

$\displaystyle\sum_{j=1}^{k} \sum_{i=1}^{n_j} (Y_{ij} - \overline{Y}..)^2$ : Total sum of squares (SSTO)

$\displaystyle\sum_{j=1}^{k} \sum_{i=1}^{n_j} (Y_{ij} - \overline{Y}._j)^2$ : Error sum of squares (SSE)

$\displaystyle\sum_{j=1}^{k} \sum_{i=1}^{n_j} (\overline{Y}._j - \overline{Y}..)^2$ : Treatment sum of squares (SSTR)

We also need to know the degrees of freedom of each of these sums of squares.

Degrees of freedom are defined as the total number of

terms in an expression minus the number of linear constraints among the observations.

For example the expression

$$\sum_{i=1}^{n} (X_i - \overline{X})^2 \qquad \text{has n terms}$$

$$\underbrace{(X_1 - \overline{X})^2 + (X_2 - \overline{X})^2 + \ldots + (X_n - \overline{X})^2 .}_{\text{n terms}}$$

Also, there is one linear constraint present;

$$\frac{\sum_{i=1}^{n} X_i}{n} = \overline{X} \qquad \text{or} \qquad \sum_{i=1}^{n} (X_i - \overline{X}) = 0.$$

Thus, there are n - 1 degrees of freedom associated with this expression.

We now proceed to find the degrees of freedom for the important sums of squares.

The expression,

SSTO: $\displaystyle\sum_{j=1}^{k} \sum_{i=1}^{n_j} (Y_{ij} - \overline{Y}..)^2$ , has $\displaystyle\sum_{j=1}^{k} n_j$ terms

and one linear constraint; $\displaystyle\sum_{j=1}^{k} \sum_{i=1}^{n_j} (Y_{ij} - \overline{Y}..) = 0$. Thus,

there are $\displaystyle\sum_{j=1}^{k} n_j$ - 1 degrees of freedom.

The expression $\displaystyle\sum_{j=1}^{k} n_j (\overline{Y}_{ij} - \overline{Y}..)^2$ , SSTR, has k terms

and one linear constraint: $\displaystyle\sum_{j=1}^{k} n_j (\overline{Y}._j - \overline{Y}..) = 0$. Thus,

there are k - 1 degrees of freedom associated with it.

The error sum of squares:

$\displaystyle\sum_{j=1}^{k} \sum_{i=1}^{n_j} (Y_{ij} - \overline{Y}._j)^2$ contains $\displaystyle\sum_{j=1}^{k} n_j$ terms and k linear

constraints. These are:

$$\sum_{i=1}^{n_j} (Y_{ij} - \overline{Y}._j) = 0 \qquad \text{for } j = 1, \ldots k.$$

774

Thus, the error sum of squares, SSE, has $\sum_{j=1}^{k} n_j - k$ degrees of freedom.

Note that just as the sums of squares are additive, so are the degrees of freedom.

(degrees of freedom for SSTO) =

(degrees of freedom for SSE) + (degrees of freedom for SSTR)

or $\sum_{j=1}^{k} n_j - 1 = (\sum_{j=1}^{k} n_j - k) + (k-1)$.

● **PROBLEM** 18-5

The following scores represent the performance in a beer drinking contest between reporters from three different newspapers

"Scores" (measured in liters)

| | |
|---|---|
| Newspaper 1 | 1, 3, 4 |
| Newspaper 2 | 4, 5, 6, 6, 7, 8, 9 |
| Newspaper 3 | 2, 3, 3, 4 |

(1)  Set up an analysis of variance table. (2) Calculate the F-statistic and test the hypothesis that newspaper affiliation has no effect on the ability to drink beer.

Solution:    An analysis of variance (or ANOVA) table is a compilation of the sums of squares and degrees of freedom used in testing the hypothesis that the population means differ.

Let  $Y_{ij} = \mu_j + \varepsilon_{ij}$    $i = 1, \ldots n_j$

$j = 1, 2, 3.$

Then $Y_{ij}$ = amount of beer consumed by the ith reporter from the jth newspaper.

If newspaper affiliation has no relationship with the ability to drink beer we would expect on the average for $Y_{ij}$ to be the same for all j.   That is, we would expect that $\mu_1 = \mu_2 = \ldots = \mu_k$.

We use the following test of this hypothesis.   Let

$$F = \frac{\dfrac{SSTR}{k-1}}{\dfrac{SSE}{n-k}} \quad .$$

It can be shown that if $\mu_1 = \mu_2 = \ldots = \mu_k$, the test statistic has the F-distribution with $k - 1$ and $n - k$ degrees of freedom in the numerator and denominator, respectively.

To justify this test, consider the expected values of the numerator and denominator separately.

It can be shown that

$$E\left[\frac{SSTR}{k-1}\right] = \frac{1}{k-1} E\left[\sum_{j=1}^{k} \sum_{i=1}^{n_j} (\overline{Y}_{.j} - \overline{Y}_{..})^2\right]$$

$$= \sum_{j=1}^{k} \frac{(\mu_j - \mu_.)^2 \, n_j}{k-1} + \sigma^2$$

where $\mu_.$, is the overall mean, and that

$$E\left[\frac{SSE}{n-k}\right] = \frac{(n-k)\sigma^2}{n-k} = \sigma^2$$

It is not true in general that $E\left(\dfrac{Y}{X}\right) = \dfrac{E(Y)}{E(X)}$ but, rather if $\mu_1 = \mu_2 = \ldots = \mu_k = \mu$. Then

$$E\left[\frac{SSTR}{k-1}\right] \approx \sigma^2 + 0 \quad \text{and} \quad E\left[\frac{SSE}{n-k}\right] \approx \sigma^2$$

and finally, $\quad E(F) \approx \dfrac{\sigma^2}{\sigma^2} = 1.$

If the $\mu_j$ are not equal, then on the average the numerator of F will be larger than $\sigma^2$ and consequently F will be larger than one.

A natural test is to reject $H_0: \mu_1 = \mu_2 = \ldots = \mu_k$, when F is too large and accept $H_0$ if F is small.

We now compute the necessary summary statistics:

| Newspaper 1 | | Newspaper 2 | | Newspaper 3 | |
|---|---|---|---|---|---|
| $Y_{i_1}$ | $Y_{i_1}^2$ | $Y_{i_2}$ | $Y_{i_2}^2$ | $Y_{i_3}$ | $Y_{i_3}^2$ |
| 1 | 1 | 4 | 16 | 2 | 4 |
| 3 | 9 | 5 | 25 | 3 | 9 |
| 4 | 16 | 6 | 36 | 3 | 9 |

| | | | 6 | 36 | 4 | 16 |
|---|---|---|---|---|---|---|
| | | | 7 | 49 | | |
| | | | 8 | 64 | | |
| | | | 9 | 81 | | |
| Column totals | 8 | 26 | 45 | 307 | 12 | 38 |

Also $n_1 = 3$, $n_2 = 7$, $n_3 = 4$

$$\bar{Y}._1 = \frac{8}{3} \qquad \bar{Y}._2 = \frac{45}{7} \qquad \bar{Y}._3 = \frac{12}{4}$$

$$\bar{Y}.. = \frac{8 + 45 + 12}{3 + 7 + 4} = \frac{65}{14}$$

$$\sum_{j=1}^{3} \sum_{i=1}^{n_j} Y_{ij}^2 = 26 + 307 + 38 = 371.$$

Computing the necessary sums of squares, we have

$$SSTO = \sum_{j=1}^{k} \sum_{i=1}^{n_j} (Y_{ij} - \bar{Y}..)^2 = \sum_{j=1}^{k} \sum_{i=1}^{n_j} Y_{ij}^2 - \bar{Y}^2. \sum_{j=1}^{k} n_j$$

$$= 371 - \left(\frac{65}{14}\right)^2 \cdot 14 = 69.21.$$

$$SSTR = \sum_{j=1}^{k} n_j(\bar{Y}._j - \bar{Y}..)^2 = \sum_{j=1}^{k} n_j \bar{Y}^2._j - \bar{Y}^2. \left(\sum_{j=1}^{k} n_j\right)$$

$$= 346.61 - \left(\frac{65}{14}\right)^2 \cdot 14 \qquad = 346.61 - 301.78 = 44.83.$$

We can now find SSE directly or from the fact that SSTO = SSTR + SSE.

$$SSE = \sum_{j=1}^{k} \sum_{i=1}^{n_j} (Y_{ij} - \bar{Y}._j)^2 = \sum_{j=1}^{k} \sum_{i=1}^{n_j} Y_{ij}^2 - \sum_{j=1}^{k} n_j \bar{Y}^2._j$$

$$= 371 - 346.61 = 24.38.$$

Thus the ANOVA table is:

| | Sum of Squares | Degrees of Freedom |
|---|---|---|
| Total | 69.2 | 13 |
| Between newspapers (treatment) | 44.83 | 2 |
| Within newspapers (error) | 24.4 | 11 |

The test statistic is

$$F = \cfrac{\cfrac{SSTR}{k - 1}}{\cfrac{SSE}{\left(\sum\limits_{j=1}^{k} n_j\right) - k}} = \cfrac{\cfrac{44.83}{2}}{\cfrac{24.4}{11}} = \frac{22.415}{2.218} = 10.158.$$

To perform this test at the level of significance $\alpha = .05$, we will reject $H_0$; treatments are equal if $F > F(.95, 2, 11)$, the 95th percentile of the F-distribution with 2 and 11 degrees of freedom. From the table, $F(.95, 2, 11) = 3.9823$. Thus, we reject $H_0$, that is newspaper affiliation does not affect beer drinking ability in favor of the hypothesis that newspaper affiliation does matter.

● **PROBLEM** 18-6

Show that the test statistic for the t-test of equality of two population means is the square root of the test statistic

$$F = \frac{\dfrac{SSTR}{k - 1}}{\dfrac{SSE}{n - k}}, \quad \text{where} \quad n = \sum_{j=1}^{k} n_j.$$

Solution:    In the case that $k = 2$, 2 populations,

$$n = n_1 + n_2 \quad \text{and} \quad F = \frac{\dfrac{SSTR}{2 - 1}}{\dfrac{SSE}{n_1 + n_2 - 2}}$$

is the appropriate test statistic.

$$F = \left(\sum_{j=1}^{2} \sum_{i=1}^{n_j} (\overline{Y}_{.j} - \overline{Y}..)^2\right) \bigg/ \left(\frac{\sum\limits_{j=1}^{2} \sum\limits_{i=1}^{n_j} (Y_{ij} - \overline{Y}_{.j})^2}{n_1 + n_2 - 2}\right)$$

$$= \left(n_1 (\overline{Y}_{.1} - \overline{Y}..)^2 + n_2 (\overline{Y}_{.2} - \overline{Y}..)^2\right) \bigg/ \left(\frac{\sum\limits_{i=1}^{n_1} (Y_{ij} - \overline{Y}_{.1})^2 + \sum\limits_{i=1}^{n_2} (Y_{ij} - \overline{Y}.}{n_1 + n_2 - 2}\right)$$

The denominator of this expression is

$$\frac{(n_1 - 1)s_1^2 + (n_2 - 1)s_2^2}{n_1 + n_2 - 2} = s_p^2,$$

the pooled estimate of the common population variance.

The numerator is    $n_1(\overline{Y}_{.1} - \overline{Y}..)^2 + n_2(\overline{Y}_{.2} - \overline{Y}..)^2$

$$= n_1 \left[\overline{Y}_{.1} - \left(\frac{n_1\overline{Y}_{.1} + n_2\overline{Y}_{.2}}{n_1 + n_2}\right)\right]^2 + n_2 \left[\overline{Y}_{.2} - \left(\frac{n_1\overline{Y}_{.1} + n_2\overline{Y}_{.2}}{n_1 + n_2}\right)\right]$$

$$= n_1 \left[ \frac{n_2 \overline{Y}_{.1} - n_2 \overline{Y}_{.2}}{n_1 + n_2} \right]^2 + n_2 \left[ \frac{n_1 \overline{Y}_{.2} - n_1 \overline{Y}_{.1}}{n_1 + n_2} \right]^2$$

$$= \frac{n_1 n_2^2}{(n_1 + n_2)^2} [\overline{Y}_{.1} - \overline{Y}_{.2}]^2 + \frac{n_2 n_1^2}{(n_1 + n_2)^2} [\overline{Y}_{.1} - \overline{Y}_{.2}]^2$$

$$= \frac{n_1 n_2 (n_1 + n_2)}{(n_1 + n_2)^2} [\overline{Y}_{.1} - \overline{Y}_{.2}]^2 \qquad = \frac{n_1 n_2}{n_1 + n_2} [\overline{Y}_{.1} - \overline{Y}_{.2}]^2 .$$

Thus, 
$$F = \frac{[\overline{Y}_{.1} - \overline{Y}_{.2}]^2}{s_p^2 \left( \frac{n_1 + n_2}{n_1 n_2} \right)} = \frac{[\overline{Y}_{.1} - \overline{Y}_{.2}]^2}{s_p^2 \left[ \frac{1}{n_1} + \frac{1}{n_2} \right]}$$

and finally, the square root of this expression is

$$t = \frac{\overline{Y}_{.1} - \overline{Y}_{.2}}{s_p \sqrt{\frac{1}{n_1} + \frac{1}{n_2}}} \quad ,$$

the t-statistic for testing the equality of two population means.

● **PROBLEM** 18-7

The following data was gathered in an experiment comparing the effects of three insecticides in controlling a certain species of parasitic beetles. Each observation represents the number of such insects found dead in a certain fixed area containing the insecticide.

| Insecticide | $n_j$ | $Y_{ij}$ | $\overline{Y}_{.j}$ | $\sum_{i=1}^{n_j} (Y_{ij} - \overline{Y}_{.j})^2$ |
|---|---|---|---|---|
| 1 | 4 | 11, 9, 13, 11 | 11 | 8 |
| 2 | 6 | 25,28,31,27,30,33 | 29 | 42 |
| 3 | 5 | 19,23,19,21,20 | 20.4 | 11.2 |

Set up the ANOVA table and test for differences in effectiveness of the three insecticides.

Solution: The error sum of squares and treatment sum of squares are respectively:

$$SSE = \sum_{j=1}^{3} \sum_{i=1}^{n_j} (Y_{ij} - \overline{Y}_{.j})^2 = \sum_{j=1}^{3} \sum_{i=1}^{n_j} Y_{ij}^2 - \sum_{j=1}^{3} n_j \overline{Y}_{.j}^2$$

$$= 8 + 42 + 11.2 = 61.2 .$$

$$SSTR = \sum_{j=1}^{3} n_j (\overline{Y}_{.j} - \overline{Y}_{..})^2 = \sum_{j=1}^{3} n_j \overline{Y}_{.j}^2 - \overline{Y}_{..}^2 \left( \sum_{j=1}^{3} n_j \right)$$

$$= 7610.8 - 6826.66 = 784.14 .$$

Thus $MSSE = \dfrac{61.2}{\substack{3 \\ \sum\limits_{j=1} n_j - 3}} = \dfrac{61.2}{15 - 3} = 5.1$,

$$MSSTR = \dfrac{784.14}{3 - 1} = 392.07 .$$

The ANOVA table is

| Source of Variation | Sum of Squares | Degrees of Freedom | Mean Squares |
|---------------------|----------------|--------------------|--------------|
| Treatment | 784.14 | $k - 1 = 2$ | 392.07 |
| Error | 61.2 | $\sum\limits_{j=1}^{3} n_j - 3 = 12$ | 5.1 |

The test statistic $F = \dfrac{MSTR}{MSE} = \dfrac{392.07}{5.1} = 76.87$

which is much larger than the 95th percentile of the F distribution with 2 degrees of freedom in the numerator and 12 degrees of freedom in the denominator. Thus, we reject the null hypothesis that the insecticides are equally effective.

● **PROBLEM** 18-8

Consider the following situation. An experimenter wants to determine which of four seat-belt designs would provide the best protection in the event of a head-on collision at speeds of 35 mph. or less. Simulated accidents are performed and the following measurements collected. Each observation is a composite index of passenger injury.

| Design 1 | Design 2 | Design 3 | Design 4 |
|----------|----------|----------|----------|
| 37 | 49 | 33 | 41 |
| 42 | 38 | 34 | 48 |
| 45 | 40 | 40 | 40 |
| 49 | 39 | 38 | 42 |
| 50 | 50 | 47 | 38 |
| 45 | 41 | 36 | 41 |

Compute the ANOVA table and test for a significant difference in design.

Solution: The summary statistics for this data set are: $n_1 = n_2 = n_3 = n_4 = 6$ , $k = 4$

$$\sum_{i=1}^{n_1} Y_{i1} = 268 \qquad\qquad \sum_{i=1}^{n_2} Y_{i2} = 257$$

$$\sum_{i=1}^{n_3} Y_{i_3} = 228 \qquad\qquad \sum_{i=1}^{n_4} Y_{i_4} = 250$$

$$\sum_{i=1}^{n_1} Y_{i_1}^2 = 12084 \qquad\qquad \sum_{i=1}^{n_2} Y_{i_2}^2 = 11147$$

$$\sum_{i=1}^{n_3} Y_{i_3}^2 = 8794 \qquad\qquad \sum_{i=1}^{n_4} Y_{i_4}^2 = 10474 \, .$$

Thus, $\quad \displaystyle\sum_{j=1}^{4} \sum_{i=1}^{n_j} Y_{ij}^2 = 42499 \quad$ and $\quad \displaystyle\sum_{j=1}^{4} \sum_{i=1}^{n_j} Y_{ij} = 1003 \, .$

The sums of squares are: $\quad SSE = \displaystyle\sum_{j=1}^{4} \sum_{i=1}^{n_j} (Y_{ij} - \bar{Y}_{.j})^2$

$$= \sum_{j=1}^{4} \sum_{i=1}^{6} Y_{ij}^2 - 6 \sum_{j=1}^{4} \bar{Y}_{.j}^2 \quad = 42499 - 6(7009.916)$$

$$= 42499 - 42059.4 \quad = 439.5.$$

Thus, the mean square error is:

$$MSE = \frac{SSE}{n - k} = \frac{439.5}{24 - 4} = 21.975.$$

And the treatment sum of squares is:

$$SSTR = \sum_{j=1}^{4} n_j (\bar{Y}_{.j} - \bar{Y}_{..})^2 = 6 \sum_{j=1}^{4} \bar{Y}_{.j}^2 - 6 \cdot 4 \, \bar{Y}_{..}^2.$$

$$= 42059.496 - 41917.036 = 142.46 \, .$$

Thus, the mean square treatment is:

$$MSTR = \frac{SSTR}{k - 1} = \frac{142.46}{3} = 47.486.$$

The ANOVA table is:

| Source of Variation | Sum of Squares | Degrees of Freedom | Mean Squares |
|---|---|---|---|
| Treatment | 142.46 | 4 - 1 = 3 | 47.486 |
| Error | 439.5 | 24 - 4 = 20 | 21.975 |

The test statistic is $\quad F = \dfrac{MSTR}{MSE} = \dfrac{47.486}{21.975} = 2.160.$

We will reject the null hypothesis $H_0\colon \mu_1 = \mu_2 = \mu_3 = \mu_4$, that is, that the seat belt designs are equally safe, if the test statistic $\dfrac{MSTR}{MSE}$ exceeds the

95th percentile of the F distribution with 3 and 20 degrees of freedom. This percentile, $F(.95, 3, 20) = 3.0984$ and $\frac{MSTR}{MSE} < 3.0984$. Therefore, we accept the null hypothesis, that the four designs are equally safe.

● **PROBLEM** 18-9

Using the table below, test at the .05 level of significance, the hypothesis

$$H_0: \mu_1 = \mu_2 = \mu_3 .$$

| Source of Variation | Sum of Squares | Degrees of Freedom |
|---|---|---|
| Between groups (treatments) | 70 | 2 |
| Within groups (error) | 30 | 12 |

Solution:     The test statistic is

$$F = \frac{\text{Treatment sum of squares} \div (\text{degrees of freedom})}{\text{Error sum of squares} \div (\text{degrees of freedom})} .$$

We usually refer to a sum of squares divided by its degrees of freedom as a mean square. For example,

$$\frac{\text{Error sum of squares}}{\text{Degrees of freedom}} = \text{Mean Square Error}$$

$$\frac{\text{Treatment or between groups sum of squares}}{\text{Degrees of freedom}}$$

$$= \text{Mean Square Treatment.}$$

These are denoted MSE and MSTR, respectively. With this terminology, the test statistic becomes $F = \frac{MSTR}{MSE}$ and under the hypothesis $\mu_1 = \mu_2 = \mu_3$ it is distributed approximately with an F-distribution with $(k - 1, n - k)$ degrees of freedom. ($k - 1$ = number of degrees of freedom associated with the treatment sum of squares and $n - k$ = number of degrees of freedom associated with error sum of squares.)

For this problem,    $MSTR = \frac{70}{2} = 35$,

$MSE = \frac{30}{12} = 2.5$;     thus    $F = \frac{MSTR}{MSE} = 14$.

We will reject $H_0: \mu_1 = \mu_2 = \mu_3$ at the level of significance .05 if $F > F(.95, 2, 12)$, the 95th percentile of the F-distribution with 2 degrees of freedom in the numerator and 12 degrees of freedom in the denominator.

$$F(.95, 2, 12) = 3.8853,$$

thus we reject $H_0: \mu_1 = \mu_2 = \mu_3$ in favor of the hypothesis that at least two of the population means differ.

● **PROBLEM** 18-10

Five different treatments of fertilizer were applied to a number of plots of corn. Treatment 1 was applied to four plots, Treatments 2 and 3 were applied to six plots. Treatment 4 was applied to seven plots and Treatment 5 was applied to three plots. The yields per acre are shown below.

| (1) | (2) | (3) | (4) | (5) |
|-----|-----|-----|-----|-----|
| 78.9 | 63.5 | 79.1 | 87.0 | 75.9 |
| 72.3 | 74.1 | 90.3 | 91.2 | 77.2 |
| 81.1 | 75.5 | 85.6 | 75.3 | 81.5 |
| 85.7 | 80.8 | 81.4 | 79.4 | |
| | 71.3 | 74.5 | 80.7 | |
| | 79.4 | 95.3 | 82.8 | |
| | | | 89.6 | |

Test the hypothesis that mean yield is the same for each fertilizer treatment at level of significance $\alpha = 0.5$.

**Solution:** If we assume that these observations are random samples from five distributions with possibly different means but equal variances, then analysis of variance is appropriate for this test.

The summary statistics from this data are: $k = 5$, $n_1 = 4$, $n_2 = n_3 = 6$, $n_4 = 7$ and $n_5 = 3$.

$$\sum_{i=1}^{n_1} Y_{i1} = 318 \qquad \sum_{i=1}^{n_4} Y_{i4} = 586.0$$

$$\sum_{i=1}^{n_2} Y_{i2} = 444.6 \qquad \sum_{i=1}^{n_5} Y_{i5} = 234.6$$

$$\sum_{i=1}^{n_3} Y_{i3} = 506.2$$

$$\sum_{j=1}^{5} \sum_{i=1}^{n_j} Y_{ij} = 2089.4, \qquad \sum_{j=1}^{5} \sum_{i=1}^{n_j} Y_{ij}^2 = 169,131.04.$$

Computing the sums of squares necessary for the ANOVA table we have:

$$SSTO = \sum_{j=1}^{5} \sum_{i=1}^{n_j} (Y_{ij} - \bar{Y}..)^2$$

783

$$= \sum_{j=1}^{5} \sum_{i=1}^{n_j} Y_{ij}^2 - \overline{Y}_{\cdot\cdot}^2 \cdot \left[ \sum_{j=1}^{5} n_j \right]$$

$$= 169{,}131.04 - \frac{(2089.4)^2}{26} = 169{,}131.04 - 167{,}907.39$$

$$= 1223.65.$$

The treatment or between columns sum of squares is

$$SSTR = \sum_{j=1}^{5} n_j \ (\overline{Y}_{\cdot j} - \overline{Y}_{\cdot\cdot})^2 = \sum_{j=1}^{5} n_j \ \overline{Y}_{\cdot j}^2 - \overline{Y}_{\cdot\cdot}^2 \cdot \left( \sum_{j=1}^{5} n_j \right)$$

$$= \frac{(318.0)^2}{4} + \ldots + \frac{(234.6)^2}{3} - 167{,}907.40$$

$$= 168{,}334.56 - 167{,}907.40 = 427.15.$$

We may now find the error sum of squares from the fact that $SSE = SSTO - SSTR$. Thus,

$$SSE = 1223.65 - 427.15 = 796.5.$$

The ANOVA table for this problem is

| Source of Variation | Sum of Squares | Degrees of Freedom | Mean Square |
|---|---|---|---|
| Treatment | 427.16 | $k - 1 = 4$ | 106.79 |
| Error | 796.48 | $n - k = 26 - 5 = 21$ | 37.92 |
| Total | 1223.64 | $26 - 1 = 25$ | |

The F-statistic for testing the hypothesis, $H_0: \mu_1 = \mu_2 = \mu_3 = \mu_4 = \mu_5$ is

$$F = \frac{MSTR}{MSE} = \frac{106.79}{37.92} = 2.816.$$

We will reject $H_0$ if

$$F > F(.95, \ k - 1, \ n - k) = F(.95, \ 4, \ 21) = 2.840.$$

Since $2.816 < 2.840$, we accept $H_0$ at level of significance $\alpha = .05$.

● **PROBLEM** 18-11

As an engineer for General Motors, you suspect that the four machines producing parts for a wind-shield wiper assembly are manufacturing parts with different mean diameters. Design a test to confirm or disprove this suspicion. What assumptions are necessary for this test to be a valid one?

Solution: An appropriate test in this situation is one-way analysis of variance. One possibility would be to take a random sample of size n, (say n = 100) from each machine. Measure the diameter of each part sampled and then conduct an analysis of variance. Compute the mean square treatment and mean square error and use this to compute an F-statistic.

The assumptions necessary for this test to be valid are the following:

(1)   Independent observations from each machine.

(2)   Approximate normality of the measurements.

(3)   Constant variance of the deviations about their true mean.

The technical term for the third assumption is homoscedasticity.

● **PROBLEM** 18-12

A new method of determining the amount of calcium oxide, CaO, in the presence of magnesium has been developed. Ten different samples containing known amounts of CaO were analyzed using this new method. Each sample was analyzed twice. Using the data below, test for the linearity of the regression line, relating known amount of CaO to amount indicated by the new technique.

(All measurements in grams)

| Known Amount of CaO $X_j$ | Amount Determined on first test $Y_{j_1}$ | Amount Determined on second test $Y_{j_2}$ |
|---|---|---|
| 20.0 | 19.8 | 19.6 |
| 22.5 | 22.8 | 22.1 |
| 25.0 | 24.5 | 24.3 |
| 28.5 | 27.3 | 28.4 |
| 31.0 | 31.0 | 30.0 |
| 33.5 | 35.0 | 33.0 |
| 35.5 | 35.1 | 35.0 |
| 37.0 | 37.1 | 36.8 |
| 38.0 | 38.5 | 38.0 |
| 40.0 | 39.0 | 40.2 |

Solution:   Linear regression in this case involves fitting the model

$$Y_{ij} = \alpha + \beta X_j + \varepsilon_{ij} \qquad\qquad i = 1, 2,$$
$$j = 1, 2, \ldots 10.$$

It can be shown that the least squares estimates for $\alpha$ and $\beta$ are:

785

$$\hat{\alpha} = \frac{\sum\limits_{j=1}^{10} \sum\limits_{i=1}^{2} Y_{ij}}{20} - \hat{\beta} \bar{X} \quad \text{and} \quad \hat{\beta} = \frac{\sum\limits_{j=1}^{10} (X_j - \bar{X})(\bar{Y}_{.j} - \bar{Y}_{..})}{\sum\limits_{j=1}^{10} (X_j - \bar{X})^2} .$$

Substituting the appropriate values of $X_j$ and $Y_{ij}$ into these equations gives:

$$\hat{\alpha} = -.6792528, \qquad \hat{\beta} = 1.0146.$$

We are interested in whether or not this regression equation is in fact linear. That is, we are testing the hypothesis,

$$H_0: \quad Y_{ij} = \alpha + \beta X_j + \varepsilon_{ij}$$

vs. $H_A$: $Y_{ij} = \mu_j + \varepsilon_{ij}$ $\qquad\qquad i = 1, 2$

$$j = 1, 2, \ldots 10.$$

The alternative hypothesis states that the means of the $Y_{ij}$ take some unspecified functional form.

A modification of analysis of variance procedures used previously will provide a test for this hypothesis.

Let $\sum\limits_{j=1}^{10} \sum\limits_{i=1}^{2} (Y_{ij} - \bar{Y}_{.j})^2 =$ Sum of squares about the sample means, $\bar{Y}_{.j}$, $j = 1, \ldots 10$. This sum of squares reflects the inherent variability of the $Y_{ij}$'s.

Let $\sum\limits_{j=1}^{10} \sum\limits_{i=1}^{2} (\bar{Y}_{.j} - \hat{Y}_{.j})^2 =$ sum of squares about the regression equation.

If linear regression is appropriate, then the mean squares of these two expressions should be close and their ratio should approach one.

Computing these sums of squares from the data, we

have $\qquad \sum\limits_{j=1}^{10} \sum\limits_{i=1}^{2} (Y_{ij} - \bar{Y}_{.j})^2 = 4.2850$ $\qquad$ and

$$\sum\limits_{j=1}^{10} \sum\limits_{i=1}^{2} (\bar{Y}_{.j} - \hat{Y}_{ij})^2 = 2(1.2024).$$

The ANOVA table for this test is:

| Source of Variation | Sums of Squares | Degrees of Freedom | Mean Squares |
|---|---|---|---|
| About the Regression line | 2.4048 | 8 | .3006 |
| About the Sample Means | 4.2850 | 10 | .4285 |

The degrees of freedom are found in the usual way.

In $\sum_{j=1}^{10} \sum_{i=1}^{2} (Y_{ij} - \overline{Y}._j)^2$ there are (2)(10) or 20 terms and

10 linear constraints. $\sum_{i=1}^{2} (Y_{ij} - \overline{Y}._j) = 0$ for $j = 1, \ldots 10$.

Thus, $20 - 10 = 10$ degrees of freedom. Now,

$\sum_{j=1}^{10} \sum_{i=1}^{2} (\overline{Y}._j - \hat{Y}._j)^2$ has 10 terms and two linear con-

straints due to estimating $\hat{\alpha}$ and $\hat{\beta}$; hence $10 - 2 = 8$ degrees of freedom.

The F-statistic is $F = \frac{.3006}{.4285} = .702$ .

We will reject $H_0$ at the .05 level of significance if $F > F(.95, 8, 10)$. However, $F(.95, 8, 10) = 3.0717 > F$. Therefore, we accept $H_0$: the regression is linear.

# TWO-WAY ANOVA

● PROBLEM 18-13

The following experiment was performed to determine the effect of two advertising campaigns on three kinds of cake mixes. Sales of each mix were recorded after the first advertising compaign and then after the second advertising campaign. This experiment was repeated 3 times for each advertising campaign with the following results:

|  | Campaign 1 | Campaign 2 |
|---|---|---|
| Mix 1 | 574, 564, 550 | 1092, 1086, 1065 |
| Mix 2 | 524, 573, 551 | 1028, 1073, 998 |
| Mix 3 | 576, 540, 592 | 1066, 1045, 1055 |

Set up an ANOVA table for this problem and find the appropriate sums of squares, degrees of freedom and mean squares.

Solution: The model describing this experiment is the following: let $Y_{ijk}$ be the dollar sales observed in the kth repetition for the ith campaign and the jth cake mix.

Then,
$$Y_{ijk} = \mu . + \alpha_i + \beta_j + \eta_{ij} + \varepsilon_{ijk} \quad \text{for } \begin{array}{l} k = 1, 2, 3 \\ i = 1, 2 \\ j = 1, 2, 3 \end{array},$$

where $\alpha_i$ is the effect on sales due to the ith campaign for some fixed j. $\beta_j$ is the effect on sales due to the jth mix for some fixed i and $\eta_{ij}$ is the effect on sales due to an interaction between mix and advertising campaign. The $\varepsilon_{ijk}$ are random variables with mean 0 and variance $\sigma^2$.

The analysis of variance procedures are similar to those used for one-way ANOVA. The total variation of an observation about the grand mean,

$$\overline{Y}... = \frac{\sum\limits_{i=1}^{2} \sum\limits_{j=1}^{3} \sum\limits_{k=1}^{3} Y_{ijk}}{3 \times 3 \times 2}$$

is decomposed into variance due to mix, the advertising, interactions and the error. The error variance is the variation within each treatment combination.

The sums of squares associated with each of these variances are:

1)
$$SSA = \sum\limits_{i=1}^{2} \sum\limits_{j=1}^{3} \sum\limits_{k=1}^{3} (\overline{Y}_{i}.. - \overline{Y}...)^2$$

$$= 3 \cdot 3 \cdot \sum\limits_{i=1}^{2} (\overline{Y}_{i}.. - \overline{Y}...)^2 \qquad \text{where}$$

$$\overline{Y}_{i}.. = \frac{\sum\limits_{j=1}^{3} \sum\limits_{k=1}^{3} Y_{ijk}}{3 \cdot 3} .$$

This is the variation in sales due to the advertising campaign.

2)
$$SSB = \sum\limits_{i=1}^{2} \sum\limits_{j=1}^{3} \sum\limits_{k=1}^{3} (\overline{Y}._{j}. - \overline{Y}...)^2$$

$$= 2 \cdot 3 \cdot \sum\limits_{j=1}^{3} (\overline{Y}._{j}. - \overline{Y}...)^2 \qquad \text{where}$$

$$\overline{Y}._{j}. = \frac{\sum\limits_{i=1}^{2} \sum\limits_{k=1}^{3} Y_{ijk}}{2 \cdot 3} .$$

This is the variation in sales due to the type of mix.

3) $\quad SSAB = \sum\limits_{i=1}^{2} \sum\limits_{j=1}^{3} \sum\limits_{k=1}^{3} (\overline{Y}_{ij\cdot} - \overline{Y}_{i\cdot\cdot} - \overline{Y}_{\cdot j\cdot} + \overline{Y}_{\cdots})^2$

$\quad\quad\quad\quad = 3 \cdot \sum\limits_{i=1}^{2} \sum\limits_{j=1}^{3} (\overline{Y}_{ij\cdot} - \overline{Y}_{i\cdot\cdot} - \overline{Y}_{\cdot j\cdot} + \overline{Y}_{\cdots})^2$

where $\quad\quad \overline{Y}_{ij\cdot} = \dfrac{\sum\limits_{k=1}^{3} Y_{ijk}}{3}$ .

This is the variation in sales due to an interaction between mix and advertising campaign.

4) $\quad SSE = \sum\limits_{i=1}^{2} \sum\limits_{j=1}^{3} \sum\limits_{k=1}^{3} (Y_{ijk} - Y_{ij\cdot})^2$ .

This is the variation in sales within each treatment combination, which is the variation in sales due to error.

Computing the necessary summary statistics we have:

$\sum\limits_{j=1}^{3} \sum\limits_{k=1}^{3} Y_{1jk} = 5044 \quad\quad\quad \sum\limits_{k=1}^{3} Y_{11k} = 1688$

$\sum\limits_{j=1}^{3} \sum\limits_{k=1}^{3} Y_{2jk} = 9508 \quad\quad\quad \sum\limits_{k=1}^{3} Y_{21k} = 3243$

$\sum\limits_{i=1}^{2} \sum\limits_{k=1}^{3} Y_{i1k} = 4931 \quad\quad\quad \sum\limits_{k=1}^{3} Y_{12K} = 1648$

$\sum\limits_{i=1}^{2} \sum\limits_{k=1}^{3} Y_{i2k} = 4747 \quad\quad\quad \sum\limits_{k=1}^{3} Y_{22k} = 3099$

$\sum\limits_{i=1}^{2} \sum\limits_{k=1}^{3} Y_{i3k} = 4874 \quad\quad\quad \sum\limits_{k=1}^{3} Y_{13k} = 1708$

$\quad\quad\quad\quad\quad\quad\quad\quad\quad\quad\quad\quad \sum\limits_{k=1}^{3} Y_{23k} = 3166$

$\sum\limits_{i=1}^{2} \sum\limits_{j=1}^{3} \sum\limits_{k=1}^{3} Y_{ijk}^2 = 12,882,026.$

$\sum\limits_{i=1}^{2} \sum\limits_{j=1}^{3} \sum\limits_{k=1}^{3} Y_{ijk} = 14,552$ .

We now compute the necessary sums of squares in the following manner:

1) $\displaystyle SSA = \sum_{i=1}^{2} \sum_{j=1}^{3} \sum_{k=1}^{3} (\overline{Y}_{i..} - \overline{Y}...)^2$

$\displaystyle = 9 \sum_{i=1}^{2} (\overline{Y}_{i..} - \overline{Y}...)^2 \quad = 9 \sum_{i=1}^{2} \overline{Y}_{i..}^2 - 9 \cdot 2 \cdot \overline{Y}_{...}^2$

$\displaystyle = 9 \left(\frac{5044}{9}\right)^2 + 9 \left(\frac{9508}{9}\right)^2 - 18 \left(\frac{14552}{18}\right)^2$

$= 12{,}871{,}553 - 11{,}764{,}484 \quad = 1{,}107{,}070.$

2) $\displaystyle SSB = \sum_{i=1}^{2} \sum_{j=1}^{3} \sum_{k=1}^{3} (\overline{Y}_{.j.} - \overline{Y}...)^2$

$\displaystyle = 6 \sum_{j=1}^{3} \overline{Y}_{.j.}^2 - 18 \overline{Y}_{...}^2$

$\displaystyle = 6 \left[ \left(\frac{4931}{6}\right)^2 + \left(\frac{4747}{6}\right)^2 + \left(\frac{4874}{6}\right)^2 \right] - 11{,}764{,}483$

$= 2957.$

3) $\displaystyle SSAB = \sum_{i=1}^{2} \sum_{j=1}^{3} \sum_{k=1}^{3} (\overline{Y}_{ij.} - \overline{Y}_{i..} - \overline{Y}_{.j.} + \overline{Y}...)^2$

$\displaystyle = 3 \cdot \sum_{i=1}^{2} \sum_{j=1}^{3} (\overline{Y}_{ij.} - \overline{Y}_{i..} - \overline{Y}_{.j.} + \overline{Y}...)^2$

$= 1126.$

4) $\displaystyle SSTO = \sum_{i=1}^{2} \sum_{j=1}^{3} \sum_{k=1}^{3} (Y_{ijk} - \overline{Y}...)^2$

$\displaystyle = \sum_{i=1}^{2} \sum_{j=1}^{3} \sum_{k=1}^{3} Y_{ijk}^2 - 18 \overline{Y}_{...}^2$

$= 12{,}882{,}026 - 11{,}764{,}484 = 1{,}117{,}542.$

The total sum of squares:

$\displaystyle SSTO = \sum_{i=1}^{2} \sum_{j=1}^{3} \sum_{k=1}^{3} (Y_{ijk} - \overline{Y}...)^2$

may be decomposed as in one-way ANOVA. The decomposition is the following:

$\displaystyle \sum_{i=1}^{2} \sum_{j=1}^{3} \sum_{k=1}^{3} (Y_{ijk} - \overline{Y}...)^2$

$$= \sum_{i=1}^{2} \sum_{j=1}^{3} \sum_{k=1}^{3} (\bar{Y}_{i}.. - \bar{Y}...)^2 + \sum_{i=1}^{2} \sum_{j=1}^{3} \sum_{k=1}^{3} (\bar{Y}._{j}. - \bar{Y}...)^2$$

$$+ \sum_{i=1}^{2} \sum_{j=1}^{3} \sum_{k=1}^{3} (\bar{Y}_{ij}. - \bar{Y}_{i}.. - \bar{Y}._{j}. + \bar{Y}...)^2 + \sum_{i=1}^{2} \sum_{j=1}^{3} \sum_{k=1}^{3} (Y_{ijk} - \bar{Y}_{ij}.)^2$$

or $\quad$ SSTO = SSA + SSB + SSAB + SSE.

Thus, SSE = SSTO - SSA - SSB - SSAB = 6389 .

The ANOVA table is

| Source of Variation | Sum of Squares | Degrees of Freedom | Mean Squares |
|---|---|---|---|
| Advertising Campaign | 1107070 | 2 - 1 = 1 | 1107070 |
| Cake mix | 2957 | 3 - 1 = 2 | 1478.5 |
| Interaction | 1126 | (2 - 1)(3 - 1) = 2 | 563 |
| Error | 6389 | 3 · 2(3 - 1) = 12 | 532.42 |

The degrees of freedom are found in the usual way. To find the number of degrees of freedom for the interaction sum of squares we use the fact that the degrees of freedom are additive. That is

$$df_A + df_B + df_{AB} + df_E = df_{total} = n - 1 .$$

Thus, $\quad df_{AB} = 18 - 1 - (2 - 1) - (3 - 1) - \left[3 \cdot 2(3 - 1)\right]$

$$= 3 \cdot 2 - (2 - 1) - (3 - 1) - 1$$

$$= (3 \cdot 2) - 2 - 3 + 1$$

$$= (3 - 1)(2 - 1) = 2 .$$

In general, $df_{AB} = (r - 1)(c - 1)$

where r = number of rows, c = number of columns.

● **PROBLEM** 18-14

Referring to the previous problem, test for the significance of the interactions at significance level $\alpha = .05$. Interpret the results in terms of the experiment.

Solution: $\quad$ We first test for the significance of the interactions. The natural test statistic, by analogy with one-way ANOVA is

$$F = \frac{MSAB}{MSE} , \quad \text{where} \quad MSAB = \frac{SSAB}{(r - 1)(c - 1)}$$

and SSAB = the sum of squares due to interaction,
r = the number of rows and c = the number of columns.

The null hypothesis $H_0$: $\eta_{ij}$ = 0 for all i and j
will be rejected at the level of significance $\alpha$ if

$$F = \frac{MSAB}{MSE} > F(1 - \alpha, (r - 1)(c - 1), rc(n - 1))$$

Choosing $\alpha$ = .05 and referring to the ANOVA table in
the previous problem we see that

$$(r - 1)(c - 1) = (3 - 1)(2 - 1) = 2$$

$$rc(n - 1) = 3 \cdot 2 (3 - 1) = 12. \qquad \text{Thus,}$$

$$F(1 - \alpha, (r - 1)(c - 1), rc(n - 1)$$

$$= F(.95, 2, 12) = 3.8853.$$

$$F = \frac{MSAB}{MSE} = \frac{563}{532.42} = 1.057 < 3.8853.$$

Therefore, accept $H_0$ that the interactions are
zero and proceed to test the main effects.

Because the interaction term is essentially zero we
may pool the sum of squares due to interaction with the
error sum of squares. This increases the number of
degrees of freedom for error and hence, increases the
precision of further testing. The new SSE is,

$$SSE = SSE_{old} + SSAB.$$

Our new ANOVA table is

| Source of Variation | Sum of Squares | Degrees of Freedom | Mean Squares |
|---|---|---|---|
| Advertising campaign | 1,107,070 | 2 - 1 = 1 | 1,107,070 |
| Cake mix | 2,957 | 3 - 1 = 2 | 563 |
| Error | 7,515 | 14 | 563,78 |

In terms of the experiment; we now have the model.

$$Y_{ijk} = \mu. + \alpha_i + \beta_j + \varepsilon_{ijk} \qquad \begin{array}{l} i = 1, 2 \\ j = 1, 2, 3 \\ k = 1, 2, 3 . \end{array}$$

This model implies that the cake mix and advertising
campaigns effect mean sales separately. There is no
interrelationship between these two factors.

Referring to the previous two problems, test for the significance of the two main effects, advertising and type of cake mix. Interpret the results of these tests. What is the most important factor in determining sales?

Solution:    First test for significance of the type of cake mix. The null hypothesis is:

$H_0$: $\beta_j = 0$                    $j = 1, 2, 3$

$H_A$: at least one $\beta_j \neq 0$.

The test statistic for this is   $F = \dfrac{MSB}{MSE}$ .

Under the null hypothesis this is F-distributed with $3 - 1 = 2$ and 14 degrees of freedom in numerator and denominator, respectively.

We will reject $H_0$ if   $F > F(.95, 2, 14) = 3.7389$.

From the ANOVA table in the previous problem we

see that   $F = \dfrac{MSB}{MSE} = \dfrac{563}{537.78} = 1.046 < 3.7389$.

Therefore, accept $H_0$, that the $\beta_j = 0$, $j = 1, 2, 3$.

To test the hypothesis that the other main effect is zero, we test the null hypothesis

$H_0$:   $\alpha_i = 0$              $i = 1, 2$

vs.   $H_A$: at least one of the $\alpha_i \neq 0$.

The test statistic for this test is $F = \dfrac{MSA}{MSE}$ . Under the null hypothesis this statistic has a F-distribution with 1 and 14 degrees of freedom.

H  will be rejected at significance level $\alpha = .05$ if

$F = \dfrac{MSA}{MSE} > F(.95, 1, 14) = 4.60$.

From the ANOVA table,      $F = \dfrac{MSA}{MSE} = \dfrac{1107070}{536.78} = 2062 > 4.60$

Therefore, reject $H_0$ and accept that the $\alpha_i$'s are not equal to zero.

Through the three hypothesis tests we have accepted $\eta_{ij} = 0$ $\beta_j = 0$ and $\alpha_i \neq 0$ for all i and j. The model of choice seems to be   $Y_{ijk} = \mu. + \alpha_i + \varepsilon_{ijk}$              i, j, k.

This model states that the only factor important in determining sales of the cake mix is the particular advertising campaign used. Of these three cakes mixes, the type of cake mix does not appreciably effect sales.

● **PROBLEM** 18-16

Blue-Green Foods Inc. wishes to enter the frozen shrimp market. They contract a researcher to investigate various methods of growing shrimp in large tanks. The researcher suspects that temperature and salinity are important factors influencing shrimp yield and conducts a factorial experiment with three levels of temperature and salinity. That is, each combination of temperature and salinity are employed and the shrimp yield for each (from identical 80 gallon tanks) is measured.

The recorded yields are given in the following chart:

Salinity (in ppm)

|  | 700 | 1400 | 2100 |
|---|---|---|---|
| Temperature 60°F | 3 | 5 | 4 |
| 70°F | 11 | 10 | 12 |
| 80°F | 16 | 21 | 17 |

Check for interactions and compute the ANOVA table for the model:

$$Y_{ijk} = \mu. + \alpha_i + \beta_j + \varepsilon_{ij} \quad i = 1, 2, 3, \; j = 1, 2, 3.$$

Solution: An interaction effect is the effect due to the combination of factors. If the interaction effect is absent, then the model

$$Y_{ijk} = \mu. + \alpha_i + \beta_j + \varepsilon_{ijk}$$

is appropriate. This model implies that main effects are independent of each other. Another implication is that given a certain level of one treatment, the effect of the other treatment is additive. If the true means of each cell are plotted, we would expect that the graph would consist of parallel line segments.

A quick check for interactions is to plot the sample means of each cell. If there is only one observation per cell, then the sample mean is that observation. For this data, the plot is:

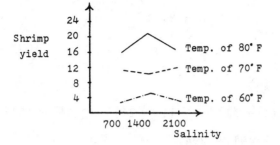

The lines are not perfectly parallel but they do not intersect and seem to indicate that the effects of temperature and salinity do not interact to influence the shrimp yield.

Assuming that the model

$$Y_{ij} = \mu. + \alpha_i + \beta_j + \varepsilon_{ij} \qquad i = 1, 2, 3,$$

$$j = 1, 2, 3$$

is appropriate, we proceed to calculate the necessary sum of squares.

If $\alpha_i$ is the effect due to temperature then we have the row averages,

$$\bar{Y}_1. = \frac{3 + 5 + 4}{3} = 4$$

$$\bar{Y}_2. = \frac{11 + 10 + 12}{3} = 11$$

$$\bar{Y}_3. = \frac{16 + 21 + 17}{3} = 18 .$$

The column averages are:

$$\bar{Y}._1 = \frac{3 + 11 + 16}{3} = 10$$

$$\bar{Y}._2 = \frac{5 + 10 + 21}{3} = 12$$

$$\bar{Y}._3 = \frac{4 + 12 + 17}{3} = 11$$

$$\bar{Y}.. = \frac{4 + 11 + 18}{3} = \frac{10 + 12 + 11}{3} = 11$$

and $\displaystyle\sum_{i=1}^{3} \sum_{j=1}^{3} Y_{ij}^2 = 3^2 + 5^2 + 4^2 + 11^2 + 10^2 + \ldots + 21^2 + 17^2$

$$= 9 + 25 + 16 + 121 + 100 + \ldots + 441 + 289$$

$$= 1401.$$

The sum of squares due to variation in temperature is:

$$SSA = \sum_{i=1}^{3} \sum_{j=1}^{3} (\overline{Y}_i. - \overline{Y}..)^2$$

$$= 3 \sum_{i=1}^{3} (\overline{Y}_i. - \overline{Y}..)^2$$

$$= 3 [(4 - 11)^2 + (11 - 11)^2 + (18 - 11)^2]$$

$$= 2[49 + 49] = 294.$$

The sum of squares due to variation in salinity is:

$$SSB = \sum_{i=1}^{3} \sum_{j=1}^{3} (\overline{Y}._j - \overline{Y}..)^2$$

$$= 3 \sum_{j=1}^{3} (\overline{Y}._j - \overline{Y}..)^2$$

$$= 3 [(10 - 11)^2 + (12 - 11)^2 + (11 - 11)^2]$$

$$= 3 [1 + 1 + 0] = 6.$$

The total sum of squares is:

$$SSTO = \sum_{i=1}^{3} \sum_{j=1}^{3} (Y_{ij} - \overline{Y}..)^2$$

$$= \sum_{i=1}^{3} \sum_{j=1}^{3} Y_{ij}^2 - 9 \cdot \overline{Y}_{..}^2$$

$$= 1401 - 9 \cdot 11^2 = 1401 - 1089$$

$$= 312.$$

Thus, the sum of squares due to error is

$$SSE = SSTO - SSA - SSB$$

$$= 312 - 6 - 294 = 12.$$

The ANOVA table becomes:

| Source of Variation | Sum of Squares | Degrees of Freedom | Mean Squares |
|---|---|---|---|
| Factor A Temperature | 294 | 3 - 1 = 2 | 147 |
| Factor B Salinity | 6 | 3 - 1 = 2 | 3 |
| Error | 12 | (9 - 1) - 4 = 4 | 3 |

Referring to the previous problem test for the significance of the main effects.  Interpret the conclusions
of these tests.

Solution:     The test for a significant difference in
shrimp  yield due to differences in salinity involves
the hypotheses:

$H_0$:  there is no significant difference in yield
due to difference in salinity

vs.  $H_1$:  there is a significant difference.

Equivalently, we are testing

$H_0$:  $\beta_j = 0$                 $j = 1, 2, 3$

vs.  $H_1$:  $\beta_j \neq 0$   for at least one value of $j$

in the model,     $Y_{ij} = \mu. + \alpha_i + \beta_j + \varepsilon_{ij}$     $i = 1, 2, 3$

$j = 1, 2, 3.$

The test statistic for a test of this hypothesis is:

$$F = \frac{MSB}{MSE} = \frac{3}{3} = 1.$$

If the null hypothesis is true this test statistic
will be approximately distributed as an F-distributed
random variable with 2 and 4 degrees of freedom.  (These
degrees of freedom are those associated with the sum of
squares used in computing F.)

A level $\alpha$ test is to reject $H_0$ if the test statistic
F exceeds $F(1 - \alpha, 2, 4)$, the $1 - \alpha$ percentile of the F-
distribution with 2 and 4 degrees of freedom.

If we arbitrarily choose $\alpha$ to be .025, then we will
reject $H_0$ if  $F > F(.975, 2, 4) = 10.649$.
    $F = 1 < 10.649.$

Therefore accept $H_0$ at level of significance $\alpha = .025$.

Next test the hypothesis that there is a significant
difference in shrimp yield due to differences in levels of
temperature.  That is test:

$H_0$:  $\alpha_i = 0$                 $i = 1, 2, 3.$

vs.  $H_1$:  $\alpha_i \neq 0$ for at least one value of $i$.

For the model,  $Y_{ij} = \mu. + \alpha_i + \beta_j + \varepsilon_{ij}$ ;  $i = 1, 2, 3$

$j = 1, 2, 3.$

For similar reasons, a test for this hypothesis is to reject $H_0$ if $\frac{MSA}{MSE} > F(1 - \alpha, 2, 4)$. Choosing $\alpha$ to be .025 and using the tabulated values of the F-distribution we see that $F(1 - .025, 2, 4) = F(.975, 2, 4) = 10.649$ and from the previous problem, $\frac{MSA}{MSE} = \frac{147}{3} = 49 > 10.649$.

Thus, we reject $H_0$ and accept that there are differences in shrimp yield due to temperature at level of significance .025.

In summary, we conclude that $\beta_j = 0$ for $j = 1, 2, 3$ and that $\alpha_i \neq 0$ for at least one value of i. The model for describing shrimp yield is thus

$$Y_{ij} = \mu. + \alpha_i + \varepsilon_{ij} \qquad i = 1, 2, 3$$
$$j = 1, 2, 3.$$

This model implies that temperature is a more important factor than salinity in influencing shrimp yield. Differences in level of salinity appear to have no effect on shrimp yield at all.

● **PROBLEM** 18-18

An investigator performed an experiment with four experimental conditions. He wanted to learn whether distracting lights, odors and touches affect a secretary's ability to take dictation. The experimenter selected four-member groups from the secretarial pool. The four subjects within each group were then matched for their auditory acuity. Each secretary was then assigned at random to each condition. The scores indicating proficiency of dictation were:

C o n d i t i o n s

| | Distracting Lights | Distracting Odors | Distracting Touches | Control |
|---|---|---|---|---|
| Group 1 (excellent auditory ability) | 25 | 30 | 25 | 25 |
| Group 2 (good auditory ability) | 23 | 22 | 23 | 21 |
| Group 3 (medium auditory ability) | 19 | 23 | 20 | 24 |

798

| Group 4 (fair auditory ability) | 15 | 17 | 16 | 21 |
| Group 5 (poor auditory ability) | 15 | 15 | 15 | 24 |

Check for interactions by plotting these observations and then compute the ANOVA table.

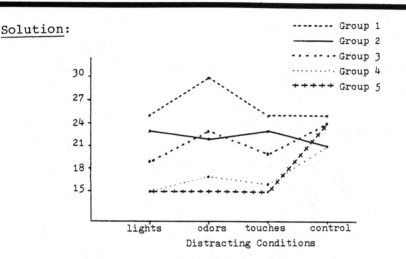

These lines are not parallel but except for two observations, the order between the groups is preserved. (Group 1 highest, Group 2 next, etc., and Group 5 the lowest.) This gives an indication that any possible interactions may be minor compared to the main effects. Because of this we may test for the main effects and ignore any variation due to interaction.

The row averages are:

$$\bar{Y}_1 \cdot = \frac{25 + 30 + 25 + 25}{4} = \frac{105}{4} = 26.25.$$

$$\bar{Y}_2 \cdot = \frac{23 + 22 + 23 + 21}{4} = \frac{89}{4} = 22.25.$$

$$\bar{Y}_3 \cdot = \frac{19 + 23 + 20 + 24}{4} = \frac{86}{4} = 21.5.$$

$$\bar{Y}_4 \cdot = \frac{15 + 17 + 16 + 21}{4} = \frac{69}{4} = 17.25.$$

$$\bar{Y}_5 \cdot = \frac{15 + 15 + 15 + 24}{4} = \frac{69}{4} = 17.25.$$

799

The column averages are:

$$\overline{Y}_{\cdot 1} = \frac{25 + 23 + 19 + 15 + 15}{5} = \frac{97}{5} = 19.4$$

$$\overline{Y}_{\cdot 2} = \frac{30 + 22 + 23 + 17 + 15}{5} = \frac{107}{5} = 21.4$$

$$\overline{Y}_{\cdot 3} = \frac{25 + 23 + 20 + 16 + 15}{5} = \frac{99}{5} = 19.8$$

$$\overline{Y}_{\cdot 4} = \frac{25 + 21 + 24 + 21 + 24}{5} = \frac{115}{5} = 23$$

and $\overline{Y}_{\cdot\cdot} = \frac{418}{20} = 20.9$.

Also $\displaystyle\sum_{i=1}^{5} \sum_{j=1}^{4} Y_{ij}^2 = 9086$.

Using these summary statistics we compute the necessary sums of squares:

SSA = sum of squares between conditions

$$= \sum_{i=1}^{5} \sum_{j=1}^{4} (\overline{Y}_i \cdot - \overline{Y}_{\cdot\cdot})^2$$

$$= 4 \sum_{i=1}^{5} (\overline{Y}_i \cdot - \overline{Y}_{\cdot\cdot})^2 \quad = 4 \sum_{i=1}^{5} \overline{Y}_i^2 \cdot - 20\, \overline{Y}_{\cdot\cdot}^2$$

$$= 4 \cdot (2241.5) - 20\,(20.9)^2$$

$$= 8966 - 8736.2 \quad = 229.8.$$

SSB = Sum of squares between groups

$$= \sum_{i=1}^{5} \sum_{j=1}^{4} (\overline{Y}_{\cdot j} - \overline{Y}_{\cdot\cdot})^2$$

$$= 5 \sum_{j=1}^{4} (\overline{Y}_{\cdot j} - \overline{Y}_{\cdot\cdot})^2 \quad = 5 \sum_{j=1}^{4} \overline{Y}_{\cdot j}^2 - 20\, \overline{Y}_{\cdot\cdot}^2$$

$$= 5(1755.36) - 20(20.9)^2$$

$$= 8776.8 - 8736.2 \quad = 40.6.$$

The total sum of squares is;

$$\text{SSTO} = \sum_{i=1}^{5} \sum_{j=1}^{4} (Y_{ij} - \overline{Y}_{\cdot\cdot})^2 \quad = \sum_{i=1}^{5} \sum_{j=1}^{4} Y_{ij}^2 - 20\, \overline{Y}_{\cdot\cdot}^2$$

$$= 9086 - 8736.2 = 349.8.$$

Thus, the error sum of squares, or residual variation is         SSE = SSTO - SSA - SSB

$$= 349.8 - 40.6 - 229.8 = 79.4 .$$

The ANOVA table is therefore:

| Source of Variation | Sum of Squares | Degrees of Freedom | Mean Squares |
|---|---|---|---|
| Group (auditory ability) | 229.8 | 5-1=4 | 57.45 |
| Condition | 40.6 | 4-1=3 | 13.53 |
| Error | 79.4 | 19-4-3=12 | 6.616 |
| Total | 349.8 | 20 - 1 = 19 | - |

● **PROBLEM** 18-19

Referring to the previous problem, test for significant differences in dictation ability due to differences in auditory ability.  Test at level of significance, $\alpha = .05$.

Solution:    Our original model is

$$Y_{ij} = \mu . + \alpha_i + \beta_j + \varepsilon_{ij} \qquad i = 1, \ldots 5$$
$$j = 1, \ldots 4 .$$

$Y_{ij}$ is the score measuring dictation proficiency. The $\alpha_i$ are the effects on dictation proficiency due to being in the ith group.

We test the null hypothesis;

$H_0$:    $\alpha_i = 0$        for i = 1, 2, 3, 4, 5

vs.    $H_1$:    $\alpha_i \neq 0$ for at least one value of i.

If the null hypothesis is true then

$$Y_{ij} = \mu . + \beta_j + \varepsilon_{ij} \qquad i = 1, 2, 3, 4, 5$$
$$j = 1, 2, 3, 4$$

and because $\varepsilon_{ij}$ are assumed to be independent, normally distributed random variables with mean 0 and variance $\sigma^2$, $E(Y_{ij}) = \mu . + \beta_j$ is constant for all values of i.  That is, we expect that a secretary's hearing ability will have no affect on dictation ability.

In addition, if $H_0$ is true then $\dfrac{MS_{group}}{MS_{error}}$ is approximately F-distributed with 4 and 14 degrees of freedom. Because of this, we will reject $H_0$ if $\dfrac{MS_{group}}{MS_{error}}$ is too large.

Specifically, we will reject $H_0$ at a level of significance of $\alpha = .05$ if $\dfrac{MS_{group}}{MS_{error}} > F(.95, 4, 12)$

where $F(.95, 4, 12)$ is the 95th percentile of the F-distribution with 4 and 12 degrees of freedom. From a table for the F-distribution this value is

$F(.95, 4, 12) = 3.2592$.

From the ANOVA table found in the previous problem we see that $\dfrac{MS_{group}}{MS_{error}} = \dfrac{57.45}{6.616} = 8.68$.

Thus, we reject $H_0$, and conclude that differences in hearing ability do have an affect on dictation proficiency.

● **PROBLEM** 18-20

From the data involving dictation ability, test for significant differences due to differences in the distracting condition. Use a level of signifigance of $\alpha = .05$.

Solution:   Our model is

$$Y_{ij} = \mu. + \alpha_i + \beta_j + \varepsilon_{ij} \qquad \begin{array}{l} i = 1, \ldots\ 5 \\ j = 1, \ldots\ 4 \end{array}$$

which has been previously described. The $\beta_j$ are the effects on dictation proficiency due to being distracted by the jth condition.

We test the null hypothesis

$H_0$:   $\beta_j = 0$      for $j = 1, 2, 3, 4$

vs.   $H_A$:   $\beta_j \neq 0$ for at least one value of j.

As before, if the null hypothesis is true, then

$$Y_{ij} = \mu. + \alpha_i + \varepsilon_{ij}, \quad i = 1, 2, 3, 4, 5$$
$$j = 1, 2, 3, 4$$

and we would expect that differences in distracting condition will have no effect on a secretary's ability to take dictation.

Our test is similar to that employed in the previous problem, but this time the test statistic involves the mean square due to differences between the distracting conditions. As in the previous problem we will reject $H_0$ if $\dfrac{MS_{condition}}{MS_{error}} > F(.95, 3, 12)$.

There are three degrees of freedom rather than four because there is one fewer column than row.

From the ANOVA table we see that

$$\frac{MS_{condition}}{MS_{error}} = \frac{13.53}{6.616} = 2.045.$$

Also, from the tables of the F-distribution we have that $F(.95, 3, 12) = 3.49$.

Since $2.045 < 3.49$ we accept $H_0$, that $\beta_j = 0$ for $j = 1, 2, 3, 4$ and finally conclude that there is no difference in dictation skills due to differences in the distracting condition.

# RANDOM EFFECTS MODEL

● PROBLEM 18-21

A certain drug is thought to have an effect on the ability to perform mental arithmetic. The quantity of the drug used may vary from 0 to 100 milligrams.

One possible experiment would be to test all possible levels of this drug on groups of subjects and then use analysis of variance to detect differences. Because of limited funds, only six levels of the drug may be tested. Describe two methods of implementing and analyzing this experiment.

Solution: One possibility would be to systematically choose a set of levels covering the range of doses. For example, one might choose 0, 20, 40, 60, 80, and 100. The differences in mental arithmetic scores could then be analyzed using one-way analysis of variance. The model analyzed would be

$$Y_{ij} = \mu. + \alpha_i + \varepsilon_{ij} \qquad i = 1, 2, 3, 4, 5, 6$$
$$j = 1, 2, \ldots n$$

where $Y_{ij}$ is the mental arithmetic test score, $\alpha_i$ is the fixed effect of dosage level i and $\varepsilon_{ij}$ is a zero-mean normally distributed random variable.

Another possibility is to choose the six dose levels randomly from the set of numbers 1 to 100. If this experiment were repeated then different levels might be chosen. The ith dosage level changes and because of this the effect of the ith treatment is a random variable. The model to be analyzed becomes

$$Y_{ij} = \mu_1 + \alpha_i + \varepsilon_{ij} \qquad i = 1, \ldots 6$$
$$j = 1, \ldots n$$

where $Y_{ij}$, $\mu_1$ and $\varepsilon_{ij}$ are as before, but $\alpha_i$ (the effect due to the ith treatment) is a random variable. This is called the random effects model. The $\alpha_i$ are usually assumed to have a mean of zero and be normally distributed with variance $\sigma_\alpha^2$.

● **PROBLEM 18-22**

There is some evidence that a new drug may be able to relieve cold symptoms more quickly than those already on the market. There is some doubt about whether different dosages have an effect on the time before relief is felt. Of many possible dosages, three are randomly chosen and administered to four adults with colds. The elapsed times (in hours) before relief was felt are:

| Dosage 1 | Dosage 2 | Dosage 3 |
|----------|----------|----------|
| 2.0 | 2.3 | 3.4 |
| 1.5 | 2.6 | 4.0 |
| 2.5 | 3.0 | 4.6 |
| 2.0 | 2.5 | 4.4 |

Describe an appropriate model for this experiment and compute an ANOVA table for this data.

Solution: The dosages constitute a random sample from a larger population. Thus, the random effects model is appropriate. We assume that the model underlying this experiment is the following

$$Y_{ij} = \mu. + \alpha_i + \varepsilon_{ij} \qquad i = 1, 2, 3$$
$$j = 1, 2, 3, 4$$

where $Y_{ij}$ = elapsed time until relief is felt

$\mu.$ = overall mean time until relief is felt

$\alpha_i$ = random effect of dosage level i (assumed to be normally distributed with mean zero and variance $\sigma_\alpha^2$)

$\varepsilon_{ij}$ = a random error term (assumed to be normally distributed with mean zero and variance $\sigma^2$).

The ANOVA table for this experiment is computed as in previous problems. The summary statistics are:

$$\overline{Y}_1. = 2$$

$$\overline{Y}_2. = 2.6$$

$$\overline{Y}_3. = 4.1$$

$$\sum_{i=1}^{3} \sum_{j=1}^{4} Y_{ij}^2 = 111.88, \qquad \overline{Y}.. = 2.9.$$

The sum of squares between dosages are

$$SSTR = \sum_{i=1}^{3} \sum_{j=1}^{4} (\overline{Y}_i. - \overline{Y}..)^2 = 4 \sum_{i=1}^{3} \overline{Y}_i.^2 - 12 \, \overline{Y}..^2.$$

$$= 4(4 + 16.81 + 6.76) - 12(2.9)^2$$

$$= 4(27.57) - 12(2.9)^2$$

$$= 110.28 - 100.92 = 9.36.$$

Total sum of squares:

$$SSTO = \sum_{i=1}^{3} \sum_{j=1}^{4} (Y_{ij} - \overline{Y}..)^2 = \sum_{i=1}^{3} \sum_{j=1}^{4} Y_{ij}^2 - 12 (\overline{Y}..)^2$$

$$= 111.88 - 100.92 = 10.96.$$

Thus, the error or residual sum of squares is

$$SSE = \sum_{i=1}^{3} \sum_{j=1}^{4} (Y_{ij} - \overline{Y}_i.)^2 = SSTO - SSTR$$

$$= 10.96 - 9.36 = 1.6.$$

The ANOVA table is

| Source of Variation | Sum of Squares | Degrees of Freedom | Mean Squares |
|---|---|---|---|
| Dosage levels | 9.36 | $3 - 1 = 2$ | 4.68 |
| Error | 1.6 | $11 - 2 = 9$ | .18 |
| Total | 10.96 | 11 | - |

● **PROBLEM** 18-23

Referring to the previous problem, devise a test for determining whether the dosage level has any effect on the time before relief is felt. Test this hypothesis at the .05 level of significance.

<u>Solution</u>:     We wish to test the null hypothesis.

$H_0$:  the effect on relief time of each dosage level is the same

vs.  $H_A$:  relief time is affected by dosage level.

In the fixed effects model we tested that $\alpha_1 = \alpha_2 = \ldots = \alpha_k = 0$. However, in the random effects model, the $\alpha_i$ are random variables and a statement about equality of random variables has little meaning for the purpose of this test.

However, if the common variance, as well as the mean of the $\alpha_i$ is zero, then the $\alpha_i$ will all be equal to zero. That is, there will be no effect of dosage level on time before relief is felt.  The null hypothesis is thus:

$H_0$:     $\sigma_\alpha^2 = 0$     vs.  $H_1$:     $\sigma_\alpha^2 \neq 0$.

The test for the fixed effects model applies only to the levels used in the test.  The results of the test for random effects may be extended to all possible levels. This is because the levels used in the random effects test constitute a random sample from the population of all possible levels and are, in a sense, representative of that population.

The student may be surprised to learn that the procedures for testing this hypothesis are the same as those previously shown.

If the null hypothesis is true, then the statistic $\frac{MSTR}{MSE}$ is approximately distributed with an F distribution with degrees of freedom;

# dosages - 1  and # observations - (#dosages - 1) - 1.

In this problem, $\frac{MSTR}{MSE} = \frac{4.68}{.18} = 26$  and the F-distribution will have $3 - 1 = 2$ and $12 - (3 - 1) - 1 = 9$ degrees of freedom.

If  $\frac{MSTR}{MSE} > F(1 - \alpha, 2, 9)$ then we will reject $H_0$ at the level of significance $\alpha$.

Setting $\alpha = .05$, we see from tables of the F-distribution that $F(.95, 2, 9) = 4.256 < 26$ ; thus we reject $H_0$ and conclude that different dosages do have an effect on the time until relief is felt.

● **PROBLEM** 18-24

A litigation-support firm wishes to determine whether

there is a significant variation in the number of
documents processed by different groups in the New York
office.  Because of the large number of groups in this
office, a sample of 4 groups is chosen and the number of
documents processed in 5 randomly selected weeks is
recorded.  The data is as follows:

| Supervisor | Documents Processed | Average |
|---|---|---|
| Jenny – | 215, 218, 175, 205, 200 | 196 |
| Joanna – | 175, 150, 225, 200, 220 | 194 |
| Dianna Lee – | 240, 210, 200, 230, 215 | 219 |
| Art – | 160, 170, 195, 200, 180 | 181 |

Test for differences in the number of documents
processed by different groups in the entire office.

Solution:    Using the random effects model we assume
that the number of documents processed in the jth week
by the ith group is

$$Y_{ij} = \mu. + \alpha_i + \varepsilon_{ij} \qquad \begin{array}{l} i = 1, 2, 3, 4 \\ j = 1, 2, 3, 4, 5 \end{array}$$

where $\alpha_i$ is the random effect of the ith group and is
normally distributed with mean 0 and variance $\sigma_\alpha^2$.  The
error term is assumed to be normally distributed with
mean 0 and variance $\sigma^2$.

The sums of squares are computed in the usual way
and we see that the sum of squares due to differences

between groups is:    $SSTR = \sum\limits_{i=1}^{4} \sum\limits_{j=1}^{5} (\overline{Y}_i. - \overline{Y}..)^2$

$= 5 \sum\limits_{i=1}^{4} (\overline{Y}_i. - \overline{Y}..)^2 = 5 \sum\limits_{i=1}^{4} \overline{Y}_i^2. - 20 \overline{Y}_.^2.$

$= 5(156,774) - 20(197.5)^2 = 783,870 - 20(39,006.25)$

$= 783,870 - 780,125 = 3745.$

The total sum of squares is:

$SSTO = \sum\limits_{i=1}^{4} \sum\limits_{j=1}^{5} (Y_{ij} - \overline{Y}..)^2 = \sum\limits_{i=1}^{4} \sum\limits_{j=1}^{5} Y_{ij}^2 - 20 \overline{Y}_.^2.$

$= 804,299 - 780,125 = 24,174.$

Thus, the error sum of squares is:

$SSE = \sum\limits_{i=1}^{4} \sum\limits_{j=1}^{5} (Y_{ij} - \overline{Y}..)^2$

$$= SSTO - SSTR$$

$$= 24,174 - 3745 = 20,429.$$

The ANOVA table is therefore:

| Source of Variation | Sum of Squares | Degrees of Freedom | Mean Squares |
|---|---|---|---|
| Between Groups | 3745 | 4 - 1 = 3 | 1248.33 |
| Error | 20,429 | 16 | 1276.81 |

To test the hypothesis that the groups do not process different numbers of documents, we reject

$$H_0: \quad \sigma_\alpha^2 = 0 \quad \text{at the .05 level if}$$

$$\frac{MSTR}{MSE} > F(.95, 3, 16).$$

$$\frac{MSTR}{MSE} = \frac{1248.33}{1276.81} = 0.9777.$$

From the tables of F-distribution, we find that the 95th percentile of the F-distribution with 3 and 16 degrees of freedom is:

$$F(.95, 3, 16) = 3.2389 > \frac{MSTR}{MSE}$$

Therefore we accept $H_0$: that there is no difference between the number of documents processed in the office.

# CHAPTER 19

# CHI-SQUARE AND CONTINGENCY TABLES

## CONTINGENCY TABLES

● PROBLEM 19-1

The results of a survey show that the 518 respondents may be categorized as

| | |
|---|---|
| Protestant - Republicans | 126 |
| Protestant - Democrats | 71 |
| Protestant - Independents | 19 |
| Catholic - Republicans | 61 |
| Catholic - Democrats | 93 |
| Catholic - Independents | 14 |
| Jewish - Republicans | 38 |
| Jewish - Democrats | 69 |
| Jewish - Independents | 27 |

Given this data construct a contingency table.

Solution:    A contingency table provides a way of simplifying the presentation of data. Each cell of such a table represents the number of observations belonging to a particular category or class of the data. The labels of this class are found in the column and row corresponding to the cell.

Contingency tables provide a useful method of comparing two variables. We are often interested in the possibility of relationship between two variables.

Also of interest are the degree or strength of relation between two variables and the significance of the relationship. Contingency tables are essential with nominal variables such as religion, political affiliation, or occupation.

The contingency table for the data in this problem is below:

Religion

| Political Party | Protestants | Catholics | Jews | Row Totals |
|---|---|---|---|---|
| Republicans | 126 | 61 | 38 | 225 |
| Democrats | 71 | 93 | 69 | 233 |
| Independents | 19 | 14 | 27 | 60 |
| Column Totals | 216 | 168 | 134 | 518 |

The row totals are formed by summing along the rows. Thus there are

| 225 | Republicans | |
|---|---|---|
| 233 | Democrats | and |
| 60 | Independents | |

in the sample.

The column totals are formed by summing down the columns. Thus there are

| 216 | Protestants | |
|---|---|---|
| 168 | Catholics | and |
| 134 | Jews | in the sample. |

The sum of the column totals equals the sum of the row totals and both are equal to the number of observations in the sample.

● **PROBLEM** 19-2

Of 12 sampled workers who are 50 years of age or over, 2 had an industrial accident last year and 10 did not. Of 18 sampled workers under 50 years of age, 8 had industrial accidents. Construct a contingency table to represent these findings.

Solution:     The contingency table is:

| | Accident | No Accident |
|---|---|---|
| Under 50 years old | 8 | 18 - 8 = 10 |
| 50 years or older | 2 | 12 - 2 = 10 |

The number of workers who are under 50 and had an accident is in the 1st cell, 8.

The number of workers who are under 50 and had no accidents is the second cell. This is 10.

The number of workers who are over 50 and had no accidents was 10 and in the lower right hand cell.

The number of workers who are over 50 and had an accident is in the lower left hand cell. This is 2.

# CHI-SQUARE TESTS AND CONTINGENCY TABLES

A die was tossed 120 times and the results are listed below.

| Upturned face | 1 | 2 | 3 | 4 | 5 | 6 |
|---|---|---|---|---|---|---|
| Frequency | 18 | 23 | 16 | 21 | 18 | 24 |

Compute the $\chi^2$ statistic for this 1 by 6 contingency table under the hypothesis that the die was fair.

Solution:    The $\chi^2$ statistic provides a means of comparing observed frequencies with expected frequencies.

This statistic is defined to be

$$\chi^2 = \sum_{i=1}^{n} \frac{(O_i - E_i)^2}{E_i}$$

where $O_i$ is the observed frequency in cell i, $E_i$ is the expected frequency found from some underlying probability model which must be assumed, and n is the number of cells.

The chi-square statistic ($\chi^2$) is approximately distributed with a chi-square distribution. This distribution is found tabulated in many statistics texts. The $\chi^2$ statistic has a parameter called degrees of freedom associated with it.

In this problem, we assume that the die is fair. That is, any face will land upturned with probability $\frac{1}{6}$. If this model is valid we would expect equal numbers of each face to appear, or $\frac{120}{6} = 20$ occurrences of each face. The expected frequencies are

| Upturned face | 1 | 2 | 3 | 4 | 5 | 6 |
|---|---|---|---|---|---|---|
| $E_i$, expected frequency if die is fair | 20 | 20 | 20 | 20 | 20 | 20 |

Thus we can compute the $\chi^2$ statistic from the observed and expected frequencies.

The degrees of freedom of a 1 by n contingency table is n - 1. In our problem n = 6 thus n - 1 = 6 - 1 = 5 degrees of freedom.

The chi-square statistic will give some idea of the difference between the hypothesized model and the observed frequencies. The $\chi^2$ statistic, with its distribution, will allow us to test the significance of the hypothesized probability model.

$$\chi^2 = \sum_{i=1}^{6} \frac{(O_i - E_i)^2}{E_i}$$

$$= \frac{(18 - 20)^2}{20} + \frac{(23 - 20)^2}{20} + \frac{(16 - 20)^2}{20}$$

$$+ \frac{(21 - 20)^2}{20} + \frac{(18 - 20)^2}{20} + \frac{(24 - 20)^2}{20}$$

$$= \frac{1}{20} [(- 2)^2 + 3^2 + (- 4)^2 + 1^2 + (- 2)^2 + 4^2]$$

$$= \frac{1}{20} [4 + 9 + 16 + 1 + 4 + 16] = \frac{50}{20}$$

$$= 2.5 \qquad \text{with 5 degrees of freedom.}$$

● **PROBLEM** 19-4

Let the result of a random experiment be classified by two attributes. Let these two attributes be eye color and hair color. One attribute of the outcome, eye color, can be divided into certain mutually exclusive and exhaustive events. Let these events be:

A₁ : Blue eyes
A₂ : Brown eyes
A₃ : Grey eyes
A₄ : Black eyes
A₅ : Green eyes

The other attribute of the outcome can also be divided into certain mutually exclusive and exhaustive events. Let these events be:

B₁ : Blond hair
B₂ : Brown hair
B₃ : Black hair

812

$B_4$ : Red hair .

The experiment is performed by observing n = 500 people and each of them are categorized according to eye color and hair color. Let $A_i \cap B_j$ be the event that a person with eye color $A_i$ and hair color $B_j$ is observed, i = 1, 2, 3, 4, 5 and j = 1, 2, 3, 4. Let $X_{ij}$ be the observed frequency of event $A_i \cap B_j$. Test the hypothesis that $A_i$ and $B_j$ are independent attributes.

Solution:     Let $p_{ij} = P(A_i \cap B_j)$.

We wish to test the hypothesis

$H_o$:   $P(A_i \cap B_j) = P(A_i)P(B_j)$           against

$H_A$: $P(A_i \cap B_j) \neq P(A_i)P(B_j)$.

Let

$$Q_{5 \cdot 4 - 1} = \sum_{j=1}^{4} \sum_{i=1}^{5} \frac{(X_{ij} - np_{ij})^2}{np_{ij}} .$$

It can be shown that this random variable is $\chi^2$ with $5 \cdot 4 - 1 = 19$ degrees of freedom.

Let     $p_i = \sum_{j=1}^{4} p_{ij}$                 and

$p_j = \sum_{i=1}^{5} p_{ij}$     . We see that

$P(A_i) = p_i$         and     $P(B_j) = p_j$ .

Our hypothesis can be reformulated as:

$H_o$:   $p_{ij} = p_i\, p_j$

$H_A$: $p_{ij} \neq p_i\, p_j$ .

To test $H_o$, we use Q with $p_{ij}$ replaced by $p_i\, p_j$. The truth of $H_o$ would make no difference in the statistic Q if we effect this change.

$p_i$ and $p_j$ are unknown and must be estimated from the observed frequencies. It is reasonable to estimate $p_{ij}$ by

813

$$\hat{p}_{ij} = \frac{X_{ij}}{n} \ .$$

Then the estimate of $p_i$ would be

$$\hat{p}_i = \sum_{j=1}^{4} \hat{p}_{ij} = \frac{\sum_{j=1}^{4} X_{ij}}{n}$$

and similarly, $p_j$ is estimated by

$$\hat{p}_j = \sum_{i=1}^{5} \hat{p}_{ij} = \frac{\sum_{i=1}^{5} X_{ij}}{n} \ .$$

If the observations were put in a contingency table with $X_{ij}$ as the frequency of observations in the i-jth cell,

$\sum_{j=1}^{4} X_{ij}$ and $\sum_{i=1}^{5} X_{ij}$ are the quantities found by summing

down the column and summing across the rows. Let the following contingency table represent the observed frequencies among the 500 people.

| Eye Color | Hair Color | | | | Row Totals |
|---|---|---|---|---|---|
| | Blond | Brown | Black | Red | |
| Blue | 50 | 87 | 5 | 8 | 150 |
| Brown | 40 | 69 | 60 | 11 | 180 |
| Grey | 15 | 13 | 42 | 5 | 75 |
| Black | 5 | 27 | 17 | 1 | 50 |
| Green | 15 | 4 | 1 | 25 | 45 |
| Totals | 125 | 200 | 125 | 50 | 500 |

Substituting $\hat{p}_i$ and $\hat{p}_j$ into Q we get

$$\hat{Q} = \sum_{j=1}^{4} \sum_{i=1}^{5} \frac{(X_{ij} - n\hat{p}_i\hat{p}_j)^2}{n\hat{p}_i\hat{p}_j}$$

where we made 5 - 1 substitutions for $p_i$, $i = 1, \ldots 5$ and
4 - 1 substitutions for $p_j$, $j = 1, \ldots 4$. Thus we lost
$(5 - 1) + (4 - 1)$ degrees of freedom by making these
substitutions. Hence $\hat{Q}$ is approximately chi-square distributed
with

$$5 \cdot 4 - 1 - (5 - 1) - (4 - 1)$$

$$= 4(5 - 1) - 5 - 1 + 1 + 1$$

$$= 4(5 - 1) - (5 - 1) = (5 - 1)(4 - 1)$$

$$= 12 .$$

Another interpretation of degrees of freedom can be
seen. In an r × c contingency table the number of degrees
of freedom is $(r - 1)(c - 1)$, the product of the number
rows minus 1 and the number of columns minus 1.

The number of degrees of freedom is the number of cells
that can vary given that the marginal column and row totals
are fixed.

The $\hat{p}_i$'s are:

$$\hat{p}_1 = \frac{150}{500} = \frac{3}{10}$$

$$\hat{p}_2 = \frac{180}{500} = \frac{9}{25}$$

$$\hat{p}_3 = \frac{75}{500} = \frac{3}{20}$$

$$\hat{p}_4 = \frac{50}{500} = \frac{1}{10}$$

$$\hat{p}_5 = \frac{45}{500} = \frac{9}{100} .$$

The $\hat{p}_j$'s are:

$$\hat{p}_1 = \frac{125}{500} = \frac{1}{4}$$

$$\hat{p}_2 = \frac{200}{500} = \frac{2}{5}$$

$$\hat{p}_3 = \frac{125}{500} = \frac{1}{4}$$

$$\hat{p}_4 = \frac{50}{500} = \frac{1}{10} .$$

The level of significance will be arbitrarily set at
$\alpha = .05$, for which the critical value is 21.026, for 12 degrees
of freedom. If the chi-square statistic is greater than
21.026, then we will reject $H_0$.

The expected observations given independence of eye
color and hair color and these marginal distributions are

|        | Blond | Brown | Black | Red |
|--------|-------|-------|-------|-----|
| Blue   | 37.5  | 60    | 37.5  | 15  |
| Brown  | 45    | 72    | 45    | 18  |
| Grey   | 18.75 | 30    | 18.75 | 7.5 |
| Black  | 12.5  | 20    | 12.5  | 5   |
| Green  | 11.25 | 18    | 11.25 | 4.5 |

The i - jth component of this table is

$$n \, \hat{p}_i \hat{p}_j = E_{ij} .$$

The test statistic is thus

$$\hat{Q} = \sum_{j=1}^{4} \sum_{i=1}^{5} \frac{(X_{ij} - E_{ij})^2}{E_{ij}}$$

$$= \frac{(50 - 37.5)^2}{37.5} + \frac{(87 - 60)^2}{60} + \ldots + \frac{(25 - 4.5)^2}{4.5}$$

$$= 4.17 + 12.15 + 28.167 + 3.27 + .55 + .125 + 5$$

$$+ 3.27 + .65 + .3 + 28.83 + .83 + 4.5 + 2.45$$

$$+ 1.62 + 3.2 + 1.25 + 12.8 + 10.58 + 93.38$$

$$= 217.$$

Thus, $\hat{Q} = 217$, thus $\hat{Q} > 21.026$ and we reject the hypothesis that these two attributes eye color and hair color are independent.

A final note of caution; the approximation of $\hat{Q}$ to the chi-square distribution is most valid if all the expected frequencies are at least 5. The approximation is less valid if the table is 2 by 2.

It is sometimes maintained that women sleep less soundly after having children than they did beforehand. Suppose we asked 60 women with children, and found:

| Number of children | Present sleep compared with before having children – | | |
| --- | --- | --- | --- |
| | Worse | Same | Better |
| 1 | 25 | 5 | 0 |
| 2 | 10 | 4 | 1 |
| 3 or more | 5 | 7 | 3 |

What inference can you draw from this data?

**Solution:**   We first compute the row and column totals for this three by three contingency table. They are:

| Number of Children | Slept worse | Slept the same | Slept better | Row totals |
| --- | --- | --- | --- | --- |
| 1 | 25 | 5 | 0 | 30 |
| 2 | 10 | 4 | 1 | 15 |
| 3 or more | 5 | 7 | 3 | 15 |
| Column totals | 40 | 16 | 4 | 60 |

We will justify and use the chi-square test.

Remember that the $\chi^2$ test is appropriate only if the expected frequencies are greater than five. In this three by three table, the expected frequencies are not all greater than five. These expected frequencies are computed and tabulated below;

$$E_{ij} = np_i p_j = \frac{\text{ith row total} \times \text{jth column total}}{\text{total number of observations}} .$$

This expected value is computed under the assumption that the two attributes making up the table are in fact independent.

For this table,

$$E_{11} = \frac{30 \times 40}{60} = 20 \qquad E_{21} = \frac{40 \times 15}{60} = 10$$

$$E_{12} = \frac{30 \times 16}{60} = 8 \qquad E_{22} = \frac{16 \times 15}{60} = 4$$

$$E_{13} = \frac{4 \times 30}{60} = 2 \qquad E_{23} = \frac{4 \times 15}{60} = 1.$$

The other expected frequencies can be computed in a similar way. We notice that there are so few respondents who slept better after having children that the expected frequencies in the third column are all less than 5. The $\chi^2$ test is thus not appropriate.

We can still investigate this question by merging two or more of the categories. If all respondents who slept better and who slept the same are put in one category the contingency table will be

| Number of Children | Sleeping Worse | Sleeping Better or Same | Row Totals |
|---|---|---|---|
| 1 | 25 | 5 + 0 = 5 | 30 |
| 2 | 10 | 4 + 1 = 5 | 15 |
| 3 or more | 5 | 7 + 3 = 10 | 15 |
| Column totals | 40 | 20 | 60 |

This pooling of categories will not effect the aim of the investigation and now the expected frequencies will all be greater than 5 so that the $\chi^2$ test is applicable. The expected frequencies have been computed in precisely the same way as before and are found in the table below.

| ith Row Total $i = 1, 2, 3$ (R) | jth Column Total $j = 1, 2$ (C) | $\frac{R \times C}{n} = E_{ij}$ |
|---|---|---|
| 30 | 40 | 20 |
| 30 | 20 | 10 |
| 15 | 40 | 10 |
| 15 | 20 | 5 |
| 15 | 40 | 10 |
| 15 | 20 | 5 |

The chi-square statistic is thus

$$\chi_2^2 = \sum_{i,j} \frac{(\text{observed}_{ij} - \text{expected}_{ij})^2}{\text{expected}_{ij}}$$

$$= \frac{(20 - 25)^2}{20} + \frac{(5 - 10)^2}{10} + \frac{(10 - 10)^2}{10} + \frac{(5 - 5)^2}{5}$$

$$+ \frac{(5 - 10)^2}{10} + \frac{(10 - 5)^2}{5}$$

$$= \frac{25}{20} + \frac{25}{10} + 0 + 0 + \frac{25}{10} + \frac{25}{5} = 5 + 5 + \frac{5}{4} = 11.25 .$$

For two degrees of freedom, we see from the chi-square table that if the attributes
of sleeping and number of children are in fact independent then we can expect such a statistic less than 1% of the time. Thus it is very unlikely that these two attributes are independent and so there is a significant relation between number of children and sleeping.

● **PROBLEM** 19-6

Often frequency data are tabulated according to two criteria, with a view toward testing whether the criteria are associated. Consider the following analysis of the 157 machine breakdowns during a given quarter.

Number of Breakdowns

| | Machine | | | | |
|---|---|---|---|---|---|
| | A | B | C | D | Total per Shift |
| Shift 1 | 10 | 6 | 13 | 13 | 41 |
| Shift 2 | 10 | 12 | 19 | 21 | 62 |
| Shift 3 | 13 | 10 | 13 | 18 | 54 |
| Total per machine | 33 | 28 | 44 | 52 | 157 |

We are interested in whether the same percentage of breakdown occurs on each machine during each shift or whether there is some difference due perhaps to untrained operators or other factors peculiar to a given shift.

Solution:    If the number of breakdowns is independent
of the shifts and machines, then the probability of a breakdown
occurring in the first shift and in the first machine can
be estimated by multiplying the proportion of first shift
breakdowns by the proportion of machine A breakdowns.

If the attributes of shift and particular machine
are independent,

Pr(Breakdown on Machine A during shift 1)

= Pr(breakdown on Machine A) ×

Pr(breakdown during shift 1)

where

Pr(Breakdown on Machine A) is estimated by

$$\frac{\text{number of breakdowns on A}}{\text{total number of breakdowns}} = \frac{33}{157}$$

and

Pr(Breakdown during shift 1)

$$= \frac{\text{number of breakdowns in shift 1}}{\text{total number of breakdowns}}$$

$$= \frac{41}{157} \quad .$$

Of the 157 breakdowns, given independence of machine
and shift, we would expect

$$(157) \left(\frac{41}{157}\right)\left(\frac{33}{157}\right) = \frac{41 \cdot 33}{157}$$

breakdowns on machine A and during the first shift.

Similarly, for the third shift and second machine, we
would expect

$$\left(\frac{54}{157}\right)\left(\frac{28}{157}\right) \cdot 157 = \frac{54 \cdot 28}{157} \quad \text{breakdowns.}$$

The expected breakdowns for different shifts and
machines are

$$E_{11} = \frac{41 \times 33}{157} = 8.62$$

$$E_{12} = \frac{28 \times 41}{157} = 7.3$$

$$E_{13} = \frac{44 \times 41}{157} = 11.5$$

$$E_{14} = \frac{52 \times 41}{157} = 13.57 \quad .$$

820

Similarly, the other expected breakdowns given independence are:

|  | A | B | C | D |
|---|---|---|---|---|
| Shift 1 | 8.62 | 7.3 | 11.5 | 13.57 |
| Shift 2 | 13.03 | 11.06 | 17.38 | 20.54 |
| Shift 3 | 11.35 | 9.63 | 15.13 | 17.88 |

We will assume that the $\chi^2$ test is applicable. There are $r = 3$ rows and $c = 4$ columns; thus, the chi-square statistic will have $(3 - 1)(4 - 1) = 6$ degrees of freedom. The level of significance of this hypothesis will be $\alpha = .05$. This is the probability of rejecting independence of attributes (the null hypothesis) given that the attributes are in fact independent.

If this statistic is greater than 12.6, then we will reject the hypothesis that the machine and shift are independent attributes in determining incidence of breakdown.

The chi-square statistic is

$$\chi_6^2 = \sum_{i=1}^{3} \sum_{j=1}^{4} \frac{(O_{ij} - E_{ij})^2}{E_{ij}} = 2.17.$$

We see that $2.17 < 12.6$. Thus we accept that the attributes of machine and shift are independent in determining incidence of breakdown.

● PROBLEM 19-7

Is there a significant relationship between the hair color of a husband and wife? A researcher observes 500 pairs and collects the following data.

| WIFE | H U S B A N D | | | | Row Total |
|---|---|---|---|---|---|
|  | Red | Blonde | Black | Brown |  |
| Red | 10 | 10 | 10 | 20 | 50 |
| Blonde | 10 | 40 | 50 | 50 | 150 |
| Black | 13 | 25 | 60 | 52 | 150 |
| Brown | 17 | 25 | 30 | 78 | 150 |
| Column total | 50 | 100 | 150 | 200 | 500 |

The researcher wishes to test the theory that people tend to select mates with the same hair color.

Test this theory at the level of significance $\alpha = .01$.

Solution: We wish to test the following hypotheses:

$H_o$: Husband's and Wife's hair color are independent

$H_A$: People tend to select mates with the same hair color. (Husband's and Wife's hair color are dependent.)

We will now determine a critical region for our $\chi^2$-statistic. The table has 4 rows and 4 columns, thus the statistic will have $(4 - 1)(4 - 1) = 9$ degrees of freedom. The critical region will be determined by a constant c such that if $\chi_9^2$ is a random variable with 9 degrees of freedom,

$$\Pr(\chi_9^2 > c) = .01.$$

From the table of the chi-square distribution we see that $c = 21.67$. If our chi-square statistic is greater than 21.67 we will reject $H_o$ and accept $H_A$. If the chi-square statistic is less than 21.67 we will accept $H_o$.

To compute the chi-square statistic we first need to compute the expected frequencies based on a sample of 500 couples if the null hypothesis is true.

If husband's and wife's hair color are independent, the expected frequencies in the cells of the table will be determined by the marginal frequencies. We have see that

$$E_{ij} = \frac{R_i \times C_j}{N}$$

where $R_i$ is the ith row total, $C_j$ is the jth column total and $N = 500$ is the total number of observations.

For example, the expected number of observations in cell $(4,1)$, the expected number of couples where the husband has red hair and the wife has brown hair is

$$\frac{50 \times 150}{500} = 15.$$

822

The expected frequencies for each cell are calculated in a similar way and are given below.

| Wife | Husband | | | |
|------|-----|--------|-------|-------|
|      | Red | Blonde | Black | Brown |
| Red    | 5  | 10 | 15 | 20 |
| Blonde | 15 | 30 | 45 | 60 |
| Black  | 15 | 30 | 45 | 60 |
| Brown  | 15 | 30 | 45 | 60 |

The chi-square statistic is

$$\chi_9^2 = \sum_{i=1}^{4} \sum_{j=1}^{4} \frac{(O_{ij} - E_{ij})^2}{E_{ij}} = 32.57.$$

Since the chi-square statistic is greater than the critical value c, we reject the null hypothesis and accept the hypothesis that people tend to select mates with the same hair color.

# FISHER'S TEST AND 2 × 2 TABLES

● PROBLEM 19-8

Suppose we wish to test whether a new drug aids the recovery of patients suffering from a mental illness when it is known that some patients recover spontaneously without any treatment at all. Starting with m + n patients, we create two groups. One group of m patients gets no treatment and thus acts as a control group for the treatment group, which contains n patients.

At the end of the experiment, the numbers of patients who recovered are j and k. If in fact that drug has no effect, then it is as if there were j + k among the n + m who were bound to recover anyway. Find the probability that k recover in the treatment group only by virtue of drawing a random sample of n from n + m.

Solution:    We wish to find the probability that a sample of n from n + m contains k of k + j and n - k of the remaining n + m - (j + k). This is the probability that the k patients who recover with treatment do so only because they happen to be in a random sample of n patients chosen from n + m.

To compute this probability, first count the number of ways n patients can be chosen from n + m. This is $\binom{n + m}{n}$. Since the drug is not effective, we now ask how many ways can the sample of n be chosen so that it contains k patients from the k + j who would have recovered anyway and thus n - k patients from the remaining n + m - (j + k) who would not have recovered. The first number is $\binom{k + j}{k}$ and the second $\binom{n + m - (j + k)}{n - k}$; thus $\binom{k + j}{k}\binom{n + m - (j + k)}{n - k}$ ways in all.

The Pr(observing k in the treatment group recover when the drug has no effect) = the number of ways n patients can be chosen containing k recoverables and n - k unrecoverables divided by the number of ways n patients can be chosen from the n + m total or

$$\frac{\binom{k + j}{k}\binom{n + m - (j + k)}{n - k}}{\binom{n + m}{n}}.$$ This equals:

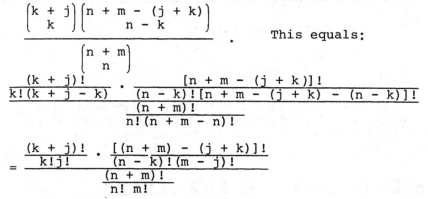

$$\frac{(k + j)!}{k!(k + j - k)} \cdot \frac{[n + m - (j + k)]!}{(n - k)![n + m - (j + k) - (n - k)]!}}{\frac{(n + m)!}{n!(n + m - n)!}}$$

$$= \frac{\frac{(k + j)!}{k!j!} \cdot \frac{[(n + m) - (j + k)]!}{(n - k)!(m - j)!}}{\frac{(n + m)!}{n!\,m!}}$$

$$= \frac{(k + j)!(n + m - j - k)!\,n!m!}{k!\,j!\,(n - k)!(m - j)!\,(n + m)!}.$$

This is sometimes known as Fisher's Test.

● **PROBLEM** 19-9

Two machines process raw materials from two different suppliers, A and B. A record of machine breakdowns is kept. This record mentions the raw material which was being processed at the time of breakdown. This record is:

| Machine | Supplier A | Supplier B | Row Totals |
|---------|-----------|-----------|-----------|
| I | 4 | 9 | 13 |
| II | 15 | 3 | 18 |
| Column total | 19 | 12 | 31 |

Is there a significant relation between the source of raw material and the occurrence of breakdowns?

**Solution:** Because this is a two by two table, the approximation of $X^2$ distribution is not appropriate. We may use Fisher's Test to calculate directly the probability that these observations are due to random factors. If the probability that these observations are due to chance alone is very small, say less than .01, we will accept the existence of a relationship between the sourceof raw materials and breakdown.

In the previous problem, this probability was found to be:

$$P = \frac{(j + k)!\,(n + m - j - k)!\,n!\,m!}{k!\,j!\,(n - k)!\,(m - j)!\,(n + m)!}$$

where in this case $k = 4$, $j = 15$, $n = 13$, $m = 18$. Thus

$$P = \frac{19!}{4!}\,\frac{12!}{15!}\,\frac{13!\,18!}{9!\,3!\,31!} = \frac{(19 \times 18 \times 17 \times 16)(12 \times 11 \times 10)}{4!\;3!\;\binom{31}{13}}$$

$$= \frac{852720}{\binom{31}{13}} = \frac{852720}{206253075} = .004 < .01.$$

Thus, it is very unlikely that these results were due to chance alone and we conclude that there is a significant relation between the source of raw material and incidence of breakdown of particular machines.

● **PROBLEM** 19-10

Consider the 'top 40' songs from the hit parade of a year ago, and let us see if there is any relationship between the number of sales of these songs and the attractiveness of their record album covers. We shall classify each record cover as being either 'good' or 'bad' according to our considered judgement, and will divide the sales of the top 40 records into those that have sold more than half a million and those that have sold less.

(a) If the results were as follows, would it indicate that a significant association existed between these 2 variables?

| | | Number of songs with – | |
| --- | --- | --- | --- |
| | | More than ½ million sales | Less than ½ million sales |
| Cover | Good | 3 | 7 |
| | Bad | 2 | 28 |

Solution:    This significance test is undertaken in a 2-by-2 table. Thus a $\chi^2$ test is not appropriate. We use Fisher's method to compute the probability that these observations are due to chance alone and not to a significant relationship between the quality of the cover and the number of albums sold. If this probability is less than .05 we will accept that the relationship is a significant one. If the probability is greater than .05 we can infer that there is no significant relation between the two variables.

The contingency table with its marginal row and column totals is:

Number of Songs

|  | | more than ½ million sales | less than ½ million sales | Row Totals |
|---|---|---|---|---|
| Cover | Good | 3 | 7 | 10 |
| | Bad | 2 | 28 | 30 |
| Column totals | | 5 | 35 | 40 |

The probability that this arrangement is due to chance alone is

$$P = \frac{(j + k)!(n + m - j - k)!\, n!\, m!}{k!\, j!\, (n - k)!(m - j)!\, (n + m)!}$$

where k = 3 j = 2 n = 10 and m = 30. Thus

$$P = \frac{5!\,(40 - 5)!\, 10!\, 30!}{3!\, 2!\, 7!\, 28!\, 40!}$$

$$= \frac{5!\, 35!\, 10!\, 30!}{3!\, 2!\, 7!\, 28!\, 40!}$$

$$= \frac{30 \cdot 29 \cdot 5!\, 10!}{3!\, 2!\, 7!\, 40 \cdot 39 \cdot 38 \cdot 37 \cdot 36} = .08 \; .$$

Thus P > .05 and we accept that there is no significant relationship between the quality of the record album cover and the number of sales of that album.

● **PROBLEM 19-11**

The dropout rate among volunteer workers in community development programs varies widely. The theory is advanced that the degree of involvement of volunteers in setting the goals of the program influences the dropout rate. In a new program 27 volunteers are selected to participate in a series of goal-setting workshops as part of their activities, whereas 23 others are simply assigned tasks. At the end of two months the results are as follows:

|                    | Remained in Program | Dropped Out | Total |
|--------------------|---------------------|-------------|-------|
| Workshop group     | 18                  | 9           | 27    |
| No workshop group  | 10                  | 13          | 23    |
| Total              | 28                  | 22          |       |

Are these results significant? Outline an appropriate statistical test and compute the necessary statistic.

Solution: Because this is a two-by-two contingency table we will calculate the probability that the observed frequencies are due to chance alone. We will use Fisher's method.

$$P = Pr(\text{observed frequencies are due to chance alone})$$

$$= \frac{(j + k)! \ (n + m - j - k)! \ n! \ m!}{k! \ j! \ (n - k)! \ (m - j)! \ (n + m)!}$$

where $k = 18$, $j = 10$, $n = 27$ and $m = 23$. Thus,

$$P = \frac{28! \ (50 - 28)! \ 27! \ 23!}{18! \ 10! \ (27 - 18)! \ (23 - 10)! \ 50!}$$

$$= \frac{28! \ 22! \ 27! \ 23!}{18! \ 10! \ 9! \ 13! \ 50!} \approx .06 \ .$$

Thus the probability that these observations are due to chance is greater than .05 and the results are therefore not significant at the .05 level.

# YATE'S CORRECTION AND 2 × 2 TABLES

● PROBLEM 19-12

At the annual shareholders' meeting of the Syntho-Diamond Company, the managing director said he was pleased to report that they had captured a further 6% of the gem market. 'How do you know?' asked a shareholder. The managing director replied, 'Last year we conducted a survey of 1,000 people who owned jewelry . They were selected quite haphazardly, so that we believe them to be a random sample. Of this group, 400, that is 40%, owned one or more of our artificial diamonds. Last week we conducted another such survey, and found 460 out of 1,000 owning our gemstones; this represents a rise to 46%.' This didn't impress the shareholder, who retaliated, 'It looks to me as though the difference might easily be due to chance.' The managing director was able to answer this doubt within a few minutes. Can you?

Solution: First formulate a contingency table representing the results of the survey:

|                      | Owned Artificial Diamonds | Owned Real Diamonds | Row Total |
|----------------------|---------------------------|---------------------|-----------|
| First Random Sample  | 400                       | 600                 | 1000      |
| Second Random Sample | 460                       | 540                 | 1000      |
|                      | 860                       | 1140                | 2000      |

This table represents the results of two surveys.

Because this contingency table has only two rows and two columns the chi-square statistic must be corrected.

This correction factor is designed to correct for the approximation of a discrete distribution by a continuous distribution. To make this correction, we compute the $\chi^2$ statistic in the following way.

Let $O_{ij}$ = observed frequency in cell ij and

$\quad E_{ij}$ = expected frequency in cell ij.

Let $Y_{ij} = \left| O_{ij} - E_{ij} \right| - .5$

Then the Yates $\chi^2$, as this corrected chi-square statistic is called, is

$$\chi^2 = \sum_{j=1}^{2} \sum_{i=1}^{2} \frac{Y_{ij}^2}{E_{ij}} \, .$$

The degrees of freedom for this statistic will be

$(2 - 1)(2 - 1) = 1.$

If the observed frequencies in this table are due to chance, then we would expect half of the 860 respondents who owned artificial diamonds to be found in each survey.

Similarly, we would expect half of the 1140 respondents to be in each survey.

Thus the expected frequencies are,

| 430 | 570 |
|-----|-----|
| 430 | 570 |

828

The Yates chi-square statistic is computed in the table below.

| $O_{ij}$ | $E_{ij}$ | $Y_{ij} = \lvert O_{ij} - E_{ij} \rvert - .5$ | $\dfrac{Y_{ij}{}^2}{E_{ij}}$ |
|------|------|------|------|
| 400 | 430 | $29.5 = \lvert 430 - 400 \rvert - .5$ | 2.02 |
| 600 | 570 | $29.5 = \lvert 600 - 570 \rvert - .5$ | 1.53 |
| 460 | 430 | $29.5 = \lvert 460 - 430 \rvert - .5$ | 2.02 |
| 540 | 570 | $29.5 = \lvert 570 - 540 \rvert - .5$ | 1.53 |

Thus, $\chi^2{}_1 = 7.10$.

The chance of observing this statistic due to chance alone is found from the table of chi-square values. The $\chi^2$-statistic will be greater than 6.63 only 1% of the time. Since $7.10 > 6.63$, there appears to be a significant increase in the company's share of the gem market.

● **PROBLEM** 19-13

Suppose a new cancer medicine, called Treatment Q134, is developed and tested on a random sample of 170 patients. Of these patients, 150 are cured and 20 die.

An almost identical group of 170 patients are tested with the older treatment Q133 and of these patients 130 are cured and 40 die.

Test the significance of these results.

Solution: The data is represented in the contingency table below;

Number of Patients

| Treatment | Cured | Died | Row Totals |
|------|------|------|------|
| Q 134 (new) | 150 | 20 | 170 |
| Q 133 (old) | 130 | 40 | 170 |
| Column Totals | 280 | 60 | 340 |

If one treatment is not significantly better than the other than we would expect the same number of patients to die and to be cured in each sample of 170. Thus we might expect:

| | Cured | Died |
|---|---|---|
| Q 134 | 140 | 30 |
| Q 133 | 140 | 30 |

We now conduct a significance test to see if the observed frequencies are significantly different from those expected. We will compute the $\chi^2$- statistic from this data using Yates correction factor to $O_{ij} - E_{ij}$ because the table has two rows and two columns and the total number of observations, n = 340, is large.

If the resulting $\chi^2$-statistic is greater than some constant c, where $Pr(\chi^2 > c) < .05$, then we will accept the significance of the relationship between the treatment used and the number of patients cured. The level of significance will be .05.

The constant c is chosen from the tabulated values of the $\chi^2$ distribution. Because our statistic is computed from a table with two rows and two columns, the statistic will have $(r - 1)(c - 1) = (2 - 1)(2 - 1) = 1$ degree of freedom. From the tables of the chi-square distribution, we see that the value of c such that $Pr(\chi^2 > c) = .05$, for a $\chi^2$ random variable with 1 degree of freedom is c = 3.84.

To compute the chi-square test statistic we use the following table.

| $E_{ij}$ = Expected Frequency of Cell i,j | $O_{ij}$ = Observed Frequency of Cell i, j | $Y_{ij} = \lvert O_{ij} - E_{ij} \rvert - .5$ | $\dfrac{Y_{ij}^2}{E_{ij}}$ |
|---|---|---|---|
| 140 | 150 | 10 - .5 = 9.5 | .65 |
| 140 | 130 | 10 - .5 = 9.5 | .65 |
| 30 | 40 | 10 - .5 = 9.5 | 3.0 |
| 30 | 20 | 10 - .5 = 9.5 | 3.0 |

830

$$\chi^2 = \sum_{j=1}^{2} \sum_{i=1}^{2} \frac{Y_{ij}^2}{E_{ij}} = .65 + .65 + 3.0 + 3.0 = 7.3.$$

Our $\chi^2$ statistic is greater than $c = 3.84$; and so there is a significant difference between the two treatments.

On the basis of this test, we should begin to use the new treatment on cancer patients of this type.

● **PROBLEM** 19-14

A large tobacco company conducts a survey to determine the percentage of white male United States citizens who are regular smokers. They question 188,000 respondents and determine that 108,000 respondents are regular smokers and 80,000 are non-smokers.
This survey is used to convince the major shareholders that smoking is not excessively prevalent and the company should cut dividends and embark on an expensive advertising campaign.

One suspicious shareholder feels that the company's sample may not have been random and hires you to use the U.S. Bureau of Census data to conduct a similar experiment with a sample that is known to be random.

You find that of 12000 white male Americans; 7000 smoke and 5000 do not smoke. Is there a significant difference between the sample used and these results?

Solution:   The data from the two investigations is compiled in the two by two contingency table below.

|                      | Non-smokers | Smokers | Row Totals |
|----------------------|-------------|---------|------------|
| True random sample   | 5,000       | 7,000   | 12,000     |
| Suspect sample       | 80,000      | 108,000 | 188,000    |
| Column Totals        | 85,000      | 115,000 | 200,000    |

The proportion of smokers in your sample is

$$\frac{7,000}{12,000} = .58$$

and the proportion in the company's sample is: $\frac{108,000}{188,000} = .57$ .

To see if this difference is significant, we will compute $\chi^2$ statistic.

If there is no significant difference between the samples we would expect that the frequency in cell i-j depends only on the marginal row total and column totals.

The expected frequency of cell (1,1) is

$$E_{11} = (200,000)\left(\frac{12,000}{200,000}\right)\left(\frac{85,000}{200,000}\right)$$

$$= \frac{(12,000)(85,000)}{200,000} = \frac{(120)(85)}{2} = 60 \cdot 85 = 5100.$$

Similarly, the other expected frequencies are:

$$E_{12} = \frac{(12,000)\quad(115,000)}{200,000} = 6,900$$

$$E_{21} = (85,000) \times \left(\frac{188,000}{200,000}\right) = 79,900$$

$$E_{22} = (115,000) \times \left(\frac{188,000}{200,000}\right) = 108,100.$$

Because there are two rows and two columns, the Yates correction can be used in computing the chi-square statistic. Also, the number of degrees of freedom this statistic will have is $(2-1)(2-1) = 1$.

The chi-square statistic is thus,

| $E_{ij}$ | $O_{ij}$ | $Y_{ij} = \left\|O_{ij} - E_{ij}\right\| - .5$ | $\dfrac{Y_{ij}^2}{E_{ij}}$ |
|---|---|---|---|
| 5100 | 5000 | 100 − .5 = 95.5 | 1.788 |
| 6900 | 7000 | 100 − .5 = 95.5 | 1.322 |
| 79,900 | 80,000 | 100 − .5 = 95.5 | .114 |
| 108,100 | 108,000 | 100 − .5 = 95.5 | .084 |

and    $\chi^2_1 = 3.308.$

From the $\chi^2$ table we see that by chance alone such a statistic will be observed more than 5% of the time. We conclude that there is no significant difference between the samples at the level of significance $p = .05$. The company's sample appears to be random and the stockholder's fears were not justified.

# CHI-SQUARE TESTS

You believe that people who die from overdoses of narcotics tend to die young. To test this theory you have obtained the following distribution of number of deaths from overdoses:

| Age | 15-19 | 20-24 | 25-29 | 30-34 | 35-39 | 40-44 | 45-49 |
|---|---|---|---|---|---|---|---|
| Number of deaths | 40 | 35 | 32 | 10 | 13 | 13 | 4 |

Total — 147

An appropriate null hypothesis for a statistical test would be that equal numbers die in all age groups. Use this theory to compute predicted frequencies for the following table. Divide the total equally among the groups.

Solution:    We formulate our hypotheses and then test. The usual steps will be:

(1) Formulate the null and alternate hypotheses.

(2) Set a level of significance.

(3) Find a critical region from a knowledge of the sampling distribution and the level of significance.

(4) Compute a test statistic and based on this test statistic accept or reject the null hypothesis.

In the case of a test involving a contingency table the test statistic is the $\chi^2$-statistic discussed earlier in this chapter.

This statistic is defined to be

$$\chi^2 = \sum_{i=1}^{n} \frac{(O_i - E_i)^2}{E_i}$$

where $O_i$ is the observed frequency in cell i, $E_i$ is the expected frequency in cell i and n is the number of cells in the table.

The degrees of freedom of a 1 by n table is n - 1.

The hypotheses for this problem are:

$H_o$: Any age group is equally likely to die from a narcotics overdose.

$H_A$: Some age group is more likely to die of a narcotics overdose than some other age group.

The level of significance will be set arbitrarily at $\alpha$ = .05. Thus

Pr(rejecting $H_o$ when $H_o$ is true) = .05.

The $\chi^2$-statistic is approximately $\chi^2$ distributed with $n - 1 = 7 - 1 = 6$ degrees of freedom. The probability that an observed $\chi^2$-statistic is greater than $c = 12.592$ is equal to .05. Thus if the test statistic is greater than 12.592, we will reject the null hypothesis, $H_o$ and accept $H_A$.

If the null hypothesis is true, we would expect equal numbers of deaths in each age category. There are 147 deaths total and 7 age groups. Thus under the null hypothesis, the expected number of deaths in each group is

$$\frac{147}{7} = 21.$$

The chi-square statistic is

$$\chi^2 = \sum_{i=1}^{7} \frac{(O_i - E_i)^2}{E_i}$$

$$= \frac{(40 - 21)^2}{21} + \frac{(35 - 21)^2}{21} + \frac{(32 - 21)^2}{21}$$

$$+ \frac{(10 - 21)^2}{21} + \frac{(13 - 21)^2}{21} + \frac{(13 - 21)^2}{21} + \frac{(4 - 21)^2}{21}$$

$$= \frac{1216}{21} = 57.90.$$

This statistic is greater than 12.592; thus we reject the null hypothesis and accept that some age group is more likely to die of a narcotics overdose than some other age group.

● **PROBLEM** 19-16

Suppose that a sales region has been divided into five territories, each of which was judged to have an equal sales potential. The actual sales volume for several sampled days is indicated below.

|  | Territory | | | | |
|---|---|---|---|---|---|
|  | A | B | C | D | E |
| Actual Sales | 110 | 130 | 70 | 90 | 100 |

What are the expected sales for each area? How many degrees of freedom does the chi-square statistic have? Compute $\chi^2$ and use the table of $\chi^2$ values to test the significance of the difference between the observed and expected levels of sales.

Solution:     If each sales area is judged to have equal sales potential we would have expected each area to show an equal number of sales.

There were

110 + 130 + 70 + 90 + 100 = 500 sales altogether

and 5 sales regions. Thus we would have expected $\frac{500}{5}$ = 100 sales per region. The expected frequencies would be:                    T e r r i t o r y

|  | A | B | C | D | E |
|---|---|---|---|---|---|
| Expected sales | 100 | 100 | 100 | 100 | 100 |

There is 1 row and 5 columns; hence there are 5 - 1 = 4 degrees of freedom.

$$\chi^2 = \sum_{i=1}^{5} \frac{(O_i - E_i)^2}{E_i}$$

$$= \frac{(110 - 100)^2}{100} + \frac{(130 - 100)^2}{100} + \frac{(70 - 100)^2}{100}$$

$$+ \frac{(90 - 100)^2}{100} + \frac{(100 - 100)^2}{100}$$

$$= \frac{1}{100} [10^2 + 30^2 + 30^2 + 10^2 + 0^2]$$

$$= \frac{100 + 900 + 900 + 100}{100} = 20.0 .$$

The computed value of $\chi^2$ with 4 degrees of freedom will be greater than 13.28 due to random factors only 1 time in 100 if the sales territories do in fact have equal sales potential.

Our calculated $\chi^2$ statistic is 20 > 13.28; thus we see it is quite unlikely that the sales territories have equal sales potentials.

● **PROBLEM** 19-17

A factory has four machines that produce molded parts. A sample of 500 parts is collected for each machine and the number of defective parts in each sample is determined:

| Machine | 1 | 2 | 3 | 4 |
|---|---|---|---|---|
| Defects/500 | 10 | 25 | 0 | 5 |

Is there a difference between the machines? Outline an appropriate statistical test and, if possible, determine if these data are significant.

<u>Solution:</u>    We use a chi-square test to determine if a significant relationship exists between the machine and the number of defective parts produced. The relevant hypotheses are:

$H_O$ :   There is no difference between machines

$H_A$ :   There is a difference between machines.

The level of significance for this test will be $\alpha$ = .01. We wish to determine the critical region of the test. The tower bound on the critical region will be the 99th percentile of the chi-square distribution with 4 - 1 = 3 degrees of freedom. There are 4 classes, hence the 4 - 1 = 3 degrees of freedom.

Under the null hypothesis, $H_O$, the machines are equally likely to produce a defective item. If this is the case, then we would expect the total number of defectives, 40, to be equally divided between the 4 machines. That is, we would expect:

| Machine | 1 | 2 | 3 | 4 |
|---------|-----|-----|-----|-----|
| Defects/500: | 10 | 10 | 10 | 10 |

The chi-square statistic is

$$\chi^2 = \sum_{i=1}^{4} \frac{(\text{Observed} - \text{Expected})^2}{\text{Expected}}$$

$$= \frac{(10 - 10)^2}{10} + \frac{(25 - 10)^2}{10} + \frac{(0 - 10)^2}{10} + \frac{(5 - 10)^2}{10}$$

$$= 0 + 22.5 + 10 + 2.5$$

$$= 35.$$

From the table of the chi-square distribution we see that

$$Pr\,(\chi_3^2 > 11.34) = .01.$$

That is, the probability that a chi-square random variable with 3 degrees of freedom is greater than 11.34 is .01. Our statistic is greater than 11.34; thus we reject $H_O$ and accept the hypothesis that there is a significant relation between particular machines and the number of defects produced.

How to become an art sleuth. Like all creative artists, composers of music develop certain personal characteristics in their works. One such characteristic is the number of melody notes in each bar of music. Now suppose you buy an old unsigned manuscript of a waltz which you suspect is an unknown work by Johann Strauss, and if so, very valuable. You count the number of melody notes per bar of several genuine Strauss waltzes and compare the frequency distribution with a similar count of the unknown work. Would the following results support your high hopes?

| | No. of Melody Notes Per Bar | | | | | | | Total Number of Bars |
|---|---|---|---|---|---|---|---|---|
| | 0 | 1 | 2 | 3 | 4 | 5 | 6 or more | |
| Strauss waltzes | 5 | 32 | 133 | 114 | 67 | 22 | 15 | 388 |
| Unknown waltz | 6 | 60 | 62 | 96 | 33 | 7 | 18 | 282 |

Solution: We will calculate a $\chi^2$ statistic for this $1 \times 7$ (1 row by 7 columns) contingency table. The chi-square statistic is

$$\chi^2 = \sum_{i=1}^{n} \frac{(O_i - E_i)^2}{E_i}$$

where $O_i$ is the observed frequency for cell i, $E_i$ is the expected frequency of cell i and n is the number of cells. In this case, $n = 1 \times 7 = 7$ cells.

The chi-square statistic will have $n - 1 = 7 - 1 = 6$ degrees of freedom.

The expected frequencies of melody notes per bar must be calculated from the estimates of frequency of melody notes per bar in Strauss waltzes. The percentages of bars in which Strauss used a certain number of melody notes per bar are

Number of Melody Notes per Bar

| 0 | 1 | 2 | 3 | 4 | 5 | 6 or more |
|---|---|---|---|---|---|---|
| $\frac{5}{388}$ | $\frac{32}{388}$ | $\frac{133}{388}$ | $\frac{114}{388}$ | $\frac{62}{388}$ | $\frac{22}{388}$ | $\frac{15}{388}$ |

Percentage (row label at left)

If the unknown waltz is written by Strauss, then of the 282 bars in the unknown waltz we would expect:

$\frac{5}{388}$ of 282 = 3.63 bars with 0 melody notes

$\frac{32}{388}$ of 282 = 23.26 bars with 1 melody note

$\frac{133}{388}$ of 282 = 96.66 bars with 2 melody notes

$\frac{114}{388}$ of 282 = 82.86 bars with 3 melody notes

$\frac{67}{388}$ of 282 = 48.70 bars with 4 melody notes

$\frac{22}{388}$ of 282 = 15.99 bars with 5 melody notes

$\frac{15}{388}$ of 282 = 10.90 bars with 6 or more melody notes.

Thus these are the expected frequencies of the cells under the hypothesis that the unknown waltz is actually written by Strauss.

Thus, the chi-square statistic is

$$\chi^2 = \frac{(6 - 3.63)^2}{3.63} + \frac{(60 - 23.26)^2}{23.26} + \frac{(62 - 96.66)^2}{96.66}$$

$$+ \frac{(96 - 82.86)^2}{82.86} + \frac{(33 - 48.70)^2}{48.70}$$

$$+ \frac{(7 - 15.99)^2}{15.99} + \frac{(18 - 10.90)^2}{10.90} = 88.83$$

with 6 degrees of freedom.

Checking the table of chi-square values we see that the chances of observing a chi-square statistic of at least 88.83 with 6 degrees of freedom due to random factors is less than 1 in a 1000.

Thus it is not likely that the unknown waltz was written by Strauss.

● **PROBLEM** 19-19

Consider two independent multinomial distributions with parameters

$n_1, p_{11}, p_{21}, \ldots p_{k1}$ and $n_2, p_{12}, p_{22}, \ldots p_{k2}$

Devise a test for the hypothesis that the parameters satisfy,

$p_{11} = p_{12}, \ldots p_{k1} = p_{k2}$

where all probabilities are unspecified.

<u>Solution:</u>    Let $X_1$ be binomially distributed with parameters $n$ and $p_1$. We have shown that the random variable

$$Q_1 = \frac{X_1 - np_1}{\sqrt{np_1(1-p_1)}}$$

is approximately normally distributed with mean zero and variance 1 if $n$ is large. We have also shown that $Y = Z^2$ where $Z$ is a standard normal is a chi-square random variable with 1 degree of freedom.

Because of this we would expect that the random variable $Y = Q_1^2$ would be approximately chi-square also with 1 degree of freedom. This is in fact true.

Now consider the random variable $X_2 = n - X_1$ and let $p_2 = 1 - p_1$. Let

$$Q_2 = Q_1^2 \qquad \text{where } Q_1 = \frac{(X_1 - np_1)}{\sqrt{np_1(1-p_1)}} \quad . \quad \text{Then}$$

$$Q_2 = \frac{(X_1 - np_1)^2}{[\sqrt{np_1(1-p_1)}]^2} = \frac{(X_1 - np_1)^2}{np_1(1-p_1)}$$

$$= \frac{(X_1 - np_1)^2}{np_1} + \frac{(X_1 - np_1)^2}{n(1-p_1)}$$

by partial fractions.

Let $X_1 = n - X_2$ and $p_1 = 1 - p_2$, then

$$\frac{(X_1 - np_1)^2}{n(1-p_1)} = \frac{(n - X_2 - n(1-p_2))^2}{np_2} = \frac{(X_2 - np_2)^2}{np_2} \quad .$$

Thus
$$Q_2 = Q_1^2 = \frac{(X_1 - np_1)^2}{np_1} + \frac{(X_2 - np_2)^2}{np_2}$$

and $Q_2$ is distributed with approximately a $\chi^2$ distribution with 1 degree of freedom.

$X_1$ and $X_2$ are observed frequencies and $np_1$ and $np_2$ are the expected frequencies. Thus $Q_2$ reduces to our familiar $\chi^2$ statistic.

Now let $X_1$, $X_2$, ... $X_{k-1}$ have a multinomial distribution with parameters $n$, $p_1$, $p_2$, ... $p_{k-1}$ .

Let $X_k = n - \sum\limits_{i=1}^{k-1} X_i$ and

$$p_k = 1 - \sum\limits_{i=1}^{k-1} p_i \quad .$$

Let
$$Q_{k-1} = \sum\limits_{i=1}^{k} \frac{(X_i - np_i)^2}{np_i} \quad .$$

By a generalization of the previous argument, $Q_{k-1}$ is approximately $\chi^2$ distributed with $k - 1$ degrees of freedom.

Now consider the hypothesis $H_o$: $p_{11} = p_{12}, \ldots p_{k1} = p_{k2}$ where $p_{11} \ldots p_{k1}$ and $p_{12} \ldots p_{k2}$ are described above.

The random variable

$$Q = \sum_{j=1}^{2} \sum_{i=1}^{k} \frac{(X_{ij} - n_j p_{ij})^2}{n_j p_{ij}}$$

is the sum of two random variables each of which is approximately chi-square with $k - 1$ degrees of freedom. Thus $Q$ is chi-square distributed with $(k - 1) + (k - 1) = 2k - 2$ degrees of freedom.

But the $p_{ij}$ for $j = 1, 2$ and $i = 1, 2, \ldots k$ are unknown and must be estimated by the observed frequencies $X_{ij}$. If the null hypothesis is true, the maximum likelihood estimates of

$$p_{i2} = p_{i1} \quad \text{are} \quad \frac{X_{i1} + X_{i2}}{n_1 + n_2} \quad \text{for } i = 1, 2, \ldots k - 1.$$

Because $k - 1$ such estimates must be used, $k - 1$ degrees of freedom are lost in computing a test statistic.

$$\hat{Q} = \sum_{j=1}^{2} \sum_{i=1}^{k} \frac{\left[ X_{ij} - n_j \left( \frac{X_{i1} + X_{i2}}{n_1 + n_2} \right) \right]^2}{n_j \left( \frac{X_{i1} + X_{i2}}{n_1 + n_2} \right)}$$

is a test statistic with a chi-square distribution with $2k - 2 - (k - 1) = k - 1$ degrees of freedom. A critical value can be found from the chi-square table and by choosing a level of significance.

If $\hat{Q} > c$ then we reject $H_o$ at the level of significance $\alpha$.

● **PROBLEM** 19-20

Monsieur Alphonse is director of Continental Mannequin Academy. He is desirous of a raise in salary, so is telling his Board of Management how his results are better than those of their competitor, Mrs. Batty's Establishment for Young Models. 'At the Institute's last examinations,' he goes on, 'we got 10 honours, 45 passes, and 5 failures, whereas Mrs. Batty's Establishment only got 4 honours, 35 passes, and had 11 failures.'

Do his figures prove his point, or might they be reasonably ascribed to chance?

| | Exam. results Honours | Passes | Failures | Row Totals |
|---|---|---|---|---|
| Alphonse | 10 | 45 | 5 | 60 |
| Batty | 4 | 35 | 11 | 50 |
| Column Totals | 14 | 80 | 16 | 110 = N |

Solution: We use a chi-square test to determine if there is a significant difference between Monsieur Alphonse's and Mrs. Batty's results.

Let

$H_o$ : There is no significant difference between Alphonse and Batty.

$H_A$: There is a significant difference between the Academy and the Establishment.

Also, let the level of significance be set at $\alpha$ = .05. Our chi-square statistic will have

$$(R - 1)(C - 1) = (2 - 1)(3 - 1) = 2$$

degrees of freedom because R = number of rows = 2 and C = number of columns = 3.

From the level of significance we may determine a critical region for the $\chi^2$-statistic. This will be a number C such if $\chi_2^2$ is a chi-square distributed random variable with 2 degrees of freedom then

$$Pr(\chi_2^2 > C) = .05.$$

The table of various chi-square values gives C = 5.99.

If $H_o$ is true and there is no significant difference between Alphonse and Batty, then the expected cell frequencies will be determined by the marginal row and column totals. Thus

$E_{11}$ = expected frequency in cell (1, 1)

$$= \frac{14 \times 60}{110} = 7.64 \qquad E_{21} = \frac{50 \times 14}{110} = 6.36$$

$$E_{12} = \frac{80 \times 60}{110} = 43.64 \qquad E_{22} = \frac{50 \times 80}{110} = 36.36$$

$$E_{13} = \frac{16 \times 60}{110} = 8.73 \qquad E_{23} = \frac{50 \times 16}{110} = 7.27 .$$

We may now compute the $\chi^2$ statistic.

841

$$\chi^2 = \sum_{i=1}^{2} \sum_{j=1}^{3} \frac{(O_{ij} - E_{ij})^2}{E_{ij}}$$

where $O_{ij}$ = the observed frequency in cell $(i, j)$.

$$\chi^2 = \frac{5.57}{7.64} + \frac{1.85}{43.64} + \frac{13.91}{8.73} + \frac{5.57}{6.36} + \frac{1.85}{36.36} + \frac{13.91}{7.27}$$

$$= 5.20.$$

The $\chi^2$-statistic is less than C = 5.99; thus we accept the null hypothesis that there is no significant difference between Alphonse and Batty. Alphonse does not get a raise.

● **PROBLEM** 19-21

Experience in a certain apple-growing region indicates that about 20 per cent of the total apple crop is classified in the best grade, about 40 per cent in the next highest rating, about 30 per cent in the next highest rating, and the remaining 10 per cent in the fourth and lowest rating. A random sample of 50 trees in a certain orchard yielded 600 bushels of apples, classified as follows: 150 bushels of the highest quality apples  290 bushels of the next highest, 140 bushels of the next highest, and 20 bushels of the lowest quality apples  Can we conclude that the apples  in this orchard are typical?

Solution:    The proportion of apples  in the four categories is represented by $p_1$, $p_2$, $p_3$ and $p_4$. We wish to test the hypothesis that $p_1 = .20$, $p_2 = .40$, $p_3 = .30$ and $p_4 = .10$ against the hypothesis that the true proportions are actually different from those above.

Thus the two hypotheses are:

$H_O$: $p_1 = .20$, $p_2 = .40$, $p_3 = .30$, $p_4 = .10$    and

$H_A$: At least one of $p_1$, $p_2$, $p_3$ and $p_4$ are different from the values specified in $H_O$.

We will perform a chi-square test. The level of significance is abitrarily set at $\alpha = .01$. We now find the critical region. If our observed $\chi^2$-statistic, falls into this region, we will reject $H_O$. Because

$\alpha = \Pr(\text{rejecting } H_O \text{ given } H_O \text{ true}) = .01$.

We wish to find a critical region such that,

$$Pr(\chi^2 > C) = .01 .$$

Thus any $\chi^2$-statistic that is greater than C will cause us to reject $H_o$ in favor of $H_A$.

There are 4 classes in this problem, thus there are $4 - 1 = 3$ degrees of freedom for the chi-square statistic.

From the table of $\chi^2$ values we see that the probability that a chi-square distributed random variable is greater than 11.3 is equal to .01, or

$$Pr(\chi_3^2 > 11.3) = .01 .$$

Thus C = 11.3 determines the critical region of this test.

If the null hypothesis is true, then the frequency of each type of apple is $np_i$, for $i = 1, 2, 3, 4$. This is because we expect 20% of the 600= 120 apples to be classified in the best grade. Similarly we expect:

40% of 600 = 240 apples in the second grade
30% of 600 = 180 apples in the third grade
10% of 600 = 60 apples in the lowest grade.

The $\chi^2$-statistic is defined to be

$$\chi_3^2 = \sum_{i=1}^{4} \frac{(O_i - E_i)^2}{E_i} .$$

This statistic has approximately a chi-square distribution with $4 - 1 = 3$ degrees of freedom.

Also,

$O_i$ = observed frequency in class i

$E_i$ = expected frequency in class i.

To compute the chi-square statistic we use the following table.

| $O_i$ | $E_i$ | $\dfrac{(O_i - E_i)^2}{E_i}$ |
|---|---|---|
| 150 | 120 | 7.5 |
| 290 | 240 | 10.42 |
| 140 | 180 | 8.89 |
| 20 | 60 | 26.67 |

Thus,   $\chi_3^2 = 53.48$   $> C = 11.34 .$

We reject $H_o$ because the observed statistic is greater than 11.34. We reject $H_o$ and accept that the proportions are not,

$$p_1 = .20, \quad p_2 = .40, \quad p_3 = .30 \quad p_4 = .10.$$

When you use a $\chi^2$ test to reject a null hypothesis, you must always look back at the data to make sure that they support your alternative. You have taken a census of the insect population of your rose garden. On the basis of several large samples you conclude that the insect population is distributed as follows:

| | |
|---|---|
| Ladybugs | 20% |
| Inch worms | 20% |
| Weevils | 30% |
| Aphids | 25% |
| Brown spiders | 5% |

Now you treat your garden with an insecticide that is supposed to control the undesirable weevils, aphids, and brown spiders without affecting ladybugs or inch worms.

To check the effect of the insecticide you collect 150 insects at random. Your sample is composed as follows:

| | |
|---|---|
| Ladybugs | 25 |
| Inch worms | 45 |
| Weevils | 45 |
| Aphids | 25 |
| Brown spiders | 10 |

Use the census to determine the predicted frequencies. Compute $\chi^2$ and answer these two questions:

1.  Has the distribution of insects changed significantly (at the 5% level)?

2.  Has the insecticide had the intended effect?

Solution:    We wish to test the following hypotheses:

$H_o$: The distribution of insects unchanged, $p_1 = .20$, $p_2 = .20$, $p_3 = .30$, $p_4 = .25$, $p_5 = .05$

$H_A$: The distribution of insects has changed in the prescribed direction.

The level of significance is $\alpha = .05$ and we will perform a $\chi^2$ test. The computed statistic will have a chi-square distribution. Because there are 5 classes there will be $5 - 1 = 4$ degrees of freedom to the test-statistic.

The critical region, the region where a test statistic will lead to rejection of the null hypothesis, is all $X > C$ where $C$ is determined such that

$$Pr(\chi_4^2 > C) = .05$$

and $\chi_4^2$ is a chi-square distributed random variable with 4 degrees of freedom.

From the table of the chi-square distributions, we see that C = 9.49. Thus if the $\chi^2$-statistic is greater than 9.49 we will accept that a significant change has been made in the insect population.

To compute the $\chi^2$-statistic, we need to know the expected numbers of insects of each type in the sample if the null hypothesis is true.

The sample consists of 150 insects. If the insect population has remained unchanged, then we would expect:

20% of 150 = 30 ladybugs
20% of 150 = 30 inch worms
30% of 150 = 45 weevils
25% of 150 = 37.5 aphids
 5% of 150 = 7.5 brown spiders.

The chi-square statistic is

$$\chi^2 = \sum_{i=1}^{5} \frac{(O_i - E_i)^2}{E_i}$$

where $O_i$ is the observed frequency of insect i in the sample and $E_i$ is the expected frequency of insect i in the sample.

|  | $O_i$ | $E_i$ | $\frac{(O_i - E_i)^2}{E_i}$ |
|---|---|---|---|
| Ladybugs | 25 | 30 | .83 |
| Inch worms | 45 | 30 | 7.50 |
| Weevils | 45 | 45 | 0 |
| Aphids | 25 | 37.5 | 4.17 |
| Brown spiders | 10 | 7.5 | .83 |

$$\chi^2 = 13.33 > C = 9.49.$$

We accept the hypothesis that the distribution of insects has changed. But the direction of change is not the one expected.

The proportion of ladybugs decreased, weevils were unaffected, and brown spiders actually increased. Only inch worms and aphids changed in the prescribed direction.

● **PROBLEM** 19-23

An experiment consists of throwing 12 dice and counting fives and sixes as successes. The number of possible successes in each experiment ranges from 0 to 12. This experiment was performed 23,306 times and the results are shown in the following table:

| Number of Successes | Frequency | Number of Successes | Frequency |
|---|---|---|---|
| 0 | 185 | 7 | 1331 |
| 1 | 1149 | 8 | 403 |
| 2 | 3265 | 9 | 105 |
| 3 | 5475 | 10 | 14 |
| 4 | 6114 | 11 | 4 |
| 5 | 5194 | 12 | 0 |
| 6 | 3067 | | |
| | | Total | 26306 |

Find the probability of success in a given experiment, p, so that this observed frequency distribution is closely "fitted" or approximated by a binomial distribution.

Solution: For each die, P(a five appears) $= \frac{1}{6}$ and P(a six appears) $= \frac{1}{6}$. Because these events are mutually exclusive, P(a five or a six appears) $= \frac{1}{6} + \frac{1}{6} = \frac{2}{6} = \frac{1}{3}$. Thus we would expect p$= \frac{1}{3}$. However, we want to estimate p from the data.

We do this by equating the theoretically <u>expected</u> number of successes with the observed <u>average</u> number of successes. The average or sample mean of the empirical frequency distribution is:

$$\overline{X} = \frac{\Sigma X_i f_i}{\Sigma f_i} \qquad \text{where } X_i = 0, 1, 2, 3, \ldots 12 \text{ and}$$

$f_i$ = frequency of $X_i$.

This expression is the method for computing the average of grouped data.

Here the "groups" consist of the single points $X_i$, for $X_i = 0, 1, 2, \ldots 12$. Also $\Sigma f_i = 26,306$.

Substituting we see that,

$$\overline{X} = [0(185) + 1(1149) + 2(3265) + 3(5475) + 4(6114)$$

$$+ 5(5194) + 6(3067) + 7(1331) + 8(403) + 9(105)$$

$$+ 10(14) + 11(4) + 12(0)] \div 26,306$$

$$= \frac{106,602}{26,306} = 4.052.$$

The probability distribution we are fitting to this data is described by;

$$Pr(X = k) = \begin{cases} \binom{12}{k} p^k (1-p)^{12-k} & k = 0, 1, \ldots 12 \\ \\ 0 & \text{otherwise.} \end{cases}$$

The theoretical mean or expected value of the binomial distribution with parameters n and p is $E(X) = np$.

In this problem, $n = 12$. Thus, $E(X) = np = 12p$. To estimate p it seems reasonable to let

$$\overline{X} = n\hat{p} \quad \text{or} \quad \hat{p} = \frac{\overline{X}}{n} = \frac{4.052}{12} = .338.$$

Thus we have as our "fit" distribution, a binomial distribution with parameters $n = 12$ and $p = .338$.

We now compute the expected frequencies based on this distribution. The expected frequency of i successes in k trials is $k \cdot Pr(X = i)$ where

$$Pr(X = i) = \binom{12}{i}(.338)^i (.662)^{12-i}.$$

Thus the expected number of zero's in 26,306 trials is $26{,}306 [Pr(X = 0)]$

$$= 26{,}306 \binom{12}{0}(.338)^0 (.662)^{12} = 187.38.$$

These expected frequencies are computed below and placed in the table. This table allows us to compare the "fit" distribution to the empirical distribution. Tests that examine the significance of these differences may be used and will be developed later in the chapter.

| Number of Successes x | Observed Frequency f | $\binom{12}{x}$ | $p^x q^{12-x}$ $(\times 10^{+8})$ | Expected Frequency $f_e$ |
|---|---|---|---|---|
| 0 | 185 | 1 | 712,307 | 187.38 |
| 1 | 1,149 | 12 | 363,194 | 1,146.50 |
| 2 | 3,265 | 66 | 185,189 | 3,215.23 |
| 3 | 5,475 | 220 | 94,425 | 5,464.70 |
| 4 | 6,114 | 495 | 48,146 | 6,269.32 |
| 5 | 5,194 | 792 | 24,559 | 5,114.63 |
| 6 | 3,067 | 924 | 12,517 | 3,042.48 |
| 7 | 1,331 | 792 | 6,382 | 1,329.65 |
| 8 | 403 | 495 | 3,224 | 423.72 |
| 9 | 105 | 220 | 1,609 | 96.01 |
| 10 | 14 | 66 | 846 | 14.69 |
| 11 | 4 | 12 | 431 | 1.36 |
| 12 | 0 | 1 | 220 | 0.06 |
| Total | 26,306 | | | 26,305.73 |

In 10 hypothetical cities over a period of twenty weeks the number of deaths per week resulting from automobile accidents are given in the following table.

| X = number of deaths | 0 | 1 | 2 | 3 | 4 |
|---|---|---|---|---|---|
| f = number of weeks when X deaths occurred | 109 | 65 | 22 | 3 | 1 |

Construct a Poisson distribution that fits this data. How do the frequencies predicted by this distribution compare with the observed frequency?

Solution: The Poisson probability mass function is of the form:

$$Pr(X = k) = \frac{\lambda^k e^{-\lambda}}{k!} \qquad k = 0, 1 \ldots$$

When X has the Poisson distribution,

$$E(X) = \sum_{k=0}^{\infty} k \, Pr(X = k) = \sum_{k=0}^{\infty} \frac{k\lambda^k e^{-\lambda}}{k!}$$

$$= 0 \cdot \frac{\lambda^0 e^{-\lambda}}{0!} + \sum_{k=1}^{\infty} \frac{k \lambda^k e^{-\lambda}}{k!} = \sum_{k=1}^{\infty} \frac{k \lambda^k e^{-\lambda}}{k \cdot (k - 1)!}$$

$$= \sum_{k=1}^{\infty} \frac{\lambda^k e^{-\lambda}}{(k - 1)!} \quad ; \quad \text{let } j = k - 1 \text{ then}$$

$$= \sum_{j=0}^{\infty} \frac{\lambda^{j+1} e^{-\lambda}}{j!} = \lambda e^{-\lambda} \sum_{j=0}^{\infty} \frac{\lambda^j}{j!} \quad .$$

But $\sum_{j=0}^{\infty} \frac{\lambda^j}{j!} = e^{\lambda}$ ; thus $E(X) = \lambda e^{-\lambda} \cdot e^{\lambda} = \lambda$ .

We must estimate $\lambda$ from our data. The "best" estimate for the mean of a distribution, by many criteria, is $\overline{X}$, the sample mean.

$$\overline{X} = \sum_{x=0}^{4} \frac{(\text{frequency of observing X accidents}) \cdot X \text{ accidents}}{\text{Total number of observations}}$$

$$= \frac{109 \cdot 0 + 65 \cdot 1 + 22 \cdot 2 + 3 \cdot 3 + 1 \cdot 4}{109 + 65 + 22 + 3 + 1}$$

$$= \frac{65 + 44 + 9 + 4}{200} = \frac{122}{200} = .61 \quad .$$

$\overline{X}$, our estimate of $\lambda$, equals .61.

Substituting this into the probability mass function gives

$$Pr(X = k) = \frac{(.61)^k e^{-.61}}{k!}.$$

The expected frequencies of accidents based on this estimate are given in the table below.

| X | Expected Frequency |
|---|---|
| 0 | $200 \, Pr(X = 0) = 200 \, \dfrac{(.61)^0 e^{-.61}}{0!} = 108.7$ |
| 1 | $200 \, Pr(X = 1) = 200 \, \dfrac{(.61)^1 e^{-.61}}{1!} = 66.3$ |
| 2 | $200 \, Pr(X = 2) = 200 \, \dfrac{(.61)^2 e^{-.61}}{2!} = 20.2$ |
| 3 | $200 \, Pr(X = 3) = 200 \, \dfrac{(.61)^3 e^{-.61}}{3!} = 4.1$ |
| 4 | $200 \, Pr(X = 4) = 200 \, \dfrac{(.61)^4 e^{-.61}}{4!} = .7$ |

Rounding the expected frequencies to the nearest integer, we have the following table.

| Expected frequencies | 109 | 66 | 20 | 4 | 1 |
|---|---|---|---|---|---|
| Observed frequencies | 109 | 65 | 22 | 3 | 1 |
| X | 0 | 1 | 2 | 3 | 4 |

The expected frequencies are very close to those actually observed.

● **PROBLEM 19-25**

Use a $\chi^2$-test to test if the empirical distribution in the previous problem is significantly close to the fitted distribution.

Solution:   We will use a $\chi^2$ test to test the following hypotheses.

$H_o$: The empirical distribution of deaths due to accidents is generated by

$$Pr(X = k) = \frac{e^{-.61}(.61)^k}{k!}$$

for k = 0, 1, 2, ...

$H_A$: The empirical distribution of deaths differs from the "fit" distribution.

We will base the test statistic on the observed and expected frequencies:

| X | 0 | 1 | 2 | 3 | 4 | 5 or more |
|---|---|---|---|---|---|-----------|
| Observed: | 109 | 65 | 22 | 3 | 1 | 0 |
| Expected: | 109 | 66 | 20 | 4 | 1 | 0 |

The expected frequency of 5 or more accidents is approximately

$$200 \cdot Pr(X \geq 5) = 200(1 - Pr(X \leq 4))$$

$$= 200(1 - 1.00) = 0.$$

Let the level of significance be $\alpha = .01$; because there are 6 classes for the data, there will be 6 - 1 = 5 degrees of freedom for the test statistic.

Because the level of significance is $\alpha = .01$, we wish to find a constant c such that $Pr(\chi^2_5 > c) = .01$ where $\chi^2_5$ is a chi-square distributed random variable with 5 degrees of freedom. From the table we see that c = 15.1 satisfies this condition.

Therefore c is the critical value for this test. If the observed chi-square statistic is less than c we will accept the null hypothesis that the two distributions are the same. If the observed chi-square statistic is greater than c we will reject the null hypothesis that the distributions are the same and accept that they are different.

The chi-square statistic is

$$\chi^2 = \sum_{i=1}^{6} \frac{(O_i - E_i)^2}{E_i}$$

where $O_i$ and $E_i$ are the observed and expected frequencies in class i.

$$\chi^2 = \frac{(109 - 109)^2}{109} + \frac{(65 - 66)^2}{66} + \frac{(22 - 20)^2}{20}$$

$$+ \frac{(3 - 4)^2}{4} + \frac{(1 - 1)^2}{1} + 0$$

$$= 0 + \frac{1}{66} + \frac{4}{20} + \frac{1}{4} + 0 = .465.$$

This statistic is less than c = 15.1 thus we accept the null hypothesis that the distribution of deaths is

$$Pr(X = k) = \frac{e^{-.61}(.61)^k}{k!} \qquad k = 0, 1, 2, \ldots$$

where X = the number of deaths due to automobile accidents in a period of a week.

This test is known as "Goodness of Fit" and can be used to make inferences about the observed frequency distributions.

Note that $Pr(\chi^2_5 < 0.465) < 0.01$. As a result of this, the Poisson fit in this case is very nearly a perfect fit.

It should also be noted that the expected frequency of the last three classes are each less than 5. Since this is so, we can combine those three giving us four classes and 4 - 1 = 3 degrees of freedom. In doing this we have: $\chi^2 = \frac{1}{66} + \frac{4}{20} + \frac{1}{5} = 0.415$.

Finally, this chi-square actually has only two degrees of freedom, not three, because it will still lose another as a result of estimating the mean by using $\overline{X}$, its maximum liklihood estimate.

From a chi-square table, we find that:

$0.10 < Pr(\chi^2 < 0.415) < 0.20$ and so the fit is still seen to be quite good.

● **PROBLEM 19-26**

Verify the validity of the chi-square test in comparing two probability distributions.

**Solution:** In comparing two distributions, each with cumulative distribution functions F(Z) and G(Z), we are testing the following hypotheses:

$H_o$: F(Z) = G(Z)          for all Z

$H_A$: F(Z) ≠ G(Z).

One way to test this hypothesis is to partition the real line into k mutually disjoint and exhaustive sets; $A_1, A_2, \ldots A_k$.

Let $p_{i1} = Pr(X \in A_i)$      i = 1, 2, ... k

where X is a random variable distribution with distribution function F(Z) and

$p_{i2} = Pr(Y \in A_i)$      i = 1, 2, ... k

where Y is a random variable distributed with distribution function G(Z).

If $F(Z) = G(Z)$ for all Z then

$$P_{i1} = P_{i2} \qquad \text{for} \qquad i = 1, 2, \ldots k .$$

But this is exactly a test of two independent multinomial distributions. The chi-square test has already been developed as appropriate for this test.

Other methods of testing the equality of two distributions will be discussed in the chapter on nonparametric statistics.

● **PROBLEM** 19-27

One hundred observations were drawn from each of two Poisson populations with the following results:

|  | 0 | 1 | 2 | 3 | 4 | 5 | 6 | 7 | 8 | 9 or more | Total |
|---|---|---|---|---|---|---|---|---|---|---|---|
| Population 1 | 11 | 25 | 28 | 20 | 9 | 3 | 3 | 0 | 1 | 0 | 100 |
| Population 2 | 13 | 27 | 28 | 17 | 11 | 1 | 2 | 1 | 0 | 0 | 100 |
| Total | 24 | 52 | 56 | 37 | 20 | | 11 | | | | 200 |

Is there strong evidence in the data to support the assertion that the two Poisson populations are the same?

Solution:     We wish to test whether these two populations are the same. One way to test this hypothesis is to first combine the two populations and then group the observations into six groups. This has been done above by adding the total number of observations of zero, one, two, three and four, then combining groups 5 through 8.

Let $X_1$ be a random observation from population 1 and $X_2$ an observation from population 2.

Let $P_{1j} = \Pr(X_1 = j)$          $j = 0, 1, 2, 3, 4, 5$

and     $P_{2j} = \Pr(X_2 = j)$          $j = 0, 1, 2, 3, 4, 5 .$

Similarly, let $N_{1j}$ be the frequency of observations in a sample of size $n$, from population 1 of type $j$, $j = 0,\ldots 5$ and $N_{2j}$ be the frequency of observations from a sample of size $n_2$ in population 2 of type $j$, $j = 0, 1, 2, 3, 4, 5.$

We have seen that

$$\sum_{j=0}^{5} \frac{(N_{ij} - n_i P_{ij})^2}{n_i P_{ij}} \qquad \text{for } i = 1, 2$$

has an approximate chi-square distribution with $6 - 1 = 5$ degrees of freedom. (The degrees of freedom is one less than the number of classes.)

Thus

$$Q = \sum_{i=1}^{2} \sum_{j=0}^{5} \frac{(N_{ij} - n_i P_{ij})^2}{n_i P_{ij}}$$

is the sum of two chi-square random variables, each with 5 degrees of freedom. Thus, Q is also chi-square with 10 degrees of freedom.

$$\Pr(X_1 = j) = \frac{e^{-\lambda_1} \lambda_1{}^j}{j!} \qquad j = 0, 1, 2 \ldots$$

$$\Pr(X_2 = j) = \frac{e^{-\lambda_2} \lambda_2{}^j}{j!} .$$

The problem is now to estimate $n_i P_{ij}$ for $i = 1, 2$ and $j = 0, 1, 2, 3, 4, 5$. $n_i P_{ij}$ is the expected number of observations of type j in population i. In this problem, $n_1 = n_2 = 100$. We also know that

$$P_{1j} = (\Pr(X_1 = j) \qquad \text{and}$$

$$P_{2j} = \Pr(X_2 = j) \qquad \text{are}$$

Poisson probabilities. Thus

Under the null hypothesis, these two populations are the same, that is $\lambda_1 = \lambda_2 = \lambda$.

If the populations are the same, the best estimate of $\lambda$ is formed by pooling the two observed samples and estimating $\lambda$ by $\overline{X}$, the sample mean. We have already seen that if X is Poisson distributed with parameter $\lambda$, then $E(X) = \lambda$. Thus $\overline{X}$ is a reasonable estimate of $\lambda$.

The sample mean of the pooled observations is

$$\overline{X} = \frac{\sum_{i=0}^{5} x_i \, (\text{frequency of } x_i)}{\sum_{i=0}^{5} (\text{frequency of } x_i)} .$$

$$\overline{X} = [0(24) + 1(52) + 2(56) + 3(37) + 4(20) + 5(4)$$

$$+ 6(5) + 7(1) + 8(1)] \div 200 = \frac{420}{200} = 2.1 .$$

Thus we expect that if the two populations are from the same distribution, this probability distribution is Poisson distributed with parameter $\lambda = 2.1$.

We are now able to compute the expected frequencies under the null hypothesis that the populations are the same.

Under the null hypothesis,

$$P_{1j} = P_{2j} = \Pr(X_i = j) \qquad\qquad i = 1, 2$$

$$= \frac{e^{-2.1} (2.1)^j}{j!} \quad .$$

Thus, the expected frequencies for either group are

| $j =$ | 0 | 1 | 2 | 3 | 4 | 5 or more |
|---|---|---|---|---|---|---|
| $N_{ij} =$ | 12.25 | 25.72 | 27.00 | 18.90 | 9.92 | 6.21 |

where for example

$$N_{i0} = \frac{100 \ (e^{-2.1}) (2.1)^0}{0!} = n_i \ P_{i0}$$

$$= \frac{100}{e^{2.1}} = 12.25 \ .$$

Substituting these values into

$$Q = \sum_{i=1}^{2} \sum_{j=0}^{5} \frac{(N_{ij} - n_i \ P_{ij})^2}{n_i P_{ij}}$$

we lose 1 degree of freedom because the $n_i P_{ij}$ are all functions of one estimated quantity $\bar{X} = \hat{\lambda} = 2.1$. Thus, the computed chi-square statistic will have $10 - 1 = 9$ degrees of freedom.

Testing at the level of significance $\alpha = .05$, we will reject that the two populations are the same if $Q > c$ where $\Pr(\chi_9^2 > c) = .05$ otherwise we will accept that the two populations are different.

From the table of the chi-square distribution we see that $c = 16.9$.

The chi-square statistic $Q$ is computed with the aid of the following table:

| $E_{ij}$ | $O_{ij}$ | $\dfrac{(O_{ij} - E_{ij})^2}{E_{ij}}$ |
|---|---|---|
| 12.25 | 11 | .128 |
| 25.72 | 25 | .020 |
| 27.00 | 28 | .037 |
| 18.90 | 20 | .064 |
| 9.92 | 9 | .085 |
| 6.21 | 7 | .100 |
| 12.25 | 13 | .046 |
| 25.72 | 27 | .064 |
| 27.00 | 28 | .037 |
| 18.90 | 17 | .191 |
| 9.92 | 11 | .118 |
| 6.21 | 4 | .786 |

Q is approximately 1.68; thus we accept that the populations are the same.

● **PROBLEM** 19-28

What is the relationship between the $\chi^2$ statistic and sample size given that everything else remains constant?

Solution:     To discover this relationship consider the following three by three contingency table:

X                                  Row Totals

|  |  |  |  |
|---|---|---|---|
| 3 | 1 | 2 | 6 |
| 2 | 3 | 1 | 6 |
| 1 | 2 | 3 | 6 |
| 6 | 6 | 6 | 18 |

Y is the label for the rows; Column totals label applies to the bottom row (6, 6, 6 and 18).

The expected frequencies in this table are computed under the assumption that the variables X and Y are independent. The expected frequencies are tabulated below.

|   |   | X |   | Row Totals |
|---|---|---|---|---|
|   | 2 | 2 | 2 | 6 |
| Y | 2 | 2 | 2 | 6 |
|   | 2 | 2 | 2 | 6 |
| Column totals | 6 | 6 | 6 | 18 |

Where $E$ = expected frequency of cell $(i,j)$

$$= \frac{6 \times 6}{18} = \frac{6}{3} = 2.$$

Thus the $\chi^2$ statistic for the observed table is

$$\chi^2 = \frac{3\ [(3-2)^2 + (1-2)^2 + (2-2)^2]}{2} = 3$$

and this statistic has $(3-1)(3-1) = 4$ degrees of freedom. Thus, the variables are not shown to have a significant relationship because $\chi^2 < 9.49$ where

$$\Pr(\chi^2_4 > 9.49) = .05.$$

If the sample size, and all the observations are increased by a power of 10, the original table becomes;

|   |   | Y |   | Row Totals |
|---|---|---|---|---|
|   | 30 | 10 | 20 | 60 |
| X | 20 | 30 | 10 | 60 |
|   | 10 | 20 | 30 | 60 |
| Column Totals | 60 | 60 | 60 | 180 |

The expected frequencies are

|   |   |   | Row Totals |
|---|---|---|---|
| 20 | 20 | 20 | 60 |
| 20 | 20 | 20 | 60 |
| 20 | 20 | 20 | 60 |
| 60 | 60 | 60 | 180 |

where $\quad E_{ij} = \dfrac{60 \times 60}{180} = \dfrac{60}{3} = 20$

$i = 1, 2, 3$

$j = 1, 2, 3$.

The $\chi^2$ statistic still has 4 degrees of freedom but the value of the statistic has become

$$\chi^2 = \frac{3 \, [(30 - 20)^2 + (20 - 20)^2 + (10 - 20)^2]}{20}$$

$$= \frac{3 \, [100 + 100]}{20} = \frac{600}{20} = 30 \; .$$

The chi-square statistic is now significant at $\alpha = .01$, even though the proportions in the table have not changed!

We see that the chi-square statistic is directly proportional to the sample size if everything is increased proportionately. Because of this property, a very slight difference in proportions may be significant if the sample size is large enough. Significance of a relationship may not be sufficient to practically describe the relationship. We also need an indication of the strength and direction by a contingency table.

Especially for large samples, an important question is: Given that a relationship exists, how strong is it.

● **PROBLEM** 19-29

Find the measure of association, $\phi^2$ for the following data relating reaction to a drug and sex.

|  | Male | Female | Row Totals |
|---|---|---|---|
| Severe reaction | 26 | 24 | 50 |
| Mild reaction | 24 | 26 | 50 |
| Column totals | 50 | 50 | 100 |

Solution: The measure of association, $\phi^2$, is most useful in 2-by-2 contingency tables.

We desire the following properties from a measure of association. A perfect relationship between two variables should have a measure of association equal to 1.0 and no relationship between two variables should have a measure of association of 0.

The measure $\phi^2$ satisfies these properties in a 2 by 2 (or 2 by k) contingency table. $\phi^2$ takes advantage of the fact that the $\chi^2$ statistic is proportional to the sample size, N. $\phi^2$ is defined to be

$$\phi^2 = \frac{\chi^2}{N} \ .$$

Thus as the sample size increases, the relationship between the two variables and $\phi$ will not change even though $\chi^2$ increases proportionally to the sample size.

Furthermore, it can be shown that in a table where a perfect relationship exists, say

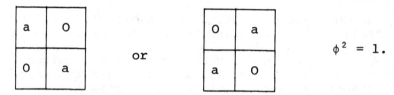

or $\qquad \phi^2 = 1.$

To see this we compute $\chi^2$ for these tables:

$$\chi^2 = 2 \ \frac{\left(a - \frac{a}{2}\right)^2}{\frac{a}{2}} + 2 \ \frac{\left(0 - \frac{a}{2}\right)^2}{\frac{a}{2}} = \frac{\frac{1}{2}a^2}{\frac{a}{2}} + \frac{\frac{1}{2}a^2}{\frac{a}{2}} = 2a$$

but the sample size is N = 2a and thus $\phi^2 = \frac{\chi^2}{N} = \frac{2a}{2a} = 1$ .

If there is no relationship between the variables, $\chi^2 = 0$ hence $\phi^2 = 0$ also.

For the table in the given problem, assuming the independence of variables,

$$\chi^2 = 2 \ \frac{(26 - 25)^2}{25} + 2 \ \frac{(24 - 25)^2}{25} = \frac{2}{25} + \frac{2}{25} = \frac{4}{25}$$

and N = 100 thus

$$\phi^2 = \frac{\chi^2}{N} = \frac{4/25}{100} = \frac{1}{(25)^2} = .0016 \ .$$

Thus $\phi^2$ is close to zero indicating practically no relationship between sex and severity of reaction to this drug.

However, there are disadvantages to $\phi^2$. If the table has r > 2 rows and c > 2 columns, $\chi^2/N$ can be greater than 1. Also we may be interested in a measure that indicates the direction of a relationship as well as the strength. $\phi^2$ only gives the strength.

Another consideration in the use of $\phi^2$ is that $\phi^2$ can only assume the value 1 if the originals for both variables are identical.

Use Cramer's V to interpret the strength of the relationship between the hair color of husbands and wives. (problem # 7 of this chapter) This table had 500 observations; 4 rows, 4 columns and a chi-square statistic of
32.57.

Solution:     Cramer's V is defined to be

$$V^2 = \frac{\chi^2}{N \min \{r - 1, c - 1\}}$$

where $\chi^2$ is the chi-square statistic, r is the number of
rows, c is the number of columns and N is the total sample
size.

This measure reduces to $V^2 = \phi^2$ in a 2 × 2 contingency
table. Cramer's V has the advantage that it will be 1.0 in
the case of a perfect relationship even if the rows and
columns are unequal. In addition, V = 0 if the variables
are completely independent.

For this problem,

$$V = \sqrt{\frac{\chi^2}{N \min (r - 1, c - 1)}} = \sqrt{\frac{32.57}{500 \cdot 3}} = .147,$$

this indicates a rather weak relationship between the hair
color of husbands and wives.

Remember that this relationship was significant. Thus
strength of a relationship and statistical significance
do not always accompany each other. This is an example of
a weak, statistically significant relationship.

● **PROBLEM** 19-31

Three insurance agents each sell three different policies.
A record of which agent sells which policy is kept over
a randomly selected time interval. This record is:

| Policy | Agent 1 | Agent 2 | Agent 3 |
|--------|---------|---------|---------|
| A      | 10      | 6       | 14      |
| B      | 5       | 2       | 2       |
| C      | 5       | 12      | 4       |

The $\chi^2$ statistic for this table, computed under the
assumption that the variables "Policy" and "Agent" are
independent, is $\chi^2 = 10.63$. Find and interpret Cramer's V.

Solution:    Cramer's V is defined to be

$$V^2 = \frac{\chi^2}{N \min \{r - 1, \, c - 1\}}$$

where N = number of observations, r and c are the numbers of rows and columns respectively and $\chi^2$ is the chi-square statistic. We see by substituting that

$$V = \sqrt{\frac{10.63}{60 \cdot 2}} = .298.$$

Thus there appears to be a slight relationship between these variables.

● **PROBLEM** 19-32

Compute and interpret Cramer's V for the contingency table relating the results of Monsieur Alphonse's Continental Mannequin Academy and Mrs. Batty's Establishment for Young Models,(problem #20 of this chapter).

The table had 2 rows, 3 columns, 110 observations and a $\chi^2$-statistic equal to 5.20.

Solution:    Cramer's V is defined to be

$$V^2 = \frac{\chi^2}{N \min \{r - 1, \, c - 1\}} .$$

Thus $V^2 = \dfrac{5.20}{110 \times 1} = .047$    and    $V = .217$ .

Thus the relationship is relatively weak but stronger than the relationship in the previous problem.

● **PROBLEM** 19-33

Compute Pearson's contingency coefficient, C, as a measure of association between the hair color of busbands and wives. (problem #7 of this chapter).    This problem had a $\chi^2$ of 32.57 and 500 observations.

Solution:    Pearson's contingency coefficient is defined as:

$$C = \sqrt{\frac{\chi^2}{\chi^2 + N}} .$$

This measure of association may be used in any r by c table but has a slightly more complex interpretation than does the other measures we have considered. In the case of complete independence, C = 0. But in the case of a perfect relationship C is not equal to one.

For example, consider a two by two contingency table. We have seen that the maximum value of $\chi^2$ (indicating a perfect relationship) is $\chi^2 = N$. Then

$$C = \sqrt{\frac{\chi^2}{\chi^2 + N}} \qquad \text{will be equal to}$$

$$= \sqrt{\frac{N}{2N}} = \sqrt{\frac{1}{2}} = .707 .$$

To adjust C to conform to the convention that C = 1 indicate a perfect relationship we must divide by .707. This is only in the case of a two by two table.

In a 4 × 4 table this correction factor is .866. Thus Pearson's contingency coefficient, C, as a measure of association between husbands' and wives' hair color is:

$$C = \frac{1}{.866} \sqrt{\frac{32.57}{32.57 + 500}} = .285,$$

this is greater than Cramer's V.

● PROBLEM 19-34

Compute and interpret C for the data compiled relating the drop-out rate among volunteers to participation in a workshop group. The contingency table was

|  | Remained in Program | Dropped Out |  |
|---|---|---|---|
| Workshop | 18 | 9 | 27 |
| No workshop | 10 | 13 | 23 |
|  | 28 | 22 | 50 |

Solution: We first compute $\chi^2$ for this table.

If the two variables are assumed independent, the expected cell frequencies for cell i, j are:

$$E_{11} = \frac{28 \cdot 27}{50} = 15.12 \qquad E_{21} = \frac{23 \cdot 28}{50} = 12.88$$

$$E_{12} = \frac{22 \cdot 27}{50} = 11.88 \qquad E_{22} = \frac{22 \cdot 23}{50} = 10.12$$

and $\chi^2 = .55 + .70 + .64 + .82 = 2.71$

Thus

$$C = \left( \sqrt{\frac{\chi^2}{\chi^2 + N}} \right) \frac{1}{(.707)} = \frac{1}{.707} \sqrt{\frac{2.71}{2.71 + 50}} = .320$$

The relationship is insignificant and is moderately weak, because C is relatively small on a scale of 0 to 1.

To find out whether there is a significant association between the sensitivity of the skin to sunlight and the color of a person's eyes, we could take a random sample of, say, 100 people, and test them all with a standard dose of ultra-violet rays, noting both their reaction to this test and their eye color. Both of these features are noted for each person in the trial, so the observations are matched. The results could then be tabulated in an association table like this

| | | Ultra-violet reaction | | | R |
|---|---|---|---|---|---|
| | | ++ | + | - | |
| Eye Color | Blue | 19 | 27 | 4 | 50 |
| | Grey or green | 7 | 8 | 5 | 20 |
| | Brown | 1 | 13 | 16 | 30 |
| | C | 27 | 48 | 25 | 100 = N |

Is this relationship significant? What are some measures of association which describe the strength of association? How strongly associated are these variables?

Solution:    To test significance, we test to see if the observed table departs significantly from what we might expect on the basis of chance alone. This is the familiar chi-square test of independence between the variables "eye color" and "ultra-violet" reaction.

If the variables are independent, we would expect the cell frequencies to depend on the marginal totals alone. Our hypotheses are:

$H_o$: The variables are independent.

$H_1$: The variables are dependent.

Previously we have seen that under the null hypothesis of independence, the expected frequencies are:

$$\frac{\text{Column Total} \times \text{Row Total}}{\text{Number of Observations}} \quad \text{for each row and column.}$$

The expected frequencies are:

$$\frac{50 \times 27}{100} = 13.5 \qquad \frac{20 \times 27}{100} = 5.4 \qquad \frac{30 \times 27}{100} = 8.1$$

$$\frac{50 \times 48}{100} = 24.0 \qquad \frac{20 \times 48}{100} = 9.6 \qquad \frac{30 \times 48}{100} = 14.4$$

$$\frac{50 \times 25}{100} = 12.5 \qquad \frac{20 \times 25}{100} = 5 \qquad \frac{30 \times 25}{100} = 7.5$$

The chi-square statistic is

$$\chi^2 = \sum_{\substack{\text{all cells} \\ \text{in table}}} \frac{(\text{observed} - \text{expected})^2}{\text{expected}}.$$

This statistic will have approximately a chi-square distribution with $(3-1)(3-1) = 4$ degrees of freedom. (Remember that degrees of freedom is equal to $(c-1)(r-1)$ where $c$ and $r$ are the number of columns and rows in the table.)

The chi-square statistic is

$$\chi^2 = \frac{(5.5)^2}{13.5} + \frac{3^2}{24} + \frac{(8.50)^2}{12.5} + \frac{(1.6)^2}{5.4} + \frac{(1.6)^2}{9.6} + \frac{0^2}{5.0}$$

$$+ \frac{(7.1)^2}{8.1} + \frac{(1.4)^2}{14.4} + \frac{(8.5)^2}{7.5}$$

$$= 25.13 \text{ with 4 degrees of freedom.}$$

From the tabulated chi-square distribution, we see that under the assumption that there is no association between eye color and ultra-violet-ray skin sensitivity, this value of $\chi^2$ could arise by chance less than once in 1,000 times. Thus we infer that the association between these variables are significant.

To measure the association between these variables we use measures such as Cramer's V or Pearson's Contingency coefficient, C.

Computing these measures we see that:

$$V = \sqrt{\frac{\chi^2}{N \min \{r-1, c-1\}}}$$

$$= \sqrt{\frac{25.13}{100 \cdot 2}} = .354$$

indicating a moderately strong association between these variables.

$$C = \sqrt{\frac{\chi^2}{\chi^2 + N}} \qquad \text{and a correction factor of .82. Thus,}$$

$$C = \frac{1}{(.82)} \sqrt{\frac{25.13}{125.13}} = (.448) \frac{1}{(.82)}$$

$$= .54.$$

The variables appear to have a relatively strong association on a scale of 0 to 1.

# CHAPTER 20

# NON-PARAMETRIC METHODS

## SIGN TEST

Consider the following data obtained from testing the breaking strength of ceramic tile manufactured by a new cheaper process: 20, 42, 18, 21, 22, 35, 19, 18, 26, 20, 21, 32, 22, 20, 24.

Suppose that experience with the old process produced a median of 25. Then test the hypothesis $H_0 : M = 25$ against $H_1 : M < 25$.

Solution:     We will use the Sign Test. M is the value

uniquely defined by $\int_m^\infty f(x) \, dx = \frac{1}{2}$ , the median.

Let $X_1, \ldots, X_n$ be a random sample of size $n$. We will devise a method for testing

$\quad H_0 : M = M_0 \quad$ against $H_1 : M < M_0$.

It follows from the definition of the median that if $H_0$ is true

$\quad Pr(X - M_0 \geq 0) = \frac{1}{2} \qquad$ and therefore

$\quad Pr(X_i - M_0 \geq 0) = \frac{1}{2}, \quad i = 1, \ldots n.$

$\quad$ Let $Z_i = \begin{cases} 1 & \text{if } X_i - M_0 \geq 0 \\ 0 & \text{if } X_i - M_0 < 0. \end{cases}$

The variable $Z_i$ is a Bernoulli random variable corresponding to a single trial for which $p = \frac{1}{2}$.

$U = \sum\limits_{i=1}^n Z_i$ will then be a binomial random variable corresponding to n independent trials of an experiment for which $p = \frac{1}{2}$ .

Under $H_1$, the $X_i$ will tend to be larger than $M_0$ and U will exceed the value expected under $H_0$. Hence a good rejection region might be $U < K$. Under $H_0$, U is distributed binomially with parameters n and $p = \frac{1}{2}$ . Thus

$$Pr(U < K) = \sum_{i=0}^{K} \binom{n}{i} \left(\frac{1}{2}\right)^n .$$

This is the probability that K or less of the $z_i = 1$. If $U = \Sigma z_i$ is less than K, it is likely that $M < M_0$, thus we reject the null hypothesis.

For very small samples it is necessary to calculate the binomial probabilities exactly until a total probability of roughly $\propto$ has been computed to obtain the critical region for the test. Here $\propto = Pr(\text{reject H given H is true})$.

For most problems it suffices to use normal approximation to the binomial. However, to use this approximation when the sample is below 30, it is best to employ a small correction of $\frac{1}{2}$ to correct for the approximation of a discrete random variable by a continuous one. The following is then approximately a standard normal random variable:

$$Z = \frac{U \pm \frac{1}{2} - np}{\sqrt{np(1 - p)}} .$$

In our problem, $p = \frac{1}{2}$, thus $Z = \dfrac{U \pm \frac{1}{2} - \frac{n}{2}}{\sqrt{\frac{n}{4}}}$

The correction $+ \frac{1}{2}$ is used for a $U < K$ type critical region and $- \frac{1}{2}$ is used for $U > K$.

Returning to our original problem, we subtract 25 from each observed value. $- 5, 17, - 7, - 4, - 3, 10, - 6, - 7, 1, - 5, - 4, 7, - 3, - 5, - 1$.

The following are the corresponding $z_i$:

0, 1, 0, 0, 0, 1, 0, 0, 1, 0, 0, 1, 0, 0, 0.

$$U = \sum_{i=1}^{n} z_i = 4 .$$

Often it is customary to record the signs of the

values $X_i - M_0$ instead.

$$- + - - - + - - + - - + - - -.$$

The total number of + signs gives the value of U. Since $n = 15$ and $U = 4$,

$$Z = \frac{4 + \frac{1}{2} - \frac{15}{2}}{\sqrt{\frac{15}{4}}} = -1.55.$$

From standard normal tables, it will be seen that

$$Pr(U < K) \overset{\sim}{\sim} Pr(Z < -1.645) = .05.$$

Because $-1.55$ is greater than $-1.645$, we accept the null hypothesis that the median is $m = 25$ and reject that the median is less than 25.

● **PROBLEM** 20-2

Let $X_1$, $X_2$, ....., $X_{10}$ be a random sample of size 10 from a distribution function $F(x)$. We wish to test the hypothesis, $H_0 : F(72) = \frac{1}{2}$ against the alternative hypothesis

$H_1 : F(72) > \frac{1}{2}$ . Let Y be the number of sample items which are less than or equal to 72. Let the observed value of Y be y, and let the test be defined by the critical region $\{y : y \geq 8\}$. Find the power function of this test.

Solution: The power function of a test is the function that yields the probability that the sample falls in the critical region of the test. The power function, $\pi(\theta)$, yields the probability of rejecting the null hypothesis under consideration when the parameter being tested equals $\theta$.

We want $Pr(Y \geq 8)$. This is a binomial probability;

$$\pi(\theta) = Pr(y \geq 8 \mid F(72) = \theta)$$

$$= \sum_{y=8}^{10} \binom{10}{y} \theta^y (1 - \theta)^{10-y}$$

where $\theta$ is the probability that a random observation attains a value greater than 72. $(\theta = Pr(X > 72))$. The domain of the function is

$$\frac{1}{2} \leq \theta < 1 \quad \text{since we are not considering the}$$

hypothesis that $\theta = F(72) < \frac{1}{2}$ .

$\pi(\theta)$ is the power function for the sign test.

The following table gives scores on equivalent forms of the same test taken before ($A_1$) and after ($A_2$) a special audio-visual instructional program. Determine whether these data support the conclusion that this special program improved test performance.

| Person | $A_1$ | $A_2$ | Person | $A_1$ | $A_2$ |
|--------|-------|-------|--------|-------|-------|
| 1  | 87 | 98 | 12 | 72 | 79 |
| 2  | 89 | 93 | 13 | 80 | 78 |
| 3  | 83 | 90 | 14 | 73 | 77 |
| 4  | 93 | 89 | 15 | 77 | 76 |
| 5  | 85 | 87 | 16 | 70 | 75 |
| 6  | 81 | 86 | 17 | 66 | 73 |
| 7  | 82 | 85 | 18 | 69 | 71 |
| 8  | 78 | 84 | 19 | 71 | 70 |
| 9  | 79 | 83 | 20 | 58 | 67 |
| 10 | 75 | 81 | 21 | 64 | 61 |
| 11 | 74 | 80 |    |    |    |

Solution:    Let $f_{A_1}$ and $f_{A_2}$ be the two continuous density functions of $A_1$ and $A_2$. Let $(X_1, Y_1)$, $(X_2, Y_2)$, ..... $(X_n, Y_n)$ denote the n paired samples drawn from the two populations. Consider the hypothesis

$$H_0 : f_{A_1}(x) = f_{A_2}(x).$$

To test this hypothesis, we can modify the sign test. Consider the differences $X_i - Y_i$, ($i = 1, 2, ......,$ n). Under $H_0$, $X_i$ and $Y_i$ form a random sample of size two from the same population. In that case,

$$Pr(X_i \geq Y_i) = Pr(Y_i < X_i) = \frac{1}{2}.$$

It follows that      $Pr(X_i - Y_i) \geq 0 = \frac{1}{2}$.

We will consider only the signs of $X_i - Y_i$ and form a nonparametric test for $H_0$.

$$\text{Let } Z_i = \begin{cases} 1, & \text{if } X_i - Y_i \geq 0 \\ 0, & \text{if } X_i - Y_i < 0. \end{cases}$$

Let $U = \sum_i Z_i$. U will be a binomial random variable with $p = \frac{1}{2}$. U also equals the number of + signs in the sample $X_i - Y_i$. Let $X = A_1$ and $Y = A_2$ and note the information in the following table.

| Person | $A_1 - A_2$ | Sign of $A_1 - A_2$ |
|--------|-------------|---------------------|
| 1      | $- 9$       | $-$                 |
| 2      | $- 4$       | $-$                 |
| 3      | $- 7$       | $-$                 |
| 4      | $4$         | $+$                 |
| 5      | $- 2$       | $-$                 |
| 6      | $- 5$       | $-$                 |
| 7      | $- 3$       | $-$                 |
| 8      | $- 6$       | $-$                 |
| 9      | $- 4$       | $-$                 |
| 10     | $- 6$       | $-$                 |
| 11     | $- 6$       | $-$                 |
| 12     | $- 7$       | $-$                 |
| 13     | $2$         | $+$                 |
| 14     | $- 4$       | $-$                 |
| 15     | $1$         | $+$                 |
| 16     | $- 5$       | $-$                 |
| 17     | $- 7$       | $-$                 |
| 18     | $- 2$       | $-$                 |
| 19     | $1$         | $+$                 |
| 20     | $- 9$       | $-$                 |
| 21     | $3$         | $+$                 |

$U$ = number of + signs = 5

A good rejection region would be of the form $U \geq K_0$ and $U \leq K_1$. Is $U = 5$ small enough to reject $H_0$?

If $U = 5$ and $n = 21$, then $Z$ is standard normal and

$$Z = \frac{U + \frac{1}{2} - \frac{n}{2}}{\sqrt{\frac{n}{4}}} = \frac{5 + \frac{1}{2} - \frac{21}{2}}{\sqrt{\frac{21}{4}}} = - 2.18 .$$

From the table, $\Pr(|Z| > 2.18) = .0292$.

This is quite improbable and would suggest a rejection of $H_0$.

The sign test when used for equality of 2 distributions uses very little information, only the sign of the difference in measurements. In testing equality of distributions, other tests, such as the Wilcoxon tests will usually be better since they use more information.

# CONFIDENCE INTERVALS FOR QUANTILES

● **PROBLEM** 20-4

For a sample of size 10, what is the confidence coefficient of the confidence interval $(Y_2, Y_q)$ which is an interval estimate of the population median?

Solution:     We can obtain a confidence interval estimate of $\xi_q$, the $q^{th}$ quantile, by using two order statistics. We are interested in computing the confidence coefficient for a pair of order statistics, i.e.,

$$Pr(Y_j \leq \xi_q \leq Y_i).$$

The confidence coefficient is the probability that a random interval contains a parameter. Note that

$$Pr(Y_j \leq \xi_q \leq Y_i) = Pr(Y_j < \xi_q) - Pr(Y_k < \xi_q). \quad \text{But}$$

$$Pr(Y_j < \xi_q) = Pr(j^{th} \text{ order statistic} < \xi_q)$$

which is the same as

Pr(j or more observations $< \xi_q$).

This probability equals

$$\sum_{i=j}^{n} Pr(\text{exactly i observations} \leq \xi_q).$$

We consider the event of having an observation $< \xi_q$ a success.

The probability of having an observation $< \xi_q$ is fixed. By definition it is $F(\xi_q)$. Putting this all together, the number of observations less than or equal to the $q^{th}$ quantile is a binomial random variable with parameters n and $F(\xi_q)$.

Hence    $Pr(Y < \xi_q)$ now becomes

$$\sum_{i=j}^{n} \binom{n}{i} F(\xi_q)^i (1 - F(\xi_q))^{n-1}.$$

By definition of $\xi_q$, $\xi_q$ is the value such that

$Pr(X \leq \xi_q) = q$. Therefore $F(\xi_q) = q$. Finally,

$$Pr(Y < \xi_q) = \sum_{i=j}^{n} \binom{n}{i} q^i (1 - q)^{n-i}. \quad \text{And}$$

$$Pr(Y_j < \xi_q < Y_k) = Pr(Y_j < \xi_q) - Pr(Y_k < \xi_q)$$

$$= \sum_{i=j}^{n} \binom{n}{i} q^i (1-q)^{n-i} - \sum_{i=k}^{n} \binom{n}{i} q^i (1-q)^{n-i}$$

869

$$= \sum_{i=j}^{n} \binom{n}{i} q^i (1-q)^{n-1} .$$

A table of the binomial distribution can be helpful in evaluating the confidence coefficient.

In our problem we are concerned with the median, $\xi_{\frac{1}{2}}$, so that $q = \frac{1}{2}$. We also want $Pr(Y < \xi_{\frac{1}{2}} < Y_q)$

which tells us $j = 2$ and $k = 9$. Hence

$$Pr(Y_2 < \xi_{\frac{1}{2}} < Y_a) = \sum_{i=2}^{9-1} \binom{n}{i} \left(\frac{1}{2}\right)^i \left(1 - \frac{1}{2}\right)^{n-i}$$

$$= \sum_{i=2}^{8} \binom{n}{i} \left(\frac{1}{2}\right)^n .$$

The sample is of size $n = 10$. We now want

$$\sum_{i=2}^{8} \binom{10}{i} \left(\frac{1}{2}\right)^{10} = \left(\frac{1}{2}\right)^{10} \sum_{i=2}^{8} \binom{10}{i}$$

$$= \frac{1}{1024} \left[ \binom{10}{2} + \binom{10}{3} + \binom{10}{4} + \binom{10}{5} + \binom{10}{6} + \binom{10}{7} + \binom{10}{8} \right]$$

$$= \frac{1}{1024} (45 + 120 + 210 + 252 + 210 + 120 + 45)$$

$$= \frac{1002}{1024} = .9785 .$$

Thus the confidence coefficient is

$$.9785 = Pr(Y_2 < \xi_{\frac{1}{2}} < Y_q) .$$

● **PROBLEM 20-5**

Let $Y_1 < Y_2 < Y_3 < Y_4$ be the order statistics of a random sample of size four from a continuous distribution. Find the probability that the interval $(Y_1, Y_4)$ includes the median.

Solution: The median is $\xi_{0.5}$ so we want

$Pr(Y_1 < \xi_{0.5} < Y_4)$. From the last problem

$$Pr(Y_j < \xi_q < Y_k) = \sum_{i=j}^{k-1} \binom{n}{i} (q)^i (1 - q)^{n-i} .$$

With the present values n = 4, j = 1, k = 4, and $q = \frac{1}{2}$ we have

$$\sum_{i=1}^{4-1} \binom{4}{i} \left(\frac{1}{2}\right)^i \left(1 - \frac{1}{2}\right)^{4-i} = \sum_{i=1}^{3} \binom{4}{i} \left(\frac{1}{2}\right)^4$$

$$= \left(\frac{1}{2}\right)^4 \left[ \binom{4}{1} + \binom{4}{2} + \binom{4}{3} \right]$$

$$= \frac{1}{16} (4 + 6 + 4) = \frac{14}{16} = .875.$$

Therefore if $Y_1$ and $Y_4$ are observed to be $y_1 = 2.8$ and $y_4 = 4.2$, the interval (2.8, 4.2) is an 87.5 percent confidence interval for the median of the distribution.

# TOLERANCE LIMITS

● **PROBLEM** 20-6

For a random sample of size 5, use the order statistics $(Y_1, Y_5)$ as a tolerance interval for 75 per cent of the population. With what probability, $\gamma$, can we expect that 75% of the population falls in the interval.

**Solution:** We now concern ourselves with a nonparametric method for estimating the variability of a random variable. In general terms, let $f(\cdot)$ be a probability density function, and on the basis of a sample of n values we want to determine two numbers, $L_1$ and $L_2$ such that at least .75 of the area under $f(\cdot)$ is between $L_1$ and $L_2$. On the basis of a sample we cannot be positive that .75 of the area under $f(\cdot)$ is between $L_1$ and $L_2$, but we can specify a probability to that effect. Our goal now is to find two functions $L_1 = \ell_1(X_1, \ldots, X_n)$ and

$L_2 = \ell_2(X_2, \ldots, X_n)$ such that

$$\Pr\left( \int_{L_1}^{L_2} f(x) \, dx \geq .75 \right) = \gamma.$$

We now recall the general definition of Tolerance Limits: Let $X_1, \ldots, X_n$ be a random sample from a continuous c.d.f $.F(\cdot)$ having a density function F $(\cdot)$. Let $L_1 = \ell_1(X_1, \ldots, X_n) < L_2 = \ell_2(X_2, \ldots, X_n)$ be two statistics satisfying:

(i) The distribution of $F(L_2) - F(L_1)$ does not depend on $F(\cdot)$, and

(ii) $\Pr(F(L_2) - F(L_1) \geq 1 - \alpha) = \gamma.$

Then $L_1$ and $L_2$ will be defined to be $100(1 - \alpha)$ percent tolerance limits at probability $\gamma$.

For continuous random variables, order statistics $Y_j$ and $Y_k$ $(j < k)$ form tolerance limits. To obtain $\beta$ and $\gamma$, where $\Pr(F(L_2) - F(L_1) > \beta) \leq \gamma$, we need the distribution of $F(L_2) - F(L_1)$. Recall that for the order statistics $Y_i$ and $Y_j$, the joint density is

$$f_{Y_j, \ Y_k}(Y_j, \ Y_k) = \frac{n!}{(j - 1)!(k - 1 - j)!(n - k)!} \times [F(Y_j)]^{j-1}$$

$$[F(Y_k) - F(Y_j)]^{k-1-j} \ [1 - F(Y_k)]^{n-k} f(Y_i) f(Y_k).$$

Now make the transformation $Z = F(Y_k) - F(Y_j)$ and $Y = F(Y_1)$. Once we find the joint distribution of $Y$ and $Z$, we can integrate with respect to $Y$ to get the marginal distribution of $Z$. We find that

$$f_Z(Z) = \frac{n!}{(k - 1 - j)!(n - k + j)!} \ z^{k-1-j} (1 - z)^{n-k+j}$$

for $0 < Z < 1$.

This is a beta distribution with parameters $k - j$ and $n - k + j + 1$. Now we define

$$\Pr(Z < \beta) = \int_0^\beta f_Z(z) \ dz = IB_\beta \ (k - j, \ n - k + j + 1),$$

the incomplete beta function, which is extensively tabulated. It can be shown that

$$IB_\beta \ (k - j, \ n - k + j + 1) = \sum_{k-j}^{n} \binom{n}{i} \beta^i (1 - \beta)^{n-i}.$$

Thus for any $\beta$, we can calculate $\gamma$. In our problem, we are given $\beta = .75$ and we need $\gamma$. By definition:

$$\gamma = \Pr[F(Y_5) - F(Y_1) \geq .75]$$

$$= 1 - \Pr[F(Y_5) - F(Y_1) < .75]$$

$$= 1 - \int_0^\beta f_Z(z) \ dz$$

$$= 1 - IB(5 - 1, \ 5 - 5 + 1 + 1)$$

$$= 1 - \sum_{i=4}^{5} \binom{5}{i} (.75)^i (.25)^{5-i}$$

$$= 1 - \binom{5}{4} (.75)^4 (.25) - \binom{5}{5} (.75)^5 \ = .3672.$$

Suppose that it is desired to determine how large a sample must be taken so that the probability is .90 that at least 99 percent of a future day's output of bearings will have diameters between the largest and smallest observations in the sample.

**Solution:** We want to know how large a sample we must take to be sure

$$Pr[F(Y_n) - F(Y_1) \geq .99] = .90.$$

In this problem we have $\beta = .99$ and $\gamma = .90$. The density of $Z = F(Y_n) - F(Y_1)$, (the range of the random sample), is

$$F_Z(z) = \frac{n!}{(k - 1 - j)!(n - k + j)!} z^{k-1-j} (1 - z)^{n-k+j}$$

$$z > 0$$

We have $j = 1$ and $k = n$, therefore

$$f_Z(z) = \frac{n!}{(n - 1 - 1)!(n - n + 1)!} z^{n-1-1} (1 - z)^{n-n+1}$$

$$z > 0$$

$$= \frac{n!}{(n - 2)!1!} z^{n-2} (1 - z)$$

$$= n(n - 1) z^{n-2} (1 - z), \qquad z > 0.$$

Since $Pr(Z \geq .99) = .90$

$$.90 = \int_{.99}^{1} f(z) \, dz = \int_{.99}^{1} n(n - 1) z^{n-2} (1 - z) \, dz$$

or $\quad .90 = \int_{.99}^{1} (n^2 - n) (z^{n-2} - z^{n-1}) \, dz$

$$= (n^2 - n) \int_{.99}^{1} (z^{n-2} - z^{n-1}) \, dz$$

$$= (n^2 - n) \left[ \frac{z^{n-1}}{n-1} - \frac{z^n}{n} \right]_{.99}^{1}$$

$$= n(n - 1) \left[ \frac{1^{n-1}}{n-1} - \frac{1^n}{n} - \frac{(.99)^{n-1}}{n-1} + \frac{(.99)^n}{n} \right]$$

$$= n - (n - 1) - n(.99)^{n-1} + (n - 1)(.99)^n$$

$$.90 = 1 - n(.99)^{n-1} + (n-1)(.99)^n$$

$$.90 = 1 - n(.99)^{n-1} + .99(n - 1)(.99)^{n-1}$$

$$- .10 = - n(.99)^{n-1} + (.99)(n - 1)(.99)^{n-1}$$

$$.10 = n (.99)^{n-1} - .99(n - 1)(.99)^{n-1}$$

$$10 = 100 \, n \, (.99)^{n-1} - 99 \, (n - 1)(.99)^{n - 1}$$

$$10 = (.99)^{n-1} (100n - 99n + 99)$$

Therefore, $\quad (.99)^{n-1} = \dfrac{10}{n + 99}$

The easiest way to solve this is by trial and error. The solution is approximately n = 388.

● **PROBLEM** 20-8

Let $Y_1 < Y_2 < Y_3 < \ldots < Y_6$ be the order statistics of a random sample of size six from a continuous distribution. We want to use the interval $(y_1, y_6)$ as an 80 percent tolerance interval for the distribution. What is the corresponding probability level for this interval?

Solution:   The problem asks us to find $\gamma$ where

$$\gamma = \Pr(F(Y_6) - F(Y_1) \geq 0.8) .$$

The distribution of $Z = F(Y_k) - F(Y_j)$ is

$$F(z) = \frac{n!}{(k - 1 - j)!(n - k + j)!} z^{k-1-j} (1 - z)^{n-k+j}.$$

In our problem $j = 1$ and $n = k = 6$, therefore

$$F(z) = \frac{6!}{(6 - 1 - 1)!(6 - 6 + 1)!} z^{6-1-1} (1 - z)^{6-6+1}$$

$$= \frac{6!}{4!1!} z^4 (1 - z) = 30 (z^4 - z^5) .$$

Now $\gamma = \Pr(Z \geq 0.8) = \displaystyle\int_{0.8}^{1} f(z)dz = \int_{0.8}^{1} 30 (z^4 - z^5) \, dz$

$$= 30 \left[ \frac{Z^5}{5} - \frac{Z^6}{6} \right]_{0.8}^{1} \quad = [6Z^5 - 5Z^6]_{0.8}^{1}$$

$$= 6 - 5 - 6(0.8)^5 + 5(0.8)^6$$

$$= 1 - 6 (0.8)^5 + 5 (0.8)^6$$

$$= 1 - 6 (.328) + 5 (.262)$$

$$\gamma = 1 - 1.97 + 1.31$$

$$\gamma = 0.34 .$$

Thus, $\Pr(F(Y_6) - F(Y_1) \geq 0.8) = .34$.

● PROBLEM 20-9

Nine economy cars were priced at $4,330; $4,287; $4,450; $4,295; $4,340; $4,407; $4,295; $4,388; and $4,356. We wish to estimate with probability .99, limits within which 90% of the economy car prices are.

Solution:    Often the quality of a manufactured product is specified by setting a range, the bounds of which are called tolerance limits. These limits have the property that a certain percentage of the product may be expected to fall within these limits. We have found in our study of confidence intervals that they can be found in the form

$$\left( \overline{X} - K \frac{Sx}{\sqrt{n}}, \quad \overline{X} + K \frac{Sn}{\sqrt{n}} \right) .$$

Tolerance limits, defined as those limits within which $100(1 - \alpha)\%$ of the product falls $(0 \leq \alpha \leq 1)$, can be of a similar form,

$$(\overline{X} - K_{\alpha/2} Sx, \overline{X} + K_{\alpha/2} Sx) .$$

Values of such K's for different conditions have been tabulated. Such tables are labelled "Tolerance Factors" for distributions.
    It should be evident that the fraction of items included in $(\overline{X} - K_{\alpha/2} Sx, \overline{X} + K_{\alpha/2} Sx)$, will not always be

$1 - \alpha$. However, it is possible to determine, from the previous table, a constant K such that in a large series of samples from a normal distribution, a fixed proportion $\gamma$ of the intervals $(\overline{X} - K Sx, \overline{X} + K Sx)$ will include $100(1 - \alpha)\%$ or more of the distribution. Thus, statistical tolerance limits for a normal distribution are given by $(L = \overline{X} - K Sx, U = \overline{X} + K Sx)$ and have the property that the probability is equal to a preassigned value $\gamma$ that the interval includes at least a specified proportion $1 - \alpha$ of the statistical distribution. In most practical situations $\gamma$ is usually a large number close to 1.

Do not confuse statistical tolerance limits with confidence intervals for a parameter of the distribution. Confidence limits for the mean of a normal distribution are such that in a given fraction, say 0.95, of the samples from which they are computed, the interval bounded by the limits will include the true mean of the distribution.

In our economy car example $n = 9$ events $\gamma = .99$ and $1 - \alpha = .90$ or $\alpha = .10$. From the tables, $K = 3.822$. All we need now is $\overline{X}$ and $Sx$.

$$\overline{X} = \frac{\Sigma X}{n}$$

$$= \frac{4330+4287+4450+4295+4340+4407+4295+4388+4356}{9}$$

$$= \frac{39,148}{9} = 4,350.$$

For $Sx = \sqrt{\dfrac{\Sigma (X - \overline{X})^2}{n - 1}}$ use the following table

| $\overline{X}$ | $X - \overline{X}$ | $(X - \overline{X})^2$ |
|---|---|---|
| 4330 | $-$ 20 | 400 |
| 4287 | $-$ 63 | 3,969 |
| 4450 | 100 | 10,000 |
| 4295 | $-$ 55 | 3,025 |
| 4340 | $-$ 10 | 100 |
| 4407 | 57 | 3,249 |
| 4295 | $-$ 55 | 3,025 |
| 4388 | 38 | 1,444 |
| 4356 | 6 | 36 |

$$\Sigma (X - \overline{X})^2 = 25,248$$

$$Sx = \sqrt{\frac{\Sigma (X - \overline{X})^2}{n - 1}} = \sqrt{\frac{25,248}{9 - 1}} = 56.18 .$$

The tolerance limits are $\overline{X} \pm K\, Sx$ .

Substituting, we obtain: $4,350 \pm (3.822)(56.18)$ .

Simplifying, our result is: $4,350 \pm 215$ .

$(\$4,350 - 215, \quad \$4,350 + 215\,)$

$= (\$4,135 \quad , \quad \$4,565\,)$ .

## KOLMOGOROV-SMIRNOV STATISTIC

● PROBLEM 20-10

Use the Kolmogorov-Smirnov Statistic to find a 95%

confidence interval for F(x). F(x) is the cumulative
distribution function of a population from which the
following ordered samples was taken: 8.2, 10.4, 10.6,
11.5, 12.6, 12.9, 13.3, 13.3, 13.4, 13.4, 13.6, 13.8,
14.0, 14.0, 14.1, 14.2, 14.6, 14.7, 14.9, 15.0, 15.4,
15.6, 15.9, 16.0, 16.2, 16.3, 17.2, 17.4, 17.7, 18.1.

<u>Solution:</u>    Let $X_1'$, $X_2'$, ....., $X_n'$ denote a random
sample from a population with distribution function F(x)
and let $x_1$, ...., $x_n$ denote the ordered sample.

The Kolmogorov-Smirnov method uses the ordered
sample to construct an upper and lower step function such
that F(x) will have a specified probability of lying
between them. Consider the sample cumulative distribution
given by

$$Sn(x) = \begin{cases} 0 & X < X_1 \\ \dfrac{K}{n} & X_K \leq X < X_{K+1} \\ 1 & X \geq X_n \end{cases}.$$

A graph of this type of function is:

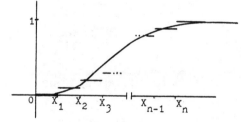

Superimposed on the above graph is a typical continuous
c.d.f.

If F(x) were a known continuous function, we could
calculate $|F(x) - Sn(x)|$ for any X. From the above sketch
we can see that the function $|F(x) - Sn(x)|$ takes on its
largest value at the endpoint of the interval $[X_i, X_{i+1}]$.

Because Sn(x) is constant over each interval $[X_i, X_{i+1}]$,

and F(x) is nondecreasing and continuous, we can assume
$|F(x) - Sn(x)|$ attains its maximum at the left endpoint
since the right endpoint is not included in the interval.
What happens at the right of the interval is of concern
too. Therefore, instead of maxima, we study the function

$$\underset{x}{Sup} \; |F(x) - Sn(x)|.$$

This gives the maximum vertical distance possible
between the graphs of F(x) and Sn(x). It can be shown that
the distribution of $\underset{x}{Sup} \; |F(x) - Sn(x)|$ does <u>not</u> depend

877

upon $F(x)$. Hence, this quantity, which we shall call $D_n$ can be used as a non-parametric variable for constructing a confidence band for $F(x)$.

Dn is a random variable. Certain critical values of this distribution are given in the table below. Let $D_n^{\alpha}$ denote such a critical value that satisfies the relation.

$$\Pr(D_n \le D_n^{\alpha}) = 1 - \alpha.$$

Critical Values for $D_n$ in the Kolmogorov-Smirnov Test

| n \ $\alpha$ | .20 | .10 | .05 | .01 |
|---|---|---|---|---|
| 5 | .45 | .51 | .56 | .67 |
| 10 | .32 | .37 | .41 | .49 |
| 15 | .27 | .26 | .34 | .40 |
| 20 | .23 | .24 | .29 | .36 |
| 25 | .21 | .22 | .27 | .32 |
| 30 | .19 | .20 | .24 | .29 |
| 35 | .18 | .19 | .23 | .27 |
| 40 | .17 | .18 | .21 | .25 |
| 45 | .16 | .17 | .20 | .24 |
| 50 | .15 | | .19 | .23 |
| Large values | $\dfrac{1.07}{\sqrt{n}}$ | $\dfrac{1.22}{\sqrt{n}}$ | $\dfrac{1.36}{\sqrt{n}}$ | $\dfrac{1.63}{\sqrt{n}}$ |

We can now write the following equalities:

$$1 - \alpha = \Pr\left(\frac{\text{Sup}}{x}|F(x) - Sn(x)| \le D_n^{\alpha}\right)$$

$$= \Pr(|F(x) - Sn(x)| \le D_n^{\alpha}) \qquad \text{for all } x$$

$$= \Pr\left(Sn(x) - D_n^{\alpha} \le F(x) \le Sn(x) + D_n^{\alpha}\right).$$

The 2 step functions $Sn(x) - D_n^{\alpha}$ and $Sn(x) + D_n^{\alpha}$ yield a $1 - \alpha$ confidence interval for $F(x)$.

In our problem, $n = 30$ and $\alpha = .05$. $D_{30}^{.05} = .24$. Therefore .24 is the value that must be added to and subtracted from $S_{30}(x)$ to yield the desired confidence interval.

| Observed Value | $S_{30}(x)$ | Intervals * Lower Bound $(S_{30}(x) - .24)$ | Intervals ** Upper Bound $(S_{30}(x) + .24)$ |
|---|---|---|---|
| 8.2 | $\dfrac{1}{30}$ | 0 | .273 |

878

| | | | |
|---|---|---|---|
| 10.4 | $\frac{2}{30}$ | 0 | .301 |
| 10.6 | $\frac{3}{30}$ | 0 | .340 |
| 11.5 | $\frac{4}{30}$ | 0 | .373 |
| 12.6 | $\frac{5}{30}$ | 0 | .401 |
| 12.9 | $\frac{6}{30}$ | 0 | .440 |
| 13.3 | – | – | – |
| 13.3 | $\frac{8}{30}$ | .027 | .501 |
| 13.4 | – | – | – |
| 13.4 | $\frac{10}{30}$ | .093 | .573 |
| 13.6 | $\frac{11}{30}$ | .127 | .601 |
| 13.8 | $\frac{12}{30}$ | 1.60 | .640 |
| 14.0 | – | – | – |
| 14.0 | $\frac{14}{30}$ | .227 | .701 |
| 14.1 | $\frac{15}{30}$ | .260 | .740 |
| 14.2 | $\frac{16}{30}$ | .293 | .773 |
| 14.6 | $\frac{17}{30}$ | .327 | .801 |
| 14.7 | $\frac{18}{30}$ | .360 | .840 |
| 14.9 | $\frac{19}{30}$ | .393 | .873 |
| 15.0 | $\frac{20}{30}$ | .427 | .901 |
| 15.4 | $\frac{21}{30}$ | .460 | .940 |
| 15.6 | $\frac{22}{30}$ | .493 | .973 |
| 15.9 | $\frac{23}{30}$ | .527 | 1 |
| 16.0 | $\frac{24}{30}$ | .560 | 1 |
| 16.2 | $\frac{25}{30}$ | .593 | 1 |
| 16.3 | $\frac{26}{30}$ | .627 | 1 |
| 17.2 | $\frac{27}{30}$ | .660 | 1 |
| 17.4 | $\frac{28}{30}$ | .693 | 1 |
| 17.7 | $\frac{29}{30}$ | .727 | 1 |
| 18.1 | $\frac{30}{30}$ | .760 | 1 |

\* The reason for the presence of zeroes is that even though $S_{30}(x)$ - .24 may be less than 0, we know F(x) never is.

\*\* The ones are there since F(x) never exceeds one no matter what $S_{30}(x)$ + .24 is.

The confidence interval is sketched below:

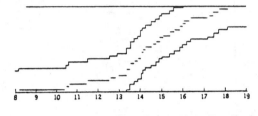

Confidence Band for a Distribution
Function

● **PROBLEM** 20-11

Test the hypothesis, by the Kolmogorov-Smirnov method, that the following sample: .36, .92, - .56, 1.86, 1.74, .56, - .95, .24, - .15, - .74, .32, .82, .70, - .10,-1.26, - 1.06, .15, .55, - .48, - .49, came from a normal distribution with mean $\frac{1}{2}$ and variance 1. Use $\alpha$ = .05.

Solution: We can use the statistic $D_n$ to test the hypothesis that a random sample came from a specified distribution. We calculate the maximum difference between Sn(x) and Fo(x), the hypothetical distribution function of x. If this difference exceeds $D_n^{\alpha}$, we must reject the hypothesis that we are dealing with the given distribution.

The following table orders the sample and gives some pertinent information.

| Sample Value | $S_{20}(X_i)$ | $Fo(X_i)$ | $S_{20}(X_i) - Fo(X_i)$ |
|---|---|---|---|
| - 1.26 | $\frac{1}{20}$ = .05 | .04 | .01 |
| - 1.06 | $\frac{2}{20}$ = .10 | .06 | .04 |
| - .95 | $\frac{3}{20}$ = .15 | .07 | .08 |
| - .74 | $\frac{4}{20}$ = .20 | .11 | .09 |
| - .56 | $\frac{5}{20}$ = .25 | .14 | .11 |
| - .49 | $\frac{6}{20}$ = .30 | .16 | .14 |
| - .48 | $\frac{7}{20}$ = .35 | .16 | .19 |

880

| | | | |
|---|---|---|---|
| - .15 | $\frac{8}{20}$ = .40 | .26 | .14 |
| - .10 | $\frac{9}{20}$ = .45 | .27 | .18 |
| .15 | $\frac{10}{20}$ = .50 | .36 | .14 |
| .24 | $\frac{11}{20}$ = .55 | .40 | .15 |
| .32 | $\frac{12}{20}$ = .60 | .43 | .17 |
| .36 | $\frac{13}{20}$ = .65 | .44 | .21 |
| .55 | $\frac{14}{20}$ = .70 | .52 | .18 |
| .56 | $\frac{15}{20}$ = .75 | .52 | .23 |
| .70 | $\frac{16}{20}$ = .80 | .58 | .22 |
| .82 | $\frac{17}{20}$ = .85 | .63 | .22 |
| .92 | $\frac{18}{20}$ = .90 | .66 | .24 |
| 1.74 | $\frac{19}{20}$ = .95 | .89 | .06 |
| 1.86 | 1 = 1 | .91 | .09 |

$Fo(X_i)$ was calculated in the following manner:

$Fo(X_i)$ is $N\left(\frac{1}{2}, 1\right)$. Hence $\dfrac{X_i - \frac{1}{2}}{\sqrt{1}} = X_i - \frac{1}{2}$

is a standard normal random variable and the figures in the $Fo(X_i)$ column were taken off the standard normal table as $Pr\left[Z \le X_i - \frac{1}{2}\right]$.

We see from the table that $D_n$ = .24; but $D_{20}^{.05}$ = .29; .24 < .29.

Therefore we accept the hypothesis that we are dealing with the hypothesized distribution.

● PROBLEM 20-12

A question of interest is the following: Are the times of birth uniformly distributed over the hours of the day? For 35 consecutive births the following times were observed: 7:02 P.M., 11:08 P.M., 3:56 A.M., 8:12 A.M., 8:40 A.M., 12:25 P.M. 1:24 A.M., 8:25 A.M., 2:02 P.M., 11:46 P.M., 10:07 A.M., 1:53 P.M., 6:45 P.M., 9:06 A.M., 3:57 P.M., 7:40 A.M., 10:45 A.M. 3:06 P.M., 6:26 A.M., 4:44 P.M., 12:26 A.M., 2:17 P.M., 11:45 P.M., 5:08 A.M., 5:49 A.M., 6:32 A.M., 12:40 P.M., 1:30 P.M., 12:55 P.M., 4:09 P.M., 7:46 P.M., 2:28 A.M., 10:06 A.M., 11:19 A.M.,

4:31 P.M. Test the hypothesis that the distribution is
uniform. Use $\alpha$ = .05.

Solution:     Use the Kolmogorov-Smirnov statistic. The
following table will be useful in solving the problem.
The first column gives the sample in order. The second
column relates the value of the step function, $S_{35}(x)$,
the sample cumulative distribution function. The third
gives the cumulative probabilities of each birth time
under the hypothesis that the birth times are uniformly
distributed. The values there are arrived at by dividing
number of minutes after midnight each birth occurred by
1440, the number of minutes in a 24-hour day.

| Birth Time | $S_{35}(x)$ | Fo(x) | $|S_{35}(x) - Fo(x)|$ |
|---|---|---|---|
| A.M. 12:26 | $\frac{1}{35}$ = .029 | .018 | .011 |
| 1:24 | $\frac{2}{35}$ = .057 | .058 | .001 |
| 2:28 | $\frac{3}{35}$ = .086 | .103 | .017 |
| 3:56 | $\frac{4}{35}$ = .114 | .164 | .050 |
| 5:08 | $\frac{5}{35}$ = .143 | .214 | .071 |
| 5:49 | $\frac{6}{35}$ = .171 | .242 | .071 |
| 6:26 | $\frac{7}{35}$ = .200 | .268 | .068 |
| 6:32 | $\frac{8}{35}$ = .229 | .272 | .043 |
| 7:40 | $\frac{9}{35}$ = .257 | .319 | .062 |
| 8:12 | $\frac{10}{35}$ = .286 | .342 | .056 |
| 8:25 | $\frac{11}{35}$ = .314 | .351 | .031 |
| 8:40 | $\frac{12}{35}$ = .343 | .361 | .018 |
| 9:06 | $\frac{13}{35}$ = .371 | .379 | .008 |
| 10:06 | $\frac{14}{35}$ = .400 | .421 | .021 |
| 10:07 | $\frac{15}{35}$ = .429 | .422 | .007 |
| 10:45 | $\frac{16}{35}$ = .457 | .448 | .009 |
| 11:19 | $\frac{17}{35}$ = .486 | .471 | .015 |
| P.M. 12:25 | $\frac{18}{35}$ = .514 | .517 | .003 |
| 12:40 | $\frac{19}{35}$ = .543 | .528 | .015 |
| 12:55 | $\frac{20}{35}$ = .571 | .531 | .040 |
| 1:30 | $\frac{21}{35}$ = .600 | .562 | .038 |

| | | | |
|---|---|---|---|
| 1:53 | $\frac{22}{35} = .629$ | .578 | .051 |
| 2:02 | $\frac{23}{35} = .657$ | .585 | .072 |
| 2:17 | $\frac{24}{35} = .686$ | .595 | .091 |
| 3:06 | $\frac{25}{35} = .714$ | .629 | .085 |
| 3:57 | $\frac{26}{35} = .743$ | .665 | .078 |
| 4:09 | $\frac{27}{35} = .771$ | .673 | .098 |
| 4:31 | $\frac{28}{35} = .800$ | .688 | .112 |
| 4:44 | $\frac{29}{35} = .829$ | .697 | (.132) |
| 6:45 | $\frac{30}{35} = .857$ | .781 | .076 |
| 7:02 | $\frac{31}{35} = .886$ | .793 | .093 |
| 7:46 | $\frac{32}{35} = .914$ | .824 | .090 |
| 11:08 | $\frac{33}{35} = .943$ | .964 | .021 |
| 11:45 | $\frac{34}{35} = .971$ | .990 | .019 |
| 11:46 | $\frac{35}{35} = 1$ | .990 | .010 |

Now $D_n = \sup\limits_x |S_{35}(x) - Fo(x)|$

$\qquad = .132 \qquad$ from the chart; but

$D_{35}^{.05} = .230 \qquad$ from the table (Critical values for $D_\alpha$ in the Kolmogorov-Smirnov test). Now $.132 < .230$:

therefore we accept the hypothesis that births are uniformly distributed.

# WILCOXON'S SUM OF RANKS TEST (MANN-WHITNEY RANK SUM TEST)

● PROBLEM 20-13

Suppose we wish to compare the recovery times of patients after 2 different versions of some operation, say removing the gallbladder. Operation A is performed through a vertical incision; Operation B through an oblique incision. Each operation is performed alternately (A, B, A, B, etc.) on a consecutive series of patients suffering from gallbladder disease, and the recovery times (say, number of days in hospital after operation, including the day of operation and the day of discharge from hospital) are then collected as follows:

| Patient # | Days to recover from operation A | Patient # | Days to recover from operation B |
|---|---|---|---|
| 1 | 16 | 2 | 18 |
| 3 | 20 | 4 | 19 |
| 5 | 25 | 6 | 15 |
| 7 | 19 | 8 | 16 |
| 9 | 22 | 10 | 21 |
| 11 | 15 | 12 | 17 |
| 13 | 22 | 14 | 17 |
| 15 | 19 | 16 | 14 |

For this test it is not necessary to know the sample averages, but just out of interest the average recovery time of the 8 patients who had Operation A is 158/8 = 19.8 days, while the 8 who had Operation B have an average of 137/8 = 17.1 days.

Now the question is: Do these 2 sets of results differ significantly or could the observed difference be reasonably attributed to chance?

Solution:    To solve this problem we will use Wilcoxon's Sum of Ranks Test, often called the Wilcoxon-Mann-Whitney Rank Sum Test.

This test applies when we are given two random samples, $X_1, \ldots, X_m$ and $Y_1, \ldots, Y_n$ from two populations with continuous c.d.f.'s $F_x(\ )$ and $F_y(\ )$.

One collects the $m + n$ observations and places them in ascending order. Then replace the smallest observation by 1, the second by 2, and so on until the largest is replaced by $m + n$. These integers are called ranks. Let $T_x$ denote the sum of the ranks of the $m$ x values; and let $T_y$ have the same meaning for the $n$ y's.

Note that    $T_x + T_y = \sum\limits_{i=1}^{m+n} i$ = Sum of all ranks.

Using an algebra formula,

$$\sum\limits_{i=1}^{m+n} i = \frac{(m + n + 1)(m + n)}{2} ,$$    we see that

$$T_x + T_y = \frac{(m + n + 1)(m + n)}{2} ,$$    or

$$T_y = -T_x + \frac{(m + n + 1)(m + n)}{2} ,$$    so that $T_y$ is

a linear function of $T_x$.

We could base a test on either statistic, $T_x$ or $T_y$. We will use $T_x$.

Define $\quad Z_{ij} = 1, \qquad X_i > Y_j$

$$= 0, \qquad X_i < Y_j$$

and consider the statistic

$$U = \sum_{j=1}^{n} \sum_{i=1}^{m} Z_{ij} \ .$$

Note that $\sum_{i=1}^{m} Z_{ij}$ counts the number of values of

X which exceeds $Y_j$. Hence U is the total number of times

an X exceeds a Y.

For a given set of observations, let $r_1, r_2, \ldots, r_m$ denote the ranks of the X values and let $X_1', \ldots\ldots, X_m'$ denote the ordered x values. $X_1$ will exceed $r_1 - 1$ Y-values, $X_2$ will exceed $r_2 - 2$ Y values, etc. Hence

$$U = \sum_{i=1}^{m} (r_i - i) = \Sigma r_i - \Sigma i = T_x - \frac{m(m+1)}{2} \ .$$

To find the mean of $T_x$ we will first find E(U).

$$E(U) = E\left(\sum_{i=1}^{m} \sum_{j=1}^{n} Z_{ij}\right) = \sum_{i=1}^{m} \sum_{j=1}^{n} Z_{ij}$$

$$E(Z_{ij}) = (1)\ \Pr(X_i > Y_j) + (0)\ \Pr(X_i < Y_j).$$

We will be testing the null hypothesis, $H_0$: the distributions of X and Y are the same. Under $H_0$,

$$\Pr(X_i > Y_j) = \Pr(X_i < Y_j) = \frac{1}{2} \ .$$

Therefore $\quad E(U) = \sum_{i=1}^{m} \sum_{j=1}^{n} \frac{1}{2} = \frac{mn}{2} \ .$

Now $\quad E(U) = E(T_x) - E\left(\frac{m(m+1)}{2}\right)$

$$E(T_x) = E(U) + E\left(\frac{m(m+1)}{2}\right)$$

$$= \frac{mn}{2} + \frac{m(m+1)}{2} = \frac{m(m+n+1)}{2} \ .$$

The computation of Var $(T_x)$ is more involved and will be omitted but    Var $(T_x) = \frac{mn(m+n+1)}{12}$ .

Mann and Whitney have shown that for large m, n (m, n $\geq$ 7) $T_x$ is approximately normally distributed.

For testing Ho: $F_x(Z) = F_y(Z)$ versus $H_1$ : $F_x(Z) \neq F_y(Z)$, the test would be the following: Reject Ho if $|T_x - E(T_x)|$ is large. That is if $|T_x - E(T_x)| \geq K$ where K is fixed by determining the test size and using an asymptotic normal distribution.

In our example, a number of measurements are tied, (e.g., 2 patients recovered in 15 days), but it would be fruitless to try to make the recovery time more precise in order to break the ties. We shall therefore award average rank values to such ties. In our problem n = m = 8.

Note the following table:

| Data Values | Tally | | Rank Values | Contributions $T_x$ | $T_y$ |
|---|---|---|---|---|---|
| 14 | | B | 1 | | 1 |
| 15 | A | B | 2, 3 = 2 $\frac{1}{2}$ | 2 $\frac{1}{2}$ | 2 $\frac{1}{2}$ |
| 16 | A | B | 4, 5 = 4 $\frac{1}{2}$ | 4 $\frac{1}{2}$ | 4 $\frac{1}{2}$ |
| 17 | | BB | 6, 7 = 6 $\frac{1}{2}$ | | 13 |
| 18 | | B | 8 | | 8 |
| 19 | AA | B | 9, 10, 11 = 10 | 20 | 10 |
| 20 | A | | 12 | 12 | |
| 21 | | B | 13 | | 13 |
| 22 | AA | | 14, 15 = 14 $\frac{1}{2}$ | 29 | |
| 23 | | | | | |
| 24 | | | | | |
| 25 | A | | 16 | 16 | |

$$T_x = 84$$

$$E(T_x) = \frac{m\ (m + n + 1)}{2} = \frac{8\ (8 + 8 + 1)}{2} = 68$$

$$Var\ (T_x) = \frac{mn\ (m + n + 1)}{2} = \frac{8 \cdot 8\ (8 + 8 + 1)}{12} = 90.67$$

$$\sqrt{Var\ (T_x)} = 9.52 .$$

$$|z| = \left| \frac{T_x - E(T_x)}{\sqrt{Var\ (T_x)}} \right| = \left| \frac{84 - 68}{9.52} \right| = 1.68 .$$

If we were testing Ho at the 5% significance level $|z|$ would have to be at least 1.96 to reject Ho. A significant difference in distributions is not proven by this experiment.

● **PROBLEM** 20-14

Random samples of 2 brands of almond candy bars were examined to see if one brand contained more almonds than the other. Altogether 18 bars of brand A and 22 of brand B were tested. The rank total of brand A, $T_x$, turned out to be 274. Does this indicate a 5% statistically significant difference between the two brands.

Solution:    We have $H_0: F_A(\ ) = F_B(\ )$ and $H_1: F_A(\ ) \neq F_B(\ )$.

We will use the Mann-Whitney-Wilcoxon Rank Sum Test

and reject Ho if    $\left| T_x - E(T_x) \right| \geq K.$

At the 5% level we will reject Ho if $\left| \dfrac{T_x - E(T_x)}{Var\ T_x} \right| \geq 1.96.$

We are given $T_x = 274.$

$E(T_x) = \dfrac{m\ (m + n + 1)}{2}$    where m = number of X's in sample and n = size of Y sample.

$$E(T_x) = \frac{18\ (18 + 22 + 1)}{2} = 369$$

$$Var\ (T_x) = \frac{mn\ (m + n + 1)}{12} = \frac{18 \cdot 22\ (18 + 22 + 1)}{12} = 1353.$$

$$\sqrt{Var\ (T_x)} = \sqrt{1353} = 36.78$$

$$\left| \frac{T_x - E(T_x)}{Var\ (T_x)} \right| = \left| \frac{274 - 369}{36.78} \right| = 2.58 .$$

887

Since 2.58 $\geq$ 1.96 we reject H₀ and assume a statistically significant difference.

Given below are the ages of 29 executives on Madison Avenue:

Men:   44, 30, 34, 47, 35, 46, 35, 47, 48, 34, 32, 42,
       43, 49, 46, 47

Women: 26, 25, 38, 33, 42, 40, 44, 26, 25, 43, 35, 48,
       37.

Test the hypothesis that the population medians are equal $M_m = M_w$ versus the hypothesis that $M_w < M_m$ .

Solution:   We will use the Wilcoxon Sum of Ranks test. First order all the ages collectively.

25, 25, 26, 26, 30, 32, 33, 34, 34, 35, 35, 35,

37, 38, 40, 42, 42, 43, 43, 44, 44, 46, 46, 47, 47,

47, 48, 48, 49.

The underlined ages are those of women.

Consider the statistic $T_w$, the total rank sum of all female ranks. Since our alternative hypothesis is $M_w < M_m$, it makes sense to eventually consider the critical region $T_w < K$. Assume we want to reject at the .05 significance level. Since

$$\frac{T_w - E(T_w)}{\sqrt{Var\ (T_w)}}$$   approximates a standard normal

statistic under the null hypothesis,

$$Pr\left[\frac{T_w - E(T_w)}{\sqrt{Var\ (T_w)}} < -1.645\right] = .05 .$$

Multiplying by $\sqrt{Var\ (T_w)}$ and adding $E(T_w)$ yields

$$Pr\left[T_w < E(T_w) - 1.645\ \sqrt{Var\ (T_w)}\right] = .05.$$

We will take $T_w < E(T_w) - 1.645\ \sqrt{Var\ (T_w)}$ as our rejection region.

$$E(T_w) = \frac{n_w\ (n_w + n_m + 1)}{2}$$

where $n_w$ = the number of women in the sample and $n_m$ = the number of men. In our example $n_w$ = 13 and $n_m$ = 16. Therefore

$$E(T_w) = \frac{13\ (13 + 16 + 1)}{2} = 195 \ .$$

Furthermore $\quad \text{Var}\ (T_w) = \dfrac{n_w\ n_m\ (n_w + n_m + 1)}{12}$

$$= \frac{13 \cdot 16 \cdot (13 + 16 + 1)}{12}$$

$$= 520.$$

$$\sqrt{\text{Var}\ (T_w)} = 22.8.$$

Our rejection region now becomes

$$T_w < 195 - (1.645)\ 22.8 \qquad\qquad \text{or}$$

$$T_w < 157.823.$$

We compute $T_w$ with the aid of the following table. Ties yield average ranks.

| Data Values | Tally | | Rank | Rank M | Rank W |
|---|---|---|---|---|---|
| 25 | | W | $1,\ 2 = 1\frac{1}{2}$ | | $1\frac{1}{2}$ |
| 25 | | W | $1,\ 2 = 1\frac{1}{2}$ | | $1\frac{1}{2}$ |
| 26 | | W | $3,\ 4 = 3\frac{1}{2}$ | | $3\frac{1}{2}$ |
| 26 | | W | $3,\ 4 = 3\frac{1}{2}$ | | $3\frac{1}{2}$ |
| 30 | M | | 5 | 5 | |
| 32 | M | | 6 | 6 | |
| 33 | | W | 7 | | 7 |
| 34 | M | | $8,\ 9 = 8\frac{1}{2}$ | $8\frac{1}{2}$ | |
| 34 | M | | $8,\ 9 = 8\frac{1}{2}$ | $8\frac{1}{2}$ | |
| 35 | M | | $10,\ 11,\ 12 = 11$ | 11 | |
| 35 | M | | $10,\ 11,\ 12 = 11$ | 11 | |
| 35 | | W | $10,\ 11,\ 12 = 11$ | | 11 |

| | M | W | | Rank M | Rank W |
|---|---|---|---|---|---|
| 37 | | W | 13 | | 13 |
| 38 | | W | 14 | | 14 |
| 40 | | W | 15 | | 15 |
| 42 | M | | $16, 17 = 16\frac{1}{2}$ | $16\frac{1}{2}$ | |
| 42 | | W | $16, 17 = 16\frac{1}{2}$ | | $16\frac{1}{2}$ |
| 43 | M | | $18, 19 = 18\frac{1}{2}$ | $18\frac{1}{2}$ | |
| 43 | | W | $18, 19 = 18\frac{1}{2}$ | | $18\frac{1}{2}$ |
| 44 | M | | $20, 21 = 20\frac{1}{2}$ | $20\frac{1}{2}$ | |
| 44 | | W | $20, 21 = 20\frac{1}{2}$ | | $20\frac{1}{2}$ |
| 46 | M | | $22, 23 = 22\frac{1}{2}$ | $22\frac{1}{2}$ | |
| 46 | M | | $22, 23 = 22\frac{1}{2}$ | $22\frac{1}{2}$ | |
| 47 | M | | $24, 25, 26 = 25$ | 25 | |
| 47 | M | | $24, 25, 26 = 25$ | 25 | |
| 47 | M | | $24, 25, 26 = 25$ | 25 | |
| 48 | | W | $27, 28 = 27\frac{1}{2}$ | | $27\frac{1}{2}$ |
| 48 | M | | $27, 28 = 27\frac{1}{2}$ | $27\frac{1}{2}$ | |
| 49 | M | | 29 | 29 | |

$T_w$ = Sum of all entries in column Rank W

= 153;

$153 < 157.823$ therefore reject $H_0$ and accept $H_1$.

● **PROBLEM** 20-16

At the University of Michigan's Graduate School of Business Administration, grades are given on a nine point scale. Ten East Coast students were chosen at random and had the following grade point averages: 4.3, 5.9, 4.9, 3.1, 5.3, 6.4, 6.2, 3.8, 7.5, 5.8. Nine Westerners had averages of 5.5, 7.9, 6.8, 9.0, 5.6, 6.3, 8.5, 4.6, and 7.1. Test by the Mann-Whitney-Wilcoxon Test the hypothesis that the distribution of Eastern grades is the same as that of Western grades. Use a .05 significance level.

Solution:   A quick glance shows that the West Coast grades appear a bit higher. In that light a good alternative hypothesis might be that the Westerners actually do receive higher grades. It would then be a wise choice to choose $T_w > K$ as a rejection region where $T_w$ is the sum of the ranks of the Western grades in the pooled sample.

We know that under the null hypothesis

$$\frac{T_w - E(T_w)}{\sqrt{Var\ (T_w)}}$$ is approximately a standard normal

statistic. Therefore $$Pr\left(\frac{T_w - E(T_w)}{\sqrt{Var\ (T_w)}} > 1.645\right) = .05.$$

or    $Pr(T_w > E(T_w) + 1.645\ \sqrt{Var\ (T_w)}) = .05.$

We choose as our rejection region

$$T_w > E(T_w) + 1.645\ \sqrt{Var\ (T_w)}$$

But   $E(T_w) = \dfrac{n_w(n_w + n_e + 1)}{2}$   where $n_w$ and $n_e$ are the sizes of the Western and Eastern samples.

$$E(T_w) = \frac{9\ (10 + 9 + 1)}{2} = 90.$$

Furthermore,  $Var\ (T_w) = \dfrac{n_w\ n_e\ (n_w + n_e + 1)}{12}$

$$= \frac{9 \cdot 10\ (9 + 10 + 1)}{12} = 150.\ \sqrt{Var\ (T_w)} = 12.25$$

Our rejection region becomes

$T_{..} > 90 + (1.645)(12.25)$           or           $T_w > 110.146.$

The first step in finding $T_w$ is to order the grades without regard to the students' homes; 3.1, 3.8, 4.3, 4.6, 4.9, 5.3, 5.5, 5.6, 5.8, 5.9, 6.2, 6.3, 6.4, 6.8, 7.1, 7.5, 7.9, 8.5, 9.0. The underlined figures are from East Coast students.

$T_w$ can be determined from the following table.

| Data Value | Tally | Rank | Rank E | Rank W |
|---|---|---|---|---|
| 3.1 | e | 1 | 1 | |
| 3.8 | e | 2 | 2 | |
| 4.3 | e | 3 | 3 | |
| 4.6 | w | 4 | | 4 |

| 4.9 | | e | 5 | 5 | |
|---|---|---|---|---|---|
| 5.3 | | e | 6 | 6 | |
| 5.5 | w | | 7 | | 7 |
| 5.6 | w | | 8 | | 8 |
| 5.8 | | e | 9 | 9 | |
| 5.9 | | e | 10 | 10 | |
| 6.2 | | e | 11 | 11 | |
| 6.3 | w | | 12 | | 12 |
| 6.4 | | e | 13 | 13 | |
| 6.8 | w | | 14 | | 14 |
| 7.1 | w | | 15 | | 15 |
| 7.5 | | e | 16 | 16 | |
| 7.9 | w | | 17 | | 17 |
| 8.5 | w | | 18 | | 18 |
| 9.0 | w | | 19 | | 19 |

$T_w$ = sum of elements in column Rank W. = 114.

114 > 110.146. Therefore we reject the null

hypothesis and assume that West Coast students actually do get higher grades.

● **PROBLEM** 20-17

The 6 honor pupils at Mother Hubbard's Cookery School had challenged the 8 honor pupils at the Good Wives' Training College to a cake-making competition. Would it indicate a significant difference between the 2 groups if the individual marks gained by the competitors were as follows:

| Mother Hubbard's | Good Wives' |
|---|---|
| 91 | 91 |
| 92 | 90 |
| 96 | 91 |
| 97 | 87 |
| 97 | 94 |
| 93 | 95 |
| | 88 |
| | 89 |

Solution: We will again use Wilcoxon's Sum of Ranks test. We have two hypotheses:

$H_0$ : The two groups have the same distribution function .

$H_1$ : The two distributions are unequal.

Consider the ordered combined sample,

87, 88, 89, 90, 91, 91, <u>91</u>, <u>92</u>, <u>93</u>, 94, 95, <u>96</u>, <u>97</u>, <u>97</u>.

The underlined scores are Mother Hubbard scores.

Since the Mother Hubbard scores are generally higher, a good rejection region might be one of the type $T_{MH} > K$, where $T_{MH}$ is the total of all Mother Hubbard ranks in the combined sample. Assume we are testing at a .05 significance level. Then, since

$$\frac{T_{MH} - E(T_{MH})}{\sqrt{Var\ (T_{MH})}} \quad \text{is approximately a standard normal}$$

random variable under $H_0$,

$$Pr\left[ \frac{T_{MH} - E(T_{MH})}{Var\ (T_{MH})} > 1.645 \right] = .05 .$$

Multiplying by $\sqrt{Var(T_{MH})}$ and adding $E(T_{MH})$ produces

$$(*)\ Pr\left[ T_{MH} > E(T_{MH}) + 1.645\ \sqrt{Var\ (T_{MH})} \right] = .05.$$

$$E(T_{MH}) = \frac{n_{MH}\ (n_{MH} + n_{GW} + 1)}{2} ,$$

where $n_{MH}$ and $n_{GW}$ are the sizes of the Mother Hubbard and Good Wives' samples. $n_{MH} = 6$ and $n_{GW} = 8$.

$$E(T_{MH}) = \frac{6\ (6 + 8 + 1)}{2} = 45. \quad \text{Furthermore,}$$

$$Var\ (T_{MH}) = \frac{n_{MH}\ n_{GW}\ (n_{MH} + n_{GW} + 1)}{12}$$

$$= \frac{6 \cdot 8\,(6 + 8 + 1)}{12} = 60$$

$$\sqrt{Var(T_{MH})} = \sqrt{60} = 7.746.$$

(*) now becomes

$$Pr(T_{MH} > 45 + (1.645)(7.746)) = .05 \qquad \text{or}$$

$$Pr(T_{MH} > 57.74) = .05.$$

We will take $T_{MH} > 57.74$ as our rejection region.

To find $T_{MH}$, we will use the following table. Tied observations yield average ranks.

| Data Value | Tally | Rank | Rank MH | Rank GW |
|---|---|---|---|---|
| 87 | GW | 1 | | 1 |
| 88 | GW | 2 | | 2 |
| 89 | GW | 3 | | 3 |
| 90 | GW | 4 | | 4 |
| 91 | GW | 5, 6, 7 = 6 | | 6 |
| 91 | GW | 5, 6, 7 = 6 | | 6 |
| 91 | MH | 5, 6, 7 = 6 | 6 | |
| 92 | MH | 8 | 8 | |
| 93 | MH | 9 | 9 | |
| 94 | GW | 10 | | 10 |
| 95 | GW | 11 | | 11 |
| 96 | MH | 12 | 12 | |
| 97 | MH | 13, 14 = $13\frac{1}{2}$ | $13\frac{1}{2}$ | |
| 97 | MH | 13, 14 = $13\frac{1}{2}$ | $13\frac{1}{2}$ | |

$T_{MH}$ = Sum of all entries in Rank MH column = 62.

62 > 57.74. Therefore we reject $H_0$ and accept $H_1$.

# THE WILCOXON SIGNED-RANK TEST

● **PROBLEM** 20-18

My wife wanted to know whether putting cut flowers into a certain chemical solution (we'll call it 'Flower-Life') would prolong their life, so we designed the following experiment. She bought 2 fresh blooms of 25 different kinds of flowers - 2 roses, 2 irises, 2 carnations, and so on
We then put one of each pair in a vase of water, and their partners in a vase containing 'Flower-Life'. Both vases were put side by side in the same room, and the length of life of each flower was noted.

We then had 2 matched samples, so the results could be tested for significance by Wilcoxon's Signed Ranks Test. This revealed a smaller rank total of 50. Is there a statistical difference between 'Flower-Life' and plain water?

Solution:    Wilcoxon's Signed Ranks Test compares 2 random samples of matched measurements.

The test depends on the fact that if no significant difference between 2 sets of paired measurements exist, then there should be equal numbers of plus and minus differences. This test not only takes into account the direction of the difference but the size as well. If there is really no significant difference the total plus and minus rank values should be about equal.

First align all pairs from set A and set B. Subtract each member in set B from its partner in set A. Mark all appropriate minus signs. If any pairs are identical, we exclude them from our test on the grounds that they contribute nothing to our search for a significant difference. This unfortunately reduces our sample and the power of our test.

Rank all differences by absolute value and then ascribe a minus sign if appropriate. For example suppose the signed differences were

$$-\frac{1}{4}, \frac{1}{2}, \frac{3}{4}, \frac{11}{10}, -2, -\frac{17}{18}, 3.$$

The signed ranks would be $-1, 2, 3, 4, -5, -6, 7$.

Let $T_x = \Sigma$ positive signed ranks

and $T_y = \Sigma$ negative signed ranks.

In the above example $T_x = 2 + 3 + 4 + 7$ and $T_y = 1 + 5 + 6$.

In general, consider either one, $T_+$ or $T_-$. Call it T. If we assume that there is no significant difference,

$$E(T) = \frac{1}{2} \times \text{the total sum of all rank absolute values}$$

$$= \frac{1}{2} \sum_{i=1}^{n} i = \frac{1}{2} \left[\frac{n(n+1)}{2}\right] = \frac{n(n+1)}{4}.$$

Var(T) can be calculated to be $\frac{n(n+1)(2n+1)}{24}$.

The computation is involved and will be omitted. It is important to note that we can use either $T_+$ or $T_-$.

For large values of n, the exact determination of T's distribution becomes tedious. Since all ranks do not have identical distributions we cannot apply the Central Limit Theorem. However, a more general theorem, due to Liapounov, states that if a random variable $U_i$ has mean $\mu_i$ and $\sigma_i^2$ (i = 1, 2, 3, ..., n) and the $U_i$ are mutually stochastically independent, if $E(|U_i - \mu_i|^3)$ is finite for all i, and if

$$\lim_{n \to \infty} \frac{\sum_{i=1}^{n} E(|U_i - \mu_i|^3)}{\left(\sum_{i=1}^{n} \sigma_i^2\right)^{\frac{3}{2}}} = 0$$

895

then 
$$\frac{\sum_{i=1}^{n} U_i - \sum_{i=1}^{n} \mu_i}{\sqrt{\sum_{i=1}^{n} \sigma_i^2}}$$
has a limiting distribution

which is standard normal. Let $U_i = R_i$, the ith signed rank, that is the appropriate rank, i, with the suitable + or - sign.

$\mu_i = E(R_i)$. Under the null hypothesis of equality of distributions, $H_0$, the positive rank sum would equal the negative rank sum and they are of opposite signs. Hence

$E(R_i) = 0$ since $\Sigma$ signed ranks $= 0$.

$E(|R_i - \mu_i|)^3 = E(|R_i|)^3 = i^3$.

$$\sum_{i=1}^{n} E(|R_i - \mu_i|)^3 = \sum_{i=1}^{n} i^3 = \frac{n^2 (n+1)^2}{4}$$

by a known algebraic formula.

Now 
$$\lim_{n \to \infty} \sum_{i=1}^{n} \frac{E(|U_i - \mu_i|)^3}{\left(\sum_{i=1}^{n} \sigma_i^2\right)^{\frac{3}{2}}}$$

$$= \frac{\sum_{i=1}^{n} E(|U_i - \mu_i|)^3}{\left(\sum_{i=1}^{n} \sigma_i^2\right)^{\frac{3}{2}}} = \frac{n^2 (n+1)^2/4}{(Var(T_+) + Var(T_-))^{\frac{3}{2}}}$$

$$= \frac{n^2 (n+1)^2/4}{(2 Var(T))^{\frac{3}{2}}} = \frac{n^2 (n+1)^2/4}{[n(n+1)(2n+6)/12]^{\frac{3}{2}}}$$

As $n \to \infty$, (1) becomes $\dfrac{n^4 + \text{other terms}}{n^{9/27} + \text{other terms}} \to 0$,

so Liapounov's Theorem holds

and 
$$\frac{\sum_{i} R_i - 0}{\sum_{i} Var(R_i)}$$
has a limiting standard normal

distribution. It can be now shown, although it won't be here, that since $(T_+) + (T_-) = \Sigma R_i$ (a constant),

$$\frac{(T_+) - \frac{n\ (n+1)}{4}}{\sqrt{\frac{n\ (n+1)\ (2n+1)}{24}}} \quad \text{and} \quad \frac{(T_-)\left[\frac{n(n+1)}{4}\right]}{\sqrt{\frac{n\ (n+1)\ (2n+1)}{24}}}$$

have approximate standard normal distributions. That we can use either $T_+$ or $T_-$ comes from the fact that either one uniquely determines the other and they therefore have "mirror" distributions. Since the normal distribution is symmetric, this mirror quality is irrelevant.

Let us examine, in our problem,

$$K = \left| \frac{T - \frac{n\ (n+1)}{4}}{\sqrt{\frac{n\ (n+1)\ (2n+1)}{24}}} \right| = \left| \frac{50 - \frac{25\ (25+1)}{4}}{\sqrt{\frac{25\ (25+1)\ (2 \cdot 25 + 1)}{24}}} \right|$$

$$= 3.03 .$$

Examination of the standard normal table shows this to indicate a random probability of .0002, if there is no difference between water and Flower-Life. We therefore reject the outside possibility.

● **PROBLEM** 20-19

Let $\xi_{0.5}$ be the median of a symmetric distribution which is of the continuous type. Use the Wilcoxon Signed Ranks Test to test, at the .01 significance level, the hypothesis $H_0: \xi_{0.5} = 75$ against $H_1: \xi_{0.5} > 75$. We have a random sample of size 18 and their deviations from 75 are the following values:

1.5, - 0.5, 1.6, 0.4, 2.3, - 0.8, 3.2, 0.9, 2.9

0.3, 1.8, - 0.1, 1.2, 2.5, 0.6, - 0.7, 1.9, 1.3.

Solution:    If we match each value in the sample with 75 and subtract we come up with deviations as above. If the null hypothesis is true the sum of the signed ranks should be close to zero. Hence the situation is conducive to the Wilcoxon Signed Ranks Test.

First arrange the deviations in ascending absolute value order.

- 0.1, 0.3, 0.4, - 0.5, 0.6, - 0.7, - 0.8, 0.9

1.2, 1.3, 1.5, 1.6, 1.8, 1.9, 2.3, 2.5, 2.9, 3.2.

The signed ranks are therefore

- 1, 2, 3, - 4, 5, - 6, - 7, 8, 9, 10, 11, 12,

$$13, 14, 15, 16, 17, 18.$$

$$T_+ = \Sigma \text{ positive ranks} = 2 + 3 + 5 + \sum_{i=8}^{18} i = 153$$

$$T_- = \Sigma |\text{negative ranks}| = 1 + 4 + 6 + 7 = 18.$$

Since we are checking $H_0: \xi_{0.5} = 75$ vs. $H_1: \xi_{0.5} > 75$, it makes sense to use as a rejection region $T_+ \geq K$. We know however that

$$\frac{(T_+) - \frac{n(n+1)}{4}}{\sqrt{\frac{n(n+1)(2n+1)}{24}}} \text{ is approximately standard normal.}$$

Therefore from the normal table

$$\text{Pr}\left[ \frac{T_+ - \frac{n(n+1)}{4}}{\sqrt{\frac{n(n+1)(2n+1)}{24}}} \geq 2.236 \right] = .01 .$$

Hence the decision rule is; reject $H_0$ if

$$\frac{T_+ - \frac{n(n+1)}{4}}{\sqrt{\frac{n(n+1)(2n+1)}{24}}} \geq 2.236.$$

$$\frac{T_+ - \frac{n(n+1)}{4}}{\sqrt{\frac{n(n+1)(2n+1)}{24}}} = \frac{153 - \frac{18(18+1)}{4}}{\sqrt{\frac{18(18+1)(2 \cdot 18 + 1)}{24}}}$$

$$= \frac{153 - 85.5}{22.96} = 2.94 > 2.236.$$

Reject $H_0: \xi_{0.5} = 75$, and accept that $\xi_{0.5} > 75$.

● **PROBLEM 20-20**

For the Wilcoxon matched-pair signed ranks test, assume
N = 9. Using a table of critical values of T, determine
the critical values for a one-tailed test when $\alpha = .025$,
$\alpha = .01$ and $\alpha = .005$. Compare these critical values to
critical values for T obtained when the normal approximation
for T is used. How good is the normal approximation when N
is as small as 9?

<u>Solution:</u>     Using a table of critical values of T, when
N = 9, critical values for a one-tailed test when $\alpha = .025$,

$\alpha = .01$ and $\alpha = .005$ are 6, 3, and 2 respectively.

Using the normal approximation, we must find

$$\mu_T = \frac{N(N+1)}{4} \quad \text{and} \quad \sigma_T = \sqrt{\frac{N(N+1)(2N+1)}{24}}.$$

For $N = 9$

$$\mu_T = \frac{(9)(10)}{4} = 22.5$$

$$\sigma_T = \sqrt{\frac{9(10)(19)}{24}} = \sqrt{\frac{1710}{24}} = 8.44.$$

Critical values for T are obtained by applying the equation $Z = \dfrac{T - \mu_T}{\sigma_T}$

for $Z = -1.96$, $-2.33$, and $-2.58$ which correspond to $\alpha = .025$, $\alpha = .001$, and $\alpha = .005$ respectively.

For $Z = 1.96$: $-1.96 = \dfrac{T - 22.5}{8.44}$.

Solving for T: $-16.54 = T - 22.5$, $T = 5.96$.

For $Z = -2.33$: $-2.33 = \dfrac{T - 22.5}{8.44}$, $T = 2.83$.

For $Z = -2.58$: $-2.58 = \dfrac{T - 22.5}{8.44}$, $T = .72$.

So the normal approximation when $N = 9$ is good except when $\alpha = .005$.

# THE WILCOXON STRATIFIED TEST

● PROBLEM 20-21

Suppose we want to compare 2 treatments for curing acne (pimples). Suppose, too, that for practical reasons we are obliged to use a presenting sample of patients. We might then decide to alternate the 2 treatments strictly according to the order in which the patients arrive (A, B, A, B, and so on). Let us agree to measure the cure in terms of weeks to reach 90% improvement (this may prove more satisfactory than awaiting 100% cure, for some patients, may not be completely cured by either treatment, and many patients might not report back for review when they are completely cured).

This design would ordinarily call for Wilcoxon's Sum of Ranks Test, but there is one more thing to be considered: severity of the disease. For it could happen that a disproportionate number of mild cases might end up, purely by chance, in one of the treatment groups, which could bias the results in favor of this group, even if there was no difference between the 2 treatments. It would clearly be better to compare the 2 treatments on comparable cases, and this can be done by stratifying the samples. Suppose we decide to group all patients into one or other of 4 categories - mild, moderate, severe, and very severe. Then all the mild cases would be given the 2 treatments alternatively and likewise with the other groups.

Given the results tabulated below (in order of size, not of their actual occurrence), is the evidence sufficient to say that one treatment is better than the other?

| Category | Treatment A Weeks | Treatment B Weeks |
|---|---|---|
| (I) Mild | 2<br>3 | 2<br>4 |
| (II) Moderate | 3<br>5<br>6<br>10 | 4<br>6<br>7<br>9 |
| (III) Severe | 6<br>8<br>11 | 9<br>14<br>14 |
| (IV) Very severe | 8<br>10<br>11 | 12<br>14<br>15 |

Solution: Wilcoxon extended his sum of ranks to compare 2 independent stratified random samples of measurements which have comparable strata. Wilcoxon's Stratified Test serves to compare the effect of 2 treatments when both are tested at various levels or when both are applied to 2 or more independent sample groups.

The first step is to divide the sample into appropriate strata. In our case this has already been done. Next assign ranks to the observations in both samples combined, for each stratum separately, working from the smallest to the largest in each case. We give average rank values to identical measurements occurring in the same stratum. Add up the 2 sets of sample ranks. Call either one T (it should be easy to see that we can construct a test also using the other total).

It can be shown that as the strata groups increase in number

$$Z = \frac{T - \dfrac{n_I(2n_I + 1)}{2} - \dfrac{n_{II}(2n_{II} + 1)}{2} - \text{etc.}}{\sqrt{\dfrac{n_I^2(2n_I + 1)}{12} + \dfrac{n_{II}^2(2n_{II} + 1)}{12} + \text{etc.}}}$$

has a distribution which approximates standard normal ($n_I$, $n_{II}$, etc. are the number of observations in each stratum).

If each of the K strata contains n measurements, the above statistic reduces to

$$Z = \frac{T - \frac{kn(2n+1)}{2}}{\sqrt{\frac{kn^2(2n+1)}{12}}}$$

The above formulae are only extensions of that given in the Wilcoxon Sum of Ranks Test.

The following extension of the problem's table should prove helpful.

| Category | Treatment A Weeks | Rank | Treatment B Weeks | Rank |
|---|---|---|---|---|
| (I) Mild | 2 | $1,2 = 1\frac{1}{2}$ | 2 | $1, 2 = 1\frac{1}{2}$ |
|  | 3 | 3 | 4 | 4 |
| (II) Moderate | 3 | 1 | 4 | 2 |
|  | 5 | 3 | 6 | $4, 5 = 4\frac{1}{2}$ |
|  | 6 | $4,5 = 4\frac{1}{2}$ | 7 | 6 |
|  | 10 | 8 | 9 | 7 |
| (III) Severe | 6 | 1 | 9 | 3 |
|  | 8 | 2 | 14 | $5, 6 = 5\frac{1}{2}$ |
|  | 11 | 4 | 14 | $5, 6 = 5\frac{1}{2}$ |
| (IV) Very severe | 8 | 1 | 12 | 4 |
|  | 10 | 2 | 14 | 5 |
|  | 11 | 3 | 15 | 6 |

Rank sum:  34          Rank sum:  54

Let T = 34

$n_I = 2$ so $n_I(2n_I + 1) = 2 \times 5 = 10$

$n_I^2(2n_I + 1) = 4 \times 5 = 20$

$n_{II} = 4$ so $n_{II}(2n_{II} + 1) = 4 \times 9 = 36$

$n_{II}^2(2n_{II} + 1) = 16 \times 9 = 144$

$$n_{III} = 3 \text{ so } n_{III} \ (2n_{III} + 1) = 3 \times 7 = 21$$

$$n_{III}^{2} \ (2n_{III} + 1) = 9 \times 7 = 63$$

$$n_{IV} = 3 \text{ so } n_{IV} \ (2n_{IV} + 1) = 3 \times 7 = 21$$

$$n_{IV}^{2} \ (2n_{IV} + 1) = 9 \times 7 = 63 \ .$$

Now our standard normal statistic Z

$$= \frac{T - \dfrac{n_I \ (2n_I + 1)}{2} - \dfrac{n_{II} \ (2n_{II} + 1)}{2} - \text{etc.}}{\sqrt{\dfrac{n_I^{2} \ (2n_I + 1) + n_{II}^{2} \ (2n_{II} + 1) + \text{etc.}}{12}}}$$

$$= \frac{34 - \dfrac{10}{2} - \dfrac{36}{2} - \dfrac{21}{2} - \dfrac{21}{2}}{\sqrt{\dfrac{20 + 144 + 63 + 63}{12}}} = \frac{-10}{4.92} = -2.03 \ .$$

A standard normal statistic will produce a value with absolute value as large as 2.03 less than 5% of the time. There probably is a significant difference between the 2 treatments.

Note that ranks do not show the size of the differences and thus the sensitivity of the test is reduced. The test of Analysis of Variance will be more precise but much more laborious.

● **PROBLEM** 20-22

When Joe got back from Bolivia, the first thing he did was to test the 'magic powder' that the natives there had claimed would prevent materials from shrinking when they were being laundered. He got 9 different sorts of cloth, cut them into strips, measured them, laundered them with the 'magic powder', and then measured them again. He did this twice with each type of cloth, and then repeated the whole process (using fresh cloths, of course) without the "magic powder", to serve as his controls. Here are the results; is there a statistically significant difference between them?

| Material | With "Magic Powder' % Shrinkage | | With ordinary detergent % Shrinkage | |
|---|---|---|---|---|
| | 1st test | 2nd test | 1st test | 2nd test |
| A | 0 | 1 | 3 | 3 |
| B | 2 | 5 | 4 | 6 |
| C | 6 | 4 | 5 | 7 |

| | | | | |
|---|---|---|---|---|
| D | 10 | 8 | 7 | 11 |
| E | 4 | 1 | 3 | 2 |
| F | 1 | 2 | 1 | 4 |
| G | 6 | 5 | 9 | 9 |
| H | 0 | 2 | 2 | 3 |
| I | 4 | 7 | 3 | 5 |

<u>Solution:</u>    We will again use Wilcoxon's Stratified Test. Since each strata, or material has n = 2 measurements in each process we can use the formula

$$Z = \frac{T - \frac{kn(2n+1)}{2}}{\sqrt{\frac{kn^2(2n+1)}{12}}}$$

as a standard normal statistic. There are k = 9 strata so

$$Z = \frac{T - \frac{9.2(2 \cdot 2 + 1)}{2}}{\sqrt{\frac{9.2^2(2 \cdot 2 + 1)}{12}}} = \frac{T - 45}{3.873} \quad .$$

We now need T.

We rewrite the table and assign ranks.

| Material | % Shrinkage with "Magic Powder" and Ranks | | % Shrinkage with detergent and Ranks | |
|---|---|---|---|---|
| A | 0 | 1 | 3 | 3, 4 = $3\frac{1}{2}$ |
| | 1 | 2 | 3 | 3, 4 = $3\frac{1}{2}$ |
| B | 2 | 1 | 4 | 2 |
| | 5 | 3 | 6 | 4 |
| C | 6 | 3 | 5 | 2 |
| | 4 | 1 | 7 | 4 |
| D | 10 | 3 | 7 | 1 |
| | 8 | 2 | 11 | 4 |
| E | 4 | 4 | 3 | 3 |
| | 1 | 1 | 2 | 2 |
| F | 1 | 1, 2 = $1\frac{1}{2}$ | 1 | 1, 2 = $1\frac{1}{2}$ |
| | 2 | 3 | 4 | 4 |

| | | | | |
|---|---|---|---|---|
| G | 6 | 2 | 9 | $3, 4 = 3\frac{1}{2}$ |
| | 5 | 1 | 9 | $3, 4 = 3\frac{1}{2}$ |
| H | 0 | 1 | 2 | $2, 3 = 2\frac{1}{2}$ |
| | 2 | $2, 3 = 2\frac{1}{2}$ | 3 | 4 |
| I | 4 | 2 | 3 | 1 |
| | 7 | 4 | 5 | 3 |

Rank sum = 38     Rank sum = 52

Let T = 38;

$$Z = \frac{38 - 45}{3.873} = -1.81 \; .$$

If we test at the 5% significance level, $|Z|$ would have to be $\geq 1.96$ to reject the hypothesis that the two distributions are not significantly different. In our case this value of Z tells us that 7% (not 5%) of the time will similar distributions yield this type of result. For a more precise, but very complicated measurement one can use Analysis of Variance. Here we will stick with the simple approximation yielded by Wilcoxon's Test.

# SPEARMAN'S RANK CORRELATION TEST

● PROBLEM 20-23

Mr. Smith was asked to judge the beauty contest. There were 8 lovely young ladies in the contest, and the results were as follows:

| Contestant | Place |
|---|---|
| Amelia, aged 17 | 1 |
| Betsy, aged 16 | =2 |
| Carolyn, aged 18 | =2 |
| Daisy, aged 20 | 4 |
| Eve, aged 18 | 5 |
| Freda, aged 18 | 6 |
| Georgina, aged 20 | 7 |
| Helen, aged 23 | 8 |

Their ages are also quoted, because I suspect that Mr. Smith shows a bias towards youth. Let us see if this apparent relationship between age and place is likely to be a mere chance correlation, or not. In other words, if Mr. Smith has shown no tendency to favor the young con-

testants, what is the probability of getting the observed
results merely by chance?

Solution:      Spearman's Rank Correlation Test is suitable.
Its purpose is to test for correlation between 2 measurable
characteristics. When considering correlation between 2
things one must be on guard against the fallacy that one
causes the other.

The test works on the following principle. Each of
the two sets of measurements is given its own set of rank
values. If the sets are perfectly correlated, there would
be no difference in the ranking order of the 2 sets, so if
we subtracted each rank value in one set from its partner
the total of differences would be zero. On the other hand,
if the 2 sets are perfectly inversely correlated the ranks
will be reversed. You can convince yourself that in this
case the total of the rank differences will be a maximum.

In testing for correlation we start by assuming the
null hypothesis $H_0$; there is no significant correlation.
We determine the probability, under $H_0$, that we can obtain
our result by chance. If the probability is remote we
usually reject the hypothesis of no correlation. We will
use 5% as our dividing line.

The procedure for the test is a bit involved. First
record all paired values of the 2 sets in question. Second
assign ranks to each set independently. In case of ties,
use average ranks.

Subtract to find the difference (d) between the rank
values of each pair of observations. Square each difference
value $(d^2)$. Add up  all the difference squares. Call this
total $D^2$. If there are any ties, a correction factor (T)
must be added to the value of $D^2$. This is needed because
each set of ties involving x observations falsely lowers
the value of $D^2$ by $\frac{x^3 - x}{12}$ . Let tx = number of ties involving x elements. Then

$$T = \sum_{x} tx \left( \frac{x^3 - x}{12} \right).$$

If n = 5 to 30, we have provided a table giving the
probabilities of observing certain values of $D^2$ + T under
the assumption of no correlation.

If n > 30

$$Z = \sqrt{n - 1} \left[ 1 - \frac{D^2 + T}{\frac{1}{6} (n^3 - n)} \right]$$

is approximately a standard normal statistic.

The following table rearranges the data for our problem.

| Contestant | Rank of Place | Age Rank | d | $d^2$ |
|---|---|---|---|---|
| Amelia | 1 | 2 | $-1$ | 1 |
| Betsy | $2, 3 = 2\frac{1}{2}$ | 1 | $1\frac{1}{2}$ | $2\frac{1}{4}$ |
| Carolyn | $2, 3 = 2\frac{1}{2}$ | $3,4,5 = 4$ | $-1\frac{1}{2}$ | $2\frac{1}{4}$ |
| Daisy | 4 | $6,7 = 6\frac{1}{2}$ | $-2\frac{1}{2}$ | $6\frac{1}{4}$ |
| Eve | 5 | $3,4,5 = 4$ | 1 | 1 |
| Freda | 6 | $3,4,5 = 4$ | 2 | 4 |
| Georgina | 7 | $6,7 = 6\frac{1}{2}$ | $\frac{1}{2}$ | $\frac{1}{4}$ |
| Helen | 8 | 8 | 0 | 0 |

$$n = 8 \qquad D^2 = \Sigma d^2 = 17$$

We have 3 sets of ties

(1) Betsy and Carolyn, for second place.

(2) Daisy and Georgina are both aged 20.

(3) Carolyn, Eve, and Freda are all aged 18.

We have 2 sets of ties involving 2 observations each ($t_2 = 2$) and 1 set involving 3 ($t_3 = 1$). Therefore

$$T = 2\,\frac{2^3 - 2}{12} + 1\,\frac{3^3 - 3}{12} = 1 + 2 = 3.$$

$$D^2 + T = 20.$$

Use a $D^2 + T$ table. Look under $n = 8$ and find that we could expect a result like this less than 5% of the time. The correlation is probably significant.

● **PROBLEM** 20-24

In the Journal of the American Dental Association (1948, pp. 28 - 36), the Director of U.S. National Institute of Dental Research, Dr. Francis Arnold, Jr., reported the incidence of tooth decay in samples of children aged 12 to 14 years, in difference areas of the U.S.A. Against each group was noted the fluoride content of the drinking water in the area. Does the following excerpt warrant any firm conclusions about the possible association between tooth decay and the fluoride content of the water supply?

| Town | No. of children examined | No. of decayed teeth found | Average number of decayed teeth per child | Flouride content of water supply (parts per million) |
|---|---|---|---|---|
| Hereford, Texas | 60 | 88 | 1.47 | 3.1 |
| Colorado Springs, Colorado | 404 | 994 | 2.46 | 2.6 |
| Elmhurst, Ill. | 170 | 428 | 2.52 | 1.8 |
| Joliet, Ill. | 447 | 1,444 | 3.23 | 1.3 |
| Kawanee, Ill. | 123 | 422 | 3.43 | 0.9 |
| Pueblo, Colo. | 614 | 2,530 | 4.12 | 0.6 |
| Marion, Ohio | 263 | 1,462 | 5.56 | 0.4 |
| Vicksburg, Miss. | 172 | 1,010 | 5.87 | 0.2 |
| Oak Park, Ill. | 329 | 2,375 | 7.22 | 0.0 |
| Elkhart, Ind. | 278 | 2,288 | 8.23 | 0.1 |
| Escabana, Mich. | 270 | 2,368 | 8.77 | 0.2 |
| Michigan City Mich. | 236 | 2,446 | 10.36 | 0.1 |

Solution: Our goal is to apply Spearman's Correlation Test. We must first rank the sample. We give tied ranks average scores.

| Town | Rank in Average Number Decayed Teeth | Rank in Fluoride | d | $d^2$ |
|---|---|---|---|---|
| Hereford | 1 | 12 | − 11 | 121 |
| Colorado Springs | 2 | 11 | − 9 | 81 |
| Elmhurst | 3 | 10 | − 7 | 49 |
| Joliet | 4 | 9 | − 5 | 25 |

| | | | |
|---|---|---|---|
| Kawanee | 5 | 8 | $-$ 3 | 9 |
| Pueblo | 6 | 7 | $-$ 1 | 1 |
| Marion | 7 | 6 | 1 | 1 |
| Vicksburg | 8 | $4, 5 = 4\frac{1}{2}$ | $3\frac{1}{2}$ | $12\frac{1}{4}$ |
| Oak Park | 9 | 1 | 8 | 64 |
| Elkhart | 10 | $2, 3 = 2\frac{1}{2}$ | $7\frac{1}{2}$ | $56\frac{1}{4}$ |
| Escanaba | 11 | $4, 5 = 4\frac{1}{2}$ | $6\frac{1}{2}$ | $42\frac{1}{4}$ |
| Michigan City | 12 | $2, 3 = 2\frac{1}{2}$ | $9\frac{1}{2}$ | $90\frac{1}{4}$ |

$n = 12$ $\qquad$ $D^2 = \Sigma d^2 = 552$

There are 2 ties of 2 observations each. Hence

$$T = \Sigma tx \frac{x^3 - x}{12} = t \frac{2^3 - 2}{12} = 2 \cdot \frac{1}{2} = 1$$

$D^2 + T = 552 + 1 = 553$ .

We have a small enough sample to use a $D^2 + T$ table. Since it appears that the 2 rank sets are in reverse order we should check for inverse correlation. A look at the table under $n = 12$ shows that a $D^2 + T$ value of 553 would be observed with a probability far less than .01 due to chance alone. Therefore the observed inverse correlation is statistically significant. However, this does not prove that fluoride prevents tooth decay.

● **PROBLEM** 20-25

Professor Solinger questioned the validity of a certain mathematical aptitude test. One time she decided to investigate whether or not there was any correlation between test scores and age. She went to a school, chose 37 children at random and recorded her data. The results are given in the following table.

| Age | Test Score |
|---|---|
| $6\frac{1}{2}$ | 16 |
| $6\frac{3}{4}$ | 28* |
| $6\frac{3}{4}$ | 46 |
| 7 | 14 |

| | |
|---|---|
| $7 \frac{1}{4}$ | 41 |
| $7 \frac{1}{2}$ | 10 |
| $7 \frac{1}{2}$ | 56 |
| $7 \frac{1}{2}$ | 43 |
| $7 \frac{1}{2}$ | 15 |
| $7 \frac{3}{4}$ | 21 |
| 8 | 20 |
| 8 | 28* |
| 8 | 57 |
| 8 | 65 |
| $8 \frac{1}{4}$ | 42 |
| $8 \frac{1}{2}$ | 36 |
| $8 \frac{3}{4}$ | 71** |
| 9 | 47*** |
| $9 \frac{1}{4}$ | 47*** |
| $9 \frac{1}{4}$ | 66 |
| $9 \frac{1}{2}$ | 71** |
| $9 \frac{1}{2}$ | 71** |
| $9 \frac{1}{2}$ | 61 |
| $9 \frac{1}{2}$ | 55 |
| 9 | 86 |
| $9 \frac{3}{4}$ | 62 |
| $9 \frac{3}{4}$ | 78**** |

| Age | Test Score |
|---|---|
| 10 | 71** |
| 10 | 59 |

909

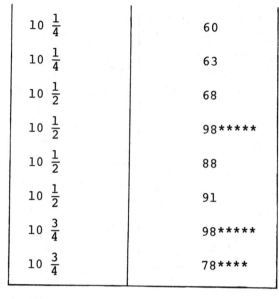

| $10\frac{1}{4}$ | 60 |
|---|---|
| $10\frac{1}{4}$ | 63 |
| $10\frac{1}{2}$ | 68 |
| $10\frac{1}{2}$ | 98***** |
| $10\frac{1}{2}$ | 88 |
| $10\frac{1}{2}$ | 91 |
| $10\frac{3}{4}$ | 98***** |
| $10\frac{3}{4}$ | 78**** |

$n = 37$

A quick glance reveals a tendency for those children who are older to score higher marks. Apply Spearman's Correlation Test to see if these effects are due to chance or significant.

Solution:    We will first expand the table to include rank values. Ties yield average ranks.

| Age | Score | Age Ranks | Score Ranks | d | $d^2$ |
|---|---|---|---|---|---|
| $6\frac{1}{2}$ | 16 | 1 | 4 | $-3$ | 9 |
| $6\frac{3}{4}$ | 28 | $2,3=2\frac{1}{2}$ | $6,7=6\frac{1}{2}$ | $-4$ | 16 |
| $6\frac{3}{4}$ | 46 | $2,3=2\frac{1}{2}$ | 12 | $-9\frac{1}{2}$ | $90\frac{1}{4}$ |
| 7 | 14 | 4 | 2 | 2 | 4 |
| $7\frac{1}{4}$ | 41 | 5 | 9 | $-4$ | 16 |
| $7\frac{1}{2}$ | 10 | $6,7,8,9=7\frac{1}{2}$ | 1 | $6\frac{1}{2}$ | $42\frac{1}{4}$ |
| $7\frac{1}{2}$ | 56 | $6,7,8,9=7\frac{1}{2}$ | 17 | $-9\frac{1}{2}$ | $90\frac{1}{4}$ |
| $7\frac{1}{2}$ | 43 | $6,7,8,9=7\frac{1}{2}$ | 11 | $-3\frac{1}{2}$ | $12\frac{1}{4}$ |
| $7\frac{1}{2}$ | 15 | $6,7,8,9=7\frac{1}{2}$ | 3 | $4\frac{1}{2}$ | $20\frac{1}{4}$ |

| | | | | | |
|---|---|---|---|---|---|
| 7 $\frac{3}{4}$ | 21 | 10 | 5 | 5 | 25 |
| 8 | 50 | 11,12,13,14 = 12 $\frac{1}{2}$ | 15 | $- 2\frac{1}{2}$ | 6 $\frac{1}{4}$ |
| 8 | 28 | 11,12,13,14 = 12 $\frac{1}{2}$ | 6,7= 6 $\frac{1}{2}$ | 6 | 36 |
| 8 | 57 | 11,12,13,14 = 12 $\frac{1}{2}$ | 18 | $- 5\frac{1}{2}$ | 30 $\frac{1}{4}$ |
| 8 | 65 | 11,12,13,14 = 12 $\frac{1}{2}$ | 24 | $-11\frac{1}{2}$ | 132 $\frac{1}{4}$ |
| 8 $\frac{1}{4}$ | 42 | 15 | 10 | 5 | 25 |
| 8 $\frac{1}{2}$ | 36 | 16 | 8 | 8 | 64 |
| 8 $\frac{3}{4}$ | 71 | 17 | 27,28,29,30=28 $\frac{1}{2}$ | $-11\frac{1}{2}$ | 132 $\frac{1}{4}$ |
| 9 | 47 | 18 | 13,14=13 $\frac{1}{2}$ | 4 $\frac{1}{2}$ | 20 $\frac{1}{4}$ |
| 9 $\frac{1}{4}$ | 47 | 19,20= 19 $\frac{1}{2}$ | 13,14=13 $\frac{1}{2}$ | 6 | 36 |
| 9 $\frac{1}{4}$ | 66 | 19,20= 19 $\frac{1}{2}$ | 25 | $- 5\frac{1}{2}$ | 30 $\frac{1}{4}$ |
| 9 $\frac{1}{2}$ | 71 | 21,22,23,24,25= 23 | 27,28,29,30=28 $\frac{1}{2}$ | $- 5\frac{1}{2}$ | 30 $\frac{1}{4}$ |
| 9 $\frac{1}{2}$ | 71 | 21,22,23,24,25= 23 | 27,28,29,30=28 $\frac{1}{2}$ | $- 5\frac{1}{2}$ | 30 $\frac{1}{4}$ |
| 9 $\frac{1}{2}$ | 61 | 21,22,23,24,25= 23 | 21 | 2 | 4 |
| 9 $\frac{1}{2}$ | 55 | 21,22,23,24,25= 23 | 16 | 7 | 49 |
| 9 $\frac{1}{2}$ | 86 | 21,22,23,24,25= 23 | 33 | -10 | 100 |
| 9 $\frac{3}{4}$ | 62 | 26,27= 26 $\frac{1}{2}$ | 22 | 4 $\frac{1}{2}$ | 20 $\frac{1}{4}$ |
| 9 $\frac{3}{4}$ | 78 | 26,27= 26 $\frac{1}{2}$ | 31,32=31 $\frac{1}{2}$ | - 5 | 25 |
| 10 | 71 | 28,29= 28 $\frac{1}{2}$ | 27,28,29,30=28 $\frac{1}{2}$ | 0 | 0 |
| 10 | 59 | 28,29= 28 $\frac{1}{2}$ | 19 | 9 $\frac{1}{2}$ | 90 $\frac{1}{4}$ |

| age | score | age rank | score rank | d | d² |
|---|---|---|---|---|---|
| $10\frac{1}{4}$ | 60 | 30,31= $30\frac{1}{2}$ | 20 | $10\frac{1}{2}$ | $110\frac{1}{4}$ |
| $10\frac{1}{4}$ | 63 | 30,31= $30\frac{1}{2}$ | 23 | $7\frac{1}{2}$ | $56\frac{1}{4}$ |
| $10\frac{1}{2}$ | 68 | 32,33,34,35= $33\frac{1}{2}$ | 26 | $7\frac{1}{2}$ | $56\frac{1}{4}$ |
| $10\frac{1}{2}$ | 98 | 32,33,34,35= $33\frac{1}{2}$ | 36,37= $36\frac{1}{2}$ | $-3$ | 9 |
| $10\frac{1}{2}$ | 88 | 32,33,34,35= $33\frac{1}{2}$ | 34 | $-\frac{1}{2}$ | $\frac{1}{4}$ |
| $10\frac{1}{2}$ | 91 | 32,33,34,35= $33\frac{1}{2}$ | 35 | $-1\frac{1}{2}$ | $2\frac{1}{4}$ |
| $10\frac{3}{4}$ | 98 | 36,37= $36\frac{1}{2}$ | 36,37= $36\frac{1}{2}$ | 0 | 0 |
| $10\frac{3}{4}$ | 78 | 36,37= $36\frac{1}{2}$ | 31,32= $31\frac{1}{2}$ | 5 | 25 |

$$n = 37 \qquad D^2 = \Sigma d^2 = 1446 .$$

Note the ties. How many ties involve 2 observations? There are 6 in age and 4 in score so $t_2 = 10$. There are no ties involving 3 observations, $t_3 = 0$. There are 3 ties involving 4 observations in age and one in score so $t_4 = 4$. Finally there is one tie involving 5 observations in age so $t_5 = 1$. Accordingly –

$$T = \sum_{x} tx \; \frac{x^3 - x}{12} = 10 \; \frac{2^3 - 2}{12} + 0 \; \frac{3^3 - 3}{12} + 4 \; \frac{4^3 - 4}{12} + 1 \; \frac{5^3 - 5}{12}$$

$$= 10 \left(\frac{1}{2}\right) + 0 \; (2) + 4 \, (5) + 1 \, (10) = 5 + 0 + 20 + 10$$

$$= 35.$$

Therefore $D^2 + T = 1446 + 35 = 1481$.

Now n = 37, which is beyond the limit of most reference tables, so we must calculate our "standard normal" statistic.

$$Z = \sqrt{n - 1} \left[ 1 - \frac{D^2 + T}{\frac{1}{6} \, (n^3 - n)} \right] = \sqrt{37 - 1} \left[ 1 - \frac{1481}{\frac{1}{6} \, (37^3 - 37)} \right]$$

$$= \sqrt{36} \left[ 1 - \frac{1481}{8436} \right] = 6 \left( \frac{6955}{8436} \right) = 4.95.$$

Referring this value to the standard normal table shows that if there was no correlation, the probability of getting the observed results is less than .002. We therefore reject

912

the hypothesis of no correlation. A statistically significant correlation probably exists.

Nine applicants for a position at Harvard University were interviewed by interviewer A. Interviewer B spoke to the same nine applicants for a similar position at Yale. Each interviewer ranked the applicants according to job suitability.

| Applicant | Rank at Harvard | Rank at Yale |
|-----------|-----------------|--------------|
| 1 | 4 | 2 |
| 2 | 3 | 4 |
| 3 | 7 | 6 |
| 4 | 2 | 1 |
| 5 | 9 | 9 |
| 6 | 8 | 8 |
| 7 | 1 | 3 |
| 8 | 5 | 7 |
| 9 | 6 | 5 |

Test the hypothesis that the rankings of the two interviewers are independent.

Solution:    We will use the Spearman Rank Correlation Test. We might hope to reject the hypothesis. If two trained interviewers should rank two sets of applicants significantly differently, then the interview method would appear to be an unsatisfactory way to evaluate people. We choose the alternative hypothesis that there is positive correlation between the sets of ranks. Formally:

$H_0$: The two sets of ranks are independent

against    $H_1$: The two sets are positively correlated.

We can rewrite the table to include the differences.

| Applicant | A rank | B rank | d | $d^2$ |
|-----------|--------|--------|-----|-------|
| 1 | 4 | 2 | 2 | 4 |
| 2 | 3 | 4 | - 1 | 1 |
| 3 | 7 | 6 | 1 | 1 |
| 4 | 2 | 1 | 1 | 1 |
| 5 | 9 | 9 | 0 | 0 |
| 6 | 8 | 8 | 0 | 0 |
| 7 | 1 | 3 | - 2 | 4 |
| 8 | 5 | 7 | - 2 | 4 |
| 9 | 6 | 5 | 1 | 1 |

$n = 9$              $D^2 = \Sigma d^2 = 16$

There were no ties in the interviewer's ratings.

Therefore $T = 0$ and $D^2 + T = 16 + 0 = 16$. Our sample size is 9, small enough so that we can use a table of $D^2 + T$ values. Looking in the row $n = 9$, we see that a $D^2 + T$ value as small as 21 can be expected by chance only 1% of the time. A value of 16 will appear even less often. Therefore we will reject $H_0$.

# THE KRUSKAL-WALLIS TEST

● PROBLEM 20-27

In their article announcing their test, Kruskal and Wallis gave the following example.

Three machines were making bottle caps. Their output on days selected at random were -

| Machine | Daily output | | | | |
|---------|------|------|------|------|------|
| A | 340 | 345 | 330 | 342 | 338 |
| B | 339 | 333 | 344 | | |
| C | 347 | 343 | 349 | 355 | |

Is there a significant difference between the output of these 3 machines?

Solution:     The Kruskal and Wallis Test extends the range of Wilcoxon's Sum of Ranks Test to cases where there are more than two sets of measurements. As before, we make the tentative assumption, $H_0$, that there is no significant difference between the samples. Any differences are (tentatively) looked upon as being the result of chance variation. As in the Wilcoxon Rank Sum Test, we pool all the measurements and assign them rank values.

If $H_0$ is correct, extracting the rank totals for each subgroup from the total ranking should reveal that they are about equal, if the number in each group is equal. If each of these subtotals is squared, and the squares are summed, the result will be minimal when the rank totals are identical. For example, $15^2 + 15^2 + 15^2 = 675$, while $13^2 + 15^2 + 17^2 = 683$.

In this test the probability of getting any particular sum of squares, under $H_0$, is determined by converting the sum of squares into a value called chi-squared, by

$$\chi^2 = \frac{12}{n^2 + n} \left[ \frac{R_1^2}{n_1} + \frac{R_2^2}{n_2} + \frac{R_3^2}{n_3} , \text{ etc.} \right] - 3(n + 1)$$

where $n$ is the size of the total samples and $n_i$ is the size of the $i$th subgroup.

The higher the value of $\chi^2$, the greater the likelihood that the observed differences are not just from chance but are due to genuine differences in the parent groups from which the samples have been drawn.

With up to five measurements in each sample, we can refer the value of $\chi^2$ to Kruskal and Wallis' table below, which shows the values that $\chi^2$ must reach so that the probability would be 5% or 1% that such a deviation was produced by chance alone.

With more than 5 measurements in each sample or with more than 3 samples of measurements, our new $\chi^2$ will follow a $\chi^2$ distribution with K-1 degrees of freedom where K is the number of samples being compared. We can obtain probabilities that way.

We use the following table to help with Kruskal and Wallis' initial problem.

| Date Values | Tally | | | Rank Values | A ranks | B ranks | C ranks |
|---|---|---|---|---|---|---|---|
| 330 | A | | | 1 | 1 | | |
| 333 | | B | | 2 | | 2 | |
| 338 | A | | | 3 | 3 | | |
| 339 | | B | | 4 | | 4 | |
| 340 | A | | | 5 | 5 | | |
| 342 | A | | | 6 | 6 | | |
| 343 | | | C | 7 | | | 7 |
| 344 | | B | | 8 | | 8 | |
| 345 | A | | | 9 | 9 | | |
| 347 | | | C | 10 | | | 10 |
| 349 | | | C | 11 | | | 11 |
| 355 | | | C | 12 | | | 12 |

$$n = 12 \qquad R_1 = 24 \qquad R_2 = 14 \qquad R_3 = 40$$

$$n_1 = 5 \qquad n_2 = 3 \qquad n_3 = 4$$

$$\chi^2 = \frac{12}{n^2 + n} \left( \frac{R_1^2}{n_1} + \frac{R_2^2}{n_2} + \frac{R_3^2}{n_3} \right) - 3(n - 1)$$

$$= \frac{12}{12^2 + 12} \left( \frac{24^2}{5} + \frac{14^2}{3} + \frac{40^2}{4} \right) - 3\ (12 + 1)$$

$$= \frac{12}{156} \left( \frac{576}{5} + \frac{196}{3} + \frac{1600}{4} \right) - 3\ (13)$$

$$= \frac{1}{13}\ (115.2 + 65.33 + 400) - 39$$

$$= \left( \frac{1}{13} \times 580.53 \right) - 39 = 44.66 - 39 = 5.66\ .$$

All three samples contain 5 or less measurements, so we refer this value of $\chi^2$ to Kruskal and Wallis' table. In the present instance $n_1 = 5$, $n_2 = 3$, and $n_3 = 4$, but for interpreting the results it does not matter which is which

- all that matters is that we have 3 samples sized 3, 4 and 5. Examine the line 3, 4, 5. This row shows that 5.66 has a probability of just less than 5% of occurring by chance. We conclude that the deviation is probably significant.

You may be interested to know that Analysis of Variance gives a probability of 5.1%. The correspondence is good.

Three brands of silver polish were tested on 3 sets of similar silver. At the conclusion of the test period measurements were made of the amount of tarnish taken off of 4 pieces of silver with each brand. The results were as follows:

| Polish | Tarnish Removed (Tenths of a gram) | | | |
|---|---|---|---|---|
| A | 7.5 | 7.4 | 7.8 | 7.1 |
| B | 6.9 | 7.2 | 7.4 | 7.1 |
| C | 6.3 | 7.0 | 6.5 | 6.8 |

Take it that under test conditions like these, previous experience has shown that there is no significant difference in tarnish removed as long as they use the same polish. Compare these measurements to determine whether there is a significant difference in the amounts of tarnish removed. If a significant difference is demonstrated, how do polishes A and B compare individually with the control polish C? Are they both significantly superior?

Solution: Kruskal and Wallis' Test is applicable. In the light of the previous problem, we can write down the following table.

| Data Value | Tally | Rank Value | Rank A | Rank B | Rank C |
|---|---|---|---|---|---|
| 6.3 | C | 1 | | | 1 |
| 6.5 | C | 2 | | | 2 |
| 6.8 | C | 3 | | | 3 |
| 6.9 | B | 4 | | 4 | |
| 7.0 | C | 5 | | | 5 |
| 7.1 | A | $6, 7 = 6\frac{1}{2}$ | $6\frac{1}{2}$ | | |

| | | | | |
|---|---|---|---|---|
| 7.1 | B | $6, 7 = 6\frac{1}{2}$ | | $6\frac{1}{2}$ |
| 7.2 | B | 8 | | 8 |
| 7.4 | A | $9, 10 = 9\frac{1}{2}$ | $9\frac{1}{2}$ | |
| 7.4 | B | $9, 10 = 9\frac{1}{2}$ | | $9\frac{1}{2}$ |
| 7.5 | A | 11 | 11 | |
| 7.8 | A | 12 | 12 | |

$$n = 12 \qquad R_1 = 39 \qquad R_2 = 28 \qquad R_3 = 11$$

$$n_1 = 4 \qquad n_2 = 4 \qquad n_3 = 4$$

$$\chi^2 = \frac{12}{n^2 + n} \left( \frac{R_1^2}{n_1} + \frac{R_2^2}{n_2} + \frac{R_3^2}{n_3} \right) - 3\,(n + 1)$$

$$= \frac{12}{12^2 + 12} \left( \frac{39^2}{4} + \frac{28^2}{4} + \frac{11^2}{4} \right) - 3\,(12 + 1)$$

$$= \frac{1}{13} \left( \frac{2426}{4} \right) - 39$$

Examining the Kruskal and Wallis table in the row 4-4-4, we see that the probability of obtaining a $\chi^2$ value as high as 7.65 is slightly less than .01. The observed differences are therefore significant. To the nearest hundredth this agrees with the result obtained by the more complicated Analysis of Variance.

In experiments which compare 3 or more unmatched samples of measurements, the difference between any 2 of the samples can be tested for significance quite easily provided that all samples contain the same numbers of measurements.

The test is accomplished by obtaining K from the following formula;

$$K = \frac{d - 0.8}{n \sqrt{n}}$$

where n is the size of each subsample and d = difference of the 2 rank totals.

The critical values of K are given in the following table, the left side of which is designed to compare any or all of the samples with one another, while the right side is reserved for comparing a number of samples individually with a control. If your calculated K equals or exceeds the value found in the body of the table, it indicates a significant difference between the samples in question, at

| Total No. of samples in experiment k | When comparing any pair of samples | | When comparing any sample with a control | |
|---|---|---|---|---|
| | Values of K indicating | | | |
| | P = 5% | P = 1% | P = 5% | P = 1% |
| 3 | 2·89 | 3·60 | 2·72 | 3·45 |
| 4 | 4·22 | 5·12 | 3·86 | 4·80 |
| 5 | 5·60 | 6·69 | 5·00 | 6·16 |
| 6 | 7·01 | 8·30 | 6·17 | 7·53 |
| 7 | 8·46 | 9·92 | 7·37 | 8·94 |
| 8 | 9·94 | 11·58 | 8·55 | 10·33 |
| 9 | 11·43 | 13·25 | 9·77 | 11·77 |
| 10 | 12·97 | 14·95 | 11·01 | 13·19 |

the probability level shown at the top of the table. (If the number of measurements is not the same in all samples, individual pairs of samples can still be compared by applying Wilcoxon's Rank Sum test.

Regarding the individual comparisons, let us deal with A and C first. Their rank total difference d = 39 - 11 = 28. Therefore

$$K = \frac{d - 0.8}{n \sqrt{n}} = \frac{28 - 0.8}{4 \sqrt{4}} = \frac{27.2}{8} = 3.40.$$

The right-hand part of the K table is relevant in this instance (because C is a control); our value of K indicates a probability of just over 1% which is a statistically significant difference.

However, with B and C, d = 28 - 11 = 17 and

$$K = \frac{17 - 0.8}{4 \sqrt{4}} = \frac{16.2}{8} = 2.02.$$

The probability of this is > 5%, hence a significant difference between B and C is not proven.

● **PROBLEM** 20-29

To compare the effectiveness of three types of pain relievers, a homogeneous group of 22 secretaries was divided into three subgroups, and each subgroup took one of these pain relievers for a period of 2 weeks. The average duration of the headaches, in minutes, during these two weeks were as follows:

| Brand A | Brand B | Brand C |
|---|---|---|
| 5.3 | 6.3 | 2.4 |
| 4.2 | 8.4 | 3.1 |
| 3.7 | 9.3 | 3.7 |
| 7.2 | 6.5 | 4.1 |
| 6.0 | 7.7 | 2.5 |
| 4.8 | 8.2 | 1.7 |
| | 9.5 | 5.3 |

| | | 4.5 |
| | | 1.3 |

Use the Kruskal-Wallis Test to test the null hypothesis that the effectiveness of the three brands is the same, against the alternative hypothesis that their effectiveness is not the same. Use a level of significance of 0.01.

Solution:    We begin by ordering the entire sample:

1.3, 1.7, 2.4, 2.5, 3.1, 3.7, 3.7, 4.1, 4.2,

4.5, 4.8, 5.3, 5.3, 6.0, 6.3, 6.5, 7.2, 7.7

8.2, 8.4, 9.3, 9.5.

We can now write the following table, giving average ranks to tied observations.

| Data Value | Tally | Rank | Rank A | Rank B | Rank C |
|---|---|---|---|---|---|
| 1.3 | C | 1 | | | 1 |
| 1.7 | C | 2 | | | 2 |
| 2.4 | C | 3 | | | 3 |
| 2.5 | C | 4 | | | 4 |
| 3.1 | C | 5 | | | 5 |
| 3.7 | A | $6,7 = 6\frac{1}{2}$ | $6\frac{1}{2}$ | | |
| 3.7 | C | $6,7 = 6\frac{1}{2}$ | | | $6\frac{1}{2}$ |
| 4.1 | C | 8 | | | 8 |
| 4.2 | A | 9 | 9 | | |
| 4.5 | C | 10 | | | 10 |
| 4.8 | A | 11 | 11 | | |
| 5.3 | C | $12,13 = 12\frac{1}{2}$ | | | $12\frac{1}{2}$ |
| 5.3 | A | $12,13 = 12\frac{1}{2}$ | $12\frac{1}{2}$ | | |
| 6.0 | A | 14 | 14 | | |
| 6.3 | B | 15 | | 15 | |

919

| | | | | |
|---|---|---|---|---|
| 6.5 | B | 16 | | 16 |
| 7.2 | A | 17 | 17 | |
| 7.7 | B | 18 | | 18 |
| 8.2 | B | 19 | | 19 |
| 8.4 | B | 20 | | 20 |
| 9.3 | B | 21 | | 21 |
| 9.5 | B | 22 | | 22 |

$$n = 22 \qquad R_1 = 70 \qquad R_2 = 131 \qquad R_3 = 52$$

$$n_1 = 6 \qquad n_2 = 7 \qquad n_3 = 9$$

$$\chi^2 = \frac{12}{n^2 + n} \left( \frac{R_1{}^2}{n_1} + \frac{R_2{}^2}{n_2} + \frac{R_3{}^2}{n_3} \right) - 3(n + 1)$$

$$= \frac{12}{22^2 + 22} \left( \frac{70^2}{6} + \frac{131^2}{7} + \frac{52^2}{9} \right) - 3(22 + 1)$$

$$= 15.63.$$

Since our subsamples contain more than five observations, we cannot use our table. Instead we assume $\chi^2$ has a chi-square distribution with $K - 1$ degrees of freedom, where $K$ is the number of subsamples being tested. In our example $K = 3$ and $K - 1 = 2$. We have a chi-square distribution with 2 degrees of freedom. According to the chi-square table,

Pr(chi-square (2) $\geq$ 9.21) = .01.

Our value 15.63 is greater than 9.21. Therefore,

Pr(chi-square (2) $\geq$ 15.63) < .01.

Hence the null hypothesis is rejected at the .01 level of significance. In other words, based on the provided information, we conclude that the effectiveness of the three pain relievers is not the same.

● **PROBLEM** 20-30

A manufacturer of chocolate peppermint creams consulted a market research firm for advice as to how he could improve his sales. One of the first things they did was to get a customer appraisal of the package in which the chocolates were sold. They designed 4 alternative packages, and devised a scheme to see if any one package appealed to customers as being 'better value' than the others. This scheme entailed having an investigator visiting 20 confectionary shops in different areas, and stopping the first person over the age of 14 emerging from each shop, showing that person one or other of the 4 packages, and asking them how much they would expect to pay for such a product. This design avoided the risk of annoying anyone, because each person was only asked a single brief question (in contrast to showing them all 4 packages and asking them to price or grade them all). In this way, 20 potential customers were interviewed, and each of the 4 packages was evaluated independently by 5 people. The results are tabuled below; is there a significant difference between the package values, or might the difference be reasonably likely to occur by chance?

| Package | Evaluations (cents) | | | | |
|---------|------|------|------|------|------|
| A | 60 | 40 | 40 | 60 | 50 |
| B | 70 | 70 | 60 | 70 | 75 |
| C | 55 | 70 | 60 | 55 | 70 |
| D | 55 | 45 | 35 | 40 | 50 |

**Solution:** Since we are dealing with four subsamples, we can use Kruskal and Wallis' Test. We can reformulate the problem's data and give ranks in the following tabular form. As always, we assign average ranks to tied values.

| Data Value | Tally | Rank | Rank A | Rank B | Rank C | Rank D |
|------------|-------|------|--------|--------|--------|--------|
| 35 | D | 1 | | | | 1 |
| 40 | D | 2,3,4= 3 | | | | 3 |
| 40 | A | 2,3,4= 3 | 3 | | | |
| 40 | A | 2,3,4= 3 | 3 | | | |
| 45 | D | 5 | | | | 5 |
| 50 | D | 6,7= $6\frac{1}{2}$ | | | | $6\frac{1}{2}$ |
| 50 | A | 6,7= $6\frac{1}{2}$ | $6\frac{1}{2}$ | | | |
| 55 | D | 8,9,10= 9 | | | | 9 |
| 55 | C | 8,9,10= 9 | | | 9 | |
| 55 | C | 8,9,10= 9 | | | 9 | |
| 60 | A | 11,12,13,14=$12\frac{1}{2}$ | $12\frac{1}{2}$ | | | |
| 60 | A | 11,12,13,14=$12\frac{1}{2}$ | $12\frac{1}{2}$ | | | |

| | | | | |
|---|---|---|---|---|
| 60 | C | $11,12,13,14=12\frac{1}{2}$ | | $12\frac{1}{2}$ |
| 60 | B | $11,12,13,14=12\frac{1}{2}$ | $12\frac{1}{2}$ | |
| 70 | C | $15,16,17,18,19=17$ | | $17$ |
| 70 | C | $15,16,17,18,19=17$ | | $17$ |
| 70 | B | $15,16,17,18,19=17$ | $17$ | |
| 70 | B | $15,16,17,18,19=17$ | $17$ | |
| 70 | B | $15,16,17,18,19=17$ | $17$ | |
| 75 | B | $20$ | $20$ | |

Here, $n_A = n_B = n_C = n_D = 5$

$$n = n_A + n_B + n_C + n_D = 20 ,$$

$R_A = \Sigma$ entries in Rank A column

$$= 3 + 3 + 6\frac{1}{2} + 12\frac{1}{2} + 12\frac{1}{2} = 37\frac{1}{2} .$$

Similarly, $R_B = 83\frac{1}{2}$, $R_C = 64.5$, and $R_D = 24\frac{1}{2}$. Now

$$\chi^2 = \frac{12}{n^2 + n} \left[ \frac{R_A^2}{n_A} + \frac{R_B^2}{n_B} + \frac{R_C^2}{n_C} + \frac{R_D^2}{n_D} \right] - 3(n+1)$$

$$= \frac{12}{20^2 + 20} \left[ \frac{(37.5)^2}{5} + \frac{(83.5)^2}{5} + \frac{(64.5)^2}{5} + \frac{(24.5)^2}{5} \right]$$
$$- 3(20 + 1)$$

$$= \frac{12}{420} \left( \frac{13,139}{5} \right) - 63 = 12.08 .$$

Since four samples are being compared, we refer to the chi-square table with $4 - 1 = 3$ degrees of freedom. We see that a $\chi^2$ value of 12.08 or more would occur by chance less than one percent of the time. The differences are significant.

A point about the ties. In their article describing the test, Kruskal and Wallis give a method for correcting the slight weakness that ensues when there are many tied observations. In this example, 17 of the 20 measurements are tied, and applying this correction will raise $\chi^2$ from 12.08 only to 12.44. The effect on the probability level is thus very small. You might wish to apply this correction if the probability is close to the significance level.

The correction consists of dividing $\chi^2$ by T where

$$T = 1 - \frac{\Sigma tx(x^3 - x)}{n^3 - n} \quad ,$$

where $tx$ = number of ties involving $x$ observations and $n$ = total number of observations in all samples. In the present case we get

$$T = 1 - \frac{(1 \times 6) + (2 \times 24) + (1 \times 60) + (1 \times 120)}{20^3 - 20}$$

$$= 1 - 0.0293 \quad = 0.9707.$$

The corrected value of $\chi^2$ is now $\frac{12.08}{.9707} = 12.44.$

● **PROBLEM** 20-31

A sports magazine reported some tests on 2 makes of outboard motors for speed-boats. Three out of 4 of Make A had pushed a trial boat along at more than 60 m.p.h., while one of the 4 of Make B managed to reach this speed (on the same boat and under the same trial conditions). Use a median test to see if this difference is significant.

Solution: Let $X_1, \ldots, X_m$ be a random sample from $F_x(\cdot)$ and $Y_1, \ldots, Y_n$ from $F_y(\cdot)$. Combine the two samples, and order them into $Z_1 < Z_2 < \ldots < Z_{m+n}$. The median test of $H_0 : F_x(u) = F_y(u)$ for all $u$ consists of finding the median, say $\tilde{Z}$ of the z values and the counting the number of x values, say $m_1$, which exceed $\tilde{Z}$ and the number of y values, say $n_1$, which exceed $\tilde{Z}$. If $H_0$ is true, $m_1$ should be approximately $\frac{m}{2}$ and $n_1$ approximately $\frac{n}{2}$. We shall use the statistic $M_1$ to construct the test; however it should be obvious that $N_1$ can be also used.

If $m + n$ is even, there are $\frac{m + n}{2}$ values greater than the median of the combined sample. Note that we can choose our $m_1$ values of X greater than the median in $\binom{m}{m_1}$ ways. The rest of the $\frac{m + n}{2}$ above median values can be chosen from the n Y's in $\binom{n}{(m + n)/2 - m_1}$ ways. Hence, by the fundamental principle of counting, we can have $m_1$ values above the median in $\binom{m}{m_1}\binom{n}{(m + n)/2 - m_1}$ ways.

By the classical model of probability:

$$P(M_1 = m_1) = \frac{\text{\# of ways getting } m_1 \text{ values above median}}{\text{Total possible ways of arranging values}}$$
above the median

$$= \frac{\binom{m}{m_1}\binom{n}{(m + n)/2 - m_1}}{\binom{m + n}{(m + n)/2}} .$$

In our problem we have 4 values above 60 m.p.h. and 4 below. We will consider 60 as the median.

It makes sense to assume a significant difference if $M_1 \geq K$. We have $m_1 = 3$ $m = n = 4$, and $n_1 = 1$. Let us find

$$Pr(M_1 \geq 3) = Pr(M_1 = 3) + Pr(M_1 = 4)$$

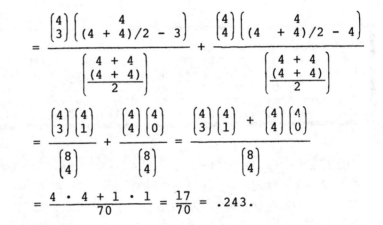

$$= \frac{4 \cdot 4 + 1 \cdot 1}{70} = \frac{17}{70} = .243.$$

This is too high a probability for us to assume a significant difference.

## COCHRAN'S TEST

● **PROBLEM** 20-32

A teacher wanted to find out the best way to demonstrate the proof of Sylow's Theorem to his class. There are three possible ways of proving this formula, but perhaps his students would not find them all equally easy to understand. He explained each of the proofs to his class of 18 students, and then asked each student to write down which of the proofs he had not understood. The results were:

| Student | | | | |
|---|---|---|---|---|
| 1 | A, B, C | 10 | - | |
| 2 | B | 11 | - | |
| 3 | B | 12 | B | |
| 4 | B | 13 | B | |
| 5 | B, C | 14 | B, C | |
| 6 | - | 15 | B | |
| 7 | B | 16 | A, B | |
| 8 | A, B | 17 | A, B, C | |

Does this represent a significant difference or might it be reasonably attributed to chance?

Solution:    We want to see if there is a significant difference between three or more sets of matched observations. When the observations can be divided into two categories, Cochran's Test is usually used.

The tentative assumption is made that there is no significant difference between the various sets of observations. On this basis, the probability of getting any observed deviation can be calculated.

The ordinary $\chi^2$ test is inapplicable in these circumstances, because the sample groups are not necessarily independent.

All observations must fall into one of the two categories, positive or negative, good or bad, etc. Note in which category each observation falls. Choose one of the 2 classes and add the total number of observations of this class in each of observations. Call these totals, $x_A$, $x_B$, $x_C$, etc. Obtain $X = x_A^2 + x_B^2 + x_C^2$, etc.

Now for every matched triple or n-tuple of observations, note how many fall into the category in question. Call these values $y_1$, $y_2$, etc. Obtain $Y = \sum\limits_{n} y_n$ . Square each $y_n$ and find $\sum\limits_{n} y_n^2 = Z$. Finally calculate $\chi^2$ from

Cochran's Formula    $\chi^2 = \dfrac{(K - 1)(KX - Y^2)}{KY - Z}$ ,

where K is the number of sets being compared.

This value has a chi-square distribution with K - 1 degrees of freedom. The higher the value of $\chi^2$, the less the likelihood of no significant difference between the three methods. The following table should aid in the application of Cochran's Test.

| Student | Failed to understand A | B | C | y | y² |
|---|---|---|---|---|---|
| 1 | ✓ | ✓ | ✓ | 3 | 9 |
| 2 | | ✓ | | 1 | 1 |
| 3 | | ✓ | | 1 | 1 |
| 4 | | ✓ | | 1 | 1 |
| 5 | | ✓ | ✓ | 2 | 4 |
| 6 | | | | 0 | 0 |
| 7 | | ✓ | | 1 | 1 |
| 8 | ✓ | ✓ | | 2 | 4 |

| | A | B | C | Y | Z |
|---|---|---|---|---|---|
| 9 | ✓ | ✓ | ✓ | 3 | 9 |
| 10 | | | | 0 | 0 |
| 11 | | | | 0 | 0 |
| 12 | | ✓ | | 1 | 1 |
| 13 | | ✓ | | 1 | 1 |
| 14 | | ✓ | ✓ | 2 | 4 |
| 15 | | ✓ | | 1 | 1 |
| 16 | ✓ | ✓ | | 2 | 4 |
| 17 | ✓ | ✓ | ✓ | 3 | 9 |
| 18 | | ✓ | | 1 | 1 |
| Column Totals | $x_A=5$ | $x_B=15$ | $x_C=5$ | $Y=25$ | $Z=51$ |

$$X = x_A^2 + x_B^2 + x_C^2 = 25 + 225 + 25 = 275.$$

We also have $Y = 25$, $Y^2 = 625$, $Z = 51$, and $K = 3$. Hence,

$$\chi^2 = \frac{(K-1)(KX - Y^2)}{KY - Z} = \frac{(3-1)(3 \cdot 275 - 625)}{3 \cdot 25 - 51}$$

$$= \frac{2(825 - 625)}{75 - 51} = \frac{2 \times 200}{24} = 16.67.$$

The degrees of freedom are $K - 1$ which thus equal 2 in the present case. Reference to the $\chi^2$ table shows that this value of $\chi^2$ with 2 d.o.f. could be expected to occur by chance, if there was no significant difference between the 3 proofs, with a probability of less than .001. We conclude, then, that a very significant difference exists between the three methods.

● **PROBLEM** 20-33

It is very inconvenient, to say the least, when sailors get seasick, so Captain McIntosh thought he should try out the latest remedy, 'Sicko' pills. He bought 200 pills (1 for each member of his crew), and 200 others that looked exactly the same but which were made of pure lactose (milk sugar). He would use the latter as a control, for he knew that they had no specific effect on seasickness. He put all the pills in his medicine cupboard, and waited for a storm.

During the first storm, Captain McIntosh did nothing except note the names of the 30 men (out of 200, remember) who became seasick.

At the first warning of the next storm, he got each and every man aboard to swallow a lactose pill (he didn't tell anyone what they were or what they were for), and again he noted the names of those who became sick.

Finally, when the next storm approached, he gave each man a 'Sicko' pill, and again noted the results.

All 3 storms being similar in severity and duration, he felt it was quite fair to compare the results of each storm with each other. So he sorted out the results and found -

15 men were sick only when they took no pill.

3 other men were sick only when they took a 'Sicko' pill.

1 other man was sick only when he took a lactose pill.

8 other men were sick both when they took no pill, and when they took a lactose pill.

4 other men were sick both when they took no pill, and when they took a 'Sicko' pill.

3 other men were sick both when they took a lactose pill, and when they took a 'Sicko' pill.

3 other men were sick on all 3 occasions.

Can you tell -

(a) Was there a significant difference between the numbers of men seasick during the 3 storms?

(b) How could this investigation have been planned so that it would have remained valid if the storms had proved unequal in severity?

Solution: (a) We want to apply Cochran's Test. We prepare the following table.

Sick with

| Sailor | No Pill | Sicko | Lactose | y | $y^2$ |
|--------|---------|-------|---------|---|-------|
| 1 | ✓ | | | 1 | 1 |
| 2 | ✓ | | | 1 | 1 |
| 3 | ✓ | | | 1 | 1 |
| 4 | ✓ | | | 1 | 1 |
| 5 | ✓ | | | 1 | 1 |
| 6 | ✓ | | | 1 | 1 |
| 7 | ✓ | | | 1 | 1 |
| 8 | ✓ | | | 1 | 1 |
| 9 | ✓ | | | 1 | 1 |
| 10 | ✓ | | | 1 | 1 |
| 11 | ✓ | | | 1 | 1 |
| 12 | ✓ | | | 1 | 1 |
| 13 | ✓ | | | 1 | 1 |
| 14 | ✓ | | | 1 | 1 |
| 15 | ✓ | | | 1 | 1 |
| 16 | | ✓ | | 1 | 1 |
| 17 | | ✓ | | 1 | 1 |
| 18 | | ✓ | | 1 | 1 |
| 19 | | | ✓ | 1 | 1 |
| 20 | ✓ | | ✓ | 2 | 4 |
| 21 | ✓ | | ✓ | 2 | 4 |
| 22 | ✓ | | ✓ | 2 | 4 |
| 23 | ✓ | | ✓ | 2 | 4 |

927

| | A | B | C | Y | Z |
|---|---|---|---|---|---|
| 24 | ✓ | | ✓ | 2 | 4 |
| 25 | ✓ | | ✓ | 2 | 4 |
| 26 | ✓ | | ✓ | 2 | 4 |
| 27 | ✓ | | ✓ | 2 | 4 |
| 28 | ✓ | ✓ | | 2 | 4 |
| 29 | ✓ | ✓ | | 2 | 4 |
| 30 | ✓ | ✓ | | 2 | 4 |
| 31 | ✓ | ✓ | | 2 | 4 |
| 32 | | ✓ | ✓ | 2 | 4 |
| 33 | | ✓ | ✓ | 2 | 4 |
| 34 | | ✓ | ✓ | 2 | 4 |
| 35 | ✓ | ✓ | ✓ | 3 | 9 |
| 36 | ✓ | ✓ | ✓ | 3 | 9 |
| 37 | ✓ | ✓ | ✓ | 3 | 9 |
| Column Totals | $x_A = 30$ | $x_B = 13$ | $x_C = 15$ | $Y = 58$ | $Z = 106$ |

$$X = x_A^2 + x_B^2 + x_C^2 = (30)^2 + (13)^2 + (15)^2 = 1294$$

Also $Y = 58$, $Y^2 = 3364$, $Z = 106$, $K = 3$. Hence,

$$\chi^2 = \frac{(K - 1)(KX - Y^2)}{KY - Z} = \frac{(3 - 1)(3 \times 1294 - 3364)}{(3 \times 58) - 106}$$

$$= \frac{2(518)}{174 - 106} = 15.24.$$

The degrees of freedom are $K - 1$, 2. From the chi-square table, a value of 15.24 with 2 d.o.f. would have a probability less than .001. The difference in numbers sick is highly significant.

(b) The design could have divided the crew into three groups by ballot; at the approach of the first storm, 1 group would get no pills, the second group a lactose pill, and the third would take the 'Sicko' pills. At the approach of each subsequent storm, the groups would be rotated, so that the group which got no pills the first time would get a lactose the second time and a 'Sicko' the third. Similar rotations would be done with the other 2 groups. At the end of the three storms, every man would have tried each of the three treatments, and the results could be analyzed by Cochran's Test. Then if one storm was appreciably milder or stronger than the others, all 3 groups would show a proportionate decrease or increase in seasickness and the experiment would not be ruined.

# RUNS TEST

● **PROBLEM** 20-34

A taxi driver kept a note of his monthly mileage for the period of a year. Do the following figures indicate a seasonal or any other periodic fluctuation, or might they reasonably be accounted to vary in a random manner?

928

| Jan. | Feb. | Mar. | Apr. | May | June |
|------|------|------|------|-----|------|
| 4,690 | 4,910 | 3,520, | 3,330 | 3,140, | 2,850 |

| July | Aug. | Sept. | Oct. | Nov. | Dec. |
|------|------|-------|------|------|------|
| 3,400 | 3,090, | 3,480 | 4,650 | 3,830, | 5,270 |

<u>Solution:</u>    As before let $X_1, \ldots, X_m$ denote a random sample from $F_x(\cdot)$ and $Y_1, \ldots, Y_n$ a random sample from $F_y(\cdot)$. A test of $H_0: F_x(z) = F_y(z)$ for all z is based on runs of values of X and values of Y. To understand the meaning of runs, combine the m x observations with the n y's and order the combined sample. For example, if m = 4 and n = 5, one might obtain

      y x x y x y y y x.

A run is a sequence of letters of the same kind bounded by letters of another kind except for the first and last position. In the above sequence, the runs are y, xx, y, x, yyy, and x. If the two samples are from the same population, the x's and y's will be well mixed and the number of runs will be quite large. If the populations are so dissimilar that their ranges do not overlap, then the number of runs will be only 2 (e.g.: <u>xxxx yyyyy</u>). In general, population differences will reduce the number of runs.

Even if the two populations have the same mean and median, but one population is dispersed while the other is concentrated, the number of runs will be small (e.g.: <u>yyyyy xxxxxxx yyy</u>).

We will perform a test by observing the total number of runs, Z, and reject $H_0$ if $Z \leq$ some specified $z_0$. Our task is now to find the distribution of Z.

If $H_0$ is true, we can see that all possible arrangements of the m x and n y values are equally likely. There are $\binom{m + n}{m}$ such arrangements. To find $\Pr(Z = z)$, it is now sufficient to count all arrangements with z runs. Suppose z is even, say 2K; then there must be K runs of x values and K runs of y values. To get K runs of x's, the m x's must be divided into K groups. These groups, or runs, can be formed by inserting K - 1 dividers into the m - 1 spaces between the m x values with no more than 1 divider per space. This can be done in $\binom{m - 1}{K - 1}$ ways. Similarly, we can construct the K runs of y values in $\binom{n - 1}{K - 1}$ ways. We can combine any particular x arrangement with any one of y. Now since the combined arrangement may begin with an x run or a y run there are a total of $2\binom{m - 1}{K - 1}\binom{n - 1}{K - 1}$

arrangements of 2 K runs. Hence

$$\Pr(Z = z) = \Pr(Z = 2K) = \frac{2\begin{pmatrix}m - 1\\K - 1\end{pmatrix}\begin{pmatrix}n - 1\\K - 1\end{pmatrix}}{\begin{pmatrix}m + n\\m\end{pmatrix}}.$$

The only difference in determining $\Pr(Z = 2K + 1)$ is to note that there must be $K + 1$ runs of one type and $K$ of the other. Using the same arguments we can obtain:

$$\Pr(Z = z) = \Pr(Z = 2k+1) = \frac{\begin{pmatrix}m - 1\\K\end{pmatrix}\begin{pmatrix}n - 1\\K - 1\end{pmatrix} + \begin{pmatrix}m - 1\\K - 1\end{pmatrix}\begin{pmatrix}n - 1\\K\end{pmatrix}}{\begin{pmatrix}m + n\\m\end{pmatrix}}.$$

To test $H_0$ at the $\alpha$ significance level, one finds the integer zo, so that as nearly as possible $\sum_{Z=2}^{z_0} \Pr(Z = z) = \alpha$.

Reject $H_0$ if $Z \leq z_0$.

The Runs Test can test for randomness. It can be used as a check to see if we can treat $X_1$, $X_2$, ..., $X_s$ as a random sample from a continuous distribution.

For the sake of argument, take s to be even. We are given the s values $X_1$, $X_2$, ..., $X_s$ in the order in which we observe them. There are $\frac{s}{2}$ of these values smaller than the remaining $\frac{s}{2}$. We have a "lower half" and an upper half. In the sequence $X_1$, $X_2$, ...., $X_s$, replace each value by either L or U, depending on whether $X_i$ is in the lower or upper half.

For s = 10, an arrangement such as

LLLLULUUUU

may suggest a trend towards increasing values of x. We can make a test of randomness and reject if $Z < c$ using the probability distributions found earlier. On the other hand if we find a sequence such as

LULULULULU,

our suspicions will be aroused that there is a cyclic effect. Here we might want to use a rejection region of $Z \geq c_2$.

In our taxi driver problem the six lower half values are in order 2,850, 3,090, 3,140, 3,330, 3,400, and 3,480. These will be assigned the letter L. the upper half, or

U, values are 3,520, 3,830, 4,650, 4,690, 4,910, 5,270.

The data in original order with the appropriate substitutions of L and U is

$$\underline{UUU}\ \ \underline{LLLLL}\ \ \underline{UUU}\ .$$

There are Z = 3 runs.

Let us determine $Pr(Z \le 3)$. We have n = m = 6.

$Pr(Z \le 3) = Pr(Z = 2) + Pr(Z = 3)$.

$Pr(Z = 2) = Pr(Z = 2 \cdot 1)$ so K = 1.

$$Pr(z=2) = \frac{2 \binom{6-1}{1-1}\binom{6-1}{1-1}}{\binom{6+6}{6}} = \frac{2\binom{5}{0}\binom{5}{0}}{\binom{12}{6}} = \frac{2}{\binom{12}{6}} = \frac{2}{924}\ .$$

$Pr(Z = 3) = Pr(Z = 2 \cdot 1 + 1)$   so K = 1

$$\frac{\binom{6-1}{1}\binom{6-1}{1-1} + \binom{6-1}{1-1}\binom{6-1}{1}}{\binom{6+6}{6}}$$

$$= \frac{\binom{5}{1}\binom{5}{0} + \binom{5}{0}\binom{5}{1}}{\binom{12}{6}} = \frac{10}{924}\ .$$

Hence    $Pr(Z \le 3) = \frac{2}{924} + \frac{10}{924} = \frac{12}{924} = .013$.

The probability of as few as 3 runs in a random process is quite small. Hence we conclude that the process is not random.

● **PROBLEM 20-35**

Would the following series of boys and girls selected haphazardly at a coeducational school, be acceptable as a random sample?

$\underline{G}\ \underline{BB}\ \underline{GG}\ \underline{B}\ \underline{G}\ \underline{BBB}\ \underline{GGGG}$

$\underline{B}\ \underline{G}\ \underline{B}\ \underline{G}\ \underline{BB}\ \underline{G}\ \underline{B}\ \underline{GGG}\ \underline{BB}$

$\underline{G}\ \underline{B}\ \underline{GG}\ \underline{B}\ \underline{GG}\ \underline{B}\ \underline{G}\ \underline{B}\ \underline{G}$

$\underline{BB}\ \underline{G}$

Solution:    There are m = 19 boys, n = 22 girls and Z = 27 runs. The computation using the formulae from the last problem would be tedious indeed. Fortunately, the distribution of Z is approximately normal for large samples, and in fact the approximation is good enough when m and n both exceed 10. If $H_0$ is true, the mean and variance of Z are

$$E(Z) = \frac{2mn}{m + n} + 1 \quad \text{and Var}(Z) = \frac{2\ mn\ (2\ mn - m - n)}{(m + n)^2 + (m + n - 1)} .$$

The asymptotic normal distribution under $H_0$ has the above mean and variance and can be used to determine a critical region.

In this example we have a lot of runs so we will use a rejection region of the form $Z \geq c$. We will use an approximate standard normal statistic $N = \dfrac{Z - E(Z)}{\sqrt{Var(Z)}}$ and reject if $N > 2.326$. This way $Pr(N \geq n)$ will be less than .01.

Let us compute

$$E(Z) = \frac{2mn}{m + n} + 1 = \frac{2 \cdot 19 \cdot 22}{19 + 22} + 1$$

$$= \frac{836}{41} + 1 = 21.39.$$

$$Var(Z) = \frac{2\ mn\ (2mn - m - n)}{(m + n)^2\ (m + n - 1)}$$

$$= \frac{2 \cdot 19 \cdot 22\ (2 \cdot 19 \cdot 22 - 19 - 22)}{(19 + 22)^2\ (19 + 22 - 1)}$$

$$= \frac{836 \cdot 795}{1681 \cdot 40} = 9.884$$

$$N = \frac{Z - E(Z)}{\sqrt{Var(Z)}} = \frac{27 - 21.39}{3.144} = 1.78.$$

1.78 < 2.326. Therefore we accept the hypothesis of a random sample.

# CHAPTER 21

# TIME-SERIES AND INDEX NUMBERS

## PERIOD RATIOS

● PROBLEM 21-1

One of the simplest ways of analyzing data over time is to choose one period as the base period and compare other periods as ratios of the base period.

Using month 1 as the base period compare the monthly sales volumes for a six-month period from the table below:

| Month | 1 | 2 | 3 | 4 | 5 | 6 |
|---|---|---|---|---|---|---|
| Sales ($) | 50,000 | 40,000 | 45,000 | 50,000 | 75,000 | 100,000 |

Solution: Let sales in month 1 be represented by 1.00. Then, sales in other months as a proportion of month 1 are given by the ratio

$$\frac{\text{Month i}}{\text{Month 1}} \qquad (1)$$

Using the given table and formula (1) we obtain the following table:

| Month: | 1 | 2 | 3 | 4 | 5 | 6 |
|---|---|---|---|---|---|---|
| Ratio: | 1.00 | .80 | .90 | 1.00 | 1.50 | 2.0 |

We see that sales volume fell at first from the base period ratio and then rose continuously until sales during the sixth month were double the amount of sales during the first month.

● PROBLEM 21-2

Compute relatives for the following data, using month 6 as the base period:

| Month | 1 | 2 | 3 | 4 | 5 | 6 |
|---|---|---|---|---|---|---|
| Sales ($) | 75,000 | 110,000 | 80,000 | 86,000 | 111,000 | 100,000 |

Solution: When the ratio of data of one period with respect to another is multiplied by 100 to give percentages, the result is called a relative (meaning relative to the base period).

In the given problem letting month 6 be the base period we obtain the following ratios:

| Month | 1 | 2 | 3 | 4 | 5 | 6 |
|-------|-----|------|-----|-----|------|------|
| Ratio | .75 | 1.10 | .80 | .86 | 1.11 | 1.00 |

(2)

Multiplying each ratio in (2) by 100 we obtain the required relatives:

| Month | 1 | 2 | 3 | 4 | 5 | 6 |
|-------|----|-----|----|----|-----|-----|
| Relatives | 75 | 110 | 80 | 86 | 111 | 100 |

These figures show the percentages of sales in each month relative to month 6.

● **PROBLEM** 21-3

Using month 3 as a base period, compute relatives for the following data:

| Month | 1 | 2 | 3 | 4 | 5 | 6 |
|-------|--------|--------|--------|--------|--------|--------|
| Sales($) | 45,000 | 50,500 | 50,000 | 60,800 | 50,400 | 60,000 |

Solution: First compute the ratios of sales in the ith month with respect to the sales in the third month. Thus,

| Month | 1 | 2 | 3 | 4 | 5 | 6 |
|-------|-----|------|------|-------|-------|-----|
| Ratio | 0.9 | 1.01 | 1.00 | 1.216 | 1.008 | 1.2 |

Next, to find the relatives, multiply each ratio by 100.

| Month | 1 | 2 | 3 | 4 | 5 | 6 |
|-------|----|-----|-----|-------|-------|-----|
| Relative | 90 | 101 | 100 | 121.6 | 100.8 | 120 |

● **PROBLEM** 21-4

Find the linked relatives for the following sales data:

| Month | 1 | 2 | 3 | 4 | 5 | 6 |
|-------|------|------|------|------|------|------|
| Sales (000) | $100 | $150 | $100 | $120 | $132 | $99 |

Solution: When relatives are computed, the change over time is measured as a function of the base period. Frequently, however, interest centers on how data change from one period to the next. Linked relatives show each period as a percentage of the preceding period.

For example, in the data above, with month 1 as the base period, the linked relative for month 2 is 150. Now, using month 2 as the base period, the linked relative for month 3 is 66.7. First, let us find the ratio of sales in the ith month with respect to sales in the preceding month. Thus,

934

| Month | 1 | 2 | 3 | 4 | 5 | 6 |
|-------|---|---|---|---|---|---|
| Ratio | 1.0 | 1.50 | .67 | 1.2 | 1.1 | .75 |

Next, to find the linked relatives, we simply multiply the above ratios by 100 (these percentage ratios are the linked relatives):

| Month | 1 | 2 | 3 | 4 | 5 | 6 |
|-------|---|---|---|---|---|---|
| Linked Relative | 100 | 150 | 67 | 120 | 110 | 75 |

The reader should note that the original data is no longer present. Sometimes, in business analysis, the original figures may completely disappear, to be replaced by refined measures.

● **PROBLEM** 21-5

A demographer is studying population growth in a rapidly expanding metropolitan area and wishes to identify those years in which the rate of growth was unusually high or unusually low. Would simple relatives or linked relatives be a more appropriate method of comparison?

Solution: Simple relatives give the values of data over time as percentages of a base period. Linked relatives, on the other hand, give the measure of data for one period as a percentage of the immediately preceding period. Since any period may be chosen as the base period when computing simple relatives, there are as many sets of simple relatives as there are observations in a given set of data. There is, however, only one sequence of linked relatives for any set of observations.

Since the expansion is rapid, it is worthwhile studying the changes from year to year. Hence the method of linked relatives is preferred.

# PRICE INDICES

● **PROBLEM** 21-6

An economist is interested in finding how the price of food changes over a period of time. He selects a sample of goods and notes their average prices in each of three years. He constructs the following table:

| | Year 1 | Year 2 | Year 3 |
|---|--------|--------|--------|
| Tomatoes ($/lb) | 0.50 | 0.70 | 0.65 |
| Potatoes ($/lb) | 0.30 | 0.15 | 0.30 |
| Cornflakes ($/box) | 0.75 | 0.75 | 0.65 |
| Hamburgers ($/lb) | 1.20 | 1.10 | 1.25 |

Using the above data, construct a simple aggregate food price index using year 1 as the base period.

Solution: The adjective 'simple' indicates the scope of the method used. We sum the prices for each year to obtain

| Year 1 | Year 2 | Year 3 |
|--------|--------|--------|
| 2.75 | 2.70 | 2.85 . |

Multiplying these sums by 100, we find

| Year 1 | Year 2 | Year 3 |
|--------|--------|--------|
| 275 | 270 | 285 . |

Since the base year is year 1, it has the value 100. The simple aggregate price index is defined as

$$p = \frac{\sum\limits_{i=1}^{n} p_{ai}}{\sum\limits_{i=1}^{n} p_{0i}} \tag{1}$$

where the subscript $0$ denotes the base period (= 100) and the subscript $a$ denotes the given year for which the price index is being computed.

Using formula (1) we find,

$$p_2 = \frac{\sum\limits_{i=1}^{n} p_{1i}}{\sum\limits_{i=1}^{n} p_{0i}} = \frac{270}{275} = 98.3$$

$$p_3 = \frac{\sum\limits_{i=1}^{n} p_{2i}}{\sum\limits_{i=1}^{n} p_{0i}} = \frac{285}{275} = 103.6 \ .$$

According to this index we see that year 3 had the highest food prices while year 2 had the lowest food prices.

● PROBLEM 2▮

After interviewing several families, an economist weighted a sample of food items in the following manner:

| Commodity | Weight | Year 1 | | Year 2 | | Year 3 | |
|-----------|--------|--------|----------|--------|----------|--------|----------|
| | | Price | Weighted Price | Price | Weighted Price | Price | Weighted Price |
| Tomatoes | 2 | 0.50 | 1.00 | 0.70 | 1.40 | 0.65 | 1.30 |
| Potatoes | 1 | 0.30 | 0.30 | 0.15 | 0.15 | 0.30 | 0.30 |
| Cornflakes | 1 | 0.75 | 0.75 | 0.75 | 0.75 | 0.65 | 0.75 |
| Hamburger | 2 | 1.20 | 2.40 | 1.10 | 2.20 | 1.25 | 2.50 |

Find the weighted aggregate price indexes for years two and three.

<u>Solution</u>: A simple aggregate price index is computed using the following formula:

$$p = \frac{\sum\limits_{i=1}^{n} P_{ai}}{\sum\limits_{i=1}^{n} P_{0i}} \tag{1}$$

where $P_{0i}$ are average prices during the base year and $P_{ai}$ are average prices during the year for which the index is being calculated. The base year sum of prices is defined as 100. The relatives for the other years are then found thereby yielding the price indexes.

An obvious defect of the simple aggregate price index is that all items receive the same importance regardless of what proportion of the budget they require. For example, suppose the families interviewed consumed more potatoes than tomatoes. Then, a change in the price of tomatoes would have less impact on the family budget than a change in the price of potatoes.

The method used to surmount this difficulty in the given problem is to weight the different items according to their importance. Then, letting $w_i$ be the weights, the weighted prices are

$$w_i P_i \ ,$$

and the sum of weighted prices is

$$\sum\limits_{i=1}^{n} w_i P_{ai} \ .$$

The weighted price index is then

$$P_w = \frac{\sum\limits_{i=1}^{n} w_i P_{ai}}{\sum\limits_{i=1}^{n} w_i P_{0i}} \ . \tag{2}$$

Note that the weights are the same in both periods. From the table, we find

$$\sum\limits_{i=1}^{n} w_i P_{1i} = 4.45$$

and

$$\sum\limits_{i=1}^{n} w_i P_{1i} \times 100 = 445.$$

Similarly,

$$\sum\limits_{i=1}^{n} w_i P_{2i} \times 100 = 450$$

and

$$\sum\limits_{i=1}^{n} w_i P_{3i} \times 100 = 485.$$

Substituting these results successively into (2) (where $P_{1i} = P_{0i}$ and $\sum_{i=1}^{n} w_i P_{0i} = 100$)

$$P_2 = \frac{450}{445} = 101.12$$

$$P_3 = \frac{485}{445} = 106.74 \ .$$

We see, using year 1 as the base year, that prices rose in both years with the greater change occurring in year 3.

Construct a Laspeyres' quantity index for the following sales data using 1966 = 100 as the base year.

| Commodity | Year | | | |  |
|---|---|---|---|---|---|
|  | 1966 | 1967 | 1968 | 1966 |  |
|  | $q_0$ | $q_1$ | $q_2$ | $P_0$ |  |
| Radio | 15 | 16 | 17 | $ 20 | (1) |
| TV sets | 20 | 22 | 24 | $ 80 |  |
| Hi-fi sets | 10 | 20 | 30 | $ 60 |  |

Solution: Index numbers may be classified as price indexes or quantity indexes. A price index number uses the quantities of goods bought as weighting factors.

The Laspeyres' quantity index uses base year prices as the weighting factors. Thus, if we are interested in finding the Laspeyres' index number of a basket of goods we use the formula

$$L = \frac{\sum_{i=1}^{n} P_{0i}\, q_{1i}}{\sum_{i=1}^{n} P_{0i}\, q_{0i}} \times 100 \ . \tag{2}$$

Note that in (2), base year prices (as indicated by the subscript 0) are used as the weights. A Laspeyres' index number (quantity, price or value) is defined as an index number that uses base year observations as the weighting factors.

Using formula (2) we wish to construct the following Laspeyres' index numbers from the data of table (1): $L_0$, $L_1$ and $L_2$.

First, however, let us find some figures necessary for further computation:

| | $q_0 P_0$ | $q_1 P_0$ | $q_2 P_0$ |
|---|---|---|---|
| Radio | 300 | 320 | 340 |
| TV sets | 1600 | 1760 | 1920 |
| Hi-fi sets | 600 | 1200 | 1800 |

Now,

$$L_0 \atop (1966) \ = \ \frac{\sum_{i=1}^{n} P_{0i}\, q_{0i}}{\sum_{i=1}^{n} P_{0i}\, q_{0i}} \times 100 = \frac{2500}{2500} \times 100 = 100$$

$$L_1 \atop (1967) \ = \ \frac{\sum_{i=1}^{n} P_{0i}\, q_{1i}}{\sum_{i=1}^{n} P_{0i}\, q_{0i}} \times 100 = \frac{3280}{2500} \times 100 = 131.2 \ .$$

$$L_2 \atop (1968) \ = \ \frac{\sum_{i=1}^{n} P_{0i}\, q_{2i}}{P_{0i}\, q_{0i}} \times 100 = \frac{4060}{2500} \times 100 = 162.4 \ .$$

The index number 162.4 indicates that output in 1968 was 62.4% greater than 1966 output.

Compute a weighted aggregate index for production wages based on the following data. Use year 1 as the base period and year 4 to establish weights.

| Skill Level | Year 1 Wage Rate ($) | Year 1 % of Workers (w) | Year 2 Wage ($) | Year 2 % of (w) | Year 3 Wage ($) | Year 3 % of (w) | Year 4 Wage ($) | Year 4 % of (w) |
|---|---|---|---|---|---|---|---|---|
| 1 | 1.50 | 20 | 1.60 | 15 | 1.75 | 20 | 1.80 | 15 |
| 2 | 2.50 | 40 | 2.50 | 45 | 2.75 | 35 | 3.00 | 30 |
| 3 | 3.50 | 30 | 4.00 | 30 | 4.50 | 35 | 5.00 | 40 |
| 4 | 5.00 | 10 | 5.50 | 10 | 6.50 | 10 | 7.50 | 15 |

Solution: We use the weighted aggregate index when some items are more important than others. The relative importance of different items is assigned through weights.

Examining the table we see that the weighting factors in this case are the percentage of workers in the different skill levels. The choice of year, year 4, for the weights is determined by two considerations: 1) the percentages do not show any radical shifts over time; 2) the last year is a natural choice viewed as the year in which the index is being prepared.

We first rewrite table 1 using only '% w' of year 4 as the weight. Thus,

| Skill Level | Weight | Wage rates Year 1 | Wage rates Year 2 | Wage rates Year 3 | Wage rates Year 4 |
|---|---|---|---|---|---|
| 1 | 15 | 1.50 | 1.60 | 1.75 | 1.80 |
| 2 | 30 | 2.50 | 2.50 | 2.75 | 3.00 |
| 3 | 40 | 3.50 | 4.00 | 4.50 | 5.00 |
| 4 | 15 | 5.00 | 5.50 | 6.50 | 7.50 |

Next we compute the weighted wage rates and find their totals. Then, using the total of year 1 as 100 we find the indexes for the other years. Thus,

| Skill Level | Weight | Weighted Wage Rates Year 1 | Weighted Wage Rates Year 2 | Weighted Wage Rates Year 3 | Weighted Wage Rates Year 4 |
|---|---|---|---|---|---|
| 1 | 15 | 22.50 | 24.00 | 26.25 | 27.00 |
| 2 | 30 | 75.00 | 75.00 | ·82.50 | 90.00 |
| 3 | 40 | 140.00 | 160.00 | 180.00 | 200.00 |
| 4 | 15 | 75.00 | 82.50 | 97.50 | 112.50 |
| Total | | 312.50 | 341.50 | 386.25 | 429.50 |
| Index | | 100 | $\frac{341.50}{312.50}$ | $\frac{386.25}{312.50}$ | $\frac{429.50}{312.50}$ |

Hence the indexes for years 2,3, and 4 are 109.3, 123.6 and 137.4 respectively.

# TIME SERIES

● PROBLEM 21-10

Consider the following table giving daily ticket sales figures for a movie theatre.

|  | Week 1 | Week 2 |
|---|---|---|
| Sunday | 900 | 800 |
| Monday | 400 | 500 |
| Tuesday | 500 | 300 |
| Wednesday | 600 | 300 |
| Thursday | 300 | 400 |
| Friday | 700 | 600 |
| Saturday | 1100 | 900 |

Compute a seven-day moving average.

Solution: We proceed in the following manner. First, find the average daily attendance from Sunday to Saturday of the first week. This figure is placed next to Wednesday. Then find the average from Monday of the first week to Sunday of the second week. Proceeding in this way we obtain the seven-day moving average for the given data. Thus,

|  | Week 1 Daily Sales | 7 day M.A. | Week 2 Daily Sales | 7-day M.A. |
|---|---|---|---|---|
| Sunday | 900 |  | 800 | 571 |
| Monday | 400 |  | 500 | 586 |
| Tuesday | 500 |  | 300 | 571 |
| Wednesday | 600 | 643 | 300 | 543 |
| Thursday | 300 | 629 | 400 |  |
| Friday | 700 | 643 | 600 |  |
| Saturday | 1100 | 614 | 900 |  |

Examining the original data we see that sales fluctuate. On weekends, the number of patrons is larger than on weekdays. Note now that these fluctuations are reduced by the moving average method. The moving average typically reduces seasonal (or in this case weekly) variability. Thus, for example, assume we have a series of monthly sales figures extending over a number of years. If we wish to identify the trend (i.e., reduce the seasonal variations), one way of doing so is to use the method of moving averages. This method involves less computation than the use of seasonal index adjustments.

● PROBLEM 21-11

The table below shows the production of passenger cars and the deliveries of motor-cycles by manufacturers in the United Kingdom.

Calculate the coefficient of linear correlation for these data.

| Year | Production of passenger cars<br><br>x | Deliveries of motor-cycles (000)<br>y |
|------|------|------|
| 1954 | 769.2 | 179.6 |
| 1955 | 897.6 | 177.2 |
| 1956 | 707.6 | 124.5 |
| 1957 | 860.8 | 173.0 |
| 1958 | 1051.6 | 139.7 |
| 1959 | 1189.9 | 248.9 |
| 1960 | 1352.7 | 203.2 |
| 1961 | 1004.0 | 145.7 |
| 1962 | 1249.4 | 106.0 |
| 1963 | 1607.9 | 107.1 |
| 1964 | 1867.6 | 111.6 |
| | $\Sigma x = 12558.3$ | $\Sigma y = 1716.5$ |

<u>Solution</u>: We first plot a scatter diagram to see whether the two series appear to be correlated.

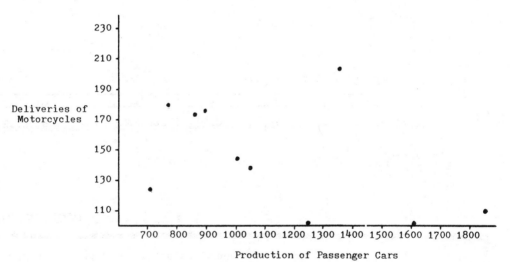

Production of Passenger Cars

The coefficient of linear correlation between two sets of observations, $x_i$ and $y_i$ ($i = 1, \ldots, n$), is

$$r = \frac{n \sum_{i=1}^{n} x_i y_i - \sum_{i=1}^{n} x_i \sum_{i=1}^{n} y_i}{\sqrt{\left[ \left\{ n \sum_{i=1}^{n} x_i^2 - \left( \sum_{i=1}^{n} x_i \right)^2 \right\} \left\{ n \sum_{i=1}^{n} y_i^2 - \left( \sum_{i=1}^{n} y_i \right)^2 \right\} \right]}} \qquad (1)$$

To simplify the calculation of (1) we construct the following table of "sum mary" statistics (using the given table):

| xy | $x^2$ | $y^2$ |
|---|---|---|
| 13814.32 | 591668.64 | 32256.16 |
| 159054.72 | 805685.76 | 31399.84 |
| 88096.20 | 500697.76 | 15500.25 |
| 148918.40 | 740976.64 | 29929.00 |
| 146908.52 | 1105862.50 | 19516.09 |
| 296166.11 | 1415862.00 | 61951.21 |
| 274868.64 | 1829797.20 | 41290.24 |
| 146282.80 | 1008016.00 | 21228.49 |
| 132436.40 | 1561000.30 | 11236.00 |
| 172206.09 | 2585342.40 | 11470.41 |
| 208424.16 | 3487929.70 | 12454.56 |

Total: 1911510.2          15632838.9          288232.25

Also,

$$\Sigma x \; \Sigma y = (12558.3)(1716.5) = 21556321$$

$$(\Sigma x)^2 = (12558.3)^2 = 157710898.9.$$

$$(\Sigma y)^2 = (1716.5)^2 = 2946372.25$$

Hence,

$$r = \frac{11[1,911,510.2] - 21,556,321}{\sqrt{[\{11(15,632,838.9) - 157,710,898.9\}\{11(288,232.25) - 2,946,372.25\}]}}$$

$$= \frac{-529708.8}{1787365.2} = -0.296.$$

● **PROBLEM** 21-12

The data below represents the annual sales of the Acme Tool Corporation for the years 1960-69. Describe this time series through the use of a trend line.

| Year | 1960 | 1961 | 1962 | 1963 | 1964 | 1965 | 1966 | 1967 | 1968 | 1969 |
|---|---|---|---|---|---|---|---|---|---|---|
| Sales | 1 | 2 | 4 | 3 | 6 | 5 | 4 | 2 | 6 | 7 |

(Millions of dollars)

Solution: A time series is a collection of data which has been observed over time. In this problem, each yearly sales figure is one observation and the sales figures for 1960-1969 form a time series.

This time series has been plotted:

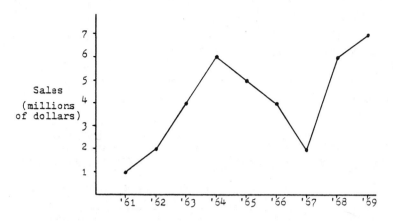

The sales for this company seem to increase over time. That is, the sales data seem to exhibit positive trend. The company may wish to describe or estimate this trend to improve its sales or to forecast future sales.

It is often assumed that the trend in sales is linear. If $Y_t$ is the sales figure at time t, then the trend line

$$Y_t = a + bt + u_t$$

is an expression relating sales at time t, $Y_t$, to time, denoted by t. The sales data is not perfectly linear in time as our graph shows. To account for this we introduce a random error term $u_t$. It is usually assumed that $E(u_t) = 0$ and the variance of $u_t$ is $\sigma^2$, a constant.

This "linear stochastic model" is very similar to the linear regression model presented in an earlier chapter. In that chapter, a relationship between a dependent variable Y and independent variable X was described and estimated through the techniques of linear regression.

In the case of a time series, the trend line is a linear relationship between some dependent variable, in this case sales, and the independent variable time.

The "values" of time are given as the years 1960, 1961... up to 1969. Each of these values differ from adjacent values by 1 unit. Because of this we may think of time as measured in periods say time 1, time 2... up to time 10. Indeed, we may scale the values that t takes on in any arbitrary way without changing the relationship between time and sales, which is of primary interest. We will choose the values of t in such a way as to simplify the computations.

Rearranging the data we have:

| Year | Time t | Sales Y |
|------|--------|---------|
| 1960 | -5 | 1 |
| 1961 | -4 | 2 |
| 1962 | -3 | 4 |
| 1963 | -2 | 3 |
| 1964 | -1 | 6 |
| 1965 | 0 | 5 |
| 1966 | 1 | 4 |
| 1967 | 2 | 2 |
| 1968 | 3 | 6 |
| 1969 | 4 | 7 |

and
$$\sum_{i=1}^{10} t = -5 + (-4) + (-3) + \ldots + 2 + 3 + 4 = -5$$

$$\sum_{i=1}^{10} Y_i = 1 + 2 + 4 + 3 + 6 + 5 + \ldots + 7 = 40 .$$

We now use the technique of linear regression to estimate the trend line between Y and t. Remember that the estimates of a and b were respectively:

$$\hat{a} = \bar{Y} - \hat{b} \bar{X} , \qquad \hat{b} = \frac{\sum_{i=1}^{n} (Y_i - \bar{Y})(X_i - \bar{X})}{\sum_{i=1}^{n} (X_i - \bar{X})^2} .$$

Our independent variable is now time, thus these equations become

$$\hat{a} = \bar{Y} - \hat{b} \bar{t} , \qquad \hat{b} = \frac{\sum_{i=1}^{n} (Y_i - \bar{Y})(t_i - \bar{t})}{\sum_{i=1}^{n} (t_i - \bar{t})^2}$$

where

$$\bar{Y} = \frac{\sum_{i=1}^{n} Y_i}{n} \quad , \quad \bar{t} = \frac{\sum_{i=1}^{n} t_i}{n} .$$

The $t_i$ were chosen to make $\bar{t}$ as small as possible. If there are an odd number of observations, it is possible to choose the values of t in such a way that $\bar{t} = 0$.

We have that $\sum_{i=1}^{n} t_i^2 = 85$ , $\sum_{i=1}^{n} Y^2 = 196$ and $\sum t_i Y_i = 17$ . Thus,

$$\hat{a} = \frac{40}{10} - \hat{b}\left(\frac{-5}{10}\right) = 4 - (.45)(-.5) = 4.23$$

$$\hat{b} = \frac{17 - 10(4)(-.5)}{85 - 10(-.5)^2} = .448 = .45 .$$

The trend line is then $Y_t = 4.23 + .45t$ .

The coefficient .45 states that on the average, annual sales increase by .45 million dollars. This line is plotted below:

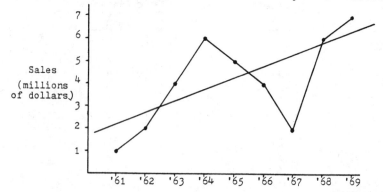

Sales
(millions
of dollars)

'61  '62  '63  '64  '65  '66  '67  '68  '69

Translate the linear trend in the previous problem into a trend line describing quarterly average sales. Find the annual quarterly average sales.

Solution: The estimated trend line for the Acme Tool Company sales data was found to be $Y = 4.23 + .45t$ where t is measured in units of a year.

If we divide both the slope and intercept by four, the trend line becomes

$$\hat{Y}_t = 1.06 + .11t .$$

This equation still has t measured in units of one year. Now $\hat{Y}_t$ is the annual quarterly average sales, that is $\hat{Y}_t$ is the quarterly average sales in year t.

To see why this is so, remember that the average annual sales is

$$\hat{Y}_t = 4.23 + .45t.$$

This is the meaning of value $\hat{Y}_t$. In year t there are four quarters, thus the average quarterly sales for year t would be $\hat{Y}_t/4$ or

$$\frac{4.23 + .45t}{4} = 1.06 + .11t .$$

Taking t = 0, we find that the annual quarterly average sales figure for 1965 is $1.06 + .11(0) = 1.06$ million dollars.

Taking t = 1, we find that the annual quarterly average sales figure for 1966 is $1.06 + .11(1) = 1.17$ million dollars.

● **PROBLEM** 21-14

Consider the following table:

| Year | Amount of Gold (Billions of Dollars) | |
|------|------|------|
| 1957 | 22.8 | |
| 1958 | 20.6 | |
| 1959 | 19.5 | |
| 1960 | 17.8 | |
| 1961 | 16.9 | (1) |
| 1962 | 16.0 | |
| 1963 | 15.6 | |
| 1964 | 15.4 | |
| 1965 | 13.8 | |
| 1966 | 13.2 | |
| 1967 | 12.0 | |

Use the method of semi-averages to estimate a trend line.

Solution: We must first clarify what the purpose of the method of semi-averages is. One of the objectives of time series analysis is to decompose a set of data into a) the trend b) seasonal variation and c) irregular variation.

The aim a) may be achieved by the method of semi-averages. Recall from elementary geometry that two points are necessary to draw a line in a plane. Given a set of data, break up the data into two equal parts, calculate the average of each part and draw the trend line by connecting the two resulting points.

For the data in the given problem, we note that the number of observations (= 11) is odd. Omitting the middle year (1962), however, results in a set of observations having an even number of members.

We then break up the data into the two sets 1957-1961 and 1963-1967, and calculate the respective means. Thus,

$$\bar{Y}_1 = \frac{22.8 + 20.6 + 19.5 + 17.8 + 16.9}{5}$$

$$= 19.52 ,$$ (2)

$$\bar{Y}_2 = \frac{15.6 + 15.4 + 13.8 + 13.2 + 12.0}{5}$$

$$= 14.00 .$$ (3)

The semi-average (2) is centered on 1959 (the mid-point of 1957-1961) and the semi-average (3) is centered on 1965. Connecting these two points we obtain the trend line:

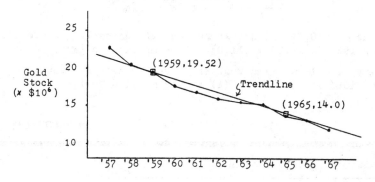

● PROBLEM 21-15

The following table lists the registration of new passenger cars in the United States for the years 1951-1970.

Use the method of least squares to identify the trend line.

| Year (1) | Annual registration in millions (2) |
|---|---|
| 1951 | 5.061 |
| 1952 | 4.158 |
| 1953 | 5.739 |
| 1954 | 5.535 |
| 1955 | 7.170 |
| 1956 | 5.955 |
| 1957 | 5.982 |
| 1958 | 4.655 |
| 1959 | 6.041 |
| 1960 | 6.577 |
| 1961 | 5.855 |
| 1962 | 6.939 |

| | | |
|---|---|---|
| 1963 | | 7.571 |
| 1964 | | 8.065 |
| 1965 | | 9.314 |
| 1966 | | 9.008 |
| 1967 | | 8.357 |
| 1968 | | 9.404 |
| 1969 | | 9.447 |
| 1970 | | 8.388 |

**Solution:** The method of least squares is used to obtain the regression
line  $y = a + bt$ ,  (1)
In the present problem, $y$ is "new cars registered" and  $t$  is time.
We wish to estimate the parameters  $a$  and  $b$  in (1).

Recall that the regression coefficient  $b$  is found by the following formula

$$b = \frac{\sum\limits_{i=1}^{n} t_i y_i - n\bar{t}\,\bar{y}}{\sum\limits_{i=1}^{n} t_i^2 - n\bar{t}^2} \tag{2}$$

The intercept term  $a$  is given by

$$a = \bar{y} - b\bar{t} . \tag{3}$$

To find (2) and (3) we must calculate  $t_i y_i$  and  $t_i^2 (i = 1,\ldots,20)$ .

Before doing this, it is advisable to code the time variable.  Let the
year 1960 = 0.  Then 1951 = -9, 1952 = -8,...,1969 = +9  and 1970 = +10.

The calculations of (2) and (3) are unaffected by this transformation.  We obtain the following figures:

| $t^*$ | $t^* y$ | $t^{*2}$ |
|---|---|---|
| -9 | -45.549 | 81 |
| -8 | -33.264 | 64 |
| -7 | -40.173 | 49 |
| -6 | -33.210 | 36 |
| -5 | -35.850 | 25 |
| -4 | -23.820 | 16 |
| -3 | -17.946 | 9 |
| -2 | - 9.310 | 4 |
| -1 | - 6.041 | 1 |
| 0 | 0 | 0 |
| 1 | 5.855 | 1 |
| 2 | 13.878 | 4 |
| 3 | 22.713 | 9 |
| 4 | 32.260 | 16 |
| 5 | 46.570 | 25 |
| 6 | 54.048 | 36 |
| 7 | 58.499 | 49 |
| 8 | 75.232 | 64 |
| 9 | 85.023 | 81 |
| 10 | 83.880 | 100 |
| 10 | 232.795 | 670 |

Hence,  $\sum\limits_{i=1}^{20} t_i^* y_i = 232.795$ ,  $\sum\limits_{i=1}^{20} t_i^{*2} = 670$  and  $\bar{t}^* = 0.50$ .

Substituting these values into (2),

$$b = \frac{232.795 - 20(0.50)(6.961)}{670 - 20(0.50)^2} = \frac{163.185}{665} = 0.245,$$ (4)

where we used $\quad \bar{y} = \frac{1}{20} \sum_{i=1}^{20} y_i = 6.961.$

Substituting (4) into (3),

$$a = 6.961 - 0.245(0.50) = 6.838.$$ (5)

Substituting (5) and (4) into (1), we obtain the required trend line

$$y = 6.838 + 0.245t$$ (6)

Suppose we wish to estimate annual registration in the year 1971. Letting $t = 11$ in (6) we find

$$y = 6.838 + 0.245(11) = 9.533 .$$

Therefore, we expect the number of cars newly registered in 1971 to be 9.533 million.

● **PROBLEM** 21-16

The following time series represents sales of imported cars for the years 1964 through 1970.

| Year | Sales of Imported Cars (in thousands) |
|------|----------------------------------------|
| 1964 | 516 |
| 1965 | 559 |
| 1966 | 913 |
| 1967 | 1021 |
| 1968 | 1620 |
| 1969 | 1847 |
| 1970 | 2013 |

Find the least squares trend line for this series.

Solution: We proceed as in the previous problem to rescale the variable time and then use linear regression to estimate the trend line.

Let $t$ be given as follows:

| Year | $t$ | Sales $Y_t$ |
|------|-----|-------------|
| 1964 | -3 | 516 |
| 1965 | -2 | 559 |
| 1966 | -1 | 913 |
| 1967 | 0 | 1021 |
| 1968 | 1 | 1620 |
| 1969 | 2 | 1847 |
| 1970 | 3 | 2013 |

Then

$$\sum_{i=1}^{n} t_i = -3 - 2 - 1 + 0 + 1 + 2 + 3 = 0$$

$$\sum_{i=1}^{n} Y_i = 8489$$

$$\sum_{i=1}^{n} t_i^2 = 28 \ , \quad \sum_{i=1}^{n} Y_i t_i = 7774 \ .$$

Thus $\hat{b} = \dfrac{7774}{28} = 277.64$ and

$$\hat{a} = \bar{Y} - \hat{b} \, \bar{t} = \frac{8489}{7} = 1212.7 \ .$$

Thus the trend line for this time series is
$$\hat{Y}_t = 1212.7 + 277.64t \ .$$

● **PROBLEM** 21-17

Compare from the data below the trend in volume of consumption of tobacco. Graph the original series and the trend. Use the trend line to predict the average volume of tobacco consumption for the year 1965.

| Year | T |
|------|------|
| 1954 | 855 |
| 1955 | 880 |
| 1956 | 935 |
| 1957 | 981 |
| 1958 | 1031 |
| 1959 | 1061 |
| 1960 | 1140 |
| 1961 | 1213 |
| 1962 | 1242 |
| 1963 | 1286 |
| 1964 | 1344 |

Solution: We first rescale the variable times so that the year 1959 corresponds to $t = 0$. Then 1954 corresponds to $t = -5$, 1955 to $t = -4$ etc. up to 1964 corresponding to $t = 5$. Then $\sum_{i=1}^{11} t_i = 0$ and also $\sum T_i = 11968$ , $\sum t_i^2 = 110$ , $\sum t_i T_i = 5413$ . Thus,

$$\hat{b} = \frac{5413}{110} = 49.2$$

$$\hat{a} = \bar{T} - \hat{b}\bar{t} = \frac{11960}{11} = 1088 \ .$$

The trend line is then $\hat{T} = 1088 + 49.2t$ . The appropriate graph is:

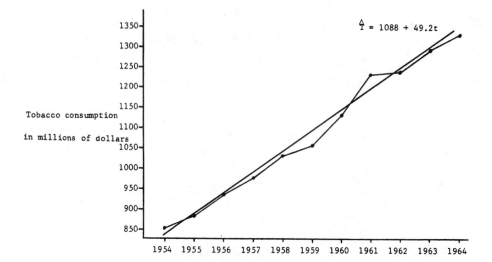

To forecast average tobacco consumption for the year 1965 we use the least squares trend line

$$\hat{T} = 1088 + 49.2t .$$

The value of $t$ corresponding to the year 1965 is $t = 6$. Thus the forecast will be

$$\hat{T} = 1088 + (49.2)6 = 1383.2 .$$

Thus on the basis of past observation we would predict that tobacco consumption for the year 1965 would be 1383.2 million dollars.

● **PROBLEM** 21-18

The following data set represents coal and oil consumption by a well-known utility in a large metropolitan area. Each figure represents a monthly average in thousands of tons.

| Year | Quarter | Coal (C) | Oil (D) |
|------|---------|----------|---------|
| 1961 | 1 | 650.7 | 212.4 |
|      | 2 | 541.5 | 184.7 |
|      | 3 | 459.0 | 157.8 |
|      | 4 | 592.3 | 216.9 |
| 1962 | 1 | 608.9 | 243.6 |
|      | 2 | 512.0 | 206.2 |
|      | 3 | 432.3 | 174.4 |
|      | 4 | 555.7 | 235.0 |
| 1963 | 1 | 586.9 | 281.7 |
|      | 2 | 476.2 | 227.5 |
|      | 3 | 392.0 | 196.0 |
|      | 4 | 528.4 | 266.6 |
| 1964 | 1 | 543.3 | 303.6 |
|      | 2 | 461.9 | 260.0 |
|      | 3 | 385.7 | 217.4 |
|      | 4 | 512.3 | 300.2 |
| 1965 | 1 | 535.2 | 336.0 |
|      | 2 | 442.1 | 281.7 |
|      | 3 | 382.6 | 239.1 |
|      | 4 | 493.4 | 317.3 |

Graph each series.  Find the trend lines and graph.  Plot each detrended series and comment on the appropriateness of the use of the trend line for forecasting.

Solution: First scale the time units so that $\Sigma_{i=1} t_i = 0$ .  This is done as follows.  Let the  t  value corresponding to the first quarter of 1961 be  t = -19, the second quarter of 1961 be  t = -17  and so on until setting the fourth quarter to be  t = 19.  Then  $\Sigma t_i = 0$  and we have

$$\sum_{i=1}^{20} C_i = 10092.4 \qquad\qquad \sum_{i=1}^{20} D_i = 4858.1$$

$$\sum_{i=1}^{20} C_i t_i = -8999.6 \qquad\qquad \sum_{i=1}^{20} D_i t_i = 7917.9$$

and

$$\sum_{i=1}^{20} t_i^2 = 2660. \qquad\qquad n = 20 .$$

Thus the trend line for the coal series is:

$$\hat{C}_t = \hat{a} + \hat{b}t \quad \text{where}$$

$$\hat{a} = \bar{C} \qquad\qquad \hat{b} = \frac{\Sigma C_i t_i}{\Sigma t_i^2} = \frac{-8999.6}{2660} = -3.38$$

$$= 504.62$$

so that $\hat{C}_t = 504.62 - 3.38t.$

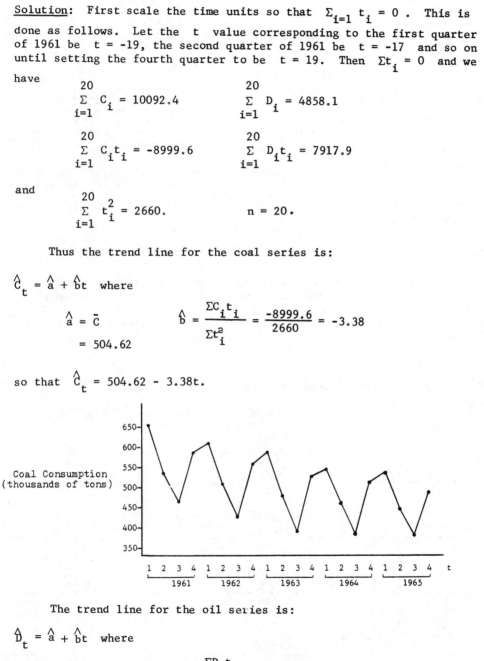

Coal Consumption (thousands of tons)

The trend line for the oil series is:

$$\hat{D}_t = \hat{a} + \hat{b}t \quad \text{where}$$

$$\hat{a} = \bar{D} \qquad\qquad \hat{b} = \frac{\Sigma D_i t_i}{\Sigma t_i^2} = \frac{7917.9}{2660} = 2.98$$

$$= 242.9$$

or $\hat{D}_t = 242.9 + 2.98t .$

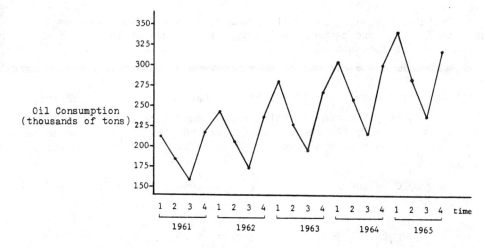

Oil Consumption
(thousands of tons)

To detrend the series we divide each observation in the series by the value of the trend line at that point. That is, if $C_t$ represents the amount of coal consumed at time $t$ , then the detrended observation at time $t$ is

$$\frac{C_t}{504.62 - 3.38t} .$$

The detrended series resulting from this division has the trend removed and hence the series does not show a net increase or decrease over time.

The detrended series for coal and oil consumption are given below along with their graphs.

| Year | Quarter | Coal consumption(detrended) | Oil consumption(detrended) |
|------|---------|-----------------------------|----------------------------|
| 1961 | 1 | 1.144 | 1.140 |
|      | 2 | .963 | .960 |
|      | 3 | .826 | .796 |
|      | 4 | 1.080 | 1.062 |
| 1962 | 1 | 1.124 | 1.159 |
|      | 2 | .957 | .954 |
|      | 3 | .818 | .785 |
|      | 4 | 1.066 | 1.031 |
| 1963 | 1 | 1.140 | 1.204 |
|      | 2 | .937 | .948 |
|      | 3 | .782 | .797 |
|      | 4 | 1.069 | 1.059 |
| 1964 | 1 | 1.114 | 1.178 |
|      | 2 | .960 | .986 |
|      | 3 | .813 | .806 |
|      | 4 | 1.096 | 1.089 |
| 1965 | 1 | 1.162 | 1.193 |
|      | 2 | .974 | .980 |
|      | 3 | .856 | .815 |
|      | 4 | 1.120 | 1.060 |

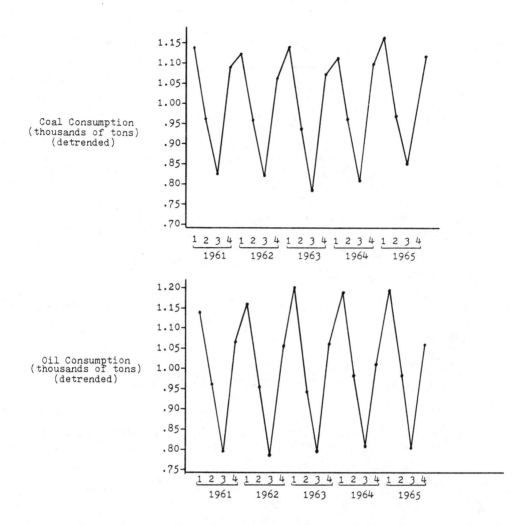

Coal Consumption
(thousands of tons)
(detrended)

Oil Consumption
(thousands of tons)
(detrended)

As we can see from these graphs, the trend line is not completely adequate for describing the behavior of these time series. There is still a great deal of fluctuation present.

For both coal and oil, the greatest consumption occurs in the first and fourth periods of each year.

Coal and oil consumption is highly related to the weather and hence the consumption pattern is seasonal. If we take account of the season in our model, the forecasts will be more accurate and useful.

● **PROBLEM** 21-19

Find the coefficient of correlation for the previous problem.

<u>Solution:</u> Let $x_i y_i$ ( i = 1,...,n) represent two sets of numbers. The Pearsonian coefficient of correlation is defined to be the ratio of the covariance of $\{x_i\}$, $\{y_i\}$ to the product of the standard deviations of $\{x_i\}$ $\{y_i\}$ . Thus,

$$r = \frac{\sum\limits_{i=1}^{n} (x_i - \bar{x})(y_i - \bar{y})}{nS_x S_y}$$

$$= \frac{n \sum\limits_{i=1}^{n} x_i y_i - \sum\limits_{i=1}^{n} x_i \sum\limits_{i=1}^{n} y_i}{\sqrt{\left[\left\{n \sum\limits_{i=1}^{n} x_i^2 - \left(\sum\limits_{i=1}^{n} x_i\right)^2\right\}\left\{n \sum\limits_{i=1}^{n} y_i^2 - \left(\sum\limits_{i=1}^{n} x_i\right)^2\right\}\right]}} \qquad (1)$$

Letting x represent coal and y represent oil, we calculate the following figures:

$$n = 20; \quad \sum_{i=1}^{n} x_i = 10092.4; \quad \sum_{i=1}^{20} y_i = 4858.1; \quad \sum_{i=1}^{20} x_i^2 = 5202270.68;$$

$$\sum_{i=1}^{20} y_i^2 = 1226531.51; \quad \sum_{i=1}^{20} x_i y_i = 2465463.30.$$

Substituting these number into (1),

$$r = \frac{(20)(2465463.30) - (10092.4)(4858.1)}{\sqrt{[\{(20)(5202270.68) - (10092.4)^2\}\{20(1226531.51 - (4858.1)^2\}]}}$$

$$= + 0.196 . \qquad (2)$$

We interpret (2) as indicating that there is little relationship between the consumptions of coal and oil. This conclusion is not very plausible.

# CHAPTER 22

# BUSINESS AND ECONOMIC APPLICATIONS

● **PROBLEM** 22-1

When BankAmericard became VISA, the vice president of a small branch bank compiled the following data:

| Accounts Outstanding ($) | Number of Accounts |
|---|---|
| Less than 100 | 28 |
| 100 - 200 | 32 |
| 200 - 300 | 17 |
| 300 - 400 | 9 |
| 400 - 500 | 6 |
| 500 - 600 | 1 |
| | 93 |

Draw a histogram for this data.

Solution: We first apportion the x-axis into equal intervals corresponding to the above account divisions. Above each division, we put a block with the same width as the division. The height of the block will correspond to the number of people in that division.

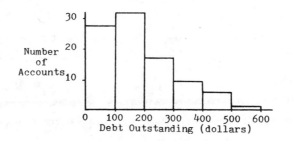

● **PROBLEM** 22-2

The following table represents a distribution of the number of shares (in thousands) of common stock in the Micheli corporation traded during the trading days of August 1976 and for 1976 altogether. Prepare cumulative frequency distributions for both.

| Number of Shares | August 1976 Number of Days | Year 1976 Number of Days |
|:---:|:---:|:---:|
| 0 - 10 | 6 | 60 |
| 11 - 20 | 12 | 168 |
| 21 - 30 | 4 | 64 |
| 31 - 40 | 1 | 12 |
| 41 - 60 | 1 | 8 |
| | 24 | 312 |

Solution: We first convert all our data into percentages by dividing in each case by the total number of days (24 or 312) and multiplying by 100%. This results in the following table:

| Number of Shares | % (August) | % (1976) |
|:---:|:---:|:---:|
| 0 - 10 | 25 | 19 |
| 11 - 20 | 50 | 54 |
| 21 - 30 | 17 | 20 |
| 31 - 40 | 4 | 4 |
| 41 - 60 | 4 | 3 |
| | 100 | 100 |

We have produced a relative frequency table for both data sets. Direct comparison is now possible, yet the relationship within and between each group has been maintained. Note that 6:12:4:1:1 is almost the same as 25:50:17:4:4, the difference being due only to rounding.

The cumulative frequency table gives what percentage of the observations lie at or below a certain value. We compute the values for the table by adding each successive frequency figure to the previous cumulative total. Using the above relative frequency distribution:

| | Number of Days | |
| Number of Shares | 1976 - August % Cumulative Frequency | 1976 - Year % Cumulative Frequency |
|:---:|:---:|:---:|
| 0 - 10 | 25 | 19 |
| 11 - 20 | 75 | 73 |
| 21 - 30 | 92 | 93 |
| 31 - 40 | 96 | 97 |
| 41 - 60 | 100 | 100 |

● PROBLEM 22-3

Plot the following time series. Use percentages for convenience.

| Year | British GNP (1958 constant prices) (millions of £ ) | British GNP percentage change compared with 1958. |
|:---:|:---:|:---:|
| 1958 | 21,768 | 0 |
| 1959 | 22,628 | 4.0 |
| 1960 | 23,719 | 9.0 |
| 1961 | 24,517 | 12.6 |
| 1962 | 24,762 | 13.8 |
| 1963 | 25,911 | 19.0 |
| 1964 | 27,289 | 25.4 |

Solution: The x-axis contains the years of interest. It is the time axis. The y-coordinate will be the GNP percentage change compared with 1958. We connect the points in order to visualize the trend.

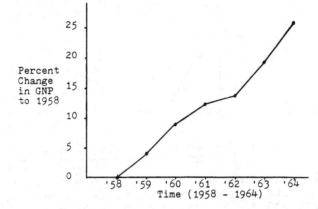

Time (1958 - 1964)

● **PROBLEM** 22-4

Graph the following time series

| Year | Soap Purity as Percentage of Total |
|------|-----------------------------------|
| 1955 | 99.0 |
| 1956 | 99.0 |
| 1957 | 98.3 |
| 1958 | 98.1 |
| 1959 | 98.2 |
| 1960 | 98.6 |
| 1961 | 98.8 |
| 1962 | 98.3 |
| 1963 | 98.0 |

Solution: Plotting this in a conventional manner (below) produces a graph of dubious value. It is almost impossible to detect the changes in soap purity.

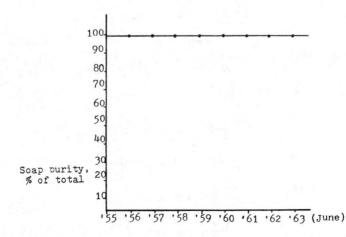

In the following graph the origin is suppressed.

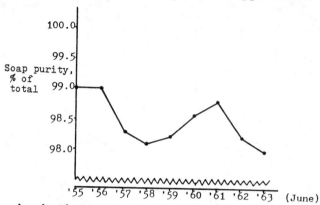

This is indicated by a jagged edge at the bottom (representing a tear). Any suitable device may be employed to illustrate the omission of a section of the vertical axis.

Plot the following two time series on the same graph and compare.

| Coal production Tons (millions) | Year | Wage earners in industry Number (thousands) |
|---|---|---|
| 210.8 | 1952 | 706.2 |
| 211.5 | 1954 | 701.8 |
| 207.4 | 1956 | 697.4 |
| 198.8 | 1958 | 692.7 |
| 183.9 | 1960 | 602.1 |
| 176.8 | 1962 | 531.0 |

Solution: There is no natural relationship between the units of measurement and thus no obvious basis of comparison. We resolve this difficulty with the use of index numbers. The index numbers used here are the percentage changes in each year of the series as compared with 1952. For example, the index number for coal production in 1954 is

$$\frac{211.5}{210.8} \times 100 = 100.3 .$$

|  | Year | Coal Production Index | Wage Earners Index |
|---|---|---|---|
| Similarly, | 1952 | $\frac{210.8}{210.8} \times 100 = 100$ | $\frac{706.2}{706.2} \times 100 = 100.0$ |
|  | 1954 | $\frac{211.5}{210.8} \times 100 = 100.3$ | $\frac{701.8}{706.2} \times 100 = 99.4$ |
|  | 1956 | $\frac{207.4}{210.8} \times 100 = 98.4$ | $\frac{697.4}{706.2} \times 100 = 98.8$ |
|  | 1958 | $\frac{198.8}{210.8} \times 100 = 94.3$ | $\frac{692.7}{706.2} \times 100 = 98.1$ |
|  | 1960 | $\frac{183.9}{210.8} \times 100 = 87.2$ | $\frac{602.1}{706.2} \times 100 = 85.3$ |
|  | 1962 | $\frac{176.8}{210.8} \times 100 = 83.9$ | $\frac{531.0}{706.2} \times 100 = 75.2$ |

We now have a basis of comparison. For each category we place the
years on the x-axis and index numbers on the y-axis. We plot the
above points and connect them with straight lines.

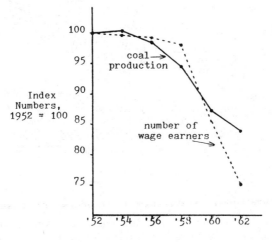

● **PROBLEM** 22-6

Plot the following data on one chart. Make sure cumulative effects
are shown.

British Current Expenditure on the Social Services (millions of £'s)

| | 1954-5 | Cumu- lative total | 1956-7 | Cumu- lative total | 1958-9 | Cumu- lative total | 1960-1 | Cumu- lative total |
|---|---|---|---|---|---|---|---|---|
| Benefits and assistance | 909-9 | 909-9 | 1063-1 | 1063-1 | 1383-7 | 1383-7 | 1494-7 | 1494-7 |
| Health and welfare | 631-0 | 1540-9 | 750-4 | 1813-5 | 825-1 | 2208-8 | 982-3 | 2477-0 |
| Education | 432-0 | 1972-9 | 546-4 | 2359-9 | 669-9 | 2878-7 | 811-7 | 3288-7 |
| Housing | 103-9 | 2076-8 | 103-8 | 2463-7 | 110-7 | 2989-4 | 121-5 | 3410-2 |
| | 2076-8 | | 2463-7 | | 2989-7 | | 3410-2 | |

Solution: Begin by placing the time periods along the x-axis. The
scale for the vertical axis is in millions of pounds.

First plot the series representing benefits and assistance. Shade the
area under the line. Now consider the series of health and welfare.
Add each observed value of this series to the corresponding value of
the benefits and assistance series in each time period. The height of
the point should be the cumulative height for benefits and assistance
and health and welfare expenditures. Connect the points to form a
line. The newly constructed area represents health and welfare.
Repeat this procedure for education and housing.

The final graph is shown below.

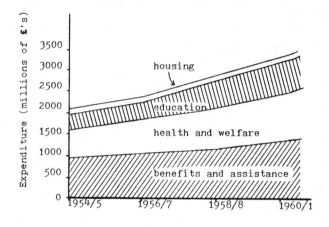

Contractor Dittmar is bidding on a job that he expects will cost him $500,000 to complete. Dittmar has excess capacity and can take on the new job. Several other contractors, including the firm of Causey and Grasso, are bidding on the same job. Dittmar has bid against this company in the past and feels that he has some knowledge about how they are likely to bid. In the following table, Dittmar has estimated the subjective probabilities of winning for any bid he makes.

PROBABILITIES OF VARIOUS BIDS

| Possible Bid | Cumulative Probability of Winning with Bid |
|---|---|
| $450,000 | 1.00 |
| 475,000 | 0.95 |
| 500,000 | 0.90 |
| 525,000 | 0.80 |
| 550,000 | 0.60 |
| 575,000 | 0.35 |
| 600,000 | 0.20 |
| 625,000 | 0.10 |
| 650,000 | 0.05 |
| 675,000 | 0.02 |

a) Sketch a graph of these probabilities.
b) What should Dittmar's optimal strategy be?

Solution:  a)

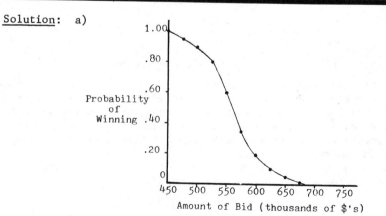

b) The situation Dittmar is in is very common. The contract is to be awarded to the lowest bidder. The higher the contractor raises his bid, the more his profit, but the less his chances of winning. He must find some balance.

Dittmar's profit if his bid wins is his bid less the $500,000 cost. For example, if his bid is $575,000, his profit would be $575,000 - $500,000 = $75,000. Furthermore, if his bid doesn't win, his profit is zero. Hence E(profit) = (profit with given bid x probability of winning at that bid) + (0 x probability of losing) = Profit if bid wins x probability of winning. We can construct the following table

| Bid | (1) Profit if bid wins (Bid-$500,000) | (2) Probability of winning | (3) Expected profit [(1)x(2)] |
|-----|-----|-----|-----|
| 450,000 | -50,000 | 1 | -50,000 |
| 475,000 | -25,000 | 0.95 | -23,750 |
| 500,000 | 0 | 0.90 | 0 |
| 525,000 | 25,000 | 0.80 | 20,000 |
| 550,000 | 50,000 | 0.60 | 30,000 |
| 575,000 | 75,000 | 0.35 | 26,250 |
| 600,000 | 100,000 | 0.20 | 20,000 |
| 625,000 | 125,000 | 0.10 | 12,500 |
| 650,000 | 150,000 | 0.05 | 7,500 |
| 675,000 | 175,000 | 0.02 | 3,500 |

We now assume that Dittmar wants to maximize his expected profit. The above table shows he should bid $550,000.

● **PROBLEM** 22-8

A contractor has found through experience that the low bid for a job (excluding his own bid) is a random variable that is uniformly distributed over the interval $(3c/4, 2c)$ where $c$ is the contractor's cost estimate (no profit or loss) of the job. If profit is defined as zero if the contractor does not get the job (his bid is greater than the low bid) and as the difference between his bid and the cost estimate $c$ if he gets the job, what should he bid, in terms of $c$, in order to maximize his expected profit?

Solution: Let $k$ be the contractor's bid. Profit $\pi$ is defined as follows:

$$\pi = \begin{cases} k - c & \text{if } k \text{ is less than lowest bid by competition .} \\ 0 & \text{if } k \text{ is greater than low bid.} \end{cases}$$

$E(\pi) = (k - c) \cdot Pr(k \text{ is less than low bid})$

$\qquad + 0 \cdot Pr(k \text{ is greater than low bid})$

$\qquad = (k - c) \cdot Pr(k \text{ is less than low bid})$ .

But the low bid follows a uniform distribution.

$$F(\text{low bid}) = \frac{1}{2c - 3/4\ c} = \frac{4}{5c}, \quad 3c/4 < \text{low bid} < 2c.$$

$Pr(k \text{ is less than low bid}) = Pr(\text{low bid is greater than } k)$

$$= \int_k^{2c} \frac{4}{5c}\ dx = \left[\frac{4}{5c}\right](2c - k) .$$

Now $E(\pi) = (k - c)\,\dfrac{4}{5c}\,(2c - k) = \dfrac{4}{5c}(2ck - 2c^2 + kc - k^2)$ .

To maximize, we set $\dfrac{dE(\pi)}{dk} = 0$ .

$$\dfrac{dE(\pi)}{dk} = \dfrac{4}{5c}\,[2c + c - 2k] = 0$$

or
$$3c - 2k = 0\ .$$

Thus the optimal bid is

$$k = \dfrac{3c}{2}\ .$$

We now need to check that we have a maximum. We do this by showing $\dfrac{d^2E(\pi)}{dk^2} < 0$:

$$\dfrac{d^2E(\pi)}{dk^2} = \dfrac{d}{dk}\!\left[\dfrac{4}{5c}(3c - 2k)\right]$$

$$= -\dfrac{8}{5c} < 0\ .$$

● **PROBLEM** 22-9

You are the president of a company that makes wrist watches. The prestige line of watches, Chronomatrix 1536 is waterproof, shockproof, dustproof and features anti-magnetic movement. This watch is sold to distributors for $25 apiece. Your vice-president suggests that a guarantee to replace watches that fail within two years of purchase would allow a price increase of $2.00 per watch without a decrease in demand.

The engineering department assures you that the lifetimes of the Chronomatrix 1536 follow some unknown probability distribution with mean $\mu = 3.5$ years and $\sigma = 0.5$ years. If sales remain constant at 100,000 watches per year and a replacement watch would cost $15.00, is this a profitable policy for your company?

Solution: We wish to find the expected profit of these ventures. Let X be the lifetime of one of these watches.

From Chebyshev's inequality, which is valid for any random variable with a mean and variance,

$$Pr(|X - \mu| \geq k\sigma) \leq 1/k^2$$

for some constant $k$.

Equivalently, this inequality states that

$$Pr(X \geq k\sigma + \mu\ ,\quad X \leq \mu - k\sigma) \leq 1/k^2\ .$$

The region, $X \geq k\sigma + \mu\ ,\ X \leq \mu - k\sigma$ is shown in the figure below:

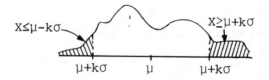

The probability of this event, $X \geq \mu + k\sigma$ or $X \leq \mu - k\sigma$ , is the combined area of the two shaded regions. Because the two regions are disjoint,

962

$$Pr(X \geq \mu + k\sigma , X \leq \mu - k\sigma)$$

$$= Pr(X \geq \mu + k\sigma) + Pr(X \leq \mu - k\sigma) < 1/k^2 .$$

Substituting for $\mu$ and $\sigma$ gives

$$Pr(X \geq 3.5 + k/2) + Pr(X \leq 3.5 - k/2) < 1/k^2 .$$

We are interested in the probability that a watch lasts for less than 2 years. If $k$ is chosen to be 3, then the inequality becomes

$$Pr(X \geq 3.5 + 3/2) + Pr(X \leq 3.5 - 3/2) < 1/3^2$$

or

$$Pr(X \geq 5) + Pr(X \leq 2) < 1/9 .$$

We do not know anything about the $Pr(X \geq 5)$ except that it is a positive number between zero and 1. Because of this,

$$Pr(X \leq 2) \leq Pr(X \geq 5) + Pr(X \leq 2) < 1/9$$

or

$$Pr(X \leq 2) < 1/9 .$$

Thus by the use of Chebyshev's inequality, we have derived an inequality about the probability that one watch will fail in 2 years or less.

Out of 100,000 watches sold we would expect that $(100,000) Pr(X \leq 2)$ of them will fail.

By Chebyshev's inequality

$$(100,000) Pr(X \leq 2) \leq (100,000) \cdot 1/9$$

or expected number of watches that fail in two years or less $\leq 11,111.11$.

The expected cost of replacing the watches under the proposed guarantee would be

$$\$15 \times \text{(Expected \# of watches that fail)}$$

which is less than

$$\$15 \times 11,111.11 = \$166,666.67.$$

Thus the expected cost of guarantee < \$166,666.67. The company will gain \$2.00 on every watch sold with an entire gain of \$100,000 $\times$ \$2.00 = \$200,000.00 gain. Thus the expected profit is

$$\$200,000 - \text{expected cost} \geq \$200,000 - \$166,666.67 \geq \$33,333.33$$

In summary, the company's profit will be on the average greater than \$33,333.34 per year. The president should conclude that the guarantee is a profitable policy and adopt it.

● **PROBLEM** 22-10

The marketing research firm of Burrows, Heller and Larimer wants to estimate the proportions of men and women who are familiar with a shoe polish. In a sample (random) of 100 men and 200 women it is found that 20 men and 60 women had used this particular shoe polish. Compute a 95% confidence interval for the difference in proportions between men and women familiar with the product. Use this to test the hypothesis that the proportions are equal.

<u>Solution</u>: Some quantities necessary for solution to this problem are:

$$\hat{P}_1 = \frac{x_1}{n_1} = \left(\frac{60}{200}\right) = 0.3 = \text{the proportion of women familiar with the product}$$

$$\overset{\wedge}{P_2} = \frac{x_2}{n_2} = \left(\frac{20}{100}\right) = 0.2 = \text{the proportion of men familiar with the product}$$

and

$$\sqrt{\frac{\overset{\wedge}{P_1}(1-\overset{\wedge}{P_1})}{n_1} + \frac{\overset{\wedge}{P_2}(1-\overset{\wedge}{P_2})}{n_2}} = \sqrt{\frac{.3(.7)}{200} + \frac{.2(.8)}{100}} = 0.0515 = \text{the estimated}$$

standard deviation of $\overset{\wedge}{P_1} - \overset{\wedge}{P_2}$ .

$n_1$ and $n_2$ are sufficiently large to apply the Central Limit Theorem to $x_1/n_1 - x_2/n_2 = \overset{\wedge}{P_1} - \overset{\wedge}{P_2}$ .

$$\text{Thus} \quad E(\overset{\wedge}{P_1} - \overset{\wedge}{P_2}) = E(\overset{\wedge}{P_1}) - E(\overset{\wedge}{P_2}) = P_1 - P_2 .$$

We can justify the use of the above estimated standard deviation by noting that we have a large sample and the Law of Large Numbers applies; hence

$$Z = \frac{(\overset{\wedge}{P_1} - \overset{\wedge}{P_2}) - (P_1 - P_2)}{\sqrt{\frac{\overset{\wedge}{P_1}(1-\overset{\wedge}{P_1})}{n_1} + \frac{\overset{\wedge}{P_2}(1-\overset{\wedge}{P_2})}{n_2}}}$$

is approximately standard normal. With our values.

$$Z = \frac{(0.3-0.2) - (P_1-P_2)}{.0515} \quad \text{is} \quad N(0,1) .$$

Therefore,

$$(0.1-(1.96)(0.0515), 0.1+(1.96)(0.0515))$$
$$= (-0.00094, 0.20094)$$

The required confidence interval is
$$(-.00094, .20094).$$

Since equal proportions mean that $p_1 - p_2 = 0$, then we see that this confidence interval covers this difference and so we conclude that the true proportions of women and men do not differ significantly, i.e., the proportions are equal.

**● PROBLEM 22-11**

A research worker was interested in racial differences in the standard of living of farm operators in the southeastern United States. He used the presence of running water in farm dwellings as a crude index of the standard of living. For each of 31 economic areas in North Carolina, South Carolina, and Georgia in 1945, he calculated two measures: X = farms operated by nonwhites per 100 white farm operators and Y = percent of farms having running water in dwellings. The following values were obtained:

$$\Sigma X = 1,860 \qquad \Sigma Y = 465 \qquad \Sigma XY = 23,400$$

$$\Sigma X^2 = 201,600 \quad \Sigma Y^2 = 7,925 \qquad n = 31$$

Compute the regression line and the correlation of X and Y.

<u>Solution</u>: The regression line is $Y = a + bX$ where a and b are found by the computation formulae

$$b = \frac{\Sigma XY - n\bar{X}\bar{Y}}{\Sigma X^2 - n\bar{X}^2}$$

$$a = \bar{Y} - b\bar{X} \ .$$

$$\bar{Y} = \frac{\Sigma Y}{n} \quad \text{and} \quad \bar{X} = \frac{\Sigma X}{n} \ .$$

$$\bar{Y} = \frac{465}{31} = 15 \quad \text{and} \quad \bar{X} = \frac{1860}{31} = 60 \ .$$

Using the formula above

$$b = \frac{23,400 - 31 \cdot 60 \cdot 15}{201,600 - 31(60)^2} = \frac{23,400 - 27,900}{201,600 - 111,600} = \frac{-4500}{90,000}$$

$$= -.05.$$

And

$$a = \bar{Y} - b\bar{X} = 15 - (-0.05)60 = 18.$$

The least-squares regression line is

$$Y = 18 - 0.05 \ X \ .$$

The computational formula for r, the correlation between x and y is:

$$r = \frac{n\Sigma XY - (\Sigma X)(\Sigma Y)}{\left(\sqrt{n\Sigma X^2 - (\Sigma X)^2}\right)\left(\sqrt{n\Sigma Y^2 - (\Sigma Y)^2}\right)}$$

In our case

$$r = \frac{(31)(23,400) - (1860)(465)}{\sqrt{31(201,600)-(1860)^2} \ \sqrt{31(7925)-(465)^2}}$$

$$= \frac{725,400 - 864,900}{\sqrt{6,249,600-3,459,600} \ \sqrt{245,675-216,225}}$$

$$= \frac{-139,500}{\sqrt{2,790,000} \ \sqrt{29,450}}$$

$$= -.4867.$$

● **PROBLEM** 22-12

The following data pertains to presidential elections of the past

| Year | New York City Registration (in 1000's) | New York State Vote (in 1000's) |
|------|----------------------------------------|---------------------------------|
| 1924 | 1500 | 3246 |
| 1928 | 2030 | 4406 |
| 1932 | 2340 | 4689 |
| 1936 | 2900 | 5596 |
| 1940 | 3390 | 6302 |
| 1944 | 3218 | 6317 |
| 1948 | 3316 | 6177 |

Compute the regression line with New York City registration as the independent variable. Compute the correlation.

**Solution:** Letting X be the registration and Y the vote we can expand the table as follows.

| Year | X | $X^2$ | Y | $Y^2$ | XY |
|------|-----|------------|--------|-------------|-------------|
| 1924 | 1500 | 2,250,000 | 3246 | 10,536,516 | 4,869,000 |
| 1928 | 2030 | 4,120,900 | 4406 | 19,412,836 | 8,944,180 |
| 1932 | 2340 | 5,475,600 | 4689 | 21,986,721 | 10,972,260 |
| 1936 | 2900 | 8,410,000 | 5596 | 31,315,216 | 16,228,400 |
| 1940 | 3390 | 11,492,100 | 6302 | 39,715,204 | 21,363,780 |
| 1944 | 3218 | 10,355,524 | 6317 | 39,904,489 | 20,328,106 |
| 1948 | 3316 | 10,995,856 | 6177 | 38,155,329 | 20,482,932 |
| Totals | 18694 | 53,099,980 | 36,733 | 201,026,311 | 103,188,658 |

Note first that

$$\bar{X} = \frac{\Sigma X}{N} = \frac{18694}{7} = 2670.57$$

and

$$\bar{Y} = \frac{\Sigma Y}{N} = \frac{36,733}{7} = 5247.57.$$

We now use the computational formulae

$$b = \frac{\Sigma XY - n\bar{X}\bar{Y}}{\Sigma X^2 - n\bar{X}^2}$$

$$a = \bar{Y} - b\bar{X} .$$

Here

$$b = \frac{103,188,658 - 7\cdot(2670.57)(5247.57)}{53,099,980 - 7(2670.57)^2}$$

$$= \frac{5,090,558}{3,176,318} = 1.603$$

$$a = 5247.57 - (1.603)(2670.57) = 967.553$$

The line is: $Y = 967.553 + 1.603X$

This line is plotted below.

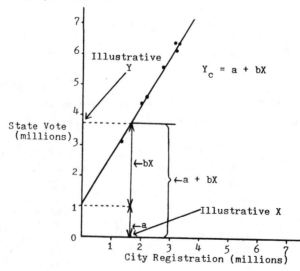

Our sample points seem to provide a good approximation to our line. Intuition tells us the correlation should be close to one. Calculating r:

966

$$r = \frac{n\Sigma XY - (\Sigma X)(\Sigma Y)}{\left(\sqrt{n\Sigma X^2 - (\Sigma X)^2}\right)\left(\sqrt{n\Sigma Y^2 - (\Sigma Y)^2}\right)}$$

$$= \frac{7(103,188,658) - (18,694)(36,733)}{\sqrt{7(53,099,980) - (18,694)^2}\sqrt{7(201,026,311) - (36,733)^2}}$$

$$= \frac{35,633,904}{(4715.32)(7607.29)}$$

$$= .993.$$

Our suspicions are confirmed.

● **PROBLEM** 22-13

The following table contains time series observations on per capita consumption of beef and the retail price of beef deflated by a consumer price index:

| Year | Consumption per Capita Q Pounds | Retail Price P cents/1b. |
|------|------|------|
| 1949 | 63.9 | 67.2 |
| 1950 | 63.4 | 73.3 |
| 1951 | 56.1 | 79.5 |
| 1952 | 62.2 | 76.3 |
| 1953 | 77.6 | 60.4 |
| 1954 | 80.1 | 59.7 |
| 1955 | 82.0 | 59.0 |
| 1956 | 85.4 | 56.8 |
| 1957 | 84.6 | 58.7 |
| 1958 | 80.5 | 65.6 |
| 1959 | 81.4 | 66.4 |
| 1960 | 85.2 | 63.8 |

a) Why is a deflated price used?
b) Find the regression line $Q = f(P)$.

Solution: a) According to consumer theory, an equal percentage change in the prices of all commodities and in money income should not disturb the pattern of quantities demanded or consumed. Hence, during a period such as 1949-1960 in which the consumer price index rose more than 20 percent, we would expect that the actual price of beef would be less closely associated with changes in its per capita consumption than would the deflated price, which shows changes in the price of beef relative to the average price level for all consumer goods and services.

b) We now expand the previous table.

| Year | Q | $Q^2$ | P | $P^2$ | PQ |
|------|------|----------|------|---------|---------|
| 1949 | 63.9 | 4083.21 | 67.2 | 4515.84 | 4294.08 |
| 1950 | 63.4 | 4019.56 | 73.3 | 5372.89 | 4647.22 |
| 1951 | 56.1 | 3147.21 | 79.5 | 6320.25 | 4459.95 |
| 1952 | 62.2 | 3868.84 | 76.3 | 5821.69 | 4745.86 |
| 1953 | 77.6 | 6021.76 | 60.4 | 3648.16 | 4687.04 |
| 1954 | 80.1 | 6416.01 | 59.7 | 3564.09 | 4781.97 |
| 1955 | 82.0 | 6724.00 | 59.0 | 3481.00 | 4838.00 |
| 1956 | 85.4 | 7293.16 | 56.8 | 3226.24 | 4850.72 |
| 1957 | 84.6 | 7157.16 | 58.7 | 3445.69 | 4966.02 |
| 1958 | 80.5 | 6480.25 | 65.6 | 4303.36 | 5280.80 |
| 1959 | 81.4 | 6625.96 | 66.4 | 4408.96 | 5404.96 |
| 1950 | 85.2 | 7259.04 | 63.8 | 4070.44 | 5435.76 |
| Totals | 902.4 | 69,096.16 | 786.7 | 52,178.61 | 58,392.38 |

The regression line will be of the form
$$Q = a + bP$$
where
$$b = \frac{\Sigma PQ - N\bar{P}\,\bar{Q}}{\Sigma P^2 - N\bar{P}^2}$$
and
$$a = \bar{Q} - b\bar{P} .$$

First $N = 12$, $\bar{P} = \frac{\Sigma P}{N} = \frac{786.7}{12} = 65.56$, and $\bar{Q} = \frac{\Sigma Q}{N} = \frac{902.4}{12} = 75.2$ .

Now
$$b = \frac{58,392.38 - 12(\ 65.56)(75.2)}{52,178.61 - 12(65.56)^2}$$
$$= \frac{-768.96}{601.25} = -1.28$$
and
$$a = 75.2 - (-1,28)(65.56) = 159.12.$$

Therefore  $Q = 159.12 - 1.28P$ .

The slope coefficient, -1.28, implies that a 1.28 pound decrease in predicted per capita consumption is associated with every one-cent increase in the deflated retail price of beef.

● **PROBLEM** 22-14

Suppose a pilot plant is run for 30 weeks in order to establish costs of production. In each period, a rate of output is established and the corresponding total costs are found. The resulting data is plotted in a scatter diagram.

Microeconomic theory and empirical investigations suggest that a linear relationship might not be best. Sketch possible linear, quadratic, and cubic regression lines.

Solution:
(1) linear
(2) quadratic
(3) cubic

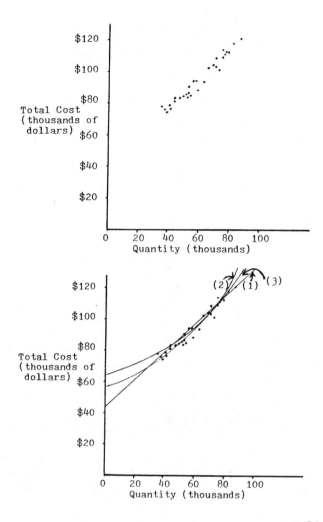

Suppose Q is a measure of output, K is a measure of capital stock in use, and L is a measure of the size of the employed labor force. Then

$$Q = AK^\beta L^\gamma$$

is a much used form of production function. When $\beta + \gamma = 1$, it is known as a Cobb-Douglas production function.

This function has many convenient properties: Marginal products of both labor and capital are positive if $\beta$ and $\gamma$ are. If $\beta + \gamma = 1$, the function has constant returns to scale. That is, if both inputs are increased in like proportion, output will increase in that same proportion. A doubling of both inputs, for example, will result in doubled output. Discuss how the concept of linear regression might be applied to estimate $\beta$ and $\gamma$.

Solution: Notice that this is a problem with two independent variables, K and L. Multiple regression is called for. But first we must obtain a linear form. We have

$$Q = AK^{\beta}L^{\gamma} .$$

Taking the natural log of both sides, we obtain

$$\ln Q = \ln (AK^{\beta}L^{\gamma})$$

or

$$\ln Q = \ln A + \beta \ln K + \gamma \ln L$$

$\ln Q$, $\ln K$, and $\ln L$ are observable .

$$\text{Let } \underline{Y} = \begin{bmatrix} \ln Q_1 \\ \ln Q_2 \\ \cdot \\ \cdot \\ \ln Q_n \end{bmatrix} \quad \text{and}$$

$$\underline{X} = \begin{bmatrix} 1 & \ln K_1 & \ln L_1 \\ \cdot & \ln K_2 & \ln L_2 \\ \cdot & \cdot & \cdot \\ \cdot & \cdot & \cdot \\ 1 & \ln K_n & \ln L_n \end{bmatrix}$$

Then by our analysis of multiple regression in an earlier chapter, we have estimates of:

$$\begin{bmatrix} \ln \hat{A} \\ \hat{\beta} \\ \hat{\gamma} \end{bmatrix} = [\underline{X}'\underline{X}]^{-1} \underline{X}' \underline{Y} .$$

Our final production function would be  $Q = e^{\ln A} K^{\beta} L^{\gamma} .$

● **PROBLEM** 22-16

XYZ Company is considering digging an oil well.  The cost of the well is $50,000.  If the well is successful XYZ will make a profit of $400,000, otherwise zero.  The probability of the well being successful is 0.1.  Is it worthwhile to dig the well?

<u>Solution</u>:  We have the following choice :

We will choose the alternative with the higher expected profit.  If we don't dig, our expected profit is zero.  If we dig, we have the following uncertainty:

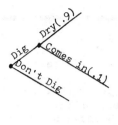

If there is oil, our profit is $400,000 - $50,000 = $350,000. If there isn't we loose the $50,000 cost of the well. Therefore our expected profit is $350,000·P ( oil ) + (-$50,000)·P (dry) = 350,000(.1) - 50,000(.9) = -$10,000. If we dig, our expected profit is less than zero. Our best bet is not to dig.

We can summarize the solution in a decision tree with the profit shown.

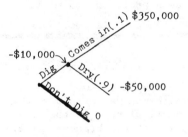

The optimal decision is indicated by the darkened line.

● **PROBLEM** 22-17

Suppose in the previous problem, the probability of striking oil if the well is dug is 0.2. Would the decision still be the same?

Solution: Our decision tree will be of the same form only with different probabilities.

The new expected profit if we dig is ($350,000)·P( oil ) + (-$50,000)·P(dry) = 350,000(.2) - 50,000(.8) = $30,000.

Our expected profit is now higher if we dig. We might now chose to dig. However, there are other sides to this problem; if the president of XYZ is adverse to risk, he still might not want to dig. For our decision, we would say the Expected Profit Criterion indicates that the firm should dig the well.

The Kannan Manufacturing Company is going to build a new plant.
Kannan can either build a large plant or a small one with the option
of expanding the small one if feasible.  Kannan is uncertain of the
demand for his product, but he does know that it will be high with a
probability of 0.6 and low with a probability of 0.4.  For a large
plant and high demand net profit is $6 million; and if the demand
is low, the payoff is $1 million.  Similarly, if a small plant is
built initially and no expansion is made the net profits are $4 mil-
lion (high demand) and $3 million (low demand).  There is a net
profit of $5 million with expansion of a small plant in the face of
high demand.  This is determined as follows:

```
Profit from high demand
    (with production ability to meet demand)              $10 million
Less: Cost of building small plant        $2 million
        Cost of expanding                  3 million
        Total cost                                         5 million
    Payoff                                               $ 5 million
```

Similarly, expanding in the face of low demand costs the $5 million
as above and only has a profit of $5 million.  The net profit is zero.

Should Kannan build a large or a small plant?

Solution:  We use a decision tree to analyze this problem.

Starting at the left, the first two lines or branches of the decision
tree represent the alternative actions for the first decision - either
build a large or a small plant.  At the end of each of the decision
branches comes a fork with two branches representing the events high
and low demand for the product.  It is unknown at the time of the
first decision (size of plant) which of these events will actually
occur.

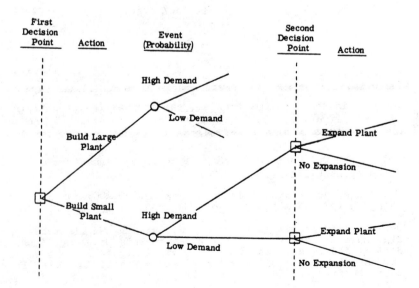

For the "build large plant" action, the tree ends after the event branches. However, for the "build small plant" action a second decision point is reached after the demand events. The decision-maker can choose between the actions expand and no expansion after he knows the market demand. These actions are represented as branches on the decision tree. Including both branches at this point may seem unnecessary at first. One would generally expect to expand the plant in response to a high demand and not to expand if a low demand occurred. But we cannot be sure of this until we include the economic information in the tree. There is always the possibility that the expansion will cost more than the additional revenue. Hence, we should retain both action alternatives at each of the second decision points.

We now augment the original decision tree with the probabilities and payoffs given in the problem,

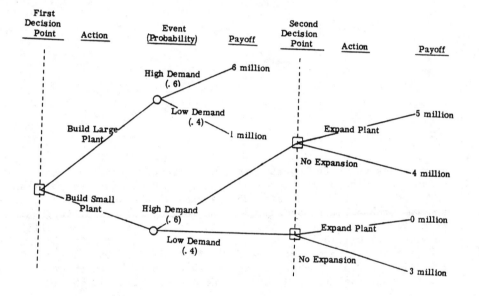

We now begin the analysis of finding that decision which is best. We proceed by working backward on the tree. The second decision point is considered first. At the end of the high demand branch is the following fork,

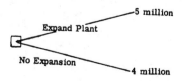

Since the action "expand the plant" leads to $5 million net profit as opposed to only $4 million for no expansion, that alternative is selected and the "no expansion" branch is removed from further consideration. Similarly, we remove the "extend plant" option at the end of the low demand branch. Our result is the following reduced decision tree.

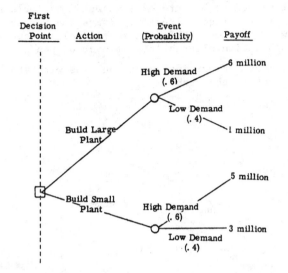

| First Decision Point | Action | Event (Probability) | Payoff |
|---|---|---|---|

We now back up to the event forks, with branches labeled "high demand" and "low demand", respectively. At each of these forks an expected value if taken using the payoffs at the ends of the branches and the probabilities shown. For the fork at the end of the "Build Large Plant" action the expected value is $4.0 million ($6 million × .6 + .4 × $1 million). For the fork at the end of the "Build Small Plant" branch, the expected value is $4.2 million ($5 million × 0.6 + $3 million × 0.4). By replacing the event forks by their expected values, the final reduced form of the decision tree is obtained.

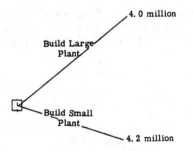

Seeing this, Kannan decides to build the small plant.

Flapjack Computers is interested in developing a new tape drive for a proposed new computer. Flapjack does not have research personnel available to develop the new drive itself and so is going to sub-contract the development to an independent research firm. Flapjack has set a fee of $250,000 for developing the new tape drive and has asked for bids from various research firms. The bid is to be awarded not on the basis of price (set at $250,000) but on the basis of both the technical plan shown in the bid and the firm's reputation.

Dyna Research Institute is considering submitting a proposal (i.e., a bid) to Flapjack to develop the new tape drive. Dyna Research Management estimated that it would cost about $50,000 to prepare a proposal; further they estimated that the chances were about 50-50 that they would be awarded the contract.

There was a major concern among Dyna Research engineers concerning exactly how they would develop the tape drive if awarded the con-tract. There were three alternative approaches that could be tried. One involved the use of certain electronic components. The engineers estimated that it would cost only $50,000 to develop a prototype of the tape drive using the electronic approach, but that there was only a 50 percent chance that the prototype would be satisfactory. A second approach involved the use of certain magnetic apparatus. The cost of developing a prototype using this approach would cost $80,000 with 70 percent chance of success. Finally, there was a mechanical approach with cost of $120,000, but the engineers were certain of success.

Dyna Research could have sufficient time to try only two approaches. Thus, if either the magnetic or the electronic approach tried and failed, the second attempt would have to use the mechanical approach in order to guarantee a successful prototype.

The management of Dyna Research was uncertain how to take all this information into account in making the immediate decision-whether to spend $50,000 to develop a proposal for Flapjack. Can you help?

Solution: Since this decision seems complex, we will build the decision tree in steps. The first decision facing Dyna Research involves the actions "Prepare a Proposal" and "Do not Prepare a Proposal". If a proposal is developed and submitted to Flapjack, then either of the events "Contract Awarded to Dyna" or "Dyna Loses Contract". Each event has probability 0.5. These choices are shown below:

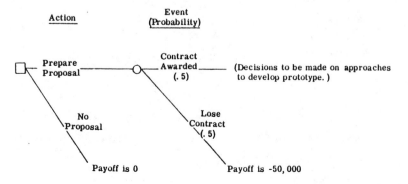

975

If Dyna Research decides not to prepare a bid, the net payoff is zero. If a bid is prepared but the contract is lost, Dyna Research loses the $50,000 cost of preparing the bid (i.e., the payoff is -$50,000). If the contract is awarded to Dyna, then the next decision, the choice between alternative methods of developing a successful tape drive, must be made.

In the second decision, Dyna Research must decide which of the three approaches - mechanical, electronic, or magnetic - to try first. This decision is shown below:

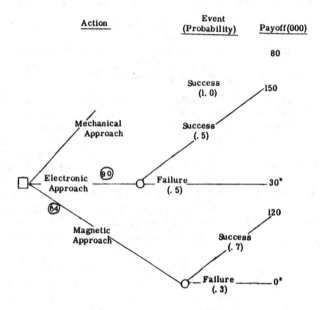

*Mechanical Approach must be used.

The payoffs in the above diagram are calculated as shown below:

| | | Payoff(thousands of dollars) | | |
|---|---|---|---|---|
| End of Branch | Fee | Cost of Proposal | Cost of Prototype Indicated | Cost of Mechanical Prototype |
| Electronic Approach | | | | |
| Success.................. | 250 - | 50 - | 50 | = 150 |
| Failure.................. | 250 - | 50 - | 50 - | 120 = 30 |
| Magnetic Approach | | | | |
| Success.................. | 250 - | 50 - | 80 | = 120 |
| Failure.................. | 250 - | 50 - | 80 - | 120 = 0 |

For the mechanical approach we take

    Fee - Cost of Proposal - Cost of Mechanical Prototype

      = 250 - 50 - 120 = 80.

The complete decision tree is shown as follows:

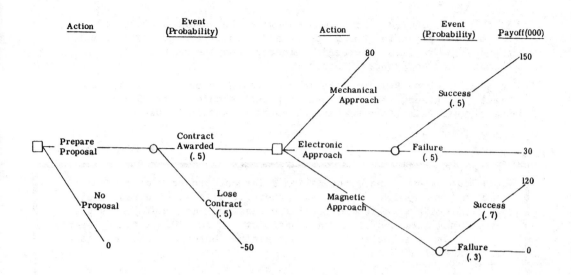

We proceed by working backwards. The expected values are calculated
for each of the event forks in the right part of the tree. Thus the
expected payoff associated with the electronic approach is $90,000
((0.5 x 150) + (0.5 x 30) = 90) and for the magnetic approach, it is
$84,000 ((0.7 x 120) + (0.3 x 0) = 84). These expected payoffs are
inserted in circles beside the appropriate forks in the following
figure:

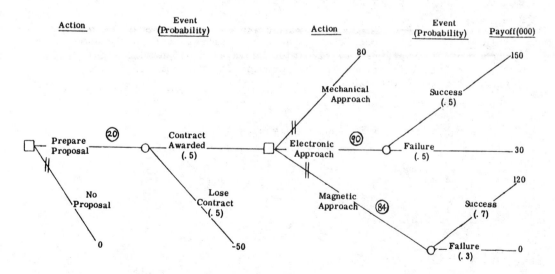

Moving left to the second decision point, we see that the electronic
approach offers the highest expected payoff ($90,000) and is the best
choice. The value $90,000 is written (circled) beside the decision
point and the nonpreferred approaches are indicated by drawing ‖ on
the branches.

The tree now has a payoff of +$90,000 if the contract is awarded
and -$50,000 if not. The expected value of preparing a proposal is
$20,000 ((0.5 x 90) + (0.5 x (-50)) = 20). This is written in a
circle beside the event fork.

Finally, the choice must be made between the expected profit of $20,000 for preparing the proposal and zero if the proposal is not prepared. The first course is selected, and the mark "||" drawn through the "No Proposal" branch.

In summary, Dyna Research should prepare the proposal. If the contract is awarded, the electronic approach should be tried first; but if this fails, the mechanical approach should be used.

● **PROBLEM** 22-20

World-Wide Vacuums Inc., the nation's largest producer of central vacuuming systems, has 5 training centers for its service personnel. Upon completion of a 10 week training session, each employee is given a competency exam and rated on a scale of 1 to 20. A random sample of size four is selected from each training center and the results of their exams given below.

| Center 1 | Center 2 | Center 3 | Center 4 | Center 5 |
|----------|----------|----------|----------|----------|
| 9 | 5 | 11 | 9 | 16 |
| 11 | 6 | 14 | 10 | 15 |
| 12 | 8 | 15 | 7 | 19 |
| 7 | 8 | 10 | 9 | 14 |

Test the hypothesis:

$$H_0: \mu_1 = \mu_2 = \mu_3 = \mu_4 = \mu_5 \quad \text{against the alternative}$$

$$H_A: \quad \text{the means are not all equal.}$$

Use $\alpha = .01$ .

**Solution:** We first note that because all samples contain the same number of observations, (a situation known as a balanced design) there are simplifications in the formulas for the sums of squares needed for the ANOVA table.

The summary statistics are

$$k = 5, \quad n = n_1 = n_2 = n_3 = n_4 = n_5 = 4$$

$$\sum_{i=1}^{4} Y_{i1} = 39 \qquad\qquad \sum_{j=1}^{5} \sum_{i=1}^{4} Y_{ij}^2 = 2575$$

$$\sum_{i=1}^{4} Y_{i2} = 27$$

$$\sum_{i=1}^{4} Y_{i3} = 50 \qquad\qquad \sum_{j=1}^{5} \sum_{i=1}^{4} Y_{ij} = 215 \; .$$

$$\sum_{i=1}^{4} Y_{i4} = 35$$

$$\sum_{i=1}^{4} Y_{i5} = 64$$

Computing the sums of squares:

$$SSTO = \sum_{j=1}^{5} \sum_{i=1}^{4} (Y_{ij} - \bar{Y}_{..})^2 = \sum_{j=1}^{5} \sum_{i=1}^{4} Y_{ij}^2 - 4 \cdot 5 \cdot \bar{Y}_{..}^2$$

$$= 2575 - 20\left(\frac{215}{20}\right)^2$$

$$= 2575 - \frac{(215)^2}{20} = 2575 - 2311.25$$

$$= 263.75 .$$

$$SSTR = \sum_{j=1}^{5} n_j (\bar{Y}_{.j} - \bar{Y}_{..})^2 = 4\left( \sum_{j=1}^{5} \bar{Y}_{.j}^2 - 5 \cdot \bar{Y}_{..}^2 \right)$$

$$= 4\left( \sum_{j=1}^{5} \bar{Y}_{.j}^2 \right) - 20 \cdot \bar{Y}_{..}^2$$

$$= 2517.75 - 2311.25$$

$$= 206.5 .$$

Thus

$$SSE = SSTO - SSTR = 263.75 - 206.5 = 57.25 .$$

The ANOVA table is thus

| Source of Variation | Sum of Squares | Degrees of Freedom | Mean Square |
|---|---|---|---|
| Between training centers | 206.5 | k-1=5-1=4 | 51.625 |
| Within training centers (error) | 57.25 | rk-k=k(r-1)=5.3=15 | 3.817 |
| Total | 263.75 | 20-1 = 19 | |

The F-statistic for testing the hypothesis that $\mu_1 = \mu_2 = \ldots = \mu_5$

is $F = \frac{MSTR}{MSE} = \frac{51.625}{3.817} = 13.52$ . The 99th percentile of the F distribution with 4 and 15 degrees of freedom is

$$F(.99, 4, 15) = 4.8932 .$$

$$F = 13.52 > F(.99, 4, 15) = 4.8932$$

thus we reject $H_0$ and accept that the population means are not all equal.

● PROBLEM 22-21

The largest manufacturer of cold breakfast cereal in Spokane, Washington notices that sales of its hottest selling cereal, Crispy Crunchy Sugar-Coated Corn Chips , are slipping. In a marketing research study, the company experiments with three new package designs in the hope of finding one that will reverse this trend. The company thinks that the area in which the cereal is marketed will have an effect on sales and thus divides the state into 4 geographical areas. Five nearly identical stores are selected in each area to be used for the experiment. After a month sales in each store are recorded and an analysis of variance table is constructed. No interactions between package design and geographical area are found. Thus the ANOVA table is

| Source of Variation | Sum of Squares | Degrees of Freedom | Mean Square |
|---|---|---|---|
| Package Design | 154.24 | 3-1=2 | 77.12 |
| Geographical Area | 218.00 | 4-1=3 | 72.66 |
| Error | 746.01 | 29-2-3=24 | 31.08 |

Test at the .025 level, for significant differences in sales due to differences in package designs and geographical area.

**Solution:** We first test the hypothesis that there is no effect on sales due to differences in package design.

The test for significant differences in sales between the 3 designs is carried out in the following manner:

1) Compute $F = \dfrac{\text{Mean Square due to Package Design}}{\text{Mean Square Error}}$ .

2) Under the null hypothesis that there is no difference between designs, F is distributed with an F-distribution having 2 and 24 degrees of freedom.

3) Set the level of significance of the test at $\alpha$ . We are given $\alpha = .025$ . Now find $F(1-\alpha, 2, 24) =$ $F(.975, 2, 24)$ the 97.5 percentile of the F-distribution with 2 and 24 degrees. From a table, we see that $F(.975, 2, 24) = 4.3187$.

4) If $F > 4.3187$, reject the null hypothesis, otherwise accept. We see that

$$F = \frac{77.12}{31.08} = 2.48 < 4.3187 \text{ ,}$$

thus accept that there is no significant effect on sales due to package design.

Similarly, we reject

$H_0$: no effect due to geographical area

if $\qquad F = \dfrac{\text{Mean Square Due to Geographical Area}}{\text{Mean Square Error}}$

is less than $F(.975, 3, 24) = 3.7211$. $F = \dfrac{72.66}{31.08} = 2.34 < 3.7211$

therefore accept the null hypothesis that there is no effect on sales due to the geographical location.

An economist wishes to estimate the relationship between the quantity demanded of a good, its price, the price of a substitute and disposable personal income. Thus he hypothesizes the following linear relationship

$$Q_i = \beta_0 + \beta_1 P_i + \beta_2 P_i' + \beta_3 Y_i + u_i , \qquad (1)$$

where Q is the quantity demanded, P is the price of the good, P' is the price of a substitute and Y is the disposable income. $\beta$ is the regression coefficient and the $u_i$ are random disturbances.

He obtains, using a sample of 30 successive time periods, the following results:

$$\begin{array}{ll} Q = 67,900 - 14,870P - 4,986P' + 146.7Y & (2) \\ \quad\;\; (20,004) \quad (1,594) \quad (4,141) \quad\; (25.8) & (3) \end{array}$$

$$R^2 = 0.7729 \qquad \bar{R}^2 = 0.7467$$

$$F = 29.50 \qquad S_e = 5646 .$$

Interpret the above results.

**Solution:** Let us first clarify the relationship (1). Since quantity demanded varies inversely with price, we expect $\beta_1 < 0$. On the other hand $\beta_2 > 0$ since the quantity demanded of a good varies proportionately with the price of a substitute good. Finally, under normal conditions $\beta_3 > 0$.

The random disturbances, $u_i$, are assumed to be independently distributed. Furthermore, they are identically distributed, the form of the distribution being

$$u_i \sim N(0, \sigma_u^2) .$$

This is the assumption of homoskedasticity. With this assumption one can prove that the least squares estimators are linearly unbiased with minimum variance.

Next, we turn to an interpretation of the regression results. First consider (2). The estimate of the intercept (i.e., when P = P' = Y = 0) is $\beta_0 = 67,900$. The three regression coefficients are

$$\beta_1 = -14,870 , \quad \beta_2 = -4,986 \quad \text{and} \quad \beta_3 = 146.7 .$$

The set of numbers in (3) gives the standard error of estimates of the regression coefficients. We use these errors to calculate confidence intervals and the significance levels of the $\beta_i$. To do this for $\beta_1$ set up the null and alternative hypotheses.

$$H_0: \quad \beta_1 = 0$$

$$H_1: \quad \beta_1 \neq 0 .$$

Using the t-test, (since the variance of the $\beta_s$ is unknown)

$$\frac{\hat{\beta} - \beta_0}{s_{\hat{\beta}}} \sim t(\alpha/2, n-k) \qquad (4)$$

where  k  denotes the number of parameters being estimated, $\alpha$  is
the significance level desired, and  n-k  are the degrees of freedom.   Substituting the given results into (4),

$$\frac{-14{,}870 - 0}{1594} = -9.33 \ .$$

Since 4 parameters are being estimated $t(\alpha/2, n-k) = t(.025, 26)$.
From a table of t-values we find

$$t(.025, 26) = 2.056 \ .$$

Since the calculated value of the t-statistic is much less than
-2.056, we reject the null hypothesis  $\beta_1 = 0$  and conclude, in accordance with economic theory, that  $\beta_1 < 0$ .

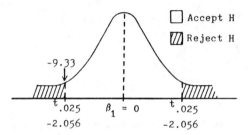

Similarly, we find that

$$\frac{\hat{\beta}_3}{s\,\hat{\beta}_3} = \frac{146.7}{25.8} = 5.69 \ ,$$

leading us to the conclusion that  $\beta_3 > 0$ .   But   $\dfrac{\hat{\beta}_2}{s\,\hat{\beta}_2} = \dfrac{-4986}{4141} = -1.20,$

indicating that we should accept the null hypothesis  $\beta_2 = 0$ .

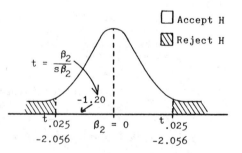

We now examine the coefficient of determination, $R^2$, and the corrected
coefficient of determination, $\bar{R}^2$ .   Let  $\hat{Y}_i$  denote the  ith value
on the regression line and  $\bar{Y} = \dfrac{1}{n} \sum\limits_{i=1}^{n} Y_i$  the mean of the observed
values of the explained variable.   Then  $R^2$  is defined to be

$$R^2 = \frac{\sum\limits_{i=1}^{n} (\hat{Y}_i - \bar{Y})^2}{\sum\limits_{i=1}^{n} (Y_i - \bar{Y})^2} \ . \qquad (5)$$

Since $Y_i - \bar{Y} = (Y_i - \hat{Y}_i) + (\hat{Y}_i - \bar{Y})$,  then,  $0 \leq R^2 \leq 1$.   Since $R^2 = 0.7729$,
we suspect that the hypothesis  $\beta_1 = \beta_2 = \beta_3 = 0$  must be rejected.

If the null-hypothesis is true,

$$\frac{\sum\limits_{i=1}^{n} (\hat{Y}_i - \bar{Y})^2/(k-1)}{\sum\limits_{i=1}^{n} (Y_i - \hat{Y})^2/(n-k)} \sim F_{k-1,n-k} \qquad (6)$$

where $F_{k-1,n-k}$ denotes a member of the family of F distributions with parameters k-1, n-k. Define

$$SSR = \sum\limits_{i=1}^{n} (\hat{Y}_i - \bar{Y})^2$$

$$SSE = \sum\limits_{i=1}^{n} (Y_i - \hat{Y})^2$$

$$SST = SSR + SSE .$$

Then (6) may be written,

$$\frac{SSR/(k-1)}{SSE/(n-k)} = \left[\frac{n-k}{k-1}\right]\left[\frac{SSR/SST}{1 - SSR/SST}\right] \qquad (7)$$

But, from (5), $R^2 = SSR/SST$ . Hence (7) becomes

$$\left[\frac{n-k}{k-1}\right]\left[\frac{R^2}{1 - R^2}\right] \qquad (8)$$

In the present problem, n = 30, k = 4. Hence, (8) becomes

$$\left(\frac{26}{3}\right)\left(\frac{0.7729}{0.2271}\right) = 29.50 .$$

This is the calculated F statistic. From (6),

$$F_{.01,3,26} = 4.64.$$

Since $F_{calculated} > F_{test}$ , we reject $H_0: \beta_1 = \beta_2 = \beta_3 = 0$ .

Quite frequently we desire a value of $R^2$ that is adjusted for the degrees of freedom lost in attempting to estimate the required parameters. Define

$$\bar{R}^2 = R^2 - \frac{(k-1)}{n-k} (1 - R^2) \qquad (9)$$

where n is the number of observations, and k is the number of parameters estimated.

(9) is called the corrected coefficient of determination. In the present problem, we find

$$\bar{R}^2 = .7729 - \frac{3}{26}(.2271)$$

$$= .7467 .$$

# CHAPTER 23

# BIOLOGICAL APPLICATIONS

● **PROBLEM** 23-1

Assume four rats are given a dose of a drug. After two days, the number of dead rats are observed. Each rat has the same probability,p, of dying. Find the binomial distribution of 0, 1, 2, 3, and 4 rats dying. Why might the binomial model fail?

Solution:    In a binomial experiment,

$$P(x = k) = \binom{n}{k} p^k (q)^{n-k}.$$

Here, $q = 1 - p$ and $n$ = the number of rats dying. We have:

$$P(4) = \binom{4}{4} p^4 = p^4 ; \quad P(3) = \binom{4}{3} p^3 q = 4p^3 q;$$

$$P(2) = \binom{4}{2} p^2 q^2 = 6 \ p^2 q^2;$$

$$P(1) = \binom{4}{1} pq^3 = 4pq^3 ; \quad P(0) = \binom{4}{0} q^4 = q^4.$$

The binomial model might fail to apply for a variety of reasons. The drug may be administered in the food and, consequently the rats may not all receive equivalent dosages of the drug, because some may eat more than others.

Those receiving a larger dose would have a higher probability of dying. P(Die) would not be the same for all four rats. Another possibility is that an undetected infectious disease might occur in the laboratory. Thus, if one rat dies of this disease the probability that the others will also die may be increased. The deaths would not be independent. Both these departures from the binomial situation are readily understandable, only because we precisely constructed the model for identical, independently repeated dichotomous experiments.

● **PROBLEM** 23-2

Consider the model below for the circulation of phosphorus in a simple pasture ecosystem:

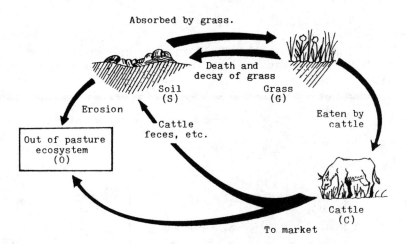

Absorbed by grass.

Death and decay of grass

Soil (S)

Grass (G)

Erosion

Eaten by cattle

Out of pasture ecosystem (0)

Cattle feces, etc.

Cattle (C)

To market

Assume further that, (1) whenever an atom of phosphorus is in the soil at the beginning of the day, then the sample space giving its location at the end of the day is

$$\left\{ S, \ G, \ O \right\}$$
$$\frac{3}{5}, \ \frac{3}{10}, \ \frac{1}{10} \ .$$

(In the case if where $O$ occurs, the molecule has been lost to the pasture by erosion.)

(2) Whenever an atom of phosphorus is in the grass at the beginning of the day, then its probable location at the end of the day is given by the sample space

$$\left\{ S, \ G, \ C \right\}$$
$$\frac{1}{10}, \frac{4}{10}, \frac{1}{2} \ ,$$

so that the probability is $\frac{1}{2}$ that the atom of phosphorus will be eaten by cattle.

(3) Similarly, whenever the atom of phosphorus starts in cattle,

$$\left\{ S, \ C, \ O \right\}$$
$$\frac{3}{4}, \frac{1}{5}, \frac{1}{20} \ ,$$

in the sample space for its location at the end of the day. (Note the high probability $\frac{3}{4}$ of the ingested phosphorus being returned to the soil via feces).

(4) Finally, if an atom of phosphorus is outside the pasture it stays outside, so that a sample space for its location at the end of the day is

$$\left\{ \begin{matrix} 0 \\ 1 \end{matrix} \right\} .$$

If an atom of phosphorus starts in the soil, what is the probability that it will be outside the system in three days?

Solution: We can construct the following tree diagram:

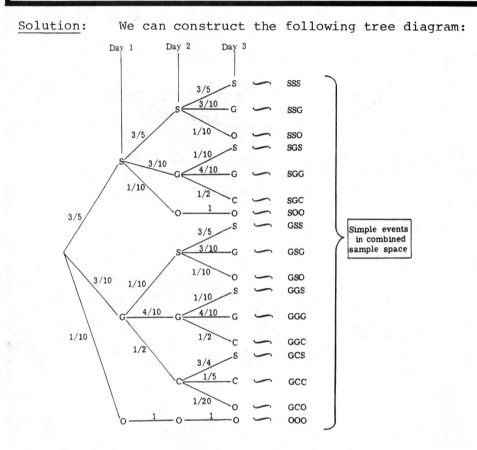

The event OUT, (the atom is outside the system after three days) is made up of the simple events, SOO, SSO, GSO, GCO, and OOO. Since all of these simple events are mutually exclusive

$$P(OUT) = P(SOO) + P(SSO) + P(GSO) + P(GCO) + P(OOO).$$

The probability of any simple event is found by multiplying the probabilities along its branch. Therefore,

$$P(OUT) = \left(\frac{3}{5}\right)\left(\frac{1}{10}\right)(1) + \left(\frac{3}{5}\right)\left(\frac{3}{5}\right)\left(\frac{1}{10}\right)$$

$$+ \left(\frac{3}{10}\right)\left(\frac{1}{10}\right)\left(\frac{1}{10}\right) + \left(\frac{3}{10}\right)\left(\frac{1}{2}\right)\left(\frac{1}{20}\right) + \left(\frac{1}{10}\right)(1)(1)$$

$$= \frac{3}{50} + \frac{9}{250} + \frac{3}{1000} + \frac{3}{400} + \frac{1}{10}$$

$$= \frac{413}{2000} .$$

986

Derive the Hardy-Weinberg probabilities in a population
with random mating.

Solution:    Assume that a sexually reproducing population
contains N males and K females.  The total population, T,
is equal to N + K.  Each individual carries two genes and
each gene is represented by one of two alleles, A or a.
The two genes together constitute that individual's
"genotype" - AA, Aa, or aa.  (Note that the genotype Aa
is the same as aA.)

In the process of mating each partner contributes
one gene to the offspring.  For example, if a male of genotype Aa mates with a female of genotype AA, the following
diagram illustrates the possible genotypes of the offspring:

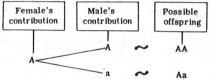

First, consider all of the male genes.  Since there
are N males, there are 2N total male genes. A certain
number of these, r, are of the type A.  The proportion
of the frequency of gene A in the males can be represented
by $p = \frac{r}{2N}$ .  The proportion of the remaining genes, type

a, can be represented by q = 1 - p, or $q = 1 - \frac{r}{2N}$ .  For

example, if there were 100 males, there would be 200 total

genes (A + a).  If r = 50, then $p = \frac{50}{200} = \frac{1}{4}$, and $q = \frac{3}{4}$ .

Similarly, realizing that the total number of female genes
is 2K we can define p' as the gene frequency of A, and q'
as the frequency of a, in females.

Note, that it is possible to have the same gene
frequencies even though the genotype proportions might
differ.  Consider the following example:  In a group of
100 organisms, we might have 50 AA, 0 Aa, and 50 aa, in
which case p = 0.5.  Another possibility is that there
might be 25 AA, 50 Aa, and 25 aa, in which case p is also
0.5.

We now turn to the subject of random mating: we are
said to have a random mating population if the determination of the genotype of an offspring obeys the following
three rules:  (1) A gene is selected simply at random
from all the male genes in the population.  (2)  A gene
is selected simply at random from all the female genes
in the population.  (3)  The two experiments are independent.

In the first experiment there are 2N male genes in
the sample space.  Since the selection is simply at random,
each gene has the probability, $\frac{1}{2N}$ of contributing to the

offspring, if there are r genes of type A. The probability, p, of choosing one is $\frac{r}{2N}$ .

Analogous reasoning holds for the second experiment: the selection of a gene from a female. There are 2K simple events in the sample space. The probability of the event "the gene chosen is A" is p'; and that of "the gene chosen is a" is q'. Since the two experiments are independent, the following tree diagram can be constructed:

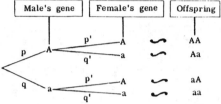

Recall that genotype Aa is the same as aA. From the diagram the probabilities of offspring genotypes are:

P(AA) = pp'; P(Aa) = pq' + qp'; P(aa) = qq'.

Usually we assume that the gene frequencies are the same in both males and females (i.e. p = p' and q = q'). Then the probabilities become:

P(AA) = $p^2$; P(Aa) = 2pq; P(aa) = $q^2$.

● **PROBLEM** 23-4

Referring to the independent random mating scheme of the previous problem, find the offspring genotype probabilities of the following two populations:

| a) | AA | Aa | aa |
|---|---|---|---|
| Males | 600 | 0 | 400 |
| Females | 400 | 400 | 200 |

| b) | AA | Aa | aa |
|---|---|---|---|
| Males | 400 | 400 | 200 |
| Females | 200 | 800 | 0 |

Solution:    Each individual has 2 genes. AA has 2 A's;
aa has 2 a's; and Aa has one of each, A and a.

a)    We must find the population gene frequencies.

Males: 600 AA → 600 × 2 A's  →   1200 A

$\qquad$ 400 aa → 400 × 2 a's  →    800 a

$\qquad\qquad\qquad$ Total =       2000     alleles

$$P(A) = p = \frac{\#\ A}{Total} = \frac{1200}{2000} = \frac{3}{5}$$

$$P(a) = q = 1 - p = \frac{2}{5}\ .$$

Females:    400 AA → 400 × 2 A's → 800 A

$\qquad\qquad$ 200 aa → 200 × 2 a's → 400 a

$\qquad\qquad$ 400 Aa → 400 × 1 A   → 400 A

$\qquad\qquad\qquad\qquad$ 400 × a      → 400 a

Totals: 1200 A; 800 a; 2000 alleles

$$p' = \frac{\#\ A}{Total} = \frac{1200}{2000} = \frac{3}{5}\ ;\ q' = 1 - p' = \frac{2}{5}\ .$$

From the Hardy-Weinberg probabilities:

$$P(AA) = pp' = \left(\frac{3}{5}\right)\left(\frac{3}{5}\right) = \frac{9}{25}$$

$$P(Aa) = pq' + p'q = \left(\frac{3}{5}\right)\left(\frac{2}{5}\right) + \left(\frac{3}{5}\right)\left(\frac{2}{5}\right) = \frac{12}{25}$$

$$P(aa) = qq' = \left(\frac{2}{5}\right)\left(\frac{2}{5}\right) = \frac{4}{25}\ .$$

b)    The same solution technique applies for the second
population. We first find the population gene frequencies.

Males:      400 AA → 400 × 2 A's → 800 A

$\qquad\qquad$ 200 aa → 200 × 2 a's → 400 a

$\qquad\qquad$ 400 Aa → 400 × 1 A   → 400 A

$\qquad\qquad\qquad\qquad$ 400 × 1 a   → 400 a

Totals: 1200 A; 800 a; 2000 overall

$$p = \frac{\#\ A}{Total} = \frac{1200}{2000} = \frac{3}{5}\ ;\ q = 1 - p = \frac{2}{5}$$

Females:    200 AA → 200 × 2 A's → 400 A

$$800 \text{ Aa} \rightarrow 800 \times 1 \text{ A} \rightarrow 800 \text{ A}$$

$$800 \times 1 \text{ a} \rightarrow 800 \text{ a}$$

Totals: 1200 A; 800 a; 2000 overall

$$p' = \frac{\# \text{ A}}{\text{Total}} = \frac{1200}{2000} = \frac{3}{5} ; \quad q' = 1 - p' = \frac{2}{5} .$$

We have the same p, p', q',q' as in part a. Therefore, the offspring genotype probabilities will be the same.

$$P(AA) = \frac{9}{25} \qquad P(Aa) = \frac{12}{25} \qquad P(aa) = \frac{4}{25} .$$

● **PROBLEM** 23-5

Consider a group of N individuals, m are smokers, and n die of lung cancer. What is the probability that x of these n are smokers? Assume smoking has no effect on lung cancer.

<u>Solution</u>: Since smoking has no effect on lung cancer, it is assumed that all combinations of n people dying from lung cancer are equally likely. There are $\binom{N}{n}$ of these. The number of ways that x smokers die of lung cancer is:

$$\left[ \begin{array}{c} \text{The number of ways of} \\ \text{choosing x from m} \\ \text{smokers, to die of} \\ \text{lung cancer} \end{array} \right] \times \left[ \begin{array}{c} \text{The number of ways of} \\ \text{choosing } (n - x) \text{ of the} \\ (N - m) \text{ nonsmokers to} \\ \text{die of lung cancer} \end{array} \right]$$

or: $\quad \binom{m}{x} \times \binom{N - m}{n - x} .$

The probability is then $\quad P(X=x) = \dfrac{\binom{m}{x} \binom{N - m}{n - x}}{\binom{N}{n}} .$

Notice that this is a hypergeometric probability.

● **PROBLEM** 23-6

In the previous problem we regarded the persons who die of lung cancer as a simple random sample of size n coming from a total population, N, comprised of m smokers and (N - m) nonsmokers. Now, regard the smokers as a simple random sample of size m from a population of n persons dying of lung cancer and regard the (N - n) nonsmokers as not dying from lung cancer. Find the probability of x smokers dying of lung cancer using this model. Show that the two probabilities are equal.

Solution:    As in the last problem, we consider equally likely combinations; but now the combinations consist of m smokers.   There are $\binom{N}{m}$ of these.

According to this model x smokers die of lung cancer in

$$
\begin{bmatrix} \text{The number of ways of} \\ \text{designating x of the} \\ \text{n individuals who died} \\ \text{from lung cancer as} \\ \text{smokers} \end{bmatrix} \times \begin{bmatrix} \text{The number of ways of} \\ \text{designating (m - x) of} \\ \text{the remaining (N - n)} \\ \text{individuals as} \\ \text{smokers} \end{bmatrix}
$$

or     $\binom{n}{x}$     $\times$     $\binom{N - n}{m - x} = \binom{n}{x}\binom{N - n}{m - x}$ .

The probability is then     $P'(X = x) = \dfrac{\binom{n}{x}\binom{N - n}{m - x}}{\binom{N}{m}}$ .

We now must show $P(X = x) = P'(X = x)$

$$
P(X = x) = \frac{\binom{m}{x}\binom{N - m}{n - x}}{\binom{N}{m}}
$$

$$
= \frac{\dfrac{m!}{x!\ (m - x)!}\ \dfrac{(N - m)!}{(n - x)!\ (N - m - n + x)!}}{\dfrac{N!}{n!\ (N - n)!}}
$$

$$
= \frac{\dfrac{m!}{x!\ (m - x)!\ (n - x)!\ (N - m - n + x)!}\ n!\ (N - n)!}{\dfrac{N!}{m!\ (N - m)!}}
$$

$$
= \frac{\dfrac{n!}{x!\ (n - x)!}\ \dfrac{(N - n)!}{(m - x)!\ (N - n - m + x)!}}{\dfrac{N!}{m!\ (N - m)!}}
$$

$$
= \frac{\binom{n}{x}\binom{N - n}{m - x}}{\binom{N}{m}} = P'(X = x) .
$$

Thus, we have demonstrated here a property of hypergeometric probabilities called duality.

A pharmaceutical company wants to test the effectiveness of a new vaccine in preventing a certain disease. It is estimated that 40 per cent of the people exposed to the disease will contract it under normal circumstances. A group of 12 persons who have been exposed to the disease volunteer to be vaccinated. Two of them later contract the disease.

An effective vaccine would reduce the probability that a person exposed to the disease will actually contract it. However, if the vaccine has no effect the probability of any given exposed person contracting the disease is p = 0.4. Use a .05 significance level to decide if the vaccine is effective.

Solution: We first notice that this is a problem in binomial probabilities with n = 12 and p = .4. Under pre-vaccine circumstances, we would expect to find np = 12(0.4) = 4.8 persons contract the disease on the average in a long series of experiments involving 12 people.

Let $H_0$: the hypothesis that the serum has no effect

$H_1$: the hypothesis that it works .

We reject $H_0$ if, P(2 or less people are affected) = $P(x \leq 2) \leq .05$

$$P(x \leq 2) = P(x = 0) + P(x = 1) + P(x = 2)$$

$$= \binom{12}{0} (1 - 0.4)^{12} + \binom{12}{1} (1 - 0.4)^{11} (0.4)$$

$$+ \binom{12}{2} (1 - 0.4)^{10} (0.4)^2$$

$$= .0022 + .0174 + .0638$$

$$= .0834.$$

We see that $P(x \leq 2) > .05$. Hence we do not reject $H_0$ and cannot conclude that the vaccine is effective.

Suppose it is desired to compare the effects of two analgesic drugs A and B in the treatment of a certain disease, and eight patients volunteer for the experiment. The following results are obtained:

Data on the effects of two analgesic drugs:

| Patients | Hours of relief with analgesic A | Hours of relief with analgesic B | Relative advantage of B in Hours (x) |
|---|---|---|---|
| 1 | 3.2 | 3.8 | +0.6 |
| 2 | 1.6 | 1.0 | -0.6 |
| 3 | 5.7 | 8.4 | +2.7 |
| 4 | 2.8 | 3.6 | +0.8 |
| 5 | 5.5 | 5.0 | -0.5 |
| 6 | 1.2 | 3.5 | +2.3 |
| 7 | 6.1 | 7.3 | +1.2 |
| 8 | 2.9 | 4.8 | +1.9 |
| Means | 3.62 | 4.67 | +1.05 |

Test the hypothesis that drugs A and B are equally effective.

Solution: Consider the random variable x in the last column. $H_0: \mu_x = 0$.

If $\mu_x = 0$, neither B nor A will have a relative advantage over the other.

We compute the following summary statistics

$$\Sigma x = 0.6 - 0.6 + 2.7 + 0.8 - 0.5 + 2.3 + 1.2 + 1.9 = 8.40$$

$$\Sigma x^2 = (0.6)^2 + (0.6)^2 + (2.7)^2 + (0.8)^2 + (0.5)^2$$
$$+ (2.3)^2 + (1.2)^2 + (1.9)^2 = 19.24$$

$$n = 8 \qquad \overline{x} = \frac{1}{n} \Sigma x = \frac{8.40}{8} = 1.05$$

$$s^2 = \frac{1}{n-1} \left[ \Sigma x^2 - \frac{1}{n} (\Sigma x)^2 \right] = \frac{1}{7} \left( 19.24 - \frac{(8.40)^2}{8} \right) = 1.489$$

$$\frac{s}{\sqrt{n}} = \sqrt{\frac{1.489}{8}} = .4314 .$$

We know that $\dfrac{\overline{x} - \mu}{\frac{s}{\sqrt{n}}}$ is a t random variable

with n - 1 degrees of freedom. In our case n - 1 = 7 and
$$\frac{\overline{x} - \mu}{\frac{s}{\sqrt{n}}} = \frac{1.05 - 0}{.4314} = 2.43 = t .$$

From a t table we see $P(|t(7)| \geq 2.43) < .05$.

Accordingly, we reject the null hypothesis.

The following figures reveal results of an experiment with ten patients on the effect of two supposedly soporific (sleep producing) drugs, A and B.

### ADDITIONAL HOURS OF SLEEP GAINED BY THE USE OF TWO TESTED DRUGS

| Patient | A. | B. | Difference (B - A). |
|---------|------|------|---------------------|
| 1 | +0.7 | +1.9 | +1.2 |
| 2 | -1.6 | +0.8 | +2.4 |
| 3 | -0.2 | +1.1 | +1.3 |
| 4 | -1.2 | +0.1 | +1.3 |
| 5 | -0.1 | -0.1 | 0.0 |
| 6 | +3.4 | +4.4 | +1.0 |
| 7 | +3.7 | +5.5 | +1.8 |
| 8 | +0.8 | +1.6 | +0.8 |
| 9 | 0.0 | +4.6 | +4.6 |
| 10 | +2.0 | +3.4 | +1.4 |
| Mean ($\bar{x}$) | + .75 | +2.33 | +1.58 |

Test the hypothesis at the 5% level that the two drugs are equally effective.

<u>Solution</u>:    If the two drugs are equally effective the true mean of the last column, the difference in hours of sleep gained, would be zero.

Test $H_0: \mu = 0$        versus        $H_1: \mu \neq 0$.

Since we have a small sample with unknown variance, we will use a t-test. With ten patients we have nine degrees of freedom. From t-tables we know that

$P(-2.262 < t(a) < 2.262) = .95.$

Let $\bar{x}$ be the mean of the last column entries.

Recall that $\dfrac{\bar{x} - \mu}{\frac{s}{\sqrt{n}}}$ has a t distribution with n - 1

(9 in this case) degrees of freedom.  Hence,

$$P\left(-2.262 < \frac{\bar{x} - \mu}{\frac{s}{\sqrt{n}}} < 2.262\right) = .95.$$

If $H_0$ is true, $\mu = 0$ and $\dfrac{\sqrt{n}\,\bar{x}}{s}$ will be t(9).  We use the following decision rule: Reject $H_0$ if $\left|\dfrac{\sqrt{n}\ \bar{x}}{s}\right| \geq 2.262$. Accept otherwise.

We must find $\quad s^2 = \dfrac{1}{n-1}\ \Sigma (X_i - \bar{X})^2$

$= \dfrac{1}{9}\ [(1.2 - 1.58)^2 + (2.4 - 1.58)^2 + (1.3 - 1.58)^2$

$\quad + (1.3 - 1.58)^2 + (0 - 1.58)^2 + (1 - 1.58)^2$

$\quad + (1.8 - 1.58)^2 + (0.8 - 1.58)^2 + (4.6 - 1.58)^2$

$\quad + (1.4 - 1.58)^2$

$= 1.513.$

$s = \sqrt{1.513} = 1.23,$

$\dfrac{\sqrt{n}\ \bar{x}}{s} = \dfrac{\sqrt{10}\ 1.58}{1.23} = 4.062.$

$4.062 > 2.262$ and we reject $H_0$.

Thus, it is concluded that the effectiveness of the two drugs is different.

● **PROBLEM** 23-10

The mean difference in length between the right and left femurs of 36 skeletons of a certain species is found to be 2.0234 cm. The sum of the squared deviations from the mean, $\Sigma (X - \bar{X})^2$, is 418.6875. Test the hypothesis that on the average the left and right femurs are of equal lengths.

Solution: We don't know the variance in this problem and therefore will use a t-test. We know that

$$t = \dfrac{\sqrt{n(n-1)}\ (\bar{X} - \mu_0)}{\sqrt{\Sigma (X - \bar{X})^2}}$$

has a t-distribution with $n - 1$ degrees of freedom. In this case, under the hypothesis that $\mu = 0$,

$$t = \dfrac{(\sqrt{36 \cdot 35})\ (2.0234)}{\sqrt{418.6875}} = \dfrac{71.8236}{20.4619} = 3.51.$$

With 35 degrees of freedom,

$P(t_{35} \geq 3.51) < .005$ from a t-table.

We conclude that 3.51 is too large a t value to be produced by chance alone. Therefore, there is a significant difference between the left and right femurs.

In experiments on the breeding of flowers of a certain species, an experimenter obtained 120 magenta flowers with a greem stigma, 48 magenta flowers with a red stigma, 36 red flowers with a green stigma and 13 red flowers with a red stigma. Theory predicts that flowers of these types should be obtained in the ratios 9 : 3 : 3 : 1. Are the experimental results compatible with the theory at a 5% level of significance?

Solution:    This is a problem of testing the hypothesis

$$H_0: p_1 = \frac{9}{16} \; ; \; p_2 = \frac{3}{16} \; ; \; p_3 = \frac{3}{16} \; ; \; p_4 = \frac{1}{16} \; ,$$

for a multinomial distribution with 4 possible outcomes, where    n = 120 + 48 + 36 + 13 = 217.

Under $H_0$, the expected frequencies, to the nearest integer, are as follows:

Magenta - Green : $\frac{9}{16} \times 217 = 122$

Magenta - Red    : $\frac{3}{16} \times 217 = 41$

Red   -  Green : $\frac{3}{16} \times 217 = 41$

Red - Red    : $\frac{1}{16} \times 217 = 13$ .

Apply a chi-square test to determine a value of

$$\chi^2 = \Sigma \; \frac{(Observed - Expected)^2}{Expected}$$

$$= \frac{(120 - 122)^2}{122} + \frac{(48 - 41)^2}{41} + \frac{(36 - 41)^2}{41} + \frac{(13 - 13)^2}{14}$$

$$= .03 + 1.20 + .61 + \quad 0 \quad = 1.84.$$

Since we have 4 categories, we            consider a chi-square distribution with 4 - 1 = 3 degrees of freedom.

For such a distribution    $P(\chi^2 (3) \geq 7.8) = .05.$

Our value 1.8 is less than the 5 percent critical value and consequently            these experimental results are compatible with the 9:3:3:1 theory.

The following table shows the observed numbers of male and female offspring  of several stallions:

| Sex of Offspring | Reference numbers of stallions | | | | | | Totals |
|---|---|---|---|---|---|---|---|
| | 1 | 2 | 3 | 4 | 5 | 6 | |
| Male | 13 | 8 | 7 | 15 | 9 | 19 | 71 |
| Female | 9 | 10 | 8 | 6 | 5 | 7 | 45 |
| Totals | 22 | 18 | 15 | 21 | 14 | 26 | 116 |

Determine whether the above variations in the ratios of male to female offspring could be explained by chance alone.

**Solution:** We would expect males and females to be born in a 1 : 1 ratio, half of the totals would be of each sex. The following table shows the expected numbers of male and female offspring.

| Sex of Offspring | Reference numbers of stallions | | | | | | Totals |
|---|---|---|---|---|---|---|---|
| | 1 | 2 | 3 | 4 | 5 | 6 | |
| Male | 11 | 9 | 7.5 | 10.5 | 7 | 13 | 58 |
| Female | 11 | 9 | 7.5 | 10.5 | 7 | 13 | 58 |
| Totals | 22 | 18 | 15 | 21 | 14 | 26 | 116 |

The null hypothesis is that 50% of each stallion's offspring will be male. Apply a chi-square test.

Calculate,

$$\chi^2 = \Sigma \ \frac{(\text{Observed} - \text{Expected})^2}{\text{Expected}}$$

$$= \frac{(13 - 11)^2}{11} + \frac{(8 - 9)^2}{11} + \frac{(7 - 7.5)^2}{7.5}$$

$$+ \frac{(15 - 10.5)^2}{10.5} + \frac{(9 - 7)^2}{7} + \frac{(19 - 13)^2}{13}$$

$$= .3636 + .0909 + .0333 + 1.9286 + .5714 + 2.7692$$

$$= 5.76.$$

We have six different stallions. Hence, we resort to a chi-square distribution with 6 - 1 = 5 degrees of freedom. We assume a .05 significance level. From a chi-square table we see

$$P(\chi^2(5) \geq 11.1) = .05. \quad \text{Since } 5.76 < 11.1,$$

$$P(\chi^2(5) \geq 5.76) > .05 \quad \text{and so we do not have}$$

reason to reject the null hypotheses.

The following table is taken from Greenwood and Yule's data for typhoid:

Observed

|  | Attacked | Not Attacked | Total |
|---|---|---|---|
| Inoculated | 56 | 6,759 | 6,815 |
| Not inoculated | 272 | 11,396 | 11,668 |
| Total | 328 | 18,155 | 18,483 |

Under the hypothesis of independence construct the expected value table for the above data.

Can we conclude whether or not the results above are from independent variables?

Solution: For independence we must have our values calculated so that in a loose sense the frequencies are in proportion. There were 18,483 people in the sample. 328 were attacked and 18,155 were not attacked. By the law of large numbers, we can state

$$P(\text{Attacked}) = \frac{328}{18,483} \qquad \text{and}$$

$$P(\text{Not Attacked}) = \frac{18,155}{18,483}.$$

If the variables were independent, we would expect the number inoculated and attacked to be equal to the number( inoculated) × P(attacked)

$$= 6815 \times \frac{328}{18,483} = 120.94.$$

Similarly, we would expect the number

inoculated and not attacked = $6815 \times \frac{18,155}{18,483} = 6,694.06,$

998

not inoculated and attacked $= 11{,}668 \times \dfrac{328}{18{,}483} = 207.06,$

not inoculated and not attacked $= 11{,}668 \times \dfrac{18{,}155}{18{,}483} = 11{,}460.94.$

The table of expected values is then

Expected

| | Attacked | Not attacked | Total |
|---|---|---|---|
| Inoculated | 120.94 | 6,694.06 | 6,815 |
| Not inoculated | 207.06 | 11,460.94 | 11,668 |
| Total | 328 | 18,155 | 18,483 |

We now turn to a chi-square test. For a 2 x 2 table, it isn't necessary to calculate

$$\Sigma \; \frac{(O_i - E_i)^2}{E_i} \; , \; \text{if you recall the formula}$$

$$\chi^2 = \frac{(ad - bc)^2 \, (a + b + c + d)}{(a + b)(c + d)(a + c)(b + d)}$$

where a, b, c, d are the four observed numbers. (If you do not recall this formula, then use $\Sigma \, (O_i - E_i)^2 / \, E,$ since the formula was derived from this.)

$$\chi^2 = \frac{(56 \cdot 11{,}396 - 6{,}759.272)^2 \, (56 + 6759 + 272 + 11{,}396)}{(56 + 6{,}759)(272 + 11{,}396)(56 + 272)(6759 + 11{,}396)}$$

$$= \frac{(1{,}200{,}272)^2 \, (18{,}483)}{(6815)(11{,}668)(328)(18{,}155)}$$

$$= 56.234.$$

We now consider a chi-square distribution with 1 degree of freedom. We use only 1 d.o.f. since we are talking about independence vs. non-independence. Our value 56.234 goes extremely off the chi-square table. There can be little doubt with a $\chi^2$ value so large that independence does not exist.

● **PROBLEM** 23-14

Four plots of land were divided into five subplots of corn. Each subplot had a different treatment assigned to it at random. Test whether the five treatments are equally effective. The following table contains relevant information:

Treatment

| | A | B | C | D | E |
|---|---|---|---|---|---|
| Plot 1 | 310 | 353 | 366 | 299 | 367 |
| Plot 2 | 284 | 293 | 335 | 264 | 314 |
| Plot 3 | 307 | 306 | 339 | 311 | 377 |
| Plot 4 | 267 | 312 | 312 | 266 | 342 |

Solution:     This problem involves a one-way analysis of variance.

The following summary statistics are easily computed:

Let $a_{ij}$ denote the element belonging to the ith row and jth column in the table. Then, $\bar{x} = \frac{1}{20} \sum_{j=1}^{5} \sum_{i=1}^{4} a_{ij}$.

Hence,    $\bar{x} = 316.2$

$$\sum_{j=1}^{5} (\bar{x}_{ij} - \bar{x})^2 = 3178; \quad \sum_{j=1}^{5} \sum_{i=1}^{4} (x_{ij} - \bar{x})^2 = 8314$$

n = the total number of measurements = 20

$n_j$ = the sample size of the jth treatment = 4 for all j

k = the number of treatments = 5.

We assume that the random variable $x_{ij}$ has a mean

$$\mu_{ij} = a_i + b_j + c.$$

We wish to test the hypothesis that all treatments are the same. If so, $b_j$ is a constant and can be absorbed into c. Hence we can assume $b_j = 0$ for all j. We now test

$$H_0: b_j = 0 \quad \text{for all } j \quad \text{versus} \quad H_1: b_j \neq 0 \text{ for some } j$$

Recall that    $r = \dfrac{\dfrac{\sum_{j=1}^{5} r_j (\bar{x}._j - \bar{x})^2}{(k-1)}}{\dfrac{\sum_{j=1}^{5} \sum_{i=1}^{5} (x_{ij} - \bar{x}._j)^2}{(n-k)}}$

is F distributed with $(k - 1, n - k) = (5 - 1, 20 - 5) = (4, 15)$ degrees of freedom.

We will reject $H_0$ if r is larger than what we would expect by chance alone.

Reject $H_0$ if $\quad r > F(.975, 4, 15) = 3.80$. Here,

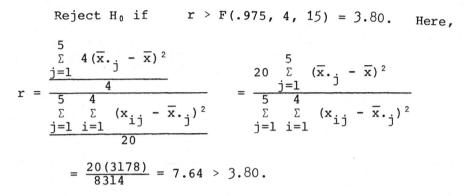

$$r = \frac{\displaystyle\sum_{j=1}^{5} \frac{4(\bar{x}._j - \bar{x})^2}{4}}{\displaystyle\sum_{j=1}^{5}\sum_{i=1}^{4} \frac{(x_{ij} - \bar{x}._j)^2}{20}} = \frac{20\displaystyle\sum_{j=1}^{5}\frac{(\bar{x}._j - \bar{x})^2}{4}}{\displaystyle\sum_{j=1}^{5}\sum_{i=1}^{4}(x_{ij} - \bar{x}._j)^2}$$

$$= \frac{20(3178)}{8314} = 7.64 > 3.80.$$

Thus, $H_0$ must be rejected and it is concluded that the treatments are not equally effective.

● **PROBLEM** 23-15

Consider the following graph showing the relationship between altitude (x), in ft., and tail-length (y) in mm of a species of African bird.

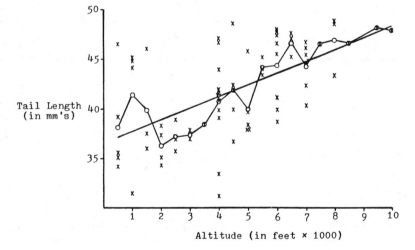

Altitude (in feet × 1000)

The data from which the graph was constructed yielded the following quantities:

$$n = 72; \quad \bar{x} = 4.46; \quad \bar{y} = 41.69;$$

$$\sum_{i=1}^{72}(x_i - \bar{x})^2 = 390.4; \quad \sum_{i=1}^{72}(y_i - \bar{y})^2 = 1526.3.$$

$$\sum_{i=1}^{n}(x_i - \bar{x})(y_i - \bar{y}) = 446.0.$$

> Find the equation of the regression line and also find the variation about the regression line.

Solution:    The population regression line has the form

$$y = \alpha + \beta x$$

where $\alpha$, $\beta$ are unknown parameters.  Using the above data, we may estimate $\alpha$ and $\beta$ using the method of least squares. The estimated regression line has the form

$$\hat{y} = \hat{\alpha} + \hat{\beta} x \qquad (1)$$

where

$$\hat{\beta} = \frac{\sum\limits_{i=1}^{n} (x_i - \bar{x})(y_i - \bar{y})}{\sum\limits_{i=1}^{n} (x_i - \bar{x})^2} \qquad (2)$$

and

$$\hat{\alpha} = \bar{y} - \hat{\beta}\bar{x}. \qquad (3)$$

Substituting the numbers 446.0 and 390.4 for $\sum\limits_{i=1}^{n} (x_i - \bar{x})(y_i - \bar{y})$ and $\sum\limits_{i=1}^{n} (x_i - \bar{x})^2$ respectively into (2), we have

$$\hat{\beta} = \frac{446.0}{390.4} = 1.142. \qquad (4)$$

Then, letting $\bar{y} = 41.69$, $\bar{x} = 4.46$ in (3),

$$\hat{\alpha} = 41.69 - (1.142)4.46$$

$$= 36.6. \qquad (5)$$

Substituting (4) and (5) into (1),

$$\hat{y} = 36.6 + 1.142\, x. \qquad (6)$$

Equation (6) gives the linear relationship between altitude and tail-length on the basis of the observed data.

Next we must find the variation about the regression line.  The formula for the variance is

$$s^2 = \sum\limits_{i=1}^{n} \frac{(y_i - (\hat{\alpha} - \hat{\beta}x_i))^2}{n - 2} \qquad (7)$$

since $E(y_i | x_i) = \hat{y} - \hat{\alpha} - \hat{\beta}x_i$.  Note that two degrees of freedom were used up in estimating $\hat{\alpha}$ and $\hat{\beta}$; hence the denominator of (7) is $n - 2$. Formula (7) can be converted into an equivalent form that is computationally simpler. Thus,

$$s^2 = \frac{1}{n - 2} \sum_{i=1}^{n} (y_i - \bar{y} + \hat{\beta}\bar{x} - \hat{\beta}x_i)^2$$

(since $\hat{\alpha} = \bar{y} - \hat{\beta}\bar{x}$),

$$= \frac{1}{n - 2} \sum_{i=1}^{n} [(y_i - \bar{y}) - \hat{\beta}(x_i - \bar{x})]^2$$

$$= \frac{1}{n - 2} \left[ \sum_{i=1}^{n} (y_i - \bar{y})^2 - 2\hat{\beta} \sum_{i=1}^{n} (x_i - \bar{x})(y_i - \bar{y}) \right.$$

$$\left. + \hat{\beta}^2 \sum_{i=1}^{n} (x_i - \bar{x})^2 \right]. \qquad (8)$$

But

$$\hat{\beta} = \frac{\sum_{i=1}^{n} (x_i - \bar{x})(y_i - \bar{y})}{\sum_{i=1}^{n} (x_i - \bar{x})^2} .$$

Hence, (8) becomes

$$s^2 = \frac{1}{n - 2} \left[ \sum_{i=1}^{n} (y_i - \bar{y})^2 - 2 \frac{\sum (x_i - \bar{x})(y_i - \bar{y})}{\sum (x_i - \bar{x})^2} \sum (x_i - \bar{x})(y_i - \bar{y}) \right.$$

$$\left. + \left[ \frac{\sum (x_i - \bar{x})(y_i - \bar{y})}{\sum (x_i - \bar{x})^2} \right]^2 \sum (x_i - \bar{x})^2 \right]$$

$$= \frac{1}{n - 2} \left[ \sum_{i=1}^{n} (y_i - \bar{y})^2 - \frac{\left[ \sum_{i=1}^{n} (x - \bar{x})(y - \bar{y}) \right]^2}{\sum (x - \bar{x})^2} \right] \qquad (9)$$

Substituting the given numbers into (9),

$$s^2 = \frac{1}{70} \left[ 1526.3 - \frac{(446)^2}{390.4} \right]$$

$$= 14.53.$$

Thus, the distribution of tail lengths for a given altitude has mean given by the corresponding point on the regression line and variance 14.53. For example, when altitude is 6000, the average tail-length is 43.45 mm with standard deviation 3.81.

# CHAPTER 24

# MISCELLANEOUS APPLICATIONS

● **PROBLEM** 24-1

A Geiger counter can be used to determine the number of alpha particles emitted in a given amount of time. The following observations of the number of particles emitted by barium-133 in one-tenth of a second were recorded.

$$
\begin{array}{cccccccccc}
7, & 4, & 3, & 6, & 4, & 4, & 5, & 3, & 5, & 3, \\
5, & 5, & 3, & 2, & 5, & 4, & 3, & 3, & 7, & 6, \\
6, & 4, & 3, & 11, & 9, & 6, & 7, & 4, & 5, & 4, \\
7, & 3, & 2, & 8, & 6, & 7, & 4, & 1, & 9, & 8, \\
4, & 8, & 9, & 3, & 9, & 7, & 7, & 9, & 3, & 10,
\end{array}
$$

Determine whether this follows a Poisson distribution using a 5% significance level.

Solution: We shall use the chi-square test to answer this question. First, we estimate the parameter $\lambda$ in the Poisson density function that the emissions are assumed to follow. The sample mean $\bar{x}$ is used to estimate $\lambda$ in

$$
f(x) = \frac{e^{-\lambda} \lambda^x}{x!} \quad ; \quad x = 0,1,\ldots \tag{1}
$$

We find

$$
\bar{x} = \frac{1}{n} \sum_{i=1}^{n} x_i = \frac{1}{50} \sum_{i=1}^{50} (x_i) = \frac{270}{50} = 5.4.
$$

For computational convenience we partition the outcomes into the mutually disjoint sets:

$$
A_1 = \{0,1,2,3\}, \ A_2 = \{4\}, \ A_3 = \{5\}, \ A_4 = \{6\},
$$
$$
A_5 = \{7\}, \text{ and } A_6 = \{8,9,10,11\} .
$$

Note that each partition contains at least five outcomes.

Substituting $x = 0,1,2$, and $3$ successively into (1) (with $\lambda = 5.4$) and adding, we find that $A_1$ has frequency 13 and probability 0.213. Proceeding in a similar manner we obtain the following table.

|  | Outcome | | | | | |
|---|---|---|---|---|---|---|
| Frequency: | $A_1$ | $A_2$ | $A_3$ | $A_4$ | $A_5$ | $A_6$ |
|  | 13 | 9 | 6 | 5 | 7 | 10 |
| Poisson Probability: | 0.213 | 0.160 | 0.173 | 0.156 | 0.120 | 0.178 |

We are now prepared to compute the chi-square statistic for the problem.

$$q_{6-1} = \sum_{i=1}^{n} \frac{(\text{obs}_i - \text{Exp}_i)^2}{\text{Exp}_i}$$

$$q_5 = \frac{[13 - 50(0.213)]^2}{50(0.213)} + \frac{[9 - 50(0.160)]^2}{50(0.160)}$$

$$+ \frac{[6 - 50(0.173)]^2}{50(0.173)} + \frac{[5 - 50(0.156)]^2}{50(0.156)}$$

$$+ \frac{[7 - 50(0.120)]^2}{50(0.120)} + \frac{[10 - 50(0.178)]^2}{50(0.178)}$$

$$= 2.763.$$

But we estimated the parameter $\lambda$ by the sample mean $\bar{x}$. Thus we lose another degree of freedom and $q_5$ becomes $q_4$. Consulting a table, $\chi^2_{.95,4} = 9.448$. Since $2.763 < 9.448$, we accept the hypothesis that the emission of particles follows a Poisson process.

● **PROBLEM** 24-2

Human mortality increases almost exponentially once a person reaches 25 years of age. Using this empirical fact, derive the distribution function and probability density function associated with the Gompertz law found in actuarial science.

Solution: We reason that as a person gets older the probability of his dying ("failure") increases. Recall that one of the assumptions of the Poisson process is that the probability of change in a sufficiently short interval of length $h$ is approximately $\lambda h$ where $\lambda$ is the parameter of the Poisson density function

$$f(x) = \frac{e^{-\lambda} \lambda^x}{x!} \quad ; \quad x = 0, 1, \ldots$$

We now modify the model implied by this process. Assume that $\lambda h$ is now no longer a parameter but is a nonnegative function of the position of the interval $h$, $\lambda = \lambda(\omega) h$. That is, if $p(x, \omega)$ represents $x$ changes in the interval $(0, \omega)$, $0 \le \omega$, $p(x+1, \omega+h) - p(x, \omega) \approx \lambda(\omega) h$. Assuming further that changes in non-overlapping intervals are independent of each other, the probability of zero changes in the interval $(0, \omega+h)$ is given by

$$p(0, \omega+h) \approx p(0, \omega)[1 - \lambda(\omega) h] \tag{1}$$

Examining (1), note that for $\lambda(\omega)$ nonnegative, $p(0, \omega+h)$ decreases as $\omega$ increases. This is a mathematical reflection of the morbid fact that as we grow older (for example), the probability of no change (from life to death) decreases. We wish to isolate $\lambda(\omega)$. Hence, dividing (1) by $h$, and rewriting,

$$p\frac{(0, \omega+h) - p(0, \omega)}{h} \approx - \lambda(\omega) p(0, \omega) .$$

In the limit, as $h \to 0$, we obtain a differential equation,

$$p'(0, \omega) = -\lambda(\omega) p(0, \omega)$$

or

$$\frac{p'(0, \omega)}{p(0, \omega)} = -\lambda(\omega) . \tag{2}$$

Noting that $\int \frac{du}{u} = \ln |u| + c$, we integrate (2),

$$\ln p(0,\omega) = -\int \lambda(\omega)\,d\omega + c$$

and

$$p(0,\omega) = c_1 \exp[-\int \lambda(\omega)\,d\omega] \qquad (3)$$

where $c_1 = e^c$.

The initial condition is $p(0) = 1$, i.e., the probability of zero changes in an interval of length zero is one. Letting $c_1 = 1$,

$$\exp[-\int \lambda(\omega)\,d\omega] = 1$$

or

$$-\int \lambda(\omega)\,d\omega = 0$$

when $\omega = 0$. Let $H(\omega) = \int \lambda(\omega)\,d\omega$ such that $H(0) = 0$. Substituting into (3),

$$p(0,\omega) = \exp[-H(\omega)].$$

Since $H'(\omega) = \lambda(\omega)$ and $H(0) = 0$,

$$H(\omega) = \int_0^\omega \lambda(t)\,dt . \qquad (4)$$

Let us use (4) to find a distribution function for modelling the exponential force of mortality. We have,

$$\lambda(\omega) = H'(\omega) = ae^{b\omega}, \quad a, b > 0 \qquad (5)$$

where $a$ and $b$ are the parameters of the distribution. Integrating (5)

$$H(\omega) = a \int e^{b\omega}\,d\omega = \frac{a}{b} e^{b\omega} + c.$$

Since $H(0) = 0$, $c = \frac{-a}{b}$. Then,

$$G(\omega) = P(W \le \omega) = 1 - e^{-H(\omega)}$$

$$= 1 - \exp[-\frac{a}{b} e^{b\omega} + \frac{a}{b}], \ 0 \le \omega . \qquad (6)$$

Differentiating (6) with respect to $\omega$,

$$g(\omega) = ae^{b\omega} \exp[-\frac{a}{b} e^{b\omega} + \frac{a}{b}] . \qquad (7)$$

Equations (6) and (7) are respectively the distribution function and probability density function of the Gompertz law.

● **PROBLEM** 24-3

In league bowling, each team member bowls three games. In one night, 63 games were recorded with regard to whether they were bowled first, second or third, and also according to the scores achieved:

SCORES

| Game | 0-162 | 163-177 | 178-300 | Total |
|------|-------|---------|---------|-------|
| 1 | 4 | 4 | 13 | 21 |
| 2 | 8 | 7 | 6 | 21 |
| 3 | 6 | 10 | 5 | 21 |
| Total | 18 | 21 | 24 | 63 |

Determine whether the scores obtained are independent of the game bowled.

**Solution:** The method applied in testing the null hypothesis, that there is no relationship between the number of the game bowled and the score achieved is a chi-square test on the given table. Such a table is known as a contingency table.

Determining the relevant probabilities:

the probability that a game bowled is the first game is $\frac{21}{63}$ ;

the probability that a game bowled is the second game is $\frac{21}{63}$ ;

the probability that a game bowled is the third game is $\frac{21}{63}$ ;

the probability that the score achieved is from 0 to 162 is $\frac{18}{63}$ ;

the probability that the score achieved is from 163–177 is $\frac{21}{63}$ ; and

the probability that the score achieved is from 178–300 is $\frac{24}{63}$ .

Now, a table to compare the observed values with the expected values can be made:

### SCORES

| Game | 0–162 obs. | 0–162 exp. | 163–177 obs. | 163–177 exp. | 178–300 obs. | 178–300 exp. | Total obs. | Total exp. |
|---|---|---|---|---|---|---|---|---|
| 1 | 4 | $(63)(\frac{21}{63})(\frac{18}{63})$ $= 6.0$ | 4 | $(63)(\frac{21}{63})(\frac{21}{63})$ $= 7.0$ | 13 | $(63)(\frac{21}{63})(\frac{24}{63})$ $= 8.0$ | 21 | 21 |
| 2 | 8 | $(63)(\frac{21}{63})(\frac{18}{63})$ $= 6.0$ | 7 | $(63)(\frac{21}{63})(\frac{21}{63})$ $= 7.0$ | 6 | $(63)(\frac{21}{63})(\frac{24}{63})$ $= 8.0$ | 21 | 21 |
| 3 | 6 | $(63)(\frac{21}{63})(\frac{18}{63})$ $= 6.0$ | 10 | $(63)(\frac{21}{63})(\frac{21}{63})$ $= 7.0$ | 5 | $(63)(\frac{21}{63})(\frac{24}{63})$ $= 8.0$ | 21 | 21 |
|  | 18 | 18 | 21 | 21 | 24 | 24 | 63 | 63 |

To calculate the value of chi-square; $Q = \Sigma \dfrac{(\text{observed–expected})^2}{\text{expected}}$ ,

for all the cells of the contingency table.

Thus,

$$Q = \frac{(4-6)^2}{6} + \frac{(4-7)^2}{7} + \frac{(13-8)^2}{8} + \frac{(8-6)^2}{6} + \frac{(7-7)^2}{7} + \frac{(6-8)^2}{8}$$

$$+ \frac{(6-6)^2}{6} + \frac{(10-7)^2}{7} + \frac{(5-8)^2}{8}$$

$$= 8.65 .$$

Now, to determine whether the null hypothesis should be rejected or not, the chi-square comparison number must be obtained from the table. To determine the number of degrees of freedom when a contingency table is used, we use the formula $df = (k - 1)(h - 1)$, where $k$ is the number of rows ($k = 3$ in our example) and $h$ is the number of columns ($h = 3$). Therefore, degrees of freedom = $(3 - 1)(3 - 1) = (2)(2) = 4$. At a 95% confidence level ($\alpha = .05$) the chi-square value is 9.49. Since $8.65 < 9.49$, then there is no reason to reject the null hypothesis that there is no relationship between the ordinal number of the game bowled and the score obtained. As a result, we can conclude that the scores are independent of when they were bowled.

Twenty cars from two comparable major brand models are selected at random. These 40 cars are subjected to accelerated life testing (they are driven many kilometers over very poor roads in a short time) and their failure times are recorded in weeks:

Brand U: 25, 31, 20, 42, 39, 19, 35, 36, 44, 26,
          38, 31, 29, 41, 43, 36, 28, 31, 25, 38 ;

Brand V: 28, 17, 33, 25, 31, 21, 16, 19, 31, 27,
          23, 19, 25, 22, 29, 32, 24, 20, 34, 26.

Determine whether the two brands of cars have equal distributions for the length of their lives under accelerated life testing.

**Solution:** The null hypothesis, $H_0$, that the 2 brands of cars have corresponding probabilities for equivalent life spans under the given conditions, is tested by a chi-square comparison test. To use the chi-square comparison test, it is necessary to divide the given data into groups. If the groups (16-23), (24-28), (29-34), and (35-44) are used, then one-fourth of the 40 cars fall into each of these four sets. Thus, the data can be summarized as:

### Groups (Failure intervals)

|  | (16-23) | (24-28) | (29-34) | (35-44) | Totals |
|---|---|---|---|---|---|
| Brand U | 2 | 4 | 4 | 10 | 20 |
| Brand V | 8 | 6 | 6 | 0 | 20 |
| Totals | 10 | 10 | 10 | 10 | 40 |

Group probabilities are determined. The probability that the car will fail between 16 and 23 weeks under accelerated life testing is $\frac{10}{40}$ or $\frac{1}{4}$; $p(16-23) = \frac{1}{4}$. Similarly,

$$p(24-28) = \frac{10}{40} = \frac{1}{4} ;$$

$$p(29-34) = \frac{10}{40} = \frac{1}{4} ;$$

$$p(35-44) = \frac{10}{40} = \frac{1}{4} .$$

Thus the expected number of cars failing, for both Brand U and Brand V, in between weeks 16 and 23 is np or $(20)(1/4) = 5$; 24 and 28 is $(20)(1/4) = 5$; 29 and 34 is $(20)(1/4) = 5$; and 35 and 44 is $(20)(1/4) = 5$.

To determine the calculated chi-square value (Q), the formula for the chi-square comparison test is used:

$$Q = \Sigma [ \frac{(observed_{category\ 1} - expected_{category\ 1})^2}{expected_{category\ 1}}$$

$$+ \frac{\Sigma [observed_{category\ 2} - expected_{category\ 2}]^2}{expected_{category\ 2}}$$

In this problem category 1 = Brand U and category 2 = Brand V. Thus,

$$Q = [\frac{(2-5)^2}{5} + \frac{(4-5)^2}{5} + \frac{(4-5)^2}{5} + \frac{(10-5)^2}{5}]$$

$$+ [\frac{(8-5)^2}{5} + \frac{(6-5)^2}{5} + \frac{(6-5)^2}{5} + \frac{(0-5)^2}{5}] .$$

$= \frac{72}{5} = 14.4$, where the numbers in the first set of brackets are representative of Brand U and those in the second set of brackets are representative of Brand V.

Now, the chi-square table value must be determined. Using a 95% confidence level ($\angle = .05$) and 3 degrees of freedom

a 7.815 value for chi-square is found. Comparing the calculated chi-square value with the table's chi-square value, we see that $14.4 > 7.8$ and so the hypothesis that the two brands of cars have equal probabilities for equivalent life spans under accelerated life testing must be rejected.

● **PROBLEM** 24-5

A student was asked to write down a string of 50 digits that seemed to him to represent a random sequence. Reasoning that when digits are written down at random, then the same digit cannot be repeated successively the student proceeded to write down the following digits:

```
5  8  3  1  9  4  6  7  9  2
6  3  0  8  7  5  1  3  6  2
1  9  5  4  8  0  3  7  1  4
6  0  4  3  8  2  1  3  9  8
5  6  1  8  7  0  3  5  2  5
```

On being questioned he broke down and confessed that he had also tried to keep successive digits at least two units apart. As penance he computed the chi-square statistic to test the hypothesis that the sequence was random. What did he find?

Solution: In a random sequence of numbers, the probability that a number will be the same as its predecessor is 1/10. The probability that two numbers next to each other differ by one is 2/10. Using these expected values we form the following table:

| | Actual Frequency | Expected Frequency |
|---|---|---|
| Same | 0 | 50(1/10) = 5 |
| one away | 8 | 50(2/10) = 10 |
| other | 42 | 50(7/10) = 35 |
| Total | 50 | 50 |

Before we compute the chi-square statistic for the data above we must first specify our level of significance. Let it be $\alpha = .05$. The degrees of freedom associated with the test is (k-1) = 3-1 = 2. Then, if the numbers are indeed a random sequence, we should obtain a value of $\chi^2$ less than 5.99.

The computed chi-square statistic is

$$\frac{(0-5)^2}{5} + \frac{(8-10)^2}{10} + \frac{(42-35)^2}{35} = 6.80 > 5.99 .$$

Hence we reject the hypothesis that the sequence was random.

An insurance agent is interested in the relationship between the number of licensed vehicles in a community and the number of accidents per year in that community. He takes a random sample of ten communities and computes the following table:

| Community | X Licensed Vehicles (in thousands) | Y # of accidents (in hundreds) | $X^2$ | $Y^2$ | XY |
|---|---|---|---|---|---|
| 1. | 4 | 1 | 16 | 1 | 4 |
| 2. | 10 | 4 | 100 | 16 | 40 |
| 3. | 15 | 5 | 225 | 25 | 75 |
| 4. | 12 | 4 | 144 | 16 | 48 |
| 5. | 8 | 3 | 64 | 9 | 24 |
| 6. | 16 | 4 | 256 | 16 | 64 |
| 7. | 5 | 2 | 25 | 4 | 10 |
| 8. | 7 | 1 | 49 | 1 | 7 |
| 9. | 9 | 4 | 81 | 16 | 36 |
| 10. | 10 | 2 | 100 | 4 | 20 |
| | 96 | 30 | 1060 | 108 | 328 |

Find the following:
a) the regression line of Y on X.
b) the sample correlation coefficient.
c) the sample variances of X and Y.
d) the predicted value of Y corresponding to X = 10.

Solution: We first draw a scatter diagram to visually grasp the data. From this diagram we can expect the slope of the regression line to be positive.

a) The equation of the regression line is

$$\hat{y} = \hat{\alpha} + \hat{\beta}x \tag{1}$$

where

$$\hat{\beta} = \frac{n \sum_{i=1}^{n} x_i y_i - \left( \sum_{i=1}^{n} x_i \right)\left( \sum_{i=1}^{n} y_i \right)}{n \sum_{i=1}^{n} x_i^2 - \left( \sum_{i=1}^{n} x_i \right)^2} \tag{2}$$

and

$$\hat{\alpha} = \bar{y} - \hat{\beta}\bar{x} = \frac{1}{n} \sum_{i=1}^{n} y_i - \hat{\beta} \frac{1}{n} \sum_{i=1}^{n} $$

$$= \frac{\sum_{i=1}^{n} y_i - \hat{\beta} \sum_{i=1}^{n} x_i}{n} . \tag{3}$$

Substituting the available data into (2) and (3) gives

$$\hat{\beta} = \frac{10(328) - (30)(96)}{10(1060) - (96)^2} = 0.289 \tag{4}$$

and

$$\hat{\alpha} = \frac{30 - 0.289(96)}{10} = 0.225 \tag{5}$$

Substituting (4) and (5) into (1),

$$\hat{y} = 0.225 + 0.289x .$$

Since $\beta$ is positive, then the correlation coefficient will be positive. If we look again at the scatter diagram, then we can conjecture that it should be closer to 1 than to 0. Let us see if we are correct.

b) The correlation coefficient is defined as

$$r = \frac{\sum_{i=1}^{n} (x_i - \bar{x})(y_i - \bar{y})}{\sqrt{\frac{\sum_{i=1}^{n} (x_i - \bar{x})^2}{n}} \sqrt{\frac{\sum_{i=1}^{n} (y_i - \bar{y})^2}{n}}} \qquad (6)$$

A computational formula that is equivalent to (6) is

$$r = \frac{n \sum_{i=1}^{n} x_i y_i - \left(\sum_{i=1}^{n} x_i\right)\left(\sum_{i=1}^{n} y_i\right)}{\sqrt{n \sum_{i=1}^{n} x_i^2 - \left(\sum_{i=1}^{n} x_i\right)^2} \sqrt{n \sum_{i=1}^{n} y_i^2 - \left(\sum_{i=1}^{n} y_i^2\right)}} \qquad (7)$$

Substituting the results of the table into (7)

$$r = \frac{10(328) - (96)(30)}{\sqrt{10(1060)-(96)^2} \sqrt{10(108)-(30)^2}} = 0.801 .$$

The sample correlation coefficient measures the degree of linear association between the two variables X and Y. Like any other statistic it is subject to variation from sample to sample.

From part (a), we have

$$\hat{y} = 0.225 + 0.289x.$$

Substituting $x = 10$, we have

$\hat{y} = 0.225 + 0.289(10) = 0.225 + 2.89 = 3.115$. This is seen to be a good predicted value for y since from the table it is seen that two communities have their x equal to 10 and the corresponding y values for these 10's are 4 and 2, which average out to 3. This differs from the predicted value of 3.115 by only about 3.8 percent.

c) The sample variance of x is defined as

$$s_x^2 = \sum_{i=1}^{N} (x_i - \bar{x})^2 . \qquad (8)$$

We now convert (8) into a form that utilizes the available computations. Thus

$$s_x^2 = \frac{1}{n} [ (x_1 - \bar{x})^2 + \ldots + (x_n - \bar{x})^2 ]$$

$$= \frac{1}{n} [ x_1^2 - 2x_1\bar{x} + (\bar{x})^2 + \ldots + x_n^2 - 2x_n\bar{x} + (\bar{x})^2 ]$$

$$= \frac{1}{n} [ \sum_{i=1}^{n} x_i^2 - 2\bar{x} \sum_{i=1}^{n} x_i + n(\bar{x})^2 ]$$

$$= \frac{1}{n} \left[ \sum_{i=1}^{n} x_i^2 - \frac{2}{n} \left( \sum_{i=1}^{n} x_i \right) \left( \sum_{i=1}^{n} x_i \right) + \frac{n}{n^2} \left( \sum_{i=1}^{n} x_i \right)^2 \right]$$

$$= \frac{1}{n} \left[ \sum_{i=1}^{n} x_i^2 - \frac{1}{n} \left( \sum_{i=1}^{n} x_i \right)^2 \right]$$

$$= \frac{n \sum_{i=1}^{n} x_i^2 - \left( \sum_{i=1}^{n} x_i \right)^2}{n^2} \qquad (9)$$

Similarly, since
$$s_y^2 = \frac{\sum_{i=1}^{n} (y_i - \bar{y})^2}{n}$$

$$s_y^2 = \frac{n \sum_{i=1}^{n} y_i^2 - \left( \sum_{i=1}^{n} x_i \right)^2}{n^2} \qquad (10)$$

Substituting the appropriate numbers into (9) and (10),

$$s_y^2 = \frac{10(1060) - (96)^2}{100} = 13.84.$$

$$s_y^2 = \frac{10(108) - (30)^2}{100} = 1.80.$$

The sample variances give an indication of the spread of values around the sample mean. But, using the regression line we can reduce the sample variance of $y$ by eliminating the variance accounted for by the linear relationship. Thus,

$$s_{y.x}^2 = s_y^2 (1 - r_{xy}^2) = 1.8(1-0.64) = 0.648,$$

where $s_{y.x}^2$ denotes the sample variance of $y$ given $x$, i.e., the variance unaccounted for by the linear relationship. The square root of $s_{y.x}^2$

$$s_{y.x} = s_y \sqrt{1 - r_{xy}^2}$$

is known as the standard error of estimate. From the above computations, the standard error of estimate is 0.805.

● PROBLEM 24-7

The packaging of breakfast cereals is done automatically. Each package is filled with a certain number of grams of cereal. Assume a package is filled with 400g of cereal and is labeled as such. The cereal processor has kept a record of his variation and found the population standard deviation to be $\sigma = 14g$. He knows that he will be satisfying the "truth-in-packaging" law if the variation about the printed weight on the package is held within 2 standard deviations 95% of the time. How can he determine whether 95% of his packages will fall within 400g $\pm$ 2$\sigma$ ?

Solution: He can do this by taking sample packages at regular intervals and constructing a control chart showing a plot of sample
means. If the population is assumed normal, then the distribution
of sample means is also normal with mean of 400g and standard deviation

$$\sigma_{\bar{x}} = \frac{\sigma}{\sqrt{n}} = \frac{14}{\sqrt{n}}$$

If 95% of the packages fall within $\pm 2\sigma$ , then 95% of the sample
means can be expected to fall within $\pm 2\sigma_{\bar{x}}$ ; i.e.,

$$\mu \pm 2\sigma_{\bar{x}} = 400 \pm 2\sigma_{\bar{x}} \; .$$

The lower bound of the control chart $(\mu - 2\sigma_{\bar{x}})$ is called the
lower control limit and the upper bound $(\mu + 2\sigma_{\bar{x}})$ is called the upper
control limit.

The processor can sample his production at regular intervals; if
the process is in normal statistical control, then about 95% of the
sample means will fall between the lower control limit and the upper
control limit. If this does not occur, then the packaging process is
not in statistical control and $\mu$ is no longer 400g. If $\mu > 400$g,
then overfilling is occurring and a loss of profits will probably
result; if $\mu < 400$g, then the "truth-in-packaging" law is being violated.

Since in our example $\sigma_{\bar{x}} = 14/\sqrt{n}$ , then the 95 percent control
limits are $400 \pm 2\left(\frac{14}{\sqrt{n}}\right)$ , i.e., $\mu_L = 400 - \frac{28}{\sqrt{n}}$ and

$$\mu_U = 400 + \frac{28}{\sqrt{n}} \; .$$

If, for example, n = 100, then

$$\mu_L = 400 - \frac{28}{\sqrt{100}} = 400 - 2.8 = 397.2$$

and

$$\mu_U = 400 + \frac{28}{\sqrt{100}} = 400 + 2.8 = 402.8 \; .$$

This means that 95% of the samples of size 100 will have a mean
mass between 397.2 and 402.8 grams.

● **PROBLEM** 24-8

Samples of 50 pieces are drawn from the production of an
automatic screw machine. The number of defective items found in 25
successive samples is given in the columns of the table below.

SCREW MACHINE DEFECTIVE ITEMS

| | | | | |
|---|---|---|---|---|
| 1 | 5 | 0 | 2 | 1 |
| 2 | 2 | 1 | 1 | 0 |
| 5 | 1 | 0 | 0 | 0 |
| 6 | 1 | 1 | 0 | 1 |
| 3 | 0 | 0 | 1 | 0 |

What might be appropriate control limits for $\bar{p}$ , the proportion of defective items produced by the machine?

Solution: The value of $\bar{p}$ for this data is given by

$$\bar{p} = \frac{\text{total number of defective items}}{\text{total number of items drawn}}$$

For this problem,

$$\bar{p} = \frac{34}{25(50)} = \frac{34}{1250} = 0.0272$$

$$\sigma_{\bar{p}} = \sqrt{\frac{pq}{n}} = \sqrt{\frac{(0.0272)(1-0.0272)}{50}}$$

$$= 0.023.$$

Our upper and lower control limits might be $\bar{p} \pm 3\sigma_{\bar{p}}$

$$\text{UCL} = 0.0272 + 3(0.023) = 0.0962$$

$$\text{LCL} = 0.0272 - 3(0.023),$$

which we take as $0$ since the calculated value is negative and it is impossible for $\bar{p}$ to be negative.

Since $0.0962(50) = 4.81$, it is seen that the third, fourth, and sixth values in the table exceed the upper control limit. In fact, examining the table further, we see that of the first 7 samples, 6 yielded more than 1 defect and this same number of defects occurred only once more in the remaining 18 samples. This would lead us to suspect that there was some assignable cause of variation present when the first samples were taken (which was not present when the later samples were taken).

Let us recompute the control limits using only those samples after the seventh sample.

$$\bar{p} = \frac{10}{18(50)} = \frac{10}{900} = 0.0111$$

$$\sigma_{\bar{p}} = \sqrt{\frac{pq}{n}} = \sqrt{\frac{(0.0111)(0.9889)}{50}} = 0.015$$

Now our control limits are

$$\text{UCL} = 0.0111 + 3(0.015) = 0.056$$

and

$$\text{LCL} = 0.011 - 3(0.015) < 0 ,$$

so we take LCL to be zero.

Now since $(0.056)(50) = 2.8$, then no points fall outside these limits and we may use them for future predictions.

● **PROBLEM** 24-9

Limits of $\pm 3\sigma_{\bar{x}}$ are customary for control charts. A control chart could for example, use $\pm 2\sigma_{\bar{x}}$ or $\pm 2.5\sigma_{\bar{x}}$. Which would keep the inspectors busier: a control chart with limits of $\pm 2\sigma_{\bar{x}}$ or one with limits of $\pm 3\sigma_{\bar{x}}$ ?

Solution: A control chart with limits of $\pm 2\sigma_{\bar{x}}$ would result in values of $\bar{x}$ falling outside of the control limits approximately 5% of the time. Limits of $\pm 3\sigma_{\bar{x}}$ would result in values of $\bar{x}$ falling outside of the limits only about 0.3% of the time, therefore, if the limits were $\pm 2\sigma_{\bar{x}}$ the inspectors would be kept busier.

The table below gives the number of missing rivets noted at final inspection on 25 airplanes.

### Data on Missing Rivets

| 10 | 14 | 21 | 15 | 12 |
|----|----|----|----|----|
| 17 | 7  | 13 | 11 | 18 |
| 16 | 14 | 10 | 12 | 6  |
| 20 | 19 | 11 | 8  | 10 |
| 10 | 16 | 25 | 30 | 8  |

Calculate the upper control limit, UCL, and the lower control limit, LCL, to determine whether the process in question is in statistical control.

**Solution:** Data such as the number of defects in a finite volume follows the Poisson distribution. For the Poisson distribution if the mean is c, then the standard deviation is $\sqrt{c}$.

As a working rule, control limits for our control chart are defined as

$$UCL = \mu + 3\sigma \; ; \; LCL = \mu - 3\sigma .$$

When the distribution is Poisson, we obtain

$$UCL = c + 3\sqrt{c} \; ; \; LCL = c - 3\sqrt{c} .$$

For this problem, the mean is

$$c = \frac{353}{25} = 14.12 \text{ and}$$

$$\sqrt{c} = \sqrt{14.12} = 3.76 .$$

Therefore,

$$UCL = 14.12 + 3(3.76) = 25.40, \text{ and}$$
$$LCL = 14.12 - 3(3.76) = 2.84.$$

However, the value of 30 in the table of Data on Missing Rivets falls outside these control limits, and it would be best to base future calculations on a value for c which does not involve this airplane. We recalculate c and $\sqrt{c}$.

$$c = \frac{323}{24} = 13.46, \text{ and}$$
$$\sqrt{c} = \sqrt{13.46} = 3.67 .$$

Now our limits for our control chart are

$$UCL = 13.46 + 3(3.67) = 24.47$$
and
$$LCL = 13.46 - 3(3.67) = 2.45.$$

Now the value of 25 in the table falls outside of the control limits, so again calculate c and $\sqrt{c}$ without this value.

$$c = \frac{298}{23} = 12.96 , \sqrt{c} = 3.6, \text{ and}$$

$$UCL = 12.96 + 3(3.6) = 23.76, \text{ and}$$

$$LCL = 12.96 - 3(3.6) = 2.16 .$$

Since all of the remaining values in the table fall within these limits, the statistical quality control chart will have 2.16 as its lower limit and 23.76 as its upper limit.

In a study of cheating among elementary-school children, 144 of 348 children from homes of 'good' socio-economic status were found to have cheated on various tests. On the same battery of tests, 133 of 265 children from homes of 'poor' socio-economic status also cheated. Is there a significant difference in the proportions of students that cheated on these tests at the 0.05 level of significance?

<u>Solution</u>: Let $P_1$ and $P_2$ represent the true fractions of students that cheated on these tests. We will test the hypothesis that there is no difference:

$$H_0: P_1 - P_2 = 0$$

vs.

$$H_A = P_1 - P_2 \neq 0 .$$

The test statistic for this test is the following:

$$\frac{\hat{P}_1 - \hat{P}_2}{\sqrt{\hat{P}(1 - \hat{P})\left[\frac{1}{n_1} + \frac{1}{n_2}\right]}}$$

where $\hat{P}_1$ and $\hat{P}_2$ are the sample proportions of cheaters observed in the two groups, and $\hat{P}$ is the sample proportion of cheaters from both groups,

$$\hat{P} = \frac{n_1 \hat{P}_1 + n_2 \hat{P}_2}{n_1 + n_2} .$$

The denominator of the test statistic is an estimate of the standard error of $\hat{P}_1 - \hat{P}_2$ when the null hypothesis is true.

When the null hypothesis is true and $n_1$ and $n_2$ are large, this test statistic is approximately standard normal. If the test statistic turns out to be much larger or smaller than we would expect on the basis of chance alone, then we will reject $H_0$. Specifically, we will reject $H_0$ at the .05 level of significance if the test statistic:

$$\frac{|\hat{P}_1 - \hat{P}_2|}{\sqrt{\hat{P}(1 - \hat{P})\left(\frac{1}{n_1} + \frac{1}{n_2}\right)}} > 1.96 .$$

(The value 1.96 is the 95th percentile of the standard normal distribution.)

From the problem, we have

$$\hat{P}_1 = \frac{144}{348} = 0.414 \quad \text{and} \quad \hat{P}_2 = \frac{133}{265} = 0.502 .$$

Thus,

$$\hat{P} = \frac{n_1 \hat{P}_1 + n_2 \hat{P}_2}{n_1 + n_2} = \frac{348\left(\frac{144}{348}\right) + 265\left(\frac{133}{265}\right)}{348 + 265}$$

$$= \frac{144 + 133}{348 + 265} = \frac{277}{613} = 0.452 \ .$$

The estimated standard error is then

$$\sigma_{\hat{P}_1 - \hat{P}_2} = \sqrt{(0.452)(1-0.452)\left(\frac{1}{348} + \frac{1}{265}\right)} = 0.040 \ .$$

and thus the test statistic is equal to

$$\frac{|0.414 - 0.502|}{0.040} = \frac{|-0.088|}{0.040} = 2.2 \ .$$

Since $2.2 > 1.96$, we reject the null hypothesis at the 0.05 level of significance and conclude that there is a significant difference between the proportions of students that cheated on these exams.

● **PROBLEM** 24-12

On an arithmetic reasoning test 31 ten-year-old boys and 42 ten-year-old girls made the following scores:

|  | Mean | SD | n | df |
|---|---|---|---|---|
| Boys: | 40.39 | 8.69 | 31 | 30 |
| Girls: | 35.81 | 8.33 | 42 | 41 |

Is the mean difference of 4.58 in favor of the boys significant at the .05 level?

<u>Solution</u>: We wish to test the following hypothesis at the 0.05 level of significance.

$$H_0: \text{mean difference} = 0$$
vs.
$$H_1: \text{mean difference} \neq 0 \ .$$

If $\mu_1 - \mu_2$ represents the true mean difference between boys' and gifls' test scores, then we wish to test the hypothesis:

$$H_0: \mu_1 - \mu_2 = 0$$
vs.
$$H_1: \mu_1 - \mu_2 > 0 \ .$$

We have shown previously that if $H_0$ is true, then the statistic

$$\frac{(\bar{x}_1 - \bar{x}_2) - (\mu_1 - \mu_2)}{s}$$

where

$$s = \sqrt{\frac{s_1^2(n_1-1) + s_2^2(n_2-1)}{n_1 + n_2 - 2}} \cdot \sqrt{\frac{1}{n_1} + \frac{1}{n_2}}$$

$s_1^2 =$ the variance in boys' test scores.

$s_2^2 =$ variance in girls' test scores, and $n_1$ and $n_2$ are the number of boys and girls respectively is approximately t-distributed

1017

with $n_1 + n_2 - 2$ degrees of freedom.

In this problem,

$$\bar{x}_1 - \bar{x}_2 = 4.58$$

$$s_1^2 = (8.69)^2 \qquad n_1 = 31$$

$$s_2^2 = (8.33)^2 \qquad n_2 = 42 .$$

Thus,

$$s = \sqrt{\frac{(8.69)^2 (30) + (8.33)^2 (41)}{71}} \cdot \sqrt{\frac{1}{31} + \frac{1}{42}}$$

$$= \sqrt{\frac{5110.4279}{71}} \cdot \sqrt{\frac{73}{1302}}$$

$$= (8.49)(0.237) = 2.01 ,$$

and thus

$$t = \frac{4.58}{2.01} = 2.28 .$$

Our test will be to reject $H_0$ if $t > t(\alpha, 71)$, the $100(1-\alpha)$ percentile of the t-distribution with 71 degrees of freedom.

Setting $\alpha = 0.05$ and using the table of the t-distribution, we find that

$$t(0.95, 71) = 1.67.$$

Since $t > t(0.95, 71)$, we reject $H_0$ and conclude that the true mean difference between the boys and girls' test score is not equal to zero, i.e., the boys did significantly better on the test.

● **PROBLEM** 24-13

---

As part of an attitude survey, a sample of men and women are asked to rate a number of statements on a scale of 1 to 5, according to whether they agree or disagree. The following are the results for the statement "Woman's place is in the home."

|  | Agree Strongly 1 | 2 | 3 | 4 | Disagree Strongly 5 | Total |
|---|---|---|---|---|---|---|
| Women | 3 | 13 | 10 | 16 | 8 | 50 |
| Men | 2 | 12 | 26 | 10 | 0 | 50 |
| Total | 5 | 25 | 36 | 26 | 8 | 100 |

Use $\chi^2$ to determine whether there is a significant difference between the answers of men and women.

---

Solution: Let $H_0$ be that there is no significant difference between male and female responses. Since half of the total people sampled are men and the other half are women, the expected frequencies for each category of answer would be ½ of the total for that category for men and the other half for women. A table of expected frequencies would then be given as follows:

|        | 1    | 2    | 3    | 4    | 5   |
|--------|------|------|------|------|-----|
| Women  | 2.5  | 12.5 | 18.0 | 13.0 | 4.0 |
| Men    | 2.5  | 12.5 | 18.0 | 13.0 | 4.0 |

Because four of these predicted frequencies are less than 5, their categories can be combined with other categories without introducing significant error. Combining categories 1 and 2 and also 4 and 5 eliminates all predicted frequencies which are less than 5. Our table of expected frequencies now becomes

|        | 1 and 2 | 3  | 4 and 5 |
|--------|---------|----|---------|
| Women  | 15      | 18 | 17      |
| Men    | 15      | 18 | 17      |

Now we may calculate our $\chi^2$ statistic. The formula for $\chi^2$ is

$$\chi^2 = \Sigma \frac{(0-e)^2}{e}, \text{ where } 0 = \text{observed and}$$
$$e = \text{expected values.}$$

We may use the table below as an aid in calculating $\chi^2$.

| 0  | e  | 0-e | $(0-e)^2$ | $(0-e)^2/e$ |
|----|----|-----|-----------|-------------|
| 16 | 15 | 1   | 1         | 0.067       |
| 14 | 15 | -1  | 1         | 0.067       |
| 10 | 18 | -8  | 64        | 3.556       |
| 26 | 18 | 8   | 64        | 3.556       |
| 24 | 17 | 7   | 49        | 2.882       |
| 10 | 17 | -7  | 49        | 2.882       |
|    |    |     |           | 13.010      |

Therefore $\chi^2 = 13.010$.

We are testing three columns so the number of degrees for our critical value of $\chi^2$ is 2. For $\alpha = .01$, our critical value of $\chi^2$, the 99th percentile of $\chi^2(2)$, is 9.210. Since our calculated value of $\chi^2$ is greater than our critical value, we would reject a null hypothesis that there is no difference between the answers of men and women and conclude that there is such a difference.

● **PROBLEM** 24-14

In a study of abstract reasoning, a sample of 83 twelfth-grade boys and a sample of 95 twelfth-grade girls scored as shown below on a test of abstract reasoning.

| Sex   | Number | Mean  | Standard Deviation |
|-------|--------|-------|--------------------|
| Girls | 95     | 29.21 | 11.56              |
| Boys  | 83     | 30.92 | 7.81               |

Test for a significant difference between these means at the 0.05 level of significance.

Solution: If we assume that our samples are random, then we may test for a difference in the following manner.

Let $\mu_1$ and $\mu_2$ represent the true mean test scores of the boys and girls, respectively. We wish to test for a significant difference,

vs.
$$H_0: \mu_1 - \mu_2 = 0$$
$$H_A: \mu_1 - \mu_2 \neq 0 .$$

If the null hypothesis is true, then the test statistic,

$$T = \frac{\bar{X}_1 - \bar{X}_2}{\text{estimated standard error of } (\bar{X}_1 - \bar{X}_2)}$$

is approximately t-distributed with $n_1 + n_2 - 2$ degrees of freedom. $\bar{X}_1$ and $\bar{X}_2$ are the sample means and $n_1$ and $n_2$ are the sample sizes of boys and girls scores, respectively.

If the null hypothesis is true, then the pooled estimate of the population variance is

$$s^2 = \frac{(n_1-1)s_1^2 + (n_2-1)s_2^2}{n_1 + n_2 - 2}$$

and the estimated standard error of $\bar{X}_1 - \bar{X}_2$ is $s\sqrt{\frac{1}{n_1} + \frac{1}{n_2}}$ .

If $|T| > t(0.975, n_1+n_2-2)$, then we reject $H_0$ at the 0.05 level of significance.

From the problem, we have

$$s^2 = \frac{83 - 1)(7.81)^2 + (95-1)(11.56)^2}{95 + 83 - 2}$$

$$= \frac{(82)(60.9961) + (94)(133.6336)}{176}$$

$$= \frac{17563.2386}{176} = 99.79.$$

Thus,

$$s\sqrt{\frac{1}{83} + \frac{1}{95}} = (9.989)(0.150) = 1.50$$

and our test statistic is

$$T = \frac{30.92 - 29.21}{1.50} = \frac{171}{150} = 1.14 .$$

The 97.5th percentile of the t-distribution with $95 + 83 - 2 = 176$ degrees of freedom is approximately $1.96 > 1.14$ . Thus, we accept $H_0$, that the mean test scores are the same.

Note: Since the number of boys and girls are each much larger than thirty, then we could have used the regular normal statistic

$$\frac{\bar{X}_1 - \bar{X}_2}{\sqrt{\frac{\sigma_1^2}{n_1} + \frac{\sigma_2^2}{n_2}}} ,$$

using $s_1^2$ and $s_2^2$ as estimates for $\sigma_1^2$ and $\sigma_2^2$ . Doing this, we find its value to be 1.16, which differs from the value obtained by the t-test by only 0.02 (or 1.75%).

A sociologist maintains that later-born children maintain closer relationships with their families than their older brothers and sisters do. To check his hypothesis, he selects a random sample of 20 college students from each of three groups. Group 1 consists of students who are youngest children, group 2 are students who have both older and younger siblings, and group 3 of students who are oldest children. He then obtains information about the number of letters written home by each student over a period of 6 months at college. The results are as follows.

| Letter frequency | Family Position | | | |
|---|---|---|---|---|
| | Youngest | Middle | Oldest | Total |
| At least 2 per mo. | 12 | 14 | 7 | 33 |
| Less than 2 per mo. | 8 | 6 | 13 | 27 |
| Total | 20 | 20 | 20 | 60 |

Calculate $\chi^2$ for this data under the hypothesis that family position has no effect on letter writing frequency. Does our value of $\chi^2$ justify the hypothesis?

Solution: In calculating $\chi^2$ we first must calculate the expected frequencies for each cell. For each cell, under the null hypothesis, this involves equal division of the row totals among the three columns.

The expected values will then be:

| | Youngest | Middle | Oldest |
|---|---|---|---|
| At least 2 per mo. | 11 | 11 | 11 |
| Less than 2 per mo. | 9 | 9 | 9 |

We calculate $\chi^2$ by using the formula

$$\chi^2 = \Sigma \frac{(0-e)^2}{e}$$ , where 0 = observed and e = expected values.

We use the table below to calculate $\chi^2$ .

| 0 | e | 0-e | $(0-e)^2$ | $(0-e)^2/e$ |
|---|---|---|---|---|
| 12 | 11 | 1 | 1 | 0.091 |
| 14 | 11 | 3 | 9 | 0.818 |
| 7 | 11 | -4 | 16 | 1.455 |
| 8 | 9 | -1 | 1 | 0.111 |
| 6 | 9 | -3 | 9 | 1.000 |
| 13 | 9 | 4 | 16 | 1.778 |
| | | | | 5.253 |

Hence $\chi^2 = 5.253$. Since df = (2-1)(3-1) = 2, we find from the chi-square table that $\chi^2_2(0.05) = 5.99$. Since our $\chi^2 < 5.99$, we conclude that position of birth had no effect on the child's frequency of writing letters.

A merchant has found that the number of items of brand XYZ that he can sell in a day follows a Poisson distribution with mean 4.

a) How many items of brand XYZ should the merchant stock in order to be at least 95 percent certain that he will have enough to last for 25 days?

b) What is the expected number of days out of 25 that the merchant will sell no items of brand XYZ?

**Solution:** The mean is 4. Hence $\lambda = 4$ and

$$P(X = K) = \frac{4^K e^{-4}}{K!} \quad , \quad K = 0,1,2,\ldots$$

a) The number of items sold in 25 days will be the sum of 25 Poisson random variables. From previous work we know this sum will be Poisson with parameter $\underbrace{4 + 4 + 4 + \ldots + 4}_{25 \text{ times}} = 100.$

If we let $Y$ = the number of items sold in 25 days, then

$$P(Y = K) = \frac{100^K e^{-100}}{K!} \quad , \quad K = 0,1,2,\ldots$$

To be 95 % certain that the merchant will not run out, we want the smallest value of $n$ such that $\sum_{K=0}^{n} P(Y = K) \geq 0.95$

$$\sum_{K=0}^{n} \frac{100^K}{K!} e^{-100} \geq 0.95$$

$$\sum_{K=0}^{n} \frac{100^K}{K!} \geq 0.95 e^{100} \approx 2.55 \times 10^{43}.$$

(The value of $n$ may be found by solving this by computer.)

b) Consider the event $E_0$ that the merchant sells no brand XYZ on a certain day.

$$P(E_0) = \frac{4^0 e^{-4}}{0!} = e^{-4}.$$

If we let $Z$ equal the number of days on which no items are sold, then $Z$ is binomial (# days total, $P(E)$). Hence,

$$E(Z) = (\text{\# days total}) \cdot P(E)$$
$$= 25e^{-4} = 0.458.$$

● **PROBLEM** 24-17

Assume a Gallup poll interviews a random sample. In California in 1948, Gallup interviewers questioned 1818 persons, 52 percent of whom expected to vote for Dewey. Within what limits could it have been said that the sample proportion approached the actual population proportion?

**Solution:** As we increase the size of a binomial sample, we approximate a normal distribution. One of the properties of a normal distribution is that in approximately 95% of the samples, the sample mean will fall within 2 sampling standard deviations of the population mean.

For a binomial sample, the standard deviation is given by the formula

$$\sqrt{\frac{pq}{n}} \; .$$

In this formula

p = the proportion of the population having a given attribute,

q = the proportion not having the attribute, and

n = the size of the sample .

Since n is large, then we can estimate p by the sample proportion. Hence,

$$\sqrt{\frac{pq}{n}} = \sqrt{\frac{(0.52)(0.48)}{1818}} = 0.0117 \quad \text{or} \quad 1.17\% \; .$$

Thus, it could be said that at the 95% confidence level, the true Dewey percentage in California was $52.0 \pm 2(1.17) = 52.0 \pm 2.34$. So, in only one out of 20 samplings would we expect the true population percentage to lie outside of the interval 49.66 to 54.34.

It is also known that in a reasonably large binomial distribution in 99 samples out of 100, the sample proportion will fall within $\pm 3$ standard deviations (i.e., sampling standard deviations) from the true population proportion. Thus, at the 99 percent confidence level, the confidence interval is $52.0 \pm 3.51$, or from 48.49 to 55.51.

Dewey's actual percentage turned out to be 47.4, which is outside the 99 percent confidence interval. We thus see that Dewey's actual percentage had a chance of occurring of less than 1 in 100!

● **PROBLEM** 24-18

In August 1952, the Iowa Poll conducted a survey of presidential preferences in Jasper County, Iowa. Of men polled, 451 of 902 preferred Eisenhower and of the women polled, 200 of 433 preferred Eisenhower. Is there a significant difference between the proportions of men and women who preferred Eisenhower?

Solution: Let $p_1$ and $p_2$ represent the true (but unknown) proportions of men and women who preferred Eisenhower. We wish to test for a significant difference; thus we test

$$H_0: p_1 - p_2 = 0$$

vs.

$$H_A: p_1 - p_2 \neq 0 \; .$$

If the null hypothesis is true and there is no significant difference between the proportions of men and women preferring Eisenhower, then the test statistic,

$$Z = \frac{\hat{p}_1 - \hat{p}_2}{\sqrt{\hat{p}(1-\hat{p})\left(\frac{1}{n_1} + \frac{1}{n_2}\right)}}$$

where $\hat{p}_1$ and $\hat{p}_2$ and $n_1$ and $n_2$ are the sample proportions and sample sizes, respectively, of men and women favoring Eisenhower and

$$\hat{p} = \frac{n_1 \hat{p}_1 + n_2 \hat{p}_2}{n_1 + n_2} \quad ,$$

is approximately normally distributed. Thus, if the null hypothesis is true, then we would expect $|Z| > 1.96$ only 5 times in 100.

Because of this, we will reject $H_0$ at the 0.05 level if the test statistic is larger in absolute value than 1.96.

From the problem, we see that

$$\hat{p}_1 = \frac{451}{902} = 0.5 \quad \text{and} \quad \hat{p}_2 = \frac{200}{433} = 0.461 \ .$$

Also

$$\hat{p} = \frac{451 + 200}{902 + 433} = \frac{651}{1335} = 0.487 \ .$$

Our test statistic is thus,

$$\frac{0.5 - 0.461}{\sqrt{(0.487)(0.513)\left(\frac{1}{902} + \frac{1}{433}\right)}} = \frac{0.039}{0.029} = 1.34.$$

Since $1.34 < 1.96$, we accept $H_0$ , i.e., there is no significant difference between the proportions of men and women preferring Eisenhower.

● PROBLEM 24-19

In an opinion survey regarding a certain political issue, there was some question as to whether or not the eligible voters under 25 years of age might view the issue differently from those over 25. Twenty-five hundred individuals were interviewed. The results were as follows.

|  | Opposed | Undecided | Favor | Total |
|---|---|---|---|---|
| Under 25 | 400 | 100 | 500 | 1000 |
| Over 25 | 600 | 400 | 500 | 1500 |
| Total | 1000 | 500 | 1000 | 2500 |

What conclusion can we draw about whether age is related to stand on this particular political issue?

Solution: We use the $\chi^2$ distribution to solve this problem. First we calculate the expected frequencies for each of the cells in the contingency table under the hypothesis that age bears no relation to political attitude. These values are found by the formula

$$\frac{\text{row total} \times \text{column total}}{\text{grand total}}$$

and are given in the following table.

|  | Opposed | Undecided | Favor |
|---|---|---|---|
| Under 25 | 400 | 200 | 400 |
| Over 25 | 600 | 300 | 600 |

We now calculate $\chi^2 = \Sigma \dfrac{(0-e)^2}{e}$ , where 0 = observed and

e = expected values.

| 0 | e | 0-e | $(0-e)^2$ | $(0-e)^2/e$ |
|---|---|---|---|---|
| 400 | 400 | 0 | 0 | 0 |
| 100 | 200 | -100 | 10000 | 50 |
| 500 | 400 | 100 | 10000 | 25 |
| 600 | 600 | 0 | 0 | 0 |
| 400 | 300 | 100 | 10000 | 33.33 |
| 500 | 600 | -100 | 10000 | 16.67 |

$\Sigma = 125$

Since we are dealing with three columns and two rows, then we have 2 degrees of freedom. But 133 is much greater than $\chi^2_{.01}(2) = 9.21$. We cannot accept the hypothesis that age bears no relation.

● **PROBLEM** 24-20

The percentage of voters in 10 counties in New Hampshire who voted for Roosevelt in 1944 and the percentage who voted for Truman in 1948 in these same counties is given in the following table.

| County | 1944(%) | 1948(%) |
|---|---|---|
| Belknap | 46.3% | 34.8% |
| Carroll | 31.9 | 23.4 |
| Cheshire | 46.0 | 41.2 |
| Coos | 58.4 | 53.1 |
| Grafton | 44.4 | 35.8 |
| Hillsborough | 62.0 | 59.7 |
| Merrimack | 47.8 | 40.2 |
| Rockingham | 43.5 | 38.7 |
| Strafford | 57.1 | 53.7 |
| Sullivan | 50.2 | 43.9 |

How well could the 1948 Democratic vote have been determined by the 1944 Democratic vote?

**Solution:** This problem is found by finding the coefficient of correlation. The formula is

$$r = \dfrac{\Sigma XY - \dfrac{(\Sigma X)(\Sigma Y)}{n}}{\sqrt{\left(\Sigma X^2 - \dfrac{(\Sigma X)^2}{n}\right)\left(\Sigma Y^2 - \dfrac{(\Sigma Y)^2}{n}\right)}}$$

Let X = percent in 1944 of voters who voted for the Democratic candidate; let Y = percent in 1948 of voters who voted for the Democratic candidate. The following table aids in the calculation of $r^2$.

| X | Y | XY | $X^2$ | $Y^2$ |
|---|---|---|---|---|
| 46.3 | 34.8 | 1611.24 | 2143.69 | 1211.04 |
| 31.9 | 23.4 | 746.46 | 1017.61 | 547.56 |
| 46.0 | 41.2 | 1895.20 | 2116 | 1697.44 |
| 58.4 | 53.1 | 3101.04 | 3410.56 | 2819.61 |
| 44.4 | 35.8 | 1589.52 | 1971.36 | 1281.64 |
| 62.0 | 59.7 | 3701.40 | 3844 | 3564.09 |
| 47.8 | 40.2 | 1921.56 | 2284.84 | 1616.04 |
| 43.5 | 38.7 | 1683.45 | 1892.25 | 1497.69 |
| 57.1 | 53.7 | 3066.27 | 3260.41 | 2883.69 |
| 50.2 | 43.9 | 2203.78 | 2520.04 | 1927.21 |
| 487.6 | 424.5 | 21,519.92 | 24,460.76 | 19,046.01 |

XY = 10

$$r = \frac{21,520 - (488)(425)/10}{\sqrt{\left(24,461 - (488)^2/10\right)\left(19,046 - \frac{(425)^2}{10}\right)}}$$

$$= \frac{21,520 - 20,740}{\sqrt{(24,461 - 23,814)(19,046 - 18,063)}}$$

$$= \frac{780}{\sqrt{(647)(983)}} = \frac{780}{797}$$

= 0.978, an extremely strong correlation indeed! As a result of this strong LINEAR correlation, the least squares line is excellent with respect to determining the 1948 vote from the 1944 vote.

● PROBLEM 24-21

At the beginning of the school year, the mean score of a group of 64 sixth-grade children on an achievement test in reading was found to be 45 with an unbiased sample variance of 36. At the end of the school year, the mean score on an equivalent form of the same test was 50 with an unbiased sample variance of 25. The correlation between scores made on the initial and final testing was 0.6. Are the mean scores on these two exams significantly different?

<u>Solution</u>: Let $\mu_1$ and $\mu_2$ be the true mean scores of the class on the first and second examinations, respectively.

The null hypothesis will be that the mean score is the same on both exams. In other words, we test

$$H_0: \mu_1 - \mu_2 = 0$$

vs.

$$H_1: \mu_1 - \mu_2 \neq 0 .$$

We are interested in the difference between the two means. Let $X_i$ = 1st test score and $Y_i$ = 2nd test score of student i. First form a new data set from the two sets of test scores. Let the ith score in the new data set be $D_i Y_i - X_i$ .

If there is no difference between the true mean scores, then this new set should have a true mean of zero. Our test becomes

$$H_0: \mu_D = \mu_1 - \mu_2 = 0$$

vs.

$$H_A: \mu_D \neq 0$$

where $\mu_D$ is the true mean of the new set of scores.

The usual test for this hypothesis is the following. Compute the test statistic:

$$\frac{\bar{D}}{S_D/\sqrt{n}}$$

where

$$\bar{D} = \frac{\sum\limits_{i=1}^{n} D_i}{n} = \frac{\sum\limits_{i=1}^{n} (Y_i - X_i)}{n} \qquad \text{and}$$

1026

$$S_D = \sqrt{\frac{\sum\limits_{i=1}^{n} (D_i - \bar{D})^2}{n-1}} = \sqrt{\frac{\sum\limits_{i=1}^{n} [(Y_i - X_i) - (\bar{Y} - \bar{X})]^2}{n-1}}$$

To compute $S_D$ note that

$$S_D^2 = \frac{\sum\limits_{i=1}^{n} [(Y_i - X_i) - (\bar{Y} - \bar{X})]^2}{n-1}$$

$$= \frac{\sum\limits_{i=1}^{n} (Y_i - \bar{Y})^2}{n-1} - \frac{2\sum\limits_{i=1}^{n} (Y_i - \bar{Y})(X_i - \bar{X})}{n-1} + \frac{\sum\limits_{i=1}^{n} (X_i - \bar{X})^2}{n-1}$$

$$= S_1^2 - 2\, r_{12}\, S_1 S_2 + S_2^2$$

where $S_1^2$ and $S_2^2$ are the unbiased sample variances of the first and second groups of test scores and $r_{12}$ is the sample correlation coefficient between the first and second sets of scores.

If $\mu_D = 0$, then this statistic is distributed with approximately a t-distribution with n-1 degrees of freedom. If this statistic is too large, that is, if

$$\frac{\sqrt{n}\ \bar{D}}{S_D} > t(0.95,\ n-1),$$

the 95th percentile of the t-distribution with n-1 degrees of freedom, then we reject $H_0$ .

From the data given in the problem, we have $\bar{D} = 50 - 45 = 5$ and $S_D = \sqrt{36 + 25 - 2(0.6)(6)(5)}$
$$= \sqrt{25} = 5.$$

Therefore, the test statistic is

$$\frac{\sqrt{n}\ \bar{D}}{S_D} = \frac{8(5)}{5} = 8.$$

The 95th percentile of the t-distribution with 64 - 1 = 63 degrees of freedom is approximately 2. Therefore, since $8 > 2$, then we reject $H_0$ and conclude that there is a significant difference between the mean scores on the two exams.

● **PROBLEM** 24-22

A highly specialized industry builds one device each month. The total monthly demand is a random variable with the following distribution.

| Demand | 0 | 1 | 2 | 3 |
|--------|-----|-----|-----|-----|
| P(D) | 1/9 | 6/9 | 1/9 | 1/9 |

When the inventory level reaches 3, production is stopped until the inventory drops to 2. Let the states of the system be the inventory level. The transition matrix is found to be

$$P = \begin{array}{c} \\ 0 \\ 1 \\ 2 \\ 3 \end{array} \begin{pmatrix} 0 & 1 & 2 & 3 \\ 8/9 & 1/9 & 0 & 0 \\ 2/9 & 6/9 & 1/9 & 0 \\ 1/9 & 1/9 & 6/9 & 1/9 \\ 1/9 & 1/9 & 6/9 & 1/9 \end{pmatrix} \qquad (1)$$

Assuming the industry starts with zero inventory find the transition matrix as $n \to \infty$.

Solution: This problem involves stochastic processes. Since both the random variable and the time intervals are discrete and there is no carry-over effect, we consider a Markov chain.

The transition matrix (1) gives the probabilities of changing from one state to another in one step. For example, the probability of the inventory level changing from 1 to 2 is 1/9. The relationship between the initial transition matrix and the transition matrix after n steps is given by the matrix equation

$$P(n) = P^n .$$

For example after two steps, the transition matrix is given by $P(2) = P^2$

$$= \begin{pmatrix} 8/9 & 1/9 & 0 & 0 \\ 2/9 & 6/9 & 1/9 & 0 \\ 1/9 & 1/9 & 6/9 & 1/9 \\ 1/9 & 1/9 & 6/9 & 1/9 \end{pmatrix} \begin{pmatrix} 8/9 & 1/9 & 0 & 0 \\ 2/9 & 6/9 & 1/9 & 0 \\ 1/9 & 1/9 & 6/9 & 1/9 \\ 1/9 & 1/9 & 6/9 & 1/9 \end{pmatrix}$$

$$= \frac{1}{81} \begin{pmatrix} 66 & 14 & 1 & 0 \\ 29 & 39 & 12 & 1 \\ 17 & 14 & 43 & 7 \\ 17 & 14 & 43 & 7 \end{pmatrix} . \qquad (2)$$

The elements of (2) give the probabilities of proceeding from the initial state to another in exactly 2 steps. Similarly, after 3 steps $P(3) = P^3$

$$= \begin{pmatrix} 8/9 & 1/9 & 0 & 0 \\ 2/9 & 6/9 & 1/9 & 0 \\ 1/9 & 1/9 & 6/9 & 1/9 \\ 1/9 & 1/9 & 6/9 & 1/9 \end{pmatrix}^3 = \frac{1}{729} \begin{pmatrix} 557 & 151 & 20 & 1 \\ 323 & 276 & 117 & 13 \\ 214 & 151 & 314 & 50 \\ 214 & 151 & 314 & 50 \end{pmatrix}$$

We are interested in finding the value of $P(n)$ as $n \to \infty$. First, however, we must include the initial inventory level in our calculations. The probabilities of reaching the various states in n steps are given by $p'(n) = p'(0)P(n)$. Thus,

$$p'(1) = (1,0,0,0) \begin{pmatrix} 8/9 & 1/9 & 0 & 0 \\ 2/9 & 6/9 & 1/9 & 0 \\ 1/9 & 1/9 & 6/9 & 1/9 \\ 1/9 & 1/9 & 6/9 & 1/9 \end{pmatrix}$$

$$= (8/9, 1/9, 0, 0)$$

$$p'(2) = (66/81, 14/81, 1/81, 0/81)$$

$$p'(3) = (557/729, 151/729, 20/729, 1/729)$$

We note that the probability of zero inventory is decreasing. Furthermore, for $n > 3$, all the elements of $P^n$ are greater than zero. For

Markov matrices having this property, $P^n$ approaches a probability matrix A, where each row of A is the same probability vector $\alpha'$ (where $\alpha'$ denotes the transpose of the row vector $\alpha$).
To find $\alpha$, we solve the equations

$$
\begin{pmatrix}
8/9 & 2/9 & 1/9 & 1/9 \\
1/9 & 6/9 & 1/9 & 1/9 \\
0 & 1/9 & 6/9 & 6/9 \\
0 & 0 & 1/9 & 1/9
\end{pmatrix}
\begin{pmatrix}
\alpha_1 \\
\alpha_2 \\
\alpha_3 \\
\alpha_4
\end{pmatrix}
=
\begin{pmatrix}
\alpha_1 \\
\alpha_2 \\
\alpha_3 \\
\alpha_4
\end{pmatrix}
\qquad (3)
$$

subject to the requirement $\alpha_i \geq 0$, $i = 1,4$ and $\sum_{i=1}^{n} \alpha_i = 1$. Using either Cramer's rule or Gauss-Jordan elimination, the solution to (3) is found to be

$$\alpha' = (45/72, 18/72, 8/72, 1/72) .$$

The limit matrix is then

$$
A = \begin{pmatrix}
45/72 & 18/72 & 8/72 & 1/72 \\
45/72 & 18/72 & 8/72 & 1/72 \\
45/72 & 18/72 & 8/72 & 1/72 \\
45/72 & 18/72 & 8/72 & 1/72
\end{pmatrix} .
$$

Thus, if the initial inventory level is zero, the system approaches the state where the probability of zero inventory is 45/72.

# INDEX

Numbers on this page refer to PROBLEM NUMBERS, not page numbers

Acceptance inspection, 4-25 to 4-29
Acceptance region, 16-26
Accidental deaths, 10-22
Airplane inspection, 24-10
Alpha particles, 24-1
Analysis of variance, 22-20 to 22-21, 23-14
Applicant rankings, 20-26
Arithmetic mean, 1-7 to 1-9, 1-23 to 1-29, 1-46 to 1-47
    grouped data, 1-48 to 1-53, 1-58, 1-60, 1-62, 1-66
Arrivals, 5-8, 12-12
Average deviation, 1-34, 1-45
    grouped data, 1-61 to 1-62
Average loss, 14-39

Base period, 21-1 to 21-3
Bayes' rule, 2-54 to 2-56
Bayesian interval, 14-73
Bayesian statistics, 15-45 to 15-46
Bernoulli random variables, 6-7
Bernoulli trials, 4-8, 10-4
Best critical region, 16-95 to 16-97
Best estimate, 14-34
Beta distribution, 15-36, 20-6
Beta function:
    relation to gamma function, 15-46
Biased estimator, 15-4
    population variance, 13-9
Biased sample, 13-2
Bidding, 22-7 to 22-8, 22-19
Binomial coefficient, 2-13
Binomial distribution, 7-32, 13-40, 15-7, 15-10, 15-28 to 15-30, 16-97, 19-23, 23-1
    normal approximation, 11-35 to 11-41, 16-55 to 16-57, 16-91, 16-92
    parameter, 14-57
Binomial event:
    most probable, 4-7
Binomial expansion, 4-3 to 4-6
Binomial experiment, 4-1
Binomial probabilities, 23-7
    cumulative, 4-30 to 4-34
Binomial random variable:
    moment generating function, 6-7
Binomial sketch, 4-2
Bivariate function, 5-9
Bivariate normal distribution, 14-73, 17-36 to 17-37
Breaking strength, 16-6
Bridge hands, 2-13, 2-35

Cards, examples involving, 2-13, 2-17, 2-19, 2-20, 2-23, 2-30 2-35, 2-36, 2-41, 2-43, 2-45, 2-47 to 2-50, 2-57, 4-12, 4-17
Cauchy distribution, 3-15, 6-22, 15-38
Central limit theorem, 13-8, 13-10 to 13-18, 14-15, 14-17 to 14-25, 14-33, 14-70 to 14-72, 16-5
Change of variable technique, 6-1 to 6-6
Chebyshev's inequality, 22-9
    proof of, 9-1
    lower bound, 9-2, 9-5, 9-6
    upper bound, 9-3, 9-4
Chi-square confidence interval, 14-44 to 14-51
Chi-square distribution, 6-10, 6-25, 16-58

additive property of, 13-38
mean, variance, moment-generating function, 13-21
moment - generating function technique, 13-22, 13-23
probabilities concerning sample variance, 13-26
Chi-square random variable, 13-24, 13-25, 14-1, 14-26, 14-30, 14-37
formation of, 13-37, 13-38
Chi-square statistic, 14-29, 16-72, 19-3, 19-4, 19-6, 19-7, 24-3 to 24-5, 24-13, 24-15, 24-19
Chi-square test, 16-59, 16-60, 16-62, 19-15 to 19-22, 19-26, 19-27, 23-11 to 23-13
fixed contingency table, 19-28
Circumference, 6-13
Cobb-Douglas production function, 22-15
Cochran's test, 20-32, 20-33
Coefficient of contingency, 19-33 to 19-35
Coefficient of correlation, 7-42, 17-11, 17-12, 17-14 to 17-19, 17-21, 17-22, 17-32, 17-34, 21-11, 21-19, 22-11, 22-12, 24-6, 24-20
confidence interval, 17-31
joint density, 7-44
significance test, 17-33, 17-35
Coefficient of determination, 17-10, 17-13, 17-19, 17-22, 17-43, 22-22
Coefficient of variation, 1-45
Coin tossing, examples involving, 2-10, 2-27, 2-34, 2-38, 2-39 4-8, 4-9, 4-15, 7-1, 10-4, 11-41, 16-57
Combinations, 2-10 to 2-13
Combining:
results of different samples, 16-72 to 16-74
sample variances, 15-25
Committees, examples involving, 2-40, 7-8
Comparison test, 8-10
Complementary events, 4-21

Conditional density, 5-14, 5-15
Conditional distribution, 5-5, 17-37, 17-47
Conditional distribution function, 5-16, 5-17
Conditional expectation, 7-27, 7-28
Conditional probability, 2-36, 5-16, 5-18, 5-19, 8-4, 10-23
Confidence interval, 24-7
difference in proportions, 22-10
proportions, 24-17
Consumer price index, 22-13
Contract bidding, 22-7, 22-8, 22-19
Convolutions, 6-26 to 6-28
Consistent estimator, 15-37, 15-38
population variance, 15-23
Contingency coefficient, 19-33 to 19-35
Contingency table, 19-1, 19-2, 19-5, 24-3

Continuous, 1-1, 1-2
Continuous random variable, 3-9, 3-13
Covariance, 7-42, 17-32
pair of sums, 7-43
Covariance matrix, 17-52
Cramer-Rao inequality, 15-40 to 15-44
Cramer's V, 19-30 to 19-32, 19-35
Critical region, 16-3 to 16-21
Critical value, 16-10, 16-24, 16-41
Cumulative density function, 3-11, 3-12, 3-14, 3-15, 3-19, 3-20
Cumulative frequency distribution, 1-5, 22-2
Cumulative frequency graph, 1-6
Cumulative percentage graph, 1-4
Cumulative probability, 2-29
Cumulative probability function, 3-3, 3-4

Dart throwing, example involving, 14-72
Decision rule, 16-14
Decision tree, 22-16 to 22-19
Defective items, examples involving, 11-43, 19-17, 24-8
Deflated price, 22-13

Degree of confidence, 14-19, 14-59
Demand, 11-23
Demography, 21-5
Dependent random variables, 5-3
Design matrix, 17-52
Detrend, 21-18
Deviation, 1-33
Dice, examples involving, 2-16,
    2-21, 2-22, 2-26, 2-28, 2-29,
    2-31 to 2-33, 4-10, 4-11,
    4-40, 5-3, 7-2, 11-35, 16-56,
    19-3
Difference between two means,
    16-23, 16-28 to 16-39, 16-69,
    16-82, 16-84, 24-12, 24-14
    confidence interval, 14-37,
    14-38
    correlated data, 24-21
    lower confidence limit, 14-11
    maximum likelihood estimate,
    14-13
Difference between two proportions,
    14-68, 14-69, 16-48 to 16-54
    24-11, 24-18
Difference between variances,
    16-63 to 16-67
Difference scores, 16-68, 16-69,
    16-90
Differential equation, 17-9
Discrete values, 1-1, 1-2
Discrete random variable, 3-1
Distribution:
    maximum random variable,
    6-18
    minimum random variable,
    6-19, 6-20
    sample means, 13-4, 13-8,
    13-9, 16-5
Distribution function, 3-3, 3-4,
    3-11, 3-12, 3-14, 3-15, 3-19,
    3-20, 6-17
Distribution function technique,
    6-11 to 6-16, 6-21 to 6-23,
    6-29
Drug effectiveness, examples
    involving, 4-23, 23-8, 23-9

Ecosystem, 23-2

Education, examples involving,
    20-25, 24-11, 24-12, 24-14,
    24-21
Efficient statistic, 15-26, 15-42 to
    15-44
Equal chance, 13-2
Error sum of squares, 18-4, 18-7
Exhaustive events, 2-52
Expectation:
    linearity properties of, 13-16,
    14-11 to 14-14, 14-68
    random variable function, 7-17
Expected committee size, 7-8
Expected defectiveness, 7-9
Expected difference between two
proportions, 11-48
Expected earnings, 7-3
Expected horizontal distance of
projectile trajectory, 7-18
Expected length of interval, 14-2
Expected lifetime of light bulb, 7-12
Expected lifetime of radio tube, 7-14
Expected loss, 7-6, 7-7
Expected profit, 7-4, 7-19, 22-7,
    22-9, 22-16, 22-17, 22-19
Expected return from lottery, 7-5

Expected revenue, 7-10
Expected Rockwell hardness, 7-11
Expected value:
    joint distribution, 7-25
    multivariate distribution, 7-26
    of product, 7-23, 7-24
    of sum, 7-21, 7-22, 7-41
    sample variance, 13-19
Explained variation, 17-10
Exponential distribution, 3-19, 3-20,
    6-4, 6-9, 6-11, 6-16, 6-20,
    6-25, 6-27, 7-12, 12-12, 13-39,
    15-40
    distribution function, 12-7,
    12-8
    expected value, 7-15
    loss of memory property, 12-9,
    12-10
    moment-generating function,
    mean and variance, 12-6
    variance, 7-47
Exponential growth, 17-9

Numbers on this page refer to **PROBLEM NUMBERS**, not page numbers

Exponential random variable:
  moment-generating function,
  8-8
Extrapolation from sample, 13-1

F distribution, 16-63, 16-64
  density function, 13-31
  expected value, 13-32
  formation of, 13-31
  reading F-table, 13-33 to
  to 13-35
  reciprocal property of, 13-34,
  13-35
F random variable, 14-52 to 14-55,
  16-63
  formation of, 13-36 to 13-38
F statistic, 18-5 to 18-9, 18-12,
  18-14, 18-15, 18-17, 18-19,
  18-20, 18-23, 18-24, 22-20 to
  22-22, 23-14
  relation to t statistic, 18-6
F test, 16-65 to 16-67, 18-3
Factor analysis, 17-52 to 17-56
Factorial experiment, 18-16
Factorial generating function, 8-5
Factorization theorem, 15-34 to
  15-36
Family, examples involving:
  attribute probabilities, 4-14
  gender probabilities, 4-13
  ties, 24-15
Fertilizers, example involving,
  18-10
Finite population correction, 7-39
Fisher-Neyman criterion, 15-32,
  15-33
Fisher's test, 19-8 to 19-11
Fisher's Z transformation, 17-28
  to 17-31, 17-33, 17-35
  table of values, 17-27
Fit distribution, 19-23, 19-24
Frequency distribution table, 1-3,
  1-5
Frequency polygon, 1-5
Functional form, 17-8
Fundamental counting principle,
  2-1 to 2-3

Gamma distribution, 6-10, 6-20,
  6-21, 6-24, 6-27, 12-12,
  13-21
  moment-generating function,
  mean, and variance, 12-11
Gamma function, 12-11
  relation to beta function, 15-46
Generating function, 8-4
Genotype probabilities, examples
  involving, 23-4
Geometric distribution, 10-4, 10-5
  loss of memory property, 12-10
  mean and variance, 10-6
Geometric series, 3-7, 6-3, 8-9,
  12-10
Geometric probability function,
  3-6, 3-7
Gompertz law, 24-2
Goodness of fit test, 19-25
Grading system, 11-28, 11-29
Grand mean, 18-1
Greenword and Yule: typhoid data,
  23-13

Hardy-Weinberg probabilities, 23-3
Harmonic mean, 1-10
Histogram, 1-3, 1-5, 1-6, 4-1, 22-1
Homoscedasticity, 18-11, 22-22
Human mortality, example involving,
  24-2
Hypergeometric distribution, 10-24,
  23-5
  duality property, 23-6
  mean and variance, 10-25
Hypothesis tests:
  binomial distribution, 16-98,
  16-99
  means, 16-3 to 16-21, 16-80
  proportions, 23-7, 23-11

Inclusion/exclusion principle, 2-30
Income and consumption, 17-8
Independence, 13-2
Independent random variables, 5-2

Independent trials, 2-32
Indicator function, 15-19
Infinite series, 3-5, 3-7

1033

Insecticides, examples involving, 7-34, 18-7, 19-22
Insurance probabilities, 4-19, 11-44
Integration by parts, 7-12 to 7-14, 7-47
Interactions, 18-13, 18-14, 18-16, 18-18
Interval length, 14-7
IQ scores, examples involving, 11-30, 14-18

Jacobian, 6-30 to 6-34, 13-27, 13-31
Joint distribution, 5-1, 5-7, 5-13, 6-34
Joint probabilities, 5-11
Joint uniform density, 5-8
Jointly complete, 15-39

Kinematics, 7-18
Kinetic energy, 6-12
Kolmogorov-Smirnov statistic:
    confidence interval, 20-10
    hypothesis test, 20-11, 20-12
Kruskal-Wallis test, 20-27 to 20-30
Kurtosis, 1-69, 1-71

Lagrange multiplier, 15-17
Large sample, 13-8
Laspeyres' index number, 21-8
Law of large numbers, 13-7, 14-9, 14-15 to 14-17, 14-43, 14-56, 14-65, 14-70
    derivation of, 13-7
Law of total probability, 10-23
Layer graph, 22-6
Least squares line, 17-1, 17-2
Leibnitz's rule, 15-39
Leptokurtic, 1-69
Level of significance, 16-27
L'Hôpital's rule, 8-10
Liapounov's theorem, 20-18
Light bulbs, examples involving, 7-12, 11-11, 11-46, 12-7 14-9, 15-21
Likelihood function, 15-7, 15-10, 15-15 to 15-17, 15-19, 15-20

Likelihood ratio test, 16-95, 16-96
Linear regression:
    maximum likelihood estimators, 17-39 to 17-41
    predicted value, 17-38
Linear transformation, 17-9
Linearity of regression line, 18-12
Linked relatives, 21-4, 21-5
Loss function, 15-20, 15-21
Lottery, 7-5
Lower confidence limit, 14-5

Machine breakdown, 19-6
Machine setting, 16-19, 16-20
MacLaurin series, 8-7
Mann-Whitney rank-sum test, 20-13 to 20-17
Marginal density, 5-10, 5-14, 5-15
Marginal distribution, 5-1, 5-2, 5-4, 5-17, 5-18, 6-33
Marginal probabilities, 5-1
Marginal probability function, 5-12
Markov chain, 24-22
Markov property, 12-10
Maximum likelihood, 15-7
Maximum likelihood decision function, 15-21
Maximum likelihood estimate, 15-8 to 15-10, 15-18, 15-19
    mean of normal distribution, 15-11, 15-13
    parameter of exponential distribution, 15-16, 15-20
    parameter of geometric distribution, 15-14, 15-15
    parameter of multinomial distribution, 15-17
    variance of normal distribution, 15-12, 15-13
Maximum likelihood estimator, 14-8
Mean, 1-7 to 1-9, 1-23 to 1-29, 1-46, 1-47
    grouped data, 1-48 to 1-53, 1-58, 1-60, 1-62, 1-66
Mean deviation, 1-34, 1-45
Mean of sample means, 13-4
Mean-square error, 15-38
Measure of association, 19-29

Numbers on this page refer to **PROBLEM NUMBERS**, not page numbers

Median, 1-4, 1-11 to 1-17, 1-23
    to 1-29, 1-46, 1-47
    grouped data, 1-54, 1-56 to
    1-58, 1-60, 1-62, 1-66
Median test, 20-31
Midrange, 1-32
Minimum variance estimator,
    15-40, 15-41
Mode, 1-18 to 1-29, 1-46
    grouped data, 1-59, 1-60
Moment-generating function, 8-1,
    8-2
    binomial distribution, 6-7
    chi-square distribution, 13-21
    exponential distribution, 8-8,
    12-6
    gamma distribution, 12-11
    joint distribution, 8-11
    non-existence of, 8-3, 8-10
    normal distribution, 8-6, 8-7
    Poisson distribution, 8-2
    uniform distribution, 12-4
    technique, 6-7 to 6-10
Moments, 1-67, 15-4, 15-6
Moving average, 21-10
Multinomial coefficient, 4-36
Multinomial distribution, 4-35 to
    4-40, 13-42, 19-5, 19-19
Multinomial expansion, 4-37, 4-38
Multiple choice test, 11-38
Multiple regression, 17-52
Multiplication rule, 4-17, 4-22
Multivariate transformation, 6-30
    to 6-34
Mutually exclusive events, 2-31,
    2-52, 2-53, 4-20, 4-23 to 4-25
    4-29
Mutually independent, 14-37


Neyman-Pearson theorem, 16-95
Non-linear regression, 17-22, 22-14
Normal distribution, 14-3, 15-31
    approximation to binomial,
    11-35 to 11-41, 14-56, 14-58,
    14-60 to 14-67
    estimation of binomial
    parameter, 11-47

maximum value, 11-6
    mean, 11-52
    median, 11-5
    mode, 11-6
    parameters, 11-27
    variance, 11-53
Normal distribution function, 11-3
    11-4
Normal population, example
    involving, 14-4
Normal random variables, 6-21,
    11-7 to 11-26, 14-2
    combinations of, 13-36 to 13-38


Object occupancy, 2-58
Objects selection, 2-18, 2-24, 2-25,
    2-42, 2-53, 2-58, 2-60
Ogive, 1-5, 1-6
One-tailed test, 16-12, 16-42,
    16-43, 16-45, 16-46, 16-51 to
    16-54, 16-62
Optimal strategy, 22-7, 22-8
Order statistics, 13-39 to 13-42,
    15-33, 15-35, 15-39
    confidence coefficient, 20-4
    confidence interval, 20-5
    sample size, 20-7
    tolerance interval, 20-6, 20-8


Pareto distribution, 6-19
    variance, 7-48
Partial fractions, 19-19
Pearson's contingency coefficient,
    19-33 to 19-35
Percentile, 1-4, 1-66, 11-31
Permutations, 2-4 to 2-8
    circular, 2-9
Platykurtic, 1-69
Poisson distribution, 3-8, 5-6, 6-5,
    6-8, 6-24, 15-5, 15-6, 15-41,
    15-43, 16-70, 16-71, 19-24,
    19-25, 19-27, 24-1, 24-2, 24-10
    24-16
    approximation to binomial,
    10-11 to 10-15
    arrival rate, 10-21
    cumulative probabilities, 10-8

to 10-10
derivation, 10-12
inequalities, 10-17
mean, 10-7
recursive relation, 10-16
variance, 10-7
Poisson parameter, 15-5, 15-6
Poisson process, 10-18 to 10-23
Poisson random variables:
moment-generating functions,
8-2
Polar coordinates, 11-51
Pooled variance, 18-1 to 18-3
Population sample, 13-1, 13-3
Population variance:
estimation of, 15-27
Posterior Bayes estimator, 15-46
Posterior probability function,
14-73, 15-45
Power function, 16-94
Power of a test, 16-91, 16-92, 16-93
Predicted value, 24-6
Price index:
simple, 21-6, 21-7
weighted, 21-7
Prior distribution, 14-73, 15-45
Prism, 5-16
Probability density function, 3-9,
3-10, 3-15 to 3-18
Probability distribution, 3-1, 3-2,
3-5 to 3-8
Proportions, 16-41 to 16-47
Psychotherapy, example involving,
17-21
Public opinion poll, 14-59, 14-67,
24-13, 24-17 to 24-19

Quadratic loss function, 15-20
Quality control, 24-7 to 24-10

Radioactive particles, 6-24
Random digits, 24-5
Random effects, 18-21 to 18-24
Random interval, 14-1 to 14-3
Random mating, 23-3, 23-4
Random sample, 13-2

Random variable:
continuous, 3-9, 3-13
discrete, 3-1
Random walk, 7-20
Range, 1-28, 1-30, 1-31, 1-42,
1-45, 1-46
Rank correlation coefficient, 17-24
to 17-26
derivation of, 17-23
Ratio test, 8-3
Ratio of variances, 14-52 to 14-54
Regression coefficients, 17-48,
22-22
confidence intervals, 17-42 to
17-44, 17-50
hypothesis tests, 17-43 to
17-46, 17-49
Regression curve, 17-37
Regression equation, 17-17
Regression line, 17-1, 17-3 to 17-6,
17-13, 17-18, 17-20 to 17-22,
17-34, 17-45, 17-47, 21-15 to
21-18, 22-11 to 22-13, 23-15,
24-6
Reliability, 6-20
Riemann-Stieljes integral, 8-9
Rocket engine, example involving,
8-4
Runs test, 20-34, 20-35

Sample mean, 13-5
minimum variance, 15-26
Sample size, 14-10, 14-24, 14-25,
16-40, 16-61, 16-62, 16-76 to
16-78, 16-81, 16-83, 16-85,
16-87, 16-89
Sampling distribution:
difference of sample means,
13-16 to 13-18
sample means, 13-4, 13-8,
13-9
Sampling variance, 7-39, 15-3
Scatter diagram, 17-2, 17-3, 17-18,
17-22, 17-34, 21-11, 21-14
Semi-averages, 21-14
Semicircle, example involving, 12-5
Sets, 2-14
Sign test, 20-1 to 20-3

Significance level, 16-1, 16-2, 16-5

Simple relatives, 21-2, 21-3, 21-5

Skewness, 1-68 to 1-70

Sleep, examples involving, 15-3, 19-5, 23-9

Spearman rank correlation test, 20-23 to 20-26

Squares of normal variables, 13-22, 13-23

Standard deviation, 1-29, 1-37 to 1-47
    grouped data, 1-55, 1-62 to 1-66
    sample means, 13-4

Standard error, 13-9
    estimate, 17-6, 17-7, 17-18 24-6
    mean, 7-39 15-1 to 15-3

Standard normal curve, 11-51

Standard normal distribution, 16-7

Standard normal random variables, 6-25, 6-28, 6-31, 6-34, 11-1, 11-2
    formation of, 13-36
    mean and variance, 8-6
    moment-generating function, 8-6, 8-7
    odd and even moments, 8-7

Standardizing, 11-18

Stochastically independent, 5-12

Subjective probability, 4-14, 4-24, 14-73, 22-7

Sufficient statistics, 15-28 to 15-33
    jointly, 15-34 to 15-36

Sum of squares:
    between columns, 18-10
    total, 18-4
    treatment, 18-4, 18-7

Summary statistics, 17-3

Symmetric bounds, 14-36

Symmetric points, 14-7

Target population, 13-3

Target shooting, 4-18, 4-34

t distribution, 14-31, 16-8, 16-9, 16-18, 16-69
    density functions, 13-27

formation of, 13-27

Telephone calls, examples involving, 10-18, 10-20, 10-23

Telescopic sum, 6-24

Tetrahedra dice, 5-3

Time series, 22-3, 22-4
    graph, 22-5

Tolerance limits, 20-9

Total variation, 17-10

t random variable, 14-30, 14-32, 14-34, 14-35, 14-37
    formation of, 13-36

Transition matrix, 24-22

Transpose, 17-52

Tree diagram, 2-51 to 2-53, 4-22, 23-2

Trend line, 21-12 to 21-18

Truncated exponential distribution:
    expected value, 7-16

t score:
    distribution of normal variables, 13-30
    using t table, 13-28, 13-29

t statistic, 14-26 to 14-29, 14-40 to 14-42, 16-21
    relation to F statistic, 18-6

t test, 16-30 to 16-39, 16-86, 16-88, 18-1, 18-2, 23-8 to 23-10, 24-12, 24-14, 24-21

Two-tailed tests, 16-13, 16-17, 16-25, 16-32, 16-44, 16-47, 16-49, 16-50, 16-65, 16-86, 16-88

Type II errors, 16-2, 16-75 to 16-79, 16-79, 16-81, 16-83, 16-85, 16-87, 16-89

Unbiased estimator:
    population mean, 15-22
    population variance, 13-20, 15-23

Unbiased sample variance, 13-24

Unexplained variation, 17-10

Uniform distribution, 3-16 to 3-18, 5-19, 6-13, 6-18, 6-23, 12-2, 12-3, 12-5, 15-8, 15-35, 22-8
    distribution function, 12-4
    mean, 12-1

moment-generating function, 12-4

variance, 12-1

Uniform probability function, 6-1, 6-2, 10-1 to 10-3

Uniform variable, function of, 6-23

Unit circle, 5-10

Vaccine effectiveness, example involving, 23-7

Variance, 1-29, 1-35, 1-36, 1-42 to 1-47, 7-29 to 7-34, 7-38, 7-39, 7-45, 7-46

grouped data, 1-55, 1-64, 1-65

product, 7-37

ratio, 14-52 to 14-54

significance tests, 16-58 to 16-61

sum, 7-36, 7-40, 7-41

sum of two dependent random variables, 7-42

sum of two independent random variables, 7-35

Venn diagrams, 2-14, 2-15

Waiting time, 12-10

Weibull distribution, 6-16, 6-25

Weighted index number, 21-9

Wilcoxon rank-sum test, 20-13 to 20-17

Wilcoxon signed-rank test, 20-18 to 20-20

Wilcoxon stratified test, 20-21, 20-22

X score, 11-15

Yates' correction, 19-12 to 19-14

Y intercept, 17-1

Z score, 11-15

Z transformation, 17-27 to 17-31, 17-33, 17-35

# The Correlation Coefficient

Values of the Correlation Coefficient for Different Levels of Significance

For a total correlation, $\nu$ is 2 less than the number of pairs in the sample; for a partial correlation, the number of eliminated variates should also be subtracted. The probabilities at the head of the columns refer to the two-tail test of significance and give the chance that $|r|$ will be greater than the tabulated values. For a single-tail test the probabilities should be halved.

|  | .1 | .05 | .02 | .01 | .001 |
|---|---|---|---|---|---|
| $\nu=1$ | .98769 | .99692 | .999507 | .999877 | .9999988 |
| 2 | .90000 | .95000 | .98000 | .990000 | .99900 |
| 3 | .8054 | .8783 | .93433 | .95873 | .99116 |
| 4 | .7293 | .8114 | .8822 | .91720 | .97406 |
| 5 | .6694 | .7545 | .8329 | .8745 | .95074 |
| 6 | .6215 | .7067 | .7887 | .8343 | .92493 |
| 7 | .5822 | .6664 | .7498 | .7977 | .8982 |
| 8 | .5494 | .6319 | .7155 | .7646 | .8721 |
| 9 | .5214 | .6021 | .6851 | .7348 | .8471 |
| 10 | .4973 | .5760 | .6581 | .7079 | .8233 |
| 11 | .4762 | .5529 | .6339 | .6835 | .8010 |
| 12 | .4575 | .5324 | .6120 | .6614 | .7800 |
| 13 | .4409 | .5139 | .5923 | .6411 | .7603 |
| 14 | .4259 | .4973 | .5742 | .6226 | .7420 |
| 15 | .4124 | .4821 | .5577 | .6055 | .7246 |
| 16 | .4000 | .4683 | .5425 | .5897 | .7084 |
| 17 | .3887 | .4555 | .5285 | .5751 | .6932 |
| 18 | .3783 | .4438 | .5155 | .5614 | .6787 |
| 19 | .3687 | .4329 | .5034 | .5487 | .6652 |
| 20 | .3598 | .4227 | .4921 | .5368 | .6524 |
| 25 | .3233 | .3809 | .4451 | .4869 | .5974 |
| 30 | .2960 | .3494 | .4093 | .4487 | .5541 |
| 35 | .2746 | .3246 | .3810 | .4182 | .5189 |
| 40 | .2573 | .3044 | .3578 | .3932 | .4896 |
| 45 | .2428 | .2875 | .3384 | .3721 | .4648 |
| 50 | .2306 | .2732 | .3218 | .3541 | .4433 |
| 60 | .2108 | .2500 | .2948 | .3248 | .4078 |
| 70 | .1954 | .2319 | .2737 | .3017 | .3799 |
| 80 | .1829 | .2172 | .2565 | .2830 | .3568 |
| 90 | .1726 | .2050 | .2422 | .2673 | .3375 |
| 100 | .1638 | .1946 | .2301 | .2540 | .3211 |

# Percentage Points of the Normal Distribution

The table gives the $100\alpha$ percentage points, $u_\alpha$, of a standardised Normal distribution where $\alpha = \frac{1}{\sqrt{2\pi}} \int_{u_\alpha}^{\infty} e^{-x^2/2}\,dx$. Thus $u_\alpha$ is the value of a standardised Normal variate which has probability $\alpha$ of being exceeded.

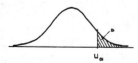

$u_\alpha$

| $\alpha$ | $u_\alpha$ | $\alpha$ | $u_\alpha$ | $\alpha$ | $u_\alpha$ | $\alpha$ | $u_\alpha$ | $\alpha$ | $u_\alpha$ | $\alpha$ | $u_\alpha$ |
|---|---|---|---|---|---|---|---|---|---|---|---|
| .50 | 0.0000 | .050 | 1.6449 | .030 | 1.8808 | .020 | 2.0537 | .010 | 2.3263 | .050 | 1.6449 |
| .45 | 0.1257 | .048 | 1.6646 | .029 | 1.8957 | .019 | 2.0749 | .009 | 2.3656 | .010 | 2.3263 |
| .40 | 0.2533 | .046 | 1.6849 | .028 | 1.9110 | .018 | 2.0969 | .008 | 2.4089 | .001 | 3.0902 |
| .35 | 0.3853 | .044 | 1.7060 | .027 | 1.9268 | .017 | 2.1201 | .007 | 2.4573 | .0001 | 3.7190 |
| .30 | 0.5244 | .042 | 1.7279 | .026 | 1.9431 | .016 | 2.1444 | .006 | 2.5121 | .00001 | 4.2649 |
| .25 | 0.6745 | .040 | 1.7507 | .025 | 1.9600 | .015 | 2.1701 | .005 | 2.5758 | .025 | 1.9600 |
| .20 | 0.8416 | .038 | 1.7744 | .024 | 1.9774 | .014 | 2.1973 | .004 | 2.6521 | .005 | 2.5758 |
| .15 | 1.0364 | .036 | 1.7991 | .023 | 1.9954 | .013 | 2.2262 | .003 | 2.7478 | .0005 | 3.2905 |
| .10 | 1.2816 | .034 | 1.8250 | .022 | 2.0141 | .012 | 2.2571 | .002 | 2.8782 | .00005 | 3.8906 |
| .05 | 1.6449 | .032 | 1.8522 | .021 | 2.0335 | .011 | 2.2904 | .001 | 3.0902 | .000005 | 4.4172 |

# Percentage Points of the F Distribution

The table gives the values of $F\alpha; \nu_1, \nu_2$ the $100\alpha$ percentage point of the F distribution having $\nu_1$ degrees of freedom in the numerator and $\nu_2$ degrees of freedom in the denominator.

For each pair of values of $\nu_1$ and $\nu_2$, $F\alpha; \nu_1,\nu_2$ is tabulated for $\alpha = 0.05, 0.025, 0.01, 0.001$, the 0.025 values being bracketed.

The lower percentage points of the distribution may be obtained from the relation:-

$$F_{1-\alpha}; \nu_1, \nu_2 = {}^1/F\alpha; \nu_2, \nu_1$$

e.g. $F_{.95;12,8} = {}^1/F_{.05; 8,12} = {}^1/_{2.85} = \underline{0.351}$

| $\nu_2$ \ $\nu_1$ | 1 | 2 | 3 | 4 | 5 | 6 | 7 | 8 | 10 | 12 | 24 | ∞ |
|---|---|---|---|---|---|---|---|---|---|---|---|---|
| 1 | 161.4 | 199.5 | 215.7 | 224.6 | 230.2 | 234.0 | 236.8 | 238.9 | 241.9 | 243.9 | 249.0 | 254.3 |
|   | (648) | (800) | (864) | (900) | (922) | (937) | (948) | (957) | (969) | (977) | (997) | (1018) |
|   | 4052 | 5000 | 5403 | 5625 | 5764 | 5859 | 5928 | 5981 | 6056 | 6106 | 6235 | 6366 |
|   | 4053* | 5000* | 5404* | 5625* | 5764* | 5859* | 5929* | 5981* | 6056* | 6107* | 6235* | 6366* |
| 2 | 18.5 | 19.0 | 19.2 | 19.2 | 19.3 | 19.3 | 19.4 | 19.4 | 19.4 | 19.4 | 19.5 | 19.5 |
|   | (38.5) | (39.0) | (39.2) | (39.2) | (39.3) | (39.3) | (39.4) | (39.4) | (39.4) | (39.4) | (39.5) | (39.5) |
|   | 98.5 | 99.0 | 99.2 | 99.2 | 99.3 | 99.3 | 99.4 | 99.4 | 99.4 | 99.4 | 99.5 | 99.5 |
|   | 998.5 | 999.0 | 999.2 | 999.2 | 999.3 | 999.3 | 999.4 | 999.4 | 999.4 | 999.4 | 999.5 | 999.5 |
| 3 | 10.13 | 9.55 | 9.28 | 9.12 | 9.01 | 8.94 | 8.89 | 8.85 | 8.79 | 8.74 | 8.64 | 8.53 |
|   | (17.4) | (16.0) | (15.4) | (15.1) | (14.9) | (14.7) | (14.6) | (14.5) | (14.4) | (14.3) | (14.1) | (13.9) |
|   | 34.1 | 30.8 | 29.5 | 28.7 | 28.2 | 27.9 | 27.7 | 27.5 | 27.2 | 27.1 | 26.6 | 26.1 |
|   | 167.0 | 148.5 | 141.1 | 137.1 | 134.6 | 132.8 | 131.5 | 130.6 | 129.2 | 128.3 | 125.9 | 123.5 |
| 4 | 7.71 | 6.94 | 6.59 | 6.39 | 6.26 | 6.16 | 6.09 | 6.04 | 5.96 | 5.91 | 5.77 | 5.63 |
|   | (12.22) | (10.65) | (9.98) | (9.60) | (9.36) | (9.20) | (9.07) | (8.98) | (8.84) | (8.75) | (8.51) | (8.26) |
|   | 21.2 | 18.0 | 16.7 | 16.0 | 15.5 | 15.2 | 15.0 | 14.8 | 14.5 | 14.4 | 13.9 | 13.5 |
|   | 74.14 | 61.25 | 56.18 | 53.44 | 51.71 | 50.53 | 49.66 | 49.00 | 48.05 | 47.41 | 45.77 | 44.05 |
| 5 | 6.61 | 5.79 | 5.41 | 5.19 | 5.05 | 4.95 | 4.88 | 4.82 | 4.74 | 4.68 | 4.53 | 4.36 |
|   | (10.01) | (8.43) | (7.76) | (7.39) | (7.15) | (6.98) | (6.85) | (6.76) | (6.62) | (6.52) | (6.28) | (6.02) |
|   | 16.26 | 13.27 | 12.06 | 11.39 | 10.97 | 10.67 | 10.46 | 10.29 | 10.05 | 9.89 | 9.47 | 9.02 |
|   | 47.18 | 37.12 | 33.20 | 31.09 | 29.75 | 28.83 | 28.16 | 27.65 | 26.92 | 26.42 | 25.14 | 23.79 |
| 6 | 5.99 | 5.14 | 4.76 | 4.53 | 4.39 | 4.28 | 4.21 | 4.15 | 4.06 | 4.00 | 3.84 | 3.67 |
|   | (8.81) | (7.26) | (6.60) | (6.23) | (5.99) | (5.82) | (5.70) | (5.60) | (5.46) | (5.37) | (5.12) | (4.85) |
|   | 13.74 | 10.92 | 9.78 | 9.15 | 8.75 | 8.47 | 8.26 | 8.10 | 7.87 | 7.72 | 7.31 | 6.88 |
|   | 35.51 | 27.00 | 23.70 | 21.92 | 20.80 | 20.03 | 19.46 | 19.03 | 18.41 | 17.99 | 16.90 | 15.75 |
| 7 | 5.59 | 4.74 | 4.35 | 4.12 | 3.97 | 3.87 | 3.79 | 3.73 | 3.64 | 3.57 | 3.41 | 3.23 |
|   | (8.07) | (6.54) | (5.89) | (5.52) | (5.29) | (5.12) | (4.99) | (4.90) | (4.76) | (4.67) | (4.42) | (4.14) |
|   | 12.25 | 9.55 | 8.45 | 7.85 | 7.46 | 7.19 | 6.99 | 6.84 | 6.62 | 6.47 | 6.07 | 5.65 |
|   | 29.25 | 21.69 | 18.77 | 17.20 | 16.21 | 15.52 | 15.02 | 14.63 | 14.08 | 13.71 | 12.73 | 11.70 |
| 8 | 5.32 | 4.46 | 4.07 | 3.84 | 3.69 | 3.58 | 3.50 | 3.44 | 3.35 | 3.28 | 3.12 | 2.93 |
|   | (7.57) | (6.06) | (5.42) | (5.05) | (4.82) | (4.65) | (4.53) | (4.43) | (4.30) | (4.20) | (3.95) | (3.67) |
|   | 11.26 | 8.65 | 7.59 | 7.01 | 6.63 | 6.37 | 6.18 | 6.03 | 5.81 | 5.67 | 5.28 | 4.86 |
|   | 25.42 | 18.49 | 15.83 | 14.39 | 13.48 | 12.86 | 12.40 | 12.05 | 11.54 | 11.19 | 10.30 | 9.34 |
| 9 | 5.12 | 4.26 | 3.86 | 3.63 | 3.48 | 3.37 | 3.29 | 3.23 | 3.14 | 3.07 | 2.90 | 2.71 |
|   | (7.21) | (5.71) | (5.08) | (4.72) | (4.48) | (4.32) | (4.20) | (4.10) | (3.96) | (3.87) | (3.61) | (3.33) |
|   | 10.56 | 8.02 | 6.99 | 6.42 | 6.06 | 5.80 | 5.61 | 5.47 | 5.26 | 5.11 | 4.73 | 4.31 |
|   | 22.86 | 16.39 | 13.90 | 12.56 | 11.71 | 11.13 | 10.69 | 10.37 | 9.87 | 9.57 | 8.72 | 7.81 |
| 10 | 4.96 | 4.10 | 3.71 | 3.48 | 3.33 | 3.22 | 3.14 | 3.07 | 2.98 | 2.91 | 2.74 | 2.54 |
|   | (6.94) | (5.46) | (4.83) | (4.47) | (4.24) | (4.07) | (3.95) | (3.85) | (3.72) | (3.62) | (3.37) | (3.08) |
|   | 10.04 | 7.56 | 6.55 | 5.99 | 5.64 | 5.39 | 5.20 | 5.06 | 4.85 | 4.71 | 4.33 | 3.91 |
|   | 21.04 | 14.91 | 12.55 | 11.28 | 10.48 | 9.93 | 9.52 | 9.20 | 8.74 | 8.44 | 7.64 | 6.76 |
| 11 | 4.84 | 3.98 | 3.59 | 3.36 | 3.20 | 3.09 | 3.01 | 2.95 | 2.85 | 2.79 | 2.61 | 2.40 |
|   | (6.72) | (5.26) | (4.63) | (4.28) | (4.04) | (3.88) | (3.76) | (3.66) | (3.53) | (3.43) | (3.17) | (2.88) |
|   | 9.65 | 7.21 | 6.22 | 5.67 | 5.32 | 5.07 | 4.89 | 4.74 | 4.54 | 4.40 | 4.02 | 3.60 |
|   | 19.69 | 13.81 | 11.56 | 10.35 | 9.58 | 9.05 | 8.66 | 8.35 | 7.92 | 7.63 | 6.85 | 6.00 |
| 12 | 4.75 | 3.89 | 3.49 | 3.26 | 3.11 | 3.00 | 2.91 | 2.85 | 2.75 | 2.69 | 2.51 | 2.30 |
|   | (6.55) | (5.10) | (4.47) | (4.12) | (3.89) | (3.73) | (3.61) | (3.51) | (3.37) | (3.28) | (3.02) | (2.72) |
|   | 9.33 | 6.93 | 5.95 | 5.41 | 5.06 | 4.82 | 4.64 | 4.50 | 4.30 | 4.16 | 3.78 | 3.36 |
|   | 18.64 | 12.97 | 10.80 | 9.63 | 8.89 | 8.38 | 8.00 | 7.71 | 7.29 | 7.00 | 6.25 | 5.42 |
| 13 | 4.67 | 3.81 | 3.41 | 3.18 | 3.03 | 2.92 | 2.83 | 2.77 | 2.67 | 2.60 | 2.42 | 2.21 |
|   | (6.41) | (4.97) | (4.35) | (4.00) | (3.77) | (3.60) | (3.48) | (3.39) | (3.25) | (3.15) | (2.89) | (2.60) |
|   | 9.07 | 6.70 | 5.74 | 5.21 | 4.86 | 4.62 | 4.44 | 4.30 | 4.10 | 3.96 | 3.59 | 3.17 |
|   | 17.82 | 12.31 | 10.21 | 9.07 | 8.35 | 7.86 | 7.49 | 7.21 | 6.80 | 6.52 | 5.78 | 4.97 |

\* Entries marked thus must be multiplied by 100

| $\nu_2$ \ $\nu_1$ | 1 | 2 | 3 | 4 | 5 | 6 | 7 | 8 | 10 | 12 | 24 | ∞ |
|---|---|---|---|---|---|---|---|---|---|---|---|---|
| 14 | 4.60 | 3.74 | 3.34 | 3.11 | 2.96 | 2.85 | 2.76 | 2.70 | 2.60 | 2.53 | 2.35 | 2.13 |
|  | (6.30) | (4.86) | (4.24) | (3.89) | (3.66) | (3.50) | (3.38) | (3.29) | (3.15) | (3.05) | (2.79) | (2.49) |
|  | 8.86 | 6.51 | 5.56 | 5.04 | 4.70 | 4.46 | 4.28 | 4.14 | 3.94 | 3.80 | 3.43 | 3.00 |
|  | 17.14 | 11.78 | 9.73 | 8.62 | 7.92 | 7.44 | 7.08 | 6.80 | 6.40 | 6.13 | 5.41 | 4.60 |
| 16 | 4.49 | 3.63 | 3.24 | 3.01 | 2.85 | 2.74 | 2.66 | 2.59 | 2.49 | 2.42 | 2.24 | 2.01 |
|  | (6.12) | (4.69) | (4.08) | (3.73) | (3.50) | (3.34) | (3.22) | (3.12) | (2.99) | (2.89) | (2.63) | (2.32) |
|  | 8.53 | 6.23 | 5.29 | 4.77 | 4.44 | 4.20 | 4.03 | 3.89 | 3.69 | 3.55 | 3.18 | 2.75 |
|  | 16.12 | 10.97 | 9.01 | 7.94 | 7.27 | 6.80 | 6.46 | 6.19 | 5.81 | 5.55 | 4.85 | 4.06 |
| 18 | 4.41 | 3.55 | 3.16 | 2.93 | 2.77 | 2.66 | 2.58 | 2.51 | 2.41 | 2.34 | 2.15 | 1.92 |
|  | (5.98) | (4.56) | (3.95) | (3.61) | (3.38) | (3.22) | (3.10) | (3.01) | (2.87) | (2.77) | (2.50) | (2.19) |
|  | 8.29 | 6.01 | 5.09 | 4.58 | 4.25 | 4.01 | 3.84 | 3.71 | 3.51 | 3.37 | 3.00 | 2.57 |
|  | 15.38 | 10.39 | 8.49 | 7.46 | 6.81 | 6.35 | 6.02 | 5.76 | 5.39 | 5.13 | 4.45 | 3.67 |
| 20 | 4.35 | 3.49 | 3.10 | 2.87 | 2.71 | 2.60 | 2.51 | 2.45 | 2.35 | 2.28 | 2.08 | 1.84 |
|  | (5.87) | (4.46) | (3.86) | (3.51) | (3.29) | (3.13) | (3.01) | (2.91) | (2.77) | (2.68) | (2.41) | (2.09) |
|  | 8.10 | 5.85 | 4.94 | 4.43 | 4.10 | 3.87 | 3.70 | 3.56 | 3.37 | 3.23 | 2.86 | 2.42 |
|  | 14.82 | 9.95 | 8.10 | 7.10 | 6.46 | 6.02 | 5.69 | 5.44 | 5.08 | 4.82 | 4.15 | 3.38 |
| 22 | 4.30 | 3.44 | 3.05 | 2.82 | 2.66 | 2.55 | 2.46 | 2.40 | 2.30 | 2.23 | 2.03 | 1.78 |
|  | (5.79) | (4.38) | (3.78) | (3.44) | (3.22) | (3.05) | (2.93) | (2.84) | (2.70) | (2.60) | (2.33) | (2.00) |
|  | 7.95 | 5.72 | 4.82 | 4.31 | 3.99 | 3.76 | 3.59 | 3.45 | 3.26 | 3.12 | 2.75 | 2.31 |
|  | 14.38 | 9.61 | 7.80 | 6.81 | 6.19 | 5.76 | 5.44 | 5.19 | 4.83 | 4.58 | 3.92 | 3.15 |
| 24 | 4.26 | 3.40 | 3.01 | 2.78 | 2.62 | 2.51 | 2.42 | 2.36 | 2.25 | 2.18 | 1.98 | 1.73 |
|  | (5.72) | (4.32) | (3.72) | (3.38) | (3.15) | (2.99) | (2.87) | (2.78) | (2.64) | (2.54) | (2.27) | (1.94) |
|  | 7.82 | 5.61 | 4.72 | 4.22 | 3.90 | 3.67 | 3.50 | 3.36 | 3.17 | 3.03 | 2.66 | 2.21 |
|  | 14.03 | 9.34 | 7.55 | 6.59 | 5.98 | 5.55 | 5.23 | 4.99 | 4.64 | 4.39 | 3.74 | 2.97 |
| 26 | 4.23 | 3.37 | 2.98 | 2.74 | 2.59 | 2.47 | 2.39 | 2.32 | 2.22 | 2.15 | 1.95 | 1.69 |
|  | (5.66) | (4.27) | (3.67) | (3.33) | (3.10) | (2.94) | (2.82) | (2.73) | (2.59) | (2.49) | (2.22) | (1.88) |
|  | 7.72 | 5.53 | 4.64 | 4.14 | 3.82 | 3.59 | 3.42 | 3.29 | 3.09 | 2.96 | 2.58 | 2.13 |
|  | 13.74 | 9.12 | 7.36 | 6.41 | 5.80 | 5.38 | 5.07 | 4.83 | 4.48 | 4.24 | 3.59 | 2.82 |
| 28 | 4.20 | 3.34 | 2.95 | 2.71 | 2.56 | 2.45 | 2.36 | 2.29 | 2.19 | 2.12 | 1.91 | 1.65 |
|  | (5.61) | (4.22) | (3.63) | (3.29) | (3.06) | (2.90) | (2.78) | (2.69) | (2.55) | (2.45) | (2.17) | (1.83) |
|  | 7.64 | 5.45 | 4.57 | 4.07 | 3.75 | 3.53 | 3.36 | 3.23 | 3.03 | 2.90 | 2.52 | 2.06 |
|  | 13.50 | 8.93 | 7.19 | 6.25 | 5.66 | 5.24 | 4.93 | 4.69 | 4.35 | 4.11 | 3.46 | 2.69 |
| 30 | 4.17 | 3.32 | 2.92 | 2.69 | 2.53 | 2.42 | 2.33 | 2.27 | 2.16 | 2.09 | 1.89 | 1.62 |
|  | (5.57) | (4.18) | (3.59) | (3.25) | (3.03) | (2.87) | (2.75) | (2.65) | (2.51) | (2.41) | (2.14) | (1.79) |
|  | 7.56 | 5.39 | 4.51 | 4.02 | 3.70 | 3.47 | 3.30 | 3.17 | 2.98 | 2.84 | 2.47 | 2.01 |
|  | 13.29 | 8.77 | 7.05 | 6.12 | 5.53 | 5.12 | 4.82 | 4.58 | 4.24 | 4.00 | 3.36 | 2.59 |
| 40 | 4.08 | 3.23 | 2.84 | 2.61 | 2.45 | 2.34 | 2.25 | 2.18 | 2.08 | 2.00 | 1.79 | 1.51 |
|  | (5.42) | (4.05) | (3.46) | (3.13) | (2.90) | (2.74) | (2.62) | (2.53) | (2.39) | (2.29) | (2.01) | (1.64) |
|  | 7.31 | 5.18 | 4.31 | 3.83 | 3.51 | 3.29 | 3.12 | 2.99 | 2.80 | 2.66 | 2.29 | 1.80 |
|  | 12.61 | 8.25 | 6.59 | 5.70 | 5.13 | 4.73 | 4.44 | 4.21 | 3.87 | 3.64 | 3.01 | 2.23 |
| 60 | 4.00 | 3.15 | 2.76 | 2.53 | 2.37 | 2.25 | 2.17 | 2.10 | 1.99 | 1.92 | 1.70 | 1.39 |
|  | (5.29) | (3.93) | (3.34) | (3.01) | (2.79) | (2.63) | (2.51) | (2.41) | (2.27) | (2.17) | (1.88) | (1.48) |
|  | 7.08 | 4.98 | 4.13 | 3.65 | 3.34 | 3.12 | 2.95 | 2.82 | 2.63 | 2.50 | 2.12 | 1.60 |
|  | 11.97 | 7.77 | 6.17 | 5.31 | 4.76 | 4.37 | 4.09 | 3.86 | 3.54 | 3.32 | 2.69 | 1.89 |
| 120 | 3.92 | 3.07 | 2.68 | 2.45 | 2.29 | 2.18 | 2.09 | 2.02 | 1.91 | 1.83 | 1.61 | 1.25 |
|  | (5.15) | (3.80) | (3.23) | (2.89) | (2.67) | (2.52) | (2.39) | (2.30) | (2.16) | (2.05) | (1.76) | (1.31) |
|  | 6.85 | 4.79 | 3.95 | 3.48 | 3.17 | 2.96 | 2.79 | 2.66 | 2.47 | 2.34 | 1.95 | 1.38 |
|  | 11.38 | 7.32 | 5.78 | 4.95 | 4.42 | 4.04 | 3.77 | 3.55 | 3.24 | 3.02 | 2.40 | 1.54 |
| ∞ | 3.84 | 3.00 | 2.60 | 2.37 | 2.21 | 2.10 | 2.01 | 1.94 | 1.83 | 1.75 | 1.52 | 1.00 |
|  | (5.02) | (3.69) | (3.12) | (2.79) | (2.57) | (2.41) | (2.29) | (2.19) | (2.05) | (1.94) | (1.64) | (1.00) |
|  | 6.63 | 4.61 | 3.78 | 3.32 | 3.02 | 2.80 | 2.64 | 2.51 | 2.32 | 2.18 | 1.79 | 1.00 |
|  | 10.83 | 6.91 | 5.42 | 4.62 | 4.10 | 3.74 | 3.47 | 3.27 | 2.96 | 2.74 | 2.13 | 1.00 |

## $D^2 + T$ TABLE FOR SPEARMAN'S CORRELATION TEST

| No. of pairs n | Direct correlation | | | Inverse correlation | | |
|---|---|---|---|---|---|---|
| | P=10% | P=5% | P=1% | P=10% | P=5% | P=1% |
| 5 | 3 | 1 | — | 37 | 39 | — |
| 6 | 8 | 5 | 1 | 62 | 65 | 69 |
| 7 | 17 | 12 | 5 | 95 | 100 | 107 |
| 8 | 31 | 23 | 11 | 137 | 145 | 157 |
| 9 | 49 | 38 | 21 | 191 | 202 | 219 |
| 10 | 73 | 59 | 35 | 257 | 271 | 295 |
| 11 | 104 | 85 | 54 | 336 | 355 | 386 |
| 12 | 144 | 121 | 84 | 428 | 451 | 488 |
| 13 | 191 | 163 | 115 | 537 | 565 | 613 |
| 14 | 247 | 213 | 154 | 663 | 697 | 756 |
| 15 | 313 | 272 | 201 | 807 | 848 | 919 |
| 16 | 390 | 342 | 257 | 970 | 1,018 | 1,103 |
| 17 | 479 | 423 | 322 | 1,153 | 1,209 | 1,310 |
| 18 | 581 | 515 | 398 | 1,357 | 1,423 | 1,540 |
| 19 | 697 | 621 | 484 | 1,583 | 1,659 | 1,796 |
| 20 | 827 | 740 | 583 | 1,833 | 1,920 | 2,077 |
| 21 | 972 | 873 | 695 | 2,108 | 2,207 | 2,385 |
| 22 | 1,134 | 1,022 | 820 | 2,408 | 2,520 | 2,722 |
| 23 | 1,313 | 1,188 | 960 | 2,735 | 2,860 | 3,088 |
| 24 | 1,509 | 1,370 | 1,115 | 3,091 | 3,230 | 3,485 |
| 25 | 1,725 | 1,570 | 1,286 | 3,475 | 3,630 | 3,914 |
| 26 | 1,961 | 1,790 | 1,475 | 3,889 | 4,060 | 4,375 |
| 27 | 2,217 | 2,028 | 1,681 | 4,335 | 4,524 | 4,871 |
| 28 | 2,495 | 2,288 | 1,906 | 4,813 | 5,020 | 5,402 |
| 29 | 2,795 | 2,569 | 2,150 | 5,325 | 5,551 | 5,970 |
| 30 | 3,119 | 2,872 | 2,414 | 5,871 | 6,118 | 6,576 |

## E TABLE FOR POISSON'S TEST

| No. in sample x | Probability when x > E | | | | Probability when x < E | | | |
|---|---|---|---|---|---|---|---|---|
| | P=10% | P=5% | P=1% | P=0.2% | P=10% | P=5% | P=1% | P=0.2% |
| 0 | 0·105 | — | — | — | 2·8 | 3·6 | 5·1 | 6·6 |
| 1 | 0·53 | 0·355 | 0·010 | 0·002 | 4·75 | 5·55 | 7·15 | 9·1 |
| 2 | 1·10 | 0·82 | 0·149 | 0·065 | 6·25 | 7·1 | 9·15 | 11·1 |
| 3 | 1·74 | 1·37 | 0·435 | 0·243 | 7·75 | 8·6 | 10·65 | 13·1 |
| 4 | 2·35 | 1·97 | 0·82 | 0·52 | 8·8 | 10·1 | 12·6 | 14·7 |
| 5 | 2·75 | 2·61 | 1·28 | 0·87 | 10·3 | 11·55 | 14·1 | 16·5 |
| 6 | 3·55 | 3·15 | 1·78 | 1·27 | 11·75 | 13·05 | 15·5 | 18·0 |
| 7 | 4·3 | 3·5 | 2·35 | 1·72 | 12·8 | 14·1 | 17·0 | 19·5 |
| 8 | 4·7 | 4·45 | 2·91 | 2·20 | 14·3 | 15·7 | 18·5 | 21·5 |
| 9 | 5·75 | 5·1 | 3·5 | 2·72 | 15·6 | 17·5 | 20·0 | 22·5 |
| 10 | 6·2 | 5·5 | 4·1 | 3·25 | 17·0 | 18·5 | 21·5 | 24·5 |
| 11 | 7·25 | 6·6 | 4·7 | 3·8 | 18·0 | 19·5 | 23·0 | 25·5 |
| 12 | 7·7 | 7·0 | 5·05 | 4·4 | 19·5 | 21·0 | 24·0 | 27·0 |
| 13 | 8·7 | 8·05 | 5·8 | 5·0 | 20·5 | 22·5 | 25·5 | 28·5 |
| 14 | 9·5 | 8·5 | 6·65 | 5·6 | 22·0 | 23·5 | 27·0 | 30·0 |
| 15 | 10·25 | 9·55 | 7·05 | 6·15 | 23·0 | 25·0 | 28·0 | 31·5 |
| 16 | 11·25 | 10·0 | 7·7 | 6·5 | 24·5 | 26·0 | 29·5 | 32·5 |
| 17 | 11·7 | 11·1 | 8·65 | 7·1 | 25·5 | 27·5 | 31·0 | 34·0 |
| 18 | 12·75 | 11·5 | 9·05 | 8·0 | 26·5 | 28·5 | 32·0 | 35·5 |
| 19 | 13·45 | 12·55 | 10·0 | 8·6 | 28·0 | 29·5 | 33·5 | 37·0 |
| 20 | 14·25 | 13·0 | 10·6 | 9·0 | 29·0 | 31·0 | 35·0 | 38·0 |
| 21 | 15·1 | 14·05 | 11·15 | 9·9 | 30·5 | 32·5 | 36·0 | 39·5 |
| 22 | 15·9 | 14·9 | 12·1 | 10·6 | 31·5 | 33·5 | 37·5 | 41·0 |
| 23 | 16·5 | 15·5 | 12·55 | 11·05 | 32·5 | 34·5 | 38·5 | 42·0 |
| 24 | 17·5 | 16·2 | 13·6 | 12·0 | 34·0 | 35·5 | 40·0 | 43·5 |
| 25 | 18·0 | 17·0 | 14·0 | 12·6 | 35·0 | 37·0 | 41·0 | 45·0 |
| 26 | 19·0 | 18·0 | 15·0 | 13·1 | 36·0 | 38·5 | 42·5 | 46·0 |
| 27 | 20·0 | 19·0 | 15·5 | 14·15 | 37·0 | 39·5 | 43·5 | 47·5 |
| 28 | 21·0 | 19·5 | 16·0 | 14·6 | 38·5 | 40·5 | 45·0 | 48·5 |
| 29 | 21·5 | 20·0 | 17·0 | 15·1 | 39·5 | 41·5 | 46·0 | 50·0 |
| 30 | 22·5 | 21·0 | 18·0 | 16·0 | 40·5 | 43·0 | 47·5 | 51·0 |
| 31 | 23·5 | 22·0 | 18·5 | 16·5 | 42·0 | 44·0 | 48·5 | 52·5 |
| 32 | 24·0 | 23·0 | 19·5 | 17·0 | 43·0 | 45·5 | 50·0 | 54·0 |
| 33 | 25·0 | 23·5 | 20·0 | 18·0 | 44·0 | 46·5 | 51·0 | 55·0 |
| 34 | 26·0 | 24·5 | 21·0 | 19·0 | 45·5 | 47·5 | 52·0 | 56·5 |
| 35 | 27·0 | 25·0 | 22·0 | 19·5 | 46·5 | 48·5 | 53·5 | 57·5 |
| 36 | 27·5 | 26·0 | 22·5 | 20·0 | 47·5 | 50·0 | 54·5 | 58·5 |
| 37 | 28·5 | 27·0 | 23·5 | 21·0 | 48·5 | 51·0 | 56·0 | 60·0 |
| 38 | 29·5 | 28·0 | 24·0 | 22·0 | 50·0 | 52·5 | 57·0 | 61·5 |
| 39 | 30·0 | 29·0 | 25·0 | 22·5 | 51·0 | 53·5 | 58·0 | 62·5 |
| 40 | 30·5 | 30·0 | 26·0 | 23·0 | 52·0 | 54·5 | 59·5 | 64·0 |

# TABLE OF RANDOM NUMBERS

| | | | | | |
|---|---|---|---|---|---|
| 251630 | 188970 | 014150 | 214129 | 067312 | 718571 |
| 595768 | 971114 | 036525 | 107629 | 372393 | 329505 |
| 870011 | 199278 | 426340 | 184776 | 562236 | 815436 |
| 251863 | 737509 | 824449 | 900504 | 921737 | 011470 |
| 793997 | 643971 | 169205 | 327821 | 622024 | 781759 |
| 451972 | 533283 | 745225 | 670451 | 525624 | 950966 |
| 794648 | 460855 | 581519 | 118782 | 169303 | 336183 |
| 761608 | 734325 | 384145 | 608332 | 598301 | 291413 |
| 492036 | 807126 | 143870 | 634580 | 854092 | 794352 |
| 906318 | 383847 | 476141 | 196374 | 805132 | 192246 |
| 800887 | 707488 | 722567 | 366616 | 494316 | 691931 |
| 678724 | 720000 | 880890 | 180029 | 481331 | 900541 |
| 558343 | 635352 | 541310 | 546655 | 306931 | 281846 |
| 474457 | 905617 | 284811 | 834799 | 826841 | 639528 |
| 724848 | 247425 | 593485 | 453524 | 718619 | 136741 |
| 861119 | 241816 | 161871 | 153342 | 442767 | 512211 |
| 724746 | 277370 | 758319 | 159970 | 758616 | 120826 |
| 412282 | 092904 | 131413 | 239219 | 763611 | 996794 |
| 090767 | 042351 | 357417 | 200699 | 026374 | 278464 |
| 225011 | 862790 | 872401 | 882819 | 329593 | 886279 |
| 497211 | 598620 | 953678 | 700441 | 589973 | 441482 |
| 157868 | 875508 | 719152 | 000231 | 230280 | 783326 |
| 246869 | 163439 | 753634 | 498916 | 822360 | 240086 |
| 776378 | 416056 | 596173 | 488670 | 490907 | 093399 |
| 455479 | 445874 | 284050 | 414980 | 720288 | 340607 |
| 949504 | 146521 | 629028 | 654158 | 342434 | 697835 |
| 482593 | 629593 | 891704 | 305520 | 473721 | 031750 |
| 519302 | 947665 | 643829 | 978293 | 478940 | 154687 |
| 432444 | 482775 | 982096 | 163646 | 542584 | 341145 |
| 428207 | 410888 | 222885 | 707401 | 525704 | 910350 |
| 175514 | 750489 | 683860 | 362880 | 878739 | 516059 |
| 221223 | 049031 | 472877 | 173343 | 928304 | 149117 |
| 481210 | 280580 | 418671 | 771059 | 621065 | 540785 |
| 073950 | 795521 | 794405 | 600604 | 780334 | 325852 |
| 589055 | 721639 | 618498 | 569932 | 666067 | 427929 |
| 504352 | 680467 | 805648 | 709971 | 594813 | 700622 |
| 186542 | 449103 | 045547 | 708185 | 984996 | 169614 |
| 592164 | 787417 | 171983 | 094557 | 589317 | 325726 |
| 047670 | 076544 | 637625 | 366947 | 464958 | 069170 |
| 374038 | 699590 | 307943 | 047180 | 326825 | 055111 |
| 245991 | 314083 | 458897 | 535841 | 857710 | 810559 |
| 987871 | 122147 | 614713 | 711812 | 776743 | 584853 |

# Table 3

## PERCENTAGE POINTS OF THE $\chi^2$-DISTRIBUTION—VALUES OF $\chi^2$ IN TERMS OF $Q$ AND $\nu$

| $\nu$ \ $Q$ | 0.995 | 0.99 | 0.975 | 0.95 | 0.9 | 0.75 | 0.5 | 0.25 |
|---|---|---|---|---|---|---|---|---|
| 1 | (−5) 3.92704 | (−4) 1.57088 | (−4) 9.82069 | (−3) 3.93214 | 0.0157908 | 0.101531 | 0.454937 | 1.32330 |
| 2 | (−2) 1.00251 | (−2) 2.01007 | (−2) 5.06356 | 0.102587 | 0.210720 | 0.575364 | 1.38629 | 2.77259 |
| 3 | (−2) 7.17212 | 0.114832 | 0.215795 | 0.351846 | 0.584375 | 1.212534 | 2.36597 | 4.10835 |
| 4 | 0.206990 | 0.297110 | 0.484419 | 0.710721 | 1.063623 | 1.92255 | 3.35670 | 5.38527 |
| 5 | 0.411740 | 0.554300 | 0.831211 | 1.145476 | 1.61031 | 2.67460 | 4.35146 | 6.62568 |
| 6 | 0.675727 | 0.872085 | 1.237347 | 1.63539 | 2.20413 | 3.45460 | 5.34812 | 7.84080 |
| 7 | 0.989265 | 1.239043 | 1.68987 | 2.16735 | 2.83311 | 4.25485 | 6.34581 | 9.03715 |
| 8 | 1.344419 | 1.646482 | 2.17973 | 2.73264 | 3.48954 | 5.07064 | 7.34412 | 10.2188 |
| 9 | 1.734926 | 2.087912 | 2.70039 | 3.32511 | 4.16816 | 5.89883 | 8.34283 | 11.3887 |
| 10 | 2.15585 | 2.55821 | 3.24697 | 3.94030 | 4.86518 | 6.73720 | 9.34182 | 12.5489 |
| 11 | 2.60321 | 3.05347 | 3.81575 | 4.57481 | 5.57779 | 7.58412 | 10.3410 | 13.7007 |
| 12 | 3.07382 | 3.57056 | 4.40379 | 5.22603 | 6.30380 | 8.43842 | 11.3403 | 14.8454 |
| 13 | 3.56503 | 4.10691 | 5.00874 | 5.89186 | 7.04150 | 9.29906 | 12.3398 | 15.9839 |
| 14 | 4.07468 | 4.66043 | 5.62872 | 6.57063 | 7.78953 | 10.1653 | 13.3393 | 17.1170 |
| 15 | 4.60094 | 5.22935 | 6.26214 | 7.26094 | 8.54675 | 11.0365 | 14.3389 | 18.2451 |
| 16 | 5.14224 | 5.81221 | 6.90766 | 7.96164 | 9.31223 | 11.9122 | 15.3385 | 19.3688 |
| 17 | 5.69724 | 6.40776 | 7.56418 | 8.67176 | 10.0852 | 12.7919 | 16.3381 | 20.4887 |
| 18 | 6.26481 | 7.01491 | 8.23075 | 9.39046 | 10.8649 | 13.6753 | 17.3379 | 21.6049 |
| 19 | 6.84398 | 7.63273 | 8.90655 | 10.1170 | 11.6509 | 14.5620 | 18.3376 | 22.7178 |
| 20 | 7.43386 | 8.26040 | 9.59083 | 10.8508 | 12.4426 | 15.4518 | 19.3374 | 23.8277 |
| 21 | 8.03366 | 8.89720 | 10.28293 | 11.5913 | 13.2396 | 16.3444 | 20.3372 | 24.9348 |
| 22 | 8.64272 | 9.54249 | 10.9823 | 12.3380 | 14.0415 | 17.2396 | 21.3370 | 26.0393 |
| 23 | 9.26042 | 10.19567 | 11.6885 | 13.0905 | 14.8479 | 18.1373 | 22.3369 | 27.1413 |
| 24 | 9.88623 | 10.8564 | 12.4011 | 13.8484 | 15.6587 | 19.0372 | 23.3367 | 28.2412 |
| 25 | 10.5197 | 11.5240 | 13.1197 | 14.6114 | 16.4734 | 19.9393 | 24.3366 | 29.3389 |
| 26 | 11.1603 | 12.1981 | 13.8439 | 15.3791 | 17.2919 | 20.8434 | 25.3364 | 30.4345 |
| 27 | 11.8076 | 12.8786 | 14.5733 | 16.1513 | 18.1138 | 21.7494 | 26.3363 | 31.5284 |
| 28 | 12.4613 | 13.5648 | 15.3079 | 16.9279 | 18.9392 | 22.6572 | 27.3363 | 32.6205 |
| 29 | 13.1211 | 14.2565 | 16.0471 | 17.7083 | 19.7677 | 23.5666 | 28.3362 | 33.7109 |
| 30 | 13.7867 | 14.9535 | 16.7908 | 18.4926 | 20.5992 | 24.4776 | 29.3360 | 34.7998 |
| 40 | 20.7065 | 22.1643 | 24.4331 | 26.5093 | 29.0505 | 33.6603 | 39.3354 | 45.6160 |
| 50 | 27.9907 | 29.7067 | 32.3574 | 34.7642 | 37.6886 | 42.9421 | 49.3349 | 56.3336 |
| 60 | 35.5346 | 37.4848 | 40.4817 | 43.1879 | 46.4589 | 52.2938 | 59.3347 | 66.9814 |
| 70 | 43.2752 | 45.4418 | 48.7576 | 51.7393 | 55.3290 | 61.6983 | 69.3344 | 77.5766 |
| 80 | 51.1720 | 53.5400 | 57.1532 | 60.3915 | 64.2778 | 71.1445 | 79.3343 | 88.1303 |
| 90 | 59.1963 | 61.7541 | 65.6466 | 69.1260 | 73.2912 | 80.6247 | 89.3342 | 98.6499 |
| 100 | 67.3276 | 70.0648 | 74.2219 | 77.9295 | 82.3581 | 90.1332 | 99.3341 | 109.141 |
| X | −2.5758 | −2.3263 | −1.9600 | −1.6449 | −1.2816 | −0.6745 | 0.0000 | 0.6745 |

$$Q(\chi^2 \mid \nu) = \left[ 2^{\frac{\nu}{2}} \Gamma\left(\frac{\nu}{2}\right) \right]^{-1} \int_{\chi^2}^{\infty} e^{-\frac{t}{2}} t^{\frac{\nu}{2}-1} \, dt$$

## Table 3

### PERCENTAGE POINTS OF THE $\chi^2$-DISTRIBUTION—VALUES OF $\chi^2$ IN TERMS OF $Q$ AND $\nu$

| $\nu \backslash Q$ | 0.1 | 0.05 | 0.025 | 0.01 | 0.005 | 0.001 | 0.0005 | 0.0001 |
|---|---|---|---|---|---|---|---|---|
| 1 | 2.70554 | 3.84146 | 5.02389 | 6.63490 | 7.87944 | 10.828 | 12.116 | 15.137 |
| 2 | 4.60517 | 5.99147 | 7.37776 | 9.21034 | 10.5966 | 13.816 | 15.202 | 18.421 |
| 3 | 6.25139 | 7.81473 | 9.34840 | 11.3449 | 12.8381 | 16.266 | 17.730 | 21.108 |
| 4 | 7.77944 | 9.48773 | 11.1433 | 13.2767 | 14.8602 | 18.467 | 19.997 | 23.513 |
| 5 | 9.23635 | 11.0705 | 12.8325 | 15.0863 | 16.7496 | 20.515 | 22.105 | 25.745 |
| 6 | 10.6446 | 12.5916 | 14.4494 | 16.8119 | 18.5476 | 22.458 | 24.103 | 27.856 |
| 7 | 12.0170 | 14.0671 | 16.0128 | 18.4753 | 20.2777 | 24.322 | 26.018 | 29.877 |
| 8 | 13.3616 | 15.5073 | 17.5346 | 20.0902 | 21.9550 | 26.125 | 27.868 | 31.828 |
| 9 | 14.6837 | 16.9190 | 19.0228 | 21.6660 | 23.5893 | 27.877 | 29.666 | 33.720 |
| 10 | 15.9871 | 18.3070 | 20.4831 | 23.2093 | 25.1882 | 29.588 | 31.420 | 35.564 |
| 11 | 17.2750 | 19.6751 | 21.9200 | 24.7250 | 26.7569 | 31.264 | 33.137 | 37.367 |
| 12 | 18.5494 | 21.0261 | 23.3367 | 26.2170 | 28.2995 | 32.909 | 34.821 | 39.134 |
| 13 | 19.8119 | 22.3621 | 24.7356 | 27.6883 | 29.8194 | 34.528 | 36.478 | 40.871 |
| 14 | 21.0642 | 23.6848 | 26.1190 | 29.1413 | 31.3193 | 36.123 | 38.109 | 42.579 |
| 15 | 22.3072 | 24.9958 | 27.4884 | 30.5779 | 32.8013 | 37.697 | 39.719 | 44.263 |
| 16 | 23.5418 | 26.2962 | 28.8454 | 31.9999 | 34.2672 | 39.252 | 41.308 | 45.925 |
| 17 | 24.7690 | 27.5871 | 30.1910 | 33.4087 | 35.7185 | 40.790 | 42.879 | 47.566 |
| 18 | 25.9894 | 28.8693 | 31.5264 | 34.8053 | 37.1564 | 42.312 | 44.434 | 49.189 |
| 19 | 27.2036 | 30.1435 | 32.8523 | 36.1908 | 38.5822 | 43.820 | 45.973 | 50.796 |
| 20 | 28.4120 | 31.4104 | 34.1696 | 37.5662 | 39.9968 | 45.315 | 47.498 | 52.386 |
| 21 | 29.6151 | 32.6705 | 35.4789 | 38.9321 | 41.4010 | 46.797 | 49.011 | 53.962 |
| 22 | 30.8133 | 33.9244 | 36.7807 | 40.2894 | 42.7956 | 48.268 | 50.511 | 55.525 |
| 23 | 32.0069 | 35.1725 | 38.0757 | 41.6384 | 44.1813 | 49.728 | 52.000 | 57.075 |
| 24 | 33.1963 | 36.4151 | 39.3641 | 42.9798 | 45.5585 | 51.179 | 53.479 | 58.613 |
| 25 | 34.3816 | 37.6525 | 40.6465 | 44.3141 | 46.9278 | 52.620 | 54.947 | 60.140 |
| 26 | 35.5631 | 38.8852 | 41.9232 | 45.6417 | 48.2899 | 54.052 | 56.407 | 61.657 |
| 27 | 36.7412 | 40.1133 | 43.1944 | 46.9630 | 49.6449 | 55.476 | 57.858 | 63.164 |
| 28 | 37.9159 | 41.3372 | 44.4607 | 48.2782 | 50.9933 | 56.892 | 59.300 | 64.662 |
| 29 | 39.0875 | 42.5569 | 45.7222 | 49.5879 | 52.3356 | 58.302 | 60.735 | 66.152 |
| 30 | 40.2560 | 43.7729 | 46.9792 | 50.8922 | 53.6720 | 59.703 | 62.162 | 67.633 |
| 40 | 51.8050 | 55.7585 | 59.3417 | 63.6907 | 66.7659 | 73.402 | 76.095 | 82.062 |
| 50 | 63.1671 | 67.5048 | 71.4202 | 76.1539 | 79.4900 | 86.661 | 89.560 | 95.969 |
| 60 | 74.3970 | 79.0819 | 83.2976 | 88.3794 | 91.9517 | 99.607 | 102.695 | 109.503 |
| 70 | 85.5271 | 90.5312 | 95.0231 | 100.425 | 104.215 | 112.317 | 115.578 | 122.755 |
| 80 | 96.5782 | 101.879 | 106.629 | 112.329 | 116.321 | 124.839 | 128.261 | 135.783 |
| 90 | 107.565 | 113.145 | 118.136 | 124.116 | 128.299 | 137.208 | 140.782 | 148.627 |
| 100 | 118.498 | 124.342 | 129.561 | 135.807 | 140.169 | 149.449 | 153.167 | 161.319 |
| X | 1.2816 | 1.6449 | 1.9600 | 2.3263 | 2.5758 | 3.0902 | 3.2905 | 3.7190 |

$$Q(\chi^2 \mid \nu) = \left[ 2^{\frac{\nu}{2}} \Gamma\left(\frac{\nu}{2}\right) \right]^{-1} \int_{\chi^2}^{\infty} e^{-\frac{t}{2}} t^{\frac{\nu}{2}-1} \, dt$$

*Available at your local bookstore or order directly from us by sending in coupon below.*

# REA's **Problem Solvers**

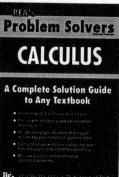

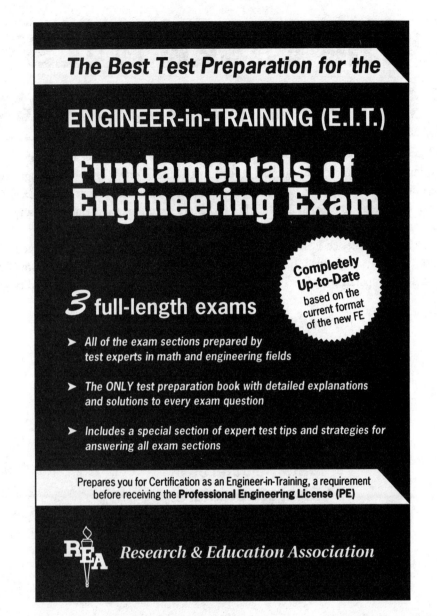

# "The ESSENTIALS" of Math & Science

Each book in the ESSENTIALS series offers all essential information of the field it covers. It summarizes what every textbook in the particular field must include, and is designed to help students in preparing for exams and doing homework. The ESSENTIALS are excellent supplements to any class text.

The ESSENTIALS are complete and concise with quick access to needed information. They serve as a handy reference source at all times. The ESSENTIALS are prepared with REA's customary concern for high professional quality and student needs.

## Available in the following titles:

Advanced Calculus I & II
Algebra & Trigonometry I & II
Anthropology
Automatic Control Systems /
    Robotics I & II
Biology I & II
Boolean Algebra
Calculus I, II & III
Chemistry
Complex Variables I & II
Data Structures I & II
Differential Equations I & II
Electric Circuits I & II
Electromagnetics I & II
Electronics I & II

Electronic
    Communications I & II
Finite & Discrete Math
Fluid Mechanics /
    Dynamics I & II
Fourier Analysis
Geometry I & II
Group Theory I & II
Heat Transfer I & II
LaPlace Transforms
Linear Algebra
Math for Engineers I & II
Mechanics I, II & III
Modern Algebra
Numerical Analysis I & II

Organic Chemistry I & II
Physical Chemistry I & II
Physics I & II
Pre-Calculus
Probability
Psychology I & II
Real Variables
Set Theory
Statistics I & II
Strength of Materials &
    Mechanics of Solids I & II
Thermodynamics I & II
Topology
Transport Phenomena I & II
Vector Analysis

*If you would like more information about any of these books,*
*complete the coupon below and return it to us or go to your local bookstore.*

---

**RESEARCH & EDUCATION ASSOCIATION**
61 Ethel Road W. • Piscataway, New Jersey 08854
Phone: (908) 819-8880

**Please send me more information about your Math & Science Essentials Books**

Name _____

Address _____

City _____ State _____ Zip _____

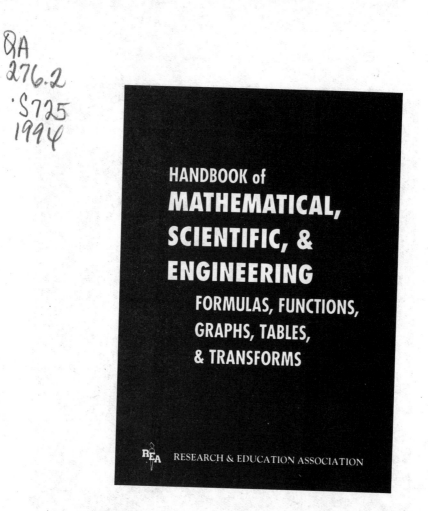

# HANDBOOK of
# MATHEMATICAL,
# SCIENTIFIC, &
# ENGINEERING
## FORMULAS, FUNCTIONS, GRAPHS, TABLES, & TRANSFORMS

**RE A** RESEARCH & EDUCATION ASSOCIATION

A particularly useful reference for those in math, science, engineering and other technical fields. Includes the most-often used formulas, tables, transforms, functions, and graphs which are needed as tools in solving problems. The entire field of special functions is also covered. A large amount of scientific data which is often of interest to scientists and engineers has been included.